Now updated and expanded—with 120 more composers than before—"The Hinson" is more useful than ever, guiding pianists to solo literature for themselves and their students. Maurice Hinson still answers the perennial questions of performers and teachers: What did a given composer write? What interesting work have I never heard of? How difficult is it? What are its special musical features? How can I reach the publisher?

Professor Hinson describes selected solo piano compositions of nearly 2,000 composers. Brief biographical sketches of major composers enhance this annotated bibliography, and pertinent facts about many of the lesser-known composers shed light on their pianistic and compositional approaches. For each entry, the author indicates the publisher(s) of the piece, the number of pages, and the performance time; he then describes the style, any individual characteristics, and the level of difficulty. There are also insightful comparisons of the various editions and collections of the standard repertoire. Many listings are followed by bibliographic references to articles about a specific work. Indexes help the user locate women composers, Black composers, and composers from a number of specific countries and regions.

(continued on back flap)

Guide to the
Pianist's Repertoire

MAURICE HINSON

GUIDE TO THE PIANIST'S REPERTOIRE

Third Edition

INDIANA UNIVERSITY PRESS

Bloomington and Indianapolis

This book is a publication of
Indiana University Press
601 North Morton Street
Bloomington, IN 47404-3797 USA

http://www.indiana.edu/~iupress

Telephone orders   800-842-6796
Fax orders   812-855-7931
e-mail orders   iuporder@indiana.edu

Manufactured in the United States of America

Library of Congress Cataloging-in-Publication Data

Hinson, Maurice.
Guide to the pianist's repertoire / Maurice Hinson. — 3rd ed.
p.   cm.
Includes bibliographical references (p.   ) and index.
ISBN 0-253-33646-5 (cloth : alk. paper) — ISBN 0-253-21348-7 (pbk. : alk. paper)
1. Piano music—Bibliography. 2. Piano music—Bibliography—Graded lists.   I. Title.

ML128.P3 H5 2000
016.7862′0263—dc21
99-058594

1 2 3 4 5   05 04 03 02 01 00

To the memory of

JANE HINSON ENOCH (1956–1996),

who was taken from us too soon.

Contents

Preface to the Third Edition

Piano repertoire continues to be one of the most exciting musical genres. Our beloved instrument is still "front and center" as we near the second millennium. Keeping up with this continually growing repertoire (what is coming out? what has gone out of print? what is worthy?) requires more and more time. It was this problem that brought about the first edition of this book.

The original purpose of the *Guide* has not changed since the first edition appeared in 1973: to make available in one practical listing the important piano literature. In this third, enlarged edition, new material has been added while some repertoire has been deleted, either because it is out of print or because the author has changed his ideas about certain pieces. It is impossible to include everything written for the piano, so the book inevitably takes on a certain amount of subjectivity.

In the decade or so since the second edition (1987), there has been a small but growing interest in minimalist music. Some avant-garde experimentation continues, but the big pendulum swing is toward tonality or, more precisely, freely tonal writing. In the past decade, interest in writing for piano and tape and for prepared piano has declined. The remnants of dodecaphonic writing are still with us. There are many fine composers who have much to say, and they say it well for our instrument. The range of American piano music has become so broad that we can only say that American music is written by an American composer, and a large amount is contained in this volume.

There are probably numerous pieces I have not been able to examine. I apologize for leaving out any qualified work and would appreciate hearing of such repertoire. I have included only published works in order to keep the material manageable.

Transcriptions are not included. Information about this fascinating genre may be found in my book *The Pianist's Guide to Transcriptions, Arrangements, and Paraphrases* (Indiana University Press, 1990).

Many people in many places have generously given me their help. I gratefully acknowledge the assistance of Ms. Martha Powell and Dr. David Gregory of The Southern Baptist Theological Seminary; Mr. and Mrs. Morton Manus of the Alfred Publishing Co.; Elmer Booze of the Library of Congress; David Fenske, Music Librarian at Indiana University; Fernando Laires, President of the American Liszt Society; my graduate assistants, Stephen Taylor and Dr. Vernon Cherrix; the faculty secretaries, especially Bev Tillman, of The Southern Baptist Theological Seminary for making possible the typing of the manuscript; and the aid of graduate assistants through the years.

Without the generous assistance of numerous publishers this volume would not be possible. Special appreciation goes to Michael Murray of Boosey & Hawkes, Inc.; George Hotton of Theodore Presser Co.; Carole Flatau of Warner Brothers Publishing Corp.; Frank Billack and Donald Gillespie of C. F. Peters Corp.; Dr. Martin Bente and Holger

Seims of G. Henle Verlag; Barry O'Neal of Carl Fischer; Dr. Corey Field of European American Music Corp.; and Ruth Serrao of Music Imports.

To those I have mentioned, and to many more, I owe gratitude forever.

Louisville, Kentucky
January 1998

MAURICE HINSON

Preface to the Second Edition

In this edition I have updated *Guide to the Pianist's Repertoire*, edited by Irwin Freundlich, which was published in 1973, and its *Supplement* of 1979. Not only is there a large amount of new material but also much of the material from the earlier versions has been refined and enlarged. For instance, in this edition the J. S. Bach section has more discussion of individual works; each sonata by Beethoven and each major opus of Chopin is described; more of the sonatas of Haydn, Scarlatti, and Soler are treated in detail; and there is more focus on separate pieces of the major composers. It seems only natural that in the intervening years—in teaching, performing, and listening to all kinds of piano music—that my ideas about certain pieces have changed, particularly with respect to grading. The purpose of this book is still the same: to make available in one practical listing the important solo piano literature. It is designed as a basic textbook for college piano literature courses and as a special reference book for performers, teachers, librarians, music dealers, and all those interested in this rich and enormous repertoire.

In selecting works for this listing I have tried to cover all the standard composers thoroughly and to introduce contemporary composers of merit, especially those of the United States (over 450 appear in this edition). I have included only published works and only those that I have been able to play through and analyze. A number of works previously listed have been dropped because they are no longer readily available; although some known to be out of print are still listed because of their merit. Some of them can be found in secondhand music stores, in the larger university or municipal libraries, or, more especially, in the Library of Congress. The time span covered is mainly from 1700 to the present, but a few works dating before 1700 are included because of their special musical interest. The listing contains some music composed before the invention of the piano, but most of this literature is effective when performed on the piano. Transcriptions of music originally written for other instruments, as a rule, are excluded, unless the arrangement was made by the composer, or, in my opinion, is highly effective. Certain outstanding ragtime works are described, as this type of music is a unique American contribution to the piano repertoire.

A certain amount of subjectivity is unavoidable in a book of this nature, but I have attempted to be as fair, objective, and clear as possible in the descriptions of the pieces.

For many of the works discussed in this volume, knowledge of the compositional processes that go into their writing would help memorization and lead to a more authentic performance. As Leonard Bernstein wrote in *The Unanswered Question*:

> A piece of music is a constant metamorphosis of given material, involving such transformational operations as inversion, augmentation, retrograde, diminution, modulation, the opposition of consonance and dissonance, the various forms of imitation (such as canon and fugue), the varieties of rhythm and meter, harmonic progressions, coloristic and dynamic changes, plus the infinite interrelations of all these with one another. These *are* the meanings of music.

I have tried to point out these elements from a pianistic viewpoint as an aid to understanding and appreciation.

We live in an *urtext* age—with good reason—and this consciousness of a fine text has made us much more sensitive to the composer's intentions. Facsimiles of autographs (manuscripts) are not difficult to come by these days (those of Bach, Beethoven, Chopin, Mozart, Schubert, Schumann, etc. are fairly common); and I am amazed to find, when encountering a piece in manuscript form for the first time, how all the layers of "tradition" peel away, so that one sees the piece fresh for the first time. I have been careful to indicate when and where facsimiles are available. The Vienna Urtext edition has introduced a masterpiece series for piano that contains a clearly printed, well-edited version for performance plus a facsimile of the autograph.

Since the 1960s (when I first began writing this book), music and, more specifically, piano music, has undergone some interesting developments. Composers of serial music, which seems to have peaked during the 1970s, now recognize their obligation to attempt to develop musical material and to unfold certain aspects of the composition. And beginning in the 1960s, many traditional composers enlarged their conceptions by including the broad field of older music, with the result that new compositions, either avant-garde or antimusic works, began to incorporate elements of earlier music in a reflective fashion by means of either direct or indirect quotation (e.g., compositions by Crumb, Ligeti, Ives earlier, and Gottschalk even earlier!). And finally, in the 1970s, younger composers spoke out against the then operative categorization of tradition as the "canon of the forbidden"; they strove to incorporate in a direct and spontaneous manner generic and idiomatic elements of tonal music, drawn most often from the late-Romantic/early modern era. This tendency has been termed the "new simplicity," and it is good to hear tunes and keys again. A few composers (including Philip Glass and Jo Kondo) are enjoying "minimal art," in which a composition uses only a few notes but they are repeated numerous times.

I find it reassuring that much of the trail-blazing formal experimentation associated with the 1960s has lately slowed to a trickle. It seems that the aim of the composer of the 1980s is more to please the listener's ear rather than to challenge it. Many of our "mainstream" contemporary composers seem to have adopted an aesthetic position that gives higher priority to traditional craftsmanship than to shock value, one that stresses quality of construction and technical correctness even if they mean the sacrifice of sound and theatrical effectiveness.

There no longer seems to be an avant-garde movement (as we had in the 1960s), since today's music is of such diversity. There is, however, an area of compositional endeavor that may earn the term "avant-garde" by virtue of its association with ideas not yet commonly known to and/or accepted by most pianists. I use the term in that sense.

Many people in many places have generously given me their help. I gratefully acknowledge the assistance of Martha Powell, Music Librarian of The Southern Baptist Theological Seminary; Elmer Booze and Rodney Mill of the Library of Congress; David Fenske, Music Librarian at Indiana University; Fernando Laires of the Peabody Conservatory of Music; my graduate assistant, Janelle Ganey; and The Southern Baptist Theological Seminary for making possible the typing of the manuscript and the aid of graduate assistants through the years.

Without the generous assistance of numerous publishers this volume would not be possible. Special appreciation goes to Michael Murray of Boosey & Hawkes, Inc.; John Pope of G. Schrimer, Inc.; George Hotton of Theodore Presser Co.; Gerard Siani of Belwin-Mills Publishing Corp.; Donald Gillespie of C. F. Peters Corp.; Susan Brailove of Oxford University Press; Ernst Hettrich of G. Henle Verlag; Barry O'Neal of Associated Music

Publishers; Mike Warren of Alphonse Leduc; Corey Field of European American Music; and Ruth Serrao of Music Imports.

   To those I have mentioned, and to many more, I owe gratitude in perpetuity.

Louisville, Kentucky   MAURICE HINSON

Preface to the First Edition

No single musician can successfully encompass the entire piano repertoire. It is, in fact, by far the largest devoted to any instrument, second only in scope to that for voice. Not only is it beyond the capability of the repertoire but it is also equally difficult to have even a cursory acquaintance with its scope and be able to sift out material for study and performance from the mass of works accumulated over the years without some organized guiding hand to lead the way. It is, indeed, a lengthy path to travel from the earlier keyboard works to the present creations of the *avant-garde* especially if, as in the present volume, one chooses to include works for harpsichord, clavichord and organ suitable for performance on the modern piano. A practicable *Guide to the Pianist's Repertoire* is, then, a necessity for student, performer and teacher alike.

The key questions for the reader are: What is there? What is it like? Where can I get it? To date the most useful efforts in English to provide answers to these question have been attempted in Ernest Hutcheson's *The Literature of the Piano* (1948, revised by Rudolph Ganz, 1964), *Music for the Piano* (1954) by James Friskin and Irwin Freundlich, and the *Short History of Keyboard Music* (1966) by F. E. Kirby. The main interest in Hutcheson's book lies in the personal viewpoints of that distinguished Australian pianist. However, it is short on the earlier and more modern repertoire since it concentrates on the traditional pianistic literature. Those gaps are only partially repaired by Ganz's interesting additions. The Friskin-Freundlich handbook is organized by periods and style groupings and has as its point of departure 1590, its cut-off date 1952. It includes not only the solo repertoire but also works for four hands at one and two pianos, and concertos. Kirby's more recent volume is an historical, chronological approach, concerned with the development of style and although not a handbook (in the sense of the Hutchenson and Frisken-Freundlich volumes) contains a wealth of material for the practical keyboardist even though clothed in a musicological garb.

Two rather unusual volumes in German must be mentioned: The *Geschichte der Klaviermusik* (1941, fourth edition 1965) of Walter Georgii and the almost unbelievable *Handbuch der Klavierliteratur* (1967, second edition 1977) of Klaus Wolters. The Georgii work was in a class by itself in terms of completeness, clarity, scope and scholarship until the appearance of Wolters' monumental volume. But it was, in fact, a history of the repertoire comparable to Kirby's opus. Wolters produced a genuine handbook of unparalleled scope in which e.g., one can find all the variant readings in all the Beethoven Sonatas in all the major editions! It also devotes much space to instructional material, methods, technical treatises and anthologies, and attempts to grade the difficulty of the material in a scale ranging from 1 to 15.*

*Three other volumes worth mentioning have appeared since this Preface was written: Albert Faurot's *Concert Piano Repertoire* (1974), which is a listing of the more advanced solo literature; Christof Rüger's *Konzerbuch Klaviermusik* (1979), which deals with the most important solo piano works; and Jaime Ingram's *Historia, Repertorio y Compositores del Piano* (1978), which presents an overview of the entire piano repertoire.—M.H.

The present volume is organized along completely different lines. First of all, it is devoted completely to the solo literature. It is alphabetical instead of chronological or stylistic in emphasis, taking on somewhat the aspect of a catalogue of catalogues supplemented by a listing of anthologies, collections and bibliographical material inserted into the text and running over into an additional appendix. The bibliography includes not only books and articles but also doctoral dissertations (both published and unpublished) pertaining to the composers and works mentioned. The inclusion of such material is unique to this volume and should prove invaluable for purposes of further self-study. The problem of style groupings and national groupings (e.g., what works are there by Canadian or Bulgarian or American composers?) has been met by an indexing system aimed to solve this problem most expeditiously for the reader. It is also hoped that the inclusion of a generous number of *avant-garde* works and listings of more than two hundred and fifty American composers will fill an obvious gap. Similar attention has been lavished on the entire spectrum of the contemporary repertoire as well as countless earlier composers never before included in any volume on the pianist's repertoire.

The huge amount of research needed to compile this book has been the responsibility of Dr. Maurice Hinson, whose indefatigable energy and industry have been exemplary and most impressive. My own contribution has been as consultant, helping to organize the material, edit it as thoroughly as possible, reformulating and rephrasing to ensure a felicitous text with, here and there, some additional contributions inserted from my own special knowledge of the repertoire. It goes without saying that even with the greatest care it is impossible to avoid an occasional error. Dr. Hinson and I would both be grateful for communications to help eliminate errata in future editions.

New York   IRWIN FREUNDLICH
September 1971

Using the Guide

Arrangement of entries. In the "Individual Composers" section, all composers are listed alphabetically. Sometimes biographies and/or stylistic comments follow the composer's name and dates of birth and death. Under each composer's name, individual compositions are listed by opus number, or by title, or by musical form, or by a combination of the three. The entries in the "Anthologies and Collections" section include the editor or compiler, the publisher, the composers, and sometimes the titles represented in the collection.

Descriptions have been limited to general style characteristic, form, particular and unusual qualities, interpretative suggestions, and pianistic problems inherent in the music. Editorial procedures found in a particular edition are mentioned. The term "large span" is used when a span larger than an octave is required in a piece, and that occurs in many contemporary works. "Octotonic" refers to lines moving in the same direction one or more octaves apart. "Shifting meters" indicates that varied time signatures are used within the space mentioned (a few bars, a movement, the entire work). "Proportional rhythmic relationships," e.g., ⌐5″4¬, indicates 5 notes are to be played in the time space for 4. "3 with 2" means 3 notes in one voice are played with (against) 2 notes in another voice. "Chance music" (aleatory, aleatoric) is described or mentioned, not analyzed, since it has no definitely ordered sequence of events. "Synthetic scale(s)" are created by the composer whose work is being discussed; the range may be less than one octave. "Stochastic techniques" refers to "a probabilistic compositional method, introduced by Iannis Xenakis, in which the overall contours of sound are specified but the inner details are left to random or chance selection" (DCM, p. 708).

Grading. An effort has been made to grade representative works of each composer. Four broad categories are used: Easy, Intermediate (Int.), Moderately Difficult (M-D), and Difficult (D). The following standard works will serve as a guide to the grading:

Easy: Bach, dance movements from the *Anna Magdalena Notebook*
           Leopold Mozart, *Notebook for Wolfgang*
           Schumann, easier pieces from *Album for the Young*
           Bartók, *Mikrokosmos*, Vols. I–II
Int.:   Bach, *Twelve Little Preludes and Fugues*
           Beethoven, *Ecossaises*
           Mendelssohn, *Children's Pieces* Op. 72
           Bartók, *Rumanian Folk Dances* 1–5
M-D: Bach, *French Suites, English Suites*
           Mozart, *Sonatas*
           Brahms, *Rhapsody* Op. 79/2
           Debussy, *La Soirée dans Granade*
D: Bach, *Partitas*
           Beethoven, *Sonata* Op. 57

Chopin, *Etudes*
Barber, *Sonata*

These categories must not be taken too strictly but are only given for general indications of technical and interpretative difficulties.

Details of entries. When known, the date of composition is given after the title of the work. Then, in parentheses, are as many of the following as apply to the particular work: the editor, the publisher, the publisher's edition number, and the copyright date. When more than one edition is available, the editions are listed in order of preference, the most desirable first. The number of pages and the performance time are frequently listed. The spelling of the composer's name and of the titles of the compositions appear as they do on the music being described. Specifically related books, dissertations or theses, and periodical articles are listed following individual compositions or at the conclusion of the discussion of a composer's works (a more extended bibliography appears at the end of the book).

Sample Entries and Explanations

C. P. E. Bach

Six Sonatas 1761 W.51 (Juanelva Rose—TP 1973).

1761 is the year of composition; W.51 stands for Wotquenne (the catalogue of C. P. E. Bach's music) and the number he assigned the pieces. Juanelva Rose is the editor. Theodore Presser is the publisher, and 1973 is the publication date.

Franz Schubert

Four Impromptus Op. 90 D.899 (Badura-Skoda—VU 50001). M-D.

Op. 90 is the opus number. D.899 stands for Deutsch (the cataloguer of Schubert's music) and the number he has assigned the pieces. Badura-Skoda is the editor. Vienna Urtext is the publisher, and 50001 is its edition number. M-D means Moderately Difficult.

Milton Babbitt

Playing for Time 1977 (Alfred) in collection *Twelve by Eleven* 12pp. D.

The date of composition is 1977; the publisher is Alfred. The piece is contained in the collection *Twelve by Eleven*; it is 12 pages long, and it is classified as Difficult. Other pieces in the collection can be checked by looking in the American section of "Anthologies and Collections" under the title *Twelve by Eleven*.

Other assistance. See "Abbreviations" for terms, publishers, books, and periodicals referred to in the text; and the directories "American Agent or Parent Companies of Music Publishers" and "Addresses of Music Publishers" to locate publishers. Five special indexes—"Alphabetical List of Composers under Nationality Designations," "Black Composers," "Women Composers," "Compositions for Piano and Tape," and "Compositions for Prepared Piano"—direct the user to entries in the text for music in these categories.

Abbreviations

A	Allemande	CMC	Canadian Music Centre
AA	Authors Agency of the Polish Music Publishers	CMP	Consolidated Music Publishing
ABRSM	Associated Board of the Royal Schools of Music	CPE	Composer/Performer Edition
ACA	American Composers Alliance	CSMP	Crystal Spring Music Publishers
AMC	American Center	CUMP	Columbia University Music Press
AME	American Music Editions		
AMP	Associated Music Publishers	D	Difficult
AMT	*American Music Teacher*	DCM	*Dictionary of Contemporary Music*, ed. John Vinton (New York: E. P. Dutton, 1974).
Anh.	Anhang (appendix)		
APS	Art Publication Society		
B	Bourrée	DDT	Denkmäler deutscher Tonkunst
B&VP	Broekmans & Van Poppel		
BB	Broude Brothers	DoB	Doblinger
BBD	Effie B. Carlson, *A Bio-Bibliographical Dictionary of Twelve-Tone and Serial Composers* (Metuchen, NJ: Scarecrow Press, 1970).	DTB	Denkmäler der Tonkunst in Bayern
		DTOe	Denkmäler der Tonkunst in Österreich
		DVFM	Deutscher Verlag für Musik
Bk(s).	Book(s)	EAM	Editorial Argentina de Música
BMC	Boston Music Co.		
BME	Brazilian Music Enterprises	EAMC	European American Music Corp. (a division of Warner Brothers)
BMI	Broadcast Music, Inc.		
Bo&Bo	Bote & Bock		
Bo&H	Boosey & Hawkes	EBM	E. B. Marks
Br	Bärenreiter	EC	Edizioni Curci
Br&H	Breitkopf & Härtel	ECIC	Editorial Cooperativa Intermericana de Compositores
C	Courante		
ca.	circa		
CAP	Composers' Autograph Publications	ECS	ECS Publishing (parent to E. C. Schirmer Music)
CeBeDeM	CeBeDeM Foundations	ELK	Elkan & Schildknecht
CF	Carl Fischer	EMB	Edition Musica Budapest
CFE	Composers Facsimile Edition	EMH	Editions Musikk-Huset
CFP	C. F. Peters	EmM	Éditions musicales du Marais
CHP	Chesky Hudebni Fond	EMM	Ediciones Mexicanas de Música
CK	*Contemporary Keyboard*		

EMT	Éditions Musicales Trans-atlantiques		Corporation of America); the former MCA/Polygram Music Publishing is now Universal Music Publishing Group
ESC	Max Eschig		
EV	Elkan-Vogel		
ff	Fortissimo		
FSF	Fast Slow Fast	M-D	Moderately Difficult
FVB	Fitzwilliam Virginial Book	Mer	Mercury Music Corp.
G	Gigue	MFTP	James Friskin and Irwin Freundlich, *Music for the Piano* (New York: Rinehart & Co., 1954; reprint New York: Dover, 1973).
Gen	General Music Publishing Co.		
GM	Gehrmans Musikförlag		
GS	G. Schirmer		
GWM	General Words and Music Co.	MGP	Music Graphics Press
Hin	Hinrichsen	MJ	*Music Journal*
HV	Heinrichshofens Verlag	MJQ	MJQ Music
IEM	Instituto de Extensión Musicale, Universidad de Chile, Calle Compañia, 1264 Santiago, Chile	ML	*Music and Letters*
		MM	*Modern Music*
		M&M	*Music and Musicians*
		MMB	MMB Music Inc.
IMC	International Music Co.	MMP	Masters Music Publications
IMI	Israel Music Institute	MMR	*Monthly Musical Record*
IMP	Israeli Music Publications	MO	*Musical Opinion*
Int.	Intermediate difficulty	MQ	*Musician Quarterly*
ITO	*In Theory Only*, Journal of the Michigan Music Theory Society, School of Music, University of Michigan, Ann Arbor, MI 48109	MR	*Music Review*
		MS(S)	manuscript(s)
		MT	*Musical Times*
		MTNA	Music Teachers National Association
IU	Music Library, Indiana University	MTP	Music Treasure Publications
JALS	*Journal of the American Liszt Society*	MVH	Musica Viva Historica (Artia)
JF	J. Fischer	Nag	Nagel's Music-Archive
JWC	J. W. Chester	NME	New Music Edition
K	Kalmus	NMO	Norsk Musikförlag
KC	*Keyboard Classics*	NMS	Nordiska Musikförlaget
KMB	Konemann Music Budapest	Nov	Novello
K&S	Kistner & Siegel	NV	Noetzel Verlag
Ku	Kultura	OBV	Oesterreischer Bundesverlag
L	Alessandra Longo	OD	Oliver Ditson
LC	Library of Congress, Washington, DC 20540	Op.	Opus
		OUP	Oxford University Press
LG	Lawson Gould	PaF	Prelude and Fugue
L'OL	L'Oiseau-Lyre	PAU	Pan American Union
M	Minuet	PIC	Peer International Corp.
MAB	Musica Antiqua Bohemica (Artia)	P&K	*Piano and Keyboard*
		PMP	Polish Music Pubications
MC	Mildly contemporary	PNM	*Perspectives of New Music*
MCA	MCA Music (Music	pp	pianissimo
		PQ	*Piano Quarterly*

PRMA	*Proceedings of the Royal Musical Association*	SKABO	Skandinavisk og Borups Musikförlag
PSM	Pennsylvania State Music Series (Pennsylvania State University Press)	SM	Skandinavisk Musikförlag
		SP	Shawnee Press
		SSB	William S. Newman, *The Sonata since Beethoven* (Chapel Hill: University of North Carolina Press, 1969; 2d ed., New York: W. W. Norton, 1972).
PWM	Polskie Wydawnictwo Muzyczne		
R&E	Ries & Erier		
Rev.	Revised		
Ric	Ricordi		
Ric Amer	Ricordi Americana S.A.	SZ	Suvini Zerboni
Ric BR	Ricordi Brazil	TM	Jeffrey Kresky, *Tonal Music* (Bloomington: Indiana University Press, 1977).
S	Sarabande		
SA	Sonata-Allegro		
Sal	Salabert	TP	Theodore Presser
SB	Summy-Birchard	TPA	*Antologia de musica antica e moderna per il pianoforte,* ed. Gino Tagliapietra, 18 vols. (Milan: Ricordi, 1931–32).
S&B	Stainer & Bell		
SBE	William S. Newman, *The Sonata in the Baroque Era* (Chapel Hill: University of North Carolina Press, 1959; rev. ed., 1966; 3d ed., New York: W. W. Norton, 1972).		
		UE	Universal Edition
		UME	Unión Musical Española
		UMKR	Unbekannte Meister der Klassik und Romantik (Boonin)
SBTS	Southern Baptist Theological Seminary School of Church Music, 2825 Lexington Road, Louisville, KY 40280	UMP	United Music Publishers
		UNC	University of North Carolina Press
		USSR	Mezhdunarodnaya Kniga (Music Publishers of the USSR). The Soviet Union no longer exists, but many former Soviet composers— and the heirs of others— have agreements for the distribution of their works in North America through G. Schirmer.
SCE	William S. Newman, *The Sonata in the Classic Era* (Chapel Hill: University of North Carolina Press, 1963; 2d ed., New York: W. W. Norton, 1972).		
SDM	Servico de Documentacão Musical da Ordem dos Musicos do Brazil, Av, Almte, Barroso, 72-7° Andar Rio de Janeiro, Brazil		
		Var(s).	Variation(s)
SFS	Slow Fast Slow	vol(s).	volume(s)
SHKY	Frank E. Kirby, *A Short History of Keyboard Music* (New York: The Free Press, 1966).	VU	Vienna Urtext Edition (UE)
		WB	Warner Brothers
		WH	Wilhelm Hansen
		WIM	Western International Music
SHV	Státní hudbeni vydavatelstí	YMP	Yorktown Music Press
SIMG	Sammelbände der Internationalen Musikgesellschaft	ZV	Zenemükiado Vállalat

American Agents or
Parent Companies of Music Publishers

[1] Alfred Publishing Company, Inc.
P.O. Box 10003
Van Nuys, CA 91410-0003
E-mail: customerservice@alfredpub.com
Tel: (818) 891-5999
Fax: (818) 892-9239

[2] Associated Music Publishers, Inc.
Music Sales Corp.
257 Park Avenue South, 20th Floor
New York, NY 10010
Website: www.musicsales.com
Tel: (212) 254-2100
Fax: (212) 254-2013

[3] Boosey & Hawkes, Inc.
35 East 21st Street
New York, NY 10010-6212
Website: www.ny.boosey.com
Tel: (212) 358-5300
Fax: (212) 358-5301

[4] Brodt Music Company
mailing address: P.O. Box 9345
Charlotte, NC 28299
street address: 1906 Commonwealth
Avenue
Charlotte, NC 28205
Website: www.brodtmusic.com
E-mail: orders@brodtmusic.com
Tel: (704) 332-2177 (local and international)
Tel: 1-800-438-4129 (U.S. and Canada)
Fax: (704) 335-7215 (local and international)
Fax: 1-800-446-0812 (U.S. and Canada)

[5] Broude Brothers, Ltd.
141 White Oaks Road
Williamstown, MA 01267

Tel: (413) 458-8131
Fax: (413) 458-5242

[6] Concordia Publishing House
3558 South Jefferson Avenue
Saint Louis, MO 63118-3968
Website: www.cph.org (homepage)
Website: www.cphmall.com (mall)
E-mail: cphorder@cph.org (for orders)
E-mail: jpkelley@cphnet.org (for information)
Tel: 1-800-325-3040 (for orders)
Tel: 1-800-325-3040, ext. 1055 or (314) 268-1055 (for information)
Fax: (314) 268-1411

[7] ECS Publishing (parent company to
E. C. Schirmer Music)
138 Ipswich Street
Boston, MA 02215
Website: www.ecspublishing.com
E-mail: office@ecspublishing.com
Tel: (617) 236-1935
Tel: 1-800-777-1919 (orders only)

[8] Elkin Music International, Inc.
16 NE 4th Street, Suite 140
Fort Lauderdale, FL 33301-3262
Website: www.elkinmusic.com
E-mail: timsloan@worldnet.att.net
Tel: (954) 522-3611
Fax: (954) 522-3609

[9] Carl Fischer, Inc.
65 Bleecker Street
New York, NY 10012
Website: www.carlfischer.com
E-mail: info@carlfischer.com
Tel: (212) 777-0900
Tel: 1-800-762-2328
Fax: (212) 477-6996

[10] Foreign Music Distributors
9 Elkay Drive
Chester, NY 10918
Fax: (914) 469-5817
(no phone orders)

[11] Mark **Foster** Music Co.
street address: 28 East Springfield Avenue
Champaign, IL 61820
mailing address: Box 4012
Champaign, IL 61824-4012
Website: www.markfostermusic.com
E-mail: info@markfostermusic.com
Tel: 1-800-359-1386
Tel: (217) 398-2790
Fax: (217) 398-2791

[12] Theodore **Front** Musical Literature, Inc.
16122 Cohasset Street
Van Nuys, CA 91406
Website: books.tfront.com/
music/home2.html
E-mail: music@tfront.com
Tel: (818) 994-1902
Fax: (818) 994-0419

[13] Hildegard Publishing Co.
P.O. Box 332
Bryn Mawr, PA 19010
Website: www.hildegard.com
E-mail: sglickman@hildegard.com
Tel: (610) 649-8649
Fax: (610) 649-8677

[14] Neil A. **Kjos** Music Co.
4380 Jutland Drive
San Diego, CA 92117-0894
E-mail: email@kjos.com
Website: www.kjos.com
Tel: 1-800-854-1592
Tel: (619) 270-9800
Fax: (619) 270-3507

[15] Hal **Leonard** Publishing Corp.
street address: 7777 West Bluemound Road
Milwaukee, WI 53213
mailing address: P.O. Box 13819
Milwaukee, WI 53213
Website: www.halleonard.com
E-mail: halinfo@halleonard.com

Tel: (414) 774-3630
Fax: (414) 774-3259

[16] Magnamusic Distributors
P.O. Box 338
Sharon, CT 06069
Website: www.magnamusic.com
E-mail: magnamusic@magnamusic.com
Tel: (203) 364-5431
Fax: (203) 364-5168

[17] MMB Music, Inc.
Contemporary Arts Building
3526 Washington Avenue
Saint Louis, MO 63103-1019
Website: www.mmbmusic.com
E-mail: mmbmusic@mmbmusic.com
Tel: 1-800-543-3771 (U.S. and Canada)
Tel: 314-531-9635
Fax: 314-531-8384

[18] Oxford University Press, Inc.
Order Department
2001 Evans Road
Cary, NC 27513
Website: www.oup-usa.org
Tel: 1-800-451-7556
Fax: (919) 677-1303

[19] J. W. **Pepper & Son**, Inc.
P.O. Box 850
Valley Forge, PA 19482
Website: www.jwpepper.com
Tel: 1-800-345-6296
Fax: 1-800-260-1482

[20] C. F. **Peters** Corp.
373 Park Avenue South
New York, NY 10016
Tel: (212) 686-4147
Fax: (212) 689-9412

[21] Theodore **Presser** Co.
1 Presser Place
Bryn Mawr, PA 19010-3490
Website: www.presser.com
E-mail: retail@presser.com (retail)
E-mail: sales@presser.com (wholesale)
Tel: (610) 525-3636
Fax: (610) 527-7841

[22] G. **Schirmer** Music Co.
Music Sales Corp.
257 Park Avenue South, 20th Floor
New York, NY 10010
Website: www.schirmer.com
Tel: (212) 254-2100
Fax: (212) 254-2013

[23] Shawnee Press, Inc.
P.O. Box 690
Delaware Water Gap, PA 18327-1099
Website: www.shawneepress.com
E-mail: shawneepress@noln.com
Tel: 1-800-962-8584 (orders)
Tel: (570) 476-0550
Fax: (570) 476-5247

[24] Warner Brothers Publications, Inc.
15800 NW 48th Avenue
Miami, FL 33014
Website:
www.warnerbrospublications.com
Tel: 1-800-327-7643
Tel: (305) 620-1500 (orders)
Fax: (305) 621-4869 (sales dept.)

[25] Location or American agent unknown, despite our efforts to find them; many of these publishers are no longer in business.

Addresses of Music Publishers

A bracketed number (e.g., **[1]**) following the name of a publisher corresponds to that of its American agent or parent company (see preceding listing, "American Agents or Parent Companies of Music Publishers"). **Boldface** has been added to help the reader find items in the alphabetical sequence. In cases where our questionnaire was not returned, the last known address for the publisher is given.

Accent Music **[25]**
Adeva Musik (*see* Bärenreiter)
Aenear Publishing Co. **[25]**
  Toronto, Canada
Africanus Editions
  3126 Shenandoah Avenue
  Saint Louis, MO 63104
  Website: members.aye.net/~africnus
  E-mail: africnus@aye.net
  Tel: (314) 773-8769
Ahn & Simrock [25]
Alacran Press, Inc.
  695 Wrelton Drive
  San Diego, CA 92109
  Website: www.alacranpress.com
Alberson [25]
J. Albert (*see* E. B. Marks)
Allans Music Australia **[8]**
ALMA, Inc. (Association for Latin-
  American Music and Art)
  10985 West Broward Blvd.
  Plantation, FL 33324
  Website: www.alma-usa.com
  E-mail: mail@alma-usa.com
  Tel: 1-888-275-2562
  Fax: (954) 915-9144
Alpeg Editions **[20]**
Alsbach [25]
Amadeus-Päuler [10]
American Composers Alliance—Compos-
  ers Facsimile Edition
  170 West 74th Street
  New York, NY 10023

Website: www.composers.com
E-mail: info@composers.com
Tel: (212) 362-8900
Fax: (212) 362-8902
American Institute of Musicology
  (includes The Corpus of Early Music
  Keyboard Music)
  c/o Tempo Music Publications, Inc.
  3773 West 95th Street
  Leawood, KS 66206
  Website: www.tempomusic.com\aim
  E-mail: aim@tempomusic.com
  Tel: (913) 381-5088
  Tel: 1-800-733-5066
  Fax: (913) 381-5081
American Music Center
  30 West 26th Street, Suite 1001
  New York, NY 10010-2011
  Website: www.amc.net
  E-mail: center@amc.net
  Tel: (212) 366-5260
American Music Editions
  263 East 7th Street
  New York, NY 10009-6049
  Fax: (212) 420-9393
Gli **Amici della Musica da Camera**
  Via Bocca di Leone 25
  Rome, Italy
Amphion Éditions Musicales **[15, 21]**
AMS Press
  56 East 13th Street
  New York, NY 10003-4686
  Tel: (212) 777-4700

Fax: (212) 995-5413
Telex: (710) 581-2302
Amsco School Publishing, Inc.
315 Hudson Street
New York, NY 10013-1085
Tel: 1-800-969-8398
Tel: (212) 886-6500
Fax: (212) 675-7010
Johann **Andre**
Frankfurterstrasse 28
Offenback am Main, Germany
Anglican (*see* William Elkin)
A-R Editions, Inc.
801 Deming Way
Madison, WI 53717
E-mail: info@areditions.com
Website: www.areditions.com
Tel: (608) 836-9000
Tel: 1-800-736-0070 (U.S. orders only)
Fax: (608) 831-8200
Groupe **Archambault**
500 Est, Rue Ste-Catherine
Montreal, Quebec, H2L 2C6 Canada
Tel: (514) 849-6201
Fax: (514) 849-1481
Ariadne [25]
Vienna, Austria
Collecion **Arion [25]**
Arno Press [25]
Arno Volk Verlag (*see* Universal Music
Publishing Group)
Arrow Music Press **[3]**
Ars Viva [10, 24]
Arsis Press
1719 Bay Street SE
Washington, DC 20003
Website: www.InstantWeb.com/~arsis
Tel: (202) 544-4817
distributed by Plymouth Music Company, Inc.
170 NE 33rd Street
Fort Lauderdale, FL 33334
Tel: (954) 563-1844
Fax: (954) 563-9006
Art Publication of St. Louis [25]
Artia [3, 10, 17, 24]
Ascherberg, Hopwood & Crew, Ltd. Music Publishers
c/o Chappell International Music
Publ. Group Ltd., c/o Mr. Thorpe

50 New Bond Street
London W1A 2BR, England
Ashdown, Edwin, Ltd. **[3, 4]**
Ashley Dealers Service **[25]**
Hermann **Assmann** Musikverlag
Franz-Werfel-Strasse 3660431
Frankfurt 50, Germany
Tel: (069) 532431/526231
**Associated Board of the Royal School of
Music** (England) **[21]**
Astoria Verlag
Brandenburgische Strasse 22
10707 Berlin, Germany
Tel: (030) 8818898
Fax: (030) 8833415
Augener [7]
Australian Music Centre, Ltd.
P.O. Box N690
Grosvenor Place
Sydney NSW 1220, Australia
Website: www.amcoz.com.au/amc
E-mail: info@amcoz.com.au
Tel: 61 2 9247 4677
Fax: 61 2 9241 2873
**Authors Agency of the Polish Music
Publishers**
ul. Hipteczna 2, 00-950
Warsaw, Poland
Autographus Musicus
Ardalavágen 158
S-124 32 Bandhagen, Sweden
Axelrod [23]
Banks Music, Ltd. **[4, 15]**
The Old Forge, Sand Hutton
York, Y04 11L13, England
Email: BanksRamsay@mcmail.com
Tel: (44) 1904 468472
Fax: (44) 1904 468679
Bardic Edition **[21]**
6 Fairfax Crescent
Aylesbury, Bucks HP20 2ES, England
Tel: (44) (1296) 28609
Fax: (44) (1296) 28609
Bärenreiter Verlag **[10, 13, 17, 24,** works
of Schoenberg dist. in U.S. by Belmont**]**
Barry & Cia (Argentina) **[3]**
M. P. **Belaieff [20]**
Belmont Music Publishers
P.O. Box 231
Pacific Palisades, CA 90272

Website: www.primenet.com/~belmus/
E-mail: belmus@primenet.com
Tel: (310) 454-1867
Fax: (310) 573-1925
Belwin-Mills [24]
Berandol Music Ltd. (Canada) **[2, 16]**
Edizioni **Bèrben [21]**
Biblioteca Central [25]
    Sección de Música
    Barcelona, Spain
Biedermann [25]
Big 3 Music Corp. **[25]**
Gerald **Billaudot**, Editeur/Editions
    Billaudot **[21]**
Black Cat Productions
    10808 124th Street
    Edmonton, AB, T5M 0H4, Canada
    Website: www.olivermusic.com
    E-mail: oliver@compusmart.ab.ca
    Tel: 1-800-661-3613 (Canada and U.S.)
    Fax: (780) 447-5337
BMI (Broadcast Music, Inc.)
    (Note that BMI is a performing-rights
    organization, not a publisher or dis-
    tributor.)
    320 West 57th Street
    New York, NY 10019
    Website: www.bmi.com
    E-mail: classical@bmi.com
    Tel: (212) 586-2000
BMI Canada, Ltd. **[25]**
Boccaccini & Spada [21]
Fred **Bock [15]**
Boelke-Bomart Music Publications (*see*
    Jerona Music Corp.)
Bomart (*see* Boelke-Bomart)
Bongiovanni Francesco Edizioni Musicali
    Via Ugo Bassi, 31/F
    40121 Bologna, Italy
    E-mail: giancarlo@bongiovanni70.com
    E-mail: andrea@bongiovanni70.com
    Tel: (39) 51 22 57 22
    Fax: (39) 51 22 61 28
Joseph **Boonin** (*see* Jerona Music Corp.)
Bosse Edition
    Postfach 417
    84 Regensburg 2, Germany
Boston Music Co.
    Publications Department
    172 Tremont Street

Boston, MA 02111-1001
E-mail: bmco@earthlink.net
Tel: (617) 528-6155
Fax: (617) 528-6199
Bosworth & Co. **[4, 23]**
Bote & Bock [2]
Bourne Company
    5 West 37th Street, 6th Floor
    New York, NY 10018
    Website: www.internationalmusicco.com
    E-mail: bournemusic@worldnet.att.net
    Tel: (212) 391-4300
    Fax: (212) 391-4306
Bowdoin College Music Press
    Bowdoin College
    Brunswick, ME 04011
Bradley Publications **[25]**
Branden Publishing Co. Inc.
    Div. of Branden Books
    Box 843
    17 Station
    Brookline Village, MA 02147
    Tel: 1-800-537-7335 (for credit-card
    orders only)
    Tel: (617) 734-2045
Bratti [25]
    Florence, Italy
Brazilian Music Enterprises
    P.O. Box 12
    Lopez, WA 98261
Breitkopf & Härtel
    Walkmühlstrasse 52
    65195 Wiesbaden, Germany
    E-mail: info@breitkopf.de /
    sales@breitkopf.com
    Tel: 49 6128 9663 20
    Tel: 49 6128 9663 21
    Fax: 49 6128 9663 50
The **British Library** Publishing Office
    96 Euston Road
    London NW1 2DB, England
    E-mail: blpublications@bl.uk
    Tel: (44) (0171) 412 7535
    Fax: (44) (0171) 412 7768
    Telex: 21462
    distributed in North America by
    University of Toronto Press
    10 St. Mary Street, Suite 700
    Toronto, Ontario M4Y 2WS, Canada
    E-mail: utpress@utoronto.ca

Tel: (416) 978-2239
Fax: (416) 978-4738
Broadbent & Dunn [21]
Broadcast Music, Inc.
320 West 57th Street, 3rd Floor
New York, NY 10019
Tel: (212) 586-2000
Broekmans & Jan Van Poppel
van Baerlestraat 92–94
1071 BB Amsterdam, Netherlands
Website: www.broekmans.com
Email: music@broekmans.com
Tel: 31 20 679 65 75 / 659 72 70
Fax: 31 20 664 6759 / 449 10 01
Editio Musica **Budapest [21]**
Cambria Publishing **[25]**
Cambridge University Press
40 West 20th Street
New York, NY 10011-4211
Tel: (212) 924-3900
Tel: 1-800-221-4512
Website: www.cup.org
Canadian Music Centre
20 St. Joseph Street
Toronto, Ontario M4Y 1J9, Canada
Website: www.culturenet.ca/cmc
E-mail: cmc@interlog.com
Tel: (416) 961-6601
Fax: (416) 961-7198
Cantext Music
19 Laval Drive
Winnipeg R3T 2XB, Canada
Website: www.geocities.com/Vienna/
Strasse/7136/
E-mail: bthad@hotmail.com
Tel: (204) 275-1598
Canyon Press **[25]**
Carisch, S.P.A. **[3]**
Carlanita Music Co. **[22]**
Valentim de **Carvalho**
R. Nova do Almada 97
Lisbon, Portugal
Casa Amarilla
San Diego 128
Santiago, Chile
Casia Publishing Co. **[13]**
Catamount Facsimile Editions
Box 245
Shaftsbury, VT 05262

CeBeDeM (Centre Belge de Documenta-
tion Musicale)
4 Boulevard de l'Empereur
B-1000 Brussels, Belgium
Century Music Publishing Co. (*see*
Ashley Dealers)
Chant du Monde (*see* Universal Music
Publishing Group)
Chappell & Co. **[15]**
Cherry Lane Music Co.
10 Midland Avenue
Port Chester, NY 10573
Website: www.cherrylane.com
Tel: (914) 935-5200
Fax: (914) 937-0614
Chesky Hudebni Fond [25]
J. W. **Chester [22, 23]**
7–9 Eagle Court
London EC1M 5QD, England
Editions **Choudens [20, 21]**
Chromattica
P.O. Box 21196
Baltimore, MD 21228
E-mail: chromm@hotmail.com
Tel: 1-800-357-9292
Fax: (410) 448-1433
Chronos Music (absorbed by Cormorant
Press; *see* Cormorant Press)
John **Church** Company **[21]**
Andrea **Coen-Zanibon [3]**
Franco **Colombo [24]**
Columbia Music Company [21]
Columbia University Press
562 West 113th Street
New York, NY 10025-8000
Website: www.cc.columbia.edu/cu/cup
Tel: (212) 666-1000
Tel: 1-800-944-8648
Fax: (212) 316-3100/9422
Telex: 75-2794
Composer/Performer Edition
330 University Avenue
Davis, CA 95616
Composers Press (*see* Seesaw Music
Corp.)
Conners Publications
503 Tahoe Street
Natchitoches, LA 71457-5718
Website: hostnet.pair.com/conners/

E-mail: ALMEI@aol.com or
almei@wnonline.net
Tel: (318) 357-0924
Consolidated Music Publishers
Music Sales Corp.
257 Park Avenue South, 20th Floor
New York, NY 10010
Website: www.musicsales.com
Tel: (212) 254-2100
Fax: (212) 254-2013
The **Consort** Press **[25]**
Continuo Music Press, Inc. (*see* Plymouth Co.)
Copa (*see* Ashley Dealers)
Cormorant Press
P.O. Box 169
Hallowell, ME 04347
Website: www.cormorantpress.com
E-mail: wlgold@gwi.net
Tel: (207) 622-5560
J. B. **Cramer** & Co., Ltd. **[3]**
Cranz [25]
Creazioni Artistiche Musicali (C.A.M.)
Via Cola di Rienzo, 152
00192 Rome, Italy
Website: www.cam-ost.it
E-mail: cam-ost@uni.net
Tel: (39) (6) 6874220/6874341
Fax: (39) (6) 6874046
Crescendo Publishing Co. **[2,** out of
business**]**
Crystal Spring Music Publishers
250 Ohua Avenue, 10E
Honolulu, HI 96815
Tel: (808) 923-6859
Culver Crest Publications
P.O. Box 4484
Culver City, CA 90231-4484
Edizioni **Curci** (*see* Big 3 Music Corp.)
Currency Press Pty Ltd.
street address: 201 Cleveland Street
Redfern 2016
mailing address: P.O. Box 2287
Strawberry Hills 2012
NSW Australia
Website: www.currency.com.au
E-mail: currency@magna.com.au
Tel: (61) (02) 9319 5877
Fax: (61) (02) 9319 3649

distributed in the U.S. by
Accents Publications Services Inc.
721 Ellsworth Drive, Suite 203-A
Silver Spring, MD 20910-4436
E-mail: accents@iamdigex.com
Tel: (301) 588-5496
Fax: (310) 588-5249
J. **Curwen** & Son (England) **[15]**
Czech State Music [25]
Da Capo Press, LLC
10 East 53rd Street, 19th Floor
New York, NY 10022
Website: www.plenum.com
Tel: 1-800-242-7737 (orders and queries)
Fax: 1-800-822-4090 (orders and queries)
distributed by
Harper Collins Publishers
Order Department
1000 Keystone Park
Scranton, PA 18512
Dantalian, Inc.
11 Pembroke Street
Newton, MA 02458
Website: www.dantalian.com
E-mail: dantinfo@dantalian.com
Tel: (617) 244-7230
De Ring [25]
Edizioni **de Santis**
Viale Mazzini 6
I-00195 Rome, Italy
Georges **Delrieu** & Cie (*see* William Elkin)
Derry Music Co. **[24]**
Desforges
Le Havre, France
Deutscher Verlag für Musik [24]
DGR Publishers (name changed to Seda Publications; *see* Seda Publications)
Oliver **Ditson** Company **[21]**
Ludwig **Doblinger [10]**
Donemus [21]
Edition **Donna [25]**
Düsseldorf, Germany
Dotesio (Spain) (*see* Union Musical Española)
Dover Publications, Inc.
31 East Second Street
Mineola, NY 11501-3582

Tel: 1-800-223-3130 (orders)
Tel: (516) 294-7000
Fax: (516) 742-6953
Telex: 12-7731
Dreililien Verlag, Richard Birnbach
Aubinger Strasse 9
82166 Gräfelfing, Germany
Tel: (49) (089) 875450
L. K. **Drew** Publishing Co.
303 Orton Road
Yellow Springs, OH 45387
E-mail: lkdrew@aol.com
Tel: (937) 767-9383
Duma Music, Inc.
580 Alden Street
Woodbridge, NJ 07095-3802
Website: www.dumamusic.com
E-mail: dumamuse@aol.com
Tel/Fax: (732) 636-5406
Durand Costallat [21]
Durand et Cie [21]
Eastman School of Music Publications **[9]**
Edition **Modern [25]**
Edition **Pan [16]**
Edition Russe de Musique [3]
Les Éditions **Bleu Blanc Rouge** (*see*
Hansen House)
**Éditions d'Etat pour la Littérature et
l'Art [25]**
Bucharest, Rumania
Éditions de la **Sirène Musicale [25]**
Paris, France
Éditions Musicales de la **Schola Can-
torum** et de la Procure Générale de
Musique & Labatiaz (*see* Labatiaz)
Éditions Musicales **des Marais [25]**
Éditions Musicales **Transatlantiques [21]**
Éditions Ray **Ventura [25]**
Paris, France
Éditions **Rideau Rouge [21]**
Editorial Argentina de Música **[21]**
**Editorial Cooperativa Interamericana de
Compositores [21]**
Editorial de **Música Española Contem-
poránea**
Alcalá, 70
28009 Madrid, Spain
Tel: (34) (91) 5770752
Fax: (34) (91) 5757645

Editorial **Politonia**
Buenos Aires, Argentina
Editura de Stat **Pentru**
Literatura si Arta
Bucharest, Rumania
Elkan & Schildknecht, Emil Carelius AB
Kungsholmsgatan 15
112 27 Stockholm, Sweden
E-mail: elkan.schildknecht@swipnet.se
Tel: (46) 8-6515421
Elkan-Vogel [21]
William **Elkin** Music Services **[In U.S.,
see 8]**
Elkin Music International Inc.
Station Road Industrial Estate
Salhouse
Norwich NR13 6NS, England
E-mail:
richard@elkinmusic.demon.co.uk
Tel: (44) (01603) 721302 (24 hours)
Fax: (44) (01603) 721801
Engström & Södring (Denmark) **[20]**
Enoch & Cie **[21]**
Erviti
San Martin, 28 bajo
20.005 San Sebastian, Spain
E-mail: erviti@euskalnet.net
Tel: (34) 943 30 04 93
Fax: (34) 943 20 03 43
Max **Eschig [15, 21]**
Eulenburg [24]
European American Music Distributors
Corp. and European American Retail
Music **[24]**
Excelsior Music Publishing **[21]**
Faber Music **[15,** also dist. by Belmont**]**
Fairfield, Ltd. (*see* Novello)
Manuel de **Falla** Ediciones, S.L.
C/ Breton de los Herreros, 55-Bajo F
28003 Madrid, Spain
Tel: (34) (91) 441 77 43
Fax: (34) (91) 442 60 96
Fallen Leaf Press [19]
P.O. Box 10034
Berkeley, CA 94709
Website: www.fallenleaf.com
E-mail: abasart@dnai.com
Tel/Fax: (510) 848-7805
Edition **Fazer [17]**

FEMA Music Publications [2, out of business]
Fentone Music (England) [21]
Finnish Information Centre [25]
J. **Fisher** & Bro. [2]
FJH Music Company, Inc.
  2525 Davie Road, Suite 360
  Fort Lauderdale, FL 33317-7424
  Website: www.fjhmusic.com
  E-mail: fjhmusic@gate.net
  Tel: 1-800-262-8744 (U.S.)
  Tel: 1-800-457-8744 (Canada)
  Fax: (954) 382-3073
FLP Music Publishing
  P.O. Box 60806
  Oklahoma City, OK 73146
  (Does business by mail only.)
A la **Flûte de Pan**
  49, rue de Rome et
  3, rue de Madrid
  Paris 8, France
Foetisch Frères, S.A. (Switzerland) [7]
Charles **Foley**, Inc. [9]
Fondazione **Carminignani Rossini** [25]
  Pesaro, Italy
Fondazione **Eugenio Bravi** [25]
  Milan, Italy
Forberg [20]
A. **Forlivesi** & Cia
  Via Roma, 4
  50123 Florence, Italy
  Tel: (39) (55) 78 44 76
  Fax: (39) (55) 70 11 86
  Telefax: 0574 81 40 99
Arnaldo **Forni**, Editore
  Via Gramsci 164, 40010 Sala
  Bologna, Italy
  Tel: (39) (51) 95 41 42 / 95 41 98
  Fax: (39) (51) 95 46 72
Forsyth Brothers, Ltd.
  126–128 Deansgate
  Manchester M3 2GR, England
  Tel: (44) (161) 834281
  Fax: (44) (161) 8340630
Sam **Fox** Music Sales Corp.
  c/o Plymouth Music Co., Inc.
  170 Northeast 33rd Street
  Fort Lauderdale, FL 33334
Frangipani Press (*see* Alfred)

Frank Music Corporation [15]
Fredonia Press-Discs
  3947 Fredonia Drive
  Hollywood, CA 90068
  Tel: (213) 851-3043
H. **Freeman** & Company [25]
Fromont [25]
Fujihara Music Company [25]
Furore Verlag [13]
  Naumberger Strasse 40
  D-34127 Kassel, Germany
  Fax: (49) 561 83 472
Adolph **Fürstner** [25]
Galaxy Music Corp. [7]
Galliard, Ltd. (England) [25]
Garland Publishing, Inc.
  717 Fifth Avenue, 25th Floor
  New York, NY 10022
  E-mail: info@garland.com
  Tel: (212) 751-7447
  Fax: (212) 308-9399
Carl **Gehrmans** Musikförlag [3]
General Music Publishing Co., Inc.
  (*see* Boston Music Company)
General Words and Music Co.
  distributed by Neil Kjos Music Co.
  4380 Jutland Drive
  San Diego, CA 92117-0894
  Website: www.kjos.com
  Tel: (619) 270-9800
Daniel **Gerard** Publications, Inc.
  5 Plain Avenue
  New Rochelle, NY
  Tel: (914) 235-2525
Musikverlag Hans **Gerig** [25]
Girard [25]
  Naples, Italy
Greenwood Press
  World Library Publications
  2145 Central Parkway
  Cincinnati, OH 45214
Gregg International
  White Swan Ho
  Godstone, Surrey RH9 8LW, England
  Tel: (44) (1883) 744214
  Fax: (44) (1883) 744024
Henri **Gregh**
  129, rue Montmartre
  Paris, France

Grupo **Renovación** [25]
    Buenos Aires, Argentina
Gulbenkian Foundation
    Parque de Sta. Gertrudes à Avda. de
    Berna
    Lisbon, Portugal
G. K. **Hall** & Co.
    c/o Simon & Schuster
    200 Old Tappan Road
    Old Tappan, NJ 07675-7095
    Tel: 1-800-257-5157
    Fax: 1-800-558-4676
Hamelle et Cie (France) [21]
Hansen House
    (Charles Hansen Publications)
    1804 West Avenue
    Miami Beach, FL 31139
    Tel: 305-672-8729
    Fax: 305-357-7768
Wilhelm **Hansen** [22, 23]
Hänssler (*see* American Institute of Musi-
    cology)
Hargail Music Press [25]
Harmonia Uitgave
    Roeltjesweg 23–25
    Hilversum, Netherlands
Frederick **Harris** Music Co., Ltd.
    (Distributed in the U.S. by FJH Music
    Company, Inc. See FJH.)
Harvard University Press
    79 Garden Street
    Cambridge, MA 02138-1499
    Email: contact__HUP@harvard.edu
    Website: www.hup.harvard.edu
    Tel: 1-800-448-2242
    Tel: (617) 495-2600
    Fax: 1-800-962-4983
Heinrichshofen Edition [20]
Helicon Music Corp. [24]
Helios Music Edition (*see* Plymouth
    Music)
G. **Henle** USA. Inc.
    P.O. Box 460127
    Saint Louis, MO 63146
    Website: www.henleusa.com
    E-mail: musicpubs@msn.com
    Tel: (314) 514-1791
    Fax: (314) 514-1269
Henmar Press (USA) [20]

Éditions **Henn**
    street address: 8, rue de Hesse
    CH-1204 Geneva, Switzerland
    mailing address: P.O. Box 5476
    CH-1211 Geneva 11, Switzerland
    E-mail: sidomusic@bluewin.ch
    Tel: 41 22 311 51 85
    Fax: 41 22 311 18 52
Heugel & Cie [21]
Editions **Heuwekemeijer** [21]
Highgate Press [7]
Hinrichsen Edition (England) [20]
Hinshaw Music, Inc. [25]
    (Hinshaw no longer publishes piano
    literature; other works available
    through William Elkin)
Hofmeister, Friedrich (Germany) [10, *see
    also* William Elkin]
Hope Publishing Co.
    380 South Main Place
    Carol Stream, IL 60188
    Website: www.hopepublishing.com
    E-mail: hope@hopepublishing.com
    Tel: 1-800-323-1049
    Tel: (630) 665-3200
    Fax: (630) 665-2552
Hudební Matice (Czech Republic) [25]
Hug (Switzerland) [16, 24]
Hyperion Press, Inc.
    45 Riverside Avenue
    Westport, CT 06880
    *Division of Disney Book Publishing
    Inc.
    114 Fifth Avenue
    New York, NY 10011
    Tel: 1-800-343-9204 (orders)
    Tel: (212) 633-4400
    Fax: (212) 633-4811
Ichthys Verlag GmbH [25]
    Postfach 834
    7000 Stuttgart I, Germany
Impero-Verlag [21]
Imprimus Music (*see* Sikesdi Press)
Indiana University
    William and Gayle Cook Music Library
    Simon Music Library & Recital Center
    200 South Jordan Avenue
    Bloomington, IN 47405
    Website: www.music.indiana.edu/

muslib.html
E-mail: libmus@indiana.edu
Tel: (812) 855-8541
Fax: (812) 855-3843
Instituto de Extensión Musicale
Calle Compañia 1274
Santiago, Chile
International Music Corporation (*see*
Bourne Co.)
Internationale Gesellschaft für Neue Musik
(International Society for Contemporary Music)
Winklerstrasse 20
1 Berlin 33, Germany
Intrepid Pixels Publishing Co.
820 West End Avenue, Box 9E
New York, NY 10025
Website: www.musicalonline.com/ipt
E-mail: info2@musicalonline.com
Tel: (212) 866-3939
Fax: (212) 280-8187
Ione Press, Inc. **[7]**
Israel Music Institute [21]
Israeli Music Publications Limited **[21]**
Japan Federation of Composers
5th Sky Building, #311
3-3-8 Sendagaya Shibuya-Ku
Tokyo 151-0051, Japan
E-mail: thejfc@ack.ne.ja
Tel: (81) 5474-1853
Fax: (81) 5474-1854
Japanese Society of Rights of Authors and Composers [25]
Jaymar Music Ltd.
P.O. Box 2191, Stn. B
London, Ontario N6A 4E3, Canada
Website: www.jaymar.com
Tel: (519) 672-7369
Fax: (519) 672-0016
Jerona Music Corp.
P.O. Box 671
Englewood, NJ 07631
Tel: (201) 568-8448
Fax: (201) 569-7023
Jean **Jobert**/Editions Jobert et Cie **[21]**
Johnson Reprint Corp.
111 Fifth Avenue
New York, NY 10003
Joshua Corp. (*see* Boston Music Company)

Joubert [25]
P. **Jürgenson**
Moscow 200, Russia
C. F. **Kahnt** (Germany) **[20]**
Edwin F. **Kalmus [24]**
Kenyon Publications **[15]**
E. C. **Kerby**, Ltd. **[15]**
The **Keys Press**
66 Clotilde Street
Mount Lawley
Western Australia 6050, Australia
Website:
www.iinet.net.au/~nick/keyspress/
Tel: (61) (8) 9271 6547
Fax: (61) (8) 9271 6581
Kistner & Siegel [6]
Kultura [3]
Kunzelmann (Switzerland) **[10]**
La Jolla Publishing Co. **[14]**
Éditions Musicales **Labatiaz**
Case postale 112
CH-1890 St-Maurice, Switzerland
E-mail: labatiaz@bluewin.ch
Tel/Fax: (41) (0) 24 485 24 80
Lawson Gould Music Publishers, Inc.
[1, *see also* William Elkin**]**
Lea Pocket Scores **[24]**
Alphonse **Leduc [21]**
175, rue Saint-Honoré
75040 Paris, France
Tel: (33) (1) 42 96 89 11
Fax: (33) (1) 42 86 02 83
Lee Roberts [15]
Leeds Music Corp. (*see* Universal Music
Publishing Group)
Leeds Music Ltd. (Canada) (*see* Universal Music Publishing Group)
Robert Owens **Lehman** Foundation **[25]**
Henry **Lemoine** et Cie **[21]**
Alfred **Lengnick** & Co. Ltd. **[22,** *see also*
William Elkin**]**
Lerolle [25]
Paris, France
Editorial **Letras Cubanas**
Calle G, No. 505
El Vedado
Ciudad de la Habana, Cuba
F. E. C. **Leuckart [25]**
Lewis Music Publishing Co. **[24]**

Library of Congress
Music Division
101 Independence Avenue SE
Washington, DC 20003
Tel: (202) 707-5000
Lingua Press
P.O. Box 1192
La Jolla, CA 92038
Collection **Litolff [20]**
Longman
1560 Broadway
New York, NY 10036
Harald **Lyche** & Co. **[25]**
Maestro (*see* Hansen House)
Pierre **Mardaga** Editeur, S.A.
Hayen, 11
B-4140 Sprimont, Belgium
Tel: (32) 4 368 42 42
Fax: (32) 4 368 42 40
Margun/Gunmar Music, Inc.
167 Dudley Road
Newton Center, MA 02459
E-mail: margunmu@aol.com
Tel: (617) 332-6398
Fax: (617) 969-1079
E. B. **Marks [15]**
Masters Music Publications
P.O. Box 810157
Boca Raton, FL 33481-0157
Tel: (561) 241-6169
Fax: (561) 241-6347
Website: www.masters-music.com
E-mail: mastersmus@aol.com
MCA Music Publishing (*see* Universal
Music Publishing Group)
McAfee Music Corp. **[24]**
McGinnis & Marx
236 West 26th Street, #11S
New York, NY 10001-6736
Tel: (212) 675-1630
Fax: (212) 675-1630
Mercury Music Corp. **[21]**
Merion Music, Inc. **[21]**
Mersburger (Germany) **[25]**
Metropolis Editions **[25]**
Ediciones **Mexicanas** de Música **[21]**
Mills Music **[24]**
Minkoff Musique et Musicologie/Éditions Minkoff

8, rue Eynard
CH-1211 Geneva 12, Switzerland
Website: www.minkoff-editions.com
E-mail: minkoff@minkoff-editions.com
Tel: (41) (022) 310 46 60
Fax: (41) (022) 310 28 57
Represented in the U.S. by OMI (*see*
OMI)
Mira Music Associates
199 Mountain Road
Wilton, CT 06897-1526
Tel: 302-762-5186
Mitteldeutscher Verlag **[25]**
MJQ Music Inc.
1697 Broadway, Suite 503
New York, NY 10019
Tel: (212) 582-6667
Fax: (212) 582-0627
Mobart Music Publications (*see* Boelke-Bomart)
Hermann **Moeck** Verlag **[24]**
Editio **Moravia [25]**
Moravian Music Foundation Press
c/o Assoc. University Presses
440 Forsgate Drive
Cranbury, NJ 08512
Tel: (609) 655-4770
Edwin H. **Morris**
39 West 54th Street
New York, NY 10019
Möseler Verlag **[25]**
Willy **Müller [25]**
Murdoch & Murdoch (London) **[25]**
Music Graphics Press
121 Washington Street
San Diego, CA 92103-2002
Tel: (619) 298-3629
Music Press [21]
Music Treasure Publications
620 Fort Washington Avenue, #1F
New York, NY 10040-3930
Musica Islandica
Iceland Music Information Centre
Sidumuli 34
108 Reykjavik, Iceland
Website: www.mic.is
E-mail: itm.mic.is
Tel: 354 568 3122
Fax: 354 568 3124

Editorial **Musica Moderna [25]**
Musica Obscura Editions
    17 Joey Road
    Merrimack, NH 03054-4549
    E-mail: musobscu@ultranet.com
    Tel: (603) 881-7210
    Fax: (603) 595-8382
Musica Rara [25]
Musical Scope Publishers **[25]**
Editions **Musikk-Huset [25]**
Musikwissenschaftlichen [20]
Editura **Muzicala**
    Calea Victoriei nr. 141
    71102 Bucharest, Romania
    E-mail: editura__muzicala@hotmail.com
    Tel/Fax: 40 1 312 98 67
Nagel's Musik-Archive **[25]**
Arthur **Napoleão [25]**
    Rio de Janeiro, Brazil
New Music Edition [21]
New Music West
    1437 Crest Drive
    Altadena, CA 91001
    Tel: (626) 794-1684
New World Music Corp. **[24]**
Pierre **Noël [25]**
    Paris, France
Otto Heinruch **Noetzel** Verlag **[25]**
Nordiska Musikförlaget [22]
Norruth Music **[17]**
Norsk Musikforläg [17]
Norton Critical Scores
    W. W. Norton Co.
    500 Fifth Avenue
    New York, NY 10110
    Website: www.wwnorton.com
    E-mail: ftp@wwnorton.com
    Tel: 1-800-233-4830 (orders & customer service)
    Tel: (212) 354-5500
    Fax: (212) 869-0856
Novello [21]
Oertel Verlag **[25]**
Oesterreichischer Bundesverlag [25]
Éditions de l'**Oiseau-Lyre [16]**
    Les Remparts, Monaco
OMI (Old Manuscripts and Incunabula)
    P.O. Box 6019 FDR Station
    New York, NY 10150

    E-mail: immels@panix.com
    Tel: (212) 758-1946
    Fax: (212) 593-6186
Ongaku-no-tomo-sha [21]
Les Éditions **Ouvrières [25]**
Pan American Union [25]
Panton [25]
Papagrigoriou-Nakas (Musical Publications Ch. Nakas—C. Papagrigoriou Co.)
    39 Panepistimiou Street
    105 64 Athens, Greece
    Tel: (30) (1) 3221786
    Tel: (30) (1) 3251144
    Fax: (30) (1) 3222742
Paragon Music Publishers
    c/o Benson Music Group
    365 Great Circle Road
    Nashville, TN 37228
    Fax: (615) 742-6911
Parnaso
    Rua N.S. Fatima, 231
    Porto, Portugal
W. **Paxton** & Co., Ltd. **[25]**
Peer International has become part of Peermusic Classical (810 Seventh Avenue, New York, NY 10019), whose publications are distributed by Theodore Presser. **[21]**
Pennsylvania State Music Series
    Publication of this series was discontinued in the 1970s; no longer available from the publisher.
Permanent Press, Music of Quality
    7508 42nd Avenue, NE
    Seattle, WA 98115
    Tel: (206) 525-6596
Philharmusica Edition [25]
Philippo Editions (France) **[25]**
Pioneer Editions (*see* American Composers Alliance)
Piwarski Verlag **[25]**
    Cracow, Poland
Plymouth Music Co., Inc.
    170 NE 33rd Street
    Fort Lauderdale, FL 33334
    Tel: (305) 563-1844
    Fax: (305) 563-9006
Polish Music Publications [15]
Polskie Wydawnictwo Muzyczne [15, 21]

al. Krasinskiego 11a
31-111 Krakow, Poland
Tel/Fax: (48) (012) 422-71-71
E-mail: pewuem@polbox.com
Poon Hill Press **[19, 12]**
Price Milburn
    Wellington, New Zealand **[25]**
Printed Editions
    P.O. Box 27
    Barrytown, NY 12507
Providence Music Press
    P.O. Box 2362
    East Side Station
    Providence, RI 02906
Keith **Prowse [25]**
D. **Rahter [21]**
Basil **Ramsey**, Publisher of Music, Ltd.
    [5, 15]
    604 Rayleigh Road
    Eastwood, Leigh-on-Sea
    Essex 559
    5HU England
    Tel: (44) (1702) 524305
Redcliffe Edition
    68 Barrowgate Road
    London W4 4HD, England
    Website: www.musicweb.force9.co.uk/
    Redcliffe/index.htm
    Tel: (44) (181) 9951223
Remick Music Corp **[24]**
Reuter & Reuter Forlags **[25]**
G. **Ricordi** & Co. (International) **[3]**
Ricordi Americana (*see* ALMA, Inc., and
    G. Ricordi & Co.)
Ricordi BA (Argentina) **[3]**
Ricordi BR (Brazil) (*see* ALMA,
    Inc.) **[3]**
Ries & Erler (Germany) **[3]**
Robbins Music (*see* Big 3 Music Corp.)
Roberton Publications **[21]**
Winthrop **Rogers** Edition **[3]**
Rongwen Music, Inc. **[5]**
E. **Rouart, Lerolle & Co.** (*see* Salabert)
Rozsavölgi [25]
Editions **Salabert [22]**
San Andreas Press
    3732 Laguna Avenue
    Palo Alto, CA 94306

Sassetti & Cia.
    R. Nova do Almada, 60
    Lisbon 2, Portugal
Richard **Schauer [21]**
Schaum Publications, Inc.
    10235 North Port Washington Road
    Mequon, WI 53092
    Website: www.schaumpiano.com
    Tel: 1-800-786-5023
    Tel: (414) 241-5013
    Fax: (414) 241-1063
Schlesinger Schemusikhandlung **[25]**
Arthur P. **Schmidt** Co. **[24]**
Schott [8; also dist. by Belmont**]**
Schott Frères **[24]**
Schroeder & Gunther [15]
Schultheiss Musikverlag, C.L. **[25]**
    Stuttgart, Germany
Schwann Musikverlag **[20]**
Charles **Scribner**'s Sons **[25]**
Seda Productions (*see* Seda Publications)
Seda Publications
    45 Common Street
    Belmont, MA 02478-3022
    E-mail: grdianne@aol.com
    Tel: (617) 489-1848
    Fax: (617) 489-6474
Maurice **Senart** (*see* Salabert)
Servico de Documentacao Musical da
    Ordem dos Musicos do Brasil
    Av. Almte. Barroso, 72-7 Andar
    Rio de Janeiro (RJ), Brazil
Sikesdi Press
    1102 Bellevue Avenue SE
    Calgary, Alberta T2G 4LI, Canada
    Website: www.cadvision.com/
    home__pages/accounts/liszt/
    SikesdiPressWebpage.html
    E-mail: rumsong@cadvision.com
    Fax: (403) 262-1201
Hans **Sikorski [22,** *see also* William Elkin**]**
    Johnsallee 23
    D-20148 Hamburg, Germany
    Tel: (040) 41 41 00-0
    Fax: (040) 41 41 00-40
N. **Simrock [21]**
Sisra Publications (*see* Arsis Press)
Skandinavisk Musikförlag **[25]**

Skandinavisk og Borups Musikförlag [25]
Smith Publications/Sonic Art Editions
  2617 Gwynndale Avenue
  Baltimore, MD 21207
  Tel: (410) 298-6509
  Fax: (410) 944-5113
Société des Nouvelles Editions
  Liègeoises (see Mardaga)
Société Française de Musicologie (see
  Minkoff)
Société Liègeoise de Musicologie [25]
  Werbomont, Belgium
Sonos Music Resources [1]
Soundings Press
  948 Canyon Road
  Sante Fe, NM 87501
Southern Baptist Theological Seminary
  School of Church Music and Worship
  2825 Lexington Road
  Louisville, KY 40280-1812
  Website: www.sbts.edu
  E-mail: chmusic@sbts.edu
  Tel: 1-800-626-5525, ext. 4115
  Tel: (502) 897-4115
Southern Music Publishing
  Southern Music Publishing has be-
  come part of Peermusic Classical,
  whose publications are distributed by
  Theodore Presser Co. [21]
Soviet Composer (Sovetskii Kompozitor)
  c/o Collet's Holdings Ltd.
  Denington Estate
  Wellingborough, Northants
  NN8 2QT England
  Tel: (1933) 224351
  Fax: (1933) 276402
Sowerby Foundation [21]
Stainer & Bell [7]
Stat hudbeni vydavateiski (see Supraphon)
Steingräber Verlag [25]
Stockhausen Verlag [25]
Thomas C. Stangland Co.
  Music Publishers
  P.O. Box 19263
  Portland, OR 97280-0263
  E-mail: tcstangland@yahoo.com
  Tel: (503) 244-0634
  Fax: (503) 244-8442

Studio P/R [24]
Subito Music Publishing [21]
Süddeutscher Musikverlag [25]
Summy-Birchard [24]
Supraphon [25]
Edizioni Suvini Zerboni
  Galleria del Corso, 4
  I-20122 Milano, Italy
  Fax: (39) 0277 07 02 61
  Fax: (39) 030 22 20 67 (mail order)
Swan & Co. (England) [25]
Templeton Publishing Co. [23]
Tempo Praha/Bote & Bock [21]
Tenuto Publications [21]
Tetra Music Corp. (see Plymouth Mu-
  sic Co.)
Thames Music Publishing Co. [21]
Gordon V. Thompson [25]
Thorpe Music Publishing Co. [21]
Tonos Verlag (see Seesaw Music Corp.)
To-oN Kikau Co.
  1-15-1 Sugamo
  Toshima-ku
  Tokyo, Japan 170
  Tel: (81) (3) 39441581
  Fax: (81) (3) 39442130
Transcontinental Music Publica-
  tions/New Jewish Music Press
  633 Third Avenue
  New York, NY 10017-6778
  Website: www.uahc.org/transmp/
  E-mail: tmp@uahc.org
  Tel: 1-800-455-5223
  Tel: (212) 650-4101
Editorial Tritone [25]
  Lima, Peru
Two-Eighteen Press
  Box 218, Village Station
  New York, NY 10014
Unión Musical Española [22]
United Music Publishers [21]
Universal Edition [24, also dist. by
  Belmont]
Universal Music Publishing Group
  2440 Sepulveda Boulevard, Suite 100
  Los Angeles, CA 90064-1712
  Website: www.mcamusicpublishing.com
  Tel: (310) 235-4700

Fax: (310) 235-4905
(*See* Hal Leonard Corporation for retail distribution, permission to arrange or copy in the U.S.)
University of California Press
2120 Berkeley Way
Berkeley, CA 94720
Website: www.ucpress.edu
E-mail: ucpress@ucpress.ucap.edu
Tel: 1-800-642-4247
Tel: (510) 642-4247
University of Washington Press
P.O. Box 50096
Seattle, Washington 98145
Website: www.washington.edu/upress
E-mail: wwpord@uwashington.edu
Tel: 1-800-441-4115
Tel: (206) 543-4050
Fax: 1-800-441-4115
University Press of Virginia
Box 3608 University Station
Charlottesville, VA 22903
Website: www.upressvirginia.edu
E-mail: upressvirginiada@virginia.edu
Tel: (804) 924-3468
Fax: (804) 982-2655
University Society Publishers
145 N. Franklin Turnpike
Ramsey, NJ 07446-1634
Tel: (201) 327-2337
Urbanek (*see* Artia)
Valley Music Press **[25]**
Northampton, MA
Van Rossum (Netherlands) **[25]**
Vereniging voor Nederlandse Muziekgeschiedenis (Dutch Society for Musicology)
Verlag für Musikalische Kultur und Wissenschaft
Wolfenbüttel, Germany
Vienna Urtext Editions **[24]**
Musikverlag C. F. **Vieweg [25]**
Viking Musikförlag
Lille Strandvej 3
2900 Hellerup
Copenhagen, Denmark
Tel: (31) 62 12 10
Editores **Vitale**
Music Imports

2571 North Oakland Avenue
Milwaukee, WI 53211
Vivace Press
P.O. Box 157
Readfield, WI 54964
Website: www.vivacepress.com
Email: yordy@vivacepress.com
Tel: 1-800-543-5429
Fax: (920) 667-5237
Arno **Volk** Verlag (*see* Universal Music Publishing Group)
Walton Music Corp. (*see* Plymouth Music; *see also* William Elkin)
Waterloo Music Co. **[4]**
Carlo **Wehrs**
Ac/de Eulenstein Musica S.A.
Rua Rute Ferreira, 258
(ZC-22-Ramos)
20000 Rio de Janeiro
RJ, Brazil
Josef **Weinberger**, Ltd. **[3,** *see also* William Elkin**]**
Weintraub Music Co. **[22]**
Westerlund [25]
Western International Music
2859 Holt Avenue
Los Angeles, CA 90034
Western Music, Ltd. (Canada) **[25]**
Joseph **Williams** Editions (England) **[25]**
Willis Music Co.
P.O. Box 548
Florence, KY 41022-0548
Website: www.willismusic.com
E-mail: orderdpt@willis-music.com
Tel: 1-800-354-9799
Tel: (606) 283-2050
Fax: (606) 283-1784
Wimbledon Music, Inc.
Trigram Music Inc./Wimbledon Music Inc.
1888 Century Park East, #1900
Century City (Los Angeles), CA 90067-1702
Website: www.wimbtri.com
Tel: (310) 284-6890
Witmark & Sons [25]
Walter **Wollenweber** Verlag **[25]**
Yorktown Music Press **[2]**
Casa Musicale G. **Zanibon**

Via Salomone, 77
20138 Milan, Italy
Tel: (39) (02) 88811
Fax: (39) (02) 5082280
Zen-on Music Co., Ltd. **[17]**
Zenmükiado Vallalat (Editio Musica
  Budapest EMB) **[3]**
Éditions du **Zephyr [25]**
  Brussels, Belgium

Edizioni Suvini **Zerboni**
  Via Quintiliano, 40
  I-20138 Milan, Italy
  (*see also* William Elkin)
Wilhelm **Zimmermann** Musikverlag (*see*
  William Elkin)
Editions Aug. **Zurfluh [21]**

Part I

Individual Composers
Their Solo Piano Works
in Various Editions
and Facsimile Reproductions

A

Marcello Abbado (1926–   ) Italy

Abbado studied at the Milan Conservatory with Ghedini and has served as principal conductor and music director of the London Symphony orchestra. He is the brother of the conductor Claudio Abbado.

Variations on a Minuet by J. S. Bach (BWV Anh. 121) 1951 (Zerboni 1953) 15pp., 12½ min. Var. I: two voices, chromatic, contrary motion between the hands. Var. II: Con decisione, rhythmic, chromatic. Var. III: Lento, full arpeggiated chords plus right-hand trills and tremolando, wide keyboard range. Var. IV: Scorrevole, veiled and subdued, melody transferred between the hands. Var. V: Allegro, hammered repeated chords, large span required, chords move over wide range of keyboard. Var. VI: Molto allegro, widely spaced two-note chords skipping over keyboard. Minuetto: Largamente, pointillistic, final eight measures suggest rising line of Bach minuet, build to large climax. M-D to D.

Louis Abbiate (1866–1933) France

Trois Pièces 1918 (Jobert 1980) 13pp. 1. Prélude; 2. Romance; 3. Diabolique. Post-Romantic style, with No. 3 showing some Prokofiev influence. Large span required. M-D.

Sonata IV Op.48 1925 (Jobert 1981) 31pp. Allegretto con moto un poco barcarola: SA, many triadic figures. Cavatina: melodic writing suggests Chopin. Vivace: triadic use in a typically French toccata style. The roots of this work stretch back to Beethoven, with a mixture of the "heroics" of Romantic composers and the less-extroverted style of the Impressionists. Conservative but effective writing. Worth investigating. M-D.

Jean Absil (1893–1974) Belgium

Many of Absil's earlier works were written in a conventional idiom, but in his later years Absil turned to a more-personal, austere style. Unconventional rhythmic procedure was the norm in his writing. See anthologies of Belgian composers for other works.

Echecs: Suite Op.96 1956 (CeBeDeM) 16 min. 1. Le roi; 2. La reine; 3. Le fou; 4. La tour; 5. Les pions; 6. Les cavaliers: effective toccata. Much variety and contrast. M-D.

Passacaille Op.101 1959 (CeBeDeM) 10pp. In memoriam Alban Berg. Required piece for the 1960 Queen Elisabeth Competition. Chromatic theme and 20 variations treated in various ways. A few variations are relieved by short episodes. A calm and expressive mood is characteristic of the four middle vatiations, while a brilliant coda concludes the work. D.

Six Bulgarian Dances Op.102 (Lemoine). Dances in ternary or variation form. Bartók influence. Driving rhythms, unusual dissonances over stable tonalities, whimsical. See especially No.6. Int.

Sonatine Op.125 1966 (Metropolis) 7pp. Allegro moderato: fresh harmonies, clever rhythms. Pavane: imitative with mildly dissonant chords. Tarentelle: 6/8, dancelike, fleeting, attractive. Int.

Pastourelle 1958 (Lemoine) 2pp. Accompanied melody, MC. Int.

Motohiko Adachi (1940–   ) Japan

Per Pianoforte (Zen-On 412 1978) 27pp. Accordo: Ostinato; Monodia. Complex rhythms, highly organized, clusters, aleatoric, avant-garde. D.

George Adams (1904–1959) USA

Sonata b 1959 (CFP 6232) 14 min. A three-movement (FSF) work written by a versatile hand. Tonal, dramatic, full sonorities. M-D.

John Adams (1947–   ) USA

Adams writes in an elegant minimalist style influenced by the popular vernacular and European mainstream art.

China Gates 1977 (AMP 7859-21983) 11pp. In collection *American Contemporary Masters* (GS 1995). Evolving patterns that should be soft and resonant throughout, never exceeding an *mf.* Both hands should be equalized so that no line is ever louder than another. Pedals should be held throughout each passage until the next gate (change of mode) occurs, minimalistic music. M-D to D.

Phrygian Gates 1977–78 (AMP 7860-2 1983) 61pp. Gradually evolving patterns; special attention should be given to equalizing the volume of both hands so that no single pattern ever dominates another. Minimalistic music. M-D to D.

Samuel Adler (1928–   ) USA, born Germany

Adler's works display enormous rhythmic vitality.

Canto VIII 1973 (CF) 5 min. String effects inside piano, harmonics. Quiet introduction is exploded by torrents of octaves, clusters, stopped notes—all make this a fun avant-garde concert etude. D.

See: David Burge, "Five New Pieces," CK, 3 (December 1977):66.

Capriccio 1954 in collection *New Music for the Piano* (LG). Flexible meters and tonal centers, cross-relations, polymodality. Makes a fine one-minute encore. Int. to M-D.

Gradus: Forty Studies 1971 (OUP). Books I and II. Twenty studies in each volume that explore contemporary techniques. Volume II is more difficult than I. Notes explain each study. Int. to M-D.

Gradus III (OUP 1981). Twenty pieces illustrating twentieth-century techniques including clusters, string strumming, harmonics, 12-tone pieces. Excellent etudes. M-D.

The Sense of Touch (TP 1983) 11pp., 12 min. Eight short pieces that introduce the young pianist to twentieth-century idioms. Int.

Sonata Brève 1963 (OUP) 11 min. Allegro grazios: Adagio con delicatezza; Allegro di bravura. Contrapuntal, freely tonal. Large span required; needs mature pianism. M-D.

The Song Expands My Spirit (TP 1983) 7pp., 4 min. Slow lyric introduction leads to main part of piece, which is energetic and introduces two new tunes. Enthusiastic ending. Short, colorful, brilliant. M-D.

Triptych for Dancing 1958 (AMC). Changing meters, colorful, three-sectioned, polytonal. Large span required. M-D.

Sonatina 1979 (GS E-3468) 20pp. Fast and brilliant: a broad-gestured introduction leads to section "even a bit faster"; varied textures, including tremolo clusters; broad-gestured coda. Slow and very gently moving: melodic, section "like a chant, very freely moving 8ths," octotonic faster section, slow-moving coda. Very fast (perpetual motion): perform as fast as possible, "make certain the 8th-notes are not all equal," carefully pedaled, brilliant, all over keyboard, coda "Fast, but heavily." D.

The Road to Terpsichore. 1989 (GS 3774) 24pp., 12½ min. A suite of dances. 1. Fast and Wild. 2. Free, quite relaxed, but stately. 3. Like a waltz. 4. Like a Tango, with verve, and very rhythmic. 5. Like a Tarantella, fast and furious. Strong rhythms, fairly thin textures, contrasting, MC. M-D.

See: Bradford Gowen, "Samuel Adler's Piano Music," AMT, 25 (January 1976): 6–8.

Denes Agay (1911–   ) USA, born Hungary

Agay's style is conservatively modern, freely tonal, and full of harmonic surprises. Agay knows how to write for the instrument; not one gesture seems contrived or dictated by formula.

Concertino Barocco (GS 1975) 15pp. Based on themes of Handel. Three contrasting movements, delightful. Int.

15 Little Pieces on Five-Note Patterns (BMC 1973). Great variety of five-finger positions. Easy to Int.

Four Dance Impressions (TP 1977) 6½ min. Night Music; Vibrations; Ballad without Words; Hommage à Joplin. Chromatic, strong rhythms, MC, sophisticated. Int. to M-D.

The Joy of the Music of Denes Agay (Yorktown 1980) 64pp. Twenty-four pieces from early published works to new compositions that illustrate Agay's attractive style and the great variety of his creative approaches, including distillations of popular idioms dating from the 1940s. Easy to Int.

Mosaics 1968 (MCA) (Six Piano Pieces on Hebrew Folk Themes) 21pp., 12½ min. Five short pieces followed by a set of eleven variations over an eight-bar melody that progresses to a brilliant but not too demanding climax. Beautifully laid out for the piano. M-D.

Petit Trianon Suite (GS). Ten tuneful short pieces in classic dance forms. M; S; Contredanse; Musette; etc. Easy.

Serenata Burlesca 1968 (Bo&H) 7pp., 2½ min. Cross-rhythms, chromatic lines, brilliant closing. Int.

Sonatina Hungarica (MCA 1967) 19pp., 9½ min. Scena; Serenata; Rondo. Changing meters, quartal harmony, cadenza passages, well put together, attractive. Int.

Two Improvisations on Hungarian Folk Songs (TP 1973) 7pp., 4 min. The Peacock. Gipsy Tune: modal, more fetching of the two, attractive. Int.

4 Popular Diversions (TP 1984) 12pp. Little Prelude in Waltz Time. Baroque Bounce. Echoes of the Blues. Ragtime Doll. Clever, contrasting, colorful. Int.

Teresa Agnesi (1720–1795) Italy
Agnesi was best known as an opera composer in European courts.

Two pieces for Solo Piano or Harpsichord (Harbach—Vivace) 12pp. Contains a *Sonata in G* and *Allegro ou Presto*: hand crossings and arpeggios, Scarlatti-like. M-D.

Roy Agnew (1891–1944) Australia
Agnew was the most outstanding of the early-twentieth-century Australian composers. His music is written in a unique style strongly influenced by Romantic-Impressionistic tendencies.

Piano Works Vol. I (Keys Press 1997) 21pp. Australian Forest Pictures: six colorful character pieces. Youthful Fancies: four pedagogical pieces, attractive. Int.

The Six Sonatas for Piano (Larry Sitsky—Keys Press 1997) 127pp. Introduction by Rita Crews. Symphonic Poème; Fantasie Sonata; Sonata (1929); Sonata Poem; Sonata Ballade; Sonata Legend (Capricornia).

See: Rita Crews, "An Analytical Study of the Piano Works of Roy Agnew, Margaret Sutherland and Dulcie Holland, including Biographical Material," diss., University of New England, Armidale, 1994.

Guido Agosti (1901–1989) Italy
Agosti wrote in a mildly contemporary style strongly influenced by Ravel. He was an outstanding pianist and teacher. Zubin Mehta and Carlo Maria Giulini studied with Agosti.

Cinque Bagatelle Op.5 1941 (SZ). 10pp. Scorrevole. Lento. Presto. Marcia Funebre per Bobolino. Allegro vivace. Grateful tonal writing, Impressionistic, varied moods. M-D.

Prelude and Toccata Op.7 1942 (SZ). Slow, expressive Prelude e, *pp* closing leads to short, brilliant Toccata E, somewhat in Ravel's style. D.

Johan Agrell (1701–1765) Sweden

Sonata B♭ Op. 2/1, *Sonata* D Op.2/5 (Autographus Musicus 1976) 20pp. Facsimile of a 1748 edition. Op.2/1: Largo; Allegro; Larghetto; Presto; Aria Andante; Menuetto I, II. Traditional eighteenth-century style, melodic, written in various clefs. Op.2/5: Adagio; Presto assai; Allegro; Aria; Tempo di Menuetto. Both works show strong Germanic influence. M-D.

Miguel del Aguila (1957–   ) USA, born Uruguay
Aguila moved to the U.S. in 1978 and received a BA degree from the San Francisco Conservatory. He spent the next ten years in Vienna, active as a composer. He now lives in southern California.

Conga 1993 (PIC 1995) 17pp. Began as the last movement of an Organ Fantasy. Changing meters, minimalistic, glissandos, motoric rhythms. Repeat the final figuration many times. M-D to D.

Julián Aguirre (1868–1924) Argentina
Aguirre taught at the Buenos Aires Conservatory for a number of years. Some of his piano works are based on Argentine idioms, while others show Spanish and French influences.

Aires Criollos (Ric 1953) 7pp. Three short contrasting pieces using traditional Latin-American tunes, rhythms, and harmonies. Int.

2 Books of Argentine National Airs (Ric). Book I: Op. 17, 5 Tristes. Book II: Op. 36, 5 Cançiones. No. 5 has text and melody. Unusual rhythms and haunting melodies. M-D.

Huella Op.49 (Ric). Tricky but effective rhythms. M-D.

Gato (Ric). Very rhythmic Argentine dance. Int.

Kalevi Aho (1949–   ) Finland
Sonata 1980 (Fazer) 15 min. First movement: kaleidoscopic, highly chromatic lines spin out eruptively and forcefully. Second movement: a nine-page perpetual-motion idea; climax of rising and falling passages is breathtaking. Finale: more than twice as long as the first two movements together; begins languidly with brief configurations reminiscent of the Barber piano sonata; eventually tremolo activity builds to a climax before the sonata ends reflectively with gentler, more melancholy trilling. There is much anxiety here—true *angst* at times. Inspired by late Scriabin style, with large leaps, cluster glissandos, hand crossings. Moves constantly over entire range of keyboard; intense feverish writing. D.

Hugh Aitken (1924–   ) USA
Piano Fantasy (OUP 1969) 20pp. 15 min. Complex, with contrasting expressive qualities. Large-scale work in two movements demanding virtuosity and mature musicianship. D.

Three Connected Pieces for Piano (OUP 1968) 4pp. Thirds. Melody: uses ostinato figures. Fifths: displays attractive contrasting writing. Changing meters, chromatic studies. M-D.

Jéhan Alain (1911–1940) France
Alain's style is characterized by rhythmic and metric flexibility and colorful, highly individualized writing. Rhythm and melody are emphasized. The music

contains great variety, ranging in difficulty from the two-line *Choral* in *Mythologies Japonaises* to the *Etude on a Four-Note-Theme* and the driving rhythms of *Taras Boulba*. The easiest works are: *Suites faciles* I-II, *Nocturne, Romance Etude de Sonorité*.

Works for Piano (Leduc). Vol. I: Chorale; Etude de sonorité; Un cercle d'argent souple; Heureusement la bonne fée; Mythologies japonaises; Romance; Nocturne; Suite facile I; Suite facile II. Vol. II: Thème varié; Ecce ancilla Domini; Etude; Togo; Lumière qui tombe d'un vasistas; Historie d'un homme; Prélude; Il pleura toute la journée. Vol. III: Etude sur un thème de 4 notes; Petite rapsodie; Dans le rêve laissé par . . . ; Taras Boulba.

Seize Pièces (Leduc 1992) 19pp.

Isaac Albéniz (1860–1909) Spain
Albéniz, a prolific composer for the piano, was one of Spain's finest pianists. His works are a composite of Lisztian pianistic techniques and the idioms and rhythms of Spanish popular music. He wrote about 250 pieces for his instrument, mostly in small form.

Alhambra Suite No. 1 1897 (ESC). La Vega (UME; K). This fairly lengthy movement is set in Granada. Colorful native rhythms and melodies. The suite contains only this movement. It was left unfinished. M-D.

Azulejos ("Mosaics" or "Tiles") 1909 (UME). 1. Prelude: this work was finished by Granados. This is the only piece in this intended set of short pieces. M-D.

A Book of Waltzes (K). Four waltzes from Op.25 to Op.170. L'Automne. Champagne. Cotillon. Six Little Waltzes. M-D.

Cantos de España (Songs of Spain) Op.232 ca. 1896. (K9218; UME; Onagaku-No-Toma-Sha). Prelude: this is the same piece as Asturias in *Suite española* Op.47/5. Imitates the guitar's flowing right-hand tremolo technique. Midsection suggests improvisation while the outer sections are full of the dramatic tension found in flamenco dance. Orientale: uses subtle chromatic elements in imitation of Eastern influences found in Spanish music. Sous le palmier (Under the Palms): a suave and pleasant tango. Córdoba: This haunting nocturne is a colorful picture of that famous Andalusian city. Sharp chords, as if plucked from the strings of a guitar, preface an oriental-type melody, which suggests the Moorish background of the city. Albéniz wrote at the beginning of this piece: "In the silence of night, interrupted by whispering breezes full of jasmine scent, the *guzlas* [a one-string instrument] intone as they accompany serenades, sending flowing melodies through the air, tones as sweet as the sound of swaying palms high overhead." Spanish dance rhythms, colorful imagination. M-D. Seguidillas: a brilliant stylish dance, one of Spain's oldest dance forms for couples, mentioned by Cervantes around 1600. Full of melodious joy and fascinating rhythms.

Collected Works Vol. I (K 09478) 60pp. *Navarra*. Op. post. *Mallorca* (Barcarola) Op.202: languid and flowing. *Sérénade Espagnole* Op.181. *Triana* from *Iberia*. *Zambra Granadina*: an oriental dance. *Serenata Arabe*. *Asturies*: short. M-D to D.

Collected Works Vol. II (K 09479) 62pp. *Barcarolle Catalane* Op.23. *Sérénade Espagnole* Op.181: this piece is the same as *Suite española*, Op.47/4 *Cadiz-Gaditana*: very similar to *Rumoreres de la caleta: Malagueña* Op.71. *Troisième Suite Ancienne*: Minuetto, Gavotta. *Rapsodia Cubana* Op.66 (the same opus number used for *6 Mazurkas de salón*). *Estudio Impromptu* Op.56. *Torre Bermeja* Op.92/12, from *Piezas Características*. This edition omits some repeat signs, as well as a whole section at the end. Print not always clear. M-D.

Suite Espagnole Op.47 (IMC; Schott 5068; Ongaku-No-Tomo-Sha). Pieces date from various years in the 1880s and 1890s. This suite, with the exception of No. 8, Cuba, is an affectionate representation of Spanish towns and regions. 1. Granada: Serenata: opening suggests guitar strumming with repeated rolled chords over a left-hand lyrical syncopated melody. This melody is shifted to the right hand and moves over some unusual harmonic modulations before ending with the opening material. 2. Cataluña: Curranda: a musical portrait of Albeniz's birthplace; majestic 6/8 rhythm supports a chromatic harmony and tender melodies. 3. Sevilla: Sevillanas: passionate piece with incisive rhythm suggesting the clicking of castanets as a background accompaniment; full of flamenco excitement. 4. Cadiz: Canción: in the style of a *saeta*, a song sung to a statue of the Virgin Mary held aloft in procession. A gentle lullaby supported by Spanish dance rhythms. 5. Asturias: Leyenda: strong guitar influence, hands work closely together, large skips, octotonic writing in mid-section, *ppp* closing. 6. Aragón: Fantasy: Introduction moves through three keys. The mid-section, Copla (a designation of stanzas of early Spanish and Italian song forms) provides some of Albeniz's most languid writing; *fff* closing. 7. Castillas: Seguidillas: Full of melodious joy and intriguing rhythms, octatonic (same as *Cantos de España* Op.232/5 Seguidillas). 8. Cuba: Capricho: suggests travel impressions from Albeniz's days as a touring virtuoso pianist; a slow and dreamy rumba. The suite contains some of Albeniz's most colorful writing. M-D.

Gavotte from Suite ancienne III 1886 (UME). A minuet with a bagpipe tune. Melodious; played over a drone pedal D. Int. to M-D.

Torre Bermeja: Serenata Op.92/12 (UME; K9218; Ongaku-No-Toma-Sha; Sal; Ashley; IMC). Strong guitar influence, passionate and exciting mood. The opening uses the two hands in close proximity to produce a striking rhythmic effect. M-D.

Cadiz-Gaditana 1886–90? (Ashley; K). Strong influence of Spanish folk music, a picture of the spirited citizens of Cadiz. Strong guitar-like strumming in opening chords, left-hand rhythmic melody; somewhat similar to *Rumores de la celeta, malagueña*. M-D.

Mallorca: Barcarola Op.202 ca. 1891 (UME; Sal; K). Celebrates the sun-drenched island where Chopin composed his *Préludes*. A lively middle part contrasts with the outer, more introspective sections. M-D.

6 Spanish Dances (K 3003) 33pp. All six dances use tango rhythm, making a somewhat monotonous impression. No titles on any of the dances. No. 4 in G is this writer's preference. Int.

Pavana-Capricho Op.12 1883 or earlier (UME 6273) 4pp. ABA, some two-against-three writing, more like a capriccio than a pavana. Int.

Seis pequeños valses (6 Little Waltzes) Op.25 before 1884 (UME; Ashley). Chopin influence, different mood and texture for each waltz, Channing. No. 6, A♭ is this writer's preference; it may have been modeled after Chopin's Waltz in A♭, Op.64/3. Int.

Il mio primo Albeniz (My First Albeniz) (Rattalino—Ric 2738). Pavana Op.83: like a rondo. Waltz A♭ Op.25/6. Curtsey. Waltz E♭ Op.25/2. Preludio Op.165/1. Capriccio catalano Op.165/5.

Serenata española Op.181 ca. 1890 (UME; Sal; K; Ashley). This is the same piece as *Suite española* Op.47/4, "Cadiz."

Zambra granadina: Danse orientale ca. 1890 (UME; K; Ashley). Many triplets followed by duplets, cross relations. M-D.

Deseo Op.40 ca. 1883–86. Estudio de concerte (K9480). Bold octaves, large chords, six pages of triplets, like a perpetual-motion study. Long, ambitious. D.

España Op.165 1890. (Six Album Leaves) (UME; CFP; Schott; IMC; Ongaku-No-Tomo-Sha) Prélude; Tango (Godowsky—CF). This protype of all tango music with its fascinating flamenco-like melody and insistent rhythm is Spanish in all aspects. The Godowsky arrangement is brilliant and complex. Malagueña available separately (Alfred); Serenata; Capricho catalan; Zortizco. M-D.

See: Douglas Riva, "Albeniz's *Malagueña*," KC, 10/4 (July–August 1990): 42–43. A master lesson on Op.165/3.

Fiesta de Aldea Op. posth. (UME 1973) 18pp. Apparently the first part of an unfinished composition intended for orchestra. M-D.

Iberia 1906–9 4 vols. (UME: K; Sal; IMC; EBM Nos. 1–9). Evocation; El Puerto; Fête-Dieu à Seville; Rondeña; Almeria; Triana; El Albaicin; El Polo; Lavapies; Malaga; Jerez; Eritaña. This pianistic marvel is Albéniz's masterpiece. The pieces are evocative of Spanish scenes and landscapes and they blend Liszt with newer and more suggestive elements of the best French music of Albeniz's times. Enormous technical demands. D.

Mallorca: Barcarola Op.202 ca. 1891 (UME: Sal; IMC; K.). Albeniz played this piece in London during the spring of 1891. M-D.

Navarra Op. posth. (EBM; IMC; Sal; UME). A poignant tonal evocation of the Spanish province below the Pyrenees. There are no direct motives of authentic popular themes in this work; rather it uses a special style of singing that is the essence of the region. The jota itself does not appear; instead Albéniz introduces its rhythm by means of a sublime stylization, full of spirit and energy, which freely transcribes the character, if not the music, of Navarra. Because of the complexity and immense wealth, it is difficult to follow the lyric melodic lines at all times. The last 26 bars were completed by Déodat de Sévérac (1872–1921). M-D to D.

12 Piezas Características Op.92 ca. 1888. (UME). Gavotte; Minuetto à Sylvia; Barcarolle; Prière; Conchita: Polka; Pilar: Waltz; Zambra; Pavana; Polonesa; Majurka; Staccato: Caprice; Torre Bermeja: Serenade. Published separately. M-D. Nos.3 and 12 (UME; K; Ashley) published separately.

Recuerdos de Viaje Op.71 ca. 1886. (Travel Impressions) (IMC; UME). En el mar (On the sea): melodic detail is tossed between the hands. Leyenda: languid. Alborada (Dawn): uses repeated large chords over arpeggio figures and a melody in the bass. En la Alhambra (In the Alhambra): insistent rhythm. Puerto de (Port of) Tierra (refers to Cadiz, a seventeenth-century fortress): a lively bolero. Rumores de la Caleta (Murmurs from the small courtyard): a sensual and emotional courting dance from Malaga (malaguena). The Lento mid-section is improvisational; available separately (BMC). En la Playa (On the beach): requires a cantabile style.

Three Sonatas No.3, Op.68 A♭; No. 4 Op. 72 A; No. 5 Op.82 G♭ (UME) separately. For a thorough discussion of these three works see Newman, SSB, 652–54.

Albeniz Album (A. Héra and J. Sármai—EMB Z. 13826 1993) 47 pp. From *España*, Op.165: Tango, Serenata, Capricho Catalan. From *Cantos de España*, Op.232: Danza Espagnola—Bajo la palma. From *Recuerdos de Viaje* (Travel Impressions) Op.71: Malagueña-Rumores de la caleta, Puerto di Tierra (bolero), En la Alhambre. Mallorca, Op.202. Serenata Arabe. Zambra Granadina: Danza Oriental. A fine introduction to Albeniz's music with some of his finest piano works. Int. to M-D.

Isaac Albeniz Piano Album (Douglas Riva—GS No. 1985). Selections from a Piano Sonata, Cantos de España, Suite Española, Recuerdos de Viaje, and others. M-D.

Selected Works for Piano Solo (Ashley 1979) 195pp. Compiled by Bradford G. Thompson. Contents: Mallorca-Barcarola Op.202. Navarra. Sérénade Espagnole Op.181. Triana. Zambra Granadina: Danse orientale. Arabe (Serenata arabe). Espagne: Souvenirs (No. 2 Asturies). Barcarolle Catalane Op.23. Sérénade Espagnola Op.181 (almost the same piece as on pp. 23–28). Cadiz—Gaditana: very similar to Rumores de la Calcta: Malagueña Op.71. Minuetto: No. 1 from [Troisième] Suite ancienne. Gavotta: No. 2 from [Troisième] Suite ancienne: written to serve as a sight-reading test for the position of assistant professor at the Escuela Nacional de Música, November 1886. Rapsodia Cubana Op.66. Estudio Impromptu Op.56. Torre Bermeja Op.92/12 (revised by John Montés). L'Automne Waltz Op.170/1–3: a three-section waltz with each section in a different key. Champagne Waltz: also called Cotillon Carte blanche and Vals de salón. Cotillian Waltz: very similar to Champagne Waltz. Six Little Waltzes Op.25. Songs of Spain Op.232: Prelude, Orientale, Sous les Palmier, Córdoba, Seguidillas. First works written while Albeniz was living in Paris. Reprint of early editions; mistakes not corrected. Int. to D.

Album of 8 Pieces (BMC). Cadiz; Cuba; Tango; Seguidilla; Curranda; Leyenda; Mazurka; Zortzico. Leyenda available separately (BMC).

Album of Isaac Albeniz Masterpieces (EBM). Cadiz from *Suite Espagnole*. El Puerto from *Iberia Suite*. Evocation from *Iberia Suite*. Fête-Dieu à Seville from *Iberia Suite*. Seguidillas, Op.232/5. Sevilla. Tango. Triana from *Iberia Suite*.

Ten Pieces (Leduc). Aragonaise; L'Automne; Berceuse; Chant d'armour; L'été; Hiver; Menuet; Le Printemps; Scherzino; Tango en la mineur. Nos. 3, 5, 7, 8, 9, 10 available separately. M-D.

See: Pola Baytelman, *Isaac Albeniz. Chronological List and Thematic Catalog of His Piano Works*. Warren, MI: Harmonie Park Press, 1993.

Sydney Grew, "The Music for Pianoforte of Albeniz," *Chesterian*, 6 (November 1924):43–48.

Mateo Albéniz (1706?–1831) Spain
Sonata D (Alfred; Editiorial Musica Moderna) 3pp. Presto, attractive, suggestion of Zapateado dance, fanfare effects. Fine program opener or encore. Int.

Sebastián Albero (1722–1756) Spain
Treinta Sonatas (S. Kastner—UME 1978) 115pp. Edited from a MS in the Biblioteca nazionale Marciana, Venice. Some charming as well as surprising works in this collection, somewhat in style of Soler. Int. to M-D.

Eugen D'Albert (1864–1932) Germany, born Scotland
D'Albert, an outstanding pianist, left a few early works, eminently pianistic and well grounded in a late-nineteenth-century idiom. He is better known for his operas and editions of keyboard works by Bach and Beethoven.
Suite d Op.1 1883 (Bo&Bo). Baroque influence plus nineteenth-century harmony. A, C, S, Gavotte and Musette, and G, A, Gavotte, and Musette (GS). The Musette shimmers over a long D pedal point, and the G is fugal and full of rhythmic vitality.
Sonata f♯ Op.10 1892 (Bo&Bo) 31pp. Brahms influence in all three movements. Cyclic construction. M-D to D.
4 Klavierstücke Op.16 (CFP Nos. 3 and 4). Waltz A♭; Scherzo f♯; Intermezzo B; Ballade b. At least the vivacious Scherzo deserves an occasional hearing; available separately (Musica Obscura). M-D.
5 Bagatelles Op.29 (Bo&Bo). Ballade; Humoresque; Nocturne; Intermezzo; Scherzo. M-D.

Domenico Alberti (ca. 1710–ca. 1740) Italy
Although Alberti probably did not invent the "Alberti Bass," he used it with such prominence that his name has become linked with this technique. He wrote about 36 sonatas.
Sonata G Op.1 No.8. (W. S. Newman—UNC) *Thirteen Keyboard Sonatas of the 18th and 19th Centuries*. From a set of eight sonatas published by Walsh in London. Thin textures, Alberti bass, elaborate ornamentation. Int. to M-D.
Toccata G (Boghen—Ric) *Toccatas by Old Italian Masters*. M-D.
Sonata B♭ (Zecchi, Fazzari—Carisch 1971) 10pp. Preface in Italian. Flowing lines, charming. Int. to M-D.

Johann Georg Albrechtsberger (1736–1809) Germany
Six Fugues, Op.7 (Imre Sulyok—EMB & Litolff 1974) 32pp. For keyboard instrument. Informative preface in English and German deals with sources and editorial procedure. These pieces are good examples of contrapuntal skill using attractive subjects. Printed score contains a few errors. M-D.

William Albright (1944–1998) USA

Albright, an outstanding performer, has presented many organ and piano recitals of contemporary music in the United States and Europe. Popular music and jazz, along with his work in the theater and film, have influenced his music. He teaches at the University of Michigan.

The Dream Rags 1979 (CFP 1995) 25pp., 18 min. Sleepwalker's Shuffle: lazy, full chords, large span required; trio leads to a "Chicken Scratch" Harlem style. The Nightmare Fantasy Rag—A Night on Rag Mountain: based loosely on Mussorgsky's *Night on Bald Mountain*, a kind of Lisztian "Mephisto Waltz rag"; wild, fantastic, involved, cadenza, coda (cruel rock tempo—a rag to end all rags!); longest and most difficult of the three pieces. Morning Reveries—A Slow Drag: highly chromatic, suggests morning recovery from the night of tortured dreams. Intriguing rhythms, colorful harmonies, out-Joplins Joplin. The set is a veritable goulash of excursions and interruptions. D.

Five Chromatic Dances 1976 (CFP 66797) 38pp., 28 min. Procession and Rounds; Masquerade; Fantasy-Mazurka; Hoedown; The Farewell. Albright refers to but does not quote from chromatic styles from the past, using passages from Bach, Chopin, Debussy, and Ellington. Relies strongly on long sections of a homogeneous nature; rhythmic ostinatos; sonorous; easily recognizable formal structures use frequent recapitulation of earlier material. Evokes the grand Romantic spirit of Chopin and Liszt. One of the finest American piano works from the 1970s. M-D to D.

See: David Burge, "William Albright," CK, 3 (March 1977): 52.

———, "Contemporary Piano—Albright's Five Chromatic Dances," CK, 7 (March 1981): 56–57.

Grand Sonata in Rag 1974 (Jobert) 21pp. Scott Joplin's Victory; Ragtime Turtledove; Behemoth Two-Step. Technically and musically demanding (especially the second movement). Each movement can be played alone. A blend of sonata form with rag characteristics. D.

Pianoagogo (Jobert 1965) 8pp., 8 min. Suggestions for performance, spatial notation, dynamic range *ppppp-fff*. Jazz element gradually becomes more important throughout. Pianistic for both hand and instrument. D.

Sweet Sixteenths (EBM 1977) in collection *Ragtime Current*. Interesting irregular left-hand part. M-D.

Three Novelty Rags 1973 (Jobert) 17pp. Written with William Bolcom. Sleight of Hand, or Legerdemain Rag; Burnt Fingers; Brass Knuckles. Clever, tricky, delightful fun for pianist and audience. M-D.

Sphaera 1985 for piano and computer-generated four-channel tape (CFP) 40pp. Tape is available from the publisher. The notation of the tape part is incomplete and serves only as an assistance for coordination of the live piano part. Some piano preparation (mutes, etc.) is necessary. Plucked strings, scrape along strings with stick-end, extended, several sections. D.

The Machine Age 1988 (CFP) 12 min. A set of short piano pieces inspired by contemporary images. The Ever-Blinking Eye; Player-Piano on Broadway; The Computer's Revenge (Scherzo); Blues for Cristofori (Lullabye Pian'e

Forte); Robot Drummers (From Hell); Prayer (after the poetry of Chris-topher Smart as presented in the oratorio *Song to David*). Some unme-tered notation, "let piano lid fall closed, piano strings should resonate," some avant-garde techniques, improvisation required. M-D.

Three Original Rags (CFP 1985) 23pp. 11 min. On the Lamb: moderate Rag Tempo, with enthusiasm and poise. Queen of Sheba: slow drag (with stomp = foot tapping), shy and relaxed. Onion Skin: lively rag tempo, infectious chromaticism. Striking examples of the contemporary rag. M-D.

Raffaele d'Alessandro (1911–1959) Switzerland

3ème Sonatine Op.39 (Henn) 8pp., 7 min. Allegro marcato: dry chords punctuated by chromatic interchange between hands. Lento: chorale-like. Allegretto molto grazioso: an "ironic" minuet. Presto: a rondo with contemporary Al-berti bass, catchy melody, rhythmic, neoclassic, extremely attractive. M-D.

Four Visions Op.49 (Gerig 1973) 8pp. Four short contrasting pieces. No.3 "Som-nambulique" has wide chord spacing. Large span required. M-D.

Fantaisie Op.59 (Bo&Bo 1950) 17pp., 12–13 min. Improvisation: introduction, recitative-like. Marcato: driving rhythmic punctuation. Lirico (Lent). Con brio Toccata: brilliant figuration with exciting close. M-D.

Haim Alexander (1915–   ) Israel

6 Israeli Dances (Israeli Music Publications). Suite of short pieces inspired by Israeli folk material. Could be played as a group or individually. Climactic ending. M-D.

Improvisation on a Persian Song 1974 (IMI 6006) 6pp., 2 min. Lyrical; repeated rhythmic figuration. M-D.

Patterns (IMI 325) 11pp., 6 min. Required piece for the first Arthur Rubinstein International Piano Competition, held in Israel in 1974. Exhibits the req-uisite variations of texture and opportunities for virtuoso display. Strong rhythmic figurations throughout; wide span required. M-D.

Soundfigures (IMI 1968). Twelve cyclic pieces in variation form. A 12-tone row and a cantus firmus form the basis of the work. Profuse use of the melodic interval of a minor second. D.

Josef Alexander (1910–   ) USA

Alexander studied at both Harvard University and the New England Conserva-tory.

12 Bagatelles for Piano (Gen 1967). These thin textured "trifles" demand a well-developed technique. Wide variety of moods with a liberal sprinkling of dissonances. All pieces are tonal. Seconds are exploited in No. 1. Most are no longer than two pages. M-D.

Games Children Play (Gen). Ten short pieces with titles such as Leap Frog; Hide-and-Go-Seek; Follow the Leader. Contemporary sonorities, clever. Int.

Of Chinese New Year (Gen 1980) 16pp. Twelve pieces for solo piano or piano and Chinese toy cymbals or wood blocks. Musical illustrations of the various animals associated with Chinese celebration. Colorful contemporary settings. Int.

Anatoly Alexandrow (1888–1982) Russia
Scriabin influenced Alexandrow's early works, but native folk song took on more importance in later compositions.
Sonata No.5 g Op.22 (UE 1922). First movement: Scriabin influence. Second movement: set of ten variations and a fugue. M-D.
Sonata No.6 Op.26 (USSR 1925) Lyric, serene opening leads to an Adagio; closes with a rhythmic Foxtrot. M-D.
Eight Pieces on USSR Folksongs Op.46 (USSR 1938). Simple settings of Armenian, Kirghiz, Russian, and Tchouvach folk tunes. Int.
Sonata No.8 B♭ Op.50 (USSR 1946). Employs tunes from Op.46 in transparent writing. A buoyant Allegretto giocoso opening, a serious Andante cantabile, and an exuberant finale make this a well-balanced work. M-D.
Sonata No.9 Op.61 (USSR 1946). Allegro moderato; Andante; Allegro. M-D.
Six Pieces of Medium Difficulty (USSR). Short character pieces in varied moods.

Alexander A. Aliabev (1787–1851) Russia
Selections from His Piano Works (USSR). Consists mainly of short pieces in a post-Mozart style with some indebtedness to John Field. Int. to M-D.

Heitor Alimonda (1922–   ) Brazil
Alimonda teaches at the School of Music in The University of Rio de Janerio.
O Estudo do Piano (Ric Brazil 1976) 10 vols. A piano course covering the main ingredients for developing a solid pianistic background. Easy to M-D.
Movimento Perpétuo (Ric BR 1966) 2pp. Ostinato treatment recalls Ibert's *The Little White Donkey*. M-D.
Estudo No.I (Ric BR 1956) 3pp. Romantic, tuneful.Int.
Estudo No.II (Wehrs 1958) 1 min.
Estudo No.III (Gerig 1957) 3pp. Moving thirds in right hand, then left hand; melody in opposite hand; contrary-motion thirds in next to last bar. M-D.
Sonatina II (SDM 1960–61) 11pp. 8 min. Three movements. M-D.

Roman Alis (1931–   ) Spain
Alis teaches in the conservatories of Seville and Madrid. He has written music for films and television.
Poemas de la Baja Andalucía Op.18 1958 (Editorial de Música Española Contemporánea 1991) 20pp. 10 min. Nubes. Canción. Niños. Siesta. Fiesta. Colorful contrasting pieces using a broadened tonality, some use of harmonic fourths, well crafted. M-D.

Charles Henri Valentin Alkan (1813–1888) France
This contemporary of Chopin, Liszt, Anton Rubinstein, and César Franck produced some of the most powerful piano music of the nineteenth century. Busoni

placed him among "the greatest of the post-Beethoven piano composers." Many of his works deserve to be rescued from oblivion. Alkan gave the same opus numbers to different compositions; he also republished some works under different opus numbers. Therefore it is impossible to provide a complete and accurate list of his works.

Allegro Barbaro (Israeli Music Publications 127) 7pp. An octave study, all on white keys, composed sixty years before Bartók's piece of the same title. Plenty of vigor; storm and stress. M-D.

Concerto da Camera I Op.10/1 a (Musica Obscura). Adagio available separately from same publisher.

Alleluia Op.25 (Billaudot; Musica Obscura) 5pp. Slow, sustained, full repeated chords. M-D.

Sonata Op.33 "Les Quatre Ages" (Billaudot; Joubert). "Twenty Years"—Very fast, Firmly. "Thirty Years"—Quasi-Faust—Quite fast, Satanically. "Forty Years"— A happy household—Slowly. "Fifty Years"—Prometheus chained—Extremely slow. This "grand" work begins with the scherzo "Twenty Years," which turns out to be a kind of introduction to a huge, virtuosic, Romantic sonata. As the work unfolds, the effect is one of gradual deceleration (getting old!). Combines flash with musical substance; continually appealing musical inventiveness. D.

12 Etudes in Major Keys Op.35 (Joubert; MMP) 32 min. Some of Alkan's finest works.

12 Etudes in Minor Keys Op.39 (Billaudot) in two suites, six pieces in each. 1. Comme le vent: 27 min. 2. Rythme molossique. 3. Scherzo diabolico. 4. Allegro moderato. 5. Marche funèbre. 6. Menuet. 7. Finale. 8. Concerto: Allegro assai. 9. Concerto: Adagio. 10. Allegro alla Barbaresca. 11. Ouverture, la. Le festin d'Esope. Nos.4–7 make up the *Symphony for Piano Solo.* No.12 is a cross between a bolero and a polonaise, an eclectic sprawling piece full of imagination, craft, and virtuosity. This set contains some of Alkan's most interesting compositions; No.12 is one of his finest achievements and shows Alkan at the height of his powers.

Réconciliation, petite caprice en forme de Zorcico Op.42 (Billaudot) 10pp. Contains some sonorous effects. M-D.

Capriccio alla solidatesca Op.50/1 (Billaudot). Left-hand clusters, fantastic writing.

Une Fusée Op.55 (Billaudot). Introduction and Impromptu.

Sonatine a Op.61 (Billaudot). Classic in its purity of form; what a piano sonata by Berlioz might have sounded like. M-D.

48 Esquisses Op.63 (Billaudot). Four suites, twelve pieces in each. Some are published separately by Billaudot. Nos.42 and 48 (Musica Obscura).

Les Mois Op.74 (Billaudot). Twelve pieces in four suites published in four books.

3 Grandes Etudes Op.76 (Billaudot). Fantaisie A♭: left hand only. Introduction, Variation, Finale: right hand only. Mouvement semblable et perpetuel: for both hands. Published separately. D.

Perpetuum Mobile (Billaudot). Preparatory to Op.76.

Deux Fugues (Musica Obscura). Jean qui pleure; Jean qui rit.

Oeuvres choises (F. M. Delaborde, I. Philipp—Billaudot 1970). Super flumina Babylonis, Op.52; Paraphrase du psaume 137, Op.52.

Alkan in Miniature (R. Smith, J. White—Billaudot 1979) 31pp. Fourteen shorter and easier pieces representing the variety of Alkan's style. See especially The Pursuit; Laus Deo (Praise to God); Song of the Mad Woman (eerie); La Vision (exquisite lyricism); Esquisses. Text in French and English. Int. to M-D.

The Piano Music of Alkan (Raymond Lewenthal—GS 1964). Contains a brief biography of Alkan, a Preface "On Recreating a Style," "General Remarks on Alkan's Style as it Affects the Interpreter," "Alkan's Treatment of the Piano," "Athletic Form," and extensive performance suggestions. Includes *Le Festin D'Esope* Op. 39/12 (the last etude in a 275-page set of studies published in 1857); *Symphonie* Op.39 (comprising Nos.4, 5, 6, 7 of the *Etudes* Op.39); *Fa* Op.38/2; *Barcarolle* Op.65/6; *Le Tambour Bat aux Champs* Op.50/2; *Etude* Op.35/8; *Quasi-Faust* Op.33 (second movement of the "Grande Sonate"); and *Esquisses* Op.63 (eleven pieces from this set of 48 short pieces through all the major and minor keys). The *Esquisses* are *La Vision* No.1, *Le Staccatissimo* No.2, *Le Legatissimo* No.3, *Les Soupirs* No.11, *Barcarolette* No.12, *Scherzettino* No.37, *Héraclite et Démocrite* No.39, *Les Enharmoniques* No.41, *Les Diablotins* No.45, *Le Premier Billet Doux* No.46, and *Scherzetto* No.47. Virtuoso techniques required for this orchestral approach to the piano. D.

SEPARATE PIECES:

Desire (Musica Obscura) 3pp. A miniature set of variations with some interesting modulations. Requires good melodic projection. M-D.

Les Omnibus: Variations Op.2. See below, "Collections," *Piano Music and the Virtuosos 1810–1860.*

The Wind (GS). Sweeping figurations. M-D.

13 Selected Works for the Piano (George Beck—Heugel). Notes in French, German, and English. Does not duplicate any of the pieces in the Lewenthal album.

Bourée D'Avergne; Etude Op.29 (Schott). Strong rhythms, full chords. M-D.

See: Henry H. Bellamann, "The Piano Works of C. V. Alkan," MQ, 10 (April 1924):251–62.

Joseph Bloch, "Charles-Valentin Alkan," thesis, Harvard University (Indianapolis: privately printed for the author, 1941).

Raymond Lewenthal, "The Berlioz of the Piano," MA, 84/2 (February 1964): 44.

Bryce Morrison, "Alkan the Mysterious," M&M, 22 (June 1974):30–32. Mainly discusses *Sonata* Op.33.

J. H. White, "Alkan the Neglected Genius," *Piano Journal*, 7 (February 1982):15–17.

Humphrey Searle, "A Plea for Alkan," ML, 18/3 (1937):276–79.

Larry Sitsky, "Summary Notes for a Study on Alkan," *Studies in Music*, 8 (1974):53–91. Twenty sections, each of which could well be the subject of a separate essay. Musical examples, including the following complete pieces: *Gigue et Air de Ballet* Op.21/1; *Trois Airs à Cinq Temps et un à Sept Temps* Op.32/2; *Cinquième Recueil de Chants* Op.70; *Ancienne Mélodie de la Synagogue.*

Douglass Allanbrook (1921–   ) USA
Allanbrook studied composition with Walter Piston and Nadia Boulanger.
40 Changes (Bo&H 1971) 22 min. Large-scale set of variations, exploits the piano's possibilities. The composer states: "Its form could be thought of as a jeweled sphere with many facets which wheels before the ear and the mind—its intensity increases until the end where it reveals itself as a song." Mature pianism required. D.
12 Preludes for All Seasons 1974 (Bo&H) 25pp. One short prelude for each month of the year. Advanced compositional and pianistic techniques are used. Linear writing interspersed with vertical sonorities. For the artist student. D.

Terence Allbright (1946–   ) Great Britain
Piano Sonata I 1974 (B. Ramsey 1978) 20pp., 12 min. Facsimile reproduction. Divided into two main sections. Requires solid technique. MC. M-D.

P. Humberto Allende (1885–1959) Chile
An Impressionistic nationalism pervades the work of Allende. Unusual metric structure also appeals to him.
6 Etudes (Sal). French influence, melodic in emphasis. M-D.
6 Miniatures Grecques (Sal). All on white keys except No.5.
2 Preludes (Sal). Subtle, expressive. Int. to M-D.
Tempo di Minuetto (Sal). Short, chromatic, lyric. Int.
12 Tonadas (Sal 1918–22). Based on popular Chilean tunes. Short pieces that go through a circle of major and minor keys. Each piece begins in a minor key, then goes to the parallel major in a faster tempo. Some of the finest piano music inspired by folk music of the region. Int. to M-D.

Hans Günther Allers (1935–   ) Germany
Eleven Bagatelles (Br&H EB8100 1980) 12pp. Preface in German and English. Pieces become progressively more difficult. They begin well but inspiration dries up toward the end of the collection. Many directions, footnotes in German only. Int.

Yardena Alotin (1931–   ) Israel
Alotin teaches at the Israel Conservatory in Tel Aviv.
Three Preludes (IMI 1978) 12pp., 7 min. 1. E, virtuosic, bitonal counterpoint. 2. Quiet, pastorale-like tune, loose rondo form. 3. Playful and lively. Contains pedaling, essential fingering, and metronome indications. M-D.

Laurence Altman (–   ) USA
Piano Poems (TP 1978) 16pp. Studies on Different Scales. Fifteen short pieces demonstrate non-Western scales, including whole-tone, an African scale, a

Japanese scale, a Greek scale, and a Korean scale. An unusual collection with MC to dissonant sonorities. M-D.

Delamar Alvarenga (1952–   ) Brazil
Since 1962 Alvarenga has lived in São Paulo and has studied with Oliver Toni.
Ah, Vous Dirai-Je, Maman 1970 (Universidade de São Paulo 1972, Escola de Communicacões e Artes, São Paulo, Brazil) 7pp. Aleatoric, improvisational, new notation. Directions are given for three different realizations. Avant-garde.
Estudo a duas vozes 1969 (Ric) 2pp. This work attempts to integrate daily sounds into the context of a musical structure in two voices. Improvisational, graphic notation. On the thirtieth repetition the pianist must decide how to bring about the climax by using anything except the glissando. Avant-garde.

William Alwyn (1905–1985) Great Britain
Alwyn was best known as a writer of music for over fifty films. He composed in an unashamed Romantic style full of instrumental color.
Sonata alla Toccata (Lengnick 1951) 21pp. Maestoso: C, basically diatonic, much rhythmic drive. Andante con moto e semplice: F, much use of thirds in melody and accompaniment. Molto vivace: F—f; triplet figuration prominent; requires good octave technique; concludes with an effective Presto furioso. M-D.
Fantasy-Waltzes (Lengnick 1956) 48pp. Eleven pieces inspired by Schubert and Ravel, cast in a MC harmonic idiom. Some charming, delectable writing, always grateful for pianist and audience. M-D.
Three Movements (JWC). Allegro appassionato; Evocation; The Devil's Reel. Pianistic writing of moderate difficulty.
Twelve Preludes (Lengnick 1959) 33pp. The *Twelve Preludes*, Alwyn said, "were written when I was experimenting with short note groups each with a strong tonal center; a different group of notes is used for each Prelude. . . ." From a Chandos compact disc. Each is written in a specific key, i.e., No.1 in E♭, No.2 in A, No. 6 in G and F♯, etc., but with no key signature. Each piece is a complete entity and "fits the hand" beautifully. An impressive set that shows there is still plenty to be said in the key of C. M-D.

André Ameller (1912–   ) France
Montreal (Leduc 1973) 3pp., 3 min. Short prelude opens with an expressive recitative. Octotonic writing interspersed with MC chords, modal. Impressionistic portrayal of Montreal, bell sonorities. M-D.

René Amengual (1911–1954) Chile
Amengual's piano works show the stylistic influences of the modern French school.
Sonatina 1938 (ECIC 1945). Three movements, the second of which contains effective melodic writing. Does not display any overt Latin-American rhyth-

mic characteristics. Shows a startling resemblance to the Ravel *Sonatine*. M-D.

Emanuel Amiran-Pougatchov (1909–   ) Poland
Lahat (Ecstasy) (IMI 1974) 20pp. A toccata for the adventurous pianist. M-D.

David Amram (1930–   ) USA
Amram is equally at home with classical music and jazz.
Sonata 1965 (CFP 6685) 18 min. Overture: rhythmic with quiet ending. Lullaby:
    song-like, requires span of ninth. Theme and Variations: variety of moods,
    brilliant climax, quiet close. Requires first-class pianism. M-D.
See: David Amram, *Vibrations; the Adventures and Musical Times of David Am-
    ram* (New York: Macmillan, 1968).

Gilbert Amy (1936–   ) France
Amy studied with Messiaen and Milhaud, but Messiaen influenced him more.
The two seemingly opposed principles of serial and aleatoric techniques exist
side by side in his piano works.
Cahiers d'Epigrammes pour Piano (Heugel 1966). Contains Formant A, Formant
    B, Formant B, second part. Directions given. Serial and aleatoric. D.
Epigramme pour piano (Heugel 1962). Issued in an envelope with one large score
    printed on both sides. Performance directions listed on outside cover. Se-
    rial and aleatoric. D.
Obliques No.3 1989 (Amphion 1994) 10pp. Requires piano with sostenuto pedal.
    Proportional rhythmic relationships, pointillistic, contrasted sonorities
    and touches, pedal indicated, frequent tempo changes, highly organized. D.
Sonate pour piano (Heugel 1961). Within its aleatoric limits this is extraordinar-
    ily fashioned music. D.
See: André Hodeir, *Since Debussy: A View of Contemporary Music* (New York:
    Grove, 1961).
H. Riley, "Aleatoric Procedures in Contemporary Piano Music," MT, 107 (April
    1966):311–12.
K. Stone, "The Piano and the Avant-Garde," PQ, 52 (Summer 1965):14–28.

Karl Andersen (1903–1970) Norway
Anderson was one of Norway's leading cellists. His style is thoroughly contem-
porary and logically thought out and developed.
Columbine and the Annoyed Harlequin (Lyche). Serial technique handled in a
    highly personal manner. D.

Thomas Jefferson Anderson (1928–   ) USA
Watermelon 1971 (Bo&Bo) 9 pp. 7 min. Based on a street huckster's song heard
    in Washington, D.C. Tune included in index. Variations on the tune use
    many contemporary techniques: pointillism, harmonics, contrary black-
    and white-key glissandos, careful pedal indications, dynamic extremes.
    M-D to D.

Volkmar Andreae (1879–1962) Switzerland
Sechs Klavierstücke Op.20 (Hug 1911). Praeludium: Bacchantischer Tanz; Frage; Catalonisches Ständchen: Adagio; Unruhige Nacht. Post-Brahms writing, well-conceived pianistic sonorities. Available separately. M-D.

Hendrik Andriessen (1892–1981) The Netherlands
The elder Andriessen's style incorporates influences of both Debussy and popular music.
Sonate (Van Rossum 1934) 10 min. Oriented toward Hindemith, polytonal. M-D.

Jurriaan Andriessen (1925–1996) The Netherlands
Andriessen studied with his father, Hendrik. Later, in Paris, he studied film music and was influenced by Olivier Messiaen. However he writes in a neoclassic style and is oriented toward Stravinsky.
Roger's Sonatine (B&VP 1237). Outside movements are lively, while the middle one is a sensitive sarabande. Refreshing. Contains no stretch larger than a seventh. Int.

Louis Andriessen (1939–   ) The Netherlands
Andriessen studied with his father, Hendrik, and later with Kees van Baaren. During 1962–63 he worked with Luciano Berio in Milan and again with Berio in Berlin in 1964 and 1965. Cage and Stockhausen have influenced Andriessen considerably.
Registers (Donemus 1963) 7 min. Written in spatial or time-notation, i.e., the duration is fixed by the space on the paper. Andriessen says this piece "is more an indication for action than a composition." Avant-garde, fascinating sonorities. D.

Jean-Henri D'Anglebert (1635–1691) France
Among the galaxy of composers who made the reign of the Sun King one of the high points in the history of music, D'Anglebert is one of the most important.
Pièces de Clavecin (Roesgen-Champion—Société Française de Musicologie 1934). Urtext edition containing all the keyboard works. Newly transcribed with preface and notes by Denise Restout.
Pièces de Clavecin (BB 1965). Facsimile of the 1689 Paris edition. Contains a Preface and a detailed Table of Ornaments. Harpischord Suites in G, g, d, and D; five fugues and a short contrapuntal Kyrie for the organ; Principles of Accompaniment; six pages of theoretical treatise, chords, intervals, etc. The harpsichord suites usually contain a prelude, A, C, S, and G. Other compositions, including transcriptions of works by Lully, follow. The final piece is D'Anglebert's tribute to his teacher, Chambonnières.
Pièces de Clavecin (K. Gilbert—Heugel 1975). This easy-to-read edition offers all of the 1689 collection plus 35 more pieces, thirteen of which were previously unpublished. M-D.
See: Beverly Scheibert, *Jean-Henri D'Anglebert and the Seventeenth-Century Clavecin School* (Bloomington: Indiana University Press, 1986).

Istvan Anhalt (1919–   ) Canada, born Hungary
Fantasia for piano (Berandol). Eloquent serial writing. D.

George Antheil (1900–1959) USA
Antheil shocked audiences in the twenties with his "machine music." His style changed remarkably since the early experimental days, and he finally seemed at home in the area of neo-romantic and Impressionist surroundings. A sense of humor often permeates his writing.

Piano Pastels (Weintraub). 15 varied short pieces, mildly dissonant. First-rate teaching pieces. Int.

Sonata II "The Airplane" 1922 (NME 1931) In two movements, the first very fast, the second slower. No dynamic markings except at the beginning and close of the first movement. Rhythms are aggressive and motoristic but also sometimes reminiscent of ragtime. Strident harmonies, clusters, deliberately noisy. Sharply contrasting ideas juxtaposed but not developed; repeats material either wholly or in fragments. M-D.

Sonata III 1947 (AMC). Allegro marcato (Heroic): chordal; dramatic; syncopated; bitonal; large gestures; static tonal planes and overused sequential devices antithetical to the style of the rest of the movement; coda based on opening material. Adagio molto expressivo (Romantic): accompanied melody in tripartite form; nocturne-like; some bitonality; sensitive pedaling required. Presto (Diabolic): full chords at fast tempo; C major pounded out in last 18 bars. Changing meters, large skips, sardonic, ironic, humorous. Not a totally integrated work. M-D to D.

Sonata IV 1948 (Weintraub). Allegro Giocoso-Ironico: frames the rhythmic and aesthetic elements of Antheil's mechanistic music of the 1920s within the formal construct of traditional forms. Andante: neo-Romantic, lyric, expressive. Allegro (Presto): a brilliant toccata activated by a continual frenzied pulse and by pounding chords. M-D.

Suite (GS). Three short pieces that provide an introduction to the contemporary idiom. M-D.

2 Toccatas 1951 (GS). Published separately. No. 2 B♭ has constant eighth-note motion and alternating chords and octaves. M-D.

La Femme 100 têtes—45 Preludes 1933 (Antheil Press, 7722 Lynn, El Cerrito, CA 94530-4133, 1985) These 44 preludes and the concluding *Percussion Dance* were inspired by Max Ernst's collage of etchings by the same name. The preludes explore many facets of Antheil's style, from percussive machinations to triadic lyricism. M-D to D.
See: David L. Albee, "George Antheil's 'La Femme 100 têtes': A Study of the Piano Preludes." Diss., University of Texas–Austin, 1977.

Theodore Antoniou (1935–   ) Greece
Antoniou teaches at Boston University. His music combines conventional and avant-garde techniques. He explores abstract relationships, such as the movements of sounds, the several ways of playing an instrument, problems of space, sound, movement, and event.

Acquarelle (Edition Modern 1967) 14pp. in a package, 15 min. Ten separate pieces. Adagio espressivo; Vivo e secco; Largo mysterioso; Allegro ritmico; Andante espressivo; Allegro brioso; Andantino calmo; Presto scherzino; Largo amoroso; Allegro barbaro. Colorful and appealing pieces written in a freely tonal idiom with use of some serial technique. MC sonorities. Entire suite or a selection of the pieces would add strong interest to any program. One suggested grouping consists of Nos.2, 3, 8, 10. Requires above-average pianistic ability. M-D.

Sil-ben (Syllables) (Gerig 1965) 4pp. in collection *Contemporary Greek Piano Music.* Six short pieces, each based on certain properties of letters or syllables in speech. Constructed on a 12-tone row that also uses parameters of serial organization. Parachesis: a sound group recurs frequently, like the recurring syllable creating this rhetoric figure in speech; dynamic extremes; hands crossed. Anagram: the position of notes is interchanged in quick passages with different quantities that always end on a stressed note; short groups of fast chromatic notes stop on a long melody note. Derivatives: a sound group or note induces others to sound as in language; addition of prefixes or suffixes leads to new words; pointillistic. Epenthesis; middle register is altered in timbre by placing a book on the strings, giving a harpischord-like sound; a motive has been transposed, transformed, and varied. Aphairesis: the Greek word means both subtraction and abstraction; glissando on string; plucked strings. Conclusion: a theme in a different style appears amid motives from the preceding movement; finally it is assimilated. Experimental. D.

Dennis ApIvor (1916–   ) Ireland
Seven Pieces Op.30 1960 (Sikesdi Press 1996) 13pp. Serial, pointillistic, contrasting. D.
Animalcules Op.35 1993 (Sikesdi Press 1996) 12pp. Twelve short pieces. Serial, pointillistic, contrasting. D.

Rafael Aponte-Ledée (1938–   ) Puerto Rico
Aponte-Ledée teaches composition at the University of Puerto Rico.
Tema y seis differencias (PIC 1963) 6pp., 3 min. Serial, six short contrasting and effective variations, frequent meter changes, contemporary treatment. M-D.

Hans Eric Apostel (1901–1972) Austria
Early works by Apostel were highly chromatic and thick textured. After he studied with Schönberg and Berg, more linear writing and thinner textures appeared in his compositions. For a while he was interested in combining traditional principles with serial technique, but after the mid-fifties he showed more interest in exploiting the possibilities of 12-tone writing.
Sonatina Ritmica Op.5 (Dob 1934). Three movements. Changing meters plus thick textures. Slow movement is most effective. M-D.
Klavierstücke Op.8 (Dob). Thick chromatic textures. M-D.

Kubiniana Op.13 (UE). Ten short pieces after drawings of Alfred Kubin. Variety of moods, serial. Some use of harmonics. D.

Suite "Concise" Op.24 1956 (UE) 11 min. L'arrivée; La promenade; La maison; Les salutations; Problème dodécaphonique; Le vin et les poissons; Le départ. Descriptive serial writing inspired by Switzerland. M-D.

Vier Kleine Klavierstücke Op.31A (Dob 1962) 4 pp., 6½ min. Bound with *Fantasie* Op.31B. Promenade; Walzer; Fantasie; Marsch. Imitation, some chromaticism. Serial. M-D.

Fantasie Op.31B (Dob 1962) 4 min. Bound with *Vier Kleine Klavierstücke*. More involved than Op.31A but employs the same techniques. M-D.

Edward Applebaum (1938–) USA

Applebaum teaches at the University of California, Santa Barbara.

Sonata (WH 1965) 16pp., 12 min. Reproduction of the MS is not very legible, and there are a number of errors in the score. Serial, contemporary idioms. Mirrors: a mixture of contrasting sounds, i.e., dissonant chords, fast passagework, moderate tempo. Gestures: pedal effects, more colorful sonorities including a tremolo passage to be played "à la Errol Garner." D.

Preludes (MMB 1984) 7pp. I: 1980 3½ min. Serial influence, slow, contrast of strict rhythmic sections with rubato sections. II: 1982 2½ min. Serial influence, frequent dynamic changes, looks more interesting than it sounds. M-D to D.

Stan Applebaum (1929–) USA

Sound World (Schroeder & Gunther 1974) 23pp. A collection of new keyboard experiences. 31 short pieces that will open new worlds of sonorities for the intermediate pianist. Each new technique explained in detail. May be played separately or grouped in sets to form a miniature suite. Ideas developed include: major seconds, bitonality, perfect fourths contrasted with augmented fourths, clusters, 12-tone piece. Int.

Frenzy-Toccata (Broude 1977) 4pp. In 6/8 with frequent hand alternations, bitonal, chromatic, thin textures, Vivace agilimente directions. M-D.

Summercloud (Broude 1980) 2pp. Lyric, freely with expression over ostinato-like left-hand eighth notes, MC. Int.

Tito Aprea (1904–) Italy

15 Dances for Piano (Ric 1973) 39 pp. Titles include Pastoral Dance; Rustic Dance; Dance of the Ant; Dance of the Elephant; Dance of the Flea; Dance of the Chicks; Pierrot's Dance; Ponchinello's Dance. Colorful illustrations ranging from folk to circus dances. Imaginative and some original writing. Int.

Pedro De Araújo (ca.1615–1684) Portugal

Five Pieces for Keyboard Instruments (Kastner—Valentim de Carvalho). Preface in Portuguese. Excellent editing. In the style of tientos and toccatas; reveal both fantasy and fluency. M-D.

Pierre Arbeau (–   ) France
Preludes, Book 4 (Choudens). Contemporary, yet quite approachable. Int. to M-D.

Violet Archer (1913–2000) Canada
Archer writes in a combination of neoclassic and serial techniques. She is a master of complex dissonant counterpoint and has often been inspired by simple folk materials.
Eleven Short Pieces 1960 (PIC) 10 min. Pedagogic material much above average. Fertile ideas; varied moods and techniques. Int.
Four Bagatelles (Waterloo 1979) 15pp. Forceful: needs strength and firmness without being harsh. Capricious: needs lightness and control, legato accompanied by staccato, rhythmic changes. Introspective: expressive cantabile playing. Festive: brilliant and light, mid-section needs smooth legato. Effective. M-D.
Four Little Studies 1964 (Waterloo) 2pp. Each piece concentrates on one contemporary technique. Int.
Habitant Sketches (TP) 5 min. Jig; Church Scene; Christmas in Quebec. Int.
Six Preludes 1976 (Waterloo) 20 min. Variety of moods and idioms. Tonal; tend toward lean textures. M-D.
Sonata 1945, rev. 1957 (CMC) 16 min. A large-scale three-movement work demanding mature pianism. D.
Sonata No. 2 1979 (Berandol 1982) 16pp. Andante moderato, amabile capriccioso. Largo a piacere, meditando e con rubato. Andante ma Energico. Dramatic ideas, well-organized, demanding for performer, easier on listener. D.
Sonatina II 1946 (Bo&H) 9 min. Three movements in neoclassic style. Final movement, Fughetta, is difficult but attractive. M-D.
Sonatina III 1973 (Waterloo) 7 min. First movement: two-part counterpoint. Second movement: quiet, tuneful, a waltz. Third movement: a cheery jig. Uses only white keys; more difficult to play than it sounds. Int. to M-D.
Three Miniatures 1963 (Waterloo) 4 min. Dreaming; Dark Mood; Determination. MC. Int.
Theme and Variations 1963 (Waterloo) 5pp., 3 min. Flowing theme, six contrasting short variations. Int.

José Ardévol (1911–1981) Cuba, born Spain
Seis Piezas (Southern 1949). Preludio; Danzon; Invencion; Habanera; Son; Rumba. Short, folk-like melodies, tricky rhythms. Int. to M-D.
Sonata No. 3 (ECIC 1944). Moderato: three basic contrasting textures alternate. Invenciones en Rondo: lengthy allegretto, two- and three-part linear treatment, deceptive rhythms. Differencias sobre la cantiga "Entre Ave et Eva" del Rey Sabio: theme and nine variations, theme da capo, homophonic and linear treatment of modal tune, quiet. Neoclassic, in the style of Scarlatti–de Falla. D.
Sonatina (NME 1934). Two short dissonant movements. Larghetto: linear and lyric. Allegro: in two and three voices. M-D.

Anton Arensky (1861–1906) Russia
Excellent material in salon style.
6 Morceaux Op.5/5 Basso ostinato D (Musica Obscura). 5/4, six pleasing variations. M-D.
3 Esquisses Op.24 (K 9905) 27pp. 1. F: Allegro, flowing figuration surrounds
embedded melody, cadenza, fleeting figures. 2. A♭: Vivace, outer sections
use broken chordal intervals (fourths, fifths, sixths, etc.): Meno mosso mid-
section is more melodic. 3. f: Presto, syncopated melody over active left
hand, conclusion is similar to No.1. M-D.
24 Morceaux Caractéristiques Op.36 (K 9904) 128pp. No.13 Etude F♯ only (Os-
terle—GS). Varied moods and figuration; Nos. 12, 16, and 21 are especially
fine. M-D.
12 Preludes Op.63 (CFP F114, 115) in two vols. Nos. 4 and 10 are of special interest. Int.
12 Etudes Op.74 (C. Sorel—EBM). Excellent preface. Each piece is in a different
key. Varied styles; fine recital material; excellent for developing flexible
wrist motion, nimble fingers, and tonal control. Carefully edited with commentary. M-D.
Piano Selections (L. Prosypalova—USSR 1976) 61pp. Contains studies and other
piano pieces. M-D.
Two Pieces (GS 139). In the Field, Op.36/24; Prelude in d, Op.63/10.
By the Sea (Musica Obscura) 6pp. Melody mostly in left hand; triplet figuration
suggests lapping waves. M-D.
Barcarolle (Musica Obscura) 4 pp. Left-hand melody printed in large notes. Undulating right-hand accompaniment. Int.
Gavotte Pastorale (Musica Obscura) 3pp. Sprightly, a few awkward spots. Int.

Isabel Aretz (1913–   ) Venezuela, born Argentina
Since 1952 Aretz has been the director of the Inter-American Institute of Ethno-
musicology and Folklore of the National Institute of Culture and Fine Arts in
Venezuela.
Sonata (PAU 1965) 27pp. Moderato agitato: textures are thin and widely spread.
Andante—Ostinato—Scherzando: mid-section scherzando breaks mono-
tony of Andante—Ostinato. Toccata—Allegro: major seventh exploited in
propulsive movement. M-D.

Rodolfo Arizaga (1926–   ) Argentina
Arizaga studied with Luis Gianneo, Olivier Messiaen, and Nadia Boulanger. He
is a well-known music critic for the newspaper *El Clarin*.
Preludio y Arietta (EAM 1946). Neoclassic. M-D.
Serranillas del Jaque Op.17 (EAM 1956) 8 min. Spanish Impressionism. M-D.
Toccata Op.5 (PIC 1947) 4 pp. In Prokofieff Toccata style, chromatic, driving
rhythm, tonal, exciting. Program closer. Large span required. M-D.

Paul Arma (1905–   ) France, born Hungary
Arma studied with Béla Bartók. In 1945 he organized the Folklore de la Résistance at the Radiodiffusion Française in Paris.
A la decouverte du passé (Lemoine 1947). Fourteen easy pieces.
Cinq Esquisses (EMT 1969) 4pp., 7 min. Parlando; Rubato; Con allegrezza;
    Lento rubato, con dolore; Con fretta. Contrasting, colorful, based on popular Hungarian melodies. Makes a fine set performed together. Int. to M-D.
Le Tour du Monde en 20 Minutes (Galazy). Varied styles, clever. Int.
Sonata da Ballo (EMT 1940). 11 min. Based on popular French themes from
    Bourgogne, Savoie, Auvergne, and Bretagne. First movement: the longest;
    has rhythmic drive, attractive melodic construction. Second movement; orchestral coloring. Third movement: builds to a tremendous climax. An appealing, unusual work. M-D.
Trois Epitaphes (EMT 1945) 9pp. 15 min. Pour Romain Roland: improvisatory,
    quietly moving harmonic sevenths with a chordal accompaniment, unbarred. Pour ceux qui ne sont jamais revenus: mes amis torturés, massacrés:
    written on four and five staffs; octotonic; chordal punctuation; builds to
    large climax, then subsides; *ppp* closing. Pour Béla Bartók, qui fut mon
    maître et mon ami: slow-moving chords, long-held sonorities; requires large
    span. Individual style. M-D.
Two Sonatinas 1937 (Lemoine 1980) 8pp. Preface in French. Sonatine I, 7 min.
    Sonatine II, 4 min. Lean textures, strong rhythms. M-D.

Thomas Arne (1710–1778) Great Britain
Arne was no mere imitator of the Handelian style but, nevertheless, Italianate
ornamental melody is characteristic of his *Sonatas* or *Lessons*. These suite-like
compositions, dating from about 1756, were the first works entitled Sonatas to be
published in England. They contain lively dance movements, vigorous toccatas,
and simple airs.
A Keyboard Allegro (C. Hogwood—OUP 1974). A graceful and melodically deft
    alternative for a Bach *Two-Part Invention*. Was originally the third movement of *Concerto* in C. Editor has added an improvised cadenza on the
    diminished seventh just before the close, which a good student could and
    should expand. Int.
Eight Keyboard Sonatas (C. Hogwood—Faber 1983; K; S&B). F; e; G; d; B♭; g; a;
    G. Arne's unique melodic gifts have long ensured popularity for these
    pieces, his only published works for solo keyboard. No. 4 has a fine fugue.
    No.8 is a set of variations on a minuet of Rameau. M-D.
Concerto II G (R. Langley—Musica Rara). May be played with or without orchestra. Two outer movements with orchestra flank three short solo movements. Scarlatti-like writing with outer movements requiring the most facility. Contains historical and performance notes. Int.
See: A.E.F. Dickinson, "Arne and the Keyboard Sonata," MMR, 85 (May
    1955):88–95.

A.M. Henderson, "Old English Keyboard Music (Byrd to Arne)," *PRMA*, 64 (1937–38).

Arthur Steiger, "Thomas Arne and His Keyboard Sonatas," *Clavier*, 16 (May 1977). Brief remarks on the eight sonatas by Arne.

Richard Arnell (1917–   ) Great Britain

Arnell writes in an eclectic style and has composed in almost all forms. "I simply believe that it is mere prejudice and unclear thinking which rejects a work of art that has attached to it the stigma of 'programme music.' Music is a complicated amalgam of meanings, an expression of man himself, and cannot be abstracted from him without becoming 'un-music' or sheer noise. Theorists and academicians who try to tear them apart would doom us to sterility and death" (composer in BHI brochure).

Siciliana and Furiante Op.8 (Music Press 1947). Siciliana (2pp.): smoothly flowing style. Furiante (Poco presto) (8pp.): imitative, thin textures, some ostinato-like writing, hand crossings, MC. M-D.

Impromptu Op.66 (PIC 1960). 4pp. Essentially diatonic, modern writing. M-D.

Malcolm Arnold (1921–   ) Great Britain

Arnold is one of the most distinctive voices in English music.

Buccaneer (Lengnick). Healthy rhythmic drive. Int.

Sonata 1942 (Roberton 1992) published in ms form. The two outer movements are strongly rhythmic interspersed with lyrical sections, much dynamic contrast. The middle movement (Andante) is calm and tranquil and leads immediately to the finale. M-D.

Variations on a Ukrainian Folk-Song (Lengnick 1944). Diatonic idiom. Expressive theme harmonized in a mildly dissonant style. Ten variations cover the gamut of contrast; Var. 10 serves as a coda to the complete work. Has much audience appeal and could add excitement to a program. M-D.

Children's Suite—Six Little Studies Op.16 (Lengnick 1948). Prelude: study in fourths and fifths. Carol: study in legato thirds for left hand. Shepherd's Lament: study in triplets and accidentals. Trumpet Tune: study in trills and rhythmic playing. Blue tune: study in rhythms and color. Folk-Song: study in touch and phrasing. Short, attractive, clever. Int.

Juan Crisostomo Arriaga (1806–1826) Spain

Precocious Spanish violinist and composer who left some astonishing works: three string quartets, a symphony, an overture, and many unpublished works.

Tres Estudios de Carácter (Dotesio). Allegro; Moderato; Risoluto. Classic style infused with some chromatic usage. Int. to M-D.

Claude Arrieu (1903–1990) France

Arrieu studied piano with Marguerite Long and composition with Jean Roger-Ducasse and Noël Gallon.

La boite à malice (Lemoine 1931). Eight pieces. Impressionistic. M-D.

Toccata pour Clavecin (ou Piano) (Leduc 1963) 7 min. Registration leads to Allegro. A mid-section Commenciando Lento (quasi Cadenza) provides contrast before a return to faster tempi. Allegro sections have numerous ritards. M-D.

Petit Récit. La Poupée Cassée (Billaudot 1976) 2pp.

Escapade et Cerf-Volant (Billaudot 1976) 4pp.

Promenade Mélancolique et Questionnaire (Billaudot 1976) 4pp.

Prélude Pastoral. L'Enfant Sage (Billaudot 1976) 2pp.

The above Billaudot publications are easy teaching pieces written in a traditional style.

Lectures 1977 (Billaudot) 8pp. Four contrasting pieces in a MC attractive idiom. Int.

Haruo Asakaua (1942–   ) Japan

Piano-Sonaro (Eterna) 1975 (Japan Federation of Composers) 11pp. Sonaro is synonymous with "sonata." Hexachord: allegro, Pentachord: andante. Heptachord (Phrygian mode): allegro (toccatina). Freely tonal. M-D.

John H. Ashton (1938–   ) USA

Theme and Five Variations (Seesaw) 19pp. Var.I: March, *pp* and staccato. Var.II: Andante, freely. Var.III: Very fast. Var.IV: Chorale Prelude. Var.V: Finale, brightly. Solid neoclassical writing. M-D.

Daniel Asia (1953–   ) USA

Asia teaches at the University of Arizona.

Piano Set I (Merion 1997) 23 min. Features a dreamlike second movement, and a strong rhythmic fourth movement of fast linear contrary motion between hands. D.

Scherzo Sonata (Merion 1995) 34 min. Seven contrasting movements, a powerful sense of expression, worth investigating. D.

Why (?) Jacob (Merion 1995). An elegy written as a memorial for a childhood friend killed in the 1973 Arab-Israeli War. M-D.

Thomas Attwood (1763–1838) Great Britain

Attwood studied in Vienna with Mozart, who said of him, "He partakes more of my style than any scholar I ever had: and I predict that he will prove a sound musician."

Easy Progressive Lessons (Four Sonatas) (R. Jones—ABRSC 1983) 16pp. G; C; F; D. Delightful, musically and technically. Would make an excellent substitute for the Clementi Op.36 sonatinas. Int.

Sonatina I G (Alfred 8050) 5pp. Attractive. Editing in gray print. Int.

Louis Aubert (1877–1968) France

Esquisse sur le nom de Fauré 1922 (Durand). In the collection *Hommage à Gabriel Fauré* (*La Revue Musicale* 23 [October 1922]) 3pp. Chromatic and harmonic writing suggestive of Fauré's style. Gentle tribute to his teacher. M-D.

Tony Aubin (1907–1981) France

Aubin wrote in a lively neoclassic style.

Prélude, Récitatif et Final (Heugel 1931). In Franckian tradition. Utilizes full resources of the keyboard. D.

Sonata b (Heugel 1930). A large three-movement (FSF) work of Romantic character. Effective pianistic writing. D.

Le Sommeil d' Iskender 1936 in *Le Tombeau de Paul Dukas* (*La Revue Musicale* 161 [May–June 1936]). 6pp. "The Sleep of Iskender" refers to a character in the ballet *La Peri* by Dukas. Material in measures 31–32 quotes from *La Peri*. Written on three staves; large hand span. M-D.

Marianna d'Auenbrugg (1759–1782) Austria

Sonata per Il Clavicembalo o Forte Piano (Hildegard Publishing Co.). First published in 1781 with an ode by her teacher Antonio Salieri. Three movements, classical style. Haydn dedicated some of his best sonatas to the d'Auenbrugg sisters. M-D.

Sonata E♭. In collection *At the Piano with Women Composers* (Hinson—Alfred 428). Rondo: allegro. The finale of the Sonata discussed above. Numerous dynamic changes show this movement was intended for the fortepiano. Editorial policy explained. M-D.

Rafal Augustyn (1951–   ) Poland

Mono Sonata (PWM 8213 1979) 23pp. Notes in Polish, German, and English. An ambitious, percussive work; a toccata. M-D.

Yoon-il Auh (1961–   ) USA

Auh is a violinist and has composed works for many different instruments. He is also active in the field of computer technology and has written a book on the subject.

Eastern Suite Op.8 1993 (Intrepid Pixels Publishing Co.) 22pp. Dawn. One Day, One Room, One Window. The Winter Bridge. Summer Breeze. Freely tonal, contrasted figuration, MC. M-D.

Micro Carnival Op.10 1993 (Intrepid Pixels Publishing Co.) 16pp. Prelude. Marching Ants. A Fire Bug. Sleepy Flea. A Spanish Lady Bug (tango rhythm). Old Spider. Colorful, clever, contrasting moods, some figures repeated "as many times as possible." Int. to M-D.

Liberty Suite Op.11 1995 (Intrepid Pixels Publishing Co.) 14pp. La Vague: rubato, long-held sonorities. The Heart of Cloister: fantasia, strongly contrasted sonorities, glissando. Autumn Leaf: contrasted styles and sections, freely tonal. M-D.

Josephine Aurenhammer (1758–1820) Austria

Aurenhammer studied with Mozart, who often played piano duets with her. She was an outstanding improviser.

Six Variations on a Hungarian Theme (Furore 118). An excellent well-crafted work in Viennese classical style. M-D.

Georges Auric (1899–1983) France
Auric was the youngest member of the group known as "Les Six." He was influenced early in his career by Satie and wrote in a style that would produce "auditory pleasure without demanding a disproportionate effort from the listener."
Adieu, New York (Editions de la Sirène 1919; MMP). Exciting foxtrot with a ragtime bass. M-D.
3 Impromptus (ESC 1940). Exploits clear ideas. M-D.
3 Pastorales (Sal 1920). No. 2 is serene, No. 3 spirited. All are short. Int. to M-D.
Petite Suite (Heugel 1927). Prélude; Danse; Villanelle et Entrée; Sarabande; Voltes. Two- and three-part writing in varied moods. Int. to M-D.
La Seine, au Matin 1937 (Sal 1975) Available separately. Light and spirited. All French words are translated into English. M-D.
Rondeau from the ballet *L'Eventail de Jeanne* 1927 (Heugel). Very rhythmic with a waltz for the mid-section. M-D.
Sonata F 1930–31 (Sal). A large four-movement virtuoso work, neoclassic, full of gestures intended to be dramatic. Subject matter is characterless, has little distinction. Thickly dissonant handling of sound texture, insufficient contrast in development. Mature pianism required. D.
Sonatine G 1922 (Sal). Allegro: rhythmic vitality. Andante: flowing. Presto: brisk. Clear, thin textures. M-D.

Larry Austin (1930–   ) USA
Austin teaches at the University of North Texas. Some of his recent works include theatrical, multimedia, and live electronic techniques.
Piano Set in Open Style (CPE 1964). Directions discuss space-time, i.e., durations of single notes and/or groups of notes are determined by the visual space between. Blank spaces are silent. Durational gradations are obtained by use of the tie. Pointillistic, expressionistic. Avant-garde. D.
Piano Variations (MJQ) 1960. Jazz influence. There is no theme for the variations in the traditional sense, but rather a set of notes and intervals serving as highly generative raw material. The term "variations" refers more to the process of composition rather than of classical form. Seven numbered sections differentiated by texture and movement. M-D.

Menahem Avidom (1908–1995) Israel, born Poland
Hommage à Schoenberg 1974 (IMI 307) 6pp., 4 1/2 min. Serial; based on a hexachord derived from Schoenberg's name; displays strong musical integrity. M-D.
Once Upon a Time 1977 (IMI 6195) 8pp., 8 min. Five MC pieces; requires subtlety. Int.
Passacaglia D-A-E-B 1973 (IMI 466) 7pp., 7 min. Six contrasting variations. M-D.

Jorge Gonzalez Avila (1925–   ) Mexico
24 Invenciones (EMM 1964) 15pp., 2 vols. I:1–9; II:10–24. Atonal; individual ideas
for each invention are well developed. Displays a fine craft. M-D.

Emil Axman (1887–1949) Czech Republic
Axman was a prolific composer and wrote in all forms except opera. His Romantic style is based on folk song.
Sonata Appassionata (Hudební Matice 1922). 36pp. Warm, Romantic, virtuoso
writing. The first of three piano sonatas, all written in the early 1920s. D.

B

Kees van Baaren (1906–1970) The Netherlands
Sonatina in memoriam Willem Pijper 1948 (B&VP 1950). No.5 in the set *Hommage à Willem Pijper*. Van Baaren studied with Pijper at the Amsterdam Conversatory. Serial style. M-D.

Arno Babadjanian (1921–   ) Armenia
Poem 1966 (USSR). Composed for the 1966 Tchaikowsky Piano Competition. A splashy, technically oriented showpiece. Style fits somewhere between Anton Rubinstein and Aram Khachaturian. Proficient and inventive. D.

Milton Babbitt (1916–   ) USA
Babbitt's pioneering work in the development of 12-tone compositional techniques and electronic music in the United States has already entered the realm of legend.
Three Compositions for Piano 1947 (Bomart) 7 min. Contains probably the earliest serialization of non-pitch elements. M-D.
    See: H. Wiley Hitchcock, *Music in the United States* (New York: Prentice-Hall, 1969), pp.232–35 for an analysis of this set.
Partitions 1963 (LG). See album *New Music for the Piano*. Serial, pointillistic, subtle use of sostenuto pedal, complex rhythms. D.
Playing for Time 1977 (Alfred) in collection *Twelve by Eleven*. 12pp., 2½ min. Employs characteristically unfamiliar rhythmic notation in a simple context (3/4 meter). The underlying "set" finally evolves and appears explicitly in (among other places) the final four measures. Highly organized musical syntax, pointillistic. Falls into place remarkably fast when read through even a few times. Contains some unique pianistic sonorities. D.
Post Partitions (CFP 1973) 4 min. To be performed immediately after *Partitions* or independently. Pitch, rhythm, and dynamics are serial. Atonal, complex. D.
Reflections (CFP) for piano and tape. 9½ min. Based on a scale of twelve dynamic values ranging from *ppppp* to *fffff* plus *mf* and *mp*. Three separate sections; in the first two the piano and tape exchange places, while in the third the basic musical and sonorous materials are superimposed on each other. The title refers to the structure and content of the work, which is composed of reflections and interchanges between the piano and the loudspeakers, as well as to the organization of 12-tone material. D.

See: *Contemporary Music Newsletter*, May-June 1975, for a thorough analysis of this complex and highly sensitive piece.

Semi-Simple Variations 1956 (TP). Although this piece seems to be a theme followed by five variations in 12-tone technique, it is actually six variations on a 12-tone set. Explanatory notes. M-D.

See: Elaine Barkin, "A Simple Approach to Milton Babbitt's Semi-Simple Variations," MR, 28/4 (November 1967):316–22.

Christopher Wintle, "Milton Babbitt's Semi-Simple Variations," PNM, 14–15 (1976):111–54.

Tableaux 1973 (CFP 66560) 30pp., 9½ min. Pointillistic, complex rhythms, constant dynamic changes, proportional rhythmic notation. Virtuoso technique required. D.

See: James M. Keller, "Conversation with Robert Taub," PQ, 159 (Fall 1992): 29–32, 34. Touches on Babbitt's piano works.

Stanley Babin (1932–   ) Israel, born Latvia

Babin received his musical training in Israel and at the Curtis Institute of Music.

Dance around the World. (MCA 1969). Twenty countries represented by characteristic dances. Mood of each nation cleverly captured. Int.

Three Piano Pieces (MCA 1968). Musette: ostinato in 7/8 meter. Fugue: modal subject, Hindemithian treatment. Presto: dramatic closing, Prokofieff-inspired. A mildly modern triptych. M-D.

Two Sonatinas (MCA). No.1 (1965). Comodo; Lento; Allegro molto. Requires span of ninth. Int. No.2 (published separately). Int. to M-D.

Victor Babin (1908–1972) USA, born Russia

Babin studied with Artur Schnabel and performed as a duo team with his wife, Vitya Vronsky. He was Director of the Cleveland Institute of Music.

Variations on a Theme of Beethoven (Augener 1960). Five variations, closing with a fugue and a coda. Contains some brilliant idiomatic writing. D.

Vytautas Bacevičius (1905–   ) Poland, born Lithuania

Poems (Mer), all published separately: *Poem contemplation* Op.5. *Poem mystique* Op.6. *Poem astral* Op.7. *Poem* No.4 Op.10. Short single movements in rhapsodic style. M-D.

Sonata No.2 Op.37 (Mer 1960). Three movements, with introduction to first movement. Traditional harmonic and tonal treatment, chromatic embellishment. Thick textures, thematic material well defined, Szymanowski influence. D.

Sonata No.3 Op.52 (Mer 1960) 23pp. Three movements (FSF). Chromatic, dramatic, tonal writing. D.

Poem cosmique Op.65 (Mer).

Sixième mot Op.72 (UE). In four parts, no bar lines. More tightly unified than the early works. D.

Trois pensées musicales Op.75 (Mer). Serious atonal works requiring sensitive pedaling. D.

Grazyna Bacewicz (1909–1969) Poland
Bacewicz was Poland's outstanding woman composer in her generation. Her music reflects the conflicts and shattering changes that took place during her lifetime.
Petit Triptyque (PWM 1966) 7pp. Three short complementary pieces using strong contemporary compositional techniques. M-D.
Rondino 1953 (PWM 1993). Tuneful with varied harmonizations, chordal, large leaps, ends with a glissando and rhythmic effect. M-D.
Sonata No.2 (PWM 1955). 21pp., 14 min. Maestoso; Largo; Toccata. Many chromatics, much rhythmic interest. Sonorous Largo, virtuoso writing in the Toccata. This work is a good example of mid-twentieth-century Polish piano writing by a moderately conservative composer. Her finest work for piano. D.
Suita Dziecieca (Suite Enfantine) 1934 (PWM 1966) 14pp. Preludium; Marsz; Walc; Kolysanka; Burleska; Menuet; Gawat; Scherzino. Clever, sparkling, charming, MC. No key signatures, chromatic. Int. to M-D.
Ten Studies (PWM 1958) 42pp. Covers pianistic problems such as leaps, extreme keyboard range, legato sixths, polyrhythms. Powerful writing. D.
See: Charlotte R. Mills, "Grazyna Bacewicz: A Stylistic Analysis and Evaluation of Selected Keyboard Works," diss., University of Northern Colorado, 1986, 139 pp.

Carl Philipp Emanuel Bach (1714–1788) Germany
The keyboard contribution of J. S. Bach's most-talented son contains over 400 works, including some 143 sonatas, approximately 50 concerti, and many separate pieces. Although there is no complete edition of his works, a comprehensive listing is to be found in MGG, I, cols. 930–35. The most extensive collection of the sonatas is in *Le Trésor des Pianistes*, which contains 65 sonatas and four rondos.

Indispensable to studying this composer is his *Essay on the True Manner of Playing Keyboard Instruments*, available in a fine English translation by William J. Mitchell (New York: W. W. Norton, 1949). Numbers preceded by W. refer to Alfred Wotquenne's *Thematisches Verzeichnis der Werke von C. P. E. Bach* (Br&H 1905). See also Eugene Helm, *Thematic Catalogue of the Works of Carl Philipp Emanuel Bach* (New Haven: Yale University Press, 1990). H. refers to *Thematic Catalogue. Complete Edition* (New York: Oxford University Press), begun in 1989. When complete this urtext edition is expected to comprise 99 volumes; coordinating editor, E. Eugene Helm.
Series I, Vol. 24, 1990. *Eight Keyboard Sonatas*, H. 176–78, 189, 92, 211–13. Claudia Widgery, ed. 127 pp.
Series II, Vol. 15, 1989. *Keyboard Concerto* No.38 in C, H. 488; *Keyboard Concerto* No. 39 in F, H. 454. Elias N. Kulukundis and Paul G. Wiley, II, eds. 112 pp.
Series II, Vol. 23, 1992. *Concertos and Sonatinas*.

SONATAS:

Clavier Sonaten und freien Fantasien, nebst einigen Rondos für Fortepiano für Kenner und Liebhaber (Connoisseurs and Amateurs) 1779–87 (Krebs—

Br&H). Vol.I: W.55/1–6. Vol.II: W.56/1–6. Vol.III: W.57/1–6. Vol.IV: W.58/1–7. Vol.V: W.59/1–6. Vol.VI: W.61/1–6. Urtext. Sonatas W.55/1 (C) and W.55/3 (A) deserve special mention. These large-scale works are eminently suitable for recitals. The fantasies contain some of Bach's most original writing. Of special interest are the Fantasia E♭ from Vol.VI and the Fantasia C from Vol.V. The other genre is the rondo, found everywhere except Vol.I. The Rondos b and G are also in *Klavierwerke* (H. Schenker—UE), Vol.II, while those in B♭ and c, from Vols.IV and V, are contained in Georgii, *Keyboard Music of the Baroque and Rococo* III.

See: E. G. Elden, "Carl Philipp Emanuel Bach's Concept of the Free Fantasia," thesis, Eastman School of Music, 1980.

William A. Koehler, "The Late Independent Keyboard Rondos of Carl Philipp Emanuel Bach," diss., University of Texas–Austin, 1986, 102 pp.

4 Leichte Sonaten (O. Vrieslander—Nag). H.56, 143, 21, and 42 in G, a, g, and D. These sonatas were not published during Bach's life. They show more buoyancy in style than many of the other sonatas. Int.

The Prussian Sonatas 1742, W.48 (Br; Steglich—Nag) 2 vols. (K). Six sonatas (each has three movements) dedicated to Frederick the Great. No.1 F: contains an Andante f, parts of which are modeled after operatic recitative; numerous dynamic indications. No.2 B♭: has a slow movement, Adagio g, with a cadenza near the end. No.6 A: the most adventurous and prophetic of the set; silence as well as sound produce much of the dramatic effect of the first movement, and one can discern a direct continuity between its development section and those of Haydn, Beethoven, and Brahms; the expressive fantasylike Adagio movement in f♯ (the favorite "Romantic" key), is followed by a Scarlattian finale. These Sonatas are among the musical high points between J. S. Bach and Haydn and firmly established Bach as a major composer. M-D.

Sonata G, W.62 (H. Albrecht—K&S) Organum, Series 5 No.2. A delightful FSF arrangement of movements. The last movement, a short Allegro, sparkles. M-D.

Sonatas and Pieces (K. Herrmann—CFP). Four sonatas, Variations on *La Folia*, Rondo E♭, and short pieces. Int. to M-D.

The Württemberg Sonatas 1744, W.49 (R. Steglich—Nag) 2 vols. (K). Six sonatas dedicated to the Duke of Württemberg. Baroque–early classic sonatas in the three-movement Italian ideal form of the time: two quick movements enclose a slow middle movement. M-D.

Sechs Sonaten mit veränderten Reprisen W.50 (Etienne Darbellay—Amadeus 1760, 1976) 72pp. Preface and critical note in German and English. Six sonatas with varied reprises in an exemplary edition including comprehensive critical material. The aphorism "Play from the soul, not like a trained bird" sums up the aesthetic approach of C. P. E. Bach, an approach that defines the style known as *Empfindsamkeit*. M-D.

Sonatas, Fantasias and Rondos (K 890). M-D.

See: M. S. Cole, "Rondos, Proper and Improper," M&L, 51 (October 1970): 388–99.

Piano Works (Herrmann—CFP 4188). Sonatas and pieces: W.50/5; 51/3; 52/3; 61/1; 65/48; 116/16, 17, 21. M-D.

Six Sonatas 1761 W.51 (Juanelva Rose—TP 1973). No.8 in Series of Early Music, University of California, Santa Barbara. These works appear here for the first time in a modern edition. They generally reflect the more conservative harmonic language favored by King Frederick. Table of ornaments and editorial notes are included. Interesting examples of works written between the Baroque and Classic periods. See especially No.6, g. M-D.

6 Sonatas (Hoffmann-Erbrecht—Br&H; Doflein—Schott, 2 vols. 2353/4) written to go with *The Essay on the True Art of Playing the Keyboard*. M-D.

6 Sonatas (K. Janelzky—Musica Rara 1958). H. 629–34.

6 Sonatas (P. Friedheim—State University of N.Y., through Galaxy). W.65/9, 16, 23; 62/19; 52/2; 53/4. Well edited. M-D.

3 Leichte Klaviersonaten (Zürcher—Schott 4707). Int.

Sonata c, W.60 1766 (F. Nagel—Eulenburg 717 1978) 6pp. Bach stated that this work is "easy and practical without any Adagio [middle movement]," adding that such slow movements were "no longer in fashion." This work could have easily been included in his *Kenner und Liebhaber* collections. It is graceful and pleasing in spite of being written in the "tragic" key of c minor. The use of dynamics shows that the work was definitely intended for a large German clavichord or a fortepiano. M.D.

MISCELLANEOUS PIECES:

Keyboard Pieces with Varied Reprises (O. Jonas—UE). Twenty-two easy pieces.

Klavierwerke (H. Schenker—UE) 2 vols. Nine sonatas, four single movements, and a rondo. A superb, interesting edition.

24 Kleine Stücke für Klavier (O. Vrieslander—Nag). Menuets, Fantasias, Polaccas, four Solfeggi, Arioso con Variazione (W.118/4, 1747), and other pieces.

Kurze und Leichte Clavierstücke (O. Vrieslander—UE). Also edited by O. Jonas (UE 1962) in Vienna Urtext Edition. Twenty-two small pieces. The word "easy" (*leichte*) is used rather loosely. These pieces are C. P. E. Bach's "Inventions." Int.

Leichte Spielstücke (Hug 1971) 12pp. Menuett D; Allegretto C; Aria B♭; Rondo b; Arioso con Variazioni A; Polonaise a. Int.

4 Fantasias (Gát—EMB) No.18 Thesaurus Musicus. M-D. Contains H.277, 278, 284, 291.

Seven Pieces (E. Caland, F. P. Goebels—Heinrichshofen 1975) 48pp. Contains pieces from various collections: Sonatas W.51/4, 5; Rondos W.53/3, W.58/1, 3; and two short pieces, *La Stahl* and *Les languers tendres*, W.117/24. Editorial notes in German; editorial additions are confusing. A few interpretations of ornaments are questionable. M-D.

Solfeggio H.220 (Alfred; Willis). Famous study in broken chords and diatonic figuration. Int.

Miscellaneous Pieces: Abschied von meinem Silbermannschen Claviere (1781). Poignant rondo, liberally laced with rubato, unusual harmonic treatment and florid melodies. See *The Character Piece* (Anthology of Music Series), and *The Bach Family* (UE). M-D.

Musikalisches Mancherlei (Musical Diversities) (Kranz—NV). Six pieces. Int. to M-D.

See the collection *Sons of Bach* for other separate pieces.

18 Probestücke W.63 (E. Döflein—Schott). Example pieces for Bach's *Essay*, organized into six sonatas, each sonata in three movements. Allegro siciliano e scherzando, a short, graceful piece in f♯; and Allegro di molto f, fast, etude-like, with contrasting lyric sections, are choice selections. Int. to M-D.

The Second Bach (O. Jonas—SB). Unusual choice and variety of material. Int. to M-D.

12 Variationen auf die "Folie d'Espagne" (Herrmann—CFP). Unusual modulations and changes of key; brilliant and expressive keyboard treatment. M-D.

Fantasia C (J. Friskin—JF 8831). Sectional; lively and humorous; anticipates boisterous pranks of Haydn and Beethoven. Int.

Keyboard Works of C. P. E. Bach (H. Ferguson—ABRSM) 4 vols. I. Short and Easy Keyboard Pieces (19), including Six New Sonatines (W.63/7–12) from Bach's *Essay*. Valuable introduction. Int. to M-D. II. Miscellaneous Keyboard Pieces. Eleven pieces including the Fantasia Allegretto in d (W.114/7) with a suggested realization by the editor. M-D. III. Five Keyboard Sonatas: W.49/2 A♭; 55/3 b; 55/5 F; 57/6 f; 60 c. M-D. IV. Six Keyboard Sonatas from the *Essay*. Int. to M-D. Excellent edition; ornaments are realized in footnotes, essential fingering is given, and sources are identified.

23 Pièces Caractéristiques (C. Hogwood—OUP 1989) 51pp. Some of Bach's most stylistically varied pieces. La Borchward: Polonaise H. 79. La Pott: Menuet H.80. La Gleim: Rondeau H. 89. La Bergius H. 90. La Prinzette H. 91. L'Auguste: Polonaise H. 122. L'Herrmann H.92. La Buchholtz H.93. La Stahl H. 94. La Boehmer H. 81. L' Aly Rupalich (La Bach) H. 95. La Complaisante H. 109. La Xénophon—La Sybille H. 123. Les Langueurs tendres H. 110. L'Irresolüe H. 111. La Journalière H. 112. La Capricieuse H. 113. La Philippine H. 96. La Gabriel H. 97. La Louise H. 114. La Gause H. 82. L'Ernestine H. 124. La Caroline H. 98. Editorial notes include discussion of person, song, or idea that inspired the piece. Int. to M-D.

Variationen "Ich schlief da traumte mir" ("I slept, then I dreamed") H. 69, W. 118:1 (Schott Ed 7335) 21 pp. Also in collection *Masters of the Theme and Variations* (Hinson—Alfred 2209). Published with set of variations on the same tune by J. P. Kirnberger, 6 pp., as No. 9 of *Journal für das Pianoforte*. Bach's set includes 24 variations, Kirnberger's ten. Int. to M-D

See: Philip Barford, *The Keyboard Music of C. P. E. Bach* (London: Barrie and Rockliff, 1965).

——"C. P. E. Bach, A Master of the Clavichord," MO, 76 (July 1953): 601–603.

Darrell M. Berg, *"The Keyboard Sonatas of C. P. E. Bach: An Expression of the Mannerist Principle,"* diss., State University of New York–Buffalo, 1975.

Paz Corazon G. Canave, *A Re-Evaluation of the Role Played by C. P. E. Bach in the Development of the Clavier Sonata.* (Washington: Catholic University Press, 1956).

Kathleen Dale, "C. P. E. Bach and the Keyboard," MMR, 76 (October 1946):187–92.

Emily R. Daymond, "C. P. E. Bach," PRMA, 33 (1907).

Frank E. Lorince, "A Study of Musical Texture in Relation to Sonata-Form as Evidenced in Selected Keyboard Sonatas from C. P. E. Bach through Beethoven," diss., University of Rochester, 1966.

William J. Mitchell, "C. P. E. Bach's 'Essay': An Introduction," MQ, 33 (1947):460–80.

Dragan Plamenac, "New Light on the Last Years of C. P. E. Bach," MQ, 35 (1949):565–87.

Eduard Reeser, *The Sons of Bach* (Stockholm: Continental Book Co., 1949).

Walter Schenkman, "Three Collections of Keyboard Works by C. P. E. Bach," Part I, *Bach*, 8 (October 1977):23–33; Part II, *Bach*, 9 (January 1978):2–14. Deals with three representative collections of keyboard works: the *Prussian* and *Württemberg Sonatas* and the *Sechs Sammlungen für Kenner und Liebhaber.*

Patricia Ann Thompson, "A Study of the Chromatic Fantasy in D Minor (J. S. Bach) and the Free Fantasia in C Minor by C. P. E. Bach," thesis, University of Washington, 1958.

Jean M. Walkinshaw, "Improvisatory Aspects of the Keyboard Music of C. P. E. Bach (1714–1788)," thesis, University of Washington, 1972.

Jan Bach (1937–   ) USA

Three Bagatelles 1963 (AMP 1979) 21pp. Emilia (for unprepared piano): "twittery." Lauretta: reflective, recitatives. Pamfilo: restless. All are thorny mazes to cut through. Unusual sonorities, Expressionist in style. Helpful suggestions to the performer, e.g.: "Use all or none depending on tightness in R. H." D.

Johann Christian Bach (1735–1782) Germany

The youngest and most successful son of J. S. Bach is one of the most important representatives of Italianate lyricism in the early development of the piano sonata. A student of Padre Martini during his stay in Italy, J. C. Bach soon became a major musical influence in London after his arrival in that world capital. Thin textures, Alberti basses, sequences, passagework, and smooth "singing melodies" are found in abundance in his works, which are of moderate difficulty. In 1768, J. C. Bach was the first musician to perform in solo on the pianoforte; and with his friend Carl Friedrich Abel, he gave concerts in London for seventeen years. J. C. Bach greatly influenced Mozart, whose admiration for him is well known. He composed 24 solo keyboard sonatas but only about half of them are readily available in modern editions.

12 Keyboard Sonatas (Christopher Hogwood—OUP). A facsimile of the original eighteenth-century editions with an excellent introduction by the editor. Set I Op.5 (1768), Six sonatas. Set II Op.17 (1779), Six sonatas. The *style galant* at its best. Both sets sound fine on the piano or harpsichord but even better on the fortepiano. Excellent preparation for Mozart sonatas. Int. to M-D.

Klaviersonaten Op.5 Vol.I (Heinemann—Henle 332 1981) with fingering by H. -M. Theopold, 53pp. Sonatas B♭; D; G; E♭; E; c. Op.17 Vol.II (Heinemann—Henle 333 1981) with fingering by H. -M. Theopold, 65pp. Sonatas G; c; E♭; G; A; B♭. The two sets make an important contribution to the advancement of classical instrumental forms, the principal movements revealing distinct features typical of the classical form. This edition is based on the first edition. Contains a Preface and remarks on each sonata. Urtext and performing edition.

10 Sonatas (L. Landschoff—CFP) 2 vols. Excellent introductory remarks.

Sonata G Op.5/3 (F. Goebels—Schott).

Le Trésor des Pianistes contains Op.5/3–6, and Op.17/2, 3, and 6 (as Op.12).

Sonata B♭ Op.17/6 (W. Newman—Mer). In *Sons of Bach*.

Sonata c Op.17/2 (W. Georgii—Arno Volk Verlag). In *Keyboard Music of the Baroque and Rococo*, Vol.III.

Leichte Spielstücke für Klavier (Hug 1971). Menuett F; Andantino F; Marsch C; Allegretto a; Menuett and Trio D; Theme and Variations G. Easy to Int.

14 Pieces (Hinson—Alfred 10153) 32pp. By J. C. Bach and Francesco P. Ricci. These pieces are part of a method that appeared in 1786 by both composers, written for a conservatory in Naples. All have thin textures, sequences, passagework, and smooth, singing melodies. This style greatly influenced W. A. Mozart. Int.

See: Maurice Hinson, "Johann Christian Bach and Francesco Pasquale Ricci Forte-Piano or Harpsichord Method," *Piano Journal*, 3/8 (June 1982):13–15.

Richard Maunder, "J. C. Bach and the Early Piano in London," *Journal of the Royal Musical Association,* 116 (1991): 201–10. Suggests the Op.5 sonatas and Op.7 concertos were written for the fortepiano.

Beth Mekota, "The Solo and Ensemble Keyboard Works of J. C. Bach," diss., University of Michigan, 1969.

S. W. Roe, *Keyboard Music of J. C. Bach: Source Problems and Stylistic Development in the Solo Ensemble Music* (New York: Garland Publishing Co., 1989). 490 pp.

Charles S. Terry, *John Christian Bach* (London: Oxford University Press, 1929).

Johann Christoph Bach (1642–1703) Germany

This Bach was a cousin of Johann Sebastian's father.

Aria a with 15 Variations (G. Birkner—Amadeus 1973) 12pp. Charming. Int. to M-D.

Sarabande mit 12 Variationen (H. Riemann—Steingräber). Overedited. M-D.

Prelude and Fugue E♭ (Steingräber). Bischoff formerly attributed this work to J. S. Bach (S.Anh.177). Effective. M-D.

Johann Christoph Friedrich Bach (1732–1795) Germany
Known as the "Bückeburg Bach" (since he was active at the Bückeburg court),
this ninth son of J. S. Bach wrote fifteen solo sonatas and smaller works for the
keyboard. His style combines German and Italian elements with a compositional technique characteristic of both baroque and classic styles.
Sechs leichte Sonaten (H. Ruf and H. Bemmann—Schott). Originally published
   in 1785. All in three movements. Simple and attractive. Int.
Variations on "Ah, vous dirai-je Maman." In collection *The Sons of Bach* (Alfred
   418). Theme and fourteen short, delightful variations. Easier than the famous Mozart set. Int. to M-D. Another edition of this work (F. Goebels—
   Schott 6916) includes a set of variations on the same tune by an anony-
   mous composer (1795). Charming and clever. M-D.
Leichte Spielstücke für Klavier (Hug 1971). Arioso F; Menuett and Trio D; An-
   dantino G; Allegretto c; Polonaise D; Andante F. Easy to Int.
Musikalische Nebenstunden (Musical Leisure Hours) (A. Kreutz—Schott). Fif-
   teen varied short pieces: Marche; Menuet; Polonaise; etc. Int. (T. Roberts—
   ABRSM) 40 pp., contains 26 short pieces.
Le Trésor des Pianistes, Vol.15. Sonatas in F, C, G, and F and various pieces. Int.
   to M-D.
See: Karl Geiringer, *The Bach Family* (New York: Oxford University Press, 1954).
Eduard Reeser, *The Sons of Bach*, translated by W. A. G. Doyle-Davidson (Stock-
   holm: The Continental Book Co., 1949).

Johann Sebastian Bach (1685–1750) Germany
The pianist must have a thorough knowledge of the keyboard works of this great
master. Henle Verlag and Alfred Publishing Co. have produced some remarkable
urtext editions for practical use. Vienna Urtext and Peters publish many fine editions of the individual works. It is best to request specific editors or individual
volume numbers of Peters, for many works are available from this publisher in
more than one edition. The Hans Bischoff edition (published by Kalmus) still
has many positive features. If tempo, dynamic, and articulation marks are disre-
garded, this edition is remarkable considering the date of its publication (1891).
The original Bach-Gesellschaft edition is now available in Lea Pocket Scores
through European American, and, in regular size, from J. W. Edwards (Ann Arbor, Michigan). See Vols. 3, 13, 14, 36, and 45 for the keyboard works. The *Neue
Ausgabe Sämtliche Werke* (Br) represents the latest scholarly thinking. S. numbers refer to Wolfgang Schmieder's *Thematisch-systematisches Verzeichnis der
musikalischen Werke von Johann Sebastian Bach* (Leipzig: Br&H, 1950).
   Helpful to the pianist is *Interpreting Bach at the Keyboard* by Paul Badura-
Skoda (Oxford University Press, 1993), and the preface to Rosalyn Tureck's *An
Introduction to the Performance of Bach* (New York: Oxford University Press,
1962). Consult the bibliography for other specific references to the performance
of Bach on the modern piano.
Fifteen Two-Part and Fifteen Three-Part Inventions S.772–801. The Alfred—Palmer edition is a fine scholarly and performing edition. Differences in the

autograph copies of 1720 and 1725 are noted. A table of tempo indications by Bischoff and by Czerny as well as tempi of recordings by Glenn Gould, Martin Galling, Ralph Kirkpatrick, Wanda Landowska, George Malcolm and Rosalyn Tureck are listed. The Landshoff—CFP urtext has a fine Preface. CFP also publishes a facsimile of the 1723 autograph with a Foreword by Ralph Kirkpatrick. See also the fine edition of Steglich and Theopold—Henle. Yale University Press publishes a facsimile (reproduced from the holograph) of the *Notebook for Wilhelm Friedemann Bach* with a Preface by Ralph Kirkpatrick. It contains the first version of the two- and three-part inventions. Other noteworthy editions are KMB; Bischoff—K; E. Fischer—WH; ABRSM; Röntgen—UE; Kreutz—Schott; J. Friskin—JF; Friedman—WH; and E. Simon—Dover, which contains a facsimile of the autograph along with a reprint of the Bach-Gesellschaft edition.

Two- and Three-Part Inventions (Georg von Dadelsen—Br 1972), from Vol. V/3 of the New Bach Edition; appendix includes six of the sinfonias in the ornamented form in which they survive in two MSS belonging to Bach's pupils; Ratz, Fussl, Jonas—VU 50042, edited and annotated from autographs and MS copies; contains charming rhythmic variant of Invention I; extensive critical notes and preface; Lajos Hernardi—EMB; Richard Jones—ABRSM; Kreutz—Schott; Snell—Kjos.

Two-Part Inventions (G. Anson—Willis, has performance suggestions and ornamentation; Banowetz—GWM 1974, contains an extensive discussion of ornamentation, fingering, rhythmic conventions, tempi; editorial suggestions in red print, excellent preface, helpful performance suggestions; Landshoff—CFP; Pestalozza—Ric 1973; Solymos—EMB 1972; ABRSM—Jones).

Three Two-Part Inventions C, E, F (S.772, 777, 779) (Ratz, Füssl, Jonas—VU). Urtext edition plus facsimile of the autographs.

See: Karl Heinz Füssl, "Bach's Secret Composition Course," PQ, 93 (Spring 1976):18–19. A discussion of the Inventions and Sinfonias as Bach's only manual on composition.

John Satterfield, "Dissonance and Emotional Content in the Bach Two-Part Inventions," MR, 17 (November 1956):273–81; 19 (August 1958):173–79.

Ruth Slenczynska, "J. S. Bach's Two-Part Invention No. 12—An Analysis for Performers," *Keyboard*, 10/9 (September 1984):44–45. Includes score and analysis on pp.48–50.

TM, Analysis of Invention in d, pp.56–67.

Bach composed nearly forty suites for various solo instruments. The best-known for keyboard are the "French" Suites, "English" Suites, and Partitas.

6 French Suites S.812–817 (Steglich, Theopold—Henle 71, based on the autographs and copies in the *Notebook for Anna Magdalena* of 1725; Durr—Br; Müller, Kahn—VU 50048; Keller—CFP; KMB; Bischoff—K; Petri—Br&H; E. Fischer—WH; Mugellini—Ric; EMB 1975). The form A, C, S, optional dances, and G is followed throughout this set.

Suite No.1 d (S.812). Allemande: three voices, requires fine voicing. Courante: French type, light and fast, contains complicated fingering problems. Sarabande:

four voices, harmonic. Minuets I and II; three voices, pseudo-contrapuntal, expressive. Gigue: unusual slow-moving type; requires precise treatment of dotted notes; 16ths and 32nds must be carefully handled. M-D.

Suite No.2 c (S.813). Allemande: duet, plucked bass. Corrente: Italian type. Sarabande: expressive. Air: attractive. Minuet: two voices, flowing. Gigue: two voices. Technically the easiest of the set. Int. to M-D.

Suite No.3 b (S.814). Allemande: highly organized. Courante: French type, some fingering problems. Sarabande: interesting counterpoint, must be carefully balanced. Minuet and Trio: tuneful. Anglaise: attractive. Gigue: challenging. Int. to M-D.

Suite No.4 E♭ (S.815). Allemande: flowing, easiest Allemande of the set. Courante: three voices, graceful. Sarabande: easier than one in S.814. Gavotte: attractive; observe the authentic slurs. Minuet: flowing. Gigue: trills require careful attention. M-D.

Suite No.5 G (S.816) (VU 51011 Müller, Kahn). Urtext edition plus facsimile of autograph. Allemande: melodious and expressive with phrasing a problem. Courante: fast and brilliant. Sarabande: Romantic; take plenty of time. Gavotte: a test of rhythmic control. Bourrée: tricky, begins on upbeat. Loure: flowing bass; needs delicate accentuation. Gigue: brilliant; bubbles with gaiety, a three-voice fugue with technical and rhythmic problems. The best of the French Suites. M-D.

Suite No.6 E (S.817). Allemande: contrapuntal. Courante: requires firm rhythmic control. Sarabande: rich and full chords. Gavotte: needs careful accentuation. Polonaise: nice rhythms. Bourrée: needs a snappy tempo. Minuet: charming. Gigue: trill passages require steady control. M-D.

6 English Suites S.806–811 (Steglich—Henle 100, and in 2 vols. 102, 103, based on copies by Bach's pupils; Dürr—Br 5165; Dehnhard—VU 5250060; Bischoff—K; Kreutz—CFP, in 2 vols. 4580A and B; Tamás—EMB; E. Fischer—WH; Petri—Br&H; Mugellini—Ric). These suites begin with a Prelude and are generally on a larger scale and more imposing than the French Suites.

Suite No.1 A (S.806). Prelude: flowing; three-voiced; improvisatory character; ABA form, as are all the Preludes. Allemande: complex part writing. Courante I: French type. Courante II: two variations (doubles). Sarabande: beautiful and expressive. Bourrée I: appealing. Bourrée II: more appealing! Gigue: vivacious but slower than some of its five companions. M-D.

Suite No.2 a (S.807). Prelude: lively, mainly two-voiced, could be used as a solo. Allemande: stately, moderate tempo. Courante: simple textures, rhythmic ambiguity. Sarabande: ornaments are written out in a second version. Bourrées I and II: lighter in mood than other movements. Gigue: has a da capo. M-D.

Suite No.3 g (S.808). Prelude: has the ritornello form of an Italian concerto, still within the ABA design. Allemande: similar in tempo and character to Nos.2, 3, and 5. Courante: care needed with the ornamentation. Sarabande: Bach provides both mildly and floridly ornamented versions. Gavottes I and II: No.II is a musette (bagpipe imitation), play *pp* on repeat. Gigue: a two-voice fugue with theme inverted for second half. M-D.

Suite No.4 F (S.809). Prelude: opens like a two-part invention, gathers force with various devices. Allemande: rolling triplets; figurative elements treated sequentially and contrapuntally. Courante: elaborate and refined. Sarabande: highly expressive. Minuets I and II: contrasting. Gigue: imitative counterpoint in two or three voices. M-D.

Suite No.5 e (S.810). Prelude: lively, energetic, fugal. Allemande: short motives treated in various ways. Courante: oscillation between pattern of two beats each divided in 3 and three beats divided by 2. Sarabande: more melodic than some of the other sarabandes. Passepieds I and II: in the form of a rondeau with three episodes. Gigue: a fugue. M-D to D.

Suite No.6 d (S.811). Prelude: fugal passages alternate with episodes. Allemande: short running figures pass through various voices. Courante: French type. Sarabande and Double: dignified and expressive. Gavottes I and II: provide mood contrast to surrounding movements. Gigue: stunning and more exacting technically than the other gigues. M-D to D.

See: Rosaline Cameron, "Bach's Six English Suites," MJ, 32 (July 1974): 6–7.

Serge De Gastyne, "Bach's English Suites: A New Approach," PQ, 116 (Winter 1981–82): 45–47.

J. Fuller-Maitland, *The Keyboard Suites of J. S. Bach* (London: Oxford University Press, 1925).

James W. McConkie, "The Keyboard Suites of Bach: A Consideration of the Horizontal and Vertical Elements Found Therein," diss., Columbia University, 1950.

KLAVIERÜBUNG:

The *Klavierübung* was one of the few works of Bach that was published during his lifetime. Its complete title was "Keyboard Practice consisting of Preludes, Allemandes, Courantes, Sarabandes, Gigues, Minuets, and Other Galanteries, Composed for Music Lovers, to Refresh Their Spirits," and it was published in four parts by Bach between 1726 and 1731.

Part I: *6 Partitas* (1731) S.825-30 (Pitch-Axenfeld—VU 50166-67; Steglich—Henle 28, or in 2 vols. 30, 31, based on the original edition of 1731; Jones—Br5165; Emery—ABRSM; Engler—VU 5250062; Soldan—CFP in 2 vols. 4463A&B; Bischoff—K; E. Fischer—WH; Petri—Br&H; EMB). Published as Bach's Op.1, these grand suites have greater diversity than the French and English suites. The introductory movements vary in each partita: Praeludium, Sinfonia, Fantasia, Overture, Praeambulum, Toccata. The dance movements become freer, as in Partita No.5, where Bach uses "Tempo di Minuetto," and in No.6, "Tempo di Gavotta." The standard suite form is changed in the Second Partita, in which Bach substitutes a Capriccio for the usual Gigue.

Partita No.1 B♭ (Palmer—Alfred). Praeludium: flowing arabesques in right hand over steadily moving eighth and quarter notes in left hand; fourth and fifth voices added to fill harmony at end. Allemande: arpeggiated chords; two measures before the double bar warns against a too-fast tempo. Corrente: Italian type, two voices, vivacious. Sarabande: elaborate melody requires a steady left-hand pulse to maintain motion. Minuets I and II: guard against too fast a tempo. Gigue: stunning; three voices that look like two; hand-crossings suggest Scarlatti; Italian influence. Discreet pedaling advised. M-D.

Partita No.2 c (S.826). Sinfonia: Andante section requires careful phrasing. Allemande: two voices, constructed on sequence of descending imitations. Courante: elaborate. Sarabande: different in texture from No.1 but has similar harmonic and rhythmic structure. Rondeau: base tempo on triplets in bars 86–87, delightful. Capriccio: brilliant; requires unflagging tempo; presents technical problems greater than any other movement in the Partitas. M-D to D.

Partita No.3 a (S.827). Fantasia: simple textures. Allemande: florid and elaborate. Corrante: Italian type, light and simple. Sarabande: austere, no character of a sarabande. Burlesca: slight but original. Scherzo: light. Gigue: three voices, fugal, inverted second subject, serious and weighty. M-D.

Partita No.4 D (S.828). Overture: imposing Grave orchestral opening and spirited contrapuntal Allegro. Allemande: one of Bach's most moving movements; requires a sustained cantabile line. Courante: French type, rhythmic and fast. Aria: two voices, simple, unhurried. Sarabande: Baroque arabesques in right hand over a steadily paced left hand. Minuet: short, simple. Gigue: brilliant, technically exacting; contrapuntal D.

Partita No.5 G (S.829). Praembulum: bright and lively rondo, requires well-controlled fingers. Allemande: weighty and complex. Corrente: technically one of the easiest. Sarabande: unusual rhythm, ornament interpretation not easy. Tempo di Minuetto: delicate, cross-rhythms. Passepied: trio has some difficult ornaments. Gigue: trills pose real problems; digital and interpretative complications. M-D.

Partita No.6 e (S.830). Toccata: a solid fugue framed in a decorative improvisatory opening and closing. Allemande: extremely rich. Corrente: abounds in rhythmic surprises. Air: light, delicate tune, full of bold keyboard devices. Sarabande: transcendentally rich ornamentation, most complex of all the sarabandes. Tempo di Gavotta: elegant and witty. Gigue: conceals beneath its mockery and banter recondite and masterly fugal writing. A fitting climax to the form as used by Bach. D.

Bach's first biographer, Forkel, expressed his appreciation for these suites as follows: "This work made in its time a great noise in the musical world. Such excellent compositions for the clavier had never been seen and heard before. Anyone who had learnt to perform well some pieces out of them could make his fortune in the world thereby; and even in our times, a young artist might gain acknowledgment by doing so, they are so brilliant, well-sounding, expressive, and always new" (Hans David and Arthur Mendel, *The Bach Reader* [New York: Norton, 1945] pp.337–38.

See: Walter Emery, "Bach's Keyboard Partitas: A set of Composer's Corrections?" MT, 93 (November 1952):495–99.

Charles Joseph, "Performing Bach on the Piano," *Clavier*, 14 (November 1975):20, 36–39. Compares the tempi of *Partita* No.3 in three editions and in three different recordings.

Arthur A. Lambert, "The Keyboard Partitas of J. S. Bach, A Study of Background, Text, and Interpretation," diss., State University of Iowa, 1961.

Joseph Ponte, "Problems in the Performance of J. S. Bach's Clavierübung," Part I, thesis, Harvard University, 1952.

Fernando Valenti, *A Performer's Guide to the Keyboard Partitas of J. S. Bach* (New Haven: Yale University Press, 1989).

Part II: *Overture nach französischer Art* b (S.831) and *Concerto nach italienischem Gusto* F (S.971) (1735) (Emery—Br 5161; Steglich and Lampe—Henle; Bischoff—K; Hans T. David—Schott; Soldan—CFP, early version in c, S.831a; Petri—Br&H).

The movements in S.831 are an Overture in the French manner with a majestic introduction, gigue-like mid-section, and a return to the opening idea; C; Gavottes I and II; Passepieds I and II; S; B I and II; G; and an Echo (which makes clever use of the two manuals of the harpsichord, but is also very effective on the piano; it is published separately by CFP). Paired dances take on greater importance than in any of the other suites.

See: Frederick Neumann, "The Question of Rhythm in the Two Versions of Bach's French Overture S.831," in *Studies in Renaissance and Baroque Music in Honor of Arthur Mendel* (Kassel: Bärenreiter, 1974), pp.183–94.

S.971 (Tureck—GS (see below); Engler—VU; Palmer—Alfred; Bischoff—K; Steglich and Lampe—Henle, based on first edition and manuscript copies of Bach's pupils; E. Fischer—WH; Kruetz—Schott; Petri—Br&H and Soldan—CFP, published with *The French Overture*; Röntgen—UE; Schungeler—Heinrichshofen, published with *Chromatic Fantasia and Fugue*). Allegro; Andante; Presto. Although this work was designed for a two-manual harpsichord, Bach provided a few dynamics marks. It is written in the style of the Italian concerto grosso, with "forte" and "piano" representing the alternation of large and small concertino groups. The Petri edition is almost a transcription for harpsichord, for it tries to reproduce pitches that instrument produces with 16', 8', and 4' stops.

Concerto in the Italian Style (R. Tureck—GS 1983) 18pp. plus 26pp. of critical notes and facsimile edition. In this very special edition the editor discusses the music text, original sources, embellishment symbols, notation style, part writing, Bach on the piano, and other topics. A superb critical and performing edition. W. Emery—Br. M-D.

See: Wha Kyung Choi, "The Italian Concerto of J. S. Bach and Its Interpretation," Master's thesis, Southern Illinois University, 1965.

Part III: *Four Duets* S. 802–805 in e, F, G, and a (1739) (M. Tessmer—Br; Steglich and Lampe—Henle, published separately and also with the rest of the *Klavierübung*; (Bischoff—K; Soldan—CFP; Petri—Br&H). These pieces are not for two players! Bach intended one part for the right hand and one part for the left hand. Other works in Part III are intended for the organ, and perhaps these Duets were also, but they sound well on the piano. Even though they are short and similar in character to the *Two-Part Inventions*, they are mature Bach and their construction is much more elaborate. M-D.

Part IV: *The Goldberg Variations* S.988 (1742) (R. Kirkpatrick—GS, excellent scholarly edition with information on many performance problems; Soldan—CFP; C. Wolff—Br; C. Wolff & H. Dreyfus—VU; Gilbert—Sal; Busoni and Petri—Br&H; Bischoff—K; Steglich and Theopold—Henle, published with the rest of the *Klavierübung*). This towering set of thirty-two variations, based on a majestic sarabande, was written for a harpsichord with two keyboards, but performances on the piano are frequent today. Wanda Landowska called this work, along with *The Art of Fugue* and *The Musical Offering*, "a dazzling secular temple erected in honor of absolute music." It is Bach's most highly organized set of variations. See Bibliography for numerous writings on this work.
See: Rosalyn Tureck, "The Goldberg Variations: Pianistic Prisms," MJ, 21 (March 1963):28, 89.

14 Canons S.1087 (C. Wolff—Br 5153). From Vol.V/2 of the New Bach Edition. Recently discovered work that is based on the main subject of *The Goldberg Variations*. Published for the first time. Contains a facsimile of the original MS and reproduces the canons in their original notation; also offers suggestions by the editor for their solution and performance. (Sal 1976, with realizations by Olivier Alain).

The Well-Tempered Clavier S.846–893 (Palmer—Alfred 1980; Durr—Br). Based on Bach's original autograph and every other important source known to exist. Includes the original as well as the final form of the preludes and fugues. 27pp. foreword. A superb edition with the editor's suggestions in lighter print. (Other editions: von Irmer and Theopold—Henle; Kroll—CFP; Tovey & R. Jones—ABRSM, contains an excellent introduction and separate notes for each Prelude and Fugue; Busoni—Br&H, 8 vols., contains interesting phrasing; K, Fugues are in open score; GS and K have Busoni edition of Vol. I; W. Dehnhard—VU 1977, fingering by Detlef Kraus; Mugellini—Br&H, judicious fingering; Bischoff—K; Hughes—GS; Kreutz & Keller—CFP; Röntgen—UE; Dover, reprint of Bach-Gesellschaft edition; Amsco, 2 vols., 8-page introduction and fingering by Glenn Gould, who presents a viable argument for performing both volumes on the piano; text is the one edited by Franz Kroll and published by CFP over a hundred years ago; Br&H, facsimile of Vol.I; O. Morgan—Ashdown, 2 vols.) Study edition (small scores) (Henle), Vols. 1 and 2; Thomson—Allans includes facsimile of autograph, 2 vols.
Available separately: Preludes and Fugues S.850, 851, 861, 871 (Schott).

Selected Preludes and Fugues from Book I (Banowetz—General Words & Music 321 1980) 61pp. Includes Preludes and Fugues 1, 2, 5, 6, 21, 22. Based on seven known MSS and copies of the work. Critical notes. Excellent edition.

Prelude and Fugue Vol.I, C (S.846) (Dehnhard, Kraus—VU 51003). Urtext edition plus facsimile of the autograph.

Well-Tempered Keyboard (Bartók—EMB 4475,4476) 2 vols. The volumes are arranged in progressive order (arabic numbers standing alone refer to Preludes and Fugues in Book I of the original edition; those followed by the indication "II" refer to Book II):

Volume I	Volume II
15/II	15
6	12/II
21	1/II
10	24/II
20/II	10/II
11	16
2	5/II
9	18/II
13	24
21/II	9/II
6/II	4/II
19/II	23
11/II	3/II
19	12
14	3
18	8/II
2/II	22
5	17/II
7	4
14/II	8
7/II	20
1	22/II
17	16/II
13/II	23/II

"The Well-Tempered Clavier or Preludes and Fugues through all the tones and semitones, both as regards the 'tertia major' or 'Ut Re Mi,' and as concerns the 'tertia minor' or 'Re Mi Fa.' For the Use and Profit of the Musical Youth Desirous of Learning, drawn up and written by Johann Sebastian Bach, Capellmeister to His Serene Highness the Prince of Anhalt-Cöthen, etc. and Director of His Chamber Music. Anno 1722" (Hans David and Arthur Mendel, *The Bach Reader* [New York: Norton, 1945], p.85). This title indicates the instructional emphasis Bach placed on this work, yet the musical world has chosen to place it among the loftiest of his creations.

Well-Tempered Clavier Vol.I (1722) Cöthen
   1. C (S.846) Prelude: modulating chords in broken figures require delicacy and evenness. Fugue: rich in strettos but contains no episodes and needs careful tonal distinction between voices played by same hand.
   2. c (S.847) Prelude: persistent animated broken-chord figuration to five

bars before the end, three tempo changes. Fugue: four episodes use fragments of the subject; requires rhythmic vitality.

3. C♯ (S.848) Prelude: dazzling; even finger technique essential. Fugue: graceful and dancelike; requires firm rhythmic control and finger independence in double-note passages.

4. c♯ (S.849) Prelude: duet between outer voices requires legato and cantabile phrasing. Fugue: five-voice triple fugue, three distinct subjects developed separately and together; climax in third section is more internal than external.

5. D (S.850) Prelude: charming; should be played leisurely, with even finger technique. Fugue: grand "Handelian style," with dignity but not too stiff or affected.

6. d (S.851) Prelude: harmonic subtleties lurk in inner voices; even finger technique required. Fugue: three voices, requires careful tonal discrimination between voices.

7. E♭ (S.852) Prelude: pastoral mood in flowing sixteenth notes interrupted once by a fugato; steady tempo but not dragging. Fugue: requires good phrasing and staccato plus rhythmic vitality and steady, even fingers.

8. e♭ (S.853) Prelude: grand; break (roll) chords solemnly; sarabande rhythm; cantabile plus steady rhythmic flow. Fugue: slow and eloquent; grasp design and point to climax.

9. E (S.854) Prelude: a three-part invention that needs legato cantabile phrasing. Fugue: high-spirited and busy; needs even fingers.

10. e (S.855) Prelude: flowing; duet-like; chordal punctuation; even finger control necessary, especially in second half. Fugue: easiest of the fugues, with energy but not too hurried; even fingers needed.

11. F (S.856) Prelude: dashing study in finger playing that needs smooth legato. Fugue: has rhythm and grace of a passepied; point up phrasing of imitative entries.

12. f (S.857) Prelude: legato; organistic; steady and reposeful tempo. Fugue: unique chromatic subject; point up contrast between thematic parts and episodes.

13. F♯ (S.858) Prelude: giguelike, transparent two-voice texture, flowing, cantabile legato. Fugue: soft and gently flowing, requires careful voice leading.

14. f♯ (S.859) Prelude: suppressed emotional content; serious; requires even fingers. Fugue: expressive; countersubject as important as subject; legato cantabile.

15. G (S.860) Prelude: broken chords; exuberant; needs strong finger technique. Fugue: multi-part subject; requires uninterrupted tempo and sharp articulation.

16. g (S.861) Prelude: three-voiced arioso; begin trills slowly then increase their speed and slacken toward the end. Fugue: quietly moving tempo; do not let the subject fall apart at the rest; differentiate between voices. Nos.15 and 16 make an excellent group.

17. A♭ (S.862) Prelude: festive and ceremonial; sarabande-like; requires

much rhythmic vitality. Fugue: warm and noble; organistic; phrasing and careful legato essential.

18. g♯ (S.863) Prelude: a three-part invention strictly worked out; cantabile; quietly moving tempo. Fugue: one of the freest, subject is legato except for repeated eighth notes, which should be slightly separated; expressive and graceful.

19. A (S.864) Prelude: three-part invention that stresses contrapuntal interest; develops three themes in triple counterpoint; reflective tempo; be careful of voice leading. Fugue: dance rhythm; strange subject; delicate; accurate tonal balance vital.

20. a (S.865) Prelude: bold; elastically resilient subject; requires much rhythmic vitality; superior to the fugue. Fugue: four voices almost throughout, monotonous rhythm; separate large sections from one another; do not emphasize all subject entries.

21. B♭ (S.866) Prelude: brilliant; a fast and lightly tossed-off small toccata that requires steady finger technique. Fugue: a capricious dance that needs much rhythmic vitality and finger independence in the double-note figuration.

22. b♭ (S.867) Prelude: dark, poignant, expressive phrasing in flowing rhythms. Fugue: songlike; full and warm choral sonorities; legato cantabile; be careful of voice-leading.

23. B (S.868) Prelude: three-part invention; quietly flowing tempo; phrasing and careful finger control essential. Fugue: all voices should be quiet and songlike; legato and careful balance of voices required.

24. b (S.869) Prelude: two-voice canon plus scale accompaniment; Bach's direction "andante" means a quiet, steady tempo, with quarter note ca.69. Fugue: longest in the *WTC*; bold subject, "largo" indicates solemnity and breadth; bring out tonal contrast in episodes not based on main subject.

Well-Tempered Clavier Vol.II (1744) Leipzig

1. C (S.870) Prelude: has much charm and fluency; legato; requires dignity and breadth. Fugue: masculine humor; should be played exactly twice as fast as the prelude to unify the two; requires even finger technique.

2. c (S.871) Prelude: a dancelike two-part invention, not too fast, but with a quiet, thoughtful delicacy; finger independence and careful phrasing required. Fugue: severe and reflective; tonal balance in voice leading important.

3. C♯ (S.872) Prelude: unusual meter change from 4/4 to 3/8; crescendo in bars 23–24 leads to the forte of the fughetta in bar 25, which needs rhythmic vitality. Fugue: many short-breathed cadences; grows in intensity toward closing; requires careful building of climax to the quarter-note augmentation.

4. c♯ (S.873) Prelude: five sections, problematic ornaments, needs an expressive legato. Fugue: double fugue; virtuosic; controlled, even finger technique required.

5. D (S.874) Prelude: brilliant; a complete SA movement; strong fingers

and articulation needed. Fugue: contains many harmonic delights; needs distinction between two voices in same hand, expressive and restrained.

6. d (S.875) Prelude: passagework and broken harmonies; lively; strongly articulated; full of tense energy. Fugue: dazzling, chromatic, elastically resilient, controlled energy.

7. E♭ (S.876) Prelude: five sections; lyrical; fluent transitions; gently flowing with expressive legato and phrasing. Fugue: like a choral fugue with careful attention to voice leading and planning of climax.

8. d♯ (S.877) Prelude: a two-part invention of 16 plus 20 bars, both parts repeated; legato and rhythmic flow are the problems. Fugue: melancholy mood; voice leading, arrival of climax, and legato cantabile present the most difficulty.

9. E (S.878) Prelude: pastoral serenity, quietly flowing, expressive phrasing and legato. Fugue: noble and stately; Palestrina-like; clear voice leading and grasp of design required.

10. e (S.879) Prelude: corrente-like; two-part and two voices; needs inner liveliness and humor. Fugue: virtuosic, requires a powerfully controlled rhythmic vitality and drive.

11. F (S.880) Prelude: four sections; restful and peaceful; sustained notes must have a clear singing quality. Fugue: fleeting and light; needs firm rhythmic control and even fingers.

12. f (S.881) Prelude: simplest and technically the easiest prelude, expressive legato phrasing. Fugue: capricious, needs even fingers and rhythmic vitality.

13. F♯ (S.882) Prelude: festive; like a French overture; needs verve, fire, and strong rhythms. Fugue: bold trill opening; gavotte-like episodes; delicacy and rhythmic vitality important.

14. f♯ (S.883) Prelude: a noble arioso that requires smooth legato and eloquent phrasing. Fugue: triple fugue with three contrasting subjects; player must understand design clearly and plan tone in relation to climax.

15. G (S.884) Prelude: keep it graceful and not too hasty; finger technique and rhythmic drive essential. Fugue: delicately moving, light staccato, two-voice countersubjects must come through clearly.

16. g (S.885) Prelude: grandioso, full sonorities, steady rhythmic flow. Fugue: cumulative rhetoric; needs careful planning of the climax and strong rhythmic vitality.

17. A♭ (S.886) Prelude: full of grandeur and dignity, builds to an impressive closing. Fugue: in two halves; second half intensifies; legato; distinguish the tonal voice leading.

18. g♯ (S.887) Prelude: close to SA design; animated; a certain elegance underlies the expressive legato phrasing. Fugue: gliding subject; requires a fluent, nimble tempo; legato; economy of tone.

19. A (S.888) Prelude: a pastorale-like three-part invention, needs a quiet legato delicacy. Fugue: same tempo as the prelude, constantly intertwining motives, rhythmic vitality.

20. a (S.889) Prelude: chromatic; two-part invention; reflective legato and phrasing required. Fugue: bold; grand; heavy and powerful; strong rhythmic drive essential.

21. B♭ (S.890) Prelude: fast; cheerful; graceful; flowing; smooth legato plus careful phrasing needed. Fugue: lightly animated, has grace and humor; requires tonal balance in playing two voices in same hand.

22. b♭ (S.891) Prelude: contrapuntal art plus intellectual discipline in prelude and fugue; expressive legato; careful voice leading important. Fugue: many contrapuntal devices; grasp of design needed; should not be too slow.

23. B (S.892) Prelude: 4 sections; toccata-like; requires fiery, richly colored performance with even finger technique. Fugue: quietly flowing, singing, steady rhythmic flow toward cadences.

24. b (S.893) Prelude: a two-voice dance; motivic elaboration resembles an invention; rhythmic drive; legato. Fugue: playful; like a passepied; controlled rhythmic vitality but with comfortable grace.

See: Eric L. Altschuler, *Bachanalia. The Essential Listener's Guide to Bach's Well-Tempered Clavier* (Waltham, MA: Little, Brown & Co., 1994).

Siglund Bruhn, *J. S. Bach's Well-Tempered Clavier, In-Depth Analysis and Interpretation.* 4 vols. (Hong Kong: Mainer International Ltd., 1993). The finest and most comprehensive analysis seen by this writer.

Laurette Goldberg, *The Well Tempered Clavier of J. S. Bach, A Handbook for Keyboard Teachers and Performers.* 2 vols. (Berkeley, CA: Music Sources, 1996).

Cecil Gray, *The Forty-Eight Preludes and Fugues of J. S. Bach* (London: Oxford University Press, 1938; Reprint New York: Da Capo Press, 1979).

Hermann Keller, *The Well-Tempered Clavier by Johann Sebastian Bach* (New York: W. W. Norton, 1976).

Ralph Kirkpatrick, *Interpreting Bach's Well-Tempered Clavier* (New Haven: Yale University Press, 1984).

Joseph Matthews, "Busoni's Contribution to Piano Pedagogy," DM diss., Indiana University, 1977, 120pp. See especially the chapter on Busoni's edition of Bach's *The Well-Tempered Clavier.*

Paul Pisk, "A New Look at the 'Great 48,'" *Bach*, 8 (April 1977):23–25.

Carl Schacter, "Bach's Fugue in B♭ Major, Well-Tempered Clavier, Book I, No.XXI," *The Music Forum*, 3 (1973):239–67. A thorough analysis oriented toward a Schenkerian approach.

Konrad Wolff, "Fugue Subjects without Leading Tone in the WTC," PQ, 100 (Winter 1977–78):11–12, 14.

Seven Toccatas f♯ (S.910), c (S.911), D (S.912) d (S.913) e (S.914), g (S.915), G (S.916) (Keller—CFP, urtext; Bischoff—K; Busoni, Petri—Br&H; Steglich and Lampe—Henle; Hughes—GS). These toccatas are the apex of this musical convention. They are multisectional works of a free and rhapsodic character employing diverse moods, rhythms, and textures. All contain at least one slow movement and one fugue. Tremolos and long trills abound. The fugues are more improvisatory than those in *The Well-Tempered Cla-*

vier. The Toccatas in f♯ and c are later than the others. All seven make fine opening numbers. M-D.

Available separately: S.912 (Kreutz—Schott), S.913 (Donath—Mitteldeutscher Verlag).

See: J. Fuller-Maitland, "The Toccatas of Bach," SIMG, 14 (1912–13):578–82. Published separately, London, 1913.

Sidney Grew, "The Clavier Toccatas of J. S. Bach," MT, 60 (1919):17–20.

Igor Kipnis, "Ornaments in Bach's Toccata in G (S.916)," *Clavier*, 23/8 (October 1984):20–25. Includes score.

The Little Notebook for Anna Magdalena Bach. Neue Ausgabe Sämtlicher Werke (Dadelsen—Br). Contains both the 1722 and the 1725 editions. From the 1722 edition: Suite d (S.812) A, C, S, M I and II, G; Suite c (S.813) A, C, S, Air, G; Suite b (S.814) A, C, S, Gavotte, G; Suite E♭ (S.815) A, C, S, Gavotte, Air, G; Suite G (S.816) A, C, S, Gavotte, B, Loure, G; Fantasia for Organ (S.573); Air c (S.991); Chorale "Jesu, meine Zuversicht" (S.728); Menuet c from Suite (S.813); Menuet and Trio b from Suite (S.814); Menuet G (S.814). From the 1725 edition: Partita a (S.827) Prelude, A, C, S, M, G; Partita e (S.830) Prelude, A, C, S, Tempo di Gavotta, G; Suite I pour le Clavessin d (S.812) A, C, S, M I & II, G; Suite II pour le Clavessin c (S.813) A, C, S; smaller works by Bach and other composers such as Couperin, C. P. E. Bach, Stoelzel (?) and Boehm. Some of the small dance movements (so popular with many piano teachers) are not by Bach. Bach himself started this collection with the two large partitas (Partita a S.827, Partita e S.830) as a form of dedication. The *Klavierbüchlein*, with its patchwork of grave and gay, spontaneity and profound art, opens a door for us to the Bachs' daily life. (Other editions: Henle; A. Schering—K, based on the 1725 edition; Keller—CFP; Imre—EMB; O. Mortensen—WH.) Selections are offered in *Twenty Easy Pieces* (Sauer—Augener), *Twelve Selected Pieces* (Philipp—IMC), *Twenty Easy Pieces* (Ludwig—Schott). *Selections* (Snell—Kjos).

Selections from Anna Magdalena Note Book (Palmer—Alfred). 22 pieces in scholarly edition. Int.

Bach I (Anson—Willis). Eighteen pieces from the *Anna Magdalena Bach Note Book*. Int.

Twenty Easy Pieces from Anna Magdalena Bach's Notebook (E. Sauer—CFP 3829). Int.

Easiest Piano Pieces—Notebook for Anna Magdalena Bach (CFP 5008). Thirteen pieces. Int.

Anna Magdalena Bach Notebook (Langrish—ABRSM) 32pp. Twenty pieces. S. Anh.113–132. Highly edited. Int.

The Little Notebook for Wilhelm Friedemann Bach (1720) *Neue Ausgabe Sämtlicher Werke* (Wolfgang Plath—Br). A scholarly edition that includes Bach's only table of ornaments and 62 pieces. This notebook contains first versions of 11 preludes from *The Well-Tempered Clavier, 15 Two-Part Inventions* (Praeambulums), *14 Three-Part Inventions* (Fantasias), and miscellaneous pieces by Bach, W. F. Bach, Richter, Telemann, and J. G. Stoelzel. The miscellaneous pieces are Applicatio C (S.944); Prelude C (S.924a); "Wir nur den lieben Gott" (S.691); Prelude d (S.926); "Jesu meine Freude" (S.753); Allemandes g (S.836 and 837); Prelude F (S.927); Prelude g (S.928); Minuet G (S.841); Minuet g (S.842); Minuet G (S.843); earlier versions (with different S. numbers) of two preludes from *The Well-Tempered Clavier*: Prelude No.1 C (S.846a), and Prelude No.5 e (S.855a); Prelude C (S.924); Prelude D (S.925); Prelude e (S.932); Prelude a (S.931); Fugue C (S.953); Suite by Telemann (S.824); Partita by Stoelzel with minuet trio by Bach (S.824). (Other editions: K; Ralph Kirkpatrick—Yale University Press, 1959, facsimile of the holograph with commentary; H. Trede—Schott, 16 selections; Palmer—Alfred 603, 22 selections.)

See: Trevor Fischer, "The Little Clavier Book for W. F. Bach," MT, 101 (February 1960):87–88.

SEPARATE PIECES:

Chromatic Fantasia and Fugue d (S.903) 1720–23 (Henle 163; Schenker, rev. Jonas—UE; Keller—CFP; Busoni—Br&H; Bischoff—K; Kreutz—Schott; E. Fischer—WH; Röntgen—UE; Huber—UE; Schenker—Longman, 128-page critical edition with commentary translated and edited by Hedi Siegel; Schungeler—Heinrichshofen, published with the *Italian Concerto*). Expansive harmonic language; highly sectionalized and free in construction. The three-voice fugue is a magnificent example of dramatic cumulative effect. M-D to D.

See: Heinrich Schenker, *J. S. Bach's Chromatic Fantasy and Fugue*. Critical edition with Commentary. Trans. and ed. by Hedi Siegel (New York and London: Longman, 1984), 101 pp. The commentary includes, among other topics, a discussion of non-legato, dynamics, and fingering. An appendix lists works of Heinrich Schenker.

Konrad Wolff, "Bach's Chromatic Fantasy S.903—An Attempt at an Analysis with Commentary and Realizations," PQ, 115 (Fall 1981):41–45.

Fantasia and Fugue a (S.904) (CFP 208; Br&H). The Fantasia is written in organ style, while the double Fugue is one of Bach's most majestic compositions. M-D.

Fugue a (S.944) (CFP 9009; Br&H; Durand). Opening arpeggiated introduction leads to one of Bach's longest fugues (198 bars) in "perpetual-motion" style. M-D.

Fantasia c (S.906) (Br 1976; CFP 9009; Br&H; Henle; Schott; JF; K). Brilliant, short, Scarlatti-like. Int. to M-D.

Prelude and Fugue a (S.894) (CFP 9009; Br&H). This large work, later transformed into the opening and closing movement of the *Triple Concerto* in a (S.1044), requires the utmost finger dexterity. The Prelude is in the style of a huge fantasy while the fugue is gigue-like. Impressive. D.

Adagio G (S.968) (CFP 9091). A beautiful transcription by Bach of the first movement of the *Sonata* C for unaccompanied violin S.1005. Very effective on the keyboard. M-D.

Two Fugues on Themes by Albinoni. A (S.950), b (S.951) (Bischoff—K; Kreutz—Schott; Friskin—JF). M-D.

Capriccio, On the Departure of a Beloved Brother (S.992) Bischoff—K; Dadelsen—Henle; Busoni—Br&H; Friskin—JF; Goldberger—GS; CFP). An early (1704?) work. Bach's only example of programmatic keyboard music. In six sections with programmatic titles. M-D.

Three Fugues on Themes by Reinken, a (S.965); C (S.966); B♭ (S.954) (Keller—Br). The first two themes are from Reinken's *Hortus Musicus.* M-D.

Sonata D (S.963) (CFP; Br&H). Two untitled movements (125 and 41 bars respectively). Adagio introduction to a fugue "all' Imitatio Gallina Cucca," imitating a hen and a cuckoo. M-D.

Sonata d (S.964) (CFP; Br&H). A transcription of a solo violin sonata a S.1003. Adagio; Fuga; Andante; Allegro. M-D.

See: Kenwyn G. Boldt, "The Solo Clavier Sonatas Attributed to J. S. Bach," DM paper, Indiana University, 1967.

Sonata C (S.966) (K) in Various Works. Vol.I: Präludium; Fuga; Adagio-Presto; Allemande; Courante; Sarabande; Gigue. Bach's transcription of a quartet by J. S. Reinken. M-D.

Suite a (S.818) (CFP 214 and 9007: A, C, S Simple, S Double, G. S.818a; Busoni, Mugellini—Br&H: Prelude, a different version of the C, a different S, M, the same A and G as S.818). In the style of the French Suites. M-D.

Suite E♭ (S.819) (CFP 214 and 9007; Busoni, Petri—Br&H). Two separate Allemandes, C, S, B, and M with Trio in e♭. M-D.

Two Suites (S.818, 819, 818a, 819a) (Durr—Br 5166). Includes second versions. M-D.

Suite f (S.823) (CFP 9007: Busoni, Petri—Br&H; Tureck—OUP, in Vol.III of *An Introduction to the Performance of Bach*). P, S, G. Lute influence. M-D.

Suite A (S.824) (Busoni, Petri—Br&H; Tureck—OUP, in Vol.III of *An Introduction to the Performance of Bach*). A, C, G. This suite is contained in the *Notebook for W. F. Bach.* Difficulty of French Suites.

Ouverture F (Suite) (S.820) (CFP 9007) (Busoni, Petri—Br&H). An untitled opening movement in the style of a French Overture, Entrée, M (Trio), B, G. M-D.

Suite B♭ (S.821) (Busoni, Petri—Br&H). Praeludium, A, C, S, Echo. M-D.

Suite g (S.822) (CFP 1959). Overture, Aria, Gavotte en Rondeau, M I and II (Trio), G. An early work. M-D.

Partita c (S.997) (CFP 9007) (Busoni, Petri—Br&H; H. Ferguson—Schott). Preludio, Fuga, S, G, Double. M-D.

Suite F (S.Anhang 80) (J. Werner—Ascherberg). A, C, S, G. Dates from around 1701. Easier than any of the French or English Suites. The autograph is at Stanford University. M-D.

Aria with Variations in the Italian Manner (S.989) 1709 (Tureck—OUP, in Vol.III of *An Introduction to the Performance of Bach*; CFP 9043; Br&H; Bischoff—K; Amadeus-Paüler; Frotscher—Mitteldeutscher Verlag). Aria with ten contrasting variations. M-D. This early set and the *Goldberg Variations* are Bach's only two separate sets of keyboard variations.

COLLECTIONS for the early grades of piano study:

Dance Forms from the Suites (Anson—Willis). Thirteen dances from the Suites and Partitas. Int. to M-D.

The Dances of J. S. Bach (Hinson—Alfred 600). These pieces are to be played before the *Two-Part Inventions*. Includes allemandes, courantes, sarabandes, 18 optional dances, and gigues. The Foreword includes a discussion of the Bach suites, standard dance movements, optional dance movements, interpretation, table of ornaments, a suggested order for studying the keyboard works of Bach, and editorial policy. Int.

  See: Natalie Jenne and Meredith Little, "Bach's Dance Music," *Clavier*, 34/9 (November 1995): 21–23.

  ——, *Dance and the Music of J. S. Bach* (Bloomington: Indiana University Press, 1991).

Bach Collection (Berlinger, Jonas—SB). Fifteen pieces, mainly from the suites, and one gigue by Telemann. Int. to M-D.

Various Short Preludes and Fugues (Bischoff—K). Int. to M-D.

The Young Bach (E. H. Davies—OUP). Twenty pieces from the two notebooks and five preparatory canonic studies. Easy to Int.

The First Bach Book (Lipsky—K). Easier pieces.

An Introduction to the Performance of Bach (R. Tureck—OUP 1960). A graded series of three volumes on Bach performance. Contains both text and music. Vol.I discusses fingering, phrasing, dynamics, touch, pedaling, ornamentation, instruments (harpsichord, clavichord, piano), and a section on playing Bach on the piano. Eight pieces from the notebooks plus Tureck's realization of the Applicatio from the W. F. Bach notebook. Easy to Int.
  Vol.II has further notes on ornamentation, fingering, phrasing, practical uses of the sustaining pedal, and suggestions for the study of contrapuntal music, especially two-, three-, and four-part counterpoint. Music includes: Invention C (S.722) with its inversion; Fantasia g (S.917); Prelude and Fugue a (S.895). Int. to M-D.
  Vol.III discusses manuscripts, editions, repeats, the Baroque dot, Bach's table of ornaments, and further questions of ornamentation. Music includes: Suite f (S.823); Suite A (S.824); Aria and Ten Variations in the Italian Style (S.989). A first-rate series by one of our foremost Bach interpreters. M-D.

Bach verklärt (P. Cox—E. C. Schirmer). Includes numerous little-known pieces. Int. to M-D.

Bach. Die kleinen Klavierstucke (Döflein—Br). Thirty-three pieces, mainly Little Preludes. Int.

Leichte Klavierstücke (H. -J. Schulze—CFP 9412 1974) 59pp. Preface and critical notes in German and English. Forty-five pieces compiled from various keyboard works. Int. to M-D.

Young Pianist's Guide to J. S. Bach (Y. Novik—Studio PR 1976) 24pp. with recording. Eleven pieces, mostly from the *Anna Magdelena Bach Notebook*. Well edited. Easy to Int.

The Young Pianist's Bach (H. Davies—OUP). Formerly titled "The Children's Bach."

Il Mio Primo Bach, Vol.I (E. Pozzoli—Ric E. R. 1951) 13pp. Minuets G, g, c, d, G, a; Musette G (from the Gavotte, English Suite g); Musette D; Polonaise g; Marches D, G; Prelude g. Easy to Int. Vol.II (Riboli—Ric 1973). Contains eight of the eighteen Short Preludes, three Two-Part Inventions. Fingering provided is used to indicate phrasing, mainly by thumb repetition. A few suggestions are given in footnotes but no dynamics or phrasing are indicated. Int.

Introduction to the Study of Bach (Mirovitch—GS 1955) 35pp. Contains a foreword, notes on interpretation, a Bach course of study (discussion of dance forms, the prelude, compositions in polyphonic form, the fugue, three-part inventions, English Suites and Partitas, Toccatas, *Well-Tempered Clavier*). Preparatory pieces by Hook, Zipoli, Chilcot, Kirnberger. Bach pieces include four Preludes and four movements from the French Suites. Int. to M-D.

Bach Easy Piano (Alfred). Seventeen easier selections of Bach's most familiar music from the suites and the *Anna Magdalena Bach Notebook*. Brief biography; notes concerning the style or origin of each piece; ornaments realized. Easy to Int.

Bach—Favorite Pieces (Alfred). Twenty-eight pieces with a few duplicates from the *Bach Easy Pieces* collection. Also includes more difficult works, such as three pieces from the *Wilhelm Friedemann Bach Notebook*, four Two-Part Inventions, two Preludes and Fugues from WTC I, dances from the suites, and transcriptions. A short biography and notes about each piece add interest. Int. to M-D.

J. S. Bach—An Introduction to His Keyboard Music (W. Palmer—Alfred). A varied selection of works with the usual fine introductory material providing a good understanding of the composer and his music. Int.

Easier Piano Pieces (H. J. Schulze—CFP 9412). A selection of 45 easy to M-D pieces and movements, either original or transcribed by Bach. With details of sources and comments by the editor in English and German.

Das Bach—Klavierbuch (Wiehmayer—Heinrichshofen 20). Fifty easy pieces.

J. S. Bach (Henry Duke—Freeman). In Keyboard Master Series. Prelude c (from *12 Short Preludes*); Courante G; Two-Part Inventions F, a, d; Three-Part Invention E; G from Partita I; Air on the G String; Prelude C from WTC I. Fingering, pedaling, and phrasing are added. Int. to M-D.

First Lessons In Bach (Carroll, Aldrich—Alfred 1977) 31pp. Many of the easier pieces. Aldrich has revised Carroll's original instructive comments from the earlier edition (GS). Phrasing, tempo indications, and dynamics are by Carroll. Easy to Int.

J. S. Bach. Easiest Piano Pieces (Steurer—CFP 5012 1980) 23pp. Eighteen short pieces plus a table of ornaments. Easy to Int.

The Very First Bach Studies (Teöke—EMB Z8865) 43pp. Thirty-six of the easiest pieces by Bach, some from the notebooks for Anna Magdelena Bach and Wilhelm Friedemann Bach. Well edited. Easy to Int.

Short Preludes and Fugues:

Unedited:

Little Preludes and Fugues (Steglich—Henle). Based on the *Notebook for Wilhelm Friedemann Bach.*

24 Little Preludes and Fugues (Keller—CFP).

Little Preludes (Edwin Fischer—WH).

12 Little Preludes (Kreutz—Schott). S.924–930; 939–942; 999.

6 Little Preludes (Kreutz—Schott). S.933–938.

6 Little Preludes (Bischoff—K).

Edited:

Little Preludes, Fughetta c, Four Duets (Busoni—Br&H).

24 Little Preludes and Fugues (Czerny—CFP).

24 Little Preludes and Fugues (Röntgen—UE).

12 Little Preludes (Anson—Willis).

Kleine Präludien und Fughetten (Denhard—VU 1973). S.895, 899, 900, 902, 924–28, 930, 933–43, 952, 953, 961, 999. Edited from autograph and MS copies. Fingering added. Preface and critical notes in German and English.

Kleine Präludien (H. Walter—Br&H 1977) Vol.I (13pp.): S.902a; 926–27; 934–35; 937. Vol.II (13pp.): S.925; 928–29; 933; 936; 940–41. Vol.I provides a link between the easy dancelike movements of the notebook for Anna Magdalena Bach and the *Two-Part Inventions*. Vol.III (13 pp.): provides practice in hand independence. Excellent preparation for the *Three-Part Inventions* and the more difficult movements of the *French Suites*. Ornaments are realized in footnotes. Fingered. Int. to M-D.

18 Little Preludes (ABRSM) 36pp. Six Little Preludes from the Notebook for Wilhelm Friedemann Bach, S.924–928, 930; Six Little Preludes for Beginners; S.933–938; Six Little Preludes from Johann Kellner's Collection, S.939–943, 999. Highly edited. Int.

MORE DIFFICULT COLLECTIONS:

Sonatas and Partitas (PWM). Well edited. Int. to M-D.

Keyboard Music (Dover) 312pp. A reprint of the Bach Gesellschaft edition, 1853 and 1863: 6 English Suites; 6 French Suites; 6 Partitas; Goldberg Variations; 15 Two-Part Inventions; 15 Three-Part Sinfonias. Clean edition. Int. to D.

14 Chorale Preludes (Zorn—Concordia). From the chorale preludes Bach wrote for the manuals alone. Int. to M-D.

Klavier und Lautenwerke (H. Eichberg, T. Kohlhase—Br 5044GA). Series V Vol.10 of the Neue Ausgabe Sämtlicher Werke. Contains the following keyboard works: Ouverture F (Suite) S.820; Suite g (S.822); Suite f (S.823); Partie A (S.832); Praeludium e Partita del Tuono Terzo F (S.833); Sonata D (S.963); Aria Variata alla maniera Italiana a (S.989); Capriccio B♭ on the Departure of His Beloved Brother (S.992); Capriccio E In Honorem Joh. Christoph. Bachii (S.992). M-D.

Bach Album für Klavier (Istvan Mariassy—EMB 1973, 1974). Vol.I (58pp): Aria variata (S.989); Capriccio B♭ (S.992); Duetto a (S.805); Fuga a (S.958); Gigue f (S.845); Menuet I G (S.841); Menuet II g (S.842); Menuet III G (S.843); Praeludium D (S.925); Praeludium F (S.928); Praeludium und Fuga A (S.896); Praeludium und Fughetta e (S.900); Praeludium und Fughetta F (S.901); Scherzo d (S.844); French Suite VI E (S.817). Clean edition. Vol.II: Duetto F (S.803); 2 Fughettas (S.679, 681); Partita a (S.827); Praeambulum d (S.875a); Sonata D (S.963); Suites a, E♭ (S.818, 819); Toccata e (S.914). M-D.

Bach, Keyboard Masterpieces (M. Gresh—GS 1976). Vol.I: English and French Suites. Vol.II: Partitas and Toccatas.

Bach: The Fugue (Charles Rosen—OUP). In Oxford Keyboard Classics series. Prelude and Fugue E (S.878); Prelude and Fugue F♯ (S.858); Contrapunctus 1, 3, 9, 10, from *The Art of Fugue* (S.1080); Fantasie and Fugue a (S.904); Ricercars a^3 and a^6 (S.1079). M-D to D.

Suiten, Sonaten, Capriccios, Variationen (Georg von Dadelsen—Henle 262). Fingering added by Hans-Martin Theopold. Preface in English, French, and German; critical notes and commentary in German. Urtext edition. Suite a (S.818a): Prelude, A, C, S, M, G. Suite a (S.818): A, C, S simple and S double, G. These two suites are similar in many ways. Suite E♭ (S.819): A (another version of this A, S.819a), C, S, B, M I & II. Ouverture F (S.820): Entrée, M, B, G. Suite f (S.823): Prélude, S en Rondeau, G. Suite A (S.832): A, Air pour les Trompettes, S, B, G. Präludium et Partita del Tuono Terzo (S.833): Präludium, A, C, S and Double, Air. 2 Menuettes from French Suites c (S.813a); E♭ (S.815a). 3 Menuettes from the Notebook for Wilhelm Friedemann Bach: I G (S.841); II g (S.842); III G (S.843). Sonata D (S.963). Sonata a (S.967). Sonata after Reinken a (S.965). Sonata after Reinken C (S.966). Sonata d (S.964, transcribed from a violin sonata). Adagio G (S.968), transcribed from a violin sonata C). Capriccio on the Departure of His Beloved Brother (S.992). Capriccio E in Honor of Johann Christoph Bachii Ohrdruf (S.993). Aria Variata a (S.989). Int. to M-D.

Einzelne Suiten und Suitensaetze (Complete Suites and Movements from Suites) (CFP 9007). Most of the movements are based on dance forms, and much of the music is relatively unknown. Int. to M-D.

Sonaten und Sonatensatze (CFP 9066). Includes four complete sonatas, S.963, 964, 965, 966, and two separate sonata movements, Adagio G (S.968), Allegro e (S.1019). Some of this material was used by Bach in other works. M-D.

Harpsichord Music. Selections (Busoni—Br&H 4314 1982 reprint) 81pp. Chromatic Fantasy and Fugue (S.903): Capriccio on the Departure of a Beloved

Brother (S.992): Fantasie, Adagio and Fugue c (S.968): Prelude, Fugue and Allegro (S.998). Preface in German. M-D.

Musikalisches Opfer S.1079 Book I: Ricercari für cembalo (C. Wolff—Br 1983) 19pp. Magnificent contrapuntal writing. M-D to D.

Claviermusik um Johann Sebastian Bach (Keyboard Music from Johann Sebastian Bach's Circle) (R. Wilhelm—Br & H 8454 1993) 45pp. Concerto del Sign. Telemann, Anonymous. Fuga G, Johann P. Kellner. Präludium c, J. P. Kirnberger. Sechs Fugen; Fantasie und Fuge g; Johann D. Kellner. Fuga B, David T. Nicolai. Fuga F, Wilhelm H. Pachelbel. Preface in English and German and critical notes in German.

Masterworks Piano Library (W. Phemister—Fred Bock Music 1994) 72pp. One of a series developed to help the church pianist locate appropriate music for preludes, offertories, interludes, solos, and postludes. Includes repertoire originally written for organ without a pedal part. Includes variations, chorale preludes from *Clavierübung*, Part III, and miscellaneous chorale preludes. Excellent front matter and choice of material. M-D.

Miscellaneous Keyboard Works. Toccatas, Fugues and Other Pieces (Dover 1991) 303 pp. From Bach-Gesellschaft (Br & H) 1890, 1894, 1897. 7 Toccatas. PaF BWV 895. Fugue from BWV 996. Fugue BWV 897. PaF BWV 899, 900. Fantasia and Fugue BWV 905, 907, 908. Concerto and Fugue BWV 909. Fantasia BWV 920, Anh. 86, BWV 921. Prelude BWV 923. 7 Little Preludes BWV 924–930. 6 Little Preludes BWV 933–938. 5 Preludes BWV 939–943. Fugues BWV 944, 949, 951, 952, 953, 954, 955, 956, 957, 958, 959, 961. Prelude, Fugue and Allegro BWV 998. Suites BWV 818, 819. Overture BWV 820. Suites BWV 821, 823. Partie BWV 832. Partitas BWV 832, 897, 1006a. Sonatas BWV 963, 964, 965, 966. Adagio BWV 968. 3 Minuets BWV 841–843. Aria variata alla maniera italiana BWV 989. Capriccio on the Departure of His Beloved Brother BWV 992. Capriccio BWV 993.

TRANSCRIPTIONS:

See: Maurice Hinson, *The Pianist's Guide to Transcriptions, Arrangements, and Paraphrases* (Bloomington: Indiana University Press, 1990).

Philip Adamson, "Problems for the Pianist in the Performance of J. S. Bach." diss., Indiana University, 1976, 66pp. See especially the chapter on the differences between harpsichord and piano technique.

Putnam Aldrich, "Bach's Technique of Transposition and Improvised Ornamentation," MQ, 35 (January 1949):26–35. You may not agree with all of Aldrich's findings but his scholarship is beyond question.

Sol Babitz, "On Using J. S. Bach's Keyboard Fingerings," ML, 43 (April 1962):123–28. Includes a discussion of "notes inégales," fingerings, ornamentation.

Paul Badura-Skoda, *Interpreting Bach at the Keyboard* (London: Oxford University Press, 1993).

L. S. Barnard, "Philip Dore's Bach Clavier Lectures," MO, 76 (May 1953):491–93,

557–59; continued in subsequent monthly issues through February 1954. Reports on a series of twenty lecture-recitals entitled "The Clavier Works of J. S. Bach."

Diane Carliner, *The Bach Sinfonias: History and Performance* (Baltimore: Musicolor Publication, 1968). In color. Different color for each voice; historical and performance commentary.

James Ching, "On the Playing of Bach's Clavier Music," MT, 91 (August 1950):299–301.

Thurston Dart, "Bach's Early Keyboard Music: A Neglected Source," AM, 42/3–4 (1970):236–38.

Robert C. Ehle, "Comments on the Goldberg Variations," AMT, 19 (November-December 1969):20–22.

Edwin Fischer, *Reflections on Music* (London: Williams and Norgate, 1951). See chapter on Bach.

J. Fuller-Maitland, *The "48": Bach's Wohltemperiertes Clavier.* 2 vols. (London: Oxford University Press, 1925).

Karl Heinz Füssl, "Bach's Secret Composition Course," PQ, 93 (Spring 1976):18–19. A discussion of the Inventions and Sinfonias.

John Horton, "A Famous Primer—J. S. Bach's Little Keyboard Book for Wilhelm Friedemann," *Music Teacher*, 60/3 (March 1981):21.

Serge de Gaslyne, "Bach's English Suites—A New Approach," PQ, 116 (Winter 1981–82):45–47.

Edwin Hughes, "'Forty-Eight' from the Player's Standpoint," MQ, 11 (July 1925):444–53.

George Kochevitsky, "The Performance of J. S. Bach's Keyboard Music," PQ, 54 (Winter 1965–66).

Wanda Landowska, *Landowska on Music.* Edited by Denise Restout. (New York: Stein & Day, 1964.)

Ray McIntyre, "On the Interpretation of Bach's Gigues," MQ, 51 (July 1965):478–92.

Fritz Rothschild, *A Handbook of the Performance of the Forty-eight Preludes and Fugues of Bach According to the Rules of the Old Tradition,* 2 vols. (London: Adam and Charles Black, 1955).

Liselotte Selbiger, "Bach on the Piano," MR, 11 (May 1950):98–108.

Howard Stephens, "Bach's French Suite No. 2 in G Minor," *Music Teacher*, 60/4 (April 1981):16.

Wadham Sutton, "J. S. Bach: The Goldberg Variations," *Music Teacher*, 54 (August 1975):11.

Dennis Todd, "Bach's Partita No. 1 in B flat Major," *Music Teacher*, 60/2 (February 1981):13.

Rosalyn Tureck, "A Revaluation of Concepts in Relation to the Interpretation and Performance of Bach," *Bulletin of the British Institute of Recorded Sound*, 1957 (Autumn):2–17.

——, "Bach in the Twentieth Century," MT, 103 (February 1962):92–94.

——, "Bach: Piano, Harpsichord or Clavichord," AMT, 11 (January-February 1962):8–9, 30.

——, "Learning to Learn Bach," *Etude* (May-June 1956):13–14, 48.

——, "Bach on the Piano? Why Not? After All, He Was a Piano Salesman," HF, 27 (October 1977):91–93.

Lory Wallfisch, "The Gigues of the Six 'French Suites' by J. S. Bach—A Performer's and Teacher's View," *Piano Journal*, 7 (February 1982):11, 13–14.

P. D. Q. Bach (1807–1742)?

Three Teeny Preludes S.001 (TP) 6pp., 2 min. Three parodies after J. S. Bach's *Short Preludes and Fugues*. The first one keeps the treble part in one hand position and is most expressively played during muscle spasms or earthquakes. The other two draw from Barber Shop, Baroque and Nashville. Twentieth-century Baroque style. Composed in Baden Baden during P. D. Q.'s "Contrition Period." Clever, fun. Int.

Notebook for Betty Sue Bach, S. 13 going on 14 (TP 1973) 23pp. Allemande Left; Corrate; Oh! Courante!; Two-Part Contraption; Three-Part Contraption; Andre Gigue; Traumarie; Capriccio Espagnole for Charles III, "The Reign in Spain." Written in P. D. Q. Bach's most gingerly style—great fun! Int.

"Goldbrick" Variations S.14 1996 (TP) 11pp., ca. 6 min. Var. I: Allegro boffo. Var. II: Lento pathetico. Var. III: Presto changio. Theme: Lento not so pathetico. Vintage P. D. Q. Bach. Great fun for all. Int. to MD.

Wilhelm Friedemann Bach (1710–1784) Germany

The oldest son of J. S. Bach combines both contrapuntal and homophonic styles in his keyboard writing. His musical language is very expressive and represents the "Empfindsamkeit" style, so popular during this age of stylistic overlapping. His keyboard works consist of sonatas, fantasias, fugues, concerti, polonaises and short pieces. F. numbers refer to the thematic index by Martin Falck, *W. F. Bach* (Leipzig: Kahnt, 1913), the accepted catalogue of this composer's works.

Nine Sonatas (F. Blume—Nag; K.). (1744–1754). Vol.I: Sonatas G (F.7), A (F.8), B♭ (F.9). Vol.II: Sonatas D (F.3), D (F.4), E♭ (F.5). Vol.III: Sonatas C (F.1), C (F.2), F (F.6). The second and third movements of F.1 and F.2 were revised and appear in a Fantasia c of 1784. Sonata E♭ (F.5) is in the Newman collection *Sons of Bach*, and Sonata G (F.7) is in the collection *The Bach Family*, edited by Geiringer (see Collections: German: Bach Family). All in three movements, FSF. Int. to M-D.

Drei Sonaten (Hänssler HE32.202 1980) Vol.II., 34pp. Vol.I in preparation.

Twelve Polonaises, F.12, 1765 (Bohnert—Henle; CFP; Epstein—UE, Wührer—OBV; PWM; K, highly edited). C, c, D, d, E♭, e♭, E, e, F, f, G, g. Arranged according to key; excellent examples of idealized dances, coupled with elements of sensitive "Empfindsamkeit" style. Varied moods. Int. to M-D.

Eight Fugues, F.31, 1778 (CFP). C, c, D, d, E♭, e, B♭, f. No.2 is in the collection *Alte Meister*, No.4 in Vol.II of *Harvard Anthology of Music*.

Six Little Fugues (F. Koschinsky—NV).

Ten Fantasias 1778. Not all are available in performing editions. *A Fantasia* C is
No. 31 in *Organum*, Series V (K&S). *Fantasia* e is in the collection *Alte
Meister*, and a *Fantasie* e is in Georgii, *400 Years of European Keyboard Mu-
sic* (see Collections).

Klavierfantasien (Schott 6122 1972). Edited with preface in French, German, and
English; playing instructions and critical notes (only in German) by Peter
Schleuning. Nine fantasias that require much finger dexterity. M-D.

Solo Concerto G (K&S, No.31 Series V, *Organum*). In the same category as *The
Italian Concerto* of J. S. Bach. Three movements, FSF. M-D.

Four Fantasias and a *Suite* are contained in Vol.X of *Le Trésor des Pianistes*.

Leichte Spielstücke für Klavier (Hug 1971). Menuetto and Trio a; Allegretto B♭;
Bourrée b; Menuetto and Trio d; Larghetto F; Largo d; Polonaise d. Easy
to Int.

Selected Keyboard Works (Andreas Böhnert—Henle 452, 1993) 69pp. Contains
Suite g (F. 24); Sonata D (F. 3); Sonata E♭ (F. 5); Sonata D (F. 4); Fantasia a
(F. 23); Fantasia c (F. 15). A mixed bag of thick polyphony mixed with con-
trasting moods. Informative commentary. Fingered. M-D.

Sven-Erik Bäck (1919–   ) Sweden

Bäck studied with Hilding Rosenberg and Goffredo Petrassi. His music has developed from a post-Nielsen style to a vital modern idiom. Bäck is fundamentally an intellectual with a strong feeling for mysticism.

Sonata alla ricercare (WH 1950). Exuberant and humorous first movement.

Expansive Preludes (WH 1949). Three atonal pieces. D.

Agathe Bäcker-Grondahl (1847–1907) Norway

Piano Music (Da Capo) 120pp. Introduction by Charles Slater. Includes many of
the composer's favorite salon pieces as well as her more ambitious works—
Ballade Op.36/5; Prelude Op.61/1; and several Etudes de Concert. In the
style of Schumann and Mendelssohn. Int. to M-D.

Song of Youth Op.45/1. In collection *At the Piano with Women Composers* (Alfred
428). Int.

Summer Song Op.45/3. In collection *At the Piano with Women Composers* (Alfred
428). M-D.

See: Jane M. L. Iverson, "Piano Music of Agathe Grandahl," diss., Greeley: University of Northern Colorado, 1993, 142pp.

Fridtjof Bäcker-Grondahl (1885–1959) Norway

Tre Klaverstykker Op.20 (NMO 1943) 10pp. Fragrance; Petite Chanson Hereuse;
Laengsel. M-D.

Dreaming Op.21 (NMO 1945). Thick harmonies, fast harmonic rhythm. M-D.

Scherzo Op.22 (NMO 1944) 11pp. "Printer's Error." M-D.

All these pieces are written in a style similar to Grieg's.

Ernst Bacon (1898–1990) USA

Flight (Bo&H 1948). Rhumba rhythm, perpetual motion, virtuoso writing. D.

Sombrero (MCA). In *USA 1946*, album of piano music. Short, light, humorous, 5/8. M-D.

Byways (GS). Twenty-four pieces based on folk tunes from various countries. Easy to Int.

My World (SB). Fourteen pieces, good introduction to contemporary sounds. Easy.

Maple Sugaring (GS). Arrangements of New England folk tunes. Easy.

The Pig-Town Fling. See Anthologies and Collections, USA, *New Music for the Piano* (LG). Fun for all. M-D.

Tekla Badarzewska (1834–1860) Poland

Composer of salon music.

The Maiden's Prayer 1851 (Schott Ed 7033 1982), published with her *Das erhärte Gebet*, 25pp. Reprint. Composed when the composer was seventeen years old, this piece "unaccountably seized the imagination not only of inhibited virgins, but of sentimental amateur pianists all over the world" (BBD, 7th ed., 1984, p. 124). The composer wrote 34 more piano pieces in the salon style but none matched "A Maiden's Prayer." Int. to M-D.

Henk Badings (1907–1987) The Netherlands, born Java

Sonata I (Schott 1934) 15½ min. First movement: full of dissonant counterpoint. Second movement: more lyrical. Third movement: scherzo; Finale: highly motoric. Oriented toward the Brahms–Reger–Hindemith tradition. D.

Arcadia VII (Schott 1945) 3 vols. Ten short MC attractive pieces in each volume. Int.

Paul Badura-Skoda (1927–   ) Austria

Elegie (Leduc 1982) 5pp., 6 min. Expressive, dramatic opening, filmy mid-section with a theme floating ethereally over a silent forearm cluster. Tranquillo denouement settles on a C♯-major chord. Dissonant, freely tonal style with strong French influences, many expressionistic clichés. Half-pedals, harmonics, surging octave runs, large chords. M-D.

Raymond Baervoets (1930–   ) Belgium

Hommage à Serge Prokofieff 1958 (Metropolis) 7pp. Secco style, strongly rhythmic, "tongue-in-cheek" melodic treatment, mildly dissonant. M-D.

Invensioni 1964 (CeBeDeM) 26pp., 12 min. Six pieces. Pointillistic writing, wide dynamic range. D.

Sonatine 1958 (Metropolis) 6pp., 5 min. Three movements with the finale, a toccata, the most successful. Int. to M-D.

Junsang Bahk (1938–   ) Korea

Mark (Litolff 1971) 10pp. Extensive explanation. Palm and forearm glissandi, clusters, trills, rolled chords, Stockhausen-inspired, rhythmically dull. Avant-garde. D.

William Baines (1899–1922) Great Britain
In his short life, this little-known Yorkshire composer wrote some unusual and evocative music, skillfully set for the piano.
Coloured Leaves (Augener). Prelude; Valse; Still Days; Purple Heights. M-D.
Four Poems (Augener). Poem-fragment; Elves; Poem-nocturne; Appassionata. M-D.
Pictures of Light (Elkin). Drift-Light: right hand ostinato, moving tune in left hand. Bursting Flames: octaves moving over keyboard. Pool-Lights: chromatic. M-D.
Seven Preludes (Elkin). Varied moods, charming. M-D.
Silverpoints (Elkin). Labyrinth: right hand has accompaniment against sweeping left-hand figuration. Water Pearles. The Burning Joss Stick. Floralia. M-D.
Twilight Pieces (Elkin). Twilight Woods; Quietude; A Pause for Thought. M-D.
See: Peter J. Pirie, "William Baines," M&M, 21 (November 1972):36–40.

Tadeusz Baird (1928–1981) Poland
Little Suite for Children (PWM 1952) 8pp., 5½ min. Four short MC movements. Int.
Sonatina II (PWM 1952) 18pp., 12 min. Vivo e giocoso: changing tempi and mood; restless; moves into an improvisatory andante. Andante molto e calmato: peaceful, tranquil, overtones used. Finale: full of drive and vitality; final chords played with massive force. Strong folksong influences. Style is reminiscent of early Lutoslawski. M-D.
See: Alistair Wightman, "Tadeusz Baird at 50," MT, 1627 (October 1978):847–50.

David A. Baker (1949–   ) USA
Five Pieces for Piano Igor Stravinsky—in memoriam. (CAP 1972) 15pp. No titles, only tempo indications. Neoclassic style, each piece has well-developed ideas. Closest in style to Stravinsky *Sonata*. No.4 is followed by "attacca." M-D.

David N. Baker (1931–   ) USA
Baker's style is distinctive for its blending of Afro-American elements with traditional European techniques and forms. It draws on jazz, serialism, electronic techniques, gospel, and folk materials. Baker teaches at Indiana University.
Sonata I 1969 (MMB) 37pp. Black Art; A Song—after Paul Lawrence Dunbar; Coltrane. Freely tonal, flexible meters, jazz influence, energetic octotonic writing, syncopation. "Coltrane" is toccata-like. M-D.
Jazz Dance Suite 1989 (Norruth Music) 32pp. 21 min. Facsimile of MS. 1. Some sort of waltz; 2. Solo Dance; 3. The Jitterbug Boogie; 4. Double Dance. Jazz idioms handled artistically throughout. Effective performance requires jazz experience. M-D to D.

Michael Baker (1941–   ) Canada
Four Piano Pieces Op.22 (F. Harris). Four untitled atonal and contrasting MC works that show a fine craft. Dissonant, demanding, some three-stave writing. M-D.

Sonata Op.31 (Harris 1977) 20pp., 15 min. In one movement. Vigorous cadenza opening (returns later), freely tonal figuration, clusterlike sonorities, Larghetto choralelike section, enormous coda. Thoroughly contemporary. Requires dextrous fingers. D.

Leonardo Balada (1933–   ) Spain
Balada teaches at Carnegie-Mellon University in Pittsburgh.
Música en Cuatro Tiempos (Gen 1967). Lento: one page, quiet mood builds to climax. Energico: changing meters, vigorous, fist and forearm clusters. Scherzando: eighth notes in continuous motion, changing meters. Tiempos variados: expressive; cross-rhythms; accents; ends fast; climactic closing. D.
Persistencies (GS 1978) 20pp., 8½ min. An energetic exposition launches this strikingly effective movement. Strong syncopated lines gradually expand to clusters through persistent rhythmic patterns. Highly percussive. Some relief is provided through a Poco più mosso section; palm clusters end work; opening motive repeated. D.
Transparency of Chopin's First Ballade 1976–77 (GS 3366 1982) 12pp., 10 min. A free fantasy based on the Chopin work using clusters, unbarred passages, and harmonics. A few fragments of the Chopin, tucked in here and there, are usually well concealed. M-D.
Preludis Obstinants 1979 (GS 48508 1983) 12pp. 9 min. Five contrasting sections. Many tremolo chords between the hands, parallel chromatic scales in minor seconds between the hands, evolving patterns, choralelike passages, arpeggiated chords (slower at every repetition), many contrasting sonorities. M-D to D.

Mili Balakirev (1837–1910) Russia
Balakirev was the guiding spirit behind the Russian group known as "The Five." He was a competent pianist but could never perform his own *Islamey*.
Complete Piano Works (Sorokin—USSR) 3 vols. Vols.I and III contain two books each. Vol.III, book 2, contains the two-piano works.
Ausgewählte Klavierstücke (Christof Ruger—CFP P 9576a 1977) Vol.I, 97pp. Selected piano works including Polka; Nocturne II; Mazurkas 1–3; Waltzes 4, 6; Scherzo II; Lullaby; Toccata. Epilogue in German and English. M-D. Vol.II (CFP P 9576b). A representative survey of Balakirev's piano music from his early Chopinesque genres to his program music. Includes remarks on the composer and the works. M-D.
Selected Piano Works (Roshchinoi—GS 8064).
The Lark (Musica Obscura; GS). Arrangement of a Glinka song. Int. to M-D.
Islamey 1865 (C. Rüger—CFP; Simrock; CF; Montes—Ric). The main theme is a tune Balakirev picked up on his travels in the Caucasus. He combined it with a Tartar melody and wove these materials into a rich pianistic fabric. It is his most famous work for piano and is based on Lisztian technique. A forbidding peak in the repertoire; accessible only to the most intrepid. D.

Nocturne No. 3 d (Zimmermann). Outer sections are pastoral and lyrical while the mid-section is dramatic. M-D.

Scherzo No.2 b♭ (Zimmermann; Musica Obscura). One of Balakirev's finest works; pianistically superb. Much easier than *Islamey*. M-D.

Sonata b♭ (Zimmermann; Musica Obscura). 34pp. Andante, Allegro assai feroce, Maestoso; Mazurka; Intermezzo; Finale. Reached final form after two revisions in 1905. Suite-like; unified. In Liszt tradition. Exploits percussive possibilities of the piano. D.

See: SSB, pp.728–29.

Gerald Abraham, "A Remarkable Piano Sonata," *Sackbut*, 11 (1931):330–34.

Waltz f♯ (Zimmermann). Elegant writing, pianistic, more a fantasy than a piece for dancing. M-D.

Complete Piano Works contains, in addition to the works listed above, Esquisses (Sonatina); Fantasiestück D♭; Humoresque b; 7 Mazurkas A♭, c♯, b, G♭, D, A♭, e♭; 3 Nocturnes b♭, b, d; Novelette; Polka; Reverie; Scherzi b, b♭, F♯; Tarantella B; Toccata C♯; Tyrolienne; Waltzes, G, F, b, B♭, D♭, f♯, g♯. The Tarantella is a perpetual-motion study and makes high virtuosic demands on the performer. D.

Scherzo 1 b 1856 (Zimmermann). A rather weak imitation of Chopin's Scherzo b; chromatic, octaves, meandering themes. M-D to D.

Scherzo 2 b♭ 1900 (Zimmermann; Music Obscura). One of Balakirev's finest works; pianistically superb. Much easier than *Islamey*. M-D.

Scherzo 3 F♯ 1901 (Zimmerman). Not as powerful as No.2 but charming, captivating and effective. M-D.

Balakirev Album (EMB Z.13 774 1990) 40pp. Polka: based on one melody, innocent charm, attractive coda. Mazurka I A♭: includes some slight changes in a later version. Mazurka II c♯: second verson. Lullaby D♭: beautiful and effective, prefaced by story, bell-like butterfly (from the story), coda. Sixth Waltz f♯: light, uneven in quality. Sonatina G: three movements, weak. M-D.

See: Vera Breheda, "The Original Solo Piano Works of Mili Balakirev," thesis, University of Washington, 1983.

Edward Garden, *Balakirev: A Critical Study of His Life and Music* (New York: St. Martin's Press, 1968). An unannotated Catalogue of Works (pp.330–39) and a large bibliography (pp.321–25) are of special interest.

Claude Balbastre (1729–1799) France

Pièces de clavecin, d'orgue et de fortepiano (Alan Curtis—Heugel) 93pp. Eighteen pieces including sonatas, sonatinas, overtures, and studies. Demonstrates a vigorous and brilliant style; Italian influence shows transition from harpsichord to pianoforte composition. The "Marche des Marseillois et l'air Ça ira" is an exciting battle piece. Excellent descriptive notes. Questionable editorial policy. M-D.

Livre de noëls (Schola Cantorum et Procure Generale) restitution J. Bonfils. 3 vols. Preface in French, two facsimiles. Int. to M-D.

Noël with Variations (J. Ohl—SB). Serves as excellent preparation for the Haydn or Mozart easier sets of variations. Int. to M-D.

Gerald Bales (1919–   ) Canada
Toccata (BMI Canada 1947). Tempo and texture changes, contemporary recital
    piece. Solid technical equipment necessary. M-D.

Louis W. Ballard (1931–   ) USA
Ballard, who is of Cherokee and Quapaw extraction, has used Indian folk music
and traditions for inspiration in a number of his compositions. He is chairman
of the music department at the Institute of American Indian Arts in Santa
Fe, NM.
American Indian Piano Preludes (New Southwest Music Publications, Box 4552,
    Santa Fe, NM 87502), six pieces. Well written. Indian influence gently per-
    meates each piece but is not obvious. M-D.
A City of Fire (New Southwest Music Publications). Dedicated to the people of
    Los Alamos, New Mexico, "where the fire of nuclear energy was released
    and exists in our society as a sort of 'sacred fire.'" Begins with a plaintive
    and maestoso introduction after which a rhythmical, somewhat whimsical,
    section suggests the innocence of spirit prior to "the discovery." Tonal sec-
    tions segue into tonal episodes, which by their disjunctive natures are in-
    tended to suggest the impending torment associated with those people
    who felt the impact of atomic fire. Moves onward relentlessly, with persis-
    tent rhythmic impulse. Double octaves and disjunctive leaps suggest spiri-
    tual upheaval. Ends with a musical question mark—where do we go from
    here? D.

Claude Ballif (1924–   ) France
Cinquième Sonate Op.32 (Choudens 1975) 32pp. One extended dramatic move-
    ment in contrasting sections. Serial, linear, arpeggi figuration, dynamic ex-
    tremes, pointillistic, harmonics, proportional rhythmic relationships, low
    register *ppp* tremolo, varied tempi and moods, many ritards, expressionistic
    and intense. The color, character, and structure of this work are apparent.
    Contains characteristics similar to those of the Boulez sonatas. Requires
    mature pianism and large span. D.

Esther Williamson Ballou (1915–1973) USA
Sonata (ACA 1955) 11 min. Allegro quasi Fantasia: effective use of trill, me-
    lodic sevenths, complete range of keyboard, harmonics. Andante sostenuto:
    bitonal. Chorale Variations: chorale in unison five octaves apart; four varia-
    tions. D.
Variations, Scherzo and Fugue on a Theme by Lou Harrison (ACA 1959) 12 min.
    Four variations on a two-part theme; each variation well defined. Scherzo:
    exploits percussive effects; plaintive trio using ostinato-like effect before
    Scherzo idea returns; good octave technique required. Fugue: excitingly
    worked out; leads to frenetic climax. Ballou's second sonata; a large work.
    Ballou knew the capabilities of the piano thoroughly. Requires mature
    pianism. D.

Ernö Balogh (1897–) Hungary
Conversation (Bo&H 1966) 2pp. In treble clef only, imitation. Easy.
Debate (Bo&H 1968) 3pp. Right hand on black keys, left hand mainly on white keys. Thin textures. Int.
Reel (Bo&H 1966) 2pp. All in treble clef, clever rhythmic combinations of 6/8 meter. Easy.

Oyo Bankole (1935–) Nigeria
Bankole had his early musical training in Lagos, followed by study in London and at UCLA.
Nigerian Suite (Chappell 1961) 11pp. Forest Rains; Ó Yá K'á Konga!; Orin Fún Òsùmàrè (Music for the Rainbow); October Winds; Warriors March. Contrasting, colorful, appealing. Unusual sonorities. Int.

Don Banks (1923–1981) Great Britain
Pezzo Drammatico 1956 (Schott) 5 min. In album *Contemporary British Piano Music*. Three-part form, 12-tone. Mood is established by ranges in dynamics, modes of attack, coloristic devices, and strong rhythmic vitality. Last two bars give retrograde of opening statement. M-D.

Francisco Xavier Baptista (?–1797) Portugal
12 Sonatas para Cravo ca.1770 (Gulbenkian 1981) 75pp. Contrasting works of one, two, or three movements. Similar in style to Soler. Interesting music that deserves investigation. Int. to M-D.

George Barati (1913–1996) USA, born Hungary
2 Piano Pieces (ACA 1948). Andantino: tonal, ABA, accompanied melody, succulent sonorities. Andante: harmonic preference for seconds, sevenths, and ninths; piquant sonorities; builds to climax then ends *mezzo forte*. Small tone-poems. Rather diffuse in style but effective. Int. to M-D.

Samuel Barber (1910–1981) USA
Barber's accessible idiom is based on a lyrical, neoclassical style. He used a broad spectrum of color in writing for both solo instruments and orchestra.
Love Song 1924 (Alfred 4628; also in collection *Masters of American Piano Music*) 1p. Flows gracefully, strong melody, an American "Song Without Words." Int.
Complete Piano Music (GS 1993) 113pp. Includes the works discussed below, as well as "A Personal Note" about Barber by Paul Wittke. M-D to D.
Excursions (GS 1944). Un poco Allegro: boogie-woogie style. In slow blues tempo. Allegretto: Western song with variations over ostinato harmonies. Allegro molto: square dance. Barber writes, "These are 'Excursions' in small classical forms into regional American idioms. Their rhythmic characteristics, as well as their source in folk material and their scoring, reminiscent of local instruments, are easily recognized." M-D.

Sonate eb Op.26 (GS 1949). Allegro energico: energetic, rhythmic vitality. Allegro vivace e leggiero: quick waltz vacillating between double and triple meter (hemiola). Adagio mesto: impressive ostinato treatment involving use of all 12 tones in a unique way; Allegro con spirito: demanding four-voice fugue; dissonant; chromatic; complex counterpoint but all set within a clearly articulated tonal framework. One of the most important piano sonatas of the twentieth century. D.

  See: Hans Tischler, "Barber's Piano Sonata, Opus 26," ML, 33 (1952): 352–54.

Souvenirs 1952 (GS) 17½ min. Originally for piano duet; solo version by the composer. Light, evokes ballroom music around the time of the First World War. Elements of the tango and the waltz sometimes collide with Prokofiev-like harmonic twists. An exploration of dance forms that is thoroughly delightful and charming; subtle humor. M-D.

Nocturne Ab Op.33 1959 (GS). 5 min. Inscribed "Homage to John Field." Some reference to the Field Nocturne e, No.10. A flexible rhythmic pattern is combined with a nineteenth-century melody and twentieth-century harmonies. M-D.

Ballade Op.46 1977 (GS) 6pp. Written for the fifth Cliburn competition. Large ABA design, rich chordal sonorities, cadenza-like passages. Builds to enormous climax with octaves in alternating hands; colorful and effective; *pp* closing. M-D.

See: James P. Fairleigh, "Serialism in Barber's Solo Piano Music," PQ, 72 (Summer 1970):13–17.

Russell E. Friedewald, "A Formal and Stylistic Analysis of the Published Music of Samuel Barber," diss., University of Iowa, 1957.

Ramon Barce (1928–   ) Spain

Estudio de Densidades (Editorial de Música Española Contemporánea 1974) 10pp. A study in densities. D.

Woldemar Bargiel (1828–1897) Germany

Bargiel was Clara Schumann's stepbrother. Stylistically, his works are related to those of the circle around Schumann, Brahms, and Joseph Joachim.

Drei Charakterstücke Op.8 1853 (Br&H EB8159 c. 1995). Dedicated to his sister, Clara Schumann. Allegro appassionato: agitated and exciting. Lento: contrasting moods. Allegro con fuoco: rambunctious but satisifying. Robert Schumann thought highly of these pieces. Int. to M-D.

Jan Bark (1934–   ) Sweden

Bark began his musical career as a jazz trombonist. His attitude toward composing is colored by his experiences in jazz, especially with regard to the improvisatory character of the music.

Sonata (NMS 1957). In four short movements. Atonal writing with strong tonal final cadence. Economic use of material, clear style. A misprint at opening of second movement: bass clef should obviously be a treble clef. M-D.

Elaine Barkin (1932–   ) USA
Six Piano Pieces (ACA 1969) 11pp. Short, flexible meters, pointillistic, extreme ranges exploited, expressionistic, rhythmic proportional relationships, percussive treatment, atonal, serial. M-D.

David Barlow (1927–1975) Great Britain
Genesis (Nov 1953) 4 min. A short fantasy in four contrasting sections built on a basic motif of four ascending notes. Somber contrapuntal writing, neo-Romantic style. M-D.

Elsa Barraine (1910–   ) France
Barraine has remained a Romantic throughout her career.
Fantaisie pour clavecin ou piano (EMT 1961) 11pp. Neoclassic writing in one movement with contrasting sections. A piano addendum is included for certain passages. Effective on the piano; lean textures. Romantic characteristics. M-D.
Hommage à Paul Dukas 1936. In *Le Tombeau de Paul Dukas, La Revue Musicale* 166 (May–June 1936), 2pp. Simple right-hand tune over left-hand accompaniment. Int. to M-D.

Jean Barraqué (1928–1973) France
A student of Jean Langlais and Olivier Messiaen, Barraqué developed a unique modification of 12-tone technique. Certain elements of tonal and atonal writing are highly synthesized in his writing.
Sonate pour Piano 1950–52 (Margun/Gunmar). A 40-minute work of enormous dimensions. In two large parts to be played without interruption. The composer warns in his preface that too fast a tempo will mar the clarity of the polyphony. Extreme organization of material: rhythm, melody, and dynamics. Silence is an integral part of the form. Goléa (see below) has described this work as "one of the most important works for piano in recent French music alongside the sonatas of Boulez." Few pianists will be able to handle this work successfully. D.
See: G. W. Hopkins, "Jean Barraqué," MT, 107 (November 1966):952–54.
Andre Hodeir, *Since Debussy: A View of Contemporary Music* (New York: Grove, 1961). See pp.193–96 for a fine discussion of this work.
Antoine Goléa, "French Music Since 1945," MQ, 51 (January 1965):22–37.

Henri Barraud (1900–   ) France
Technically, Barraud is an eclectic. His originality lies in the expressive content of his music.
6 Impromptus (Amphion). Souple et Calme: short, chordal. Rapide: long melodic

line with flowing eighths as substructure. Lent et Grave: quiet opening, contrasting sections, large climax, quiet close. Modéré: short, melody in tenor. Sans Trainer: bass ostinato rhythms, dirgelike. Cursif: two voices. M-D.

Histoires pour les Enfants (Durand 1930). Four simple pieces. Int.

Premiers Pas (ESC). Five pieces for young people. Int.

Richard Barrett (1959–   ) Great Britian

Invention 6 1982 (UMP 1985) 8pp. Tremendously complicated writing, much use of proportional rhythmic relationships, difficult to make much sense of the musicality of the piece. D.

Gerald Barry (1952–   ) Ireland

Triorchic Blues 1991 (OUP) 8pp. "This piece should be played with great rhythmic drive and a generally detached and punchy articulation. Use of the pedal should always be absolutely clean and should never blur the harmonies. The title refers to the castrato Ferdinando Tenducci, who was reputedly triorchic" (from the score). Thin textures, changing meters, persistent throughout. M-D.

Sur les Pointes (OUP 1988) 18pp. 13 min. Up to p. 4 may be performed on any keyboard instrument with the correct range. Contrasting sonorities; full chords, many octaves; last section is entitled "Like a mad pianola." The title is a ballet term describing the raising of the body on the tips of the toes. M-D to D.

Cecilia Barthelemon (1770– ?) Great Britain

Barthelemon was considered one of London's outstanding musicians.

Three Sonatas (Harbach—Vivace) 56pp. Multi-movement works, late classical style. Rich harmonies and good sense of form. Op.1/1C; Op.1/3E; Op. 3G. M-D.

Béla Bartók (1881–1945) Hungary

Bartók is one of the half-dozen major composers of the twentieth century. He was a marvelous pianist, and his piano works mirror this great talent. His early works are derivative of both Debussy and Richard Strauss, but in late 1904 Bartók began to explore Hungarian folk music. He published nearly 2,000 folk tunes collected in his research, and he developed a style using rhythmic, melodic, and harmonic patterns from these native tunes. His piano works can be roughly divided into three periods: early (1907–1917), in which the music is clearly tied to folk materials; middle (1918–1935), which shows Bartók at his most dissonant and rhythmically explosive style; and late (1936–1945), in which he is more mellow, the music more spiritual and sublime. When studying Bartók's piano music, three aspects must be taken into account: his belonging to the Hungarian people, his authentically revolutionary spirit, and his own piano technique. The first two aspects are largely responsible for his highly original approach to the instrument, which, in turn, allowed him to give concrete shape to the ideas germinating in his mind. Bartók recorded about a dozen long-playing records of his own works, which are of inestimable value when studying his music.

In addition to the publishers listed below, Bo&H has published all of Bartók's piano music. The designations "Dover I" and "Dover II" refer to respective parts of a two-volume set.

4 Pieces 1905 (K; Dover I; EMB). Study for the Left Hand: sonata-rondo. First Phantasy: wistful. Second Phantasy. Scherzo: zestful. All show harmonic experimentation. M-D.

Rhapsody Op.1 1904 (Dover I; MMP). Later arranged for piano and orchestra. In the style of Liszt. D.

See: Colin Mason, "Bartók's Rhapsodies," ML, 30 (1949):26–36.

3 Popular Hungarian Songs 1907 (K). Simple treatment of the tunes. Int. to M-D.

14 Bagatelles Op.6 1908 (K; Dover I). Short, original treatment of sonorous materials; require quick changes in tempo, articulation, dynamics, and dramatic gestures. Only the last two have titles: "Elle est Morte" and "Valse. Ma mie qui dance." Int. to M-D.

See: Elliott Antokoletz, "The Musical Language of Bartók's 14 Bagatelles for Piano," *Tempo*, 137 (June 1981):8–16.

Young People at the Piano. 2 vols. 12 pieces in Vol.I, 10 pieces in Vol.II. Short, interesting and varied pieces for the 2nd and 3rd years of instruction. Easy to Int.

Ten Easy Piano Pieces 1908 (MCA; Schott; Alfred; K; Maestro; Dover I) 17 min. Bartók intended this set to be a complement to the *Bagatelles* Op.6, but with pedagogical intentions, "to supply piano students with easy contemporary pieces." Like the character cycles of Schumann, they display a variety of musical styles. None are "easy," and No.10 is the most difficult. Bartók recorded Nos.5 and 10. 1. Paraszti nota (Peasant song): Dorian mode. 2. Lassú vergödés (Painful wrestling): tritone emphasis. 3. Tót legényak tánca (Slovak dance): tempo gradations. 4. Sostenuto: much melodic interplay. 5. Este a székelyeknél (Evening in the country): pentatonic melodies; form is ABABA. 6. 'Gödölle! piactérre leesett a-hó' (Hungarian folk song): rhythm is most interesting point. 7. Hajnal (Dawn): Debussy influence; subtle tonal and pedal effects. 8. 'Azt mondják, nem adnak' (Folksong): requires careful gauging of dynamics. 9. Ujjgyakorlat (Finger exercise): inspired by Clementi and Czerny etudes. 10. Medvetánc (Bear dance): repeated-note ostinato with chords in parallel motion. Int.

See: Robert Dumm, "Teaching Bartok's *Aurora*" (Dawn, No. 7), *Clavier*, 33/9 (November 1994): 25–26, 28, music on p.29.

2 Rumanian Dances Op.8a 1909–10 (K; EMB). Thick textures, skips, rhapsodic, long and brilliant. D.

2 Elegies Op.8b 1908–1909 (Schott; K). Related stylistically to Op.1. M-D.

3 Burlesques Op.8c 1908–10 (K; Dover II). Lively scherzos in varied moods; Impressionistic; no folk influence. Brilliant. 1. Quarrel: a dispute, two opposing characters grimacing and teasing. The unison first subject and the waltz of the quasi-trio are character-variations of the same motif; an unprogrammatic scherzo. 2. Slightly Tipsy: programmatic, tipsy staggering with bits of a sentimental melody in thirds in the trio. Musically the staggering is brought about by parallel white key triads bouncing up and down in melodic fourths supported by minor second grace-note chords. 3. Molto vivo, capriccioso: a grotesque scherzo that points toward the grotesque puppet dance in the late opera *The Wooden Prince*. M-D.

For Children 1908–1909 (GS, 2 vols.; Dover II; Banowetz—GWM, Vol.I in an authoritative edition; MMP). Eighty-five short pieces, 79 without octaves. Delightful pieces showing ingenious treatment of traditional Hungarian (Vol.I) and Slovakian (Vol.II) children's songs and folk songs. Superb examples of the genre. Int.

See: Denes Agay, "Bartók's 'For Children' Which Edition? Original? . . . Revised?" *Clavier* 10 (March 1971):18–23.

Dale Topp, "Bartók's 'For Children,'" PQ, 143 (Fall 1988): 35–40.

7 Sketches Op.9B 1908–10 (EBM; K). 11 min. Andante (Portrait d'une jeune fille). Commodo (Balançoire). Lento. Non troppo lento: most difficult of the set. Andante (Mélodie populaire Roumaine). Allegretto (À la manière valaque). Poco lento. Short pieces, thin textures. Int. to M-D.

4 Nénies (Dirges) Op.9A 1910 (K; Dover II; EMB). 9 min. Short, stark, deceptively simple, Impressionistic. Refined pedaling required. M-D.

Allegro Barbaro 1911. (Alfred; UE; MMP). 3½ min. Dancelike, barbaric, dogged stress in unexpected places; bravura and strength demanded. Phrygian and lydian modes mixed. Uses the piano as a drum. M-D.

First Term at the Piano 1913. (K; Dover II; Schott). 18 pieces from the Bartók-Reschofsky *Piano Method* published in a separate volume under this title in 1929. All by Bartók. Contains folk song adaptations and original compositions. Not intended for concert performance; some are stylistically reminiscent of easy folk song adaptations in *For Children* (1908–09). Easy to Int.

15 Hungarian Peasant Songs and Dances 1914–17 (UE; MMP). 12 min. A connected cycle of short folktunes, simply harmonized. Boisterous "Bagpipe" concludes set. Int. to M-D.

See: Robert Dumm, "A Bartók Ballad," *Clavier*, 15 (March 1976):33–37. Discusses "Ballad" from this set.

Sonatina 1915 (Alfred; IMC; Dover II; GS separately and in collection *Selected Works for the Piano*). Bagpipe; Bear Dance; Finale. Based on Rumanian folk tunes, picturesque miniatures. One of the finest sonatinas ever written. Int.

See: Guy Wuellner, "Béla Bartók's Sonatine: A Survey of Editions and Transcriptions," AMT, 25 (April-May 1976):28–31.

Three Hungarian Folk Tunes 1914–17 "Homage to Paderewski" (Bo&H 1942).

This set was probably intended for inclusion in *Fifteen Hungarian Peasant Songs*, which was written about the same time. It is an effective recital-opener or companion set to one of the folk dance cycles. Int. to M-D.

Rumanian Folk Dances 1915 (Alfred; UE; MMP). Rev. ed. by Peter Bartók (Bo&H). 4 min. 6 short pieces. Bot-tánc (The Stick Dance); Brâul (Braul); Topogó (In One Spot); Bucsumi tánc (Dance from Bucsum); Roman (Rumanian polka); Aprozó (Lively dance). One of Bartók's most popular sets. Charming, graceful, and poignant. Int. to M-D.

Rumanian Christmas Songs 1915 (UE; MMP) 2 series, 10 in each, to be played as connected cycles. Modal, asymmetrical phrasing.

See: Ingrid Arauco, "Bartók's *Rumanian Christmas Carols*: Changes from the Folk Sources and Their Significance," *The Journal of Musicology*, V/2 (Spring 1987):191–225.

Angeline Schmid, "Bartók's Rumanian Christmas Carols," *Clavier* 20 (October 1981):30–31.

Suite Op.14 1916 (UE). Allegretto: jesting. Scherzo: sturdy. Allegro molto: driving. Sostenuto: short, Impressionistic. M-D.

See: Diana K. Oki, "Performance Problems in Béla Bartók's Suite Opus 14 and 'Out of Doors,'" thesis, Long Beach: California State University, 1993.

3 Etudes Op.18 1918. (MMP) 7½ min. Allegro molto: expansion and contraction of the hand, ninths and tenths. Andante sostenuto: Impressionistic sonorities, double notes in cadenza. Tempo giusto: left-hand figuration against staccato chords, irregular meters, motoric drive. Virtuoso works, much dissonance, hard driving, colorful, highly original. D.

Improvisations on Hungarian Peasant Songs Op.20 1920. 12 min. Eight tunes in a connected cycle, anything but improvised, carefully unified and developed construction, very dissonant, highly individual. The end point of Bartók's folksong settings. No.7 is in memory of Debussy; quiet clusters. M-D.

See: Stuart Thyne, "Bartók's Improvisations," ML, 31/1, (1950):30–45.

Dance Suite 1923 (Peter Bartók—Bo&H, UE) 18 min. Originally written for orchestra, transcribed for piano by Bartók. Moderato; Allegro molto; Allegro vivace; Molto tranquillo; Commodo; Finale (Allegro). Contains some of Bartók's most arresting and invigorating writing. M-D to D.

Sonata 1926 (UE; EMB has a three-color facsimile of the autograph). 13 min. Allegro moderato; Sostenuto e pesante; Allegro molto. Classical forms plus tight motivic unity. Repeated notes throughout, intricate embellishments. Bartók's longest work for solo piano, a twentieth-century classic. Requires brittle tone, power, rhythmic drive, virtuosity. Composed as a virtuoso piece for Bartók's own concerts. D.

See: David Burge, "Contemporary Piano—Bartók's Piano Sonata," CK, 4 (September 1978):56. A discussion of the first movement.

Out of Doors 1926 (UE) 13 min. With Drums and Pipes: percussive, rhythmic, short. Barcarolla: plastic, chromatic, linear, swaying barcarolle figure, melancholy. Musettes: major-minor sonorities mixed; drone decorated with trills.

Night's Music: hypnotic; an eerie nocturnal picture that includes crickets, croaking frogs, twittering, chirping, fluttering of bat wings; cluster chords. The Chase: wild ostinato, wide skips, octaves, parallel ninths, dissonant, burst of frightening power. More concerned with color than structure. D. See: Oki entry under Suite Op.14.

9 Little Pieces 1926 (UE) 3 books. No.1. Four short dialogues in two- and three-part counterpoint. Bachlike. No.2. Menuetto, Air, Marcia delle Bestie, Tambour de Basque. No.3. Preludío—All'Ungherese: a genuine Magyar rhapsody, slow introduction leads to a lively dance section. Int. to M-D.

3 Rondos on Folk Tunes 1916–1927 (UE). 7 min. No.1 is the easiest. Light, clever, playful. Int. to M-D.

Little Suite 1936 (UE). 6 min. Six adaptations from *44 Duos for 2 Violins*. Slow Melody; Walachian Dance; Whirling Dance; Quasi Pizzicato; Ukrainian Song; Bagpipe. Excellent on the piano, picturesque. M-D.

Mikrokosmos, 153 progressive piano pieces 1926–37. 6 vols. Bartók began writing these pieces for his son Peter. When completed, they constituted one of the most comprehensive collections of contemporary techniques and idioms for the piano ever assembled. They are full of exquisite miniature masterpieces. The title means "the universe is small."

Vol. 1: Hands in unison. Independence developed by simple two-part counterpoint, including canon. Modal melodies. 1–6. Unison melodies; 7. Dotted notes; 8. Repetition; 9. Syncopation; 10. With alternate hands; 11. Parallel motion; 12. Reflection; 13. Change of position; 14. Question and answer; 15. Village song; 16. Parallel motion and change of position; 17. Contrary motion; 18.–21. Unison melodies; 22. Imitation and counterpoint; 23. Imitation and inversion; 24. Pastorale; 25. Imitation and inversion; 26. Repetition; 27. Syncopation; 28. Canon at the octave; 29. Imitation reflected; 30. Canon at the lower fifth; 31. Little dance in canon form; 32. In Dorian mode; 33. Slow dance; 34. In Phrygian mode; 35. Chorale; 36. Free canon.

Vol. 2: Two-part writing, varied homophonic accompaniments, legato and staccato dynamics, pieces for two pianos, some chromaticism, more difficult key signatures. Technical exercises. 37. In Lydian mode; 38. Staccato and legato; 39. Staccato and legato; 40. In Yugoslav mode; 41. Melody with accompaniment; 42. Accompaniment in broken triads; 43. In Hungarian style (duet 2 pianos); 44. Contrary motion (duet 2 pianos); 45. Méditation; 46. Increasing—diminishing; 47. Big fair; 48. In Mixolydian mode; 49. Crescendo—diminuendo; 50. Minuetto; 51. Waves; 52. Unison divided; 53. In Transylvanian style; 54. Chromatic; 55. Triplets in Lydian mode (duet 2 pianos); 56. Melody in tenths; 57. Accents; 58. In oriental style; 59. Major and minor; 60. Canon with sustained notes; 61. Pentatonic melody; 62. Minor sixths in parallel motion; 63. Buzzing; 64. Line and point; 65. Dialogue: song; 66. Melody divided.

Vol. 3: Double notes, chord studies, irregular rhythmic groupings, inventions, changing meters, technical exercises. 67. Thirds against a single voice; 68. Hungarian dance (2 pianos, 4 hands); 69. Chord study; 70. Melody against double notes; 71. Thirds; 72. Dragon's dance; 73. Sixths and triads; 74. Hungarian song; 75. Triplets; 76. In three parts; 77. Little study; 78. Five-tone scale; 79. Hommage à J. S. B.; 80. Hommage à R. Sch.; 81. Wandering; 82. Scherzo; 83. Melody with interruptions; 84. Merriment; 85. Broken chords; 86. Two major pentachords; 87. Variations; 88. Duet for pipes; 89. In four parts; 90. In Russian style; 91. Chromatic invention; 92. Chromatic invention; 93. In four parts; 94. Tale; 95. Song of the fox; 96. Stumblings.

Vol. 4: More-complicated problems, studies in clashing dissonances, Bulgarian rhythms. 97. Notturno; 98. Thumb under; 99. Crossed hands; 100. In the style of a folksong; 101. Diminished fifths; 102. Harmonies; 103. Minor and major; 104. Through the keys; 105. Playsong; 106. Children's song; 107. Melody in the mist; 108. Wrestling; 109. From the island of Bali; 110. Clashing sounds; 111. Intermezzo; 112. Variations on a folk tune; 113. Bulgarian rhythm; 114. Theme and inversion; 115. Bulgarian rhythm; 116. Melody; 117. Bourrée; 118. Triplets in 9/8 time; 119. Dance in 3/4 time; 120. Fifth chords; 121. Two-part study.

Vol. 5: Double notes, chord studies, thirds, fourths, major and minor seconds, whole-tone scales, syncopations, changing meters. 122. Chords together and opposed; 123. Staccato and legato; 124. Staccato; 125. Boating; 126. Change of time; 127. New Hungarian folksong; 128. Peasant dance; 129. Alternating thirds; 130. Village joke; 131. Fourths; 132. Major seconds broken and together; 133. Syncopation; 134. Studies in double notes; 135. Perpetuum mobile; 136. Whole-tone scale; 137. Unison; 138. Bagpipe; 139. Merry Andrew.

Vol. 6: More extended treatment of the foregoing problems, culminating in six dances in Bulgarian rhythms. Vols.5 and 6 are suitable for concert use. 140. Free variations; 141. Subject and reflection; 142. From the diary of a fly; 143. Divided arpeggios; 144. Minor seconds, major sevenths; 145. Chromatic invention; 146. Ostinato; 147. March; 148–153. Six dances in Bulgarian rhythm. In the popular Nos.148–53, Bartók combines Bulgarian rhythms in two-, three-, and four-note units and shapes them into enchanting and haunting pieces. M-D.

See: Adele Franklin, "Bartók: Mikrokosmos, Book II," *Music Teacher*, 55 (November 1976):7–8; "Bartók: Mikrokosmos, Book III," *Music Teacher*, 55 (December 1976):12–13; "Bartók: Mikrokosmos, Book IV," *Music Teacher*, 56 (January 1977):17–18, and 56 (February 1977):15–16.

Mary E. Parker, "Bartók's 'Mikrokosmos': A Survey of Pedagogical and Compositional Techniques," diss., University of Texas–Austin, 1987.

Benjamin Suchoff, *Guide to the Mikrokosmos* (New York: Boosey & Hawkes, 1971; reprint, New York: Da Capo Press, 1982, with a new introduction by György Sandor).

———, "Bartók's Musical Microcosm," *Clavier*, 16 (May-June 1977):18–20 (pp.22–25 contain Nos.57 [Accente] and 140 [Free Variation] from the *Mikrokosmos*).

Stuart Thyne, "Bartók's Mikrokosmos—A Reexamination," PQ, 107 (Fall 1979):43–46. Discusses errors between printed text and Bartók's recordings.

Margit Varro, "Bartók's Mikrokosmos in Retrospect," in *Selections from the Piano Teacher, 1958–1963* (Evanston: Summy-Birchard, 1964).

COLLECTIONS:

Allegro Barbaro and Other Short Works for Solo Piano (Dover 1998). Includes: Allegro Barbaro, Romanian Folk Dances, Romanian Christmas Carols, 15 Hungarian Peasant Songs, Improvisations on Hungarian Peasant Songs, Op.20, Suite Op.14, and Etudes Op.18. A fine survey. Int. to D.

Bartók Album (Bo&H) Vol.1: Bagatelles Nos.2, 3, 5, 10, and 14; Burlesque Nos.1 and 2; Danse roumaine; Esquisses Nos.1, 2, 5, and 6; Soir à la campagne; Danse de l'ours. Vol.2: Aurora; Bagatelles Nos.1, 6, 8, and 11; Dirge No.3; Folksong; Rumanian Dance No.2; Sketch No.7; Slovak Peasant's Dance; Sostenuto; Three Folksongs from the Country of Csik; Village Dance.

Selected works for the piano (GS). Funeral march from the symphonic poem "Kossuth"; Rhapsody Op.1; 14 Bagatelles Op.6; 2 Elegies Op.8b; Sketches Op.9; 4 Dirges; 2 Rumanian Dances Op.8a; 3 Burlesques Op.8c; Sonatina.

Bartók Album (K). 3 Hungarian Folksongs; Fantasy (1903); 2 Rumanian Dances; Scherzo (1903); Sonatina; Sketches Op.9; 14 Bagatelles Op.6; Bear Dance.

Bartók Easy Piano (Alfred). Twenty-four pieces selected from various educational collections. Contains a brief biography and introductory notes for the pieces. Easy to Int.

Bartók—Favorite Piano (Alfred). Twenty-four pieces including the *Sonatina* and pieces from other collections by Bartók. Contains a short biography and notes on each piece. Int. to M-D.

The Easy Piano Music of Béla Bartók (D. Goldberger—Schroeder & Gunther). Twenty-four pieces that provide a fine introduction to a fundamental twentieth-century style.

Young Pianist's Guide to Bartók (Y. Novik—WB) 24pp. with recording of sixteen of the easier pieces. Well edited. Easy to Int.

The Story of Béla Bartók (Hinson, Glover—Belwin-Mills 1971) in collection *Contemporary Piano Repertoire*, level 5. Contains biography of Bartók, discussion of his piano works, and four short easy pieces: Let's Dance; Peasant Dance; The Fox; Scaredy Cat!

Bartók—His Greatest (Ashley) 192pp. Contains both volumes of *For Children, Ten Easy Pieces, Bagatelles* Op.6, and other selected works. Int. to M-D.

Bartók—An Introduction to His Piano Works (Palmer—Alfred) 64pp. A most informative foreword includes information about Bartók, about the selections, on wrist and finger action, and on touch; and studies in finger staccato, wrist staccato, staccatissimo, portato, tenuto, legato, accents, syncopation, and legato-staccato. Contains pieces from *The First Term at*

the Piano, For Children, 10 Easy Pieces, and *7 Sketches.* Editorial additions in light gray print. Int.
Compositions for Piano (GS). Suite Op.14; *Rumanian Folk Dances; Rumanian Christmas Carols.* M-D.
Piano Music of Bela Bartok (Dover). Series I: *Funeral March; Four Piano Pieces; Rhapsody* Op.1; *Three Folk Songs; 14 Bagatelles* Op.6; *Ten Easy Pieces; Two Elegies* Op.8B.; *Seven Sketches* Op.9B; *Two Rumanian Dances* Op.8A. Series II: 85 short pieces from *For Children.* Excellent introduction. Int. To D.
See: Christine Brown, "Bartók the Teacher," *Music Teacher,* 60/3 (March 1981): 16–17.
Elizabeth Buday, "Focus on Bartók," *Clavier,* 20 (October 1981):21–22.
Anthony Cross, "Debussy and Bartók," MT, 108 (February 1967): 125–31.
Andor Foldes, "Bartók as Pianist," JR, 2 (1955):18–22.
David Hamilton, "Bartók at the Piano," HF (March 1981):39–41. A survey of the recordings made by Bartók.
Joan Pursewell, "Bartók's Early Music: Forecasting the Future," *Clavier,* 20 (October 1981):23–27. A discussion of the *Bagatelles* Op.6 (including No.5 printed), *Three Burlesques* Op.8, and *Sketches* Op.9B.
György Sandor, "Béla Bartók—Extending the Piano's Vocabulary," CK, 1 (September-October 1975):16–18, 34.
Tamas Vasary, "Vasary Teaches Bartók," *Clavier,* 17 (May-June 1978):17–20. A lesson on *Suite* Op.14.
David Yeomans, *Bartók for Piano. A Survey of His Solo Literature.* Bloomington: Indiana University Press, 1998.

Jan Z. Bartoš (1908–1981) Czechoslovakia
Bartoš was a prolific and gifted composer. Contemporary events in his country inspired some of his latest compositions.
Sonata Op.70 (Artia 1953). Allegro—Piu animato; Adagio; Tarantella (Presto).
Sonata Op.82 (Artia 1959). Allegro molto; Largo; Allegro molto.
Both sonatas display a fine compositional technique and could only have been written by a pianist. Both are tonal, yet liberally sprinkled with dissonance. Highly effective. M-D.

Nevett Bartow (1934–1973) USA
Toccata (SP 1972) 6pp. Tricky rhythms, dissonant. Meter and mood change in mid-section; off-beat accentuations give jazzy rhythmic effect; concludes with cluster chords. Showy and effective. M-D.
6 Character Pieces Op.13 posth. (SP 41) 8pp. Toccata: bitonal. March: pompous. American Dance: jazzy. The Cuckoo: flowing lines interrupted by bird call. Chaconne Maestoso: syncopated melody, octotonic, cheerful. Int.

Leonid Bashmakov (1927–   ) Finland, born Russia
Six Preludes 1974 (Fazer) 13pp. 10 min. Short, contrasting, MC except for No.6, which is filled with dissonance. M-D.

Leslie Bassett (1923–   ) USA

Bassett's style is based on textural sounds and colors that help to convey a specific mood. The composer uses various kinds of tones and groupings of instruments to achieve his methods of counterpoint. He teaches at the University of Michigan.

Six Piano Pieces (ACA 1951). Allegro moderato: mainly 2 voices, imitative, tonal. Allegro: thin textures, melodic, chromatic coloring. Andante cantabile: long melodic idea well developed, unusual sonorities. Allegro brilliante: bitonal, perpetual motion, breathless. Adagio, ma non troppo: ethereal, melodic. Allegro assai: Toccata-like, moving freely into closely related tonalities. A refreshing set, effective as a group. M-D.

Hommage à Arthur Honegger (ACA 1951). Andantino: a two-voice Nocturne employing linear writing with a quote from Honegger's *King David*. Piquant. M-D.

Elaborations (CFP 1966). 11pp. Fast: scalar passages punctuated by chordal gestures, thin textures, ornamented by trills, *pp* close. Slow: great freedom, long crescendo leads to a dynamic climax. Quiet: more harmonically treated, incisive rhythmic punctuation relaxes to a calm close. Brilliant: broad chromatic line, martellato effects, trill produces stunning sonorities; dramatic close. Wide range of keyboard and dynamics exploited throughout in these facile works. Basic patterns unfold inconspicuously. D.

Mobile (Hinson—Alfred 1978) in collection *Twelve by Eleven*. Lyrical yet intense, constantly unfolding, rich in color and range. The chromatic language is enhanced by several varied repetitions that, as it were, assume new perspectives as they turn in the wind. Expressionistic, effective. M-D.

Configurations (CFP 1988) 1. Whirling Triplets: no bar lines, nonfunctional harmonic texture, triplets divided between hands. 2. Lines: no bar lines, two-part counterpoint, chromatic. 3. In Balance: no bar lines, chromatic, eighth notes grouped into fours and further grouped by the Fibonacci number series. 4. Climbing: changing meters, chromatic melody, pedal study. 5. Spirals: minimalist style, repeated eight times, arpeggio groupings, fast, loud. A fine set to introduce contemporary techniques. Int.

James Bastien (1934–   ) USA

Toccata (GWM 1975). A sophisticated, contemporary, dashing recital piece that would make a good substitute for the overworked Khachaturian *Toccata*. Pianist needs good octaves and plenty of stamina. M-D.

Stanley Bate (1913–1959) Great Britain

Bate's works reveal the direct influence of his teacher Hindemith and also Vaughan Williams.

7 Pieces 1940 (Schott 10012). Prelude; Romance; Chanson Populaire; Moment Musical; Polka; Valse. Short works of moderate difficulty, influenced by Shostakovitch. Int. to M-D.

6 Pieces for an Infant Prodigy Op.13 (Mer). Short, unpretentious. Int.

Sonatina No.6 E♭ (AMP 1943). Moderato; Andante; Allegro. Quartal and quintal harmonies; clear, facile writing. M-D.
Sonatina No.7 C 1949 (Schott). Bright, smaller in dimensions than No.6. Int. to M-D.
Sonatina No.8 C (AMP 1945). Prelude; Valentine; Toccata. Alternating hands, tremolos, repeated notes and scales. Short movements. M-D.

Yves Baudrier (1906–1988) France
Baudrier was one of the group of "La Jeune France," formed in 1936. It also included O. Messiaen, A. Jolivet, and D. Lesur.
La Dame à la Licorne (Amphion 1935). The title refers to the tapestries "The Lady and the Unicorn" in the Musée de Cluny in Paris. MC with Impressionistic overtones. M-D.

Marion Bauer (1887–1955) USA
Turbulence Op.17/2 (EBM). Octaves, vigorous, brief motives, sonorous. M-D.
A Fancy (Axelrod). Short, Impressionistic. Int.
Eight Diversions (Chappell). Varied moods and styles. Int.
Four Piano Pieces Op.21 (Arrow Music Press). Chromaticon; Ostinato; Toccata; Syncope. Short; varied compositional techniques. M-D.
Dance Sonata Op.24 (ACA). Allegro Appassionata: very chromatic. Sarabande: five variations. Allegretto giocoso. Graceful writing. M-D.
Patterns Op.41 (ACA). Five 12-tone pieces: Allegretto in two voices; quick Waltz; Scherzo; eloquent slow movement; Toccata. M-D.
See: Nancy L. Stewart, "The Solo Piano Music of Marion Bauer," diss., University of Cincinnati, 1990.

Raymond Bauer (–   ) USA
Sonatina (CF 1971) 13pp. Allegro animato; Andantino; Allegro vivace. In the style of Kabalevsky. Int.

Jürg Baur (1918–   ) Germany
Baur studied under Philipp Jarnach at the University of Cologne. He has taught at the Robert Schumann Conservatory in Düsseldorf since 1946 and became director in 1965. In his serial writing he is fond of mirror structures.
Aphorismen (Br&H 1957). 17 min. Twelve pieces. M-D.
Capriccio (Br&H 1953). 5 min. One of Baur's earliest serial works. M-D.
Heptameron (Br&H 1964–65). Dedicated to Anton von Webern. Seven pieces in serial technique with well-contrasted, attractive sonorities. M-D.

Arnold Bax (1883–1953) Great Britain
Bax wrote prolifically for the piano. His style always shows great facility and a Romantic temperament. A love of the great Irish poets and Celtic folklore plus an early visit to Russia proved to be major influences.
2 Russian Tone Poems 1912 (J. Williams). Nocturne (May night in the Ukraine):

imaginative writing requiring keyboard facility. M-D. Gopak (National Dance): strong rhythmic drive, masterful piano writing. M-D.

Country Tune (Murdoch). Needs careful balance of tone. Easy.

Lullaby 1920 (Murdoch). Melody treated with varied harmonies, two contrasting cantabile sections. M-D.

Toccata D♭ 1913 (Murdoch 1920). Double-note technique in right hand, brilliant. M-D.

Nereid (JWC; MMP). Poetic, flowing, recurring rhythmic figure. M-D.

Winter Waters (JWC). "Tragic Landscape" achieved by a four-note ground bass. Effective. M-D.

Whirligig (JWC; MMP 1919). Ostinato passed between the hands. Clever, needs digital facility. M-D.

Sonata No.1 f♯ 1910, rev. 1917–21 (Murdoch 1922). One movement, varied moods and tempi. Advanced pianism required. M-D to D.

Sonata No.2 G 1919 (Murdoch 1921). One movement; overall mood is grim and menacing; rhapsodic in character. Five themes, folk-song influence, thick textures. Large span required. D.

Sonata No.3 g♯ 1926 (Murdoch). Three movements, not easy for performer or audience. Advanced pianism required. D.

Sonata No.4 G 1932 (Chappell). Perhaps the most attractive of the sonatas. M-D.

7 Selected Piano Solos (Chappell 1915–43). Available separately. A fine varied album including Lullaby; Mediterranean; Country-Tune; A Hill Tune; Serpent Dance; In a Vodka Shop. Int. to M-D.

Selected Works for Piano (Thames). An interesting collection of short pieces written between 1897 and 1945. Includes the exquisite *Nereid*. M-D.

Irwin Bazelon (1922–1995) USA

Sonatina (Weintraub 1952). 11pp. Outside movements are quick, without clearly defined tonal centers. Shifting tonality in middle movement. D.

Five Pieces for Piano (Weintraub 1956). Miniatures with disjunct melody, much dissonance and complex rhythmic ideas. Polyphonic texture. Difficult for performer and listener. M-D.

Suite for Young People (PIC 1954). Part 1: Little Serenade; Christmas Carol; Dance for a Tomboy; Lullaby; Cowboy Tune; Prayer. Int. Part 2: Prelude; The Clown and the Puppet; Circus Parade; The Haunted Chateau; Dance of an Elf; Goblins and Ghosts; Int. to M-D. "The purpose in writing these pieces was to acquaint young pianists with style and character of contemporary music as early as possible in their musical training" (from the score).

Imprints . . . On Ivory and Strings (Nov 10023107 1982) 24pp., 12 min. Preface. Dissonant chords, tone clusters, strings plucked and strummed, large paper pad inserted in strings, flexible tempi, careful pedal instructions, harmonics, spatial rhythmic notation. Exploits the resonant resources of the instrument; music from beyond the fringe! M-D.

Sunday Silence 1989 (TP 1993) 16pp. 15 min. Inspired by a race horse named "Sunday Silence," this recital piece is full of rhythmic vitality. Serial, wide dynamic range, expressionistic, dazzling, performance notes: S.H.=Short Hold; V.S.H.=Very Short Hold, etc., changing tempos, harmonics, plucked strings, proportional rhythmic relationships. D.

Mrs. H. H. A. Beach (Amy Marcy Cheney) (1867–1944) USA
The forward-moving drive throughout Mrs. Beach's writing seems to be the essence of early-twentieth-century optimism. Amy Beach is finally being recognized as one of the greatest women composers in the United States, perhaps our greatest!

Piano Music (Da Capo 1982) 150pp. Introduction by Sylvia Glickman. Includes Valse Caprice Op.4; Ballade Op.6; Sketches Op.15: In Autumn, Phantoms, Dreaming, Fireflies; three pieces from Op.28: Barcarolle, Menuet Italien, Danse des Fleurs; Variations on a Balkan Theme Op.60: powerful and refreshingly original; Prelude and Fugue Op.81; Fantasia Fugata Op.87; Nocturne Op.107; A Cradle Song of the Lonely Mother Op.108; Tyrolean Valse Fantaisie Op.116; three Pianoforte Pieces Op.128: Scherzino, Young Birches, A Humming Bird. Also includes a complete list of Beach's solo piano works and chamber music including piano. Her piano music falls into three categories: elementary teaching pieces, intermediate works, and virtuoso compositions. This anthology "deals only with the last category and presents a superb survey of her pianistic style. The renaissance of interest in her music today coincides with the revival of Romantic-style composition that attracts many contemporary composers" (from the preface).

Valse-Caprice Op.4 (Schmidt 1889; MMP). Laced with difficulties, graceful figuration, diminished chords, subtle modulations. Lighthearted, Saint-Säens colored. M-D to D.

Ballad Op.6 (Schmidt 1894; MMP). Fauré-like introduction leads to a larger Liszt-like section. M-D.

Four Sketches Op.15 (Schmidt 1892; MMP). In Autumn; Phantoms; Dreaming; Fireflies. Intriguing writing. M-D. In Autumn is in collection *Masters of American Piano Music* (Alfred 4603). 5pp. Melancholy, numerous tempo changes.

Morceaux Caractéristiques Op.28 (Schmidt 1894). Barcarolle; Menuet Italian; Danse de Fleurs. Reprint from original publication. Traditional forms, Romantic harmonies. M-D.

Scottish Legend Op.54/1 (E. Gold—McAfee) in collection *American Keyboard Music*. Int. to M-D. In collection *At the Piano With Women Composers* (Alfred 428).

Prelude and Fugue. Op.81 (GS 1918). Academic. M-D.

Hermit Thrush at Eve Op.92/1 (Schmidt 1922). Tuneful, based on bird calls. M-D.

Hermit Thrush at Morn Op.92/2 (Schmidt). M-D.

Nocturne Op.107 (J. Church 1924). Lovely Romantic writing. M-D.

Five Improvisations Op.148 (Seesaw 1938). Introspective, reflective. More modern idiom than the other listed works. M-D.

Farewell, Summer. Dancing Leaves Op.102 (Ditson 1924). Int.

Variations on a Balkan Theme Op.60 1904 (MMP). Longest and most difficult of all Beach's solo piano works. Eight variations, long cadenza, superb writing. Includes composer's preface. M-D to D.

Young People's Carnival Op.25 (Alfred 3576) 19pp. Six programmatic movements that depict the characters of early European pantomine popular in America in the late nineteenth century. Promenade; Columbine; Pantalon; Pierrot and Pierrette; Secrets; Harlequin. Int.

Young People's Album Op.36 (Alfred 3573) 18pp. Minuet; Gavotte; Waltz; March; Polka. Five dance pieces, all notated in the treble clef; thin textures. Some of the better pedogogical pieces written around this time (1897). Int.

Collection of Piano Music (Sylvia Glickman—Hildegard 1994). Ballade Op.6; Fireflies Op.15; Barcarolle Op.28; Scottish Legend and Gavotte Fantastique Op.54; Les Réves de Columbine Op.65; From Grandmother's Garden Op.97. M-D.

The Life and Music of Amy Beach: The First Woman Composer of America (G. Smith—Creative Keyboard Publications 1992) 103pp. 15 pp. of biography with some early unusual pictures of Beach; 83 pp. of music, including *Summer Dreams* Op.47 for piano duet (28pp.). Solo music includes Mamma's Waltz; Menuetto; Romanzo; Petit Valse; Pierrot and Pierrette, Harlequin, Secrets Op.25/4, 6, 5; Waltz, Minuet F, Gavotte Op.36/3, 1, 2; Canoeing, Sliding on the Ice Op.54/1, 2; Menuet Italian Op.28/2; Fireflies Op.15/4. Wide variety of Beach's piano music. Int. to M-D.

See: Dean Elder, "Where Was Amy Beach All These Years?" *Clavier*, 15 (December 1976):14–17. Includes "Out of the Depths" Op.130 for piano; and "Twilight" Op.47/3 for piano duet.

Marmaduke S. Miles. "The Solo Piano Works of Mrs. H. H. A. Beach," diss., Peabody Conservatory of Music, 1985, 175 pp.

Burnet C. Tuthill, "Mrs. H. H. A. Beach," MQ, 26 (1941):197–310.

Marcelle Vernazza, "Amy Beach and Her Music for Children," AMT, 30/6 (June-July 1981):20–21. Discusses the piano collections *Young People's Album* Op.36 and *Young People's Carnival* Op.25.

James Beale (1924–   ) USA

Beale teaches at the University of Washington, Seattle. All the sonatas are well written for the piano by a composer who obviously knows the possibilities and limitations of the instrument.

Sonata No.2 Op.8 (University of Washington Press 1953). Five movements that exploit a wide range of sonorities and techniques. Lyrical aspects and fluid handling of the instrument emphasized. M-D.

Sonata No.3 Op.9 (ACA 1952) 15 min. Allegretto espressivo. Allegro pesante. Allegro misterioso: exploits extreme ranges, prestissimo coda. Some use of harmonics, neoclassic style. M-D.

Sonata No.6 Op.13 (ACA 1956). Adagietto; Presto; Andante; Presto con impeto. Least involved of the four piano sonatas. M-D.

Sonata No.7 Op.20 (ACA 1956). 23 min. Slow-Moderate-Slow; Fast; Moderate-Slow; Slow-Fast-Slow. These tempos are suggested for program printing.

Few tempo indications appear in the work, usually only metronome marks. Many "start and stopping" effects. Tremolandos and long pedal effects are effectively used. D.

Robert Beaser (1954–   ) USA
Beaser teaches at The Juilliard School.
Landscape with Bells 1986. In collection *Changing Faces* (EAMC 1987). 4pp. Pedal used to produce colorful bell-like sonorities, changing meters. Follow accents closely at indicated levels so the bell-like ringing tone will be produced. "Fast, light, and ringing tempo I." M-D.

Dan Beaty (1937–   ) USA
Beaty teaches piano and composition at Stephen F. Austin State University in Nacogdoches, Texas.
Seven Bagatelles (GWM 320 1980) 23pp. Seconds; Thirds; Fourths; Fifths; Sixths; Sevenths; Octaves. Each piece exploits the interval of its title. MC. Int. to M-D.
Woodsprite and Waterbug Collection (Kjos 1977). 1. Woodsprite: pentatonic, polytonal, wide leaps. 2. Red Dog: whole-tone, ostinato. 3. Doodling: touch and dynamic contrasts, meter changes, polytonal. 4. Mists: pedal study, choice of octave placement of melody. 5. Hobby Horse: polytonal, whole-tone, two-note slurs. 6. Pagoda: glissando, pedal, pentatonic plus chromatics. 7. Thunderheads: forearm clusters, tritones, glissando. 8. Jump: alternating hands, staccato, pentatonic. 9. All Twelve: 12-tone, legato balance, pedal. 10. Morning Song: 5/8 meter, modal, melody tossed between hands. 11. Bells: pedal, chords, tritone. 12. Water Bug: polytonal, whole-tone, hands widely spaced. Excellent set (all are short) for introducing contemporary techniques. Int.

Conrad Beck (1901–1989) Switzerland
Beck lived in Paris from 1925 to 1933 and was closely acquainted with Roussel, Ibert, and Honegger. Many of his works show their influence.
Klavierstücke (Schott 1920–30). Books I and II contain eleven pieces. Atonal. M-D.
Dance (ESC 1929). Strong rhythms, not as dissonant as other works. M-D.
Sonatine II (Schott 1947). Large three-movement atonal work, serial. M-D to D.
Fox-trot in *Hommage à Albert Roussel, La Revue Musicale* 94 (April 1929), 4pp. Written in honor of Roussel's 60th birthday. Beck studied with Roussel in 1924–33. Delightful dance piece. M-D.
Prélude (Heugel 1948). This piece and the *Sonatine II* show more emphasis on a unified French-German style. Contrapuntal texture underlies both works. M-D.

John Becker (1886–1961) USA
Becker developed a personal harmonic style and was quite adventurous as a composer. He wrote articles for numerous music journals and was associate editor of the quarterly *New Music*.

2 Architectural Impressions (ACA 1924) 4 min. Romantic-Impressionistic idiom. M-D.

2 Chinese Miniatures (GS 1926) 4 min. Attractive, even if a little "dated" sounding. M-D.

Soundpiece No. 5 (new edition, J. Gillespie—CFP 1996). (Short Sonata for Piano). 8 min. A one-movement work in four contrasting sections utilizing arpeggio figuration, chorale and toccata treatment, plus a fugue, MC. M-D.

4 Modern Dances (CFE) 5 min. More complex dissonant idiom, percussive. M-D.

John Beckwith (1927–   ) Canada
Beckwith studied piano with Alberto Guerrero, at the Royal Conservatory of Music in Toronto, and composition with Nadia Boulanger, in Paris. He is the music critic for the *Toronto Daily Star*, associate editor of the *Canadian Music Journal*, and on the music faculty at the University of Toronto.

4 Conceits (CMC 1945–48). Contrasting short pieces in Impressionistic style. M-D.

Novelette (BMI Canada 1954). Pungent sonorities. Requires broad span and good sense of driving rhythmic syncopation. M-D.

New Mobiles (Waterloo 1973) 6pp. Wind-harp: hands play independently and freely. Machine: perpetual motion. Tough Beans Charlie: repeated chords, skips, arpeggi. Int.

White Black (Waterloo 1973). One hand plays white keys while the other plays black keys. Glissandi. Int.

David Bedford (1937–   ) Great Britain
Bedford studied with both Lennox Berkeley and Luigi Nono. His music is influenced by Schönberg.

Piano Piece I 1965 (UE) 4 min. Bars lasting 5 seconds are marked off. Values are only approximate, and much is left to the performer to decide. Staccato and legato elements are cleverly used, dramatic. Based on a single chord, may be a reaction to the abstruseness of serial technique. John Cage and Morton Feldman influence. D.

Piano Piece II 1968 (UE) 6pp., 7½ min. Larger in scope than *Piano Piece I*; form is repetitive rather than developmental. Much emphasis on dynamics and silences. Among other preparations, six notes must be fitted with rubber wedges, and four milk bottles are to be placed on strings. Avant-garde. M-D.

Sonata in One Movement 1981 (UE) 18 min. Sections are bound together tightly; well unified. Opens with the presentation of a group of seven pitches, with only one pitch in each two-bar segment, varied meters. Second group of seven pitches is a permutation of the first set of metric changes; five groups of seven notes are presented altogether. Fast moving, dramatic cumulative effect, very quiet and haunting ending. D.

See: David Burge, "Contemporary Piano," *Keyboard*, 8 (April 1982):58, 74, for a discussion of this work.

Toccata d 1981 (UE) 12 min. Driving, serial influence, contains some highly effective moments. M-D to D.

Jack Beeson (1921–   ) USA
Beeson is a graduate of the Eastman School of Music and Columbia University.
He studied privately with Bartók in New York in 1944.
Fourth Piano Sonata 1945, rev. 1951 (TP 1984) 16pp., 11 min. Slowly, with freedom: freely tonal with much chromatic coloring, corky rhythmic figure
contrasted with more cantabile sections, quiet closing. Squarely: fughetta-
like, thin textures, quiet and "warmly" section, logically built climax, excit-
ing ending. Pedal indications are suggestive and incomplete. M-D to D.
Fifth Piano Sonata 1946, rev. 1951 (TP 1973) 11pp., facsimile edition. Edited by
John Kirkpatrick. Allegro moderato: shifting meters and emotions, restless, unstable tonality. Adagio: free, ornate, irregular rhythmic flow. Marziale:
audacious, daring, strong rhythmic drive, dissonant percussive harmonies.
Short, tightly knit. D.
See: Janet E. Seitzer, "The Solo Piano Works of Jack Beeson," diss., Baltimore:
Peabody Institute of The Johns Hopkins University, 1986.

Ludwig van Beethoven (1770–1827) Germany
Beethoven's piano works occupy a unique place in keyboard literature and demand the detailed attention of both the teacher and the serious student. Works
without opus number (WoO) are numbered in accordance with Georg Kinsky,
*Das Werk Beethovens, thematisch-bibliographisches Verzeichnis seiner sämtlichen
vollendeten Kompositionen*, completed by Hans Halm (Munich: G. Henle Verlag,
1955).

EDITIONS OF THE SONATAS:

From work to work, within this genre, the music takes many—and frequently
abrupt—turns of character. More often than not, almost schizophrenic changes
occur from movement to movement. What an enormous difference there is between Op.106 and Op.110, or even between Op.10/2 and Op.10/3.

There have been more editions of the sonatas than of any other body
of works in the keyboard literature. B. Wellner—Henle has an urtext edition.
GS and K have reprinted the old Br&H edition, which is also available in five
volumes in Lea Pocket Scores (LPS 11–15) and Kalmus miniature scores. The
Heinrich Schenker—UE edition, newly revised by Erwin Ratz, in two volumes,
is based on solid research and scholarship and is very reliable. Dover has reprinted the Heinrich Schenker edition, which is excellent although it has a few
minor flaws; Schenker's fingering is very illuminating. Hans Schmidt—Henle is
part of the Neue Ausgabe sämtlicher Werke, Vol.I: Opp.2–26; Vol.II: Opp.27–57;
Vol.III: Opp. 79–111; critical commentary volume forthcoming. Claudio Arrau,
L. Hoffmann-Erbrecht—CFP combines research, based on authentic sources of
revision, with the experience of international concert practice and established

academic principles. Measures are numbered; contains fingering and metronome marks by Czerny as well as by Arrau, whose fingering is unusually interesting. A very personal conception is the edition by Artur Schnabel—Belwin-Mills, available in two volumes or as separate sonatas; compare with Schnabel's recordings! The fingering is one of the finest attributes of this edition. Other editions with merit are: Martienssen—CFP; Koehler, Ruthardt—CFP; Lamond—Br&H; Liszt—Zen-On (Liszt expressed not only the *urtext* of the music but the *urgeist* [spirit] of the music as well); d'Albert—CF; Casella—Ric; Dukas—Durand; L. Weiner—EMB; D. Geoffroy—Lemoine; Germer—Litolff; Peter Solymos— EMB; Tovey, Craxton—ABRSM; Kendall Taylor (Allans Music Australia 1985), 4 vols., complete with notes on performance and interpretation I. Mariássy, T. Zaszkalicsy—KMB, 3 vols. Hauschild—VU: Vol. I, contains Opp.2/1–3; 7; 10/1–3; 13; 14/1, 2; 22; Vol. II contains Opp. 26; 27/1, 2; 28; 31/1–3; 49/1, 2; 53; 54; Vol. III contains Opp. 57; 78; 79; 81a; 90; 101; 106; 109; 110; 111.

Available separately: Every sonata from Op.2/1 through Op.111 (Tovey, Craxton—ABRSM; Bülow and Lebert—GS, use with care; notes are changed).

See: William Drabkin, "The Beethoven Sonatas," MT (April 1985):216–20. Discusses six editions presently available.

Kenneth Drake, *The Sonatas of Beethoven as He Played and Taught Them* (Cincinnati: MTNA, 1972). 209pp. Reprint, Indiana University Press, 1981.

————. *The Beethoven Sonatas and the Creative Experience.* Bloomington: Indiana University Press, 1994, 320 pp.

Ernest Walker, "The Associated Board's Edition of Beethoven's Pianoforte Sonatas," ML, 13/1 (1932):11–18.

————. "The (Beethoven) Pianoforte Sonatas: Some Textural Problems," ML, 8/2 (1927):211–17.

Facsimiles available: Op.27/2 (H. Schenker—UE); Op.53 (Beethovenhaus, Bonn); Op.57 (CFP; GS; Kesei Sakka—Ongaku-No-Tomo-Sha); Op.109 (Robert O. Lehman Foundation); Op.111 (CFP; Dover).

An order of progressive difficulty in the sonatas might be: Op.49, 2/1, Op.79, Op.14/1, Op.2/1 (last movement more difficult), Op.14/2, Op.10/2, Op.10/1, Op.10/3, Op.13, Op.26, Op.27/1, Op.28, Op.22, Op.2/2, Op.2/3, Op.78, Op.90, Op.7, Op.31/3, Op.54, Op.31/2, Op.27/2, Op.31/1, Op.109, Op.110, Op.81a, Op.53, Op.57, Op.101, Op.111, Op.106.

Sonata C (Ates Orga—Roberton Publications 1978) 16pp. 12 min. This little-known sonata, consisting in MS of a complete first movement and 25 bars of a second, prompted Tovey to the conclusion that: "it cannot have been written long before the sonatas in Op.2 (1795) and the first movement, for all its slenderness in dimensions and sound, is as masterly as anything in that opus" (from the score). It is published here in a scholarly and practical edition, with a completion of the second movement and a projected third movement based on contemporary sketchbooks of the composer. Int. to M-D.

Sonata f Op.2/1 1795 (Hoehn—Schott; Wallner—Henle; Hinson—Alfred 8052; Ching—Prowse; d'Albert—CF; K; Heugel; Scionti—Ric). Allegro; Adagio;

Minuetto—Allegretto; Prestissimo. A dramatic work of moderate technical demands. Retains the classic minuet. Triplet basses of the finale require
a flexible left hand.

See: Garrick Ohlsson, "Beethoven's Sonata No.1 (Op.2/1)—A Performer's
Analysis," *Keyboard*, 8/10 (October 1982):22-27.

Sonata A Op.2/2 1795 (Hoehn—Schott). Allegro vivace; Largo appassionato;
Scherzo—Allegretto; Rondo—Grazioso. The most interesting of the three
sonatas in this opus. Brilliant outer movements. The beautiful slow movement presents tonal problems, while the third is a lively scherzo full of
staccato humor.

Sonata C Op.2/3 1796 (Hoehn—Schott; d'Albert—CF). Allegro con brio: broken-chord and broken-octave required. Adagio: deeply moving. Scherzo—
Allegro: strong rhythmic control necessary for the groups of three eighth-
notes. Allegro assai: many staccato chords and octaves, scintillating. A
large-scale work, the most difficult of this opus.

Sonata Eb Op.7 1796 (VU). Allegro molto e con brio: difficult legato octaves in
the second half of the exposition, fast broken octaves later. Largo, con gran
espressione: requires a fine rhythmic sense. Allegro: folksy; naive; flowing
legato required. Rondo—Poco Allegretto e grazioso: graceful theme, leaping left hand shares melody.

See: Roger Kamien, "Chromatic Details in Beethoven's Piano Sonata in E
Flat Major, Op.7," MR, 35 (August 1974):149-56.

Sonata c Op.10/1 1796? (Hoehn—Schott; Wallner—Henle; Ching—Prowse;
d'Albert—CF; K). Allegro molto e con brio: first-rate musical and technical material. Adagio Molto: varied ornamental version of the second subject but be in tempo when it returns. Finale—Prestissimo: needs firm fingers, accurate staccato, a stunning SA design.

Sonata F Op.10/2 1797? (VU; Hoehn—Schott; d'Albert—CF; K). Allegro: gracious. Allegretto: cantabile, chorale in Db. Presto: fuguelike opening; needs
fluent fingers, accurate staccato, and firm rhythmic control.

Sonata D Op.10/3 1798 (VU; Hoehn—Schott). Presto: requires good rotation
technique and strong fingers; needs to race along. Largo e mesto: one of
the most eloquent of all the slow movements; has emotional depth. Menuetto—Allegro: match triplet tempo in the Trio with the Menuetto. Rondo—
Allegro: elaborate working-out of the opening three-note motif, humorous
throughout with many starts and stops.

Sonata c ("Pathétique") Op.13 1789? (Wallner-Henle; Hinson—Alfred 6352;
Banowetz—GWM, available with cassette; Hoehn—Schott; Schenker,
Ratz—UE; Ching—Prowse; d'Albert—CF; K; Fischer—CFP; Lympany—
Hansen House). Grave—Allegro di molto e con brio—Tempo I—Allegro
molto e con brio: young players who attempt this movement are not
equipped for its difficulties, such as the left-hand tremolo passages. Adagio
cantabile: one basic tempo throughout, although careful rubato will point
out melodic nuances. Rondo—Allegro: not as demanding as the opening
movement but should not sound anti-climactic. M-D.

See: Kenneth Drake, "Beethoven's Sonata Pathétique," PQ, 107 (Fall 1979):51–54.

Miriam Hyde, "Beethoven Sonata No.13 (Pathétique)," *MTA of New South Wales Quarterly Magazine* (August 1993):13–17.

William S. Newman, "K.457 and Op.13—Two Related Masterpieces in C Minor," PQ, 57 (Fall 1966):11–15; revised and enlarged version, MR, 28 (1967):46–52.

TM, "Analysis of Beethoven: Piano Sonata in c minor, Op.13 ('Pathétique'), Second Movement," pp.92–107.

Sonata E Op.14/1 1799 (Wallner—Henle; Hoehn—Schott; K). Op.14/1, 2 published together (Köhler/Kann—Schott). Allegro: tricky broken thirds. Allegretto: scherzo-like substitute for the usual central slow movement. Rondo—Allegro commodo: joyous.

See: Forbes Watson, "Beethoven's Op.14 No.1," MT, 86 (1945):108–11. A discussion of Beethoven's arrangement of this sonata for string quartet.

Sonata G Op.14/2 1799 (Wallner—Henle; Hoehn—Schott; K; Ching—Prowse). Allegro: be careful of the repeated D in measures 9 and 11; left-hand staccatos in the development are problems. Andante: variations on a chorale; be careful of tonal balance in the first variation. Scherzo—Allegro assai: in rondo form; opening bars must be clearly accented.

Sonata B♭ Op.22 1800. Allegro con brio: rotation passages require a free forearm. Adagio con molta espressione: must have a warm singing tone. Menuetto: rhythmic swing; requires clean finger articulation in the alternative G minor section. Rondo—Allegretto: beautiful Schubertian tune requires smooth legato. Beethoven showed a special fondness for this work.

Sonata A♭ Op.26 1801 (Hauschild—VU; Wallner—Henle; Hoehn—Schott; Heugel; Schenker—UE). Andante con Variazioni: needs a consistent tempo to unite all five variations. Scherzo—Allegro molto: difficult legato thirds. Marcia funebre sulla morte d'un Eroe—Maestoso andante: distinguish carefully between tenuto and staccato and be careful of pedaling. Allegro: this busy rondo requires a fine rotation technique. None of the movements are written in SA design.

Sonata E♭ Op.27/1 1801 (Fischer—CFP with Op.27/2; Hoehn—Schott; K). Andante—Allegro—Tempo I: firm rhythmic and tonal control essential. Allegro molto e vivace: dance form, has bright Trio. Adagio con espressione: not a separate movement but an introduction to the final movement. Allegro vivace: rondo with a development; interrupted near the end to reintroduce the melody of the slow introduction. The subtitle of this work, *Sonata quasi una Fantasia*, is amply justified, for Beethoven seems not to be overly concerned with the sonata's traditional structure. His capacity for wit is stunningly revealed in this subtle yet stalwart work.

Sonata c♯ ("Moonlight") Op.27/2 1801 (Palmer—Alfred 2502; J. Fischer—CFP with Op.27/1; Wallner—Henle; Schenker, Ratz—UE; M. Lympany—Hansen House; Ching—Prowse; K). Adagio sostenuto: an expressive, lyric cantabile line, pianissimo, is necessary for this magnificent movement. Allegretto; Liszt called this movement "a flower between abysses," but it is actually a spontaneous scherzo and trio that requires a fine rhythmic swing. Presto agitato: dramatic, animated, tumultuous, SA design with two themes, fiery broken chords, tremolos and staccato chord passages.

See: Irwin Fischer, "A Note in Opus 27, No.2", ML, 32 (January 1951):45–46.

Sonata D ("Pastorale") Op.28 1801 (Schenker, Ratz—UE; Hoehn—Schott; K). Allegro: various sections closely unified. Andante: one of Beethoven's favorites. Scherzo—Allegro vivace: use the left-hand part of the Trio to establish the tempo for the Scherzo. Rondo—Allegro, ma non troppo: the opening has the most "pastoral" sound in the entire sonata. The subtitle "Pastorale" was not original with Beethoven.

See: James Callahan, "Arrau vs. Schnabel in Beethoven's Op.28," PQ, 93 (Spring 1976):46–52.

Sonata G Op.31/1 1802. Allegro vivace: requires a good finger technique. Adagio grazioso: elegant graces. Rondo—Allegretto: difficult left-hand passages for a small hand.

Sonata d ("Tempest") Op.31/2 1802 (Wallner—Henle; Hoehn—Schott; L. Weiner—EMB; Heugel). Largo—Allegro: storm and stress; tricky two-note slurs; the two ghostly recitatives require careful pedaling. Adagio: rhythmic continuity is the greatest problem. Allegretto: melancholy; wistful; agitated interruptions; persistent use of opening four-note motive must never sound mechanical. One of the greatest Romantic sonatas.

See: Tedd Joselson, "Master Class—Beethoven's 'Tempest' Sonata," CK, 5 (August 1979):65.

Barry Cooper, "The Origins of Beethoven's D Minor Sonata Op.31 No.2," M&L, 62/3–4 (July-October 1981):261–80.

Ludwig Misch, *Beethoven Studies* (Norman: University of Oklahoma Press, 1953). Chapter 5 discusses "The 'Problem' of the D Minor Sonata." Suggests a new interpretation of the form.

Sonata Eb Op.31/3 1802 (Heugel). Allegro: Liszt wrote over the opening motive the words "Liebst du mich?" and Tobias Matthay used the word "lov-ing-ly" to underscore the gentle rhythm and touch; requires a good trill and careful definition of the slurs in the second theme. Scherzo—Allegretto vivace: an excellent hand-staccato study. Menuetto—Moderato e grazioso: keep the same tempo for the Menuetto and Trio. Presto con fuoco: fast tempo presents problems of coordination between the hands; requires fine left-hand staccato; contagious gaiety abounds.

Sonata g Op.49/1 1795–96 (Alfred, with Op.49/2; Henle, with Op.49/2; K; Hoehn—Schott; Ratz—UE; Ching—Prowse; Lemoine). Andante: requires smooth thirds in the left hand at opening. Rondo—Allegro: main theme must be a good staccato. Beethoven probably did not intend to publish the Op.49 sonatas, as he used a *menuetto* section from Op.49/2 in his *Septet* Op.20. It is believed that his brother Karl found the works and sent them to a publisher. They were published in 1805. Both works have clear forms and charming moments and are excellent for introducing Beethoven to young pianists.

See: Stefan Bardas, "Sonata Op.49/1—A Beethoven Master Class," *Clavier*, 22/8 (October 1983):26–33. Includes music.

Sonata G Op.49/2 1795–96 (same editions as for Op.49/1). Allegro ma non troppo; Tempo di Menuetto. Easier than Op.49/1. Both sonatas seem out of place, situated between the highly progressive sonatas of Op.31 and the virtuoso "Waldstein" Op.53.

Sonata C ("Waldstein") Op.53 1804 (Wallner—Henle; Schenker, Ratz—UE; L. Weiner—EMB; K; Hoehn—Schott; M. Lympany—Hansen House; Heugel; Lemoine). Allegro con brio: virtuosic; needs careful attention to its larger shape with very little tempo change at the E-major second subject. Introduzione—Adagio molto: exact time values required in this short, slow, and sonorous introduction. Rondo—Allegretto moderato: contains transformed statements of the basic theme, long trills, and glissando octaves; point up the moderato, especially in the lyric main theme; requires utmost control. One of the greatest sonatas.

See: Barry Cooper, "The Evolution of the First Movement of Beethoven's 'Waldstein' Sonata," M&L, 58 (April 1977):170–91.

Anthony J. Crain, "Problems in the Beethoven Literature," *Clavier*, 9 (January 1970):30–36. Mainly a discussion of trouble spots with special reference to Sonata C, Op.53.

Elizabeth N. McKay, "Abbe Vogler, Beethoven and the Waldstein Sonata," *The Beethoven Newsletter* (Spring 1993):7.

Sonata F Op.54 1804. In tempo d'un menuetto: two alternating subjects; second one requires endurance in vigorous staccato octaves and sixths. Allegretto: toccata based on one theme; requires a smooth delivery. This work has much to recommend it and is frequently overlooked.

See: James C. Kidd, "Wit and Humor in Tonal Syntax," *Current Musicology*, 21 (1976):70–82. Discusses the first movement of Op.54 from the viewpoint of a subtle and comprehensive use of wit and humor by Beethoven.

Sonata f ("Appassionata") Op.57 1804–5 (J. Fischer—CFP contains epilogue in German and English, critical notes in German, and bars 340–66 of the first version of the last movement; Wallner—Henle; Schenker, Ratz—UE; M. Lympany—Hansen House; d'Albert—CF; Hoehn—Schott; K; Heugel; WH). Allegro assai: emotional and dramatic qualities; difficult articulation problems, especially in the second part of the second subject, which requires great speed and large tone. Andante con moto: short set of variations using one of Beethoven's most beautiful melodies. Allegro ma non troppo: must have an intense emotional drive in the tremendous sweep of the movement. Beethoven thought this his best sonata.

See: Martha Frohlich, *Beethoven's 'Appassionata' Sonata* (Oxford: Clarendon Press, 1991). In the series "Studies in Musical Genesis and Structure."

Sonata F♯ Op.78 1809 (Höpfel—Schott, with preface and critical notes in German and English; Hinson—Alfred 6327). Adagio cantabile—Allegro ma non troppo: leisurely; lyric; tempo should not be too fast. Allegro vivace: clear articulation of the two-note slurs should restrain the tempo of this scherzo-like vivace; graceful caprice.

Sonata G Op.79 1809 (Wallner—Henle; WH; Hoehn—Schott; K). Presto alla tedesca: hand crossings help the lilt of this German dance. Andante: simple and beautiful Neapolitan barcarolle. Vivace: a fun movement; briefly worked out; has no difficulties.

See: Ludwig Misch, *Beethoven Studies* (Norman: Oklahoma University Press, 1953). Chapter 2, "Alla danza tedesca," throws light on the original sketches of this movement.

Sonata E♭ ("Sonate caractéristique: Les Adieux; l'absence et le retour") Op.81a 1809 (K; Heugel). Adagio—Allegro: treacherous legato double notes and fast staccato chords. Andante espressivo: do not play too slowly, especially in comparison with the Adagio of the first movement, but bend the tempo slightly when the melodic turns appear. Vivacissimamente: triumphant; slurs in bars 9 and 10 should restrain the fast tempo. This sonata was inspired by Archduke Rudolph, friend and student of Beethoven, who left Vienna shortly before the French occupation of 1809.

Sonata e Op.90 1814 (Wallner—Henle; K; Heugel). Mit Lebhaftigkeit und durchaus mit Empfindung und Ausdruch: requires smooth left-hand sixteenth-note accompaniment of the second subject (difficult for a small hand). Nicht zu geschwind und sehr singbar vorgetragen: a leisurely rondo with Schubertian overtones; must have a beautiful legato. More difficult than it looks, this sonata balances intellect and cool emotion. It is mercurial, almost capricious. Modulations and expressive counterpoint in the first movement contrast with gentle lyricism in the Rondo. This sonata stands on the threshold of Beethoven's last "metaphysical" works.

Sonata A Op.101 1816. Etwas Lebhaft, und mit der innigsten Empfindung (Allegretto, ma non troppo): difficult to decide on the correct tempo for this quiet reverie (lively, but with innermost feeling). Lebhaft. Marschmässig (Vivace alla marcia): usually played too fast; heroic mood needs dignity and extreme rhythmic accuracy. Langsam und sehnsuchtsvoll (Adagio, ma non troppo, con affetto): opening reverie heard again; take the fast turns at a very sustained pace; serves as introduction to the finale. Geschwinde, doch nicht zu sehr, und mit Entschlossenheit (Allegro): expansive, too fast a tempo turns this movement into trivia.

See: Marta Schermerhorn, "An Historical and Analytical Study of Beethoven's Fortepiano Sonata in A Major, Opus 101," thesis, San Jose State University, 1991.

Sonata B♭ ("Hammerklavier") Op.106 1817–18 (J. Fischer—CFP: epilogue in German and English, critical notes in German, fingered; Hoehn—Schott). Allegro: Beethoven's metronome indications are impractical; a flexible

tempo with the half note approximately 92 is suggested; formidable technical problems; grandiose; SA with two contrasting themes; much contrapuntal use in the development. Scherzo—Assai vivace: brusque contrasts; rhythmic figures must be accurate but delicate in their accentuation. Adagio sostenuto: the longest Adagio Beethoven wrote for a sonata; meditative and melancholy; amazingly expressive ornamentation. Largo: an improvisatory introduction to the finale fugue. Allegro risoluto: extended fugue subject; many deviations in the fugue; develops a fugue within a fugue (*sempre dolce cantabile*); requires great finger control. A colossal work, the longest and most difficult of the sonatas, an apocalyptic masterpiece.
See: Alan Tyson, "The Hammerklavier and Its English Editions," MT, 103 (April 1962):235–37.

Sonata E Op.109 1820 (Schenker—UE; K; Henle 362). Vivace, ma non troppo: short; like a prelude; introspective; amiable; SA design with two contrasted key centers of E and B presented in two contrasted tempos. Prestissimo: condensed SA design; restless; like an interlude connecting the outer movements; similar in texture to the first movement of Op.101. Gesangvoll, mit innigster Empfindung (Andante molto cantabile ed espressivo): theme and six variations, including a fugato, that reveal changes in character while progressing to a climatic point and then subsiding into a quiet return of the theme. In many ways this work seems like a *Sonata quasi una Fantasia* in all but name.
See: Russell Bliss, "Late Beethoven—Playing Piano Sonata Op.109," *Clavier*, 15 (January 1976):19–22.
Allen Forte, *The Compositional Matrix* (Cincinnati: Music Teachers National Association, 1961; reprint, New York: Da Capo Press, 1973). On the sketches for Beethoven's Op.109.
Nicholas Marston, *Beethoven's Piano Sonata in E, Op.109* (New York: Clarendon Press, 1995), 230 pp.

Sonata A♭ Op.110 1821 (Henle 363; Höpfel—Schott 09715; K). Moderato cantabile molto espressivo: SA design treated freely; keep a generally uniform tempo for all of the pieces of material; songlike; amiable. Allegro molto: scherzo-like; the right-hand figuration in the central section must not be hurried. Adagio ma non troppo: short lyric introduction leads to Fuga—Allegro, ma non troppo: smooth counterpoint, a friendly fugue that gradually arrives at a full conclusion. Much more difficult than it looks, especially in the voice leadings.

Sonata c Op.111 1822 (Henle 364; K; Hoehn—Schott; Schenker—UE). Maestos—Allegro con brio ed appassionato: stormy, powerful, and potent. Arietta—Adagio molto semplice e cantabile: deeply moving; maintain the basic tempo throughout the variations; Var. 4 is frequently taken too fast; Beethoven seems to have found the peace of God in this movement.
See: Philip Barford, "Beethoven's Last Sonata," ML, 35 (October 1954):320–31.

William Drabkin, "Some Relationships between the Autographs of Beethoven's Sonata in C minor, Op.111," *Current Musicology*, 13 (1972):38–47.
Johanna Goldstein, *A Beethoven Enigma: Performance Practice and the Piano Sonata, Opus 111* (New York: Peter Lang, 1988).
Willis H. Hackman, "Rhythmic Analysis as a Clue to Articulation in the Arietta of Beethoven's Op.111," PQ, 93 (Spring 1976):26–37.
Charles Timbrell, "Notes on the Sources of Beethoven's Op.111," M&L, 58 (April 1977):204–15.
The Titled Sonatas (I. Kolodin—GS). Includes eight dramatic and programmatic sonatas: Pathétique, Moonlight, Pastorale, Tempest, Waldstein, Appassionata, Les Adieux, Hammerklavier. A most interesting and illuminating preface defends the use of these names. Urtext edition (the old Br&H) reprinted.
Selected Easiest Sonata Movements for Piano, Vol. 1 (Alfred 4841).
Selected Easiest Sonata Movements for Piano, Vol. 2 (Alfred 4842).
See: David Breitman, "The Damper Pedal and the Beethoven Piano Sonatas: A Historical Perspective," diss., Cornell University, 1993.
Cassandra Irene Carr, "Wit and Humor as a Dramatic Force in the Beethoven Piano Sonatas," diss., University of Washington, 1985.
Shiow-Lih L. Shieh, "A Pianist's Reference Guide to Beethoven's Piano Sonatas," diss., University of North Carolina at Greensboro, 1992.

EDITIONS OF THE VARIATIONS:

Twenty-two sets of variations make up another large group of Beethoven's keyboard writing. They date from 1782 to 1823 and cover even a larger span of years than the sonatas (1782–1822). Opus numbers were used with only a few sets. Interpretative problems vary from easy to the most formidable.
Joseph Schmidt-Görg—Henle: All 22 sets including: 9 Variations on a March of E. Chr. Dressler WoO 63; 6 Variations on a Swiss Air WoO 64; 24 Variations on "Vieni Amore" by V. Righini WoO 65; 13 Variations on "Es war einmal" by K. Ditters von Dittersdorf WoO 66; 12 Variations on the Minuet à la Vigano by J. Haibel WoO 68; 9 Variations on "Quant' è più bello" by G. Paisiello WoO 69; 12 Variations on a Russian Dance by P. Wranitzky WoO 71; 8 Variations on "Une fièvre brûlante" by A. E. M. Gretry WoO 72; 10 Variations on "La stessa la stessissima" by A. Salieri WoO 73; 7 Variations on "Kind, willst du ruhig schlafen" by P. Winter WoO 75; 8 Variations on "Tändeln und Scherzen" by F. X. Sussmayr WoO 76; 6 Easy Variations G WoO 77; 6 Variations F Op.34; 15 Variations and Fugue E♭ Op.35; 7 Variations on "God Save the King" WoO 78; 5 Variations on "Rule Britannia" WoO 79; 32 Variations c WoO 80; 6 Variations D Op.76; 33 Variations on a Waltz by A. Diabelli Op.120; 9 Variations on a March of E. Chr. Dressler (2d version) WoO 63: 8 Variations on "Ich hab' ein kleines Hüttchen nur" Anhang 10.

Monike Holl, Bruno Seidlhofer—VU 1973; Vol.I: WoO 64, 65, 70, 71, 77, 80; Opp.34, 35, 76, 120. Vol.II: WoO 63, 66, 68, 69, 72, 73, 75, 76, 78, 79. Urtext, performing format edition, fingered.

Peter Hauschild—CFP 1970: Vol.I: Opp.34, 35, 76, 120; WoO 65, 80. Vol.II: remaining variations. Urtext, preface in German and English, fingered by Gerhard Erber.

Complete Variations (Dover 1986) 228pp. From the Br&H complete edition 1862–65. Contains 21 sets of variations. Missing are *9 Variations on a March of E. Chr. Dressler* (2d version) WoO 63.

See: Steven M. Whiting, "To the 'New Manner' Born: A Study of Beethoven's Early Variations," University of Illinois, 1991. Covers the Dressler Variations of 1782 to the Süssmayer Variations of 1799.

Variationen über Volkweisen Opp.105, 107 (Gerschon Jarecki—VU) Although an *ad libitum* flute part is included, these are mainly piano variations making less than usual demands on the pianist. There are numerous unexplained articulation and dynamic marks in this edition.

Selected Variations WoO 70, 64, 77 (Henle). Available separately: Variations c WoO 80 (Henle; Schott; Ric; Agosti-Curci). "Nel cor più non mi sento" WoO 70 (Schott; Heinrichshofen; Ric; WH). Op.120 C (Kuhlmann—CFP; Schnabel—CF). Variations F Op.34 (Schott). Swiss Air Variations WoO 64 (Heinrichshofen). 6 Easy Variations G WoO 77 (Schott). Variations Op.105/3 and 4 (Schott). Variations on a Russian Folksong Op.107 (Schott). 10 Variierte Themen Op.107 (Br&H) 2 vols.

Variations on "Kind, Willst du Ruhig Schlafen.," WoO 75 (Ruthardt—CFP 7232) 15pp. Charming, attractive. Int.

Variations on a Swiss Song WoO 64 and *Variations on the Duet "Nell cor più mi sento"* WoO 70. In collection *Masters of the Theme and Variations* (Alfred 2209).

LARGER SETS OF VARIATIONS:

Variations in F, Op.34 1802. Six variations, only the theme and last variation are in F, the others each move down a third (D, B♭, G, E♭, c). Each variation has its own personality: Var.1: graceful roulades. Var.2: a scherzo. Var.3: pastoral. Var.4: a minuet. Var.5: a funeral march. Var.6: in rondo style. An interesting experiment that Beethoven never repeated. M-D.

Variations and Fugue on a Theme from "Prometheus" Op.35 1802. The theme is from the *Prometheus* ballet and was used later for the *Eroica* symphony finale. Demands are similar to those of the sonatas from this time, such as the Opp.53 and 57; more difficult than *Variations* Op.34. A unique work in that it combines elements of fugue, sonata, and suite in one movement. The main part of the work encompasses 15 variations handled with a kaleidoscopic display of keyboard figuration. The final variation is a long, highly ornamented Largo. The light-hearted fugue has an unsuccessful conclusion. D.

See: Ellwood Derr, "Beethoven's Long-Term Memory of C. P. E. Bach's Rondo in E Flat, W.61/1 (1787), Manifest in the Variations in E Flat for Piano, Op.35 (1802)," MQ, 70/1 (Winter 1984):45–76.

Thirty-Two Variations in c Minor WoO 80 1806 (Alfred 1153; Henle). An attractive eight-bar chaconne provides the harmonic basis for (actually) 35 variations, which partake of some wonderfully contrasted techniques. Vars.12–17 serve as the equivalent to a slow movement, with the coda beginning at Var.31. Probably the most often performed set of variations and the favorite of many audiences. M-D.

See: George A. Kochevitsky, "Beethoven's Variations in C Minor," *Clavier* (September 1967).

Variations in D Major Op.76 1809. In collection *Masters of the Classical Period* Alfred 1199. The theme is from the familiar Turkish March of the *Ruins of Athens*. The six variations display all of Beethoven's later style characteristics infused with humorous touches. Easier than any of the other discussed sets. Int. to M-D.

Thirty-Three Variations on a Waltz by Diabelli Op.120 1823 (CFP 4476). This set is a masterpiece because of the novelty of its ideas, care in working them out, and beauty in the most artful of their transitions. It is a sort of cosmos unto itself in its spectrum of moods and its endless inventiveness. Diabelli's fun theme sets Beethoven free to build recognizable variations in every conceivable way, and it is in that instant recognizability that this giant set of variations becomes possible. Alfred Brendel considers this set the greatest work in all piano literature. It invites comparison with Bach's *Goldberg Variations*. D.

See: Stephen A. Berquist, "Beethoven's Diabelli Variations: Early Performance History," *The Beethoven Newsletter*, 7/2 (Summer 1992):38–41.

Eric Blom, "Beethoven's Diabelli Variations," in *Classics Major and Minor* (London: J. M. Dent, 1958) pp.48–78.

Karl Geiringer, "The Structure of Beethoven's Diabelli Variations," MQ, 50 (October 1964):496–503.

William Kinderman *Beethoven's Diabelli Variations* (New York: Oxford University Press 1987), 244 pp.

William Yeomans, "Problems of Beethoven's Diabelli Variations," MMR, 89, No.991 (January-February 1959):8–13.

PIANO PIECES:

Collections containing miscellaneous works, such as bagatelles, rondos, and ecossaises.

Klavierstücke (Brendel—VU). Contains Rondo G Op.129; Rondo C Op.51/1; Allegretto c WoO 53; Rondo G Op.51/2; 7 Bagatelles Op.33; Andante F WoO 57; 6 Ecossaisen WoO 83; Fantasie Op.77; Für Elise WoO 59; Polonaise Op.89; Klavierstück B♭ WoO 60; 11 Bagatelles Op.119; 6 Bagatelles Op.126. Excellent scholarship; part of the Wiener Urtext Ausgabe.

Klavierstücke (H. Keller—CFP). Vol.I: Bagatelles and Rondos. Vol.II: Andante F
WoO 57; Fantasie Op.77; Polonaise Op.89; Allegretto c (1797); Presto C
(1797); Allegretto C (1804); Lustig und traurig; Für Elise; Klavierstück B♭;
Allegretto for F. Piringer; Menuett E♭; Allemande A; Walzer D, E♭; Ecos-
saisen, Fuge D (1817; Op.137 original for string quartet), Praeludium f, 2
Praeludien through all keys.

Klavierstücke (Kohler, Ruthardt—CFP; K). Opp.33, 39, 51/1–2, 77, 89, 119, 126,
129, Andante F WoO 57.

Piano Pieces (Irmer, Lampe—Henle 12). Based on autographs and original editions. Alla Ingharese (The Rage Over the Lost Penny), Op.129; Allegretto
c WoO 53; Andante F WoO 57; Bagatelles WoO 52, WoO 56, Opp.33, 119,
126; Fantasy Op.77; Piano Pieces (Lustig und Traurig) WoO 54; WoO 59
(Für Elise); in B♭ WoO 60; in b, WoO 61 (for Piringer); in g, WoO 61a; Minuet E♭ WoO 82; Polonaise C Op.89; Preludes Op.39 and WoO 55; Rondos
in C, WoO 48; in A, WoO 49; in C, G, Op.51/1, 2; in B♭, Appendix 6; 3 (Kur-
fürsten-) Sonatas, WoO 47; Easy Sonata C WoO 51; 2 Sonatinas, Appendix
5; 2 Sonatina movements, WoO 50. Appendix—Andante C; Minuet F.

Complete Bagatelles (von Irmer—Henle).

14 Bagatelles (Frickert—CFP). In progressive order: Op.33/1–6; Op.119/1, 3–4, 9–
11; Op.126/2, 5.

Bagatelles Opp.33, 119, 126 (VU; ABRSM). In one volume.

Seven Bagatelles Op.33 (von Irmer—Henle; Scholz—Dob; Hoehn—Schott; WH;
Ric). All are fairly easy with the exception of No.5 (brilliant). Int. to M-D.

Bagatelles Op.119 (Alfred; IMC; CFP). Eleven short trifles. Int.

Bagatelles Op.126 (IMC; Hoehn—Schott). Profound, late style characteristics,
the finest of this genre. M-D.

See: Philip Barford, "Bagatelles or Variations?" MO, 76 (February 1953):
277–79. A discussion of the origin of Beethoven's Bagatelles Op.119/7
and 8.

Margaret Lorince, "The Beethoven Bagatelles," AMT, 32/1 (September–
October 1982):8–11.

Three Bagatelles (B. Cooper—Nov 1991) 10pp. Three "new" bagatelles edited
from holographs in the Beethoven-Archive, Bonn. Int.

Bagatelles, Rondos and Other Shorter Works for Piano (Dover 1987) 124pp. From
complete edition (Br&H) 1862–65. Bagatelles Opp.33, 119, and 126. 2 Pre-
ludes through all 12 Major Keys Op.39. Rondos Op.51/1/2. Fantasia Op.77.
Polonaise Op.89. Rondo a Capriccio Op.129. Andante favori WoO 57.
Minuet WoO 82. 6 Minuets WoO 10. Prelude WoO 55. Rondo WoO 49. 6
Ländler. 7 Ländler WoO 11. Int. to M-D.

Two Preludes in All Major Tonalities Op. 39 1789 (CFP 287). For piano or organ.
The first prelude is built on the pyramid principle with a brilliant climax
in the middle section. The second is more academic, but careful use of its
antiphonal construction can make it surprisingly impressive. Int. to M-D.

Rondo C Op.51/1 (Henle; Dob; Ric; Zen-On; Heinrichshofen). About the same
difficulty as Sonata E Op.14.

Rondo G Op.51/2 (Zen-On; Hoehn—Schott, with Op.51/1). More extended work than Op.51/1; requires refined touch, subtety, and sensitivity.

Andante Favori WoO 57 (von Irmer—Henle; Hoehn—Schott; WH). This was the original slow movement for the "Waldstein" Sonata, Op.53. It has some of the same style characteristics as the *Rondo* G Op.51/2 and concludes with brilliant octaves. M-D.

Fantasia Op.77 (IMC). Improvisatory; moves through numerous keys; passages of excitement alternate with those of a more expressive nature. M-D.
See: Michael R. Sutton, "Beethoven's Op.77 Fantasy: An Improvisational Document?," *AMT*, 36/6 (June–July 1987):25–28.

EASIER COLLECTIONS AND PIECES:

Seven Sonatinas WoO 47 Nos.1–3, E♭, f, D; WoO 51, C; Anh.5/1, G; Anh.5/2, F; WoO 50, F (Alfred; ABRSM). Display strong hints of future formal development. Int.

Six Sonatinas All of the above except WoO 50 (Hoehn—Schott; Kohler—CFP; EMB Z8648; Hauschild—CFP 9420; K; Heinrichshofen; Frugatti—Ric).

Three Sonatinas WoO 47 Nos.1–3 (Belwin-Mills).

Fourteen Easy Pieces (Schott). Easy to Int.

Easy Pieces (Br&H). Sonatine for Mandoline and Klavier (arranged); Lustig-Traurig; Für Elise; Dances; Bagatelles F, E♭, Op.33/3,1; Rondos C, G, Op.51/1,2.

The Easiest Original Pieces (Rowley—Hin). Dance; Adagio/Sonatine C, WoO 51; Bagatelles Op.33/3, Op.119/2–4, 9, 10; Variations on "God Save the King" WoO 78. Int.

Pieces for the Young (Ric). Bagatelles Op.33; Rondo Op.51/1; Variations G, WoO 77; Variations G, WoO 70; Sonatas Op.49/1–2, Op.79. Int.

Beethoven for the Young Musician (EBM). 6 Country Dances; 6 German Dances; 6 Minuets; Sonatinas G, E♭; 6 Easy Variations on a Swiss Song. Int.

Für Elise WoO 59 (Alfred; Henle; Brendel—VU). This often-played charming little rondo still has much to recommend it. Keep one basic tempo throughout. Int.
See: John Horton, "The Girl Who Never Was?—Beethoven's Für Elise," *Music Teacher*, 60/4 (April 1981):21.

Music for a Knightly Ballet (Hess—Br&H). Eight short pieces by Count Ferdinand of Walstein but put together by Beethoven. The German Song is repeated after each number like a refrain. Marsch; Deutscher Gesang; Jagalied; Minnelied; Kriegslied; Trinklied; Tanzlied and Coda. A charming set that provides good sight-reading material with some historical interest. Int.

Beethoven Album (EMB) Vol.I: 7 Bagatelles Op.33; Rondo Op.51/1; Für Elise; Six Easy Variations on a Swiss Song; Seven Variations on "Nel cor più non me sento"; 6 Ecossaises; 2 Minuets; 3 Contradances. Vol.II: Rondo Op.51/2; 11 Bagatelles Op.119; 6 Bagatelles Op.126; Rondo a Capriccio Op.129; Andante Favori. Int. to M-D.

Beethoven—An Introduction to His Piano Works (W. Palmer—Alfred 1970) 64pp. 3 Bagatelles; 3 Country Dances; 2 Ecossaises; Für Elise; Lustig, Traurig; 3 Menuets; Theme from Rondo a Capriccio, Op.129; Sonata G Op.49/2; Sonatina G, Variations on a Swiss Song. Excellent introductory materials. Int.

Il Mio Primo Beethoven (Pozzoli—Ric E. R. 1952) 18pp. Three Country Dances D; Moderato semplice from Sonatina G; Scottish Tune; Romance from Sonatina G; Minuets C, G; Waltz D; Allegro from Sonatina F; Allemanda A; Rondo from Sonatina F. Int.

Beethoven—Easier Favorites (Heinrichshofen N4046) 49pp. Ten pieces that range from Seven Country Dances to Air Autrichien—Theme and Six Variations. Int. to M-D.

Beethoven—Easiest Piano Pieces (Steurer—CFP 5005) 24pp. Twelve short pieces such as Ecossaises, German Dances, Waltz, Minuets, Sonatina F. Int.

Beethoven—The First Book for Young Pianists (Palmer—Alfred) 24pp. Contains some of the easiest pieces plus a discussion of ornamentation in Beethoven's works. Easy to Int.

Beethoven Selected Works (Snell—Kjos 1995) 64pp. Sonatinas F and G; Bagatelles Op.119/9, 3, 1; 6 Variations on a Swiss Song. For Elise; Minuet G; Sonatas Op.49/1, 2; 6 Variations on "Nel cor più non mi sento"; Bagatelle Op.33/3; 6 Variations on an Original Theme; Rondo Op.51/1. Int. to M-D.

Sonatinen und Leichte Sonaten (Peter Hauschild—CFP 1973) 87pp. Fingering by Gerhard Erber. Contains Op.49; Op.79; WoO 47, 50–55; Kinsky Anhang 5. Preface in German and English, critical note in German.

A First Beethoven Book (K 3204) 16pp. German Dances F, D; Ecossaise Eb; Allemanda A; 3 Ländler D; Sonatina G: Moderato semplice; Rondo from Sonatina F; Six Easy Variations on a Swiss Air. Int.

Little Known Piano Pieces (P. Zeitlin, D. Goldberger—BMC 1972). Rondo (1783); Easy Sonata C; Two Bagatelles (1797, 1804); Two Piano Pieces (1821, 1818) are the most interesting. Int.

Beethoven Easy Piano (Alfred). Sixteen pieces, including the two possibly spurious Sonatinas, dance forms, and other familiar works. A short biography and notes on each piece are included. Easy to Int.

The Beethoven Sketch Books (Jack Werner—Chappell) 6 vols. Edited and arranged from the original MSS in a manner closely allied to Beethoven's own settings and style. 55 pieces arranged in order of difficulty. Helpful notes from the editor throughout. Easy to Int.

Young Pianist's Guide to Beethoven (Y. Novik—Studio P/R). Includes easier pieces plus a recording by the editor. Int.

Two Sonatinas, G, F (Henle 365). These two well-known pieces still have much to recommend them. Int.

Seven Sonatinas (Hinson—Alfred 639; Craxton, Tovey—ABRSM) 62pp. WoO 47/1–3: 50, 51, Anh.5/1–2. WoO 50 was composed by Beethoven in his late teens for a friend in Bonn. Int. to M-D.

Sonatina F (Alfred 8070). Int. In collection *World's Greatest Sonatinas* (Alfred 4617).

Sonatina G (Alfred 2149). Int. In collection *World's Greatest Sonatinas* (Alfred 4617).

Easy Piano Pieces and Dances (Töpel—Br 6560 1996) 32pp. Varied miniatures, attractive. Int.

DANCE COLLECTIONS:

Dances of Beethoven. Pieces to Play Before His Sonatinas (Hinson—Alfred 2092). Includes allemandes, country dances, ecossaises, German dances, ländler, minuets, and waltzes. Includes a discussion of performance practices relating to the dances. Int.

Six Ecossaises (Georgii—Schott; Parlow—WH; Ric; Busoni—Br&H). Int.

Ecossaises and German Dances (Niemann—CFP). Int.

12 German Dances (Lutz—Schott). Int.

Six German Dances (K). Int.

Contradances (WH). Int.

Kleine Tänze (Frey—Schott). 20 Menuette; Ländler; Ecossaises; Kontretänze. Int.

Eleven Little Dances (Schott; Br&H). Int.

Six Contretänze (Frickert—Schott). Int.

Fifteen Walzer (Kuhlstrom—Schott). Int.

Six Waltzes (Vitali—Ric). Int.

Allemandes, Waltzes and Songs (BMC). Int.

A Book of Dances WoO 81–86 (Ferguson—ABRSM). Charming and well edited. Int.

Deutsche Tänze (Walter—Br&H). Int.

Twelve German Dances (Kreutzer—Brodt). Int.

Fifteen Waltzes (Allans 1161) 24pp. No.15 is by Franz Schubert, the second of the 36 Waltzes of his Op.8 (Deutsch 365). Int.

BEETHOVENS SÄMTLICHE WERKE, SUPPLEMENTE:

In 1957 under the editorial direction of Willy Hess, Breitkopf and Härtel began issuing *Supplemente zur Gesamtausgabe*, supplements to the first and only "critical" and "complete" edition of *Ludwig van Beethovens Werke* (1864–90). Hess has listed some 335 items not included in the first critical edition. Two volumes of piano works have so far come out in the series: Vol.VIII (1964) contains arrangements for piano by Beethoven of works for two and four hands originally written for other media. Solo works include Musik zu einem Ritterballet WoO 1 (1791) (8 sections); Scherzo from Klaviertrio Op.1/2 (Fragment); Menuett A♭ for String Quartet (ca.1794); 12 German Dances for Orchestra WoO 8; 12 Menuette for Orchestra WoO 7; 12 German Dances for Orchestra WoO 13; 6 Contradances for Orchestra (1802); The Creatures of Prometheus Op.43—Ballet music (Overture and 18 numbers), Wellington's Victory Op.91. Vol.IX (1965) contains solo piano works and chamber works with piano. Many of these are not listed in Kinsky/Halm (p.74). Includes Rondo C WoO 48; Sonatine F WoO 50; Zwei Klavierübungen C, B♭; Menuett C; Drei kleine Nachahmungssätze; Dreistimmige Fuge; Allegretto WoO 53; Allegretto (ca. 1797); Zwei Bagatellen C, E♭ (1800); Anglaise; Zweistimmiger Kanon G (1802); Ländler c; Zweistimmiger Kanon A♭; Thema mit Variationen A (1803); Zwei "Deutsche" F, f (1811–12); Thema für Erzherzog Rudolph (1818); Kleines Konzertfinale (1820); Allegretto (18 Feb. 1821); Bagatelle C (1823–24); Bagatelle g (27 Sept. 1825).

See: Claudio Arrau, "The [Beethoven] Piano Sonatas—Performance Insights," as told to Dean Elder, *Clavier*, 9 (January 1970):18–23.

Jeanne Bamberger, "The Musical Significance of Beethoven's Fingerings in the Piano Sonatas," *Music Forum*, IV (1976): 237–80.

Malcolm Bilson, "Beethoven and the Piano," *Clavier*, 22/8 (October 1983):18–21. The author believes that the piano music of Beethoven is the most compromised, as compared with that of Haydn, Mozart, and Schubert, when performed on a modern piano.

John V. Cockshoot, *The Fugue in Beethoven's Piano Music* (London: Routledge & Paul, 1959).

Carl Czerny, *On the Proper Performance of All Beethoven's Works for the Piano*. Edited with a commentary by Paul Badura-Skoda (Vienna: Universal Edition, 1970).

George Dyson, "Beethoven and the Piano," ML, 8/2 (1927):206–10.

Edwin Fischer, *Beethoven's Piano Sonatas* (London: Faber, 1959).

Robert K. Formsma, "The Use of Pedal in Beethoven's Sonatas," PQ, 93 (Spring 1976):38–45.

J. A. Fuller-Maitland, "Random Notes on the [Beethoven Piano] Sonatas and Their Interpreters," ML, 8/2 (1927):218–23.

William Glock, "A Note on Beethoven's Pedal Marks," *Score*, 2 (January 1950):24–25.

H. A. Harding, *Analysis of Form as Displayed in Beethoven's 32 Pianoforte Sonatas* (London: Novello, 1890), 67pp.

Rudolf Kastner, *Beethoven's Piano Sonatas* (London: Reeves, 1935). A commentary on the sonatas in the light of Schnabel's interpretations; gives an aesthetic appreciation of each sonata, with an outline of the development of the sonata form in Beethoven's hands. Also contains a biographical sketch of Schnabel and an account of his activity as an executant, composer and teacher. Translated by Gerald Abraham.

George Kochevitsky, "Controversial Pedaling in Beethoven's Piano Sonatas," PQ, 40 (Summer 1962):24–28.

Rudolf Kolisch, "Tempo and Character in Beethoven's Music," MQ, 29 (1943):169–87, 291–312. Updated version appears in MQ, 77/1 (Spring 1993):90–131.

George Langley, "The Triune Element in Beethoven as Specially Exemplified in His Piano Sonatas," PRMA, 23 (1896–97):67–84.

E. H. W. Meyerstein, "The Problem of Evil and Suffering in Beethoven's Piano Sonatas," MR, 5 (1944):96–111.

Ludwig Misch, *Beethoven Studies* (Norman: University of Oklahoma Press, 1953). Deals only partly with the piano works but contains fine observations.

———, "Fugue and Fugato in Beethoven's Variation Form," MQ, 42 (1956):14–27.

William S. Newman, "Beethoven's Fingerings as Interpretive Clues," *The Journal of Musicology*, 1/2 (April 1982):171–97.

——, "A Chronological Checklist of Collected Editions of Beethoven's Solo Piano Sonatas Since His Own Day," *NOTES*, 33 (March 1977):503–30. Includes all editions of at least six of the 32 piano sonatas. Entries contain annotations.

——, *Performance Practices in Beethoven's Piano Sonatas* (New York: Norton, 1971).

——, "The Performance of Beethoven's Trills," JAMS, 29 (Fall 1976):439–62.

——, "Performance Practices in Beethoven's Time—A Selected Bibliographic Survey," PQ, 93 (Spring 1976):53–57. The single largest bibliography of sources on Beethoven performance practices that has yet been published.

——, "Tempo in Beethoven's Instrumental Music—Its Choice and Its Flexibility," Part I, PQ, 116 (Winter 1981):22–24, 26–29. Part II, PQ 117 (Spring 1982):22, 24–31.

——, "Some 19th-Century Consequences of Beethoven's 'Hammerklavier' Sonata, Op. 106," PQ, 67 (Spring 1969):12–18; 68 (Summer 1969):12–17.

Cecil B. Oldman, "Beethoven's Variations on National Themes; The Composition and First Publication," MR, 12 (February 1951):45–51.

David Ossenkop, "Editions of Beethoven's Easy Piano Pieces," PQ, 38 (1961–62):17–20.

Ernst Oster, "The Fantasie-Impromptu—A Tribute to Beethoven," *Musicology*, 1/4 (1947):407–29.

Rudolph Reti, *Thematic Patterns in Sonatas of Beethoven* (New York: Macmillan, 1967).

William Rothstein. "Heinrich Schenker as an Interpreter of Beethoven's Piano Sonatas." *19th Century Music*, VIII/1 (Summer 1984):3–27. Discusses Schenker's annotations of the Beethoven sonatas.

Peter Stadlen, "Beethoven and the Metronome," ML, 48 (October 1967):330–49.

Donald Francis Tovey, *A Companion to Beethoven's Pianoforte Sonatas* (London: Associated Board of the Royal Schools of Music, 1948). A measure-by-measure analysis of each sonata.

Alan Tyson, *The Authentic English Editions of Beethoven* (London: Faber, 1963).

——, ed. *Beethoven Studies* (London: Oxford University Press, 1974). 260pp.

Herbert Westerby, *Beethoven and His Piano Works* (London: W. Reeves, 1931).

Robert Winter, "Commentary II: And Even More Thoughts on the Beethoven Trill," MQ, 65/1 (January 1979):111–16.

Konrad Wolff, "Asides on Beethoven's Trills," PQ, 98 (Summer 1977):37–39.

Richard Zimdars, "Hans von Bülow Explores Beethoven's Piano Music," PQ, 125 (Spring 1984):59–63. Nineteenth-century attitudes toward Beethoven, women, and teacher-pupil relationships.

Nicolas Antoine Le Bègue (1631–1702) France

Oeuvres de Clavecin (N. Dufourcq—l'OL 1956). Livre I (1677): Suites in D, G, A, C, F. Livre II (1687): Suites in d, g, a, A, F, G. All the suites but two include an unmeasured prelude. Le Bègue is considered the first French composer to maintain the order of the suite as A, C, S, G with optional dances added. Norbert Dufourcq's description of Le Bègue, "the man had little genius, but a great knowledge and talent," is a terse summation. Int. to M-D.

See: Norbert Dufourcq, *La Musique d'Orgue Française* (Paris: Librairie Fleury, 1949), p.70.

Nöels variés (Br). These variations on Christmas carols resemble folksongs in their simplicity. Int. to M-D.

See: John Edward Gillespie, "The Harpsichord Works of Nicolas Le Bègue," diss., University of Southern California, 1951.

Jeanne Behrend (1911–1988) USA

Behrend was an outstanding musician who made important contributions to American music.

The Scissors Grinder (TP). Constant figuration suggests the title. Very popular in the 1930s and 40s. M-D.

See: Elizabeth A. Hostetter, "Jeanne Behrend: Pioneer Performer of American Music, Pianist, Teacher, Musicologist, and Composer," diss., Arizona State University, 1990.

Jack Behrens (1935–   ) Canada, born USA.

Events for Piano Op.28b (CMC 1961–63). Celebration; Meditation; Anticipation; Joy; Praise. Short character pieces, mostly one page each, in clear, tonal writing. Int. to M-D.

Passacaglia Op.36 (CMC). Approximate difficulty of Copland *Passacaglia*.

Victor Belyi (1904–1968) USSR

3 Miniatures (MCA 1939). 2 lyric, 1 dancelike. M-D.

Sonata No.3 (MCA 1942). One movement of energetic, dissonant writing. M-D.

Sonata No.4 (MCA 1947). Allegretto semplice; Moderato sostenuto; Andante con moto—Allegro appassionato. Advanced pianism required. D.

Anton Bemetzrieder (1743–1817) Germany

Leçons de Clavecin, et Principes d'Harmonie Paris 1771 (BB). In "Monuments of Music and Music Literature in Facsimile," Second Series—Music Literature, XVIII. This collection was written for Denis Diderot's daughter, a pupil of Bemetzrieder. Contains numerous helpful examples of fingering. Published in English as *Music Made Easy* (1778).

Georg Antonin Benda (1722–1795) Bohemia

The historical importance of Benda lies in the fact that his compositions created a link between the late Baroque and the Viennese Classical music. He was a close friend of C. P. E. Bach, whose influence can be seen in many of Benda's keyboard works, and he was greatly appreciated by Mozart. Benda wrote at least 55 sonatas.

Sonatas I-XVI (MAB Vol.24—Artia). M-D.

Twelve Sonatas (R. Jones—ABRSM). Contrasting moods. Int. to M-D.

34 Sonatinen (MAB Vol.37—Artia). Int. to M-D.

Seven Sonatinas (Kreutzer—Brodt 1976) 16pp. Sonatinas a; F; C (Theme and Variations): D; G; G; g. Delightful and well written. Int.

Twelve Sonatinas (MMP). A broad selection. Int.

Sonatina a (Alfred 8047). Some hand crossings, attractive. Int.

See collection *German Keyboard Music of the 17th and 18th Centuries* (Fischer, Oberdoerffer—Vieweg), Vol.6.

Paul Ben-Haim (1897–1984) Israel

Ben-Haim wrote in a colorful folkloristic style that was especially well adapted for the keyboard.

5 Pieces for Piano Op.34 (MCA 1948). Pastorale: improvisational exotic melody. Intermezzo: siciliano rhythms. Capriccio agitato: bravura writing. Canzonetta: melodic. Toccata: repeated-note figuration, similar to the Prokofieff and Ravel Toccatas. M-D.

Sonatina a Op.38 (MCA 1946). Allegretto grazioso: varied moods. Improvisazione: melodic. Molto vivo: driving rhythms culminating in a rigorous finale based on the national dance, Hora. M-D.

Piano Sonata 1954 rev. ed. (IMP 1955) 24pp. 13½ min. Preamble—Fast; Fugue—Quiet; Variations—Moderately fast. Thick chromatic sonorities, ends *pppp*. M-D to D.

Arthur Benjamin (1893–1960) Great Britain, born Australia

Benjamin, a prolific composer in many forms, taught in Sidney, Australia for a few years before moving to London, where he was on the faculty of the Royal College of Music.

Tambourin (Bo&H 1927). Quartal and quintal harmonies. Int.

3 Little Pieces (Bo&H 1929). Easy.

Fantasies (Bo&H 1933). Moderately easy. Two books, three pieces in each book.

Let's Go Hiking (Bo&H 1936). Int.

Chinoiserie (Bo&H 1936). Gavotte and Musette. Int. to M-D.

3 New Fantasies (Bo&H 1938). M-D.

Jamaican Rumba (Bo&H 1938). A light accompaniment in bright rumba rhythm supports a saucy melody and attractive countersubject, changing meters. Benjamin's most popular piano work. M-D.

Elegiac Mazurka 1941 (Bo&H) in *Homage to Paderewsky*, 5pp. No.2 of a set of 16 pieces written as a "musical offering from composers living in the Americas in 1941 for the 50th anniversary of Paderewsky's New York debut." M-D.

Pastorale, Arioso and Finale (Bo&H 1943) 14 min. Virtuoso but unpretentious writing. M-D to D.

George Benjamin (1960–   ) Great Britain

Sonata 1977–78 (Faber FO 578) 57pp. 21 min. Vivace; Lento; Allegro straziando. An exuberant and dramatic virtuoso piece written while Benjamin was studying with Messiaen in 1977–78. Unmistakable Messiaen influences in the type of chording, "added" values, and simulated bells and gongs. Effective piano sonorities supported by a fine sense of formal proportion. Sostenuto pedal required. D.

Sortilèges 1981 (Faber FO 671) 25pp. 11 min. Effective textures; scrunchy chords; long pedals; uses sostenuto pedal; sudden tempo changes; dynamic extremes; expressionistic. Many directions like "wild," "menacing," "as fast and as soft as possible." Long pause; ends in a gentle, hypnotic, extreme pianissimo; like a spellbinding dream. D.

Richard Rodney Bennett (1936–   ) Great Britain

Total serialization appeals to Bennett, and this technique appears frequently in his piano works. Jazz elements show some influence from time to time.

Three Diversions (UE). Two of these are in collection *The Century of Invention* (Hinson—EAMC 1996). Outstanding works for children, excellent for small hands. Easy to Int.

Five Studies 1965 (UE) 10 min. Fluent ideas, many time signature changes, witty, rich textures, serial. Basic set is used in all but Study II, where it is slightly rearranged. D.

Fantasy for Piano 1962 (Belwin-Mills) 10½ min. Three-movement serial work with some delicate and unusual sonorities. Short motives are constantly repeated in varied form; uses mirror relationships. Bennett's best work for solo piano. D.

Sonata 1954 (UE) 8 min. A three-movement serial work that produces unusual expressionistic sonorities and fine pianistic writing. The Grave is extremely expressive. Bartókian influence in the percussive quality and clear-cut rhythmic figures. Inventive and vital. D.

Scena I 1975 (Nov) 14pp. 7½ min. A short, three-movement sonata in all but name. Clear, concise, plenty of contrast, harmonics, fragmented style, unusual sonorities, half-pedal effects, musically vigorous. D.

Theme from Estace and Hilda (Nov). From the BBC TV trilogy. Pleasant, flowing, a few octaves, chording over left-hand arpeggi figures. Int.

Noctuary: Variations on a Theme of Scott Joplin (Nov 1992) 43pp. 27 min. Originally written in 1981 for the ballet in one act by Kenneth Macmillan; based on three sections of Joplin's *Solace—A Mexican Serenade* (1909). D.

Partridge Pie (Nov). Book 1 1990, 11pp.; Book 2, 13pp. Each book contains six pieces "inspired by the popular rhyme *The Twelve Days of Christmas* in which the 'true love's' various gifts are characterized with the composer's familiar grace, wit and skill" (from the score). Int. to M-D.

Tender Is the Night (Nov). Two short pieces in an accessible, atmospheric salon style written as incidental music for the BBC dramatization of the novel by F. Scott Fitzgerald. Nicole's Theme; Rosemary's Waltz. Int.

Tango after Syrinx and Impromptu on the Name of Haydn (Nov). *Tango* is the fourth in a series of pieces based on Debussy's *Syrinx* (1912) for solo flute. *Impromptu* was commissioned by the BBC for a 1982 broadcast commemorating the 250th anniversary of Haydn's birth. M-D to D.

See: Laura Holleran, "Richard Rodney Bennett's Surprising *Partridge Pie.*" *Clavier* 37:10 (December 1998): 21–23. Also includes "Four Calling Birds" from *Partridge Pie* (Book I) and a brief survey of Bennett's other piano music.

William Sterndale Bennett (1816–1875) Great Britain
Bennett studied in Leipzig and later was the director of the Royal Conservatory of Music. His style of writing was greatly influenced by Felix Mendelssohn.
Piano and Chamber Music (Geoffrey Bush—S&B 1972) 165pp. Edited from original English editions, the composer's MSS., and the German editions. Contains: Sonata I, Op.13; Suite de Pièces, Op.24 (available separately); Chamber Trio for violin, cello, piano, Op.26; Sonata—Duo for piano and cello, Op.32. Sonata Op.13 is a four-movement work in f with the two middle movements entitled Scherzo and Serenata. Dramatic and lyric contrasts are evident in each movement. Suite Op.24 (also available separately—S&B) contains six movements, each of which displays some aspect of piano technique. The final movement, Lento—Bravura is sonatalike and the most expansive. M-D.
Sonata I Op.13 (Ashdown) 28 min. Four movements on a grand scale, inner movements of most interest. Shows Bennett's mastery of musical design. Concentrated themes; pianistically dazzling. D.
3 Romances Op.14 (McFarren—Ashdown). Shows Bennett's lyrical invention at its best. M-D.
Fantasia A Op.16 (McFarren—Ashdown). In all but name a second sonata, with four continuous movements. D.
Suite de Pièces Op.24 (McFarren—Ashdown). Six contrasting and imaginative movements in c♯, E, d, f♯, B. The thunderous Scherzo in f♯ and the Alla Fantasia in A are the finest in the set. M-D.
Toccata c Op.38 (Augener). Abundance of right-hand figuration. M-D.
See: *The London Pianoforte School 1770–1860*, in Anthologies and Collections section.
Geoffrey Bush, "William Sterndale Bennett (1816–75)," M&M, 23 (February 1975):32–34.

Warren Benson (1924-   ) USA
Three Macedonian Miniatures 1951 (TP 1995) 5pp. An Old Olive Tree; The Ride to the Vineyards; Village Dance. Colorful and contrasting. Int.
If I Could Be . . . Four Daydreams 1963 (TP 1995) 5pp. 3 min. Four small pieces evoking images of a child's fancies. Clever. Int.

Jørgen Bentzon (1897–1951) Denmark
A pupil of Carl Nielsen, Bentzon wrote in a modern contrapuntal style tempered with an expressive lyric quality.
Sonata No.1 Op.43 (SKABO 1946). First movement: SA design, chromatically colored, *pp* ending. Second movement: ABA design with B section con-

taining some dramatic writing. Third movement: changing meters, many octaves, brilliant ending. M-D.

Niels Viggo Bentzon (1919–2000) Denmark
Bentzon is probably the most prolific composer in all of Scandinavia. The major influences in his music are Brahms, Nielsen, and Hindemith. In fact, his large piano works can be regarded as direct successors of Carl Nielsen's big keyboard compositions. Bentzon is from an old Danish musical family and was first interested in jazz. It is difficult to classify him with any "school" of composition; his works are distinguished by compact contrapuntalism and harmonic clarity. He is one of Europe's most individual talents, and his contribution to twentieth-century piano literature has been large. His sonatas probably represent the finest piano works to come out of Scandinavia since Nielsen. Bentzon has been active as a music critic and has appeared widely as virtuoso pianist.

Unless otherwise indicated, all Bentzon's works are published by WH.

7 Small Piano Pieces Op.3. Melodious, in a Hindemithian harmonic style. M-D.

Toccata Op.10 1941. Virtuosic. D.

Passacaglia Op.31 1944. 19pp. Exceptional contemporary handling of a Baroque form. M-D to D.

Partita Op.38 1945. Praeambulum; Allegro; Intermezzo I and II; Fanfare. A brilliant piece of pianistic writing requiring virtuoso technique. Ends *fffff*. D.

Koncert etude Op.40 1947. A "tour de force." D.

Sonata No.2 Op.42 1942. 24pp. Allegro; Adagio; Allegro. Bitonal writing in bravura Liszt tradition. D.

Sonata No.3 Op.44. Requires tremendous concentration and displays strong intellectual vitality. D.

Dance Pieces Op.45. (Published separately.) Valse subtile: full of clever metrical fluctuations. Polonaise: uses Polonaise rhythm only at selected places. Danza burlesca; written in bravura style, octaves everywhere. M-D.

Sonata No.4 Op.57. 23 min.

Woodcuts Op.65 1951. Eleven pieces of varying difficulty. The art form of the title is reflected in the simple but well-defined motives, developed with much economy. Int. to M-D.

Sonata No.5 Op.77 1951, 20 min. Compact, full of controlled vitality, impressive. D.

Sonata No.6 Op.90 56 pp. 18 min. Includes some powerful and muscular fugal writing. Traces of serial procedure, à la Prokofiev, with Lisztian pianism. D.

Sonata No.7 Op.121 1959 40pp. 15 min. Three movements in the style of Nielsen's progressive tonality. Movements begin in one key, progress, and end in another key. D.

Das Temperierte Klavier Op.157. 24 preludes and fugues that proceed upward chromatically from C, major then minor. Some fugues are very short (No.9 E is 5½ bars long), and some are loosely constructed. No dynamics, slurs, or touch indications are given. Harmonic relationships are especially interesting. Not as inspired as the sonatas. M-D.

Fifteen Two-Part Inventions Op.159 (JWC). These pieces are colored with so much chromaticism that key feeling is often lost, although each piece has the key listed. Sometimes more than two parts. The inventions in G and B♭ are outstanding. Int. to M-D.

2 Frederiksberg Suites Opp.173, 174. Suite I: Praeludium; A; C; Sarabande; Passepied; M I and II; Capriccio. Suite II: Praeludium; A; C; Sarabande; B; Gavotte; G. ". . . and the wind came over from Brønshoj, crept past Godthabsvej Station and spread itself over the low terrain" (from the Introduction). No dynamic or metronome indications given. Varied moods. D.

Paganini Variations "In Memoriam." Op.241 1968 16pp. Dramatic, powerful. M-D to D.

Hydraulic Structures. Commissioned by Carlisle (England) Festival, 1973. For prepared piano. Title alludes to the up-and-down movement of its patterns; improvisatory. M-D to D.

Short Pieces for Piano Op.436 1980 (WH 4396) 7pp. Ten short pieces, some only two or three lines long. Freely tonal, thin textures, varied moods. Int. to M-D.

See: Klaus Møllerhøj, *Niels Viggo Bentzons Kompositioner* (Copenhagen: Edition Wilhelm Hansen, 1980), 160pp. Mainly a list of works from Op.1 (1939) to Op.429 (1979). Includes bibliographical references and indexes.

Cathy Berberian (1925–1983) USA

Berberian was a versatile singer, best known as an exponent of contemporary music.

Morsicat(h)y (UE 1969) 11pp. For piano or harpsichord. "A musical action (Morse code) based on my interest in onomatopoeia" (from the score). Includes detailed instructions for performer, a drawing, and two cards requesting receipt of performance code from the composer in a back cover pocket. The right hand simulates the sound of a mosquito while the left hand attempts to swat it with clusters. Aleatoric. A joke; could be very funny and fascinating, given the proper performance. Avant-garde. M-D.

Alban Berg (1885–1935) Austria

Sonata Op.1 1908 (UE). This minor masterpiece dates from the time Berg was still studying with Schönberg. It is a one-movement SA design, highly chromatic, thick-textured, and demands advanced pianism. All its ideas grow from the opening measures. Its contrapuntal web requires a focus on the polyphonic, which shares little affinity with nineteenth-century pianism. New ideas are wrested out of old materials. Haunted by overripe yet fastidious romanticism. M-D to D.

See: Robert Turnbull, "Alban Berg Piano Sonata Op.1," *Piano Journal*, 13 (February 1984):8–9 for an analysis.

12 Variationen über ein eignes Theme C 1908 (UE 18146 1985) 16pp. Written as part of Berg's composition studies with Schönberg. The major influences are Brahms, Beethoven, and Schumann. A simple theme lends itself to wide-ranging variation treatment. These contrasting variations are delicate and full of melodic invention. Var.12 is a Presto Finale, which builds to a climax before ending quietly. M-D.

Klavierstück b 1907. In collection *The Century of Invention* (EAM 1996). Style is close to late Brahms. M-D.

Menuette F 1907. In collection *The Century of Invention* (EAM 1996). Three voices, tonal, contrapuntal. Int.

Arthur Berger (1912–) USA

"Clarity, refinement, perfect timing and impeccably clean workmanship are the keynotes to Berger's style," wrote Alfred Frankenstein in the June 6, 1948 *San Francisco Chronicle*.

Two Episodes 1933 (LG) in collection *New Music for the Piano*. Contrasting, atonal. M-D.

Three Bagatelles 1946 (EBM). Risoluto con moto; Poco andante; Allegro brillante. Dry sonorities, rhythmic punctuation, moderate length. M-D.

Suite for Piano 1946 (ACA). Capriccio; Intermezzo; Rondo (Rondo available through Mer). Flowing, expressive writing requiring careful tonal balance. M-D.

Fantasy (ACA). Moderato opening, flowing scherzo, short meno mosso leads to a quick close. M-D.

Partita 1947 (Boelke-Bomart 1980) 19pp. Intonazione; Aria; Capriccio; Intermezzo; Serenade. Short movements; Stravinsky-oriented. M-D.

Five Pieces 1969 (CFP 1975) 30pp. 13 min. Extensive preface. Pointillistic, complicated skips, finger-picking effects, harmonics, special pedal effects. A few notes are prepared for the first two pieces. Avant-garde. D.

Improvisation for A. C. (Aaron Copland) PNM, Vol.19. Berger describes this piece as "a good, simple demonstration of my latest techniques." MT, 123 (May 1982):325.

See: Bayan Northcott, "Arthur Berger: An Introduction at 70," MT, 124 (May 1982):323–26.

Jean Berger (1909–) USA, born Germany

Fandango Brazileiro (EBM 1942). Contains a biographical sketch of the composer.

Sonatina (TP 1952). 12pp. Allegro; Andante; Molto vivo. Shows a high order of craftsmanship. Style is post-Debussy.

Diversions for Keyboard (GWM 323 1980) 14pp. For piano or harpsichord. Neoclassic, thin textures, Stravinsky-inspired, stiff canons. Int.

More Diversions for Keyboard (GWM 325 1980) 16pp. Five pieces. Fluent writing; pieces are a little longer and harmonies are fuller than in *Diversions for Keyboard*. Int. to M-D.

Country Sketches (GWM 1982) 15pp. Seven descriptive pieces that provide impressions of the countryside. Clever rhythms, unusual harmonies, varied pianistic gestures. Int.

Seven Inventions (SP). 2 pp. each. Contrapuntal contemporary sonorities.

Sverre Bergh (1915–   ) Norway
To Norske Danser (NMO 1944) 7pp. Bjönnes'n: contrasting sections, lively.
Gamel-Holin: subtle, flowing triplets, *ppp* ending. In style of Grieg. Int.
Gubben Noah (NMO 1946) 11pp. Theme and ten contrasting variations. Clever,
delightful, attractive set based on story of Noah's Ark. Int. to M-D.

Erik Bergman (1911–   ) Finland
Bergman is an exponent of serial technique, one of the few Finnish composers
who has adopted this style of writing to any degree.
Intervalles Op.34 1964 (Fazer) 24pp. Each of the 7 pieces exploits a different interval: 2nds, 3rds, 4ths, 5ths, 6ths, 7ths, unison, and octaves. Variety of style
and mood. M-D.
Aspekte 1968–69 (NMO) 15pp. Spektrum; Meditation; Metamorfos. Annotations
in Norwegian, English, and German. Harmonics, aleatoric, pointillistic. D.

William Bergsma (1921–1994) USA
Bergsma's style involves dissonant counterpoint infused with a strong lyric quality.
Three Fantasies 1943 (Plymouth 1980, rev. ed.) 12pp. 1. This is the way an eagle
feels: agitated opening, bass pedal tones. 2. March by night: relaxed melody
over pizzicato basses. 3. Toccata: energetic rondo in perpetual motion. M-D.
Tangents 1950 (CF) Two books. 33 mins. Book I: Prologue; Prophecies; De Rerum
Natura. Book II: Masques; Pieces for Nickie; Epilogue. Bergsma says "Although the pieces can be played separately, *Tangents* is planned as a contrasting set and specifically for the second half of a program." Both books
display an unusual mixture of styles, pianistic figuration, and strongly contrasted moods. M-D.

Luciano Berio (1925–   ) Italy
Berio studied with Giorgio Ghedini and Luigi Dallapiccola. He helped establish
the Studio di Fonologia di Musicale of the Italian Radiotelevision in Milan and
became its director. His interest in electronic music has broadened tremendously
in the last few years, and he has incorporated serial principles in composing electronic music. He is one of Italy's leading composers.
Cinque variazioni per Pianoforte (SZ 1953). Berio's excellent serial craft shows
through in all these variations. Nos. 3 and 5 have codas; No.3 also has a
cadenza. An exciting vitality is evidenced in this work. It is full of interesting sonorities and written in a style that shows some influence of Stravinsky. Dynamic range: *ppppp* to *fff*. M-D.
Sequenza IV (UE 1967) 7pp. Lyric, colorful, and grateful to performer. This
work is a series of constantly changing chords (continual variation). Much
use is made of the sustaining pedal. The score is a reproduction of the MS
but it is fairly easy to read. M-D.
See: David Burge, "Luciano Berio's Sequenza IV," CK, 2 (September–October 1976):42. A fine discussion of this composition, surely one of the
most original piano works of the 1970s.

Erdenklavier (UE 1969) 2pp. "Pastorale." Performance directions. Dynamics appear to be serialized. Unharmonized melody. Avant-garde. M-D.

Wasserklavier (UE 1965) 2pp. Also in collection *The Century of Invention* (Hinson—EAMC 1996). Tonal, key signature, arpeggi. Entire piece is *ppp*. Large span required. M-D.

Family Album (UE 15950 1975) 30pp. A collection of works by Berio's father, Ernesto (a song); his grandfather, Adolfo (Maria Isabella—a waltz for piano duet); and Berio's own *Petite Suite* for solo piano, written in 1947. This neoclassical suite is the finest work in the collection, but it demonstrates little or nothing of Berio's present style. M-D.

Six Encores (UE). Collection of six piano solos. Available separately.

Leaf (UE 19590 1990) 1p., 1½ min. Sostenuto pedal held throughout, harmonics kept sounding by short staccato chords. M-D.

Brin (UE 19591 1990) 2pp. *pppp,* fast notes to be played without accents, thin textures until final line when textures thicken. M-D.

Wasserklavier. See description above.

Erdenklavier. See description above.

Luftklavier 1985, 4pp. 3 min. Always *ppp*, to be played as fast and evenly as possible; melody embedded in busy figurations. Large span required. D.

Feuerklavier 1989, 7pp. Always *ppp* (until indicated otherwise) and legatissimo; sostenuto and damper pedals indicated, fast figures, pointillistic, clusters. D.

Lennox Berkeley (1903–1989) Great Britain

Berkeley's style incorporates thin textures, delicate instrumentation, and a lyric emphasis found all too seldom in twentieth-century works.

5 Short Pieces Op.4 (JWC 1937; MMP). All are easily accessible. Nos.1 and 5 have rhythmic problems. Int. to M-D.

Polka Op.5 (JWC). Infectious rhythm and melody. M-D.

3 Impromptus Op.7 (W. Rogers 1937). Short contrasted works. Make a convincing suite. M-D.

Sonata A Op.20 (JWC; MMP). 25 min. Dedicated to Clifford Curzon. 2d ed. 1974. Moderato: lyric first subject contrasted with a kind of two-part invention for second subject; development employs bravura writing. Presto: a scherzo that fits the fingers well. Adagio: easy to play; miniature character piece. Allegro (Rondo): slow introduction before main theme; the eighth note in the Allegro is twice as fast as in the Introduction. M-D to D.

3 Pieces (Augener 1937). Etude; Berceuse; Capriccio. M-D.

6 Preludes Op.23 1948 (JWC) Varied and contrasting moods. M-D.
See: Dennis Todd, "Berkeley: Six Preludes," *Music Teacher,* 57 (April 1978):14–15. A discussion and analysis of these pieces.

3 Mazurkas (Hommage à Chopin) Op.32/1 1949 (JWC) 8½ min. Short, effective, chromatic, clever modulations, MC. M-D.

Scherzo D Op.32/2 1949 (JWC) 3 min. Rapid repeated single and double notes. M-D to D.

4 Concert Studies 1940 (Schott). Op.48 E♭; Op.14/2 e; Op.14/3 c; Op.14/4 F. M-D to D.

Improvisation on a Theme of Manuel de Falla Op.55/2 1960 (JWC) 2 min. Short character piece, fast mid-section, quiet ending. M-D.

4 Piano Studies Op.82 1972 (JWC 55076 1976) 15pp. 10 min. Varied technical purposes for each study; musical. M-D.

Mazurka Op.101B (WC 55582 1983) 4pp. Fresh and attractive sounds. M-D.

Michael Berkeley (1948–   ) Great Britain

"*Strange Meeting*" 1974–78 (OUP 1980) 13pp. 15 min. Preface in English. Inspired by a poem of Wilfred Owen. In three sections: The Strangeness of the Meeting. The Viciousness of War: fine pianistic show piece; resolves into finale. Peace Is Attained: fragmentary variation of material from the first movement. Martellato, expressing the agony and horror of war. Written in a well-worn tonal language, with thematic transformation, and in a nineteenth-century imaginative piano idiom. D.

Dark Sleep (OUP 1995) 11pp., 9 min. Exploits low register of keyboard. Recurring treble figuration, expressionistic, gloomy, repressive, atmospheric. M-D to D.

Sol Berkowitz (1922–   ) USA

Berkowitz studied composition with Karol Rathaus and Otto Luening and piano with Abby Whitesides. Since 1960 he has written mainly for theater and television.

Syncopations (LG 1958) in collection *New Music for the Piano.* Jazz influence, chromatic. M-D.

Twelve Easy Blues (BMC). Varied blues style; good for developing rhythmic flexibility. Int.

Four Blues for Lefty (TP 1976) 7pp. One-Sided Conversation; The Tired Bugler; A Quiet Song; Movin' Along. Intriguing descriptive pieces featuring left-hand melodies. Freely chromatic. Int. to M-D.

Nine Folk Song Preludes (Frank Music 1972) 21pp. Tunes are treated to MC and modal harmonies; some are clever. Int.

Johann Daniel Berlin (1714–1787) Norway

Sonatina d (Lyche 1953) 9pp. Capricetto; Arietta; Gavotta; Menuet; Giga. Eighteenth-century style, attractive. Int.

Hector Berlioz (1803–1869) France

Berlioz is best known for his orchestral works and has been called the "father of modern orchestration," but he did compose three works for the keyboard.

Piano Works (Hinson—Alfred 10157) Rustic serenade: based on the same "Theme of the Roman Pifferari" that is found in the D. Scarlatti Sonata C, K.513; more expansive than the Scarlatti. Hymne: flowing linear theme is worked out in a most efficient contrapuntal manner. Toccata: moves with motoric steadiness throughout until the final five bars, where an interesting series of chords slows the motion and brings the work to a firm close. Int. to M-D.

Miguel Bernal Jiménez (1910–1946) Mexico

Antigua Valladolid (The Ancient City) (PIC). A pleasant suite for an intermediate student. Toccatina for RH alone; Double Minuet; Gavotte; Pleasantry.

Cartels (Pastels) (PIC 1957) 20pp. Eight pieces that employ Mexican folk rhythms and tunes. See especially Danza Maya and Sandunga. Int. to M-D.

Lord Gerald Tyrwhitt Berners (1883–1950) Great Britain

Berners was a wit, an eccentric, a composer, a painter, and a man of letters who during his lifetime served as a "missionary of the arts" for English society. His sense of humor caused him to be called "the English Satie."

Trois Petites Marches Funèbres 1914 (JWC). Pour un Homme d'Etat: slow and pompous. Pour un Canari: clever, whimsical. Pour une Tante à Héritage: Allegro giocoso. Satirical, effective, not difficult. Int.

Trois Fragments psychologiques 1915–16 (JWC). Three representations of psychological states of mind: Hate; Laughter; Sighing. M-D.

Poissons d'or 1919 (JWC). Difficult Impressionistic study illustrating the movement of fish. M-D to D.

The Triumph of Neptune 1926 (JWC 1975) 12pp. Edition for piano. Three pieces that were originally part of a ballet: Harlequinade; Intermezzo; Hornpipe. Witty, humorous, MC. M-D.

The Collected Music for Solo Piano (Dickinson—JWC 55283 1982) 48pp. Le poisson d'or; Dispute entre le papillon et le crapaud; Trois petites marches funèbres; Fragments psychologiques; Polka; Valse; March; The Expulsion from Paradise. "All earlier editions of the piano music and songs of Lord Berners are inaccurate" (from the score). Int. to D.

Leonard Bernstein (1918–1990) USA

Bernstein's style was a mixture of Broadway and Mahler's chromaticism.

Seven Anniversaries 1944 (Witmark). For Aaron Copland: quiet. For My Sister Shirley: Light. In Memoriam: Alfred Eisner: elegiac. For Paul Bowles: ground bass followed by four variations and coda. In Memoriam: Natalie Koussevitsky: slow elegy. For Serge Koussevitsky: declamatory. For William Schuman: energetic. Int. to M-D.

Four Anniversaries 1945 (Bo&H). For Felicia Montealegre: lyric. For Johnny Mehegan: jazzy scherzo. For David Diamond: flowing. For Helen Coates: boisterous. M-D.

Five Anniversaries 1949–51 (Bo&H). For Elizabeth Rudolf; For Lukas Foss; For Elizabeth Ehrman; For Sandy Gillhorn; For Susanna Kyle. M-D.

Thirteen Anniversaries 1989 (Bo&H). Short, well-unified, ostinati. M-D.

See: Conwell R. Harris, Jr., "Unifying Techniques in the Anniversaries of Leonard Bernstein," diss., Louisiana State University, 1993.

Jane Magrath, "Bernstein's Anniversaries and Other Works for Solo Piano," *AMT*, 38/1 (September–October 1988):66–67.

Touches—Chorale, Eight Variations and Coda 1980 (Bo&H) 15pp. 9 min. Commissioned for the Sixth Van Cliburn International Piano Competition. A serial subject undergoes various contrasted treatments. The coda provides the climax (written on four staves) but ends *ppp*. Lean textures, rhythmically vigorous, open sonorities. Copland influence. Bernstein explains the title of this short but ambitious piece: *"Touches="* (French) the keys of the keyboard; different 'feels' of the fingers, hands and arms—deep, light, percussive, gliding, floating, prolonged caressing; small bits (cf., 'a *touch* of garlic')—each variation is a *soupçon*, lasting from 20 to 100 seconds apiece; vignettes of discreet emotions—brief musical manifestations of being 'touched', or moved; gestures of love, especially between composer and performer, performer and listener" (from record jacket of Etcetera ETC 1019). M-D to D.

See: James Tocco, "Playing Bernstein's Piano Music," *Keyboard Classics* (November–December 1983):40.

Seymour Bernstein (1927–   ) USA

Bernstein is an outstanding teacher who has composed a unique repertoire for the piano. His writing is always expressive and eminently pianistic.

Birds (Schroeder & Gunther 1972). A suite of eight impressionistic studies, each named after a feathered friend: Purple Finch; Hummingbird; Woodpecker; Sea Gull; Chickadee; Vulture; Penguin; Eagle. Complicated notation. M-D.

Birds II (Schroeder & Gunther). Nine descriptive pieces of birds: Myna Bird; Swan; Robin; Owl; Roadrunner; Condor; Nightingale; Guinea Hen; Phoenix. Helpful foreword and notes on performance. With added narration, this would make a diverting collection for a student recital. M-D.

Insects (A. Broude). Eight characteristic studies: Carpenter Ant; Cockroach; Mosquito; Dying Moth; Humbug; Praying Mantis; Centipede; Black Fly. Witty, atonal, imaginative. Performing directions included. Hilarious introduction relates the insects' origins. Player must clap hands, slap legs, etc. Int. to M-D.

Lullaby for Carrieann (A. Broude) 5pp. A reverie. Freely changing tonalities, meters, and tempi; restless at spots; contemporary sonorities. M-D.

Raccoons (A. Broude 1977) A musical adventure with nine descriptive pieces. Also includes a story and unusual photographs taken by Bernstein. M-D.

New Pictures at an Exhibition (A. Broude 1977) 40pp. Combining masterpieces of art, poetry by Owen Lewis, and music, this elegant book stimulates aural and visual senses. Nine pieces to be played as a suite although a few (Chagall, especially) can be extracted and performed separately. M-D.

Warblers and Flutters (A. Broude 1977). Book I of The Earth Music Series, an introduction to the trill. Nine short pieces that teach the student how to play this ornament. Presented in order of difficulty. Excellent performance commentary. "What better way to learn the trill than to think of birds whose trills are the envy of all instrumentalists!" (from the preface). Easy to Int.

Out of the Nest (A. Broude 1977). Book II of The Earth Music Series. An introduction to the mordent. Eight short pieces with same approach as Book I in this series. Clever and effective. Easy to Int.

Early Birds (Schroeder & Gunther 1984) 21pp. Book III of The Earth Music Series. An introduction to the appoggiatura. Ten short pieces. Easy to Int.

The Pedals (Schroeder & Gunther 1984) 24pp. Book IV of The Earth Music Series. An introduction to the pedals. Eight short pieces. Int.

Dragons (Schroeder & Gunther 1984) 14pp. Book V of The Earth Music Series. An introduction to the contemporary idiom. Eight short pieces, each with a brief discussion. Clever, resourceful writing. Int. to M-D.

Fantasy on a Theme by Francisco (GS 1995). Francisco J. Nuñez was a pupil of Bernstein. The opening eight-note theme in the left hand is from his choral work *Balloons.* Imaginative writing, expressive, pianistic, MC. M-D.

Toccata Française (CF 1969) 11pp. Quasi-cadenza opening leads to Allegro Tempestoso section; a Cantando mid-section is followed by a return to the Allegro tempestoso section; builds to strong climax and ends *fff con abbandone e strepitoso.* A stunning piece in freely tonal style. Special pedal effects are indicated. M-D.

Trees. Five Hymns and Poems to the Miracles of Nature (GS 1988) 15pp. The Young Maple; The Willow; The Magnolia; The Dying Birch; The Sequoias. Tonal. Lovely painting and poem with each piece. Int.

Köchel and Sheila (GS 1988) 15pp. A musical adventure about two Siamese cats. Clever and attractive. Story and photos by the composer. Int.

Belinda the Chipmunk (GS 1986) 27pp. Twelve pieces inspired by a pet chipmunk. Story and photos by the composer. Int.

Henri Bertini (1798–1876) France
See below, "Collections," *Piano Music of the Parisian Virtuosos 1810–1860.*

Gérard Bertouille (1898–   ) Belgium
Bertouille's music is basically tonal and expressed in classical form with great emphasis on melodic clarity.

Six Preludes and Fugues (CeBeDeM 1940–42) 2 vols. Imitation extensively employed. Varied moods, effective. All require solid pianistic equipment. M-D.

Sonata (Schott Frères 1945) 13pp. 12 min. Allegro; Nocturne; Final. Tonal, neoclassic; Nocturne is the most effective. M-D.

Introduction et Final (CeBeDeM 1970) 11pp. 8 min. Quiet opening, chromatic. Moves to contrapuntal development, dramatic conclusion. In Franck tradition. M-D.

Franz Berwald (1796–1868) Sweden
Berwald was a violinist but devoted much of his life to composition. He spent time in Berlin, Vienna, and Paris. He was not recognized during his day, but now he is considered Sweden's most important nineteenth-century composer.
Keyboard Music (Bengt Edlund—Br) 201pp. Complete works, XV. Includes: Three Fantasias, 1816–17, written for the melodicon, a Danish invention whose tone somewhat resembled that of the glass harmonica. These pieces contain variations on themes from *Don Giovanni* and *Die Zauberflöte*. Sixteen of the remaining pieces come from the *Musical Journals* that Berwald published in 1818–20. Most of these are salon pieces, many of them anonymous. Fantasia c on two Swedish Folk Melodies is one of the better Berwald works. The later pieces display a genuine individuality. Beautifully produced volume. Int. to M-D.

Charles Bestor (1924–   ) USA
Sonata (Gen 1977) 11pp. One movement, vigorous rhythms, flexible meters, mood shifts, dissonant. M-D.

Bruno Bettinelli (1913–   ) Italy
Bettinelli studied in Milan and Siena. In 1941 he became Professor of Harmony at the Milan Conservatory and music critic for the Milan paper *Italia*. He has edited works of classic Italian masters. His style is mainly linear and dominated by a strong rhythmic pulse.
Tre Ricercari e Toccata (SZ 1948) 21pp. 11 min. Ricercare is not used in the strict sense of the word. Toccata requires agile fingers. A well-made group that could also be played separately. M-D.
Fantasia (Ric 1955) 20pp. 12 min. Preambolo; Ritmico; Notturno; Intermezzo; Fugato. M-D.
Suite C (A. Drago 1945) Preludio; Sarabande; Minuetto; Siciliana; Giga. M-D.
Sei Bagatelles (Sal). Six atonal pieces with varied textures, inventive rhythms. D.

Brian Bevelander (1942–   ) USA
Sonata Op.2 (Branden Press 1966) 14pp. First movement: agitated, numerous meter changes, based on motivic development, rhapsodic pianistic style. Second movement: rondo, wide skips in left hand; returns to the opening section are treated in variation, scherzo style. No key signature but tonal. M-D.
Scherzo (Branden Press) 11pp. Flexible tempi, light and playful, slower expressive mid-section, sprightly ending. Requires fast shifts of hand position; large chords throughout. M-D.

Philip Bezanson (1916–1975) USA
Sonata (ACA). A large three-movement work in neoclassic style. The slow movement is especially attractive: variations over an ostinato bass. Last movement (Toccata) is demanding with full chords in wide skips. D.

Piano Sonatina (ACA). A well constructed one-movement work with plenty of pianistic problems. Accidentals are numerous, thin textures prevalent, and change of mood corresponds to tempo changes. M-D.

Gunter Bialas (1907–1995) Germany

Bialas's early works were written in neoclassical style. His recent style includes 12-note serialism, African music, and Medieval music.

Lamento, vier Intermezzi und Marsch 1983–86 (Br 7111) 28pp., ca. 18 min. Serial influence, widely spread sonorities. Wide span required. D.

Antonio Bibalo (1922–   ) Norway, born Trieste

Bibalo has never made style the principal factor in his works, but in all of them one recognizes his personality immediately.

Four Balkan Dances (JWC 1956) 7½ min. Bartók influence. I. Allegro deciso e ben ritmato: left-hand chordal octaves open and close the piece; 3+3+2 rhythms; toccata-like figurations alternate between hands. II. Andantino semplice: 5/4 meter, chromatic melodic line over chordal (second and seventh) accompaniment; lines sometimes three or four octaves apart; quasi echo effects. III. Adagio: a spun-out murmuring effect in upper register provides accompaniment; chordal punctuation in left hand adds rhythmic interest. IV. Presto: Sciolto e brillante in an ABABA design; tarantella-like rhythm with embedded melodic line worked into fabric; B sections rely on chromatic triplet for coloration; driving modal descending scales in right hand provide dramatic conclusion. M-D.

Fire Miniaturer (WH 1966). Four miniatures with folk-song and dance influence. Written in honor of Bartók. Reverie: vacillates between tonic major and minor third. Allegretto con spirito: a fine left-hand study in perpetual motion. Lonesome Doll. Little Finale. Int. to M-D.

Trois Hommages à de Falla, Schönberg, and Bartók 1957 (WH 4148 1969) 13pp. Aubade: guitar style found in de Falla's piano works, ABA form. Nocturne: 12-tone, extreme registers. Bulgara: alternates octotonic writing with gypsy style and Bulgarian rhythms. M-D to D.

John Biggs (1932–   ) USA

Theme and Variations (Consort 1959) 10pp. 8 min. A nine-bar theme and six variations with final variation serving as an exciting coda, neoclassic style. Highly pianistic, variations well contrasted. Good octave technique necessary for Var. 4. The composer's penchant for linear and unencumbered writing is obvious. M-D.

Invention for Piano and Tape (Consort 1970) 7½ min. Tape available from publisher. Tape cues notated on staff above piano staff. Changing meters, imitative, chromatic. Up to bar 112, tape sounds are made entirely with a piano with strings and hammers prepared in different ways. Following this is a live recording of a Kansas thunderstorm, with a train whistle faintly heard in the background. Explanation of closing section is included. M-D.

Sonatina "Clementiana" (Consort 1974) 8pp. 5½ min.
Sonatina II (Consort 1975) 11pp. 8½ min.
Both sonatinas are in three short movements, with much imitation. Tonal and
    freely chromatic. Well-turned and attractive writing. Int.

Marie Bigot (1786–1820) France
Bigot was a fine pianist and composer who taught Felix and Fanny Mendelssohn.
Sonata Op.1 (Adagio; Allegro espessivo; Andantino; Rondo: Allegro) is in collec-
    tion *Historical Women Composers for the Piano* (Johnson—Vivace Press
    1992). 56pp. This collection also contains her *Suite d'études*, consisting of
    six studies written in an early Romantic style firmly built on classic formal
    construction. Int. to M-D.
See: Calvert Johnson. "Marie Bigot. Schubert's Piano Teacher," KC, 12/6 (No-
    vember–December 1992):12. Contains the Andantino from her piano *So-
    nate* Op.1.

Elizabeth Weichsell Billington (ca. 1768–1818) Great Britain
Billington was a fine singer who studied with J. C. Bach and J. S. Schroeter.
Three Sonatas Op.1 (Harbach—Vivace Press) 28pp. Composed when she was
    eight years old. Idiomatic, each movement uses a different form, two move-
    ments in each sonata. Int. M-D.
Six Sonatas Op.2 (Harbach—Vivace Press) 60pp. Composed when she was eleven
    years old. Varied movements with a preference for rondo and variation
    form. Classic style. Int. to M-D.

Gordon Binkerd (1916–   ) USA
Binkerd's music is often contrapuntal but great care is taken with vertical so-
norities. Texture is frequently thick but a lyric impulse is usually present.
Sonata 1955 (Bo&H 1968) 51pp. 22 min. First movement: modified SA design;
    plaintive theme returns in various guises throughout the sonata as a uni-
    fying device. Second movement: demonstrates great power coupled with
    grand sonorities. Scherzo: jazz-influenced. Fourth movement: motoric re-
    petitiveness; concludes dramatically; Stravinsky-inspired. Fine craftsman-
    ship with well-developed ideas permeate this formidable work. D.
Entertainments (Bo&H). Seven pieces opening with Brief Encounter and closing
    with Graceful Exit. No.6 needs a sensitive rubato. Fun to play, contempo-
    rary. Int.
Concert Set (Bo&H). Witch Doctor; Legend; Etude; Mice. Short pieces that make
    for an unusual and successful group, exciting pianism. M-D.
The Young Pianist (Bo&H). Ten short pieces bristling with contemporary ideas. Int.
Piano Miscellany (Bo&H). Lake Lonely; Rough and Tumble; Something Serious;
    For the Union Dead; Country Dance. Varied techniques, interpretational
    directions. Int. to M-D.
Essays 1976 (Bo&H) 32pp. Intermezzo: parodies Brahms's Op.118/1; a kind of
    recasting of the whole piece. Adagietto. Allegresse. Lightly Like Music

Running. She, to Him. Shut Out that Moon. These pieces are Binkerd's Lisztian transformations of some of his own songs—somewhat in the manner of Liszt's *Années de Pèlerinage*, Book II. Fanciful and imaginative writing. D.

See: David Burge, "New Pieces, Part II," CK, 4 (January 1978):50.

Five Pieces 1973 (Bo&H). Preambulum; Fugue à la Gigue; Zarabanda; Toccata; Fantasia. Highly contemporary writing. Demands pianistic expertise in all pieces. D.

Suite for Piano (Bo&H 1978) 33pp. Five Fantasies: Capriccio; Intermezzo on *Meine Lieder* (Brahms Op.106/4); Intermezzo on *Wenn du nur zuweilen lächelst* (Brahms Op.57/2); Intermezzo on *Jungfraülein, soll ich mit euch gehn* (Brahms *49 Deutsche Volkslieder*, Bk.II/11); Rhapsody. Style and approach similar to that of *Essays*, discussed above. The outer movements are especially concentrated. M-D to D.

Juan Carlos Biondo (1933–   ) Brazil

Sonata I (Providence 1971) 16pp. Short, one movement. Contrasting sections; recurring Presto unifies work; cadenza-like sections; freely tonal. M-D.

Preludio Op.12/1 (Providence 1966) 2pp. Vision Fugaz. Fleeting, chromatic. Large span required. M-D.

Harrison Birtwistle (1934–   ) Great Britain

Précis for Piano Solo 1959 (UE) 2 min. Five short sections that mirror each other, plus two interludes. Open textures, delicate sonorities, post-Webernian pointillistic style. D.

Chester Biscardi (1948–   ) USA

Biscardi teaches at Sarah Lawrence College, Bronxville, NY.

Mestiere 1979 (Merion 1980) 10pp. 5 min. The title, from the Italian, means "craft." A one-movement work, delicate yet powerful. Diverse sonorities integrated into a compelling structure. Dissonant, exploits entire keyboard range; florid, cadenza-like. Contains detailed performance instructions. Debussy influence. D.

Incitation to Desire 1984 (CFP 1996) 6pp., ca. 3 min. After a free and catchy introduction the subtitle appears: "In the style of a tango canción." A flowing melody over tango rhythms is featured in the main part of the piece; concludes with an effective driving coda. Performance notes. M-D.

Companion Piece 1989–91 (CFP 1995) 7pp., 6½ min. "In this work, I am commenting muscially on Morton Feldman's *Extensions 3*, written for solo piano in 1952" (from the score). Chorale-like sections punctuated with short fast notes, quiet sonorities. Large span required. M-D.

Sonata 1986–87 (CFP 1989) 24pp. 10 min. One movement in three sections "based on Jasper Johns' *Voice 2* [painting]. Since the early 1970's, I have been interested in the ways literature and painting influence musical ideas and form—how literary images or use of color can inspire everything from the smallest melodic shape to a work's overall structure" (from the score). Each section reflects a different musical texture: "angular and pulsating; fast runs and chords; and lyrical" (from the score). Performance notes. D.

Keith Bissell (1912–1992) Canada
Variations on a Folk Song (Waterloo 1970) 8pp. Asymmetrical theme, six variations plus coda. MC with a few rhythmic problems. Int.
Three Preludes (Harris 1973) 7pp. MC. Int.

Marcel Bitsch (1921–   ) France
Hommage à Domenico Scarlatti (Leduc 1967) 13pp. 7½ min: Three one-movement sonatinas for harpsichord or piano. More effective on the harpsichord. Excellent craftsmanship. M-D.
Sonatine (Leduc 1960) 15pp. 8 min. Ravel influence. Well-written. D.
12 Easy Pieces (Marvelous Dreams) (Leduc). Short, above-the-average pedagogy material.
Le Livre de Noémie ("For Naomi") (Leduc 1949). Ten studies: Duet; The Little Railroad; When There Were Coaches; On the Water; Invention; In the Meadow; Lullaby; Chase; Fanfare; Ring for Matins. Each piece is devoted to some technical problem. Int.

Georges Bizet (1838–1875) France
Variations Chromatiques Op.3 1868 (Choudens; Editions musicales du Marais). Chaconne-like theme is a chromatic scale over a pedal; 14 variations and a coda. This masterpiece was revised by Felix Weingartner in a later edition (Choudens 1933). The style is Romantic, à la Liszt and Schumann. M-D.
Trois Esquisses Musicales (Heugel 1905). Freely transcribed by I. Philipp. Light, airy. M-D.
6 Chants du Rhin (Heugel; MMP). Nos.1 and 6 (Augener). Mendelssohn and Schumann influence. M-D.
Bilder vom Rhein; 6 Lieder ohne Wörte (CFP 1920). 36pp. German edition of the above. Morgenstimmung. Fröhliche Fahrt. Träumerei: contained in *Album of French Composers* (EBM). Die Zigeunerin. Nachklänge. Heimfahrt. Int. to M-D.
Romance sans Paroles (Kann—Zen-On 350) 5pp. C, flowing Andantino expressivo melody over sixteenth-note accompaniment. Builds to climax and subsides. Int. to M-D.
L'Arlesienne Suites I and II 1872 (K 9906) 60pp. Transcribed by the composer. I: Prelude; Minuetto; Adagietto; Carillon. II: Pastorale; Intermezzo; Menuet; Farandole. Written for a mélodrame; more effective in their original context, but each piece contains a primary dramatic intensity. The second suite was put together by Ernest Guiraud after Bizet's death. M-D.
Nocturne I (MMP). Flowing lines, expressive. M-D.

Jean Bizet (1924–   ) France

Quatre Etudes (EMT 1980) 18pp. 10 min. Four well-varied studies in MC style. Strong rhythms in No.4. Includes some fingering. Style reminiscent of a chromatic Milhaud. M-D.

Le Singe Vert (E. C. Kerby). This "Green Monkey" moves along in fourths and sevenths; contains some dry syncopated seventh chords, à la *Minstrels* by Debussy. Int.

Nils Björkander (1893–1972) Sweden

3 Pianostychen Op.1 (NMS 1934) 9pp. Preludium; Capriccio; Humoresk. Written in a post-Brahms idiom. M-D.

Glimtar (AL). Published separately. Pastoral (1938); Danslek (1938); Visa i Folkton (1949); Ganglat (1949). Each piece is two pages long. Same idiom and difficulty as Grieg *Lyric Pieces*. Excellent pedagogic material. Int.

Sonatine Op.20 (NMS 1950). Allegro moderato e cantabile: angular melody, big closing, difficult. Andantino con grazia (Serenata Carezzante): melodic emphasis, romantic harmony. Vivace ma marcando (Rondo rustico): toccata-like. Mature pianism required. M-D.

Arni Björnsson (1905–   ) Iceland

Sonata Op.3 (Musica Islandica 1963) 17pp. Allegro con fuoco: SA, dramatic, much two with three. Andante cantabile: chordal, melodic; careful legato required. Rondo—Allegro ma non troppo: dancelike, contrasting sections and keys. Written in a somewhat updated Romantic style. M-D.

Boris Blacher (1903–1975) Germany

Major influences in Blacher's music have been Schönberg and the rhythmic innovations of Stravinsky. Jazz has also found its way into some of Blacher's compositions. His use of serial technique is very personal; it differs considerably from that of Boulez and Stockhausen. Blacher developed a system of variable meters, a technique that governed most of his compositions written during the 1950s and 1960s.

Zwei Sonatinen Op.14 1955 (Bo&Bo). Main interest lies in the asymmetrical rhythms. M-D.

Trois Pièces pour Piano Op.18 1943 (Bo&Bo). No.2 displays jazz harmonies and rhythms. M-D.

Ornamente Op.37 1950 (Bo&Bo). Seven pieces, each built on a tone-row, but not applied to pitch. Each measure is in a different meter; thin textures; short. The variable meters provide an enrichment of rhythm and form. M-D.

Sonate für Klavier Op.39 1951 (Bo&Bo). Allegro ma non troppo leads to somber Andante; inversion of the Andante leads to light Vivace. Ostinati beautifully worked out in the variable meter technique, sparse textures, vague tonality. M-D.

24 Preludes 1974 (Bo&Bo) 32pp. Short, contrasting, varied textures, subdivided rhythms emphasized (345678/8, 87 . . . 43/8, etc.). Nos.12 and 19 have special interest. M-D.

Richard Blackford (1954–   ) Great Britain
Blackford was an honor graduate of the Royal College of Music, where he studied with John Lambert. He also worked privately with Elisabeth Lutyens and Hans Werner Henze.
Sonata 1975 (GS 1977) 22pp. 11 min. Molto vivace; Andante. The second movement has numerous contrasting sections. Pointillistic, expressionistic, many repeated notes, serial influence. Large span required. D.
Three Cornish Pieces (OUP 1981) 5pp. Skillywidden's Dance; River Song; Lullaby. Rhythmic ostinatos under free, colorful harmony. Easy to Int.

Easley Blackwood (1933–   ) USA
Blackwood writes astringent dissonances that penetrate essentially simple diatonic textures.
Three Short Fantasies Op.16 (GS 1965). Serial, metric changes, wide skips, unusual sonorities. D.

Leopoldine Blahetka (1811–1887) Austria
Blahetka studied with Joseph Czerny, Kalkbrenner, and Moscheles.
Music for Piano (Lydia H. Ledeen—Hildegard Publishers). Introduction. Includes variations, a fantasie, and a polonaise. M-D.
See below, "Collections," *Piano Music of the Parisian Virtuosos 1810–1860.*

David Blake (1936–   ) Great Britain
Variations for Piano Op.1 (OUP 1964) 8pp. 6 min. Linear theme, eight contrasting variations and a finale in four sections. Freely tonal; large span required. M-D.

Eubie Blake (1884–1983) USA
Sincerely, Eubie Blake (Belwin-Mills 1975) 72pp. Transcribed by Terry Waldo. The Charleston Rag; Eubie's Classical Rag; Rhapsody in Ragtime; Eubie Dubie; Brittwood Rag; Kitchen Tom; Poor Katie Redd; The Baltimore Todolo; Poor Jimmy Green. Original rags covering Blake's entire career. More sophisticated and difficult than the Joplin rags. Interesting foreword includes a discussion of the pieces and a biography of Blake. M-D.

Ran Blake (1935–   ) USA
Third Stream Compositions (Margun) 40pp. Jinxey's; Vanguard; Wende; Thursday; Breakthru; Silver Fox; Field Cry; Jim Crow; Three Personalities; East Wind; How 'bout That; Aftermath; Arline. "Third Stream" is used to describe works that join complex, dissonant jazz with complex, dissonant classical materials through shrewd, intricate transitions. Blake's style shows

influences of Ives, T. Monk, Theodorakis, and others. Blake is chairman of a Third Stream Department at the New England Conservatory of Music. Each piece has a few words about its background. Highly appealing but difficult writing. M-D to D.

Alberto Blancafort (1929–   ) Spain

Sonata para Piano 1960 (UME). Allegro vivace: mainly lyric with much sixteenth-note accompaniment; some flexible metric changes. Lento: A B A, songlike. Prestissimo: very scalar, punctuated chords, exciting. D.

Emile R. Blanchet (1877–1943) Switzerland

Variations sur un thème de Mendelssohn Op.22 (Ric 1917). M-D.

64 Preludes Op.41 (ESC 1926). Preface and explanatory notes in French, German, and English. Fourth Book is devoted to the left hand. M-D.

10 Nouvelles Etudes (Henn 1920). Polyphonic and polyrhythmic problems. M-D.

Olga de Blanck (1916–   ) Cuba

De Blanck was state advisor on music education in Cuba for a number of years.

Homage to the Cuban Dance (EMB). Manuel Saumell: shortest movement, fanfare, soaring melody. Ignacio Cervantes: lush sentimental flavor. Ernesto Lecuona: bolero-like left hand shifts from e to e♭ to a and A; hypnotic rhythms; syncopation; cascading 64th notes. Steamily written. M-D.

Allan Blank (1925–   ) USA

Music for Piano (ACA 1962). Unusual meters, athletic textures, and melodic notes used harmonically add up to some interesting sonorities. M-D.

4 Easy Pieces (ACA). Overture (In the Style of a Fanfare); Play; Song; Dance: Appealing set. About same difficulty as Vol.II of *Mikrokosmos*. Some notes can be left out if hand is too small. Int.

6 Miniatures and a Fantasia (ACA 1967). Varied moods in these mildly contemporary pieces. No.4 (Anapests) and No.6 (Dactyls) have more interest. The Fantasia: 4pp., exploits broad gestures; some clusters. M-D.

Expansions and Contractions (ACA 1966). 6pp. As the title would suggest, much emphasis on contrary-motion writing. Chromatic coloring, extremes in range, fluctuating tempi. D.

2 Pieces (ACA 1966). 5pp. No titles, only metronome markings. No.1 exploits interval of fourth. No.2 uses imitation in a short-long rhythmic scheme. M-D.

4 Pieces (ACA 1965) 5pp. No.1: tonal, melodic line against syncopated accompaniment. No.2: a staccato study, exploits minor seconds. No.3: phrases in 4 plus 3 arrangement. No.4: equality of hands in this little syncopation study. Int.

A Short Invention (ACA 1965) 2pp. Thin textures punctuated with thicker ones. D.

Rotation: A Study for Piano (ACA 1959–60). Rhythmic divisions are difficult. Effective sonorities. Technical and musical problems abound. Requires large span and broad dynamic range. M-D.

Brenno Blauth (1931–   ) Brazil
Duas Peças Breves (Ric Brazil 1969) 4pp. Atonal, monothematic. Various timbres
explored on the instrument. Second piece is aleatoric. Must be played as a
group. M-D.
Suite Paulistinha (Ric Brazil 1968) 12pp. 12 min. 1. Tarde de Garôa. 2. A Cape-
linha de Juquitiba. 3. Nisseizinha. 4. A Valsa do Brotinho. Int.

Blind Tom (1849–1908) (Thomas Green Bethune) USA
The Battle of Manassas (Musica Obscura) in collection *Piano Music in Nineteenth
Century America* (Alfred 10102). Vol.I: A musical description of this fa-
mous battle. Variable keys, meters, and tempos. Uses patriotic tunes of the
period, including "The Girl I Left behind Me," "Dixie," "Yankee Doodle,"
"The Marseillaise." Clusters are used to simulate cannon fire; pianist must
whistle and make locomotive noises. A fun piece from beginning to end.
M-D. The Music Obscura edition also contains *The Downfall of Paris*.
See: Geneva H. Southall, "Blind Tom: A Misrepresented and Neglected Composer-
Pianist," *The Black Perspective in Music*, 3 (May 1975):141–59.
——, *Blind Tom: The Post–Civil War Enslavement of a Musical Genius* (Chal-
lenge Productions, P.O. Box 9624 Minneapolis, MN 55440, 1979).
——, *Blind Tom, the Black Pianist-Composer* (Challenge Productions, 1983).

Arthur Bliss (1891–1975) Great Britain
Bliss wrote in a neoclassic style that leaned toward English Romanticism.
Masks 1925 (Curwen; MMP) 24pp. 35 min. Four pieces that exploit the full range
of the piano. M-D.
Two Interludes 1925 (Nov 10024910 1982) 10pp. Contrasting, colorful. M-D.
Toccata 1926 (Curwen). Effective concert piece. M-D.
Suite 1926 (Curwen) 31pp. Overture; Polonaise; Elegy; Finale. Clever but in-
volved. M-D.
Sonata 1953 (Nov) 21 min. Three movements (FSF), difficult but rather tame. The
first movement (Moderato marcato) is the most coherent. Slow movement
is chaconne-like. A certain "steely brilliance" to much of this piece. A few
places attempt a kind of Prokofievian acerbity and bravura. M-D to D.
Miniature Scherzo 1969 (Nov) 2 min. Based on a phrase from the Mendelssohn
Violin Concerto; in e, chromatic, toccata-like octaves, *pp* ending. M-D.
Two Piano Pieces (Nov 10021908 1982) 9pp. One-step; The Rout Trot (from the
revue of "White Birds"). Jazz-oriented, delightful pastiches, ragtime idiom,
light-hearted. M-D.
Triptych 1970 (Nov) 20pp. 14 min. Meditation; Dramatic Recitative; Capriccio.
Excellent craft, pianistic. Second movement has the most interest. M-D.

Augustyn Bloch (1929–   ) Poland
Wariacje ni fortepian (Variations for Piano) (PWM 1962) 13pp. 10 min. Romantic
theme with seven variations that differ widely in tempi, meter, and dynamics. Final variation is the most contemporary sounding. M-D.

Ernest Bloch (1880–1959) USA, born Switzerland
Bloch's piano music is largely Impressionistic. The damper pedal is used profusely to connect rich sonorities. Many of his works are modal and rhapsodic.
Ex-Voto 1914 (BB). 2pp. Short, expressive. Int.
Poems of the Sea 1922 (GS). Waves: modal, uses ostinato. Chanty: short, folkloric.
     At Sea: undulating figuration, hornpipe-like melody. M-D.
Enfantines 1923 (GS; CF). Ten colorful pieces for young people. Int.
     See: David Kushner, "Ernest Bloch's *Enfantines*," *College Music Symposium*, 23/2 (Fall 1983):103–12.
Nirvana 1923 (GS). Short, colorful, mystic poem. Ostinato harmonies, unusual
     timbres. Int.
In the Night 1923 (GS). An atmospheric "love-poem." M-D.
Five Sketches in Sepia 1925 (GS). Prélude; Fumées sur la ville; Lucioles; Incertitude; Epilogue. The final piece quotes from the others. Short pieces. Impressionistic; sensitive sonorities. Int. to M-D.
Sonata 1935 (Carisch). A cyclic work in three large connected movements. Maestoso ed energico; Pastorale; Moderato alla Marcia. Requires stamina, power and drive, advanced pianism. Bloch's most important work for piano. D.
Visions et Prophéties 1940 (GS). Five short rhapsodic pieces that are intense and achieve a telling effect. M-D.
See: Cassandra I. Carr, "Ernest Bloch: the Piano Music," thesis, University of Washington, 1978.
Joan Purswell, "Ernest Bloch—Composer, Conductor, Educator," *Clavier*, 19 (November 1980):26–31. Includes lesson and music of "Joyous March" from *Enfantines*.
Charles Lynn Wheeler, "Ernest Bloch's Solo Piano Music," AMT, 30 (November-December 1980):22–24.

Waldemar Bloch (1906–1984) Austria
Sonata E (Dob 1970) 19pp. Traditional forms SA and Rondo are used to give direction to the work. Strong tonal passages are interspersed with more MC lines. M-D.

Michel Block (1937–   ) Belgium
Block made his debut as a pianist at age nine and completed his training at The Juilliard School. He teaches piano at Indiana University.
Un beau jour (One Fine Day) (Alfred 1994) 19pp. Tell Me; Do You Remember?; Highway to the South; The Rendezvous We Missed; Come; The Perfect Hour. Six descriptive pieces depicting scenes and impressions of France. Impressionistic style, excellent preparation for playing more difficult French music. Int. to M-D.

John Blow (1648–1708) Great Britain
Blow was probably the most important contemporary of Purcell. His style is simple and direct.
Six Suites (Ferguson—S&B 1965) Excellent edition. M-D.

Contemporaries of Purcell (Fuller-Maitland—JWC 1921) First two volumes of
this series. Vol.I: *Suite* I: A,C,M. *Suite* II: A, Ayre, S. *Suite* III: Andante, C.
Suite IV: Ayre, C I and II; same keys throughout the entire Suite. Miscellaneous pieces. Vol.II: other miscellaneous pieces, a Fugue, Prelude, Ayre,
Theater Tune, Ground, and The Hay's a Ground. Int. to M-D.

12 Compositions for the Harpsichord or Virginal (Pauer—K). Transcribed for
piano and realized in the taste of Pauer's day but over-edited by today's
standards. No sources listed. Some works probably doubtful. M-D.

The Second Part of Musick's Handmaid (Dart—S&B) revised and corrected by
H. Purcell. First published in 1689, re-issued in 1705. 35 easy keyboard
pieces, mostly by J. Blow and H. Purcell. Pieces vary in length from two
lines to two pages. Mainly dances with much ornamentation. Int. to M-D.

Gavot in Gamut. Short, brisk, two voices. In *Musick's Handmaid* pt. II; *Contemporaries of Purcell*, vol. I. Int.

Ground in g. Variations on a four-bar harmonic structure. In *Contemporaries of
Purcell*, vol.II. M-D.

Compositions (K). Selected works. Int. to M-D.

Ground in e (Dart—S&B) in collection *John Blow's Anthology*. M-D.

Felix Blumenfeld (1863–1931) Russia
Blumenfeld's music is fluent and ripples agreeably; his pianistic felicity makes
even his less-interesting pieces attractive to play.

24 Preludes Op.17 (Musica Obscura) 4 books. Nos.3, 4, 5 also published separately. In the same key sequence as the Chopin *Preludes*. Melodious, extremely pianistic. All are worthy of consideration. M-D.

Impromptu G♭ Op.13/2 (Musica Obscura) 6pp. Flowing chordal melody over
left-hand accompaniment, suggestive Impressionistic qualities, surprising
fff ending. M-D.

Etude d Op.29/1 (Musica Obscura) 4pp. Melody worked into sweeping triplets;
much interplay between hands. Sonorities reminiscent of Rachmaninoff
and Scriabin. Effective. M-D.

Two Etude Fantasies Op.25 (Musica Obscura) 19pp. Allegro tempestuoso: g; dramatic; driving outer sections enclose a chorale-like middle section; *ppp*
closing. M-D. Allegro appassionato: e♭; form similar to first etude; *disperato*
(desperate) *fff* closing. D.

Etude de Concert f♯ Op.24 (Musica obscura) 9pp. Allegro non troppo: Chopin
influence noted, chromatic, soaring melodies. Large span required. M-D to
D.

Moment Lyrique e♭ Op.27/1 (Musica Obscura) 1pp. Andante, Molto expressivo e
legato. Lush harmonies, lyrical, builds to *ff* climax, chromatic, *pp* ending.
M-D.

Moment Lyrique e Op.27/4 (Musica Obscura) 2pp. Andante. Mesto. Tempo rubato. Alternating melody between hands in thirds, chromatic, 2 against 3,
ff climax, *ppp* ending. M-D.

Près de l'Eau (By the Sea) E Op.38/3 (Musica Obscura) 1p. Lento, ma non troppo.
A short "song without words"; exploits upper-register sonorities. M-D.

L'Isle Abandonnée c♯ (The Abandoned Island) (Musica Obscura) 7pp. Andante mesto. Murmuring left-hand figuration supports a glorious upward moving melody. Shades of Impressionistic sonorities. M-D.

Saules pleureurs (Weeping Willows) Op.35/5 (Musica Obscura) 2pp. Rocking right-hand chordal figure accompanies cantabile left-hand melody. Melody is eventually transferred to right-hand. Perdendosi closing. M-D.

Valse Brillante Op.22/2 (Musica Obscura) 13pp. Luminous writing contrasted with grazioso flowing style. Meno mosso section features lush tenor melody. Large span required. M-D to D.

Christopher Bochmann (1950–   ) Great Britain

Sonata (OUP 1974) 17pp. 15 min. In two parts: Preludio and Variazioni (written on four staves), then an Aria followed by a Postludio, to be played without a break between movements. Clusters, sharp dissonances, enormous skips, and wide dynamic range. Thematic material evolves from a five-note pattern. Skillful pedalling is essential. D.

Konrad Boehmer (1941–   ) Germany

Potential (Tonos 1961) 29pp. 10½ min. Instructions in German. Versions I, II, III. Pointillistic, highly organized, proportional rhythmic relationships, many dynamic indications, clusters, unmeasured tempo at places, extreme ranges exploited, avant-garde. Virtuoso technique required. D.

Alexandre-Pierre-François Böely (1785–1858) France

Böely was one of the first French organists to play and appreciate J. S. Bach. He had some influence on Franck. Böely wrote etudes, sonatas, and short pieces for the piano, many of which are published by Sal.

Anthologie de Pièces pour Piano (Choudens). Contains some interesting, original, and even startling material. Individual Romantic writing. An unimpressive Capriccio opens the collection; the sixteen other short pieces that follow are all somewhat better than the opening work. A contrapuntal flavor appears in most of the pieces, and they resemble J. B. Cramer's studies in this respect. Int. to M-D.

41 Pièces (Senart 1915). Revised and annotated by M. Brenet. Int. to M-D.

L'Ecole Française de Piano (1784–1845) (M. Cauchie—l'OL 1957).

Georg Böhm (1661–1733) Germany

Complete Piano and Organ Works (G. Wolgast—Br&H). Vol.1: 5 Preludes and Fugues: Capriccio D; 11 Suites, in c, D, d, d, E♭, E♭, F, f, f, G, a; M in G; Partita on the air "Jesu du bist allzu schöne." M-D. Vol.II: organ compositions.

Adrien Boieldieu (1775–1834) France

Best known for his operas, Boieldieu was professor of piano and later professor of composition at the Paris Conservatory.

Sonates pour le piano-forte (Société Française de Musicologie, 1944), Vols.11 and

12. Edited for the first time with a historical introduction by George Favre. Vol.11: 2nd Sonata Op.1 (1795); 1st Sonate Op.2 (1795?). Vol.12: 3rd Sonate Op.2; 2 Sonatas Op.4; Grande Sonate Op.6. Written in the "Grand Style." Long, dramatic gestures; some melodic beauty; pianistic. M-D to D.

Joseph Bodin de Boismortier (ca. 1682–1765) France

Quatre Suites de Pièces de Clavecin Op.59 1736 (E. Jacobi-Leuckart 1960). These suites contain 18 short movements, each descriptive of female characters. Every one sounds well on the piano, and only one calls for two keyboards. Editor has done an excellent job. Important collection of unusual repertoire. Contains three pages of facsimile and a Table of Ornaments. Int. to M-D.

William Bolcom (1938–   ) USA

Bolcom's works have incorporated a wide variety of influences and techniques ranging from serialism to popular music (ragtime), improvisation, collage, and microtones. Bolcom teaches at the University of Michigan.

Twelve Etudes (Merion 1964). This set of pieces "while dealing with almost all aspects of piano technique, concentrates on control of textures, dynamics, pedals and the use of the strings of the piano" (from the preface). Each etude is devoted to one specific problem. No.1 concentrates on touch and dynamics; over- and under-hand technique in a small area. No.2 promotes smoothness and evenness of passagework in both hands. Notation is proportional. Avant-garde. Performance directions provided. Pushes twentieth-century piano technique to the limits of texture and sonority. D.

Seabiscuits Rag 1970 (EBM 1974) 7pp. Cakewalk tempo, syncopation, swing. M-D.

The Garden of Eden 1968 (EBM 1974) 20pp. Four rags based on Genesis. A blend of rag characteristics with fine contemporary compositional techniques. Includes comments on the style of rag performance. Old Adam: a vigorous two-step in bouncy dotted rhythms. The Eternal Feminine: slow, languorous, elegantly shaped. The Serpent's Kiss: changing tempi and mood; slap the piano, stop time, click the tongue; two fingers tap dance; a virtuoso "Rag Fantasy." Through Eden's Gates: a casual cakewalk. M-D to D.

Raggin' Rudi 1972 (EBM 1974) 3pp. Clever. Large span required. M-D.

Three Ghost Rags 1970 (EBM 1981). Published separately. Graceful Ghost Rag 1971, 4pp.: moderate rag-tempo, full chords, chromatic, intriguing rhythms, large span required. M-D to D. The Poltergeist 1971, 10pp. 4 min.: fleeting; not too fast; insouciantly, arpeggiated chordal melody. Large span required. M-D. Dream Shadows 1970, 7pp. 6½ min.: caressing; similar in style but more tender and lyric than No.2; tenths in left hand to be unbroken if possible. M-D.

Monsterpieces 1980 (and Others) (EBM 1981) 16pp. Ten short, clever descriptive pieces with monsters, misters, ministers, and other characters. Big Mountain: Henry Cowell influence with left forearm clusters. The Big Bad Mr.

Monster Strikes Again: left-hand black and white key clusters. Appropriate illustrations. Int.

Nine Bagatelles (EBM 1997) 16pp. Commissioned for the Tenth Van Cliburn International Piano Competition. 1. The ghost mazurka: quote from Chopin Op.33/4, mixed style. 2. . . . aimai-je un rêve? (Mallarmé): slowly, light, ghostly. 3. . . . forgotten prayers: fast upper-register material contrasted with chorale-like chords. 4. . . . cycle de l'universe: opening idea (14 measures) repeated 3 times at different dynamic levels; less aggressive concluding section (9 measures). 5. . . . la belle rouquine: tonal, lyrical, moving chordal sonorities. 6. . . . Pegasus: prestissimo triplets fly over keyboard; silently depressed cluster; careful pedal markings. 7. . . . this endernight: 6 measures long, misterioso, widely spread sonorities. 8. . . . recess in hell: very precise punctuated sonorities; *ffz* chords. 9. . . . Circus Galop: quick march, ragtime influence, rolled chords, *fffz* conclusion. All 9 must be performed together. M-D to D.

12 New Etudes 1977–1986 (EBM). Winner of 1988 Pulitzer Prize in Music. These pieces sound like improvisations but are extremely difficult to play. Varied pianistic and compositional techniques are cleverly explored with numerous performance directions. Tonal and atonal mixture. This set and the earlier set discussed above are major contributions to the repertoire. D.
See: Linda Holzer, "William Bolcom. From Rags to Riches." P&K, 184 (January–February 1997):39–44, for a detailed discussion of *12 New Etudes*.

Three Dance Portraits 1986 (EBM). A tango, a soft shoe, and a jazz-influenced finale. M-D.

William Bolcom Piano Rags (EBM). Contains 15 of his best original rags in the classic sense, including "Graceful Ghost Rag" and some published for the first time. M-D to D.
See: Dan R. McAlexander, "Works for Piano by William Bolcom: A Study in the Development of Musical Postmodernism," diss., University of Cincinnati, 1994.

Claude Bolling (1930–   ) France
Jazz History "With the Help of My Friends" (Editions Bleu Blanc 1980). Twelve original piano pieces written in the style of Duke Ellington, Erroll Garner, Thelonius Monk, and others. M-D.
See: Allan Kozinn, "Claude Bolling—French Pianist and Jazz-Baroque Composer," *Keyboard* 8/6 (June 1982):30, 32, 34, 36.

Harriet Bolz (1912–   ) USA
Two Profiles for Piano 1974 (Sisra 1980) 10pp. 3½ min. Simple, graceful: linear; chromatic; builds to climax in octaves, subsides, ends *p*. Gay, debonair: linear, fuller textures, freely tonal. M-D.
Floret 1965 (Sisra 1980) 10pp. 4 min. "A mood caprice for piano." More developed than *Two Profiles*. Contrasting moods, neat textures. M-D.

João Domingos Bomtempo (1775–1842) Portugal
Sonatas Op.18 (Doderer—W. Müller 1982) 42pp. Preface in German and Portuguese. Expressive melodies, Alberti basses, broken octaves, quick arpeggi, cadenza passages, well crafted and attractive. Int. to M-D.

Anna Bon (1738– ?) Italy
Six Sonatas Op.2 (Jane Hettrick—Hildegard Publishing; Edition Donna 1991) 24pp. Reprint of Nürnberg edition, 1757, for harpsichord or piano. Active at the court of Frederick the Great, Bon composed these works during her teenage years. Preface. Facsimile edition. Rococo style, three movements each. Also available (Harbach—Vivace) 52 pp. Int. to M-D.

Margaret Bonds (1913–1972) USA
Bonds was a student of Florence Price.
Troubled Water (Sam Fox 1967). A demanding fantasy on the spiritual "Wade in the Water." Requires rhythmic drive, strong accentuation, gospel music underpinning, jazz orientation. M-D to D.

Mel Bonis (1858–1937) France
Pseudonym of Mrs. Albert Domange. She studied with Guiraud and Franck. About 200 of her works were published.
Six Pièces pour le piano (Lemoine 1993) 27pp. Cache-cache; Gai Printemps; Le Moustique; Romance sans Paroles; Marionnettes; L'Escarpolette. Late-nineteenth-century style, pianistic, colorful, varied moods. Int.

Bruno Bontempelli (1948–) Italy
Touches (Billaudot 1977) 2 vols. each 13pp. Eighteen pieces that present various rhythmic and phrasing patterns. Clusters. Int.

Charles Bordes (1863–1909) France
A pupil of Franck, Bordes was one of the founders, with d'Indy and Guilmant, of the Schola Cantorum. His reputation rests mainly on his musicological studies. He collected and published old church music and Basque folktunes.
Caprice à cinq temps (Edition Musicales de la Schola Cantorum). Changing meters, a small "tour de force." M-D.
Quatre fantaisies rythmiques (Heugel 1889). Interesting rhythmic and metric subdivisions. Significant writing for 1883–1901, when these pieces were composed. M-D.

Benjamin Boretz (1934–) USA
(". . . my chart shines high where the blue milks upset. . .") (Lingua Press 1978; PNM, 14–15 [1976]:337–423). 87pp. 19 min. Highly organized, complex. Requires more musicianship than technique. M-D.

Alexander Borodin (1833–1887) Russia

Borodin's small amount of piano music is worth investigating.

Petite Suite (CFP; GS; EBM; Leduc). In the Monastery (GS); Intermezzo; 2 Mazurkas; Reverie; Serenade; Nocturne (Anson—Willis). Picturesque Romantic writing. No unifying theme. Int. to M-D.

Scherzo A♭ (IMC; Br&H). Kind of a Polovstian dance tamed down for the drawing room. Effective. M-D.

Borodin: Album for Piano (EMB Z 13975). Contains *Petite Suite* and *Scherzo* A♭.

Sergey Eduardovich Bortikievich (1877–1952) USSR

Bortikievich's compositions are partly Russian, partly Oriental, and influenced by Chopin and Liszt. Many of his smaller works are excellent and are approximately late-intermediate level.

Seven Impressions Op.4 (Rahter 1907). Old Picture; Bird's Study; Storm; After the Rain; Shepherds and Shepherdesses; By Moonlight; Fancy-Dress Ball. Requires a certain amount of maturity for proper interpretation. Int. to M-D.

Sonata B Op.9 1909 (Rahter) 31pp. Allegro ma non troppo; Andante mesto e molto espressivo; Presto. A large work, well constructed. Late-nineteenth-century idiom, highly pianistic with predictable passage work; beautiful melodic writing infuses entire work. Does not sound too dated. D.

Six Pensées Lyriques Op.11 (Rahter 1909). Colorful short character pieces with Russian overtones. Int. to M-D.

From My Childhood Op.14 (Rahter 1911) 27pp. What the Nurse Sang; The Dark Room; The Dancing Lesson; First Love; First Sorrow; When I Am a Man. Int.

Ten Etudes Op.15 (Rahter 1911) 45pp. In Chopin tradition. All "sound" and are effective. M-D.

The Little Wanderer Op.21 (Rahter 1922). Eighteen pieces that take the little wanderer to many lands. The characteristics of each country are incorporated in the piece. Would make an attractive group project. Int.

Three Waltzes Op.27 (Rahter Elite Ed.108). La Gracieuse; La Mélancolique; La Viennoise. Delightful, attractive; titles indicate character and style. M-D.

From Andersen's Fairy Tales Op.30 (Rahter). Twelve musical pictures. Some Impressionistic devices. Unusually attractive collection that could be performed as a whole, integrating some of the prose from Hans Christian Andersen. Int.

Ten Preludes Op.33 (Rahter 1926) 34pp. Contrasting moods and sonorities. Suggest early Rachmaninoff style. Tend toward thick textures. M-D.

Ballade Op.42 and *Elegie* Op.46 (CFP 8543). Published together. M-D.

Marionettes Op.54 (Simrock 1938) 15pp. Nine short pieces. Int.

Lyrica Nova Op.59 (UE 1941) 10 min. Four character pieces. Con moto affettuoso; Andantino; Andantino; Con slancio. All are written in either five or six sharps. Mainly Romantic style with some Impressionistic influence. M-D.

See: Laura Holleran and B. N. Thadani, "Discovering the Music of Sergei Bortikiewicz," *Clavier*, 35/1 (January 1996):27–31. Includes music to "Lyrica Nova," Op.59/3.

Pieter Joseph Van Den Bosch (1736–1803) The Netherlands
Sonatine G (Metropolis E.M. 4720). Similar in style and length to the Kuhlau
   Sonatinas Op.55. Published with Three Sonatinas by F. Staes. Int.

Alexander Boscovich (1907–1964) Israel, born Transylvania
Semitic Suite (IMP). Allegretto: dancelike. Andantino: songful. Folk Dance:
   lively, syncopated. Andantino: recitative-like. Pastorale: quiet. Dance: vigorous. Entire suite has a bare, non-romantic quality, modeled after folk idioms of the Near East. Other versions for four hands at one or two pianos
   and for orchestra. M-D.

Arturo Bosmans (1908–   ) Brazil, born Belgium
Sonatina Lusitana (ECIC 1947). Based on Portuguese folk tunes. Allegro vivace:
   popular treatment of two tunes, interludes. Cantiga do Cêgo (Ballad of the
   Blind): quartal harmony over pedal point, open sonorities. Allegro non
   troppo: cheerful, rhythmic, fast double notes, animated closing. M-D.
Sonata en Colores 1944 (ECIC). Rojo: spirited broken-chord figuration, etude
   style. Gris: Melody in parallel fourths, quiet. Verde: rhythmic, some linear
   writing, Impressionistic parallel chords. M-D.
Clavinecdotes 1955 (Metropolis) 15pp. Five anecdotas for piano. Short, clever,
   colorful, freely tonal, MC. M-D.

Henriette Bosmans (1895–1952) The Netherlands
Vieille Chanson 1948 (Br&VP 1950) in *Hommage à Willem Pijper*, 3pp. Bosmans
   studied with Pijper in 1927. M-D.

Will Gay Bottje (1925–   ) USA
Sonata No.1 (AMC 1958). Three movements (moderate FSF) in neoclassical
   style. Tonal writing with much dissonance. Lines move according to their
   own melodic function. The slow movement is built on an ostinato. Third
   movement bristles with octaves. Brilliant and effective piano writing. D.

Carlos Botto (1923–   ) Chile
Tres Caprichos Op.10 (IEM 1959). Tonal but freely chromatic. Int. to M-D.

André Boucourechliev (1925–1988) France, born Bulgaria
Archipel 4 (Leduc 1970). "Archipelago" is a mobile work, i.e., changing in shape,
   character, articulation, and duration at each performance. In four sections,
   aleatoric; shown to best advantage in a concert performance in two different versions. Great piles of tone alternate with ringing sonorities; improvisation is as important as the written notes; hangs together remarkably well.
   Notation is almost unbelievable! Wildest sounds imaginable; extensive directions for performer; performer must literally chart his own course in
   this work. Avant-garde. D.
Six études d'après Piranese (Sal 1975) 7 leaves, photostat. Explanations in French. D.

Lili Boulanger (1893–1918) France
Sister of the famous French composition teacher Nadia Boulanger, and a fine composer.
Theme and Variations 1914 (Selma Epstein—Chromattica 1993). Written in a
    late French Romantic style that borders on Impressionism. M-D.
Trois Morceaux 1914 (GS 1979) 13pp. D'un Vieux Jardin; D'un Jardin Clair;
    Cortège. Subtle expressive writing; chromatic and somewhat impression-
    istic. Requires large span. No. 1 is in collection *The Century of Invention*
    (EAMC 1996). M-D.

Pierre Boulez (1925–   ) France
No matter how variable and complex the organization of his music may be,
Boulez sticks tenaciously to the basic elements that have always characterized
his art. One work grows out of another in his creativity, and so too does Boulez
stand before us today as a protagonist of a rightly comprehended link between
tradition and progress.
Première Sonate (Amphion 1946) 9 min. Lent; Assez large. Twelve-tone, many
    tempo changes, difficult for ear to comprehend, wide leaps, Messiaen in-
    fluence especially noticeable in rhythmic practice. Much originality and vi-
    tality, full of knotty, uncompromising logic. D.
    See: David Burge, "Untying Rhythmic Knots," CK, 3 (September 1977):52,
    for a discussion of the problem of meterless music, as related to this work.
    ———, "Renotation," CK, 3 (October 1977):58, on the more complex pas-
    sages from the same sonata.
Deuxième Sonate 1948 (Heugel) 48pp. 30 min. Extrêmement rapide; Lent; Mo-
    déré; Presque vif, Vif. Wide range of musical textures. Serialized "closed"
    structure, spasmodic outbursts. Shows influence of some of the rhythmic
    organizations of Messiaen, lean keyboard acrobatics. Complex and very
    difficult.
    See: David Burge, "Renotation revisited," CK, 4 (March 1978):66.
    ———, "Boulez Second Sonata," *Keyboard*, 7/12 (December 1981):69.
    William Heiles, "The Second Piano Sonata of Pierre Boulez," AMT, 22
    (January 1973):34–37.
    André Hodeir, *Since Debussy: A View of Contemporary Music* (New York:
    Grove Press, 1961) pp.129–33, for a thorough discussion of this work.
Troisième Sonate (UE 1961) 19 min. Begun in 1957 and still not complete. Only
    two of the proposed five movements have been published: Trope: Texte-
    Parenthèse-Commentaire-Glose-Commentaire and Constellation-Miroir.
    The second movement contains six major sections—mélange (mixture),
    points 3, blocs 2, points 2, blocs 1, points 1. One may begin with either
    movement and continue in several different orders. Serialized "open" struc-
    ture; quasi-extempore freedom; intricate dynamics, pedaling, rhythms, and
    touch. Sonorities vary from refined expression to violent outbursts. The
    most remote in musical expression of the three sonatas; one of the greatest

pianistic creations of this century. Virtuoso pianism required, and even this may not overcome the lack of discernible continuity. D.

See: Robert Black, "Boulez's Third Piano Sonata: Surface and Sensibility," PNM (Fall/Winter 1981, Spring/Summer 1982):182ff.

Anne Trenkamp, "The Concept of 'Alea' in Boulez's Constellation-Miroir," M&L, 57 (January 1976):1–10.

Mark Wait, "Aspects of Literary and Musical Structure as Reflected by the Third Piano Sonata of Pierre Boulez," diss., Peabody Conservatory, 1976, 81pp. Contains a very enlightening analysis.

Douze Notations (UE 18310, 1985) 11pp. 8 min. 1. Fantasque—Modéré: scampers over keyboard, strict tempo. 2. Tres vif: glassandi, clusters, repeated patterns. 3. Assez lent: intense; large span required. 4. Rythmique: chromatic pattern repeated, accents. 5. Doux et improvisé: long pedals, widely spread gestures. 6. Rapide: two different touches possible, wide keyboard range. 7. Hiératique: short punctuated gestures, dynamic contrast. 8. Modéré jusqu'a très vif: piled up sonorities. 9. Lointoin—Calme: pedal study. 10. Mecanique et très sec: martelé throughout, no pedal. 11. Scintillant: flying gestures over keyboard, *pp-p*. 12. Lent—Puissant et âpre: biting sonorities; large span required; *fff*. M-D to D.

See: Pierre Boulez, *Notes of an Apprenticeship* (New York: Knopf, 1968). Early critical writings of Boulez.

———, *Boulez on Music* (Cambridge: Harvard University Press, 1971). A highly technical, abstract, philosophic treatise on basic problems in contemporary composition.

Josse Boutmy (1697–1779) Flemish, Belgium

Werken voor klavecimbel. Vol.5 of *Monumenta Musicae Belgicae* with a short biography by Susanne Clercx. *Troisième Livre de Pièces de clavecin* contains six suites, optional dance movements with colorful titles (La Martiale, Fanfarinette, La Brillante, L'Obstinée, 1st and 2nd Tambourine) as well as the standard suite movements, A, C, S, G. More than interesting writing. M-D.

Roger Boutry (1932–   ) France

Boutry is professor of harmony at the Conservatoire de Paris.

Sonate—Scherzo (Leduc 1962) 16pp. 7½ min. Allegro con fuoco: driving rhythms (2/2 + 3/8); leads to more lyric section involving wide sweeps across the keyboard; opening section returns. Andante: sostenuto (quasi recitativo) leads to big climax, subsides, then leads through an octave stringendo to Allegro vivace: toccata-like, concludes vivacissimo. Effective virtuoso contemporary writing. D.

York Bowen (1884–1961) Great Britain

Bowen was a fine pianist and wrote a great deal for the piano. His pedagogical editions are highly regarded in Great Britain.

Sonata f Op.72 1923 (Swan) 34pp. FSF plus introduction to first movement. Solid musical writing in a post-Brahms idiom. M-D.

24 Preludes Op.102 1950 (JWC) 30 min. 4 books. In all major and minor keys. Rachmaninoff influence. These works are highly pianistic and contain some impressive sonorities. M-D.

Sonatina C Op.144 1956 (JWC) 16pp. 10 min. Colorful work. M-D.

4 Bagatelles Op.147 1956 (JWC). Ideas not too interesting but pianistic and fun to play. M-D.

Paul Bowles (1910–1999) USA

Bowles lived in Spain, Morocco, Central and South America, and Mexico for a number of years. These experiences have added a unique quality to his music. He was also a successful writer of novels.

El Indio (Mer). Employs Mexican Indian material. An arrangement from Bowles ballet *Pastorelas*. Int.

El Bejuco (Mer). Same inspiration as above, based on a popular song. Int.

Huapango Nos.1 and 2 (Axelrod 1937). Short, changing meters, Mexican dance style. No.1 uses actual folk material. Int.

Sayula (Hargail 1946). Inspired by dance hall. M-D.

Six Preludes (Mer 1933–1944). Short, mainly lyric; brief comments on nostalgic states. Popular style. Int.

Two Portraits (Axelrod). Short, Int.

Sonatina (EV 1947). Allegro ritmico; Andante cantabile; Allegro. Less use of exotic elements. Int.

Carretera de Estepona (EBM). Rhythmic, octaves, syncopation. M-D.

Folk Preludes (TP). Six charming settings. Int.

Anne Boyd (1946–   ) Australia

Angklung (Faber 1974) 6pp. Reproduced from holograph. To be played as slowly as possible. No bar lines; only dynamic direction is "sempre *p* poss." Static harmonies built around E and b. M-D.

Martin Boykan (1913–   ) USA

Fantasy-Sonata (CFP 67374) 12 min. One movement. Wide dynamic range, requires enormous rhythmic flexibility. D.

Piano Sonata II (CFP 67513) 15 min. Three movements of pointillistic and expressionistic writing. Restful sections contrasted with clangorous sonorities. D.

Attila Bozay (1939–1999) Hungary

Bagatelle Op.4 1961 (EMB) 11pp. 7 min. Andantino tranquillo: preference for seconds, grace notes, chromaticism. Sostenuto: long effective pedal usage. Agitato, fugato: rhythmic, driving non-strict fugue. M-D.

Intervalli Op.15 1969 (EMB) 15pp. Impressionistic, reminiscent of "Night Music" from Bartók's *Out of Doors* suite. M-D.

Medailles (Bo&H). 36 varried short pieces from which the performer selects own suite. Excellent introduction to twentieth-century techniques. Easy to M-D.

Eugène Bozza (1905–1991) France
Allegro de Concert (Leduc 1974) 10pp. 7 min. A big concert etude with full chromatic chords, fast octaves, alternation of hands, flexible meters, glissando at conclusion. Sounds more difficult than it actually is. M-D.
Esquisses (Leduc 1979) 3pp. 2 min. Moves through several keys, beginning and returning in G Dorian and closing in F. Interesting dynamics and fingering. Int.
Toccata (Leduc). A real "show-piece." M-D.

Susan Bradshaw (1931–   ) Great Britain
8 Hungarian Melodies 1961 (JWC) 11pp. Comparable to Book V of *Mikrokosmos*, these pieces have a flair for rhythm and harmony. Not as easy as they seem to be. Int. to M-D.

Johannes Brahms (1833–1897) Germany
A severe critic of all his compositions, Brahms left us little that is not of fine quality for the piano. Therefore, the pianist should aim for a comprehensive acquaintance with the complete piano works. They span Brahms's entire career and offer a panoramic view of his development. The piano was the instrument of his choice for his earliest works—the three sonatas and the Scherzo—and his next to last works, the groups of short character pieces of Opp.116–119.

EDITIONS:

In the New Johannes Brahms Complete Edition (Br) Series III will include the piano music.
Klavierwerke (Carl Seemann, Kurt Stephenson—CFP 1974) Vol.I: Sonatas Opp.1, 2, 5. Vol.II: Variations Opp.9, 21, 24, 35. Vol.III: Piano Pieces Opp.4, 10, 39, 76. Vol.IV: Piano Pieces Opp.79, 116, 117, 118, 119. Vol.V: Variations, Piano Pieces, Studies: Variations in d from Op.18; Sarabandes and Gigues; Waltzes, Op.39 (easy version): Hungarian Dances, Nos.1–10; Gavotte after Gluck; 5 Studies after Chopin, Weber, and J. S. Bach; 51 Exercises. This urtext edition is based on the Mandyczewski edition of the *Complete Works*. Contains interesting suggestions for distributing the material between the hands (Op.10/3) as well as for positioning the hands wherever they interlock. Editorial suggestions are indicated by use of brackets and dotted slurs. Brahms's original fingering appears in italics. Preface in German, English, and French.
Complete Works for Piano Solo (Mandyczewski—GS). 3 vols.
Complete Works for Piano Solo (Mandyczewski—Dover). Vol.I: Complete Transcriptions, Cadenzas and Exercises. Vol.II: Shorter Works. Vol.III: Complete Sonatas and Variations.

Piano Works (Sauer—CFP; GS). Vol.I: Opp.1, 2, 4, 5, 9, 10, 21, 24. Vol.II: Opp.76, 79, 116–119; 5 Studies. Other works available separately.

Complete Piano Works (Mandyczewski—Br&H). Vol.I: Opp.1, 2, 5, 9, 21, 24, 35. Vol.II: Opp.4, 10, 39, 39 (simplified version), 76, 79, 116–119. Vol.III: Works without opus numbers.

Piano Works (Sauer—K). Vol.I: Opp.1–24. Vol.II: Opp.76–119. Vol.III: Opp.35, 39; Concertos.

Complete Piano Works (IMC). Vol.I: Opp.1, 2, 5, 9, 21, 24, 35. Vol.II: Opp.4, 10, 39, 39 (simplified version), 76, 79, 116–119. Vol.III: Works without opus numbers.

Piano Works (Kalmus miniature study scores 725, 726). Vol.I: Opp.4, 10, 24, 35, 56b. Vol.II: Opp.76, 79, 116–119.

Sonatas, Scherzi, and Ballades (Giorgii—Henle 38).

Piano Pieces Opp.76–119 (Steegmann, Georgii—Henle 36). Other works available separately.

Sonata C, Op.1 1853 (VU; Br&H). Allegro: SA design; opening idea recalls Beethoven's "Hammerklavier" Sonata Op.106; orchestral scoring. Andante (Nach einem altdeutschen Minnelied): written when Brahms was fourteen years old; theme, three variations, and coda. Scherzo—Allegro molto e con fuoco: 6/8 meter, with rhythmic accents shifting between 2 and 3, was to become a Brahms trademark; grand sweep; needs big technical equipment. Allegro con fuoco: rondo treatment, great vigor, requires an energetic drive. M-D to D.

Sonata f♯ Op.2 1853 (Br&H). Allegro non troppo ma energico: requires a powerful octave technique; Schumann influence in opening octaves figure; dramatic second subject. Andante con espressione: rich harmonies and lyric melodies require a warm tone. Scherzo—Allegro: thick textures in the trio; large span required. Finale—Introduzione—Allegro non troppo e rubato: weakest movement; closes with a cadenza of trills and scales; unusual for Brahms (scale passages especially). Written before Op.1. M-D to D.

Sonata f Op.5 1854 (Cortot—EC; Steuermann—UE; Br&H; WH; Bauer—GS; Klasen—UE; Ric). Allegro maestoso; powerful, concise, some awkward writing. Andante espressivo: duet effect of melody; much use of the interval of a sixth; with three lines from the poet Sternau appearing at the beginning of the movement, we come as close to program music as we ever do in Brahms. Scherzo—Allegro energico: energetic opening theme; devotional Trio in long melodic curves. Intermezzo—Andante molto: unexpected (Retrospect), returns to theme of the Andante, canonic imitation in middle in D♭ middle theme. Finale—Allegro moderato ma rubato: effective large movement; rich varied themes well developed; modified rondo. The finest and longest of the three sonatas. D.

In these early sonatas, the sprawling framework of the traditional Classical sonata was congenial to Brahms, and in many ways these prove to be his most derivative works.

See: Wadham Sutton, "Brahms: Sonata in F minor, Op.5," *Music Teacher*, 52 (August 1973):12–13.

Colin Mason, "Brahms' Piano Sonatas," MR, 5 (May 1944):112–18.

Frank E. Kirby, "Brahms and the Piano Sonata" in *Paul A. Pisk: Essays in His Honor* (Austin: University of Texas Press, 1967); pp.163–80.

Harold Truscott, "Brahms and Sonata Style," MR, 25 (1964):186–201.

Scherzo e♭ Op.4 1854 (Br&H; Klasen—UE; Deis—GS). No humor here. Bristling with youthful impulse. Requires much stamina. Both Schumann and Liszt liked this work. M-D.

Variations on a Theme by Robert Schumann Op.9 1854 (Henle; Br&H; Ric). The theme is No.4 of Schumann's *Bunte Blätter* Op.99 followed by 16 variations, full of much beauty and poetry. The identity of the bass persists throughout and is the connecting link between variations. M-D.

See: Oliver Neighbor, "Brahms and Schumann: Two Opus Nines and Beyond," *Nineteenth-Century Music* (April 1984):266ff. General notes on Schumann's influence on Brahms as revealed in Brahms's Op.9.

Four Ballades Op.10 1856 (Hinson—Alfred 4820; Steuermann—UE; Mayer-Mahr—Schott; GS; Alnaes—WH). 1. Andante: d, inspired by the grisly Scottish Ballad "Edward"; ghostly march rhythm ends in a whisper. 2. Andante: D; gentle; winning themes; lush harmonies; staccato in mid-section needs careful attention. 3. Intermezzo—Allegro: b; scherzo-like; fast passages *pp*; imaginative writing; resembles in conception No.3 of Op.117, also titled "Intermezzo." 4. Andante con moto: B; beautiful romanza with an outstanding cantabile melody; mid-section suggests Schumann influence. These four pieces could be viewed as components of a dramatic sonata structure in which the third ballade begins a transition from darkness into light that is fully realized in the last one, whose meditative concluding section is illumined with convincing serenity. M-D.

Variations Op.18 1860 (CFP; Dover) 6pp. This transcription of the variations from the string sextet Op.18 was intended for concert performance. It was written as a birthday present for Clara Schumann. The six variations exploit numerous characteristics of the composer. Var.3 contains numerous scale passages for the left hand, which support the syncopated chordal right-hand melody. Theme returns at conclusion and quietly ends in D. A beautiful set that deserves more performance. M-D.

Variations on an Original Theme Op.21/1 1861 (Br&H; Ric). Op. 21, 1/2 (Henle 439). Brahms's theme is so beautiful and well constructed that it is difficult for the eleven variations that follow to improve on it. Var.1 shows a faint trace of Chopin's Prelude Op.28/5. This set is slightly more difficult than Op.9.

Variations on a Hungarian Theme Op.21/2 1861 (Br&H; Ric). Shorter and easier than Op.21/1 but not as interesting. Each variation has a distinct melody, and the harmony departs freely from the theme. Vars.5, 6, and 9 display the most Hungarian flavor. M-D.

Variations on a Theme by Schumann Op.23 1861 arranged for solo piano by Theodore Kirchner (Goebels—Schott 09735 1982) 23pp. 15 min. This work was originally written for one piano, four hands but this arrangement for solo piano is so exquisite that it must be included. The Schumann theme was composed during the night of February 17, 1854 and was his last musical thought. He claimed to have heard it from the spirits of Schubert and Mendelssohn. The piece is like a requiem. The theme is worked out differently in each variation, and the final variation, bathed in sadness and resignation, is like a death march. Ends with the return of the theme accompanied by poignant harmonies. M-D.

Variations and Fugue on a Theme by Handel Op.24 1862 (Henle; CFP 3926A; Cortot—EC; Br&H; Ric; WH; GS) 24 min. One of the greatest masterpieces of variation form; 25 superbly developed variations climaxing with an enormously successful fugue. The simple Handel theme comes from the first *Leçon* in B♭, but what Brahms does with it is extraordinary. The fugue-subject is clearly derived from Handel's theme, and the intermingling of fugal and developmental techniques brings the work to a most impressive conclusion. D.

See: Jane A. Bernstein, "An Autograph of the Brahms-Handel Variations," MR, 34 (August–November 1974):272–81.

Variations on a Theme by Paganini Op.35 Books I and II 1866 (Cortot—EC; Foldes—CF; Sauer—CFP; Br&H; Hughes—GS; K; Ric; IMC). Each book contains 14 variations on the theme. These pieces grew out of lengthy discussions and demonstrations of piano technique which Brahms had with Carl Tausig. They remain a challenge to virtuosity that has seldom if ever been surpassed. The second set is slightly easier than the first. A performance possibility is a selection of variations from both books rather than one complete book or both books complete. D.

Variationen für Klavier (Henle 440 1988) 156pp. Preface and critical report in English, French, and German. Variations on a Theme of Schumann Op.9; Variations on an Original Theme Op.21/1; Variations on a Hungarian Song Op.21/2; Variations on a Theme of Handel Op.24; Variations on a Theme of Paganini Op.35; Variations from String Sextet Op.18, arranged by Brahms; Variations for Four Hands Op.23, arranged for two hands by Theodor Kirchner.

Sixteen Waltzes Op.39 1866 (Georgii—Henle; Höpfel—VU; Seemann—CFP; Sauer—UE; Schott; Lympany—Hansen House; Br&H; K; WH; Ric; IMC; Levine—Alfred). The Alfred and VU editions contain both the original solo versions and Brahms's simplified version. Simplified version available separately (Henle 43). Originally written for four hands. In the solo version Nos.14, 15, and 16 are transposed down a half-step. Inspired by Schubert but contains more subtle phrasing. Pleasantly transparent sound. When the complete set is performed, a repetition of the familiar No.15 after No.16 ends the set more successfully. Int. to M-D.

Waltz Op.39/15 (Höpfel—VU 51005). Both piano solo versions, A and A♭. Urtext edition plus facsimile of the autograph. Int.

See: Henry Levine, "Brahms Simplifies Brahms," *Clavier*, 13/2 (February 1974):14–20.

Santiago Rodriguez, "Brahms's Waltzes, Op.39," KC, 10/3 (May–June 1990): 40–41.

LATER SHORT PIECES:

With the exception of the *Two Rhapsodies* Op.79, the pieces from Op.76 on are highly expressive works in which certain moods or characters can be evoked. They represent a more intimate approach to the keyboard and all display uniformly finished workmanship.

The Shorter Piano Pieces (Hinson—Alfred 677). Includes Opp. 76, 79, 116, 118, and 119.

Eight Piano Pieces Op.76 1879 (Peterson-Kämmerling—VU; Georgii—Henle; Br&H; Sauer—CFP; Mayer-Mahr—Schott; IMC; Ric and WH, Nos. 1–4 only). 1. Capriccio f♯: cantabile melody alternates with sweeping arpeggios; deep, warm tone required. 2. Capriccio b: cheerful; requires a delicate staccato. 3. Intermezzo A♭: legato syncopated chords against staccato left-hand accompaniment. 4. Intermezzo B♭: melody with figural accompaniment, gracious and dark. 5. Capriccio c♯: more complex rhythms, powerful and broad. 6. Intermezzo A: lyric; in two sections with Codetta; serene, calm, and restful. 7. Intermezzo a: binary theme with repeats; textural balance is important. 8. Capriccio C: whirling; exploits remote keys; complicated rhythms; needs mature musicianship. M-D.
See: David Lewin, "On Harmony and Meter in Brahms's Op.76, No.8," *Nineteenth-Century Music*, IV/3 (Spring 1981):261–65.

Two Rhapsodies Op.79 1880 (Stockman—VU; H. Ferguson—ABRSM; Hinson—Alfred 6386; Steegman—Henle; Klasen—UE; Br&H; Ric; WH; Heinrichshofen; Schott, available separately). 1. b: longest of the 30 late works, turbulent, difficult for small hands. 2. g: fatalistic character; requires broad contrasts of dynamics; inspired by the Scottish ballad "Archibald Douglas." These works are among the most popular of the late piano works. They are the most extended and extroverted, and they are noted for their harmonic wealth and boldness. M-D.
See: Edwin Smith, "Brahms: Two Rhapsodies for Piano Op.79," *Music Teacher*, 55 (May 1976):13–14, for analysis and discussion of these works.
Beth Greenberg, "Brahms Rhapsody in G Minor, Op.79/2: A Study of Analyses by Schenker, Schoenberg, and Jonas," ITO, 1/9–10 (1975–76):21–29.

Seven Fantasies Op.116 1892 (Stockman, Pressler—VU 5L50072; Henle; Ferguson—ABRSM; UE; Sauer—CFP; WH, in two vols.). The VU edition contains an excellent preface by Stockman, extensive performance suggestions by Pressler, and practical fingerings. 1. Capriccio d: persistent syncopations; fiery; energetic 3/8 Presto is larded with sequences of hemiola; shifted accents and chromatic chords; requires a controlled virtuosity. 2. Intermezzo a: introspective; verges on a sarabande; a slow movement with an episode or "trio" that shimmers with right-hand broken octaves underpinned with delicate chromatic suggestions. 3. Capriccio g: passionate and impulsive, reminiscent of the younger Brahms; needs full tone and power. 4. Intermezzo E: Brahms originally thought of calling this "Nocturne," improvisatory; melody and accompaniment must be carefully balanced. 5. Intermezzo e: some anguished dissonances mirrored between the hands; warm mid-section and coda resolve tensions generated in outer parts. 6. Intermezzo E: the g♯ mid-section, with its pulsating hemiolas, contains one of the loveliest duets between the tenor and soprano parts that Brahms ever conceived; one of the most popular of all his Intermezzi. 7. Capriccio d: restless and stormy, much diminished-seventh harmony; mid-section bristles with cross-rhythmic effects. The "Capricci" in this opus provide the greatest contrast, but it is the Intermezzi that display the essence of the true late Brahms. M-D.

See: Camilla Cai, "Brahms's Short, Late Piano Pieces—Opus Numbers 116–119: A Source Study, an Analysis and Performance Practice," diss., Boston University, 1986.

William S. Newman, "About Brahms' Seven Fantasien, Op.116," PQ, 23 (Spring 1958):13.

Three Intermezzi Op.117 1892 (Palmer—Alfred 2417; Müller—VU; VU 51015, urtext edition and facsimile of the autograph; Georgii—Henle; Alfred; UE; K; Schott; Ric; WH; IMC; Bèrben). 1. E♭: folk tune; charming and lilting; poetic superscription is a Scots folk poem; requires clear distinctive line from the surrounding octaves in the same hand. 2. b♭: SA design, most elaborate of the three; same theme is used for first and second subjects; needs warm full tone in the D♭ thematic transformation. 3. c♯: dark and bleak opening, colorful distribution of texture. M-D.

See: Kerry Gripe, "An Analysis of the Three Intermezzi, Op.117 by Johannes Brahms," DM document, Indiana University, 1980, 57pp. The final chapter discusses motivic unity in Op.117, influence of Op.117, and performance suggestions.

Harold Zabrack, "Projecting Emotion," *Clavier*, 16 (September 1975):27–34. Contains a lesson on Op.117/2.

Six Piano Pieces Op.118 1893 (Fellinger—VU; Georgii—Henle; UE; K; Sauer—CFP; Schott; WH; IMC; Ric, Schott, No.3). 1. Intermezzo a: full of sweep and power, SA design, optimistic and enthusiastic. 2. Intermezzo A: an exquisite and melodious andante teneremente, beautiful canons at bars 50 and 66. 3. Ballade g: five-bar phrases throughout the first part, gentle rocking counter subject; requires fiery delivery in the outer sections and careful legato in the duet-like mid-section. 4. Intermezzo f: colorful effects, canonic structure, little melodic distinction. 5. Romanze F: elusive melodic line, ABA with the B section comprising continuous variations over a rocking bass that requires great delicacy. 6. Intermezzo e♭: based on the "Dies Irae," this great mournful masterpiece is full of mystery; powerful central section; careful pedaling is absolutely essential; proper tempo is andante, not adagio. M-D.

Four Piano Pieces Op.119 1893 (Fellinger—VU; Georgii—Henle; UE; K; Schott; Br&H; WH; IMC; Ric has No.4). 1. Intermezzo b: falling thirds add to this "so sadly sweet" piece, as Clara Schumann said of it; canons; requires full singing tone carefully balanced against the accompaniment. 2. Intermezzo

e: monothematic, restless; E section transforms the melodic contours into a graceful and leisurely waltz. 3. Intermezzo C: subtle cross-rhythm (3/4 against 6/8); more like a miniature scherzo; witty and playful but a lyrical tenderness emerges on the final page; requires a light touch, grace, and humor. 4. Rhapsody E♭: block chords recall the Sonata Op.1; grand manner; arch form; requires power, especially in the coda; A♭ section should be played with as little pedal as possible; find correct tempo and hold it. D. Brahms called these last four pieces the "lullabies of my pain." They give us a rare insight into his innermost feelings.
See: Peter J. Clements, "Johannes Brahms: Intermezzo, Op.119 No.1," *Canadian Association of University Schools of Music*, 7, 1977:31–51. A thorough analysis.
Brian Newbould, "A New Analysis of Brahms's Intermezzo in B minor, Op.119 No.1," MR, 38 (February 1977):33–43.
Robert Dumm, "Performer's Analysis" [of Op.119/2], *Clavier*, 13/2 (February 1974):24–32.

Five Studies Arranged from the Works of Other Composers (Ric; Simrock; Br&H, separately). 1. Etude after Chopin 1869: Op.25/2 f arranged with thirds and sixths in the right hand; Chopin's bass is left intact. 2. Weber Rondo 1869: consists of an inversion of the parts for right and left hands in the Finale of the Weber Sonata I, Op.24; has some awkward moments. 3. Presto from J. S. Bach (first arrangement 1879): taken from Bach's g Sonata for solo violin; "moto perpetuo" consisting of single notes for each hand; contrary motion and crossing of hands occur frequently. 4. Presto from J. S. Bach (second arrangement 1879): an inversion of No.3; Brahms seems to have liked these arrangements better than the Chopin and Weber movements. 5. Chaconne after J. S. Bach, arranged for the Left Hand 1879: closer to the original and more valid than Busoni's setting of Bach's famous Chaconne. M-D.

Gavotte after Glück 1871 (CFP; Ric; Schott). From Glück's *Iphigenia in Aulis*. Frequent use of three staves makes the middle part easier to read. Requires a good technique, especially a "singing" power by the weaker fingers. M-D.

Two Sarabandes 1855 and *Two Gigues* 1855 (CFP; *Two Sarabandes* only, Schott; Simrock). All four of these pieces are compositional exercises the youthful Brahms surely wrote quite often. On the first Gigue he wrote: "worth while practicing"; he thus also saw it as an exercise in three-part piano playing. The second Gigue is lightly crossed out in pencil in the MS; perhaps it was to have been replaced by another. Both Sarabandes show Brahms's interest in Bach's style. Int.

Fifty-One Exercises 1893 (Alfred; K; GS; Br&H; IMC; Ric; Durand). Could be described as the "88," as there are 37 extra exercises that appear in the guise of offshoots from the 51 numbered ones. The passage-formation on which the exercises are based is most characteristic of Brahms. Many seem to come directly "out of his music." M-D.

Kleine Stücke (Pascall—Dob DM819 1979) 7pp. First publication of three brief works. Sarabande und Gavotte: Sarabande in A, 16 bars; Gavotte I, in tonic minor with left-hand broken octaves; Gavotte II, tonic major, a variation of Gavotte I. Klavierstück: perhaps a fragment or a complete piece in the nature of a joke. Kanon 1864: two realizations are possible; the one offered here has clear part-writing and more characteristic harmony. Preface in German and English. M-D.

Hungarian Dances (Henle; Schott; Ric; CFP; Heinrichshofen; WH; Br&H; GS; UE). Originally written for piano duet. Brahms made the solo piano arrangement after the dances became so popular. They are among the happiest products of Brahms's flair for folk music. Int. to M-D.

COLLECTIONS:

At the Piano with Brahms (Hinson—Alfred 1093) 64pp. Includes descriptive material on Brahms and his music, as well as suggestion for further reading. Contains Capriccio b Op.76/2; Hungarian Dance No. 3; Intermezzo E Op. 116/6; Rhapsody g Op.79/2; Romance F Op.118/5; Sarabande and Gavotte a; Theme and Variations Op.18; Waltzes Op.39/2, 4, 6, 8, 11, 15 (original version), 15 (simplified version). Int. to M-D.

Dances of Brahms. Pieces to Play Before His Larger Works (Hinson—Alfred 4592) 60pp. Includes descriptive material and pedagogical advice. Contains Hungarian Dance No. 1; Gavotte a; Hungarian Dance No. 3; Sarabande b; Gavotte from Gluck's *Iphigenie en Aulide* transcribed by Brahms; Sarabande a; Hungarian Dance No. 7; Waltzes Op.39/1–16 (simplified version by Brahms). Int. to M-D.

Easiest Piano Pieces (Niemann—CFP 5058) 24pp. Simplified keyboard arrangements of some of the songs plus Waltzes Op.39/2, 3, 5, 10, 15, as simplified by Brahms. Int.

20 Favorite Pieces (GS) Andante from Op.1; Op.10/3; Op.39/2–15; Op.76/2–4, 6; Op.116/5; Op.117/1; Op.118/2–3, 5–6; Op.119/1, 3–4; Gavotte after Glück; Hungarian Dances Nos.3, 16.

Pezzi Scelti (A. Cortot—EC). Elucidating remarks in French, Italian, and English. Includes practice suggestions. Capriccio b Op.76/2; Intermezzo A Op.118/2; Ballad g Op.118/3; Intermezzo eb Op.118/6; Intermezzo C Op.119/3; Rhapsody Eb Op.119/4. Exceptional edition.

Brahms Album (EMB 1966). Fine edition, clear printing. Waltz Op.39/15; 2 Rhapsodies Op.79; Fantasies Op.116/1, 3, 4, 5, 6, 7; 3 Intermezzi Op.117; Romance Op.118/5; Hungarian Dances Nos.5, 6; Rhapsody Op.119/4.

Johannes Brahms Piano Compositions (Tucker—WB 1992) 32pp. Intermezzi Opp.76/7, 117/1, 118/2. Romanze Op.118/5. Scherzo from Sonata Op.5. Variations on a Theme of Paganini (Theme and Var. 6). Waltzes Op.39/3, 15 in both solo and duet versions. No distinction between composer's and editor's markings. Int. to M-D.

Selected Works (Levine—Alfred) 95pp. A brief introduction comments on Brahms the composer and his piano writing. Includes: Ballades Op.10/1, Op.118/3;

Intermezzos Op.117/1, 2, Op.118/1, 2, 6, Op.119/3; Rhapsodies Op.79/1, 2, Op.119/4; Waltz Op.39/15; Gavotte in A by C. W. von Glück transcribed by Brahms; Hungarian Dance No.7 in F. Int. to M-D.
See: Edwin Evans, *Handbook to the Pianoforte Works of J. Brahms* (London: Reeves, 1936): 327pp. Reprint: New York: B. Franklin, 1970.
Albion Gruber, "Understanding Rhythm in the [Brahms] Piano Music," *Clavier*, 13 (February 1974):9–13.
Evlyn Howard-Jones, "Brahms in His Pianoforte Music," PRMA, 37 (1910–11).
Denis Matthews, *Brahms Piano Music* (Seattle: University of Washington Press, 1978) 76pp. BBC Music Guides series.
William Murdoch, *Brahms* (London: Rich and Cowan, 1933). Contains an analytical study of the complete piano works.
Garrick Ohlsson, "Cross-Rhythms in the Music of Brahms," *Keyboard*, 8/9 (September 1982):56.

Theo Brandmüller (1948–   ) Germany
Five Details 1975 (Bo&Bo) 8pp. 8 min. Dramatic and violent tonal contrasts require strong percussive technique. D.

Wim Brandse (1933–   ) The Netherlands
Postcards from Holland (GS). A picturesque group of scenes including: An Old Abbey; Fields of Tulips; Windmills; Sailing on a Lake; An Old Church; Market Day. Mixture of Romantic and MC sonorities. Int.

Henry Brant (1913–   ) USA, born Canada
An avowed experimenter, Brant has said, "No two of my works have any surface resemblance in technique and style." His interest in Ives is not reflected in any of the following works.
Four Short Nature Pieces 1942 (MCA). Sand; Stars; Sun; Sky. Colorful, short (one page each), MC. Int.

François Brassard (1908–   ) Canada
Oratoire à la Croisée des Chemins (BMI Canada). From the suite "Orleanaises." Two picturesque lyric pieces in post-Romantic style. M-D.

Yehezkiel Braun (1922–   ) Israel, born Germany
Sonata 1957 (IMI 067) 28pp. 10 min. Allegro con brio: two thematically related subjects are carefully developed. Adagio: ABA. Presto: rondo, closes with a condensed recapitulation of the slow movement theme and a short coda in the form of a chorale. Freely tonal around d-D. M-D.

Robert Bremner (?–1789) USA, born Great Britain
The Harpsichord or Spinnet Miscellany (J. S. Darling—University Press of Virginia) 32pp. Facsimile of original 1765 edition. The title page of this collection of popular eighteenth-century keyboard music describes it as "Be-

ing a Graduation of *Proper* Lessons from the Beginner to the tollerable Performer / Chiefly intended to save Masters the trouble of writing for their pupils. / To which are prefixed some Rules for Time." Includes dances, folksongs, grounds, and compositions by contemporary composers, Corelli among them, and "God Save the King." Contains music "that Jefferson and Washington enjoyed at Monticello and Mount Vernon" (from the preface). Informative preface by the editor. Int. to M-D.

Cesar Bresgen (1913–1988) Austria, born Italy

Holbein-Suite 1946 (Dob 01594 1980) 11pp. Commentary in German and English. Eight pieces inspired by the composer's intensive exposure to *Pictures of Death*, woodcuts by Hans Holbein. Each movement is related to a Holbein woodcut of the same title but the pieces are not musical illustrations and the Suite is not program music; they merely provide the inspiration for composition. An unusual set with metronome markings but no fingering. M-D.

Studies VII Romanesca (Dob 1971) 15pp. Seven varied pieces, neo-Classic orientation. Int.

Pierre de Breville (1861–1949) France

Breville was a pupil of both Dubois and Franck. He composed in a very refined style. All the pieces listed below are interesting and well worth examining.

Fantaisie: Introduction, Fugue et Finale 1888 (Lerolle). Franckian influence. Well planned for the piano. M-D.

Stamboul 1894–95 (Lerolle). Four movements, each depicting a section of Istanbul. An extra movement was added in 1913. M-D.

Sonata d♭ 1923 (Lerolle) 28pp. A fresh and spontaneous-sounding one-movement work displaying fine lyric cantabile writing. M-D.

Frank Bridge (1879–1941) Great Britain

Bridge wrote a large number of works for piano. Most are short and are effectively conceived for the instrument.

Three Sketches (GS). April; Rosemary; Valse Capricieuse. Contrasting romantic moods. M-D.

Capriccio f♯ (Augener). Clever and brilliant writing. Good facility required. M-D.

Gargoyle (Thames 1977). An original, whimsical, and impressive scherzo. Bridge's last piano work. M-D.

Miniature Pastorales Bk.3 (Cramer). Delightful. Int.

Vignettes de Marseilles 1925 (Cramer; Thames). Carmelita; Nicolette; Zoraida; En Fête. An extensive suite with a Mediterranean flavor. M-D.

Three Poems (Augener). Solitude; Ecstasy; Sunset. Impressionistic, varied moods. M-D.

The Hour Glass (Augener; MMP). Dusk: delicate and legato. The Dew Fairy: rapid pianissimo figuration. The Midnight Tide: thick textures. M-D.

In Autumn (Augener). Retrospect: austere chromatic writing. Through the Eaves: short, exploits upper register, twittering figuration in right hand. M-D.

Lament for Catherine 1915 (Thames 1992) 3pp. Lyrical, nostalgic. M-D.

Sonata 1925 (Augener; S&B 1979) 46pp. 30 min. Three movements. Serious, dissonant writing; heroic in scope. Superimposed triads and shifting chromaticism bring Scriabin to mind. One of the most ambitious British piano compositions of its period. Advanced pianism required. D.

See: Peter J. Pirie, "Frank Bridge's Piano Sonata," M&M, 24 (January 1976):28–30, 32.

Todd Brief (1953–   ) USA

Concert Etude (UE). Extremely involved, numerous advanced techniques. D.

Allen Brings (1934–   ) USA

Variations on an American Folk Theme 1954 (Mira). 3 min. An unpretentious work employing a clever rhythmic and melodic theme. Needs well-rounded pianistic equipment. Would make a suitable substitute for the overworked Barber *Excursions*. M-D.

Sonata 1961 (Mira). A large-scale work in four movements. Demanding both technically and musically. Well organized but many thorny passages must be patiently analyzed. M-D to D.

Petite Suite 1956 (Mira 1976) 8pp. 6 min. March; Sarabande; Ragaudon; Musette; Burlesca. 11 levels of dynamics; mildly dissonant; changing meters. M-D.

Five Pieces 1980 (Mira) 29 pp. 14 min. Untitled. Contrasting, fine craftsmanship. M-D.

Benjamin Britten (1913–1976) Great Britain

Britten possessed a remarkable melodic gift. His style was characterized by thin textures that added clarity and zest to his writing.

Holiday Diary 1934 (Bo&H). Suite in four movements. Early Morning Bathe: fast sixteenth-note figuration. Sailing: flexible melody, lively middle section. Fun-Fair: brilliant bravura rondo, sharply accented rhythms, chords, octaves. Night: melody unwinds surrounded by widely spaced tranquil accompaniment. M-D.

Night Piece (Bo&H) 5 min. Composed for the Leeds International Piano Competition, 1963. Lento tranquillo: a Nocturne in B♭, with changing meters, orchestrally conceived. Requires fine control and balance. Middle section is reminiscent of "Night's Music" from Bartók *Out of Doors Suite*.

Walztes [sic] Op.3 1923–25 (Faber 1970). Five tonal, eclectic pieces. Nos.1–4 have contrasting trios. No.5 is a theme with four variations and a coda. Int.

Moderato and *Nocturne* 1940 (Faber 1986) 8pp. Two movements from *Sonatina Romantica*, which Britten refused to release as a complete work. Both movements are colorful and complement each other, MC. Int. to M-D.

Twelve Variations 1931 (Faber 1986) 14pp. Composed during Britten's first year at the Royal College of Music. Twelve-measure Allegretto A theme. Var. I: *più lento*, flowing elaboration of theme. Var. II: L'istesso tempo, quartal harmony, molto legato. Var. III: molto marcato theme, syncopation. Var. IV: Allegro molto, contrary motion figuration. Var. V: *Molto più lento*, pesante octaves, chordal figuration. Var. VI: Andante grazioso, nocturne-like. Var. VII: Allegro, pp, molto legato, no pedal. Var. VIII: flowing legato lines interrupted with staccato sixteenth-note figures. Var. IX: Chordal theme punctuated with broken-chord figuration. Var. X: Andante, four flats, chromatic. Var. XI: Allegro, staccato figuration. Var. XII: A; fughetta, expanded finale. Colorful writing but not vintage Britten. M-D to D.

Three Character Pieces 1930 (Faber 1989) 17pp. John; Daphne; Michael. Suggest influence of Ravel and Scriabin. M-D.

Jane Brockman (1949–   ) USA

Tell-tale Fantasy 1978 (Arsis 1982) 10pp. 4½ min. Precise notation but creates an illusion of improvisation. "It is as though the pianist, intending to play a 'contemporary' composition, becomes sidetracked in wistful thought about masterworks of the early twentieth century. At each digression, a sonority in the music initiates reflection on an earlier work. The first digression begins with a paraphrase of the first few bars of Scriabin's *Prometheus Symphony*. This is juxtaposed with the very similar chords of the sixth movement of Schoenberg's *Six Little Piano Pieces*, Op.19 and the third movement 'Farben' of his *Five Pieces for Orchestra*, Op.16. Other paraphrases include the melody (reharmonized) from the third movement ('The Alcotts') of Ives's *Concord Sonata* and gestures reminiscent of *Dr. Gradus ad Parnassum* of Debussy. In addition to these interruptions, the work does have a clear formal plan based on transformations of two contrasting types of thematic material" (from the score). Expressionistic. D.

Gerard Brophy (1953–   ) Australia

Brophy studied composition with Richard Toop at the Sydney Conservatorium of Music and graduated in 1981. He has won many prizes and fellowships.

Spiked Heels 1992 (Australian Music Center) 5pp. "A Carmen Fantasy." A few bits and pieces of the opera *Carmen* are woven into a fluid chromatic texture; changing dynamics, contrasted touches. M-D to D.

Léo Brouwer (1939–   ) Germany

Sonata "pian e forte" (Ars Viva 1970). One folded loose leaf. About 10 min. Explanations in English, German, and Spanish. In addition to playing the piano, the performer is asked to play in and around the instrument. Calls for taped segments of the Gabrieli original and some improvisation by the performer. Aleatoric, avant-garde. D.

Earle Brown (1926–   ) USA

Brown studied mathematics and engineering at Northwestern University but eventually turned to music. He has been associated with John Cage and David Tudor on *Project for Music and Magnetic Tape*. Brown is very interested in aleatory techniques and the relationship of sound, space, and time.

3 Pieces for Piano (Schott 1951). Serial, two rows in double counterpoint. M-D.

Perspectives for Piano (Schott 1952). Chromatic, free 12-tone writing. M-D.

Folio and Four Systems (AMP 1952–54). Six movements as follows: Oct. 1952; Nov. 1952 (Synergy); Dec. 1952; MM 87; MM 135; Music for Trio for 5 Dancers. Graphic notation, open form. Avante-garde. M-D to D.

Twentyfive Pages for 1 to 25 pianos (UE 15587). Explanations in German and English, 1–25 leaves. "The *Twentyfive Pages* may be played in any sequence; each page may be performed either side up; events within each two-line system may be read as either treble or bass clef; the total time duration of the piece is between eight minutes and 25 minutes, based on 5 seconds and 15 seconds per two-line system as probable but not compulsory time extremities. After the 'Folio' experiments of 1952–3, this is the first extended work using what I call 'time notation' (durations extended in space relative to time, rather than expressed in metric symbols as in traditional notation) and which has since been called proportional notation" (from the score). Aleatoric, clusters, dynamic extremes, ten different attacks, performance directions, avant-garde. D.

See: David Burge, "Two Indeterminate Pieces," CK, 3 (January 1977):46, a discussion of Brown's "Twentyfive Pages" and John Cage's "Etudes Australes."

Merton Brown (1913–   ) USA

Arioso (NME 1949) 7pp. Chromatic, flexible meters, constant moving figuration, expressionistic. Second half to be played "sans nuance." M-D.

Raynor Brown (1912–   ) USA

Sonata Breve (WIM 1974) 10pp. Allegretto: sharply dotted rhythms as in a French Overture. Adagio: chordal, repeated parallel seventh chords. Prelude and Fugue: three voices, mood contrasts, well constructed. M-D.

Rosemary Brown (1917–   ) Great Britain

Brown is an English medium who claims to have communicated with some of the world's great composers "from beyond." The music speaks for itself.

The Rosemary Brown Piano Album (Nov 1973). Seven pieces inspired by Beethoven, Brahms, Chopin, Liszt, Schubert, and Schumann, claims Brown. Opinion is still divided about her claim to have taken down pieces by the composers listed. The compositions look and sound like good imitations of their respective styles but they have yet to be fully explained. An unusual collection. Int. to M-D.

Music from Beyond (Basil Ramsey 1977). Seven more pieces said to be inspired by J. S. Bach (Prelude), Beethoven (Scherzo), Brahms (Intermezzo), Chopin (Prelude), Liszt (Sonata movement), Rachmaninoff (Prelude), Schubert (Moment Musical). Brown is still being "visited" by a host of music's immortals, who, she says, have dictated these pieces to her. Try them and judge for yourself. Int. to M-D.

Le Paon (B. Ramsey 1978) 2pp. The Peacock. Inspired by Debussy 15 Oct. 1967. Int.

Intermezzo A♭ inspired by Brahms on August 18, 1977 (Ramsey) 3pp. ABA, slower mid-section. Musical; has much to recommend it but lacking in rhythmic originality. M-D.

Eight Pieces for Children of All Ages (Ramsey) 22pp. Brown received these pieces in little more than a month toward the end of 1978. They were inspired by Liszt (A Rainy Day); Rachmaninoff (Sleigh Ride); Debussy (Chicklings: the scampering of tiny birds is evident); Beethoven (A Little Carol); Chopin; and others. Int.

Six Mazurkas from Frédéric Chopin as dictated to Rosemary Brown (Ramsey 1981) 12pp. "Chopin offers these little Mazurkas as a sign of his continuing existence in the world beyond death, and continuing ability to compose in his own characteristic style" (from the foreword). Int. to M-D.

Twelve Cameos from Robert Schumann as dictated to Rosemary Brown (Ramsey 1980) 20pp. Foreword by Franz Liszt, dated November 1980. Titles and performance directions in German. Many resemblances to Schumann's pianistic writing, including octaves and large chords. Pedaling but not fingering given. Int. to M-D.

Woodland Waters (Ramsey) 14pp. Inspired by Liszt on July 7, 1977. Numerous Romantic clichés but not much Liszt in this listless work. Some phrases have unusual shape and direction. M-D.

See: Rosemary Brown, *Unfinished Symphonies* (London: Souvenir Press, 1971).

Ian Parrott, *The Music of Rosemary Brown* (London: Regency Press, 1978).

Basil Ramsey, "Music from Beyond," KC, 9/4 (July–August 1989):12–14. Includes Mazurka f♯ by Chopin, dictated to Rosemary Brown!

David Brubeck (1920–   ) USA
Brubeck was one of the first jazz musicians to use classical music concepts, as well as twentieth-century idioms, in his music. He studied with Darius Milhaud at Mills College.

Reminiscences of the Cattle Country 1946 (AMP 1980) 18pp. Sun Up; Breaking a Wild Horse; The Fairgrounds; Look at My Pony; The Chicken and the Ducklings; Dad Plays the Harmonica. Brubeck was raised on a cattle ranch in northern California. In 1946 he was studying with Darius Milhaud at Mills College, and that influence is reflected in these pieces. M-D.

Dave's Diary (WB 1995) 56pp. A collection of pieces inspired by events in Brubeck's life from 1942 to 1994. Int. to M-D.

Glances (WB 1995) 26pp. Overture; Blue Aria; Struttin'; Doing the Charleston. Four-movement suite. "When performed as a ballet, the tempos must remain strict. If performed as a piano solo, more freedom of expression and tempo can be given to the 'Blue Aria' movement" (from the score). M-D.

They All Sang Yankee Doodle 1976. In collection *American Contemporary Masters* (GS 1995) 22 pp. Fantasy-like, sectional, contrasting textures, glissandi, imitation between hands, jig rhythms, chime-like sonorities, bitonal writing. Large span required; cluster chords. Dedicated to Charles Ives. D.

The Genius of Dave Brubeck. Book 1 (WB 1984) 78pp. Fourteen pieces by Bru-

beck plus his transcription of Paul Desmond's "Take Five." Large span required. M-D.

Book 2 (WB 1984) 76 pp. Twelve pieces. M-D.

At the Piano With Dave Brubeck (CPP/Belwin 1993) 63pp. Eighteen pieces composed from the 1950s to the present. Brubeck includes a brief description
of his inspiration for each piece. Listed as intermediate level, but some of
the complicated rhythms are more like M-D. An outstanding late intermediate student might be able to handle them. Clever, sophisticated settings.

Quiet as the Moon 1988 (CPP/Belwin 1992) 32pp. Eleven pieces matching the
album of the same title; the sound track for the *Peanuts* cartoon series.
Catchy rhythms. Int.

Time Out 1960 (CPP/Belwin 1992) 48pp. Eight pieces that blend the formalism
of Western classical music, the freedom of jazz improvisation, and the complex pulse of African folk music. M-D.

Time Further Out 1961–62 (CPP/Belwin 1992) 48pp. Eight pieces based on the
12-bar blues. M-D.

Chromatic Fantasy Sonata (Derry Music Co. 1993) 35pp. Inspired by J. S. Bach.
Opens with a few measures of Bach; contains quotes from Bach's *Chromatic Fantasy* as well as the German musical notation of his name. D.

See: Rosemary Hallum, "The Best of Times for Dave Brubeck," *Clavier*, 35/4
(April 1996):8–12.

Danny R. Zirpoli, "An Evaluation of the Work of Jazz Pianist/Composer Dave
Brubeck," diss., University of Florida, 1990.

Robert Bruce (1962–   ) Canada

Bruce was born in Hamilton, Ontario. He has played in bands and ensembles
and has worked as a pianist, church organist, and choir director. Most of his
piano music is for younger students.

Miniatures (Black Cat Productions 1990, 1992, 1995). Three books of six short
pieces each. They range from Int. in Book I to M-D in Book IV. The style
is fresh and MC, and each piece explores different textures and colors and
one or two specific musical elements. Bruce suggests making each piece
musical, magical, and effective. "Imagination will get you everywhere"
(from the score).

Max Bruch (1838–1920) Germany

Bruch worked in Classic forms using a Romantic harmonic language, but he also
favored folk material.

Six Piano Pieces Op.12 1861 (Br&H 1980). 1. B♭; 2. g; 3. Impromptu; 4. d; 5. Walzer
F♭; 6. E. Tuneful and folklike with full chords. Naive in their workmanship
and harmonic content but beautifully written for the piano. M-D.

Swedish Dances Op.63 (MMP). Tunes are folklike; clever rhythms. M-D.

Bruckner, Anton (1824–1896) Austria

Works for Piano Solo (W. Litschauer—Musikwissenschaftlicher Verlag 1988)
39pp. Lancier-Quadrille, ca. 1850. Steiermärker, ca. 1850. Klavierstück in

E♭, ca. 1856. Stille Betrachtung an einem Herbstabend (Quiet Contemplation on an Autumn Evening), 1863. Erinnerung (Memory), ca. 1868: the best piece in the collection; elegant, melodic grandeur. Available separately from (Dob). Sonata g (one movement) (1862). Bruckner's path as a symphonist can be forecast in some of these miniatures. Int. to M-D.

Mark Brunswick (1902–1971) USA
Six Bagatelles (LG 1958) in collection *New Music for the Piano*. Brief, attractive. Astringent contemporary style. M-D.

Joanna Bruzdowicz (1943–   ) Poland
Erotiques (Sal 1966) 8pp. 7½ min. Five short colorful sketches. Clusters are used in the second piece. M-D.

Albertus Bryne (ca.1621–ca.1670) Great Britain
Musicks Handmaide (T. Dart—S&B 1969). Contains Bryne's only published keyboard music, five short pieces (in 1678 edition): Ayre, Corante, Sarabande, Ayre, Allemande, all in a. Bryne wrote several unpublished suites which have been overlooked until now. Three four-movement suites (almand, corant, sarabande, and "Jigg Allmaine") in Bodleian MS Mus. Sch. d.219 are among the finest English examples of their time. Of Bryne's English contemporaries only Matthew Locke has more surviving keyboard pieces. Bryne influenced many younger composers, particularly John Blow, and a suite ascribed to Blow in Brit. Mus. Add.31465, ff.36v-39, was actually written by Bryne.
See: Barry Cooper, "Albertus Bryne's Keyboard Music," MT, 113, No.1548 (February 1972):142–43.

Walter Buczynski (1933–   ) Canada
Eight Epigrams for Young Pianists (Bo&H 1969) 10pp. Cheerful and forward-looking studies to help develop cantabile playing. MC harmony and compositional techniques. Analytical and performance directions. Int.

Carolyn Bull (–   ) USA
Music for Haiku (CF 1971) 16pp. Inspired by Japanese poetry and music. Six musical postcards with a poem based on the Japanese verse form of *haiku*. Modal, MC. Int.
From Here to There (CF 1972) 23pp. Ten pieces, each stressing a specific interval. Clever, attractive. Int.

John Bull (1562–1628) Great Britain
Immense finger dexterity is required for some of this master's works.
Keyboard Music, Musica Britannica Vol.XIV (J. Steele, F. Cameron) and XIX (T. Dart—S&B 1963). Vol.XIV contains 61 works, and Vol.XIX contains 82 works. As Thurston Dart says in the preface, "the music itself is extrava-

gant and artificial, in the best sense of those words." These two volumes reveal Bull as a versatile composer, gentle as well as flamboyant. Some remarkable music here. M-D to D.

Ten Pieces (Steele, Cameron—S&B). Reprint from *Musica Britannica* with a short discussion of the music by T. Dart, including critical commentary and calendar of Bull's life. M-D.

Selected Works of John Bull (M. H. Glyn—S&B) 60 works in the following arrangement: Vol.I: Dances and Fancy Pieces. Vol.II: Folksong Variations. Vol.III: Pavans and Galliards. Vol.IV: Plainsong and other Fantasies. M-D.

Harpsichord Pieces from Dr. John Bull's Flemish Tabulatura (H. F. Redlich—NV 1958). Pavane; Gagliarda; Courante Alarme; Corante The Princess; and Het Jewel. These pieces date from Bull's stay at Antwerp and are contained in a Tabulatura of 1629. In this Tabulatura a clear distinction is made between organ style and harpsichord style. These pieces are definitely written for the harpsichord. M-D to D.

The King's Hunt FVB, II, 116. Vivid sounds of a hunt are reproduced by trills, syncopations, and repeated notes. Excellent program music, brilliant figuration. M-D.

In Nomine FVB, II, 34. An "In Nomine" is a fantasy built on prolonged notes of a plainsong melody. The plainsong serves as a skeleton around which the melody and harmony revolve. This remarkable piece has 11 quarter notes to the bar and produces an asymmetrical effect. Suspensions are plentiful. M-D.

Parthenia (K. Stone-BB 1951) (T. Dart-S&B 1960) contains 7 pieces by Bull. M-D.

Popular Pieces (Augener; K). Pavans and Gagliards, Preludium, The King's Hunting Jigg, Les Bouffons, Courante Jewel. Practical edition. M-D.

Dr. Bull's My Self FVB, II, 116. Short, dotted rhythms. Int. to M-D.

Twelve Pieces (T. Dart—S&B 1977) selected by John Steele from Volume XIX of *Musica Britannica*. A fine choice of works including: Chromatic Pavan; Prince's Galliard; Revenant; My Jewell; Bull's Goodnight. M-D.

Walsingham FVB, I, 1. Set of 30 variations on old tune "As I went to Walsingham." Amazing piece. Sums up idiomatic keyboard advances made by English virginalists. D.

See: G. W. Whittaker, "Byrd and Bull's Walsingham Variations," 3 MR (1942).

See: Wilfrid Mellers, "John Bull and English Keyboard Music," MQ, 40 (1954):364–83, 548–71.

Alan Bullard (1947–   ) Great Britain

Air and Gigue (OUP 1974) 6pp. 3½ min. For clavichord or piano. Air: melodic, cantabile, freely tonal around G. Gigue: driving rhythms, broken seventh chords. Int.

Hans Von Bülow (1830–1894) Germany

Marche Heroique Op.3 (Musica Obscura) 7pp. Octotonic intervals of broken ninths, bombastic, martellato. Concludes with a section marked "quasi tamburo roulante," which uses fast, repeated chords in alternating hands. M-D to D.

See: Walter Schenkman, "Hans von Bülow in America," *Clavier*, 29/10 (December 1990):14–19, 48.

Arne Steinberg, "Hans von Bülow," PQ, 151 (Fall 1990):40, 42–47.

Richard Zimdars, *The Piano Master Classes of Hans von Bülow* (Bloomington: Indiana University Press, 1993).

Richard Bunger (1942–   ) USA

Bunger is an outstanding pianist. He has given many premiere performances of contemporary and *avant-garde* piano works.

Hommage for Pianoforte 1967 (CF 1982) 7pp. For prepared piano. 1. J. C. (John Cage): directions are given to prepare the piano with bamboo slit and penny, etc.; contains some fascinating sonorities. 2. A. S. (Arnold Schönberg): serial writing; pointillistic technique. 3. V. H. (Vladimir Horowitz): indicated "Faster than possible"! Two bars long, requires about four seconds; double glissandi up and down in white and black keys. 4. C. I. (Charles Ives): reharmonized version of "America." 5. S. R. (Sergei Rachmaninoff): pianistically in the Rachmaninoff tradition but definitely more contemporary both melodically and harmonically. Short pieces. Designed for an advanced high school student as an initial exploration of twentieth-century idioms. M-D to D.

Pianography (Fantasy on a theme by Fibonacci) (Broude). "Utilizes contact mike, tape loop, a chord-playing bar, soft mallets, hand-damped notes, several preparations and, as an option, a ring modulator. The central section makes deliberate references to past piano literature within a clearly sectionalized progression of aurally-diverse fantasy scenes" (letter from composer, June 1, 1971). M-D to D.

Two Pieces for Prepared Piano (Highgate 1977) 2pp. Preparations for both pieces include: plastic credit card, felt strip, clothespin wedges, screws, rubber erasers, dimes, bamboo wedge, vinyl tubing. I. Aria, 2½ min.: cantando; motivic figures sound over more-sustained sonorities in left hand; long pedals; subtle; sensitive. II. Rondo for CK, 4 min. (published in *Contemporary Keyboard*, August 1977); ritmico; short, two–three-bar ideas frequently repeated; repeat to sign; flexible meters; thin textures; piece gradually fades away while repeating final three bars seven or more times. M-D.

Three Bolts Out of the Blue (Highgate 1977) 4pp. For prepared piano. Preparations are the same as listed above for *Two Pieces*. I. Eleven Bolt Bebop, 1 min.: syncopated, legato left-hand chords. II. One Bolt Blues, 2 min.: long pedals, quick chromatic arpeggi figures, slow closing. III. Stovebolt Boogie, 1½ min.: perpetual-motion boogie figures with each measure repeated the number of times indicated, tremolo closing in upper range of keyboard. M-D.

Money Music (Music of Change) 1978 (CF 1982) 12pp. For prepared piano. Uses coins as well as paper money woven onto and into the strings. Oligopoly:

mechanically, like clockwork. Uncommon Cents. Small Changes. Widgets. Clever. M-D.
See: Richard Bunger, "Prepared Piano—Its History, Development, and Practice," Part I, CK 3 (July 1977):26–28. Part II, CK, 3 (August 1977):14–16.

David Burge (1930–   ) USA
Eclipse II (CPE 1967). New notation, pointillistic, dynamic extremes exploited, expressionistic, serial, initially exposed set transformed, avant-garde. D.

Friedrich Burgmüller (1806–1874) Germany
Burgmüller wrote mainly light salon music, but some of his studies, especially Opp.100 and 105, are useful.
25 Progressive Pieces (Alfred). All are interesting. Int.
25 Easy and Progressive Studies Op.100 (Alfred; UE; VU; GS; ABRSM). Worth investigating. Int.
12 Brilliant and Melodious Studies Op.105 (Hinson—Alfred 4828; GS). See especially Nos.6 and 9. M-D.
12 Character Studies Op.109 (Hinson—Alfred 4829; GS). *18 Character Studies* Op.109 (CFP). Two-page pieces; try "Thunder-Storm" for dramatic sonorities. A fine collection. The Alfred edition includes fingerings and pedaling. Int. to M-D.
See: Jane McGrath, "Teaching Burgmüller's Progressive Etudes," *Clavier*, 34/4 (April 1995):12–18.
Rondo alla Turca Op.68/3 (GS). Colorful rhythms. Int.

Norbert Burgmüller (1810–1836) Germany
Younger brother of Friedrich Burgmüller. Robert Schumann valued Norbert greatly; he begins a memorial notice of him by saying that Burgmüller's death was the most deplorable that had happened since Schubert's early death (*Gesammelte Schriften*, Vol.III, p.145).
Rhapsodie b 1836 (UMKR No.26 1975) 7pp. An agitato section marked by an accented melody in the inner voices is contrasted with a Poco adagio, flowing, arpeggiated B section. Strong Romantic writing, colorful atmospheric closing. Would make a fine substitute for the Brahms *Rhapsodie* in g, Op.79/2. M-D.
See: Eric F. Jensen, "Norbert Burgmüller and Robert Schumann," MQ, 74/4 (1990):550–565.

Willi Burkhard (1900–1955) Switzerland
These works are Reger- and Hindemith-oriented and tonally dissonant. They display a mastery of traditional techniques.
Variationen über ein Volkslied Op.8 (Br 1971) 12pp. Ten variations follow a simple theme. M-D.
Drei Präludien und Fugen Op.16 (Br 1971) 24pp.

Variationen über ein Menuett von Joseph Haydn Op.29 1930 (Br 1971) 12pp.

Sonate Op.66 (UE 1945) 14 min. FSF. All three movements oriented toward Hindemith. Large span required in the second movement. M-D.

Christmas Sonatina Op.71/1 (Br 1947). 6pp. FSF. Based on well-camouflaged carols. Not easy. Int. to M-D.

Acht leichte Klavierstücke (Br 1948). Short character pieces. Int. to M-D.

6 Preludes Op.99 (Br 1956). Short, varied, idiomatic. Int. to M-D.

Was die Hirten Alles erlebten (Br). Six Christmas carols simply arranged in a little "notebook" format. Int.

Kleine Toccata (Hug 1976) 2pp. A flicker of almost unbroken sixteenth notes; no key signature but obviously in E. Int. to M-D.

Warren Burt (1949–   ) USA

Aardvarks II: Mr. Natural Encounters Flakey Foont! (Lingua Press 1977) 10pp. 5 min. In memoriam Carl Ruggles. Dissonant but colorful. M-D.

Edward Bury (1919–   ) Poland

Variations and Fugue Op.35 (PWM). Theme, 14 variations, and fugue. Highly chromatic, canonic, dramatic in style. Karol Szymanowski seems to have been the inspiration for this work. Great contrast in individual variations. Lengthy, D.

Alan Bush (1900–1995) Great Britain

Bush taught composition at the Royal Academy of Music in London.

Suite Op.54 (CFP) for harpsichord or piano. Neoclassic. M-D.

Variations, Nocturne, and Finale Op.60 (Nov). Diatonic, fine rhythmic vocabulary. Ornate decoration permeates all movements. Theme of all three movements is "Blow, ye winds." M-D.

Geoffrey Bush (1920–1998) Great Britain

Sonatina II 1969 (Elkin 1974) 15pp. 7½ min. Reproduction of composer's MS; no fingering or pedaling indicated. Designed as an introduction to contemporary techniques. Neoclassic, contrapuntal. The three movements are based on a nine-note series. D.

Toccata (Galaxy). Presto, alla giga. Good-humored, moves over keyboard, propulsive rhythm. MC. Sounds more difficult than it is. Int. to M-D.

Ferruccio Busoni (1866–1924) Germany, born Italy

One of the greatest and most creative pianists of all times, Busoni was constantly torn between composing and performing. Born in Italy but educated in Germany, he was always pulled between these two traditions. Belonging to neither, in many ways he belonged to both. A new evaluation of his work is taking place, and it is the belief of this writer that Busoni will fare much better in the future than he did during the second third of this century. For a complete listing of Busoni's works see: E. J. Dent, *Ferruccio Busoni, A Biography* (London: Oxford

University Press, 1933; reprint, 1966, 384pp.; reprint, London: Ernst Eulenburg Ltd., 1974).

Macchiette Medioevali Op.33 1882–83 (Br&H 8129 1982) 19pp. Dama (Lady): courtly, gallant piece which favors five-beat metric groupings. Cavaliere (Knight): dancelike; middle section, in major mode, should be played more forcefully; monophonic transition emphasizes the tritone. Guerriero (Warrior): march; begins playfully but becomes menacing through a steady crescendo to the end. Astrologo (Astrologist): mysterious, brooding, chromatic, and imitative; J. S. Bach influence unmistakable. Trovatore (Troubadour): Busoni wrote: "I imagine the troubadour standing in front of the lady, the knight and the page with a lute in his hand; or improvising in a 'court of love.' To introduce his improvisation, he strikes several vigorous chords, forte, and softly modulates to A♭, thereby anticipating the rhythm that will form the accompaniment of his song. One could say that he is singing the praise of an intense and spiritual love. His song reaches a peak of proud and knightly excitement at the *ff sost. e marcato*. . . . I want you to note that the introduction in F (which also serves as the coda) is the harmonic structure of an authentic troubadour song of the thirteenth century." Busoni probably became familiar with the medieval figures in his youth thanks to the strolling players who sang and enacted tales of chivalry and brought to life the figures of the commedia dell'arte. It is not surprising that the young composer sought to depict these figures in music. M-D.

Sonata f Op.20a 1883 (Br&H) 61pp. Allegro risoluto: in the style of early Brahms, sparse notation, considerable use of unison writing. Andante con moto: 3/2, expansive mood continued from first movement, left-hand extended arpeggio accompaniments, chordal passages in climaxes. Finale: after an initial improvisatory introduction, leads into an Allegro fugato in two-part writing with a quasi-cadenza episode at the end and a presto coda. An interesting example of the seminal ideas of the budding Busoni. D.

Zweite Ballettszene Op.20 1884 (Br&H 1997). Reprint. Virtuosic.

Sonatina No.1 1910 (Zimmermann). Contains ideas borrowed from an earlier composition. *An die Jugend* (To Youth), published in 1909. There are four principal sections in the piece, beginning at bars 1, 100, 230, and 274. Variation technique is used as opposed to development. Schönberg influence, a true precursor of serial technique. This Sonatina is perhaps the easiest of the six. M-D.

Sonatina No.2 1912 (Br&H; MMP). Two movements. Ten different melodic and harmonic ideas are presented as subjects for variation, combination, and recombination in ever-changing accompanimental context. Demanding, most radical of the sonatinas. Proselike free metric background with barlines occurring mainly as guides to phrase articulations. Atonal, remarkable formal concentration, unusual harmonic progressions, unrelieved tension. M-D to D.

Sonatina No.3 ('ad usum infantis') 1916 (Br&H). M-D.

Sonatina No.4 (In diem Nativitatis Christi MCMXVII) 1917 (Br&H; Ric). This

"Christmas Sonatina" has four sections and is a classic study in organic unity. It is also a fine example of Busoni's blending the old (Classical forms of music) and the new (expanded tonality, new harmony and counterpoint, new or revived rhythmic complexities) as a means of achieving his new classicism. ABCA' design in a one-movement form. M-D.

Sonatina No.5 (after J. S. Bach) 1919 (Br&H; Ric). A free transcription of Bach's "little" *Fantasia and Fugue d*, S.905. M-D.

Sonatina No.6 1920 (Br&H). Fantasy on themes from Bizet's *Carmen*. In the tradition of the Liszt fantasies but subtler than Horowitz's treatment of some of the same themes. Ends quietly. M-D to D.

The term *sonatina* did not mean "small sonata" to Busoni. He used it to denote a piece to be played on the piano, that is, a piece to be sounded rather than sung, *sonata* as opposed to *cantata*. All six sonatinas embody the principles outlined in Busoni's *New Aesthetic*. All are characterized by great economy and restraint, clear textures, emphasis on contrapuntal construction with many explicitly fugal passages. The harmonic inventiveness, involving unusual modal combinations, is especially striking, as are the fascinating rhythmic experiments with combinations of conflicting beat subdivisions.

See: Larry Sitsky, "The Six Sonatinas for Piano of Ferruccio Busoni," *Studies in Music*, 2 (1968):66–85.

Suite Campestre 1878 (Br&H 8127 1981) 17pp. Preface in German and English. Published here for the first time. Song of a Fresh Summer Morning–Allegro Vivace: much use of C tonic drone. The Hunt. Village Bustle: many left-hand broken octaves. The Return. Evening Prayer: low opening in c. Subtle character pieces depicting aspects of country life. They already display stylistic elements that appeared in Busoni's later works. Int. to M-D.

Twenty-Four Preludes Op.37 1879–81 (Tagliapietra—Ric) 2 vols. Covers many aspects of piano technique. See especially the preludes in c♯ and A. Strong Bach influence. M-D.

Trois Morceaux 1877 (Dob). Scherzo Op.4: lively, compound quadruple time. Prelude and Fugue Op.5: easy Prelude C, more difficult Fugue. Scène de Ballet Op.6: needs strong left-hand octaves; full chords in right hand. Polished writing. M-D.

Fantasia and Fugue on "Ad nos ad salutarem undam" 1897 (Br&H). This transcription of Liszt's arrangement for two players on the organ or pedal-piano is an awe-inspiring example of the Romantic imagination in full flower. Eminently pianistic. D.

Variations on the Chopin Prelude c (Op.28/20) Op.22 1884 (Br&H) 8½ min. One of Busoni's most ingenious works. Opens with the Prelude as Chopin wrote it, but from then on we have a catalogue of Busonian pianistic and contrapuntal complexities. D.

Seven Elegies 1907 (Br&H; MMP). Nach der Wendung–Recueillement. All' Italia–In modo napolitano. Meine Selle bangt und hofft zu dir–Choralvorspiel. Turandots Fraugengemach—Intermezzo: a fantasy on "Greensleeves," one of the most appealing. Die Nächtlichen-Walzer: a virtual *danse macabre*. Erscheinung—Notturno. Berceuse: published separately and later added to the *Elegies*. Intellectually stimulating and musical writing; written in a rather free concept of harmony for its time, but does not contain much dissonance. With the exception of the first piece, each of the *Elegies* is either a piano arrangement of material borrowed from earlier works in other media or a study providing material for a later reworking. Each piece represents a study in expanded tonality wherein tonal centers are only suggested rather than clearly established, as in traditional practice. M-D.

Fantasia nach J. S. Bach alla Memoria di mio Padre Ferdinando Busoni 1909 (Br&H) 15pp. Written in honor of Busoni's father, who died in 1909. Tranquil, serious opening leads to sonorous chordal section based on a Bach chorale. Figurative treatment of single voice chorale follows and leads to section based on "In Dulci Jubilo," Mancando conclusion. Holds together well in spite of sectionalization. M-D.

Nuit de Noël 1909 (Durand). Impressionistic. M-D.

Sech kurze Stücke zur Pflege des polyphonen Spiels 1922 (Br&H) 14 min. These six short pieces for the development of polyphonic playing are based on nineteenth-century virtuoso concepts. D.

Die Nächtlichen (MS reproduced in Brazilian periodical *Musica Viva*, April 1936) 6pp. A chromatic, melodic, character piece. M-D.

Fantasia contrapuntistica 1910 (Br&H). One of Busoni's major works, scholarly, and baroque-inspired. Several musical forms are combined that require virtuosity and concentration of a high degree. There are four versions. First version: contains an appendix showing an earlier sketch of part of the fourth fugue (p.37). Second version: described as a definitive edition; earlier sketch of part of the fourth fugue appears in the main text, and an introduction which is essentially the *Third Elegy* prefaces this version. Third version: simplified version, published as a chorale prelude and fugue on a Bach fragment. Fourth version is arranged for two pianos. This work represents a summing up of Busoni's interest in Bach. D.

Indianisches Tagebuch Op.47 1915 (Br&H). This "Indian Diary" consists of four short works based on American Indian themes. Rather complex improvisations with the melodic line supported with free harmonizations. M-D. See: Joseph Smith, "Indian Diary No. 3," KC, 13/3 (May–June 1993):49–52. Includes music of No. 3 plus the folk tune (Blue Bird Song) No. 3 is based on.

Toccata (Preludio, Fantasia, Ciaconna) 1920 (Br&H). Preludio: a three-page opening virtuoso fantasy based on "The Ballad of Lippold the Jew-Coiner" from Busoni's musical-fantastical comedy; glittering figuration, restless primary motive, unstable tonality in search of a tonality, rhapsodic; previews melodic and rhythmic motives that appear in other two movements. Fantasia: most complex movement; divided into seven sections, ABCDCBA, thematic transformation; irregular phrase construction, cross-rhythms. Ciaconna: 17 variations, monolithic construction, orchestral pianism; perpetual motion is not motoristic but creates momentum through the driving quest for tonality. Three interconnected movements, all subsumed under the overall title of *Toccata,* recall Baroque practice. Projecting the varying textures is the pianist's essential task. D.

Prélude et Etude en Arpèges 1923 (Heugel). Busoni's last piano work. Written for Isidore Phillip's *School of Arpeggio Playing.* A complex study in whirlwind arpeggios. M-D.

Piano Pieces Op.33b (CFP; MMP). Set of six piano pieces. D.

Five Character Pieces Op. posth. (Br&H). Composed when Busoni was twelve years old. The Hunt; Song of a Fresh Summer Morning; Village Bustle; The Return; Evening Prayer. Fine writing for a young boy. Int.

Canto e Valse 1922 (Ronald Stevenson—Bardic Edition 1990) 3½ min. This "song and waltz" is based on Chopin's "Prelude in C Minor," Op.28/20. Originally included in Busoni's *Variationen über ein Präludium von Chopin* (1922), a revision of his Op.22, but the Canto was omitted in the published version; the Valse was included but is presented in this edition in a different version. "The Canto and Valse are musically connected and in the composer's ms do not contain a title" (from the score). Appendixes include studies and exercises pertaining to the Valse by the editor, the composer, and others. D.

Three Piano Studies and Preludes 1917–18 (Klavierübung, Part 2) (MMP). Composed in the style of earlier composers: Beethoven, Gounod, Liszt, Schubert, and others. Reprint from original publication. M-D.

The Complete Elegies, The Six Sonatinas and Other Original Works for Solo Piano (Dover 1997). Also includes Fantasia Contrapuntistica. M-D to D.

Piano Works (USSR 1969) 112pp. Contains Six Etudes Op.16; Op.33b (four pieces); All' Italia (in modo napoletano); Turandots Frauengemach (Intermezzo); Giga, Bolero and Variation (study after Mozart); Paganiniana. D.

The New Busoni (F. P. Goebels—Br&H). A selection from the five-volume *Klavierübungen* (1918–21) expanded to ten volumes in 1925. Part I: scales, changing fingers, arpeggios, etc. Part II: exercises and studies in the style of Bach, Mozart, Beethoven, Chopin, and Cramer. Goebels quotes several of Busoni's still-valid remarks on technique.

See: Virginia A. Englund, "Musical Idealism in Ferruccio Busoni's 'Klavierübung'," diss., University of Alabama, 1991.

See: Ferruccio Busoni, *The Essence of Music and Other Papers* (London: Rockliff, 1957; Reprint, New York: Dover, 1965).

PQ, 108 (Winter 1979–80), special issue devoted to Busoni. Includes the following articles: "Guido Agosti—Busoni Pupil," interviewed by Daniel M. Raessler. Peter Armstrong, "Why Play and Teach Busoni?" Antony Beaumont, "Busoni and Schoenberg." Dolores M. Hsu, "The Paradox of Busoni." Gunnar Johansen, "Busoni the Pianist—In Perspective." Daniel M. Raessler, "Ferruccio Busoni as Experimental Keyboard Composer."

Antony Beaumont, *Busoni the Composer* (Bloomington: Indiana University Press, 1985).

Runolfur Thordarson, "Ferruccio Busoni and His Records," JALS, 34 (July–December 1993): 51–60.

Sylvano Bussotti (1931–   ) Italy
Bussotti makes radical use of the resources of the piano.
5 Pieces for David Tudor 1959 (UE). The score is a maze of marks! Aleatory technique is used for the pianist to realize his impressions of three abstract paintings. One piece is to be played with the fingertips on the surface of the keys without depressing them. Strings are to be grabbed inside, the lid slammed, the piano case struck, and gloves are requested for one particularly violent portion. The pianist is asked to be a co-composer. One of John Cage's comments is pertinent here: "The composer resembles a camera who allows someone else to take the picture." D.
Musica per amici 1957, revised 1971 (Ric). Highly fragmented bits and pieces, variable meters, dynamic extremes, fists used on keys, avant-garde. D.
Foglio d'album 1970 (Ric). One folded loose leaf. M-D.
Novelleta 1973 (Ric). Pianist plays up and down the keyboard, on the cover of the keyboard, on his leg, on his arm, etc. All the clichés of contemporary piano writing, entertaining. M-D.

Martin Butler (1960–   ) Great Britain
On the Rocks 1992 (OUP 1995) 7pp. 10 min. Inspired by "a. cocktail lounge piano styles, b. the thought of Debussy writing part of *La Mer* in Eastbourne, c. the sound of Debussy playing on a phonograph . . . serve stirred, not shaken" (from the score). Clever, witty, and difficult. Requires sensitive pedaling and touch. Facsimile of ms. D.

Nigel Butterley (1935–   ) Australia
Letter from Hardy's Bay (J. Albert 224 1970) 8pp. 11½ min. Strings of four notes are to be prepared with eight metal bolts. Preparation directions included. Stemless notes indicate irregular rhythms. Clusters; harmonics; pointillistic; recurring gong-like chord halts the flow of the piece every time it appears; player stands to finish this highly abstract piece. Avant-garde. D.
Arioso (J. Albert 1960) 2pp. Freely dissonant moving lines. Int.

Dietrich Buxtehude (1637–1707) Germany, born Denmark
Although known primarily as a composer for organ, Buxtehude did leave twenty-one suites for clavier and a few sets of variations. Most of the pieces are M-D.
Keyboard Works (Bangert—WH; K). Contains 19 suites, 6 sets of variations, and 3 anonymous pieces. Suites 1–5 C, 6–8 d, 9 D, 10–12 e, 13 F, 14–16 g, 17 G, 18 a, 19 A. The suites are short and normally in the order A, C, S, G.
Suite on the Choral "Auf meinen lieben Gott" (Herrmann—Hug). Also contained in Georgii *400 Years of European Keyboard Music*. Contains an A with Double, S, C, and G. Each movement is actually a variation on the chorale.
Sämtliche Suiten und Variationen (K. Beckmann—Br&H 8077 1980). Complete

suites; five arias with variations to each; a courante; a further fragment of a suite; and Symphonie. In this performing edition the editor attempts to reconstruct the original form of the fragment. Notes on the edition, sources, critical text, and ornamentation details in German. M-D.

Collected Piano Works Vol. I (Bangert—MMP).

Collected Piano Works Vol. II (Bangert—MMP).

Collected Piano Works Vol. III (Bangert—MMP). Variations and anonymous works.

William Byrd (1543–1623) Great Britain

Byrd, the greatest of the virginal composers, tried his hand at all kinds of composition and was remarkably successful. Simple dance tunes and complex contrapuntal pieces point up the extremes in his compositional style. This "Father of Musicke" had more influence than any other composer on the development of English music.

The Collected Works of William Byrd (E. H. Fellowes—S&B 1937–1950) Vols.18–20, *Keyboard orks* (1950). Vol.18: Preludes, Fancies, Voluntaries, Dance Measures, Almans, Corantos, Jigs, Lavoltas, and The Battell, a suite of fourteen pieces. Vol.19: 40 Pavans and Galliards. Vol.20: contains Airs and Variations, Grounds, Fantasies on Plainsong, 2 adaptations. Int. to M-D.

Keyboard Music I, Musica Britannica Vol.XXVII (A. Brown—S&B 1969). Vol.XXVIII (1971) *Keyboard Music II*. The most trustworthy text. Takes into account all the known sources. Complete in 2 vols. Int. to M-D.

15 Pieces (T. Dart—S&B 1956). Newly transcribed and selected from the FVB and *Parthenia*. M-D.

45 Pieces for Keyboard Instruments (S. D. Tuttle—1'OL). Scholarly edition. M-D.

Parthenia (K. Stone—BB 1951; T. Dart—S&B 1960). Eight pieces. M-D.

14 Pieces for Keyed Instruments (Fuller—Maitland, B. Squire—S&B). M-D.

My Ladye Nevells Booke (H. Andrews—J. Curwen; BB; Dover). A scholarly edition of 42 pieces dating from 1591. Critical commentary, notes, sources. Beautiful example of what a scholarly performing edition should be. M-D.

9 Pieces from *"My Ladye Nevells Booke"* (A. Brown—S&B). Suggested directions. Int. to M-D.

See: E. H. Fellowes, "My Ladye Nevells Book" ML, 30 (1949): 1–7.

Dances Grave and Gay (M. H. Glyn—Winthrop Rogers Edition). Contains Pavans and Gagliardas, The Earle of Salisbury, Gigg, La Volta, Coranto C, Martin Said to His Man, The Queen's Almand, Medley, Irish Marche, La Volta (Morley). Suggested dynamics and phrasings; not fingered. M-D.

Popular Pieces (Augener; K). Preludes, Pavans, Gagliardas, Sellenger's Round, The Carman's Whistle. Practical edition. Int. to M-D.

The Bells. FVB, I, 274. Picturesque variations employing a ground-bass. M-D.

Walsingham Variations, My Ladye Nevells Booke, 173; FVB, I, 267. Based on the tune "Have With Yow to Walsingame." M-D.

See: Gilles W. Whittaker, "Byrd's and Bull's 'Walsingham Variations'," MR, 3 (1942):270–79.

6 Sets of Variations (A. Brown—S&B) from vols.27 and 28 of *Musica Britannica*. Contains notes on history and performance. M-D.

3 Anonymous Keyboard Pieces attributed to William Byrd (O. Neighbour—Nov 1973). Prelude G: from Will Forster's Virginal Book. Prelude F. Alman C: especially attractive. Int.

The Carman's Whistle (FVB, I, 214; Augener; other reprints). Eight variations on a popular song. Followed by a conclusion in which a new subject is treated. M-D.

Victoria; *The Carman's Whistle*; *Pavana: Mr. W. Petre*; in Vol.II of *Le Trésor des Pianistes* (Farrenc—Leduc).

See: Hilda Andrews, "Elizabethan Keyboard Music," MQ, 16 (1930):59–71.

C

Roberto Caamaño (1923–1993) Argentina

Caamaño teaches courses in instrumentation, orchestration, and advanced piano at the National Conservatory in Buenos Aires.

6 Preludes Op.6 (Barry & Cia 1948) 12 min. Vol.1:I–IV; Vol.2:V,VI. MC. Require large span and facility. M-D.

Variaciones Gregorianas para Piano Op.15 (Ric 1953). Theme and six variations. Last variation leads to a Toccata with much rhythmic emphasis. Effective close. M-D.

Juan Cabanilles (1644–1712) Portugal

Cabanilles is one of the great masters of the Baroque era in Portugal.

Complete Edition (H. Anglès—Biblioteca Central, Sección de música, 1927, 1933, 1936, 1956). *Musici organici* (in progress) in vols.4, 8, 13, 17. Vol.4 contains *16 Tientos*. Scholarly edition. All seven MS variants have been carefully noted. M-D.

See: Murray C. Bradshaw, "Juan Cabanilles: The Toccatas and Tientos," MQ, 59 (April 1973):285–301.

Antonio de Cabezón (1510–1566) Spain

Obras de música para tecla arpa y vihuela. (Revised and edited by M. S. Kastner —Schott 1951). Contains eight compositions from this collection of 1578. A cross-section of Cabezón's art in capsule form. M-D.

4 Tientos für Orgel, Kleinorgel, Harmonium oder Klavier (M. Drischer—C. L. Schultheiss Musikverlag 1953). Built on three or four themes. M-D.

Obras de música (complete) in vols.3, 4, 7, and 8 of *Hispaniae Schola Musica Sacra* (Felipe Pedrell—J. B. Pujol, 1895–98).

Peter Cabus (1923–   ) Belgium

Deux Danses (Metropolis 1965) 8pp. Introduction: Lento: rather leisurely, chromatic. Danse: alternating hands, *pp* opening, full chords, strong rhythmic drive. M-D.

John Cage (1912–1992) USA

Cage is a composer whose style is difficult to categorize. He moved along experimental paths first followed by Cowell and Varese, assimilated elements of the twelve-tone school, and was influenced by Oriental philosophy. A period of activity related to the "prepared piano" occupied him for some time. Toward the end of his life his interest in the aleatoric, or "random," element was supreme. He had a remarkable influence on his generation and pointed to new directions for contemporary music.

Quest 1935 (CFP 66757) 2 min. (second movement). Intriguing if sometimes puzzling writing. M-D.

Two Pieces for Piano ca.1935 (CFP 6813). Irregular barring. M-D.

Bacchanale 1938 (CFP) 6 min. Cage's earliest work for prepared piano: shifting, repeated rhythmic patterns. The sound of the instrument needed to be changed in order to provide an accompaniment without employing percussion instruments. Composed for a dance by Syvilla Fort. M-D.

A Metamorphosis 1938 (CFP) 15 min. Five movements in various moods, 12-tone. Row fragments never varied. M-D.

Amores 1943 (Henmar Press). 4 works. The first and last are for prepared piano and require 9 screws, 8 bolts, 2 nuts, and 3 strips of rubber, acting as mutes. The second piece is for 3 beaters on 3 tom-toms apiece. In the third piece the same players change to woodblocks. Studied unpretentiousness!

Our Spring Will Come 1943 (Bunger—CFP 66763) 16pp. Music for a dance by Pearl Primus. For prepared piano. M-D.

The Perilous Night (CFP 1943–44). Suite for prepared piano, six movements. Preparation requires weather stripping, flat pieces of bamboo, and an assortment of nuts, bolts, and washers between the strings. The effects are reminiscent of the Balinese gamelan. M-D.

A Valentine Out of Season 1944 (CFP 6766) 9pp. 4 min. Suite of three movements; the most dance-like is placed in the middle. Easiest of the prepared-piano pieces. Int. to M-D.

Prelude for Meditation 1944 (CFP) ½ min. For prepared piano, easy preparations. An interesting prelude to program before another larger prepared work. Int. to M-D.

Daughters of the Lonesome Isle 1945 (CFP 6785) 12 min. Atmospheric, conventionally notated, for dance. M-D.

Mysterious Adventure 1945 (CFP 1982) 19pp. 8 min. For prepared piano. Written for dance, following the rhythmical structure given by Merce Cunningham. Conventional notation. M-D.

Ophelia: Music for the Dance 1946 (CFP 6788) 9pp. 5 min. Reproduced from MS. Dramatic character; phraseology corresponds to that of the dance by Jean Erdman. M-D.

Two Pieces for Piano 1946 (CFP 6814). Explores rhythmic structures. M-D.

Sonatas and Interludes 1946–48 (CFP) 70 min. For prepared piano. Includes a kit to prepare 45 tones. Sonatas are one page in length. 4 Sonatas. First Interlude: 3pp. 4 more Sonatas. Second Interlude: 3pp. Third Interlude: 1p. 4 more Sonatas. Fourth Interlude. 4 more Sonatas. The sonatas attempt to express the permanent emotions of the Indian tradition. The prepared piano produces some interesting Far Eastern sonorities. Gentle percussive patterns. This set of pieces is Cage's "Well Tampered Piano." M-D.

The Seasons 1947 (Henmar). Ballet in one act, piano transcription by Cage. Winter; Spring; Summer; Fall. Preludes are separate pieces and are short and contain fascinating sonorities.

Music for Marcel Duchamp 1947 (CFP) 5 min. For prepared piano. Uses eight pitches on a single staff, repeated figures contrasted with measured silence. M-D.

Dream 1948 (CFP 6707) 5 min. For dance. Uses a fixed gamut of tones and depends on the sustaining of resonances either manually or with the pedal. M-D.

In a Landscape 1948 (CFP 6720) 8 min. Much sustaining of resonances with the pedal. M-D.

Suite for Toy Piano 1948 (CFP) 4pp. 8 min. Five pieces. Uses only nine tones. Int. to M-D.

Music of Changes 1951 (CFP) Vols.1–4. 43 min. To write this piece, Cage tossed coins to select the tempos, dynamics, durations, and silences. He says of this work, "It will be found in many places that the notation is irrational; in such instances the performer is to employ his own discretion." Sounds fragmentary and short-of-breath; too little varied in content; contrived. Lethally uninvolving! M-D to D.

For M. C. and D. T. 1952 (CFP) 2 min. The page itself is taken to be a "canvas" of time. M-D.

4′ 33″ 1952 (CFP 6777). Three movements. Tacet, any instrument or combination of instruments. No sounds are intentionally produced. Lengths of time were determined by chance operations. Performer might wish to have several repeats and a da capo of this work! The perfect example of antimusic: the expression of ideas that negates the traditional concept of music.

7 Haiku 1952 (CFP 6745) 3 min. The musical events for this work were derived by chance operations of the *I Ching*, the Chinese Book of Changes. Each of the small pieces represents the transference to musical time-space of the 17-syllable Japanese poem structure. M-D.

Music for Piano 4–19 1953 (Henmar Press). Directions: "these pieces may be played as separate pieces or continuously as 1 piece or!!" 16 pages, some pages have only one note per page.

34′46.776″ 1954 (CFP 6781) 58pp. For prepared piano. Lists the number of minutes and seconds in the title. Calls for a variety of whistles and horns plus the usual assortment of trinkets inserted between the strings (nuts, bolts, plastic spoons, etc.). Demands a virtuoso performance. D.

31′57.9864″ 1954 (CFP 6780) 23pp. Chance composition, for prepared piano. Instructions (one leaf) inserted. Graphic notation used for the graphing of force, distance, and speed of attack. M-D.

Winter Music 1957 (CFP 6775) 20 leaves. Chance composition for 1–20 pianists. Spatial notation, may be freely interpreted as to time. M-D.

Music Walk 1958 (CFP 6739) 10 leaves. For one or more pianists at a single piano plus radio and/or recordings. A performance lasts an agreed-upon length of time. Indeterminate composition. M-D.

Music for Amplified Toy Pianos 1960 (CFP). Part to be prepared from score by performer for any number of toy pianos. M-D.

TV Köln 1960 (CFP) 32 seconds. An early example of graphic music notation, and thus subject to varying realizations by different performers. Its name comes from the television station in Cologne, Germany, which commissioned the work. Leaves the listener with the wispiest of sensory impressions. Suggest it be played twice. Once one learns to read the notation, the piece is about M-D.

Water Music 1960 (CFP 6770) 10 leaves, 6 min. Chance composition, for a pianist also using radio, whistles, water containers, deck of cards; score to be mounted as a large poster.

Cheap Imitation 1970 (CFP). 16 photocopied sides in a cover. 20 min. Three movements. Melody from Erik Satie's *Socrate* is used with the *I Ching* determinator. Some melodic doubling, sustaining pedal little used, effective. Avant-garde. M-D.

One (CFP). The score consists of a set of ten time brackets with instructions for playing each in the indicated durations. Avant-garde.

Etudes Australes 1975 (CFP) Four books of 32 etudes published in two volumes. Fascinating format involving eight systems notated on two pages, with each system having four staves. Extensive directions, MS reproduction. Title comes from *Atlas Australis*, a book of star maps used when writing these pieces. Terribly involved at places; austere, pointillistic, expansive range; tremendous leaps; both hands required to play all over the keyboard at the same time. Avant-garde. Almost three hours. D.

See: David Burge, "Two Indeterminate Pieces," CK, 3 (January 1977):46, for a discussion of Cage's *Etudes Australes* and Earle Brown's *Twentyfive Pages*.

See: Tom Darter, "The Piano Music of John Cage," *Keyboard*, 8/9 (September 1982):23–29.

Doris M. Hering, "John Cage and the 'Prepared Piano,'" *Dance Magazine*, 20 (March 1946).

Louis Calabro (1926–   ) USA
Since 1955 Calabro has taught composition at Bennington College.

Young People's Sonatine (EV 1957) 7pp. Allegretto grazioso: mildly dissonant lines. Lento assai: chordal, syncopated. Allegro: changing meters, strong accents. Int.

Sonatina (EV 1959) 10pp. Allegro: freely tonal around B♭, expressive lines, subito gestures, thin textures. Adagio: dissonant counterpoint between hands. Allegro molto: driving rhythms in outer sections, calm melodic mid-section. M-D.

Five for a Nickle Pie (EV 1975) 8pp. Fresh, original pieces using contemporary and modal harmonies. Int.

Otello Calbi (1917–   ) Italy
Divagazione Op.58/4 1958 (EC 10159) 8pp. 4½ min. Neoclassic, scalar, chromatic, linear, freely tonal. M-D.

James Callihou (?–1941) Canada

Suite Canadiènne (Archambault 1955). Rigaudon: in Ravel idiom similar to the *Tombeau de Couperin*, theme and variation pattern. Chanson: charming but contains a tricky mid-section. Gigue: clever adaptation of a familiar tune. M-D.

Constantine Callinicos (1913–   ) USA

2 Greek Dances (MCA). Published separately. Laludi; Nerantzula. Based on Greek folksongs. Follow a free theme and variation pattern. M-D.

Charles Camilleri (1931–   ) Great Britain, born Malta

Camilleri writes in a style that is essentially new but at the same time very old. He expresses himself in a contemporary approach based on well-tried musical formulas used for centuries. His works for piano are prolific.

African Dreams Op.9 (Roberton 1965) 3 min. Six colorful pieces, explanations in English. Hymn to Morning; Rain Forest Fantasy; Experience of Conflict; Festival Drumming; Children's Lagoon; A Dance—Ritual Celebration. M-D.

Three African Sketches Op.11 (Roberton) 7½ min. Invocation and Dance; Ulumbundu; Lament for an African Drummer. Pentatonic, thin textures, ostinati, contemporary Alberti bass treatment. Based on original material, not African melodies. A folklike melody is introduced near the end of the third movement. Monotony sets in before piece concludes. Int. to M-D.

3 Popular Maltese Dances (Curwen). Carnival Dance; The Danse and the Kiss; Dance of Youth. All three are based on the Maltese national dance tune known as "Il Maltija." Simple, diatonic. Int.

Trois Pièces pour Piano Op.7 (Fairfield 1947). Prelude; Toccata; Scherzo. M-D.

Sonata No.2 Op.15 (Fairfield 1969). Three movements of compelling writing, especially the second movement, Funèbre. M-D.

Little African Suite (Nov). Based on genuine African tunes and rhythms. Slow movements are easier than the fast ones. Int. to M-D.

Due Canti (Roberton). Arabesque: decorated melodic line, modal harmonies. Cantilena: less-decorated melody, good for small hands. Int.

Etudes Op.8 (Roberton). Book I: In Folk Song Style; Contrasts; Fantasy Waltz. Chords and broken chords, atonal; requires strong rhythmic control. Book II: Repliement; A Tranquil Song; Réjouissance; Chorale Prelude; Rondo. Technical problems explored are octaves, complex rhythms and chords, broken chords especially. Book III: "The Picasso Set." Composed as a response to an exhibition of Picasso's paintings. For Camilleri, Picasso represents in his art the dilemma facing all twentieth-century artists: the pull between representative and abstract art. Each piece in this book has a distinct flavor. Blues: the Blue period. Foxtrot. Gavotte. Mural. Primitif: very dissonant, with African rhythms. Circus Waltz: slightly chromatic. All are short and nondevelopmental. Int. to M-D.

Four Ragamats 1967–70 (Roberton) 26 min. The title is a combination of two musical forms: the Indian Raga and the oriental Maqamat. However the *Ragamats* do not try to emulate non-Western music. On the contrary, they try to fuse within themselves the philosophy of various different cultures. They use a technique that is concerned with widening the scope of rhythm, melody, and harmony. In this technique the beat is "atomized" into self-contained units that in themselves form part of the overall rhythmic and melodic form of the work involved. Small, innumerable, different, quick and slow melodic figures, each with a life of its own, may flow in a free, improvisatory manner while the metric beat remains steady—thus shifting the accents beyond the confines of any imaginary bar line. In their texture, fragments of ancient and modern scales, fragments of folk music, and other sources common to the music of the Mediterranean are to be found. But influences covering the music of Africa, the Orient, and the Americas are not uncommon. The pieces are freely tonal and may be played separately or together. No.1 centers around d, No.2 around F, No.3 B♭, No.4 around E♭. They may also be related to special times of day—morning, noon, evening, night. Highly chromatic; pointillistic in a few places.

Pieces for Anya (Roberton 1975) 6½ min. Morning Playtime (Hopscotch): delightful, staccato and legato. A Tender Melody. A Carol of Charms: all in treble clef. A Sad Folk Song: expressive. Little Caprice: rhythms make it the most difficult of the set. Int. to M-D.

Five Children's Dances Op.9 (Fairfield 1969) 12pp. For piano, voice and piano, or voices alone—with English and Maltese words. Boy's Football; One Two Three; Merry-go-round; The Children's Band; In Hyde Park. Int.

Sonatina Classica (Roberton 1974). Dedicated to the memory of the Maltese composer Nicolo Isouard (1775–1818). Three movements written in a style to suggest the period; an eighteenth-century pastiche. Int.

Times of Day—Five Southern Impressions Op.5 (Roberton 1958) 4 min. These five short pieces crystallize the mood of "A village island, primitive, earthy and timeless," of the Maltese poet Dun Karn. Aubade: warm melismatic chords in left hand and a shimmering right hand, which possibly suggest a warm Mediterranean dawn with sunlight sparkling on the water. Interlude I: short, octaves with disjointed rhythms, improvisatory. Silent Noon: opens with a tolling bell; heavy chords bring siesta as the A tonic chord is repeated fifteen times. Interlude II: a lively presto with the right hand doing most of the work. Evening Meditation: opening "Aubade" warm chords return; calm and lethargic mood. The pieces are fitted together in an arch form. The entire work has a meditative and ritual effect. Notes in the preface describe sources used for the pieces. M-D.

Sonatina I Op.6 (Roberton 1960) 7½ min. The subtle first movement is developed from the first Interlude in the *Times of Day* suite. The second and third movements are more linearly conceived. Folklike melody is introduced near the end of the third movement, which is a set of variations. M-D.

Hemda Op.7 (Nov 1962) 6 min. A quiet miniature aimed at capturing a sense of magical stillness and tranquility evocative of sunrise on the island of

Malta. The middle section is a cantilena-type melody over a guitar-like accompaniment. M-D.

Mantra Op.12 (Nov 1969) 12 min. Camilleri tries to evoke the ethos and spiritual state that is suggested by the oriental element "Mantra"—the study and manipulation of sounds according to various planes of consciousness. The beat remains steady while constantly fluctuating patterns of melodic and rhythmic particles undergo a form of continual variation. D.

Concerto Americana 1976 (Roberton 5545). Influences of Ives, Gershwin, and Schönberg. Large chords, complex rhythms. Closing section indicates neither dynamics nor note values—these are left to the performer's discretion. M-D.

Petite Suite for Young Pianists (Bo&H Canada 1978) 6pp. Three short contrasting movements, somewhat experimental (duration of notes left to interpretation of performer). Int.

Little English Suite (Cramer 1981) 7pp. Country Rides; Derby Trot; Scottish Border; Sherwood Forest; Scoutmaster's Bugle. Contrasting short pieces. Each one is built on a restricted number of notes for each hand. Easy to Int.

Sonatina Semplice (Bo&H Canada 1978) 7pp. Three short movements that are anything but simple. Echoes of Milhaud and Poulenc. M-D.

Four Pieces for Young Pianists (Cramer 1980) 7pp. Pays homage to Bartók, Ravel, Milhaud, and Stravinsky in clever imitation of their styles. Int.

Chemins (Pathways) 1980 (Cramer) 5 min. Five short pieces in contemporary style, some rhythmic freedom. One piece consists of 8 fragments to be arranged in any order. Int.

Sonata Breve (Cramer 1982) 7pp. An economical one-movement work with strong Bartók and Boulez influence. More emphasis on dynamics, rhythm, and harmony than on melody. The frantic activities of the piece are only relaxed at the closing in a free Lento section. M-D.

See: Michael Bonello, ed., *The Piano Music of Camilleri* (Malta: Andrew Rupert Publishing, 1990), 73pp. Discusses most of the piano music to 1990.

Ates Orga, "Camilleri Premiere," M&M, 25 (November 1975):22, 24, 26, for a discussion of many of the piano works.

————"Charles Camilleri," *Musical Opinion*, 103 (January 1980):129–32.

Christopher Palmer, *Introduction to the Music of Charles Camilleri* (London: Robert Publications, 1974), 80pp. Illustrates Camilleri's technique of composition.

Héctor Campos-Parsi (1922–   ) Puerto Rico

Sonata G 1952–53 (PAU) Calmo-Allegro. Mesto—grave e sostenuto: linear and canonic. Vivo: alternates duple and triple rhythms; four-voice chorale in middle of development. Reflects twentieth-century compositional techniques in combination with Negro rhythmic elements, neoclassic. M-D.

Bruno Canino (1935–   ) Italy

9 Esercizi per la Nuova Musica (Ric 1970–71) 16pp. Includes performance instructions in English, German, and Italian. 1. The Same Sound. 2. Play with the Stop Watch. 3. Play the Tempo, Well Counting the Eighth Notes. 4. Accelerando, Ritardando. 5. Quintuplets: requires two or three players. 6. As Fast As Possible. 7. The Three Pedals. 8. Secco, Morbido: *pp, ff*. 9. Little Maze. All pieces are designed to acquaint the pianist with avant-garde techniques. D.

Philip Cannon (1929–   ) Great Britain
L'Enfant s'amuse Op.6 (Nov) 21pp. 15 min. L'Aube; Pas Seul; Pique-Nique des Marionettes; Berceuse pour une Souris; À Tricyclette. Attractive, MC, with a flair for interesting effects. M-D.
Sonatine Champêtre Op.17 (Galliard 1960). 19pp. 12 min. Three sparkling movements: Musette; Le Lac Gris; Colombine et Arlequin.

Joseph Canteloube (1879–1957) France
Danses Roumaines (MMP). Strong rhythms, fetching tunes. M-D.

Cornelius Cardew (1936–1981) Great Britain
Cardew was concerned mainly with graphic and experimental notation and with indeterminate or partly determined composition.
February Pieces 1959–61 (CFP). Cardew said: "Either play each or any of the 'February Pieces' separately—start with any section and play round the piece, joining the end to the beginning (In III read each section normally —forwards—but reverse the order of the sections—i.e., turn over pages backward and join the beginning to the end)" (from preface). His system for notating decaying sound is most unusual. Individual tones assert themselves through increasing occurrence. Avant-garde. M-D.
Octet "61" for Jasper Johns 1961 (CFP). Not necessarily for piano. Can be played on any instrument. A cycle of 60 graphic images. Avant-garde. M-D.
Three Winter Potatoes 1961–65 (UE) 15 min. Written in the months of February of 1959–61. Title refers to the fact that "they had been in the ground for a long time." Prepared piano called for in Nos. 1 and 2. No.2 is of cyclic construction, and any barline may be used as the starting point. Other interpretive directions are given. D.
Volo Solo 1965 (CFP 7129A) for piano or prepared piano. 16 pages in ring-bound plastic folder. Instructions in English. Uses numbers, lines, and shapes and admits a variety of interpretations. Negates the piano's expressive capabilities. Performer is required to play as many notes as possible as fast as possible. Virtuoso performance required. Avant-garde. D.
Memories of You 1964 (UE 15447). Avant-garde notation. Sounds are "relative" to a grand piano. Durations and dynamics are free. Any three objects may be used to create sounds (matchbox, comb, hand, etc.). Approaches maximum flexibility without resorting to mindless aleatoricism. M-D.

Cláudio Carneyro (1895–1963) Portugal
Carneyro's style is a combination of classicism, folklore, and contemporary techniques.

Arpa-Eólea (Sassetti 1959). Harp-like study in fast-changing chromatic harmony. M-D.

Raiana (Sassetti 1938) 6 pp. Dance with unusual rhythmic interest. Int. to M-D.

Poemas em Prosa Op.27 Nos.1–3 (1933) (Sassetti). Published separately. Three extended works using sonorous writing. No.2 shows French influence. M-D.

Fábulas (Sassetti). Charming. Int.

Paciências de Ana-Maria (Sassetti 1960). Piano Pieces for Children. Nursery Tale. Blind Man Bluff: three flats, B, A and G!. Music-Box. Transfer-Picture: most difficult. Int.

John Alden Carpenter (1876–1951) USA

Carpenter was from Chicago and combined the careers of businessman and composer. He showed a special gift for descriptions of the American scene.

Impromptu: July 1913 (GS). An excellent example of American Impressionism with jazz influence. M-D.

Danza 1935 (GS).

Little Dancer 1917 (GS). Quick, staccato, parallel chords. Int.

Little Indian 1916 (GS). Lento, melodic, serious pentatonic melodies, open fifths in left hand. Int.

Polonaise Américaine 1912 (GS). Uses Hispanic rhythms, harmonies, and melodies. Moderate length. M-D.

Diversions 1923 (GS). Five varied individual pieces, informal moods. M-D.

Tango Américain 1920 (GS) 4½ min. Added sixths, Spanish influence. M-D.

Piano Pieces (MMP). Polonaise Américaine; Impromptu.

Pieces (MMP). Little Indian; Little Dancer

See: Olin Downs, "John Alden Carpenter, American Craftsman," MQ, 16 (October 1930):443–48.

T. C. Pierson, "The Life and Music of John Alden Carpenter," diss., University of Rochester, 1952.

Benjamin Carr (1768–1831) USA, born Great Britain

Carr was one of the most important early American composers. He had a varied musical career in colonial America and played a major role in the development of music culture in Philadelphia.

Federal Overture (1974) (Musical Americana). A beautiful edition of this historic work edited by Irving Lowens. The pieces are a potpourri of eight different tunes of Revolutionary times, including the earliest printing of "Yankee Doodle." Written in the style of the period, crude at some points, but delightful to play and hear. Excellent contribution to early musical Americana. Int. to M-D.

The Maid of Lodi. Four Pieces from 'Mélange': Moderate; Waltz; Hornpipe; Gavotte (McClenny, Hinson—Belwin-Mills) in collection *Early American Music.* Also includes biographical material. Int.

Musical Journal (Scholarly Resources, Inc., 1508 Pennsylvania Ave., Wilmington, Delaware 19806). 2 vols. This valuable collection of pieces (piano, voice, chamber music) provides a close look at the literature performed and heard during the last part of the eighteenth and early part of the nine-teenth century in America. It was the *Etude* of its day. Int. to M-D.

Musical Miscellany 1815–25 (Da Capo 1979) 300pp. This collection, issued in oc-casional numbers over a ten-year period, contained a large variety of mu-sical types, reflecting the vogues and interests of the time: works by En-glish composers and those popular in England—such as Hook, Haydn, Pleyel, Bishop, and Kelly; French and Italian songs; Scottish ballads and folklore. The series was almost evenly divided between vocal and instru-mental music—the piano at this time was gaining popularity—and also con-tained a significant amount of sacred music by Carr as well as other com-posers, including Handel. The new introduction by Eve Meyer places both the *Miscellany* and Carr's career in historical perspective. This series is valu-able not only for the picture it provides of American musical taste of the period but also as a collection whose artistic quality and range make it as useful for performance today as when the series first appeared. Int. to M-D. See: Eve R. Meyer, "Benjamin Carr's Musical Miscellany," *Notes* 33 (De-cember 1976):253–65.

Yankee Doodle Arranged as a Rondo from Op.4 (Alfred 4603). In collection *Mas-ters of American Piano Music*. 4 pp. The final section of Carr's battle sonata *The Siege of Tripoli, An Historical Naval Sonata*, Op. 4. The famous tune is prominently featured. Int.

Edwin Carr (1926–   ) Great Britain, born New Zealand
Five Pieces for Piano (Ric 1966) 11 min. Toccata; Aria 1; Sonata; Aria 2; Finale. Built on a twelve-note series. Large, solid hands needed. M-D.

Gordon Carr (–   ) Great Britain
Five Creatures (Broadbent & Dunn 1994) 15pp. Goldfish; Dragonfly; Baby Ele-phant; Snail Nocturne; Happy Hedgehog. Each piece cleverly suggests its title; MC. Int. to M-D.

Paul Carr (1961–   ) Australia, born England.
Carr studied at the Guildhall College of Art and Design in London. In 1987 he moved to Australia to become stage manager with the Australian Opera.
Sails and Beach Games (Allans 1271 1989) 20pp. Seven untitled contrasting pieces suggesting scenes from the title. Freely tonal. Int. to M-D.

Manuel Carra (1931–   ) Spain
Cuatro piezas breves (UME 1960). Prestissimo: Webern style. Presto: based on a palindromic figure dynamically, rhythmically, and texturally. Lento: strict canon. Prestissimo: exciting perpetual-motion idea. Brilliant, pianistic, co-hesive. M.D.

Antonio Carreira (1520?–1597) Portugal
Drei Fantasien für orgel, clavichord (M. S. Kastner—Harmonia Uitgave). Kastner surmises the MS originated about 1586 in a Monastery of Santa Cruz at

Coimbra. It is one of the two most important Portuguese keyboard collections of the period. Preface in Dutch and English includes a brief discussion of Carreira's life and comments on the performance and structure of the works. M-D.

Teresa Carreño (1853–1917) Venezuela
Carreño's music is reminiscent of that of her mentor, Louis Moreau Gottschalk.

Le Sommeil de l'enfant (The Sleeping Child) (Berceuse) Op.35. In collection *At the Piano with Women Composers* (Alfred 428). Rocking rhythm, tranquil mood, firm and attractive texture. Int. to M-D.

Music for Piano (C. Rodriquez-Penalto—Hildegard Publishing). Includes La Corbeille de Fleurs Op.9; Plainte Op.17; Le Printemps Op.25; Une Revue à Prague Op.27; Venise Op.33; Highland Op.38; Kleiner Waltz. Int. to M-D.

Polonaise Op.35 (Ditson 1873). Eminently idiomatic for the instrument. M-D.

Springtime. Valse de Salon (Musica Obscura) 10pp. Infectious, contains refreshing wit and vigor. M-D.

Selected Works: Piano Music and String Quartet (Da Capo 1984) 235pp. The piano works combine elements of Chopin and Gottschalk, with an operatic melodic flair and Latin rhythms. They also show musical intelligence, in particular a firm control over structural elements. Wide left-hand leaps, complex ornamentation. M-D to D.

See: Maurice Hinson, "Teresa Carreño," *Clavier*, 27/4 (April 1988):16–19.

James McKeller, "Teresa Carreño Returns to the Stage," PQ, 151 (Fall 1990):18–22, 24, 26–27.

Elliott Carter (1908–   ) USA
Carter is a composer of penetrating insight and provocative technique. Though he has written little for the piano, he has given us one of the most important piano sonatas written by an American.

Sonata 1945, rev.1982 (Mer) 20 min. Large-scale two-movement work. Maestoso introductory section alternates with fast sections, with changing meters; another flowing legato section fits into this movement. Sonorous Andante misterioso leads to fugal Allegro, which is capped with a large climax. Demonstrates how flowing changes of textures and speed have replaced thematicism as the basis of the language. Colorful use of harmonics. Virtuoso pianism and musicianship required. In the revised edition there are approximately two dozen refinements in dynamics or rhythmic indications and some clarification concerning the use of the sostenuto pedal. The only pitch change is the addition of three notes to one of the chords of harmonics to create more resonance. "With new editorial markings by the composer" would be more accurate than "Revised." D.

See: Robert Below, "Elliott Carter's Piano Sonata," MR, 34 (August–November 1974):282–93.

Night Fantasies 1979–80 (AMP 7852-2) 48pp. 20 min. An elaborate, episodic score with deliberate virtuosic intent. A major piano work of this century.

Constructed with a rigorous intricacy, in performance it presents an image of improvisatory spontaneity. Based on a set of 88 twelve-note, all-interval chords connected by pivot tones. Rhythmically, it contains two pulse rates—10.8 and 8.75. Carter has called this work a "sort of contemporary *Kriesleriana*" and has likened it to the visions of an insomniac trying vainly to sleep. Tranquil sections alternate spasmodically with scampering "Fantastico" gyrations. Rest is never the rule in this anxious work. Much of the writing uses huge expanses of keyboard for two "voices" moving in contrary motion, constantly dovetailing. Varied and unusual keyboard textures, disjunct melodies, polyrhythms, always unpredictable. This pianistic nightmare requires vibrant, tensile strength coupled with great agility. D.

See: John F. Link, "Composition of Elliott Carter's *Night Fantasies*," *Sonus* (Spring 1994): 67.

George Pappastavrou, "Carter's Piano Sonata and *Night Fantasies*," AMT, 38/2 (November–December 1988):18–19.

90+ 1994 (Hendon Music 1994) 9 pp. 5½ min. Written in honor of Goffredo Petrassi's 90th birthday. Carter says this work "is built around 90 short, accented notes played in a slow regular beat. Against these the context changes character continually." Pointillistic, fragmented, proportional rhythmic relationships, short sections. Impossible to hear the 90 short notes as they run the gamut of the piece. This author questions: "is the piece worth the effort to learn it, and the answer is no!" Carter seems to be writing only for himself. D.

See: Richard Franko Goldman, "The Music of Elliott Carter," MQ, 43 (April 1957):151–70.

Eleazar de Carvalho (1912–1996) Brazil
Carvalho came to the United States in 1946 and was conductor of the St. Louis Symphony for a number of years.
Brazilian Dancing Tune (Ric). Uses extreme registers of keyboard. Vigorous, very rhythmic. M-D.

Robert Casadesus (1899–1972) France
All of Casadesus's writing is pianistic and exploits the piano's possibilities to their ultimate.
24 Preludes Op.5 1924 (ESC) 4 vols. Dedicated to Ravel, whose influence is apparent. Preludes in all the keys. Two are in old dance forms, one is Spanish, another is a funeral march. Various moods. Excellent concert and advanced teaching material. M-D.
See: Gaby Casadesus, "Robert Casadesus' Prelude 9," *Clavier*, 23/9 (November 1984) 10–14. Includes music and a master lesson.
Trois Berceuses Op.8 1925–31 (Sal) 8pp. Piquant, bluesy, quiet but contrasted, colorful, Romantic harmonies, nice. M-D.
8 Etudes Op.28 1941 (GS; Durand) 17 min. Problems in thirds, octaves, reso-

nance, fourth and fifths, two against three, left-hand chords, lightness of touch. Facile dexterity required. M-D.

Toccata Op.40 1950 (Durand). Double notes, octaves; requires bravura technique. D.

Sonata No.1 Op.14 1947 (Sal). FSF, many ideas, MC. M-D.

Sonata No.2 Op.31 1953 (Durand). Large three-movement work. The second movement, Adagietto grazioso, is especially beautiful. M-D.

Sonata No.3 Op.44 1948 (Durand). Three movements. The last, Rondo giocoso, is a wild "romp." M-D.

Sonata No.4 Op.56 1957 (Durand). Published together with *Sonata* No.3. Four movements. First movement, Allegro impetuoso, is dramatic, driving and especially difficult. D.

Variations d'après "Hommage à Debussy" de Manuel de Falla Op.47 1960 (Ric). An exciting set of variations fully exploiting the sonorities of the piano. M-D.

6 Enfantines Op.48 1955 (Durand). Charming short pedagogic material. Int.

Trois Berceuses Op.67 (Durand 1979) 9pp. Selections, contains Nos.3, 2, and 5. M-D.

See: John Owings, "The Composer—The Four Piano Sonatas," PQ, 118 (Fall 1982):30–32. Special issue devoted to Casadesus.

Robert J. Silverman, "A Short Talk with Gaby Casadesus," PQ, 80 (Winter 1972–73):4–5. Includes a list of Casadesus's compositions.

Sacha Stookes, *The Art of Robert Casadesus* (London: The Fortune Press, 1960). Includes a biography and an analysis of his works to that time.

Patrick Widhalm. "*Le Voyage Imaginaire*. The Piano Music of Robert Casadesus," PQ, 158 (Summer 1992):38–39. Includes music of *Italie*, from an unpublished set of pieces.

Alfredo Casella (1883–1947) Italy

Casella experimented with new styles and techniques throughout his life. He began as a Romanticist, then tried Impressionism and polytonal writing in various combinations. At the end of his life, he became interested in twelve-tone techniques. Perhaps he was more at home in a neoclassic style, which he adopted for many of his works. He was an ardent champion of contemporary music. Essential to a thorough understanding of his music is his book *Music in My Time*, translated by Spencer Norton (Norman: University of Oklahoma Press, 1955).

Toccata Op.6 1904 (Ric). Broken chords, octaves, long. D.

Sarabande Op.10 1908 (Sal; MMP). Chromatic figuration, lyric, sonorous, long. M-D.

A la Manière de . . . Op.17 (Sal). Short works "in the style of . . ." Vol. I, 1911 (MMP): R. Wagner, Prelude to a "3rd Act." G. Fauré, Romance sans Paroles: lyric. J. Brahms, Intermezzo: full textures. C. Debussy, Entr'acte pour un drame en préparation. R. Strauss, symphonia molestica: a symphonic transcription, includes colorful directives. C. Franck, Aria: Franckian harmony. Vol. II, 1914: V. d'Indy, Prélude à l'aprés-midi d'un Ascète. M. Ravel, Almanzor ou le mariage d'Adélaide. Two pieces in imitation of Borodin and Chabrier, composed and contributed by Maurice Ravel. Delightful. M-D.

Nove Pezzi Op.24 1919 (Ric; MMP). Nine pieces in contrasting moods: barbaric,

burlesque, elegiac, exotic, funereal, in "nenia" style, minuet, tango, in rustic
vein. Large span required. D.

Sonatina Op.28 1916 (Ric). Allegro con spirito; Minuetto; Finale. Long, difficult,
interesting sonorities. Finely wrought musical workmanship. M-D.

Deux Contrastes Op.31 1916–18 (JWC). Grazioso; Hommage à Chopin. Distorted treatment of Prelude A, Op.28/7. Anti-Grazioso, grotesque dance,
short. M-D.

A notte alta 1917 (Ric). Impressionistic, poetic, big climax, quiet close. One of
Casella's most important pieces. M-D.

Inezie Op.32 1918 (JWC; MMP). Preludio; Serenata; Berceuse. Short, simple,
contrasted. Int.

11 Pièces Enfantines Op.35 1920 (UE). Prélude; Waltz; Canon; Bolero; Hommage
à Clementi; Siciliana; Giga; Minuetto; Carillon; Berceuse; Galop. MC. Excellent pedagogic material. Int.

Due Ricercari sul nome di B.A.C.H. Op.52 1932 (Ric) 6 min. Funèbre: three
and four voices, intense, short, effective, ethereal. Ostinato: more difficult,
marchlike, percussive, vigorous. M-D.

Sinfonia, Arioso and Toccata Op. 59 1936 (Carisch). Sinfonia: dramatic, large gestures. Arioso: sensitive, supported by varying textures. Toccata: virtuosic
with pesante and festoso ending, thematic transformation. Advanced pianism required. D.

6 Studies Op.70 1944 (EC). Contains a piece based on thirds, on fourths, and another on major and minor sevenths; a Toccata; an Homage to Chopin; and
a fast repeated-note study. D.

Joseph F. Castaldo (1927–   ) USA

Moments (GS 1973) 5pp. Avant-garde writing that exploits the piano by damping
strings and using a rubber mallet, fingernail glissandi, forearm clusters.
Wide dynamic range, exact pedal directions, economy of material. D.

Sonata 1961 (PIC 1976) 20pp. One movement, Con rabbia: serial, pesante, non-
metered, intense. Interrupted by contrasting sections such as Largo (misterioso), calmato, calmo, meno mosso. Nervous Presto coda. Requires firm
rhythmic control plus ability to move over keyboard quickly and accurately. D.

Sonatina (Hin). Four short contrasting movements, freely tonal, vigorous finale.
M-D.

Toccata (Hin). Brilliant and dissonant, continuous sixteenth-note figuration,
dashing close. Requires virtuoso pianism. D.

Mario Castelnuovo-Tedesco (1895–1968) Italy

Melody is the essence of Castelnuovo-Tedesco's style.

English Suite 1909 (Mills 1962). Preludio, quasi un improvisazione; Andante;
Giga. Has an innocent and piquant charm. Int.

Il Raggio verde (The Ray of Green) 1916 (Forlivesi; MMP). Long, fast figuration.
The composer's most controversial work. D.

I Naviganti (The Seafarers) 1919 (Forlivesi). Romantic poem that works to large climax. M-D to D.

Cipressi 1920 (Forlivesi). Broad gestures, undulating motion, sonorous. An Impressionistic evocation of the serene and stately cypresses that are native to Florence, the composer's birthplace. M-D.

Alt Wien 1923 (Forlivesi). A Viennese rhapsody, clever, like some apparition of Old Vienna, appealing, fox trot finale. M-D.

Piedigrotta (Ric 1924). A difficult Neapolitan rhapsody.

Tre Corali su Melodie ebraiche (UE 1926). Three lengthy pieces on Hebrew melodies. D.

Candide (MCA 1944). Six musical illustrations for the Voltaire novel. Programmatic suite. M-D.

Sonata (UE 1928) 44pp. A striking work. M-D.

Six Canons Op.142 (MCA). Clear and incisive writing.

Ricercare sul nome di Luigi Dallapiccola (Forlivesi 1958).

Evangelion; the story of Jesus, narrated to the children in 28 little piano pieces (Forlivesi 1959). 4 vol. Certain portions of scripture are suggested for each piece. M-D.

Sonatina Zoologica Op.187 (Ric 1961). Four movements, based on characteristics of small winged and creeping animals. Excellent recital material. M-D.

Suite nello Stil Italiano Op.138 1947 (Ric). Preludio; Gagliarda; Siciliana; Tarantella. Displays the composer's facility and sense of effectiveness. Idiom is not forbiddingly dissonant or complex. Brilliant figuration. M-D.

Alghe 1919 (Forlivesi). The title refers to seaweeds that retain the perfume of the Italian seashores. M-D.

Questo fu il carro della Morte ("The House of Death") Op.2 1913 (Forlivesi). A descriptive work with a long quotation from Giorgio Vasari's "Vita di Pier di Cosimo" on the title page. M-D.

La Sirenetta e il pesce turchino ("The Little Mermaid and Dark Blue Fish") 1920 (Forlivesi). A fable of the sea. M-D.

Vitalba e Biancospino ("Clematis and Hawthorn") 1921 (Forlivesi). A sylvan fable. M-D.

La Danza del Re David (Forlivesi). Rhapsody on Jewish traditional themes. Strongly Impressionistic. M-D.

Epigrafe (Forlivesi). A gentle work. M-D.

Greeting Cards Op.170 1954 (Gen) Based on motives from the names of friends and colleagues. 1. Andre Previn: Tempo da Tango. 4. Walter Gieseking: Mirages, quiet and dreamy. 9. Amparo Iturbi: Tempo di Fandango. Op.170/2 (c.1975) is slow, with variations, on the name of Nicholas Slonimsky. M-D.

Hommage à Paderewski 1941 (Bo&H 1942) 7pp. Published as third piece in the set *Homage to Paderewski*. Mazurka rhythms plus clever right-hand figurations. M-D.

See: Nick Rossi, "Mario Castelnuovo-Tedesco: Modern Master of Melody," AMT, 25 (February–March 1976):13–14, 16.

————, ed. *Catalogue of Works by Mario Castelnuovo-Tedesco* (International Castelnuovo-Tedesco Society [55 W. 73 St., New York, NY 10023], 1977).

David Reeves, "The Piano Works of Mario Castlenuovo-Tedesco—A Centennial Survey," P&K, 176 (October 1995): 29–33.

Jacques Castérède (1926–   ) France
Quatre Etudes (Sal 1958) 23pp. Brilliant virtuoso writing. M-D to D.
Diagrammes (Sal 1953) 24pp. Prelude: Vivo, ma non troppo: fleeting, murmuring, perpetual motion. Nocturne: Lento: built around perfect and diminished fifths. Toccata: Vivo: Ravel influence. M-D.
Sonate (Editions Rideau Rouge 1969). One large-scale movement. Mixture of styles: Impressionism, expressionism. Clusterlike chords, freely chromatic, big climax, quiet ending. D.
Hommage à Thelonious Monk 1983 (Leduc) 25pp. 14½ min. 1. Portrait: improvisational, dynamic extremes, harmonics, embellishments. 2. Apocalypsis Rock: rock tempo, motoric, fast-moving chords over keyboard, clusters, by far the most intriguing, combining elements of boogie-woogie with the letters of Monk's name, derived through permutation and alteration. Includes performance directions. Some avant-garde techniques. D.
L'éscharpe d'iris 1975 (Zurfluh 1993) 3 min., 35 sec. The melody sings a rippling LH accompaniment, short. Last figure repeats until sound is gone. MC. M-D.
Pour un Tombeau de Frédéric Chopin (Billaudot 1994) 60 pp., ca. 30 min. Prélude; Valse; Scherzo; Nocturne; Etude. This work "was conceived as an entity. That is why it is preferable that it should be played in its entirety. If the work appears too long, the first three indissociable movements (Prélude, Valse, Scherzo) may be played or the Nocturne may be played separately" (from the score). The passages without bar lines are to be played freely (Prélude and Études); blank spaces correspond to periods of silence. Virtuosic writing, difficult to hold together, numerous performance suggestions. D.

Niccolo Castiglioni (1932–1996) Italy
Inizio di movimento (SZ 1958) 8pp. 3 min. The unusual compositional vocabulary in this work is a synthesis of the styles of Cage, Debussy, Messiaen, and Webern. M-D.
Cangianti (SZ 1959) 31pp. 10 min. Performance directions. Pointillistic writing. Organization is difficult for ear to comprehend. Unusual sonorities. Title means "changes," and three rows are announced at the same time. D.

Ricardo Castillo (1894–1967) Guatemala
Most of Castillo's piano works have an impressionist quality.
Suite D (PAU 1938). Four short movements, contrasting moods. Clear textures neatly handled. Biographical sketch included. M-D.
Huit Préludes (Henri Elkan 1950). Short, delicate. M-D.

Alexis de Castillon (1838–1875) France
Castillon worked with Franck and was a gifted composer with high ideals.
8 Fugues dans le Style Libre Op.2 (G. Hartmann) 28pp. Many moods in this set.
    Fine pianism required. M-D.
24 Pensées Fugitives (Huegel 1900). All published separately. An interesting col-
    lection of turn-of-the-century character pieces. See especially No.2 Toc-
    cata, No.4 Carillon, and No.15 Feux Follets. M-D.

José María Castro (1892–1964) Argentina
Sonata de Primavera (PIC 1939). Allegro moderato: smooth, easy-going, rich
    sonorities. Andante: flowing eighths contrasted with dotted rhythms, bi-
    tonal atmospheric coda. Allegro: bright, toccata-like, alternating hands. Se-
    rious. D.
Ten Short Pieces (Barry 1955). Estudio; La fuente; Canción de cuña; Canción
    triste; Danza; Circo; Marcha fúnebre a la tristeza criolla; Vals de la calle;
    Moto perpetuo; Campanas. Contemporary techniques including plenty of
    dissonance. Four of these are contained in the collection *Latin-American
    Art Music for the Piano* (GS). Int.
Pequeña Marcha (PIC). Short, staccato, two voices, for children. Easy.
Vals Miniatura (PIC). Pungent dissonances, two voices, for children. Easy.
Sonata (Grupo Renovacion, 1931). Allegro moderato; Arietta con Variazioni (6);
    Finale. Clear textures throughout. On the quiet and flowing side. M-D.

Juan José Castro (1895–1968) Argentina
The three Castro brothers are highly respected musicians within, as well as out-
side, their native Argentina.
Toccata (PIC 1940). Conventional harmonic idiom, approximate difficulty of
    Ravel or Prokofieff toccatas. D.
Quasi Polka (PIC 1946). Grotesque, polytonal. For children. Int.
Corales Criollos No.1 (PIC 1948) 17pp. Chorale and 8 variations. Colorful figu-
    ration. Large span required. M-D.
Five Tangos (PIC 1941) 18pp. Tango rhythm exploited in five different moods;
    kind of a "Bachianas Argentinanas." M-D.
Bear Dance (CF). Modal, vague tonality. Int.
Playful Lamb (CF). Legato–staccato contrast, irregular phrasing. Int.
Sonatina Española (UE 1956) 29pp. 14 min. Allegretto comodo: uses 12-tone
    technique. Poco lento: sensitive and lyric. Allegro: built on Carl Maria von
    Weber's *Perpetual Motion* C in right hand while left hand plays a spirited
    Scherzo F♯. Effective. D.

Washington Castro (1909–   ) Argentina
Four Pieces on Children's Themes (PIC 1942) Juegos (Jugglers): clever, brilliant,
    varied rhythms. Haciendo Nonito: a lullaby, three against two. Era un paja-
    rito . . . : facile technique required. Rondo: energetic; clarity needed. M-D.

Three Intermezzi (PIC 1947). Andante serio; Allegretto placido; Molto appassionato. Interesting sonorities, well-developed ideas, contrasting moods. M-D.

Cinco Preludios (Pic Americana 1954) 10 min. Andante grave; Allegro scherzando; Andante dramatico; Appassionato; Allegro giubiloso. M-D.

Alfredo Catalani (1854–1893) Italy

Catalani's piano works occupy an important place in late-nineteenth-century Italian piano literature.

Nocturne g♯ (Boccaccini & Spada 1994) 4pp. Moonlight and melancholy mood, works up to a strong climax followed by a *pp* closing. Influence of Chopin, Wagner, and Rachmaninoff noted. Effective. M-D.

Norman Cazden (1914–1980) USA

Sonatina Op.7 (NME 1935). Three movements. Requires large span. Dissonant and difficult. D.

8 Preludes Op.11 (Bo&H 1937). Originally part of the series "Music for Study," intended as a comprehensive course of piano study. All are short and mainly in two voices. No.6 is a "Sonatina." Sophisticated and clever. M-D.

5 American Dances Op.14 (AMC 1941). Written for the New Dance Group. M-D.

Variations Op.26 (Mer 1940). Separate variations not clearly defined. Builds to climax and subsides. Pedal-point technique effectively used. M-D.

Music for Study: 21 Evolutions for Piano Op.4 (Arrow 1933–36). 21 short melodies intended to provide an elementary foundation for musical and pianistic study. Most are in two voices. Int.

Sonata Op.53/2 (LG 1958) In collection *New Music for the Piano*. Varied textures, bitonal. M-D to D.

Josef Ceremuga (1930–   ) Czechoslovakia

Toccata 1963 (Panton AP 2046 1979) 20pp. 4½ min. Lento introduction is followed by Allegro marcato. Style is a mixture of Ravel and Prokofiev. M-D.

Ignacio Cervantes (1847–1905) Cuba

Cervantes studied piano with Louis M. Gottschalk and also attended the Paris Conservatoire. He wrote numerous drawing-room pieces in a popular French style. His piano suite *Danzas Cubanas* was the first work by a Cuban composer to incorporate native rhythms in a concert form.

Six Cuban Dances (MMP). Strong rhythmic Spanish folkdance style. M-D.

Two Cuban Dances (JWC 1900). Gran Señora; Porque, Eh? 2pp. each. Appealing, with characteristic Cuban rhythms and folklike melodies. M-D.

Three Dances (JWC 1898). La Celosa; El Veloria; La Carcajada. 2pp. each. Latin American rhythms. El Veloria is subtitled "Veillée funèbre," while the third dance is a brilliant "L'éclat de rire" with a quickly diminishing piano closing. M-D.

Ignacio Cervantes, a highlight collection of his best-loved original works (C. Hansen 1976) 48pp. Includes detachable portrait of the composer.

Emmanuel Chabrier (1841–1894) France

Chabrier, an amateur composer, wrote music that has a certain uninhibited quality and is easily accessible. All his compositions are vigorous, unpretentious, expressive, and pianistic. His piano works foreshadow his larger efforts and contain strikingly original approaches that attracted such later composers as Satie, Debussy, Ravel, and Poulenc. His music is a bridge between Saint-Saëns and Impressionism.

Pièces pittoresques 1881 (E. Klemm—CFP; B. Webster—IMC; Enoch; EmM; MMP). Paysage. Mélancholie. Tourbillon: anticipates Stravinsky with abruptly changing meters. Sous bois: evokes a whispering forest. Mauresque. Idylle: the most delicate jewel in the collection. Danse villageoise. Improvisation. Menuet pompeux: orchestrated by Ravel and influenced Ravel's Minuet Antique. Scherzo—valse. Musical pictures of nature and French and Spanish landscapes. Lithe rhythms and irregular phrases add much interest. A landmark in French piano literature and an influence on composers for the following decades. M-D. Available separately: Idylle (IMC); Scherzo—Valse (EBM).

Habanera 1885 (IMC; BMC). ABA coda, lilting rhythm and languorous melody, pseudo-exotic, dancelike. M-D.

Bourrée fantasque 1891 (EBM; Billaudot; Enoch: MMP). Loose SA design (exposition: bars 1–132; development: bars 133–99; recapitulation: bars 200–358; coda beginning at bar 336). Chabrier treats the piano almost like an orchestra, as regards timbre and tone-color. Much percussive use; colorful harmonic clashes, spicy melodies. Athletic pianism required, brilliant. M-D to D.

Joyeuse Marche (MMP). Exhuberant and challenging. M-D.

España 1883 (Enoch). A rhapsody on original Spanish airs heard during a holiday in Spain; a synthesis of all Chabrier's impressions of the Spanish *jota*. Originally a piano solo but better known in the ballet arrangement. M-D. Available separately: *Waltz* from *España* (Schott).

Impromptu C 1873 (Enoch). ABA plus coda. Highly contrasted thematic material uses hemiola, syncopation, displaced accents and ostinatos, modal shifts, pedal point, and a few unusually pungent chords. From bar 209 forward (coda) melodic and rhythmic elements combined in the manner Ravel used in *Valses nobles et sentimentales*. M-D.

Pièces Posthumes 1891 (Enoch 1927). Aubade: Spanish influence in characteristic rhythmic patterns and guitar effects; modal; chromatic; hemiola; pedal points; opens and closes with a six-bar ritornello. Ballabile: short, three-part form based on a single motive in 3/4 time, which perpetually moves to the beat of a pulsating, staccato accompaniment. Caprice: recitative followed by ABA design. Feuillet d'album: AA^1A^2 form, seventh- and ninth-chord progressions; lilting, barcarolle rhythm; tonal instability through use of modal inflections. Ronde Champêtre: country dance in a five-part design (ABACA); sprightly rhythm, reminiscent of the forlane; 12-bar refrain; modal inflection of melodic line. M-D.

Air de Ballet (Billaudot) 7pp. Allegretto scherzando, sectionalized, ebullient rhythms, varied figurations. Much fun for all, especially the Vivo conclusion. M-D.

Chabrier Album (Ongaku-No-Tomo-Sha) 137pp. Impromptu; Pièces pittoresques; Bourée fantasque; España; Joyeuse Marche; 5 Pièces posthumes. M-D.

Works for Piano (Roy Howat—Dover 1995) 128pp. Piano music composed between 1870 and 1891. 20 pieces including Impromptu; Ronde champêtre; Petite valse; Pieces pittoresques (10 pieces); Aubade; Habanera; Ballabile; Caprice; Feuillet d'album; Joyeuse Marche; Bourrée fantasque. Also includes glossary of French terms, Introduction, Notes on the Music, Chabrier's tempos, sources, and variants. Int. to D.

See: Alfred Cortot, *French Piano Music* (New York: Da Capo Press, 1977), pp. 140–77.

W. Wright Roberts, "The Pianoforte Works of Chabrier," ML, 4/2 (April 1923): 133–43.

Joel Chadabe (1938–   ) USA

Three Ways of Looking at a Square (CPE 1967). New notation, avant-garde. Numbers with fermatas refer to seconds of silence. Numbers with dashes refer to seconds of holding sounds with the pedal. In either case they may be read freely, according to the piano, acoustics, etc. Pointillistic. D.

Peter I. Chaikovsky. See Tchaikowsky

Jacques Chailley (1910–1999) France

Sketchbook (Martin Canin—Sal 1972) 20 easy pieces. Careful writing and titles, e.g., Lament of the Three Little Children; The Brooding Bagpipe; Prelude to the Evening of a Nymph; Three Hens Headed for the Fields. First ten pieces are based on French folk songs; second ten are original. Easy to Int.

Luciano Chailly (1920–   ) Italy

Variazioni nel sogno (Ric 1971) 14pp. 9 min. Theme, 12 variations, and coda. Complex and thorny avant-garde sonorities utilizing most of the keyboard. Traditional notation. D.

David Chaitkin (1938–   ) USA

Etudes 1974 (Columbia University Music Press) 9 min. Three delicate movements with no pause between them. Sparse but frequently changing textures, widely spaced sonorities, nonrepetitive rhythms, dynamic extremes. Makes great demands on performer and listeners. Similar in style to the Schönberg Op.11 and Op.19 sets. D.

Julius Chajes (1910–   ) USA, born Poland

Sonata d (Transcontinental 1959) 35pp. 15 min. A three-movement work filled
with parallelism, many metric changes, and a variety of rhythms. A three-
voice fugue is contained in the final movement. Not especially pianistic yet
a brilliant-sounding work in the hands of an advanced pianist. M-D.

Air Varié (Transcontinental). Theme, 4 variations, and coda. Int.

Jacques Champion de Chambonnières (ca. 1602–1672) France

The founder of the French clavecin school.

Deux livres de clavecin (T. Dart—l'OL). Earliest printed sources and manuscripts
were consulted. Contains 11 ordres (60 pieces), dedication, original preface, and table of ornaments. Any variants from the manuscripts are shown
above or below the staves.

Complete Keyboard Works (P. Brunold, A. Tessier—Senart). 30 suites. M-D.

Complete Keyboard Works (BB). Facsimile of 1670 Paris Edition. 30 suites. Uses
soprano and baritone clefs. English translation and new preface by Denise
Restout. M-D.

Antologia di musica antica e moderna per il pianoforte (G. Tagliapietra—Ric
1931–32). Vol.VII includes 6 suites.

Art of the Suite (Y. Pessl—EMB). Int. to M-D.

Le Trésor des Pianistes (A. & L. Farrenc—Leduc) Vol.II contains two books of
keyboard pieces. Int. to M-D.

See: Robert Lee Neill, "Seventeenth-Century French Clavier Style as Found in
the *Pièces de Clavecin* of Jacques Champion de Chambonnières," diss.,
University of Colorado, 1965. A thorough study of all available information about Chambonnières. Draws some conclusions that define his contribution to the development of keyboard music. Also contains an English
translation of a four-section treatise concerning the life of Chambonnières
by Henri Quittard, a noted French scholar.

Cécile Chaminade (1857–1944) France

Chaminade traditionally—if erroneously—has been identified as a composer of
charming salon pieces. But her output also includes two piano trios, a choral
symphony, and the *Concertstück* Op.40. She was one of the first women to make
a career of composing.

La Lisonjira ("The Flatterer") (Century). Delicate and imaginative with some
unexpected happenings. Int. to M-D.

Sonata c Op.21 (Da Capo) Bound together with *Six Concert Etudes* Op.35 and
Etude Symphonique Op.28 (Enoch separately). The powerful Sonata exudes a late-Romantic flavor within its classical structure. The first movement combines prelude/fugue and SA design, while the second displays an
arching lyricism. The brisk perpetual motion finale seems somewhat disap-
pointing. Opp.28 and 35 are character pieces of impressive scale and imagination. M-D.

Selected Compositions (GS; K; MMP). Includes portrait and biographical sketch.
Vol.I: Sérénade; Minuetto; Air de ballet; Pas des amphores; Callirhoe; Lolita; Scarf Dance; Pièce romantique; Gavotte. Vol.II; Pierrette; La lison-jira; La morena; Les sylvains; Arabesque; Valse caprice; Dance pastorale; Arlequine. Int. to M-D.
Children's Album (Enoch 1934; MMP). Vol.I. Op.123: Twelve very easy pieces. Vol.II. Op.126: Twelve easy pieces. Some of Chaminade's most appealing writing. Easy to Int.
Available separately: Autumn Op.35/2; Spinning-wheel Op.35/3; The Fauns Op.60; Scarf Dance (GS).
Scarf Dance Op.37/3 (Alfred 428). In collection *At the Piano With Women Composers*. Her most famous piano piece. Int. to M-D.
Toccata c Op.39 (Enoch; Musica Obscura) 6pp. Virtuosic. Paderewski performed this piece frequently. D.
Le Prétemps—Valse de Salon (Musica Obscura) 9pp. Refined salon style. M-D.
Six Etudes de Concert Op.35 (MMP). Virtuosic concert studies. M-D.
En Automne—Etude de Concert Op. 35/2 (Musica Obscura) 9pp. Requires nimble fingers. M-D.
Two Pieces (MMP) Automne Op.35. Expansion Op.106. M-D.
Six Romances Sans Paroles Op.76 (MMP). Flowing melodies, lucid harmonies. Int. to M-D.
See: Cecile Chaminade, "How to Play My Best Known Pieces," *Etude*, 26 (December 1906):759.
John Jerrould, "Piano Music Cecile Chaminade," AMT, 37/3 (January 1988):22.

Claude Champagne (1891–1965) Canada
Quadrilha Brasileira (BMI Canada 1942). Based on a theme from Marajo Island. Exciting rhythms, frequent use of sevenths. M-D.
Prélude et Filigrane Op.5 (BMI Canada) 3 min. Two short, Romantic miniatures. Int. to M-D.

Theodore Chanler (1902–1961) USA
Chanler's style is characterized by strong lyrical writing and polytonal harmonies.
A Child in the House (Mer). 11 charming and witty pieces, a contemporary *Scenes from Childhood*. Int.
Aftermath 1942 (Bo&H) 1p. In collection *Homage to Paderewski*. Uneasy mood. Int. to M-D.
Three Short Pieces (Arrow). Andante sciolto; Andante con moto; Allegramente. Short, lyric, expressive, tonal. M-D.
Toccata (Mer 1939). Two voices in perpetual motion (à la Paradisi *Toccata*). Square-dance mood, traditional style. M-D.
Pas de Trois (AMC). Originally for piano and two dancers, but the piano part alone is effective. Two contrasting, sophisticated movements. The second is more difficult. M-D.

Brian Chapple (1945–   ) Great Britain
Trees Revisited (JWC 1970) 16pp. 5½ min. Inspired by Oscar Rasbach's *Trees*. Introductory bravura passage over long pedal note conceals original melody. Widely spaced chords, some dissonant and rich sonorities. M-D.

Aaron Charloff (1941–   ) Israel, born Canada
Etude 1967 (IMI 270) 3 min. Short (35 bars), atonal, 12-tone, flexible meters, repeated melodic and rhythmic fragments. Generally on the quiet side. M-D.

Jacques Charpentier (1933–   ) France
72 Etudes Karnatiques (Leduc 1960). Each study uses one of 72 Karnatic modes of 7 notes each, which are listed in the Indian musical system known as the Karnatic. In this system the octave comprises 7 main notes as well as 12 "regions" within which each note may move. Compared to dodecaphonic or tonal writing, the style of these Studies is extremely free. In 12 cycles, 6 pieces per volume. M-D. to D.
Toccata (Leduc 1961) 11pp. Varied groupings of 16th notes; alternating hands; widely spaced sonorities. D.
Allegro de Concert (Leduc 1965) 9pp. 6½ min. No meter or key signatures. A broad introduction (Vif) leads to a dolce *pp* section; increased intensity leads to section of trills in upper register, Dolce, *pp*; material from introduction rounds off the work. D.

Abram Chasins (1903–1987) USA
Chasins's piano music is ingratiatingly effective and excellently written for the instrument.
Three Chinese Pieces (JF 1926) reissued 1974, slightly revised. 16pp. A Shanghai Tragedy: opens quietly, builds to climax, subsides. Flirtation in a Chinese Garden: on white keys only, graceful, quiet. Rush Hour in Hong Kong: depicts a busy traffic scene, much activity. MC, interlaced with semi-oriental flavor (quartal and quintal harmonies), attractive. M-D.
24 Preludes Op.10 (OD 1928). 4 vols., 6 preludes in each. Each prelude has its own mood, is constructed on one or two pianistic figurations and successfully completes its intended purpose. Rachmaninoff hovers pleasantly over the entire set. M-D.
Fairy Tale Op.16/1 (Cramer). Still has a kind of faded charm. M-D.

Ernest Chausson (1855–1899) France
Although Chausson studied with Franck and Massenet, his style has individuality. There is some refined and sensitive, if not always pianistic, writing in the works listed below.
Piano Music (H. Haufrecht—Sal 1978) 26pp. Paysage Op.38: easier than the Debussy *Arabesque I*; Interlude from *Poème de l'amour et de la mer*; Quelques Danses Op.26.
Quelques Danses (Some Dances) Op.26 (K). 1. Dédicace and 2. Sarabande: both

show Franckian influence. 3. Pavane. 4. Forlane: most demanding. All four display a harmonic quality and neoclassical spirit that anticipates Debussy. M-D.

See: Joseph Smith, "Chausson's Sarabande," *Piano Today*, 16/1 (January–February 1996):13–17. Includes the music.

Carlos Chávez (1899–1978) Mexico
The style exhibited in the piano works of Chávez is characterized by lean, biting dissonances; complex rhythms; motivic fragmentation; and concentrated forms. His music is steeped in the native Indian tunes of Mexico. It demands more than an initial hearing to be appreciated.

Sonata No.2 Op.21 (Bo&Bo 1920) 27 min. Allegro doloroso; Andante; Molto inquieto. Large-scale work employing much bravura writing. D.

Sonatina 1924 (Bo&H) 5 min. Moderato; Andantino; Allegretto; Vivo; Lento. Modal, dissonant, three and four voices. Requires fine tonal balance and careful attention to sonorities. M-D.

See: Maria Rodriguez, "Recollections of Carlos Chávez," *Clavier*, 21/4 (April 1982):23–29. Includes music of this piece.

Sonata No.3 1928 (NME; Colección Arion 1972) 13 min. Moderato; Un poco mosso; Lentamente; Claro y conciso. Changing meters, cross-rhythms, percussive, biting harmonies, mainly on white keys, jazz influence, open textures. D.

Seven Pieces for Piano (NME). Poligonos (1925): powerful, sonorous. Solo (1926): short, diatonic melody, dissonant counterpoint. 36 (1925): percussive, perpetual motion, bravura writing. Blues (1928): two voices, wide intervals, little blues syncopation. Fox (1928): syncopated, wide skips, percussive. Paisaje (1930): short, melodic. Unidad (1930): longest of the set; bravura writing; repeated notes; cross-rhythms; mature pianism required. Int. to D.

Ten Preludes (GS 1937). Modal, varied moods, some dissonance, mildly exotic, pandiatonic, cross-rhythms, highly usable. Int. to M-D.

Estudio (Homenaje à Chopin) 1949–50 (PIC). Nocturne-like, flowing lines, dissonant, dramatic closing. M-D.

Invención (Bo&H 1960). A large-scale work in linear style. Contrasted moods, various techniques, dramatic closing. D.

Sonata No.6 (Belwin-Mills 1965) 28 min. In "classical" style. First movement: A♭. Second movement: Andantino D♭. Third movement: theme and 12 variations; theme is folklike. D.

Estudio a Rubinstein (GS 1976) 10pp. Brilliant, based on leaping conjunct seconds. D.

Three Etudes 1949 (Belwin-Mills 1969) 16pp. 7½ min. 1. Chromatic triads in one hand against single line in the other; contrary motion triads conclude the piece. 2. Melodic, freely tonal, sectionalized. 3. Based on hemiola, chromatic. Makes a good MC recital group. M-D.

Five Caprichos (GS 3334 1983) 24pp. 14½ min. 1. Animato, serial. 2. Lentissimo, exploits lower register of keyboard. 3. Vivo, mildly pointillistic, trills. 4.

Adagio, melodic, long trills, long pedals. 5. Mosso, builds to dramatic climax. To be played as a group. Difficult to digest. M-D to D.

Four New Etudes 1952 (Carlanita 1985) 26pp. 1: Large skips, two- and three-note slurs, with dynamic range. 2: Rapido, chromatic, disjunct melody. 3: For major seconds. 4: For the left hand, no use of pedal; impossible to play as written. D.

Brian Cherney (1953–   ) Canada

Intervals, Patterns, Shapes (Waterloo). Varied contemporary sonorities. Int.

Jest (Jaymar) 3pp. A clever scherzo. M-D.

Pieces for Young Pianists (Jaymar) 3 books. Book II: four pieces, musically demanding; Int. Book III: three contrasting pieces, only the last of which is titled—Dance for a Light Hearted Elephant; M-D.

Six Miniatures (Jaymar). Untitled, clever, MC. Int.

Luigi Cherubini (1760–1842) Italy

Cherubini's only extant piano works were thought to be the sonatas composed in Florence in his youth. In 1977 his *Caprice ou Etude pour le Fortepiano* was discovered.

Sei Sonate per Cembalo (T. Alati—Carisch 1958). F, C, B♭, G, D, E♭. Composed around 1780, all are two-movement works and all second movements are rondos. The first movements have the most interest, generally speaking, and are in SA design. Classic style, Alberti bass, ornamented melodic lines, standard tonal treatment in formal structure. Int. to M-D.

Sonata No.3 B♭ (Br&H 8107) 13pp. Allegro comodo; Andantino (Rondo). Combines pianistic fulfillment with simplicity of means. Requires flexible hands and fingers and would serve as an excellent introduction to the sonatas of Clementi. M-D.

Caprice ou Etude pour le Fortepiano 1789 (Boccaccini & Spada 1982) 63pp. Various sections (995 measures) exploit different ideas and figurations of the period: scales, arpeggios, triplets, chorale style. M-D.

Thomas Chilcot (ca. 1700–1766) Great Britain

Chilcot wrote two sets of harpsichord concerti and other works. He was also an organist.

Two Suites for Harpsichord (Pennsylvania State University Press, 1969). A number of printing errors in this otherwise fine edition. Suite I: Overture; Aria I; Siciliano; C; Jigge; M. M-D. Suite II: Allemanda and Presto; Aria; Jigge; M. M-D.

Six Suites of Lessons (D. Moroney—Heugel LP 60 1981) 77pp. g, A, B♭, c, d, e. Excellent introduction by the editor. Contains some charming and effective writing that shows strong Handel influence. M-D.

See: Gwilym Beechey, "Thomas Chilcot and His Music," M&L, 54 (April 1973): 179–96, for a discussion of the suites and concerti.

Barney Childs (1926–   ) USA
37 Songs (ACA 1971) 5 min. A juxtaposition of short, simple ideas like leitmo-
   tivs. Piano is prepared with a rubber eraser, a dime, and a blackboard
   eraser. Specific instructions, e.g., "tap with knuckles on keyboard cover behind keys"; "with left hand reach inside and push eraser firmly against
   strings." Performer reads a given text to audience at conclusion of piece.
   Sensitive musicianship more important than pianistic equipment. Will not
   work on a Baldwin grand because the construction of the frame is such
   that one of the preparations cannot be accomplished. Flexible meters, wide
   dynamic range, effective use of pedals. Mystifying and enchanting. Int.
   to M-D.
J. D. (ACA) for piano and tape. The tape consists of random extracts from John
   Dowland's lute song "I Saw My Lady Weep," sung a capella. M-D.

Gabriel Chmura (1946–   ) Israel, born Poland
Piece for Piano (IMI 182 1963) 10pp. 6 min. Avant-garde notation, clusters, improvisational, free rhythms, atmospheric. Large span required. M-D.

Frédéric Chopin (1810–1849) Poland
The faultless grace of Chopin's piano writing, its personal stamp, and his preemi-
nent position as a composer make his works a *sine qua non* for all pianists and
piano teachers. His highly original writing has made a unique contribution to
the literature of the piano. BI (Brown Index) refers to Maurice J. E. Brown,
Chopin: An Index of His Works in Chronological Order, 2d ed. (New York: Da
Capo Press, 1972). KK refers to the Chopin catalog by Krystyna Kobylanska,
Thematisch-bibliographisches Werkverzeichnis (Henle 1979). It presents an ex-
haustive survey of Chopin's complete works, including all preserved manuscripts
and printed sources.

EDITIONS:

No "ultimate" edition of Chopin's works has yet appeared. The Henle Verlag
edition seems to be upholding some of the highest standards in what has been
issued. The Vienna Urtext Edition is also continuing to expand its Chopin catalog. These two scholarly and urtext editions are gradually supplanting the older
editions. The Chopin Institute edition (PWM) is complete but it does not distinguish clearly between the editor's and the composer's markings. (PWM) has announced a New National Edition but as of 1996 only four volumes had appeared:
Nocturnes, Polonaises, Ballades, and Preludes. They contain performance suggestions but lack critical notes.
Piano Works (Zimmermann, Keller, Herttrich, Keller—Henle). Ballades; Etudes;
   Impromptus; Mazurkas; Nocturnes; Piano Pieces (2 vols.); Polonaises; Preludes; Scherzos; Waltzes.
   Available separately: Sonatas, Opp.35, 58; Fantasy f, Op.49; Berceuse Db,

Op.57; Prelude D♭, Op.28/15; Funeral March from Sonata Op.35. Authentic, scholarly texts with added practical fingering.

Piano Works (Badura-Skoda, Ekier, Hansen, Demus—VU). Ballades; Etudes (Opp.10 and 25 available separately); Impromptus; Nocturnes; Preludes; Scherzos. Scholarly edition for practical musicians.

Complete Works for Piano (Bronarski, Paderewski, Turczynski—PWM). Vol.1: Preludes. Vol.2: Etudes. Vol.3: Ballades. Vol.4: Impromptus. Vol.5: Scherzos. Vol.6: Sonatas. Vol.7: Nocturnes. Vol.8: Polonaises. Vol.9: Waltzes. Vol.10: Mazurkas. Vol.11: Fantasia; Berceuse; Barcarolle. Vol.12: Rondos. Vol.13: Concert allegro; Variations. Vol.14: Concertos (two pianos). Vol.15: works for piano and orchestra (two pianos). Vol.16: chamber music. Vol.17: songs. Vol.18: minor works: Bolero; Tarantelle; March Funèbre, Op.72/2 (two versions); Trois Ecossaises, Op.72/3. Vol.19: Concerto No.1 (orchestra score). Vol.20: Concerto No.2 (orchestra score). Vol.21: works for piano and orchestra (orchestra score); Variations on "La ci darem," Op.2; Polonaise Brillante Op.22.

Selected Easy Pieces, An Introduction to Chopin (PWM). Includes: Preludes Op.28/2, 4, 6–8, 15, 20; Mazurkas Op.17/4, Op.24/1, Op.33/3, Op.67/2; Polonaises g, B♭ Op. posth; Nocturnes Op.9/2, Op.37/1, Op.72/1; Waltzes Op.34/2, Op.64/1, 2, Op.69/1, 2.

Facsimiles: Ballades A♭, f; Krakowiak-Grand Rondeau de Concert; 24 Preludes; Scherzo E; Fantasie f.

Vols.5, 8, 9, and 11 are available in study scores. Dover also reprints much of this edition. It is not reliable in a number of areas. No distinction is made between Chopin's markings and those of the editors.

Complete Works (Bargiel, Brahms, Franchomme, Liszt, Reinecke, Rudorff—K). 10 vols. Considered the first critical edition, 1878–1880.

Piano Works (Scholtz—CFP). Vol.1: Waltzes, Mazurkas, Polonaises, Nocturnes. Vol.2: Ballads, Impromptus, Scherzos, Fantasy. Vol.3: Sonatas, Piano Pieces, Concertos, Concert Pieces. Available also separately in 12 vols. Excellent for its fingering.

Piano Works (Mikuli—GS). Ballades; Four Concert Pieces; Etudes; Impromptus; Mazurkas, Miscellaneous Compositions; Nocturnes; Polonaises; Preludes, Rondos; Scherzos. Fantasy Op.49; Sonatas; Waltzes. With historical and analytical comments by James Huneker. Some textual errors.

Piano Works (Joseffy—GS). Album (33 Favorite Compositions); Ballades; Impromptus; Mazurkas; Miscellaneous Compositions; Nocturnes; Preludes; Scherzos, Fantasy Op.49; Waltzes.

Piano Works (Debussy—Durand). Ballades and Impromptus; Berceuse; Barcarolle; variations; 6 Chants Polonaises (transcribed by Liszt); Etudes; Mazurkas; Polonaises; Preludes and Rondos; Scherzos and Fantasy, Op.49; Sonatas; other separate pieces. Interesting edition, especially since Debussy studied with a pupil of Chopin and greatly admired Chopin's works throughout his life.

Piano Works (Cortot—Sal). Ballades; Etudes (Opp.10 and 25 separately); Impromptus; Mazurkas (3 vols.); Nocturnes (2 vols.); Preludes; Polonaises; Rondos; Scherzos; Sonata Op.35; Sonata Op.58; Valses; Miscellaneous Pieces (2 albums); Posthumous Works. Includes exercise to help solve problems. A fine practical edition.

Piano Works (Mertke—K). Barcarolle; Bolero; Nocturnes; Polonaises; Preludes; Waltzes. Serviceable edition with interesting fingerings.

Piano Works (Pugno—UE). Ballades and Impromptus; Etudes; Mazurkas; Nocturnes; Waltzes. Highly edited.

Piano Works (various editors—WH). Album of 26 Selected Pieces; Mazurkas (Mikuli); Nocturnes (Alnaes); Polonaises (Knudsen); Studies (Knudsen); Waltzes (Richartz).

Four Ballades (Zimmermann—Henle; Ekier—PWM, National Edition; Cortot—Sal, with English text; Palmer—Alfred; Casella—EC, with Fantasia Op.49; Agosti—EC; Brugnoli, Montani—Ric, and separately). No.1, Op.23; No.2, Op.38; No.3, Op.47; No.4, Op.52. The Henle edition contains Chopin's fingering in italics as well as fingering added by H.-M. Theopold. Preface in French, German, and English.

Complete Ballades, Impromptus, and Sonatas (Dover). Reprint of the PWM edition.

Ballade No.1 g, Op.23 1831. This work is constructed more like a narrative than are the others. Tonal ambiguity permeates the first 30 bars or so, which are technically fairly easy. But later, fast legato octaves and a big coda require advanced pianism. M-D.

Ballade No.2 f, Op.38 1839. The opening folk-like material and its return require great musical sensitiveness. It is followed by outbursts of great cascades of sonorities. This alteration of material, repeated several times with thematic variations, ends with violence triumphant. Requires drive, much technical skill, and strong, enduring fingers. M-D.

Ballade No.3 A♭, Op.47 1841. The least difficult of the four, almost a sonata, with development section in c♯. Liszt said this work was improvised on the spot for Heinrich Heine. The second subject in F requires careful phrasing and pedaling. Chopin's pedal indications in this section are especially helpful. See: Mark De Voto, "Chopin, Ballade A♭, Op.47," ITO, 1/5 (1975): 31 (bars 140–43).
Garrick Ohlsson, "Chopin Pedaling: The Ballade in A♭, Op.47," CK 7 (May 1981):54.

Ballade No.4 f, Op.52 1842. Tumultuous and dramatic; among the finest of Chopin's later pieces. Many extremely difficult double-note passages, with especially tricky ones in the strenuous coda. There is a master stroke toward the end, when, as tension reaches the breaking-point, five *pp* chords quell the fury (although only briefly), like a voice from another world. D
See: Carol Montparker, "Interpretations of Chopin's Ballade No. 4," *Clavier*, 33/10 (December 1994):10–16. Five pianists discuss how they approach

this piece. Part 2: *Clavier,* 34/1 (January 1995):16–21. Garrick Ohlsson and Harris Goldsmith comment on the challenges of this work.

The four Ballades contain some of Chopin's most poetic and inspired ideas. All are of considerable difficulty. The range of emotion is broad. They were an attempt to create a free form through which Chopin might carry several thematic ideas.

See: Lubov Keefer, "The Influence of Adam Mickiewicz on the Ballades of Chopin," *The American Slavic and East European Review,* 5/12–13 (May 1946):38–50.

12 Etudes Op.10 1828–32 (Badura-Skoda—VU; J. Ekier—PWM Esteban–Alfred; Zen-On). *12 Etudes* Op.25 1832–36 (Badura-Skoda—VU; Esteban—Alfred; Zen-On). *Etudes* Opp.10 and 25 (Zimmermann—Henle; Cortot—Sal, with English text; Friedheim—GS; Casella—EC; Oborin, Milstein—USSR; Brugnoli, Montani—Ric; Sternberg—CF; Scholtz—CFP; Thomson—Allans). The *Etudes* Opp.10 and 25 are brilliant treatments of 24 different technical problems and yet are inspired music. They exhibit the whole range of Chopin's genius.

Etudes, Book I, Op.10. Dedicated to Franz Liszt.

Etude No.1 C. Broken-chord passages alternately contract and expand the hand. Long pedals support the magnificent bass octave melody.

Etude No.2, a. Chromatic scales develop the third, fourth, and fifth fingers of the right hand, which must also play chords with the first and second fingers. One of the most difficult.

Etude No.3 E (Badura-Skoda—VU 51007, urtext and facsimile; Palmer—Alfred). Outer sections contain a cantabile melody; mid-section has a cadenza in double notes that require a good span. Do not overdo the rubato.

Etude No.4 c♯. An exciting and excellent finger study for both hands; kind of a toccata that aims at developing agility and velocity.

Etude No.5 G♭. A study on black keys. Requires free rotation, careful pedaling, nuance, and rubato.

Etude No.6 e♭. Helps to develop a delicate touch and legato playing. Seamless melody must be kept independent of the serpentine counterfiguration.

Etude No.7 C. A brilliant toccata in double notes requiring powerful fingers. Articulation of the melodic line with the fifth finger presents a problem.

Etude No.8 F. A brilliant arpeggio study for the right hand. Lilting bass melody requires careful pedaling.

Etude No.9 f. Left-hand accompaniment requires continuously rotating forearm. Chromatic shifts, molto rubato, wide extensions. Less difficult than some of the the the other études.

Etude No.10 A♭. A difficult chord study for the right hand; has numerous variations of touch and rhythm.

Etude No.11 E♭. Widely spread arpeggiated chords for both hands; hidden melody needs careful phrasing.

Etude No.12 c (PWM, facsimile). The "Revolutionary Etude" keeps the left hand very busy, but the right hand must dominate with fiery and dramatic statements. Reverses the technical problems of No.8.

Etudes, Book II, Op.25. Dedicated to Marie d'Agoult.

Etude No.1 A♭. This "Aeolean Harp" study is deceiving for its melodic skips. An even touch, clear melodies, and careful phrasing are necessary.

Etude No.2 f. This delicate finger study requires mastery of playing quarter-note triplets in one hand against eighth-note triplets in the other.

Etude No.3 F. A clarity and speed study requiring a very light touch.

Etude No.4, a. Leaping chords in the left hand and contrasting legato-staccato in the right hand help distinguish the main idea.

Etude No.5 e. Various touches must be applied to the main thematic material. The E mid-section should be broad and cantabile.

Etude No.6 g♯. Difficult study in thirds requires independent fingers, rotational flexibility in the forearm, and an accurately positioned upper arm. Sustained trills and chromatic scales in the right hand also present problems.

Etude No.7 c♯. Like a nocturne, with a duet between a cantabile melody in the left hand and a subordinate melody in the right hand, which also accompanies with quiet chords. Sometimes called "The Cello," after the opening recitative. A melting smorzando concludes.

Etude No.8 D♭. A study in sixths, technical requirements similar to those of No.6. Difficult for a small hand.

Etude No.9 G♭. This "Butterfly" study requires much endurance to maintain its delicate figuration.

Etude No.10 b. An octave study that requires much endurance and power. The legato cantabile mid-section is also taxing and difficult. Small hands should forget this one!

Etude No.11 a. This "Winter Wind" study is full of chromatic figuration in the right hand. The left hand has a strong chordal bass and at a few places must master the right-hand figuration. A whirlwind of sound; violent and passionate.

Etude No.12 c. A series of parallel arpeggios builds to a mighty climax. The right thumb brings out the booming B-A-C-H chorale theme. Requires powerful weight for the lowest notes. Orchestral in scope.

See: Emile Baume, "The Oxford Edition of the Chopin Etudes," MTNA Proceedings (1940):388–94.

Dean Elder, "Ian Hobson on the Chopin Etudes," *Clavier*, 23/7 (September 1984):18–23; 23/8 (October 1984):26–31.

Trois Nouvelles Etudes 1839. Composed for the instruction book of Moscheles and Fetis. They have no opus number. No. 1 f: right-hand melody in quarter-note triplets over a left-hand accompaniment in eighths. No.2 A♭: melody is in the top note of the right-hand chords; left-hand accompaniment in eighths of two against three. No.3 D♭: combines legato and staccato in same hand.

See: Jonathan Bellman, "Redefining the Study. Chopin's *Trois Nouvelles*

Etudes." *Piano & Keyboard,* 164 (September–October 1993):38–43. Includes the music of No. 1 These études are at least as important as the other 24.

Complete Preludes and Etudes (Dover). Reprint of the PWM edition.

See: Edward Rothchild, "Slenczynska: On Playing the Chopin Etudes," *Clavier,* 15 (February 1976):14–21.

Felix Salzer, "Chopin's Etude in F Major, Op.25, No.3. The Scope of Tonality," *Music Forum,* 3 (1973):281–90, which is mainly devoted to explaining the B mid-section of this piece.

4 Impromptus (Zimmerman—Henle; Ekier—VU; Cortot—Sal; Casella—EC; Joseffy—GS; Mikuli—GS). Henle edition contains Impromptus Op.29 A♭, Op.36 f♯, Op.51 G♭; and the Fantaisie-Impromptu Op.66 c♯ in both the Chopin and Fontana versions. These two versions show that we have been playing a great deal of Fontana for many years in the Op.66. VU edition has a preface and critical notes in French, English, and German and added fingering.

Impromptu No.1 A♭ Op.29 1837. Most passages lie easily under the fingers; two bars of double-note technique present a small problem.

Impromptu No.2 F♯ Op.36 1839. Half nocturne, half ballade. Melody is carried in top of left hand during the first half of the work. Key changes to F then returns to F♯. Pleasant but not distinguished. The most difficult of the four.

Impromptu No.3 G♭ Op.51 1842. This charming salon piece may be regarded as the forerunner of the Liszt "Legierezza." Some legato thirds and sixths are awkward for a small hand. Running figure of the outer sections contrasts with the calm, monophonic mid-section.

Impromptu No.4 c♯ (Fantaisie-Impromptu) Op.66 1835 (Hinson—Alfred 1048; Brugnoli, Montani—Ric; Rubinstein—GS, manuscript edition from the collection of Artur Rubinstein; contains detailed preface by Rubinstein, facsimile of the autograph, fingering and performance suggestions by Rubinstein). It is not known why Chopin did not publish this work during his lifetime. The Alfred edition contains both Chopin's and Fontana's editions. Comparison raises provocative questions. Grateful figuration alternates with a lyric mid-section, effective coda combines first and second themes.

The word *impromptu* literally means "improvisation." This title permits these works a certain amount of freedom, but they all use ABA design. All M-D.

See: Donald Alfano, "The Four Chopin Impromptus—Two Levels of Improvisation," *Quarterly Magazine* of the M.T.A. of New South Wales (May 1993): 2, 4–6.

57 Mazurkas (Zimmermann—Henle; Palmer—Alfred; Cortot—Sal, in 3 vols.; D. N. Kaoua—Lemoine; Agosti—EC; EMB). Study edition (Henle 9264). Henle edition contains 57 mazurkas: Nos.1–49 were given opus numbers by Chopin; Nos.50–53 were published without opus numbers during Chopin's lifetime; and Nos.54–57 were published after his death. Fingering has been added by Hans-Martin Theopold. Early versions of some of the mazurkas that were later revised are given in the Supplement. Critical notes in German. This outstanding practical urtext edition is the most complete collection of mazurkas available. Op.7/1,2 (Friedman—CF; Köhler—Litolff; Reinecke—Br&H; Fielden, Craxton—ABRSM; Sauer—Schott). Opp.17/2, 24/1, 33/1, 67/4, 68/2 (Brugnoli, Montani—Ric; Dover, reprint of Paderewski edition).

17 Selected Chopin Mazurkas (H. Levine—BMC). Highly edited. The following mazurkas have outstanding features: Op.6/3 E: vigorous, colorful bass theme, drums and drone effect. Op.7/1 F: one of the most popular, with a bagpipe trio. Op.17/1: full of zestful joy with a mid-section that contrasts a 2/4 bass against a triple-meter theme. Op.17/2 e: an example of the slow *kujawiak*; soulful sobs; repeats must be subtly varied.

Mazurka a Op.17/4: Lydian mode; plaintive melody that ends in the air on an inverted triad; drone bass.

Mazurka C Op.24/2: Lydian mode, uses a B natural with a tonic F.

Mazurka b♭ Op.24/4: One of the most dramatic; original two-voice main idea; mournful coda with new material.

Mazurka c♯ Op.30/4: chromatic descent of seventh chords before final fade-out.

Mazurka D Op.33/2: simple harmony, strong character, primitive and rustic flavor.

Mazurka c♯ Op.41/4: persistent Phrygian D natural adds much color.

Mazurka c♯ Op.50/3: contrapuntal opening and closing; mid-section has a simple harmonized melody.

Mazurka B Op.56/1: unusual succession of keys: B, E♭ (D♯, the mediant), B, G (submediant), B.

Mazurka a Op.59/1: contrapuntal; needs imaginative melodic nuance, rhythmic precision, and clear ornaments.

Mazurka A♭ Op.59/2: contains one of the most interesting melodies in all the mazurkas; a flourish of chromatic harmony leads to a refreshing coda.

Mazurka f♯ Op.59/3: contrapuntal, sophisticated rhythmic character, spirited main theme.

Mazurka B Op.63/1: begins boldly; changes character and key for next theme; question–answer section; coda displays a chromatic melisma smorzando; concludes with two big surprise chords.

Mazurka f Op.59/4: sad and beautiful; chromatic; modulation to A is striking; Chopin's last composition (R. Smith—Hansen House has a completely new realization of this work).

Robert Schumann wrote: "If the mighty autocrat of the North [the Czar of Russia] knew what a dangerous enemy threatened him in Chopin's works, in the simple melodies of his mazurkas, he would forbid this music. Chopin's works are guns buried in flowers." Chopin lifted the spontaneity of the mazurka triple dance rhythms, with emphasis on the second and third beats as well as the first, out of their origins into the charm of the lighted ballroom. The mazurkas are all beautiful tone poems that show Chopin to be a harmonic innovator. It was

Chopin who established the mazurka as an art form, and he is the only composer whose name is closely linked to it. Liszt called the mazurkas "imperious, fantastic, and impulsive."

See: TM, Analysis of Mazurka, Op.68/3, pp.80–91.

Ruth Slenczynska, "Chopin's Mazurka, Op.30/2," *Keyboard*, 10 (June 1984):85

Sigismond Stojowski, "On Performing a Chopin Mazurka," *Clavier* 9/9 (December 1970):20–21. A master lesson on Mazurka Op.30/1; includes the music.

21 Nocturnes (Zimmermann—Henle, including two versions of Nocturne c♯ BI 49, posth; Ekier—VU 50065; Ekier—PWM; Palmer—Alfred; G. Kovats—EMB; Cortot—Sal, in 2 vols., English text; Casella—EC; Bowen—Br&H; Pinter—CF; M. Lympany—Hansen House; D. Geoffrey—Lemoine). *18 Nocturnes* (Gibbs—Augener). Available separately: Nocturne E♭ Op.9/2 (Palmer—Alfred); Op.55/1 (Anson—Willis/Ekier—VU); Posthumous Nocturne c♯ (Henle; IMC; De Raco—Barry; Mertke—K); c Posthumous (Werner—Elkin; S. Akenase—Heuwekemeijer).

Nocturnes (19) *and Polonaises* (16) (Dover). Reprint of Paderewski edition.

3 Nocturnes (Cortot—Sal). Nocturnes c♯ BI 49 (posth.); Op.9/2 E♭; Op.55/1 f. English translation by Jerome Lowenthal.

Nocturne No.1 b♭ Op.9/1 1830–31. Single notes and octaves require singing legato. Nocturnal calm of the left-hand arpeggios is disturbed by an outburst of passion in the right hand that creates dramatic grandeur.

Nocturne No.2 E♭ Op.9/2 1830–31 (Palmer—Alfred 2153). Shortest, one of the most popular, graceful but not too difficult. Do not drag tempo.

Nocturne No.3 B Op.9/3 1830–31. Wide range of emotion; restless accompanimental figure in mid-section adds to stormy character. Melodic and harmonic chromaticism, key shifts, and vocal fiorituras make this a particularly original work. Most Field-like of the three.

Nocturne No.4 F Op.15/1 1830–31. Tranquil cantilena opening section with some daring harmony. Turbulent mid-section requires a powerful left hand. Serene closing.

Nocturne No.5 F♯ Op.15/2 1830–31. Two themes in opening section, elaborate ornamentation. Agitated, restless mid-section contains some unusual figuration. Marvelous coda.

Nocturne No.6 g Op.15/3 1833. Lighter in substance and one of the easier nocturnes. Exploits legato chord playing in the second half; another fine coda.

Nocturne No.7 c♯ Op.27/1 1835. Opening section exploits wide-spread extension of the left hand. Mid-section rises to an exultant climax, drops back and bursts into a lively mazurka. Octave cadenza requires a big tone.

Nocturne No.8 D♭ Op. 27/2 1835. This intensely expressive example contains a long sweeping melody in varied presentations, no contrasting mid-section, many fiorituras. Difficult to maintain mood.

Nocturne No.9 B Op.32/1 1836–37. Shorter and easier than most of the other nocturnes. Subtle tapping bass, histrionic chordal gestures, original and dramatic closing in B minor.

Nocturne No.10 A♭ Op.32/2 1836–37. Limited tonic–diminished–dominant harmony. Agitated 12/8 mid-section requires melodic line to be maintained in the outer fingers while playing accompanying chords in the same hand.

Nocturne No.11 g Op.37/1 1838. One of the easier nocturnes. Move the chorale-like passage in E♭ but keep the chords legato.

Nocturne No.12 G Op.37/2 1839. A lovely barcarolle with a rocking bass. Venetian tune alternates with the opening phrases in legato thirds and sixths that require even tone control.

Nocturne No.13 c Op.48/1 1841. Lisztian octaves, imposing effect, unique mid-section. Agitated recapitulation presents problems of control and tonal balance. The greatest of the nocturnes.

Nocturne No.14 f♯ Op.48/2 1841. Nostalgic mood; dreamily swaying. Individual character and original treatment of the recapitulation, which is cut short and leads to a beautiful coda.

Nocturne No.15 f Op.55/1 1843 (Ekier—VU 51006, urtext edition and facsimile of autograph). The melodic line is of extreme simplicity, similar to a Polish folk song of the "dumka" (elegy) type. Fairly easy except for the cadenza-like coda.

Nocturne No.16 E♭ Op.55/2 1843. Duet-like passages for the right hand present a problem. Imaginative variations of the theme, interesting counter melodies. Reflects Chopin's increased contrapuntal interest as seen in his later works.

Nocturne No.17 B Op.62/1 1846. Opening has free rhythmic structure, requires careful distinction between upper and lower voices. Shortened recapitulation; poetic coda.

Nocturne No.18 E Op.62/2 1846. Grand grief with a broad cantilena. Agitated and intense mid-section with melody carried in the outer fingers. Coda is melting and melodious. Op.62 contains two masterpieces that display a remarkable expressive force.

Nocturne No.19 e Op.72/1 (posth.) 1827. Sustained cantabile opening and closing sections; florid and passionate version of the main theme provides the mid-section. Unpretentious and not too difficult. Chopin was just beginning to sense his powers in this early work.

Nocturne No.20 c♯ (posth.) 1830. In collection *At the Piano with Chopin* (Alfred 2484). Contains some of Chopin's most beautiful writing. Related to his Piano Concerto f.

Nocturne No.21 c (posth.) 1837. Has some of the same qualities as Op.32, as it dates from the same year. Mid-section is not as contrasted as usual, numerous fiorituras, quiet ending. In collection *Chopin—Unknown Pieces* (Montani—Ric 2623).

The nocturnes are the most introspective and subjective of all Chopin's works. They require an expressive cantabile style, with a wide range of tone, and a carefully adjusted and balanced rubato to support the emotional content.

See: Daniel Ericourt with the collaboration of Robert Erickson, "Melodic Elements in the Chopin Nocturnes," *Clavier*, 16 (September 1977):35–39.

Polonaises (Ekier—PWM; Zimmermann—Henle; Palmer—Alfred; Cortot—Sal;

Agosti—EC; Biehl—Bosworth; Montani—Ric; Mertke—K). Henle edition contains Polonaises Op.26/1 c♯, 2 e♭; Op.40/1 A ("Militaire"), 2 c; Op.44 f♯; Op.53 A♭; Op.61 A♭ (Polonaise-Fantaisie); Op.71/1 (posth.) d, 2 B♭, 3 f (2 versions); g BI 1; B♭ BI 3; A♭ BI 5; g♯ BI 6; b♭ BI 13; G♭ BI 36. Based on autographs and first and early editions. Critical note in German.

Available separately: Opp.26/1, 40/1, 53 (Sauer—Schott). Opp.22, 40/2, 44 (Brugnoli, Montani—Ric). Opp.40/1, 53 (Dob). Opp.26/1, 40/1, 53 (WH). Op.53 (de Pachmann—Auguener).

Polonaise c♯ Op.26/1. Bold opening figure keeps returning in a piece that is mainly lyric in character. Tuneful theme in D♭ is laced with chromatic slides.

See: Howard Aibel, "Playing Chopin's Polonaise Op.26/1," KC, 12/5 (September–October 1992):42–44. Includes music on pp. 36–41.

Polonaise e♭ Op.26/2. Agitated and tragic mood; rhythmic chord passages. Not very difficult.

Polonaise A Op.40/1 (Palmer—Alfred 2155). This "Military Polonaise" requires rhythmic chord playing and is usually played too fast.

Polonaise c Op.40/2. Broad left-hand octave melody is supported by full chords in the right hand. Chromatic mid-section exploits motivic repetition.

Polonaise f♯ Op.44. The best of the polonaises. Much rhythmic drive, mazurka in mid-section, majestic climax, material well developed.

Polonaise A♭ Op.53 (PWM). The best known of the polonaises. A superb epic with an aristocratic march theme. Arpeggiated chords open the trio, which is full of a rhythmic melodic theme; lyric passage leads back to the noble opening idea. Requires a majestic tempo.

Polonaise d, B♭, f, Op.71/1–3. These early works, published posthumously, are not very interesting musically. Not difficult.

Polonaise g (posth.). Varied note values, numerous melodic ideas.

Polonaise B♭ (posth.). Composed when Chopin was seven years old. Not easy but easier than the other Polonaises.

Polonaise-Fantaisie A♭ Op.61 1845–46. None of the Polonaises comes nearer to the style of a tone-poem than this great work, with its extraordinary forward-looking chromatic harmony and self-generating melody. While preserving essential rhythmic characteristics of this dance form and basically adhering to the traditional ternary plan, the work creates an impression of continuous organic growth from the initial chordal challenge of the imposing, improvisatory introduction. This work has the strong rhythmic drive of the polonaises plus the poetic qualities of the ballades. A meditative mid-section supplies part of the material for the coda. Loose formal structure makes the work difficult to "hold together."

Andante Spianato and Grand Polonaise Brillante E♭ Op.22 1830–31, rev. 1834. In style, the exquisitely delicate, idyllic introduction in G is more related to Chopin's Nocturnes than to anything else. Over a rippling arpeggio accompaniment, the right hand sings a simple yet eloquent melody embellished with characteristic filigree ornamentation. A 16-bar modulatory bridge leads into the Polonaise, a brilliant *jeu d'esprit* around the rhythms of this stately old national dance. Brilliantly effective and not as difficult as it sounds.

Perhaps inspired by Bach's *Well-Tempered Clavier* Chopin wrote a prelude for each of the 24 keys. In terms of musical structure and pianistic expertise, these aphoristic compositions are some of the most original works of the nineteenth century.

24 Preludes Op.28 (Ekier—PWM; Zimmerman—Henle; Thomas Higgins—Norton Critical Scores 1974; Cortot—Sal, with English text, includes descriptions of each prelude in English; Casella—EC; G. E. Moroni—Carisch; Hansen, Demus—VU; Palmer—Alfred; Casella—Heugel; Brugnoli, Montani—Ric; Y. Bowen—British and Continental; M. Lympany—Hansen House; Dover, reprint of Paderewski edition). The Henle edition also contains Op.45 and BI 86 (*Prelude* A♭). The Norton edition contains the Henle text (but not Op.45 and BI 86) plus analytical essays and historical background, which are supplemented by contemporary assessments by many of Chopin's champions and critics. In the VU edition, alterations are not always noted in the musical text; and the critical notes must be read very closely to see where variations occur. The Alfred edition also includes Op.45 and the posthumous (1918) A♭ *Prelude* (BI 86). It has a scholarly introduction; it is based on the 1839 autograph; and all editorial suggestions are in lighter print. Hansen House contains Opp.28 and 45.

Available separately: Nos.1, 9, 10 (Kjos). Nos.4, 6, 7, 20 (Palmer—Alfred 2152). No.15 (Hansen—VU 51008, urtext edition and facsimile of the autograph). Nos.15, 24 (Brugnoli, Montani—Ric).

Complete Preludes and Etudes (Dover) 216pp. Reprint of the Polish Chopin Institute edition.

Prelude No.1 C. In this piece the performer must establish the underlying agitation and restlessness of the entire Opus. Requires free forearm rotation and a singing tone to be produced by the right thumb.

Prelude No.2 a. Dissonance is taken to unprecedented and exquisite heights. Though marked *Lento*, it is alla breve and must not be taken too slow.

Prelude No.3 G. Etude-like, combines virtuoso light left-hand running accompanimental figuration with a legato right-hand melody. Evenness is a problem.

Prelude No.4 e. A melancholy contrast; rises archlike to a central climax; played at Chopin's funeral. Should not be played too slowly.

Prelude No.5 D. Contains brevity and wit in each rapid twist and turn; needs flexible lateral adjustment at wrist joint.

Prelude No.6 b. Beguiling melodies require expansive phrasing, cell-like left-hand melody. Follow Chopin's pedal indications closely; avoid overpedaling.

Prelude No.7 A. Difficult to capture its natural simplicity; should have a slight lilt to its motion.

Prelude No.8 f♯. Rippling filigree figurations. Needs cantabile technique in right thumb. Cross-rhythms and inner voices must all be evident.

Prelude No.9 E. An austere largo; needs a rich, singing sonority. Duet between bass and upper right hand. Handelian majesty!

Prelude No.10 c♯. Needs sparkling finger work; note leggiero marking.

Prelude No.11 B. Improvisatory, must flow freely. Hemiola melody provides lilt and shape.

Prelude No.12 g♯. This presto whirlwind requires much momentum; do not sacrifice clarity. One of the most difficult preludes; needs powerful hands.

Prelude No.13 F♯. An idyllic nocturne. Main problem is maintaining the correct tonal balance between the different textures in the mid-section.

Prelude No.14 e♭. Pesante triplets require good rotation.

Prelude No.15 D♭. Longest of the preludes, and plausibly called "Raindrop." Be sure the ostinato figure which occurs throughout never sounds monotonous. Should be played with great sensitivity, dramatic crescendo in mid-section.

Prelude No.16 b♭. Virtuoso fuoco scamperings. Requires powerful fingers. Follow the composer's pedal markings carefully for some of the most cacophonous sounds ever composed by Chopin.

Prelude No.17 A♭. A song without words, poetic. Final section with 11 sumptuous pedal notes is almost Impressionistic.

Prelude No.18 f. A fantastic creation that needs power, rhythmic drive, and strong fingers.

Prelude No.19 E♭. Melody must be skillfully phrased; "limpidity" is key word. Graceful and difficult.

Prelude No.20 c. Massive and majestic chords dissolve to tranquil calm. Chopin originally ended the piece at bar 9; a grand chorale chord study.

Prelude No.21 B♭. Songlike with restless undercurrent. This slow waltz requires legato double notes in the accompaniment.

Prelude No.22 g. Dramatic; rhythmically complex. Left-hand bravura octave solo.

Prelude No.23 F. Decorous and purling flow; lowered seventh in the next to last bar adds a colorful touch.

Prelude No.24 d. An angry and defiant mood permeates this bold and cataclysmic conclusion. Requires great rotational freedom for the accompaniment. Use at least three fingers on the final three resonant D's!

Prelude No.25 c♯ Op.45. Idyllic, requires limpid tone, anticipates Brahms. Double-note cadenza is most difficult part.

See: Jean-Jacques Eigeldinger, "Chopin and 'La Note Bleue': An Interpretation of the Prelude Op.45," M&L, 78/2 (May 1987):233–53.

Prelude No.26 A♭ Op. posth. (BI86) (Novello; Henn). Dashing, teasing, and enigmatic. Similar in style to the "Butterfly" *Etude* Op.25/9.

Like Bach's "Forty-eight," these preludes investigate every key, following a pattern of major–relative minor. Within their short lengths can be heard touches of Debussy, Scriabin, and Wagner. A set of miniature gems.

See: Maurice J. E. Brown, "The Chronology of the Chopin Preludes," MT, 98 (August 1957):423–44.

Richmond Browne, "Chopin Preludes Forum: Back to Chopin," ITO, 1/4:3–4.

Ronald Cole, "Analysis of the Chopin Preludes, Op.28," Master's Thesis, Florida State University, 1967.

TM, Analysis of Op.28/4, pp.41–55.

Michael R. Rogers, "Chopin, Prelude in A Minor, Op.28, No.2," *Nineteenth-Century Music*, IV/3 (Spring 1981):245–50.

Douglas Weeks, "The Unity within Chopin's *Préludes*," *Clavier*, 34/7 (September 1995):23–24, 26–29.

3 Rondos (Cortot—Sal; Pugno—UE; Scholtz—CFP; K; Biehl—Bosworth). No.1 c, Op.1 (1825): not of much interest, being the immature work of a 15-year-old boy. No.2 F Op.5 ("Rondo a la Mazur," 1826): still retains the original name of *mazur*, not mazurka. No.3 E♭ Op.16 (1832): Probably meant as a bravura piece for one of his students. These three pieces represent Chopin's weakest genre.

4 Scherzos (E. Zimmermann—Henle; Cortot—Sal; Agosti—EC; Ekier—VU 50061; Sauer—Schott; Bowen—Br&H, Nos.1, 2; WH 2; Biehl—Bosworth; Köhler—Litolff; Brugnoli, Montani—Ric, also separately, Nos. 1,2). No.1 b Op.20 (1831–32): first section is restless and recalls the opening movement of the Sonata b♭ Op.35; theme in the contrasting lyric section is taken directly from a Polish *Noel*; fiery coda contains some taxing passages. No.2 b♭ Op.31 (1837): the most popular of the four; opening three bars provide the questioning figure that plays such a large part in this piece; contrasting motive intrudes and leads to the first melody; mid-section Trio contains thin textures; leads to a lengthy dramatic passage that returns to the opening initial idea; brilliant finger technique. No.3 c♯ Op.39 (1839): the most dramatic of the set; opening octaves in both hands followed by a chorale-like melody in D♭ with falling sprays of *leggierissimo* arpeggios interspersed among the sostenuto chords; ABA design; dashing con fuoco finale; requires strong fingers. No.4 E Op.54 (1842): the most joyous of the four, less dramatic but more poetic than the others; lyric mid-section in c♯; waltz character permeates this work although it concludes triumphantly; requires great delicacy in finger technique and chord playing.

All the scherzos are in ABA design with a contrasting "B" mid-section. They are among Chopin's greatest works and tend to exploit the element of instrumental brilliance more than do the Ballades.

See: Dean Elder, "Ivan Moravec: Conquering Chopin's Scherzo in c♯ minor," *Clavier*, 24/2 (February 1985):6–11.

3 Sonatas Opp.4, 35, 58 (Zimmermann—Henle, Opp.35 and 58 published separately; Cortot—Sal; PWM, has facsimile of the original autograph; Brugnoli, Montani—Ric, plus Op.35 separately; Agosti—EC, Opp.35 and 58, with analytical and interpretative notes in French, English and Italian).

Sonata No.1 c Op.4 (1828). Allegro maestoso; Minuetto—Allegretto; Larghetto; Finale—Presto. An elaborate student essay, dully sequential and repetitive, but in the right hands its tired gestures can be miraculously revitalized. The 5/4 Larghetto requires careful but flexible rubatos. D.

Sonata No.2 b♭ Op.35 (1837, 1839). Grave—Doppio movimento: SA design; presents some of Chopin's most compact writing; powerfully wrought development; closing is a magnificent statement that makes the movement an entity in itself. Scherzo: superbly pianistic; lyric Trio. Marche Funèbre ("Funeral March") (Henle 366): this renowned movement was composed two years earlier than the rest of the sonata. Finale—Presto: eerie and ghostly; *pp* and unison throughout, "winds of night sweeping over churchyard graves" (Anton Rubinstein); almost atonal in its sonority and chromaticism; its mysticism casts an inexorable spell, its querying finally clarified by the ultimate fortissimo b-flat chord. Probably Chopin's most successful work in a large form. D.

Sonata No.3 b Op.58 (1844). Allegro maestoso: marvelous ideas developed in Chopin's unique manner. Scherzo—Molto vivace: requires most fluent fingers; nostalgic Trio provides a welcome contrast. Largo: truly inspired; song form. Finale—Presto non tanto: is vigorous and strongly rhythmic, in rondo form with three statements. Brilliant finger technique and firm rhythmic control are basics for this work. It is another of Chopin's masterpieces. D.

Sonatas Opp.35 and 58 (Ekier—PWM 510-04041).

Waltzes (Palmer—Alfred 2483 1984) 96pp. 17 waltzes. Interesting discussion of ornamentation. Well-researched, practical edition.

Waltzes (E. Zimmermann—Henle; Cortot—Sal, with English translation by John Schneider; Casella—EC; Casella—Heugel; Bowen—Br&H; Mertke—K; Brugnoli, Montani—Ric; ABRSM, annotated by Thomas Fielding; CF). Henle edition contains 18 waltzes with two versions each of Op.69/2, Op.70/1,2. Appendix contains Waltzes E♭ BI 133 and E♭ BI 46, which are of questionable authenticity. Opp.18, 34/1,2, 64/1,2, 69/1, 2, 70/1–3, e Op. posth. (Sauer—Schott). Opp.34/3, 42, 64/3 (Brugnoli-Montani—Ric). Op.42 (Reinecke—Br&H; MacFarren—Ashdown). Op.64 (Speidel—Cotta). Op.64/1 (Samuel—Paxton; Dunhill—Lengnick). Opp.34/1, 62/2 transcribed by L. Godowsky (CF; de Pachmann—Augener).
Available separately: Op.64, 1, 2, Op.69, 1 (Palmer—Alfred).

3 Valses Op.64, Op.69/1,2 (Cortot—Sal). With English translation.

Valse f♯ (M. Dumesnil—Schroeder & Gunther). Not found in any collection. Effective, sounds like Chopin. M-D.

Waltz E♭ Op.18. Effective, brilliant, pianistic. Makes a fine effect.

Waltz A♭ Op.34/1. Brilliant, salon style.

Waltz a Op.34/2. A slow expressive type; opening theme cello-like.

Waltz A♭ Op.42. Brilliant. Trill introduction, hemiola between hands, a series of waltzes, effective and exciting closing.

Waltz D♭ Op.64/1. The famous "Minute Waltz." The word "minute" does not refer to the 60 seconds supposedly required to play the piece, but to the term "minute" meaning small.

Waltz c♯ Op.64/2. Slow, langorous, aristocratic.

Waltz A♭ Op.64/3. Bold and dashing; bass solo in mid-section.

Waltzes A♭, b Op.69/1,2. Easy, expressive, chromatic.

Waltzes G♭, A♭, D♭ Op.70/1,2,3. Early works; fluent and effective.

Waltz e (posth.) Brilliant and effective.

Waltz Op.70/1 G♭ and *Grand Valse Brillante* Op.18 E♭ (Byron Janis—Edutainment, through GS). Contains two separate versions and facsimile of these pieces. A few differences exist between these versions and other printed editions.

See: Muriel Brooks, "Chopin/Janis," AMT, 28 (April–May 1979):7–8. A discussion of Janis's discovery of two waltz MSS at Yale University, Op.70 Waltz G♭; Op.18 Grand Valse Brilliant.

Jan Drath, *Waltzes of Fryderyk Chopin: Sources* (Kingsville, TX: Texas A&I University Publications, 1979), 319pp. Contains a thematic catalogue, discussion of each waltz, bibliography.

Waltz a (posth.) 1843? BI 150. One of the easiest but needs careful attention to ornaments. Int.

Valse Melancolique KK Anh. Ia/7 1838? In collection *At the Piano With Chopin* (Alfred 2484). Seems to date from the time that Chopin and George Sand spent the winter and spring in Majorca, Spain. This expressive piece should exhibit simplicity and a plaintive character. M-D.

SEPARATE PIECES:

Variations B♭ on "Je vends des scapulaires" Op.12 1833 (Br&H; CFP; Cramer; Cranz). This set is based on the "Ronde" theme from Herold's *Ludovic*. Introduction and 4 variations. Attractive, technically effective. M-D.

Bolero a Op.19 1833 (K; Ric). Known in England in Wessel's edition as "Souvenirs d'Andalousie." Effective, same musical quality as Op.12. Superficially Spanish, rhythm resembles a Polonaise. M-D.

Tarantelle A♭ Op.43 1841 (Bèrben). Owes much to Rossini's "La Danza." Brilliant, effective, less musical than Opp.12 and 19. M-D.

Allegro de Concert Op.46. Sketched in 1832, revised and completed in 1841. Contains material originally conceived for a third piano concerto. M-D to D.

Fantaisie f Op.49 1841 (Henle; Ric; Schott). This brilliant and difficult masterpiece is structurally one of Chopin's most successful designs. Begins in march time and includes a two-bar motive of a Polish folk song. Improvisatory and march-like passages repeated in three different keys, followed by a short Lento sostenuto. Ending is quiet until the final keyboard sweep. D.

Berceuse D♭ Op.57 1843–44 (Hinson—Alfred 3579; S&B R 0228; Ric; Schott; Lengnick). Rocking ostinato figure in the bass, series of continuous ascending and descending arabesques in the right hand. Requires great delicacy in the intricate figuration and subtle pedaling. M-D.

See: Miriam Hyde, "Chopin's Berceuse," *Quarterly Magazine* of the M. T. A. of New South Wales (November 1989):45–47.

Barcarolle F♯ Op.60 1846 (Schott; K; Ric; PWM facsimile). With its Italianate melody, this piece is less intimate, more expansive than the Nocturnes, though it still belongs more to their world than to any other. Remarkably successful work with easy harmonies and arabesque-like melodic contours. On the same scale as the Ballades and Scherzos. Undulating theme suggests the Venetian gondoliers. The greatest barcarolle ever written. D.

Three Ecossaises D, G, D♭ Op.72 (posth). 1826. Delightful trifles related to the character of the waltz. Schubert influence. Int.

Marche Funèbre c Op.72/2 (posth.) 1827 (CFP D-2796; Heuwekemeijer). This work with dotted rhythms is similar to the slow movement of Sonata Op.35 B♭. Trio section is in major key. Octaves and large chords. M-D.

Album Leaf BI 151 1843. Appealing melody. Int.

Cantabile BI 84 1834. Flowing melody, vocally inspired. Int.

Souvenir de Paganini A BI 37 1829 (Werner—Elkin; in collection *Chopin—Unknown Pieces*, Ric 2625). Theme is the Venetian air "Le Carnaval de Venise," used by Paganini himself as the basis of variations in his Op.10. Four variations and closing. Florid, fast skips of tenths, chromatic melodic figuration over broken-chord accompaniment in left hand. M-D.

Contradanse G♭ 1827? (in collection *Chopin—Unknown Pieces*, Ric 2625). 27 bars. ABA, Allegretto cantabile with Trio in C♭. Ecossaise-like, contains a few ornaments. Int. to M-D.

Gallop Marquis KK p 1240a. In collection *95 Early/Late Intermediate Miniatures* (Alfred 4619). Inspired by George Sand's two pet dogs, Marquis and Dib. Int.

Largo BI 109 1837? Full chords support melody. Int.

Sostenuto BI 133 1840. A miniature waltz. Int.

Two Bourrées BI 160B 1846. These two delightful dance tunes from Berry (a region of central France) were harmonized by Chopin for use in a play by George Sand. Int.

Variations on a German Folk Song BI 14 1826. In collection *Masters of the Romantic Period* (Alfred 1183). Pianistically gratifying and effective. Theme and four contrasting variations. M-D.

Variation No. 6 from the *Hexameron* BI 113 1837. In collection *At the Piano with Chopin* (Alfred 2484). A lovely nocturne-like piece; requires pedal sensitivity and careful control of rubato. M-D.

COLLECTIONS:

Album Chopina—L'Album de Chopin 1828–1831 (Jerzy Maria Smoter—PWM 1975) 61pp. Polish and French. Bibliography, pp.61–62.

Chopin Album I (PWM). 5 preludes from Op.28; 7 mazurkas; 3 polonaises (g, c♯, A♭); 5 valses; 4 nocturnes; Revolutionary Etude. Fingering and pedal added.

Chopin—An Introduction to His Piano Works (W. Palmer—Alfred). The 13-page introduction treats Chopin's style and rubato, but concentrates on a thorough explanation of Chopin's use of ornaments, with many musical examples. Urtext edition with editorial additions in gray print.

Chopin—14 of His Easiest Piano Selections (Alfred 397). 14 pieces including 6 mazurkas, 3 preludes, 3 waltzes, 2 unfamiliar posthumous works, plus a biography and notes about each piece. Int. to M-D.

Chopin—Selected Favorites (Alfred). 19 pieces including 4 mazurkas, 4 waltzes, Etude Op.10/5 E, Nocturne Op.9/2 E♭, Fantaisie-Impromptu. Biography and notes about each piece. Int. to M-D.

Frederic Chopin Piano Compositions (Tucker—WB 1992) 32pp. Ecossaise II; Marche Funebre; Mazurkas Opp.63/2, 68/3; Nocturne Op.9/2; Preludes Op.28/4, 6, 15; Valse Op.64/1; Valse Brillante Op.34/2. No distinction between composer's and editor's marks. Int. to M-D.

Il mio primo Chopin (Pozzoli—Ric ER2446) 14pp. Preludes Op.28/4 e, 6 b, 7 A; Mazurkas Op.7/5 C, part of Op.7/2 a, Op.67/2 B♭; Waltzes O.69/1 A♭, Op.69/2 b. Int.

Diverse Pieces (Cortot—Sal) Vol.I: Fantaisie; Barcarolle; Berceuse; Tarentelle. Vol.II: Allegro de Concert; Bolero; 3 Nouvelles Etudes; Prelude c; Variations Brillantes.

Fantasy in F Minor, Barcarolle, Berceuse and Other Works for Solo Piano (Dover, reprint of Paderewski edition). Also includes Rondo Op.1; Introduction and Rondo Op.16; Introduction and Variations Op.12; Tarantella Op.43; Funeral March Op.72/2; Rondo à la Mazur Op.5; Introduction and Variations on a German Air; Bolero Op.19; Allegro Concert Op.46; Three Ecossaises Op.72/3; Andante spianato Op.22. Int. to D.

Introduction to the Cortot Editions of Chopin (Sal) 64pp. A sampler in English of Cortot's annotated editions. 4 preludes, 3 mazurkas, 3 nocturnes, 3 waltzes, ecossaises, Polonaise A.

Posthumous Works (Cortot—Sal). Sonata Op.4; Variations; 3 polonaises; 2 nocturnes; Marche Funèbre; 3 ecossaises; Polonaise g♯.

Klavierstücke (E. Herttrich, H.-M. Theopold—Henle 318). Includes Variations Op.12 B♭; Bolero Op.19; Tarantella Op.43; Allegro de Concert Op.46; Fantaisie Op.49; Berceuse Op.57; Barcarolle Op.60; Variations on a German National Air (Der Schweizerbub) BI 14; 3 Ecossaises Op.72. Based on autographs and first and early editions.

Young Pianist's Guide to Chopin (Y. Novik—WB). Includes record of the contents. Int.

Piano Pieces (Scholtz, Pozniak—CFP). *Variations brillantes* B♭ on "Je vends des scapulaires" Op.12; *Bolero* Op.19; *Tarantelle* Op.43; *Allegro de Concert* Op.46; *Berceuse* Op.57; *Barcarolle* Op.60; *Funeral March* Op.72/2; *Ecossaises* Op.72/3–5; *Variations on a German Air* Op. posth. Int. to M-D.

Introduction to Chopin (A. Mirovitch—GS 1959) 2 vols. Graded works ranging from the Prelude c Op.28/20 to the Ballade g Op.23. Main emphasis is on the "use of the pedal." Helpful prefatory remarks on each piece. Int.

Chopin Album (Friedman—Br&H). Vol. I: Ballade A♭; Berceuse; Etudes Op.25/1, 7; Fantaisie-Impromptu; Mazurkas Opp. 24/3, 33/3,4, 7/1, 56/1; Nocturnes Opp. 15/2, 32/1, 37/1, 27/2. M-D. Vol.II: Polonaises A, c♯, Preludes D♭, A; Scherzo b; Funeral March from Op.35; Waltzes Opp. 34/2, 70/2, 42, 70/1, e Op. posth. M-D.

The Easiest Original Chopin Pieces for the Piano (Rowley—Hin). Preludes A, e, b, c, D♭; Mazurkas Opp. 63/2, 68/3, 7/2; Nocturne Op.15/3; Waltz a. Int.

Chopin Album (Scholz—CFP) 32 pieces. Waltzes Opp. 18, 34/1–2, 42, 64/1–2, e; Mazurkas Opp. 7/1–2, 33/1, 3–4; Polonaises c♯, A; Etudes Opp. 25/1, 7, 9; Scherzo b; Prelude D♭; Fantaisie-Impromptu; Berceuse; Funeral March Op.35. M-D.

Chopin Album (Sauer—Schott). Vol.I: Waltzes Opp. 34/2, 64/1–2; Mazurkas Opp. 7/1, 17/1, 24/3; Nocturnes, Opp. 9/2, 15/2, 31/1, 37/2; Polonaises c♯, A; Preludes e, b, A, D♭, c; Funeral March Op.35; Impromptu A♭; Berceuse; Ballade g; Fantaisie-Impromptu. M-D. Vol.II: Waltzes Opp. 18, 34/1, 69/1; Mazurkas Opp. 7/2, 33/3–4; Nocturnes Opp. 27/2, 37/1, 55/1; Etude Op. 10/5; Scherzo b; Ballade A♭; Ecossaises. Int. to M-D.

Chopin Pastels (H. Kreutzer—BMC 1962). Eight original pieces including Mazurka B♭ (1832); Valse A♭ (posth.); Contredanse G (1827?) originally G♭; Cantabile B♭ (1834); Album Leaf E (1843); Largo E♭. Admirable collection, clear editing with measure numbers. Int. to M-D.

Album 28 Original Piano Works (WH). Preludes C, e, A, c, b, D♭; 3 Ecossaises; Mazurkas Opp. 7/1, 67/3, 33/2; Polonaises A, c♯; Nocturnes Opp. 9/2, 32/3, 15/2; Fantaisie-Impromptu; Waltzes Opp. 34/2, 64/1–2; Berceuse; Etudes Opp. 25/1,2, 10/3, 12; Scherzo b; Ballade g. Int. to M-D.

Piano Music Selections (Ekier—PWM National Edition 1992) 100pp. Variations B♭ Op.12; Bolero Op.19; Tarantella Op.43; Allegro de Concert Op.46; Fantasy Op.49; Berceuse Op.57; Barcarolle Op.60. M-D to D.

Pezzi sconosciuti (Montani—Ric 1959). 13 of these 15 unknown pieces are contained in the Paderewski edition distributed among five different volumes. Mazurka D, Waltz a, Souvenir de Paganini (a set of variations in the style of Paganini based on "Carnival of Venice" melody), polonaises, and other works. Clean edition with some new repertoire. Int. to M-D.

Antologia de 21 Pezzi (Brugnoli, Montani—Ric). Contains mainly familiar works: Preludes Op.28/4, 6, 7, 15, 20, 22; Mazurkas Opp. 33/1, 68/2, 3, 7/1, 2; Waltzes Opp. 34/2, 64/1,2, 69/1,2; Nocturnes Op.9/1–2; Fantasia Impromptu Op.66; Polonaise Op.40/1; and the rarely found Nocturne c♯ Op. posth. M-D.

Easiest Piano Pieces (Scholtz—CFP 5002) 23pp. Contains Preludes Op.28/6,7,20; Waltz, Op.34/2; Mazurkas Opp. 7/2, 17/2. Int.

Selections (Zimmermann, Theopold—Henle 348) 114pp. Contains Waltzes Opp. 34/2, 64/1,2, 69/1; KK IVa Nr.15, IV b Nr.11. Mazurkas Opp.7/1, 17/1,2, 33/1,3, 41/4, 63/2, 67/2, 68/2. Preludes Op.28,4, 6, 7, 9, 14, 15, 20, 23. Polonaises Opp. 26/1, 40/1,2; Nocturnes Opp. 15/3, 27/1, 32/1, 37/1, KK IVa Nr.16 (the Op. posth. in c♯). Fantaisie-Impromptu Op. posth. 66 (Fontana version). Preface in English, French, and German; critical notes in German. This volume of popular pieces provides an excellent introduction to Chopin in a performing/urtext edition. Int. to M-D.

Preludes and Ballades Vol. II (Escandon—WB 1994) 138pp. This edition is based on the teaching and performance of Jorge Bolet. Eight rules are discussed. Int. to M-D.

21 Favorite Chopin Mazurkas (K. Roundtree—WB 1995) 75pp. Opp.6/1, 3; 7/1, 2, 4; 17/1, 2, 4; 24/1, 4; 30/2, 3; 33/1; 59/2, 3; 63/2; 67/1, 2, 3; 68/2, 3. Comments on the mazurka and the mazurka in the life of Chopin. Int. to M-D.

See: Gerald Abraham, *Chopin's Musical Style* (London: Oxford University Press, 1939; reprint, Oxford, 1960).

Jonathan Bellman, "Chopin and the Cantabile Style," *Historical Performance*, 2/2 (Winter 1989):63–71.

Edward Blickstein, "The Lost Art of Chopin Interpretation," *International Piano Library*, 1 (Fall–Winter 1967):2–10.

Alfred Cortot, *In Search of Chopin* (New York: P. Nevill, 1951; reprint, Westport, CT; Greenwood Press, 1975).

J. P. Dunn, *Ornamentation in the Works of Chopin* (London: Novello, 1921; reprint, New York; Da Capo Press, 1970).

Thomas Higgins, "Chopin Interpretation: A Study of Directions in Selected Autographs and Other Sources," diss., University of Iowa, 1966.

——, "Tempo and Character in Chopin," MQ, 59 (January 1973):106–20.

——, "Chopin's Music and Fashions of Performing It: Some Crucial Differences," AMT, 29 (February–March 1980):12–14.

Maurice Hinson, "Pedaling the Piano Works of Chopin," in Joseph Banowetz, *The Pianist's Guide to Pedaling* (Bloomington: Indiana University Press, 1985), pp.179–98.

Jan Holcman, "The Labyrinth of Chopin Ornamentation," JR, 5 (Spring 1958): 23–41.

Jeffrey Kallberg, "Compatibility in Chopin's Multipartite Publications," *The Journal of Musicology*, 2/4 (Fall 1983):391–417.

Frank Merrick, "Some Editions of Chopin," MT, 97 (November 1956):575–77.

Garrick Ohlsson, "Pedaling Chopin," Part I, CK, 7 (April 1981):50.

Sandra P. Rosenblum, "Some Enigmas of Chopin's Pedal Indications: What Do the Sources Tell Us?" *Journal of Musicological Research,* 16 (1996): 41–61.

Felix Salzer, "Chopin's Nocturne in C♯ Minor, Op.27, No.1," *The Music Forum*, 2 (1970):283–97.

Jim Samson, ed. *The Cambridge Companion to Chopin.* Cambridge: Cambridge University Press, 1992. 341pp.

Bruce Simonds, "Chopin's Use of the Term 'Con Anima,'" *MTNA Proceedings* (1948):151–57.

Helen Walker-Hill, "Some Thoughts on the Interpretation of Chopin," AMT, 33/2 (November–December 1983):46–47. Suggests silent study (inner listening) of the music.

PQ, 113 (Spring 1981), a special issue devoted to the piano works of Chopin.

Alan Walker, ed. *Frederic Chopin: Profiles of the Man and Musician* (New York: Taplinger, 1967).

Edward N. Waters, "Chopin by Liszt," MQ, 47 (April 1961):170–94.

Wen-chung Chou (1923–   ) USA, born China

Chou's early works were based on traditional Chinese music and folk songs, but his later works used these only as a "point of departure." Characteristic of his style are delicate coloring and weaving of unique textures.

The Willows Are New (CFP 1957) 7pp. 6 min. A broad range of color and delicacy evokes the oriental spirit. The half-step is greatly exploited. Thin textured lines are similar to the fine brush strokes of Chinese painting. Non-tonal harmonization of an ancient Chinese melody, realized in a conservative, homophonic style. Effective. M-D.

Domenico Cimarosa (1749–1801) Italy

Cimarosa's sonatas provide excellent alternatives to some of the overworked Clementi and Kuhlau sonatinas.

32 Sonatas (Boghen—ESC 1925–26). 3 vols. These one-movement works are thin-textured and homophonic. They employ scalar passages and broken-chord figurations in early classic style with an admixture of Domenico Scarlatti's temperament. A wealth of unusual and usable material. Varied lengths and moods.

62 Sonatas (Crudeli—Carisch). Revised and fingered by the editor.

Sonatas (Arturo Sacchetti—Bèrben 1974) 19pp. Preface and performance notes in English. No.1 G is in the PWM collection listed below; Sonatas in F, F, C, B♭, and A are published here for the first time. These are not the finest works by Cimarosa. All use much Alberti bass. Int.

24 Sonatas (Ligteliyn, Ruperink—B&VP) 3 vols. Contains 24 of the sonatas from the Boghen collection.

Selected Harpsichord Sonatas (Z. Sliwinski—PWM 1971) 63pp. Preface in Polish only. Contains 20 sonatas, two of which are not in the Boghen collection. Well fingered; ornamentation written out.

31 Sonatas (V. Vitale, C. Brunno—Carisch) 2 vols. An edited "instructive" edition that duplicates only one sonata (No.27) in the Boghen edition. Uses MS numbers.

88 Keyboard Sonatas (Coen—Zanibon 1995). Vol. I. Sonatas 1–44; Vol. II. Sonatas 45–88.

Comparison of Sonatas by Cimarosa
in the ESC, B&VP, and PWM Editions

	Eschig	Broekmans & Van Poppel	Polskie Wydawnictwo Muzyczne
Vols.I & II:	1	21	—
	2	17	5
	3	2	—
	4	22	1
	5	3	10
	6	20	3
	7	7	—
	8	19	—
	9	1	—
	10	23	—
	11	10	9
	12	18	—
	13	5	8
	14	4	7
	15	12	—
	16	8	16
	17	16	—
	18	14	—

*Comparison of Sonatas by Cimarosa
in the ESC, B&VP, and PWM Editions (cont.)*

	Eschig	Broekmans & Van Poppel	Polskie Wydawnictwo Muzyczne
	19	11	—
	20	24	18
Vol.III:	1(21)	—	19
	2(22)	—	4
	3(23)	13	13
	4(24)	—	15
	5(25)	—	6
	6(26)	—	2
	7=MS 27	9	11
	8(28)	—	—
	9(29)	15	—
	10(30)	—	20
	11(31)	6	—
	12(32)	—	14
	—	—	12
	—	—	17
	Total: 32	Total: 24	Total: 20

(Courtesy Rita Fucez)

Eugene Cines (–) USA
Abbreviations (Bo&H 1974) 7pp. Three short works in contemporary idiom. Flexible meters, expressionistic. Requires large span. M-D.

Mikolajus Konstantinas Ciurlionis (1875–1911) Lithuania
Album (PWM) 32pp. Short variations, preludes, and a fugue testify to an extraordinary if scarcely developed Scriabin-like ability. M-D.

Jeremiah Clarke (ca.1673–1707) Great Britain
Selected Works for Keyboard (Eve Marsham—OUP 1975) 21pp. Preface and sources in English. Contains 27 short pieces. See especially the expressive "Farewell," with its unusual dissonance. Int.
Contemporaries of Purcell (Fuller-Maitland—JWC) Vol.V in this series. Suites G, A, b, c, D. Some pieces available separately (JWC).
Trumpet Voluntary (The Prince of Denmark's March) (Palmer—Alfred 3296). For years this piece was attributed to Henry Purcell. It is effective on both piano and organ. Int.

Aldo Clementi (1925–) Italy
Clementi works with serial technique in a free manner. He has added innovations to this procedure.

Composizione No.1 per Pianoforte (SZ 1957). Begins with an 18-note "row" and reduces it by one note on each repetition. D.

Intavolatura per Clavicembalo (SZ 1963). Built on three simultaneous rows, presented together. M-D.

B. A. C. H. (SZ 1973). One page of notes and one of directions. BACH motive is held in top voice over skipping left-hand figures. The piece can be repeated indefinitely until the "Fine," but not less than three times. Avant-garde. M-D.

Muzio Clementi (1752–1832) Italy

Clementi's music is essentially Classical in spirit, the result of disciplined studies and an exceptional command of polyphonic technique and form combined with typical nineteenth-century restlessness. His compositions profoundly influenced Beethoven and, in many ways, foreshadowed Verdi and Brahms. Clementi is also regarded as the originator of the proper technique for the modern pianoforte, as distinguished from the harpsichord. His skill as a musician and teacher left a profound mark on nineteenth-century composers and pianists. Alan Walker Tyson has completed *Thematic Catalogue of the Works of Muzio Clementi* (Tutzing: Hans Schneider, 1967).

Collected Works (Br&H 1802–5, reprint Da Capo 1973) 13 vols. in 5 collections plus one fascicle of violin and flute parts and one fascicle of cello parts. Published during the composer's lifetime, this anthology of Clementi's accomplishments was one of the earliest undertakings of the great Leipzig publisher Breitkopf and Härtel. It contains more than 100 sonatas plus a variety of other works. Collection I (2 vols.): 12 sonatas; 9 sonatas. Collection II (2 vols.): 9 sonatas; 6 sonatas, four hands; sonata for two pianos, four hands. Collection III (3 vols.): 17 sonatas; 7 sonatas; toccata; 2 caprices; 8 sonatas with accompaniment. Collection IV (3 vols.): 4 sonatas; 3 sonatas with accompaniment; 3 sonatas; 3 sonatas with accompaniment; 3 sonatas; 5 sonatas with accompaniment. Collection V (3 vols.): sonata and miscellaneous pieces; 4 sonatas for piano and violin; miscellaneous other works; 11 sonatas with accompaniment.

THE PIANO SONATAS:

It should come as no surprise to pianists that, although the piano sonatas of Muzio Clementi have been neglected for many years, they are among the most beautiful of the Classic period. Clementi's sonatas employ both virtuosity and an intense quality of expression, elements that distinguish them somewhat from the works of Haydn and Mozart and that are forerunners of Beethoven's style. Born in Rome, Clementi lived in England for most of his life and was head of a leading London publishing firm for some thirty years. As one might expect, the great majority of his authentic editions are indeed the English ones. Unfortunately, anyone studying Clementi's sonatas will quickly find that a problem exists with the use of different opus numbers to represent many of the sonatas. This confusing state of affairs, as Tyson puts it in his *Thematic Catalogue*, is a reflection largely of the popularity of Clementi's music throughout Europe after 1780 and of the consequent proliferation of arbitrarily numbered *Nachdrücke*, or reprintings of these works. The chart below is a collation of the many opus numbers used by selected editions compared with the original order and numbering of the sonatas according to Tyson.

The editions in this collation are the incomplete *Oeuvres complettes* issued by Breitkopf und Härtel, 13 vols.; the Peters and Kalmus edited by Ruthardt, 4 vols.; Schirmer, 2 vols., which are simply reprints of the first two volumes of Peters; Ricordi, edited by Cesi, 2 vols.; and Henle, Vol.I (No.317) and Vol.II (No.330) edited by A. Tyson and S. Gerlach with fingering by Hans-Martin Theopold. Tyson's catalogue lists a total of 71 published sonatas that are either for piano solo or may, as Clementi says, be performed as such. There is only one known sonata that remains unpublished (WO 13 in A♭); the manuscript is preserved at the Bibliothèque Nationale in Paris.

Clementi's Keyboard Sonatas as Numbered in Tyson and Five Editions

Tyson's Thematic Catalogue	Breitkopf und Härtel (Vol./No.)	Kalmus and Peters (Op./No.)	Schirmer (Op./No.)	Ricordi (Op./No.)	Henle 317 Vol.I	Henle 330 Vol.II
Op. 1/1, E♭						
1/2, G						
1/3, B♭						
1/4, F						
1/5, A						
1/6 E						
Oeuvre 1/1, F¹	V/15					
1/2, B♭					1/2	
1/3, G	V/16					
1/4, A						
1/5, a²						
Op. 2/2, C³	III/4	2/1	2/1	2/1		
2/4, A⁴	III/5					2/4
2/6, B♭	III/6					
Op. 7/1, E♭	I/11					
7/2, C	III/7					
7/3, g	I/12	7/3			7/3	
Op. 8/1, g	I/8				8/1	
8/2, E♭	I/9					
8/3, B♭	I/10				8/3	
Op. 9/1, B♭	VI/3					
9/2, C	VI/4					
9/3, E♭	VI/5				9/3	
Op. 10/1, A	VIII/2				10/1	
10/2, D	VIII/3					
10/3, B♭	VIII/4					
Op. 11, E♭⁵	VI/7					

Clementi's Keyboard Sonatas as Numbered in Tyson and Five Editions (cont.)

Tyson's Thematic Catalogue	Breitkopf und Härtel (Vol./No.)	Kalmus and Peters (Op./No.)	Schirmer (Op./No.)	Ricordi (Op./No.)	Henle 317 Vol.I	Henle 330 Vol.II
Op. 12/1, B♭	I/1	12/1	12/1			
12/2, E♭	I/2	12/2				
12/3, F	I/3					
12/4, E♭	I/4	12/4		12/4		
Op. 13/4, B♭	X/1					
13/5, F	X/2					
13/6, f	X/3				13/6	
Op. 16, D^6	XI/4					
Op. 20, C	VI/6					
Op. 23/1, E♭	I/5					
23/2, F	I/6	24/2				
23/3, E♭	I/7	24/3				
Op. 24/1, F						
24/2, B♭	VI/2	47/2	47/2	47/2	24/2	
Op. 25/1, C	II/4	25/1				
25/2, G	II/5	25/2		25/2		
25/3, B♭	II/6					
25/4, A	II/1	26/1		26/1		
25/5, f♯	II/2	26/2	26/2	26/2		25/5
25/6, D	II/3	26/3	26/3	26/3		25/6
Op. 26, F	XI/8					
Op. 32/1, F^7	VII/8					
32/2, D						
32/3, C	VII/7					
Op. 33/1, A	II/7	36/1	36/1	36/1		
33/2, F	II/8	36/2	36/2			
33/3, C	II/9	36/3	36/3			
Op. 34/1, C	V/1	34/1	34/1	34/1		
34/2, g	V/2					34/2
Op. 35/1, C^8	XIII/9					
35/2, G	XIII/10					
35/3, D	XIII/11					
Op. 37/1, C	IX/1	39/1				
37/2, G	IX/2	39/2		39/2		37/2
37/3, D	IX/3	39/3				
Op. 40/1, G	III/1	40/1	40/1			40/1
40/2, b	III/2	40/2	40/2	40/2		40/2
40/3, d & D	III/3	40/3	40/3	40/3		
Op. 41, E♭	VI/1					41
46, B♭						
Op. 50/1, A						50/1
50/2, d						
50/3, g		50/3				

Clementi's Keyboard Sonatas as Numbered in Tyson and Five Editions (cont.)

Tyson's *Thematic Catalogue*	Breitkopf und Härtel (Vol./No.)	Kalmus and Peters (Op./No.)	Schirmer (Op./No.)	Ricordi (Op./No.)	Henle 317 Vol.I	Henle 330 Vol.II
WO 3, F	III/8					
WO 14, G					WO 14	

1. This is the revised version of Op.1. Tyson calls this revision "Oeuvre 1" to distinguish it from the original. The revised opus preserves very little of the original material.

2. This sonata is actually a fugue.

3. Op.2/1, 3, and 5 are for harpsichord or pianoforte with an accompaniment for flute or violin. Op.2/2 was later revised as Op.30 for pianoforte or harpsichord and violin accompaniment, with an added slow movement. It was revised a third time years later using the original opus number.

4. This sonata was later revised as Op.31, with a new introduction of 32 bars, for harpsichord or pianoforte and flute accompaniment. It too was revised a third time years later using the original opus number.

5. Op.11 also contains a Toccata in B♭, which is in an Ediciones Lux edition as well as one by Hinshaw.

6. Titled "La Chasse"; this work is actually a sonata with three movements.

7. All three sonatas of Op.32 were composed for pianoforte, flute, and violoncello and were marked "ad libitum," which would seem to indicate that they could be performed as piano solos.

8. As with Op.32, all three sonatas of Op.35 were composed for pianoforte, flute, and violoncello and were marked "ad libitum," which would seem to indicate that they too could be performed as piano solos.

(The author is indebted to Wesley Roberts for the collated chart and its related material.)

Eighteen Sonatas (Piccioli—Curci). This edition is not faithful to the original text, but Piccioli does explain his editorial procedure in the preface. Vol.I: Opp. 25/2 G; 26/3 D; 34/1 C; 36/1 A; 39/2 G; 47/2 B♭. Vol.II: Opp.2/1 C; 12/4 E♭; 26/1 f♯; 40/2, 3 b, D. Vol.III: Opp.7/3 g; 24/1–3 E♭, F, E♭; 35/1 F; 50/3 g.

Piano Sonatas (Dover 1992) 157pp. A fine collection, reprinted from the Peters edition. Contains Op.7/3 g; Op.13/6 f (Op.14/3, 1785, rev. ca. 1807); Op.25/2 G; Op.15/5 f♯ (Op.26/2, 1790); Op.25/6 D (Op.26/3, 1790); Op.33/1 A; Op.40/1 G; Op.40/2 b; Op.40/3 D minor and major; Op.50/3 g: Didone abbandonata. Int. to M-D.

Twelve Sonatas (GS). Vol.I (also K): Opp.2/1 C; 12/1 B♭: 26/2, 3 f♯, D; 34/1 C; 36/1 A; 36/2 F. Vol.II: Opp.33/3 C; 40/1–3 G, b, d; 41/2 B♭.

Eight Sonatas (Heugel). Opp.10/3 b♭; 30/1 g; 33/3 A; 40/1–3 G, b, D; 50/1, 3 A, g.

Five Sonatas (Ric). Op.21/2, 3; Op.22/2; Op.32/1, 3. Editorial fingerings and metronome marks identified. Op.32/1 is this writer's favorite of the collection. Int. to M-D.

Six Sonatas Op.4 1780 (Palmer—Alfred 2421 1984) 64pp. Sonatas D, E♭, C, G, B♭, f. These works were published under the erroneous title Sonatinas Opp.37, 38. Each sonata consists of two contrasting movements. They fall into the classification of "pre-Classical," and baroque influence, as far as form is concerned, is much in evidence. Int.

Sonata E♭ Op.11 (Spada—Boccaccini & Spada 1100 1982) 15pp. Allegro: flowing triplets. Largo con espressione: single-line melody mixed with moving chords. Rondeau—Allegro di molto: upper register exploited, "misplaced" dynamics. M-D.

Sonata E♭ Op.12/2 10½ min. Presto; Largo; Rondo—Allegro assai. Op.12 consisted of four solo sonatas and one for two pianos. All require the sort of flashy virtuosity that Mozart had scoffed at during his encounter with Clementi in Vienna in 1781; glittering runs, brilliant arpeggios, fast broken octaves in both hands, etc. But in Op.12/2 there is also a revelling in sensuous sound in the unusually rich harmonies of the Largo. M-D.

Sonata f Op.14/3 1785 (S. Rosenblum—ECS) 24pp. Allegro agitato; Largo e sostenuto; Presto. An outstanding study edition based on the autograph. This sonata shows an affinity with certain phases of Beethoven's style. It is Beethoven-like in its terse intensity and insistence. It is possible to recognize in this sonata the closing strains of the Scherzo of Beethoven Op.31/3, composed 20 years later. And in the last movement we hear the famous melody written by Beethoven as a contredanse in 1798 and later used as the main theme of the finale of his "Eroica" Symphony. Clementi's Op.14/3, in its entirety, forms a tight, gripping little three-act drama, convincing both emotionally and logically. Listed in Tyson's *Thematic Catalogue* as Op.13/6 and published under this opus by Boccaccini & Spada, edited by Spada, 1994. M-D.

Sonata C Op.20 (Spada—Boccaccini & Spada 1099 1982) 17pp. Allegro: octotonic, much question-answer usage. Larghetto con espressione: chromatic, "Beethoven sound." Allegro molto: a romping rondo, much Alberti bass. M-D.

Sonata D, Op.25/6 1790 (E. Barsham—ABRSM 1994) 15pp. Presto: SA design. Un poco andante: ternary form. Allegro assai: rondo. Conservative but effective writing, numerous dynamic marks. Rondo contains a choice of two cadenzas. Int. to M-D.

Sonata C Op.33/3 (Br&H; CFP; K; GS). Conceived as a concerto around 1793, revised as a solo sonata a few years later. It engagingly suggests some elements of Beethoven's extroverted Sonata C Op.2/3 (e.g., rising chords over an ostinato trill, as in Beethoven's finale) but, on the whole, it looks forward to Berlioz in its garish theatricalness. Large-scale scope and content. M-D.

Sonata G Op.40/1 (Cranz; CFP; K; GS). Adagio: richly ornamented lines. Minuet and Trio: each a two-voice canon; Trio is in contrary motion. M-D.

Sonata A Op.50/1 (Henle 330). Long movements demonstrate an impressive range of keyboard styles from Bach to the nineteenth century. The Adagio movement is intense and contains stylistic influence of both Bach and Mendelssohn. A superb work. M-D.

Sonata g Op.50/3 (Henle; CFP; K; Ric) "Didone abbandonata." Clementi's final piano sonata. The sole example of a programmatic piece; based loosely on the operatic text of Metastasio, which relates the tragedy of Dido and Aeneas. Paints the series of emotions undergone by Dido after her abandonment—rage, jealousy, yearning, etc. Within this framework, Clementi uses sonata forms. M-D.

Other sonatas available separately: Opp.2/1 C (WH); 7/3 g (K&S; K); 9/3 E♭ (Schott); 10/3 B♭ (K&S); 12/4 E♭ (WH); 14/1 B♭ (K&S); 20 E♭ (WH); 26/2 f♯ (Ric; K); 26/3 D (Ric); 34/2 g (Schott); 29/1 C (K&S); 34/2 g (Schott); 36/3 (Cranz); 39/2 G in *Collected Piano Sonatas by Classical Composers* (Henle) Vol.I; 39/3 D in *Collected Piano Sonatas by Classical Composers* (Henle) Vol.II; 40/2 b (K&S); 40/3 d (ABRSM); 47/2 b *Capriccio in forma di Sonata* (Cranz); 47/2 C (Schott).

See: Philip Barford, "Formalism in Clementi's Pianoforte Sonatas," MMR, 82 (October 1952):205–208; (November 1952):238–41.

Joseph Bloch, "A Forgotten Clementi Sonata," PQ 79 (Fall 1972): 24–31. Facsimile of the 1803 Longman, Clementi Co. printing of the piano sonata in g, Op.8/1 (first published in 1782) with historical data about its composition and publication, formal analysis, performance suggestions, and brief discussion of Clementi's piano sonatas and his importance.

Rosemary Clark, "Clarifying Clementi—Realizing the Ornaments in Sonata Op.2/1," *Clavier*, 15 (January 1976):31.

SONATINAS:

6 Sonatinas Op.36 (1st ed.) (Palmer—Alfred; K; GS; CFP; Br&H; Ric; Schott; CF; WH; Kjos). These pieces represent the prototype of the classical sonatina. Int.

12 Sonatinas Opp.36, 37, 38 (K; GS; CFP; Br&H; Ric; Durand; CF). These have a clarity of form, precision of thought, and freshness of spirit that endear them to the performer and listener. Int.

Gradus ad Parnassum (Steps to Perfection—The Art of Playing the Pianoforte) (Da Capo). Published in three volumes in 1817, 1819, and 1826. These 100 pieces were composed by Clementi during various periods of his life and assembled for the *Gradus*. They are totally diverse in style, intended for advanced students, and unique in that they cover almost every aspect of piano technique. In the 18 fugues and canons Clementi shows his mastery of contrapuntal writing. Most of the studies are fairly short; many are linked together into "suites" of five or six pieces, usually in the same or related keys. Nos.38 and 39 are high points in the *Gradus*. Both are long sonata movements, improvisatory, and very expressive. M-D.

Preludes and Exercises Op.43 (Zen-On 141030; EC 4194) 72pp. Contains preludes and exercises in all keys. Most of the exercises are preceded by one or more preludes, which consist of only 3 to 18 bars. They are short but beautiful, just like the "recitativo" of Italian opera, and were to be played before larger works to set the key and mood to follow. Int. to M-D.

Preludes Op.43 (Bishop—CF). 28 short technical but beautiful pieces in all keys, some transposed by the editor. Variety of styles. Int.

18 Monferrine Op.49 1821 (Allorto—Ric 132499). These Italian dances in 6/8 had a vogue in England around 1800. They are moderate in tempo and similar to the minuet and trio in form. Ingeniously varied rhythmic patterns in these brief bagatelles exploit the upper register of the keyboard (which Clementi had greatly improved in his own pianos) and treat the meter with unexpected variety and spontaneous charm. One of Clementi's last keyboard works, lilting and charming; Clementi succeeds in avoiding monotony with a wealth of melodic invention. Int.

Five Capriccios (Allorto—Ric 133153 1981) in *Italian Masters of the Keyboard*, 115pp. Preface and critical commentary in Italian, English, and German. Op.17 B♭; Op.34/1 A; Op.34/2 F; Op.47/1 e; Op.47/2 C. Int. to M-D.

67 Little Pieces (Rattalino—Ric 2805). Taken from Clementi's *Method*, first published in London in 1801. Many interesting footnotes. Includes Clementi's fingerings. Easy to Int.

A Selection of Waltzes and Monferrine (Bo&H). Includes five waltzes from Op.38, three from Op.39, and four Monferrine from Op.49. Int. to M-D.

Fantasia con Variazione sull' aria "Au Clair de la lune" Op.48 (Omodeo—Dob). Appealing, charming, not involved. Int. to M-D.

Works for Pianoforte (Dawes—Schott) 4 vols. Sonatas Op.9/3; Op.13/6; Op.34/2; Capriccio C, Op.47/2. M-D.

Sei Arie Russe e Tarantelle (P. Spada—Bèrben 1972). These six Russian Airs are harmonizations and pianistic adaptations of popular Russian tunes. Preface in English and Italian. Int.

Introduction to the Art of Playing on the Pianoforte 1801 (Sandra Rosenblum—Da Capo) 63pp. This work is among the earliest keyboard methods written specifically for the pianoforte. The most popular tutor of its day, it was published in eleven English editions by Clementi's firm and was translated into French, German, Spanish, and Italian. Designed to meet the needs of relatively inexperienced students and amateurs, this work presents a succinct introduction to the new technical skills and interpretative knowledge needed for the performance of the emerging piano literature. Varied pieces by well-known composers are used instead of the usual short practice pieces written by the author. These pieces reflect both the musical attitudes in England at the time and the taste of the compiler. A new introduction by Rosenblum discusses the *Introduction* in relation to other contemporary piano tutors and the musical practices of the times. She also deals with Clementi's use of ornamentation, tempo, pedaling, and fingering, and provides detailed bibliographic information on all known editions of the book.

Clementi—An Introduction to His Piano Works (Schneider—Alfred) 64pp. An opening section includes a discussion of Clementi, the new "legato school," Clementi's fingering, ornamentation, pedaling, list of sources. Includes shorter works from Clementi's *An Introduction to the Art of Playing on the Pianoforte*, movements from the Op.36 Sonatinas and from the Sonatas, two waltzes from Op.38, and a waltz from Op.39. Editorial additions in light print. Int.

Clementi's Selection of Practical Harmony for the Organ or Piano-Forte, containing voluntaries, fugues, canons, and other ingenious pieces by the most eminent composers, to which is prefixed an epitome of counterpoint by the editor (London: Clementi, Banger, Collard, Davis & Collard, 4 vols., 1803–15; reprint Forni, 1974), 145pp.

Clementi—Rediscovered Masterworks (Mirovitch—EBM). Vol.I: Arietta; Allegretto; Rondo; Waltzes Op.38/1,2; Monferrine (country dance of solo type) Nos.2, 3, 5–9. Vol.II: Sonata Op.7/3 g (1782); Sonata Op.26/2 f♯ (1788); Rondo Op.34/1 g (c.1788). Op.7/3 has Adagio movement from Op.14/1 substituted. Original slow movement of Op.7/3 is contained in appendix. Vol.III: Sonatas Op.22/3 C (1787); Op.5/3 E♭ (1780); Op.14/3 (1784).

Le Trésor des Pianistes: Vol.XVI: 3 Sonatas Op.2; 2 Sonatas Op.7; 3 Sonatas Op.8; 4 Sonatas and a Toccata from Opp.9, 10, 14.

Musical Characteristics or *A Collection of Preludes and Cadenzas* Op.19 1787 (Br&H). 18 pieces in the styles of contemporaries of Clementi: Haydn, Kozeluch, Mozart, Sterkel, and Vaňhal. Some of the earliest piano portraits. Int. to M-D.

Toccata B♭ Op.11 1781 (Hinson—Alfred 10127) 6pp. This work was performed by Clementi on Dec. 24, 1781 in Vienna before the Emperor Joseph II in a sort of musical tournament with W. A. Mozart. It exploits thirds, fourths, fifths, and sixths in the right hand. Fine musical quality and finished workmanship entitle this work to be performed much more than it is. Makes a superb program opener. M-D.

See: *The London Pianoforte School 1770–1860*, in collections and anthologies.

Otto E. Albrecht, *A Census of Autograph Music Manuscripts of European Composers in American Libraries* (Philadelphia: University of Pennsylvania Press, 1953). See pp. 89–92 for a discussion of Clementi piano sonatas. Of special interest are Albrecht's observations and conclusions concerning Clementi's performance directions and their relevance to present-day performance practices.

Eva Badura-Skoda, "Clementi's *Musical Characteristics* Op.19," in *Studies in 18th-Century Music* (New York: Oxford University Press, 1970). Pp. 53–67.

Kathleen Dale, "Hours with Muzio Clementi: with a Classified List," ML, 24/3 (1943):144–54.

Joseph A. Dipiazza, "The Piano Sonatas of Clementi," DMA diss. University of Wisconsin–Madison, 1977, 115pp.

Leon Plantinga, "Clementi, Virtuosity and the 'German' Manner," JAMS, 25 (Fall 1972):303–30. Discusses different influences and styles of Clementi's keyboard writing with special emphasis on J. S. Bach's influence, the "German" Manner. This "German" Manner became a permanent element of his style, and his best music continued to reflect his study of J. S. Bach.

———, *Clementi: His Life and Music* (London: Oxford University Press, 1977).

Joan Pursewell, "Muzio Clementi: Rediscovered Genius," AMT, 30 (September–October 1980):12, 14, 16.

Walter Schenkman, "Beyond the Sonatinas: Music of Muzio Clementi," *Clavier*, 19 (October 1980):20–25. Includes the score to "Preludio alla Haydn." A look into some of the lesser-known works.

Alan Tyson, "Clementi's Viennese Compositions, 1781–82," MR, 27 (1966):16–24.

Hugh Williamson, "Clementi and the English School of Piano Playing," MTNA Proceedings (1939):290–98.

Louis-Nicholas Clérambault (1676–1749) France

Pièces de Clavecin (1704) (P. Brunold-l'OL 1938) Revised by Thurston Dart in 1964. Two suites of 14 pieces. One of the suites is in c and contains a Prelude. A, C, S, and G. M-D.

Eric Coates (1886–1957) Great Britain

Composer of lighter music with superb craftsmanship.

Entr'acte à la Gavotte (MMP). Attractive in an "old-fashioned" way. M-D.

Miniature Suite (MMP). Appealing, pianistic. Int. M-D.

Short Pieces Without Octaves (MMP). Six pieces for small hands. Int.

Collection (Chappell 1978) 96pp. Contains 11 piano solos and 5 songs. By the Sleepy Lagoon; Covent Garden; The Dam Busters; Calling All Workers; Oxford Street; London Bridge; Knightsbridge; Dance in the Twilight; In a Country Lane; At the Dance; Northwards. Tuneful. M-D.

Ruy Coelho (1891–1986) Portugal

6 Promenades Enfantines (Leduc). 3 books. Descriptive pieces of visits to different places near Paris. No.3 is bitonal, while the rest are MC. Int.

Sonatina (Senart) 10 min. Allegro; Expressivo; Allegro vivo. Impressionist, effective writing. M-D.

Randolph Coleman (1937–   ) USA

Coleman teaches at Oberlin College.

Quodlibet on a Theme by Claude Bolling 1977–78 (Smith Publications) 10pp. Performance notes. Theme is from Bolling's *Concerto for Classic Guitar and Jazz Piano*. May be performed in two versions: one commencing in the middle of p.1 (marked theme) and including all written material, and one commencing on p.3. May also be executed as a piano trio, including double-bass and percussion. Theme is bouncy, vivacious, light, yet driving in a jazzy manner. Flexible meters, thin textures, quiet dynamics, delicate sonorities, pointillistic. Some bars may be repeated 10–15 times; a humor comes through. D.

Samuel Coleridge-Taylor (1875–1912) Great Britain

24 Negro Melodies Op.59 1904 (Da Capo 1980) 127pp. Folk element predominant. Uses the theme of each of these pieces like a motto so that it can be quickly recognized. Based on authoritative sources. M-D.

Deep River Op.59/10 (Alfred 4891). Arpeggiated chords support the opening four-bar tune, which returns twice more before a climax is reached; quiet close. M-D.

Humoresques Op.31 1897 (MMP). Three pieces, clever, late-nineteenth-century harmonies. M-D.

Moorish Dance Op.55 1904 (MMP). Strong rhythms, catchy. M-D.

Giuseppe Concone (1810–1861) Italy

Thirty Brilliant Preludes Op.37 (G. Anson—Willis 1962) 27pp. In all the major and minor keys, edited, plus six original preludes by the editor. Int. to M-D.

Yannis Constantinidis (1903–   ) Greece

Greek Miniatures (Rongwen 1957). 3 vols. Varied moods, Eastern flavor, folk-song element. An interesting rhythmic vocabulary. Easy to M-D.

   See: Stephen Brown, "Four Greek Miniatures," *Clavier* (December 1993): 33–39.

Barry Conyngham (1944–   ) Australia

Snowflake 1973 (UE 29082) 16 min. For one player on piano, harpsichord, electric piano, and celeste. Uses vocal sounds (four vowels and two consonants). The performer is also equipped with various kinds of sticks and mallets as well as a plastic ruler. Score is made of arrows and dotted lines that link nine musical systems, each comprising four fragments. Includes instructions of how to move from one system to another and how to "jump from one instrument to the next." The music demonstrates a certain aural sensitivity but the style is dry. Many cliché gestures such as clusters, repeated chords, and rapid arpeggiations. Avant-garde. D.

Arnold Cooke (1906–   ) Great Britain

Suite C (OUP 1943) 10pp. Capriccio; Sarabande; Finale: Allegro con spiritoso. Neoclassic style with fresh sonorities. M-D.

Joseph Cooper (1912–   ) Great Britain

Hidden Melodies (Paxton 1975). Six improvisations, from BBC Television's "Face the Music." While Shepherds Watched Their Flocks by Night, in the style of J. S. Bach. John Peel, in the style of Mozart. Loch Lomond, in the style of Grieg. Come Landlord Fill the Flowing Bowl, in the style of Schubert. The Lincolnshire Poacher, in the style of Tchaikovsky. Yes, We Have No Bananas, in the style of Schumann. Clever, humorous characterizations with delightful cartoons. Int. to M-D.

More Hidden Melodies (Paxton) Six improvisations. Three Blind Mice, in the style of J. S. Bach. Waltzing Matilda, in the style of D. Scarlatti. When Johnny Comes Marching Home, in the style of Schubert. For He's a Jolly Good Fellow, in the style of Chopin. Londonderry Air, in the style of Brahms. I Saw Three Ships, in the style of Schumann. Clever, fun. Int. to M-D.

Paul Cooper (1926–1996) USA

Cooper's music ranges from the quiet and contemplative to the highly dissonant; it displays superb craft.

Sonata 1962 (JWC) 14pp. A one-movement sectionalized work. Tranquillo diventando agitato: proportional rhythmic relationships; serial; figuration increases to a *fff* level, then thins out, relaxes, and melts into a Grave with harmonics and some chords to be "half depressed." Intensity develops, textures are reduced, and Grave section leads to a Vivace that is pointillistic and moves over keyboard. This section gives way to a Molto agitato diventando tranquillo (*mf* a *ff* ad libitum ma con bravura), which builds to an enormous climax, then fades away to a Tranquillo *pppp* closing. Large span, solid musicianship, and mature pianistic expertise required. D.

Partimento 1967 (JWC) 10 min. Changing meters; sections to be freely improvised; harmonics exploited by use of silent clusters. Significant writing. M-D.

Cycles 1969 (JWC) 12 min. Twelve short pieces that exploit clusters, free rhythmic interpretation, strings dampened by the left hand, aleatoric writing, unusual notation, fascinating sonorities. Numerous footnotes provided. M-D.

Changes 1973 (JWC) 6–12 min. Time variable. Five easy pieces. Contemporary techniques put to musical ends; superb pieces to usher students into the last quarter of this century, and they make structural sense! Int.

Four Intermezzi 1980 (JWC) 10 min. Contrasting movements that capture the quintessence of a particular character, all consistent with Cooper's distinctive musical personality. Each is a musical gem that radiates warmth and love—the sort of pristine innocence that few composers have captured since Debussy. Some improvisation required. M-D.

David Cope (1941–   ) USA

Sonata No.4 1968 (Seesaw). Dissonant, declamatory, loudly and insistently percussive. M-D to D.

Parallax 1976 (CF). Calls for the slamming down hard on the lowest strings with the metal edge of a ruler. M-D.

Iceberg Meadow 1969 (CF) 5pp. Facsimile edition. For partially prepared piano, with performer choosing among several parameters. Various procedures are employed on the strings. Pitches are notated in relation to a single horizontal line, as in medieval music; tempo is indicated by seconds and linear distance. M-D.

Aaron Copland (1900–1990) USA

Copland's contribution to piano literature is not large but is important. His style, which is a blend of classical, folk, and jazz elements, has gradually and naturally evolved from the early French-inspired *Scherzo Humoristique* to the 12-tone *Piano Fantasy*. Copland was always inspired by the idea of composing music for and about young people.

Scherzo Humoristique (The Cat and the Mouse) 1920 (Durand). A fragmentary descriptive pianistic frolic. Shows Debussy influence. Int.

See: Celia Mae Bryant, "Musical Drama—The Cat and the Mouse," *Clavier,* 7 (December 1968):16–18.

Three Moods 1920–21 (Bo&H 1981) 8pp. Embittered: rash; rhythmic; big chords move quickly over the keyboard. Wistful: expressive, motivic. Jazz: a foxtrot with a bluesy mid-section. Int. to M-D.

Passacaglia 1922 (Senart). 8-bar theme, varied treatment, big climax, exciting. In the French tradition. M-D.

See: Richard Coolidge, "Aaron Copland's Passacaglia: An Analysis," *Musical Analysis*, 2 (Summer 1974):33–36.

Petit Portrait (ABE) 1921 (Bo&H 1981) 1p. A somber, brooding miniature based on the notes ABE, which represent the name (Abraham) of a friend of 60 years ago. M-D.

Sentimental Melody 1929 (Bo&H) 2pp. Also in collection *The Century of Invention* (Hinson—EAMC 1996). Slow bluesy dance, bitonal usage, captivating. Int. to M-D.

Variations 1930 (Bo&H). Slow and simple 10-bar theme; 20 variations, which depart progressively from the theme toward more-complex, rapidly moving textures; coda. Severe dissonance in a tentative serial style. Masterful culmination of short, tight, economically built episodes. A landmark in American repertoire. D.

See: David Burge, "Aaron Copland's Piano Variations," CK, 3 (April 1977): 44.

Michael Remson, "Copland's Piano Variations: A Forgotten Masterpiece," P&K, 178 (January–February 1996):31–35.

The Young Pioneers 1935 (Bo&H). In 7/8, canonic, a rhythm study. Int.

Sunday Afternoon Music 1935 (Bo&H). Built around a single harmonic progression. Int.

Sonata 1939–41 (Bo&H) 29pp. Molto moderato: freely developed SA, exploits interval of third. Vivace: spasmodic, irregular meters based on combination groupings of 2 + 3 eighth notes; derived rhythmically from jazz-source idioms although no jazz motifs are used. Andante sostenuto: folk-like theme over pedal point. Quiet closing. D.

See: John Kirkpatrick, "Aaron Copland's Piano Sonata," MM, 19 (May–June 1942):246–50.

Resting-Place on the Hill from *Our Town*, arranged by the composer, 1945 (Bo&H) 3pp. Melody and texture Satie-like. Large span required. M-D.

Saturday-Night Waltz from *Rodeo*, arranged by the composer, 1946 (Bo&H). Hoe-down warm-up introduction, slow waltz section, pedal points, syncopation. M-D.

4 Piano Blues (Bo&H 1948). Freely Poetic (1947); Soft and Languid (1943); Muted and Sensuous (1948); With Bounce (1926). Sophisticated jazz, can help develop spontaneity and relaxation. M-D.

Piano Fantasy 1955–57 (Bo&H). A strong 10-note idea heard at the beginning is used freely and dominates much of the work. Juxtaposes brilliantly sonorous declamation, lyricism, subtle Impressionistic colors, and breathless staccato passages. Free serial technique. Copland's most extended work for piano, massive, large-scale. D.

See: Arthur Berger, "Aaron Copland's Piano Fantasy," JR, 5 (Winter 1957–58):13–27.

Down a Country Lane 1962 (Bo&H) 2pp. Expressive pastoral style. Int.

4 Dance Episodes from *Rodeo* (Bo&H). Arranged by Copland. Buckaroo Holiday; Corral Nocturne; Saturday-Night Waltz; Hoe Down. Strong rhythms. M-D.

In Evening Air 1971 (Bo&H) 3pp. Melodic, pastoral, freely tonal around g, rather plain writing. Well fingered and pedaled. Good for teaching cantabile touch and balance of tone in chord playing. Int.

Night Thoughts (Homage to Ives) 1972 (Bo&H). Commissioned by the Van Cliburn International Piano Competition, 1973. 5pp. Bell-like opening and closing; built on interval of ascending third; many directions, e.g., sharp and clear, bell-like, simply sung, firmly sung, violent (on each chord), tenderly, etc.; con tutta forza mid-section; Impressionistic closing. Moody; interpretation problems but notes are not difficult to cover; changing meters and tempi; wide stretches. Copland says: "What I would hope for would be that *Night Thoughts* would bring out the essential musicality of the contestants and perhaps give the judges more to think about than technical brilliance and display features." M-D.

Midsummer Nocturne 1977 (Bo&H) 2pp. "Slowly, poetically (and somewhat thoughtfully)" (from the score). Melodic, thin textures, tonal around A. Int.

Midday Thoughts 1983 (Bo&H) 3pp. Based on sketches for the slow movement of a projected *Ballade* for piano and orchestra from early 1944, when Copland was finishing *Appalachian Spring*. Easy flowing melodies and gentle dissonant harmonies, as in *Appalachian Spring*. Int. to M-D.

Proclamation for Piano 1982 (Bo&H) 3pp. 2 min. Based on a sketch dating from 1972. Stern sounding with strong dissonance. Requires large span but redistribution of a few spots will help the average hand. M-D.

Piano Album (Bo&H 1981) 31pp. Petit Portrait; Down a Country Lane; Midsummer Nocturne; In Evening Air; Piano Blues Nos.1 and 4; Saturday-Night Waltz; Sentimental Melody; The Resting-Place on the Hill; The Young Pioneers; Sunday Afternoon Music. Outstanding collection. Int. to M-D.

See: David Burge, "Copland's Piano Music," CK, 6 (November 1980):37, 40, 42.

Dika Newlin, "Aaron Copland—Survey of His Piano Music," PQ, 111, (Fall 1980):6, 8, 10–12.

Vivian Perlis, "Aaron Copland and the Piano," AMT, 40/2 (October–November 1990): 12–15, 46–47.

Douglas Young, "The Piano Music" [of Aaron Copland], *Tempo*, 95 (Winter 1970–71):15–22.

Roque Cordero (1917–   ) Panama

Cordera makes very free use of serial techniques.

Sonatina Rítmica 1943 (PIC) 16pp. Presto con furia: exhibits a furious intensity; changing meters; percussive effects. Adagietto: hands crossed throughout with the right hand singing the melody in the bass. Allegro deciso: driving;

fits the hand well. A short, exciting work. Written while the composer was studying with Ernst Krenek. Tonal, but moments of tonal ambiguity add to the interest. Influences of Panamanian dances felt in the rhythmic treatment; 12-tone experimentation in occasional short passages. Brilliant, effective writing. M-D.

See: Jerry Benjamin, "Sonatina Ritmica," 1963, IU, 9pp., for a thorough analysis of this work.

Sonata Breve (PIC). Three short connected movements. Exciting introduction, more-relaxed first movement, flexible second movement, dramatic concluding movement exploiting the complete keyboard. Dissonant contemporary style, effective. D.

John Corigliano (1938–   ) USA

Corigliano writes in a brilliant and accessible updated Romantic style. It is somewhat dissonant but it retains a strong tonal foundation. Incisive rhythms and lyrical lines are characteristic of his compositions.

Adagio from *Gazebo Dances* 1978 in collection *American Contemporary Masters* (GS 1995) 6pp. Freely atonal, flowing melody, three staves required part of the time, *ppp* closing. M-D.

Etude Fantasy 1976 (GS) 18 min. 1. For the Left Hand Alone. 2. Legato. 3. Fifths to Thirds: tricky crossed-hand figures support an upper-register theme. 4. Ornaments: clusters, trills, tremolos, and glissandi of the ornaments. 5. Melody. Five virtuoso etudes worked into a fantasy without a break between them. The pianistic palate is indebted to Liszt and Debussy. Contains diatonic fragments, triadic references, implied tonal centers, dramatic gestures, much exploration of the interval of a second. Basic material from Etude I, for the left hand alone, is worked over in the other etudes. D.

Fantasia on an Ostinato 1985 (GS) 12 min. Commissioned by the Seventh Van Cliburn Competition. Intense emotional expression, energetic sections, strong minimalist structure, superb craftsmanship, colorful keyboard textures, atmospheric. Based on the repeated-note theme from Beethoven's Seventh Symphony. "The performer's sense of fantasy and, in the central section, his or her decisions concerning durations of the repeated patterns will exert considerable influence on the work's final shape (which is intended to vary from performance to performance)" (from the score).

See: Dolores Fredrickson, "The Piano Music of John Corigliano," *Clavier*, 32/9 (November 1993):20–22.

Arcangelo Corelli (1653–1713) Italy

24 Pieces (K). Vol.I: 3 Sarabandes; 2 Adagios; 2 Präludium; Corrente; Largo; Gavotte; Allegro; Gigue. Vol.II: 5 Gavottes; Präludium; Sarabande; Menuett; Corrente; Allegro; Folies d'Espagne. Over-edited. Int.

Angelo Corradini (1914–   ) Italy

Corradini writes in an accessible neoclassic style.

5 Pezzi Brevi (Ric 1960) 11 pp. Preludio; Studio sugli accordi; Toccatina; Recitativo; Danza. Impressionist style. Effective separately or as a group. Very pianistic. M-D.

Preludio e Toccata (Ric (1964). M-D. Romantic Preludio coupled with a Toccata. Repeated single notes and chords, slow mid-section, returns to opening idea, slow *ff* closing.

Suite (Ric 1967) 13pp. Preludio; Danza; Spiritual; Toccata: ostinato. Excellent recital material. The Toccata has three contrasting moods that fit well together. M-D.

9 Improvisazioni (Ric 1970). Short character pieces, varied moods, Impressionist. M-D.

Sérgio Oliveira de Vasconcellos Corrêa (1934–   ) Brazil

Corrêa is a member of the music faculty of the University of Campinas, Sao Paulo, Brazil.

Contrastes—Variações sôbre um tema popular (Ric Brazil 1969) 10pp. 4½ min. Theme and 6 variations that alternate expressive elements, rhythms, dynamics, and agogic accents. Some contrapuntal elements present. Opens and closes in a savage, hammered character. M-D.

Introdução e Chôros (Ric Brazil 1972) 12pp. 6 min. Introduction is a two-part invention. Chôro I, II, and III. M-D.

Tocatina (Ric Brazil 1971) 4pp. 2 min. Transfer of lines between hands. More lyric than most tocatinas. M-D.

Variações sôbre um tema de Cana-Fita (Ric Brazil 1961) 11pp. 6 min. Theme: canon. Var. I, Acalanto: song, two voices. Var. II, Dança. Var. III, Modinha: popular song. Var. IV, Pregão: sad, crying mood. Var. V, Valsa. Var. VI, Miudinho: popular dance. Var. VII, Baião: folk dance. Thin textures, clever treatment. Int.

Michel Corrette (1709–1795) France

Organist at the Jesuit College in Paris (1738) and later to the Duc d'Angoulême, Corrette wrote masses, motets, instrumental pieces, and several methods, including *Le Maître de Clavecin* (1753) (BB) Facsimile edition.

Premier Livre de Pièces de Clavecin Op.12 1734 (Ruf, Bemmann—Schott 6939) 35pp. Four multi-movement suites that show strong Italian influence. Suite I: 7 movements. Suite II: 5 movements. Suite III: 5 movements. Suite IV: 3 movements. Most movements have colorful titles. Includes ornament table. M-D.

Ramiro Cortés (1933–1984) USA

Suite (EV 1955) 14pp. Sinfonia; Capriccio; Arioso Sentimentale; Finale. Shows a fine craft. Similar melodic and rhythmic figures are juxtaposed in a free linear style. Chromatic, spiky metric patterns, à la Ragtime section in finale. Requires large span. M-D.

The Genie of the Waters (TP 1956) 3pp. Centers around F♯, evocative, veiled, mysterious arpeggi. M-D.

Benjamin Cosyn (early 17th century) Great Britain
Cosyn was a "famous composer of lessons for the harpsichord, and probably an excellent performer on that instrument, . . . there are many of his lessons extant that seem in no respect inferior to those of Bull"—John Hawkins, *A General History of the Science and Practice of Music,* new ed. (London: Novello, 1875), II, 522.
25 Pieces for Keyed Instruments from Benjamin Cosyn's Virginal Book (Fuller-Maitland, B. Squire—JWC). Works by Bull, Byrd, Gibbons, Cosyn, and others. Dates from ca. 1600–10. Int. to M-D.
8 Dances from Benjamin Cosyn's Second Virginal Book (F. Cameron—Schott). Delightful, appealing music. Int. to M-D.

Fred Coulter (1934–   ) USA
Variations for Agnes (Hinson—Alfred 10114) in collection *Twelve by Eleven—Piano Music of 20th Century America.* Fresh approaches to the durable and delightful folk tune "Twinkle, Twinkle, Little Star." The style is intentionally simple orally and technically. Careful attention should be paid to cross-phrasing between the voices. Int. to M-D.

Jean Coulthard (1908–2000) Canada
Aegean Sketches (BMI Canada). The Valley of the Butterflies: interesting figuration. Wine Dark Sea: a singing barcarolle with colorful use of the trill. Legend (The Palace of Knossos): resonant chords move to large climax. Fine Impressionist pieces. Large span required. Int. to M-D.
4 Etudes (BMI Canada 1945). Published separately. Well written and not overly difficult. See especially No.3, Toccata. M-D.
3 Preludes (BMI Canada). Published separately. Leggiero; Torment; Quest. Short character pieces with well-defined ideas. Int. to M-D.
Sonata (BMI Canada 1948). A fine printed photostat of the manuscript. Three movements, FSF, of well-organized and contrasted ideas. Some ninths. Carefully marked scores. Tonally oriented although no key signatures are present. M-D.
Pieces for the Present (Waterloo). 9 original pieces, MC, varied in mood and style. Int.
Variations on BACH 1971 (Nov 1972) 12pp. 10 min. No.8 in Virtuoso Series. John Ogdon, the editor, points out the meditative quality of the work with contrasting scherzando and drammatico interludes. A 16-bar theme provides a good basis for this neo-Romantic work of seven well-contrasted and well worked-out variations. Chromatic; mainly slow tempi exploited. D.
White Caps (BMI Canada). 5pp. Toccata-like, MC. Much variety. Small hands could manage it well. Int.
See: Patricia Taylor Lee, "Discovering Jean Coulthard," AMT, 45/2 (October–November 1995):16–19, 62–63.

François Couperin (1668–1733) France
Twenty-seven Ordres (suites), over 220 pieces, make up the four books of *Pièces de Clavecin.* These suites had a wide influence on the keyboard style of Bach and

Handel as well as on many of Couperin's younger contemporaries. Couperin was a most original and versatile composer. A gesture toward almost every emotion is seen in these works, and untold pleasures lie on every page. Couperin gave programmatic titles to many of his pieces. His works include nine character portraits of his friends, students, and royal masters: Ordres 2, Nos. 14, 16; 7, No. 1; 8, No. 10; 15, No. 8; 17, Nos. 1 and 4; 21, No. 3 (of Couperin himself). Couperin was very careful to notate precisely what he intended. He was always worried that players would not perform his music as he wished. His treatise, *L'Art de toucher le Clavecin*, is indispensable to a better understanding of his style. A table of ornaments is also contained in this treatise.

Complete Works (Gilbert—l'OL 1981) 12 vols. Vol.I contains *L'Art de toucher le Clavecin*; Vol.II, *Pièces de Clavecin* (4 vols.). Reprint of the 1932 edition with a few introductory comments and emendations to the revised text. Int. to M-D.

Pièces de Clavecin (Brahms, Chrysander—Augener; Dover, 1988). 4 vols. Vol.I (1713): Ordres 1–5. Vol.II (1717): Ordres 6–12. Vol.III (1722): Ordres 13–19. Vol.IV (1730): Ordres 20–27. Fine edition.

See: Kevin Bazzana, "The Uses and Limits of Performance Practice in François Couperin's *Huitième Ordre*," MQ, 75/1 (Spring 1991):12–30.

Pièces de Clavecin (Diemer—Durand). 4 vols. Added dynamics and realized ornaments.

Pièces de Clavecin (Gilbert—Heugel). 4 vols. Vol.I contains a facsimile of Couperin's table of ornaments; an alphabetical list of the contents of all four books; a general introduction, in which performance practice, instruments, and sources are discussed; and Couperin's preface of 1713.

Pièces de Clavecin (K). Vol.I: Ordres 1 and 4. Vol.II: Ordres 5 and 6.

The Music of Couperin (JWC). Keyboard, vocal, organ, and instrumental music.

The Graded Couperin (Motchand—F. Colombo). 29 selected short pieces graded from easiest to more difficult. Also gives a summary of Couperin's rules of interpretation.

Pièces de Clavecin (BB). A facsimile of the 1713, 1717, 1722, and 1730 editions.

Les Clavecinistes Français (Diemer—Durand) Vol.III. Contains 4 ordres.

Selected Pieces (PWM). Varied selection from the Ordres. Includes Couperin's original ornaments together with detailed instructions for their execution. Fingering also included. Int. to M-D.

Selected Harpsichord Music (S. Marlowe—GS). Contains 41 pieces from the 4 Books of Harpsichord Pieces. Scholarly, performance-oriented edition. A thorough introduction covers the areas of Couperin's keyboard instruments, rondeau form, ornamentation and signs, tempo, rhythmic alterations, glossary of tempo markings, and comments on the pieces. An appendix suggests ways to vary the ornamentation of the rondeau sections slightly. Beautiful edition. Int. to M-D.

Pièces de Clavecin (J. Gat—EMB). Vol.I: Ordres 1–5. Vol.II: Ordres 6–12. Vol.III: Ordres 13–19. Vol.IV: Ordres 20–27. Fine, clean edition; editorial additions easily identified; includes table of ornaments and their realization and measure numbers.

Couperin Album (J. Gat—EMB Z.7377) 52pp. Contains: L'Amphibie; L'Anguille; L'Audacieuse; Les Bergeries; Les Chinois; La Florentine; Les Jeunes Seigneurs; Les Moissonneurs; La Muse-Plantine; Passacaille; Soeur Monique; Les Timbres; La Triomphante; La Voluptueuse. Well fingered, especially the many ornaments. M-D.

L'Art de toucher le clavecin (The Art of Playing the Harpsichord). (Alfred 1975). This magnificent edition, edited by Margery Halford, of the great eighteenth-century treatise on keyboard playing, has much to recommend it. The French text of both the first and second versions (1716 and 1717) has been reproduced alongside a new English translation by the editor. Five beautiful facsimiles from the 1716 edition together with two portraits of Couperin add to this valuable edition. Excellent editorial introduction covers many aspects of performance. It describes the sources and deals with early traditions in music writing, the variable dot in Baroque music, notés inégales, ornamentation, fingering, phrasing and articulation, and expression and style. Includes a helpful summary of Couperin's rules and a bibliography. Useful footnotes throughout. Clears up the old Breitkopf and Härtel edition and Arnold Dolmetsch's transcription in a scholarly way. F and G clefs are substituted for the moveable C clefs in the original edition, and the use of lighter print for all editorial suggestions is outstanding. Also contains the eight Preludes Couperin intended to be played before each of his suites in the corresponding key. This practice should be revived.

L'Art de toucher le clavecin (Br&H 1933). Original French with German and English translations in parallel columns. A more recent translation by Dorothy Packard is available in *Clavier*, 7 (April 1968):20–25.

8 Preludes and *Allemande* (J. A. Fuller-Maitland—JWC). These pieces illustrate the principles in *L'Art de toucher le clavecin*. Overedited.

See: Thurston Dart, "On Couperin's Harpsichord Music," MT, 110 (June 1969):590–94.

Wilfrid Mellers, "Couperin on the Harpsichord," MT, 109 (November 1968):1010.

———, *François Couperin and the French Classical Tradition* (London: Dobson, 1950; reprint, New York: Dover, 1966).

———, "The Clavecin Works of François Couperin," ML 7 (1946):233–48.

Louis Couperin (ca. 1626–1661) France

Louis Couperin's musical subleties are as satisfying as those of his nephew François.

Complete Keyboard Works (P. Brunold—l'OL). Contains unbarred preludes, numerous dance movements, passacailles, chaconnes, a fantaisie, and a tombeau. Int. to M-D.

Pièces de Clavecin (P. Brunold, T. Dart—l'OL 1959). Same as the above with added ornaments by Thurston Dart.

Pièces de Clavecin (Alan Curtis—Heugel). Based on a recently discovered manuscript that brings to light not only new pieces but also works previously known in a different form. 100 pieces, arranged in 15 suites by the editor. Preface in French, English, and German; table of ornaments. Int. to M-D.

Henry Cowell (1897–1965) USA

Henry Cowell was a founding father of twentieth-century American music and multiculturism. He composed over 1,000 works, including many short piano pieces. Close to 100 of the works are incomplete fragments. He wrote a great deal of "occasional" music—music inspired by, or composed for, a specific event. His music covers an enormous range, both in technique and expression. Cowell tended to disregard musical trends and fashions and went his own way. His music was often reaction; he composed the way most of us speak, as the natural medium through which he responded to the world. Cowell's clusters are well known, and his technique of manipulating the strings directly has become standard fare with many contemporary composers. Most of Cowell's piano music is based on folk materials, either American or Celtic. If his output and compositional facility is any indication, he seems not to have shared with his colleagues the Romantic ethos of self-consciousness, nor did he agonize over his scores. He recorded 20 of his works written between 1911 and 1930 on Folkways disc FG 3349.

Album of Piano Music (AMP). The Tides of Manaunaun; Exultation; The Banshee (played entirely on the strings inside the grand piano); The Aeolian Harp; Fabric; Episode; 2-Part Invention; Tiger; Advertisement. Written over a 40-year span, these pieces include a wide range of techniques and expressions. Five of them use clusters. Playing instructions and a note on the music and its composer by Oliver Daniel. Int. to M-D.

Piano Music of Henry Cowell Vol.II (AMP 1982) 65pp. Contains 22 pieces, including from Vol.I: Advertisement, as one of Five Encores to Dynamic Motion; The Tides of Manaunaun, as one of Three Irish Legends. Also includes: Nine Ings; Dynamic Motion and Four of Its Five Encores (What's This; Amiable Conservation; Advertisement; Antinomy); Sinister Resonance; Anger Dance; The Lilt of the Reel; Three Irish Legends; Vestiges; Whisking; Sneaking; Swaying; The Fairy Bells; Time Table; Piece for Piano with Strings (for piano solo). Polytonal, polyrhythms, clusters, some inside-the-piano sounds. Contains an explanation of symbols. M-D.

Dynamic Motion (AMP). Short, wide clusters; vigorous rhythmic treatment. M-D.

Amerind Suite (SP). Based on American Indian music. Int. to M-D.

The Harp of Life (AMP). Forearm clusters for both arms, triadic harmonization, harmonic effects, large climax. M-D.

Hilarious Curtain Opener and Ritournelle (NME, Oct. 1945). Taken from incidental music for a Jean Cocteau play. The Ritournelle is an example of elastic form, a kind of prescribed "aleatory" music, where the length can be varied by omitting certain portions. M-D.

The Snows of Fuji-Yama (AMP 1927). Atmospheric, built on pentatonic scale. Int.

The Irishman Dances (CF 1936). Easy.

The Irish Minstrel Sings (CF 1936). Easy.

Two Woofs (Merion). Short; bitonal writing, fresh-sounding little gems. M-D.

Sway Dance (TP). Easy.

Bounce Dance (Merion). Easy.

Maestoso (NME Oct. 1940) 7pp. Three staves are used most of the time. M-D.

Pa Jigs Them All Down (Century). Clever. M-D.

Pegleg Dance (Century). Int.

Rhythmicana 1938 (AMP 1975) 11pp. Three untitled pieces that explore and exploit unusual rhythms, rubato feeling. This is the last and longest of Cowell's experimental piano works. D.

Set of Four 1960 (AMP). 15½ min. For harpsichord or piano. A pseudo-Baroque suite consisting of Rondo; Ostinato; Chorale; Fugue and Resume. M-D.

Sinister Resonance (AMP). Violinistic treatment of the piano with muted and stopped strings as well as pizzicato. M-D.

Three Irish Legends (Br&H 1922). New notation.

Six Ings (AMP 1950). Composed early in Cowell's career. Bitonal, dissonant. Need a well-developed pianism. M-D.

Anger Dance (AMP). Int.

The Lilt of the Reel (AMP). Int.

What's This (AMP). M-D.

See: Michael Hicks, "Cowell's Clusters," MQ, 77/3 (Fall 1993):428–458.

Hugo Weisgall, "The Music of Henry Cowell," MQ, 45 (1959):484–507.

Edward Cowie (1943–   ) Great Britain

Cowie is a Senior Lecturer at Lancaster University, a professional painter, and a serious ornithologist.

Kelly Variations Op.7 1976, rev.1981–82 (Schott) 15 min. These variations are a rehearsal-model for the composer's opera *Ned Kelly*. Op.7 comprises a toccata and theme with four cleverly contrived variations written in an entirely convincing traditional style, with frequent use of triads, and employs genuinely pianistic colorations. Abstractly conceived; deliberately static use of tonality. M-D.

See: Anthony Burton, "Places, People, Pictures—The Recent Music of Edward Cowie," MT, 1668 (February 1982):99, 101–103.

Johann Baptist Cramer (1771–1858) Germany

A pupil of Clementi, Cramer had a successful career touring as a virtuoso. Beethoven met Cramer in a competition and was quoted by Ries as saying that "Cramer was the only pianist of his time. 'All the rest count for nothing'" (Harold Schonberg, *The Great Pianists* [New York: Simon & Schuster, 1963], p.60). Cramer was one of the first pianists to feature works by other composers in his recitals. His own compositions are characterized by solid musical taste.

La Parodie Sonate Op.43 (Schott 1913). Two movements. The first movement is the stronger. M-D.

See: Alan Tyson, "A Feud between Clementi and Cramer," ML, 54 (1973): 281–88.

Jerald C. Graue, "The Clementi-Cramer Dispute Revisited," ML, 56 (January 1975):47–54.

Les Menus Plaisirs (K&S) 15pp. Divertimento in two movements: Allegro con brio: serves as an introduction. Rondo: Allegretto moderato. Facile writing. M-D.

Cramer-Beethoven Studies (Shedlock—Augener). 21 Cramer etudes with annotations of Beethoven made by Anton Schindler. Newman suggests these etudes were perhaps to be used in Beethoven's projected "Klavierschule" (SCE, 517). The New York Public Library has a copy of this Shedlock edition of 1893. M-D.

21 Etüden (Hans Kann—UE 1974) xvii+43pp. Preface in German. This edition, prepared from a copy stemming from Anton Schindler's library, contains annotations and finger exercises by Beethoven. M-D.

See: William S. Newman, "On the Rhythmic Significance of Beethoven's Annotations in Cramer's Etudes," Kongressbericht of the International Musicological Society in Bonn, Germany, September 5–7, 1970.

————. "Yet Another Major Beethoven Forgery by Schindler?" *The Journal of Musicology*, 3/4 (Fall 1984):397–422.

84 Studies (CFP; K; Schott Frères, 4 vols.; Heugel, 2 vols.). These studies have been used profitably by pianists since the first 42 were published in 1804. They show Cramer's proficiency as a technical teacher as well as a lyrical and poetic writer. The ability to have complete and separate control over the hands to differentiate between the melodic line and inner voices (Nos.20, 25, 41, 80 and 84), to shape a melodic line from note groupings that initially appear to be mere repetitive patterns (Nos.3, 7, 21, 28, 33, 34 and 38), to provide clear voicing regardless of complicated left-hand and inner parts (Nos.15, 26, 37, 41, 67, 76 and 77), as well as evenness and accuracy are demanded of the pianist and demonstrate Cramer's technical aims. M-D.

50 Selected Studies (von Bülow, Hinson—Alfred 4854) 135pp. Based on the von Bülow edition of 1868 with added commentary by M. Hinson. Von Bülow selected the 50 studies he felt were the most important and arranged them in a more logical order (a systematically graded succession). He also added fingerings. Int. to M-D.

Short Studies Op.100 (J. Biggs—Cramer). Bk. I: Nos. 1–50. Bk. II: Nos. 51–100. Intricate patterns, demands concentration, never exceeds an octave. Phrasing, articulation, dynamics, and fingering are as found in the first editions. Alternative fingerings are offered for small hands. Editor gives his suggestions for working on these pieces. Int. to M-D.

60 Selected Studies (Bülow—UE; Ric). 4 vols. published as one.

50 and 84 Studies from Op. 100 (GS). 2 vols.

See: *The London Pianoforte School 1770–1860*, in collections and anthologies section.

J. B. Brocklehurst, "The Studies of J. B. Cramer and His Predecessors," ML, 39 (July 1958):256–61.

Ruth Crawford Seeger (1901–1953) USA

Crawford Seeger was one of America's finest women composers.

Etude in Mixed Accents 1930 (NME) 5pp. Various groupings of 16th notes, octotonic. Includes three sets of dynamics; performer must select one and adhere to it throughout a performance. Somewhat similar in style and difficulty to the Bartók *Etude* Op.18/3. M-D.

Four Preludes 1927–28 (NME) 15pp. No. 6. Andante mistico: consists of long, legato lines and flowing double notes as it builds to a climax. No. 7. Intensivo: extremely dramatic, surging work. No. 8. Leggiero: a darting, staccato piece of continually shifting meters; gracious, lilting middle part forms a fine contrast to the opening section. No. 9. Tranquillo: peaceful, yet it has great inner tension. Shows equal influence of Scriabin and Schoenberg. Meritorious in craft and style. M-D.

Preludes 1–5 1924–25 (R. Platt—Hildegard Publishing). The first five of Crawford's nine *Preludes for Piano*, never before published. M-D.

See: Maurice Hinson, "Remember Ruth Crawford," *Clavier*, 15 (December 1976):29. Includes *Prelude* 6 (pp. 26–28).

Paul Creston (1906–1985) USA

Creston's style, which has generally evolved from traditional compositional procedures, has a strong Romantic feeling colored by Impressionism and modal harmonies. Elements of song and dance have fascinated Creston and have often influenced the forms his works have taken. His writing for the piano is idiomatic and usually effective.

Five Dances Op.1 1932 (SP). Varied, tonal, MC, well-defined ideas. No.5 (Tarantella) is the longest and most attractive of the set. Int. to M-D.

Seven Theses Op.3 1933 (Templeton). Complex contrapuntal pieces with changing meters, thick textures. D.

Five Dances Op.7 (MGP). Varied moods and techniques. Int. to M-D.

Sonata Op.9 1936 (MGP). 4 movements, dissonant, lively rhythmic usage, pianistic, strong closing. D.

Five 2-Part Inventions Op.14 (MGP). Contrapuntal, dissonant, moderate length. M-D.

Prelude and Dance Op.29/1 (Mer 1942). Moderate length. M-D.

Prelude and Dance Op.29/2 (Templeton). Prelude: meditative. Dance: with passion. Moderate length. M-D.

Five Little Dances Op.24 (GS 1940). Short; varied moods, attractive. Int.

Six Preludes Op.38 1949 (MCA). Various metric and rhythmic problems. Facility required. M-D.

Metamorphoses (MGP). 20 pieces based on a fertile tone-row. Large design requiring mature pianism. D.

Rumba Tarantella (Belwin-Mills 1964). Int.

Pony Rondo 1964 (MGP). Tonal, chromatic, clever rhythmic treatment. Int. to M-D.

Virtuoso Technique (MGP). 2 vols. M-D. to D.

Rhythmicon (Belwin-Mills). "A practical dictionary of rhythms, its main purpose is to present a clear concept of meters and rhythms through explanatory notes, practice drills and short pieces leading to mastery of execution." 10 vols., elementary to lower intermediate (composer's grading). The pieces can be performed in recitals individually or in various combinations as suites. Easy to D.

Three Narratives Op.79 (MGP) about 9 min. each. Each piece is written for a different pianist (Mildred Victor, Claudette Sorel, Earl Wild). D.

Romanza Op.110 (MGP). Flexible meters and keys, many accidentals. Expressive. M-D.

Offertory Op.133 (MGP 1980) 8pp. Changing meters and tempos but mostly slow and in a contemplative and intense mood. Title refers to an "offering," paying tribute to an individual's memory. M-D.

See: Carol Walgren, "Paul Creston: Solo Piano Music," AMT, 24 (April–May 1975):6–9.

Donald Crockett (1951–   ) USA

Crockett is Professor of Composition at the University of Southern California.

Pilgrimage 1988 (Norruth Music) 29pp. 11½ min. Changing meters and tempos, complex rhythms, serial influence, harmonic, bell-like sonorities, contrasting moods ("hushed but jaunty"), widely arpeggiated chords, *pp* opening and closing. M-D to D.

William Croft (1678–1727) Great Britain

Croft's suite movements are in French style, especially the ornamentation.

Contemporaries of Purcell (Fuller-Maitland—JWC). Vols. III and IV in this series. Six suites in each volume. Most of the suites contain three or four movements. Suite No.1 c: A; S; C; Aire. Suite No.3 c: Ground; A, C. Suite No.7: Ground; Minuet.

Complete Harpsichord Works (S&B 1974). 2 books. Newly transcribed and edited by Howard Ferguson and Christopher Hogwood. Includes editorial and textual notes. Vol.I: 10 suites. Vol.II: 7 suites. The suites are short and use dance forms. M-D.

Randell Croley (1946–   ) USA

Quattro Espressioni (Philharmusica 1968) 4pp. Short, fleeting, expressionistic, serial, subtle dynamics. D.

George Crumb (1929–   ) USA

Crumb constantly seeks new sonorities from both the keyboard and the interior of the piano. He is one of the most original voices in new music.

Five Piano Pieces 1962 (CFP 1973) 11pp. 8 min. Plucked strings, harmonics, stopped strings, fascinating sonorities. Includes instructions for performance. To be played as a group. M-D.

See: David Burge, "Contemporary Piano—George Crumb's *Five Pieces*," *Keyboard*, 9/7 (July 1983):66. An analysis of the pieces.

Dream Images (Love-Death Music) in collection *12 by 11* (Hinson—Hinshaw 1978). From Vol.I of *Makrokosmos*. Elegant sonorities are created with varied vertical and horizontal densities. Chopin's *Fantaisie-Impromptu* excerpts must enter and leave as the character directions at the beginning of the piece state: "Musingly, like the gentle caress of a faintly remembered music." Highly effective writing. M-D.

Makrokosmos I. Twelve Fantasy-Pieces (CFP 1973). For amplified piano. 14pp. 33 min. Highly eclectic style including singing, whistling, speaking, and groaning as well as playing both inside the piano and on the keyboard. Micro-phone should be placed near bass strings inside piano. A powerful work and a major addition to twentieth-century piano literature. D.

Makrokosmos II. Twelve Fantasy-Pieces after the Zodiac for amplified piano (CFP 1974) 14pp. 30 min. This completes the sequence of 24 fantasy-pieces (12 in Vol.I) inspired partially by Debussy's *24 Preludes* and Bartók's *Mikrokos-mos.* As in Vol.I, each piece carries a sign of the zodiac and the initials of a person born under that sign. Some pieces are notated symbolically: No.4, "Twin Suns," has two circular staves; No.8, "A Prophecy of Nostradamus," has two opposing quarter circles surrounding a short horizontal staff, etc. The two volumes share such musical materials as the notes A, B, and F and a great emphasis on chromatic lines. The last two pieces in Vol.II contain brief quotes from Vol.I., and the subtitles "Genesis" and "Night-Spell" ap-pear in both volumes. Unusual timbre and sonorities are produced by plucking and muting strings, placing paper on and sliding glass tumblers over strings, rapping the piano frame with the knuckles. Moaning, shout-ing, singing, and whistling are also called for by the pianist. Long pedals and electronic amplification add effectively to the pieces. In spite of the avant-garde tendencies of this work, references to Beethoven's *Hammer-klavier* Sonata and Crumb's earlier *Madrigals*, plus other aspects, tie it to musical tradition. Highly effective works for the avant-garde pianist. D.

A Little Suite for Christmas, A.D. 1979 (after Giotto's Nativity frescos in the Arena Chapel at Padua) (CFP 66833 1978) 13pp. The Visitation; Berceuse for the Infant Jesus; The Shepherd's Noël; Adoration of the Magi; Nativity Dance; Canticle of the Holy Night; Carol of the Bells. More classic, shorter, and more accessible than Crumb's other piano works. Includes some strumming, plucking, and thumping of the strings. The only piano piece of Crumb's that ends loud. M-D.

Gnomic Variations 1981 (CFP 66905) 18 min. A conservative theme and 18 varia-tions presents Crumb in the less-familiar role of classicist and ascetic. The highly organized variations fall clearly into three sections of six each. The first section stays close to the theme, exploring some of its rhythmic and harmonic possibilities. The next six variations, more reflective in charac-ter, serve as a slow movement; and the last six provide a brilliant closing. "Gnomic" refers to the aphoristic style of the variations, their pithiness. Much is implied with hints of Beethoven slow movements and Lisztian elaboration. Some inside-the-piano sonorities (muted and plucked strings) are integrated with usual piano technique. Much vitality and drive are found in this energetic set. In this work, Crumb drops the extramusical trappings that were part of the earlier *Makrokosmos* cycle. D.
See: David Burge, *Keyboard*, 9/11 (December 1983):71, 96, for further analysis.

Processional 1983 (CFP 66991) 8 min. "The title of the work was suggested by the music's obsessive reiteration of pulse ('sempre pulsando, estaticamente') and broad 'unfolding' gestures. Perhaps the music suggests more a 'proces-sional of nature' rather than any sort of festival or somber 'human' processional" (from the score). Tonal plus chromatic, modal, and whole-tone elements; six descending tones heard at the beginning make up the basic harmonic cell, later varied by clusters, repetitions, and permutations. Small melodic fragments enter and leave and provide articulation contrast to the sustained legato seen throughout most of the piece. Some avant-garde techniques. D.

See: David Burge, "Contemporary Piano," CK, 2 (May–June 1976):48. Discusses the piano music of Crumb.

——, "Performing the piano music of George Crumb," CK, 2 (July–August 1976):20–21, 36–37. Devoted mainly to *Makrokosmos* volumes 1 and 2.

Renee Norris, "George Crumb's *Five Pieces for Piano.*" *Clavier* 37:8 (October 1998): 22, 24, 26.

Richard Steinitz, "George Crumb," MT, 1627 (October 1978):844–45, 847.

Thomas Warburton, "New Piano Techniques for Crumb's Piano Music," PQ, 87 (Fall 1974):15–16.

Ivo Cruz (1901–1985) Portugal, born Brazil

Aguarelas (Water Colors) 1921 (Sassetti). Dancam Moiras Encantadas, 5pp.: dance rhythms; changing meters; big climax; ends *pp*; arpeggi, seconds, and big chords exploited. Caem Miosotis, 8pp: syncopation; mid-section uses a chordal melody over arpeggi bass; *ppp* ending. Canto de Luar, 4pp.: easiest of the group; accompanied melody. Palacio em Ruinas, 8pp.: best in the set; octaves, full range of keyboard used; rubato Andantino grazioso section contrasts with outer sections. Virtuoso writing. M-D.

Hommages 1955 (Sassetti). A Strauss: to Richard Strauss; reminiscences of *Til Eulenspiegel* and *Rosenkavalier* permeate this graceful piece. A Manuel de Falla: guitar-like effects interspersed with melodic writing; big chordal climax, much use of trill, ends *pp*. A Oscar da Silva: takes as its inspiration "Coquetterie" from da Silva's *Images*, Op.6; bravura writing, glissandi, brilliant closing section. M-D.

Suite (Valentim de Carvalho 1974) 16pp. Preludio; Valsa Romantica; Marcha. Colorful, Impressionistic, attractive. M-D.

César Cui (1855–1918) Russia

Least typically Russian of the group of Five, Cui wrote a number of piano works mainly in salon style.

Three pieces (MCA). Moderato; Andante; Moderato. Int.

Four Spanish Marionettes (Nov). Fast, carefree, playful. Int.

À Argenteau Op.40 (Bessel). 9 pièces caractéristiques. Int. to M-D.

Album of Piano Works by César Cui (B. Tours—Nov). Op.20/1–12, Op.21/3,4, Op.22/1–4, Op.30/1, Op.31/2, OP.35/1,2, Op.39/1–6, Op.40/2,4. All small pieces, miniatures, two movements from a suite, Polonaise, Waltz, Impromptus, etc. Int. to M-D.

Causerie (Conversation) Op.40/6 (D. Stearns—Willis 1984) 9pp. A clever etude in the crossing of hands, flowing melody over alternating sixths, contrasting mid-section, bravura ending. M-D.

A César Cui Album (G. Kováts—EMB 1991) 38pp. Bagatelle italienne; Berceuse; Valse Op.81/2; Esquisse—Polka Op.8/3; Intermezzo; Nocturne; Impromptu; Scherzino. Int. to M-D.

Two Mazurkas Op.70 (MMP). Chopin influence. Int. to M-D.

Richard Cumming (1928–   ) USA, born China

Sonata 1951 (JWC) 30pp. 18 min. Dedicated to Rudolf Firkusny. Allegro deciso. Scherzo: perpetual motion. Andante: modal, harmonic treatment of a 12-tone row. Passacaglia: Allegro molto moderato; motive serves as the backbone for complete sonata; 15 variations; closes with same idea sonata opened. Strong thematic usage, utilizes entire keyboard. M-D to D.

24 Preludes 1968 (Bo&H) 43pp. 29 min. Written as a birthday present for John Browning, who has recorded them. Various contemporary techniques are exploited. Groupings are possible without playing all 24. Contains one Prelude for right hand only and one for left hand only. Large span required. Int. to D.

Geoffrey Cummings-Knight (–   ) Great Britain

24 Preludes (Roberton 1987). Appealing melodies, pianistic, improvisational. Some are overly long for what they have to offer. M-D.

Arthur Custer (1923–   ) USA

Custer's music is largely serially oriented.

4 Etudes 1964 (Pioneer Editions) 8 min. Deliberately, but Freely: blurred quality desired, many seconds; mid-section asks for a melody to be improvised using only pitches within indicated compass, accompanied by clusters; plucked strings used at conclusion; some half-pedaling. Scherzoso: large skips, *fff*, trill in left hand over five bars; more seconds; vigorous writing. Grave: interesting trill and arpeggio study. Spiritoso: syncopated, motoric, and percussive. M-D.

4 Ideas (Gen). Clusters, aleatory usage, but basically neo-Romantic. Contrasted works. M-D

Rhapsodicality Brown (Gen). Popular styles, jazz, improvisation. M-D.

Arthur Cunningham (1928–1997) USA

Cunningham has written in both tonal and atonal styles, making use of both traditional Western scales and modal and serial techniques.

Harlem Suite: Engrams (TP 1978) 11pp. 6 min. Atonal. Multisections vary between slow and fast, different thematic materials and moods. M-D.

Michael G. Cunningham (1937–   ) USA

Piano Suite Op.8 (Seesaw) 4 min.

Three Impressions (Seesaw 1964) 3pp. Prelude: Allegretto, chromatic. Prelude Variant: Rubato. Landscape: Slowly, chordal, Impressionistic. Int. to M-D.

Sonata II Op.33 (Seesaw 1970) 10 min. Excitation: large chromatic gestures; simultaneous white and black glissandi; large span required. Highly Sustained: broad dynamic range. Fast: dry, percussive, linear, extremes in range. Thoroughly contemporary idiom. D.

American Folk Songs (Seesaw) 24pp. 30 min. Contains a total of 61 folksong settings from various states including a U.S. sea chantey. Most are short (two lines or less) and are attractively presented with the tunes easily identified; MC harmonies. Int. to M-D.

Portraits for Modern Dance 1964 (Seesaw) 17pp. 3 suites published separately. 1. *Suite Montage:* The Event; Incitement; Undertow; Lyric; Demonia; Resolvae. 2. *Three Impressions:* Icon; Dark Vista; Improvisation on a Spiritual. 3. *Haiku Suite:* Fujiami; Creaking Cricket; Purpling Sky; Ambling Cat. Clever, colorful, programmatic, appealing. MC. Int. to M-D.

Curtis Curtis-Smith (1942–) USA

Rhapsodies 1973 (Sal). For prepared piano. I . . . a swift pure cry . . . II But wait! Low in dark middle earth. Embedded ore. III And a call, pure, long and throbbing, longindying call. IV Listen! The spiked and winding cold seahorn. Requires extensive inside-the-piano work (like bowing the strings with fishline); produces some incredible sounds. Highly original and effective. D.

See: David Burge, "Curtis Curtis-Smith's Rhapsodies," CK, 3 (May 1977): 44.

Warren Cytron (1944–) USA

Three Bagatelles 1968 (McGinnis & Marx) 3pp. Webernesque, enigmatic. M-D.

Sonata 1969 (McGinnis & Marx) 8pp. Quarter note = 76; Quarter note = 66; Muscularly; Expansive. Expressionistic, dynamic extremes, pointillistic, serial. D.

Carl Czerny (1791–1857) Austria

Czerny's greatest contribution to music may have been through his training of such students as Liszt and Leschetizky. He was a prolific composer and wrote approximately 1,000 printed compositions, some with 50 or more parts. His scholastic studies of Opp.299, 300, 335, 355, 399, 400, and 500, published under the title *Complete Theoretical and Practical Pianoforte School,* are the best in this category. As Igor Stravinsky has reminded us: "In Czerny I have always admired the full-blooded musician much more than the eminent pedagogue." Czerny's eleven piano sonatas are well worth investigating.

Sonata A♭ Op.7 1810 (Ernst Sauter—UMKR 1971) No.99 in series, 43pp. The first movement—Andante, Allegro moderato ed espressivo—develops a main idea with the Andante section closing the movement. Prestissimo agitato in c♯ exploits a short-long figure and moves through closely related keys. Adagio espressivo e cantabile is in SA design and based on a stately marchlike rhythm. The Rondo—Allegretto is a playful romp. The fifth movement, Capriccio Fugato, is a four-voice fugue in a♭; the final four bars bring back the Andante theme of the first movement. A highly interesting work that precedes by a number of years the musical style and character we associate with late Beethoven, Mendelssohn, Schubert, and Schumann. M-D.

See: Anton Kuerti, "Genius or Tinkler? The Riddle of Carl Czerny," *Piano Today* (July–August 1995):6–8, 60, 66. Focuses on Czerny's serious piano music, especially his Sonata A♭ Op. 7.

Variations on a Beloved Vienna Trauer-Walzer of Franz Schubert Op.12 (Musica Obscura) 8pp. Introduzione a Capriccio: brilliant; leads directly to the simple theme. Four variations, with the last the most extensive and serving as a coda. M-D.

Variations on a theme by Rode Op.33 "La Ricordanza" (IMC). Five variations, three with florid figuration. M-D.

Valses di Bravura Op.35 (UE) in Album *Viennese Masters for Piano Solo*. M-D.

Toccata Op.92 (CFP; GS; Musica Obscura). Uses 16th-note figuration throughout, looks forward to the Schumann Toccata and probably inspired that more-famous work. Op.92 is remarkable for the balance of its design and interest of its figuration. It achieves a powerfully cumulative impact by emphasizing the 16th-note rhythm of the opening bars through increasingly sonorous dispositions. Many double thirds and sixths. M-D to D.

Capriccio Op.200 (Arno Volk Verlag) see *Anthology of Music* volume on *Improvisation*, 155–57. M-D.

Introduction, Variations Brillantes et Rondeau de Chasse Op.202 (Dob; Kunzelmann GM 915 1982) 15pp. Five variations plus a seven-page finale. Well written in a likeable salon style. Uses a number of different keys. M-D.

Variations sur la Valse Charmante de Johann Strauss "Le Duc de Reichstadt" Op.249 (Musica Obscura) 17pp. Straightforward theme, 5 variations, and Finale—Allegro molto. Concludes in a burst of brilliant figurations. M-D.

Sonate d'étude Op.268 (CFP 3239). Technical problems of every sort, flamboyant dexterity required. M-D to D.

Nocturne B♭ Op.368/8 (Musica Obscura) 2pp. Flowing Allegretto con anima. Brief cadenza at mid-point. Cantabile melody. M-D.

Variations on "La ci darem" from Mozart's Don Giovanni Op.825/17 (Musica Obscura) 3pp. Four-bar introduction leads to theme. Variation of the melody plus an Allegro in 6/8 follows. M-D.

SCHOLASTIC STUDIES:

Basic Elements of Piano Technique (von Irmer—GS) 97pp. 34 pieces selected to develop an advanced technique. Int. to M-D.

The School of Velocity Op.299 (Alfred; CFP; GS; Ric). 40 studies. Nos.6 C, 19 F, and 21 c have musical as well as technical interest. Int. to M-D.

100 Progressive Studies Without Octaves Op.139 (Hinson—Alfred 4839). Begins with easier pieces and gradually increases in difficulty. Int. to M-D.

125 Exercises in Passage Playing Op.261 (Hinson—Alfred 4838). Short pieces (8–16 measures) exploring all types of passages. Int. to M-D. No. 33 is an octave etude that has the right hand hopping all over the keyboard. Josef

Lhévinne, who had a fabulous octave technique, often played this as an encore.

Czerny at Its Best (Podolsky—Belwin-Mills). A selection of 19 studies from Op.299.

The School of Legato and Staccato Op.335 (CFP). Fingered and pedaled. Int. to M-D.

40 Daily Exercises Op.337 (Hinson—Alfred 4830). Each piece consists of various sections of one to several measures. Czerny advises to repeat each one 20 times without interruption. Study one or more a day. Easy to M-D.

First Teacher of the Piano Op.599 (Palmer—Alfred; Sikorski). Int.

First Teacher of the Piano Op.599 (Sikorski). Int.

Preliminary School of Finger Dexterity Op.636 (Palmer—Alfred). 24 progressive studies. Nos.4 B♭, 7 C, 8 a, and 13 B♭ are highly effective and musical. M-D.

24 Studies for the Left Hand Op.718 (Hinson—Alfred 4831; GS). Contain some of Czerny's finest musical writing. Students enjoy these pieces. Int. to M-D.

The Art of Finger Dexterity Op.740 (Palmer—Alfred; Ric; Artia). Int. to M-D.

Czerny at Its Best (Podolsky—Belwin-Mills). A selection of 19 studies from Op.740.

L'Infatigable—Grand étude de Vélocité Op.779 (Eulenburg). 15pp. Long, brilliant cascades of scales, broken octaves, and arpeggi. Requires solid technique. M-D.

See: Garola Grindea, "An Interview with Carl Czerny," *Piano Journal,* 13/30 (October 1992):5–6, 9, 11–12.

Maurice Hinson, "Carl Czerny Remembered," *Clavier,* 24/8 (October 1985):15–19.

D

François Dagincourt (1684–1758) France
Dagincourt studied with Lebègue in Paris and later became a disciple of François Couperin, who exerted a great influence on him.
Pièces de clavecin (H. Feguson—Heugel). 43 short pieces, highly ornamented. Fine edition. M-D.

Ingolf Dahl (1912–1970), USA, born Germany
Sonata Seria 1955 (TP). Allegro energico: exciting SA. Largo and Presto scorrevole: interior fantasies on the opening theme of the first movement. Adagio Cantabile e Coda: lyrical; tender reflections of the cantabile second theme of the first movement. Modal, much use of the whole step and minor seventh, weighty material, ideas convincingly handled, free dissonant counterpoint. D.
First, Second, Third march (TP). Published separately. Interesting form. *Third March* has an indefinite tonal center. M-D.
Fanfares. See Anthologies and Collections, U.S.A., *New Music for the Piano* (LG).
Hymn and Toccata (Boonin 1943–47) Hymn 7½ min. Toccata 4½ min. Hymn is chordal with big, gonglike sonorities; syncopation helps delineate melodic line. Much eighth-note figuration throughout Toccata; a slower, dramatic mid-section provides contrast before eighth-note figuration returns. Both works use chromaticism freely. D.
Pastorale Montano (Boonin 1936–43). An alpine landscape. Strong tonal organization. M-D.
Reflections (Boonin 1967). A miniature, based on an 11-note row that suggests A, with transpositions to D and E. M-D.
Sonata Pastorale (PIC 1959). Moderato—Allegretto comodo; Elegia—Adagio ma non troppo; Scherzino—Allegretto leggiero; Fête champêtre—Allegro con brio. Infectious tunes; jazzy rhythms; movements spaced a fifth apart; variation technique combined with free association of ideas; constantly evolving phrases. M-D to D.

Martin Dalby (1942–   ) Scotland
Sonata (Nov). A four-movement work, MC idiom. M-D to D.

Luigi Dallapiccola (1904–1975) Italy
Dallapiccola uses the 12-tone system in a highly personal manner. He exploits the sensuous qualities of sound more insistently than do most other dodecaphonic composers. Some of his melodies contain elements of great beauty.

Sonatina Canonica on Paganini Caprices 1942 (SZ) 9 ½ min. Four movements in
   a "tour de force" of contemporary canonic writing. Highly effective work.
   M-D.
Quaderno Musicale Di Annalibera 1953 (SZ; MMP) 14 min. Eleven pieces conceived as one large work, based on a lyrically conceived row. The intervallic structure of the row permits the interlacing of Impressionistic sounds
   with free or strict contrapuntal devices. One of the finest serial works
   for piano. Dedicated to the composer's daughter for her eighth birthday.
   M-D.
   See: David Burge, "Dallapiccola's Quaderno Musicale," *Keyboard*, 9 (April
   1983):61, 80.

Jean-Michel Damase (1928–   ) France
Damase was a piano and composition student at the Paris Conservatory. In 1947
he won the Prix de Rome and made his piano debut; his American debut was in
1954.
Introduction et Allegro 1992 (ESC 1992) 17pp. 8 min. Written for the Concours
   International Marguerite Long 1992. A five-page Introduction filled with
   right-hand arpeggio figurations and full left-hand chords leads to the Allegro: broken chord figuration, fughetto-like, strong rhythms, repeated chords,
   freely tonal, like a toccata. Broad arpeggio gestures end the piece. D.

Jean François Dandrieu (1682–1738) France
Music for Harpsichord (J. White—Br). Contains three suites: Nos. 1 and 4 from
   the *Pièces de Clavecin* of 1728, and No.6 from Dandrieu's last volume of 1734.
   The first three movements are entitled La Lully, La Corelli, and Double la
   Corelli. M-D.
Les Clavecinistes Français (L. Diemer—Durand) Vol.II. Over-edited. M-D.
Trois Livres de Clavecin de Jeunesse 1701–13 (François-Sappey—Heugel). Less
   than ideal edition. Int. to M-D.

Richard Danielpour (1964–   ) USA
Danielpour received his doctorate at The Juilliard School and teaches at the
Manhattan School of Music.
The Enchanted Garden 1992 (GS) Five piano preludes. "The composer acknowl-
   edges that he had [his Piano Concerto II] in mind as he tilled the *Garden*.
   Several passages in the concerto's piano part use the stride bass and mo-
   tivic and rhythmic patterns of *Garden*'s "Mardi Gras" (Patrick Widhalm,
   P&K 169 [July–August 1994]: 20).
Mardi Gras from *The Enchanted Garden* 1992. In collection *American Contemporary Masters* (GS 1995). 8pp. This effective wild and uninhibited piece
   uses stride bass (large left-hand skips), lots of strong rhythmic patterns,
   quartal fourths, syncopation, quieter contrasting sections, octatonic writing, "scat-singing," and subito con forza chords. D.
Sonata 1986, rev. 1992 (CFP) 22pp., ca. 14 min. A one-movement sectionalized
   work with many tempo and mood changes; thematic ideas undergo consid-

erable transformations; textures are generally thin; *ppp* ending. An outstanding work requiring superb pianistic and interpretative abilities. D.

Psalms 1985 (CFP 1989) 15pp., ca. 15 min. I. Morning: lyrical, rubato, expressive, atonal, builds to violent climax, then tenderly dies away to a final A with staccatissimo *pp* chords. II. Afternoon: strongly rhythmic, marcato, more tonal than opening movement, dramatic conclusion. III. Evening: misterioso, large span contrasting Agitato mid-section, harmonics, sostenuto pedal indicated; large span required. M-D to D.

Ram Da-Oz (1929–   ) Israel, born Germany

Capriccio (IMI). Large-scale bravura piece written in an eclectic style. Stormy, with relief offered by middle-section slow variations. D.

Prologue, Variations and Epilogue (IMI 1966). Prize winner in the Israel Music Institute's competition for a piano piece in 1966. Both Prologue and Epilogue are variations on the theme of the middle movement. Large-scale work demanding musicianship and bravura. D.

Five Contrasts (IMI 618) 19pp. Hands in Contrast; Ostinato; Invention; Meditation; Moto Perpetuo. Well written and effective. M-D.

Aspects 1969 (IMI) 12pp. Contains a variety of textures from linear to dissonant chordal, spasmodic arpeggio figurations and interlocking chords. Large span required. D.

Louis-Claude Daquin (1694–1772) France

Pièces de Clavecin (Hogwood—Faber 1983) 74pp. The first complete modern edition of Daquin's four harpsichord suites, containing 28 individual pieces, many characterized by descriptive titles such as La Guitarre and the famous Le Coucou. Contains an introduction, table of ornaments, and editorial notes. M-D.

See: Kathleen Dale, "The Keyboard Music of Daquin," MMR (August 1946).

Alexander Sergeyevich Dargomizhsky (1813—1869) Russia

Collected Piano Works (M. Pekeleese—USSR 1954). Almost all are in the salon style of the period and contain such titles as Valse mélancholique; Cosaque; Variations sur l'air russe "People all blame me"; Le rêve de la Esmeralda; Nouvelles mazurkas; Polka; Scherzo, Song without Words. Int. to M-D.

Gyula David (1913–   ) Hungary

Szonata Zongorara (EMB 1957). The dimensions of this sonata are more like those of a sonatina. Influence of Ravel shows in the melodic spontaneity. Expert craft and expressiveness throughout. M-D.

Thomas Christian David (1925–   ) Austria

Sonate (Dob 1967) 21pp. Vivace: contains much rhythmic and harmonic repetition. Adagio: developed with arpeggi and full chords. Allegro assai: thin texture in constant eighth-note motion. Chromatic, neoclassic. Complex but knowledgeable writing. D.

Mario Davidovsky (1933–   ) USA, born Argentina
Davidovsky's music is characterized by its breadth and concentration, a balance between craftsmanship and spontaneity of development, imagination, and, when needed, simplicity.
Synchronisms VI for Piano and Electronic Sounds (EBM 1970) 23pp. 7½ min. "The electronic sounds in many instances modulate the acoustical characteristics of the piano, by affecting its decay and attack characteristics. The electronic segment should perhaps not be viewed as an independent polyphonic line, but rather as if it were inlaid into the piano part. A coherent musical continuum is sought while trying to respect the idiosyncracies of each medium" (supplied by the composer). The sparkling electronic sounds do indeed modify the piano acoustics rather than present an independent part. The piece is characterized by skillfully integrated bursts of virtuosity and delicate lyricism. It is one of a series of compositions for electronically synthesized sounds in combination with the more conventional instruments. Awarded the 1971 Pulitzer prize. M-D.

Peter Maxwell Davies (1934–   ) Great Britain
Davies writes in a sophisticated and complex style.
5 Pieces for Piano Op.2 1955–56 (Schott) 15 min. The influence of Webern is seen in both texture and technique, while the musical character and quality show more Schönberg influence. Nos.1 and 4 are the easiest. No.5 is a theme and 4 variations. Communicative serial works. M-D.
5 Little Pieces 1960–64 (Bo&H) 5 min. 3pp. Stylistically these pieces are close to Webern but they do recall Schönberg Op.19 *Little Pieces*. Sparse textures but diverting. Plenty of vitality in these serially conceived works. M-D.
Stevie's Ferry to Hoy (Bo&H 1978) 3pp. 1. Calm Water. 2. Choppy Seas. 3. Safe Landing. Colorful, descriptive. Easy to Int.
Farewell to Stromness and *Yesnaby Ground* 1980 (Bo&H) 5pp. Two Interludes from "The Yellow Cake Revue" that evoke Celtic melodies from the Orkney Islands. A few syncopation problems. Int.
Sub tuam protectionem. Ut re mi 1969, 1971 (JWC 1980) 12pp. 5½ min. The first piece is a free transcription of a motet by John Dunstable. Original notation; pieces more difficult than they appear. Note in English. M-D.
Sonata 1980–81 (JWC) 25 min. The first three movements are: Allegro; Vivace; Larghetto. The last movement is very similar in form to the last movement of Beethoven's Op.110. It is divided into four parts and labeled movements 4–7: Sostenuto—Allegro ma non troppo: sonata-like in its strenuous driving force. Scherzo: harmonically ambiguous, whole-tone usage. Larghetto: a passacaglia, chromatic. Cantabile moto: strongly influenced by Beethoven's Op.110, as seen in its cantabile phrasing, festoons of arpeggios, and its plainly presented polyphony.
See: Paul Griffiths, "Maxwell Davies' Piano Sonata," *Tempo*, 140 (March 1982):5–9.
See: Robert Henderson, "Peter Maxwell Davies," MT, 102 (October 1961):624–26.

Allan Davis (1922–   ) USA
Razorback Reel (OUP 93.211 1963) 5pp. A good MC hoedown. Requires strong rhythmic drive. M-D.

Anthony Davis (–   ) USA
Middle Passage 1983. In collection *American Contemporary Masters* (GS 1995). 9pp. Expressionistic, harsh, discordant, intense. Same note repeated many times; improvisation required: "Improvise, high energy, alternating clusters with lines ca. 1 minute" (from the score), plus other improvisation requests. Fiercely personal writing. Large span required. D.

John Davye (1929–   ) USA
Davye teachers at Old Dominion University in Norfolk, VA.
Partita Piccola (Short Suite) 1982 (CSMP) 4 pp. Allemande; Courante; Sarabande; Gigue. Built on the Dorian mode on B♭ and/or F. Twentieth-century sonorities and procedures, fresh-sounding. Int.

Emil Debusman (1921–   ) USA
Sonata No.1 Op.17 (AME 1958) 16pp. Short. First movement is no more difficult than the Clementi Sonatinas. Second and third movements require a larger span, up to an 11th. Idiomatic and very exciting final movement. Good right-hand octave technique and a crisp touch are required. Int. to M-D.
Four Sonatinas Op.27 (AME 1957). Sonatina Fanfare. Gregorian Sonatina. Chromatic Sonatina. Sonatina for a Birthday. All are short and MC, and exploit various sonorities. Int.

Claude Debussy (1862–1918) France
Claude Debussy, a seminal figure in twentieth-century music, developed a keyboard style characterized by parallel chordal treatment, layers of refined sound, unresolved harmonies, unusual pedal effects, free modulatory procedures, and full exploitation of the piano's resources. He extended the heritage of Liszt in his daring exploitation of the keyboard. Much of Debussy's piano music is made more difficult because no fingerings and only very few pedal markings were indicated. Debussy left fewer than twenty pedal marks in his entire piano music, but he did notate additional indications via long notes plus slurs. Durand & Co. and Fromont were the original publishers of Debussy's piano music, but with the copyright running out on many of his works, numerous companies are presently publishing his piano compositions. A new Oeuvres Complètes (Complete Edition), edited by Roy Howat published by Durand-Costallat, began to appear in 1985. A helpful article, regarding the various editions, is Arthur B. Wenk, "Checklist of Errors in Debussy's Piano Music," PQ, 68 (Summer 1969):18–21. Alfred and GS editions contain English translations of Debussy's indications. CFP has English titles but retains the French directions. Alfred, IMC, Ric, K, and B&VP have a number of works available.

EARLY WORKS:

Danse bohémienne 1880 (Schott; B&VP; CFP). Syncopated, mid-section more melodic and in parallel major. Int.

Arabesque I E 1888 (Henle; GS; CFP; IMC; Bo&H; K; UMP; CF: B&VP; Ric; Waterloo) 3½ min. Legato triplets in right hand plus flowing melodic lines, delicate imagery. Int.

Arabesque II G 1888 (Henle; GS; CFP; IMC; Bo&H; K; UMP; CF; B&VP; Schott; Ric; Waterloo) 2½ min. Persistent figuration, staccato touch, dance-like. Int.

Nocturne Db 1890 (CFP; EBM; CF; ESC; B&VP) 5½ min. Flowing ABA design, late-Romantic style. Int. to M-D.

Rêverie 1890 (Hinson—Alfred 6301; Choudens; Fromont; Jobert; GS; CF; CFP; B&VP) 3½ min. Melody requires a cantabile legato; ninth chords; atmospheric. Int. to M-D.

Danse (Tarantelle Styrienne) 1890 (Henle; K; Jobert; Durand; B&VP; CFP) 4½ min. Contrasted meters of 3/4 and 6/8, interesting voice leading. One of Debussy's most brilliant early works. M-D.

Valse Romantique 1890 (EBM; B&VP; CFP; Jobert) 3 min. Experimental; Chopin influence. Int.

Ballade 1890 (K; CFP; B&VP; Jobert; EBM) 6 min. Chromatic, experimental, repetitious melody. M-D.
See: Maurice Dumesnil, "Debussy's Ballade," *Etude* (February 1948):68.

Mazurka f♯ 1891 (EBM; CFP; B&VP; Jobert) 2 min. Reflects influence of Mme. Mauté de Fleurville, Debussy's piano teacher, who was a pupil of Chopin. Int. to M-D.

Suite Bergamasque 1890 (VU; Henle; Alfred; Ric; CFP; GS; IMC; EBM; SP; B&VP; Waterloo; Jobert) 15½ min. Prélude: archaic mood; brilliant but easy; legato double thirds. Menuet: contrast of phrasing, staccato chords, archaic. Clair de lune (VU51009, urtext edition and facsimile of autograph; IMC; K; B&VP; GS; Henle; CFP; UMP; Hansen House; SP): flowing melodic passage-work, legato thirds, clear textures. Passepied: busy nonlegato accompaniment, modal, constant motion, evocative. A dance suite built on the heritage of the clavecinistes. M-D.
See: Daniel Ericourt, "Master Class—a Lesson on Debussy's Clair de lune," *Piano Teacher*, 6 (1962):2–4.
Robert Spillman, "Music Does Not Start in a Vacuum," AMT, 43/5 (April–May 1994): 10–13 for a discussion of the word "Bergamasque."

Images (oubliées) 1894 (PQ 102 [Summer 1978]: 15–19, 103 [Fall 1978]:31–42; TP 1978). Three previously unpublished works appear under this collective title. The autograph of the *Images* contains the dedication and the following recommendation: "These pieces would fare poorly in 'les salons brillamment illuminés' where people who do not like music usually congregate. They are rather 'conversations' between the piano and one's self; it is not forbidden furthermore to apply one's small sensibility to them on nice rainy days." A few annotations are sprinkled throughout the scores, à la Satie. Lent: preludelike; subtle harmonies; maintains a dreamlike grace in the gait of its supple rhythms. In the Rhythm of a "Sarabande": the first version of the future Sarabande of the suite *Pour le piano* of 1901; interesting harmonic changes compared to the final version. Nous n'irons plus au bois: contains melody and figuration in alternating hands, similar to the Prélude in *Pour le piano*; hand crossings; harplike sonorities; duplets with triplets; *ppp* ending. M-D.

See: Arthur Hoérée, "Images (oubliées)," PQ, 102 (Summer 1978):15. Translated by Barry S. Brook.

See: John K. Adams, "Debussy: The Early Piano Works," Part 1, PQ, 137 (Spring 1987): 36–40.

TRANSITIONAL WORKS:

Suite pour le piano 1896–1901 (Alfred 360; Henle; GS; K; IMC; B&VP; CFP; UMP; Ric; PWM; Jobert) 13 min. Prélude (Jobert): brilliant, bravura-like, glissandi, whole-tone scales and harmonies, stunning cadenza. Sarabande: parallel solemn chordal treatment, stately and ethereal; Satie influence; sensitive rhythmic control needed. Toccata: neoclassic, perpetual motion, exacting throughout; demands clarity in the steady and brilliant 16th notes; large ternary form; the most difficult of the three movements. M-D.

See: Charles M. Joseph, "The original Version of Debussy's Sarabande," PQ, 118 (Summer 1982):48–50. Compares the original and first published versions of the second movement of *Suite pour le piano*.

Virginia Raad, "Claude Debussy's Sarabande," AMT, 30/6 (June-July 1981):22–23.

D'un cahier d'esquisses (From a Sketchbook) 1903 (Alfred 599; Durand-Costallat; EBM; CFP; JWC; B&VP; Schott Frères) 4½ min. Sketch for *La Mer*, charming and ethereal. Mixture of styles. M-D.

Masques 1904 (Durand-Costallat; Henle K; CFP; B&VP; EC) 4 min. Brilliant, similar to vivacious treatment of material in *Danse*. M-D.

L'Isle joyeuse 1904 (Alfred 6349; Durand-Costallat; GS; K; Ric; IMC; B&VP; CFP; EC; PWM; UMP) 5 min. Inspired by Watteau's painting "Embarkation for Cythere." Orchestrally conceived with great animation. Unrelenting rhythmic drive, dazzling coda, complex SA design. Advanced pianism required. D.

See: Roy Howat, "En Route for L'Isle Joyeuse: The Restoration of a Triptych." *Cahiers Debussy* No. 19, 1995, pp.37–52. Suggests *Masques, D'un cahier d'esquisses,* and *L'Isle joyeuse* were originally conceived as a three-movement suite.

Morceau de Concours 1904 (Howat—Durand 1980) 3pp. Composed for a special composer identification competition in the Parisian magazine *Musica*. Its impish, scherzo-like flavor is reflective of the most interesting fact about the piece—the inclusion of 11 bars from Debussy's sketches for his uncompleted opera based on the short story by Edgar Allan Poe, "The Devil in the Belfrey." Augmented chords, whole-tone scale. Clever and rhythmic. Excellent preparation for *Golliwog's Cake Walk*. M-D.

MATURE WORKS:

Estampes (Prints) 1903 (Alfred 4607; Henle; Durand-Costallat; IMC; K; CFP; PWM; B&VP) 12½ min. Title refers to images (engravings) printed from engraved copper or wood plates. Pagodes (Durand): pentatonic scale, atmospheric pedal effects, booming gongs (gamelan) in duple beat, exotic piano washes; light clear touch required. Soirée dans Grenade (Durand; CFP; UMP; K): one of Debussy's three "Spanish" pieces for piano; habanera rhythm permeates the whole piece; five short ideas are punctuated by guitar-like interruptions; clicking castenets; rich melodies, lush harmonies; fast, soft staccato chords require great control; one of Debussy's greatest pieces. Jardins sous la pluie (GS; Durand; Ric; CFP; UMP; EBM): fast, 16th-note figuration; broad tonal and dynamic range; simultaneous multiple melodic levels; stamina required to maintain excitement. M-D.
See: Patricia W. Harpole, "Debussy and the Javanese Gamelan," AMT, 35/3 (January 1986):8–9, 41. Focuses on gamelan influence seen in "Pagodes."
Virginia Raad, "Debussy and the Magic of Spain," *Clavier*, 18 (March 1979):13–21. Includes the music of "La soirée dans Grenade."

Images (Pictures) 1905 (Hinson—Alfred 4611; Durand-Costallat; IMC; K; CFP; UMP; PWM; B&VP) 15½ min. Reflet dans l'eau (Reflections in the water) (GS; CF; Ric; Durand; K): suggests the *impression* stimulated by a scene, not the scene itself; cascading arpeggios and sweeping figuration; demands complete facility, delicate touch, and careful timing. Hommage à Rameau (Durand): noble lyric expressive quality reminiscent of the *Suite Bergamasque* and the Sarabande from *Pour le Piano*; a slow and complex sarabande; steady rhythm necessary. Mouvement (Durand; PWM): vigorous ceaseless motion in triplet 16th notes; "an impression of animation"; needs a capricious lightness but precision. M-D.
See: T. P. Currier, "Debussy's Reflet dans l'eau," *Musician* (April 1912):278.
Maurice Dumesnil, "Dripping Dew Drops: Interpretation of Reflections in the Water," *Etude* (May 1949):282.
———, "Reflections in the Water: Detail Concerning Tone Production and Pedaling," *Etude* (August 1949):462.

Images (Pictures) 1907 (Hinson—Alfred 4612; CFP; Durand-Costallat; B&VP; PWM) 12½ min. Displays even more evocative titles than the first set of *Images*, and these titles provide indications of the nature of the music. This set is generally more difficult than the 1905 set and comes off better in a small hall. Three staves are used to indicate layers of sound more clearly. Cloches à travers les feuilles (Bells through the Leaves) (Durand): transparent textures, chime effects, whole-tone usage, atmospheric sonorities, fluttering figures, revels in rhythmic polyphony. Et la lune descend sur le temple qui fut (And the Moon Descends on the Ruined Temple) (Durand):

songlike; difficult to project; sensitive pedal technique required. Poissons d'or (Gold Fish) (Ric; Durand): inspired by a Japanese lacquer painting in Debussy's collection: overlapping tremolo figures, floating melodies in thirds, fluid arpeggios, stunning coda; fast, delicate *pp* passages are the most demanding. M-D to D.

Children's Corner 1908 (Hinson—Alfred 667; Henle; VU; Alfred; Ric; EC; CFP; PWM; UMP, B&VP; CF; Paxton) 14½ min. This exquisite set suggests a comparison with Schumann's *Kinderscenen* and Fauré's *Dolly Suite*. Composed for Debussy's daughter, Chouchou, when she was three years old. Doctor Gradus ad Parnassum (B&VP; CFP): characterization of a youngster's technical practice session; builds to a fine toccata conclusion; fast harmonic rhythms require clear chordal outlines. Jimbo's Lullaby: awkward pentatonic theme with smashed seconds; humorous; limited dynamic range; varied touches and proper relation of the two tempi are necessary. Serenade for the Doll (Ric): a strummed mandolin piece, *una corda* to be used throughout, legato and staccato contrast. The Snow Is Dancing: subtle; delicate atmospheric painting; haunting melody; distinguish between dots and dashes over notes; the most demanding of the set. The Little Shepherd (EMB): many nuances and rubato; quiet; expressive; simple; "maintain the rhythm" (from score). Golliwog's Cake Walk (Alfred; B&VP; VU; EMB; CFP; Ric; CF; Waterloo): a jazzy conclusion (ragtime) spiced with syncopated harmony; accents, dynamic contrasts, and a short, witty reference to Wagner's prelude to *Tristan und Isolde* add to the fun. M-D. All movements available separately (Durand).

See: Harold Bauer, "Children's Corner," *New York Times* (December 21, 1930).

Joyce Gault, "The Style of Debussy as Seen through the Children's Corner," *Iowa Music Teacher*, 42/1 (February 1985):4–6.

John Horton, "With Affectionate Apologies—Debussy's *Children's Corner*," *Music Teacher*, 60/1 (January 1981):15.

Le petit nègre 1909 (Alfred; Leduc; CFP 7285) 1½ min. Composed for Theodore Lack's *Methode élémentaire de Piano*, Op.269. *Golliwog's Cake Walk* was the model for this piece. The first tune of *Le petit nègre* is almost an inversion of that of *Golliwog's Cake Walk*, and the relationship between the central, trio-like sections, as well as the resemblance in construction of the two pieces, is inescapable. In 1913 Debussy used the first 16 bars in his children's ballet *La boite à joujoux*, in the key of F, with the title *Le soldat anglais*.

See: Maurice Dumesnil, "Little Nigar," *Etude* (June 1949):348, for the story of its publication.

Hommage à Haydn 1909 (CFP; B&VP) 1½ min. Originally written for a collection published by the Société Internationale de Musique in honor of the centenary of Haydn's death. Six pieces were contributed by Debussy, Dukas, Hahn, d'Indy, Ravel, and Widor. Debussy's piece is built on a distillation of the letters in Haydn's name, BADDG. This motif undergoes many subtle transformations. Int. to M-D.

La plus que Lente 1910 (Alfred 889; EBM; CFP; Durand; EC; PWM; Ric; B&VP) 4½ min. The humorous title (slower than slow) does not seem to fit the character of this charming waltz. It requires the subtle rubato carefully indicated by Debussy. Int. to M-D.

Préludes Book I 1910 (Durand-Costallat; Alfred; B&VP; Ric; CFP; PWM; EC) 32½ min. These pieces look back to Bach and Chopin and were influenced by Wagner's *Tristan and Isolde* in their psychic and programmatic characteristics. Each of the 24 musical paintings in Books I and II has its own unifying mood or character, closely relating the musical materials to the poetic intent suggested by the titles, which appear at the end of each Prélude. All are available separately (Durand).

Danseuses de Delphes (Delphic Dancers) (Ric). A statue in the Louvre inspired this piece. Five-bar phrases and subtle changes of time. Simultaneous lines must be characterized individually. Steady, flowing metric shifts in this slow, hypnotic dance.

Voiles (Sails). Oscillates between whole-tone and pentatonic harmonies; this oscillation also exists in the melodic ideas. Requires careful legato for whole-tone double thirds and a sensitive tonal balance.
See: Joseph Bloch, "Debussy's *Violes*," KC, 10/2 (March–April 1990):42–43, 47.

Le vent dans la plaine (The Wind in the Plain). Six-note pianissimo figure dominated by half-step construction needs firm technical command. Alto melody is interrupted by trills and leaping chords.

Les sons et les parfums tournent dans l'air du soir (Sounds and Scents Mingle in the Evening Air). This seductive waltz (3/4 + 2/4) was inspired by a line from Charles Baudelaire's *Les Fleurs du Mal*. It evolves from three themes that refuse to modulate. Ironically caricatured rhythm and melody. Imaginative tonal balance required.

Les collines d'Anacapri (The Hills of Anacapri) (Ric). Brilliant writing that leans considerably on a tarantella rhythm. Some folklike material employed in a brightly colored palette, the liveliest of the entire first book.

Des pas sur la neige (Footsteps in the Snow) (Ric; CFP). Persistent, stumbling rhythm. Evokes a gray horizon over a pale expanse of ice. A simple yet expressive and sustained legato is required throughout.
See: Marion A. Guck, "Tracing Debussy's 'Des pas sur la neige,'" ITO, 1/8 (November 1975):4–12.

Ce qu'a vu le vent d'Ouest (What the West Wind Saw). Takes its title from Hans Christian Andersen. Brilliant Lisztian show-piece, technically the most demanding in Book I. Sonorous chords, broken octaves, fast tremolos, and alternating passage-work create strenuous problems.

La fille aux cheveux de lin (The Girl with Flaxen Hair) (Alfred 893; Ric; B&VP; EBM; CFP). Title comes from the *Scottish Song* of Leconte de Lisle. Archaic-sounding melody. Extreme delicacy, careful legato, and flexible phrasing required. An exquisite portrait.
See: Maurice Dumesnil, "Puzzling Notation in *Maid with Flaxen Hair*," *Etude* (July 1947):23.

TM, Analysis of La Fille aux cheveux de lin, pp.151–63.

La sérénade interrompue (The Interrupted Serenade) (Ric). This effective Spanish piece, with a trace of gypsy, calls for a light staccato in a guitar-like character plus sudden dynamic contrasts.

La Cathédrale engloutie (The Sunken Cathedral) (Alfred; Ric; EBM; B&VP; CFP; Waterloo). This piece pays homage to Wagner by suggesting the lost Celtic city of Ys, birthplace of Isolde. A vision in sound of the submerged Cathedral of Ys. Impressive sense of stillness, medieval harmonies. Spans almost the entire keyboard. Needs precise pedaling, tempo continuity, and wide tonal range.

See: Charles Burkhart, "Debussy plays *La Cathédrale Engloutie* and Solves Musical Mystery," PQ, 65 (Fall 1968):14–16. A discussion of Debussy's recording of this work.

Maurice Dumesnil, "From an Old Legend: *La cathédrale engloutie*," *Etude* (July 1947):368.

Reginald Haché, "The Legendary Cathedral of Brittany," JALS, 19 (June 1986):67–76.

Dennis Todd, "Three Preludes of Debussy," *Music Teacher*, 56 (April 1977):13–14, for analysis and discussions of Voiles, La Fille aux cheveux de lin, and La Cathédral engloutie.

La danse de Puck (Puck's Dance) (Ric). This is the airy and elfish Puck of *A Midsummer Night's Dream*. Witty, whirling little dance, full of capricious rhythms. Requires a delicate touch. D.

Minstrels (Hinson—Alfred 6354; Ric). Sarcastic music hall parody that looks forward to Stravinsky. Captivating study in staccato to be played "nerveux et avec humour." Contrasting moods and a precise clarity make this one of the most attractive pieces.

Préludes Book II 1913 (Alfred; VU; EC; Ric; CFP; B&VP; PWM; Durand) 32½ min.

Brouillards (Mists) (Ric). Atmospheric figuration accompanies a vague melodic line. Exquisite control required; negate polytonal implications.

See: Dieter Schnebel, "*Brouillards*—Tendencies in Debussy," *Die Reihe*, 6 (1960), Universal Edition; English edition 1964, Theodore Presser.

Feuilles mortes (Dead Leaves). New use is made of the theme from *Les sons et les parfums*. Sustain legato at opening, do not play too fast. Requires even tonal balance in chords.

La Puerta del Vino (The Wine Gate). One of the gates to the Alhambra Palace in Granada. (Ric). Another superb Spanish piece, marked "in the motion of a habanera." Broad spectrum of tone. Observe dynamics carefully.

See: Albert Brussee, "Debussy's La Puerta del Vino," *Piano Journal*, 11 (June 1983):17–18.

Les fées sont d'exquises danseuses (The Fairies Are Exquisite Dancers). Needs delicate touch and great clarity. Use *una corda* pedal at the beginning.

Bruyères (Heaths) (Ric). This idyllic landscape requires a flexible and smooth legato. Easier than most of the preludes. May be regarded as a companion piece to the well-known "Girl with the Flaxen Hair," No.8 in Book I.

These two pieces are related musically as well as by their similarity of mood.

General Lavine—Eccentric. Portrays the famous American juggler in sharp rhythms and contrasting dynamic extremes. In same vein as *Minstrels.*

La terrasse des audiences du clair de lune (The Terrace for Moonlight Audiences). A phrase from "Au Clair de la Lune" forms the main motive of this imaginative work. Subtle mood changes must be underlined.

Ondine. Expressive, scherzo-like changes of mood characterize the legendary water sprite.

Hommage à S. Pickwick, Esq., P.P.M.P.C. Quotes from "God Save the King" and alludes to Sam Weller's whistling. Depicts the glitter and noise of the English music hall. Comical, jaunty.

Canope. An Egyptian burial urn, mysterious, atmospheric. Slow chords, haunting melody.

Tierces alternées (Alternating Thirds). This brilliant study uses rapid alternation of hands, one more static than the other. Make contrast with dynamics, not tempo. Foreshadows the *Etudes.* Compare this prelude with Bartók's study in Alternating Thirds (*Mikrokosmos V*).

Feux d'artifice (Fireworks) (Ric; EMB). Depicts an exciting illumination over Paris. Notice the "moderately animated" tempo indication. Glittering arpeggios and trills, explosive chords. A reference to "La Marseillaise" brings this festive and dazzling virtuoso finale to a close. Most difficult piece in the two books.

See: Gwilym Beechey, "The Originality of Debussy," MO, 109/1236 (October 1980):10–12. Some notes on selected preludes.

Nadia Boulanger, "Debussy: The Preludes," *Rice Institute Pamphlet*, 13 (April 1926):153–77.

Irwin Freundlich, "Random Thoughts on the Preludes of Claude Debussy," Otto Deri Memorial Issue, *Current Musicology*, 13 (1972).

J. Matthews, "Debussy's Preludes," MO (September 1910):833.

L. M. Peppercorn, "The Piano Style in Debussy's Preludes," MO (August 1937):952.

Peter Hugh Reed, "Debussy's Piano Preludes," *American Music Lover* (August 1938).

La Boite à Joujoux 1913 (Durand; CFP 9247; MMP) 30 min. Danse de la poupée; Polka finale; Ronde. A children's ballet inspired by the dolls of Debussy's daughter, Chouchou. Debussy told his publishers that he intended the work "to be clear and amusing without poses or pointless acrobatics." Charming and delightful. Int. to M-D.

Available separately: all three pieces (Durand); Danse de la poupée (Ric).

See: Robert Orledge, "Another Look Inside Debussy's Toybox," MT, 1606 (December 1976):987–89.

Six Epigraphes Antiques 1914 (Henle 402; MMP; Durand; CFP) 14½ min. Originally for piano, four hands; Debussy made a two-hand version in 1915. Pour Invoquer Pan, dieu du vent d'été (For invoking Pan, God of the summer wind): ABCBA; idyllic; themes capture the spirits of the two personages of the poem languishing in the torpor of a summer day. Pour un tombeau sans nom (For a tomb, without a name): elegy, formalized grief, highly refined, whole-tone, chromatic embroidery, parallel diminished chords. Pour que la nuit soit propice (So that the night may be propitious): a nocturne suspending murmuring voices above the sounds of the night; one musical idea; binary form with statement and development; whole-tone; ostinato unifies the piece. Pour la danseuse aux crotales (For the dancer with rattles): thrusts of groups of notes depict the dancer's rattles; harplike scoring; pentatonic; quiet closing. Pour l'Egyptienne (For the Egyptian): oriental element, improvisation, long drone pedal, exotic figuration, parallel tone clusters, varied levels of timbre sounding simultaneously in various keyboard registers. Pour remercier la pluie au matin (For thanking the morning rain): Impressionistic tone painting; loose formal design; opening figure permeates the texture and generates the drive for the entire piece; numerous thematic materials. M-D.

Berceuse Héroïque (Durand; CFP; B&VP; MMP). Written toward the end of 1914 as a tribute to King Albert of Belgium and his soldiers. Alfred Cortot says: "The accent of Moussorgsky speaks in its tragic simplicity, as the voice of the homely Brabançonne attains sublime powers and re-echoes as the mighty clarion of a struggling people." Int. to M-D.

12 Etudes 1915 (Durand-Costallat; Henle 390; B&VP; CFP; PWN; MMP) 39 min. These last piano works deal with the most varied technical and musical problems. Contrasting moods vary from the most tender to the most ferocious. Grace, beauty of timbre, and digital skills need to be happily balanced. Debussy gives the performer many interpretative directions, verbally as well as graphically. He himself said concerning these pieces: "I must confess that I am glad to have successfully completed a work which, I may say without vanity, will occupy a special place of its own. Apart from the question of technique, these 'Etudes' will be a useful warning to pianists not to take up the musical profession unless they have remarkable hands" (Léon Vallas, *Claude Debussy: His Life and Works*, translated by Maire and Grace O'Brien [London: Oxford University Press, 1933], p.259).

pour les "cinq doigts" d'après Monsieur Czerny (5-Finger Exercise). A take-off on Czerny's style. A five-finger exercise is transformed into a gigue. Differing scales are juxtaposed. Mainly on white keys.

pour les Tierces (Study in Thirds). Problems of double thirds. Complements the prelude *Les tierces alternées*. Frequent modulation, wide dynamic range, basically moderato and lyric.

pour les Quartes (Study in Fourths). Double fourths, sharp mood contrasts. Calls for a flexible legato.

pour les Sixtes (Study in Sixths). Very different from Chopin's treatment of this interval (Op.25/8). Sostenuto pedal necessary for pedal points.

pour les Octaves (Study in Octaves). Brilliant piece. Effective syncopation; chromatic and whole-tone usage.

pour les huit doigts (Study for Eight Fingers). Debussy suggests that this piece be played without thumbs, but careful use of the thumb can facilitate the performance. Rapid scale figuration, flexible meters, subtle phrasing.

pour les Degrés chromatiques (Study in Chromatic Steps). A chromatic perpetual motion with a diatonic melody. Chromatic scales in thirds.
   See: Ian Hobson, "Debussy's 'Chromatic' Etude," *Clavier*, 28/5 (May–June 1988):14–17. Includes information from Jeffrey Swann on this Etude.

pour les Agréments (Study in Ornaments). Like a barcarolle. Many embellishments in the melody. Contains a great variety of note values; their proper relationships must be maintained.

pour les Notes répétées (Study in Repeated Notes). Virtuoso toccata recalls the earlier *Masques*. Restrained use of the pedal is essential for clarity.

pour les Sonorités opposées (Study in Opposed Sonorities). Exploits contrasts of touches, dynamics, accents, etc.

pour les Arpèges composés (For Composite Arpeggios). Delicate arpeggi study based on Lisztian technique. Musical pianism at its best.

pour les Accords (For Chords). A taxing piece that requires a well-developed topographical sense. Vigorous rhythmic activity. Fine conclusion to the set.
   See: Maurice Dumesnil, "Debussy Etudes: Correct Approach as to Pedaling, Phrase and Tonal Colours," *Etude* (October 1947):552.
   John Schneider, "The Debussy Etudes—A Challenge to Mind and Fingers," JALS, 14 (December 1983):59–63.

Etude Retrouvée (Howat—TP). A preparatory draft for one of the *Etudes* of 1915 that was never published. Reconstructed by Roy Howet from the MS, which is included in this edition. Title in the MS is *Pour les arpèges composés*, but except for the presence of arpeggios and the A♭ tonality, the piece bears no resemblance to the previously published etude of the same title. Excellent preface. M-D.
   See: Marina Horak, "Claude Debussy: *Etude Retrouvée*," *Piano Journal*, 6 (1982):48–50.
   Roy Howat, "A Thirteenth Etude of 1915; the Original Version of *Pour les arpèges composés*," *Cahiers Debussy* (nouvelle série) (1977):16–24.

Page d'Album (Album Leaf) (Howat—TP). Also contained in collection *At the Piano with Debussy* (Alfred 2596). A brief and charming waltz written in 1915. Excellent for students not yet ready for the first Arabesque or other favorite "first Debussy pieces." Large span (ninth) required. Int.

Elégie 1915 (Jobert). The last piano solo by Debussy. Doleful and sad throughout all 21 bars; austere writing; modal melody. M-D.

Assez animé et tres rythme 1904. In collection *At the Piano with Debussy* (Alfred 2596). Short, whimsical, and coquettish; strong climax followed by a pixie-ish coda. M-D.

See: John K. Adams, "Debussy: The Late Piano Works," Part II, PQ, 138 (Summer 1987):48–50, 52–53. "Debussy: Sketches, manuscripts and the Preludes and Etudes," Part III, PQ, 139 (Fall 1987):40–43.

COLLECTIONS:

Album de six morceaux choisis (Durand). Arabesque E; En bateau (Petite suite); Menuet; Serenade for the Doll; La Fille aux cheveux de lin; La plus que lente. Int. to M-D.

Modern Piano Music of Debussy and Ravel (CF). D'un Cahier d'Esquisses; Nocturne; Rêverie; Dance; 4 works by Ravel. M-D.

Album (K). Clair de lune; Arabesques E, g; Soirée en Grenade; Jardins sous la pluie; Reflets dans l'eau; Prélude (*Pour le piano*); L'isle joyeuse; Danse. Int. to D.

Album of Claude Debussy Masterpieces (EBM). Clair de lune; Ballade; D'un cahier d'esquisses; Fêtes (*Three Nocturnes*); Marionettes; Mazurka; Nuages (*Three Nocturnes*); Prélude (*Afternoon of a Faun*); Rêverie. M-D.

Il mio primo Debussy (J. Demus—Ric 1975) 32pp. La Fille aux cheveux de lin; 1st Arabesque; The Little Negro; The Little Shepherd; Serenade for the Doll; Page d'album; Clair de lune; Rêverie. Int. to M-D.

Album of Five Pieces (BMC). Mazurka; Ballade; Danse; Rêverie; Valse Romantique. M-D.

Three Albums (Forsyth). I. La Fille aux cheveux de lin; The Little Shepherd; Jimbo's Lullaby. II. Clair de lune; Des pas sur la neige; The Snow Is Dancing. III. Serenade of the Doll; La Puerta del Vino; Sarabande (from *Pour le piano*).

Piano Works (E. Klemm—CFP). Vol.I: 2 Arabesques; Suite Bergamasque; Children's Corner. Preface in German, French, and English, critical note in German. Vol.II: Préludes, Book I. Vol.III: Préludes, Book II. Vol.IV: Images. Vol.V: Etudes. Edited with preface in German, French, and English and critical note in German.

Claude Debussy—An Introduction to the Composer and His Music (Banowetz—GWM). Two Arabesques; Rêverie; Valse Romantique; Mazurka; Suite Bergamasque. Informative preface. Interpretative suggestions. M-D.

Supplementary Volume (H. Swarsenski—CFP 7250). Contains preface, chronological list, glossary of French terms, La Fille aux cheveux de lin, and color reproduction of the composer by Jacques-Emil Blanche.

Piano Music (1888–1905) (Dover). Deux Arabesques; Suite Bergamasque; Rêverie; Danse; Ballade; Pour le Piano; D'un cahier d'esquisses; Estampes; Mazurka; Valse Romantique; Masques; L'Isle joyeuse; Images (first series); Reflets dans l'eau; Hommage à Rameau; Mouvement. Int. to D.

Piano Music (1888–1905) of Claude Debussy (Dover) 182pp. Deux Arabesques; Suite bergamasque; Rêverie; Danse; Ballade; Masques; Images I; Pour le piano; D'un cahier d'esquisses; Estampes; Mazurka; Valse romantique; L'Isle joyeuse. M-D to D.

Selected Works (GS L1813). Arabesques I and II; Rêverie; Mazurka; Danse Tarantelle Styrienne; Sarabande from *Pour le Piano*; Clair de lune; La Soirée dans Grenade; Jardins sous la pluie; Masques; L'isle joyeuse; Reflets dans l'eau; Hommage à Rameau. Int. to D.

Debussy—An Introduction to His Piano Music (Halford—Alfred) 64pp. Includes a fine foreword that discusses, among other subjects, performance, pedaling, Impressionism in music, and information about the pieces. Includes Children's Corner; Clair de lune; Le Petit Nègre; Rêverie; Sarabande (Suite pour le Piano). An excellent collection. Int. to M-D.

The Joy of Claude Debussy (YMP 1983). Contains the complete Children's Corner plus 8 other selections from the various suites and solo compositions. Int. to M-D.

Debussy—Selected Favorites (Olson—Alfred) 111pp. Rêverie; Le Petit Nègre; Deux Arabesques; from *Suite Bergamasque*: Prélude, Clair de lune, Passepied; Children's Corner; from *Pour le piano*: Prélude, Sarabande; Nocturne D♭; Jardins sous la pluie; En bateau. Also includes French glossary and translation. No editorial suggestions. Clean edition. Int. to M-D.

At the Piano with Debussy (Hinson—Alfred). Danse bohémienne; Ballade; Danse; Valse romantique; Mazurka; D'un cahier d'esquisses; Assez animé et très rythmé; Hommage à Haydn; La plus que lent; Minstrels; La fille aux cheveux de lin; Album Leaf. Also includes sections on Debussy and the piano, performance instructions (English translation of French terms), suggestions for teaching and performing the pieces, and notes on individual pieces. Pedal, fingering, and metronome indications by the editor. Int. to M-D.

Debussy: Easiest Piano Pieces (CFP 5097) 23pp. Arabesque I: Clair de lune. Int. to M-D.

Selected Debussy Preludes (Hinson—Alfred 4975) 40pp. Includes Canope; Danseuse de Delphes; Des pas sur la neige; Feuilles mortes; La Cathédrale engloutie; La fille aux cheveux de lin; La Puerta del Vino; Minstrels. These are the easiest Preludes from both books. Editorial pedal marks, fingerings, and metronome marks are suggested; helpful prefatory material. Int. to M-D.

Debussy. Selected Easy Piano Pieces (P. Roggenkamp—UE 18584) 29pp. Includes Jimbo's Lullaby; The Little Shepherd; Rêverie; The Little Negro; Des pas sur la neige; La fille aux cheveux de lin; Minstrels; Clair de lune; Première Arabesque. The title of the collection is a misnomer, as Debussy did not compose any easy pieces for the piano. Int. to-D.

Five Piano Selections with Ragtime Characteristics (Hinson—Alfred 4606) 36pp. Général Lavine—eccentric; Golliwog's Cakewalk; The Toy Box; Le petit Nègre; Minstrels. Includes sections on "Debussy and Ragtime," "Musical Characteristics of Ragtime," and performance suggestions for each piece. Int. to M-D.

Etudes, Children's Corner, Images II, and Other Works for Piano (Dover). Also contains Nocturne; Hommage à Haydn; Le Petit Nègre; La Plus que Lente; Berceuse Héroïque; Elegie; and Six Epigraphes Antiques. Reprint from original editions. Mistakes not corrected. Int. to M-D.

Selected Works (Wilhelm Ohmer—Schott ED 7665 1992) 64pp. Includes the complete *Children's Corner* suite; 3 preludes; Danse bohémienne; Arabesque I; Rêverie; The Little Negro; Danse de la Poupée. Int. to M-D.

Debussy. Selected Works for Piano (Snell—Kjos 1995) 64pp. Le Petit Noir; Two Arabesques; Rêverie; The Girl with the Flaxen Hair; The Sunken Cathedral; Children's Corner; Clair de lune. Glossary of French terms. Int. to M-D.

Claude Debussy Piano Compositions (D.Tucker—WB 1992) 32pp. Clair de lune; En Bateau; Golliwog's Cake Walk; La Plus que Lente; Le Petit Berger; La fille aux cheveux de lin. No distinction between composer's and editor's marks. No sources listed. Int. To M-D.

See: Joseph Banowetz, "Reflections on Playing Debussy," PQ, 119 (Fall 1982):42–46. Discusses the Debussy performances of Viñes, Cortot, E. R. Schmitz, M. Long, and R. Casadesus.

Gwilym Beechey, "A New Edition of Debussy's Piano Works," MO, 101 (October 1977):25–27, 35. A discussion of the C. F. Peters edition edited by H. Swarsenski.

Alfred Cortot, *French Piano Music* (London: Oxford University Press, 1932; reprint, New York: Da Capo Press, 1977).

———, *Studies in Musical Interpretation* (New York: Harrap, 1937).

Frank Dawes, *Debussy Piano Music* (London: BBC Publications, 1969).

Maurice Dumesnil, *How to Play and Teach Debussy* (New York: Schroeder & Gunther, 1932).

———, "Debussy's Principles in Pianoforte Playing," *Etude*, 56 (March 1938):153.

———, "Debussy's Influence on Piano Writing and Playing," MTNA Proceedings, 1945:39–42.

———, "Coaching with Debussy," *The Piano Teacher*, 5/1 (September–October 1962):10–13. Quotes Debussy concerning the piano works.

Dean Elder, "The Enduring Legend of Walter Gieseking," *Clavier*, 34/9 (November 1995): 6–13. The section on "Interpretive Ideas from Gieseking" (pp. 9–13) are especially helpful for Debussy.

Guido Maria Gatti, "The Piano Music of Claude Debussy," MQ, 7 (1921):418–60.

Roy Howat, "Debussy, Ravel and Bartók: Towards Some New Concepts of Form," M&L, 58 (July 1977):185–293. Includes a penetrating analysis of *Reflet dans l'eau*.

Virginia Raad, "Claude Debussy's Use of Piano Sonority," Part I, AMT, 26 (September–October 1976):6–9; Part II, AMT, 26 (January 1977):7–14; Part III, AMT 26 (April–May 1977):9–13.

———, "Musical Quotations in Claude Debussy," AMT, 18 (January 1968):22–23, 34.

Paul Roberts, *Images: The Piano Music of Claude Debussy*. Portland, OR: Amadeus Press, 1996. 370pp. Includes bibliographical references and index.

Charles Rosen, "When Ravel Ends and Debussy Begins," HF, 9/5 (May 1959): 42–44, 117–21.

E. Robert Schmitz, "Piano Music of Debussy and Ravel," MTNA Proceedings, 1949:231–35.

——, *The Piano Works of Claude Debussy* (New York: Duell, Sloan & Pearce, 1950; reprint, New York: Dover, 1966).
Arnold Whittall, "Tonality and the Whole-Tone Scale in the Music of Claude Debussy," MR, 36 (November 1975):261–71.

Abel Decaux (1869–1941) France
Four Clairs de Lune 1901–1907 (L. Philippo) 16 min. Minuit Passée; La Ruelle; Le Cimetière; La Mer. The fourth is the least venturesome but the most pianistic. These are the only pieces Decaux ever wrote. They foreshadow techniques of the 12-tone school. Intensely expressive with an intimacy reminiscent of Satie; grey-hued, misty sonorities; obsessively claustrophobic. M-D.

Helmut Degen (1911–1995) Germany
3 Sonatinen (Süddeutscher Musikverlag 1944). Three-movement works; excellent teaching material. A good introduction to easy contemporary sounds. Contrapuntal; neoclassic. Int.
Kleine Klavierstücke für Kinder (Süddeutscher Musikverlag). Delightful pedagogic material. Int.
Suite (Süddeutscher Musikverlag 1936–38). Hindemith influence. M-D.

Reinbert de Leeuw. See Leeuw, Reinbert de

Ton de Leeuw. See Leeuw, Ton de

Frederick Delius (1862–1934) Great Britain
Delius was often called the "English Debussy" although he wrote very little for the piano.
Three Preludes (OUP 1923) 9pp. Impressionistic, lyrical. Colorful patterns in symmetrical phrasing. Much use of arpeggios. Int. to M-D.
Five Piano Pieces (Bo&H). Mazurka and Waltz for a Little Girl; Waltz; Waltz; Lullaby for a Modern Baby; Toccata. Int. to M-D.
Album of Piano Works (Bo&H 20409) 48pp. Preface in English. Zum Carnival; Dance for Harpsichord; Five Piano Pieces; Air and Dance; Hassan-Serenade; Koanga—La Calinda; A Village Romeo and Juliet: The Walk to the Paradise Garden (arrangement); Imerlin: Prelude (arrangement); Sleigh Ride. Int. to M-D.
See: Maurice Hinson, "Frederick Delius—Individualist and Student of Nature," *Clavier*, 20/7 (September 1981):26–31. Also contains the music of *Zum Carnival* and a lesson on this earliest of Delius's solo piano works.

Azzolino Bernardino Della Ciaja (1671–1755) Italy
As an experimenter in technical features, Della Ciaja was unusual for his time. Large skips, elaborate ornamentation, false relations, and dissonantal treatment characterize his works.

Six Sonatas Op.4 (1727). Three are available (Buonamici—Bratti 1912). Each sonata includes a toccata, a canzone, and two short loosely connected sections called "tempi." Unusual style in the toccatas. M-D.
Available separately: Sonata G (Buonamici—Edizioni R. Maurri of Florence).

Justin Dello Joio (1955–   ) USA
Dello Joio received his doctorate from The Juilliard School and teaches at New
York University.
Sonata (TP). Theme and Variations; Romance; Finale Fantasie. Neo-romantic
style. According to critic Paul Hume, "The new music is conservative in
style but wholly original in sound, solidly set in ways that make the finest
piano music. . . ." M-D to D.
Two Concert Etudes 1998 (TP 1999) commissioned by the New York Music Teachers Association. 1. Momentum, 4′ 27″. Repeated notes with trills, contrasting alternating sections, chromatic and atonal sections with tonal chordal
pauses, dynamic range = ppp to sffz, dramatic and effective, toccata-like
passages. D. 2. Et Farvel . . . (A farewell) in memory of my dear friend Poul
Bundgaard, 5′ 49″. Slow, sonorous, lower register exploited with quick moving grace notes as quiet as possible, moving melody, forte climax, subtleties
throughout, atonal with tonal ending. D.

Norman Dello Joio (1913–   ) USA
Dello Joio's style emphasizes strong melodies, vigorous rhythmic practice, and
great communication. None of the piano works are overly demanding yet some
of the movements call for a much-above-average technique and fine musical
equipment.
Prelude: To a Young Musician (GS 1944). Sensitive melodic line over flexible ac-
companiment. M-D.
Prelude: To a Young Dancer (GS 1945). Works to large climax then ends *pp*. M-D.
Suite (GS 1940) 11pp. Four movements. Int. except for a more difficult last move-
ment.
Nocturne E (CF 1946). Four-part writing, contrasting mid-section with melodic
emphasis. M-D.
Nocturne f♯ (CF 1946). Calm opening, more exuberant mid-section. Large span
required. M-D.
On Stage (GS 1946). Suite arranged by composer from ballet of same name.
Much rhythmic emphasis. M-D.
Sonata No.1 (Hargail 1943). Chorale Prelude; Canon; Capriccio. Final movement
(with double notes and fast octaves) presents most problems. M-D.
Sonata No.2 (GS 1943). Presto martellato; Adagio; Vivace spiritoso. Each movement has a big climax and requires fast octaves and chords. More difficult
than No.1. M-D.
Sonata No.3 (CF 1948). Five variations and coda on a Gregorian chant. Presto e
leggiero; short scherzo with jazz influence. Adagio: extends the mood of

the opening theme in melodic fashion. Allegro vivo e ritmico: compelling rhythms; melodic invention. M-D.

Capriccio (EBM 1969). "On the interval of a second." 12pp. Written for the Third Van Cliburn International Piano Competition, 1969. A virtuoso show-piece that exploits the interval of a second both harmonically and melodically. D.

Suite for the Young (EBM). 10 pedagogic pieces. Int.

Lyric Pieces for the Young (EBM 1971). 6 pieces. Int.

Diversions (EBM 1975) 16pp. 9 min. Five pieces in a gentle modern idiom, effective as a group or as individual pieces. Preludio: solemn. Arietta: rich melody. Caccia: bright horn sounds. Chorale: based on "Good Christian Men Rejoice." Giga: brilliant closing. Int.

Salute to Scarlatti (AMP 1981). 11 pp., 9 min. A suite of sonatas in the spirit of Scarlatti's keyboard sonatas. Four short, one-movement works: a ceremonial allegretto; an andante pastorale song; a grazioso intermezzo-like contrapuntal piece; a bravura perpetual-motion finale. Tonal, pianistic, cross-handed acrobatics. Good hand span required. M-D.

Concert Variants (AMP 7856-2 1983) 20pp. Theme and 5 variations (variants). Andante amabile theme flows gently amid enough accidentals to add color. Variant I: Andantino; warm expressive lines move over entire keyboard; *pp* closing. Variant II: Andante moderato, deciso; cantando melodic thirds and sixths build to "con più intensita" climax, *ff* closing. Variant III: Allegro, molto animato, sempre spumante; staccato octave melody over nonlegato figuration; more chordal mid-section (Meno mosso); feroce; chordal tremolos, *ffff* closing. Variant IV: Lento funebre; funeral march, *pp* closing. Variant V: Allegro, molto animato; driving rhythms in toccata style. Freely tonal, basically conservative idiom, lyrical emphasis, effective pianistic writing. M-D.

Short Intervallic Etudes for Well Tempered Pianists (AMP 7987 1988) 14pp. Features 4ths and 5ths; Features 2nds; Features 6ths; Features 7ths; Features octaves and unisons. Attractive, MC. M-D.

See: Edward Downes, "The Music of Norman Dello Joio," MQ, 48 (April 1962): 149–72.

Maurice Hinson, "The Solo Piano Music of Norman Dello Joio," AMT, 19 (January 1970):34, 48.

David Del Tredici (1937–   ) USA

Del Tredici has been called the reviver of tonality in American music.

Fantasy Pieces (Bo&H 1959–60) 18pp. 6 min. Adagio, Espressivo; Poco allegretto; Allegro minacciando; Largo, senza tempo. Complex; dramatic appeal; well organized; emphasis on augmented and diminished octaves; widely spaced textures; fragments grow into broader lines. Sensitive pedaling required throughout. M-D.

See: Richard Zimdars, "Fantasy Pieces by David Del Tredici," *Clavier*, 23/9 (November 1984):33–35.

Soliloquy 1958 (Bo&H 1975) 10pp. 7 min. A major contribution. Great cohesion achieved through close motivic control. Debussy-like sonorities, freely chromatic and dissonant, pointillistic. Simultaneous lines require great tonal control. Large span required. D.

Virtuoso Alice 1988 (Bo&H). This extended work is a set of variations on the folklike tune used in the composer's orchestral work *Final Alice*. Demanding, bravura writing. M-D to D.

Claude Delvincourt (1888–1954) France

Boccacerie (Leduc 1926) 37pp. Five pieces. Each piece is dedicated to a different pianist. No.5 (Buffalmacco), one of the most accessible, is dedicated to Beveridge Webster. Varying moods, long, neoclassic, full of rhythmic accentuations. M-D.

Croquembouches (Leduc 1931) 33pp. 12 pieces, published separately. Traditional and MC harmonic language. M-D.

Cinq Pièces pour le Piano (Leduc 1926) 25pp. Prélude; Danse pour rire; Tempo di Minuetto; Berceuse; Danse hollandaise. Mildly impressionistic. Contains some glittering pianistic writing. M-D.

Edisson Denisov (1929–1996) Russia

Denisov was professor of composition and orchestration at the Moscow Conservatory.

Variations on a Theme of Handel (GS Rental Library c. 1990) 59 leaves of music. Based on a theme from Handel's Suite in g, HWV 432. M-D to D.

Reflets 1995 (Leduc) 17 min. Clear linear textures. Cross-rhythms (3 vs. 10, 5 vs. 7, etc.) produce clever polyrhythmic situations. Gentle poetic rubato usage. Sensitivity to line and color are prerequisites. D.

Pour Daniel 1989 (Leduc 1995) 3 min. Dedicated to Daniel Barenboim. Thin textures, colorful sonorities, quiet emotional intensity. Makes a good preparation piece for *Reflets*. M-D.

Trois Preludes (Leduc). The first piece is an agitated *pianissimo* of contrary motion between the hands. It is balanced by the third piece, also a fluid *pianissimo*. M-D to D.

Luis de Pablo. See Pablo, Luis de

Yvonne Desportes (1907–1993) France

Hommage à Maurice Emmanuel 1972 (Billaudot 3498 1984) 33pp. 34 min. "One long fresco illustrating the evolution of music from ancient Greece to Pop Music" (from the Preface). 28 style sections are labeled in the score. M-D to D.

Felix Despréaux (1746–1813) France

Romance avec variations (on Ah! Vous dirai-je maman) (Paul van Reijen—Schott ED. 7806 1991) 31pp. Published with C. H. Müller (fl. ca. 1800).

Seize nouvelles variations sur L'air Ah! vous dirai-je maman. Journal für das Pianoforte Heft 12. The Despréaux set (9 variations) contains some character variations: Var. 5, movement de Menuet; Var. 6, Très gay (Siciliano rhythm). Lively and varied writing style, attractive. Int. to M-D.

Paul Dessau (1894–1979) Germany

Fantasietta in Cis (Bo&Bo 1972) 7pp. Varied meters and tempi, broad gestures, expressionistic, complex notation. Extreme ranges exploited; a few fists are used; some improvisation required. D.

Sonatina II (Bo&Bo 1977) 7pp. Three short movements in a flexible and eclectic style. M-D.

Guernica: Klavierstück nach Pablo Picasso 1938 (Br&H) 3pp. Tone clusters. Written in the same year as Picasso's politically inspired painting *Guernica.* M-D.

Robert Nathaniel Dett (1882–1943) USA

Dett's music ranges from short melodic pieces to extended virtuoso works. Although his work became more complex as Dett became more involved in the craft of composition, he never broke from his strong roots in the lyricism of the Negro spiritual.

The Collected Piano Works (SB 1973) 208pp. Informative foreword includes a short biography and a brief analysis of the music. The music is a reprint of the original plates. This collection is not complete but contains a sizable portion of Dett's piano works. Six suites containing 32 pieces. *Magnolia:* Magnolias; Deserted Cabin; My Lady Love; Mammy; The Place Where the Rainbow Ends. *In the Bottoms:* Prelude; His Song; Honey; Barcarolle; Dance (Juba). *Enchantment:* Incantation; Song of the Shrine; Dance of Desire; Beyond the Dream. *Cinnamon Grove:* Moderato molto grazioso; Adagio cantabile; Ritmo moderato e con sentimento—Quasi Gavotte. *Tropic Winter:* The Daybreak Charioteer; A Bayou Garden; Pompons and Fans; Legend of the Atoll; To a Closed Casement; Noon Siesta; Parade of the Jasmine Banners. *Eight Bible Vignettes:* Father Abraham; Desert Interlude; As His Own Soul; Barcarolle of Tears; I Am the True Vine; Martha Complained; Other Sheep; Madrigal Divine. Int. to M-D.

Eight Bible Vignettes (Belwin-Mills). Descriptive, Romantic style, program notes. M-D.

In the Bottoms (SB). Suite containing the popular *Juba Dance.* Int.

See: Anne Kay Simpson, *Follow Me: The Life and Music of R. Nathaniel Dett* (Metuchen, NJ: Scarecrow Press, 1993). Contains brief musical analyses of Dett's piano works.

Albert De Vito (1919–   ) USA

In a Canon Style (Kenyon). Careful, musical handling of Baroque technique. Attractive writing that fits the hand beautifully. Int.

Sonata I (Kenyon) 16pp. Allegro con brio; Lent amente; Animando. Late-Romantic style, broken chords, scales, hand-crossings, double-note figures. Int. to M-D.

Godefroid Devreese (1893–1972) Belgium

Sixième Sonatine 1945 (CeBeDeM 1972) 20pp. 11 min. Allegro vivo (Hommage à Claude Debussy): similar techniques used by Debussy in the first movement of his *Pour le piano*. Andante (Hommage à Johannes Brahms): theme, 4 variations, return of theme. Allegro (Hommage à Paul Gilson): somewhat in the style of Poulenc. M-D.

Anton Diabelli (1781–1858) Austria

Diabelli's style includes all the techniques of the Classic period: triadic harmony, tuneful melodies, and catchy rhythms. All the keyboard works display his pianistic expertise.

Selected Piano Pieces (Hinson—Alfred 10143) 32pp. Includes: 10 short pieces; Sonatina G, Op.168/2; Valse C; Rondeau Militaire (duet). Charming pedagogic works. Easy to Int.

11 Sonatinas (CFP; Ric; Heugel; GS; Alfred). Op.151 G, C, F, C; Op.168 F, G, C, B♭, D, G, a. Excellent material for intermediate level.

Variations on a theme of Diabelli (W. Newman—Music Treasure). 16 variations by as many composers, all contemporaries of Diabelli, including Schubert and Liszt. 50 were originally asked for and were supplied. All 50(!) were originally published in 1824 (Adeva Musik).

See: Douglas Riva, "The Forgotten Files of Anton Diabelli," KC, (May 1994): 4–6.

David Diamond (1915–   ) USA

A Romantic element, vitality, and a personal lyric quality are present in Diamond's writing.

Sonatina (Mer 1947). Short movements. Largo assai; Allegretto; Allegro vivace. M-D.

8 Piano Pieces (GS). Illustrates familiar nursery rhymes. Easy.

The Tomb of Melville 1949–50 (MCA 1950). Extended development, intense, slow, expressive, sonorous. M-D. Written as a tribute to Herman Melville, author of *Moby Dick*.

Sonata (PIC 1947) 66pp. 30 min. 3 movements. Constant modulation and meter changes. Near end of first movement a fugue appears, then a vigorous coda. The last movement is interrupted by a double fugue and proceeds to an exciting coda. Advanced pianism required. D.

Then and Now (PIC 1962). 11 sophisticated pieces for the young pianist, preferably one who has had some experience with contemporary sounds. Int.

A Private World (PIC). 13 pieces for young pianists. Int.

Alone at the Piano (PIC). Book 1: 11 pieces. Book 2: 10 pieces. Book 3: 13 pieces. All three books are subtitled "Pieces for Beginners," but the material ranges from elementary to Int. and all are very contemporary sounding.

Gambit (PIC 1967). Dedicated to Rudolf Serkin. Changing meters and tempi, broad climax in low register, quiet atmospheric ending. M-D.

Album for the Young (EV 1946). 10 short excellent pedagogic pieces. Easy to Int.

A Myriologue 1935, rev. 1969 (PIC) 5pp. A short, slow, funereal dance, rhythmic patterns, composed for Martha Graham. M-D.

Prelude and Fugue (Hinson—Alfred 10114) in collection *Twelve by Eleven*. Clearly structured, tightly knit, neoclassic. The cantando lyric lines of the Prelude go their graceful individual way and finally arrive at a colorful cadence. The three-voiced Fugue is basically tonal but uses chromaticism freely and builds to a strong emotional climax. A rhythmic subject with strong off-beat accents adds excitement to a forceful work that is constantly idiomatic for the piano. Int. to M-D.

Hilda Dianda (1925–   ) Argentina

Tres Sonatas (Ric 1956). Armonica 2pp. Melodica 2pp. Ritmica 4pp. Each is short, in the same vein as the Scarlatti Sonatas. Large span required; big octave technique necessary; some rhythmic problems.

Josef Dichler (1912–   ) Austria

Intermezzo and Capriccio (Dob 01597 1980) for left hand alone, 16pp. Written on 3 staffs. Beautiful Lento section in Capriccio leads back to the lively Allegro; bravura conclusion. Large span required for octaves and full chords. D.

Peter Dickinson (1934–   ) Great Britain

Dickinson's style shows the influence of Schönberg and Ives as well as an interest in indeterminacy.

Paraphrase II (Nov 1967) 14 min. Based on Dickinson's motet, *Mark*; transforms and extends ideas from the motet. Seven varied sections. Repeated notes, octaves, skips, harmonic pedals and canonic figures, bitonal, straight and retrograded phrases. Large span required. D.

See: Roger Norrington, "Peter Dickinson," MT, 106 (1965):109–10.

Edward Diemente (1923–   ) USA

Clavier Sonata (Greenwood Press 1966) 14pp. Attractive, short, three-movement work employing imitation and clear tonal centers. Neoclassic style. M-D.

Sarcasms (AMC 1947). Short, bright, percussive, somewhat in style of Prokofiev. M-D.

Regina Coeli 1956 (TP). Short, built on a chorale and a Gregorian chant. Int.

Emma Lou Diemer (1927–   ) USA

Diemer is professor of theory and composition at the University of California, Santa Barbara.

Time Pictures (Bo&H 1962) 4 min. Gavotte; Gigue; Invention; Serenade. Each emphasizes special technical problems: 5-note scale figures in both hands, 2-note slow trills, 4-note chords in each hand, staccato in one hand, legato in other, etc. Attractive. Int.

Seven Etudes (CF 1966) 16 min. Facsimile edition. Energetic; Slow; Fast; Slow (much use of tremolo); Fast "Hommage à Schönberg" (serial, disjunct); Very Slow "Hommage à Rachmaninoff"; Spirited. Well conceived for the instrument. Makes a most convincing set. M-D.

Sound Pictures (Bo&H 1971) 11pp. Clusters and dots; Circles; Contraction and Expansion; Double Dots; Incline and Plateau; Parallels; Strata; Angles; Particles; Infinity. Accepted twentieth-century techniques cleverly employed. Precocious teenager would enjoy these. Int.

Four on a Row (Scribner's). In Vol.4 of the *New Scribner Music Library*. Serial. Int. to M-D.

Toccata 1979 (Arsis Press) 15pp. 6 min. Percussive and strong rhythms but not noisy. Reiterated figurations, gently motoric, jagged themes, carefully pedaled. Hands and arms placed on strings. M-D to D.

Encore 1981 (Sisra) 6 min. This is a "finale," a virtuoso piece in which the pianist is not permitted to relax for one moment in the declamatory, rhythmic, and insistent statement of material. The principal motives, heard at the beginning, are a disjunct, accented idea followed by a rapid, constant 16th-note repetitive pattern in which the hands do not synchronize. Later, a monodic rhythmic section (the left hand dampening the strings while the right hand plays) supplies textural contrast and serves as the "B" part of the large ABA1B1A2 form. D.

Space Suite (Plymouth 1989). Billions of Stars: twelve-tone, five eighths in the time of four, quiet playing, pedal. Out in Space: strings plucked and strummed, no bar lines. The Rings of Saturn: alternating hands, arpeggiated seventh chords. Space People Dancing: glissando on string, fingernails tap strings, rhythmic study. Space Monkey: modal, steady eighth notes grouped in threes and fours. Dance in the Light Year: modal, hemiola, legato double notes. The Surface of the Moon: glissando on strings, patting strings, quiet. Frequency Bands: measured tremolo, clusters in fourths, forearm rotation. Radio Waves: quiet, rotation, measured trills and tremolo. Walkie-Talkie: chromatic melody, no meter, fast staccato contrasted with slow legato. Data Bass (and Treble): jazzy, no meter, strings dampened, fast tapping, touch contrast. Toward Mars: ostinato, parallel clusters and triads, legato and staccato chords. Excellent set for introducing contemporary techniques. Int.

Fantasy (Plymouth). One movement with several constrasting sections in mood and tempo. To be performed with much dramatic contrast and freedom. M-D to D.

John Diercks (1927–   ) USA

Diercks was head of the music department at Hollins College, Virginia, for many years. He now lives in Honolulu. Diercks is an outstanding pianist.

Theme and Variations 1948 (CSMP) 18pp. Theme and 7 variations. Each variation well developed. Exploits coloristic and textural capabilities of the instrument. Each variation a kind of character piece, yet relates closely to the theme in melodic outline, choice of harmony, and/or musical design. Final variation is free (in rondo form), conforming to classic practice. M-D.

Twelve Sonatinas Series I 1978 (CSMP) published separately. Fast; Precipitate; Flowing; Moderately slow with much rubato; Moderate, simply; Scurrying, with rubato; Moderate; Slow—Fast; As fast as possible; Slow; Fast, march-like; Fast. A set of outstanding sonatinas conceived as a group, but any number may be extracted and played in any order. My favorite is No.4, and I also like a grouping of Nos.2, 10, and 1. All are well crafted, using contemporary idioms in an imaginative and appealing manner. Diercks's knowledge of the piano and piano technique gives this music a special authority and winsomeness. Int. to M-D.

Six Waltzes (CSMP 1994) 14pp. "As in a Dream" and "Bittersweet" appeared in *Clavier* 34/3 (March 1995):24–27. The others are Caprice; A Tender Movement; A Cello Waltz (requires some sophistication); Arabesque. Attractive, appealing melodies. MC. Int.

Six Imperatives (CSMP). Delightful, five-finger position, imitative, clever descriptive words in score, à la Satie. Easy.

Bernhard van Dieren (1884–1936) Great Britain, born The Netherlands
Tema con Variazione (OUP 1928) 12pp. Chromatic theme, 14 variations. Lines are polyphonically textured with the harmonies created by the part writing. Harmonics, wide dynamic range, tumultuous closing. Widely arpeggiated chords require a large span. D.

Charles Dieupart (c.1670–1740) France
Six Suites pour Clavecin (P. Brunold—l'OL). A, D, b, e, F, f. All suites contain an A, C, S, and G with optional dances M, Gavotte, Passepied. Each suite contains 7 movements. A corrected issue of this edition with Thurston Dart as editor came out in 1969 (l'OL). M-D.
The Art of the Suite (Y. Pessl—EBM) contains Suite f (copied by J. S. Bach in his own hand): Ouverture. A, C, S, Gavotte, M, and G. M-D.

Jan van Dijk (1918–   ) The Netherlands
Sonatine No.3 1949 (Br&VP 1950) Tenth piece in the set *Hommage à Willem Pijper.* MC. Int. to M-D.

Girolamo Diruta (ca. 1550–after 1610) Italy
Il Transilvano: I, 1593; II, 1609 (EMB 1981) Foreword in English, German, and Hungarian, 17pp. Score, 98pp. Commentary, pp.99–114. The famous treatise on keyboard playing containing toccatas and ricercari by Diruta, Banchieri, Quagliati, Bell'haver, Fattorini, Mortaro, Romanini, and others. Int. to M-D.

Hugo Distler (1908–1942) Germany
Distler was one of Germany's most important twentieth-century composers of church music.
Elf kleine Klavierstücke für die Jugend Op.15B (Br). Eleven short pieces in neo-

Baroque style. Not easy. Very detailed pedaling, fingering, metronome, and other performance directions. Int. to M-D.

Karl Ditters von Dittersdorf (1739–1799) Austria
Dittersdorf composed 72 piano preludes, 14 sonatas for four hands, 2 solo sonatas, and other short pieces.
20 Englische Tänze (Herrmann—Schott). Charming if predictable. Int.
Sonata No.2 A (Newman—UNC) in *13 Keyboard Sonatas of the 18th and 19th Centuries*. Allegro; Minuetto; Allegro. Contrasting themes, fluent and pianistic, some unusual modulations. M-D.

William Dobbins (–   ) USA
Evolutionary Etude (Ludwig). A concert piece that seeks to trace the evolution of jazz and classical piano styles. M-D.

Andrzej Dobrowolski (1921–   ) Poland
Dobrowolski teaches at the State College of Music in Warsaw.
Music for Magnetic Tape and Piano Solo (PWM 1971) 22pp. 11 min. Explanations in German and English. Space is crucial to this work, for the recording of the tape in stereo allows for transference of sound from one side to another. Chance plays its part in the improvised chords and runs at certain points in the work, for which the composer has given directions. M-D.

Charles Dodge (1942–   ) USA
Sonata for Piano (ACA 1962). 4 movements. Thorny serial work. Pointillistic writing. D.

Stephen Dodgson (1924–   ) Great Britain
Suite I C for clavichord (Chappell 1974) 16pp. Little Fanfare; First Air; Plaint; Pantomime; Greater Fanfare; Second Air; Tambourin; Last Fanfare. Freely tonal, neoclassic short movements. M-D.
Suite II E♭ for clavichord (Chappell 1974) 15pp. Overture; First Fanfare; A Dream; Second Fanfare; A Fancy; Round Dance. M-D.

Friedhelm Doehl (1936–   ) Germany
Sieben Haiku 1979 (Moeck 5227) 7 sheet-like cards, 14 min. Performance instructions in German. Cards are divided into squares; each square is labeled with an approximate number of seconds required for performance. Clusters, strumming of strings, avant-garde. D.

Martin Doernberg (1920–   ) Germany
Klaviersonate (Vieweg 1973) 12pp. 4 movements. 12-tone; row contains many whole tones, which produce fairly tame sonorities. Opening of the third movement is the most imaginative section (somewhat atmospheric) of the entire sonata. M-D.

Théodor Döhler (1814–1856) Italy
See below, "Collections," *Piano Music of the Parisian Virtuosos 1810–1860.*

Ernst von Dohnányi (1877–1960) Hungary
Dohnányi was first known as an international virtuoso of the highest order. Most of his good-natured and well-constructed music is in the Brahms tradition, pianistic and effective but not always very original.

4 Clavierstücke Op.2 1897 (Dob; Weinberger; MMP; K). Scherzo c#; Intermezzo a; Intermezzo f; Capriccio b. Full, rich sonorities, cross-rhythms, thick bass textures, parallel thirds and sixths. M-D.

Variations and Fugue on a Theme of E. G. Op.4 1897 (K 9554; UE). Theme for this work was composed by Emma Gruber. A set of 13 variations, classical formal structure, followed by a lively, four-voice fugue. M-D.

Gavotte and Musette 1898 (Dob). Written for a Hapsburg Archduchess who wished for something easy to play. This charming set was not easy enough for her. M-D.

Passacaglia Op.6 1898 (Dob; Weinberger). 36 variations on a ground bass organized as a rondo (ABACABA Coda). Full chordal structures, pedal points, complex contrapuntal fabrics, double octaves, chromatic double-note passages. D.

Albumleaf 1899 (EMB 1977) 3pp. First edition. Colorful short character piece. Int.

4 Rhapsodies Op.11 1902 (Dob; K; EBM; UE; Weinberger; Willis, Nos.2, 3). Related like the movements of a sonata in cyclic form, so all four can be performed together. No.1 g: free SA form, colorful, one of Dohnányi's favorites. No.2 f#: serves as the slow movement of the set. No.3 C: scherzo character. No.4 eb: begins and ends with variations on the *Dies Irae* theme. Liszt inspiration. M-D.

Winterreigen Op.13 1905 (EBM; GS; Weinberger; MMP; Dob). Widmung (EBM): uses the opening motive of Schumann's *Papillons* Op.2 as a bass ostinato figure. Marsh der lüstigen Brüder. An Ada: uses the notes A D A throughout, like an ostinato. Freund Victors Mazurka. Sphärenmusik (Music of the Spheres): ethereal tone poem composed after a balloon ride into space. Valse aimable. Um Mitternacht. Tolle Gesellschaft. Postludium (EBM): charged with lyrical feeling, perhaps inspired by the opening of Schumann's *Fantasy* Op.15. This set of 10 Bagatelles (as they are subtitled) is full of spontaneous keyboard improvisation. M-D.

Humoresken (in the form of a suite) Op.17 1907 (UE; Simrock; MMP; Lengnick). March: ABA form built over a four-note ground bass. Toccata: calls for a subcontra G, which is available only on the largest Bösendorfer piano. Pavane and Variations: on a 16th-century lute theme. Pastorale: strict two-voice canon opening; mid-section has the canon inverted; a third voice is added in the recapitulation. Introduction and Fugue: introduction contains the quadruple augmentation of the fugue subject; chromatic four-voice fugue.

Three Piano Pieces Op.23 1916 (Simrock). Aria: lyric melody over triplet accompaniment. Valse Impromptu. Capriccio: effective virtuoso piece. M-D.

Suite in the Olden Style Op.24 1916 (Lengnick). Prelude; Allemande; Courante; Sarabande; Menuet; Gigue. Careful part-writing. Displays high spirits with bright clear sounds. M-D.

Six Concert Etudes Op.28 1916 (EMB) 2 vols; (Bo&H; MMP) 1 vol. No.6 (EBM; BMC). a, D♭, e♭, b♭, E, f. Descendents of the Chopin Etudes and the Liszt Transcendental Etudes. Various technical problems are exploited in each etude. No.6, Capriccio, is the most popular of the set. M-D to D.

Variations on a Hungarian Folk Song Op.29 1916 (EMB). 10 variations in classical form. M-D.

Ruralia Hungarica Op.32a 1923–24 (EMB). 7 pieces based on various types of Hungarian folk music. Nos.1 and 5 are reproduced and discussed in *Clavier*, 16 (February 1977):37–40. M-D.

Valse Boiteuse Op.39b (Lengnick). Charming. M-D.

Six Piano Pieces Op.41 1945 (Lengnick 1947). Impromptu: reproduced and discussed in Clavier, 16 (February 1977):25–28. Scherzino: a little staccato toccata. Canzonetta: a miniature Hungarian Rhapsody. Cascades: rippling legato arpeggios. Ländler: a dressed-up version of a peasant dance. Cloches: depicts bells ringing in the New Year, variation form. M-D.

Three Singular Pieces Op.44 1951 (AMP). Burletta: scherzo-like, more contemporary sounding than most of Dohnányi's works. Nocturne—Cats on the Roof: realistic imitation of cats meowing. Perpetuum Mobile: a percussive toccata.

Twelve Short Studies for the Advanced Pianist 1951 (AMP). Intended to fill the gap between Clementi's *Gradus ad Parnassum* and the Chopin *Etudes*. Each study is devoted to a different pianistic problem. M-D.

Three Concert Transcriptions on themes of Schubert, J. Strauss and Delibes (Rosavölgyi). Concert versions that were typical though outstanding products of the period—when love of the piano and its sound was an aesthetic tradition *per se*. M-D to D.

Available separately: Naila Waltz by Delibes (Allans).

COLLECTIONS:

Selected Piano Compositions (Kultura). Six Concert Etudes Op.28; Variations on a Hungarian Folk Song Op.29; Ruralia Hungarica; Pastorale on a Hungarian Christmas Song. M-D to D.

Album of Dohnányi Masterpieces (EBM). A Dedication Op.13/1; A Joyous Party Op.13/8; Capriccio b Op.2/4; Intermezzo a Op.2/2; Postludium Op.13/10; Rhapsodies Op.11/2, 3, 4; Scherzo c♯ Op.2/1. M-D.

Dohnanyi Album I (EMB Z7464). 6 Concert Etudes Op.28; Variations on a Hungarian Folksong Op.29. M-D.

Dohnanyi Album II (EMB Z7465). Pastorale (Hungarian Cradle Song); Ruralia Hungarica Op.32a. M-D to D.

See: George Mintz, "Dohnányi's Piano Works," *Clavier*, 16 (February 1977). A survey of all Dohnányi's piano works that have been published. Indicates which ones are still in print.

Samuel Dolin (1917–   ) Canada
Little Toccata (BMI Canada). Fast staccato repeated notes. Int.
Sonatina (BMI Canada 1960). Resembles easier Prokofieff with some legato melodic writing. Int.

Misael Domingues (1857–1932) Brazil
Domingues was one of Brazil's best-known Romantic composers.
Misael Domigues' Piano Works, Vol. I (BME 1995). A Beira-Mar (By the Seaside); Alaide-Polka; Aline-gavotte; Relento (In the Open); Em Pleno Luar (Under the Full Moon); Gentil (Graciously); Impetuoso (Passionately); Lágrimas de um Anjo (Angel's Tears); Mimo do Céu (Heavenly Dainty); Vacilante (Hesitantly)—gavotte. Broad gestures, rich harmonies, folk and popular influence. M-D.

José Antonio Donastía (1886–1956) Spain
Donastía was a noted Basque musicologist and composer. He studied fugue and instrumentation in Paris, where he resided from 1920 to 1923.
Preludios Vascos (Basque Preludes) 1912–23 (Casa Erviti). 21 pieces in four books with titles such as Improvisation, Diálogo, Canción triste, Dolor. Romantic salon style, colorful. Some large, full chords with added seconds and sixths. Int. to M-D.

Franco Donatoni (1927–   ) Italy
Donatoni has experimented in combining serial and aleatory techniques.
Composizione (Schott 1955) 4 movements. The row is used both harmonically and melodically. Pointillistic writing. Strict control combined with great variety of freedom. M-D to D.
Doubles: Essercizi per Clavicembalo (SZ 1961). Special notation system used. 3-note sections of the row keep recurring. Complex. D.
Babi per Clavicembalo (SZ 1964). Graphic notation. A revision of *Doubles*. Wooden prongs attached to the piano necessary for performance. M-D to D.

Gaetano Donizetti (1797–1848) Italy
Donizetti left 26 pieces for piano, two hands, classical in language but not particularly inventive or distinctive.
Klavierwerke I(Irene Patay—Eulenburg 1974) 39pp. Guido Zavadini has catalogued Donizetti's works. Contains: Vivace G, Z.295; Larghetto, Tema con variazioni, Z.300; Drei Walzer, Z.200 and 311; Allegro vivace C, Z.294. These pieces were probably written between 1813 and 1821. They provide a broad sample of Donizetti's keyboard style, which is a combination of classic figuration with Romantic harmonies. Haydn seems to be the model for most of this music. The Larghetto, Tema con variazioni is the finest piece and displays real mastery of keyboard technique. Melodic ornamentation is Mozartian. Mistakes noted in this edition are omitted ledger lines, incorrect notes (they are easy to spot as they create a dissonance com-

pletely foreign to this style), Waltz III should return to bar 19, not to the Introduction. Int. to M-D.

Allegro f (Raymond Meylan—CFP 1971). Short preface by editor. Fingered, Romantic figuration, miniature operatic overture with superficial brilliance. Recently discovered. M-D.

La Guiseppina (Girard). A polka-mazurka. Int. to M-D.

Tre Valzer Z.299 and 311 (Ric 1971) 15pp. Two waltzes and Invito. Int. to M-D.

Capriccio in Sinfonia 1817 (Boccaccini & Spada 1982) 8pp. Influenced by Rossini, whose crescendo formulas are easily recognizable. Dark tragic opening, naive and interesting second theme. Tremolos; unpianistic in places. M-D.

Larghetto a (Una furtiva lagrima) (Boccaccini & Spada 1982) 3pp. Complete piano version of the famous aria sung by Nemorino in the opera *The Elixir of Love*. It was rapidly sketched as a short nocturne for piano. Int.

Giuseppini Polka-Mazurka (Boccaccini & Spada 1994) 3pp. Barcarolle introduction leads to the Polka Mazurka; captivating. M-D.

Grande Offertorio (Boccaccini & Spada 1994) 12pp. Solemn Adagio leads to a theatrical Allegro. M-D.

Allegro in C (Spada—Boccaccini & Spada 1983) 12pp. Barcarolle-like, vague modulations, expressive. M-D.

Richard Donovan (1891–1970) USA

Suite for Piano (NME 1932). Prelude; Hornpipe; Air; Jig. Effective writing. Phrasing in Hornpipe is more difficult than it looks. M-D.

Suite No.2 (ACA 1953) 11½ min. Invention; Intermezzo; Elegy; Toccata. In neoclassic style. Most problems are found in the tender Elegy and jazz-colored Toccata. M-D

Josef Friedrich Doppelbauer (1918–1986) Austria

10 Kleine Klavierstücke (Dob 1956) 16pp. Uses such compositional devices as quartal harmony, repeated notes, staccato study. Neoclassic orientation. Int. to M-D.

William Doppmann (1934–   ) USA

Doppmann is known as an outstanding pianist, but recently his interest in composition has grown.

Four Short Pieces 1988 (Divers 1996) 10pp. 6 min. A Charmed Entrance: changing meters, thin textures. Lost in a Maze: dreamlike, steady connected eighths, gently nuanced, no bar lines. Pique!: right hand written for black keys, left hand for white keys, whimsical, some violent clusters. For a Rainy Afternoon: languid, pensive, brief melodic fragments accompanied by *p* arpeggiated chords. Int. to M-D.

Fantasy I "Winter Dreams". In memorium Vladimir Horowitz 1991–1995 (Divers 1996) 15pp. 13 min. "The Polonaise-Fantasy, Op.61 of Chopin is, in a general way, the parent work for this first Fantasy. This accounts for the startling eruption of a grandiose 'Polacca' at bar 77, leading the work into other brief dance atmospheres—the Andalusian 'polo,' jazz 'polka,' a melancholy waltz, a fast ('hyper') waltz, a march and a 'dance of fury' in the high treble (the opening and closing sections also are highly elaborated evocations of the Saraband). Though poor in 'tunes,' the work in large measure is lyric and melodic. Voice leading is important to follow and delineate even in disjunct textures, as with Chopin. Bravura sections need all the virtuosity one can bring to them" (from the score). Expressisonistic, chords depressed silently (overtones), glissandi, "ice chimes", brief quotes from Tchaikovsky "A Winter Morning" and "Curious Story," from Schumann's *Album for the Young.* Highly colorful and effective. D.

Distance from a Remembered Ground 1982 (GunMar) 12 min. A set of fantasy variations on Chopin's last Mazurka for the left hand; that is, only the left hand plays on the keys, while the right hand is busy producing effects on the strings or on the outside frame. Requires an off-stage piano or tape. The composer says of this piece: "*Distances* . . . is a set of fantasy-variations about—rather than on—Chopin's haunting last work, the *Mazurka in F minor,* Op.68/4. Written for the left hand, the work asks the pianist to use his or her right hand occasionally to mute, pluck or strum the strings inside the piano creating coloristic effects that help to punctuate the work's structure. *Distances* subdivides into twelve sections. These are organized into repeating groups of three: first, a short series of fragmentary gestures, organized serially; next, a passage of incessancy—a steady beat or a reiterated background rhythm based on the free mirroring of intervals derived from the bass line, harmonies or melody of the Mazurka; finally, a 'statement'—contrapuntal, sometimes canonic—a 'summing up.' Moods fluctuate accordingly, from violence to whimsy to nostalgia."

Antal Doráti (1906–1988) Hungary
Variations for Piano on a theme by Béla Bartók (EMB 8315 1977) 24pp. 30 variations based on a theme from *Mikrokosmos* I, No.15. M-D.

Daniel Dorff (1956–   ) USA
Dorff received degrees from Cornell University and the University of Pennsylvania.
Romanza on a Theme of Rochberg 1987 (TP 1996) 4pp. Based on tiny fragments of the opening motive from Rochberg's 1985 Piano Trio. *Romanza* begins freely "and builds to a climax where the Rochberg motive is presented in its full form, as indicated in the score with quotation marks" (from the score). Tonal, flowing lines. M-D.

Joseph Dorfman (1940–   ) Israel, born Russia
Diversions 1965 (IMI 1978) 8pp. 4 min. Short pieces. Joke: staccato thirds in right hand against seconds in left hand. Recorder: legato melodic lines. Lead Soldiers: a brisk march. Water Streams: light staccato repeated notes. Teddy

Bear: legato-staccato short phrases. Dance: bright; staccato thirds and a quirky off-beat that appears every third bar. No fingering or pedaling. Int.

Sonata I 1967 (IMI 312) 23pp. 11 min. Adagio: lyrical; based on 12 notes; subject constructed as a free development of variations interrupted by virtuoso cadenzas. Allegro moderato: SA; a virtuoso main theme clashes with a singing arioso second theme; freely tonal around E♭. Careful pedal instructions. M-D.

The Modern Pianist—Young People's Delight in a Modern Idiom (IMP 691 1981). The Cap of the Clown; Pastorale; A Trip into Space. Written with children 9–12 years old in mind. Clusters, play on strings, etc. A fine introduction to contemporary techniques. Int.

Jaroslav Doubrava (1909–1960) Czech Republic

Sonata pro Klavir (Artia 1948–49). Allegro molto; Andante mesto; Allegro molto ed impeto. Bravura writing, biting dissonance, representative of mid-twentieth-century Czech piano writing. M-D to D.

John Downey (1927–   ) USA

Pyramids (TP). Improvisatory; strong dissonances; flexible meters, tempos, and dynamics. Requires a powerful percussive touch. D.

Eastlake Terrace 1959 (TP 1984) 6pp. 4½ min. "Depicts the moods and impressions of a large body of water as experienced by the composer. Water birds, and seagulls in particular, hovering and then plunging into the wavy cold water were a point of fascination. Water, its sounds and smells, birds and their flight, air illuminated by both the rising and setting sun, all filtered by a touch of jazz, were the materials from which this improvisation-like composition in free form was woven" (from the score). Chromatic, large chords, wide dynamic range, colorful pedal effects. M-D.

Sabin V. Dragoi (1894–1968) Rumania

Little Suite of Rumanian Folk Dances (Simrock). Dedicated to memory of Béla Bartók. 7 short pieces, Bartók influence. Varied moods. Int. to M-D.

Miniatures (Artia 1956). 8 short pieces, a present-day Rumanian "Album for the Young." Int.

Sem Dresden (1881–1957) The Netherlands

Dresden was Director of the Amsterdam Conservatory (1924–37) and the Royal Conservatory in The Hague (1937–49).

Hor ai dolor 1950 (B&VP). Second piece in set *Hommage à Willem Pijper.* Nostalgic, MC. Int. to M-D.

James Drew (1929–   ) USA

Primero libro de referencia laberinto (TP 1974) 6pp. on 1 leaf. Directions for performer. Avant-garde writing; only for the bravest pianist. Terribly complex,

large skips, rhythmic inequalities, new notation. Certain sections to be repeated a number of times. This is probably a powerful work if it can be
successfully realized. Title is appropriate. D.

Alexander Dreyschock (1818–1896) France
See below, "Collections," *Piano Music of the Parisian Virtuosos 1810–1860.*

Madeleine Dring (1923–1977) Great Britain
Three Dances (Cambria 1981) 12pp. Mazurka; Pavane; Ländler. Easily accessible
    with minimal dissonance and maximum sweeps of melody and rhythm;
    blue notes and jazzy vein. Int.
Fantasy Sonata (Lengnick). One movement, sectionalized, MC. M-D.

Jacob Druckman (1928–1996) USA
Druckman handles complex means with a fundamentally simple end in view—to
communicate, whether it be a sense of drama, conflict, humor, or nostalgia.
The Seven Deadly Sins 1955 (Bo&H 1980) 28pp. 16 min. A set of variations in 3
    movements: 1. Pride, Envy, Anger; 2. Sloth; 3. Avarice, Gluttony, Carnality.
    "Pride" is portentious; "Sloth" is slothful and amusingly lives up to its title,
    with a languid tune that twice accelerates and then slides back to the
    original tempo as if overcome by its own inertia. "Avarice" is a virtuoso
    frolic; "Gluttony" an agreeable pastorale. Ends with a restatement of open-
    ing material. Triadic references and implied tonal centers. D.

Pierre Max Dubois (1930–1995) France
Dubois studied with Darius Milhaud at the Paris Conservatory. Influences of
Milhaud, Françaix, Prokofiev, and Debussy are found in his piano works.
Sonata pour Piano (Billaudot) 16 min. Allegro malinconia: SA, new theme in de-
    velopment, incomplete recapitulation, closes with opening material. Scherzo:
    based on two contrasting melodic motives in contrasting meter; harmonic
    shifts and meter changes. Adagio espressivo: opening is chorale-like, chordal
    theme, *ff* entrance of dramatic rhythmic material; ends in serene mood. Al-
    legro moderato: perpetual motion dominated by rhythmic-melodic pat-
    tern; three short motives make up thematic material combined in a free
    form. D.
Dix Études de Concert (Leduc 1960) 2 vols., 39 min. Continues the nineteenth-
    century virtuoso tradition of contrasting short studies and character
    pieces. Well written. 1. Presto con fuoca. 2. *Air à Danser,* Allegretto. 3.
    Prélude, Alla breve et *Fugue,* Presto vigoroso. 4. *Aria,* Andante molto e
    molto espressivo. 5. Maestoso. 6. *Parade,* Allegro pompeux. 7. Allegro agi-
    tato. 8. Scherzando. 9. *Balançoires.* 10. *Oubanghi.* M-D to D.
Dix Préludes 1992 (Billaudot 1994) 32pp. 30 min. Series I: La triste saison; Le
    valet de nuit; La glycine tendre; La tourterelle; Les bosquets touffes. To
    be played without nuances in harpsichord style. Series II: Poco adagio;

Cinglant; Remake; Marche royale; Andante espressivo. To be played in traditional piano style. Much articulation and numerous dynamics. Chromatic and freely tonal. M-D to D.

Toccata (Leduc) 4½ min. Fast figuration, capricious mood interrupted by strongly accented chords. Mid-section is more relaxed than the outer sections; introductory material returns in *Prestissimo* coda. D.

Pour les belles écouteuses: Serenade (Leduc) 3½ min. A perpetual motion accompaniment supports an unhurried melody; contrasting theme appears in mid-section; opening mood returns for a dramatic closing. M-D to D.

10 Etudes de Concert (Leduc 1960). 2 vols. Effective. D.

Esquisses (Leduc 1961) 22pp. 10 pieces. Moderately easy.

Arlequin et Pantalon (Leduc 1964) 11pp. 6 min. Arlequin: pastoral, Impressionistic harmonies, fluctuating tempi. Pantalon: toccata-like, presto leggiero, glissandi, effective program-closer. M-D.

Partita pour Clavecin (*or Piano*) (ESC 1963) 14pp. Prélude; Pavane; Toccata. Neoclassic idioms. M-D.

Les Fous de Bassan (Leduc). Improvisatory beginning and closing with a "Scherzo" mid-section. M-D.

Au Pays Tourangeau, Suite pour Piano (Sal 1948) 15pp. Ouverture; Sarabande; Improvisation; Intermède; Berceuse; Rondo. Full chords, facile writing, Impressionistic devices. Large span required. M-D.

Contes de Nourrices (Leduc 1964). Fourteen short, clever, MC pieces. Int.

Pour Ma Mieux Aimée (Leduc 1956) For My Best Beloved Just So Stories. Ten pieces. Published separately and in a collection. MC. Int. to M-D.

Pour Anne (Rideau Rouge 1971) 4pp. Three small pieces. Int.

Strepitosso 3—Toccata pour piano (ESC) 5½ min. D.

Simple Sonatine (Rideau Rouge 1977) 3pp. One movement, ABA, flowing, peaceful, unusual twists in harmonic structure. Int.

Hommage à Poulenc 1963 (Leduc) 4pp. 3 min. Uses Phrygian mode considerably, sombre chords, flowing diatonic melodies. M-D.

Variations Sur Un Air Connu (Rideau Rouge 1977) 6pp. Theme and 4 variations. Scalar, broken chords, vigorous marchlike final variation. Int.

Marvin Duchow (1914–   ) Canada
Passacaglia (BMI Canada 1961). A 12-note subject makes artistic and varied rounds before the final statement resolves into a *pp* ending. M-D.

William Duckworth (1943–   ) USA
The Time Curve Preludes 1977–78 (CFP 66881a, b). Book I: 45pp. 29 min. Book II: 43pp. 28 min. 24 Preludes, 12 in each book. Each Prelude requires that certain bass notes be depressed by means of weights and tape before the playing begins, allowing sympathetic vibrations that reinforce the tonality —an effective dronelike device. Ravel, Satie, and minimalist influences; many repeated figurations; tranquil. M-D to D.

Paul Dukas (1865–1935) France

Sonata e♭ 1899–1900 (Durand; K) 55pp. 65 min. Modérément vite; Calme—un peu lent—très soutenu; Vivement, avec légèreté; Très lent—Animé, mais sans hâte et bien scandé. Imposing dimensions. Inspired by Beethoven; employs a Franckian keyboard technique with sensitive taste and elegant style. M-D to D.

Variations, Interlude et Finale sur un thème de Rameau 1901–1902 (Durand; MMP) 27pp. 11 variations, improvisatory interlude, animated finale (actually Var.12). M-D.

Prélude élégiaque sur le nom de Haydn 1909 (Durand). Peaceful, sensitive elegy, flowing. M-D.

La plainte, au loin du Faune 1921 (Durand). In *Le Tombeau de Claude Debussy*. Plaintive melody over pedal tones and sustained harmonies, mysterious. An elegy using the opening theme of *Prélude à l'après-midi d'un Faune*, in memory of Debussy. Short and surrealistic. M-D.

See: Alfred Cortot, *French Piano Music* (New York: Da Capo Press, 1977), pp. 178–208.

Vernon Duke (Vladimir Dukelsky) (1903–1969) USA, born Russia

Sonata (Souvenir de Venise) (BB 1955). For piano or harpsichord. One movement in unusual form, SFS. Large span necessary. M-D.

Parisian Suite (BB 1956). 10 pieces. MC. M-D.

Sonata E♭ (Bo&H). Written under the name Dukelsky. M-D.

Louis Dumas (1877–1952) France

Theme et Variations (EMT 1971) 16pp. Sixteen-bar theme in e; eight variations using triplets, 16ths, 32nds, double notes, trills, octaves. Varied moods; short coda; *pp* ending, MC. M-D.

Henri Dumont (1610–1684) France

L'Oeuvre pour Clavecin (Editions Musicales de la Schola Cantorum 1956). 17 works including 11 A's and a C. Influence of the French lutenists, the "style brisé" or broken (arpeggio) playing. M-D.

Jacques Duphly (1715–1789) France

Duphly made his living by giving lessons and concerts on the harpsichord, without holding an official position. This is the first modern edition of his music. Much charm and spirit are to be found in these works.

Pièces pour Clavecin 1744–1768 (F. Petit—Heugel). Fascinating kaleidoscope of brilliant keyboard writing. Throws interesting light on the period during which the piano began to supersede the harpsichord. Some dance titles are used (A, C) but generally descriptive titles are employed. Book I: 15 pieces. Book II: 14 pieces. Book III: 11 pieces (including an extended chaconne). Book IV: 6 pieces. Biographical introduction on the composer indicates historic and musical sources. Int. to M-D.

Marcel Dupré (1886–1971) France
One of France's most renowned organists.
4 Pièces Op.19 (Leduc 1923). Etude e♭. Cortège et litanie: later arranged for
    organ; effective on piano. Chanson: Romantic harmonic and melodic treat-
    ment. Air de ballet: brilliant closing. This group could be divided and num-
    bers played separately. M-D.
Variations in c♯ Op.22 (Leduc 1924) 22pp. Theme, 19 variations, and Final. Most
    variations are short, with many devices used: fourths, octaves, perpetual
    motion, chromatic harmony. Well suited for the piano. M-D.

Marie-Auguste Durand (1830–1909) France
Durand was a music critic, composer, and founder of the music publishing firm
of A. Durand and Fils in Paris.
Waltz E♭ Op. 83 (Lancaster—Alfred 4626; WB). An effective piece using figura-
    tions that fit the hand perfectly. Sounds more difficult than it is. Int.
Chaconne Op.62 (GS). Facile and pianistic. Int.
Valse A♭ Op.86 (GS). Needs good fingers and a sense of rubato. Int.

Pierre Durand (1939–   ) France
22 Leçons de Lecture de rythme et d'indépendance (Rideau Rouge 1974) 22pp. Ex-
    plores such contemporary techniques as unusual notation, clusters, hand in-
    dependence; rhythmic problems. Performance directions in French. Int. to
    M-D.

Francesco Durante (1684–1755) Italy
Durante achieved a fine reputation during his lifetime. Expert craftsmanship
plus a combination of old and new make him an above-average composer.
Sonate per Cembalo divise in Studii e Divertimenti (1732) (Paumgartner—Nag
    241). Six Studii and six Divertimenti paired together, Studii in duple and
    Divertimenti in triple meter. The Studii are more polyphonic, the Diverti-
    menti more homophonic. Scarlatti influence. M-D.
4 Toccatas (I Classici della musica italiana) Vol.11. See Anthologies and collec-
    tions, Italian. Some are reprinted in *Old Masters of the 16th, 17th and 18th
    Centuries*, (K); TPA Vol.18; and *Le Trésor des Pianistes* Vol.9. Nos.1, 2, and
    3 are perpetual motion pieces; No.4 is a calm allegretto; all are one-move-
    ment works. M-D.
Sonate (Degrada—Ric 1978). Two sonatas, each consisting of a more extended
    and serious "Studio" followed by a lighter "Divertimento," often in jig
    rhythm. Contrapuntal flair; well-developed harmonic sense. Durante was
    praised by Rousseau as "the greatest harmonist in Italy, indeed the world."
    The editor admits "an extraordinary freshness." Int. to M-D.
Le Quattro Stagioni Dell'Anno (Iesuè—Boccaccini & Spada 1983) 9pp. This re-
    cently discovered work uses the seasons of the year as titles. Four contrast-
    ing movements. Autumn ("Amabile") is especially lovely. Preface in En-
    glish, Italian, French, and German. M-D.

Louis Durey (1888–1979) France
Première Sonatine C (Heugel). Modérément animé; Lent; Très animé. Int. to M-D.
Dix Inventions (Heugel). Graceful two-voice writing, mixture of homophonic and contrapuntal textures. M-D.
Romance Sans Paroles (ESC). Judicious use of dissonance. Int. to M-D.

Zsolt Durko (1934–1997) Hungary
Psicogramma 1964 (Kultura) 15pp. 9½ min. Prologo; Double Psicogramma I; Motto; Psicogramma II; Canone all prima (Logicogramma); Anti-Evidenze; Un enfant terrible; Psicogramma III; Epilogo. This work balances two elements—one static and expressive, the other dynamic. A shattering climax is reached in "Un enfant terrible," with a five-octave tritone glissando. Ostentatious sonorities plus some string strumming help dramatize states of mind, as the title suggests. Durko is eclectic, yet resourceful and convincing in his melodic treatment. Intense musical feeling. D.
        See: David Burge, CF, 5 (September 1979):66, for a more thorough analysis.
Dwarfs and Giants (EMB 1974) 15pp. Eight short pieces. New notation, palm and forearm clusters, suitelike, Hungarian flavor, dissonant. Titles and descriptions in Hungarian and English. Int.

Frantisek Xaver Dušek (Dussek, Duschek, etc.) (1731–1799) Bohemia
Dušek was not related to J. L. Dussek. He was a pupil of Wagenseil and taught Kozeluch. Dušek left a set of eight sonatas, more sonatina-like in proportion, all in three movements, FSF. Written in the "galant" style of the period, they show some similarities to Mozart.
Eight Sonatas (Aria). Vol.8 of MAB. M-D. Four separate sonata-movements (more technically involved than the 8 Sonatas) are found in vols.14 and 17 of the same series.

Johann Ladislav Dussek (1760–1812) Bohemia
Dussek was the first pianist to sit with his right side to the audience. He was also one of the first to include pedal instructions in his own compositions. He truly exploited the piano, and in some ways (harmony and tonality), he anticipates later Romantic traits. Howard Allen Craw, "A Biography and Thematic Catalog of the Works of Dussek (1760–1812)" (diss., University of Southern California, 1964), contains an extended thematic catalog of approximately 300 works by Dussek. Musica Antiqua Bohemia (MAB) (Raeck, Sykora—Artia) has 29 sonatas available in Vols.46, 53, 59, and 63. William S. Newman discusses the sonatas (SSB, pp.658–75) and gives a concordance of 42 sonatas (pp.664–65), which is very helpful, since much confusion exists about opus numbers.
Collected Works (Da Capo). Twelve volumes in six with a new introduction by Orin Grossman. Vol.I: 6 Sonatas Op.9; Variations Op.10; Romance favorite. Vol.II: 4 Sonatas Opp.35, 43. Vol.III: 12 sets of Variations Opp.71, 6, Vol.IV; 12 Sonatas with accompaniment Opp.46, 28; 3 Sonatas, 4-hands Op.67. Vol.V: 4 sonatas Opp.44, 45. Vol.VI: 3 Sonatas with accompaniment, Op.8; La

Chasse and Rondeau. Vol.VII: 3 Sonatas, 4-hands Opp.32, 48, 74. Vol.VIII: 6 Sonatas Opp.39, 47, 23; 3 Rondos. Vol.IX: Sonata Op.72; 3 Fugues, 4-hands. Vol.X: 6 Sonatas, 5 with accompaniment Opp.25, 51. Vol. XI: Fantasia and Fugue Op.55; 2 Sonatas Opp.70, 75. Vol.XII: Fantasia Op.76; 3 Sonatas with accompaniment Op.12. The sonatas are frequently loosely structured, sometimes wander, and are difficult to hold together, but they all have interest and are worth studying.

MAB Vol.46: *Sonatas* 1–7: Opp.9/1–3, 10/1–3, 18/2. Appeared in Paris before 1769. Op.10/2 g (K&S, Organum, Series 5, No.4). M-D.

MAB Vol.53: *Sonatas* 8–16: Opp.23, 25/2, 31/2, 35/1–3, 39/1–3. Written between 1790 and 1800 in England. Op.35/3 c is sometimes suggested as having influenced Beethoven's Op.13 in the same key (K&S, Organum, Series 5, No.22). M-D.

MAB Vol.59: *Sonatas* 17–23: Opp.43, 44, 45/1–3, 47/1, 2. Op.44 *The Farewell*, 1800 (K&S; Artia). Op.45/1 (K&S; Br). M-D.

MAB Vol.63: *Sonatas* 24–29: Opp.61, 69/3, 70, 75, 77. Op.61 f♯, 1806, "Elégie harmonique sur la mort de Prince Louis Ferdinand" (CFP). The prince (1778–1806) was a gifted composer and pianist and had been a student and patron of Dussek. He died in battle. Op.61 contains some sublime beauty. Op.77 is melodramatic but displays some highly effective writing. M-D.

Two Piano Sonatas 1788 (F. Marvin—UE 18581) 34pp. Sonata G c.v. 40 16pp. Larghetto con espressione; Allegro. Sonata A♭ c.v.43 18pp. Allegro; Allegro non tanto e con spirito. Attractive melodies and daring harmonies make these sonatas worth investigating. M-D.

6 Sonatinas for Harp MAB Vol.22. Preface in English. Well suited to the piano. Int. to M-D.

12 Melodic Etudes Op.16 MAB Vol.21. Poetic tenderness, solid technical brilliance, and a keen sense of timbre make every one of these pieces extremely attractive. Anticipates Chopin's and Schumann's romanticism. M-D.

The Sufferings of the Queen of France Op.23 (Igor Kipnis—Alfred). An unusual piece of program music in ten movements that expresses the feelings of Marie Antoinette during her imprisonment. Excellent preface. Int. to M-D.

6 Sonatinas Op.20 (CFP; GS; Ric; Heugel). Published as Op.19 by the ABRSM. Fluently flowing. Int.

Selected Piano Works (Craw—A-R Editions 1979). Vol.I: Sonatas for piano, four hands. Long preface contains biographical details, discussion of Dussek's music in general, analytical comments about each piece, notes on performance practice, and critical notes. Vol.II: Fantasy and Fugue f Op.55; Variations Op.71; Fantasy F Op.76 (8 contrasting sections). These works seem to have been selected to show Dussek's talents in the less-usual forms. The fantasies contain much pianistic rambling and show a mixture of Classic and Romantic tendencies. Op.71 provides six sets of variations on six different themes, all popular melodies around 1800. All the pieces contain virtuoso elements and, in places, even suggest an orchestral fabric. M-D.

See: Eric Blom, "The Prophecies of Dussek," MO, 51 (1927–28):271–73, 385–86,

495–96, 602, 807–808, 990–91, 1080–81. Reprinted in Blom, *Classics Major and Minor* (London: J. M. Dent, 1958), pp.88–117.

Kenneth Emmanuel Rudolf, "The Piano Sonatas of J. L. Dussek and Ludwig van Beethoven; a Comparative Study," thesis, University of Washington, 1975.

Heino Schwarting, "The Piano Sonatas of Johann Ladislav Dussek," PQ, 91 (Fall 1975):41–45.

Henri Dutilleux (1916–   ) France
Dutilleux writes in a rich, expressionistic style that is balanced with classical forms and a subdued lyricism plus a perfect sense of instrumental nuance.

Au Gré des Ondes (Leduc). 6 petites pièces. Prélude en berceuse; Claquettes; Improvisation; Mouvement perpétuel; Hommage à Bach; Etude. Int.

Sonata 1949 (Durand) 55pp. 22 min. Allegro con moto: SA design, placid beginning. Lied—Assez lent: flowing melodic song with mildly dissonant accompaniment. Finale: chorale with four variations full of rhythmic vitality. Many added notes and rich lyricism. Neoclassic in style. This work has become something of a classic in France. D.

Three Préludes 1974 (Leduc). Exquisite sonority studies that exploit varied tone and timbre; pedal effects used to produce subtle overtones. M-D to D.

Résonances 1965 (Choudens) in collection *Nouveaux musiciens français,* ed. Lucette Descave. Uses writing close to Baroque acciaccatura technique: dissonant note(s) (chords) or resonant interference is played together with sustained chord and quickly released. Refined sonorities. M-D to D.

See: Ken Johansen, "Sound and Illusion." *P&K* 190 (January–February 1998): 35–39. A discussion of Dutilleux's more recent (1970s and 1980s) piano music, including the special effects and riches of his scores.

Andrzej Dutkiewicz (1942–   ) Poland
Dutkiewicz specializes in performing twentieth-century music.

Suite (Kjos) 1973 13pp. Preludium: freely barred; a study in thirds, double thirds, triads, full bitonal chords built of thirds. Aria: seconds and octaves are emphasized, clusters. Toccata: single notes; octaves; ninths; forearm clusters; molto crescendo plus clusters and octaves provide a tumultuous conclusion. M-D.

Toccatina 1970 (Kjos) 10pp., 2½ min. Alternates hands with black and white keys, extension of Prokofieff "Toccata" techniques, subito *pp* ending. M-D.

Jean Baptiste Duvernoy (1802–1880) France
March of the Greeks from "The Siege of Corinth" by Rossini, with Variations (Musica Obscura) 4pp. Three variations and finale on an uninspired march. Int.

25 Elementary Studies Op.176 (Palmer—Alfred). Deal with basic problems for the elementary student. Attractive.

Antonín Dvořák (1841–1904) Czech Republic
Dvořák's music has a natural freshness supported by fine craftsmanship and an engaging spontaneity. Smetana, Czech folk song, and Brahms were the main in-

fluences on his music. Most of Dvořák's piano compositions are character pieces with a pronounced nationalistic element. The piano works are found in the complete edition. Series V, Vols.I–VI published by Artia. Works without opus numbers are numbered according to Jarmil Burghaser, *Antonín Dvořák: Thematic Catalogue, Bibliography, Survey of Life and Work* (in Czech, German, and English) (Prague: Artia. 1960).

Album Leaves B.109 1880 (Hudební Matice). Nos.2 and 3 Souvenirs; No.4 Impromptu G. M-D.

Dumka (Elegy) Op.35 1876 (Artia; MMP). Sudden mood changes characterize the Dumka. M-D.

8 Humoresques Op.101 (SHV; MMP). Critical edition. Preface and critical note in Czech, German, English, and French. No.7 is the most familiar piece. Rhythmic originality and highly interesting pianistic textures. M-D.

6 Piano Pieces Op.52 1880 (Artia; MMP). Impromptu g; Intermezzo c; Gigue B♭; Eclogue g; Allegro molto g; Tempo di Marcia E♭. Nos.1, 2 (UE). M-D.

13 Poetic Tone Pictures Op.85 1889 (Henle 492: Artia; K; Simrock; Ric). Nos.3, 4, 9, 13 (GS). Twilight Way; Toying; In the Old Castle; Spring Song; Peasant's Ballad; Sorrowful Reverie; Goblin's Dance; A Dance (Furiant); Serenade C; Bachanale; Tittle-tattle; At the Hero's Grave; On the Holy Mount. Programmatic writing. M-D.

12 Silhouettes Op.8 1879 (Bo&H; Br; MMP). Attractive; some of Dvořák's easier pieces. Int. to M-D.

Suite A (American Suite) Op.98 1894 (Artia; MMP). Moderato; Molto vivace; Allegretto; Andante; Allegro. Genial and accessible writing permeated by folk idiom but not specifically based on folk music. M-D.

Tema con Variazioni A♭ Op.36 1876 (MMP). Dvořák's most substantial work for piano. The theme resembles Beethoven's variation theme in his Sonata in A♭, Op.26. M-D.

COLLECTIONS:

24 Selected Piano Pieces (CFP) 5 Humoresques from Op.101; 4 Mazurkas Op.56; 3 Waltzes Op.54; Sousedska from Two Pearls; Andante from Op.98; Impromptu No.1; 2 Silhouettes from Op.8; 2 Poetic Mood-Pictures from Op.85; Eclogues Nos.1,4; Album Leaves Nos.2, 3; Dumka Op.12. M-D.

Selected Works (Schwerdtner—Schott 6882 1980) 48pp. Impromptu Op.52/1; Menuettes from Op.28; Silhouettes Op.8/2, 3, 7; Mazurka Op.56/3; Waltzes Op.54/1,4,7; Humoreske Op.10/3; Erennerungen Op.85; 2 Memories (Schubertian) and a Capriccio without opus number. An outstanding collection of lovely works. Int. to M-D.

Leichte Spielstücke (Easy Piano Works) (Heilbut—Hug GH 11155) 12pp. Silhouette D Op.8/7; Silhouette G Op.8/3; Mazurka B♭ Op.56/3; Humoreske G Op.101/7 (transposed): Silhouette D♭ Op.8/2. Int. to M-D.

Humoresque and Other Miniatures (S. Szpinalski—PWM). Humoresque Op.101/7; Furiant F Op.42/2; Furiant Op.12; Waltzes Op.54/1,4.

Piano Works—Selections (Supraphon AP 569 1973) 44pp. Preface and critical note in Czech, German, English, and French. Contents: Eclogues; Album Leaves; untitled compositions; fragments. M-D.

Easy Original Pieces for Piano (UE 18587 1992) 25pp. Ten pieces arranged according to difficulty. Easiest piece is Grandpa Dances with Grandma; the most difficult is Walzer Op.54, No.4. Also includes the familiar Humoreske, Op.107, No.3, in its original version; mazurkas; silhouettes; and minuets. Int. to M-D.

Humoresques and Other Works for Solo Piano (R.Firkušný–Dover 1994) 153pp. 8 Humoresques Op.101. 12 Silhouettes Op.8. Slavonic Dances Op.46/1, 2, 4, 6. Poetic tone pictures Op.85/9, 5, 3, 8. Furianty Op.42/1. Theme and Variations Op.36. An excellent sampling of Dvořák's piano music. M-D.

Light Pieces for Piano (Hug) Three short pieces; Three Silhouettes from Op.8; Mazurka from Op.56; Humoresque Op.101. Large hand required. Int. to M-D.

Dvorak Album (Hera, Sármai—EMB 1991) 55pp. Silhouettes Op.8/11, 12; Impromptu Op.52; Valses Op. 54/1, 3, 7; Mazurkas Op.56/1, 2, 3: Auf der alten Burg; Humoresques Op.110/4, 5, 7, 8. Int. to M-D.

Maria Dziewulska (1909–   ) Poland
Inventions (PWM 1959). Eight short polyphonic works intended to introduce young musicians to the problems of contemporary polyphony by bold treatment of horizontal chords and free rhythms, often expressed by nontraditional musical notation. M-D.

E

John Eaton (1935–   ) USA
Variations 1958 (SP 1964). Written in a brilliant Romantic idiom with the variations recognizable only by changes of texture and meter. The opening material returns at the close. M-D.

Horst Ebenhöh (1930–   ) Austria
Programme 13 Op.22/2 (Dob 1975) 14pp. Many of the movements are only a
page long, but of fiendish difficulty.

Anton Franz Josef Eberl (1765–1807) Austria
Eberl was a pupil of W. A. Mozart and an outstanding pianist. He was highly re-
spected in his home town of Vienna.
Sonatine C Op.6 1796 (Giegling—Arno Volk) in collection *The Solo Sonata*. Al-
legro; Andante; Rondo. Strict sonata form in Mozart style. M-D.
Sonata c Op.1 1792 (Geiringer—UE 10672) in collection *Wiener Meister um
Mozart und Beethoven*. Contains only the third (and final) movement, Allegro. M-D.
Grand Sonata Caractéristique f Op.12 1802 (CFP). Grave maestoso; Allegro agitato; Andantino; Allegro assai. Tuneful, facile writing. M-D.
Grande Sonata Op.27 1805 (Dob Diletto Musicale 887 1985) 28 pp. Three contrasting movements. Excellent part writing, explores sound potential of the
instrument, sounds more difficult than it is. A few Romantic tendencies,
especially harmonic devices. Editorial suggestions placed in brackets. A
fine work. M-D.
Piano Sonatas (D. White—A-R Editions). These seven sonatas and one sonatina
reveal Mozart's influence on Eberl's early style as well as the later developments of his Romantic style. Int. to M-D.

Johann Gottfried Eckard (1735–1809) Germany
Mozart apparently admired Eckard's writing, for he used a movement from one
of Eckard's sonatas in the third (K. 40) of the four composite keyboard concer-
tos of 1767.
Oeuvres Complètes pour le Clavecin ou le Pianoforte (E. Reeser—Edition Heu-
wekemeijer 1956) 94pp. Introduction by Eduard Reeser, annotations by
Johan Ligtelijn. Contains: Six sonatas pour le clavecin ou le pianoforte.
IIème Oeuvre; Menuet d'Exaudet, avec des variations, pour le clavecin.

These were the first sonatas composed in Paris specifically for the piano-forte and date from 1763. M-D.
See: Paul Badura-Skoda, M&M, 17 (February 1969):70.

S. C. Eckhardt-Gramatté (1902–1974) Canada, born Russia
Klavierstück (Sonata No.5) (International Gesellschaft für neue Musik 1950). 15 min. A three-movement work in thick polyphonic texture. The second movement uses harmonics, the final movement octave glissandi. M-D.
Suite for Piano No.1 (Sonata C) (Simrock 1923). Allegro moderato; Andante; Allegro. M-D.
14 Alphabet Pieces (Waterloo). Composed between the ages of 6 and 7, but lyrical and technically sophisticated. Each piece expresses the composer's own colorful and imaginative rendering of different musical styles and forms. Int.

Yitzchak Edel (1896–1973) Israel, born Poland
Edel was on the teaching faculty of the Lewinsky Seminar for Music Teachers in Tel Aviv for thirty-six years. He was active in the Israel Composer's League and also wrote extensively on musical subjects.
Capriccio (IMI 1946). Vigorous large-scale piece requiring vigor and strong articulation. In mixolydian mode. Rondo-sonata form. M-D.
Triptyque (IMI 1963). Invention (Sostenuto) Quiet: brief theme with variations. Scherzino (Fresco) Dry: staccato, double counterpoint at various intervals. Toccata (Presto): Driving rondo. M-D.

Helmut Eder (1916–   ) Austria
Sonata No.1 (Br&H 1950). 3 movements of solid linear writing. The final movement, Marschmässig, is the most accessible. M-D.
Sonatina Op.13 (Dob 1960). 3 movements in neoclassic style. The second movement, Lento con espressione, is more difficult than it appears. Changing meter in final movement, Allegro scherzando, has an engaging lilt. M-D.
Zwei Aphorismen um ein Nachtstück Op.52 (Bosse 341). Serial. M-D.

Christopher Edmunds (1899–   ) Great Britain
Sonata b 1955 (Lengnick) 15 min. First movement: b; a Romantic rhapsody. Second movement: e; elegaic. Allegro scherzando: a; dashing. Fervent writing. M-D.

George Edwards (1943–   ) USA
Draconian Measures (Mobart 1977) 27pp. 11 min. Reproduced from holograph. Pointillistic, expressionistic, rhythmic proportional relationships, involved layers of sounds, frantic at spots. For the most venturesome pianists only. D.

Ross Edwards (1943–   ) Australia
Monos II (J. Albert 212 1970) 12pp. Facsimile of composer's MS. Pointillistic, fast changing meters and dynamics, serial, proportional rhythmic notation, expressionistic. D.

Kumari 1980 (Faber F0660) 6pp. 10 min. Two untitled movements. Pointillistic, serial influence, exploits keyboard extremes, expressionistic, proportional rhythmic relationships, long pedals. Large span required. D.

Etymalong 1984 (UE 29282 1990) 7pp. Half to three-quarter pedal sustained throughout. Exploits extremes of keyboard and *p-pp* dynamics, no meters, many repetitions of same sonorities, minimal influence. Large span required. M-D to D.

Florin Eftimescu (1919–   ) Rumania

Sonata, Pentru Pian (Editura Muzicala 1964) 23pp. Allegro moderato; Andante con moto; Allegretto. Virtuoso writing, much chromaticism but generally tonal in conception. Interesting harmonic vocabulary. M-D to D.

Klaus Egge (1906–1979) Norway

Egge's style is polyphonic, dissonant, and stamped with a vigorous rhythmic technique.

2 Klaverstykker Op.1 (NMO). Valse Dolce; Arkvarell.

Draumkvede Sonate Op.4 (EMH 1942). Based on Draumkvede tunes. Four-movement, well-contrasted work. M-D.

Fantasie I Halling Op.12A (EMH). Based on a familiar Norwegian folk dance. A richly intertwined contrapuntal movement is developed from this tune.

Fantasie I Springar Op.12B (Lyche). Spring Rhythm: full of strange and jagged melismas found in Norwegian folk music. M-D.

Fantasie I Gangar Op.12C (Norwegian Information Service).

Gukkoslatten (Lyche 1944). Goathorn-Dance. M-D.

Sonata No.2 (Patética) Op.27 (Lyche 1956). A large, impassioned work in three movements, FSF, with a Grave stentato introduction. Extensive use of sevenths and ninths. Extreme dynamic contrasts. Freely tonal, powerful writing. M-D.

Werner Egk (1901–1983) Germany

Sonata 1947 (Schott). Andante; Allegro; Andante; Allegro molto. Written in a diatonic style with fresh coloration. M-D.

Robert Ehle (1939–   ) USA

Hypersonde (CF 1972) 4pp. For electronically prepared piano. Five microphones are attached close to the strings to modify the sound electronically. Contains performing directions. Written so that a particular note on the upper staff stands for a microphone placed close to the string sounding that pitch. Experimental, avant-garde. M-D.

Gottfried von Einem (1918–1996) Austria, born Switzerland

Vier Klavierstücke Op.3 1943 (UE) 11pp. 4 short character pieces, rhythmically interesting. No.4 is most appealing. M-D.

Two Sonatinas Op.7 1947 (UE) 20pp. No.1: Molto allegro; Moderato. No.2: Allegro; Adagio; Molto allegro. Neoclassic style. M-D.

Jan Ekier (1913–   ) Poland
Melodies in Color (PWM 1948) 16pp. 9½ min. Nine contrasting settings of Polish and Pomeranian folk songs, freely tonal, appealing. Int.

Halim El-Dabh (1921–   ) Egypt
Mekta in The Art of Kita (CFP 1959). (Microcosm in The Art of Macrocosm). Books I, II, III. Fascinating. Many repetitions of simple material, melodic and rhythmic variations. M-D.

Edward Elgar (1857–1934) Great Britain
Elgar was England's great Romantic composer.
Presto 1889, *Griffinesque* 1884 (Kent—Nov 1981) 4pp. Two miniatures, first publication. These pieces show that during the 1880s Elgar's evolving style was significantly influenced by Schumann's conservative Romanticism. The *Presto* is a little clumsy and rather ambitious while *Griffinesque* is a delicate trifle.
Allegro Op.46 1901 (Nov 1982) 19pp. 11 min. Uneven ideas but enthusiastic writing. Broad tune returns at close. Powerful chordal figures and genuinely pianistic cadenza-type passages are sufficiently dramatic to counteract the weakness of structure and thinness of some of the quieter passages. Good chord and octave technique required. M-D.
Two Piano Pieces (Nov 1976) 8pp. In Smyrna: gently evocative of the Middle East. Skizze: quiet; expressive allegretto requiring careful pedaling. M-D.
Four Pieces (MMP). May song; Carissima; Echo's Dance (from ballet *Sanguine Fan*); Rosemary. Int. to M-D.
Music for Piano (Elkin 1980) 24pp. May Song; Carissima; Echos's Dance; Rosemary; Beau Brummel. Charming trifles. Int. to M-D.
Complete Edition (Nov). The piano works are found in Vol.35, Series V, Instrumental Works.

Brian Elias (1948–   ) Great Britain
Five Piano Pieces for Right Hand (JWC 1969) 4pp. Each piece is very short, with sparse textures, a few large chords, and rhythmic surprises; Webernesque. Pedal carefully exploited. Directions incorporated into score. To be played as a set. Pieces work just as well for the left hand alone. M-D.

Noam Elkies (1966–   ) USA
Four of My First 1974–75 (IMP 664) 7pp. Four short serial pieces, amazingly well constructed for an 8- or 9-year-old. M-D.

Jósef Elsner (1769–1854) Poland, born Germany.
Teacher of Chopin.
Sonata No.2, D (1805) (PWM 1964). Allegro; Andantino—Allegro—Andantino —Allegro. Average writing for the period. The Andantino section (d) is most interesting. Biographical notes in English and Polish. M-D.

Herbert Elwell (1898–1974) USA
Elwell's style is somewhat similar to that of Gabriel Fauré.
Plaint (TP). Interesting modulation. Easy.
Busy Day (TP). Modal. M-D.
Procession (TP). No key signature. M-D.
Sonata (OUP). Allegro; Andante espressivo; Allegro con brio. Requires good
    cantabile, tonal balance, octave facility especially in last movement. M-D.

Maurice Emmanuel (1862–1938) France
Emmanuel's style was influenced by folksong, plainchant, and modality.
Première Sonatine Bourguignonne 1893 (Heugel) 13pp. Allegro con spirito; Branle
    à la manière de Bourgogne; Andante semplice: ostinato; Ronde à la ma-
    nière Morvandelle. Delightful, based on Burgundian folk dances. M-D.
Deuxième Sonatine (Pastorale) (Heugel 1897). La Caille; Le Rossignol; Le Cou-
    cou. M-D.
Troisième Sonatine (Heugel 1920). Impressionistic. M-D.
Sonatina IV sur des modes hindous (Durand 1920) 19pp. 3 movements. Colorful.
    M-D.
Sonatina V alla francese (Lemoine 1926) 15pp. Ouverture (in the French Style,
    SFS), C, S, Gavotte, Pavane et Gaillarde, G. Attractive, Impressionistic. M-D.
Sonatina VI A (Lemoine 1926) 10pp. M-D.

Georges Enesco (1881–1955) Rumania
Enesco's style features expressive modal melodies, parlando rhythmic treatment,
complex polyphony, and a fluid, gliding harmony.
Suite in Ancient Style Op.3 (Enoch 1898; MMP) 16pp. Prelude; Fugue; Adagio;
    Finale. M-D.
Suite pour Piano Op.10 (Editura de Stat Pentru Literatură Si Artă 1956) 34pp.,
    22½ min. Toccata, S, Pavane, B. Virtuoso writing. D.
Sonata f♯ Op.24/1 1924 (MMP). Allegro molto moderato e grave; Presto vivace;
    Andante molto expressivo. A difficult work to hold together. Requires ad-
    vanced pianism. D.
Sonata No.3 D, Op.24/3 1933–35 (Sal). Vivace con brio; Andantino cantabile; Al-
    legro con spirito. A poetic, lengthy work permeated with Rumanian ele-
    ments. Changing tempos, textures. This edition is a reproduction of the
    composer's autograph. D.
Prélude et Fugue No.3 D 1903 (Sal) 9 min. The three-voice fugue uses short trills
    and is heavy with notes. M-D to D.
Pièce pour piano sur le nom de Fauré. In set *Hommage à Gabriel Fauré* (*La Revue
    Musicale*, 23 [October 1992]). 3 pp. Lyrical melody using F–A–G–D–E mo-
    tive over a flowing left-hand accompaniment. M-D.

David Engle (1938–   ) USA
Engle holds a master's degree in piano from the University of Cincinnati School
of Music. He is editor at the Willis Music Co. and writes under two pseudonyms,
Geoffrey Carroll and Christopher Davidson.

Colloquy (Willis 1996) 7pp. Based on a music fragment by C. Michael Ehrhardt. Outer polyphonic sections enclose accompanied melody mid-section. Int.

Elegy (Willis 1990) 6pp. Written under the name of Geoffrey Carroll. Slow, expressive, chromatic, freely tonal, cadenza. M-D.

Soliloquy (Willis 1994) 3pp. Tonal with chromatic additions, flowing melody, nostalgic mood. Int.

Variations on a Plaintive Melody (Willis 1988) 11pp. Theme and eight contrasting variations; freely tonal, chromatic à la Rachmaninoff *Variations on a Theme of Paganini, pp* closing. M-D.

Einar Englund (1916–1999) Finland, born Sweden

Introduzione e Toccata (Fazer 1950) 11pp. 5½ min. Large chords and arpeggi in Introduzione; martellato touch in Toccata, plenty of driving rhythms, like the Prokofieff "Toccata." D.

Manuel Enríquez (1926–1994) Mexico

Enríquez teaches composition and chamber music at the National Conservatory of Music in Mexico City.

A Lápiz, tres apuntes para piano (Collecion Arion 1965) 11pp. Trazos—Molto libero: impulsive. Deleneadno—Brillante: sparkling. Figuras—Molto tranquillo: five short parts to be arranged by performer. Three short sketches containing many directions in Spanish. Dissonant; rhythmic and textural problems. D.

Para Alicia (PIC 1970) 3pp. Diagrammatic notation, aleatoric. Ten segmented schemes to be played in any order. Many sounds are to be made inside the piano: plucking; striking strings with fingernails, open hand, and knuckles. Explanatory notes not always clear. Sonorities range from brutal to delicate. Colorful. M-D.

Donald Erb (1927–   ) USA

Erb has helped to pioneer the acceptance of electronic sounds in conventional music circles and is known for works that extend the use of conventional instruments beyond their normal limits.

Summermusic (Merion 1975) 8pp. 6 min. Strings are to be plucked and tapped with a mallet while playing clusters. Dynamic extremes, experimental notation. Facile fingers required. D.

Nightmusic II 1979 in PQ, 107 (Fall 1979):34–35. Presents some of the techniques and sounds of twentieth-century piano music. Clusters, harmonics, plucked strings. Must remove music rack. The work poses very few technical problems, but does ask the performer to be flexible and use sonic imagination. Int. to M-D.

Heimo Erbse (1924–   ) Germany

Erbse studied with Boris Blacher. His works show a lusty vitality.

Sonata Op.6 1953 (Bo&Bo). Allegro moderato: tricky rhythms and figuration. Vivace: biting dissonances, Tarantella, fast triplets. D.

Vier Rhapsodien Op.40 (Dob 01599 1980) 19pp. Well crafted. Nos.1, 2, and 4; lyrical and witty; free chromatic style. No.3, Adagio pathetico: requires accurate sense of rhythm. Style is a kind of up-dated Hindemith. M-D.

Daniel Ericourt (1903–1998) France
Fantaisie (Leduc 1924) 8pp. Varied tempi and figuration, Impressionistic, some flamboyant writing. M-D.

Rudolf Escher (1912–1980) The Netherlands
Arcana Musae Dona (B&VP 1944). One of the most important piano works in Dutch piano literature. Long and difficult.
Habanera 1945 (Donemus 1980) 4pp. 4 min. Written on three staves to show the rhythmic construction. Many pedal markings, full chords. M-D.

Aylton Escobar (1943–   ) Brazil
Escobar has conducted experiments in creativity with audience participation, particularly among young people.
Assembly (SDM 1972) for piano and tape. 2pp. 5 min. Performer must make tape according to detailed directions contained in the score (in English). Aleatoric, clusters. Piano is amplified from Structure D to the end; strings are plucked and scraped with nails; a glass is to be used to slash the central strings. Avant-garde. D.
Mini Suite das Três Máquinas (SDM 1970) 6pp. Mini-Suite for Three Machines. A Máquina de Escrever ("Typewriter"): clusters, glissandi. A. Caixinha de Musica ("Music Box"): blurred pedal effects, improvisation. O Coração da Gente ("Your Heart!"): aleatoric; sections titled Childhood, Youth, Adult, Death (pulsating in agony with clusters). Avant-garde. D.
Quatro Pequenos Trabalhos (SDM 1968) 15pp. Devaneio (Nocturne); Chorinho (invention for two voices and two free canons); Seresta (Valsa chôro); Cantos (Recitativo e coral). Highly complex writing. Canons are the most accessible. Recitativo on "Lacrimosa dies Illa." Coral in clusters. D.

Luis A. Escobar (1925–   ) Colombia
Sonatine No.2 (PAU 1952) 14pp. Three movements. Easy, gay, accessible contemporary idiom. Hemiola rhythms prevalent. Spanish influence. Contains a biographical sketch of the composer. M-D.

Oscar Esplá (1886–1976) Spain
Esplá's style is a combination of Romantic and German scholasticism.
Impressiones musicales Op.2 (Cuentos infantiles) (MMP). Mixture of impressionistic and Spanish folk music influences. Int.
Sonata Española Op.53 (UME 1944). Written in homage to Chopin. Andante romantico; Mazurka sopra un tema popolare; Allegro brioso. M-D.
Lírica Española Op.54 (UME 1952). 5 books. Book I: Esquisses Levantines. Book II: Tonadas antiguas (Airs anciens). Book V: Suite característica 1954:

Habanera; Ronda Serrana; Sonnatina Playera. Spanish temperament permeates these three works. Int. to M-D.

Akin Euba (1935–   ) Nigeria

Euba is editor of the series *Ife Music Editions*, published by the University of Ife Press in Nigeria.

Scenes from Traditional Life 1970 (University of Ife Press, Ile-Ife, Nigeria 1975). Three scenes "based on a 12-tone row whose notes are systematically assigned to a series of predetermined rhythmic phrases" (from the score). Displays Schönberg influence with Nigerian roots. Strong dissonance in mainly two-voice textures, some notational complexities. M-D.

Rachel Amelia Eubanks (–   ) USA

Eubanks is a pianist, lecturer, and composer. She received her BA degree from the University of California, an MA from Columbia University, and the DMA from Pacific Western University. She studied with Nadia Boulanger during the summer of 1977.

Five Interludes 1984 (Vivace) 12pp. Moderato; Moderato; Moderato; Larghetto; Larghetto. Tense atonal writing, contrapuntal textures, unified by similar intervals in all pieces. M-D.

Franco Evangelisti (1926–1980) Italy

Proiezioni Sonore (Tonos 1955–56) 2 folded sheets. Two pieces. Instructions in Italian and German. Clusters, pointillistic, proportional rhythmic relationships, flexible meters, new notation. M-D.

Robert Evett (1922–1975) USA

Sonata No.2 1952–53 (PAU) 18 min. Allegretto alla breve; Vivace; Chorale en Rondeau (Adagio). Strong neoclassic style, solid writing throughout, harsh sonorities. M-D.

F

Marco Facoli (ca.1588) Italy

Balli d'Arpicordo 1588 (Friedrich Cerha—Dob 1975). Contains 2 pavans, 4 arias, a napolitana, 2 tedescas, and an unidentified piece. Mainly homophonic style with occasional imitation. Fresh modal harmonies and varied rhythmic treatment. Ornamentation places demands on the performer. The complete set is available in the edition by Willi Apel, Vol.II of *Corpus of Early Keyboard Music* (American Institute of Musicology).

Richard Faith (1926–   ) USA

Faith writes in a freely tonal and neo-Romantic style. His broad, beautiful melodies naturally unfold into stunning textured sonorities.

Finger Paintings (SP 1968). 12 imaginative miniatures employing many resources of the instrument. The two hands are of equal importance. MC. Int.

5 Preludes and Nocturne (SP 1969). Tonal, contemporary treatment, varied moods. Ideas evolve naturally. The Nocturne is a slowly flowing lyrical work with a faster mid-section. Chromatic. M-D.

Sonata No.1 (SP 1970) 17pp. Allegro grazioso: unison writing, much chromaticism, B♭. Allegro: repeated notes (chords), imitation, scherzo effect; centers around C. Lento and Mesto: Romantic harmonies, F. Allegro Maestoso: rhythmic motives carefully developed, B♭. M-D.

The Dark Riders (Toccata) (SP 1970) 7pp. Brief introduction leads directly to perpetual motion open fifths in left hand, single note in right. Punctuated with longer note values and rhythmic drive. Long pedal effects. M-D.

Night Songs (SP 1975) 8pp. Andantino; Andante, poco rubato, espressivo. Two expressive nocturnes that could be played separately. The second is freer in form, has lush harmonies and Romantic melodies. M-D.

Recollections (SP 1974) 16pp. The Hunt; Fountains: Monastery; Masks; Autumn; Coach Ride; Reflection; Cavaliers; Sailor's Dance. MC, descriptive, attractive. Int.

Souvenir (Alfred 10114) in collection *Twelve by Eleven*. The title suggests a remembrance of a sad and tender nature, a recollection of something in the distant past. Bitonal shifting from a to F is colored with chromatics that add interest to the flowing melodic lines. Rich sonorities coupled with upper-register textures make for a beautiful work. Int. to M-D.

Dances (SP 1977) 8pp. Five untitled imaginative pieces. Int.

Moments in a Child's World (SP 1978) 23pp. Eighteen pieces, all one page except the last one, which is two pages. Appealing, colorful. Int.

Three Sonatinas (GS 1971). Three movements each, short, appealing. Easy to Int.

Two Nocturnes (SP 250 1980) 11pp. Espressivo, con moto: flowing melody; midsection exploits left hand over right hand in upper register; ravishing conclusion. Andante, espressivo: use of 16th notes in melody and accompaniment, contains some inner restless voices. Subtle pedal effects required. M-D.

Fantasy No.2 (SP 251 1982) 8pp. Thickly dissonant but tonally conservative, virtuosic, energetic, neo-Romantic, linear melodies, expressive and idiomatic. M-D.

Pastoral Suite (SP 1985) 31pp. Galliard; Chase; Ballad; Saraband; Oviedo; Apparition; Jester; Lugano; Festival. Subtle modal usage, unresolved mild discords, special coloristic effects, precisely articulated melodies, neoclassical influence. Attractive writing throughout. Int. to M-D.

Islands (SP 1985) 24pp. Four contrasting movements that exploit the instrument beautifully. First-rate pianism required, MC. M-D to D.

Russian Folk Tale (WB 1990) 9pp. Six untitled contrasting pieces. Colorful, fresh harmonies. Int.

Carrousels (WB 1991) 8pp. 1. Vivace; 2. Andantino, con rubato; 3. Allegro. Three contrasting pieces. Nos. 1 and 3 suggest the title; No. 2 is a lovely flowing character piece. Int.

Sonatina (WB 1987) 8pp. Three contrasting movements, freely tonal. Int.

Masquerades (WB 1989) 7pp. Three contrasting pieces. Int.

Pipes (WB 1986) 11pp. Seven contrasting pieces: at various times melancholy, haunting, lighthearted, jovial. Interesting melodies and rhythms. Int.

Sketches (WB 1986) 17pp. 12 miniatures in 12 keys. "Chase" and "Night" are two of the best. Int.

See: Theodore Guerrant, "An Introduction to Intermediate Faith," AMT, 45/5 (April–May 1996):10–17. A discussion of some of Faith's intermediate piano works.

Julien Falk (1902–   ) France

Dix études atonales, dont deux de concert, selon la technique de l'atonalisme intégral pour le piano (Leduc 1972) 29pp. Ten atonal studies: Prelude; Valse: Dactyle; Chords; Broken Chords; Prelude 2; Trills; Canon for two voices; and two concert pieces—Etude Caprice and Toccata—which are based on atonal writing. Solid technique required. M-D to D.

Manuel de Falla (1876–1946) Spain

The piano was Falla's own instrument, and it was a vehicle for profound compositional statements. Falla studied piano in Madrid with José Tragó and, later, composition with the powerful nationalist composer Felipe Pedrell, who strongly affected his aesthetic orientation.

Allegro de concierto 1902 (JWC 1986) 14pp. First publication. De Falla's entry in a 1905 competition for a Conservatory test piece. It was performed by him and received honorable mention. Granados was the winner. M-D to D.

Pièces espagnoles 1908 (Durand) 15 min. Aragonesa: based on the triple rhythm of the jota, a highly popular north Spanish dance closely associated with Aragon. Cubana: a seductive evocation of Colonial Spain, in which Spanish-type motifs blend with elements more indigenously Latin American; rhythmic piquancy derives from a subtle interplay of 3/4 and 6/8. Montañesa (Paysage): keyboard style reminiscent of Debussy; quiet opening and closing sections dominated by a rocking bell-like motif and a snatch of song; middle section brings a livelier folklike tune. In collection *Masters of Spanish Piano Music* (Alfred 434). Andaluza: inspired by the southern province of Andalusia and its rich Gypsy traditions; crisp opening dance theme, accented by clicking castanets; tempo slackens for a mid-section that imitates the more improvisational and emotionally charged flamenco style. This piece is the freest and most spontaneous of the four. M-D.

See: Julio Esteban, "Andaluza, A Master Lesson," *Clavier* 15 (October 1976):19–27.

Fantasia Baetica 1918 (JWC) 12 min. Though this most demanding of Falla's solo piano works is a brilliant and evocative show-piece, its local color is expressed with more harmonic and textural astringency than anything found in the *Pièces espagnoles*. The opening is full of twanging guitars and rattling castanets competing for attention with snatches of dance rhythm and melody; activity eventually subsides so that a Gypsy singer can take the stage in a remarkable keyboard evocation of the rhythmically free, lavishly ornamented style of *cante hondo*. Before the free recapitulation, we hear the briefly contrasting central Intermezzo (Andante), with a modally tinged g♯. D.

See: David Burge, "Contemporary Piano—Manuel de Falla's Fantasia Baetica," *Keyboard* 8/2 (February 1981):69.

Homenaje 1920 (JWC). "For the death of Debussy," a guitar piece arranged by Falla. Rhythmic treatment punctuated with staccato figuration. Based on motive from Debussy's "Soirée dans Grenade" and quotes from the Debussy piece in the final measures. M-D.

Nocturne f 1900 (UME). In the Chopin tradition, contains none of Falla's usual accent. Tuneful, minor tonality. Int.

Mazurka ca. 1900 (de Falla Ediciones) 11pp. First publication. Rondo, salon style, Chopin and Grieg influence, catchy rhythms, tuneful. M-D.

Vals—Capricho 1900 (UME). An early salon style pianistic snapshot. M-D.

Pour le tombeau de Paul Dukas 1935 (Ric 1974) 3pp. The composer's version of his original setting for guitar. 42 bars of dark f minor harmonies with a poignant, unresolved tonic chord addition. No Spanish atmosphere. M-D.

Works—Selections, Vol.3 (UME 22238 1980) 11pp. Cancion 1900: c, sad, 3/8, more animated mid-section with counter melodies. Danza de Gnomos 1901: opens in D, lyrical, changes to f♯, chromatic, opening idea returns, ends *pppp*. Canto a los Remeros del Volga: based on Russian air "Song of the Volga Boatman"; most difficult of the pieces; uses octaves and large chords; in Spanish style. M-D.

See: Gilbert Chase, "Falla's Music for Solo Piano," *The Chesterian*, 21 (1940):43.

David C. Cooper, "A Survey of the Solo Piano Works of Manuel de Falla," diss., University of Kentucky, 1991, 199 pp.

Carlos Farinas (1934–   ) Cuba
Sones Sencillos (Tonos) 7 separate sheets. Four pieces utilizing many harmonic sixths. Freely tonal, syncopated. Imitation in No.4. M-D.

Ferenc Farkas (1905–   ) Hungary
Farkas writes in a freely tonal style with intricate but logical rhythmic patterns. His melodies are strong, and a Latin clarity and Hungarian flavor permeate all of his music.
3 Burlesques (Artia 1949). Energetic writing in Bartók idiom. Nos.1 and 3 are brilliant and vigorous, while No.2 is slower with unusual left-hand melodic figuration. D.
Kit Akvarell Zongorara (EMB 1955) Geburtstagsgrüss: 3pp., slow, declamatory, chromatic. Aprilwind: 7pp., fast, polytonal, scalar over open fifths. M-D.
5 Hungarian Danses (ZV 1952). Transcribed by F. Farkas. Unusual group; less modal than Bartók's *Hungarian Dances*. Int.
Quaderno Romano 1931 (Zenmukiado 1967). Preludio; Cavatina; Dialogo; Caccia; Passeggiata; Epilogo. A fine MC suite; contrasting movements have much color. M-D.
Holiday Excursions 1975 (EMB Z7908) 12pp. Six pieces for young people. Int.
Ballade 1955 (EMB 1980) 12pp. Expanded tonal idiom, variety of textures. M-D.
Correspondances (EMB 1980) 16pp. 8 pieces that exploit MC sonorities and textures. Int.
Hybrides 1960 (EMB 1980) 14pp. Short pieces; most are based on a row. March; Minuet; Tarantella; Notturno; Valsette; Fughetta; Cadenza; Moto Perpetuo. Expressive, exacting. Learn the piece, then go back and figure out how Farkas put the notes together. Int. to M-D.
Journal 1986 (EMB Z.13802 ca. 1993) 19pp. 14 short varied pieces with titles in Hungarian and French. Much chromatic usage. Int.
Journal 1987 (EMB Z.13804 c. 1993) 15pp. 10 short varied pieces with titles in Hungarian and French. Similar styles as above. Int.

Giles Farnaby (ca.1560–ca.1620) Great Britain
Although untrained, Farnaby was an instinctive musician whose spontaneous simplicity lends a freshness to his compositions.
Keyboard Music of Giles and Richard Farnaby, Musica Britannica XXIV (R. Marlow—S&B). Contains 53 works by Giles Farnaby, 4 works by Richard, and a doubtful Coranto by Giles (?). Int. to M-D.
Selected Works (H. H. Glyn—S&B) 25 works. Vol.I: Selected Pieces. Vol.II: Folksong Variations.
17 Pieces Selected from the Fitzwilliam Virginal Book (T. Dart—S&B).
Tower Hill in collection *Keyboard Music of the Baroque and Rococo*, Vol.I. M-D.
Masque. FVB, II, 264. Grave and severe feeling of the pavan, minor mode, virtuosity out of place. M-D.

Woodycock Variations. FVB, II, 138. Six variations based on a popular Elizabethan dance tune. First part of Var.5, with its rapid and animated thirds in
the middle range of the keyboard, is charming and unique in the literature
of this period. The second part of this variation, with the subject brought
out in augmentation on counterpoint in triplets, requires a virtuoso technique if the tempo is to be maintained. M-D.
His Humor. FVB, II, 262. 4 episodes, A B C D. M-D.
See: Richard Marlow, "The Keyboard Music of Giles Farnaby," PRMA, 92(1965–
66):107–20.

David Andross Farquhar (1928–   ) New Zealand
And One Makes Ten (Price Milburn). Ten pieces that make an interesting suite.
Each piece begins where the previous one concluded, therefore the end
of Epilogue leads back to the beginning of the opening Prelude. Prelude;
Toccata; Scherzo; Procession; Bell Dance; A Weird Waltz; Nocturne; An-
tiphony; Fantasy; Epilogue. Austere style with influences of Bartók and
Stravinsky. M-D.

Louise Farrenc (1804–1875) France
Farrenc studied with Moscheles, Hummel, and Reicha and was a highly admired
pianist in her day. She was Professor of Piano at the Paris Conservatory from
1842 to 1872.
Impromptu. In collection *At the Piano with Women Composers*—Alfred 428.
Uses much imitation, interesting accompaniment figuration. Int.
See below, "Collections," *Piano Music of the Parisian Virtuosos 1810–1860.*

Arthur Farwell (1872–1952) USA
A great champion of American music, Farwell was at his best in working with
American Indian material.
The Domain of Hurakon (Wa-Wan 1902) 13pp. A large work based on three In-
dian melodies of widely divergent origin. Our word "hurricane" comes
from the Indian Word "Hurakon." Well worth reviving. M-D.
Navajo War Dance No.2 (Mer). Ostinato figures, bravura octaves and chords. M-D.
Pawnee Horses (GS). Short Omaha melody treated in a galloping figuration.
M-D.
Sourwood Mountain (GS). In *51 Piano Pieces from the Modern Repertoire.* A
"Rip-snorting development of a good old American tune." Virtuoso treat-
ment. M-D.
Approach of the Thunder God from *American Indian Melodies* 1902. In collection
Essential Keyboard Repertoire Requiring a Hand Span of an Octave or Less
(Alfred 4574). An original Indian melody harmonized by Farwell. Int.
See: *Guide to the Music of Arthur Farwell and to the Microfilm Collection of
His Work.* Compiled by his children and issued by his estate, 5 Deer Trail,
Briarcliff Manor, NY 10510.
Maurice Hinson, "Piano Solos Inspired by American Indian Melodies," *Clavier,*
17 (May–June 1978):22–23. Discusses Farwell and his *American Indian
Melodies*; includes "Song of the Ghost Dance," p.21.

Marjorie A. Ziprick, "Arthur Farwell—American Composer Rediscovered," *The California Music Teacher*, 2/3 (February–March 1979):4–5, 12.

Gabriel Fauré (1845–1924) France

Melodic spontaneity, rhythmic subtlety, harmonic reticence, and restraint are characteristic of Fauré, one of the finest and most creative French composers. Many of his 57 original piano works have a seeming similarity, but closer examination and greater familiarity reveal a striking originality. His nocturnes, preludes, barcarolles, and impromptus were inspired by Chopin, but Fauré's individual and instinctive pianism make him one of the great nineteenth-century composers for the piano. The piano works demand musicianship and pianistic maturity.

Ballade Op.19 (1881) (Hamelle; G. Johannesen—IMC). Original solo piano version of the *Ballade* for Piano and Orchestra. Begins quietly with a lyrical cantabile theme; builds to a fine climax midway, then fades away to a close in the poetic style of Chopin. A beautiful tone, a sure sense of rubato, and poetry are strong interpretative requirements. M-D.

13 Barcarolles 1883–1921 (IMC, publishes 6; K, publishes 6; Hamelle, Nos.1–6; Heugel, Nos.7–9; Durand, Nos. 10–13). 1. Op.26 a. 2. Op. 41 G: elegant salon style, interesting rhythms. 3. Op.42 G♭. 4. Op.44 A♭: a sicilienne 5. Op.66 f♯: change in style, chromatic, varied rhythms. 6. Op.70 E♭: tranquil and controlled feeling. 7. Op.90 d: has some Debussyesque chords. 8. Op.96 D♭: cheerful, strong rhythms. 9. Op.101 a: subtle rhythm and harmonies. 10. Op.104/2 a: ethereal and delicate, like a nocturne. 11. Op.105 g. 12. Op.106 E♭ (MMP): charming and joyous. 13. Op.116 C. Rhythm and texture have special significance. 6/8 meter is predominant in all but two, and allegretto tempo in all but one. Texture is typically "boat song" over "boat motion," lyrical melody over rocking broken-chord accompaniment, and it is continuously sustained throughout large areas of these pieces. Linear and coloristic elements are beautifully intertwined. M-D.

Berceuse Op.56/1 (GS; Leduc; Hamelle). Flowing melody over rocking bass figure. Int. to M-D.

Impromptus (IMC, Nos.1–3; K, Nos.1–3; Hamelle, Nos.1–3; BMC, No.1; PWM, No.2; Heugel, Nos.4, 5): full of whimsical freshness and joyous vigor. 1. Op.25 E♭ (1883): sensual harmonic coloring. 2. Op.31 (1883): opens with scale and arpeggiated passages; rhythm like a tarantella; mid-section melody is typically French; one of Fauré's most popular pieces. 3. Op.34 A♭ (1883): skillful, graceful, tasteful and well-proportioned. 4. Op.91 D♭ (1906): a midsection Andante is framed by two Allegro outer sections. 5. Op.102 f♯ (1910): augmented chords, long descending and ascending whole-tone scale appears just before the end. The style of the Impromptus is often indistinguishable from that of the Barcarolles. M-D.

Mazurka Op.32 B (Hamelle; Leduc; MMP). Salon piece; colorful French version of this Polish dance. M-D.

13 Nocturnes (IMC, publishes 8; Hamelle, Nos.1–8; Heugel, Nos.9, 10; Durand,

Nos.11–13). 1. Op.33/1 e♭. 2. Op.33/2 B. 3. Op.33/3 A♭. 4. Op.36 E♭. 5. Op.37 B♭. 6. Op.63 D♭. 7. Op.74 c♯. 8. Op.84/8 D♭. 9. Op.97 b. 10. Op.99 e. 11. Op.104/1 f♯. 12. Op.107 e. 13. Op.119 b.

Available separately: Nos.1–6 (Leduc). Op.36/4, Op.37 (IMC).

In the Nocturnes, Fauré shows a clear preference for large ternary structures with highly contrasting middle sections. More often than not, first themes are dreamy, reflective, and slower, while middle themes are more urgent, agitated, and faster. However, Fauré also wrote smaller ternary pieces in this genre with little contrast of mood in the middle sections. No.6 contains some Scriabinesque passages, so unlike No.2, but all are full of the musical idiosyncracies so often associated with Fauré. Nos. 3 and 6 are sublimely satisfying pieces and a good place to begin this genre. No. 11 is grave and emotional. No. 12 is agonized and poignant. No.13 was Fauré's last composition for piano. It is a work of intense meditation with wondrous sequences of suspensions and appoggiaturas; calm coda; a masterpiece. M-D to D.

Nocturnes and Barcarolles (Dover). 24 pieces. A 40-year survey of Fauré's piano works.

8 Pièces Brèves Op.84 (1898–1902) (IMC; K; Leduc; Hamelle). The titles were added later by the publisher, against Fauré's advice. But they do suggest the character of each piece. Capriccio: simple style, no complex technicalities. Fantaisie: short and pleasant. Fugue: of interest since Fauré did not usually write in stricter forms. Adagietto: appealing and serious style. Improvisation: originally written for a sight-reading test at the Paris Conservatory, but a fine piece. Fugue: attractive and effective academic writing. Allégresse (Gaiety): expressive and exhilarating. Nocturne: interesting fast and effective transition from opening key of D♭ to the Phrygian mode on C. Int. to M-D.

See: Robert Dumm, "A Fauré Improvisation," *Clavier*, 15 (April 1976):20–23. Contains Op. 84/5 and an analysis of it.

9 Preludes Op.103 (1910–11) (Heugel separately and in collection). Short, concentrated masterpieces full of color and imagination; varied and ingenious approach to piano technique. 1. D♭: quiet lyric mood, unique harmonies, subtle, transparent writing. 2. C♯: etudelike, moto perpetuo in fast triplets. 3. g: barcarolle style, cantabile melody. 4. F: pastorale character. 5. d: emotional, violent, mirror of anger. 6. e♭: legato canon style, one of the best. 7. A: a quiet but intense opening leads to an effective closing. 8. c: staccato repeated notes, scherzo style. 9. e: expressive, impressive mode change at measure 8, eloquent descending sequence leads to final candence. Int. to M-D.

Complete Preludes, Impromptus and Valses-Caprices (Dover; MMP).

3 Romances sans Paroles Op.17 (K; IMC; Leduc; Hamelle; MMP). No. 3 is flowing and Chopinesque, arpeggiated bass, 3 vs. 2 rhythm in two places, a few "flavoring" accidentals. Int.

See: Ken Frerichs, "Gabriel Fauré: Herald of French Impressionism," *Cla-*

vier, 20 (February 1981):23–28. Includes music and lesson on *Romance Sans Paroles*, Op.17/3.

Charles Timbrell, "Fauré's Piano Music," *Piano Today*, 15/5 (September–October 1995):60–61. The Romance sans paroles is printed in this issue (p. 32) and the article is a master class on this piece.

Theme and Variations Op.73 (1897) (IMC; K; Hamelle). A beautifully polished set (11 contrasting variations) considered a classic by the French, exemplifying all of Fauré's subtlety, grace, and reticence to the nth degree. D.

3 Valse-Caprices (Hamelle). Op.30 A; Op.59 G♭; Op.62 A♭. M-D.

4 Valses Caprices (K). These works are among Fauré's most individual pieces. All are bright, animated, and full of sensuous charm and impassioned tenderness. 1. A, Op.30 (1883): melodic sweep, interesting harmonies, has considerable individuality. 2. D♭, Op.38 (1884): two contrasting moods—melancholy and strong rhythms. 3. G♭, Op.59 (1887–93): flowing pianistic style, a sinewy rhythm and a firm line. 4. A♭, Op.62 (1893–94): wistfully tender, vivacious second theme, ebullient coda. Int. to M-D. Fauré recorded Nos.1, 3, and 4 on piano rolls for Hupfeld and Welte & Söhne. They show that he was an admirable performer of his own works.

Piano Works (Eberhardt Klemm—CFP P-9560a, 9560b). Vol.I: 9 Preludes Op.103; 6 Impromptus Opp.25, 31, 34, 86b, 91, 102. Vol.II: 13 Barcarolles.

Fauré: An Album of Piano Pieces (I. Philipp—GS). Romance sans Paroles Op.17/3. Barcarolles Nos.1, 4, 6. Impromptu III Op.34. Clair de lune Op.46/2: delicate, charming, hauntingly beautiful melody with arpeggiated chordal accompaniment, atmospheric; some transfer of melody between hands. Nocturne IV Op.36. Improvisation Op.84/5. Berceuse Op.56/1. M-D.

Gabriel Fauré—His Greatest Piano Solos (Copa 1973) 191pp. A comprehensive collection of his works in their original form. Compiled by Alexander Shealy. Contains: Romance sans Paroles Op.17. Capriccio Op.84/1. Fantasia Op.84/2. Fugue a Op.84/3. Adagietto Op.84/4. Improvisation Op.84/5. Allegresse Op.84/6. Fugue Op.84/7. Barcarolles 1–5. Nocturnes 1–8. Impromptus 1–3. Theme with Variations Op.73.

Les Petits Morceaux Faciles (Zen-On 109) 31pp. 3 Romance Sans Paroles Op.17/3. Pièces Brèves Op.84/5 (Improvisation). Sicilienne Op.78. Dolly Op.56/1 (Berceuse). Pavane Op.50. These are technically the easiest of Fauré's piano pieces. Int. to M-D.

Selected Pieces (Robin de Smet—Cramer). Transcriptions: Berceuse and Kitty Waltz from Dolly Suite Op.56/1,4; Romance without Words Op.17/3. Original works: Nocturnes II B Op.33, IV E♭ Op.36; Pavane f♯ Op.50; Barcarolles IV A♭ Op.44, VI E♭ Op.70; Improvisation c♯ Op.85/5; Fugue e Op.84/6. Metronome marks given; no fingering; little pedaling. Int. to M-D.

Selected Works (K 09960). Contains Barcarolles No.7, Op.90; No.8, Op.96; No.9, Op.101; No.10, Op.104/2. Impromptu No.6, Op.86 (after the *Impromptu* for Harp). Nocturne No.11, Op.104/1. All contain a charming individuality and are a refreshing change to less-known repertoire. Int. to M-D.

See: Jeffrey Chappell, "Civilized Passion. The Piano Music of Gabriel Fauré," P&K, 174 (May–June 1995): 38–40.

Aaron Copland, "Gabriel Fauré, a Neglected Master," *MQ*, 10 (October 1924): 573–86.

Alfred Cortot, *French Piano Music* (New York: Da Capo Press, 1977), pp. 109–39.

Collection (Heugel). Contains Barcarolles Opp.90, 96, and 101. Impromptus Opp.91 and 102; Nocturnes Opp.97 and 99. M-D.

See: John M. Arnn, "The Harmonic Language of Selected Piano Works of Fauré," thesis, Indiana University, 1969.

Gwilym Beechey, "Gabriel Fauré—His Piano Music and Songs," MO, 1165 (November 1974):61–66.

Sara Feigin (1928–   ) Israel

Toccata 1972 (IMI 258 1978) 18pp. 7 min. Divided into several sections with changes metronomically indicated. Motoric rhythms, interlocking fourths, repeated notes. Folk-like melody, brilliant but not demanding as some of the famous virtuosic toccatas. M-D.

Samuel Feinberg (1890–1962) Russia

Feinberg's early works were similar in style to Scriabin. The later works become more diatonic. Feinberg concentrated on the piano sonata.

Sonata No.2 Op.2 (MCA 1916). One-movement work, Scriabinesque, dramatic, D.

Fantasy E♭ Op.5 (MCA 1917). One movement, dramatic. M-D.

Fantasy e Op.9 (MCA 1919). Somber, melancholy. M-D.

Suite Op.11 (MCA). 4 short lyric pieces. M-D.

Sonata No.5 a Op.10 (MCA 1921). One movement, complex. M-D to D.

Sonata No.6 b Op.13 (UE 1923). One movement, many tempi changes, thick textures, involved. M-D.

Sonata No.9 (MCA). One movement, lyric, sonorous ending. M-D.

Morton Feldman (1926–1987) USA

"Feldman's music has always dealt with actual sound, produced by actual instruments, but the sounds he produced were always exceedingly quiet. . . . His is a vocabulary that may be linked to Impressionist painting without subject matter. Only the hazy, diffused light may be equated to the imperceptible aural language of Feldman's music. It is a music of deep intimacy. One must really listen to a Feldman work, or it might easily slip by without being heard at all" (John Gruen, *Vogue*, December 1968). Feldman was a disciple of John Cage.

Illusions for Piano (NME 1950). Very Fast; Slow and Tranquil; Very Fast; Very Fast. Short pieces. Changing meters, extreme dynamic range (*fff* to *ppppp*), fascinating timbres. Debussy and Schönberg flavor. Advanced pianism required. M-D.

Intersection II, III (CFP). Graphs. Great contrasts. M-D.

Piano Pieces (CFP 1952, 1955, 1956a,b, 1963). Slow, quiet. M-D to D.

Last Pieces (CFP 1959). Four short pieces with directions such as "Slow. Soft." "Durations are free for each hand." Only pitch notated. M-D.

Extensions III 1952 (CFP). Upper register exploited. M-D.

Piano 1977 (UE 16516) 29pp., 25 min. Single movement, lacks musical development, plods slowly. Intensely quiet, comments on timbral contrasts between upper and lower registers, luscious chords in middle register, delicate fragments float into audibility. *ff* chords jolt the listener about 2/3rds through the piece. Exhibits great care and knowledge about the piano; sostenuto pedal important throughout. Persuades listener to give close attention to each individual sound. Requires subtlety and skill on the part of the pianist plus a large hand span. D.

Triadic Memories 1981 (UE 17326) 90 min. *ppp* throughout; minimalist influence. M-D.

Palais de Mari 1986 (UE 18497) 20 min. Precise notation, constant rhythmic changes. D.

For Bunita Marcus 1985 (UE 18966) 59pp. Constantly changing meters, slow proportional rhythmic relationships, *ppp* and moderately slow throughout, sparcity of notes, held over silences, avant-garde. D.

Vittorio Fellegara (1927–   ) Italy

Omaggio a Bach, tema e variazioni 1975 (SZ 1978) 15pp. 11½ min. A tough-minded and pianistically exacting set of variations based on a theme from an early J. S. Bach capriccio. Each of the 8 variations exploits compositional techniques that seem to emerge from the original theme. Webernesque, austere, but rewarding writing. D.

Ramon Femenia-Sanchez (1936–   ) Spain

Homenaje (Homage) Preludio (UME 1973) 10pp. Varied meters and tempos. Contrasting sections, whole-tone and quartal harmonies, MC. M-D.

Per Tierra de Asturias ("The Land of Asturias") (UME 1973) 4pp. Andante: requires singing tone; followed by an Allegro that uses plenty of rubato. Andante returns with an accelerando to the end. Romantic writing. M-D.

Recuerdo ("Remembrance") (UME 1973) 3pp. Interval of the fourth is exploited. Bell-like sonorities at opening and closing; mid-section is nocturnelike. Some Flamenco characteristics; Romantic style. M-D.

Brian Fennelly (1937–   ) USA

Sonata Seria 1976 (Joshua) 31pp. reproduced from MS. Three sections plus an epilogue, fantasy-like sections between contrapuntal structures. Combines SA design with canonic structures and variations. Stuttering rhythmic pulse, heavy chording, and an atonal garb. Little textural variety except in the double-mirror scherzo movement. Thoroughly contemporary, freely atonal, serial influence, uncompromising. D.

Howard Ferguson (1908–1999) Great Britain

Ferguson is basically a twentieth-century Romantic. His works are built on a strong classical structure, both formally and harmonically.

Sonata f Op.8 1938–40 (Bo&H). Lento: declamatory, stark. Allegro inquieto: restless undercurrent. Poco adagio: florid, the still center of the work. Allegro non troppo: scampering, opening Introduction returns with crushing intensity. Advanced pianism required for this work of tragic grandeur. M-D.

5 Bagatelles Op.9 1944 (Bo&H). A cycle of varied sketches built on themes by the composer's friends, careful thematic integration. M-D.

See: Andrew Burn, "The Music of Howard Ferguson," MT, 124 (August 1983): 480–82.

Armando José Fernandes (1906–1983) Portugal

Fernandes's style leans toward neoclassicism.

Sonatina (Sassetti 1941) 9pp. Allegretto grazioso: dancelike. Tempo di Folia: leads to an Andante espressivo that requires span of a ninth. Allegro non troppo: fugal. M-D.

Scherzino (Sassetti 1960) 6pp. Chromatic, arpeggi, broad dynamic range, Moderato mid-section, effective. M-D.

Oscar Lorenzo Fernandez (1897–1948) Brazil

Fernandez is not afraid to write an old-fashioned melody and use characteristic South American rhythms.

First Brazilian Suite (PIC, each movement published separately) 5½ min. Old Song; Sweet Cradle Song; Serenade. Folk-like, lyric, Romantic harmony. M-D.

Second Brazilian Suite (PIC 1938, each piece published separately) 7½ min. Prelude; Song; Dance. Based on original themes. M-D.

Third Brazilian Suite (PIC 1938, each piece published separately). Song: rich harmonization, fine climax. Serenade: constant right-hand double notes; effective, difficult. Negro Dance: a "tour de force" in rhythm and dynamic control. Large span required, full dynamic range. The composer's largest work for piano. M-D.

Sonata Breve 1947 (PIC) 12 min. Energico. Largo e Pesante. Impetuoso: right hand mainly has seventh chords. An effective, forceful work requiring facile technique. M-D.

Suite das 5 Notas (PIC 1942) 8 min. Eight short movements. Easy.

Dolls (PIC 1945, published separately). Spanish Ballerina; Portuguese Shepherdess; Italian Peasant Girl; Russian Girl Woodcutter; Chocolate Cake Girl Vendor. Int.

Children's Visions (PIC 1942, published separately). Little Cortège; Nocturnal Round; Mysterious Dance. Int.

Yaya, the Doll (PIC 1946). Dancing Yaya; Dreaming Yaya; Jumping Yaya. Int.

Brian Ferneyhough (1943–   ) Great Britain

Three Pieces (Hin 1971) 19pp. 15 min. Plastic ring-bound. Many different tempi, thick contrapuntal complex textures, frequent meter changes, extreme dynamic range. D.

Lemma-Icon-Epigram (CFP 7233) 14 min. An extended single movement. Obsessive attention to detail and complete fastidiousness combine to make Ferneyhough's work distinctive. Highly complex, much tension, extremes of pitch, powerful rhythmic structures, continual movement across the complete dynamic range of the instrument, total absorption with technical complexities. The title refers to a literary verse form. D.

Pierre-Octave Ferroud (1900–1936) France
Au parc Monceau (Rouart, Lerolle 1921) 18pp. Chat jouant avec des moineaux; Sur le banc; Nonchalante; Bambins. Int.
Prélude et Forlane (Durand 1924) 9pp. Ravel influence in this charming set. M-D.
Types (Rouart, Lerolle 1922–24). Some brilliant pianistic writing, especially in the third movement. M-D.

François Joseph Fétis (1784–1871) and **Ignaz Moscheles** (1794–1870)
Méthode des méthodes de piano (Minkoff Reprint 1973) 54pp. Reprint of the Paris edition (Schlesinger 1840). Contains 18 études de perfectionnement pour le piano, composées par Bénédict et al.

George Fiala (1921–   ) Canada, born Russia
Fiala is considered one of Canada's leading composers.
Sonatina Op.1 (BMI Canada 1960) A clever 3-movement work in neoclassical style. The third movement, Tarantella, is much more difficult than the other two. M-D.
Dix Postludes Op.7 (Waterloo 1968). All are short, one page each, tonal and MC. No.6, À la Shostakovitch, is particularly evocative of that composer's style. M-D.
Australian Suite (BMI Canada). Birds and Beasts like the Emu; Kookaburra; Lyre Bird; Kangaroo; Platypus; Koala. Imaginative set. Int.
Miniature Suite (BMI Canada). Overture; Almost a Waltz; Ancient Story; Spinning Wheel. Clear forms, some dissonance, flowing, pianistic. Easy.
Children's Suite (Waterloo 1976) 16pp. Titles in English, French, and Russian. Instead of an Overture; What the Youngster Whistled Gathering Chestnuts in the Grass; Little Bear's Minuet; Moorish Doll Offended; March. Contrasting, MC, humorous and clever. Large span required. Int. to M-D.

Zdenko Fibich (1850–1900) Czechoslovakia
Fibich's use of dynamics was one of the most interesting facets of his style. His preference was for the softer levels, *pp-ppp*, etc.
Sonatina d (Urbanek 1947). In Dvořák style. Int.
Detem (Vera Koubkova-Artia 1960). 11 solo pieces and 5 duets. Excellent, interesting pedagogic material, all colorful. Int.
Scherzos I and II Op.4 (Hudebni; Supraphon). e; Ab. Delightful, somewhat in Mendelssohn style, pianistic, make excellent encores. M-D.
Poem (Artía). The composer's best-known work in the U.S.A. Int. to M-D.

Nálady, dojmy a upomínky (Urbanek). Published separately: Op.41 ("Moods, Impressions and Recollections.") 4 vols. of 46 pieces (1891–94). Op.44 ("Novella") 4 vols. of 33 pieces (1895). Op.47, 10 vols. of 148 pieces ranging in difficulty from easy to M-D (1895–97). Op.57, 2 vols. of 17 pieces (after 1897). A wonderful range of delightful sounds. Traditional piano techniques.

Mario Ficarelli (1937–   ) Brazil
Ficarelli has been very active as teacher, choir director, and pianist. He composes pedagogical pieces.
Estudio No. 3 (BME 1995). Challenging, well-crafted. M-D.

Jacobo Ficher (1896–1978) Argentina, born Russia
Ficher came to Argentina in 1923 and assumed a leading role in the Argentine musical scene. His music is characterized by rhapsodic development and rich harmonic texture.
5 Canciones Sin Palabras Op.1 (Ric). 5 Songs Without Words. Lyrical, expressive. M-D.
6 Animal Fables Op.38 (Axelrod 1942). Short descriptive barnyard pieces including an arrogant rooster, a humble hen, a pussy cat, a nanny goat, two sparrows, and some bears. Last three most difficult. M-D.
Sonata No.1 Op.44 1943 (CF). Lento—Allegro; Andantino; Allegro molto. Essentially non-nationalistic; contains consistent polytonality. M-D.
Sonata No.3 Op.71 1950 (EAM) 30pp. Allegro: syncopation and shifting accents. Second movement: rhythmic groups do not correspond with the bar lines, i.e., left hand is in 3/4 while right hand is in 3/8 all superimposed on a 5/4 meter. Third movement: straightforward rondo in 3/4. M-D.
Sonata No.4 Op.72 1950 (Ric). In 3 movements written to be played without pause. Expanded tonal idiom with various meter, texture, and tempi changes. Large span required. M-D.
6 Fables (PIC). Attractive, descriptive. M-D.
Tres Danzas (PIC). En Estilo de Zamba. En Estilo de Vidalita. En Estilo de Gato: most difficult. Popular Argentinian style, colored by polytonal treatment. M-D.

Corey Field (1956–   ) USA
Music publisher and composer Corey Field was born in Los Angeles. He studied at the University of California at Santa Barbara; the Aspen Music School; the University of Edinburgh, Scotland; and the Univeristy of York, England, where he received a doctorate in 1983. His compositions have been performed and broadcast throughout the world, and his writings on music have been published in international journals and magazines.
The Bright Shape of Sleep (Helicon 1989) 3pp., 5 min. This little nocturne uses an extended range, half pedals, a quiet dynamic range, and large skips. At-

mospheric, haunting quality. Large span required. "The title comes from a passage in William Faulkner's novel *The Sound and the Fury*. It describes a fireplace which lulls one of the characters to sleep" (from a letter to the author, June 15, 1995). M-D.

John Field (1782–1837) Ireland

John Field opened a completely original path in his piano writing. He dedicated his Op.1 (three piano sonatas) to his famous teacher, Muzio Clementi, but the nocturnes, not the sonatas, established Field's reputation as a composer. These nocturnes, with ornate melodies accompanied by widely spaced left hand chords, were written between 1814 and 1835 and make a fine introduction to the Chopin nocturnes. Liszt edited Field's nocturnes and wrote a highly appreciative fore- word, which was published in 1859. Both the GS and Augener editions still retain this preface. A complete edition of the piano works is being published by Boc- caccini & Spada in Rome, Italy.

Complete Works for Piano Solo 1795–1815. In collection *The London Pianoforte School 1770–1860*, Vols. 12 and 13 (Garland). See below, "Anthologies and Collections."

18 Nocturnes (Liszt—GS; CFP; Ric; Augener). E♭, c, A♭, A, B♭, F, C (Rêverie-Nocturne), A, E♭, e, E♭, G, d (Song without words), C, C, F, E (Grande Pas- torale), E (Nocturne caractéristique "Noontide").

Published separately: No.5 (GS; Century). No.10 (Willis). No.12 in an- thology *Romanticism in Music*, 85–86. No.18 (APS).

9 Nocturnes (K).

7 Nocturnes (PWM).

Nocturne No.1 E♭: Simple flowing melody in right hand over broken-chord figu- ration in left hand. Int. to M-D.

Nocturne No.4 A. One of the best nocturnes. Wide emotional range and more harmonic and melodic interest than most of the others. M-D.

Nocturne No.5 B♭. Short, most popular of the nocturnes, exciting contrasting chordal passages. Int. to M-D.

Nocturne No.7 A. Thematic material is beautifully varied; simple harmonies. M-D. See: Nicholas Temperley, "John Field and the First Nocturne," M&L, 56 (July–October 1975):335–40.

Nocturne No. 8 e. Reminiscent of first movement of Beethoven's "Moonlight So- nata." Int. to M-D.

Come Again, Come Again ca. 1832 (Boccaccini & Spada 1994) 11pp. An Intro- duction and Rondo on Jonathan Blewitt's (1780–1853) well-known cava- tina "Come Again." Opening Adagio (nocturne style) followed by a cen- tral Allegretto, improvisatory; abbreviated return of opening section. M-D.

Rondo A♭ (Boccaccini & Spada 1994) 14pp. An arrangement by Field of a Rondo for piano and string quartet that was published in St. Petersburg in 1813 or 1814. A brief waltz concludes the work. Interesting key changes. M-D.

Rondo E♭ (Bülow—GS). Larger form, lively, contrasting sections. M-D.

Fantasy G on "Ah! Quel dommage" 1805 (Boccaccini & Spada 1994) 13pp. The aria is from Boildieu's opera *Calife de Bagdad*. One of Field's finest works; cantabile lines, Romantic harmonies, unique form. M-D.

Fantasia on "Guardami un poco dal capo al piede" 1795 (Spada—Boccaccini & Spada 1994) 16pp. Aria from the opera *La scuola de maritati* by Vincente Martin y Solar (1754–1806). An early Field work that displays ornate pianism and cantabile style. Field's variants and corrections are listed separately, with suggested cuts. M-D.

3 Sonatas Op.1 1801 (Kite—S&B R900). E♭, A, c. Written in the style of Clementi, to whom they are dedicated. All are in two movements, mainly a fast first movement and a rondo second movement, with no slow movements or key contrasts. No.1 is the best, with fresh melodies, surprising harmonies, compact and fluent writing. M-D.

Sonata B 1812 (Br&H). Moderato: evokes the nocturne in form. Rondo: ingratiating. No masterpiece but shows more maturity than Op.1. M-D.

4 Sonatas (Langley, H.-M. Theopold—Henle 338 1983) 63pp. Includes the three Sonatas of Op.1 and Sonata B. All belong to Field's earlier years.

Chanson Russe variée (Variations d) ca. 1818 (Boccaccini & Spada 1992) 6pp. Delightful dancelike theme and seven contrasting variations. Glittering figuration. M-D.

Variations in A minor on the song "Vive Henry Quatre" 1814 (Boccaccini & Spada 1994) 4pp. Five contrasting variations, expressive. One of Field's finest sets of variations. M-D.

Selected Piano Works (Branson—CF 05051 1979) 40pp. Includes: Sehnsüchts-Walzer; Nocturne (Romance); Nocturne "The Troubadour"; Sonata No.4, first movement, Moderato cantabile; Air du Bon Roi Henri IV Varié; March Triomphale; Exercises Nos.1, 2; Andante (Andante Inédit). The last three pieces are published for the first time in the West. Int. to M-D.

See: W. H. Grattan Flood, *John Field of Dublin, the Inventor of the Nocturne: A Brief Memoir* (Dublin: M. Lester, 1921).

The International Piano Library Bulletin 2 (September 1968), special issue devoted entirely to Field. Contains: David Doscher, "John Field, The Pianoforte's First Modern Composer," "Life of John Field," "The Nocturne," "4 Unpublished Manuscripts," "Ferruccio Busoni on John Field." Franz Liszt on John Field, Robert Schumann on John Field, "A Field Discography."

Robin Langley, "John Field and the Genesis of a Style," MT, 1668 (February 1982):92–93, 95–99.

Jack W. Thames, "John Field: The Nearly Forgotten Irishman," AMT, 31 (September–October 1981):34–37.

Alan Tyson, "John Field's Earliest Compositions," ML, 47 (July 1966):239–48.

Irving Fine (1914–1962) USA

Lullaby for a Baby Panda (GS). Vague key center. Easy.

Victory March of the Elephants (GS). Modal. Easy.

Music for Piano 1947 (GS 1985). Prelude; Waltz-Gavotte; Variations; Interlude—Finale. Stravinsky oriented. M-D.

Hommage à Mozart 1957 (GS) 2pp. Theme, three variations, and coda; neoclassic. Int.

Vivian Fine (1913–2000) USA

Linear writing and harmonic dissonance are important characteristics of Fine's style.

Suite E♭ 1940 (ACA). Prelude: lyric. S: stately. Gavotte: delicate. Air: hushed. G: short, lively. Baroque inspired. M-D.

Four Polyphonic Pieces 1931–32 (CFE) 11pp. 7 min. Moderato; Non allegro, intensivo (canon); Scherzando; Vivace. Atonal; tight rhythmic structure. Great emotional intensity expressed with an intellectualized technique. D.

Sinfonia and Fugato 1952 (LG) 6 min. In collection *New Music for the Piano.* M-D.

Children's Suite 1938 (CFE) 5½ min. Seven short pieces in freely tonal style. Int. No.2, "The Small Sad Sparrow," is in collection *American Composers of Today* (EBM).

Five Preludes 1939–41 (CFE) 4½ min. Changing meters, complex rhythms. Nos. 4 and 5 are virtuosic and toccata-like. D.

Chaconne 1947 (CFE) 15 min. 15 variations based on a serial ground bass. No barlines or meters. D.

Momenti 1978 (Margun/Gunmar 1983). Inspired by the *Moments Musicaux* of Schubert. Atonal, dissonant. D.

Double Variations 1982 (CFE). Two themes, complex rhythms, exploits entire range of keyboard, atonal. D.

Toccatas and Arias 1987 (CFE) 12 min. Three vigorous toccatas contrasted with two lyric arias. M-D to D.

See: Leslie Jones, "The Solo Music of Vivian Fine," diss., University of Cincinnati, 1994, 299 pp.

———. "Seventy Years of Composing: An Interview with Vivian Fine," *Contemporary Music Review*, 16/1, 2 (January 1997). (The author is indebted to Leslie Jones for her assistance with this section.)

Ross Lee Finney (1906–1997) USA

Finney's earlier works had their roots in our American heritage, but during the 1950s his tonal language became more chromatic and dissonant. More recently serial technique has interested Finney. His sonatas and smaller sets of pieces are a notable contribution to American piano literature.

Sonata No.1 d (NME, Oct. 1937). Adagio Cantabile, Allegro; Aria; Toccata. Composed in 1933, this sonata shows great clarity both in texture and form. Obvious in the entire work is the composer's preference for unison and octave writing. The Toccata is in a perpetual motion style but is interrupted by a short lyric section. M-D.

Fantasy (Bo&H 1939). This is, in reality, the second sonata and although written in a number of sections it gives the impression of a large three-movement work. Numerous homophonic textures are present, including arpeggi figuration, agitated unison-writing, syncopated chords, singing melodic lines supported by broken figuration. Fast repeated notes characterize the toccata-like finale with harmonics required in the final bars. D.

Sonata No.3 E (Valley Music Press 1942). Allegro giusto; Lento; Prestissimo. A rhythmic motive in tonic-dominant relationship generates the first movement. Scale passages are used extensively, especially in the coda. Contrasted melodies in chorale style make up the second movement. Fast repeated-note motive in 7/8 generates the final movement and brings it to a stunning climax. D.

Sonata No.4 E (Mer 1945). Hymn; Invention; Nocturne; Toccata; Hymn. Subtitled "Christmastime 1945," this is one of the few pieces that came into existence during the Second World War. Varied pianistic treatment in this compact piece: chorale-like writing, imitation, double-note passage work, octave playing. D.

Nostalgic Waltzes (Mer 1947). Chattery; Intimate; Capricious; Conversational; Boisterous. Although inspired by the Chopin Mazurkas, they provide a clever commentary on the Romantic waltz. Picturesque directions are used as well as change of mode, ostinato, and some brilliant passagework. A delightful and rewarding set. M-D.

See: Robert Dumm, "Performer's Analysis: A Lesson on the first Nostalgic Waltz by Ross Lee Finney," *Clavier*, VI/5 (1967):21; includes score.

Inventions (CFP 1971). A collection of 24 pieces where "the name of the pieces rarely gives any clue as to the game that is being played with the notes." Most of the pieces involve the chromatic scale. A few use 12-tone techniques. These works wear well with both children and adults. Int.

Sonata No.5 (CFP 1961). Entitled "Sonata quasi una Fantasia," this is Finney's major piano contribution in serial technique. Even so, tonality is never abandoned, and a tremendous gamut of sounds, register, and dynamics is exposed. Virile and dramatic writing in all three movements. The most involved of the sonatas. D.

Games (CFP 1969). Finney declared that the object of this collection "is to introduce children to the entire sonority and articulation of the piano and to the types of notation that contemporary composers use." These 32 short pieces assume "that the child can reach the two extremes of the piano keyboard, and that he can reach the pedal." Improvisation is encouraged; unconventional notation. Easy to Int.

Medley (Campfire on the Ice) (Alfred 10114). In collection *Twelve by Eleven*. Finney has dipped into American folk tunes for this piece ("Red River Valley" and "Dinah, Won't You Blow Your Horn?"). Develops naturally. Charm of sheer sound is enhanced with a harmonic translucency. Strong tonal functions support this brightly colored piece. Int.

Variations on a Theme by Alban Berg 1952 (J. Kirkpatrick—CFP 1977) 12pp. 8 min. Slow chromatic theme (the opening theme of Berg's *Violin Concerto*) followed by 7 variations. Freely tonal around g, strong pianistic figurations, *pp* closing. M-D.

Youth's Companion 1981 (CFP 66446) 14pp. Hawk over the Prairie. Pasque-flowers. Jack Rabbitt: clear tonal patterns; dizzy dashes, sudden leaps, and frozen pauses. The Town Dump. Riddle Song: familiar folk tune with tonal accompaniment based on a predetermined hexachord. Short pieces based on groupings of six tones, which are later inverted from a new interval to produce a 12-tone row. "The surface of these little pieces reflect the memory of my childhood in North Dakota" (from the preface). Int.
See: *Clavier*, 20 (September 1981):37–38 for a discussion of "Jack Rabbitt" with the music.

Narrative in Retrospect 1983 (CFP 66982) 8 min. Terse, intense, dissonant, tightly organized, one movement. D.

Narrative in Argument 1989 (CFP 67230) 8 min. One movement, many tempo changes; illustrates the use of hexachords. D.

See: Maurice Hinson, "The Solo Keyboard Works of Ross Lee Finney," AMT, 20 (June–July 1971):16–18, 40.

Michael Finnissy (1946–   ) Great Britain

Finnissy studied at the Royal College of Music, London, and with Roman Vlad in Italy. He has held various academic posts; presently he is a Research Fellow at the University of Sussex and teaches at the Royal Academy of Music, London. He is a much-respected pianist, and has commissioned and performed works by several contemporary British composers. Finnissy is writing an enormous work, *The History of Photography,* around 4 hours long, and divided into 5 books and numerous chapters.

Song 9 1968 (International Music Co., Ltd. 16 Mortimer St., London W1N 8BU England) 8pp. Terribly involved writing with notes flying all over the staff. Only for the most adventuresome pianist, with a real flair for the avant-garde. D.

All.Fall.Down. 1977 (UE 16192) 15pp. Widely spread over keyboard, proportional rhythmic relationships, carefully pedaled, wide dynamic range, virtuosic. This writer doubts anyone could play this work, except for the composer. D.

Jazz 1976 (UE 16191) 11pp. Proportional rhythmic relationships, clusters, widely spread over keyboard, strong syncopation, tempo changes, *ppp* to *ffffff,* virtuosic. D.

Collected Shorter Piano Pieces Vol. 1 (OUP 1991). Some pieces written between 1957 and 1989. Mazurka Op.142/2; Two Pasodobles; Autumnal; Freightrain Bruise; Kemp's Morris. Short but; GFH; BS; Taja; Lylyly li; Pimmel; 3 Transcriptions of Strauss waltzes. Many of Finnissy's concerns in his major works are found in these smaller works. D.

Reels 1980–81 (UMP 1984) 15pp. Six short pieces. All use proportional rhythmic relationships; complex writing produces complex sounds; serial influences. Facsimile of ms. D.

Wee saw footprints (OUP 1993) 32pp. "These pieces are for children, to play or
to listen to—most of them are easily within a child's technical grasp, even
if the rhythms are sometimes unusual. I did not write them as 'teaching
material,' but as somewhat simplified versions of my usual compositional
preoccupations" (from the score). Nine short untitled pieces followed by
an appendix—"of stops on the journey which led to the writings of *Wee
saw footprints*. The appendix includes 4 pieces for beginners and 5 pieces
from my own youth (aged seven to twelve)" (from the score). The composer's "children" must be very precocious. Int. to M-D.
English Country Tunes 1977 (UMP 1986) 63pp. Green Meadows; Midsummer
Morn; I'll Give my Love a Garland; May and December; Lies and Marvels;
The Seeds of Love; My Bonny Boy; Come Beat the Drums and Sound the
Fifes. Outrageous passages spread all over the keyboard; the original tunes
are so atomized they are not recognizible. Transcendentally difficult. D.

Joseph-Hector Fiocco (1703–1741) Belgium (Flemish)
Fiocco was born in Brussels of an Italian family and worked in both Antwerp,
where he was director of music at the Cathedral, and his home city. François
Couperin was a strong influence on Fiocco's keyboard music.
Eight Keyboard Pieces (E. Barsham—ABRSM 1988) 19pp. From Fiocco's two
harpsichord suites, Op.1: No.1 in G with movements also in e and g; No.2
in D with movements also in d. La Villageoise; Andante; L'Italiene; La
Musette; La Légère; L'Angloise; Allegro; Gigue. Some of the ornaments
"could be omitted if desired in order to preserve reasonable tempo" (edi-
tor). *Notes inégales* might be observed in some of the movements. Int.
to M-D.
Pièces légères pour clavecin (Schott Frères). Easy to Int.
Werken voor Clavecimbel (ca. 1730) (BB). Facsimile edition.
Werken voor Clavecimbel (J. Watelet—De Ring). Vol.III in *Monumenta Musicae
Belgicae*. Suite I: L'Angloise; L'Armonieuse; La Plaintive; La Villageoise;
Les Promenades; L'Inconstante; L'Italienne; La Françoise; Adagio; An-
dante; Vivace. Suite II: Allemande; La Légère; G; S; L'Inquiète; Gavotte; M;
Les Sauterelles; L'Agitée; Les Zéphirs; La Musette; La Fringante. François
Couperin appears to be the main inspiration for the format of these suites.
Excellent craftsmanship. Int. to M-D.

Edwin Fischer (1886–1960) Switzerland
Sonatine C (Ries & Erler 1958) 9pp. Three movements. Classic style, efficient
fingering, clever, attractive. Int.

Johann Kaspar Ferdinand Fischer (1665–1746) Germany
Fischer was one of the important predecessors of J. S. Bach. His music shows
French influence, and his interest in the suite must be noted. His *Complete Works
for Keyboard* (clavier and organ) was published in 1901 by Br&H and was re-

printed in 1965 by BB. Selections of his works can be found in *Old Masters* (Niemann—K), *The Art of the Suite* (Y. Pessl—EBM), and *Selected Keyboard Pieces*
(Döflein—Schott), including Partitas in D and C and Preludes and Fugues.

Musicalisches Blumen-Büschlein 1698. Selections (L. J. Beer—HV). 8 suites, each
     preceded by a Prelude (among the earliest to do so), including A, C, S, Ga-
     votte, M, Gigues, Ballet, Canaries, Passepied, Passacaille, B, Branle, Ame-
     ner, Chaconne, Plainte.

Notenbüchlein (Notebook) (F. Ludwig—Schott). Includes 17 short pieces, among
     them Menuetts, Bourrées, Gavottes, Gigue, Marche, Sarabande.

Musikalischer Parnassus 1738 (Schott). 9 suites, each named after one of the
     Muses. Opening movements are titled Praeludium, Overture, Tastada, Toc-
     cata, Toccatina, Harpeggio. Usual dance movements plus Ballet anglois,
     Air anglois, and Rigaudon.

Ariadne Musica 1702 (Schott; D. Townsend—Sam Fox). A collection of 20 short
     preludes and fugues in as many different keys, a forerunner of the *Well-
     Tempered Clavier*. Also includes 5 short ricercari for different festivals of
     the church year, based on chorales.

Musikalischer Blumenstrauss 1733 (Schott). This "musical nosegay" contains 8
     small suites, each containing a prelude, 8 fugues, and a finale. Fischer in-
     cluded a table of ornaments in this collection. Intended for the organ.

See: Vivian Chiu, "What Bach Borrowed from Johann Kasper Ferdinand Fis-
     cher," *Clavier*, 33/8 (October 1994):28–30, 32.

     Anita H. Plotinsky, "The Keyboard Music of Johann Kaspar Ferdinand
     Fischer," Ph.D. diss., City University of New York, 1978, 221pp.

Jerzy Fitelberg (1903–1951) Poland

Sonate No.1 (ESC). One movement. Free tonal writing, toccata-like. Staccato re-
     peated chords, fast broken octaves, and sevenths require an advanced tech-
     nique. M-D to D.

Nicolas Flagello (1928–1994) USA

Piano Sonata (Gen 1962) 38pp. Andante con moto e rubato. Rubato quasi reci-
     tativo: flexible tempo, large gestures. Allegro Vivace quanto possibile: per-
     petual motion, advanced pianism required. M-D to D.

Episodes (BMC). March; Lullaby; Pulcinella. Int.

Prelude, Ostinato and Fugue 1960 (Gen). Organ-like Prelude over pedal points.
     Homophonic textures appear in the Fugue. Brilliant figuration. M-D.

3 Dances (BMC 1945). Abstract Dance: motoric rhythms. Ceremonial Dance:
     melodic. Tarantella: lively. Ostinato figures. Int. to M-D.

Petite Pastels (Gen). 7 drawings for young pianists. Int.

William Flanagan (1926–1969) USA

Sonata for Piano (PIC 1950) 12pp. 12 min. 3 movements, the first two movements
     are linked "attacca." Open harmonic texture; varying moods with abrupt

dynamic and metric changes. Fluctuating tonal centers. Technical and interpretative problems. M-D.

Robert Fleming (1921–1976) Canada

Sonatina (OUP 1941) 4 min. First movement: makes much use of chordal triplets, chromaticism for coloration, and a free lyricism. Second movement: exploits constant eighth-note figuration within clearly flowing harmonies. Pleasant writing. M-D.

Bag-o-Tricks (Waterloo 1968) 9pp. Four pieces for young pianists. Short, contrasting, MC. Int.

Toccatina (Waterloo 1968) 3pp. Brisk and rhythmic; changing meters. Two-line texture until end, where chords in left hand reinforce sonorities. Freely tonal around C. Prestissimo closing. Int.

Carlisle Floyd (1926–   ) USA

Sonata (Bo&H 1958). Three movements. Tonal, clever pianistic figuration with contrapuntal texture, brilliant closing. Large-scale. Demands virtuosity. D.

Episodes (Bo&H). 2 vols. 15 pieces, short and interesting. Int.

George Flynn (1937–   ) USA

Flynn studied at Columbia University with Vladimir Ussachevsky, Jack Beeson, Chou Wen-Chung, and Otto Luening. Since 1977 he has chaired the Composition Department at De Paul University's School of Music, Chicago.

American Icon 1988 (Sikesdi Press) 47pp. 30 min. Treats America as monument or symbol. "Juxtaposes a small number of sonorities and textures to create a rough and volatile fabric of explanatory and unconventional piano sounds against a predominately collage-like form" (from the program notes). D.

Three Preludes 1967, 1981, 1991 (Sikesdi Press) 16pp. 1. Thick textures, chromatic. 2. Minimalist influence noted. 3. Clusters, body trills (very rapid whole-body movement). A "Bruce Lee" piece! (Quoted from a letter to the author from Kenneth Derus, April 1, 1996.) M-D to D.

Toward the Light 1980, 1987, 1991 (Imprimis Music 1995) 21pp. 13 min. Begins "in the piano's middle register and eventually expands to the piano's registral extremes. Its title acknowledges Scriabin's *Vers la flamme*" (from the score). D.

Salvage 1993 (Imprimis Music 1996) 50pp., ca. 30 min. The third and last of a series of piano solos (*Kanal, Wound, Salvage*). "These works may be performed separately or as a single 90-minute work, titled *Trinity*. Although many of the pitch groupings, aggregates and textures established and revisited in *Kanal* (1976) and *Wound* (1968) reappeared in *Salvage*, the latter ultimately seeks to resolve the violent poetics of the earlier works" (from the score). Virtuosity required. D.

Derus Simples 1995 (Imprimis Music) 80pp., 45 min. Influenced by the writings of Kenneth Derus and the music of Kaikhosru Sorabji. This work "grows out of, embellishes, extends and eventually returns to a 'simple' (in this case a tritone), and exploits textual, gestural and formal growth and decline, in a variety of circumstances, within a simple and coherent, yet internally complex shape" (from the score). Enormously involved writing, virtuosic treatment. D.

Andor Foldes (1913–1992) USA, born Hungary

Foldes was an outstanding pianist. He composed a number of pedagogic pieces published by Century Music Publishing Co.

2 Miniatures (CF). No.1: folklike, thin textures, bitonal. No.2: more melodic. Accidentals are plentiful. Require good finger technique. Int. to M-D.

Four Short Pieces (EV). Bear Dance; Hommage à Robert Schumann; Simple Story; Toy Soldiers' Parade. Int.

Jacqueline Fontyn (1930–1987) Belgium

Ballade (CeBeDeM 1963) 21pp. 6½ min. Required piece for the Concours International Reine Elisabeth 1964. Rhapsodic, freely tonal; virtuoso technique required. D.

Capriccio (CeBeDeM 1954) 12pp. 4½ min. Chromatic, expressionistic, chords in alternating hands, varied figuration. D.

Mosaici (Metropolis 1964) 16pp. 10 min. Eight short contrasting pieces that may be performed in 13 different orders (listed in the score). Pointillistic, expressionistic, large gestures, dissonant. D.

Aura 1982 (PIC) 7pp. Based on Brahms Intermezzo Op.119/1. Begins with the opening notes of the Intermezzo, heard in new registers. At the close the last line of music contains the international spelling of "Brahms": B (the German B♭)–Re–A–H (the German B♮)–Mi S (= es, E♭), followed by Fontyn's initials: G (=J)–F. The final chord is the exact end of the Intermezzo. Includes an unmeasured section and performance notes. Atonal idiom. D.

Antoine Forqueray (1671–1745) France

One of a family of musicians, Antoine Forqueray was violist to Louis XIV. These are his viol pieces, skillfully transcribed for the harpsichord by his son Jean-Baptiste (1699–1782), who has added to the edition three pieces of his own.

Pièces de clavecin (Tilney—Heugel). 22 pieces arranged in 5 suites. Preface and performance suggestions in French, English, and German. Colorful titles. Int. to M-D.

John Väinö Forsman (1924–   ) Denmark, born Finland

Sonata No.1 Op.3 (WH 1950) 16pp. Adagio espressivo; Presto scherzando (with a Trio: Andante cantabile); Allegro con fuoco. Forsman mentions the lack of phrasing in this sonata. He contends that its absence gives the performer more freedom to decide his own. M-D.

5 Improvisations Op.6/3 (WH 1950). This suite is reminiscent of Poulenc's *Mouvements Perpetuels*. M-D.

Piano Ideas (Suite No.1) Op.4 (WH 1949) 9pp. Preludio; Scherzo; Intermezzo;
Polka; Humoresque; Andantino; Burlesca; Impressionisme; Pastorale; Fan-
tasia. Neoclassic style. A usable grouping might be; Intermezzo, Scherzo,
Impressionisme, Humoresque. Int. to M-D.

Wolfgang Fortner (1907–1987) Germany

Kammer-musik 1944 (Schott). Praeludium; Passacaglia; Fuga a 3; Lied; Interludium; Sonata à la Gigue. Neo-Baroque style. M-D.

Sieben Elegien für Klavier 1950 (Schott). Neo-Baroque style combined with 12-
tone technique. All 7 pieces are based on the same row. M-D.

Epigramme 1964 (Schott). Mature serial writing utilizing several contrapuntal
techniques. M-D.

Lukas Foss (1922–   ) USA, born Germany

Foss began writing in a conservative neoclassic style, then rigid serialism, and
has moved to experimenting with electronic, repetitive minimalism, post-modern
eclecticism, as well as avant-garde techniques.

Four 2-Part Inventions 1938 (CF). Imaginative rhythms and melodies. To be performed as a group. Lengthy. M-D.

Grotesque Dance 1938 (CF). A tongue-in-cheek Andante is inserted between the
lively outer sections. Strong rhythms. M-D.

Also available in *51 Piano Pieces from the Modern Repertoire* (GS 1940).

Fantasy Rondo 1944 (CF). Jazz, half-moon symbol used over appropriate eighth
notes to designate "swing" passages, driving rhythms, quartal harmonies,
polytonal, canons. Will tempt the "foot tappers." M-D to D.

Passacaglia 1940 (GS). A 4-bar bass, 22 variations; builds to sonorous climax,
quiet ending. M-D.

Solo 1981 (CF) 32pp. 15 min. Although a 12-note row is featured and undergoes
constant development, this is not truly a serial work. Toward the end the
performer sings as he plays. While the actual material is concluded at one
point on the final page, it is followed by a short passage representing the
"piano playing on without its master or the phonograph needle returning
to the opening automatically"—an indication of the work's fundamentally
mechanical nature. Has the drive of a frenetic toccata with its intensity under wraps. M-D to D.

Stephen C. Foster (1826–1864) USA

Although best known for his immortal songs, Foster also composed a few piano
pieces. They evoke a nostalgia and crinoline charm of a youthful United States.
These American "primitives" not only have a musical-historical interest but also
provide pianists with a pleasurable experience.

Complete Piano Music (E. List—GS 3455 1984) 34pp. The Tioga Waltz (1841): in-

nocent and charming. Soirée Polka: gentle and pleasant; versions for piano solo, and for piano duet. The Village Bells: a lively polka. The Holliday Schottisch: a round dance, slower than the polka. Santa Anna's Retreat from Buena Vista: written in commemoration of an important victory in the Mexican War (1846–47); fast march in quick-step. Old Folks at Home (Theme and variations): theme and 3 variations—Polka, Quadrille, and Hornpipe. The Old Folks Quadrilles: presents 5 of Foster's tunes in simplified versions, including Old Folks at Home; Oh! Boys, Carry Me Long; Nelly Bly; Farewell, My Lilly Dear; Cane Brake Jig. Int. to M-D.
See: Joseph Smith, "A Stephen Foster Curiosity," KC (March–April 1995): 10, 59. Discusses the piano variations on "Old Folks at Home."

Wolfgang Fraenkel (1897–1983) Austria
Variations and Fantasies on a Theme by Schönberg Op.19/3 (UE 1954) 23pp. 15 min. 10 variations and 3 fantasies. First fantasie is a fugue while the last one is a passacaglia. Chromatic, involved. D.

Antonio Fragoso (1897–1918) Portugal
Composicies para Piano (Valentim de Carvalho). Vol.1, 27pp. Contains: Petite Suite: Preludio; Berceuse; Dance. 7 Preludios. Some of the most interesting "period" piano music written in Portugal. Int. to M-D.
Composicies para Piano, Vol.2 (Valentim de Carvalho). 21pp. 2 Noturnos. Preludio. Pensées Extatiques (2 short character pieces). M-D.
Sonata em Mi Menor (Valentim de Carvalho 1971) 28pp. Muito agitado; Calmo e cantando com doçura. Post-Romantic techniques, dashing figurations. M-D.
Cancão e dança Portuguesas (Valentim de Carvalho 1912) 5pp. Contrasting, MC, and colorful. M-D.
Três Peças do Seculo XVIII (Valentim de Carvalho) 3pp. Minueto; Aria; Gavotte. Int.

Jean Françaix (1912–1997) France
Françaix limited himself to a small but effective harmonic vocabulary. His shorter works are his most effective.
Scherzo 1932 (Schott) 3pp. A delectable featherweight staccato etude; mainly exploits upper register of keyboard. Thin textures. M-D.
See: Joseph Bloch, "A Lesson on Scherzo by Jean Françaix," KC, 12/6 (November–December 1992):44, 47. Includes music on pp. 29–31.
Danse de Trois Arlequins 1955 (EMT) 3 min. Salon style, chromatic, effective. M-D.
Sonata 1960 (Schott) 7½ min. Prélude; Elégie; Scherzo; Toccata. More like a suite than a sonata; abounds in dance rhythms. M-D.
Cinq Bis 1965 (Five Encores) (Schott) 10 min. To Entice the Audience; For Romantic Ladies; In Case of Success; In Case of Triumph; In Case of Delirium. Requires a big technique. M-D.
Six Grandes Marches dans le Style de Ier Empire 1957 (EMT). Marche Française;

Marche Autrichienne; Marche Polonaise; March du Sacre; Marche Russe; March Européenne. Witty, elegant, suite-like. M-D.

Si Versailles m'etait contre (Suite pour piano) 1954 (Editions Ray Ventura). Henry IV; Louis XIII; Monsieur de Montespan; La Voisin; Le Grand Trianon; Jeune fille; Ronde Louis XV (for 4 hands); Napoléon; Les Cent Marches. Technically easier and shorter than most of the other works. Int. to M-D.

Zehn Stücke für Kinder zum Spielen und Träumen 1975 (Schott 6665). Portrays 10 stages in the development of a boy, from The Newly Born Child (Easy) to The Emancipated Young Man (D).

Variations on the Name of Johannes Gutenberg 1982 (Schott) 10 min. 8 variations that show wit and ingenuity, colorful and entertaining. Above the final bars Françaix has written "Gutenberg se déclare satisfait de ses Variations!" M-D.

Cinq portraits de jeunes filles 1936 (Schott ED 2483) 13 min. Five character pieces. The Capricious One; The Tender One; The Pretentious One; The Pensive One; The Modern One. Charm personified. Int. to M-D.

The Françaix collection (Hinson—Schott 1993) 43pp. 17 pieces with introductions. 1. Newborn; 2. Baby; 3. Twins; 4. Lost; 5. Good Behavior; 6. Dreamy; 7. Free and Easy; 8. Playing Soldier; 9. Dancer; 10. Little Upstart; 11. Elegy; 12. Allegretto; 13. Andantino; 14. The Tender One; 15. Hommage à F. Chopin; 16. Hommage à M. Ravel; 17. In Case of Success. Refreshing and rewarding to play. Early to late Int. Nos. 6, 8 and 14 are in the collection *The Century of Invention* (EAMC 772).

Arnold Franchetti (1906–1993) USA, born Italy

Sonata I (Bongiovanni 1954) 12pp. Allegrissimo: SA. Lento e dolce: ABA, pastorale quality. Fuga a tre voci: not literally three voices; leads to a quasi cadenza. Mosso e dolce: rondo. M-D.

César Franck (1822–1890) France

Although he began his career as a concert pianist writing piano works of a showy nature, Franck soon turned to the organ and to composing for other instruments. Nearly 40 years passed before he wrote the few great piano works that still remain in the repertoire.

7 Traditional French Noëls (Werner—Curwen). Easy pedagogical pieces. Int.

18 Short Pieces (CFP). An excellent introduction to Franck's piano style. Nos.1 and 10 are more suited to the piano. Int.

46 Short Pieces for Piano (D. Agay—TP). Some charming unknown miniatures. Int.

Grand Caprice No.1 Op.5 (Lemoine). One of the early virtuoso works, bravura chord playing, cadenza, fast octaves, cantabile melody, brilliant closing. D.

Prélude, Chorale et Fugue 1884 (Henle; CFP; Cortot—EC; K; PWM; WH Schott; Zen-On). One of the greatest works for piano. It was originally conceived as a prelude and fugue in the style of J. S. Bach, but Franck felt that a transition between the two movements was necessary. The chorale gradually expanded to become the focal point of the work. The whole piece is largely constructed on a single melodic idea, different facets of which are modified and illustrated in the course of the three movements. Franck has used all the possibilities of expression inherent in late Romantic piano technique. Requires superb legato; the fugue, especially, needs a well-developed sense of voice delineation. D.

Prélude, Aria et Finale 1886–87 (Henle; CFP; Cortot—EC; WH; Schott; Zen-On; Hamelle, Bauer—BMC; MMP). A sonata in one movement that uses cyclic form and is predominantly chordal. Prélude: three distinct themes that reappear throughout in different forms. Aria: spiritual; leads to Finale: opens with a rhythmic and forceful theme whose momentum does not let up until the conclusion. Requires solid musicianship and fluent octave technique. M-D.

Prélude, Fuge et Variation Op.18 (Durand; WH). Effectively transcribed from the organ solo by Harold Bauer. Contains some of the best Franck characteristics, gently expressive. Easier than the two preceding works. M-D.

Fantaisie sur deux Airs Polonais Op.15. See below, "Anthologies and Collections," *Piano Music of the Parisian Virtuosos 1810–1860.*

Trois oeuvres de jeunesse pour le piano (Société liegeoise de musicologie 1990). Preface by José Qiutin. Reproduced from holographs. *Grande sonata* Op.10 (1835); *2e Fantaisie* Op.14 (1836); *Trois petits riens*, Op.16 (1846). 1 vol., various pagings. The young Franck shows a few signs of later greatness. Int. to M-D.

25 Short Pieces from L'Organiste (ABRSM). Varied selection from the larger work. Int.

Selected Piano Compositions (Vincent d'Indy—Dover) 138pp. This collection contains ten pieces, evenly divided between early germinal compositions and important late pieces. 3 early compositions (written at age 14); Eglogue Op.3; Premier Grand Caprice Op.5; Ballade Op.9; The Doll's Lament; Danse lente; Prelude, Chorale and Fugue; Prelude, Aria and Finale. Each work is analyzed by the editor in his Introduction. Int. to M-D.

Danse lente 1885 (Lemoine). Flowing syncopated accompaniment, ABA, sensitive miniature. Int.

See: Alfred Cortot, *French Piano Music* (New York: Da Capo Press, 1977), pp. 37–108.

Johan Franco (1908–   ) USA

3 Temple Dances (ACA 1948) 9 min. Allegro con spirito: pentatonic influence, imitation, bitonal, thin textures. Andante: chorale-like, preference for major sevenths; colorful; careful legato needed. Allegretto molto gracioso: rondo, terse dissonance, most dance-like of group. Imitation, interesting chord progressions, abundance of accidentals. M-D.

Partita No.6 (ACA 1952). Four movements. "Blues" influence, contrasted movements, inspiration not consistent throughout, added-note technique used. First and last movements most effective. M-D.

3 Piano Sketches (TP 1954). Church Bells; Playing Tag; Barcarolle. Short pedagogic works. Int.

Toccata (OD) Short. Repeated accented notes. M-D.

Andrew Frank (1946–   ) USA

3 Preludes 1981 (Boelke-Bomart) 11pp. Dolce, ma ansioso: recitative-like, chromatic, rhythmic proportional relationships. "From the Floating World": dreamlike, mixture of Impressionistic and expressionistic elements. Molto lirico: changing meters and textures, *ppp* ending. M-D to D.

Jane Frasier (1951–   ) USA

Festivous Sonata 1980 (Arsis Press 180) 16pp. 14½ min. Waltz; Hymne; Dance. Full of rhythmic swing and jagged harmonies. Bitonal, quartal harmonies, distinct style, logical structure. D.

Isadore Freed (1900–1960) USA

Sonorités Rythmiques (Sal 1931). Six studies. Rhythmic problems, contrasting sonorities, chromatic. M-D.

Une Fête fantasque (Sal). Colorful, Impressionistic. M-D.

Five Pieces 1928–1930 (ESC). Sophisticated writing, moderately long, varied. M-D.

Sonata (ESC 1933). Allegro non troppo e ardente: irregular meters. Andante sostenuto: open harmonies, big climax. Allegro e ben ritmato; shifting accents, repeated notes, octaves, quiet closing. D.

Pastorales (ESC). 8 small pieces for young people. Mild modern flavor. Int.

Intrada and Fugue (Axelrod). Sonorous opening, sensitive 3-voiced fugue, flowing. M-D.

Sonata No.1 (PIC 1954). 3 short movements, pleasant. M-D.

Toccatina (TP). Modal, harmonic fluctuation. Int.

Sonatina No.1 (PIC 1954). Three movements, dissonant, 12-tone. Int. to M-D.

Jane Freer (fl. 1770s) Great Britain

Freer was blind and was educated and raised by London's Foundling Hopital.

Six Sonatas for Piano and Harpsichord (Harbach—Vivace). Classic style; most are in three movements. Int. to M-D.

Frederico de Freitas (1902–1980) Portugal

The music of Freitas shows a combination of various styles and influences such as Romantic, Impressionistic, and Contemporary.

10 Bagatelas (Gulbenkian Foundation). Photograph of autograph. Short, varied, mixture of styles. M-D.

O livro do Maria Frederica (Sassetti 1960). A contemporary Portuguese "Album for the Young" with a variety of difficulty. 36 short pieces that explore contemporary idioms. Folk element present. Most pieces are a page in length. Int.

Ciranda (Schott 1944) 11pp. Extended rhapsodic poem. Varied moods and textures, large gestures. M-D.

Six Morceaux (WH 1950) 19pp. Varied collection of teaching pieces, superbly contrasted. No.6 "The Dance of the Gypsy Girl" is the most difficult. Portuguese folk elements shine through these more than interesting works. Int.

Ingenuidades (Sassetti 1960). A berceuse. Arpeggio accompanimental figuration, chromatic. Voicing of line is a problem. M-D.

Dança (A. Moraes) 2pp. Short, strong rhythms, attractive. M-D.

Luis de Freitas Branco (1890–1955) Portugal

15 Prelúdios (Sassetti 1961). Varied moods and difficulty, beautifully laid out for the piano, Impressionistic. Int. to M-D.

Sonatina (Sassetti) 5pp. Allegro moderato; Andante; Rondo: Allegretto. Charming intermediate writing in a mild neoclassic style. Rondo presents the most problems. Would make an excellent program "opener." M-D.

Girolamo Frescobaldi (1583–1643) Italy

Frescobaldi was the dominant figure in Italian keyboard music of the early seventeenth century and one of the boldest innovators in the history of keyboard music in general. A mixture of scholar and artist pervades his highly individual style. His keyboard works are mainly of three types: fugal pieces, toccatas, and variations. The fugal pieces are the ricercari and canzonas, capriccios, and versets. The toccatas, sectional and frequently virtuoso-like, have a pulsing restlessness about them due, in part, to the unstable harmonic relationships that characterize this pre-tonal music. Frescobaldi's Preface to the 1614 edition of the toccatas contains some remarkable and necessary instructions for performance.

Complete Keyboard Works (P. Pidoux—Br) Vol.I. Fantasie 1608, Canzoni alla Francese 1645. Vol.II. Capricci, Ricercari and Canzoni alla Francese 1626. Vol.III. Toccate, Partite, Balletti, Ciaconne e Passacaglie 1626. Vol.IV. Toccata Partite, etc. 1637. Vol.V. *Fiori Musicali* 1635.

Three Volumes of Keyboard Works (F. Germani—De Santis). Vol.I. 12 Toccatas from the first book of toccatas, 1614–16. Vol.II. 11 Toccatas from the second book of toccatas, 1627. Vol.III. *Fiori Musicali*, includes toccatas, kyrie, canzoni, capricci, ricercari in open score using the C clefs.

Partitas I, II (K).

First Book of Toccatas (Darbellay—SZ).

Second Book of Toccatas (Darbellay—SZ).

Toccatas (K).

Fiori Musicali (CFP). Mainly liturgical compositions. M-D.

25 Canzoni, Correnti and Balletti, 5 Partite, 16 Ricercari, Sette Toccate, Nove Toccate (F. Boghen—Ric) 6 vols. Heavily edited. The Partitas are sets of variations, some quite long. Cuts may be made as sanctioned by Frescobaldi in the Preface of 1614. A wealth of beautiful and unusual music awaits the inquiring student and performer.

15 Capricci (F. Boghen—Senart). Imitative contrapuntal works. M-D.

Other reprints are contained in *L'Arte Musicale in Italia*, III; TPA, IV and V; *Trésor des Pianistes*, II.

9 Toccatas. Monumenti di Musica Italiana (Mischiati, Scarpat, Tagliavini— Br&H). Series I, Vol.II (S. D. Libera 1962).

See: Willi Apel, "Neapolitan Links between Cabezon and Frescobaldi," MQ, 24 (October 1938):419–37.

Georges Friboulet (1910–   ) France

Gestes et sentiments ("Gestures and Feelings") (Lemoine 1972) 16pp. Album of 14 pieces. M-D.

Le Pré aux Loups ("Wolves' Meadow") (Lemoine 1975) 11pp. A Romantic and descriptive suite with the following miniature movements: Wolves' Meadow; The Squirrels; On the Road to the Val-au-Cesne; Strolling in the Henry IV Forest; The Beech Grove; On the Mall at Yvetot. Int. to M-D.

Nous (Lemoine). Suite of short contrasting pieces: Ourselves; Baroque; Phrase; Caprice; Me without You; Paris Morsang. M-D.

Peter Racine Fricker (1920–1990) Great Britain

Serial composition and jazz have both influenced Fricker's writing.

4 Impromptus Op.17 1950–52 (Schott). Original pianistic writing. Effective as a group or performed individually. M-D to D.

12 Studies Op.38 1962 (Schott) 23 min. Studies in piano texture. Each one concentrates on some device, e.g., mirror-chords, Toccata (minor seconds and fourths), cantabile for left-hand octaves. Free serialism. D.

Variations Op.31 1958 (Schott) 12½ min. The opening bars are really 5 thematic ideas, presented as one paragraph. Then a variation is based on each one, but now expanded. Var.5 becomes very extended as the pianistic climax of the work; it is followed by a serene postlude. M-D to D.

14 Aubades 1963 (Schott). Excellent introduction to contemporary techniques and textures. M-D.

4 Sonnets 1956 (Schott). 12-tone. Each Sonnet is based on one of the forms of the row. M-D.

Diversions (Fentone). Six strongly characterized pieces that require performance sophistication and subtleties. M-D.

Ignaz Friedman (1882–1948) Poland

Friedman was one of the twentieth century's greatest pianists. Many considered his playing of Chopin's mazurkas to be unequaled. He composed about 100 piano pieces of startling keyboard originality.

Passacaglia Op.44 1911 (Musica Obscura). An impressive large work, conceived on broad lines, suggests a thorough knowledge of harmonic resources and much originality in the treatment of a single theme. M-D to D.

Studies on a Theme of Paganini Op.47b 1913 (UE; Musica Obscura) 17pp. Theme is the 24th Caprice of Paganini; 17 variations with the last one con spirito, vivo. Numerous lyrical slow variations. In Brahms style. Pianistic individuality. M-D to D.

La Tendre Fanchon: Rondeau de F. Couperin (Musica Obscura) 6pp. Effective concert arrangement in excellent taste. M-D.

Viennese Dances on Motifs by Gärtner 1916–25 (UE 8585). G♭, G, D♭, F, A♭, C. Friedman availed himself of themes written by the prominent Austrian baritone Eduard Gärtner. My favorite is No.3. Dense textures, thoroughly charming. Richard Strauss is the dominating influence—post *Rosenkavalier*. M-D.

Johann Jakob Froberger (1616–1667) Germany

Froberger combined the warm harmony of his teacher Frescobaldi with French style and German melodic treatment. He is probably best known as the composer who solidified the suite arrangement of dances as A, C, S, G, although the G was not always last in this organization. The emotional range of his music is great. Both Händel and Bach greatly respected Froberger.

Complete Keyboard Works Vols.VIII, XIII, and XXI of DTOe, 1901—reprinted, Graz, 1960. Contains 25 toccatas, 8 fantasias, 6 canzoni, 18 capricci, 15 ricercari, and 30 suites. Int. to M-D.

Keyboard Works (H. Schott—Heugel LP 57 1979) Vol.I of *Oeuvres complètes*. Books of 1649, 1656, and 1658. Preface in French and English. Int. to M-D.

Suite "auf die Maÿerin" (Provincetown Bookshop Editions, 246 Commercial St., Provincetown, MA 02675). 6 variations, 2 dances, and a *double*, all based on a lovely springtime tune. Partita chromatica is the last variation. English and Italian influence. M-D.

See Anthologies and Collections: *Le Trésor des Pianistes*, Vol.III; *Klaviermusik des 17. und 18. Jahrhunderts*, Vol.I; *Old Masters; Keyboard Music of the Baroque and Rococo* (Georgii), Vol.I.

Herbert Fromm (1905–1995) USA, born Germany

Sonata 1978 (Transcontinental) 23pp. Based on a Sephardic hymn. Introduction and theme with variations; Slow; Fantasy fugue. Thin textures, changing meters; the last movement has much rhythmic vitality. M-D.

Gerhard Frommel (1906–   ) Germany

Sonata No.1 F (Schott 1955) 19pp. Allegro: exploits triplet figuration. Andante cantabile: ostinato-like. Allegro (quasi una grotesca): dramatic gestures add to a rousing climax. Unusual work, fantasy-like, engaging for performer and audience. M-D.

Sonata f♯ Op.6 (Süddeutscher Musikverlag 1942). Post-Romantic harmonies, linear. M-D.

Sonata No. 5 1951 (Süddeutscher Musikverlag 1996). Stravinsky influence. M-D.

Gunnar de Frumerie (1908–1987) Sweden
Frumerie studied in Paris with Cortot. His works have a Gallic flavor.
Circulus Quintus Op.62 (GM). 24 piano pieces. Int. to M-D.
Sonatina No.2 (GM 1950). 3 movements. 9½ min. Thin textures. Second movement is a theme with 4 variations. M-D.
Piano Suite No.2 (NMS 1936). Toccata; M; S; Rigaudon. M-D.
Piano Suite No.3 (NMS 1948). Introduction; Fuga; S; Gavotte; Musette; Tarantella. M-D to D.
Chaconne Op.8 1932 (WH; NMS) 8pp. Theme and 8 variations. Solemn, beautiful sonorities in heavy chromaticism. Heroic mood, abrupt ending. Many technical demands. M-D to D.

Robert Fuchs (1847–1927) Austria
Johannes Brahms admired the compositions of Fuchs.
Children's Pieces from Opp.32 and 47 (ABRSM 1986) 24pp. Morning Song; Heartache; Proud Horseman; Mother Tells a Story; Prayer; Smiles after Tears; A Great Mystery; Drizzling Rain, etc. Colorful, musical miniatures. Int.

Sandro Fuga (1906–1994) Italy
Altri 5 Studi (Another Five Studies) 1978–79 (Bocciccini & Spada 1991) 22pp. Each study focuses on specific pianistic problems. Neoclassic. M-D.
Sonata 1957 (Ric). Large-scale four-movement work in neoclassic style. M-D.
Sonatina 1936 (Ric). Allegro vivo: two themes well developed. Largo: sarabande, unusual harmonies, octotonic. Fughetta: four voices cleverly worked out. Int.
Toccata 1935 (Ric). Freely tonal around C, triplets juxtaposed against chords and melodies in varied patterns. M-D.
Variazioni Gioconde 1957 (Ric). Theme and 12 well-developed variations. Audience appeal. M-D.

Kazuo Fukushima (1930–   ) Japan
Suien (Ongaku-No-Tomo-Sha 1972) 16pp. 6½ min. The title refers to a hazy mist from waterfalls. Contains performance directions. Aleatoric, fast arpeggi with palm and fingers of right hand; harmonics; spatial notation. Avantgarde. M-D.

Anis Fuleihan (1900–1970) USA, born Cyprus
Fuleihan was strongly influenced by his recollections of and eventual research into Mediterranean music.
Cypriana (PIC). The Girl from Paphos: staccato dance alternating with a florid song accompanied with guitar-like effects. Syrtós: rhythmic dance. Kyrenía: slow melody accompanied with broken-chord figures. Serenade: habanera or tango style. Café Dancer: like a jota in fast 3/8, drum and guitar effects. Colorful pieces exploiting melodic and harmonic resources from the island of Cyprus. M-D.

Sonatina No.1 (MCA 1949). Three movements using open sonorities, modal scales, march in 5/4, folk melody. M-D.

Sonatina No.2 (MCA 1946). First movement: melody surrounded by flowing figuration. Slow movement: features two voices. Finale: energetic, quasi-fugal. Short. M-D.

Sonata No.1 (PIC 1940). Allegro con brio e energico. Molto moderato: lengthy theme with variations. Extended movements. Mature pianism required. D.

Sonata No.2 (PIC 1953). Allegro: driving first theme contrasted with lyric second theme. Moderato: parallel chords. Allegro marciale: martellato theme, brilliant cadenza, pianistic throughout. D.

Sonata No.3 (PIC 1971). Allegro: linear textures, clear sectional form; opening theme foreshadows transparent treatment for entire movement; tonal, modal, scalar, and chordal patterns. Andantino, semplice: simple melodic accompaniment; numerous meter changes; calm, modal setting. Presto: forward moving 6/8 meter; Andantino mid-section provides contrast; imitation and pandiatonic treatment frequently used; con fuoco conclusion M-D.

From the Aegean (PIC 1950) Serenade; Tango; Sicilienne; Greek Dance. Short dances with biting dissonances and shifting pulses. M-D.

Harvest Chant (PIC). Short, simple tune accompanied by bell-like harmonies. Int.

Fifteen Short Pieces (CF). Each is 1 or 2 pages long. Varied problems in linear writing: changing meters, octaves, double notes, etc. Int.

Five Tributes 1947 (PIC 1951). Prelude; M; Gavotte; Sicilienne; Capriccio. M-D.

Sonata No.4 (PIC 1951). Allegro moderato; Andantino mesto; leads directly to a contrapuntal Intermezzo. Allegro molto, ritmico (à la grecque): a driving syncopated finale. Large work. D.

Around the Clock (PIC 1964). 12 Preludes for young pianists, short. Int.

Sonata No.9 (PIC) Four movements, MC. M-D.

Sonata No.11 (Bo&H 1970). Allegro giusto; Allegro, molto ritmico; Andantino; Allegro frenetico, e molto ritmico. Varied figuration, freely chromatic, quartal writing used in second movement, driving rhythmic closing movement, octaves. M-D.

Sonata No.12 (Bo&H 1969). Allegro molto vivace: thin textures, homophonic. Andantino: lyric and expressive; large span required. Presto: driving, cadenza-like closing. M-D.

Sonata No.14 (Bo&H 1968). Allegro vivace; Tempo giusto, misurato, molto ritmico; Allegretto grazioso; Allegro vivace. Numerous tempo changes within the movements are skillfully carried out. Bravura sections, brilliant conclusion. M-D.

Five Very Short Pieces for Talented Young Bipeds (PIC). Int.

Ionian Pentagon (Bo&H 1970). Allegretto; Moderato; Molto vivace; Largamente; Allegro grazioso. Mainly thin textures, varied moods, tonal. Int.

Norman Fulton (1909–   ) Great Britain

Prelude, Elegy and Toccata (Lengnick 1955) 23pp. Freely tonal; accessible to the student with enough technique to handle it but who has not had much experience with MC music. M-D.

Wilhelm Furtwängler (1886–1954) Germany

Drei Klavierstücke 1902–03 (Amadeus 1991) 15pp. Three contrasting pieces, strong Beethoven influence, especially late Beethoven. M-D.

Johann Joseph Fux (1660–1741) Germany

Fux was a daring and vital composer who could write in a lyric and highly poetic style.

Selected Works for Keyboard Instruments (Friedrich Riedel—Nag 1972) 31pp. Includes a multi-movement Capriccio; 3 Partitas; 3 Menuets. Facsimile of an ornamentation table by Gottlieb Muffat is included. Int. to M-D.

Capriccio and Fugue K. V. 404 (I. Ahlgrimm—Dob). Excellent edition, fine preface. Editorial comment clearly distinguished from composer's markings. There are short movements after the fugue. M-D.

12 Minuets (Schenk—OBV). Int.

3 Pieces (Schenk—OBV). Ciacona; Harpeggio e Fuga; Aria passegiata. M-D.

Sonata No.4. See collection: *Anthology of Baroque Piano Music*. M-D.

See: Ludwig von Köchel, *J. J. Fux* (Vienna, 1872), with thematic catalogue of all his works.

G

Jenö Gaál (1906–   ) Hungary
Piano Sonata (ZV 1958). Three movements, FSF. A short-long rhythmic idea is
exploited in the first two movements. The third movement utilizes nineteenth-century pianistic techniques, including arpeggio accompaniment to
chordal melodies. Dramatic work. M-D.

Andrea Gabrieli (ca.1510–1586) Italy
Gabrieli's main contribution to keyboard music was a more idiomatic style free
of vocal traits.
Complete Keyboard Works (P. Pidoux—Br). Vol.I: Intonazioni. Vols.II–III: Ricercari, 1595, 1596. Vol.IV: Canzoni and Ricercari ariosi. Vol.V: Canzoni alla
Francese. The Intonazioni are liturgical preludes, usually from 12 to 16
bars, that begin chordally and gradually introduce passage-work in faster
motion. The Ricercari are contained in the two books; 7 are monothematic, and 12 polythematic. Other reprints are found in TPA, I. M-D.

Ossip Gabrilowitsch (1878–1936) Russia
Caprice-Burlesque Op.3/1 (Musica Obscura) 10pp. Short salon piece. Chordal,
octaves, lyric mid-section, brilliant. M-D.
Meditation; Intermezzo appassionato Op.9 (Roszavölgyi). His best-known works,
in the style of Chopin and Brahms, two masters of whose works Gabrilowitsch was a distinguished interpreter. M-D.

Niels W. Gade (1817–1890) Denmark
Although Gade was strongly influenced by Mendelssohn and Schumann, he re-
tained a distinct Scandinavian character, especially in his early works.
Aquarellen (Water Colors) Op.19 (GS; CFP; WH; K&S; ABRSM). 10 pieces,
Gade's most familiar set. A second set of 5 pieces, Op.57 appeared in 1881
(WH). Similar to the Mendelssohn "Songs without Words." M-D.
Sonata e Op.28 1840 rev. 1854 (Br&H 8104; MMP). Allegro con fuoco: strident
octaves lead to a sustained melody in the right hand with arpeggio figures
in the left hand, full rich chords. Andante: G, suave melody in right-hand
octaves. Allegretto: b, many broken octaves. Molto Allegro e appassionato:
lengthy, brilliant, many triplets for left hand. The inner movements have
the most interest. Liszt and Chopin influence. M-D.
4 Fantastic Pieces Op.41 1862 (K 9897; WH). In the Woods; Fairy Tale; Mignon;

At the Festival. Spontaneous and melodic, tinged with the simple beauty of folk songs. Int. to M-D.

The Children's Christmas Eve Op.36 (K 3458; GS; WH; ABRSM). 6 charming pieces. Int.

Three Pieces (K 9898) 55pp. Includes: Arabeske, Op.27: 4 short character pieces whose technical requirements are definitely pianistic; Schumann influence. Sonata e Op.28 (see discussion above). Volkstänze Op.31: 4 lively and somewhat virtuosic dances. M-D.

Hans Gál (1890–1988) Great Britain, born Austria

Sonate Op.28 (Simrock 1927). A large 4-movement work, with the second movement, Quasi menuetto, cast in an unusual form. Captivating. M-D.

24 Preludes (UE 1965). In all the major and minor keys, Romantic style. Each piece has at least one characteristic idea. Int. to M-D.

Drei Skizzen Op.7 (UE 1921). Short character pieces in Brahms idiom. Int.

24 Fugues Op.108 (Simrock 3182). Paired in major-minor keys in chromatic ascending order. Metronome marks included. Explores much inventiveness in form and shows variety in texture, construction, and sonority. M-D.

Blas Galindo-Dimas (1910–1993) Mexico

Cinco Preludios (Ediciones Mexicanas 1945). M-D.

Siete Piezas (Ediciones Mexicanas 1952). Both sets contain subtle influences of Indian folk music cast in a modal and linear idiom. Int. to M-D.

Raymond Gallois-Montbrun (1918–   ) France

Gallois-Montbrun is Director of the Paris Conservatoire.

Trois Pièces pour Piano (Leduc 1944). Prélude; Menuet; Danse. Neoclassic style. Menuet is in 5/4. M-D.

Noël Gallon (1891–1966) France

Sonatine (Leduc 1931) 20pp. A charming work, Fauré influence. M-D.

Ker an Diskouiz (Lemoine 1928). 6 pieces. See especially No.5 Escargots et Papillons. M-D.

Tout en Canon (Durand). 30 musical canons in all major and minor keys. Int. to M-D.

Baldassare Galuppi (1706–1785) Italy

The Venetian composer Galuppi, although primarily known for his "opere buffe," left approximately 90 keyboard sonatas. Some are in two and three movements, while a very few are in one, four, and five movements. Motivic development and *galant* melodic treatment characterize these works. "I." stands for Hedda Illy, who is bringing out a complete edition of the sonatas, being published by De Santis.

6 Sonatas (E. Woodcock—Galliard 1963). I.10, 18, 32, 34/3, 41, and 43.

Dodici sonate (I. Caruana—Zanibon 1974) 73pp. I.30, 45, 50, 1, 2, 3, 56, 57, 60 (third movement omitted), 68, 6, 18. I.45 and I.57 are of fine recital quality; the others make fine teaching material. Fine editorial policy followed. Int. to M-D.

Dieci sonate (Iris Caruana—Zanibon 1972). Revised with introduction (in Italian and English) and transcribed into modern notation: 8 sonatas and 2 divertimenti.

Sonate per il Cembalo (Heddy Illy—De Santis). Contains: I.7, 8, 19, 23, 24, 32, 36–41, 49, 53, 95.

Passatempo al Cembalo-Sonate (Franco Piva—Istituto per la Collaborazione Culturale, Venice 1964). Vol. VI of the *Cembalo collana di musiche veneziane, Inedite o Rare* (TP). Six multi-movement sonatas dating from 1781 (?), late works. These sonatas differ in many ways from Galuppi's other keyboard works, suggesting a later date of composition. They are cast in sonata design, employing binary forms within a three-part thematic tonal organization. Sonata No.1 in three movements, the others in two. Lyric melodic treatment; sequential passage-work and brusque cadences are abundant. Discrepancies between the holograph manuscript and this edition are not always explained. Int. to M-D.

Sonata D (Georgii—Arno Volk). Vol. III of *Keyboard Music of the Baroque and Rococo*. Adagio; Allegro; Staccato; Giga. Expressive, elegant, and melodious. M-D.

Sonata C Op.1/1 (Holmes—OUP 1980) 11pp. Adagio; Andantino; Allegro. I.30 was first published in 1756 as a two-movement sonata. In 1760 it was reprinted with a middle movement inserted. It exemplifies the pre-classical *galant* style of grace and lyric beauty. Contains historical notes, guidelines for performance, and a bibliography; edited. M-D.

Six Keyboard Sonatas (Serafine—CF 1980) 47pp. Contains: I.5, 11, 15, 50, 61, and 66. Short, containing one, two, or three movements. About the same difficulty as some of the little early Haydn sonatas. Clear and compact classic form, clean urtext copy. Includes helpful interpretative notes. Of special interest is the single extended movement of No.2 d, which anticipates Haydn in form. Int. to M-D.

See: Ruth Jane Holmes, "The Keyboard Sonatas of Baldassare Galuppi: Pedagogical Alternatives to the Standard Repertoire," AMT 34/6 (June–July 1985):16–17, 19.

Elisabetta de Gambarini (1731–1765) Great Britain

De Gambarini was a versatile English composer, singer, and orchestral conductor.

Six Sonatas for Harpsichord or Piano (B. Harbach—Vivace Press 1994) 36 pp. Printed privately in 1740. Mostly two and three short movements in fluent straightforward writing. J. C. Bach and Handel influence noted. Int. to M-D.

Lessons for the Harpsichord Opp.1 and 2. (M. Asti—Hildegarde). Thin textures, short movements. Int. to M-D.

Gigue. Tambourin. In collection *At the Piano With Women Composers* (Alfred 428). Short suite movements. Int.

John Gambold (1760–1795) Great Britain
Rondo ca. 1788 (Moravian Music Foundation Publications No.7). Edited and arranged, with commentary by Karl Kroeger, 1974. Gambold wrote this piece while he was teaching at the Moravian School in Niesky, Germany. The Rondo is designed mainly for instructional purposes but its well-developed classic style and charm make it suitable for concert use. Editorial performance instructions have been added in brackets or with dotted lines. Int., but M-D up to the indicated Presto marking.

Carlton Gamer (1929–   ) USA
Piano Rāga Music (1962–70). Published in PNM, Fall–Winter 1973 and Spring–Summer 1974:191–216. "Notes on the Structure of Piano Rāga Music" by composer is found in same issue, pp.217–30. The music employs 48 setforms. Highly organized tonal and rhythmic structures. D.

Rudolph Ganz (1877–1972) USA, born Switzerland
Peasant Danse Op.24/3 1912 (EBM 1946). Humorous, rhythmic, sectional, MC, surprise ending, effective. M-D.
Scherzino Op.29/2 (CF). Short and brilliant. M-D.
Idée Mélancolique, Idée Rythmique Op.30 (Art Publication Society of St. Louis 1932). Well written, pianistic. Int. to M-D.
Little Sphinx, Little Elf Op.31 (Remick 1934). Ganz says: "The Sphinx is for good players, the Elf for better ones." Int.
Animal Pictures (CF 1932). 20 pieces for children. Int.
4 Compositions for Piano Op.27 (CF 1909). After moonlight; Louis XV; On the Lake; Hoffmannesque. Picturesque writing. M-D.
Exercises for Piano—Contemporary and Special (SB). "It is to train students' ears as well as their hands for the new sounds in the 20th-century music that I have devised this book." Int. to M-D.
Three Rubes (Gerig) in collection *Contemporary Swiss Piano Music*. Eclectic style, unusual sonorities. M-D.

Alejandro García-Caturla (1906–1940) Cuba
García-Caturla's music blends Afro-Hispanic tunes and rhythms in a unique style.
Comparsa (NME 1930). Negro dance, bravura writing, rich sonorities, syncopated rhythm, ostinato basses. D.
Sonata Corta (NME 1927). One short movement, 2-part linear writing, allegro con brio. M-D.
Berceuse Campesina (CF 1939). Short, folk lullaby. Int.
Preludio Corta No.1 (NME 1927). To the memory of Erik Satie. Simple melody, open textures, unbarred. Int.

Juan Gabriel Garcia-Escobar (1934–   ) Spain

Suite Popular (UME 1970) 30pp. Six Spanish dances, including Zapateado, Sequidilla, Farruca. Strong rhythmic interest, MC. M-D.

Roberto García-Morillo (1911–   ) Argentina

García-Morillo's style is characterized by stringent harmonies, forceful rhythmic treatment, and primitive qualities.

Tres Piezas Op.2 (Ric 1933). Cortejo Barbaro: tumultuous, energetic, drum-like bass built on ostinato, sonorous. Poema: chromatic introduction, lyric, long pedal points, improvisatory. Danza de los animales al salir del Arca de Noe (Dance of the animals leaving Noah's ark): "Homage to Stravinsky," driving, grotesque. Excellent recital group; requires large span. M-D.

Conjuros Op.3 Incantations. (ECIC 1934). Tchaka: stark opening, builds to large climax over ostinato basses. El Genio de las Aguas: primitive melodies, gruff bass treatment, contrasted second half. Schango, el Genio del Trueno: animated, driving, incisive. El Primogénito del Cielo y de la Tierra: descending chromatic fourths under quiet trills; leads to a marcha funebre with ostinato bass; dissonant accented melody. Atmospheric suite; primitive. M-D.

Sonata del Sur Op.4 (EAM 1935). Danza, Marcha funebre; Scherzo; Danza, Himno, Coda. Much rhythmic drive throughout entire piece. M-D.

Variaciones Op.10 (Ric 1942). Six variations on four three-bar phrases. Parallel seventh chords, astringent, bare, fine craft, climax, finale. M-D.

Variaciones Op.13 (ECIC 1944) 5 min. Seventeen variations on a three-measure theme. Stark sonorities, major seventh and minor ninth featured; reminiscent of the variations of Aaron Copland, to whom these variations are dedicated. D.

Sonata No.3 Op.14 (Ric 1944–45). 10 min. Allegro; Lento; Allegro.

Cuentos para Niños Traviesos (Ric 1953). Second series. 12 min. Caperucita Rosa; Amazonas; Gladiadores. Int.

Sonata No.4 Op.26 (Ric 1959) 12 min. Allegro: brisk 7/8 with lyric second theme. Lento: mildly dissonant. Toccata: 8/8 (3, 3, 2), brilliant; lyric second theme of first movement returns treated differently; tumultuous conclusion. D.

Janina Garścia (1920–   ) Poland

2 Sonatiny for fortepiano Op.4/1, 2 (PWM 1947). Interesting writing. Also contains Polish Folksong Op.26/9, harmonized. Fun to play. Int.

Favorite Tunes Op.27 (PWM 1973) 23pp. 20 pieces, attractively set. Includes colorful drawings. Int.

Miniatures Op.5 (PWM 1971). 13 pieces, colorful, varied. Int.

Teasers (PWM). Easy.

Very Easy Pieces for Children Op.3 (PWM). 8 imaginative pieces, not "very easy." Int.

Winter Fun (PWM). Easy.

Irena Garztecka (1913–1963) Poland
Polish Dances (PWM). Six miniatures that evoke the atmosphere and rhythms of typical Polish folk dances. Mazur; Kujawiak; Krakowiak; Oberek; Zbójnicki; Polonez. Int.
Suite (PWM). Five Movements; each may be performed separately. Simplicity of construction, serious, concentrated. M-D.

Gérard Gasparian (–   ) France
Scherzo 1990 (ESC 1995) 7pp. 2½ min. A required piece at L'Ecole Normale de Musique in Paris. Vivacissimamente, brioso leggiero, changing meters. After Moderato mid-section, Scherzo is repeated. Freely tonal around B♭. M-D.
Intermezzo 1986 (ESC 1995) 4 pp., 1½ min. Contrapuntal, more chordal mid-section, textures thicken toward ending. M-D.

Serge de Gastyne (1930–   ) USA, born France
Proem (EV 1958) 5pp. Flexible meters, freely tonal, thematic development from opening idea, più mosso mid-section, lyric orientation. Large span required. M-D.

Stephanos Gasuleas (1931–   ) Greece
11 Aphorisms (UE 1961) 8pp. Vol.II in a series edited by Hanns Jelinek called *Libelli Dodecaphonic*. The preface states that all the pieces are by pupils of the editor, Gasuleas being one of them. The pieces are 2 or 3 lines long and introduce a variety of contemporary techniques. Int. to M-D.

Walther Geiser (1897–1993) Switzerland
The music of Geiser shows strong neoclassic tendencies. He studied at the Berlin Academy of Arts in the master class of Busoni, who greatly influenced his style.
Suite Op.41 (Br 1952). 5 formal structures in contrapuntal technique. D.

Fritz Geissler (1921–1984) Germany
Sonata (DVFM 1968) 24pp. Individual writing up to final pages, where a thick Regerian chromatic quality emerges. D.
Zweite Klaviersonate (DVFM 8037 1976) 17pp. Sehr ruhige: no bar lines, spatial notation, serial, palm and arm clusters. Sehr lebhafte: secco style, skips, chordal tremolo, percussive; requires large span. Expressionistic, avantgarde. D.

Arthur Gelbrun (1913–   ) Israel, born Poland
Four Preludes (IMI 1959). Molto lento: quiet, lyric. Vivace assai: toccata-like. Languido: Impressionistic. Tranquillo: thoughtful. Constructed on a 12-tone row. M-D.
5 Caprices 1957 (IMI 430) 15pp. Based on one tone-row with permutations. M-D.

Francesco Geminiani (1687–1762) Italy

Pièces de clavecin, tirées des differences ouvrages de M. F. Geminiani (Bibliotheca Musica Bunoniensis, through Arnaldo Forni Editore 1975). 59pp. Originally published London 1743.

The Second Collection of Pieces for the Harpsichord (Bibliotheca Musica Bunoniensis, through Arnaldo Forni Editore). Originally published London 1752. Most of the pieces in these collections are string sonata movements arranged as keyboard sonatas by the composer. Geminiani usually assigns the solo part to the right hand and lets the left hand carry the accompaniment, which came from the basso continuo part. Int. to M-D.

Armando Gentilucci (1939–1989) Italy

Iter (Ric 1969) 7pp. 5 min. Involved figuration and chordal sonorities splashed over keyboard. Some aleatoric sections, dynamic extremes, highly percussive and dissonant. D.

Harald Genzmer (1909–   ) Germany

Genzmer's style shows the influence of Hindemith's contrapuntal writing plus a colorful expressiveness.

Studies (CFP). Vol.I: 11 pieces. Vol.II: 10 pieces. Complex but grateful to the pianist. Vol.II more difficult.

Sonata No.2 (Schott 1942). 4 movements. Neoclassic style. Final fugue works to great climax. D.

Sonatinas Nos. 1 and 3 (Schott). Reminiscent of Hindemith. M-D.

Capriccio (Second Sonatina) (Schott 1954). A concise 4-movement work, well proportioned, careful attention to details. M-D.

Dialogues (Litolff 1963) 26pp. 22 min. Twelve contrapuntal studies of great ingenuity and musicality. Twentieth-century equivalents of Bach *Inventions*, one for each key. M-D.

Suite C (Schott 1951). Moderato: introductory and with full chords. Allegro: pseudo contrapuntal, large gestures, clever ending. Andante: ostinato-like. Presto: toccata style with syncopated chords. M-D.

Sonata No. 3 (R&E 1987) 30 pp. Well crafted; Hindemithean approach. M-D.

Roberto Gerhard (1897–1970) Spain

Gerhard was skillful at mixing styles but 12-tone technique appealed to him greatly.

Dances from Don Quixote 1957 (K. Prowse; B&H). From the ballet of the same name. Introduction. Dance of the Muleteers: virtuosic concert piece. The Golden Age. In the Cave of Montesinos. Epilogue. Dance rhythms and fiery, colorful style recall Gerhard's teacher, Granados. Evokes a Spanish atmosphere. The dances are associated with episodes from the famous story. Their sense of drama and color make for lively piano music. Thematic interrelations unify the work. M-D.

Edwin Gerschefski (1909–   ) USA

Gerschefski's style contains elements of humor, rhythmic strength, and lyricism. His harmonies tend to be rather dense and rugged.

Concert Minuet Op.4D (CFE) 4pp. From Classic Symphony. Neoclassic. Int.

Six Preludes Op.6 (CFE) 18pp. Varied sonorities and moods, MC. M-D. No.6 available separately (CFE) in a revised version. 6pp.

Nocturne Op.6/7 (Pioneer) 2pp. Highly independent lines. M-D.

The Portrait of an Artist Op.13 1961 (CFE) 4pp. Four short contrasting pieces, subtle sonorities. M-D.

Lullaby Op.13/6 (CFE 1934) 1p. Two-voice lines. Int.

Eight Variations Op.14 (CFE 1961) 8pp. Contains an especially colorful Recitative near the beginning and at the end. M-D.

Lullaby to a Child Unborn Op.14/9 (CFE 1965) 6pp. 5 min. Sectionalized, chromatic, on quiet side. M-D.

Suite for Left Hand Alone Op.15 (CFE) 11pp. Allegro moderato; Largo; Allegretto. D.

Second Sonatine Op.20/2 (Pioneer 1961) 8pp. Lento ma non troppo; Allegro con brio. Strong independent lines, chromatic. M-D.

New Music Op.23 (Pioneer 1937) 7pp. Four pieces. All except No. 4 are thin textured. M-D.

South Carolina Waltz Op.27/4 (Pioneer) 1p. Freely tonal. Int.

Prairie Hymn Op.30/3A; *Prairie Nocturne* Op.30/3B (Pioneer) 2pp. The Nocturne is a variation of the Hymn. Int.

Waltz Nocturne Op.31/3 (CFE 1945) 3pp. Formerly titled "Schillinger Nocturne." 9/8, freely tonal around E, ends in B. M-D.

Invention Op.34/3; *Teletype Etude* Op.34/4 (Pioneer 1961) 4pp. Invention: chromatic, flowing lines. Etude: Presto energico, motoric in 5/8. M-D.

Seven Piano Pieces Op.47 (Pioneer 1964) 15pp. Contrasting, complementary. Would make a nice suite. M-D.

Six Piano Pieces Op.48 (CFE) 6pp. Short, two-voice textures, linear. Easy to Int.

Twelve Etudes Op.58 (Pioneer 1966) 15pp. Contrasting, craggy textures. Large span required. M-D.

Three Inventions Op.59 (CFE 1964) 9pp. Free dissonant counterpoint. M-D.

Hommage à Chopin Op.60 1966 (CFE) 28pp. Fourteen contrasting variations, each one built on techniques used by Chopin in his *Préludes*. Clever; effective; contains some pleasantly surprising results. Int. to M-D.

George Gershwin (1898–1937) USA

Gershwin was one of the most gifted American composers in terms of pure native endowment. Out of the elements of jazz, ragtime, and the blues he wove a musical language that is fresh, spontaneous, and, above all, American. He is known throughout the world as our most famous composer.

Rhapsody in Blue 1923 (New World Music) 16 min. Opens with an ascending line followed by the first theme, which sets a jaunty mood for the whole piece.

A second theme appears and leads to the central section, which contains material from the opening. Ends brilliantly with a short coda. This solo version is what Gershwin actually wrote. It stands complete on its own. The piano writing requires above all a strong sense of rhythm, to project the music properly. M-D.

Rhapsody in Blue (Zizzo—WB) Contains both the fully restored solo piano version and an orchestral addendum that shows the conductor where the additions to the solo version recur.

See: Alicia Zizzo, "Seeking Gershwin's True Rhapsody in Blue," *Clavier,* 36/6 (July–August 1997):18–24, 29–31.

The Complete Gershwin Preludes (Zizzo—WB 1995) 33pp. Includes seven preludes. *Prelude I* 1926: No.1 of the familiar *Three Preludes. Prelude* (Melody No.17): a 1925–26 version of "Sleepless Night" (No.7 in this collection). *Prelude* (Rubato 1923): rolled left-hand chords, tempo changes. *Prelude II* (Blue Lullaby 1926): No.2 of *Three Preludes. Prelude* (Novelette in Fourths, ca. 1919): short introduction followed by predictable rhythms in fourths; melodic mid-section suggests early Debussy influence. *Prelude III* (Spanish Prelude): No. 3 of *Three Preludes. Prelude* (used as the opening of the third movement of *Concerto in F*; 1925): strong rhythms, repeated notes alternate between hands. *Prelude* (Sleepless Night 1946, written in Kay Swift's hand): another version of *Prelude* (Melody No.17) (pp. 11–13). Light-colored type indicates editorial additions. Performance notes explain much of the background of these pieces. Int. to M-D.

See: Robert Wyatt, "The Seven Jazz Preludes of George Gershwin," *American Music,* 7 (1989): 68–85.

———, "The Seven Jazz Preludes of George Gershwin," AMT, 43/2 (October–November 1993):24–29, 63.

Melody No. 17—Sleepless Night 1925–26 (WB 1993) 2pp. Considered to be the "lost" prelude Gershwin performed in Boston in 1927. The original version is in Gershwin's handwriting; a reworked one is in the handwriting of Kay Swift (1935), for whom, presumably, Gershwin was recomposing the prelude as a song. The original version is easier. Slow, jazzy, rubato appropriate, jagged interruption in middle of the piece. The music is found is P&K, 167 (March–April 1994):30–31.

See: Alicia Zizzo, "Gershwin's 'Sleepless Night,' the 'lost' prelude returns," P&K, 167 (March–April 1994):24–25, 28.

———, "A Piano Lesson with Alicia Zizzo—The Gershwin Preludes," P&K, 167 (March–April 1994):29.

Preludes 1934 (New World Music). Allegro ben ritmato e deciso: mainly rhythmic, syncopated rhythms, bravura playing. Andante con moto e poco rubato: lyric blues with ostinato-like accompaniment, interspersed with bridge material of shorter length. Allegro ben ritmato e deciso: craggy rhythms, syncopated, brilliant closing for the group. Gershwin called it a "Spanish Prelude." These three short pieces show Gershwin's mastery of the melding of jazz idioms with concert forms. M-D.

Music by Gershwin (University Society 1975) 185pp. Includes: Rhapsody in Blue.

3 Preludes. Impromptu in 2 Keys. Two Waltzes C. 18 transcriptions of songs made by the composer. Also includes photographs of Gershwin and his circle of friends, bibliography, discography, and indexes of titles and first lines. Also includes a small 33⅓ LP of Gershwin playing the solo version of Rhapsody in Blue. A revealing performance! Int. to M-D.

Gershwin at the Keyboard (New World Music). Eighteen song hits arranged by the composer. Delightful, short. M-D.

Impromptu in Two Keys (New World Music 1973) 2pp. Jazzy melodic line over punctuated bass. M-D.

Two Waltzes C 1933 (New World Music) adapted by Saul Chaplin. Introduction, Waltz I, Waltz II, then both waltzes combined. Attractive. Int. to M-D.

Promenade (Chappell) 4pp. 3 min. Published with *Merry Andrew* and *Three-Quarter Blues*. Originally composed for the 1936 film *Shall We Dance,* with Fred Astaire and Ginger Rogers. It was to accompany the "Walking the Dog" sequence and is Gershwin's last piano work. Somewhat jazzy with a few dissonances. M-D.

Merry Andrew 1927 (Chappell) 3pp. Published with *Promenade*. Originally written as a happy-go lucky piece for Fred Astaire in *Funny Face*. Int. to M-D.

Three-Quarter Blues 1920s (Chappell) 2pp. Ira Gershwin referred to this as "Irish Waltz" and also "Melody." Delightful tune. Int.

George Gershwin for Piano (Chappell 1974). Includes: Merry Andrew; Three-quarter Blues; Promenade. M-D.

Blue Monday 1922 arr. by Alicia Zizzo (WB 1993). An Afro-American setting. Arranged from an opera. Int. to M-D.

See: Julia Peña. "Gershwin's *Blue Monday,*" KC, 12/5 (September–October 1992):12. Contains an excerpt of the piece on pp. 13–15.

See: Laura W. Holleran, "Gershwin 's' Wonderful for Students," *Clavier* 21/7 (September 1982):27–29. A discussion of his piano works. Includes "Impromptu in Two Keys."

Margory Irvin, "It's George, Not Jazz: Gershwin's Influence in Piano Music," AMT, 23 (November–December 1973):31–34.

Stuart Isacoff, "Fascinatin' Gershwin," *Keyboard Classics* (January–February 1984):6ff. General remarks on Gershwin's music and its stylistic relationship to the music of Ravel and Berg; focuses on his piano output.

Matthias van den Gheyn (1721–1785) Flemish, Belgium

Van den Gheyn's works resemble those of Handel and Arne.

Collection d'oeuvres composées par d'anciens et de célèbres Clavecinistes Flamands (van Elewyck—Schott Frères). Contains 6 *Divertimenti* (about 1760) and *6 Suites*, Op.3. Int. to M-D.

Sonata f: in collection *L'Arte Antica e Moderna* (Ric). Vol.III. Graceful and grateful. M-D.

Rita Ghosn (–   ) France

Sur un Fil 1991 (ESC 1992) 4pp. Flashy, mildly contemporary recital piece, short and effective. Int. to M-D.

Luis Gianneo (1897–1968) Argentina
Gianneo's piano pieces are written in a fluent and graceful style. They combine rhythmic elements relating to folk dances with tonally based but often dissonant harmonies to create appealing nationalistic works.

Cuatro Composiciones 1916–17 (Ric Amer) 13 min. Vieja cancíon; Berceuse; Arabesca; En bateau. Fresh folklike spirit. Int. to M-D.

Sonatina (PIC 1938) Tempo di Minuetto; quartal harmonies. Allegro vivo: dance-like rondo, florid passage-work, staccato texture. An extended work, charming, gentle. Contains syncopations in the Brazilian batucada rhythms. M-D.

Three Argentine Dances (PIC 1939). Gato; Tango; Chacarera. FSF, tonal, attractive harmonies and syncopated rhythms. Int.

Música para Niños (PIC 1941). Ten delightful pieces in many styles. Some are based on Southern American tunes and rhythms. Int.

Cinco pequeñas Piezas (ESC 1938). Five short pieces: Coquetry; Cradle Song; March; Waltz; Perpetual Motion. Int.

Sonata No.2 b♭ 1943 (CF) 28 min. Allegro: loose variation form, in *chacarera* rhythm with bitonal usage, running 6/8. Romanza: a simple Andante accompanied melody, florid da capo, short. Allegro molto: a brilliant 6/8 movement, some dissonance, extensive syncopation, dramatic closing. M-D.

Villancico (EAM 1946). Melancholy 3/4, sensitive use of chromaticism. Int.

Caminito de Belén (EAM 1946). Marchlike, simple staccato clusters. Int.

Sonata No.3 (Ric Amer 1957) 18 min. Allegro impetuoso; Adagio sostenuto; Allegro deciso.

Siete Piezas Infantiles (7 Children's Pieces) (PIC) 13pp. Rondo: Lydian mode on C. Cradle Song: Lento sequential tune. Pampean Sunset: asymmetrical phrases, fresh harmonies. Little Hat: syncopated melody. Tango: melody transferred to left hand. Small Drum: staccato study. Rustic Dance: hemiola rhythms, syncopated melody, the best in the set. Attractive tunes and rhythms cleverly handled. Easy to Int.

Vittorio Giannini (1903–1966) USA
Giannini had a superlative craft that always expressed a warmth of feeling.

Prelude and Fughetta (TP). Modal, interesting modulations, pedal point, contrapuntal neoclassic style. Prelude in crisp toccata style; 2-voice fughetta. M-D.

Variations on a Cantus Firmus (EV). Moderato Var. 1–10; Aria Var. 11–12; Toccata Var. 13–22; Interlude Var. 23–24. Published in four parts. Can be played in groups or as a whole. Large work, varied pianistic demands, requiring some virtuoso playing. D.

Sonata (Ric 1966) 24pp. Three movements. The first movement is a vigorous and exciting allegro, the second movement a lovely slow song, the last movement is fast with ostinato bass figures. Good left-hand octave technique is necessary. Pianistic. D.

Walter Giannini (1917–   ) USA
Sonatina (AME 1958). Cantabile: flowing melody. Chorale: many accidentals, sophisticated writing. Dance Finale: gigue-like, thin textures, effective, MC. M-D.

Modal Variations (AME 1951). Theme and 7 variations based on first 6 tones of the mixolydian mode beginning on E♭. Unusual sonorities. Var. 3 calls for a fine legato octave technique. M-D.

Remo Giazotto (1910–   ) Italy
Au tombeau de Ravel 1959 (Ric 129762) 20pp. Introduzione: Alla Gavotta. Minuetto e trio. Valzer lento. Toccata. Dedicated to pianist Pietro Scarpini (b. 1911). MC, M-D.

Orlando Gibbons (1583–1625) Great Britain
In addition to the six pieces in *Parthenia*, there are some forty surviving manuscripts containing keyboard works of Gibbons. The keyboard music, with the exception of the variations and dance tunes, is reserved and austere. Although Gibbons was one of the finest performers of his day, virtuosity plays a relatively small role in these works.
Keyboard Music, Musica Britannica XX (Hendrie—S&B 1962). 45 works (5 doubtful) and incipits of 9 spurious works. Int. to M-D.
Complete Keyboard Works (Glyn—S&B) 52 works. Vol.1: Masks and Dances. Vol.2: Variations. Vol.3: Pavans and Galliards. Vols.4 and 5: Fancies. Int. to M-D.
A Collection of 8 Keyboard Pieces selected from Volume XX of *Musica Britannica* (Hendrie—S&B). M-D.
A Selection of Short Dances (S&B). Excellent variety. Int. to M-D.
The King's Juell. An Allmaine consisting of variations on a double theme. In *Complete Keyboard Works* Vol.2 and *Benjamin Cosyn's Virginal Book* (JWC). M-D.
Fancy A re. Fugal, sustained, noble. In *Complete Keyboard Works* Vol.IV.
The Woods so Wilde. Gibbon's most extended set of variations developed differently from Byrd's, on the same tune. FVB, I, 144. Incomplete in this volume. No.29 in *Complete Keyboard Music.* M-D.
See: "The Keyboard Music of Orlando Gibbons (1583–1625)," PRMA, 89(1962–63):1–15.

Miriam Gideon (1906–1996) USA
Every note is meaningful in Miriam Gideon's music, a music which has both style and polish.
6 Cuckoos in Quest of a Composer (ACA) 15 min. Il Cuculo Nel Rinascimento: 3-voice ricercar, short (17 bars). Kleines Praeludium in Barockstil: delightful two-voice writing. Klassische Sonatina auf ein berühmtes Motiv: extended first movement, difficulty of Clementi Op.36 *Sonatinas*; second movement is a theme and 4 contrasted variations; third movement is a Rondo. Le Coucou au Dix-Neuvième Siècle: Prélude sentimental, chromatic harmony. Impression d'un Coucou: more difficult than other movements. The Bird: contemporary idioms. A clever suite tracing the development of musical composition from the Renaissance to the present using the "Cucu" theme in various guises. Int. to M-D.

Piano Suite No.3 (LG 1951). 3 brief atonal movements. M-D. In collection *New Music for the Piano.*

Canzona (NME, Jan. 1947). One movement, two-voice texture, wide skips, crisp touch, energetic, atonal. M-D.

Of Shadows Numberless (CFE—ACA 1966) 12 min. Suite for piano based on Keats's "Ode to a Nightingale." 5 movements, each headed by a short quotation from the poem. M-D.

Walter Gieseking (1895–1956) Germany

Jazz Improvisation (Schaum Publications) in collection *Composer-Pianists.* Short and fun. Int.

Drei tanz-improvisationen (A. Fürstner 1926) 11pp. More involved than the above-listed piece, complex rhythms. Would make a fine recital closing group. M-D.

Anthony Gilbert (1932–   ) Great Britain

Sonata Op.1 1961–62 (Schott) 19pp. 14 min. First movement: SA design. Second movement: a sensitive cantilena. Third movement: a scherzo with two trios. Post-Webern style, serial, with the basic row subject to variation. Many subtle effects; staccato bass notes half caught by the pedal; harmonics; sensitive use of sostenuto pedal. Percussive treatment is highly effective. D.

Little Piano Pieces Op.20B 1972(Schott) 6 min. From *String Quartet with Piano Pieces,* Op.20. Pieces look more difficult than they are. Chance composition. M-D.

Jacob Gilboa (1920–   ) Israel, born Czechoslovakia

Reflections on Three Chords of Alban Berg 1979 (IMP 678) 16pp. Inspired by three chords from Act 1 of *Wozzeck.* "A kind of Rhapsody on 3 chords" (from the score). Expressionistic. D.

7 Little Insects (IMP 1972) 20pp. Ant; Dragonfly; Spider; Grasshopper; Cockschafer; Caterpillar; Butterfly. Descriptive miniatures. MC. M-D.

Alberto Ginastera (1916–1983) Argentina

Ginastera was trained in his native country and developed a personal style, a Pan-American (rather than a Latin) language, that combines certain nationalistic traits with advanced contemporary techniques. His contribution to piano literature, while not large, is significant.

Danzas Argentinas Op.2 1937 (Durand). Danzas del viejo boyero: polytonal with right hand on white keys, left hand on black keys. Danza de la moza donosa: swinging motion, attractive. Danza del gaucho matrero: energetic, driving motion. M-D.

　　See: Barbara Nissman, "Ginastera's 'Dance of the Graceful Maiden,'" KC, 6/5 (September–October 1986):23–25, 36–37. Masterclass on this piece; includes music.

Tres Piezas Op.6 1940 (Ric Amer). Cuyana: flowing, lyric, melodic. Norteña: involved rhythms, atmospheric. Criolla: driving, propulsive. M-D.

Malambo Op.7 1940 (Ric Amer). Driving rhythmic dance in 6/8, ostinato, dissonant. M-D.

Twelve American Preludes Op.12 1944 (CF). These pieces are Ginastera's vision (in miniature) of Pan-America, a sort of Latin *Mikrokosmos.* Vol. I: For Accents: bitonal, broken chords, arpeggi. Sadness: melodic, single accompanying voice. Creole Dance: rhythmic, dissonant, violent. Vidala: melodic, flowing dissonance in 3/8. In the First Pentatonic Minor Mode: two-part counterpoint, Andante, in 7/8. Tribute to Roberto García Morillo: presto alternating hands, 16th notes. Vol.II: Octaves: skips, etude style. Tribute to J. J. Castro: short, melodic, tango tempo. Tribute to Aaron Copland: bravura playing required. Pastorale: lento soprano melody, alto ostinato, open texture in bass. Tribute to Heitor Villa-Lobos: wild, unison writing, skips, syncopated. In the First Pentatonic Mode: pedal point under bell sonorities, *ffff* ending. Int. to M-D.

Suite de danzas criollas Op.15 1946 (Barry) 12pp. 8 min. A set of five varied dances in Creole style. Clusters are called for in No.2, span of ninth required, unusual rhythmic treatment. M-D.

Rondo on Argentine Children's Folk Tunes Op.19 1947 (B&H) 4pp. 3 min. Delightful reharmonizations, clever rhythmic treatment, glissando, crashing close. Int.

Sonata No.1 Op.22 1952 (Bo&H). 16 min. This is now an established standard work. Allegro marcato: changing meters, contrasted textures, great motor excitement. Presto misterioso: neo-expressionistic, freely built around a 12-tone row, rondo form, double octaves spread three octaves apart proceed in a breathless 3/8. Adagio molto appassionato: rhapsodic, three sections. Ruvido ed ostinato: frenetic but tightly controlled dance, toccata-like, percussive, hemiola usage brilliantly executed. Post-Romantic, dramatic tradition. Nationalistic character within an abstract form. D.

Milonga 1948 (Ric) 2pp. Slow dance, some tricky rhythmic problems. Int.

Piezas Infantiles 1942 (GS) in collection *Latin-American Art Music for the Piano.* Attractive, charming, clever. Int. to M-D.

Sonata No.2 Op.53 1981. Rev. ed., 1995 (Bo&H) 25pp. 12 min. Allegramente: draws from strong native dance rhythms. Changing meters, some notation on 4 staves, cluster-like sonorities. Adagio sereno: source is ancient love songs with vocal inflections of primitive civilizations; tinged with melancholy, the mood of the outdoors is established variously by bird calls, trills and arpeggios; provocative; not joyful. Ostinato aymara: inspired by native dances and songs, rhythmic, ferocious crashing chords, fast runs, cluster sonorities, changing meters; the wild fast rhythms recall the South American dance *karnavalito*; some four-stave notation; glissandos on white and black keys simultaneously; sforzatissimo ending. An exciting, tightly structured work that will surely join the first sonata in popularity. The composer wrote the following about this work: "The sonata was inspired by the music of the northern part of my country, of 'aymara' and 'kechus' origins with its pentatonic scales, its sad melodies and joyful rhythms. The first movement has a main subject, a quasi introduction and conclusion, framing developments based on different dances and songs, among them the Argentinian 'Pala-pala.' The second movement has a nocturnal character. The first part is a 'harawi,' a melancholic love song, with the characteristic vocal inflections of primitive civilizations. The central section evokes murmurs of the night in the lonely Andean 'punas.' The third movement takes the form of a toccata whose rhythm comes from a dance called 'karnavalito.'" D.

Sonata No.3 Op.55 1982 (Bo&H) 9pp. 4 min. Reproduced from holograph. In one movement; uses binary form with two main sections and a coda. "The initial tempo indication 'Impetuosamente' sets the pace of the entire work whose rhythmic textures are based on American Indian and colonial dances of Latin America" (from the score). Strong driving rhythms, fast-moving chords and octaves in both hands, motoric, toccata-like, glissando-cluster conclusion. D.

See: Mary Ann Hanley, CSJ, "The Solo Piano Music of Alberto Ginastera," Part I, AMT, 24 (June–July 1975):17–20; Part II, AMT, 25 (September–October 1975):6–9.

Lodovico Giustini (18th cen., fl. 1736) Italy

Sonate da cimbalo de piano e forte (Florence, 1732), facsimile, with preface by Rosamond E. M. Harding (Cambridge University Press, 1933; Minkoff). Contains 12 sonatas: 8 in four movements and 4 in five movements. Some movements have dance titles, others have only tempo indications. This is the first known published music that specified the use of the pianoforte. Contains bibliographical notes. Int. to M-D.

See: Joseph Bloch, "Lodovico Giustini and the First Published Piano Sonatas," PQ, 86 (Summer 1974):20–24. Includes the complete Sonata IV in facsimile with performance suggestions. M-D.

Peggy Glanville-Hicks (1912–1990) USA, born Australia

Glanville-Hicks studied with Vaughan Williams in London and was later a music critic for the *New York Herald Tribune*.

Prelude for a Pensive Student. In collection *The Century of Invention* (EAMC 772 1991). Flowing left-hand triplets; melody carries some harmonic accompaniment; impressionistic influence. M-D.

Philip Glass (1937–   ) USA

Glass studied at the University of Chicago, The Juilliard School, and with Nadia Boulanger in Paris. He also worked with Ravi Shankar in Paris. Indian music inspired his working with ostinato patterns in forms of slow change (minimalist music).

Opening (TP 1982) 2pp. 6 min. Minimal music, much repetition. Contains drones and slowly overlapping ideas. Utilizes triplets in right hand and duplets in left hand throughout. M-D.

The Olympian—Lighting of the Torch (TP 1984) 6pp. Majestically; Smoothly; Majestically. Minimal music, many repetitions of chords and figuration, syncopation, tonal. Int. to M-D.

Modern Love Waltz (CFP 66735). In collection *Waltzes by 25 Contemporary Composers*. Minimalist characteristics, charming. Int.

Solo Piano (Amsco). Includes among others *Five Metamorphosis* (1988) and *Mad Rush,* which was originally composed for organ for the entrance of the Dalai Lama at St. John the Divine Cathedral in New York. Repeated rhythms, evolving patterns. M-D to D.

Wichita Vortex-Sutra 1989. In collection *American Contemporary Masters* (GS 1995) 9pp. Flowing introduction introduces ostinato pattern used throughout the piece; patterns slowly change. Introduction returns at end. Minimalist. M-D.

Alexander Glazunov (1865–1936) Russia

Glazunov, a pupil of Rimsky-Korsakov and later greatly influenced by Liszt, Wagner, and Brahms, was more successful with smaller forms than with the sonata. He was a master craftsman whose music sometimes lacks direction, even though beautiful melodies and original harmonic treatment abound at every turn.

Complete Piano Works (USSR, 1 vol.; K, 2 vols.)

Suite on the Theme "S-a-s-c-h-a" Op.2 1882–83. 32pp. Introduction; Prelude; Scherzo; Nocturne; Valse. "Sascha" is a diminutive of Glazunov's own name, Alexander. Charming melodies and harmonies, well crafted. M-D.

3 Concert Studies Op.31 1899. No.1: 16th-note repetition from beginning to end in thirds, fourths, fifths, and single line. No.3, La Nuit (Belaieff): the best known; melodious and flowing. M-D.

Nocturne D♭ Op.37. Rich harmonies, interesting inner voices, influenced by Liszt. M-D.

Prelude and Fugue d Op.62 1899. 10 min. Chromatic, dramatic. M-D.

Theme and 15 Variations f♯ Op.72 1900 (IMC; Belaieff). Imitation of styles of various composers. M-D.

Prelude and Fugue e (GS). Impressive Prelude, complex Fugue. M-D.

First Sonata b♭ Op.74 1901 (Belaieff; USSR) 39pp. 3 movements. M-D. See: SSB, pp.714–15.

Second Sonata E Op.75 1901 (Belaieff; GS) 39pp. First movement: SA design with an interesting development section; leads to Scherzo: ABA design. Finale: employs thick chordal structures throughout until fugue begins 6 pages before end; brilliant close. Large work. M-D to D.

Reinhold Glière (1875–1956) Russia

Most of these pieces require well-developed finger dexterity.

5 Esquisses Op.17 (Jurgenson). B♭, e♭, A, C, F♯. Int. to M-D.

2 Esquisses Op.40 (USSR). D♭, c♯. M-D.

3 Morceaux Op.19 (Jurgenson). Mazurka a; Intermezzo B; Mazurka b. Int. to M-D.

3 Morceaux Op.21 (Jurgenson). Tristesse; Joie; Chagrin. M-D.

6 Morceaux Op.26 (Jurgenson). Préludes Bb, Eb, b; Chanson simple. (JWC); Mazurka c♯; Feuille d'album. Int. to M-D.

25 Preludes Op.30 (Jurgenson). Int. to M-D.

3 Mazurkas (CF). Colorful, unusual. Int. to M-D.

12 Student Pieces Op.31 (Mirovitch—MCA; CFP). Excellent recital material. Int.

Prelude Db Op.43/1 (Lancaster—Alfred). Flowing accompaniment, lyric melody, broken chords passed between the hands. Int.

Michael Glinka (1804–1857) Russia

Glinka is regarded as the founder of the nationalistic Russian idiom. He studied in Germany and Italy. His operas are more characteristic of the Russian school than is his piano music.

Complete Piano Works in vol.6 of *Complete Edition* (N. Zagornie—USSR 1958).

Variations on an Original Theme F 1824. Cadenza-like introduction, theme, 4 variations. M-D.

Variations on a Theme from Mozart's Don Giovanni Eb. For harp or piano, 2 versions 1854 and 1856. Theme and 5 variations. M-D.

Variations on Benedetta siá la madre E 1826. Theme and 6 variations. Variation 6 is fantasy-like, in Tempo di polacca a capriccio, and extended. A second set is entitled *Romance Variations*. M-D.

Variations on a Russian Air, Mid Gentle Dales 1826; written down 1854. Theme and 5 variations. M-D.

Variations on a Theme from Cherubini's Opera "Faniska" 1827. 4 variations and a Brilliante Finale. M-D.

Nocturne Eb for piano or harp 1828. ABA and extended coda. M-D.

Variations on a Theme from Donizetti's "Anna Bolena." 1831. Theme and 4 variations. Var. 3 is in two parts: Un poco piu vivo, and Andante. M-D.

Variations on 2 Themes from the Ballet "Chao-Kang" 1831. Theme and 4 variations. M-D.

Rondino brillante on a Theme from Bellini's "I Montecchi ed i Capuleti." In Mendelssohn style, brilliant, glittering, showy. M-D.

Nocturne "La Separation" (Musica Obscura; GS) 3pp. Hemiola, similar to John Field style, span of tenth required in left hand. Int. to M-D.

11 Variations on a Theme by Glinka (AMP). A collection of eleven variations by some of the leading Soviet composers on a theme from Glinka's "Vanya's Song" from the opera *Ivan Susanin*. Contains one variation each by Dmitri Kabalevsky, Eugen Kapp, Andrei Eshapy, Rodion Shchedrin, Georgi Sviridov, and Yuri Levtin; two by Vassarion Shebalin; and three by Dmitri Shostakovitch. Contains some brilliant and highly interesting writing. M-D.

Benjamin Godard (1849–1895) France

Godard entered the Paris Conservatory at age 14 and by the time he was 16 had already composed some violin sonatas, chamber works, and piano solos. He was strongly influenced by Robert Schumann and orchestrated that composer's

Scenes of Childhood in 1876. The popular "Berceuse," from Godard's opera *Jocelyn* (1888), is one of the pieces for which he is remembered today.

Studies for Children (Etudes Enfantines) Op.149 Book I (ABRSM—T. Johnson 1985) 30pp. Prelude; March of the Little Boys; March of the Little Girls; See-saw; We shall go no more to the wood; First Sorrow; Teasing; Fear of the Inferno; Be Good! Children's Minuet. All contain graceful melodic qualities. Int.

Sonata Fantastique Op.63 ca. 1880 (Hamelle). More like a four-movement suite with programmatic titles for each movement. Highly polished, salon style, facile. M-D.

18 Selected Pieces with portrait and biographical sketch (GS). Vol.I: Gavotte Op.16; 1st Valse; 1st Mazurka; Les hirondelles; Pan; En valsant; Novellozza; Chopin; Le cavalier fantastique; Alfred de Musset. Vol.II: 2nd Mazurka; 2nd Valse; Au matin; Valse chromatique; Venitiènne; Française; Guirlandes; 4th Mazurka. Int. to M-D.

Leopold Godowsky (1870–1938) Poland

Godowsky is considered by many authorities to have possessed one of the most perfect pianistic mechanisms of all times. His piano compositions are unique in many ways, and their contrapuntal complexities and elaborate detail make many of them very difficult.

53 Studies Based on Chopin Etudes (CFP) 5 vols. These pieces push piano technique beyond the frontiers established by Liszt. Godowsky explained his transcriptions of these Etudes as follows: "The fifty-three studies based upon twenty-six Etudes of Chopin have manifold purposes. Their aim is to develop the mechanical, technical and musical possibilities of pianoforte playing, to expand the peculiarly adapted nature of the instrument to polyphonic, polyrhythmic and polydynamic work, and to widen the range of possibilities in tone colouring. The unusual mental and physical demands made upon the performer by the above mentioned work must invariably lead to a much higher proficiency in the command of the instrument, while the composer for the piano will find a number of suggestions regarding the treatment of the instrument, and its musical utterance in general. Special attention must be drawn to the fact, that owing to innumerable contrapuntal devices, which frequently encompass almost the whole range of the keyboard, the fingering and pedalling are often of a revolutionary character, particularly in the twenty-two studies for the left hand alone. The preparatory exercises included in a number of the studies will be found helpful in developing a mechanical mastery over the pianoforte by applying them to the original Chopin studies as well as to the above mentioned versions. The fifty-three studies are to be considered in an equal degree suitable for concert purposes and private study." Harold Schonberg says: "And despite the enormous difficulties, the *Paraphrases* (Studies) were not intended to be played as bravura stunts. Godowsky had musical aims in mind . . . they . . . represent a philosophy where the piano itself was the be-all and the end-all, less a musical instrument than a way of life, and the paraphrases end up not music for the sake of music but music for the sake of the piano" (*The Great Pianists*, p.323).

See: James McKeever, "Godowsky Studies on the Chopin Etudes," *Clavier*, 19 (March 1980):21–29. Includes Godowsky's study on the Chopin Etude Op.25/4.

Sonata e 1911 (Musica Obscura; Schlesinger) 58pp. 5 movements, great range of emotional and technical difficulties; much use of counterpoint, especially in the last 3 movements.

See: SSB, pp.419–20, for a thorough discussion.

Triakontameron 1920 (GS) 6 vols. 30 moods and scenes in triple time. Picturesque, graceful writing. Not overly difficult. *Alt-Wien* (Old Vienna), Vol. 3/11, is probably his most famous piece. M-D.

Phonoramas 1925 (CF) 4 vols. 12 pieces of descriptive Javanese music. D.

Toccata G♭ Op.13 1899 (Musica Obscura) 9pp. Constantly moving 16th-note in right hand over a chordal melody in left hand. D.

Miniatures 1918–20 (CF). Humoresque; Rigaudon; The Milller's Song; Processional March; Arabian Chant (Orientale). All are tuneful and colorful, but not easy. Available separately. Int. to M-D.

Meditation 1930 (Schaum Publications) in collection *Composer-Pianists*. Solemn. Int.

Walzermasken 1912 (Musica Obscura) 4 vols., all in 1 vol., 85pp. 25 Tone-Fantasies in 3/4 time. Karneval; Pastell; Skizze; Momento capriccioso; Berceuse; Kontraste; Profile; Silhouette; Satire; Karikatur; Tyll Ulenspegel; Legend; Humoreske (on 4 notes); Französisch; Elegie; Perpetuum Mobile; Menuett; Schuhplatter; Valse; Macabre; Abendglocken; Orientale; Wienerisch; Eine Sage; Portrait. Varied moods, figurations, attractive studies. Int. to M-D.

Passacaglia b 1928 (CF). 44 variations, cadenza, and fugue. A huge work on the bass theme from the opening of Schubert's *Unfinished Symphony*. D.

Melodie Meditative Op.15/1 1899 (Musica Obscura) 2pp. Charming and somewhat sentimental character piece. M-D.

See: Donald Manildi, "Guides to Godowsky," P&K 190 (January–February 1998):40–41. A guide to recordings, books about Godowsky and his works in print.

L. S. Saxe, "The Published Music of Leopold Godowsky," *Notes*, 14 (March 1957): 165ff.

R. H. Widder, "Godowsky and His Pianistic Philosophy," *Musical Courier*, 141 (September 1950):7.

Artis Wodehous, "Leopold Godowsky Comes of Age," P&K, 187 (July–August 1997):31–36. Focuses on the original piano music.

Hugo Godron (1900–1971) The Netherlands

24 Chansonnettes (Donemus 1973) Livres I–IV. Charming, gentle and elegant, jazz-oriented, many seventh chords. Some pieces in form of dances (gavotte, minuet, waltz, etc.). Impressionistic influences. M-D.

Roger Goeb (1914–1997) USA
Goeb's style reflects a melodic-rhythmic line that is lyric and expressive. His harmonic practice can be absorbed without too much difficulty.
Dance Suite (ACA) 14 min. Martial: steady march in fourths and fifths, crisp staccato required. Largo: built on an ostinato-like bass in octaves, many accidentals. Grazioso: flexible ostinato-like figure, needs steady rhythmic drive. Blues: "slow and swinging" mood, boogie bass in mid-section. Reminiscent of Second Gershwin *Prelude.* Animato: lively rhythmic melodic line throughout, scale passages, shifts from 3/8 to 2/8. Strong energetic ending. M-D.
Fuga Contraria (ACA 1950). Five 12-tone fugues, problems in clarity of texture. D.
Fantasia (ACA 1950). Broad-scale work, dissonant and percussive. D.

Alexander F. Goedicke (1877–1957) Russia
Goedicke is mainly remembered for his melodious instructional piano pieces.
Sechzig Klavierstücke Op.36 (CFP) Book I: 30 pieces consisting of Etudes, Russian Songs, Dances, Cradle Song, Polka, etc. Essential fingering indicated. Easy. Book II: carefully graded; more difficult than Book I. Easy-Int.

Alexander Goehr (1932–   ) Great Britain, born Germany
Goehr uses dissonance to a high degree, and his rhythmic procedure is complex. Serial writing appeals to him; all the works listed below employ this technique.
Sonata Op.2 1951–52 (Schott) 12 min. A three-sectioned one-movement work using clusters at climaxes, octave doubling, and ostinati. Developmental motivic progressions, uses Messiaen-like retrogradable and non-retrogradable rhythms. D.
Capriccio Op.6 1958 (Schott) 5 min. Complex rhythmic subleties produce sensitive expressive nuances; most tightly serial of Goehr's piano works. D.
Three Pieces Op.18 1964 (Schott) 10 min. Cantus firmus techniques used in all three, all based on same motive. No.3 is a set of 15 variations. Colorful. M-D to D.
Nonomiya Op.27 1968–69. (Schott) 13pp. 13 min. A Noh play in which the main character presents an aria in the first part, reappears as a ghost in the second, and finally dances before leaving. Epitomizes the personalization of serial technique. Entire work is based on four 3-note groups. Musical imitation of poetry. Exotic decoration in the first part, dance elements in the second part. Subtle sonorities, dreamlike qualities, repeated harmonic gestures. D.
. . . In Real Time Op.50 1989 (Schott 12395) 41pp. 30 min. Five large pieces. Serial influence but not serial; atonal; proportional rhythmic relationships. Large span required, virtuosic, wide dynamic range. The pieces appear to be difficult to hold together. D.

Johann Gottlieb Goldberg (1727–1756) Germany
Goldberg studied with J. S. Bach and W. F. Bach.
24 Polonaises in All Keys (Wolff—Schott). These miniatures are similar to those in Bach's *Notebook for Anna Magdalena Bach.* Int.

William B. Goldberg (1917–   ) USA

Chorale Prelude (Now Thank We All Our God) (Chronos Music 1989) 6pp. The chorale tune unfolds under a patter of sixteenth notes. Effective. M-D.

Perpetual Motions (Chronos Music 1989) 18pp. 1. Simple chromatic figuration in eighth notes gradually thickens in a restricted dynamic range. 2. Left-hand ostinato supports free right-hand melody. 3. Changing meters, thin textures thicken, dramatic conclusion. M-D.

Richard Franko Goldman (1910–1980) USA

Nine Bagatelles (Axelrod). Small pieces for children illustrated by Alexandra Rienzi. Easy.

Sonatina 1942 (Mer). Three contrasted movements. Energetic opening movement with a contrasting lyric theme; rich harmonies are present in the slow movement; fast finale in 5/8 with hornpipe qualities. Large span plus rhythmic agility required. M-D.

Etude on White Notes 1973 (Bo&H) 4pp. Groups of 4 eighth notes against groups of 3 eighth notes, flowing thirds, cantabile and molto rubato mid-section, subito large *ff* chords, strongly accented closing, much dissonance. M-D.

Aubades (Mer). Four short pieces. Nos.1 and 3 are melodic; Nos.2 and 4 contain running figuration. M-D.

Francisca Gonzaga (1847–1935) Brazil

Gaucho 1897 (Ca e La-o Corta Jaca) (An After Thought) (Vitale) 2pp. A little Brazilian tango with a charming melody and plenty of tango rhythms. Large span (full octave chords) required. Int.

Dianne Goolkasian-Rahbee (1938–   ) USA

Goolkasian-Rahbee was trained at The Juilliard School in piano and composition. She also studied at The Mozarteum in Salzburg, Austria.

Pictures Op.3 1980 (BMC). 11 pieces, full of ingenuity. Sound more difficult than they are. Easy.

Phantasie Variations Op.12 1980 (Seda Productions) 5pp. Based on two 12-tone rows (listed at end), contrasted sections, changing meters, "floating freely in space (note lengths may vary ad lib.), the division of notes between hands may be decided by the performer" (from the score). Wide dynamic range, pointillistic, strong ending. D.

Sonata I Op.25 1985 (DGR Publishers) 33pp., ca. 15 min. 1. With furious energy: octatonic, thin textures, wide range of keyboard. 2. Scherzando: changing meters, requires rhythmic precision, quiet ending. 3. As if asking a question (with anguish. Why? Why must it be so?): bitonal chords, subito dynamic changes, mid-section drifts off in a peaceful daydream, conclusion comes back to reality. 4. Toccata: with tremendous energy, fire, and wildly driven strong rhythm; arm and finger clusters; exciting conclusion. Extremely pianistic throughout. D.

Sonata II Op.31 1988 (Seda Productions) 15pp. Allegro Maestoso: fleeting opening idea, molto espressione contrasting material, *pp* closing. Scherzando: much quartal harmony, thin textures. Intermezzo: nocturne-like, left-hand spread figuration, flowing melody. Allegro enerico: driving rhythms, dramatic conclusion. D.

Eugene Goossens (1893–1962) Great Britain
Concert Study Op.10 (JWC). Broken chords, staccato 16ths in both hands. D.
Kaleidoscope Op.18 (JWC). 12 short pieces, chromatic harmony. Int.
Four Conceits Op.20 1917 (JWC). Gargoyle; Dance Memories; Marionette Show; Walking Tune: chordal treatment. Short pieces; first three are grotesque in character. M-D.
Nature Poems Op.25 1919 (JWC). Awakening; Pastorale; Bacchanal. Lengthy works, chordal treatment, chromatic harmony. M-D.
Homage to Debussy Op.29 (JWC). A blend of Impressionistic harmonies and neo-classical polyphony, clear tonal outline. M-D.
Two Studies Op.38 (JWC). Folk Tune: quiet harmonization, chromatic harmony. Scherzo: lively, lyric mid-section. M-D.
Homage 1941 (Bo&H 1942) 2pp. The sixth piece in collection *Homage to Paderewski*. "Based on the C minor Prélude (Op. 28/20) of Chopin" (note in the score). Final three measures are similar to the Chopin Prélude. M-D.
Ships: 3 Preludes (Curwen). The Tug; The Tramp; The Liner. Clever character sketches. M-D.

Henryk Górecki (1933–   ) Poland
Four Preludes (Bo&H). Simple, straightforward late Romantic style. Interesting textures. M-D.

Héctor Melo Gorigoytia (1899–   ) Chile
Manchas de Color (PIC). Prelude: large chords. Spring: melodic. This Age a King: shifting chords. Short pieces in dissonant idiom. M-D.

Louis Moreau Gottschalk (1829–1869) USA
Gottschalk was one of the most flamboyant figures in nineteenth-century American music. Known as the American Liszt, he ranked with the greatest European virtuosi of his time. His piano compositions, over 100, require a solid technique and display vitality, beauty, and charm. Many demand virtuosity of the highest degree, and all are well laid out for the piano. Gottschalk drew on Afro-American and Creole sources for much of his inspiration. All his piano works are delightful, tuneful, brilliant, and full of rhythm.
The Piano Works of Louis Moreau Gottschalk with a biographical essay by Robert Offergeld (1969) (Arno Press), 5 vols., 112 pieces, 1520pp.
Piano Music of Louis M. Gottschalk (J. Behrend—TP 1956). Brief notes and biography. Bamboula Op.2; Le Bananier; The Banjo Op.15 (his most famous piano piece); Berceuse Op.47; The Last Hope Op.16; L'Union Op.48; Pasquinade Op.59; Ricordati Op.26. M-D to D.

A Compendium of Piano Music compiled and edited by Eugene List (CF 1971). The Banjo Op.15; La Savane; Souvenir de Porto Rico; Danza Op.33; Ojos Criollos Op.37; Minuet a Seville Op.30; La Mancenillier Op.11. M-D to D.

Compositions for Pianoforte (Amiram Rigai—Chappell 1972). The Banjo; La Scintilla; Souvenir de Porto Rico; Morte!!; Marche Funèbre; Bamboula; Minuit à Séville; Ballade Op.6; Tournament Galop; Pasquinade. Contains notes about the composer's life and works. M-D to D.

Gottschalk Album (K). Le Banjo; Pasquinade; Valse Poétique; Pastorella e Cavalhere; Tremolo. M-D.

Piano Music (Dover) 301pp. Edited with an Introduction by Richard Jackson. Divided into four categories: I. United States Ethnic and Patriotic Music: Bamboula; Le Bananier; The Banjo; La Savane; Ballade Creole; Union. II. Music from Spain: La Jota Aragonesa; Manchega; Minuit à Séville; Souvenirs d'Andalousie. III. West Indian Souvenirs: Danza; La Gallina; Le Mancenillier; O, Ma Charmante, Epargnez Moi!; Ojos Criollos; Souvenir de la Havane; Souvenir de Porto Rico; Suis Moi!. IV. Concert and Salon Music: Sixième Ballade; Berceuse; The Dying Poet; Grand Scherzo; The Last Hope; Morte!!; Pasquinade; Ses Yeux; Tournament Galop. M-D to D.

Creole and Caribbean Piano Pieces (Eberhardt Klemm—CFP 1974) 74pp. Preface in German, French, and English; critical notes in German. Contains: Bamboula Op.2; La Savane Op.3; Le Bananier Op.5; Le Banjo Op.15; Souvenir de Porto Rico Op.31; Les Yeux Creoles Op.37; Souvenir de la Havane Op.39; Pasquinade. M-D.

See: P. Smith, "Gottschalk's 'The Banjo, Op.15' and the Banjo in the Nineteenth Century," *Current Musicology,* 50 (1992):47–61.

The Little Book of Louis Moreau Gottschalk (Richard Jackson, Neil Ratliff—Continuo Music Press 1975). A performing edition based on materials at the New York Public Library. Preface by Gilbert Chase. Includes: Romance; Ballade; Polka B♭; Chanson du gitano; Polka A♭; Mazurk; Ynés. Also includes the manuscripts in facsimile. These are all previously unpublished works and form what could be called a suite of songs and dances. They are well balanced and have great variety and mood contrast. A fine introduction with notes about each piece makes for interesting reading. The Mazurk is a real find! M-D.

See: Joseph Smith, "Gottschalk's Ynés," *Piano Today,* 16/2 (March–April 1996):11, with the music on pp. 12–13.

Orfa Grande Polka (OD). Introduction, polka, màrziale section; all sparkle and dash. M-D.

Souvenir de Porto Rico (Mer). Introduction, theme and refrain, continuous variations. M-D.

Ojos Criollos (Creole Eyes) (Paxton). In collection *Masters of American Piano Music* (Alfred 4603). A Cuban dance: polka-tango. M-D.

Le Poète Mourant (Paxton). One of Gottschalk's most popular works. M-D.

La Bananier (CFP 7185). This lively folksong transcription (The Banana Tree) has a much-repeated bass plus many chromatic scales and arpeggios. M-D.

Bamboula Op.2 (TP). The stomping of the Negroes mixed with the delicate arabesques of Chopin. A brilliant rondo on "Sweet Potatoes," which captivated contemporary audiences. M-D.

Berceuse Op.47 (APS). Based on a French folk tune. Rocking bass, melody crosses over with left hand in upper register, murmurando effect required for the accompaniment. M-D.

Souvenir de Porto Rico 1859 (Mer). After a mysterious opening, the Caribbean folklike theme is treated to a series of increasingly exciting variations, which die away to the same mysterious opening. M-D.

O My Charmer, Spare Me 1862 (Banowetz—GWM) in collection *The Pianist's Book of Early Romantic Treasures*. Habanera and cinquilo rhythms, mingled sadness and restless passion. Int.

Mazurka A Op.6/1 1846 (Banowetz—GWM) in collection *The Pianist's Book of Early Romantic Treasures*. From a set of pieces entitled *Colliers d'or* (Chains of Gold), and perhaps composed as a result of Gottschalk's meeting Chopin the year before. Int.

Collected Works (GS 2024). Collected from various G. Schirmer editions. M-D.

See: John G. Doyle, *Louis Moreau Gottschalk, 1829–1869: A bibliographical study and catalog of works* (Detroit: Information Coordinators, 1983).

Louis M. Gottschalk, *Notes of a Pianist*, edited by Jeanne Behrend (New York: Knopf, 1964; reprint, New York: Da Capo Press, 1975).

Robert Offergeld, *The Centennial Catalogue of the Published and Unpublished Compositions of Louis Moreau Gottschalk* (New York: *Stereo Review*, 1970).

———, see review in *Stereo* (December 1975):120 for a discussion of some lesser-known works.

Peter J. Rabinowitz, "With Our Own Dominant Passions: Gottschalk, Gender, and the Power of Listening," *19th Century Music*, XVI/3 (Spring 1993): 242–51.

Glenn Gould (1932–1982) Canada

This remarkable pianist composed these pieces while under the strong influence of Schoenberg's music. Gould was a great defender of twelve-tone music. All the pieces are interesting, but I am grateful that Gould was primarily a pianist.

Klavierstücke (C. Morey—Schott 8319 1995) 19pp. 5 short pieces (1951): Nos.1 and 2 (1951–52) exploit 12-tone rows; strict serial writing. Nos.3 and 4 are not serial but highly chromatic and atonal (No.3 is a canon and No.4 a two-part invention). No.5 is a brief improvisational fantasy. M-D.

See: Glenn Gould, *Selected Letters* edited and compiled by John P. L. Roberts and Ghyslaine Guertin (Toronto: Oxford University Press, 1992), 260 pp. Over 200 letters covering a wide range of Gould's artistic activities. His detailed thoughts about piano repertoire are of special interest. Includes index.

Morton Gould (1913–1996) USA

Gould's versatility is not well known. His identification with popular music is balanced by more serious works of a vigorous nature.

Americana (CF). Corn-cob: barn dance. Indian nocturne. Hillbilly. Night song. Music hall. Mood sketches. Clever, attractive, folk inspired. Int. to M-D.

Prologue—1945 (Belwin-Mills). A celebration piece in honor of the founding of the United Nations. Chordal, dissonant, sonorous. M-D.

Boogie the Woogie 1941 (WB) 7pp. Classic boogie treatment in a rocking tempo. M-D.

Boogie-Woogie Etude 1943 (Belwin-Mills). Brilliant, energetic, percussive ostinato. Requires endurance and drive. D.

Sonatina (Belwin-Mills 1939). Moderately fast-spirited: driving, energetic, non-legato eighths in alla breve. Spiritual: flowing melody, homophonic accompaniment. Minuet: crisp, caricature-like. Finale: fast driving, satirical, requires strong fingers. M-D.

Dance Gallery (Chappell 1952). Six movements. M-D.

At The Piano (Chappell). Two books, 8 and 9 pedagogic pieces. Easy.

Ten for Deborah (Chappell). Ten short pieces, MC, varied keys and meters. Int.

Abby Variations (Chappell 1964) 9 pp. Theme and 12 clever variations on ABBE. Suggestions of "Happy Birthday" appear near end. Int.

Pavanne (Belwin-Mills). Easy moving, needs loose wrists. Int.

Prelude and Toccata (Belwin-Mills). M-D.

Rag—Blues—Rag (LG) in collection *New Music for the Piano*. M-D.

Ghost Waltzes 1991 (GS 1992) 20pp. 11 min. Commissioned for the ninth Van Cliburn International Piano Competition (1993). "The first musical sounds I heard in my early years came from my parents' player piano. The music on those piano rolls reflected the taste of that period, with a preponderance of waltzes of all kinds—Viennese, Russian, American, Chopin, Strauss, etc. This piece, therefore, is a distillation of these dance forms in three-quarter time—nostalgic, poignant, assertive, reflective, brash, sentimental, celebrative, elegiac. It is a fantasy collage of my waltz memories filtered through time, with haunting 'pianola' sounds intertwining throughout. I thought it appropriate for the Van Cliburn International Piano Competition to attempt a virtuosic piece that enables the performer to rhapsodize these many contrasting textures and moods that are unique to the waltz" (from the score). Highly fragmented material, hemiola, many key changes, unexpected modulations, spectacular pianistic writing. D.

Patterns 1984 (GS). Jazz inspired. M-D.

Patterns 1 and 7 1984. In collection *American Contemporary Masters* (GS 1995) 6 pp. No.1: molto presto, a contemporary "Two-Part Invention." M-D. No.7: slowly moving, nocturne style, M-C. M-D.

Pieces of China 1985 (GS). Jazz inspired. M-D.

China Chip from *Pieces of China* 1985. In collection *American Contemporary Masters* (GS 1995) 5 pp., 2 min., 45 sec. Jazz inspired, octatonic, shifting meters, wide skips, octaves in alternating hands, *sffz* conclusion. M-D to D.

Alfred Gradstein (1904–1954) Poland

Hommage à Chopin 1940–45 (Rouart, Lerolle) 75pp. Twelve etudes in three books; inspired by Chopin's etudes. Nos.8 "La Cracovienne" and 11 "Barcarolle" are especially interesting. M-D to D.

Guillermo Graetzer (1914–   ) Argentina, born Austria

Tres Toccatas (ECIC 1937–38). Lengthy works employing a contemporary harmonic and pianistic vocabulary. Allegro: syncopated rhythms, fast unison writing, dramatic closing. Con brio: alternating hands, double-note octaves, quick chordal passages, rhetorical section, dramatic closing. Allegro ma non troppo: lyric, but drives to enormous closing. D.

Five Bagatelles (EAM 1943–1946). Short, unmetered, varied, all atonal except No.5, interesting sonorities. M-D.

Sonatina (Ric Amer 1945) 12 min. Allegro Moderato; Andante; Allegro non troppo. No meter signatures, Latin American rhythms. M-D.

Rondo para niños (EAM 1947). Mainly two voices, light allegretto, swinging, free C tonality, for children. Int.

Ulf Grahn (1942–   ) Sweden

Snapshots (Frank 1975) 11pp. Eight pieces. Includes performance directions, introduction and contemporary techniques, optical and graphic notation. Aleatoric, improvisatory, clusters, multiple activity. Avant-garde. M-D.

To Barbo (Frank). Short contemporary character piece. Int.

Percy Grainger (1882–1961) Australia, came to USA in 1914

Grainger was an outstanding pianist but is best known for his fresh and highly pianistic arrangements of English songs and dances.

The Music of Percy Grainger (GS). 15 pieces that provide contrast in style. A broad sampling of his piano compositions. Int. to M-D.

The Young Pianist's Grainger (R. Stevenson—Schott 1967; GS). Some of the pieces are by Grainger, others are settings by Grainger of folksongs and pieces by Bach and Dowland. Notes on the music, as well as some photographs of Grainger throughout his career. Contains: Country Gardens; Shepherd's Hey; Molly on the Shore; Mock Morris; Beautiful Fresh Flower; Australian Up-Country Song; Irish Tune from County Derry; Walking; Hill-Song; To a Nordic Princess; One More Day; My John; Spoon River; Blithe Bells; Over the Hills and Far Away; Now, O Now, I Need Must Part. A charming and interesting collection. Easy to Int.

Percy Grainger Piano Album (GS 2436 1982) 139pp. Children's March "Over the hills and far away"; Colonial Song; Country Gardens; Eastern Intermezzo; "Handel in the Strand" Clog Dance; Harvest Hymn; Irish Tune from County Derry; Jutish Medley; Molly on the Shore; Scotch Strathspey and Reel; Shepherd's Hey; Spoon River; The Gum-Suckers March; The Hunter in His Career; The Immovable Do (or the Cyphering C); To a Nordic Princess. This music is direct, uncomplicated, childlike, poetic, and prone to rambunctious humor. Int. to M-D.

Sailor's Song 1954 (Gillespie—CFP 1982) 5pp. 2½ min. Tuneful, many large chords, octaves. M-D.

3 Scotch Folksongs 1900–54 (CFP 66925 1983) 15pp. 4 min. Will ye gang to the Hielands, Leezie Lindsay?; Mo Nighean Dubh; O gin I were where Gadie rins (concert version), simple version by the editor Ronald Stevenson. Inspired by a visit to Scotland in 1900. Full chords, dotted rhythms, tuneful, some of the finest settings in Grainger's harvest of folk music. M-D.

Lullaby from "Tribute to Foster" 1915 (MMP). Inspired by Stephen Foster's song "Camptown Races." Based on a work for chorus, orchestra, and musical glasses. Grainger's own version for solo piano. M-D.

See: Bob Doerschuk, "The Grainger Piano Repertoire," *Keyboard*, 8/8 (August 1982):25–26, 28, 30, 32.

Leslie Howard, "The (Percy Grainger) Keyboard Music," *Studies in Music* (Percy Grainger Centennial Vol.), 16 (1982):62–68.

Harold Gramatges (1918–   ) Cuba

Dos Danzas Cubanas (PIC 1953). Montuna: fast 2/4 syncopation, rhythmic, ends quietly on dominant. Sonera: more rhythmic drive, brilliant close. M-D.

Movil I (Bo&H). Events timed by seconds, directions (in Spanish) tell player to play keys, touch strings, fluctuate tempo, improvise freely. Uses entire keyboard and dynamic range, avant-garde. Int. to M-D.

Enrique Granados (1867–1916) Spain

A fine pianist and teacher, Granados composed numerous works for his favorite instrument. The earlier works (many are picture postcards in sound) show influences of Chopin, Grieg, and Liszt and are built on a traditional pianism. The two books of *Goyescas* (1911), inspired by the painter Goya, reveal a highly developed and exuberant piano style. These piano tone-poems are extended and show a facile improvisator rather than a master craftsman.

Allegro de concierto 1904 (MMP; UME). A bravura work; haunting melodies and some surprise harmonic twists. Opening material is repeated too often but this can be an exciting piece. M-D to D.

12 Spanish Dances (GS; K; EBM; UME; IMC) 4 books. Minuet G (also in *Masters of Spanish Piano Music,* Alfred 434); Oriental d; Zarabanda D; Villanesca G; Andaluza, Playera e (Alfred; CF; BMC); Jota-Rondalla Aragonesa D; Valenciana G; Asturiana C; Majurca Bb; Danza triste G; Zambra g; Arabesca a. These "Poems on the Piano" are inspired by the color and rhythm of Spanish folklore. They vibrate like living organisms, pulsating with sun-drenched energies. Immediately accessible. M-D.

Bocetos (Sketches) Op.20 (UME). Desperta del Cazador (The Wakening of the Hunter); El Hada y el Niño (The Child's Fairy Godmother); Vals muy lento (Very Slow Waltz); La Campana de la Tarde (The Bell of the Afternoon; also in *Masters of Spanish Piano Music,* Alfred 434). Int.

Goyescas 1911 (IMC; K; UME) 53 min. Los Requiebros (Flattery): double-note technique required. Coloquio en la Reja (Love Duet): complex melodic line. El Fandango de Candil: double-note technique required. Quejas ó la Maja y el Ruiseñor (Laments, or the Lady and the Nightingale): romantic rhapsody; GS publishes this piece with a translation of the first stanza of the verses sung to this music in the opera *Goyescas*; helps increase the understanding of this lovely extemporization. El Amor y la Muerte (Love and Death): difficult interpretative problems. Epilogo (Serenade of the Spectre): this "dance of death" contains the Dies Irae in the middle section, staccato fabric. Granados's most grandiose piano compositions. M-D to D.

Intermezzo from the opera *Goyescas* 1916 (MMP) 3 min. Arranged by the composer. Strong opening, melody with staccato accompaniment, nationalistic flavor. Effective by itself. M-D.

See: Charles Wilson, "The Two Versions of *Goyescas*," MMR, 81 (October 1951):203–207.

Cuentos de la Juventud (Stories of the Young) Op.1 1910 (ABRCM) 20pp. Ten pieces, kind of an *Album for the Young*. 1. Dedication; 2. The Beggar Woman; 3. May Song; 4. Old Man's Tale; 5. Coming from the Fountain; 6. Untitled; 7. Childhood Memories; 8. The Phantom; 9. The Orphan Girl; 10. March. Early to late Int. Nos. 3, 4, 5, 8, and 10 are in collection *Masters of Spanish Piano Music* (Alfred 434). No. 3 *May Song* (Alfred 6370).

Escenas poéticas Op.27/1. First series ca. 1905 (UME; Dover). 1. Berceuse; 2. Eva y Walter; 3. Danza de la Rosa. Colorful miniatures. No.2 has a reference to *Die Meistersinger von Nürnberg,* which was produced in Madrid in 1905. No.3 is in collection *Masters of Spanish Piano Music* (Alfred 434). Int.

Escenas Poéticas Libro de Horas (UME 1923) Segunda Serie. Recuerdo de países lejanos; El Angel de los claustros; Canción de Margarita; Sueños del poeta. Colorful miniatures. Int.

6 Estudios Expresivos (MMP; UME). Tema con variaciones y final; Allegro moderato; El caminante; Pastorale; La última pavana; María. Int.

6 Pieces on Spanish Folk Songs 1888–90 (UME). Published separately. Añoranza; Ecos de la Parrando; Vascongada; Marcha Oriental; Zambra; Zapateado. Contains some of the composer's finest nationalistic writing. M-D.

Danza Característica (UME 1973) Op. posth. 4pp. Three contrasting sections. Large span required. M-D.

Danza Lenta Op.37/1 (UME). Probably one of Granados's last works. Int. to M-D.

El Pelele (GS; MMP). The Dummy. Based on music from the opening scene of the opera *Goyescas*. Lively and strongly rhythmic, depicting the "man of straw" being tossed in the air by the "Majas." Although composed last, it is really a kind of introduction to the piano suite *Goyescas*. M-D.

Escenas Románticas (UME; Dover; IMC). Mazurka; Berceuse; Lento con estasi; Allegretto; Allegro appassionata; Epilogo. This suite of six "Romantic Scenes" is not as Spanish-sounding as most of the other piano works but they are as pianistic as Chopin's. Int. to M-D.

Los soldados de cartón ("The Cardboard Soldiers") (UME 1973). Op. posth. 4pp. Shifts from minor to parallel major. Int. to M-D.

Mazurka alla polacca Op.2 (UME) 3pp. Chopin-inspired, tuneful, and rhythmic. Int.

Oriental. Canción variada, intermedio y final (UME 1973) 12pp. M-D.

7 Valses poéticos 1887 (MMP; UME). Prelude: Vivace molto 1. Melódico; 2. Tempo de Vals noble; 3. Tempo de Vals lento; 4. Allegro humoristico; 5. Allegretto (Elegante); 6. Quasi ad libitum (Sentimental); 7. Vivo. Postlude: Presto. Does not contain as much Spanish flavor as some of the other works; more salon style. Succinct writing that casts a glance toward Ravel. Similar in length and structure to Ravel's set, *Valses Nobles et Sentimentales*, composed 24 years later. Moods range from gaiety to melancholy. Int. to M-D.

Reverie—Improvisation 1916 (published in *Clavier*, 6 [October 1967]:29–33). Recorded by Granados when he was in the USA and notated by Henry Levine and Samuel Randlett. Romantic, attractive, easily accessible. Int. to M-D.

Rapsodia Aragonesa 1901 (UME) 16pp. Glittering Romantic salon writing with splashes of Spanish dance rhythms. Sounds more difficult than it is. M-D.

La Sirena (The Mermaid) KC, 10/6 (November–December 1989):38–39. A charming salon waltz originally published in an old Spanish magazine. Int.

Paisaje (Landscapes) Op.35 1913 (MMP; UME) 7pp. Noble and serene outer sections enclose a midsection featuring right-hand undulating triplet figuration over a flowing left-hand melody. More chromatic than most of Granados's other piano works. M-D.

Países Soñados (Dreams of Faraway Places) Op.20 (UME). Published with *Bocetos* Op.20. Contains only one piece: "Enchanted Palace in the Sea" (Legend). Also available in *Masters of Piano Program Music* (Alfred 4572). Conjures up the image of a palace rising out of the sea, then submerging again to the bottom—much like the story associated with Debussy's *The Sunken Cathedral*. M-D.

Goyescas, Spanish Dances and Other Works for Solo Piano (Dover 1987) 164pp. The other works are *Romantic Scenes*; *Poetical Scenes* Book I. Int. to D.

Pieces (MMP 1633) Valse de concert Op.35; A la Cubano Op.36; Spanish Dances Op.37; Marche militaire Op.38; Impromptu Op.39. M-D.

Sketches; Landscapes; Caressa (Waltz) (MMP 1236). Int. to M-D.

See: Alicia de Larrocha, "Goya of Music: Alicia de Larrocha Talks about Granados," *Opera News*, 32/6 (1967):6–7.

——. "Granados," *High Fidelity Magazine* 17 (1967):56–58.

——. "Granados, the Composer," translated from the Spanish by Joan Kerlow, *Clavier*, 6/7 (1967):21–23.

Carol A. Hess, *Enrique Granados. A Bio-Bibliography* (New York: Greenwood Press, 1991), 192 pp.

Annemarie Schuessler, "Piano Music of Granados," *Clavier*, 31/8 (October 1992):16.

Parks Grant (1910–   ) USA

Sonata No.2 Op.45 (ACA 1953). About 17 min. Molto moderato e tranquillo: cross rhythms, tertial writing, begins quietly. Lento quasi andante: chorale-like, needs fine legato. Allegro assai e giocoso: gigue-like perpetual motion idea works to climax. M-D.

The World of Muse Op.55/2 (ACA 1965) 4½ min. Wistful short mood-piece, bitonal, chromatic. Not technically difficult but requires a sensitive pianist to probe past the notes. M-D.

Carl Heinrich Graun (ca. 1701–1759) Germany

Sonata d, Vol.1 *German Keyboard Music of the 17th and 18th Centuries* (H. Fischer, F. Oberdoerffer—Vieweg). Dramatic and expressive. Int. to M-D.

Concerto F, Vol.9 *German Keyboard Music of the 17th and 18th Centuries* (Fischer, Oberdoerffer—Vieweg). An attractive solo work. M-D.

Gigue b♭ (CF) and in *Old Masters* (K). Fine recital opener. Int.

Johann Christoph Graupner (1683–1760) Germany

8 Partitas (Br&H; Möseler). Graupner's only extant set of two known sets of partitas. Unusual movements found in dance suites of the period with the exception of an occasional aria or menuet in place of the gigue. Numerous optional dances. Int. to M-D.

Monatliche Klavierfrüchte (A. Küster—Möseler). Consists of allemandes, courantes, sarabandes, minuets, and gigues. M-D.

Klavierfrüchte (W. Frickert—Litolff). A collection of dances and pieces including an Entree C, Polonaise F, M I&II A, B in e, Le Sommeille, Aria con variazioni c, Chaconne e, and Suite C in 13 movements, from the larger work *Monatliche Klavierfrüchte*, 1722. Int. to M-D.

Giovanni Battista Grazioli (ca. 1746–1820) Italy

Graceful melodic writing, standardized organization, Alberti bass, chromatic appoggiaturas, and feminine cadences add interest to these works.

Dodici Sonate per Cembalo (R. Gerlin—Fondazione Eugenio Bravi 1941–43). Vol. XII of *I Classici Musicali Italiani*. No.11 G (Kohler—Litolff). All 12 of these sonatas are in 3 movements, FSF. Int. to M-D.

Sonata G. *Alte Meister* (Pauer—Br&H). Vol. IV has a reprint of the second movement, Adagio (L. Podolsky—CF). Int.

Variazioni per cembalo (Iesuè—Boccaccini & Spada 1983) 6pp. Theme is followed by 8 innocuous short variations, each one using shorter (and faster) note values and building to a brilliant scalar variation conclusion. Similar in structure and difficulty to the Handel "Harmonious Blacksmith Variations." M-D.

Harold Bellman Green (1921–   ) USA

The Diabolic Fiddler (Schroeder & Gunther 1975) 3pp. Many fifths, rhythmic, MC, *pppp* ending. Int.

Summer Sketch Book (Providence Music Press 1974) 12pp. Six short colorful pieces. Int.

Three Old Rhymes and Three French Folk Tunes (Waterloo 1968) 8pp. London
Bridge; Tom, Tom, the Piper's Son; Hickory, Dickory Dock; Frère Jacques;
Sur le pont d'Avignon; Pierrot. Clever; colorful MC settings; familiar
melodies embellished with delicate sounds. Int.

Variations in Phrygian (Providence Music Press 1970) 16pp. Theme in Phrygian
mode and twelve variations, mostly short, well contrasted, and contrapuntal, with individual titles. Final variation is a toccata. Brilliant and effective
for recitals. M-D.

Ray Green (1908–   ) USA
Green has been very active in supporting American music through his American
Music Editions.

Sonate Brevis (AME). Tempo giusto; Andante con moto; Adagio cantabile; Allegro vivo; Maestoso. The style resembles serial writing. This is a revision of
Sonatina published in *New Music* (April 1934). M-D.

12 Inventions (AME 1955). Key-scheme is based on a circle of fourths; C, F, B♭,
etc. Can be performed as a group or separately. Variety of moods, idioms,
and techniques; emphasis on linear writing. Int. to M-D.

Quartet: 4 Preludes (AME 1964). Short colorful tone pictures in contemporary
atonal sonorities. Large span (ninth) required. M-D.

Short Sonata C (AME 1965). Three effective movements. Contemporary "Alberti Bass" with freely moving melodic line. M-D.

Pieces for Children (AME). Four pieces "to introduce contemporary music materials to children—and to adults who hear or play them." Thoroughly attractive writing. Int.

Festival Fugues (An American Toccata) (Arrow). Prelude Promenade; Holiday
Fugue; Fugal Song; Prelude Pastoral; Jubilant Fugue. American folk elements present. M-D.

Arthur Greene (1945–   ) USA
7 Wild Mushrooms and a Waltz 1976 (Galaxy). Easy pieces for prepared piano.
These ingenious little pieces make the experience easy and memorable. A
rubber eraser and some wood screws are required. They will not hurt the
piano. The resulting percussion sounds will generate much interest in the
young student. Int.

Maurice Greene (1695–1755) Great Britain
Greene's style shows strong Italian influence with careful use of contrapuntal
material and fluent melodies.

A Collection of Lessons for the Harpsichord (S&B 1977) 73pp. A facsimile of the
original edition with an introduction by Davitt Moroney. Contains 48
pieces, first published in 1750, arranged in groupings by keys, 7 groups on
either side of a central Aria con Variationi in d. Suite and sonata characteristics are present. Attractive. Int. to M-D.

5 Pieces from Harpsichord Works (P. Williams—Bosworth). Contains Prelude F; Gigue F; Minuet D; Scherzando F; Courante D. Added fingering; ornamentation adequately realized. M-D.

Alexander Gretchaninoff (1864–1956) Russia
Gretchaninoff's eclectic style covers a broad gamut of the standard forms, including some charming pieces for young people. He worked as a piano teacher and folk song arranger.

Five Little Pieces Op. 3 (WB). Popular teaching pieces. Int.

Brimborions (Galaxy). Brimborions means "knick-knacks" in French. There are delights for everyone in this charming suite. Int.

Eight Pastels Op.61 (K). Has some pleasing qualities. Int.

Historiettes Op.118 (Leduc 1930). 12 pieces. Int.

Kinder-Album Op.98 (Alfred; CFP). Fifteen short, varied pieces. Not graded progressively; little fingering given. Int.

Glass Beads Op.123 (Alfred). Lyric and attractive. Int.

The Gretchaninoff Collection (Schott 536) 39pp. Contains 20 pieces selected and introduced by Maurice Hinson and grouped by level of difficulty. Early to late Int.

Russian Folk Dances Op.130 1930 (Schott) 2 vols. Vol. I: In My Garden: varied articulation, melodic transfer between hands. In the Sun-Clad Plain Stands a Birch Tree: sectional, left hand uses drone, awkward writing, colorful use of grace notes. Mid the Tow'ring Rocks: octave introduction, chromatic, boisterous style. In the Fields: introduction, melody featured in different registers, varied meters. Peasant Dance: introduction, ostinato bass, uses wide range of keyboard, sostenuto pedal required. On the Hill an Oak: variation-like treatment of melody. Vol. II: The Capricious "Barinya": simple folklike melody. Sometimes in the Garden, Sometimes in the Fields: grace notes embellish melody. O Ivan Mine, O Ivan: hands overlap. The Long Trail Is Ended: clever rhythmic usage, scalar figuration. Kastachok: thin textures, fast, tricky. "Kamarinskaia": melody decorated with grace notes, chordal, chromatic. Int.

Suite Miniature Op.145 (Leduc 1948). Ten pieces. Int.

Sonata No.2 Op.174 (Axelrod 1947). 2 movements with the second being a set of variations. Romantic harmonies and techniques. M-D.

Edvard Grieg (1843–1907) Norway
Nationalistic elements play a large part in the piano works of Grieg, especially the smaller character pieces, Grieg's finest contribution to the piano repertoire.

Complete Piano Works (CFP). Vol.I: Lyric Pieces, all 10 books; also available separately in 13 volumes. Vol.II: Opp.1, 3, 6, 19, 24, 28, 29, 41, 52, 73. Vol.III: Opp.17, 34, 35, 37, 40, 46, 50, 56, 63, 66, 53, 55.

Complete Works (CFP) edited by the Edvard Grieg Committee under the auspices of the Institute of Musicology, University of Oslo. Piano Solo: 1. Lyric

Pieces I–X. 2. Other original compositions. 3. Arrangements of Norwegian Folk Music. 4. Arrangements of own works.

Lyric Pieces 13 vols. (CFP).

Book I: Op.12 (Alfred; Henle; KMB; Ric; CF; ABRSM, with Op.3; WH; K; Supraphon). Arietta; Waltz; Watchman's Song; Fairy Dance; Popular Melody; Norwegian Melody; Album Leaf; National Song.

Book II; Op.38 (Schott; K; Supraphon). Cradle Song; Folksong; Melodie; Halling; Springdance; Elegie; Waltz; Canon.

Book III: Op.43 (K; Supraphon). Butterfly; Lonely Wanderer; In the Native Country; Little Bird; Erotik; To the Spring.

Book IV: Op.47. Valse-Impromptu; Album Leaf; Melodie; Halling; Melancholy; Springdance; Elegie.

Book V: Op.54. Bells; March of the Dwarfs; Norwegian Peasant March; Notturno; Scherzo; Shepherd Boy.

Book VI: Op.57 2 vols. Vanished Days; Gade; Illusion; Secrecy; She Dances; Home-Sickness.

Book VII: Op.62, 2 vols. Sylph; Gratitude; French Serenade; Brooklet; Phantom; Homeward.

Book VIII: Op.65, 2 vols. From Years of Youth; Peasant's Song; Melancholy; Salon; In Ballad Vein; Wedding-Day at Troldhaugen.

Book IX: Op.68. Sailor's Song; Grandmother's Minuet; At Thy Feet; Evening in the Mountains; At the Cradle; Valse mélancolique.

Book X: Op.71. Once upon a Time; Summer Evening; Puck; Peace of the Woods; Halling; Gone; Remembrances.

Lyric Pieces (CFP) in *Complete Works*. Preface indicates that Grieg's *Lyric Pieces* comprise 66 pieces for piano two-hands, which were published in ten sets between 1867 and 1901 with the opus numbers 12, 38, 43, 47, 54, 57, 62, 65, 68, and 71. Opp.12 and 38 each contain eight pieces; Opp.43 and 71 seven pieces each; all other sets six each.

Lyric Pieces (K 9549) complete in 1 vol.

Lyric Pieces (GS). Complete in 5 vols.

Lyric Pieces (Alfred 4835). Books 1 and 2.

Lyric Pieces (Schott 9011). Books 1–3.

See: Brian Schlotel, "Grieg's Lyric Pieces: Teaching Material and So Much More," *Music Teacher*, 55 (January 1976):12–13.

———. "Grieg's Other Piano Music—A Mine of Interest for the Piano Student," *Music Teacher*, 55 (February 1976):12–13.

OTHER SMALLER SETS:

6 Poetic Tone-Pictures Op.3 1863 (CFP; WH; ABRSM, with Op.12). The spirit of the smaller Schumann piano pieces is evident here, especially in No.4. Int. to M-D.

4 Humoresques Op.6 1865 (CFP; MMP). These are in effect "Norwegian Dances." Int. to M-D.

Norwegian Dances and Songs Op.17 1870 (CFP). Also contained in *Norwegian Notebook* (CFP), 16 pieces from Opp.17 and 66. Excellent introduction to Grieg for intermediate student. Int. to M-D.

4 Album Leaves Op.28 1864 (CFP; WH). Folk dances. Int. to M-D.

Improvisations on 2 Norwegian Folk Songs Op.29 1878 (CFP). A Grieg version of Liszt's *Hungarian Rhapsodies.* M-D.

Norwegian Dances Op.35 (MMP). These four dances are Grieg's arrangements for solo piano of the original Op.35 for piano duet. No.2 (A) is the most popular of the set and was made famous in the Broadway musical *Song of Norway.* M-D.

Slätter Op.72 1902 (Henle; CFP). These are the most original pieces based on Norwegian folk music. 17 dances arranged by Grieg from his peasant dances for violin. Int. to M-D.

See: John Horton, "Grieg's 'Slätter' for Piano," ML, 26/4 (1945): 229–35.

Moods Op.73 1905 (CFP). Resignation; Scherzo—Impromptu; A Ride at Night; Popular Air; Hommage à Chopin: figurations suggest Chopin's first and third etudes from his *Trois Nouvelles Etudes*; Student's Serenade; The Mountaineers Song. Int. to M-D.

LARGER WORKS:

Sonata e Op.7 1865 (Alfred 4836; Henle; CFP; Br&H; Schott; GS; PWM; MMP). This early 4-movement work is well constructed and more demanding than the short pieces. Movements are broken up into short sections, imaginative contrast; finale is the weakest movement. M-D.

See: Wadham Sutton, "Grieg: Sonata in E Minor, Op.7," *Music Teacher*, 52 (May 1973):13–14.

Ballad g Op.24 1875 (Henle; CFP; GS). Based on a Norwegian folk song "the northern peasantry"; 14 variations. Grieg's most difficult solo piano work. D.

Holberg Suite Op.40 1884 (Henle; CFP; K) 20 min. Prelude; S; Air; Gavotte; Rigaudon. Neoclassical. An idiomatic and brilliant work. M-D.

COLLECTIONS:

38 Pieces (A. Morrison—ABRSM) Vol.I: Easy to Int. Vol.II: M-D.

Grieg—An Introduction to His Piano Works (M. Halford—Alfred). 22 pieces in progressive order. Informative foreword. The editor suggests playing most of the ornaments on the beat, an instruction that might be questioned. Some of the unusual pieces are: A King Rules in the East, Op.66/3; Bell-Ringing, Op.54/6. Int. to M-D.

Selected Works (H. Levine—Alfred 1974) 144pp. 44 of the shorter works. Contains fine biographical information. Editorial additions shown in light print.

Selected Piano Works (Bo&H). Includes selections from Peer Gynt suites and the Norwegian Dances. Int. to M-D.

45 Selected Compositions (GS) 2 books. Int. to M-D.

Il mio primo Grieg (Pozzoli—Ric ER 2600) 12pp. Contains: National Song Op.12/8; Popular Melody; Waltz Op.12/2; Arietta Op.12/1; Dance of the Nymphs Op.12/4; The Lonely Wanderer Op.43/2. Little Bird Op.43/4. Int. to M-D.

Easiest Piano Pieces (Keller—CFP 5049) 19pp. Contains: Norwegian Melody Op.17/8; Watchman's Song Op.12/3; Dance of the Fairies Op.12/4; Patriotic Song Op.12/8; Waltz Op.12/2; Sailor's Song Op.68/1; The Song of Siri Dale Op.66/4; Arietta Op.12/1; Waltz Op.38/7; Norwegian Melody Op.6/3. Int.

Grieg—The First Book for Young Pianists (Halford—Alfred 1977) 24pp. Contains: Arietta Op.12/1; Cradle Song Op.66/7; Elfin Dance Op.12/4; Gjendine's Lullaby Op.66/19; Grandmother's Minuet Op.68/2; National Song Op.12/8; Waltz Op.12/2. Watchman's Song Op.12/3. Editor's additions in light print. Int.

Selections for Piano Vol.1 (Zen-On 195 1982) 79pp. Notes in Japanese and English. Includes: Op.12/1,2,3,4,6,8; Op.47/4; Op.38/2,3,4,6,7; Op.3/4,5; Op.68/1; Op.28/3; Op.43/1,2,4,5,6; Op.57/3; Op.54/3,4,6; Op.65/6. Clean edition. Int.

Norwegian Dances and Other Works for Piano (Dover 1991) 214pp. 25 Norwegian Folk Songs and Dances Op.17; Scenes of Country Life Op.19; Ballade g Op.24; Improvisation on Norwegian Folk Tunes Op.29; 4 Norwegian Dances, arr. of Op.35; Valses-Caprices, arr. of Op.37; Prayer and Temple Dance from *Olav Trygavason*, arr. from Op.50; 3 Orchestral Pieces from *Sigund Jorsalfar*, arr. of Op.56; 2 Nordic Melodies, arr. of Op.63; 19 Norwegian Folk Tunes Op.66; Slåtter (Norwegian Peasant Dances) Op.72.

Grieg Piano Album (GS 1957) 30pp. *Poetic Tone Pictures*, Op.3/4, 5; *Humoreskes* Op.6/2, 3; *Norwegian Bridal Procession* Op.19/2; *Album Leaves* Op.28/1–4; *The Last Spring* Op.34/2; *Album Leaf* (no opus number). Int. to M-D.

Peer Gynt Suite, Holberg Suite and Other Works for Piano Solo (Dover). Also includes Grieg's solo arrangement of his Piano Concerto.

Selections for Piano Vol.2 (Zen-On 1982) 120pp. 23 pieces, including: Cradle song Op.38/1; Melody Op.47/3; Album-Leaf Op.47/2; From Early Years Op.65/1; Norwegian March Op.54/2; Remembrances Op.71/7; Puck Op.71/3; Sonata Op.7. Int. to M-D.

15 Pezzi Lirici (Bèrben 1981) 30pp. 15 selections from Opp.12, 33, 43, 47, 54, 65, and 71. Fingered and pedaled. Excellent preparation for Chopin waltzes. Int.

Grieg the World Loves (Willis 1981) 48pp. Includes; Butterfly Op.43/1; March of the Dwarfs Op.54/3; Birdling Op.43/4; Nocturne Op.54/4; Peer Gynt Suite No.1; Solvejg's Song, from Peer Gynt Suite No.2; Norwegian Dance Op.35/2; Wedding Day at Troldhaugen Op.65/6. Int. to M-D.

See: Eleanor Bailie, *Grieg: The Pianist's Repertoire: A Graded Practical Guide* (London: Valhalla, 1993), 584pp.

Einar Steen-Nøkleberg, *Onstage with Grieg,* trans. William H. Halverson (Bloomington: Indiana University Press, 1997), 424pp.

Charles Tomlinson Griffes (1884–1920) USA

Love of oriental subjects and a preoccupation with Impressionist techniques were the major influences on Griffes's music. His stature continues to grow. His

Piano Sonata was one of the most important works in that genre to appear in America during the first quarter of the twentieth century.

Three Tone Poems Op.5 1910–12 (GS; MMP). The Lake at Evening: has an eerie, compelling effect, produced by the insistent repetition of a rhythmic figure throughout, suggesting the lapping lake water. Night Winds: uses swirling arpeggiated figures based on the whole-tone scale. The Vale of Dreams: loops fascinating thirds about an attractive main theme; very chromatic; has no concord until the final chord. M-D.

See: Joseph Smith, "Griffes' *The Vale of Dreams*," KC, 12/1 (January–February 1992):4–5, 42–43. Includes the music, pp.38–41. A lesson on this piece.

Fantasy Pieces Op.6 1912–15 (GS; MMP). Barcarolle: delicate, highly varied treatment of theme, including an expression of it in canon form, atmospheric. Nocturne: sensitive; has extraordinary chromatic harmonies, some polytonal; poetic. Scherzo: bravura writing. M-D.

Four Roman Sketches Op.7 1915–19 (GS). The White Peacock (Alfred) 1915: best known of the set; legato chords, running arpeggi. Nightfall 1916: uses overlapping hand formations and a stunning black-key glissando; minor seconds; an aura of mystery permeates the piece. The Fountain of the Acqua Paola 1916: reminds one of Ravel's *Jeux d'eau* but Griffes's daring and individual experimentation with complex new harmonies is very interesting; nostalgic melodies; dramatic arpeggios. Clouds 1916: bitonal ostinato chords and unresolved appoggiaturas over a swaying drone. M-D to D.

See: Reginald Haché, "Charles Tomlinson Griffes Revisited: An Essay on the Music of Charles Griffes," JALS, 34 (December–July 1993):32–42. Analyzes the four pieces in this set.

De Profundis 1915 (Donna Anderson—CFP 6647 1978) 8pp. 6 min. The editor suggests Tempo rubato throughout. Changing meters. Broken-chord and arpeggi figuration in left hand supports chords; melody in right hand. Contains some dissonant and quartal harmonies. Style is similar to Griffes's *Piano Sonata*. M-D.

Legend 1915 (C. Scribner's Sons 1972) 3 min. Based on exotic scale; waltz meter supports colorful harmonies. M-D.

Three Preludes 1919 (CFP 1967). Different mood in each piece. No titles, tempo marks, or dynamics. Enigmatic and strange, dark and brooding, in many ways reminiscent of the last works of Liszt; harmonically atonal and spare in texture. M-D.

Sonata 1917–18 (GS). Feroce-Allegro con Moto: driving 12/8, varied textures. Molto tranquillo: more melodically oriented. Allegro vivace: energetic 6/8, dramatic presto close. Lucid in structure, precise in expression, and fierce in feeling, a bold and assertive statement. Based on scale of c♯, d, e♭, f, g♯, a, b♭, c♯. A peak of neo-Romantic expression in American piano music. D.

Rhapsody b 1912–15 (Donna Anderson—CFP). First publication of this piece. Brilliant and technically demanding, several sections with contrasting mood, melodic material and tempo. D.

A Winter Landscape (D. K. Anderson—CFP 67629 c. 1997) 3pp., ca. 5 min. This character piece was probably composed "around 1912, or earlier, since it exhibits strong evidence of Griffes' Germanic style, which gave way to a more impressionistic idiom in the early 1910's" (from the score). Accompanied melody, repeated chords, works to impassioned climax and ends *ppp*. M-D.

The Pleasure Dome of Kubla Khan 1912 (in press GS 1995) c. 8½ min. A solo piano work that Griffes orchestrated in 1915; it has been known only in this version until now. Griffes wrote about this piece: "I have taken as a basis for my work those lines of Coleridge's poem describing the stately pleasure-dome, the 'sunny pleasure-dome with caves of ice,' the 'miracle of rare device.' Therefore I call the work *The Pleasure-Dome of Kubla Khan* rather than *Kubla Khan*. . . . As to argument, I have given my imagination free rein in the description of this strange palace as well as of purely imaginary revelry which might take place there. The vague, foggy beginning suggests the sacred river, running 'through caverns measureless to man down to a sunless sea.' The gardens with fountains and 'sunny spots of greenery' are next suggested. From inside come sounds of dancing and revelry which increase to a wild climax and then suddenly break off. There is a return to the original mood suggesting the sacred river and the 'caves of ice.' "

See: David Burge, "The Piano Music of Charles Griffes," *Keyboard*, 9/2 (February 1983):64. Discusses the Piano Sonata primarily.

Beth J. Eggers, "Charles Tomlinson Griffes: Portrait of an American Impressionist," AMT, 32/1 (September–October 1982):28–29.

Michael Lewin, "Rediscovering Griffes," P&K, 186 (May–June 1997):33–38.

Aldo Mancinelli, "Charles Griffes: An American Enigma," *Clavier*, 24/6 (July–August 1985):12–14. Also includes the music to "The Lake at Evening," Op.5/1.

H. M. K. Pratt, "The Complete Piano Works of Charles T. Griffes," diss., Boston University, 1975.

George P. Sanders, "The Piano Compositions of Charles Tomlinson Griffes," AMT, 35/1 (September–October 1985):28–29.

Cor de Groot (1914–   ) The Netherlands
De Groot is best known as a pianist. He has concertized throughout the world and has recorded extensively.

Cloches dans la martin (Donemus 1972). Bell sonorities, pedal study, 5/4 meter, Impressionistic. Int.

In Any Direction (Donemus 1974) 4pp. A poem for the right hand only, uses two pedals. M-D.

Wilhelm Grosz (1894–1939) Austria
Symphonische Variationen über ein Eigenes Thema Op.9 (UE 1921). Theme and 15 variations in a post-Romantic idiom. Thick textures, chromatic writing. Big technique is required. D.

Sonate No.3 Op.21 (UE 1927) 24pp. Allegretto: numerous tempo changes, cheerful. Andantino con grazia (Siziliana). Allegro molto: biting dissonances, triplet accompaniment. D.

Gabriel Grovlez (1879–1944) France
Grovlez's style is somewhat similar to Gabriel Fauré's.
7 Fancies (Augener 1915). See especially Nos.1, 2, and 5. Int.
A Child's Garden (JWC). 6 short imaginative pieces. Int.
Sarabande (Durand 1921). Chordal, chromatic, stately. M-D.
L'Almanach aux Images (Augener). 8 pieces with accompanying poems. Int. to M-D.
Improvisations on London (Augener). Interesting writing. M-D.
2 Impressions (Heugel). Nostalgique; Joyeuse. M-D.
Le Royaume Puérii (Heugel). Eight pieces for children. Easy to Int.

Heinz Karl Gruber (1943–   ) Austria
6 Episodes from a Discontinued Chronicle Op.20 1966 (Bo&H) 18pp. Each piece bears a date for a title, e.g., 5 August 1966, 15 December 1966. A musical presentation of six days from a "discontinued chronicle." Lyrical polyphonic writing, jazz influence, strong motives, and tonal control for the general effects of improvisation. Different moods and feelings, which correspond to seasonal changes, are presented in this challenging set. D.
See: David Drew, "H. K. Gruber—A Formal Introduction from Two Sides," *Tempo*, 126 (September 1978):14–23.

Rudolph Gruen (1900–   ) USA
Sonata Op.29 (GS 1941). 3 movements. Based on artificial scale, mainly pentatonic: D, F, G♭, C plus 2 auxiliary tones E♭ and B, polytonal or atonal in effect. Traditional forms: first movement SA; second movement song form; third movement rondo, perpetual motion idea. D.
Classical Variations on an Original Theme Op.51 (ACA). 17 variations, differing styles and textures: Sicilienne, minuet, canon, ostinato, etc. Virtuoso writing with some exciting moments. D.

Louis Gruenberg (1884–1964) USA, born Russia
Gruenberg was one of the earliest American composers to incorporate jazz in his writing.
Jazzberries Op.25 (UE). Fox-trot; Blues; Waltz; Syncopep. Effective. M-D.
Polychromatics (UE 1924). An effective light suite, wittily conceived if not strikingly original. Adroit and brilliant piano writing. M-D.
Jazz Masks Op.30a (UE 9644) 11pp. A jazz version of Chopin's *Valse* Op.64/2. Clever. M-D.
See: Robert F. Nisbett, "Louis Gruenberg: A Forgotten Figure of American Music," *Current Musicology*, 18 (1974):90–95.

Gottfried Grünewald (1673–1739) Germany
2 Partitas (H. Ruf—Ric) G, A. These two works are from five Partitas, the only extant works of Grünewald. Int. to M-D.

Jean-Jacques Grünewald (1911–   ) France
Suite de danses (Sal 1948). Spirit of clavecin dances permeates this set. M-D.
Partita (Rideau Rouge). Written as "pièce imposée" for the 1971 Marguérite
Long Piano Competition in Paris. D.

Camargo Guarnieri (1907–1993) Brazil
Guarnieri's style is characterized by subtle nationalistic influences coupled with
a complete command of the general technical resources of composition. An elastic counterpoint permeates many of his more extended compositions. His piano
works vary from simple lyric pieces like *Maria Lucia* to pianistic virtuosity of
the highest order, as found in *Danza Selvagem* or the *Toccata*.
Dansa Brasileira 1928 (AMP). Samba rhythms, repeated octaves, popular flavor,
   rich sonorities. M-D.
Primeira Sonatina 1928 (Ric Amer). Molengamente; Ponteado e bem dengoso;
   bem depressa.
Chôro torturado 1930 (AMP). Agitated, chromatic, chords, octaves, cross-rhythms,
   displays numerous moods. Mature pianism required. D.
Ponteios (Ric). Vol.I: 1–10 (1931–1935). Vol.II: 11–20 (1947–1949). Vol.III: 21–30
   (1954–55). Vol.IV: 31–40 (1956–57). Vol.V: 41–50 (1958–59). One of the most
   significant additions to piano literature written by any Brazilian composer
   since the death of Villa Lobos in 1959. *Ponteio* comes from the verb *Pon-
   tear,* "to strum," as on a guitar. Guarnieri uses the word for short prelude-
   type pieces. In the books of *Ponteios* a slow, nostalgic piece is generally followed by a short piece of brilliant or virtuosic character. Musical, well
   written; has a special appeal. Int. to D.
      See: David Appleby, "Capturing Brazilian Flavor," *Clavier*, 16 (January
   1977):19–20. Discusses the *Ponteios* and has a lesson on No.18.
Dansa Selvagem 1931 (Ric). A savage jungle dance, drumbeats imitative with
   open fifths and seventh chords, bravura style. D.
Little Horse with the Broken Leg 1932 (AMP). Limping figuration, syncopated,
   3-voice texture. Int.
Lundú 1935 (Ric). Brazilian song-dance, fast, rhythmic, 4 against 3, exotic. M-D.
Toccata 1935 (AMP). Chromatic, double-note technique. D.
Sonatina No.3 1937 (Ric) 12 min. Allegro: asymmetrical rhythms, 3 voices. Con
   tenerezza: grazioso, melody over broken-chord figuration. Two-Part Fugue:
   rhythmic, moving 16th notes, forte conclusion. M-D.
Maria Lucia 1944 (Music Press). Short, calm lyric piece, smoothly flowing eighth
   notes. Int.
Dansa Negra 1946 (Ric; AMP). Mournful, intense, blues element, resonant mid-
   section. M-D.
Ficarós Sosinha 1939 (Music Press). Based on a Brazilian children's game. Short,
   graceful, peaceful. Easy.
5 Estudos 1949–50, 1954 (Ric) Vol.I, Nos.1–5. Extensive, involved. Each study is
   devoted to a compositional technique that focuses on a specific pianistic
   problem. An important series. M-D to D.

5 Peças Infantis 1935 (Ric). Estudando piano; Criança triste; Valsinha manhosa; A criança adormece; Polka. Int.

Cançao Sertaneja 1928 (Ric). Emotional, subtle syncopation. M-D.

Sonatina IV 1958 (AMP) 19pp. 14 min. Com Alegria; Melancolio; Gracioso. No key signatures, many accidentals, asymmetrical rhythms, uniform figurations. Concluding flowing movement with polyrhythms and countermelodies is most effective. M-D.

Sonatina V 1962 (Ric Brazil) 19pp. Com humor: changing meters, melodies have little folk character. Second movement: thin textures, modal. Com alegria: changing accents and meters with a *samba* rhythm predominating in the B section. M-D.

Sonatina VI 1965 (AMP) 14 min. A major work, a sonata in content and length. Represents some of Guarnieri's most involved thinking. Recalls some of the ideas presented in the *Estudos*. Gracioso: SA; intense; angular lines; left hand has much thematic activity. Etéreo: ABA, bitonal, much use of thirds. Humoristico, molto ritmato: a two-voice fugue; Etéreo theme of second movement returns at climax of fugue; fugue subject returns for a majestic closing. D.

Improviso 1 1948 (Ric Brazil) 4pp. 3 min. A calm, wistful, Brazilian "Song without Words." M-D. Nos. 2, 3, 4 (Ric 1970).

Acalanto 1954 (Ric Brazil) 2 min. Two-voice texture; lovely expressive little lullaby. From Suite IV Centario 1954. Uses only treble clef. Int.

As Tres Gracas 1963–71 (Ric Brazil) 3 min. Acalanto para Tânia; Tanguinho para Miriam; Toada para Daniel Paulo. A short suite in linear design. Folk elements seemingly permeate the pieces with a melancholy Spanish character, but no folk tunes are quoted. Int.

Valsas 1–5 (Ric Brazil). Lentemente; Preguicoso; Com Molesa; Calmo e Saudoso; Calmo. Published together. M-D.

5 Estudos, Vol.II, Nos. 6–10 (Ric Brazil 1962) 12 min. Impetuoso: ABABA; much unison writing two octaves apart; preference for melodic interval of fourth; moves over most of keyboard in angular lines; atonal. Sem Pressa (expressivo): 2 with 3 in same and both hands; polymeters; melodic; chain phrases repeated in groups; right-hand legato is vital. Comodo: ABABA; left-hand study; highly chromatic; varied textures; enormous conclusion; mirror writing in final measures; large span required. Furioso: ABA; 16th-note figures; bitonal; flexible meters are imperceptible; parallel motion between hands a ninth apart. Movido: ABA; melody in left hand with conflicting rhythmic groupings in each hand. Well-written pieces. M-D to D. Vol.III, Nos. 11–15, 1968–70, pending.

Toada 1929 (K) 3 min. Opening and closing sections a warm con muita saudade. Mid-section is a nemm rhythmado; dancelike. M-D.

Toada Triste 1936 (GS) in collection *Latin American Art Music*. 5 min.

See: Sister Marion Verhaalen, "Guarnieri—Brazilian Nationalist," *Clavier,* 16 (January 1977):18–19.

——, "The Music of Camargo Guarnieri," *Clavier*, 27/10 (December 1988):27–30. Contains music of second movement of *Sonatina* No. 4.

Carlos Guastavino (1914–   ) Argentina

Tres Sonatinas 1949 (Ric). Three one-movement post-Impressionist works. Published together. Movimiento; Retama; Danza. Based on Argentine rhythms. M-D.

Diez Preludios 1952 (Ric). Short pieces based on themes of Argentine children's songs. Int. to M-D.

Sonata 1947 (Ric) 16 min. Allegretto Intimo. Scherzo—Molto vivace. Recitativo —Lento. Fuga y Final: based on a Riojana popular melody. Solid craftsmanship, interesting sonorities. D.

Pelle Gudmundsen-Holmgreen (1932–   ) Denmark

Udstillingsbilleder (WH 1968) 13pp. Seven short pieces are contained in this "Picture Gallery." Clusters and contemporary compositional techniques are used. A large hand span plus adroit pedal techniques are requirements. D.

César Guerra-Peixe (1914–1993) Brazil

Guerra-Peixe's early works were influenced by the 12-tone system. Around 1949 he changed course and returned to his Brazilian heritage using folksong resources.

7 Preludios Tropicais (Vitale 1979–82). Published separately. Cantiga de Folia de Reis; Marcha Abaianada; Persistencia; Ponteado de Viola; Pequena Bailado; Reza-de-Defunto; Tocata. Strong folksong influence, some very effective and beautiful writing. Should be investigated. M-D.

Elisabeth Jacquet de la Guerre (1669–1729) France

Pièces de Clavecin 1707 (Brunold, Dart—l'OL 1956; Carol Gates—Heugel 1986). 12 rich dance pieces of austere dignity and intricate detail showing an awareness of some contemporaneous Italian keyboard techniques. All have individual interest. Int. to M-D.

See: Edith Borroff, *An Introduction to Elisabeth Jacquet de la Guerre* (Brooklyn: Institute of Mediaeval Music, 1966).

Jean Guillou (1930–   ) France

Sonata I (Amphion 1974) 36pp. One unwinding movement that builds to an enormous climax. The final section unleashes blazing sonorities all over the keyboard. Strong dissonances. D.

Toccata (Leduc 1971) 16pp. 9 min. Some writing spread over four staves, triple trills, widely spaced, chromatic. D.

Alexandre Guilmant (1837–1911) France

Guilmant was one of the most famous organists of his time and composed mainly for the organ. Among his few works for piano are these six pieces, possibly written for his young daughter.

Six Short Pieces Op. 48 (T. Johnson—ABRSM 1985) 16pp. Child's Song; Alla Siciliana; Fughetta; Little March; Scherzettino; Tarantella. Colorful, contrasting character pieces. Int.

David Guion (1892–1981) USA

Guion studied for three years with Leopold Godowsky in Vienna. His most successful works use naive and folkish material, but with his sophisticated imagination and musical technique he transformed them into something far from naive.

Piano Album (GS 1983) 69pp. 24 pieces. Arkansas Traveler: an old folk tune
heard by Guion as a fiddle "breakdown"; often performed by Percy Grainger. Minuet: elegant and stately; shows Godowsky influence. Sheep and
Goat Walkin' to the Pasture: uses bits and pieces of other old cowboy
breakdowns and some original ideas. The Lonesome Whistler: a lyrical
pianistic description of a boy ambling down an alley late at night. The Scissors Grinder: Impressionistic. Valse Arabesque: in a grand waltz style.
Mother Goose Suite: 17 short, descriptive movements; the first and last are
the most difficult. The first, Hey, Diddle, Diddle, uses an original Guion
tune; the rest are based on nursery tunes of J. W. Elliott. In the score Guion
noted that many of the pieces require "the technical skill and artistic finish
of the concert pianist." A highly appealing collection. Int. to M-D.

Friedrich Gulda (1930–2000) Austria

Gulda had an extensive career as an acclaimed concert pianist and performed
over most of the globe. Since 1962 he performed and wrote in a jazz idiom.

Play Piano Play (Br 8049 1971) 4pp. No.1 from *10 Pieces for Yuko*. Jazz style, unequal notes (notes inégales), moderato, quiet ending. Int. to. M-D.

Klavier Kompositionen (Weinberger). Gulda's eclectic style shows influences of
classic to impressionistic characteristics and Viennese folksongs. Each
piece is "laid out" well for the instrument. M-D.

Georges I. Gurdjieff (1877–1949) Russia. Thomas de Hartmann (1885–1956) France, born Russia.

In 1922 Gurdjieff opened an Institute for the Harmonious Development of Man
in France. Its aim was to offer to those who studied there the means to discover
their essential nature and to develop its hidden possibilities. Physical and intellectual work and a great variety of exercises, dances, and movements were all
part of an intense activity at this Institute. Hartmann worked closely with Gurdjieff in composing the music listed below.

Music for the Piano. Vol. I: *Asian Songs and Rhythms* (Schott 7841 1996) 140pp.
49 pieces that evoke the atmosphere of the peoples of the Near East and
Central Asia, particularly of Gurdjieff's own Armenian and Greek ances-
try. Some of the most interesting pieces are Greek Round Dance, Oriental
Song, Tibetan Melody, Chant of the Molokans, Kurd Shepherd's Dance.
Vol. II: *Music of the Sayyids and the Dervishes* (Schott 7842 1996) 152pp.
These pieces reflect the musical idiom of the Middle East. The Sayyids are
considered descendants of the prophet Mohammed. Dervishes belong to

different Islamic orders in which devotional and spiritual exercises are linked to musical forms. 42 pieces. Some of the most interesting are Sayyid Chant and Dance (No. 3), Dervish Dance, Persian Dervish, Kurdo-Greek Melody. Most of the pieces are harmonized in a nineteenth-century style. Int. to M-D.

Jesús Guridi (1886–1961) Spain
Guridi studied with d'Indy and Joseph Jongen.
Ocho Apuntes (UME 1954) 19pp. Amanecer; Canción Vasca; Danza Rústica; Canto de Arriero; Romanza; Cortejo Funebre; Rumor de Agua; Marcha Humorística. Short, varied pieces written in a late-nineteenth-century style. Int.
Tres Piezas Breves 1910 (UME 1956) 11pp. Amanecer: written-out trills with melody embedded in the line. Nostalgia: 6/8 in right hand with 2/4 in left; Romantic harmonies. Serenata: dancelike, alternating hands, colorful. Int.
Vasconia (UME). Three pieces on popular Basque themes. M-D.

Cornelius Gurlitt (1820–1901) Germany
Much of Gurlitt's style shows the influence of Robert Schumann.
A First Book (K 3497). Easy character pieces.
The Classicality Op.115 (Augener). Variations on "Ach, du lieber Augustin" in the style of various composers. Int. to M-D.
First Lessons Op.117 (K 3498). Attractive pieces. Easy to Int.
O Sanctissima Op.135/1 (Kuhlstrom—Augener). Variations on a Sicilian Air. Fluent and pianistic. M-D.
Album for the Young Op.140 (Alfred). An excellent set of 20 pieces. Some of Gurlitt's best. Int.
Six Sonatinas Op.54 (Alfred). Pleasing ideas. Int.
Musical Sketches Op.182 (Ashdown). Beguiling felicity and balanced reticence. M-D.
Little Flowers Op.205 (ABRSM) 19pp. 12 pieces that display particular charm and character. Each piece is named after a flower. Int.
Humorous Transcriptions (Variations) on "Ach de lieber Augustin," in the style of various composers, Op.115 (Schott ED 7165 1983) 15pp. Published with Siegfrid Ochs (1858–1929) *S'kommt ein Vogel geflogen*, 13pp. Gurlitt treats the famous tune in the style of Mozart, Haydn, Beethoven, J. S. Bach, Handel, Schubert, Weber, Mendelssohn, Chopin, and Schumann. Remarkable incorporation of each composer's main style characteristics. Delightful. M-D.

Serge Gut (–   ) France
Scènes villageoises (Billaudot 510-03486). Six musical scenes in different musical styles. Several emphasize light staccato in the left hand. Int.

Gene Gutche (1907–   ) USA, born Germany
Gutche has referred to his work as "a blending of the most modern language and techniques with a genuinely classical feeling for structure."

Sonata No.6 (Highgate). A one-movement work, complex harmonic idiom, unusual notation, a few tone clusters. D.

Sonata Op.32/1 (Highgate) 11 min. 24pp. Repeated notes, percussive, numerous meter changes, sophisticated craft. D.

Sonata Op.32/2 (Highgate 1973) 23pp. 18 min. One movement, intriguing Romantic sonorities, virtuoso writing. D.

H

Pavel Haas (1899–1944) Czech Republic

Haas studied with Janáček at the Brno Conservatory. Haas died at Auschwitz.

Suite Op.13 1935 (Tempo Praha/Bote & Bock). 1. Praeludium; 2. Con Molta espressione; 3. Danza; 4. Pastorale; 5. Postludium. Movements 1, 3, and 5 are flashy and contrast with No. 2 (dreamy) and No. 4 (meditative). Polymetric; interesting rhythms. M-D.

Alois Hába (1893–1973) Czech Republic

Around 1920 Hába evolved a system of quarter-tone and sixth-tone music based on equal temperament. He had microtonic instruments constructed, including a quarter-tone piano, and he has written a number of treatises about his experiments.

Sonata d Op.3 1919 (UE) 28pp. Thick, chromatic idiom in all three movements; contains some lovely moments. D.

Toccata Op.38 Quasi una fantasia 1931 (CHF 1962) 17pp. Sectional; many types of figuration and mood; changing meters; ending only has motoric rhythmic drive. Freely tonal. M-D.

Sech Stimmungen (Six Moods) Op.102 (Artia 1817; Panton) 13pp. 18 min. Contrasting character pieces, MC. M-D.

Yoshio Hachimura (1938–　　) Japan

Improvisation (Ongaku-No-Tomo-Sha 1964) 8pp. Five short pieces (sections) with variable meters, some "senza tempo." Pointillistic, harmonics, clusters, dynamic extremes. M-D.

Manos Hadjidakis (1925–1994) Greece

Hadjidakis is best known for his film score *Never on Sunday.*

For a Little White Seashell (Papagrigorious—H. Nakes Co.). Five preludes and dances. "Calamatianos," from this set, appears in KC, 13/5 (September–October 1993): 53–56. This dance comes from the city of Kalamata: 7/8 meter (3 + 4), structured in four-measure melodic phrases. Int. to M-D.

Six Popular Pictures; Ionian Suite; Rhythmology (H. Nakes Co.).

Reynaldo Hahn (1875–1947) France

These works are all delightful confections that cannot be indulged too excessively.

Chanson de Midi (Heugel). A pretty trifle. Int. to M-D.

Premières Valses (10) 1898 (Heugel). Simple and tuneful. Int. to M-D.

Deux Etudes (Heugel 1927). 1. A♭: sixteenth-note accompaniment over melody in left hand. 2. d: triplet study. M-D.

Portraits de Peintres 1896 (Hengel) 18pp. Four colorful pieces after the poetry of Marcel Proust. Musical pictures of Albert Cuyp, Paulus Potter, Anton van Dyck, and Antoine Watteau. A portrait of each honored painter and a Proust poem precede each piece. M-D.

Thème Varié 1909 (Durand) 4pp. Theme with five variations, neoclassic style; good finger facility required. M-D.

Alexei Haieff (1914–1994) USA, born Russia

Haieff writes in a neoclassic style that has much vitality and is naturally attractive.

Five Pieces (Bo&H 1946) 15 min. Allegro; Andantino; Vivace scherzando; Lento molto; Allegro molto. Ranges from M-D imitative counterpoint to bravura writing in the final piece.

Four Juke Box Pieces (Bo&H 1952). Waltz: you can whistle an ad lib cornet obbligato. March: with 2/4 and 3/8 juxaposed. Nocturne. Polka. Humorous. M-D.

11 Bagatelles (EMM 1950). Short; exploit contemporary idioms. M-D.

Gifts and Semblances (Bo&H 1954). 4 pieces. Int. to M-D.

Sonata (Chappell 1956). 3 movements. A large MC work with more interpretative problems than technical, tonal ambiguity, large skips in melody, contrasting textures. M-D.

Sonata No.2 (PAU 1955). 4 movements. Transparent textures. Effective bitonal final movement. M-D.

Notes of Thanks (Chappell 1961). 6 short pieces, jazz influence. Numerous pianistic problems, especially wide skips. M-D.

Saint's Wheel (Gen 1960). Variations on a circle of fifths. In reality, a fine contemporary chaconne. Looks more difficult than it is but requires sensitive voicing of lines. Contemporary sounds; trill plays an important part; left-hand skips. Requires mature musicianship.

Children's Pieces (Gen). 10 short pieces, contemporary sonorities, each piece titled. Int.

André Hajdu (1932–   ) Israel, born Hungary

Journal from Sidi-Bou-Said (IMI 204) 10pp. 4 min. Composed in 1960 during "an intense and malevolent moment of my life" (from note in score). Short, fragmentary, strong and intense writing, complex rhythms, harmonics, pointillistic. M-D.

Two Prayer Songs 1974–75 (IMI 423) 5pp. Andantino: based on a Hassidic song, "From Egypt Didst Thou Deliver Us," in d, 30 bars long. Andante: set to a hymn tune sung at the New Moon; moves along relentlessly in e; incessant theme. Int.

Two Hassidic Tunes 1975 (IMI 424) 4pp. 4½ min. Tune of Yohanan the Cobbler: lyric, rhythmic mid-section. Ve'hee She'amada: sonorous, glissando. Colorful mid-Eastern flavor. Int.

Mihály Hajdu (1909–   ) Hungary

Hajdu is one of the few contemporary Hungarian composers not noticeably influenced by Bartók.

5 Piano Pieces (EMB). Prelude; Meditation; Scherzo; Improvisation; Toccata. All well developed. M-D.

Sonatina (EMB 1962). 3 movements. Unique personal style. M-D.

Talib Rasul Hakim (1940–1988) USA

Sound-Gone 1967 (Bo&Bo) 6pp. 10 min. Relies on decaying sonorities. Uses a metal cylinder and a drinking glass. "Both damper-sustaining pedals are employed quite extensively throughout the work. The performer should aspire to a 'loose-lingering-like' approach to the work. The over-all performance should be that of an 'introspective-like involvement' in creating atmospheres of sound; only where indicated is a precision-like execution desired" (from the score). Arm clusters; plucked strings; palms strike strings. Dynamics-duration-sequence pulse is left to the performer. Avantgarde. M-D.

Cristobal Halffter (1930–   ) Spain

Halffter's earlier style was atonal with strong Bartók and Stravinsky influence. Since the mid-1950s he has used serial techniques.

Sonata para Piano (UME 1951). One movement. Neoclassic style, influenced by Bartók and Stravinsky. M-D.

Introducción, Fuga y Final Op.15 (UME 1957). Carefully worked-out serial technique. Thin textures contrasted with thicker octave doublings. Registers are widely separated. 12-tone. D.

Ernesto Halffter (1905–1989) Spain

Halffter studied with Falla and was strongly influenced by the critic Adolfo Salazar and the composer Oscar Esplá. He has championed modern music in his role as conductor in Spain and in South America.

Pregón. Cuba (ESC). Effective salon piece. M-D.

Dance of the Shepherdess (ESC 1927). Broken chords, sixteenth-note motion. Fine encore. M-D.

Sérénade à Dulcinée (ESC 1951). Spanish coloration. M-D.

Habanera (ESC 1950). Interesting rhythmic and melodic ideas. M-D.

Sonata D (ESC 1926–32). One movement. French and Spanish influence. Tertial harmonies, fugal section, full sonorities. M-D.

Dance of the Gypsy (ESC). Double thirds, exotic. M-D.

Rodolfo Halffter (1900–1987) Mexico, born Spain

Halffter's style is basically tonal with occasional use of bitonality. Frequent changes of meter are normal, and contrapuntal voices are clearly defined.

Sonata No.1 Op.16 1948 (EMM; UME) 18 min. Three movements. Tonal, added-note technique used in last movement (Allegro con spirito), which is light-hearted and dancelike. Cross-rhythms and alternation of duple and triple meters. M-D.

Sonata No.2 Op.20 1951 (PIC) 33pp. Four movements. Thin textures, pianistic, musical. Final movement, a rondo, has a dancelike quality, alternating meters. M-D.

See: David Burge, "Three Recent Piano Sonatas," *Keyboard,* 10/4 (April 1984):64–65, for a discussion of *Sonata* No.2.

Once Bagatelles Op.19 (UME 1947) 26pp. 11 short pieces. Lively rhythms, canonic imitation, colorful effects. M-D.

Homenaje a Antonio Machado (UME 1944) 22pp. Fascinating four-movement suite. M-D.

Tres Hojas de Album Op.22 (UME 1964). Elegy: somber and moving. Scherzo and Trio. March: clever and amusing. Well constructed. M-D.

Dos Sonatas de El Escorial Op.2 (UME 1930). Reflects the spirit of D. Scarlatti and Soler with piquant bitonal vocabulary. M-D.

See: L. E. Powell, Jr., "Rodolfo Halffter, Domenico Scarlatti, and Kirkpatrick's Crux," AMT, 26 (June–July 1976):4–7. A discussion of the "Dos Sonatas de El Escorial" and the "Danza de Avila."

Homenaje a Arturo Rubinstein. Nocturno Op.36 (UME 1974) 14pp.

Labertino Op.34 (Coleccion Arion 1972) 19pp. Labyrinth, Four Attempts to Locate the Exit. One page of symbol descriptions; also uses conventional notation. Aleatoric, disjunct, harmonics. Same basic material used throughout but disguised. D.

Tercera Sonata Op.30 (Coleccion Arion 1968) 22pp. Allegro; Moderato cantabile; Liberamente—Lento molto espressivo; Impetuoso. Twelve-tone, indeterminate note values, clusters, some avant-garde notation, good introduction to duodecaphonic technique. Constantly changing meters, complex rhythms. D.

Richard Hall (1903–1982) Great Britain
Hall was a composition teacher of the concert pianist John Ogdon.

Suite 1967 (Nov) No.7 in Virtuoso series. Prelude; Ostinato; Intermezzo; Scherzo (with two trios); Second Ostinato; Recitative and Chorale. "In the best sense neo-classical and suffused with a deeply-felt mysticism" (John Ogdon, editor of the series). M-D.

Charles Hallé (1819–1895) Great Britain, born Germany
See below, "Collections," *Piano Music of the Parisian Virtuosos 1810–1860.*

Haflioi Hallgrimsson (1941–   ) Iceland
Sketches in Time 1993 (JWC). Seven short pieces, varied styles, asymmetric rhythms, well written. Int.

Iain Hamilton (1922–   ) Scotland
Even though Hamilton uses serial techniques in most of his works, he has never abandoned tonality.

Sonata I (TP 1973) 24pp. 15 min. Originally published as Op.13 (Schott 1951). Three movements. Rhythmic and contrapuntal motives combined in a swirling chromatic texture. Bartók influence. D.

Three Pieces Op.30 1955 (Schott) 5 min. Tonal, exhibits fine usage of 12-tone technique. M-D.

Nocturnes with Cadenzas 1963 (Schott) 7 min. A cycle of pieces, Impressionistic yet firmly controlled by an underlying serial technique. D.

Sonata II (TP 1976) 20pp. 12 min. Five short continuous sections: Placido; Con bravura; Sospeso; Espansivo; Moto perpetuo. Elaborate, dazzling; combines florid figuration with driving rhythms. Strong dissonances, clusters, brilliant cadenza. Large span required. D.

Palinodes 1972 (TP 1975) 22pp. 15 min. Seven imaginative studies after lines of Rimbaud (1854–1891), the famous French poet. A quotation from Rimbaud precedes each work. Some of the music seems to be programmatically connected to the poems and contains wild images, dreams, etc. Strong complex writing involving clusters, pointillistic treatment, pliable rhythms, glissandi, fast atonal figuration. Highly original pieces. Require virtuoso technique and superb musicianship. D.
See: David Burge, "Five New Pieces," CK, 3 (December 1977):66. Discusses "Palinodes."

Sonata III, B 1978 (TP) 31pp. 23 min. A subtly structured, hauntingly beautiful, six-movement work in which variants of the first two movements return as part of the final two movements. Between these pairs is an eloquent slow movement and a brilliant cadenza. The uncomplicated harmonic language is quite neoclassical, and full advantage is taken of the piano's virtuoso and coloristic possibilities. D.

A Field of Butterflies 1990 (TP 1992) 16pp., ca. 12 min. The Fritillary; The Emperor; The Orange Tip; The Nevada Blue; The Peacock; The Red Admiral. Changing meters, glissandi, MC, chromatic, tonally oriented. M-D.

A Book of Watercolors 1993 (TP 1996) 24pp., 17 min. Moonlit Sea; Water Melodies; Highland Rivulets; Winter Landscape with Birds; March Winds; Summer Noon; Spring Fountain. Colorful and contrasted writing, MC, effective as a group or individually. Mixture of tonal and atonal sections. Full of evocative musical imagery. M-D.

George Frederic Handel (1685–1759) Germany

During his lifetime, Handel was equally famous as a composer and as a keyboard player of unsurpassed ability.

SUITES:

Although Handel wrote other keyboard music, his suites are the most important contribution to the medium. They reach back to the Italian chamber sonata, from which he took over a number of forms. Along with the standard dances—A, C, S, G, and others—we find movements titled Andante, Allegro, Largo, etc. The numbering and order of movements (Serauky—CFP) are as follows: No.1 A: Prelude; A; C; G. No.2 F: Adagio; Allegro; Adagio; Fuga. No.3 d: Prelude; fuga; A; C; Air (with variations); Presto. No.4 e: Fuga; A; C; S; G. No.5 E: Prelude; A; C; Air con variazioni (Harmonious Blacksmith). No.6 f♯: Prelude; Largo; Fuga; G. No.7 g: Ouverture; Andante; Allegro; S; G; Passacaglia. No.8 f: A; C; G. No.9 g: A; C; G. No.10 d: A; Allegro; Air; G. No.11 d: A; S; C; G. No.12 e: A; S; G. No.13 B♭: A; C; S; G. No.14 G: A; Allegro; C; Air; M; Gavotte with variations. No.15 d: A; C; S; G. No.16 g: A; C; S; G. The eight suites of 1720 are remarkable works, no two alike. The second set, published in 1733, does not have the same variety and uniqueness.

Keyboard Works (Serauky—CFP) 5 vols. Contains 16 suites in first three volumes. Urtext.

Keyboard Works (G. Ropartz—Durand) 4 vols. Contains 16 suites in two volumes.

Hallischer Händel-Ausgabe (BR) Series IV. Vol.1 (Steglich—Br 4224): 1720 set of suites. Vol.2 (Northway—Br 4221): 7 suites of 1733; 2 chaconnes. Vol.3 (Best—Br 4222): miscellaneous suites and pieces; scholarly edition. Vol.4 (Br 4223): 37 miscellaneous suites and pieces. Introduction in German. Contains tasty chips from Handel's workshop known only from contemporary MS copies, including the Aylesford pieces. No.19, Air, is very lovely; No.30, Air, is delightful; and No.34, Courante, is as fine as any in the "Eight Great" suites. Int. to M-D.

Sixteen Suites (K 3508, 3509).

Klavierwerke I (Peter Williams—VU 50118 a & b). Part a: Suite C HWV 443; Suite G HWV 450; Suite d HWV 448; Suite d HWV 437; Suite G HWV 441. Part b: Suite c HWV 445; Suite B♭ HWV 440; Suite e HWV 438; Suite d HWV 436; Suite d HWV 447; Suite g HWV 452. Includes sources, fingering, and notes on interpretation. These pieces are sometimes called *Miscellaneous Suites.*

8 Suites 1720 HWV 426–433 (Sal; Hicks, H.-M. Theopold—Henle 336 1983; Peter Williams—VU 50119 1993 *Klavierwerke II*; R. Jones—ABRSM). Henle edition is 101pp.; fine preface lists sources and gives performance suggestions. VU edition gives advice on sources and interpretation by Terence Best.

Klavierwerke III, Selected Miscellaneous Pieces (Peter Williams—VU 50120 1995). Free preludes, separate suite movements not a part of completed suites, several sets of variations, fugues including the *Six Fugues* of 1735. Includes fingerings and notes on interpretation. Int. to M-D.

Suites for Harpsichord (Kite—S&B 6502c, 6502d, 1979). Book I: Suites 1, 3, 5, 7. Book II; Suites 2, 4, 6, 8. Accurate text, many editorial suggestions. Occasional fingerings, some debatable and visually distracting. M-D.

Suite IX g (Ruthardt—CFP). Contains photograph of Handel's Rucker harpsichord. Overedited.

Suite No.3 d (James Erber—CFP 7215). Includes notes and a table of ornaments with realizations. Improvisatory Prelude leads to Allegro (fuga); Allemand; Courante; Air with 5 Doubles; Presto. The Air is a rare case where Handel wrote out the full ornamented line. Florid passagework. Not for small hands. M-D.

Air & Variations "The Harmonious Blacksmith" from Suite No.5 (Palmer—Alfred). Includes background on the piece, a section on ornamentation, and facsimile of the original edition. M-D.

Aria with Variations B♭ (Voss—Schott 0470½) 4pp. The Aria is the theme Brahms used in his *Variations and Fugue on a Theme of Handel*, Op. 24. I: Features sixteenth notes in right hand. Var. II: Features sixteenth notes in left hand. Var. III: Features triplets in right hand. Var. IV: Features triplets in left hand. Var. V: Features sixteenth notes in right hand with octaves in the left. Int. to M-D.

Suite 6 f♯ (J. Erber—CFP 7226) 9pp. Prelude; Largo; Allegro; Gigue. First two movements are in the French style; Allegro has two subjects. Editor's note includes useful table of ornaments. Good for small hands. Int. to M-D.

See: Phyllis K. Rueb, "Handel's Keyboard Suites: A Comparison with those of J. S. Bach," AMT, 20 (April–May 1971):33–36.

OTHER WORKS AND COLLECTIONS:

Piano Works (Ruthardt—CFP). 4 vols. Includes the 16 suites, Leçons, 7 pieces, 6 Grande Fugues, 2 Chaconnes, and Fughettas.

Ausgewählte Klavierwerke (Döflein—Schott). Contains 11 works: C, Aria, Allegro, Ouverture, Praeludium, Suite d, A, Fuga, Sonata. This collection is intended as an introduction to Handel's style and the many forms of composition characteristic of his time.

Pieces for Harpsichord (F. Brodszky—ZV 1964). Contains five works published for the first time. Includes solo concerto F with a virtuoso Allegro opening movement, an Adagio, and a Tempo di Menuet; Prelude, Introduzione e Capriccio; Badinage; Prelude e capriccio; Allemande e canzona. Fascinating collection. Int. to M-D.

Chaconne G (T. Best—OUP 1979) 18pp. (Versions 1 and 4). The first publication of Handel's final definitive version of this work, which exists in five versions. Also contains, for purposes of comparison, the earliest form. Octaves and full chords require a good handspan. M-D.

16 Small Pieces (Lajos Hernadi—EMB). Embellishments realized, well edited. Int.

Handel—An Introduction to His Keyboard Works (G. Lucktenberg—Alfred). Contains, in addition to the music, biographical information, bibliography, hints on interpretation, and information about Handel's instruments. Most of the pieces in the first half of the collection are taken from the Aylesford MSS and represent Handel's teaching pieces in a variety of moods and types. From p.28 to the end of the book, pieces are grouped according to key so that they may be played in sequence as "suites" of two or more movements if desired, in accordance with eighteenth-century practice. Easy to M-D.

A Handel Album (E. C. Scholz—UE 1959) 17 short, well-edited, easy pieces.

Handel—A First Book (K 3507) 25pp. Corrente F. Menuetto I and II. Sonatina B♭. Sarabanda d and variation. Giga d. Sonata C. Gavotta C. Air G. Allemande g. Gavotta con (5) Variazioni G. Corrente G. Int.

Il Mio Primo Handel (Pozzoli—Ric E. R. 1954) 19pp. Menuets F, F. Sonatine B♭. Corrente F. Sarabanda g. Gigue B♭. Fughetta C. Sarabanda d with variations. Fughetta D. Preludio G. Allegro g. Allemande g. Int. to M-D.

Handel, The First Book for Young Pianists (G. Lucktenberg—Alfred 1977) 24pp. Int.

Easy Graded Handel (J. Ching—K. Prowse) 32pp. Air G from Suite No.14. Allegro d from Suite No.10. Allegro F from Suite No.2. Allemande f from Suite No.8. Chaconne G with Variations. Courante G from Suite No.14. Gavotte G. Gigue e from Suite No.4. Minuet d from Suite No.11. Minuet I F, and II F from "Seven Pieces." Prelude G from "Seven Pieces." Sarabande d with Variations from Suite 11. Highly edited. Int. to M-D.

Concerto in "Judas Maccabaeus" (Frederick Hudson—Br 6212) for organ, harpsichord, or piano. First edition. Preface provides a detailed account of the sources, history, and background of the various stages of the Concerto as summarized in the essay "Das 'Concerto' in Judas Maccabaeus identifiziert," *Händel-Jahrbuch* 1974–75.

Handel Album Vol.I (EMB 6990): Corrente e due menuetti F. Fantaisie C. Fugues a, G. Praeludium a, D. Sonata C. Suites G, G. Vol.II (EMB 6991): Chaconne G. Fugues b, B♭, c. Suites B♭, C, g. Clear, unencumbered edition. Int. to M-D.

Light Piano Pieces (Walter—Br&H 6797) Designed to introduce Handel's keyboard style. Courante F. 2 Minuets and a Fugue. Fantasia Chaconne. Sonata A. The editor suggests that this volume be introduced when the student has mastered Bach's *Two Part Inventions*. Ornaments written out, some octaves, large chords. Int.

Handel—Easier Favorites (Heinrichshofen N4080 1980) 39pp. 22 pieces ranging from an easy Minuet to the "Harmonious Blacksmith" variations. Easy to M-D.

Handel—Easiest Piano Pieces (Pfeiffer—CFP 5019 1980) 22pp. 23 short pieces such as minuets, sarabands, March, Toccata, Sonatina B♭. Easy to Int.

Keyboard Works for Solo Instrument (Dover 1982) 169pp. From Vol.II of the 1859 complete edition edited by F. Chrysander. Includes 35 pieces, including the 8 Great Suites; Harmonious Blacksmith Air; Passacaille g, a work in which Handel most nearly approaches the monumental style of his choral writing; Fugue a; Sonatina B♭; Sonatas C; Fantasia C; Capriccio F; Chaconne F; Suite (Partita) G; Minuet g; Prelude and Sonata g. Int. to M-D.

Short Pieces and 'Harmonious Blacksmith' Air and Variations (R. Jones—ABRSM). The first of four projected volumes of Selected Keyboard Works of Handel. Contains 22 well-chosen pieces, ranging from the technically simplest to the most famous and brilliant of all. Jones's introduction, annotations, and interpretative markings offer the inexperienced player guidance to their stylish performance. Also includes a detailed critical report on textual sources. Int. to M-D.

76 Pieces (Fuller-Maitland, Squire—Schott). Small pieces of many moods. Excellent for use in the early grades of piano study. Int. to M-D.

20 Little Dances (Frey—Schott). Int.

Little Piano Book (K. Herrmann—Schott). 17 smaller pieces. Int.

Easier Pieces (Rowley—Hin). 14 pieces including Sonatina B♭. Int. to M-D.

14 Easy Original Pieces (O. Beringer—Augener). Arranged in progressive order.

The Young Pianist's Handel (M. Aldridge—OUP 1969) Book I, 21 pieces, well edited, excellent preface, mainly unknown works. Int.

See: Gerald Abraham, "Handel's Clavier Music," ML, 16/4 (1935):278–85.

———, ed., *Handel. A Symposium* (London: OUP 1954).

Terence Best, "Handel's Keyboard Music," MT, 112 (September 1971):845–48.

Robert Dumm, "Performer's Analysis of a Handel Capriccio," *Clavier*, 14 (November 1975):24–28. Includes score.

Eiji Hashimoto, "G. F. Handel's Keyboard Works," AMT, 35/2 (November–December 1985):26–27, 60.

Graham Pont, "French Overtures at the Keyboard: 'How Handel Rendered the Playing of Them,'" *Musicology* 4 (1980):29–50.

Charles-Louis Hanon (1819–1900) France

Known primarily for his pedagogical etudes, Hanon composed some pieces for his favorite instrument. Most are out of print.

Les Delices des jeunes pianistes 1866. No.1, "L'Aurore," appears in P&K, 174 (May–June 1995):30. Consists of scale passages and accompanied melody. Int.

See: Charles Timbrell, "Who Was Hanon?" P&K, 174 (May–June 1995):31.

Howard Hanson (1896–1981) USA

Hanson was a neo-Romantic and used clear forms.

The Bell (CF). 4 pieces, also in *Masters of Our Day* series. Each has its individual mood and quality. Easy to Int.

Clog Dance Op.13 (CF). From *Scandinavian Suite*. 6/8, quintal harmony, rhythmic bounce. Int.

Three Miniatures (CF). Reminiscence; Lullaby; Longing. More advanced than the above pieces. Require more than average sensitivity. M-D.

For the First Time (CF) 31pp. A suite of twelve evocative pieces written in varied style with diverse tonal vocabulary. Includes commentary on the pieces. Int. to M-D.

Hiroshi Hara (1933–   ) Japan

21 Etudes (Ongaku-No-Tomo-Sha 1967) 69pp. Each etude is titled: Boîte à musique; Berceuse de Blanche Neige; Pinocchio; March pour Don Quichotte; Valse pour la Traviata; Le fils d' "Erlkönig"; etc. Programmatic, thin textures, tonal, special technical emphasis and treatment in each etude. Int. to M-D.

Toccata (Zen-On 301 1971) 8pp. Strong rhythms; freely chromatic around a. M-D.

Sonata III (Zen-On 414 1976) 16pp. Allegro; Andantino; Allegro vivace. Modal, octotonic, neoclassic. M-D.

John Harbison (1938–   ) USA
Harbison is a member of the music faculty at MIT.
Parody Fantasia 1968 (McGinnis & Marx 1980) 16pp. 7 min. Part of Harbison's major work, *December Music*, a difficult and expressionistic sonorous movement. Six connected sections, each with its own characteristic material. Unusual handling of rhythm. D.
Sonata I (AMP) 1985 16min. Four compelling contrasted movements. Virtuosic, energetic passages erupt unexpectedly, and the music is shaped by its natural development. Dense contemporary writing. Peaceful ending. Requires much variety of tone and touch. D.
Gospel Shout from *Four Occasional Pieces* 1978. In collection *American Contemporary Masters* (GS 1995) 3pp. Jazz inspired, freely tonal. Large span required. M-D.
Two Part Invention from *Four Occasional Pieces* 1983. In collection *American Contemporary Masters* (GS 1995) 2pp. Freely tonal around C, chromatic, nicely shaped melody. M-D.
Minuet from *Four More Occasional Pieces* 1987. In collection *American Contemporary Masters* (GS 1995) 2pp. Sprightly rhythms, trills, freely tonal. M-D.
Anniversary Waltz 1987 from *Four More Occasional Pieces.* In collection *American Contemporary Masters* (GS 1995) 2pp. Graceful, abstruse melodic writing. M-D.
Four More Occasional Pieces 1987–90 (AMP 1991) 15pp. Minuet; Gavotte; Waltz; Tango. Motifs, thematic networks well developed, eclectic style. M-D.
See: L. Schwartz, "Music: Hard-won Directness," *Atlantic Monthly*, ccliii/3 (1984): 116.

Elizabeth Hardin (18th Century) Great Britain
Hardin was a church organist in London.
Six Lessons for Harpsichord or Piano (B. Harbach—Vivace Press) 52pp. Printed privately in 1770. Mainly in two short movements, with two- and three-voice writing, Scarlatti influence, especially in crossing hands; early classic style. Int. to M-D.

John Hare (–   ) Great Britain
4 Romantic Pieces Op. 4 (Broadbent & Dunn 1994) 12pp. Elegy; Amorphony (Homage to Maurice Ravel); Canzonetta; Idyll. Tonal with much chromatic usage, flowing lines, attractive melodies. M-D.

Donald Harris (1931–   ) USA
Sonata (Jobert) 13 min. Four movements. Numerous meter changes, 12-tone techniques. The last movement, a theme and set of variations, shows a fine grasp of variation technique. Pianistic, unusual sonorities. D.
Balladen 1979 (TP) 14pp. 8½ min. Lento assai, widely spread figuration, large

chords, proportional rhythmic relationships, expressionistic, dramatic arpeggiated gestures, "Das Lebewohl" at conclusion. Requires 4 staffs to notate some sections. Moody, dark tonal shadings. D.

Roy Harris (1898–1979) USA
Harris's style was basically tonal with frequent use of polychords in dissonant combinations, with fourths and fifths predominating. Long-lined melodies, modal scales, and folklike rhythms are important parts of his distinctive idiom.

Sonata Op.1 1928 (AMP). To be played without pause. Prelude: majestic, chordal, varied rhythmic treatment, clashing dissonance. Andante Ostinato: slow, homophonic, broken chords, abrupt key shifts. Scherzo: jazz influence, partly contrapuntal, mainly two voices, leads through a cadenza to a closing; number of voices increases in preparation for the Coda: recalls grandeur (musical material) of opening movement. D.
See: Arthur Farwell, "Roy Harris," MQ, 18 (January 1932):18–32 for a discussion of this work.

Little Suite for Piano (GS 1938). Bells; Sad News; Children at Play; Slumber. Short pieces. Sonority and rhythmic problems, quartal harmony, changing meters. M-D.

American Ballads (CF 1946). Five settings of American folk tunes; Kirby says they "are American equivalents of Bartók's folk-song arrangements" (SHKY, 455). Varied pianistic treatment, mainly homophonic. Int. to M-D.
See: Maurice Hinson, "An American Tune for Today's Student," *Clavier,* 10 (September 1971):24–27. Discusses No.1, *Streets of Laredo*, in this set.

Suite for Piano (Mills 1944). Occupation: driving octaves, changing meters, sonorous. Contemplation: varied textures support folklike tunes, slow. Recreation: spritely 6/8 motion, energetic. M-D.

Toccata (CF 1949). Improvisatory, sustained chordal textures, two-voice fugato, cadenza finale, open sonorities. Melody in octaves or double octaves. M-D.

Lou Harrison (1917–   ) USA
Harrison's music ranges from the almost primitive through the ecclesiastically archaic, the saucily pleasant, and the more serious twelve-tone, to the delicacies of scales in pure, nontempered intonation and microtonal divisions of utmost sensitivity. Harrison has been called "the father of American minimalism." Ives has been his model.

Suite for Piano 1943 (CFP) 20½ min. Prelude. Aria: has a most expressive lyricism with harmonic support. Conductus: presents the row beginning each time with the next note in all four arrangements or 48 short variations. Interlude. Rondo. Serial writing throughout. M-D to D.

Prelude and Sarabande 1937 (NME July 1938). The gritty Prelude is more demanding; the Sarabande is hypnotic, somber. Octotonic, dramatic. Large chords, plucked strings, harmonics. M-D.

Six Sonatas 1943 (PIC) for harpsichord or piano. One-movement works. Thin textures, chamber style, modest dimensions. No.3 is like three related etudes based on a sparse system of intervallic control. M-D.

Homage to Milhaud (Alfred 10114) in collection *Twelve by Eleven*. Flexible meters, simple flowing lines, motivic extension, tonal, thin textures. Int.

Reel, Homage to Henry Cowell (Alfred 10114) in collection *Twelve by Eleven*. A fine Irish-like tune is treated with all black keys in right hand, white keys in left hand, except where indicated. Sixteenth-note palm and arm clusters. Thin textures contrast with thick clusters. Cowell would have approved of this piece. Harrison studied with Cowell in 1934–35. Int. to M-D.
See: Michael Boriskin, "An American Original: Lou Harrison," P&K, 173 (March–April 1995):30–34.

Tibor Harsányi (1898–1954) Hungary
Harsányi's style is characterized by lightness of touch and clarity.

Suite (Sal 1930). 12pp. Prélude; Romance; Intermezzo; Nocturne. See especially Nocturne. M-D.

Sonata (UE 1926). 4 movements. Changing meters, thick chromaticism. M-D.

Trois Pièces de Danse (Heugel 1928). Mouvement de Tango: clusters, bitonality. Mouvement de Boston. Mouvement de Fox trot. M-D.

Pastorales (ESC 1934). Prélude; Elegy; Musette; Danse. See especially Danse. M-D.

La Semaine (Heugel 1924) 20pp. 7 pieces, one for each day of the week. Impressionistic. M-D.

Deux Burlesques (Heugel 1927). No.1: scalar, broad gestures, dramatic. No.2: Bartók influence, varied meters. M-D.

Bagatelles (Leduc 1929). 5 pieces. See especially No.5. M-D.

Baby Dancing (Sal 1930). In jazz style. M-D.

Trois Impromptus (Heugel 1948–52). Mouvement: toccata-like. Flânerie (Burlesque). Nocturne: chordal and chromatic. M-D.
See: J. S. Weissman, "Tribor Harsányi: A General Survey," *Chesterian*, 27 (July 1952):14–17.

Stephen Hartke (1952–   ) USA
Post-Modern Homages Set I (Norruth Music) 25pp. 1. Sonatina-Fantasia 1985, 3½ min. In honor of George Rochberg's 70th birthday. Makes free use of opening material of Hartke's *String Quartet No.1*; 12-tone; contrasted textures and sections. 2. Retumbante (Thunderous) 1985, 3 min. Based on melody of the Brazilian national anthem, "treated in an eccentric but faithfully serial manner" (from the score). 3. Template 1985: in homage to Brazilian composer Henrique Oswald (1852–1913). Based on Oswald's *Etude-Scherzo*, "kind of a shadow of the original in which the non-harmonic tones become the principal tonal axes" (from the score). M-D to D.

Post-Modern Homages Set II (Norruth Music) 10pp. 1. *Sonatina DCXL* 1991: Boppin' along, jazz influence, changing meters, fuguelike section, large span required. 2. *Gymnopedie No. 4* 1984: Updated Satie style. M-D.

The Piano Dreams of Empire 1994 (MMB 1995) 20pp. 7 min. Exploits entire keyboard, clever use of silence, irregular metric and rhythmic groups, "Imperiously" (opening character term) effective. M-D.

Walter S. Hartley (1927–   ) USA
Sonata No.2 (Tenuto 1968) 11 min. Manuscript beautifully reproduced. A two-movement work, changing tempi in the second movement. Fast, large leaps, big chords, tremolandos, dramatic. Effective writing, requires fine pianistic equipment. D.

Karl Amadeus Hartmann (1905–1963) Germany
Jazz-Toccata and Fugue (Schott 1928) 19pp. Toccata opens with a boogie ostinato; fugal-coda in the Charleston concludes fugue. Hindemith-oriented. M-D.
Sonatine (Schott 1931) 12pp. One short, atonal movement. Percussive, Stravinsky-oriented. Glissandi, tremolando effects, changing meters. D.
Sonata "27th April 1945" (Schott 6870 1983) 51pp. The date refers to Hartmann's postwar experience, when he became active again after a self-imposed silence throughout the Nazi years. Bewegt. Presto assai: a frantic Scherzo, thin texture throughout. Funeral March: reminiscent of Reger. Allegro: there are two versions of this movement. Strong chromatic idiom, varied textural densities. D.
Kleine Suite I (Schott 1989) 8pp. Five short contrasted movements. M-D.
Kleine Suite II (Schott 1989) 8pp. Four short contrasted movements, last one entitled "Jazz." Strong polyphonic tendencies in both suites. M-D.

Peter Emil Hartmann (1805–1900) Denmark
Sonatine Op.48 (WH). Three movements. Charming nineteenth-century traditional writing. M-D.
Sonata No.2 Op.80 (WH) 29pp. Four movements, nineteenth-century bravura writing. D.

Thomas de Hartmann (1885–1956) France, born Russia
Hartmann was a versatile composer with strong leanings toward nationalism.
Sonata No.2 Op.82 (Beliaeff 1956). A three-movement work, eclectic in style. Bitonal writing and parallel harmonies are integrated into a picturesque work. D.
See also: Georges I. Gurdjieff

Jonathan Harvey (1939–   ) Great Britain
Four Images after Yeats 1969 (Nov) 25 min. The first three are short 2- and 3-page mood pieces, untitled, with no time signatures or no bar lines. Quotes from Yeats's poetry have been inserted into the score. The final image, "Purgatory," is based on a quote from *A Vision*. We are led through 25 pages covering the entire gamut of keyboard range, dynamics, pedaling, expression, rhythmic patterns, clusters, and silences. Explores an unusual tonal and rhythmic universe. D.
Tombeau de Messiaen 1994 (Faber) 17 pp. 9 min. For piano and digital audio tape. A sound diffusionist is needed to maintain the balance. Numerous directions, 12-tone orientation, colorful, impressionistic overtones. M-D to D.

Johann Adolf Hasse (1699–1783) Germany
Two Sonatas B♭; Op.7 d (H. Ruf—Ric; Kohler—Litolff).
Sonata F (Englander—K&SO).
Sonata E♭ (R. Steglich—Wolfenbüttel: Verlag für musikalische Kultur und Wissenschaft 1936). The Sonatas are attractive, excellent for teaching and/or performance. Int. See also under Collections: *Classic Sonatas for Piano* (Podolsky) and *Sonatas of the Pre-Classic Period* (M. Frey).
See: SBE, pp.278–79, for a discussion of the Sonatas.
Sechs Konzerte (Weger—Forberg 1978). Solo keyboard concertos, originally composed for harpsichord or organ but come off well on the piano. No.1 F: Allegro; Andante; Minuet-Allegro. No.2 G: Allegro; Grave; Allegro assai. The original thin, two-voice texture has been filled out chordally, mostly through added parallel thirds in the upper voices and free embellishments similar to continuo realization. M-D.

Johann Wilhelm Hässler (1747–1822) Germany
Hässler's earlier keyboard style shows a preference for the clavichord idiom, but his later works make use of the colors and techniques of the pianoforte. He was active in Moscow for many years, writing numerous easy, short works for a large amateur public.
6 Easy Sonatas (1780) (Döflein—CFP). All are three-movement works, except the last sonata, which has two movements. Pianistic, expressive. Fine preparatory works to Haydn and Mozart. Helpful preface. Int. to M-D.
24 Studies in Waltz Form (Schott). Fine pieces through all keys, very pianistic. Int.
Der Tonkreis (Schott). Pieces in all keys arranged in order of difficulty. Easy to Int.
Fantasia I c (Farrenc—Leduc) 7pp. Allegro-Presto-Andante. M-D.
Fantasia II E♭ (Farrenc—Leduc) 4pp. Allegretto moderato; Minuetto. Int.
2 Solos (Farrenc—Leduc) in e, F. Each is three movements; could have been titled sonatas. M-D.
Sonata A (Farrenc—Leduc). Untitled first movement; Adagio; Allegro. M-D.
Five Sonatas 1758–90 (Oberdoerffer—CFP 66799) 49pp. In G; a; B♭; a; C. Two- and three-movement works; interesting harmonies for the period. Style is close to the "expressive style" of C. P. E. Bach. Contains some obvious note mistakes. M-D.
Fifty Pieces for Beginners Op.38 (H. Ferguson—ABRSM) 40pp. Short, delightful. Contain much musical interest. Easy to Int.
See: Helen S. Walker, "Johann Wilhelm Hässler (1747–1822): 18th Century Solo Keyboard Literature for Amateurs," thesis, Smith College, 1968. "Hässler's keyboard works reveal his awareness of local contemporary styles, the shift from a neatly articulated clavichord idiom to the broader sweep, proportions, and colors of the pianoforte style, and his responsiveness to the needs of his amateur public for short, easy works and effective practice drills."

Roman Haubenstock-Ramati (1919–1994) Austria, born Poland
After traditional training in theory, composition, and musicology, Haubenstock-Ramati embraced avant-garde techniques, including *musique concrète*. He was music adviser to Universal Edition in Vienna.

Decisions (UE 1960). May be played right side up or upside down by one or two pianists. Can be taped and subjected to electronic distortions. Interpretation of the graphics is left to the performer. Can be played any number of times (aleatory). D.

5 Klavierstücke (UE 1966). Wide intervals and skips interspersed with tone clusters. No.2 is the same as No.5 but rearranged. Unusual notation and instructions for performance. D.

Pour Piano (Ariadne 80039 1980) 2 leaves. Chance composition. M-D.

Josef Matthias Hauer (1883–1959) Germany
Hauer was an early exponent of tone-row composition and wrote several books on the subject.

Nomos Op.19 1919 (Dob 1976) 18pp. 12-tone; row unwinds in numerous guises but not always strictly. Complete metronomic details are listed. M-D.

See: Joseph Smith, "The Mysterious Mr. Hauer," *Piano Today*, 15/5 (September–October 1995):28–29.

Herbert Haufrecht (1909–1998) USA
Five Etudes in Blue (AMP 1956). Toccata; Quasi Ostinato; Dialogue; Nocturne; Capriccio. Unpretentious, fun to play. M-D.

Three Nocturnes (AMP 1957) 8 min. M-D.

Sicilian Suite (ACA 1944). Preludio: etude figuration. Siciliana: graceful siciliano rhythms contrasted with changing meters. Tarantella: brilliant, short. Tarantella published separately (EBM). M-D.

Sonata (ACA 1956). Fine craft in all four movements. M-D.

Passacaglia and Fugue (ACA 1947). Large work, 16 variations. Advanced pianism required. D.

Toccata on Familiar Tunes (Schroeder & Gunther 1969). Folklike, bitonal. Good octave technique required. M-D.

Lukas Haug (1921–   ) Germany
Diatonisch—Dodekaphonisch (Noetzel 1972) 10pp. 2 × 4 easy studies for youth. Four pieces in diatonic writing. Four pieces in 12-tone writing. Good introduction to easy 12-tone writing. Int.

John Haussermann (1909–   ) USA
Préludes Symphoniques Op.2 (Senart 1934) 47pp. 24 contrasting pieces in a style reminiscent of Dupré, Roger-Ducasse, and Charles Griffes. A group such as Nos.2, 6, 9, and 18 could be extracted. Colorful and well crafted throughout. M-D.

Gerhardus Havingha (1696–1753) The Netherlands
Werken voor Clavecimbel. Monumenta Musicae Belgicae, Vol.7, 1951. Includes
short biography by Susan Clercx. Contains 8 suites (1722) and Havingha's
own table of ornamentation. The suites contain Overtures, some in French
style. These movements are always the most involved and longest. There
are also Allemandas, Correntes, Sarabandas, and Gigas, some optional
dances, Marsch, Air met d'Agréments, M, Entrée, Fantasia. Some unusual
keys: one suite b♭, another A♯. Very original writing. M-D.

Mitsuaki Hayama (1932–   ) Japan
Piano Sonata (Ongaku-No-Tomo-Sha 1960) 32pp. 18 min. Allegro assai; Lento;
Allegro molto. Large dramatic gestures, freely chromatic, big chordal skips,
virtuoso character. D.

Azusa Hayashi (1936–   ) Japan
Preludes (Japan Federation of Composers 1972) "Mai" (Movement) 71pp. Seven
extensive pieces written in an improvisational, Impressionistic, modal style.
MS is beautiful and easy to read. M-D.
Suite (Japan Federation of Composers 1967) 39pp. Playing a Ball; Whirling a Pin-
wheel; Song of a Turtledove; Tag; Tune of a Strawpipe. Based on children's
songs. Similar to a five-movement sonatine. MC. M-D.

Hikaru Hayashi (1931–   ) Japan
Hayashi studied composition with Hisatada Otaka and Tomojiro Ikenouchi.
Sonata (Ongaku-No-Tomo-Sha 1965) 15pp. Fluid motivic development in each
movement, freely chromatic. Andante: extreme dynamic range. Allegro:
much rhythmic drive. Sostenuto e pesante: sonorous, free metric usage,
many octaves. D.

Franz Joseph Haydn (1732–1809) Austria
Haydn's keyboard works are finally being recognized as a major contribution to
the repertoire. Indeed, some of his Sonatas are masterpieces that cast their shadows into the nineteenth century and display astonishing formal and stylistic diversity. The difficulties are as great and sometimes greater than those encountered in the Mozart Sonatas, especially from a musical viewpoint.

SONATAS:

Complete Sonatas for Piano (Christa Landon—UE). Vol.1 (UE 50026): Nos.1–18.
Vol.2 (UE 50027): Nos.19–35. Vol.3 (UE 50028): Nos.36–52. Vol.4 (UE
50029): Nos.53–62. This edition is based on the most authentic, scholarly
sources and an eminently musical approach (fingered by Oswald Jonas).
Pushes the number of known Haydn sonatas to 62 (seven lost). Prefatory
material discussing performance, ornamentation, and related matters.

Sonatas (Georg Feder—Henle). Vol.I, 1971; Vols.II and III, 1972. Complete sonatas. Fingering added by Hans-Martin Theopold. Preface in German, French, and English. This is the same edition as the sonatas in the Complete Edition of the Haydn Works (Henle), Series XVIII, vols.1, 2, and 3. See chart below for identification of sonatas in individual volumes. Also available in study-size smaller scores.

The Complete Piano Sonatas (Hinson—Alfred). Vol. I (Alfred 21): Nos.1–22. Vol. II (Alfred 22): Nos.23–41. Vol. III (Alfred 24): Nos.42–54. Pedagogical edition. Prefatory material discusses ornamentation, pedaling, phrasing and articulation, dynamics, chronology and authenticity, and analysis of each sonata. See chart below for identification of sonatas in individual volumes.

The 52 Piano Sonatas (Lea Pocket Scores) 4 vols. A reprint of the original Collected Edition (Karl Päsler—Br&H 1918).

Sonatas (Martienssen—CFP) 4 vols. Contains editorial additions. 43 Sonatas. A fifth volume contains 6 Divertimenti.

Sonatas (Zilcher—Br&H) 4 vols. Indications from Haydn's time in heavy type, additions of the editor in light type. 42 Sonatas.

Complete Piano Sonatas (Dover 1984). Vol.I: Nos.1–29. Vol.II: Nos.30–52. A reprint of the 1918 Collected Edition (Karl Päsler—Br&H). Not all 52 sonatas included are universally accepted as authentic works by Haydn.

Selected Keyboard Sonatas (H. Ferguson—ABRSM) 23 sonatas in 4 vols. Vol. I: Sonata G, H.XVI/8; Sonata C, H.XVI/1; Sonata D, H.XVI/4; Sonata C, H.XVI/3; Sonata F, H.XVI/9; Sonata A, H.XVI/12; Sonata G, H.XVI/G1; Sonata C, H.XVI/10; Sonata G, H.XVI/6. Vol. II: Sonata D, H.XVI/14; Sonata G, H.XVI/27; Sonata Eb, H.XVI/38; Sonata Ab, H.XVI/43; Sonata e (early version), H.XVI/57. Vol. III: Sonata E, H.XVI/31; Sonata b, H.XVI/32; Sonata D, H.XVI/37; Sonata F, H.XVI/23; Sonata Eb, H.XVI/25. Vol. IV: Sonata g, H.XVI/44; Sonata C, H.XVI/50; Sonata F, H.XVI/29; Sonata Ab, H.XVI/46. Critical edition. Editor's additions carefully indicated. Int. to M-D.

Five Sonatas (Arthur Loesser—Music Press). Interesting choice, painstakingly edited.

Selected Sonatas (Lajos Hernadi—EMB) 2 vols. A superb student edition meticulously fingered and discreetly edited by a leading professor at the Liszt Academy in Budapest.

4 Sonatas (Badura-Skoda—Leduc 1982). Published separately, study edition. Includes Partita G, H.XVI/6; Sonata Ab, H.XVI/46; Sonata c, H.XVI/20; Sonata F, H.XVI/23. Critical notes in French, German, and English. All editorial suggestions are printed in blue. Provides great insights into the classic keyboard style. M-D.

Tre Sonati Facile (Lorenzini—SZ 1979) 14pp. Three easier sonatas: C, H.XVI/1; G, H.XVI/8; D, H.XVI/D[1]. Short preface in Italian, French, German, and English; suggestions for ornaments. Int.

Sonata Movements (Walter—Br&H 6760). Selections from five of Haydn's easier piano sonatas. Fingered. Int.

Selected Sonatas (Sliwinski—PWM 1974). Contains Sonata D, H.XVI/19; Sonata C, H.XVI/20; Sonata F, H.XVI/23; Sonata E♭, H.XVI/28; Sonata b, H.XVI/32; Sonata A♭, H.XVI/43; Sonata G, H.XVI/40; Sonata E♭, H.XVI/49. Includes notes on sources, ornamentation, and articulation. Ornaments are frequently realized, and alternate readings from other sources are shown. Essential fingering given. M-D.

Sonatinas (R. Dumm—BMC) 28pp. G, H.XVI/8; G, H.XVI/11; C, H.XVI/7; F, H.XVI/9; C, H.XVI/10; D, XVI/4. Six of the early Divertimenti dating from around 1760. The editor has realized ornaments in a most tasteful manner. Also includes a helpful foreword and editorial notes. Int.

Six Sonatinas (Palmer—Alfred 618) 48pp. Same works as listed above. None of these pieces were originally called *Sonatina*. Nos.4, 7, and 8 were originally named *Divertimentos*; Nos.9, 10, and 11 were called *Sonatas*. Includes a discussion of ornamentation. Editorial additions in light print. Int.

SEPARATE SONATAS:

Sonata A, H.XVI/26 (Henle). Facsimile edition with notes in German by Jens Peter Larsen.

Sonata E♭, H.XVI/52 (Badura-Skoda—Dob). Fine edition.

Sonatas A♭, H.XVI/46; C, H.XVI/15; C, H.XVI/35; c, H.XVI/20; c♯, H.XVI/36; D, H.XVI/19; D, H.XVI/37; E, H.XVI/34; E♭, H.XVI/49; E♭, H.XVI/52; F, H.XVI/23; G, H.XVI/27 (Franzpeter Goebels—Schott).

Sonata C, H.XVI/35 (Hinson—Alfred 6387).

Sonatas D, H.XVI/19; c, H.XVI/20; F, H.XVI/23; e, H.XVI/34; C, H.XVI/35; c♯, H.XVI/36; D, H.XVI/37; E♭, H.XVI/38; G, H.XVI/39; A♭, H.XVI/46; C, H.XVI/48; E♭, H.XVI/49; E♭, H.XVI/52 (Martienssen—CFP).

Sonata D, H.XVI/4 (CFP 7230; Zen-On 327).

Sonata D, H.XVI/37 (Hinson—Alfred 6388).

Sonata G, H.XVI/6 (Zen-On 328).

Sonata G, H.XVI/8 (Zen-On 326).

Sonatas G, H.XVI/40; E♭, H.XVI/49 (Feder—Henle).

Sonata G, H.XVI/8 before 1766. Allegro: lively, two-voice texture, rhythmic problems. Menuet; more rhythmic problems. Andante; charming and warm. Allegro; fast and jovial, broken interval figuration. Int.
   See: Arthur Steiger, "Exploring an Early Haydn Sonata," *Clavier*, 20 (May–June 1981):15–19. Contains discussion and print of the sonata.

Sonata E, H.XVI/13 before 1766. Moderato: many ornaments, repeated notes, scales; must have rhythmic precision and creative articulation. Menuet and Trio: Trio is a fine trill etude. Finale: brilliant; cheerful; double thirds; finger independence and evenness required. Int. to M-D.

Sonata g, H.XVI/44 ca. 1768–70. Moderato: rich harmonies, piquant appoggiaturas, dramatic, ornaments must not sound rushed. Allegretto: difficult ornamentation, lighter than the *Moderato* but still profound. M-D.
   See: Hans Kann, "A Master Lesson on Haydn's Sonata in G minor No.32, Hob.XVI/44," *Clavier*, 21/4 (April 1982):18–22.

Haydn's Keyboard Sonatas
As Numbered in Hoboken Catalogue and Nine Editions

Key	Universal (Vienna Urtext) (C. Landon)	Haydn Urtext (Henle) (Feder)	Alfred (Hinson)	Breitkopf & Härtel; Dover (Päsler)	Schirmer (Klee and Lebert) and Presser	Peters (Martienssen)	Breitkopf & Härtel (Zilcher)	Universal (Rauch)	Associated (Raymar)	Augener (Pauer)	Hoboken Catalogue
G	1	Vol. I	I	8		D.4					XVI/8
C	2	I	I	7		D.5					XVI/7
F	3	I	I	9		D.6	42				XVI/9
G	4	I	I								XVI/G1
G	5	I App. mvts. 2,3	I	11		11	31				XVI/11
C	6	I	I	10		43					XVI/10
D	7	I	I								XVII/D1
A	8	I	I	5		23	41				XVI/5
D	9	I	I	4		D.3					XVI/4
C	10	I	I	1		D.1					XVI/1
B♭	11	I	I	2		22	40		3		XVI/2
A	12	I	I	12		29	28	5		11	XVI/12
G	13	I	I	6		37	36	22		15	XVI/6
C	14	I	I	3		D.2					XVI/3
E	15	I	I	13	17	18	18	4		7	XVI/13
D	16	I	I	14	14	15	15	3	2	4	XVI/14
E♭	17	I	I								
E♭	18	I									
E	19	I	I								XVI/47ii, iii, iv
B♭	20	I	I	18	18	19	19	28		8	XVI/18
d	21	I App.									XVI/2a lost
A	22	I App.									XVI/2b lost
B	23	I App.									XVI/2c lost
B♭	24	I App.									XVI/2d lost
e	25	I App.									XVI/2e lost
C	26	I App.									XVI/2g lost
A	27	I App.									XVI/2h lost
D	28	I									XVI/5 fragment survives
E♭	29	I	III	45		26	25	30		21	XVI/45
D	30	I	I	19	9	9	9	16		20	XVI/19
A♭	31	I	III	46	8	8	8	31		28	XVI/46
g	32	I	III	44	4	4	4	33		23	XVI/44
c	33	II		20		25	24	26		27	XVI/20
D	34	III	II	33	19	20	20	11		9	XVI/33
A♭	35	III	III	43		41	11				XVI/43
C	36	II	II	21	15	16	16	23		5	XVI/21
E	37	II	II	22		40	39	19	8	26	XVI/22
F	38	II	II	23	20	21	21	10		10	XVI/23
D	39	II	II	24		31	32		6		XVI/24
E♭	40	II	II	25		32					XVI/25

Haydn's Keyboard Sonatas
As Numbered in Hoboken Catalogue and Nine Editions (cont.)

Key	Universal (Vienna Urtext) (C. Landon)	Haydn Urtext (Henle) (Feder)	Alfred (Hinson)	Breitkopf & Härtel; Dover (Päsler)	Schirmer (Klee and Lebert) and Presser	Peters (Martienssen)	Breitkopf & Härtel (Zilcher)	Universal (Rauch)	Associated (Raymar)	Augener (Pauer)	Hoboken Catalogue
A	41	II	II	26		33					XVI/26
G	42	II	II	27	11	12	12	1		1	XVI/27
E♭	43	II	II	28	12	13	13	9		2	XVI/28
F	44	II	II	29	13	14	14	21		3	XVI/29
A	45	II	II	30		36	35	6	7	14	XVI/30
E	46	II	II	31		30	29	15		25	XVI/31
b	47	II	II	32		39	38	18	5	13	XVI/32
C	48	II	II	35	5	5	5	2		22	XVI/35
c♯	49	II	II	36	6	6	6	20		31	XVI/36
D	50	II	II	37	7	7	7	17		30	XVI/37
E♭	51	II	II	38		35	34	32		29	XVI/38
G	52	II	II	39	16	17	17	24		6	XVI/39
e	53	III	II	34	2	2	2	14		33	XVI/34
G	54	III	III	40	10	10	10	8	4	19	XVI/40
B♭	55	III	III	41		27	26	13		18	XVI/41
D	56	III	III	42		28	27	27		17	XVI/42
F	57		III	47		34	33	7		16	XVI/47
C	58	III	III	48		24	23	29		24	XVI/48
E♭	59	III	III	49	3	3	3	25		32	XVI/49
C	60	III	III	50		42	22				XVI/50
D	61	III	III	51		38	37	12		12	XVI/51
E♭	62	III	III	52	1	1	1	34		34	XVI/52
				Appendix							
C			I	15							XVI/15
E♭		I	I	16							XVI/16
B♭				17			30				XVI/17
D	Allegro molto	I App.									
F		I App.									XVII/F1
f♯		I App.									IX/26

(This table is based in part on research by A. Peter Brown.)

Sonata c♯, H.XVI/36 ca.1777–79. Moderato: dramatic parallel octaves provide surprise opening, pungent harmonies, bravura figuration. Scherzando: playful tunes, excellent scale study. Menuet and Trio: somber Menuet, more cheerful Trio; scales, octaves, and ornaments. M-D.

Sonata c, H.XVI/20 1771. Moderato: emotional, intense, changing textures, full of pathos and dramatic gestures; requires careful use of dynamics and articulation. Andante con moto: still dramatic but lighter; some syncopation adds piquant rhythmic quality. Finale: moody and dark but full of motion. One of Haydn's most profound sonatas. M-D.

Sonata C, H.XVI/48 1789. Andante con Espressione: romantic theme and variations; varied note values require careful counting; improvisatory effect in cadenzalike runs. Rondo: numerous figurations require plenty of gusto; dashing and witty; full of double notes, arpeggios, octave chords, and broken intervals. M-D.

Sonata E♭, H.XVI/49 1789–90 (Landon, Jonas—VU 51016). Urtext edition plus facsimile of the autograph. Allegro: double thirds, scales, broken thirds, octaves, hand-crossings, cadenza; a very beautiful movement full of fermatas, varied textures, off-beat accents, and rich chromatic harmonies. Adagio e Cantabile: varied moods, figurations, and melodies; one of Haydn's greatest slow movements; difficult articulation, intense B♭ minor mid-section. Finale: double thirds, 2 against 3, ornaments, scales, and arpeggios make this Tempo di Menuet a charming movement. M-D.

Sonata C, H.XVI/50 ca.1794–95. Allegro: one of the most difficult movements in all the sonatas; includes original pedal markings, which create a slightly blurred effect. Adagio: exquisite, improvisational sounding; requires great subtlety. Allegro molto: humorous, abrupt modulations, rolled chords, brilliant closing. M-D to D.

Sonata D, H.XVI/51 ca.1794–95. Andante: technical brilliance, scalar passages in thirds, double notes, 4 against 3, 2 against 3. Finale: brilliant and scherzo-like, Beethoven "sounds," suspensions, misplaced accents, chromatic, involved phrasing. M-D to D.

Sonata E♭, H.XVI/52 1794 (Dob 168). Allegro: dramatic opening, lyric and virtuosic, quick double thirds, hand-crossings. Adagio: profoundly beautiful, doubly dotted notes, rhythmically complex. Finale: formidable complexity, repeated note figures, double notes. An extraordinary sonata to conclude the series. D.

Selected Keyboard Sonatas (Ferguson—ABRSM 1984) 4 vols. Vol.1: H.XVI/8; XVI/1; XVI/4; XVI/3; XVI/9; XVI/12; XVI/G1; XVI/10; XVI/6. Vol.2: XVI/14; XVI/27; XVI/38; XVI/43; XVI/57, early version. Vol.3: XVI/31; XVI/32; XVI/37; XVI/23; XVI/25. Vol.4: XVI/44; XVI/50; XVI/29; XVI/46. This selection favors the earlier and easier works. The editor's introduction contains sound and sane advice on the interpretation of early Classical keyboard music on the piano, especially regarding articulation and ornamentation. Int. to M-D.

See: A. Peter Brown, "A Re-Introduction to Joseph Haydn's Keyboard Works," PQ, 79 (Fall 1972):42–47. Recent research and editions of works from Hoboken's groups XIV, XV, XVI, XVII, and XVIIa are reviewed. Two tables collate the numberings of the solo sonatas and piano trios in the Hoboken catalogue and major editions.

——, "Problems of Authenticity in two Haydn Keyboard Works" (H.XVI/47 and H.XVI/7), JAMS, 25 (Spring 1972):85–97.

——, "The Structure of the Expositions in Haydn's Keyboard Sonatas," MR, 36 (May 1975):102–29.

Fred Fisher, "Humor in the Haydn Sonatas," *Piano Teacher* (September–October 1964):13–17.

Paul Henry Lang, "Haydn at the Keyboard," HF (January 1977):106–108. A most perceptive review of recordings of the piano sonatas.

John McCabe, *Haydn's Piano Sonatas* (London: BBC Publications, 1986), 91pp.

Timothy Miller, "Haydn Sonatas," diss., Indiana University, 1957. A compilation with detailed analyses of the sonatas.

Beth Shamgar, "Rhythmic Interplay in the Retransitions of Haydn's Piano Sonatas," *The Journal of Musicology*, 3/1 (Winter 1984):55–68.

James L. Taggart, *Franz Joseph Haydn's Keyboard Sonatas. An Untapped Gold Mine* (Lewiston, NY: The Edwin Mellen Press, 1988).

MISCELLANEOUS WORKS:

Piano Pieces. Piano Variations (Gerlach—Henle 224). Contains: Capriccio G, H.XVII/1; Variations E♭, H.XVII/3; Variations A, H.XVII/2; Variations C, H.XVII/5; Fantasia C, H.XVII/4; Variations f, H.XVII/6; Variations D, H.XVII/7; Adagio F, H.XVII/9. Authoritative collection.

Piano Pieces (VU UT50047). Edited from autographs, MS copies, and first editions. Fingering added by Franz Eibner and Gerschon Jarecki. Informative preface and critical notes. This is the largest collection of Haydn piano pieces so far, including transcriptions as well as original works. Contents: Capriccio G, H.XVII/1; Fantasia C, H.XVII/4; 20 Variations G, H.XVII/2; Arietta I E♭, H.XVII/3; Arietta II a, H.XVII/2; 6 Easy Variations C, H.XVII/5; Andante con Variazioni f, H.XVII/6; Variations on "Gott erhalte" after H.III/77[II]; Adagio F, H.XVII/9; Adagio G, H.XV/22[II]; Allegretto G, H.XVII/10; Allegretto G, H.III/41[IV]; Il Maestro e Scolare (Sonata for 4 hands), H.XVIIa/1; piano setting of song "Gotterhalte," H.XXVIa/43. A superb volume in spite of some curious editorial policies. Int. to M-D.

Eight Various Compositions (K).

Haydn (H. Ferguson—OUP 1972) 62pp. Part of the Oxford Keyboard Classics series. Includes: Variations f, H.XVII/6; Fantasia C, H.XVII/4; Sonatas c, H.XVI/20 and A, H.XVI/26; Divertimento G, H.XVI/8; Adagio, H.XVI/6; Allegretto, H.XVI/40; and Menuet, H.XIX/9. Discusses instruments of the period as well as dynamics, pedaling, phrasing, and articulation. Includes comments on the specific works. Int. to M-D.

Original Compositions (Soldan—CFP 4392). Arietta con Variazioni A; Arietta con Variazioni E♭; Capriccio G; Fantasia C; Tema con Variazioni C; Variations (Andante Variée f). M-D.

Variations for Piano (Sliwinski—PWM 7811) 86pp. Contains H.XVI/30 from Sonata A. H.XVII/2–3, 5–8, 12, 15, A3, D1, and three pieces without H. number. Epilogue in Polish, English, and German. Int. to M-D.

Adagio F, H.XVII/9 1786. Elegant *galant* style; requires careful attention to rhythm; must have great simplicity and elegance in the performance. Int. to M-D.

Capriccio G, H.XVII/1 1765 (Soldan—CFP). This excellent sportive piece is a modified rondo that uses a minuetlike folk tune in five- and three-bar phrases; many related but surprising and captivating episodes and excursions. M-D.

Fantasia C, H.XVII/4 1789 (Hinson—Alfred 4631; Georgii—Henle) 5 min. A light-hearted rondo that makes a wonderful recital opener (as does the *Capriccio* above). Daring harmonies, clever modulations, cadenzas, virtuosic passages. A superb example of Haydn's facile keyboard writing. M-D.

See: David Owen Norris, "Haydn's Hidden Rhythms," *Clavier*, 32/1 (January 1993):24–26. Discusses rhythmic usage in the Fantasy C, H.XVII/4.

Variations f, H.XVII/6 1793 (Alfred; Georgii—Henle; Eibner, Jerecki—VU 5250077). This expressive and brilliant work is one of Haydn's finest. A beautifully balanced double theme is followed by two elaborate variations and coda. Hand-crossings, elegant harmonies, irregular and free bar-groupings. Haydn designated this piece a "Sonata" in his own catalogue. M-D.

12 Minuets (Nana Krieger—UE). Based on early editions and autographs. Short. Easy to Int.

Il mio primo Haydn ("My First Haydn") (Rattalino—Ric) 21pp. Based on MS and first editions; no editing except fingering. Quadrille C, from H.IX/29. Country Dance B♭, from H.IX/29. German Dances 8–10, from H.IX/10. Gypsy Dance D, from H.IX/28. Gypsy Dance d, from H.IX/28. Minuet E♭, from H.IX/3. Minuet D, from H.IX/3. Minuet D, from H.IX/8. 12 New German Dances, H.IX/12. Contains mainly dances. Provides an excellent approach to the composer for the young pianist. More suitable for an introduction to Haydn than the Sonatas and Variations. Easy to Int.

32 Pieces for Musical Clock (Schmid—Nag). *Galant* style, charming. Some are delightfully pianistic. Int.

Pieces for Musical Clock 1789, 1792, 1793 (Salter—ABRSM) 24pp. 16 pieces based on the aural evidence provided by recordings of the clocks, which are still in existence, from which it has been possible to determine how the ornamentation was to be performed. Editorial additions in brackets. "Trills begin on the main note except where otherwise indicated" (from the introduction). A fascinating collection. Int. to M-D.

See: Walter Robert, "Flute-Clocks: Source of Timely Keyboard Music," *Clavier*, 16/9 (December 1977):14–15. Discusses the flute-clocks for which Haydn composed.

Joseph Smith, "For Mechanical Clock . . . As Played on the Piano," KC, 14/2 (April 1994):49, 64.

Egon Willfort, "Haydn's Compositions for Mechanical Instruments," MT, 63 (1932):510.

The Easiest Original Haydn Pieces for the Piano (A. Rowley—Hin 4) 22pp. Divertimento D, H.XVI/4; Minuet and Finale from Sonata A, H.XVI/26; Minuetto from Sonata B♭, H.XVI/2; Arietta con Variazioni E♭, H.XVII/3;

Adagio from Sonata G, H.XVI/6; Finale from Sonata D, H.XVI/24. Int. to M-D.

A Digest of Short Piano Works (P. Zeitlin, D. Goldberger—BMC 1972) 32pp. Fourteen original pieces and pieces based on Haydn's transcriptions of movements from his symphonies and string quartets. Unfamiliar and familiar works. Outstanding preface. Int.

A First Haydn Book (K 3523) 12pp. 6 German Dances; 6 pieces from "12 Easy Pieces"; Arietta con Variazioni E♭ (only the Arietta); Finale from Sonata C; Arietta con Variazioni A (Arietta and Var.2). Easy-Int.

The Young Pianist's Guide to Haydn (Y. Novik—Studio P/R 1978) 24pp. Includes 6 German Dances; 2 Minuets; and 2 Prestos, a Scherzo, and Andante movements from various sonatas. Edited for the piano tastefully. Record of the contents included. Int.

Easy Graded Haydn (J. Ching—K. Prowse) 32pp. Air and Variations (La Roxolane); Allegro from Sonata C; Allegro from Sonata e; Allegro from Sonata G; Arietta e♭; Finale from Sonata D; Larghetto from Sonata F; 2 Minuets C; Theme and Variations from Sonata A. Int. to M-D.

Anson Introduces Haydn (Willis). Twelve German Dances, all in binary form. Int.

Andante B♭ with (4) Variations H.XVII/12 (Robert Taylor—TP 1974). Based on an 1870 edition. Attributed to Haydn. Charming classical style with ornamentation and running figuration. Helpful editorial notes by the editor. Int. to M-D.

See: Robert S. Taylor, "An Unknown Theme and Variations by Haydn," AMT, 24/6 (June–July 1975):33–35.

12 Short Piano Pieces (Palmer—Alfred 627) 31pp. This collection was brought together in the early part of the nineteenth century. Some of the pieces are transcriptions of instrumental works, but all are admirably suited to keyboard performance. Masterfully constructed miniatures which overflow with a wealth of musical ideas and harmonic invention. Int.

Haydn, An Introduction to His Works (Lucktenberg—Alfred). 11 pieces, some complete sonata movements. Excellent background material, photographs and documents. Well edited. Int.

Haydn Easier Pieces (Heinrichshofen 4049) 39pp. 22 pieces including dance forms, variations, an early Divertimento, and a Fantasia. Int. to M-D.

Haydn—Easiest Piano Pieces (Weitzmann—CFP 5004). Easy dances and pieces: German Dances C, C. Allemandes G, E. Minuets A, F, E♭. Allegretto G. Andante A. Adagio F. Rondo E♭. Variations en Rondeau D. Sonatina G. National Hymn. Int.

Haydn—15 of His Easiest Pieces (Alfred 466) 32pp. Allegro from Divertimento G; Allegro from Sonata C; Andante from *Surprise Symphony*; Andantino E♭; Aria F; 2 Menuets and Trios; Menuet C for Musical Clock; Menuetto Giocoso; "Reversible" Menuet and Trio; Scherzo F; St. Anthony Chorale; 3 German Dances. All are in their original form except for a few transcriptions from Haydn's symphonic works. Int.

24 Minuets H.IX/8, 10 1785, 1793 (Salter—ABRSM 1822 1984) 20pp. Transcriptions of now lost orchestral originals. Charming and quite beautiful. Int.

The Easier Haydn (Barsham—Elkin 1984) 34pp. A graded album of short original piano pieces. Includes single complete pieces as well as easier movements from some of the sonatas. Int. to M-D.

Haydn Piano Compositions (Tucker—CPP/Belwin 1993) 32pp. Air and Variation; Andantino; Fantasia C; Finale, from Sonata No.43; La Roxelane (Air and Variations); Menuetto, from Sonata No. 23; Sonata No. 5 C, first movement. Works not properly identified. No distinction between composer's and editor's markings. A few ornaments realized. Int. to M-D.

Haydn. The First Book for Pianists (Lucktenberg—Alfred 1718). Contains the easier pieces from the collection *Haydn. An Introduction to His Keyboard Works* (Lucktenberg—Alfred 486).

Haydn. Easy Piano Pieces and Dances (Töpel—Br 4631 1996) 32pp. Varied miniatures, attractive. Int. to M-D.

See: Paul Badura-Skoda, "On Ornamentation in Haydn," PQ, 135 (Fall 1986):38–48.

Eleanor Bailie, *The Pianist's Repertoire. Haydn.* London: Novello, 1989.

A. Peter Brown, *Joseph Haydn's Keyboard Music: Sources and Style* (Bloomington: Indiana University Press, 1986).

Raymond Dudley, "Haydn's Knee Pedal Revealed," MJ, 26 (February 1968):33. A more thorough article by the same author is contained in "Harpsichord News," *The Diapason,* 60 (January 1969):10–11.

Carolyn Maxwell, *Haydn Solo Piano Literature* (Boulder, CO: Maxwell Music Evaluation Books, 1983).

Carl Parrish, "Haydn and the Piano," JAMS, 1 (Fall 1948):27–34.

Marcella Branagan, "Some Women in Haydn's Musical Life," P&K, 186 (May–June 1997):43–47. Looks at the social situation and the music Haydn composed for them.

H. Pollack, "Some Thoughts on 'Clavier' in Haydn's Solo Sonatas," *Journal of Musicology* 9 (1991):74–91.

Michael Haydn (1737–1806) Austria
Younger brother of Joseph Haydn.

Sechs Menuette (NV). Written in Salzburg in 1784. Easy to Int.

Easy Pieces for Piano (Heilbut—Hug 11035) 12pp. 5 Variations C. Divertimento D (Marsch). Menuett mit Trio D. Theme with (3) Variations D. Polonaise C. Flowing style, pleasing melodies. Int.

Jack Hawes (1916–   ) Great Britain

Toccata (CF). Lively and attractive "toccata" writing in traditional techniques. Rapid octaves, full chords. A technically rewarding excursion that "sounds" and will dazzle an audience. M-D.

Nocturne (CF). Mixed meters, Impressionistic, expressive. Uses some whole-tone writing. Int.

Christopher Headington (1930–1996) Great Britain
Toccata 1962 (JWC) 4½ min. A 12-tone row is incorporated into the framework of the piece in a thematic rather than an organizing sense. The 12-note sections set up a startling contrast to the diatonic toccata-like passages, producing a pleasantly heterogeneous effect. M-D.

Bernhard Heiden (1910–2000) USA, born Germany
Heiden's works are characterized by skill and melodic fluency.
Sonata No.2 (AMP 1952) 16½ min. Four movements, difficult, tonal, well-contrasted themes. Neo-classic orientation, many meter changes. D.

Werner Heider (1930–   ) Germany
Landschaftspartitur (Litolff 1968) 10 leaves. 6 min. Explanations of symbols in English and German. Stockhausen influence, traditional piano techniques, unusual construction and musical content. Avant-garde. D.
Modi (Ahn & Simrock 1959) 12pp. 9 min. Punkte; Linien; Fläcken; Räume. Serial, expressionistic, pointillistic. M-D.
Toccata 1952 (Ahn & Simrock) 15pp. 8½ min. Energico e vivace: driving triplets, freely tonal. Tranquillo mid-section: octotonic. M-D.

Paavo Heininen (1938–   ) Finland
Toccata Op.1 (Finnish Music Centre 1956) 10pp. 4 min. Constant eighth-note motion. Harmonic interval of fourth is present by itself and in many chordal structures. Freely tonal and centers around C. Martial quality in some sections, changing meters, effective. D.
Sonatine Op.2 (Westerlund 1957) 15pp. 9 min. Allegro; Largo lugubre; Presto. Freely chromatic, no time signatures, large chords plus octotonic writing, atonal. M-D.
Libretto della primavera Op.28 (Finnish Music Centre 1971). Op.28a: Sonatine della primavera: 11 min. Five contrasting movements, serial, thin textures, linear, atonal, pointillistic. D. Op.28b: Due danze della primavera: 6 min. Op.28c: Piccola poesia della primavera: 5 min.
Preludes—Etudes—Poèms Op.32b 1974 (Edition Pan 1978) 10pp. Same material used in the composer's *Piano Sonata* Op.32 and his *String Quartet* Op.32c. The Op.32b miniatures are "flashes of the growth possibilities of the same material in other directions, which are perpendiculars of the sonata-quartet-axis concerning both time scale and character" (from the score). Clusters, harmonics, plucked and damped strings. Avant-garde. M-D.

Anton Philip Heinrich (1781–1861) USA, born Bohemia
Called the "Beethoven of America," Heinrich was completely untrained musically, but wrote some of the most original music of his day. In many ways Heinrich's accomplishments can be equated with those of Charles Ives.
The Dawning of Music in Kentucky, or the Pleasures of Harmony in the Solitudes

of Nature (opera prima); *The Western Minstrel* (opera secunda) (Da Capo) Earlier Music Series, Vol.10, edited by H. Wiley Hitchcock. Both works were originally printed in Philadelphia in 1820. Surely the most daring first opus ever written. The pieces range all the way from simple tunes set at about Int. level to virtuoso settings. Deserves more investigation.

Song Without Words 1850 (Alfred 10102) in collection *Piano Music in Nineteenth Century America*, Vol.I. Written in honor of Jenny Lind's first tour of the USA. Charming, elegant, and hauntingly beautiful. Int. to M-D.

The Debarkation March (A-R Editions) in collection *Anthology of Early American Keyboard Music 1787–1830*.

The Philadelphia Waltz Op.2/2 1820. In collection *Masters of American Piano Music* (Alfred 4603). Gentle, flowing; coda is a variation and works to big climax. Int.

Toccatina capriciosa (A-R Editions) in collection *Anthology of Early American Keyboard Music 1787–1830*. Contains examples of the adventurousness and quixotic turns of phrase present in many of the works of this fascinating composer. M-D.

The Sylviad, or Minstrelsy of North America (Connors Publications) Earlier American Music Series, Vol.28. "Opus 3 by this Bohemian-born musician, who taught himself composition in Kentucky, is no less extraordinary than his opus 1, *The Dawning of Music in Kentucky* of 1820 (reprinted with *The Western Minstrel*, opus 2, in the Da Capo E. A. M. Series). Originally published in Boston in two sets, 1823 and 1825–26. *The Sylviad* was published to impress the Royal Academy of Music, to which it is dedicated, before Heinrich traveled to London in 1826 to advance his career. The thirty-four works—for piano, solo voice, or vocal ensemble—are sometimes amusing, sometimes simple, sometimes fiendishly difficult—especially the two toccatas for piano" (from the new introduction by J. Bunker Clark).

See: Neely Bruce, "The Piano Pieces of A. P. Heinrich Contained in *The Dawning of Music in Kentucky* and *The Western Wind*," diss., University of Illinois at Champaign-Urbana, 1975.

Howard Carpenter, "Kentucky Minstrel," AMT, 31 (April–May 1982):367. A discussion of Heinrich's musical contribution to Kentucky.

J. Bunker Clark, "The Solo Piano Sonata in Early America: Hewitt to Heinrich," *American Music*, 2/3 (Fall 1984):27–46.

John Heiss (1938–   ) USA

Four Short Pieces (Bo&H 1975). One page each. Schönberg idiom. Tightly compressed writing, slow tempi. Interpretive problems require mature pianism. Would make a good preparatory study for the Schönberg Op.19. M-D.

Hallgrimur Helgason (1914–1994) Iceland

Sonata II (Edition Gigjan, P. O. Box 121, Reykjavik, Iceland) 16pp. Allegro arctico: freely tonal, nineteenth-century figuration, contrasting ideas, big conclusion. Adagio non troppo: melody treated in various guises; fast harmonic rhythm. Rondo: contrasted sections in 4/4, 6/8, 2/4. Folk-tune element present. M-D.

Rondo Islandia (Edition Gigjan 1954) 7pp. A jiglike dance, flexible meters, freely tonal, Hindemithean, folklike tunes. Int. to M-D.

Stephen Heller (1813–1888) born Hungary, lived mostly in France

Although old-fashioned by today's standards, Heller's works include plenty of fine pedagogical material readily available. Like Grieg, Heller was a great small composer.

The Art of Phrasing Op.16 (GS) 2 books. 26 melodious studies. Int. to M-D.

25 Studies Op.45 (Alfred; UE; GS; CFP; Ric). These pieces originally served as an introduction to Heller's *Art of Phrasing*. Op.45 has cyclic overtones, and Debussy may possibly be indebted to the first of these studies for "Dr. Gradus ad Parnassum" in his *Children's Corner* suite. The famous *L'avalanche* is the second piece in this set. Int. to M-D.

Flower and Thorn Pieces Op.82 (GS; K). 18 characteristic pieces. Int. to M-D.

24 Preludes Op.81 (GS). Fluent, inventive, easy on ears and fingers. Int.

The Heller Collection (Hinson—UE 30108 1994) 60pp. 34 selections divided into early intermediate and late intermediate from Opp. 45, 46, 47, and 125. Contains analysis of each piece.

30 Etudes Op.46 (UE; MMP). About the same difficulty as Op.45. Int. to M-D.

33 Variations on a Theme by Beethoven Op.130 1871 (Br&H 1985) 31pp. The theme is from the C Minor Variations and there are quotes from other Beethoven masterpieces. Pianistic and excellent for a student with a sense of humor. M-D to D.

Ausgewählte Klavierwerke (Selected Piano Pieces) (Kersten—Henle 372 1987) 87pp. Character pieces from Opp.29, 40, 79, 80, 81, 82, 121, 124, 128, 134, 138, and 150. Excellent variety of Heller's output. Int. to M-D.

Tarantelle Op.85/2 (Schott) 8pp. Dedicated to Clara Schumann. Octotonic, skipping 6/8 meter, flowing melody in one section. M-D.

23 Miscellaneous Pieces (Alexander—ABRSM 1962) 40pp. Contains 23 pieces included in an earlier ABRSM publication, *56 Studies and Pieces* (1931) by Stephen Heller, Books I and II, selected and edited by Arthur Alexander. Includes Prelude Op.119/9; Scabious Op.138/14; Prelude Op.119/1; Prelude Op.119/28; Prelude Op.119/2; Do not forget me Op.138/15; Waltz Op.97/1; Waltz Op.97/6; Prelude Op.119/10; Canzonetta Op.16/3; Gypsy Dance Op.136/19; Album Leaf Op.83/4; Song Without Words Op.120/1; Prelude Op.119/14; Oberon's Horn Call Op.138/22; Prelude Op.119/12; Prelude Op.119/16; Prelude Op.119/30; Sleepless Nights Op.82/13; Prelude Op.119/19; Prelude Op.81/17; Dream Pictures Op.74/3; Prelude Op.81/12. Some of Heller's finest pieces; charming ingenuity. Int.

Selected Progressive Etudes (Olson—Alfred 598) 48pp. 18 etudes, Curious Story and Prelude, Op.81/3. First-rate pedagogical material. Int.

See below, "Collections," *Piano Music of the Parisian Virtuosos 1810–1860.*

Heller Rediscovered (Alec Rowley—Lengnick) Book 1, Miniatures. Book 2, Preludes. Book 3, Mood Pictures. Book 4, Dances. Book 5, Nature Sketches. Selected from the best of the composer's entire works. The pianist who dips into these attractive collections, whether in the course of study or merely for recreation, has a real treat in store. Heller's music is ageless. Freedom from sentimentality, impeccable workmanship, and refinement and simplicity of outlook characterize this miniaturist, whose sole object was to perpetuate beauty. Int.

56 Studies and Pieces (A. Alexander—ABRSM) Vol.I. Easy to Int. Vol.II. M-D. Contains some of Heller's best works.

William Hellerman (1939–   ) USA

Row Music: Tip of the Iceberg (Merion) 21 min. A serial work in avant-garde notation, concerned with dreams. Based on a theme from Berg's *Lyric Suite.* "The prime concern is with orderly disorder or more correctly the letting things be what they are by systematically directing their appearance. Thus the nature of the musical intervals can sink in until the listener is involved only with musical material and its contained beauty and power . . ." (note from the score). Detailed performance notes. M-D.

David Hellewell (1932–   ) Hungary

Micro-Music (EMB 1979) 18pp. A set of 14 miniatures in contemporary idiom. Avant-garde techniques. Int. to M-D.

See: Jeffrey Joseph, "David Hellewell—a Profile," *Music Teacher*, 62/3 (March 1983):16.

Everett Helm (1913–1999) USA

Helm's style blends linear clarity with dissonant counterpoint and lively rhythmic treatment.

Sonata Brevis (Hargail 1945). Easily moving: flowing chromatic lines over ostinato-like bass. Slow and Contemplative: flexible, colorful melodic writing. Vigorous: driving idea, slower mid-section that recalls main idea of first movement. Presto coda. M-D.

Brasiliana Suite (CF). I Would Flee Thee: slow, colorful, melody based on folksong. Pardon Emilia: slow, melodic. Toccata Brasileira: driving, syncopated, requires good octaves. In the AMC library there is a fourth movement entitled "Vernca, meuanjo"; shorter than the other movements, only 2 pages. Attractive. M-D.

Dance Suite (AMC). 7 pieces for piano, each 2pp. Arranged in order of difficulty. No.4 is the most sophisticated of the set. Variety of moods, idioms, and techniques. Clever writing. Int. to M-D.

New Horizons (GS 1964). Twelve pieces intended to help the piano student bridge the gap between traditional and contemporary music. Notes on each piece explain the technique of modern composition employed. Also contains an excellent introduction to the styles and practice of contemporary music, within the scope of well-trained high school students. Int. to M-D.

Charles-Joseph van Helmont (1715–1790) Belgium
Werken voor orgel en/of voor Clavicimbel. Monumenta Musicae Belgicae, vol. 6 (1948), with a short biography by Suzanne Clercx. Contains *Pièces de Clavecin* and Helmont's own table of ornaments, which is similar to F. Couperin's. Suite I: La Françoise (rondeau), La Moderne, La Caille, Le Barc, La Boulonnoise. Helmont was a great admirer of the French style. *Doubles* are written for some of the movements. 4 fugues are also included from his *6 Fugues*. Int. to M-D.

Robert Helps (1928–   ) USA
Helps has a tendency to exploit the extremes of the keyboard. His piano music is demanding and his style reflects the French piano tradition of Fauré and Ravel in particular.
Portrait (CFP) 6½ min. A self portrait? A lyric mood picture. Broken-octave technique, *pppp* closing. Structured around two texturally contrasting sections. M-D to D.
3 Etudes (CFP) 6 min. Preference for seconds, fourths, fifths, sevenths, and ninths. No.2 contains interesting pedal effects. No.3 is a program closer. For virtuoso pianists.
3 Recollections 1968 (CFP) 15 min. In Memoriam; Interlude; Epilogue. Difficult character pieces. Bloch influence. Interlude is especially colorful.
Image. See Anthologies and Collections, USA, *New Music for Piano* (LG).
Nocturne (CFP 1973) 16pp. 9 min. "All expressive indications, including tempo, dynamics and pedal, are to be viewed freely; rubato is hardly indicated but should be allowed extensively. The printed page suggests only one possibility, approximately notated" (from notes in score). Varied tempi, moods, and meters; climaxes; colorful pedal effects; complex; wide keyboard range; triplet followed by duplet figuration gives "rocking" motion; chromatic; rhythm treated flexibly throughout. D.
    See: David Burge, "New Pieces, Part II," CK, 4 (January 1978):50.
Quartet 1962 (CFP 1972) 22pp. 20 min. Prelude: Lento; intervals gradually increase from a unison to a ninth; hypnotic effect. Confrontation: Con passione, dramatic sweeping gestures, pointillistic, chromatic, syncopation, ostinati. Intermezzo: Tempo rubato; quiet; interval of second exploited. Postlude: Andante; wide-skipping right hand over chordal left hand; midsection more expressionistically treated; four staves required to notate last three pages, which include some highly refined sonorities. D.
Trois Hommages (CFP 1975) 17pp. 9 min. Hommage à Fauré; Hommage à Rachmaninoff; Hommage à Ravel. Written in each composer's style, slightly modernized by Helps. An eminently attractive pianistic group. M-D.

In Retrospect—Five Pieces that Form a Suite 1977 (AMP 7775) 12pp. Prelude; Dance; Song; Pastoral; Toccata. Recalls childhood? Expressive and melodic, thin textures, atonal, simple style of writing. M-D.

Shall We Dance? 1994 (CFP). A large elegant waltz, full of impatient arabesques. D.

Valse Mirage. In collection *Waltzes by 25 Contemporary Composers* (CFP 667351). Consistent harmonic usage logically integrated. M-D.

See: Jed Distler, "Robert Helps, Radical Pianist, Maverick Composer," P&K, 182 (September–October 1996):45–47.

Sicco Albertus Hempenius (1785–1849) The Netherlands
    See C. F. Ruppe.

Hans Henkemans (1913–1995) The Netherlands
A fondness for Debussy is seen in Henkemans's compositions.

Sonate (Donemus 1958) 11 min. 21pp. Allegro molto moderato: undulating, triplet figuration, *pp* closing leads directly to Molto adagio: light broken chords used in a brush-stroke technique, leads directly to Allegro ma non troppo: motivic development, driving, tumultuous closing. Dark and foreboding mood, dense chromaticism. D.

See: David Burge, "Three Recent Piano Sonatas," *Keyboard*, 10/4 (April 1984): 64–65.

Michael Hennagin (1936–1993) USA

Sonata (Walton Music Corp. 1977) 20pp. One movement of solid contemporary writing. Wide skips, jazz influence, frantic movement around the keyboard, quiet closing. Displays a strong compositional talent. Virtuoso demands are made on the performer, and the results provide a fine new work for the repertoire. D.

Swan Hennessy (1866–1929) USA
Hennessy lived most of his life in Paris and wrote in an impressionistic style.

À la manière de . . . 1927–28 (ESC). 30 pastiches for piano. Short style portraits. Book 1: Brahms, Franck, Dvořák, Grieg, Schumann, Fauré. Book 2: Strauss, Heller, Debussy, Godard, Reger, Demet. Book 3: Mendelssohn, d'Indy, Clementi, Jeune Génie of the avant-garde, Turina, Rossini. Book 4: Weber, Liszt, Scarlatti, Verdi, Chopin, Chabrier. Book 5: Schubert, Handel, Massenet, J. Strauss, Ravel, Wolf. M-D.

Fanny Mendelssohn Hensel (1805–1847) Germany
Hensel was the older sister of Felix Mendelssohn. She composed over 400 works. She and her brother had similar training, and they wrote in a similar style. Hensel was greatly admired and encouraged by Charles Gounod.

Two Piano Sonatas (Hildegard 1992) 67pp. *Sonata* c, 15½ min. Allegro moderato e con espressione: strong lyricism with pathos, contrasted agitated second

theme appears in recapitulation as a fugato. Andante con moto: quiet melodic lines mixed with dramatic modulations. Finale-Presto: perpetual motion in triplets and sixteenths, fiery ending. M-D to D. *Sonata* g 1843, 18
min. The movements follow each other immediately. Allegro molto agitato:
gloomy opening leads to a dramatic first and lyric second themes. Scherzo:
elfin, shimmering, rondo form. Adagio: a barcarolle recalling Fanny's visit
to Italy. Finale-Presto: scherzo-like opening leads to the rondo melodic
theme. Demonstrates stronger craft than *Sonata* c. M-D to D.

O Traum der Jugend, O Goldner Stern Op.6/3 (O Dream of Youth, O Golden
   Star) 1846. In collection *Selected Piano Works* (Henle 392) 3pp. An atmospheric and expressive Song without Words. M-D.

Notturno g 1838. In collection *Selected Piano Works* (Henle 392) 6pp. A section:
   lilting melody floats over an arpeggio-like accompaniment; B section
   builds to a climax before the return of the A section. One of Hensel's finest
   works. M-D.

Sonatensatz E 1822 (Furore Edition 1991) 35pp. 6½ min. Introduction and commentary in German with English translation. Improvisatory, SA design,
   cadenza introduces recapitulation, cantabile and virtuoso passages alternate. M-D.

Prelude e (Furore Edition 1989) 3pp. Lyrical, well crafted. Int. to M-D.

Das Jahr (The Year) (Furore Edition 138, 1989). 12 character pieces (kind of a
   12-part suite with a postlude), one for each month of the year. Composed
   in 1841, after Hensel's year of travel and living in Italy. Extensive preface
   in German. Vol. I, 50pp.: January: A Dream, alternates parlando and chorale (Vom Himmel hoch) style. February: Scherzo, lively and exuberant,
   Roman Carnival time. March: Dark opening, chorale (Christ ist erstanden)
   followed by variations. April: Capriccio, tempo and mood changes suggest
   varied weather in this month. May: Spring Song, reflects Fanny's mixed
   feelings about this month. June: Serenade, melancholy, mood change. July:
   Larghetto, mixed emotions, suggestion of sad experiences ahead. Vol. II:
   August: Allegro, Opens with a lively bugle call that introduces a march;
   a new section has a merry tune in sixteenth notes. September: At the
   River, constant sixteenths suggest flow of the river. October: Allegro con
   spiritoso, joyful reaction to Venice. November: Mesto, slow opening gives
   way to fast passages; elegiac. December: Allegro molto, agitated opening, mood becomes quieter and introduces chorale "Vom Himmel hoch"
   and two variations. Postlude: Chorale, "The Past Year is Gone" series as
   basis.

Vier Lieder ohne Worte Op.8 1840 (Rieger—Furore 142) 20pp. 1. b, rhapsodic, octave leaps, dotted rhythms. 2. a, chorale-like, pedal points. 3. D♭, "Lied,"
   possibly inspired by a poem of Lenau; mid-section contains a few unusual
   harmonic twists. 4. "Wunderlied," accompanied melody. M-D.

Six Pieces from 1824–1827 (Radell—Hildegarde) Capriccio F♯; Allegro ma non
   troppo f; Fugata E♭; Andante con espressione c; Andante con moto c; Alle-

gro c. These pieces date from Hensel's early adult years and display a broad variety of well-developed ideas. M-D.

Songs for Pianoforte 1836–37 (Cai—A-R Editions 1994) 101pp. Ten pieces plus two in an Appendix. Allegretto grazioso; Andante; Prestissimo; Allegro con brio; Allegro con spirito; Allegro con brio; Allegro agitato; Allegro moderato; Largo con espressione; Capriccio: Allegro ma non troppo. The second piece in the Appendix is the first version of No. 1. Includes critical notes, sources, and discussion of the compositional process. M-D.

Selected Piano Works (Henle 392) 45pp. Notturno; Abschied von Rom; O Traum der Jungend; O Goldner Stern; and four untitled pieces. A fine introduction to Hensel's style. M-D.

(Furore) has seven volumes of Hensel's piano works (character pieces, etudes).

See: Camilla Cai, "Fanny Hensel's 'Songs for Pianoforte' of 1836–37: Stylistic Interaction with Felix Mendelssohn," *Journal of Musicological Research,* 14 (1994).

———. "Fanny Mendelssohn Hensel as Composer and Pianist," PQ, 35/139 (1987):46–53.

Joseph Smith, "The Other Mendelssohn," *Piano Today,* 16/3 (May–June 1996):11; also includes Hensel's *Song*, Op.6/3 (without words), pp.12–13.

Adolf Henselt (1814–1889) Germany
One of the great pianists of the nineteenth century, Henselt composed mainly "studies" for his instrument. These still have value, especially in his approach to stretches and wide extensions of the hand.

12 Etudes Op.2 (GS). No.6, *Si oiseau j'etais,* is the most popular of this set. Available separately (Augener; Schott; Paxton). M-D.

Piano Concerto f Op.16 (Musical Scope Publishers). Original solo version by the composer. M-D to D.

Etude a (Musica Obscura) 2pp. Staccato melody in upper voice, repeated sixteenths throughout in one inside voice, legato melody in another inside voice, sustained bass line. Fine voicing (touch) study. M-D.

Petite Valse (Musica Obscura) 2pp. From Ignaz Friedman's Concert Repertoire No.1. Enlarged by Friedman. Charming; requires subtle rubato. Int. to M-D.

Romance Op.10, *Impromptu* Op.7 (Zen On 373) published together. Makes a nice combination, or could be performed separately. Int. to M-D.

Spring Song (Musica Obscura) 3pp. An arpeggio study plus facile melody. Int. to M-D.

Toccatina Op.25 (Musica Obscura) 7pp. Constant flowing sixteenths with a melodic line that appears in various voices, *pp* closing. M-D.

24 Preludes in All Keys (Musica Obscura). Short pieces, some only one line long. These short pieces were played before a larger work to prepare the audience for the mood and key to follow. This practice was very popular in the nineteenth century but has now almost disappeared.

See: Raymond Lewenthal, "Henselt—A Look at a Fantastic Romanticist," *Clavier*, 13 (April 1974):17–20. The piano pieces *La Fontaine* Op.6/2 and *Petite Valse* Op.28/1 are contained in this issue.

Hans Werner Henze (1926–) Germany

Henze's works display a variety of forms, as well as atonality, polytonality, and tonality.

Variationen Op.13 1949 (Schott) 9pp. Nine short variations, many of them rhap-sodic in strict 12-tone technique. Treatment of the row becomes increas-ingly more complicated. D.

Sonata 1959 (Schott) 24pp. Written in an overall three-movement form. Rows are used constantly, freely producing continuous changes in pitch and dynam-ics. Pointillistic, with rhythmic complexities; very expressive in an abstract idiom. D.

Une petite phrase 1984 (Schott 7293) 2pp. From the film *Un amour de Swann*. In-cludes facsimile of autograph. Syncopated melody, atonal. Large span re-quired. M-D.

Cherubino 1980–81 (Schott 7032) 12pp. 7½ min. Three contrasting miniatures, dense harmonies, atonal, dramatic conclusion. M-D.

Toccata mistica 1994 (Schott 8380) 12pp., ca. 5 min. Thick atonal textures, chang-ing meters and tempi, wide dynamic range. D.

6 Pieces for Young Pianists (Schott). Excerpted from Henze's children's opera *Pollicino* and arranged by the composer. Demand much experience in con-temporary technique, rhythm, and sonorities; hardly for "young pian-ists." M-D.

Eduardo Hernandez-Moncada (1899–) Mexico

Costeña (PIC 1962). Cross-rhythms, bitonal writing, interesting sonorities. M-D.

Cinco Piezas Bailables (PIC). Colorful contemporary idiom, dance forms. M-D.

Manuel Herrarte (1924–) Guatemala

6 Sketches (EV 1953). Valsante; Melancolico; Vivo; Simple; Sombrio; Festivo. M-D.

3 Dances (PAU 1957). Allegro; Andantino; Presto. Latin American rhythms. Sound easier than they are. Int. to M-D.

Hugo Herrmann (1896–1967) Germany

Cherubinische Sonate (Sikorski 396 1956) 11pp. Toccata epiphania: short intro-duction; rest of movement based on chorale "Veni creator"; single line with parallel chords; freely centered around G. Choralvariationen: theme based on Advent song "O Heiland reiss den Himmel auf"; followed by six short contrasting variations; big chordal conclusion. Festiva resurrectionis: based on an Easter alleluia; octotonic; parallel chords; freely tonal around e-E; neoclassic. M-D.

Liturgische Fantasien (Tonos 1966) 14pp. 13 min. Litanei; Offertorium; Credo; Flagellation; Mette; Abendmahl; Gloria. Freely tonal, quartal and quintal harmonies, colorful contrasts. Large span required. M-D.

Johann Wilhelm Hertel (1727–1789) Germany

Sonata d Op.1 (H. Erdmann—Br). Vol. 49 of *Hortus Musicus*. Three movements. An attractive work. Slow movement contains some lovely passages, as expressive and surprising as almost anything found in Hertel's contemporary C. P. E. Bach. M-D.

Henri Herz (1803–1888) Germany

Herz was regarded by Schumann as the model of musical philistinism.

24 Exercises and Preludes Op.21 (CFP). In all major and minor keys. M-D.

Variations brillantes sur "The Last Rose of Summer" Op.159 (Musica Obscura) 8pp. Introduction presents fragments of theme before the theme is heard Andantino espressivo. Three variations and a finale of repeated notes, tremolos, and a glissando in thirds round out the set. M-D.

Variations on Rossini's "Non più mesta" from La Cenerentola (MTP). Foreword by Earl Wild. Originally published in 1831. Contrasting keys, meters, tempi and clichés. Ingenious pianistically. Brilliant, lightweight, blazing octaves, effective. M-D.

The Flower of the Prairie Waltz (Musica Obscura) 2pp. Short rondo, salon style. Int.

Bagatelles Op.85 (CFP 1067) 26pp. 6 pieces. No.4, Rondo turc, is the most interesting. M-D.

See below, "Collections," *Piano Music of the Parisian Virtuosos 1810–1860*.

Heinrich von Herzogenberg (1843–1900) Austria

Eight Variations Op.3 (UMKR 41 1975) 15pp. Similar in character and design to the Brahms "Variations on an Original Theme" Op.21/1. M-D.

Variations on the Minuet from Don Giovanni Op.58 (J. Rieter—Biedermann 1889) 19pp. Independent style; fades out quietly with a hauntingly beautiful coda. A remarkable set, well able to stand among other similar masterpieces from this period. M-D.

Capricien Op.107 (J. Rieter—Biedermann 1900) 17pp. A set of variations based on a theme formed from the initials of a friend's name. Ends with a fugue similar to a Reger double fugue. M-D to D.

Jacques Hétu (1938–   ) Canada

Petite Suite Op.7 (CMC 1962). Six movements using much disjunct motion. Broad dynamic range; extremes of keyboard exploited. D.

Variations pour Piano (Berandol 1970). 12-tone writing, ebullient, brilliant. D.

James Hewitt (1770–1827) USA, born Great Britain

Hewitt was a leader of the Court Orchestra of George III before coming to America in 1792. He was active in New York as a music publisher, concert violinist, director of theater orchestras, and organist of Trinity Church.

The Battle of Trenton (M. Hinson—WB). Dedicated to George Washington. Pictorial subtitles (à la Satie) indicate the musical intention for the various sections. M-D. Also found in abbreviated form in collection *Music from the Days of George Washington* (AMS Press).

Mark My Alford With Variations in *A Collection of Early American Keyboard Music* (Willis). Printed in New York in 1808; based on the tune we know as "Twinkle, Twinkle, Little Star," the same tune used by Mozart for his famous set, K.265. Both sets are full of charm and childlike humor. The Hewitt set contains ten variations. Int. to M-D.

The Fourth of July. A Grand Military Sonata 1801 (Hinson—WB). More a medley-potpourri than a sonata; descriptive titles used for various sections. Uses the familiar tune "Hail Columbia," but rest of the piece is original. Performer could call out names of the various sections as they are reached in the score. M-D.

Selected Compositions (Wagner—A-R Editions 1980) 106pp. Includes 10 keyboard and 21 vocal pieces from Hewitt's 167 surviving works. Keyboard pieces include: Sonata C; Sonata D; variations, Mark My Alford; various marches; The Augusta Waltz; New Medley Overture; New Federal Overture; The Battle of Trenton. Int. to M-D.

See: J. Bunker Clark, "The Solo Piano Sonata in Early America: Hewitt to Heinrich," *American Music*, 2/3 (Fall 1984):27–46.

David Hicks (1949–   ) USA

Fantasy (CUMP 1995) 12pp. A single movement in four sections, spare in texture and rubato in character. M-D to D.

Dick Higgins (1938–1998) USA

Piano Album 1980 (Printed Editions) 34pp. Includes graphic notation as well as conventional and verbal ones. Has relevance to both music and literature; its iconoclastic scores make it fit into belles lettres as well as pianist's libraries. Avant-garde. M-D.

Sonata II 1982 (Printed Editions) 4-page folder. Uses four overlays in different colors, each of which is placed over a different sheet of existing piano music. On the overlays are arrows, and the pianist's hands, either separately or together, follow the arrows, transforming the music that is read through them. Aleatoric, avant-garde. M-D.

Sonata for Prepared Piano 1983 (Printed Editions) 8pp. 13 min. Four movements, each using a different method of interpreting its materials—a set of four photo-montages using natural imagery (tree, roots, rocks, branches, and nudes)! Avant-garde. M-D.

Ferdinand Hiller (1811–1885) Germany

See below, "Collections," *Piano Music of the Parisian Virtuosos 1810–1860*.

Lejaren Hiller (1924–1994) USA

Twelve-Tone Variations for Piano 1954 (TP 1971) 63pp. Six different rows are worked out in five movements. The theme is based on a combination of the six rows followed by a variation based on one row, a variation based on two rows, etc. Copious analytical and performance notes by the composer point up the row construction and utilization in each variation. D.

Scherzo 1958 (TP 1973) 30pp. Opens with a slow Prologue followed by an Epilogue, the Prologue in retrograde. The Scherzo proper is a series of nine scherzi with eight interlacing trios. Scherzo II employs only the odd-numbered bars of Scherzo I, and the compression idea continues until the last Scherzo is one measure long. Clever inventive atonal writing. D.

Wilfried Hiller (1941–   ) Germany

Phantasie on a theme of Johann Adam Hiller (1728–1804) after a picturebook of Wilhelm Busch (Schott ED 7190) 17pp. No.8 of the *Journal für das Pianoforte*. The "fun" tune is given at the beginning followed by an Introduction, Scherzo, Adagio, Adagio con sentimento, Piano, Smorzando, Maëstoso, Capriccioso, Passagio chromatico, Fuga del diavola, Forte vivace, Fortissimo vivacissimo, Finale furioso. This twentieth-century parody of an eighteenth-century tune is fun for audiences familiar with the theme. Includes the pictures of Wilhelm Busch that inspired the piece. D.

Paul Hindemith (1895–1963) Germany

Hindemith was one of the major composers of our century. His enormous output has contributed to the repertoire of every instrument. Hindemith approached composition through linear writing, and his expanded tonal concept is unique. For a thorough understanding of his ideas on this subject *The Craft of Musical Composition* (AMP) should be consulted. All his piano works are published by Schott.

In einer Nacht . . . Op.15 1919. 14 highly variegated short character pieces. Subtitled "dreams and experiences," they display Hindemith's romantic tendencies, despite attempts at disguising them with irony and fugal techniques. Nonvirtuosic to the point that the message completely overrides the medium. M-D.

Sonate Op. 17 1920 (Billeter—Schott ED 7951 1992) 31pp. This work was thought to be lost but the editor reconstructed it with the help of Hindemith's complete sketches. It is important because we can examine Hindemith's earliest use of new compositional methods and the different stylistic levels of the post-war years in a large-scale work. The first movement is an easily recognized sonata-allegro form, with the development section beginning as a fugue, probably Hindemith's earliest serious fugue. The second movement is a set of three variations that concludes with an imposing Stretta (Basso ostinato). A strong addition to Hindemith's piano catalogue. D.

Tanzstücke Op.19 1920. Eight dance pieces, all requiring vigorous octave and chord playing. The last five are grouped under the heading *Pantomime*. Bitonal writing, varied metrical patterns propel the music forward. An effective collection. M-D to D.

Suite "1922" Op.26. Marsch; Schimmy; Nachtstück; Boston; Ragtime. Old dances of the suite are replaced by parodies of early-twentieth-century dance styles. Concerning the Ragtime Hindemith says, "Forget everything you have learned in your piano lessons. Don't worry whether you must play D sharp with the fourth or the sixth finger. Play this piece wildly but in strict rhythm, like a machine. Use the piano as an interesting kind of percussion instrument and treat it accordingly." The lyric Nachtstück is effective performed separately. Subtle rubato is called for in Boston. M-D to D.

Sonata No.1 1936. Inspired by Friedrich Hölderlin's poem *Der Main*, this large-scale work is in five movements and requires textural clarity and solid chord playing. D.

Sonata No.2 1936. Smaller in dimensions than the other sonatas. First movement is in SA design; the second is a bright Scherzo; and the finale is a rondo with a short, slow introduction. M-D.

See: Felix Salzer, *Structural Analysis*, Vol.II (New York: Charles Boni, 1952), pp.298–305 for an analysis.

Sonata No.3 1936. Four movements. Large-scale work that closes with a powerful double fugue. Sonorous passages add to the excitement of the close. Modeled after Beethoven's Sonata Op.110? Mature pianism required. D.

Übung in drei Stücken Op.37 Part 1 1925. No.1: energetic two-part writing, changing meters, colorful jazzy mid-section. No.2: calm melody with involved figuration proceeds to prestissimo close over ostinato bass. No.3: rhythmic problems permeate this brilliant rondo. Aggressive writing throughout. M-D.

Reihe Kleine Stücke Op.37 Part 2 1927. 13 fairly complex short pieces. Varied moods and titles. M-D.

Kleine Klaviermusik (1929). Twelve five-tone pieces. Various moods, severe polyphonic writing. Int.

Wir bauen eine Stadt (1931). Six pieces from the cantata *Let's Build a City*. Int.

Ludus Tonalis (1942). *Studies in Counterpoint Tonal Organization and Piano Playing*. Twelve Fugues, in as many keys, connected by Interludes in free lyric and dance forms, old and new, and framed by a Prelude and Postlude that have more in common than meets the casual ear. This contemporary *Well-Tempered Clavier* is a cyclical whole arranged in a key sequence based on Hindemith's ranking of tonalities as given in his *Craft of Musical Composition*. The Fugues (all in three and four voices) as well as the interludes exhibit a great variety of moods and difficulty. Int. to D. Also available in a separate version, entitled *Ludi Leonum* (Schott 8200), illustrated in cartoon style (showing the form of the pieces) by the composer for his wife's 50th birthday (1950).

See: Jane Carlson, "Hindemith's *Ludus Tonalis*, A Personal Experience," PQ, 65 (Fall 1968):17–21. A descriptive survey of the entire work from a pianist's point of view.

Käbi Laretei, "Hindemith's *Ludus Tonalis*: Play with Animation!" MJ, 29 (December 1971):32, 61, 67–68.

Hans Tischler, "Remarks on Hindemith's Contrapuntal Technique. Based on his *Ludus Tonalis* of 1942." In *Essays in Musicology—A Birthday Offering for Willi Apel* (Bloomington: Indiana University, 1968), pp.175–84.

——, "Hindemith's *Ludus Tonalis* and Bach's WTC—A Comparison," MR, 20 (1959):217–27.

Variations 1936. Was originally the second movement of Piano Sonata No.1, but was replaced with the movement entitled "Im Veitmass eines sehr lang-samen Marsches" (In the tempo of a very slow march). These four superbly crafted variations are inspired by a slowly unfolding chordal theme basically centered around D♭. Requires a secure rhythmic sense. M-D.

Easy Pieces for Piano (Heilbut—Hug GH 11156 1977) 12pp. Drei leichte Fünf-tonstücke. Marsch from "Wir bauen eine Stadt" (leichte bewegte ganze Takte from "Reihe kleiner Stücke"); Interludium und Fuga sexta B♭ from "Ludus Tonalis"; Pastorale from "Ludus Tonalis." Int. to M-D.

The Hindemith Collection (Hinson—Schott 533) 51pp. Four pieces at the intermediate level; six at the moderate to difficult level. Includes an analysis of each piece plus an annotated list of Hindemith's solo piano works. Interpretative notes in English, French, and German.

Marsch from *Let's Build a Town* and *Foxtrot* from *Tuttifaentaschen*. In collection *The Century of Invention* (EAMC 772).

See: Peter Evans, "Hindemith's Keyboard Music," MT, 97 (November 1956):572–75.

Maurice Hinson, "The Piano Music of Paul Hindemith," *Music and the Teacher*, Part I, 22/3 (September 1996):11–13; Parts II and III, 23/1 (March 1997): 10–13.

Bruce Hobson (–   ) USA

Two Movements for Piano 1977 (Mobart) 26pp. 9 min. Movement I: serial, thin textures, highly concentrated but no main climax is ever achieved. Movement II: thinner textures, slower, flabby melodic lines. M-D.

Alun Hoddinott (1929–   ) Wales

Hoddinott has, with the exception of one short character piece, composed only sonatas for the piano—the only major British composer to have done so.

Second Nocturne Op.16 1964 (Nov). Impressionistic, quasi-atonal style. Wide dynamic range, no key signatures. Requires a good sense of rubato. M-D.

Sonata No.1 Op.17 1959 (OUP) 44pp. 17 min. Andante; Allegro; Adagio; Allegro assai. Some serial technique present but tonal centers are easily recognizable. Rhythmic vitality, much dissonance, linear textures. M-D.

Sonata No.2 Op.27 1960 (Nov) 20pp. 12 min. First movement: all craft and little inspiration; frequent use of palindromes; exhaustively examines, transforms, and returns to its opening fugue. Second movement: lyric and poetic. Third movement: full of rhythmic drive. M-D to D.

Sonatina for Clavichord or Piano Op.18 1959 (S&B) 11pp. Prelude; Scherzo; Elegy; Finale. Thin textures, ornaments, MC. Int. to M-D.

Sonata No.3 Op.40 1966 (Nov) 14pp. 10 min. (See Anthologies and Collections: General; Contemporary). Adagio: expressive, free, declamatory. Allegro: energetic and driving. M-D to D.

Sonata No.4 Op.49 1966 (OUP) 21pp. 11 min. Five concise movements. Toccata 1. Toccata 2: in the form of a scherzo and trio. Aria. Notturno: six lines, largely atonal, serial, Impressionistic. Toccata 3: brings together material of the first four movements. Much use of pedal. Powerfully written work. D.

Sonata No.5 1968 (OUP) 28pp. 14 min. Begins with a cadenza, which is developed. Moves to two contrasting Aria movements. Ends with a Toccata, which is a mirror canon. Unusual form, serial. D.
Sonata No.6 Op.78/3 1974 (OUP) 15pp. 10 min. One movement. Strong dissonance in bitonal setting, large dynamic contrasts, fierce rhythmic treatment, cadenza, colorful closing of soft sad chords. Virtuosic and effective. D.
Sonata No. 7 Op. 114 (University College Cardiff Press 1986) 28pp. 14 min. Highly chromatic; vigorous and forceful. D.

Richard Hoffman (1831–1909) USA, born Great Britain
Hoffman came to the USA as a lad of sixteen after having reportedly studied with Liszt, Moscheles, Rubinstein, and Thalberg. He settled in New York and made an outstanding contribution to the musical life of that city. He was a close personal friend of Louis Moreau Gottschalk.
In Memoriam LMG in collection *Piano Music in Nineteenth Century America*, Vol.I (Hinson—Alfred 10102). Written in 1869 on the occasion of Gottschalk's death. A nocturne in style; effective; one of the better pieces from this decade. M-D.
Dixiana ("Caprice for the Pianoforte on the Popular Negro Minstrel's Melody *Dixie's Land*") 1861. In collection *Masters of American Piano Music* (Alfred 4603) 7pp. Opens grandly, fuguelike, soon resolves into melodic hammered triplets, ragtime bass enters at measure 129 (25 years before ragtime). President Lincoln was fond of this setting. A grand paraphrase. M-D.
See: Richard Hoffman, *Some Musical Recollections of Fifty Years* (New York: Charles Scribner's Sons, 1910; reprint, Detroit: Detroit Reprints in Music, 1975).

E. T. A. Hoffmann (1776–1822) Germany
Hoffman wrote six piano sonatas. Four were published in 1922 by Kistner and Siegel, edited by Becking: No.1 f, No.2 F, No.3 f, No.4 c♯. No.4 is contained in the collection *Thirteen Keyboard Sonatas of the 18th and 19th Centuries* (W. S. Newman—UNC).
Sonata A 1804–1805 (Schnapp—Br). Andante. Two Minuets. Allegro assai: a bright rondo; most interesting of the movements. Not technically difficult. Serves as good introduction to nineteenth-century piano literature, although not as interesting as some of the later sonatas. Int. to M-D.
Sonata c♯ 1805. From *Anthology of Music*, Vol.21, *Romanticism in Music*, pp.71–72. Scherzo: five-note main theme dominates entire movement. M-D.
Sonata Op.57 (Wollenweber). Thick textures, poor voice leading, awkward writing. M-D.
See: L. A. Whitesell, "E. T. A. Hoffman and Robert Schumann," JALS 13 (June 1983):73–101.

Richard Hoffmann (1925–   ) USA, born Austria
Variations for Piano No.2 1957 (Mobart 1980) 20pp. 12 min. Grave: dramatic, much use of tremolo, moves over complete range of keyboard. Presto Giocoso

(Scherzo and Trio): imitative; in the da capo the dynamics of the Scherzo are reversed. Theme and eight variations: tempo increases. 12-tone virtuoso writing. Holds together well. Entire work presents a strong cumulative effect. D.

Heinrich Karl Johann Hofmann (1842–1902) Germany
Hofmann is best known today for his miniatures and chamber music with keyboard.
17 Miscellaneous Pieces from Opp. 11, 37, 77, 85, and 88 (Johnson—ABRSM 1986) 32pp. Short character pieces with charming Schumann influence. Melodie; In the Evening; Country Waltz; Little Wood-bird; Lyric song; Elves; Go to Sleep!, On the Lake; Rogue; By the Mountain Torrent; etc. Int.

Josef Hofmann (1876–1957) USA, born Poland
Hofmann was one of the greatest piano virtuosi of all times. He composed a few works (some under the pen name of Michael Dvorsky) in a fluent and florid post-Romantic style.
Elegy (TP 1943) 3pp. A short melodic character-piece. Int. to M-D.
Nocturne—Complaint (Musica Obscura) 2pp. Expressive melody over accompaniment similar to Chopin Nocturne E♭ Op.9/2. Int. to M-D.
Charakterskizzen Op.40 1908 (Musica Obscura) 37pp. Vision: light and fleet outer sections, dotted note chords in skips for the mid-section. Jadis: melodic, choralelike, chromatic. Nenien: expressive somber melody over arpeggiated accompaniment. Kaleidoskop (published separately by same publisher): presto elfinlike study, sweeping flourish concludes the piece. M-D.
The Sanctuary (Musica Obscura) 8pp. Bell-like opening and closing; Allegro arpeggiated section with hand-crossings; melody tucked into figuration. M-D.
See: Stephen Husarik, "Musical Expression in Piano Roll Performance of Josef Hofmann," PQ, 125 (Spring 1984):45–46, 48–52. Compares Hofmann's editions with his performances on Duo Art piano rolls. The results are revealing.
———, "Josef Hofmann's Approach to Musical Dynamics," JALS 15 (June 1984):139–51.
Abbey Simon, "Master Class—Josef Hofmann's 'Berceuse'," *Keyboard Classics* (September 1983):40. Analytical notes; the music is included.

Lee Hoiby (1926–   ) USA
Hoiby writes in a contemporary Romantic, lyrical style.
Toccata Op.1 1953 (GS). A concert study; driving rhythms. M-D.
Nocturne Op.6 e♭ 1981. Contrasting melodies and more dramatic sections.
5 Preludes Op.7 rev. ed. (Plymouth 1977) 22pp. Andante con moto; Allegro vivo; Moderato con moto; Allegro; Allegro ma non troppo. Not harsh on the ears or too hard on the hands. Large span required. M-D.
Capriccio on 5 Notes Op.23 (Bo&H 1962). Commissioned for the first Van Cliburn International Piano Competition, 1962. Advanced harmonic idiom, designed to show off many sides of the pianist's technical and musical abili-

ties. A mixture of styles, broad dynamic range, restless rhythmic motion, breathless coda. D.

Ten Variations on a Schubert Ländler (the A minor from D. 366) (GS 1981) Op.35, 1980. A monumental set of varied intensity. Schubert's Ländler returns at the end. D.

Narrative Op.41, 1983 (GS) 13pp. 9 min. Also in collection *American Contemporary Masters* (GS 1995). This large Romantic multisectional work is generated from its opening two-note motive. Structurally it bears some relationship to the Chopin ballades. Pianissimo ending. A solid contribution to the repertoire. D.

Jan Holcman (1922–   ) USA, born Poland

Three Echoes (TP 1973). Like a Polish Folksong; Almost Classical; Somewhat jazzy. Wry contemporary harmonies; straightforward rhythms; three different styles reflected. Int.

Trevor Hold (1939–   ) Great Britain

The Lilford Owl (Ramsey 1980) 38pp. 20 min. Short improvisations or meditations on British folk tunes. Suited for recreational purposes or students' concerts. Inspired by Grieg and Grainger. Int. to M-D.

Kemp's Nine Daies Wonder (Ramsey) 46pp. 23 min. These pieces are an homage to Will Kemp (a colleague of Shakespeare) who performed his remarkable nine-day Morris Dance from London to Norwich in 1599. Large chords, MC, polytonality, fast passage-work. M-D.

Karl Höller (1907–1987) Germany

Drei kleine Sonaten Op.41 (Sikorski 113, 114, 115 1950). Available separately. Op.41/1 d, 15pp.: Allegro molto; Un poco vivace; Andante con espressione; Molto Allegro. Op.41/2 G, 19pp.: Un poco Allegro amabile; Molto vivace; Andante con espressione; Allegro con spirito. Op.41/3 b, 15pp.: Allegro moderato, Vivo e leggiero; Un poco lento; Allegro molto. All three sonatas are neoclassic in style, show a preference for thin textures, and are freely tonal with a few Impressionistic techniques (parallel chords, unresolved dissonances). M-D.

York Höller (1944–   ) Germany

Sonata No. 2 Hommage à Franz Liszt 1986 (Bo&H 1991) 35pp. Sectionalized, virtuosic one-movement work developed (via the "projection method") from measures 7–8 of Liszt's *Feux Follets*. Two other themes are used from this Liszt etude. "Everything is development" (from the score). An extension of Lisztian technique. D.

Heinz Holliger (1939–   ) Switzerland

Elis 1961 (Schott 5383) 7pp. 5 min. Three expressionistic nocturnes in the Webern tradition. Harmonics, glissando on strings. Employs eight Indian rhythmic ragas. D.

Vagn Holmboe (1909–1996) Denmark, born Africa
Holmboe's music is strongly influenced by Carl Nielsen and Béla Bartók. He leans toward linear textures.
Suono da bardo Op.49 (Viking 1949). Toccata; Interlude; Fantasia; Metamorfosi; Finale; Posludio. A symphonic suite, employs unusual development technique. Nielsen's influence is especially seen in this work. D.
Rumainsk Suite Op.12/1 (Viking). Holmboe's wife is a Rumanian pianist with whom he explored folk music in many remote villages of Rumania. This suite dates from that period. M-D.
See: Paul Rapoport, *Vagn Holmboe: A Catalogue of His Music, Discography, Bibliographical Essays* (London: Triad Press, 1975).

Gustav Holst (1874–1934) Great Britain
Nocturne (Faber 1965). Colorful writing. Impressionistic, contrasting quiet and lively moods. Int.
Jig (Curwen). Animated, rhythmic, cross-rhythms. M-D.
Toccata (Curwen). On the tune "Newburn lads." More contemporary than the above works.
2 Folksong Fragments Op.46/2, 3 (OUP) 3 min. O! I hae seen the roses blaw; The Shoemakker. Imaginative vitality in No.2. Int.
The Solo Piano Music 1924–32 (Faber 1982) 26pp. Toccata: hornpipe; ambiguous tonality; exploits upper register of keyboard. Chrissemas Day in the Morning. O! I Hae Seen the Roses Blaw. Shoemakker: three folksong settings, subtle textures. Nocturne: Impressionistic. Jig: more complex and dissonant than the folk tunes. These six short pieces comprise Holst's entire contribution to solo piano. Int. to M-D.
Chrissemas Day in the Morning Op.46/1 (MMP).
Two Pieces (MMP). Nocturne; Jig.
Toccata (MMP).

Adriana Hölszky (–   ) Germany
Hörfenster für Franz Liszt 1986–87 (Astoria 1993) 50pp. 15 min. First movement is for prepared piano; second is for unprepared piano with electronics. In the second movement the pianist also plays percussion and sings. M-D to D.

Simeon ten Holt (1923–   ) The Netherlands
Sekwensen for 1 or 2 pianos (Donemus 1965). Six pieces, avant-garde. Directions in Dutch and French. M-D to D.
Sonata (diagonal) (Donemus 1959). Agitato; Allegretto scorrendo; Adagio lamentoso; Allegro vivace. Freely chromatic, some bitonal writing, changing meters, broad dynamic range. Octave facility required. D.

Rudolph Holzmann (1910–1992) Peru, born Germany
Cuarta Pequeña Suite (ECIC 1942). Based on Peruvian folk materials. Preludio Pastorale: peaceful, melodic. Bailan las Muchachas: little girl's dance, stac-

cato, syncopated. Melodía triste: melancholy moderato. Fanfarria Campestre (Country Fanfare): horn calls. Interludio Evocativo: atmospheric, nocturne-like. Danza Final: octaves, fast double notes, energetic 3/8, most difficult of set. Int. to M-D.

Niñerías 1947 (Editorial Tritone). Six short pieces. Int.

Remembranzas 1949 (Editorial Tritone). Nostalgic, pianistic. M-D.

Sonatina sobre motivos del folklore peruviano (PIC). Colorful, mixture of popular and art music. Int.

Arthur Honegger (1892–1955) Switzerland, born France
More at home in the larger than smaller forms, Honegger did not pour his finest efforts into his piano works. Nevertheless, his compositions show a certain substance that many of his contemporaries lacked.

Trois Pièces (Sal 1915–19). Prélude: intense, large climax. Hommage à Ravel: flowing, lyric. Danse; repeated intervals, brilliant, driving. M-D.

Toccata et Variations (Sal 1916) 17 min. Contrasted sections in the Toccata, facile. Variation theme is chorale-like; double notes, serious, more involved than Toccata. M-D.

Sept Pièces Brèves (ESC 1919–20). Souplement; Vif; Très lent; Legèrement; Lent; Rythmique; Violent. Short; contrasted moods and techniques. M-D.

Le Cahier Romand (Sal 1921–23). Five sensitive pieces, mainly lyric except No.4. M-D.

Hommage à Albert Roussel (Sal 1928) 2 min. Short; chordal; syncopated melody. Includes two themes by Roussel. Int.

Prélude, Arioso et Fughetta sur le nom de BACH (Sal 1932). 4½ min. Prelude: broken-chord pattern. Arioso: improvisatory with an ostinato bass. Fugue: three voices. M-D.

Souvenir de Chopin (Choudens 1947). Chopin style, persistent repeated note in tenor voice. Int.

Deux Esquisses (Durand 1943). No.1: rhapsodic. No.2: wistful. M-D.

La Neige sur Rome 1925 (Sal) 2pp. Arranged by Honegger from the incidental music score for *L'Impératrice aux Rochers*. Lent et doux. M-D.

Sarabande 1920 (ESC) No.2 in the *Album des Six pour Piano*. M-D.

Trois Pièces 1910 (Desforges). Scherzo; Humoresque; Adagio espressivo. M-D.

James Hook (1746–1827) Great Britain
Guida di Musica London 1785, Part I, Op.37 (BB) Facsimile edition. "Being a complete book of instructions for beginners on the harpsichord or piano forte . . . to which is added 24 progressive lessons." Part II, 1794, "consisting of several hundred examples of fingering . . . and 6 excercises . . . to which is added, a short . . . method of learning thoro bass . . . Op.75." Int.

A James Hook Album (Eve Barsham—Elkin 1975) 29pp. 22 easy pieces from "Guida di Musica." A graded selection from the 52 pieces contained in Op.37 and Op.81. Admirable teaching material, well fingered. Easy to Int.

The Precepter London 1785 (BB) "for piano-forte, the organ or harpsichord to which is added 2 celebrated lessons by James Hook." Facsimile edition.

Anthony Hopkins (1921–   ) Great Britain

Sonata No.3 c♯ (JWC 1948) 24pp. 14 min. Allegro vigoroso: SA, well-contrasted material, clearly defined sections, many dynamic changes. Largo: harmonic opening leads to contrapuntal section; slow fugato leads to rhythmic Allegro giusto. Coda requires utmost rhythmic precision. M-D to D.

For Talented Beginners (OUP) 2 vols. Displays a highly creative approach to basic keyboard skills. Easy.

Sonatine (OUP 1970) 11pp. Allegro assai: fresh melodies and harmonies. Quasi adagio: Impressionistic chordal sonorities. Capriccioso: introduction to an alla marcia, delightful. Int. to M-D.

Nightlong (Banks). Six variations on the lovely Welsh hymn tune, *Ar hyd nos*. Contains some palatable and imaginative sonorities. The beauty of the melody lies in its innocent simplicity, but the variations do not sit comfortably alongside it. M-D.

Francis Hopkinson (1737–1791) USA

Hopkinson was the first known American composer and a personal friend of George Washington. His music is couched in the conventional English style and modeled after pieces by Thomas Arne.

Lessons: A facsimile edition of Hopkinson's personal keyboard book (McKay—C. T. Wagner 1979, available through European American Music). Anthology of keyboard compositions and arrangements copied in Hopkinson's own hand; photographic facsimile of the MS at the University of Pennsylvania. Int.

Seven Songs (Hinson, Krauss—Alfred 10166). The first collection of secular music by a native-born American composer published in America. There are actually eight songs—the eighth was added after the title page had been engraved. These pieces can be performed as solo keyboard music or as songs using the text. Int.

Robert von Hornstein (1833–1890) Germany

Hornstein was a close friend of Richard Wagner.

Minnelied (Musica Obscura) 1p. Nocturne-like, salon style. Int.

Alan Hovhaness (1911–2000) USA

The Orient has had a profound effect on this American-born composer, yet his music is based on classical forms. Strict discipline, great freedom, consonance and dissonance, tonality and atonality, while seeming to be opposites, are all woven into his style.

Pastorale No.1 Op.3/2 (PIC). Marimba and timpanum stick required for glissandi. Int. to M-D.

Hymn to a Celestial Musician Op.3/3 (PIC). Soft plectrum required for circular glissandi. M-D.

Toccata and Fugue Op.6 (CFP) 5 min. Toccata: many repeated notes create a shimmering effect. Fugue: relies on much use of dynamics. M-D.

Sonata Ricercare Op.12 (CFP) 8 min. Three movements of imitative writing. M-D.

Fantasy Op.16 (CFP) 8 min. Various objects are used to contact the strings. M-D.

Mystic Flute Op.22 (CFP) 2 min. 7/8 meter, open fifths, melodic augmented seconds, hypnotic. Int.

Mazert Nman Rehani (Thy Hair Is Like Basil Leaf) Op.38 (CFP) 5 min. Imitates ancient Oriental instruments. M-D.

12 Armenian Folk Songs Op.43 (CFP) 9 min. Charming, of special interest. Int.

Slumber Song; Siris' Dance Op.52/2,3 (MCA). Easy.

Farewell to the Mountains Op.55/2 (CFP) 2 min. Rapid, like an Oud, flexible meters, repeated notes and rhythms. M-D.

Achtamar Op.64/1 (PIC). Adagio (imitating the Tmpoong, a clay drum); Allegro (imitating the Kanoon, a zither, and Oud, a lute). Exotic, programmatic, based on the biblical legend of Tamar. M-D.

Fantasy on an Ossetin Tune Op.85/6 (PIC). In two parts. Plaintive wails, lively dance. Ossetin is a district in Armenia. M-D.

Jhala Op.103 (PIC). Virtuoso writing, deep bell tones played with timpani mallet on bass strings. M-D.

Suite Op.96 (CFP) 7 min. Prelude; Fugue; Dance; Aria; Madrigal. M-D.

Orbit No.2 Op.102/2 (PIC). Calls for timpanum stick to play bass strings. M-D.

Allegro on a Pakistan Lute Tune Op.104/6 (LG). In collection *New Music for the Piano*. Int. to M-D.

Haiku Op.113/1, 2, 3 (CFP) 1 min. each. Int. to M-D.

Sonatina Op.120 (CFP) 6 min. Three movements. Expressive, based on Japanese pentatonic scale. M-D.

Macedonian Mountain Dance Op.144b/1 (CFP) 3 min. Restless, simple harmonies, big climax. M-D.

Do You Remember the Last Silence? Op.152 (CFP) 5 min. Thin melody accompanied by thick harmonies. Effective contemporary character piece. Alternates sustained chords and uses a conjunct line of single pitches, all in the bass clef. M-D.

Madras Sonata Op.176 (CFP) 10 min. Three movements. A three-voice fugue concludes this work. M-D.

Shalimar Op.177 (CFP) 11 min. Suite in eight movements. Irregular repeated-note figures alternate with contrapuntal interludes. M-D.

Poseidon Sonata Op.191 (CFP) 10 min. Two movements. Span of ninth required. M-D.

Bardo Sonata Op.192 (CFP) 7 min. Three movements. Interesting use of harmonics. "Bardo" refers to the "After Death State" described in the Tibetan Book of the Dead, and the sonata is introduced by a quotation from it. M-D.

Bare November Day Op.210 (CFP) 2 min. For clavichord, piano, organ, or harpsichord. Three movements. M-D.

Dark River and Distant Bell Op.212 (CFP) 5 min. For harpsichord but can be played on piano, organ, or clavichord. Four movements. M-D.

Visionary Landscapes Op.214 (CFP) 12 min. A group of descriptive pieces. "Midnight Bell" uses extra-keyboard sonorities. Int.

Komachi Op.240 (CFP) 11 min. Seven short descriptive pieces in a suite that honors Kamanchi, the great Japanese woman poet. Impressionistic, pentatonic, melodic with many arpeggiated chords. Adept pedaling required. The notes are easy but beautiful imagery makes them appealing to a mature performer. See especially No. 5, Flight of Dawn Birds, and No.7, Moon Harp. M-D.

Lullaby (EBM). In album *American Composers of Today*. Easy.

Mountain Idylls (AMP). Moon Lullaby; Mood Dance; Mountain Lullaby. Pedal studies. Int.

Sonata "Ananda" Op.303 (Fujihara Music 1981) 20pp. 20 min. Andante: nocturne-like. Vision of Volcano Mountain: chordal legato espressivo section alternates with an Allegro senza misura section with repeated notes "like a giant Kannoon" (a zither-like instrument). Allegro assai: a flowing 7/8 section is followed by a fugue. Vision of a Starry Night: Allegretto espressivo; lyric; contrasts with an Andante misterioso section with bell-like sounds; Impressionistic. M-D.

Sketchbook of Mr. Purple Poverty Vol.I (A. Broude 1980) 15pp. 13 short witty and humorous pieces in an easy-to-understand contemporary modal style. No key signatures. Easy.

See: Maurice Hinson, "The Piano Works of Alan Hovhaness," AMT, 16 (January 1967):22–24, 44.

Mary Howe (1882–1964) USA

Stars (Composer's Press 1938) 3pp. Sonorous, Impressionistic, large climax, *ppp* closing. M-D.

Whimsy (Composer's Press 1938) 2pp. Clever, staccato touch, a few fast octaves, abrupt *fff* ending. Int.

Herbert Howells (1892–1983) Great Britain

The music of Howells is strongly English in character without being consciously "national." He made an attempt to revive the use of the clavichord in his two sets of pieces including the instrument's name.

Howells's Clavichord 1961 (Nov). Twenty character pieces used to pay tribute to Howells's musical friends. Uses old forms and titles, MC. M-D.

Lambert's Clavichord Op.41 (OUP). Character pieces named after friends: Lambert's Fireside; Fellowe's Delight; Hughe's Ballet; Wortham's Grounde; Sargent's Fantastic Sprite; Foss' Dump; My Lord Sandwich's Dreame; Samuel's Air; De la Mare's Pavane; Sir Hugh's Galliard; H. H. His Fancy; Sir Richard's Toy. Sophisticated writing. Int. to M-D.

Sonatina (ABRSM). Vivo-inquieto: lively, wide dynamic contrasts. Quasi adagio, serioso ma teneramente: in a cantabile style. Finale: requires agility and verve. Large span necessary. M-D.

Country Pageant and *A Little Book of Dances* (ABRSM 1825) 28pp. *Country Pageant*: Merry Andrew's Procession; Kings and Queens; There Was a Most Beautiful Lady; The Mummers' Dance. *A Little Book of Dances*: Minuet;

Gavotte; Pavane; Galliard; Ragadoon; Jig. These two sets of pieces date from 1928 and reflect Howells's feeling for the English tradition. Int.

Alexandru Hrisanide (1936–   ) Rumania
Piano Piece No.8 (Gerig) 12pp. 4½ min. A toccata using clusters and numerous contemporary techniques. Great facility required. D.

Nicolas-Joseph Hüllmandel (1756–1823) Germany
Hüllmandel studied with C. P. E. Bach in Hamburg. He went to Paris in 1776. After the French revolution he went to London, where he lived the rest of his life.
Piano Pieces and Sonatas (Oberdoerffer—CFP 6981). These pieces are typical of the time. Mozart expressed appreciation of Hüllmandel's sonatas in a letter to his father. Int. to M-D.

Keith Humble (1927–1995) Australia
Arcade II (UE 1969) 4 loose sheets. Includes instructions for performance. Four sections, produced on four separate sheets A-D. Material was derived from a computer research program. Boulez-inspired. D.

Bertold Hummel (1925–   ) Germany
Invocation 52 (Simrock 1972) 6pp. Much tremolo, large gestures of fleet passage-work, extensive dynamic and keyboard range, carefully pedaled. D.
Sonatina Op.56 (Simrock 1979) 8pp. Three short contrasting movements (FSF). Second movement, Elesie, is nice enough. Last movement, Vivace, is considerably more difficult than the first two. Hindemithean fourths add dry character. Int.

Johann Nepomuk Hummel (1778–1837) Hungary
During his life Hummel was considered by many to be the greatest pianist in Europe and an outstanding composer. He was also a fine improviser. Chopin said: "Mozart, Beethoven and Hummel—the masters of us all."
Complete Piano Sonatas (Musica Rara 1975; Sachs—Garland 1989). Long and informative introduction by Harold Truscott. Vol.I, 89pp: Sonatas Op.2/3 C; Op.13 E♭; Op.20 f; Op.38 C. Vol.II, 91pp: Sonatas Op.81 f♯; Op.106 D; VII G, VIII A♭, IX C. These last three works are more like sonatinas. The Opp.81 and 106 Sonatas display Hummel's pianistic skills admirably. All of these works are important documents in the history of the form and in the evolution of Romantic piano music. They display both classical and Romantic characteristics, with florid runs and glittering figurations. Also available in 2 vols. (Hänssler 41.813, 41.814). The Garland edition is *The Collected Works*, Vol. 1, and contains seven pieces, including a hitherto unpublished work, a two-hand arrangement of Sonata Op. 92 for four hands. 225 pp. of facsimiles. M-D to D.
Sonatas and Piano Pieces (UE; K) reprint of the C. De Bériot edition. Bériot

has written a long preface on the attributes of the piano pedals. Fingering and pedaling are clearly indicated. Vol.1 (UE 91; K9894): Sonatas Op.13 (dedicated to Haydn; engagingly and appropriately Haydnesque with some early Beethoven thrown in) and Op.20; Rondo E♭ Op.11; Fantasia Op.18; Polonaise (La bella capriciosa) Op.55. Vol.2 (UE 92; K9895): Sonatas Op.81 (this work had an epochal influence on both Chopin and Schumann) and Op.106; Rondo-Fantasie Op.19; Rondo brillante Op.109. Vol.3 (UE 93): Caprice Op.49; Variations Op.57; 24 Preludes Op.67; La Contemplazione Op.107/3; Rondo all' Ungherese Op.107/6; La Galante Rondeau Op.120. M-D.

Oeuvres Choises (N. Lee—Heugel 1982) Le Pupitre No.61, 161pp. Rondo quasi una fantasia Op.19; Fantaisie en mi bémol majeur Op.18; Six Bagatelles Op.107; Rondeau brillant Op.109. Quatre Grandes Etudes Op.125. "The pieces chosen here are those which we find the most personal and the most varied instrumentally, on the one hand, and those, on the other, which are not already available elsewhere, either in older editions or in more recent ones" (from the preface). No fingering. Includes a complete catalogue of all Hummel's opus numbers. This collection shows off Hummel as a composer of originality and beauty. M-D.

Rondo E♭ Op.11 (GS; CFP; PWM). Scales, octaves, broken thirds, complicated trills with extra notes in them, ostinato-work for left hand. M-D.

Scherzo (Willis). Fine encore or recital piece, moderately adventurous. M-D.

Variations on a Gavotte by Gluck Op.57 (CF; K&S). Vocal fiorituras and decorative figures that anticipate Chopin. Fluent and naive. M-D.

24 Preludes in all the keys Op.67 1815 (Musica Obscura). Some are only three or four bars. Sketchy, undeveloped ideas, improvisatory. Key sequence is similar to Chopin's in his *Préludes*. To be played before a larger work to establish the key and mood to follow. Int. to M-D.

24 Etudes Op.125 1833 (Leduc). These works are a summation of the late classical style, which was going out of fashion in the 1830s. They lack the novelty and fire that Schumann expressed about them, but they compensate with their variety and delicacy. They demonstrate that melodiousness and counterpoint were compatible. The great resonance of the modern piano deprives the music of some of its natural transparency. M-D to D.

Etüden (UE 760). 17 Studies from Op.125. M-D.

Variations for the Piano (Introduction by Joel Sachs—Garland 1989). *The Collected Works*, Vol. 2, 225pp., facsimiles. 23 compositions, five of which are reproduced from contemporary mss.

Shorter Compositions for Piano, Most from the Viennese Years (Introduction by Joel Sachs—Garland 1989). *The Collected Works*, Vol. 3, 310pp. of the first edition. Includes the rondos, fantasies, bagatelles, fugues, etudes, preludes, and other smaller works.

Shorter Compositions for Piano, Most from the Weimar Years (Introduction by Joel Sachs—Garland 1989). *The Collected Works*, Vol. 4, 410pp., facsimiles of the first edition. Continuation of previous volume.

Dances for Piano Solo Sonatas and Other Works for Piano Solo Four Hands and Two Hands (Introduction by Joel Sachs—Garland 1989). *The Collected Works*, Vol. 5, 310 facsimiles of the first edition. 15 sets of minuets, German dances, and waltzes, along with the sonatas and variations for piano four-hands.

16 Short Pieces (Roberts—ABRSM 1984) 32pp. Four pieces come from Hummel's *6 pièces très faciles* Op.52, composed around 1815. The rest come from his huge piano method *Klavierschule* 1828. Andante; Allegretto; Gigue; Romance; Rondo; Tempo di Minuetto; To Alexis; All Polacca; etc. Attractive and poetic miniatures. Int.

Variations on an Austrian National Song, Op.8 (Artaria ca. 1801). (The "Emperor's Hymn" by Haydn.) Hummel had studied with Salieri and Albrechtsberger just before these variations were composed, and their influence is apparent. M-D.

Six Polonaises Favorites Op.70 (Kunzelmann GM 1379 1992) 12pp. Good examples of the polonaise rhythm. Appealing. Int.

Sonatas, Rondos, Fantasies, and Other Works for Solo Piano (Dover). 115 pieces. Int. to M-D.

See: Richard Davis, "The Music of J. N. Hummel, Its Derivations and Development," MR, 26 (1965):169–91.

Joel Sachs, *Kapellmeister Hummel in England and France* (Detroit: Information Coordinators, 1978).

François Hünten (1793–1878) France, born Germany.
See below, "Collections," *Piano Music of the Parisian Virtuosos 1810–1860*.

Conrad F. Hurlebusch (1696–1765) Germany
Keyboard Sonatas (A. Jambor—EV 1963) 2 vols. 6 sonatas in each. Hurlebusch's "style of writing was so progressive that it may have aroused controversial reactions among his contemporaries. He was searching for new harmonies, strange modulations, lyricism and pathos, and application of German, French and Italian musical styles. His courageous experimentation put him far ahead of his time" (from the Preface). Worthy music; moments of inspiration; use of numerous dance movements (M, Gavotta, G) lend a suite character. Editorial policy not always clear. Int. to M-D.

Karel Husa (1921–   ) USA, born Czechoslovakia
Working from within an essentially classical orientation, Husa compounds elements of the past and present, using his own distinctly individual recipe.

Élégie 1957 (Mercury 1968) 2pp. 4½ min. Simple opening theme resembles a tone row; grows to great intensity, quiet opening and closing, agitato and dramatic mid-section. M-D.

Sonatina Op.1 1943 (AMP 7709) 23pp. 12 min. Allegretto moderato; Andante cantabile; Allegretto marciale. Classical sonatina form, polytonal, delightful and remarkably fresh. M-D.

Sonata Op.11 (Schott 1949) 23 min. Three movements. "Misterioso" introduction leads to an Allegro moderato. A powerful structure, full of expressive dissonance. Requires advanced pianism. D.

Sonata No.2 1975 (AMP 1980) 18 min. Introduction, SFS movements, virtuosic style, changing tone qualities, exploits extreme registers of keyboard, extensive use of pedals (sostenuto especially), some playing on the strings. Stirring and effective. D.

Jere Hutcheson (1938–   ) USA

Fantaisie-Impromptu 1974 (Seesaw) 12 min. Much colorful glitter, requires virtuosic performance. D.

Anselm Hüttenbrenner (1794–1868) Austria

Hüttenbrenner was a close friend of Franz Schubert.

Nachruf an Schubert in Trauertonen am Pianoforte 1828 (Schott 6874 1980) 1p. In a set of three pieces entitled *Hommage à Franz Schubert*. Schubert style. M-D. Also in collection *Masters of the Character Piece* (Alfred 1856) as *Lamentation on Schubert's Death by His Friend*.

Elek Huzella (1915–   ) Hungary

Cambiate per pianoforte (EMB 1968) 6pp. Short suite. Invocazione: legato seconds, thirds, and fourths; chromatic, contrary and parallel motion. Esclamazione: quartal broken chords, some triadic sonorities. Nenia (canone enigmatico): rubato, large span required, both musical and technical problems. M-D.

Miriam Hyde (1913–   ) Australia

After graduating from the Adelaide Conservatorium, Hyde spent three years in London at the Royal College of Music. She has written two piano concertos, orchestral works, chamber music, and songs. She is best known for her piano music, which is eminently pianistic. Her style is grounded on nineteenth-century harmonic and rhythmic use but colorfully infused with unique handling of mildly contemporary techniques. Hyde knows how to end a piece, and no "padding" is found in her writing. Her autobiography, *Complete Accord*, was published by Currency.

The Piano Works of Miriam Hyde (Allans 1995). Eight graded pieces. Final section is devoted to analysis and performance suggestions by the composer. Int. to M-D.

Magpies at Sunrise 1946 (Chappell) 3 min. Built on a six-note motif of a Magpie song. It was recorded by Walter Gieseling in the early 1950s. M-D.

Reflected Reeds 1956 (Allans) 4½ min. Shows the composer's love of nature and her ability to capture a specific scene in music. Here, "it is an impression of a marshy area through which the coogee tram used to run" (from notes in recording "Brownhill Creek in Spring," Southern Cross SCCD 1027).

Hyde writes: "The reeds standing straight, or bending in various directions with geometric mirror images, produced an entrancing effect." M-D.

Valley of Rocks 1975 (Albert) 5 min. A strong, brooding, and compelling work; probably Hyde's best-known piano piece. It was inspired by an unforgettable evening when she and her husband came upon the Valley of Rocks while touring in Lynton, North Devon, in 1974. This effective piece achieved great prominence at the 1988 Sydney International Piano Competition. M-D to D.

I

Anthony Iannaccone (1943–   ) USA
Partita 1967 (ECS 695). Prelude: lively and fanciful. Sarabande: broad and lyric. Burlesca: boisterous and sassy. Gigue: dashing, meter changes. Mainly homophonic, tricky, MC. M-D.

Michael A. Iatauro (–   ) USA
Children's Pieces for Adults (PIC 1975). A charming and whimsical set of seven pieces with unusual titles such as "A Stuffed Lion Called Jonathan," "The Toy Donkey." MC and freely dissonant, clever. M-D.

Jacques Ibert (1890–1962) France
Ibert writes with clarity and Gallic wit.
Le Vent dans les Ruines 1915 (The Wind in the Ruins) (MMP). Written during the First World War; suggests the sound of wind howling through destroyed buildings. M-D.
Noël en Picardie (MMP). Colorful. M-D.
Histoires 1922 (Leduc). Published separately. La Meneuse de tortues d'Or: melancholy, tender. Le petit âne blanc (Alfred; EBM): humorous, charming staccato study. Le vieux mendiant: somber. A Giddy Girl (Alfred; EBM): sentimental. Dans la maison triste: slow and plaintive. Le palais abandonné: serious, sustained. Baja la mesa: dancelike, rhythmic. La Cage de cristal: light, cheerful. La Marchande d'eau fraîche: humorous. Le Cortège de Balkis: dancelike, light, piquant ending. Int.
See: Wesley Roberts, "Reliving Jacques Ibert's *Histoires*," *Piano Journal,* 22 (February 1987):9, 11–12.
Petite Suite en Quinze Images 1943 (Foetisch). Prélude; Ronde; Le gai vigneron; Berceuse aux étoiles; Le cavalier sans-souci; Parade; La promenade en traineau; Romance; Quadrille; Sérénade sur l'eau; La machine à coudre; L'adieu; Les crocus; Premier bal; Danse de cocher. Colorful sketches. Int.
Les Rencontres 1924 (Leduc). Les bouquetières; Les créoles; Les mignardes; Les bergères; Les bavards. A small suite in the form of a ballet, style and difficulty related to the Ravel *Valse Nobles et Sentimentales*. M-D.
Toccata sur le nom d'Albert Roussel 1929 (Leduc) 1 min. Fast, steady sixteenth-note motion throughout, difficult hand-crossings. Internal ostinatos and chromatic lines form the connective tissue of the piece. Only part of the name Albert Roussel is used. M-D.

Valse from ballet *"L'enentail de Jeanne"* 1927 (Heugel). Requires a good octave technique. Int. to M-D.
See: Wesley Roberts, "Ibert's Piano Music," *Clavier,* 29/9 (November 1990):15.

Toschi Ichiyanagi (1933–   ) Japan
Music for Piano Nos.2, 4, 7, (CFP). Published separately. Aleatoric, detailed directions, avant-garde notation. M-D to D.
Piano Media (Zen-On 370 1972) 16pp. Constant buildup of unbarred eighth notes (=1/9 second or faster) from beginning to end. A *tour de force* for performer and listener. D.
Time Sequence 1976 (Zen-On 410) 23pp. Lengthy, much repetition of patterns and sequences at a constant fast tempo. Proportional rhythmic notation. Endurance required for performer and listener. D.
Inter Konzert (Schott) 12 min. Three movements, virtuosic. D.

Andrew Imbrie (1921–   ) USA
Sonata 1947 (SP). Allegro nervoso: linear, driving, dramatic. Adagio quasi elegiaco: impassioned, dynamic central climax. Presto con brio: percussive, dissonant, dramatic closing. Serious compact work requiring advanced pianism. D.
Daedalus 1986 (Fallen Leaf Press 1993) 9 min. Strong gestures, thin textures, pointillistic, dramatic dynamic contrasts, quiet ending. Title (from Greek mythology) does not seem related to the music. D.

Kamran Ince (1960–   ) USA
Ince teaches at The University of Memphis, Tennessee.
My Friend Mozart. In collection *Changing Faces* (EAMC 1987) 3pp., ca. 3 min. Atmospheric; contrasting textures produce contrasting sections; octotonic; mildly dissonant; excellent motivic development, balance, and overall shaping of lines. Much pedal use indicated. M-D.
An Unavoidable Obsession 1988 (EAMC) 4pp., 5 min., 15 sec. Strong rhythmic chordal opening is contrasted with widely spaced thin textures; these two ideas, which return frequently, are the subject of the title. Rhythmic proportional notation, tempo changes, sectional. Much pedal use indicated. D.

Carlo de Incontrera (1937–   ) Italy
. . . Und in sich hinein (Ric 1972) 3pp. For piano and the external noise of the hall in which it is performed. Contains only sounds from *p* to *ppppp*. Strict pedal indications. To be played very freely and very slowly. Approximate rhythmic notation. In Cage tradition, many symbols explained. Preface in Italian, English, and German. Only for the adventurous. D.

Vincent d'Indy (1851–1931) France
The cyclic form of Liszt and Franck as well as use of the leitmotiv were important in the organization of d'Indy's music.

Mountain Poems Op.15 (Hamelle). Three connected movements with ten tableaux unified by leitmotiv, inspired by d'Indy's courtship, marriage, and honeymoon with a "theme of the beloved." Salon style. M-D.

Helvetia: Trois Valses Op.17 1882 (Hamelle). Named after three Swiss villages: Aarau, Schinznach, Laufenburg. Lengthy, uninteresting. M-D.

Tableaux de Voyage Op.33 1888 (Leduc). 13 descriptive travel pictures, uneven in quality but worth playing. Written to commemorate d'Indy's travels in the Black Forest and along the banks of the Rhine. Excellent substitute for Schumann *Forest Scenes* and Mendelssohn *Songs Without Words*. Int. to M-D.

Sonata E Op.63 1907 (Durand). First movement: introductory section followed by a set of variations. Second movement: brilliant, scherzo-like, contrasting trio in 5/4. Finale: uses the theme of the first movement. Cyclic construction. D.

Thème varié, Fugue et Chanson Op.85 1925 (Sal). Exceptional set of variations. M-D.

Fantasia on an Old French Air Op.99 1930 (Heugel). Introduction, six variations, finale. One of d'Indy's most delightful and successful works. M-D.

Menuet sur le nom d'Haydn 1909 (Durand) 2pp. Classical dance form. M-D.

Pour les Enfants de tout age Op.74 1919 (Rouart-Lerolle). 24 pieces in three books, arranged in order of difficulty. "An abridged chronology of music, its forms and styles." Includes a fugue, a suite, a sonata movement, as well as pieces with style traits of other composers (Haydn, Weber, Schubert, Bach, Chopin, Beethoven, Liszt, Scarlatti, Debussy, etc.). Int. to M-D.

Schumanniana Op. 30 1888 (Hamelle 2846) 10pp. Three "Songs without Words" showing certain characteristics of Schumann's style: melodic development, modulatory sequences, contrasting sections in ABA form. Requires good legato and voicing techniques for subtle contrapuntal writing. M-D.

3 French Folk Dances (OUP). Charming. Int.

Manuel Infante (1883–1958) Spain

Gitanerías (Sal 1923). Varied moods in virtuoso Spanish dance style. Exciting close. M-D.

Sevillana (Sal 1922). A fantasy of impressions of the Fête at Seville. Traditional harmonic treatment, virtuoso writing. D.

El Vito (Sal). Six variations on a popular theme in virtuoso style. A brilliant "Danse Andalouse" closes the work. M-D.

Pochades Andalouses (Gregh). Canto flamenco; Danse gitane; Aniers sur la route de Séville; Tientos. The first two are also published by Leduc. M-D.

Désirée-Émile Inghelbrecht (1880–1965) France

La Nursery (Sal). 6 vols., six pieces in each. French nursery tunes, clear textures. Also available in four-hand version for teacher and student. Int. to M-D.

Paysages (JWC). Five Impressionistic pieces. M-D.

Suite Petite-Russiènne (ESC). Five pieces based on popular tunes. M-D.

Pastourelles (Durand 1949). Nazareth; Le départ pour Bethléem; Prière de Marie; Danse des bergers; Berceuse du boeuf et de l'âne; La Marche à l'Etoile; Les bergers à le crèche. M-D.

Peter Inness (1946–   ) Great Britain

Five Pieces 1972 (November 1984) 22pp., ca. 13 min. Not overly demanding technically and MC. No. 2, Nocturne, seems to be inspired by Bartók; while No. 5, Homage to Copland, is based on material from Copland's Piano Variations. M-D.

John Ireland (1879–1962) Great Britain

Most of Ireland's piano works have a mildly contemporary sound, are well written for the instrument, and have unusually relevant and interesting titles.

The Collected Piano Works of John Ireland (S&B) 315pp. Five books with some 50 pieces that reveal Ireland in all aspects as a fine keyboard composer. Vol.I: In Those Days: Daydream, Meridian. A Sea Idyll. The Almond Trees. Decorations: The Island Spell, Moonglade, The Scarlet Ceremonies. Three Dances: Gipsy Dance, Country Dance, Reapers' Dance. Preludes: The Undertone, Obsession, The Holy Boy, Fire of Spring. Rhapsody. Vol.II: London Pieces: Chelsea Reach, Ragamuffin, Soho Forenoons. Leaves from A Child's Sketchbook: By the Mere, In the Meadow, The Hunt's Up. Merry Andrew. The Towering-Path. Summer Evening. The Darkened Valley. Two Pieces: For Remembrance (perhaps the best work in all 5 vols.), Amberley Wild Brooks. Equinox. On a Birthday Morning. Soliloquy. Vol.III: Prelude in E♭. Two Pieces: April, Bergomask. Sonatina. Spring Will Not Wait. Ballade. Two Pieces: February's Child. Aubade. Ballade of London Nights. Vol.IV: Month's Mind. Greenways: The Cherry Tree, Cypress, The Palm and May. Sarnia: Le Catioroc, In a May Morning, Song of the Springtides. Three Pastels: A Grecian Lad, The Boy Bishop, Puck's Birthday. Columbine. Vol.V: Piano Sonata.

Decorations (MMP). The Island Spell: evocative melody over restless figuration, builds to a climax then subsides. Moon-glade: mesmerizing and lyric. The Scarlet Ceremonies: mysterious and brilliant. M-D.

Four Preludes (Bo&H). The Undertone; Obsession; The Holy Boy; Fire of Spring. More dissonant and rhythmically freer than some of the other works from this period. M-D.

Ballade of London Nights (S&B). Large three-part design, gossamer quality. M-D.

London Pieces (S&B). Depicts hustle and bustle of city life. M-D.

Equinox (S&B). Continuous motion etude. M-D.

Sonata e 1918–20 (S&B). Three contrasting movements in late-Romantic style, impressive harmonies, rhapsodic, brilliant octave passages and double-note figures. M-D.

Sonatina (OUP) 15pp. First movement: flowing moderato. Second movement: atmospheric. Third movement: moto perpetuo rondo, gigue rhythm, taut writing. M-D.

Rhapsody (Bo&H). Similar in score to a Chopin Ballade; builds to a furious closing. M-D to D.

Sarnia, An Island Sequence (Bo&H 1940). Sarnia is the Roman name for the Island of Guernsey. Ireland is at his most colorful in this splashing and ebullient suite. M-D.

Spring Will Not Wait (OUP 1927). The final part of Ireland's song cycle "We'll to the Woods No More." Full, rich chords and long, sustained phrases are its main characteristics. Impressionistic. A large span and ability to bring out inside melodies are necessary. No fingering or pedaling. M-D.

Dances (MMP). Gypsy Dance; Country Dance; Reaper's Dance. M-D.

Leaves from a Child's Sketchbook (MMP).

Pieces (MMP). Merry-Andrew; The Towing-Path.

3 Preludes (MMP). The Undertone; Obsession; The Holy Boy.

See: Eric Parkin, "John Ireland and the Piano," *Music Teacher*, 53 (1974) June:11–12; July:15–16; August:12–13; September:13.

Maki Ishii (1936–   ) Japan

Aphorismen II (Ongaku-No-Tomo-Sha 1972) 8 loose leaves, explanation of symbols. The seven parts are performed in whatever order the player chooses. Glockenspiel, tam tam, maracas, and claves needed for special percussive effects. Avant-garde notation, pointillistic, clusters. D.

Beyond a Distance Op.41 1980 (Zen-On 430) 12pp. Harmonics; clusters; fast ascending scalar passages require deft fingers. Avant-garde. D.

Black Intention III 1977 "Piano etude for breath" (Zen-On 411) 9pp. The length of each phrase and figure is determined by the "breath" of the player. Each deep breath of *ppp* and each intense breath of *fff* contributes to the time structure of the piece and directly influences the shades of tone color. Some preparation of piano required (screw nails). Performance directions. Avant-garde. D.

Páll Isolfsson (1893–1974) Iceland

Three Piano Pieces Op.5 (Iceland Music Information Center). Burlesca; Intermezzo; Capriccio. Pleasant; reminiscent of Grieg. M-D.

Charles Ives (1874–1954) USA

In American music, the figure of Charles Ives dominates the twentieth century. This crusty Yankee refused to follow any rules he did not make up himself. His piano music is exceedingly complex, and only pianists with complete equipment should grapple with it. Ives's *Essays Before a Sonata and Other Writings* (New York: W. W. Norton, 1961) reveals his intellect and imagination on a variety of subjects and should be read by anyone who contemplates exploring this highly problematic music.

First Piano Sonata 1902–10 (PIC) 50pp. 42 min. Adagio con moto; Allegro moderato—"In the Inn"; Largo; No tempo indication for fourth movement; Andante maestoso. Intricate and complex patterns, hymn tunes, polyrhythms,
   polytonality, Romantic colorations, and ragtime—all are present in this
   work of depth and grandeur. This landmark of American piano literature
   has more cohesion and motival impetus than the *"Concord" Sonata*. D.
Second Piano Sonata "Concord, Mass., 1840–1860" 1909–15 (AMP) 68pp. Four
   pragmatic movements: Emerson; Hawthorne; The Alcotts; Thoreau. "A
   group of four pieces called a sonata for want of a more exact name. The
   whole is an attempt to present one person's impression of the spirit of
   transcendentalism that is associated in the minds of many with Concord,
   Mass. of over a half century ago . . . impressionistic pictures of Emerson
   and Thoreau, a sketch of the Alcotts, and a scherzo supposed to reflect a
   lighter quality which is found in the fantastic side of Hawthorne" (from
   Ives's note on the work). Virtuoso musicianship and technique required
   throughout. D.
   See: Sondra Rae Scholder Clark, "The Element of Choice in Ives' *Concord
   Sonata*," MQ, 60 (April 1974):167–86.
   Fred Fischer, "Ives' *Concord Sonata*," PQ, 92 (Winter 1975–76):23–27.
   Ann Ghandar, "Charles Ives: Organization in Emerson," *Musicology*, 4
   (1980):111–27.
Three Protests 1910? (NME). Tiny sketches, enigmatic writing. M-D to D.
Study No.20 "Even Durations Unevenly Divided" 1908 (Merion) 18pp. Ives
   wrote 27 studies for the piano; approximately 11 survive. This piece is a
   take-off on a march, boisterous and tuneful. A strenuous challenge, mind-
   bender and finger-breaker for every one of the 187 bars. Riddled with dissonance, clogged with accidentals and rich Americanisms, including a brief
   and delightfully harmonized bit of "I've Been Working on the Railroad."
   At bar 57 a march appears; it returns at the conclusion "as marching off in
   the distance." The editor, John Kirkpatrick, has added 7 pages of analysis
   notes. D.
Study 21: Some South-Paw Pitching 1908 (Mer) 5pp. In spite of the title, the right
   hand has just as much work as the left hand! Several passages are based on
   "Down in the Cornfield." More accessible than the other works discussed
   but still difficult. Most of the piece is adapted from Ives's *Second Symphony*. Uses phrases from "Massa's in de Cold Ground," "Joy to the World,"
   "The Son of God Goes forth to War," and jazzes up part of Bach's Three-
   Part Invention in F. M-D.
Etude No.22 1912 (Merion). Named for the page number in Ives's music notebook on which this piece was written. Three-part structure, witty B sec-
   tion. M-D.
   See: Robert Dumm, "Performer's Analysis of an Ives Piano Piece," *Clavier*,
   13 (October 1974):21–25.
Three-Page Sonata 1905 (Mer) 12pp. 7½ min. The original manuscript was three

pages in length. Makes fun of traditional sonata design. Uses the BACH motive over 40 times. Includes extensive editorial notes. Large span required. D.

See: Sondra Rae Clark, "Ives and the Assistant Soloist," *Clavier*, 13 (October 1974):17–20.

The Anti-Abolitionist Riots in Boston in the 1850's 1908 (Mer). Short Adagio maestoso with no bar lines. Thick textures, *fff* climax, quiet closing. D.

March: See the Conquering Hero Comes 1893 (PIC) 4pp. Full of wide leaps and large chords. M-D to D.

Varied Air and Variations 1914–23 (Merion 1971) 92 bars subtitled "Study No.2 for Ears or Aural and Mental Exercise." Theme and five through-composed variations, which are connected by short contrasting episodes. In essence, the work is a take-off of a piano recital parallel to "The One Way" (1923), a take-off on a voice recital. The programmatic content determines the form. Serial, wide variety of styles and forms. Contains valuable analytical notes. D.

Waltz-Rondo (AMP 1978) 15pp. A romp with the hands disagreeing about whether it is in D or D♭, and with Ives's comical marginalia. Monotonous rondo form, lumpy piano writing, ear-stretching. D.

Three Improvisations (AMP 1984). These brief pieces were recorded by Ives privately, probably in 1938. Transcribed from the recording by Gail and James Dapogny, who say in their editorial note, "Analysts will find much about these improvisations that is orderly." M-D.

Five Piano Pieces (Merion 1925). Contains: Varied Air and Variations. Study No.22. The Antiabolitionist Riots. Three-Page Sonata. Some South Paw Pitching. Includes photographs, illustrations, and biographical information. No musicological notes are included here, although the single publications, especially the *Varied Air and Variations*, have extensive notes. D.

Set of Five Take-Offs ca. 1906 (PIC 1991) 17pp. First edition. The Seen and Unseen?; Rough and Ready et al. and/or The Jumping Frog; Song without (good) words; Scene Episode; Bad Resolutions and Good WAN. Each piece has a parody idea; angular style. Critical edition. M-D to D.

Three Improvisations 1938 (Transcribed and edited by Gailand James Dopogny —AMP 1984) 8 pp. Transcribed from an Ives recording. I. Centers around "a phrase that sounds as if it might be part of the lost *Autumn Landscapes from Pine Mountain* (1904)"; II. "suggests perhaps one of the lost [piano] *Studies*"; III. "has chords somewhat like those in the *Waltz-Rondo*" (From the preface, quoting John Kirkpatrick). Craggy writing. M-D.

The Ives Society has commissioned editions of the following compositions, and editorial work on them is proceeding: *London Bridge Is Falling Down* (Singleton —PIC). *Four Transcriptions from "Emerson"* (J. Kirkpatrick—AMP). *The Celestial Railroad* (J. Kirkpatrick—AMP). *Piano Marches Nos.1–6* (Kirkpatrick, Singleton—AMP/PIC).

See: James M. Burke, "Ives Innovations in Piano Music," *Clavier*, 13 (October 1974):14–16.

Maurice Hinson, "The Solo Piano Music of Charles Ives," PQ, 88 (Winter 1974–75):32–35.

H. Wiley Hitchcock, *Ives*, Oxford Studies of Composers, 14 (London: Oxford University Press, 1977), 95pp.

Elizabeth McCrae, "The Piano Music (of Charles Ives)," *MENC Journal*, 61 (October 1974):53–57.

Jane E. Rasmussen, "Charles Ives's Music for Piano," *Student Musicologists at Minnesota*, 6:201–17. Capsule analyses of many of Ives's pieces for piano, both published and unpublished.

Guy S. Wuellner, "The Smaller Piano Works of Charles Ives," AMT, 22 (April–May 1973):14–16.

Jean Eichelberger Ivey (1923–   ) USA

Ivey is a composer, pianist, and electronic music specialist. She is Director of the Electronic Music Laboratory at the Peabody Conservatory of Music.

Theme and Variations (AMC 1952). A single short subject and 26 variations that fall into three groups: lyrical, humorous, and dramatic. Thoroughly contemporary in idiom; makes full use of the instrument's technical possibilities. M-D.

Prelude and Passacaglia (AMC 1955). The Prelude is a burst of fireworks which suggests motives that are to be developed in the Passacaglia. The Passacaglia subject uses all 12 tones, although no attempt is made to treat the work in dodecaphonic style. Continuous variations tend to group themselves into an overall rondo form, ABACA. M-D.

Sonata (AMC). 4 movements. Well organized, neoclassic in form and style. Coloristic potentialities of the piano are carefully explored. Demands complete pianistic equipment. M-D.

Sleepy Time and *Water Wheel* (Lee Roberts). Two easy works on black keys.

Skaniadaryo (CF 1973) 14pp. 11 min. Facsimile edition. For piano and tape. Contains performance directions and explanation of symbols for special effects. Tape plays continuously from the beginning of the piece to the end. "Skaniadaryo (Handsome Lake) was a Seneca Indian who lived in western New York from about 1749 to 1815. Inspired by visions, and mingling old and new elements, he founded a reformed version of the traditional Iroquois religion, which became widespread among his people, and persists today among the Iroquois. To me Skaniadaryo symbolizes New York's heroic past—the times celebrated, for instance, in the novels of James Fenimore Cooper—as well as the mingling of two heritages, and a way of life more intimate with nature. In this composition, which in its way also blends new and traditional elements, and suggests sounds of nature with pure electronics, I have tried to convey some of this complex of feelings" (from the score). Pointillistic, long pedal effects, proportional rhythmic relationships, sudden dynamic extremes, many harmonic seconds, clusterlike sonorities, glissandi, harmonics, strings damped at one place. Guided improvisation required. Piano and tape sonorities well blended. M-D.

Koji Izumi (1947–   ) Japan

Izumi is a graduate of the Kunitachi College of Music.

3 Africas (Japan Federation of Composers 1994) ca. 21 min. The Faraway Drumming Sounds; A Song; We Were Born on this Planet. Based on four types of pentatonic scales (beginning on four different notes), impressions of vast African scenes. M-D to D.

J

Hanley Jackson (1939–   ) USA
Tangents (SP 1974) 11pp. 4½ min. For piano and prerecorded tape. The piano
score notates tape sounds. Tape, which contains both electronic and piano
sounds, is in two versions: tape part by itself, tape in a performance with
Margaret Walker, pianist. Divided sections: Very slow—Slow—Rhythmic.
Colorful, rhythmic, octotonic, pointillistic. M-D.

Maurice Jacobson (1896–1976) Great Britain
Carousal (Lengnick 1946) 16pp. A colorful tone poem. Freely tonal. Highly attractive Alla Musette mid-section. M-D.
Romantic Theme and Variations (Lengnick 1946) 18pp. Theme dates from 1910,
variations from 1944. Six well-constructed and developed variations that
have an MC flavor reminiscent of Rachmaninoff. Effective. M-D.

Rhené Jacque (1918–   ) Canada
This is the pen name of Soeur Jacque-René, who teaches at the École Vincent
d'Indy in Outrement, Quebec.
Suite pour Piano Op.11 (BMI Canada 1961) Five short contrasted movements,
neoclassic in style. The last movement, G, is colorfully written. Int.
Deuxième Suite (BMI Canada 1964). Prélude: light, airy, graceful. Impressions:
introspective. Toccate: brilliant, fits fingers well, requires a good octave
technique. M-D.

Marie Jaëll (1846–1925) France
Jaëll studied with Moscheles in Stuttgart; Herz, Franck, and St. Saëns in Paris;
and Liszt in Weimar. In 1893, in Paris, she was the first to play all 32 of Beethoven's sonatas in a series.
Piano Sonata (L. Schmidt-Rogers—Hildegard Publishing Co.) Dedicated to Liszt.
Essentially written in Romantic style, this work shows that Jaëll was familiar with the most recent compositional thinking of her day. M-D to D.

Agi Jambor (1909–1997) USA, born Hungary
Sonata (Hildegard 1997) 22pp. Allegro appassionata; Epitaph-Andante teneremente; Allegro. Full of tension throughout; MC. M-D.

Leoš Janáček (1854–1928) Czechoslovakia
Janáček's study of his native Moravian folk music formed the character of all his
thematic invention. His music skillfully integrates folk materials into valid artis-

tic entities. The piano works are refreshingly far from the gigantism of much of the piano writing of their time.

Sonata der Strasse: I-X. 1905 (Artia; MMP) 13 min. The Presentment: fluid lines. The Death: processional rhythms. Inspired by the death of a worker in a demonstration. Romantic in tone, declamatory in manner. Full of lyric feeling and dark, reflective lament. M-D.

The Overgrown Path 1901–1908 (Artia; MMP) 53pp. 22 min. Ten pieces inspired by memories of childhood. According to the composer, who described them in a letter to his fiancée, "They are quite nice, and I consider them my first entirely correct works." In nineteenth-century character-piece tradition. Int. to M-D.

In the Mist 1912 (Hudební Matice 1938; MMP) 21pp. 14 min. Andante; Molto adagio; Andantino; Presto. More concentrated and more concise in motif and mood than *The Overgrown Path*. Uses the whole-tone scale; fragmented melodic lines, infrequent angry explosions. Veiled in Impressionistic floating chords of mystical beauty. Some of Janáček's finest piano writing. All four pieces are pervaded by a melancholy mood, clear-cut form. Each has a contrasting middle section. M-D.

12 Popular Moravian Dances (Ric). Short pieces. Folk dances with strong rhythms. Words for the songs are in Czech. All commentaries and instructions are in Italian. Left hand required to leap from low octaves to full chords and therefore demands a good hand span. Int. to M-D.

Zedenka Variations Op.1 1880 (MMP). Schumannesque, well controlled, imaginative technique. M-D.

National Dances of Moravia (MMP). 23 pieces, settings of Moravian dance tunes. Notes in Czech. Int. to M-D.

Piano Miniatures Book I. *Intime Skizzen* (Editio Moravia). 13 pieces: some sketches, some incomplete. Int. to M-D.

Piano Miniatures Book II. *Moravian Dances* (Editio Moravia). 25 dances. M-D.

Complete Works, Vol.I, Piano Works (Edition Supraphon and Br, available in USA through European American Music) 160pp. Preface in Czech, German, English, French, and Russian. Critical note in Czech and Russian. Includes an essay on the origin of the works in English, Czech, and German. Variations for Zedenka, Op.1; 3 Moravian Dances; X. 1905; On an Overgrown Path I, II; In the Mist; A Recollection; Music for Exercise with Clubs; The Madonna of Frýdek, version for harmonium. These pieces follow more the poetic tradition of Schumann than the Liszt or Chopin tradition.

See: Lorna Tedesco, "The Piano Music of Janáček," *Clavier*, 31/4 (April 1992):14. Brief commentary on *October 1, 1905* and *On an Overgrown Path*. Includes music of "Our Evenings" from *On An Overgrown Path*.

Guus Janssen (1951–   ) The Netherlands

Brake 1974 (Donemus) 5pp. partly folded, 4 min. Many tempo changes are meticulously indicated by metronome speeds. Contemporary style. A brilliant single-idea piece with plenty of fireworks. Large chords and stretches require large span. D.

Emile Jaques-Dalcroze (1865–1950) Switzerland
Dix Miniatures (Foetisch 1958) 12pp. Short, colorful, contrasting pieces; traditional harmonies. Int.
Esquisses Rythmiques (Foetisch 1528, 1536) 2 vols., 16 pieces in each. MC with Impressionistic sonorities, rhythmically oriented. Int. to M-D.
Six Danses Romandes Op.32 (Foetisch 411) 16pp. Rhythmic pieces for piano. Varied, Impressionistic tonal style. See No.2, Allegro moderato, especially. Int.

Philipp Jarnach (1892–1982) France, active in Germany
Jarnach's style is freely tonal, and his piano works are demanding but pianistic.
Drei Klavierstücke Op.17 (Schott). Three dances. Ballabile: grotesque. Sarabande: rhythmic. Burlesca: vivacious. M-D.
Sonatina Op.18 1925 (Schott). Subtitled "Romancero I." Allegretto vivace; Concitato; Sostenuto assai quasi largo e con summa espressione. Chromatic, changing textures, introspective moods. Intense. M-D.
Kleine Klavierstücke Op.27 (Schott). 10 short sketches, mainly in linear two- and three-part writing. M-D.
Das Amrumer Tagebuch Op.30 1947 (Schott). An unusual diary. Hymnus: chordal. Elegie: ethereal but builds to an imposing mid-section. Sturmreigen (Storm Dance): furious finale with a quiet closing. M-D.
Sonata No.2 1952 (Schott) 28pp. Large three-movement work. First movement: linear, unassuming. Second movement: dramatic, intense. Scherzo: interrupted by an ethereal passage, big ending. M-D to D.

Hanns Jelinek (1901–1969) Austria
Jelinek studied with Schönberg and Berg and was one of the main supporters of strict adherence to the Schönberg technique. Since his Op.13, all works were written in the 12-tone idiom.
Sonatine Op.9/4 1951 (UE) 9 min. Four movements. Second movement, Menuett, is the easiest and most accessible of this well-written work. M-D.
Zwölftonwerk (12-Tone Music) Op.15 1949–51 (UE) 5 vols. Vol.1: 4 Two-part Inventions: uses the row in different treatment, retrograde, inversion, etc. Light and transparent. Vol.2: 6 Short Character-Sketches. More difficult than Vol.1. Vol.3: 3 Dances: Walzer, Sarabande, March. Vol.4: 4 Toccatas: solenne, burlesca, funèbre, frizzante. All based on same row. Vol.5: Suite: contains 9 movements. All the pieces are short; some require only 30 seconds to perform. A clever and fascinating introduction to serial technique. Int. to M-D.
Zwölftonfibel Op.21 1953–55 (Moseler) 12 vols. bound in 6 vols. A "Twelve-Tone Primer." 12 times 12 easy to intermediate studies and pieces. Vol.1/2: Preliminary Studies. Vol.3/4: Elementary Studies. Vol.5/6: Easy 2-Voice Stud-

ies. Vol.7/8: Little Concert Pieces. Vol.9/10: Intermediate Studies. Vol.11/12: Recital Pieces.

Valarie Jelobinsky (1912–1946) Russia

Nocturne Op.19/2 (Anson—Willis). Poetic and long lines, in the post-Rachmaninoff tradition. M-D.

Scenes of Childhood. Op.19 (MCA). Toccata; Nocturne; Valse; Reminiscence; Danse; Recitatif. All are well written, original, melodic. Excellent contrasting moods, freely tonal with nice dissonance. Int. to M-D.

Sándor Jemnitz (1899–1963) Hungary

Complex contrapuntal textures are found in much of Jemnitz's writing.

Sonata No.5 Op.64 (EMB 1961). Allegretto poco sostenuto: folk influence, much repetition of opening rhythmic and melodic idea. Agitato: Two-voice texture in tenths, mid-section more chordal. Andantino sereno: serious quality, syncopation, tempo changes, ends quietly. D.

Zoltán Jeney (1943–   ) Hungary

Something Lost 1975 (EMB) 4pp.

Arthur Rimbaud in the Desert (EMB Z8907 1980) 3pp., for any keyboard instrument.

Both works have a repetitive rhythmic approach which may ultimately derive from some of John Cage's early ideas about formal structure generated by durations. M-D.

Donald Jenni (1937–   ) USA

10 Laconic Variations (ACA 1952). Short, terse, pianistic, pleasant. M-D.

Sonatine (BMI 1954). Won the BMI Young Composers Radio Award in 1952. Short, appealing, MC. M-D.

A Game of Dates 1974 (AMP). For Dancer; For Conductor; For Percussionist; For Composer. An interrelated set of character pieces; birthday presents to four of the composer's friends. Each piece is a brilliant musical portrait. Much dissonance, convincing, pianistic. Large span required. M-D.

Adolf Jensen (1837–1879) Germany

Jensen's music has a freshness about it that adds a special interest.

Scenes of Travel Op.17 (CFP; Ric). No.3, The Mill, and No.11, Will-o'-the-Wisp, are the best from this set. Int.

20 Lieder und Tänze Op.33 (WH). No.5, Elfin Dance, and No.16, Barcarolle, are two of the best. Int. to M-D.

Waldvöglein (Forest Birds) Op.43 (Musica Obscura). Romantic, charming, and pleasant. Int. to M-D.

Jörgen Jersild (1913–   ) Denmark

Trois Pièces en Concert 1945 (WH). Tambourin: dramatic gestures. Romanesque with 10 variations. Farandole: brilliant closing. Influenced by Couperin and Rameau. M-D.

Karel Jirák (1891–1972) Czechoslovakia
Little Piano Suite Op.12 1916 (Artia). Five movements, varied moods. M-D.
At the Crossroad Op.24 1924 (UE). Six short polytonal pieces. M-D.
Sonata Op.30 1924 (UE) 32pp. Three movements in a dissonant style. M-D.
Sonata No.2 Op.64 1950 (Panton) 17 min. Notes in English concerning Jirák and
   his work. Allegro appassionato: two themes, movement dominated by second theme, parallel seventh-chords, heroic in character. Tempo di marcia
   funèbre: similar (heroic idea) in opening movement. Allegro risoluto: passionate; energetic; three themes; after development section all three themes
   are recapitulated and climaxed by an exciting coda. D.
See: Alice Tischler, *Karel Boleslav Jirák: A Catalogue of His Works* (Detroit): Detroit Information Coordinators, 1975) 32pp.

Ivan Jirko (1926–1978) Czechoslovakia
Variace na Tema Johannes Brahms 1964 (Panton AP 3051) 19pp. Based on a waltz
   variation from Brahms's second book of *Variations on a Theme of Paganini*, hence this is a set of variations on a variation. Begins by quoting
   Brahms with its original harmony; in further variations the harmony becomes more rigorously dodecaphonic. Quotes Brahms again at conclusion. M-D.

Grant Johannesen (1921–   ) USA
Johannesen is one of the greatest American pianists.
Improvisation on a Mormon Hymn (OUP). "Come, Come, Ye Saints." Quiet reflective melody with sonorous harmonies that intensifies the hymn's impression of simple faith and frontier hardihood. Large chords require good
   hand span. M-D.

Gunnar Johansen (1906–1991) USA, born Denmark
Johansen was a unique voice and was best known as an outstanding pianist. He
was also a composer, scholar, educator, and humanist. A few of his compositions
have recently become available.
Affection 1972 (Sikesdi Press 1992) 6pp. For Tina Lear on her birthday 1972.
   ABA, tonal, lovely character piece. Editorial report by Gordon Rumson.
   M-D.
Atonal Sonatina 1943 (Sikesdi Press 1992) 8pp. Ricercare; Tranquillissimo, velato;
   Sfumare. Incomplete series (less than 12 tones), mixture of vertical and
   polyphonic writing. Editorial report by Gordon Rumson. M-D to D.
Ballade for Lorraine 1942 (Sikesdi Press 1995) 9pp. Tonal, sectional, builds to *fff*
   climax, *ppp* ending. Editorial report by Gordon Rumson. M-D to D.
Canzona II 1932 (Sikesdi Press 1992) 9pp. Tonal, melody accompanied by chang-
   ing chords. Editorial report by Gordon Rumson. M-D.
Like a Lullaby 1943 (Sikesdi Press 1992) 4pp. Dedicated to Lorraine Johansen.
   Quartal and seventh chord harmony support flowing melody. Editorial re-
   port by Gordon Rumson. M-D.
Sonata II "Pearl Harbor" (Sikesdi Press 1992) 58pp. Finished December 6, 1941.

Non allegro, con suppresso agitazion, Allegro tempestuoso; Grave ma non Lento; Finale. All three movements exploit resources of the keyboard. Finale uses jazz and the Dies Irae, with suggestion of a victory motif based on the opening of Beethoven's Fifth Symphony. Editorial report (10 pp.) by Gordon Rumson. D.

Hunter Johnson (1906–   ) USA

Sonata 1933–34 (Mer). Revised in 1936 and 1947–48. Allegro molto e dinamico; Andante cantabile; Allegro giusto. Large-scale cyclic work. The apotheosis of the blues. Johnson says of the work, "my spirit was teeming defiantly with America. . . . It is an intensive expression of the South . . . the nostalgia, dark brooding, frenzied gaiety, high rhetoric and brutal realism are all intermingled." Varied textures and sonorities, changing meters, driving rhythms, conclusion refers to thematics from previous movements. Requires advanced pianism. D.

See: Joseph Bloch, "Some American Piano Sonatas," JR, 3 (Fall 1956): 9–14.

Robert Sherlaw Johnson (1932–   ) Great Britain

Johnson has established a considerable reputation as a concert pianist specializing in performance of piano music by major twentieth-century composers.

Sonata No.1 1963 (OUP) 14½ min. A set of variations with an intervening Cadenza and Coda. Messiaen influence, strong rhythmic writing, clearly defined themes, atonal. Concludes with an imposing Coda. D.

Sonata No.2 1967 (OUP) 19 min. Three movements with cyclic overtones. New notation symbols; formidable. Strummed strings in the second and third movements provide an orchestral palette. Supple handling of serial technique. Avant-garde. D.

7 Short Piano Pieces 1968–69 (OUP) 10 min. Prelude; Catena; Chameleon (the possibilities can be greatly extended by the uses of any kind of stick or a wire brush); Phoenix; Acanthus; Bleak Ecstasies; Epilogue; Chameleon 2. Imaginative mixture of traditional and avant-garde techniques. Combines an intimate knowledge of the piano with a search for new kinds of sonority. M-D to D.

Asterogenesis (OUP 1974) 19pp. 10 min. Explanations in English. Used as a test piece in the 1975 Leeds International Piano Competition. Astrological significance; influence of Varèse and Messiaen felt; clear architectural lines missing. Exploits keyboard alone; no inside-piano techniques, as in Johnson's earlier works. Makes use of extended bass range of the Bösendorfer piano but can be adapted for performance on a regular concert grand. Vigorous atonal melody, complex rhythms, clusters, extensive dynamic range. D.

Sonata No. 3 (OUP 1978) 12 min. Based on a more traditional tonal and metrical scheme than is *Asterogenesis*, with individual notes used as tonal centers. Four clearly defined sections are played without pause, with the most intriguing being the second, in which a richly colored sea of sound rides above a series of sustained bass pedal points. D.

See: Meirion Bowen, "Robert Sherlaw Johnson," M&M, 19 (June 1971):34–36.

Tom Johnson (1939–   ) USA
Johnson received degrees from Yale University and studied privately with Morton Feldman. "He is considered a minimalist, since he works with simple forms, limited scales, and generally reduced materials, but he proceeds in a more logical way than most of the other American minimalists, often using formulas, permutations and predictable sequences." P&K, 180 (May–June 1996):13.
Cosinus Pour Piano 1994 (Two-Eighteen Press) 6 min. Four movements with mathematical melody in one, two, three, and finally four voices. M-D.
Music for 88 1988 (Two-Eighteen Press). 9 pieces written for the 88 keys of the piano, including "The Mersenne Numbers," "Pascal's Triangle," and "The Multiplication Table." Performance by the composer on CD. D.
Tango 1984 (Two-Eighteen Press) 5 min. 120 permutations of the five-note melody in an Argentine rhythm. M-D.
Triple Threat 1979 (Two-Eighteen Press) 10 min. A challenge for the pianist/ actor/technician, who must record one channel and then a second channel, all on stage. M-D to D.
Septapede (Two-Eighteen Press) 7pp. 159 fragments to be arranged by the performer in an aleatory manner. Each fragment may be repeated as many times as performer wishes. Performance should sound improvised, and no two performances should ever sound alike. Pianist will need to plan some arrangement until confidence is attained. Avant-garde. M-D. to D.
See: David Burge, "Five New Pieces," CK, 3 (December 1977):66.
Spaces 1969 (AMP 1975) 10pp. 12 min. Varied types of music are combined. No meters, bar lines, or key signatures. Slow opening with highly dissonant chords that lead to almost inaudible figurations that become more obvious. Dynamics and pedaling are vitally important. Demanding and diverting. Ives and Feldman influence. M-D.
Scene for Piano and Tape 1969 (Two-Eighteen Press) tape with score and directions are available. The tape contains a series of spoken phrases and musical fragments punctuated by pauses of appropriate duration. In these pauses the pianist says or plays his part, which is carefully outlined in Johnson's script score. There is conversation, persuasion, explanation, etc. M-D to D.
See: David Burge, "Theater Pieces of the 60s," *Keyboard*, 8/1 (January 1982):69.

Ben Johnston (1926–   ) USA
Johnston teaches at the University of Illinois.
Knocking Piece (Smith Publications). For piano interior. One or two players required, who seem to be destroying the piano, but they don't, and that's all part of the fun. Avant-garde. M-D.
Sonata for Microtonal Piano 1965 published with *Grindlemusic* 1976 (Smith Publications) 21pp. Both works consist of the same music. Movement numbers

and page numbers labeled "G" refer to the version called *Grindlemusic*. Those labeled "S" refer to the version called *Sonata for Microtonal Piano*. "Deploys chains of just-tuned (untempered) triadic intervals over the whole piano range in interlocked consonant patterns. . . . The *Sonata*, whether presented as beauty or as the beast, is a monstrous parody-enigma, allusive, referential, sometimes derisive, distorted, a tissue of familiarity in radically strange garb" (from the score). Avant-garde. D.

Betsy Jolas (1926–   ) France, born USA
Jolas is a pupil of Messiaen and a protégée of Pierre Boulez.
B for Sonata (Heugel 1973) 30pp. 20 min. One movement of diverse material well laid out over the keyboard, with octaves used in an interesting manner. Momentum is lost about halfway through, and the piece tends to drift to a conclusion. Study in sonorities, no relationship to sonata form. Three pages of directions in French, German, and English. Some sections require four staves to notate. Avant-garde. D.
Chanson d'approche (Heugel 1972) 11pp. 8½ min. Avant-garde notation; bars are measured in seconds of duration. Numerous pedal markings including half-pedals. Strong contrasts, silently depressed clusters. Instrument's sonorities exploited. D.
Mon Ami 1974 (Heugel) 4pp. For a singer-pianist who is either a woman or a child. The performer sings a simple, folklike melody in French and must accompany herself some of the time (easy passages) and play solo passages at other times (not easy!). Jolas has arranged five versions of the piece in different lengths. Performed with taste, the work will surprise you. Contains some exquisite sonorities. M-D.
See: David Burge, "Five New Pieces," CK, 3 (December 1977):66.
Three Bell Studies for Piano or Keyboard Carillon (Leduc). Originally written for the keyboard carillon; when played on the piano this work challenges the performer's linear sense and requires much suppleness in pedaling so as not to sound like a piano. M-D.

André Jolivet (1905–1974) France
Jolivet reacted against the lightness of "Les Six" and wrote large works that were dense in texture and intense emotionally.
Algeria—Tango 1934 (Billandot). A colorful dance. In collection *Pièces pour Piano*. M-D.
Deux mouvements pour piano 1930 (Billandot 1991) 12pp. 8 min. Thick textures. M-D to D.
Suite Mana 1935 (Costallat). Six pieces with rhythmic complexities developed from a linear treatment. Strongly percussive. D.
Cinq Danses Rituelles (Durand 1947). Danse initiatique: decorated melodic line, imposing climax, quiet close. Danse du Héros: bold, furious, percussive. Danse nuptiale: arched climax, flexible, quiet close. Danse funèraire: pro-

cessional, intense. Danse du rapt: drumlike basses, rumbling effects, quick passages. Colorful, dynamic, exotic set. D.

3 Temps: No.1 (Sal 1931). Invention; Air; Rondeau. Freely tonal. M-D.

Etude sur des modes antiques 1944 (Durand) 4pp. Very free tempo and nuances; built on three Karnatique modes indicated in score; freely tonal. M-D.

Prélude (Cosmogonie) 1938 (ESC) 8pp. Sectional, lutelike, flexible meters, chromatic, many ritards and a tempos, chordal plus arpeggio figuration, on the quiet side. M-D.

Chanson Naïves 1951 (P. Noël). Six children's pieces. Fresh sounds, appealing. Int.

Sonata No.1 1945 (UE) 22 min. Three movements. A tribute to Bartók, but sounds more like Prokofieff, percussive, driving, strong modal language with free polytonal writing. D.

Sonata No.2 1957 (Heugel) 33pp. Three movements. Complete and partial tone-rows. Asymmetrical rhythms add to the excitement and difficulty. The finale is horrendously complex. Idiom is further advanced than *Sonata* No.1. D.

Richard Jones (before 1730–1744) Great Britain

Pièces de clavecin 1732 (Stoddard Lincoln—Heugel 1974) 79pp. Six suites or sets of lessons for harpsichord or spinnet. Consisting of a great variety of movements, such as preludes, aires, toccats, all'mands, jiggs, corrents, borees, sarabands, gavots, minuets. Preface in French, English, and German. One of the most attractive collections among the repertoire of English harpsichord music but still little known. Most of the pieces sound well on the piano. Int. to M-D.

Three Keyboard Pieces (G. Beechey—Banks). Minuet; Boree; Giga. Taken from a "Suite of Lessons" published in 1732. A few octaves and large chords. No fingering, interpretation, or ornaments included. Int. to M-D.

Keyboard Dances (R. Jones—ABRSM 1985) 32pp. 16 attractive dances including Allemandes, Borees, Minuet, Scotch Air, Sarabandes, Gavotte, Gigas, and Brisk Air. Published originally (1732) as Suite or Sets of Lessons. Int.

Joseph Jongen (1873–1953) Belgium

Jongen was greatly influenced by César Franck and the Impressionists.

Sérénade Op.19 (Sal 1901) 7pp. Lyric, contrasting sections, quiet. M-D.

13 Préludes Op.69 1930 (Schott). 2 vols. Many moods and pianistic effects in this unusual polished collection. M-D.

Second Ballade 1941 (CeBeDeM) 16pp. 8 min. Tonal, rhapsodic, tasteful, Impressionistic. M-D.

Scott Joplin (1868–1917) USA

Joplin's works are an original contribution to American piano literature. This gifted American has told our story in a certain age as no one else could.

The Complete Works of Scott Joplin for Solo Piano (Vera Brodsky Lawrence–New York Public Library 1971 through Belwin-Mills, 2d edition, 1981). 352

pages. Contains 54 works—rags, marches, waltzes—pieces written in collaboration with other composers, and the *School of Ragtime*. Also included are a rollography and a discography of 78 rpm recordings of Joplin compositions.

Original works: Antoinette—March and Two-Step (1906), Augustan Club Waltz (1901), Bethena—A Concert Waltz (1905), Binks' Waltz (1905), The Cascades—A Rag (1904), Breeze from Alabama, A—A Ragtime Two Step (1902), The Chrysanthemum—An Afro-Intermezzo (1904), Cleopha—March and Two Step (1902), Combination March (1896), Country Club—Rag Time Two-Step (1909), The Easy Winners—A Ragtime Two-Step (1901), Elite Syncopations (1902), The Entertainer—A Ragtime Two Step (1902), Eugenia (1905), Euphonic Sounds—A Syncopated Novelty (1909), The Favorite—Ragtime Two Step (1904), Gladiolus Rag (1907), Great Crush Collision—March (1896), Harmony Club Waltz (1896), Leola—Two Step (1905), Magnetic Rag (1914), Maple Leaf Rag (1899), March Majestic (1902), Nonpareil (None to Equal) (1907), Original Rags (arranged by Charles N. Daniels) (1899), Palm Leaf Rag—A Slow Drag (1903), Paragon Rag (1909), Peacherine Rag (1901), Pine Apple Rag (1908), Pleasant Moments—Ragtime Waltz (1909), The Ragtime Dance (1906), Reflection Rag—Syncopated Musings (1917), Rosebud—Two-Step (1905), Scott Joplin's New Rag (1912), Solace—A Mexican Serenade (1909), Stoptime Rag (1910), The Strenuous Life—A Ragtime Two Step (1902), Sugar Cane—A Ragtime Classic Two-Step (1908), The Sycamore—A Concert Rag (1904), Wall Street Rag (1909), Weeping Willow—Ragtime Two-Step (1903), Searchlight Rag (1907), Rose Leaf Rag (1907), Fig Leaf Rag (1908).

Collaborative Works: Felicity Rag (with Scott Hayden) (1911), Heliotrope Bouquet—A Slow Drag Two-Step (with Louis Chauvin) (1907), Kismet Rag (with Scott Hayden) (1913), Lily Queen—A Ragtime Two-Step (with Arthur Marshall) (1907), Something Doing—Cake Walk March (with Scott Hayden) (1903), Sunflower Slow Drag—A Rag Time Two Step (with Scott Hayden) (1901), Swipesy—Cake Walk (with Arthur Marshall) (1900).

Miscellaneous Works: School of Ragtime—6 Exercises for Piano (1908), Sensation—A Rag (by Joseph F. Lamb, arranged by Scott Joplin) (1908), Silver Swan Rag (attributed to Scott Joplin) (1971). Most all of these works are M-D.

At the Piano with Scott Joplin (Hinson—Alfred 445). The Cascades; The Chrysanthemum; The Easy Winners; The Entertainer; Heliotrope Bouquet; Maple Leaf Rag; Rag-Time Dance; Solace; The Strenuous Life; Sun Flower; Slow Drag; Swipesy. Text includes Background and Development of Ragtime; Musical Characteristics of Ragtime; Scott Joplin's "School of Ragtime"; Interpreting Ragtime; About This Collection; About the Music (analysis of each piece); For Further Reading. M-D.

Best of Ragtime (Cuellar—CPP/Belwin). 43 rags, Joplin's "School of Ragtime," Joplin's notes defending ragtime. M-D.

Scott Joplin Piano Rags (Paxton 1974) 32pp. Vol.I: Maple Leaf Rag; The Entertainer; Ragtime Dance; Gladiolus Rag; Fig Leaf Rag; Scott Joplin's New Rag; Euphonic Sounds; Magnetic Rag. Some pieces are fingered and have pedal indications. M-D. Vol.II: Elite Syncopations; Eugenia; Leola; Rose Leaf Rag; Bethena (a concert waltz); Paragon Rag; Solace; Pine Apple Rag. M-D. Vol.III: Original Rags; Weeping Willow; The Cascades; The Chrysanthemum; Sugar Cane; The Nonpareil; Country Club; Stoptime Rag. M-D.

The Missouri Rags (Max Morath—GS 1975) 66pp. Seventeen rags written while Joplin lived in Missouri. Unedited, helpful preface. Maple Leaf; Original Rags, Peacherine; Easy Winners; A Breeze from Alabama; Elite Syncopations; Strenuous Life; Entertainer; Weeping Willow; Palm Leaf; The Favorite; The Chrysanthemum; The Sycamore; The Cascades; Bethena; Eugenia; Ragtime Dance. M-D.

Complete Ragtime Piano Solos (C. Hansen) 177pp. Includes waltzes, marches, songs, and a vocal and original piano solo of The Entertainer. M-D.

Scott Joplin, King of Ragtime (Compiled by Albert Gamse—Lewis Music Publishing Co. 1972) 159pp. Piano solos and songs.

Solace (MCA). A very slow march. M-D.

An Adventure in Ragtime (M. Hinson, D. C. Glover—Belwin-Mills) 32pp. Gay Ninety Rag; The Entertainer; "The Story of Scott Joplin"; Maple Leaf Rag; The Strenuous Life; The Easy Winners; Cascades (encore duet). An informative picture about Ragtime; features the music of Joplin. Easy to Int.

The Easy Winners (Alfred 8064).

Elite Syncopations (Alfred 8062).

The Entertainer (Alfred 16804).

Maple Leaf Rag (Alfred 16803).

Three Piano Rags (Alfred 3580). The Entertainer; Maple Leaf Rag; Solace. Includes a discussion of the music.

Gladious Rag. In collection *Masters of American Piano Music* (Alfred 4603).

Wilfred Josephs (1927–1997) Great Britain

Second Piano Sonata Op.40 (Weinberger 1965) 22pp. 14 min. 8 sections played as one movement. Trills and tremolos, exploits minor ninths and major sevenths. Well-integrated writing, shows excellent command of keyboard resources. D.

14 Studies Op.53 (OUP 1969). 2 books, 28 min. Influenced by Debussy *Etudes*: seconds, thirds, octaves, ninths, etc. Numerous kinds of piano technique called for, written in an advanced pianistic idiom. No.3, A Spectral Waltz, No.5, and No.7 are especially attractive. M-D.

Pièces pour ma belle-mere Op.18 1958–59 (Bo&H 1974) 7 min. Three short pieces. Int.

John Joubert (1927–   ) Union of South Africa

Dance Suite Op.21 (Nov 1958) 10 min. Five short studies contrasted in style juxtaposing regular and irregular rhythms. No.5 is especially dramatic and closes with a powerful climax. M-D.

Sonata I Op.24 (Nov 1959). 20pp. 12 min. One movement. A long tarantella appears between the exposition and recapitulation but first and second exposition subjects are in usual key relationships. Changing meters and tonalities, well-timed large gestures. Good rotational technique will help. D.

Sonata II Op.71 (Nov 10023009 1977) 49pp. 20 min. Moderato—Poco Allegro: chromatic, trills, triplets, 8/8 divided 3+3+2/8, full chords, Bartók influence, *ppp* closing; large span required. Presto: octotonic, freely tonal, poco lento mid-section more chordal. Poco lento: secco *pp* octaves and tremolo open the movement; repeated chords; broken chordal figuration; leads to an Allegro Vivace section in bravura style followed by a tranquillo section; Lento and serene *ppp* closing. Solid and exciting contemporary writing. D.

See: Peter Dickinson, "John Joubert Today," MT 112 (January 1971):20–22.

Clifford A. Julstrom (1907–1991) USA

Julstrom graduated from Augustana College, Rock Island, IL and received his doctorate at the Eastman School of Music. He studied with Bernard Rogers and Howard Hanson. He was chairman of the Music Department of Western Illinois University for many years. Julstrom had a fine understanding of the piano, and his writing combines Romantic, impressionistic, and dissonance characteristics in a unique style. The following pieces and others are published by Julstrom Enterprises, 226 East Grant Street, Macomb, IL 61455.

Con Brio (1979) 9pp. Ravel influence noted, midsection contains some oriental color, brilliant conclusion. M-D.

Gershwinesque (1983) 5pp. Rocking mood, parallel seventh chords, bluesy, *pp* closing. M-D.

Whimsy (1981) 11pp. Varied moods, scherzando, heavy chords, changing tonal centers. Big conclusion quickly subsides to *pp* ending. Very effective. M-D.

Paul Juon (1872–1940) Germany, born Russia

Juon's mature musical style suggests a combined Germanic-Slavonic heritage from Tchaikovsky and Dvořák.

Little Suite Op.20 1902 (MMP). Trotzig-Zärtlich; Traurig; Geschwätzig; Lustig. This early work suggests a "Russian-Brahms" heritage. M-D.

K

Dmitri Kabalevsky (1904–1987) Russia

Kabalevsky's writing is designed for immediate utility and popular consumption. His music for young people is unusually appealing.

Four Preludes Op.5 1927–28 (Bo&H; GS; MCA). Short, lyric, varied moods. Int. to M-D.

Sonata No.1 Op.6 (Bo&H; CFP; K; MCA). Three contrasting movements, post-Romantic style, brilliant closing. M-D.

Sonatina C Op.13/1 (Bo&H; Alfred; GS; K; CFP; MCA; IMC). Three movements. Cheerful, bright, outside movements brilliant, neoclassic style. Int.

Sonatina G Op.13/2 (Alfred; K; MCA). *Sonatina* Op.13/1 is overplayed, while many teachers do not know the very tuneful one in G, which is of the same difficulty, more serious, and longer. Int.

Four Little Pieces Op.14 (MCA). Charming pedagogic works. Int.

Fifteen Children's Pieces Op.27 Book I (IMC; K; MCA). Easy teaching pieces of the first rank.

Ten Children's Pieces Op.27 Book II (MCA). Each is finely wrought. Int.

17 Selected Children's Pieces from Op.27 (CFP; K).

3 Rondos from the opera *Colas Breugnon* Op.30 (Sikorski). Sparkling and imaginative. Int. to M-D.

24 Preludes Op.38 1947 (CFP; K; IMC; MCA). Arranged in Chopin's order of keys. Range from Int. to M-D.

24 Little Pieces Op.39 (MCA; CFP; IMC; GS; K; Ric). Easy teaching pieces.

Variations Op.40/1,2 (IMC, MCA). Two easy sets: I (Zen-On; K): 12 variations. II: 5 variations.

Sonata No.2 E♭ Op.45 (Bo&H; CFP; MCA; IMC; GS; K; MMP). Festivamente: pompous and rhythmic. Second movement: Romantic. Finale: sparkling and vivacious. M-D.

Sonata No.3 F Op.46 (CFP; MCA; GS; Bo&H; K; IMC). Allegro: delightful, imaginative bridge passage. Second movement: cantabile and sentimental, weakest of the movements. Finale: scintillating. Tonal with some bitonality. M-D.

5 Easy Sets of Variations Op.51 (MCA; Zen-On; Ric). Based on Russian, Slovakian, and Ukrainian folksongs. All attractive. Int.

Rondo a Op.59 (CFP; MCA; K; IMC). Much dissonance and rhythmic drive, in 3/8, slow mid-section. M-D.

4 Rondos Op.60 1959 (MCA; IMC). March: dotted rhythms, sixths. Dance: needs light touch. Song: singing tone required. Toccata: staccato study. M-D.

6 Preludes and Fugues Op.61 (MCA; IMC). Neobaroque orientation. Contains two two-voice fugues, three three-voice fugues, and one four-voice fugue. M-D.

Spring Games and Dances Op.81 1965 (CFP; MCA; Zen-On; GS; Sikorski). Free-form suite in playful dancelike character. M-D.

Variations on an American Folksong 1966 (MCA). Theme and six variations.

Lyric Tunes Op.91 (Zen-On). A suite designed to be played complete. M-D.

At the Piano with Kabalevsky (Hinson—Alfred 431) 63pp. Selections from Opp.5, 14, 27, 39, 40, 51, and 60. Performance suggestion on each of the 23 pieces. Includes sections on The Composer and Music for Young People, Characteristics of Kabalevsky's Piano Music, About This Collection, For Further Reading. Int. to M-D.

Kabalevsky for the Young Pianist (D. Goldberger—GS). 21 pieces from Opp.14, 27, 39, 51. Fingered and pedaled. Int.

Kabalevsky for the Young (EBM). 25 pieces from Op.27, books 1 and 2, and Op.39. Easy to Int.

30 Pieces for Children (GS).

Kabalevsky—An Introduction to His Piano Works (Palmer—Alfred) 64pp. Selections from Opp.27, 39, and 40. Comments on each piece. Int.

Young Pianist's Guide to Kabalevsky (Y. Novik–WB) 24pp. with recording. 14 of the easier teaching pieces. Tastefully edited. Easy to Int.

Easy Piano Compositions (Bo&H 1985) 84pp. With introduction and teaching notes by Narine Haroutiunian and Alfred Mirovitch. Contains 4 Little Pieces, Op.14; 15 Children's Pieces, Op.27; 24 Little Pieces, Op.39; 5 Easy Variations, Op.51; 4 Rondos, Op.60. Contains many outstanding sets under one cover. Easy to Int.

28 Piano Pieces by Dmitri Kabalevsky (T. Dubrovskaya, M. Kabalevskaya—Hal Leonard) 110pp. Sections from Opp.13, 27, 30, 39, 51, 60, 61, 88, 89, and 91. Selected editing but not identified. Easy to M-D.

Music for Children and Young People (MMP) Book 1: Preludes and Fugues, Op.61. Book 2: 3 Rondos Op.30; 4 Rondos Op.60. Book 3: Variations Opp.40, 51, and 87.

See: Mervyn Coles, "Kabalevsky's Piano Music," *Music Teacher*, 57 (July 1978):22.

Cortland M. Koots, "Kabalevsky for the Piano," AMT, 20 (April–May 1971):26, 46.

Guy Wuellner, "The Simple Elegance of Dmitri Kabalevsky's Piano Music," *The Iowa Music Teacher*, LVI (Winter–February 1994):7–12.

Miloslav Kabelac (1908–   ) Czechoslovakia

8 Preludes Op.30 1955–56 (Supraphon). Imaginative and original writing, worth exploring, MC. M-D.

16 Easy Preludes (GS 1979). Satie and Bartók influence in the hypnotic rhythmic variations and modal melodies. Fine introduction to modern music. Progressively difficult. Int.

Pal Kadosa (1903–1983) Hungary

Kadosa's music is characterized by harsh dissonances, pounding rhythms, and instrumental melodic practice.

Suite I Op.1/1 (EMB) 11pp. Four contrasting movements. Intricate rhythms and sonorities. M-D.

Suite II Op.1/2 (EMB). Based on Hungarian folk elements, driving rhythms. M-D.

Suite III Op.1/3 (EMB 1972) 4pp. Three short movements, introspective. Fourths and fifths exploited in last movement, Allegro giusto. M-D.

Epigramme Op.8 (Bo&H). Eight short pieces. Int. to M-D.

Sonata II Op.9 (ZV 1965) 15pp. Four short movements. M-D.

Al Fresco Op.11a (Bo&H). Based on folk songs collected by Bartók and Kodály. Rhythmic vitality; requires good octave technique. M-D.

Sonatina Op.11b (ZV 1927). First movement, Con Fiducia, needs steady rhythmic drive and much intensity. Last movement, Triste (1 page), is slow, sad, but equally intense. Broad dynamic range, *ppp-fff.* Large span required. M-D.

Folksong Suite Op.21 (EMB 1933) 11pp. In Bartók style. M-D.

Five Studies Op.23F (EMB). Each study is devoted to a particular problem. Int. to M-D.

Rhapsodie Op.28a (UE 1937). Driving rhythms in style of Bartók's *Allegro Barbaro.* M-D.

Sonata IV Op.54 (ZV) 26pp. A powerful four-movement work, fine craft. Requires excellent pianistic facility. Dissonant. D.

4 Capriccios Op.57 (Bo&H). Bartók influence present. M-D.

55 Small Piano Pieces (EMB). A miniature *Mikrokosmos,* not so modal or dissonant. Appealing. Int.

7 Bagatelles (EMB). Short, in folk style. Some fast octaves; large span needed for No.6. M-D.

Snapshots Op.69 (EMB 1971) 7pp. Five short pieces. Clashing dissonance and cimbalon effects. Good hand span required. Int. to M-D.

Mauricio Kagel (1931–   ) Germany, born Argentina

Metapiece (Mimetics) (UE 1961). 13 pages folded into one long accordion-like page. Detailed explanation; can be performed as solo, by two pianos, as piano duet, or with other instruments. Diagrammatic notation in part. Stones can be placed on the strings and/or on the keyboard. Many clusters and pointillistic figurations. More interesting for performer than listener. Avant-garde. D.

MM 51: Ein Stueck Filmmusik fuer Klavier 1976 (UE 16651) 1 portfolio, 20 leaves, 8 pp. Preface in German and English. Subtitled "A Piece of Film Music," this piece evokes "the threat of unspoken fears and dangers" through various stereotyped formulas drawn from movie music. A metronome is required for performance. M-D.

An Tasten 1977 (UE 16753) 20pp. 16 min. Based on the four basic types of triads —major, minor, diminished, augmented—in root position and their inversions. Changing meters, a few free sections. Performance instructions. Based exclusively on a single arpeggiation pattern of the chord sequence, so accompaniment and main voice are no longer separable from one another. Avant-garde. M-D to D.

Erich Itor Kahn (1905–1956) Germany

Ciaccona dei tempi di guerra Op.10 1943 (Bomart) 25 min. This Chaconne "in time of war" is a large-scale work in non-strict serial technique that is powerful in its combination of anger, strength, and poignance. The straight row is presented between the fantasy-like Introduction and the beginning of the Ciaccona proper. 40 variations of ingenious invention follow. Very pianistic but will challenge the finest performers. D.
See: Russell Smith, "Erich Itor Kahn," *ACA Bulletin*, 9/2 (1960): 8–9 for a discussion of this work.

3 Bagatelles 1938 (CFE) 11 min. 12-tone materials not used strictly. Stunning sonorities, pianistic. No.1 dates from 1935–36. Interpretative problems in all three require a sensitive pianist. D.

Huit Inventions Op.7 1937 (ACA). No.3, Sur un thème de Brahms, and No.6, Hommage à Ravel, are the most attractive. Mature pianism required. M-D to D.

Nachiko Kai (1932–   ) Japan

Essai pour le Piano 1971 (Zen-On 320) 6pp. 4 min. Expressionistic, large span required. M-D.

Music for Piano (Zen-On 1974) 10pp. Serial influence, expressionistic, aleatoric, harmonics; pluck and mute strings, make noise with piano stool, etc. Avant-garde. D.

Viktor Kalabis (1923–   ) Czechoslovakia

Entrata, Aria e Toccata Op.41 1975 (Supraphon) 10 min. Dissonant, atonal, transparent, contrasting movements. M-D.

Friedrich Kalkbrenner (1785–1849) Germany

Traité d'harmonie du pianiste Op.185 (Heuwekemeijer 1970). Reprint of 1849 Paris edition. Contains etudes, fugues, and preludes with an introduction by the composer. Int. to M-D.

László Kalmar (1931–   ) Hungary

Invenzioni 1974 (EMB Z7613). Nine pieces without fixed order. Some are in free meter, others recall Baroque dance types (Gigue, Reminiscence de sarabandes englouties), yet others are constructive (Sereno) or expressive (Lento). M-D.

Hans Kann (1927–   ) Austria

Zehn Klavierstücke ohne Bassschlüssel (Dob 1971) 15pp. Ten short pieces without bass clef. Close proximity of hands, varied styles. M-D.

Abschnitt 37 (Dob 1966) 3pp. Ostinati, free section, changing meters, low register clusters, strong accents. M-D to D.

Sonatine 1954 (Dob 1961) 8pp. Allegro leggiero. Gleichmässig ausdrucksvoll. Andante leggiero. Rondino: moderato. Freely tonal, parallel chords, many staccatos. Large span required. Int. to M-D.

Yoshihiro Kanno (1953–   ) Japan

The Remains of the Light I—Signals to Those Unknown (Ongaku No Tomo Sha
    1993) 19 min. Widely spread colorful sonorities suggest twinkling lights in
    the distance; pedal notes, pointillistic, impressionistic influence, changing
    tempos, avant-garde. D.

Génari Karganov (1858–1890) Russia

Karganov composed mainly for the piano, and most of his works were of an instructional nature.

Album for the Young Op.25 (ABRSM 1983) 15pp. Eight short picturesque pieces
    with Russian flavor. Int.

Sigfrid Karg-Elert (1877–1933) Germany

Poetic Bagatelles Op.77 (Br&H 8120/1). 6 pieces in Vol.I. 4 pieces in Vol.II. Facile,
    original, and charming. Int. to M-D.

Maurice Karkoff (1927–   ) Sweden

Miniature Suite Op.39 1960 (GM) 7pp. Preludietto doloroso; Intermezzo 1 and 2;
    Toccatino. Pleasant MC sounds. M-D.

Capriccio on Football 1960 (GM). Pointillistic. M-D.

Pál Károlyi (1934–   ) Hungary

Toccata Furiosa (EBM 1969) 12pp. Avant-garde notation; clusters; string glis-
    sandi, sometimes with fingernail or with stick; palm tremolo, plucked
    strings. Barbaric handling of the keyboard. Dies away to *pp* ending. D.

24 Pieces for Children (EMB). Hungarian flavor. Easy to Int.

David Karp (1940–   ) USA

Karp is a composer of inexhaustible imagination and energy with an amazing
insight into what students enjoy playing. He has made a significant contribution to the musical awakening of countless young people. He teaches at Southern Methodist University and is director of the National Piano Teacher's Institute.

Adventures in Sound (Willis 10390). An excellent introduction to twentieth-cen-
    tury styles. Int.

Escapades (SP). 11 two-page pieces. Near East influence, melancholy, clever and
    fluent writing. Int.

The Inverted Row Boat (Brodt 1977). 12-tone, clever. Int.

Jazz Suite II (SP 1981) 31pp. Ten small and attractive pieces. Int.

Lady Margaret's Suite (Alfred 1994) 17pp. Eight pieces in the style of Bach: Pre-
    lude, A, S, B, M, Gavotte, Air, G. Uses many devices from Baroque period.
    More ornaments can be added as the student becomes more proficient in
    this area. Attractive. Int.

Shades of Time (Alfred 6544) 24pp. Eight impressionistic pieces that provide a
    superb introduction to the style. Int.

Lucrecia R. Kasilag (1918–   ) Philippines

Theme and Variations based on a Filipino Folk Tune "Walay Angay" (PIC 1950). Simple theme followed by 11 variations and Finale. Nineteenth-century pianistic devices, closely related key signatures. Balance between harmonic and melodic variations. M-D.

Elena Kats-Chernin (1957–   ) Australia, born Russia

Kats-Chernin was born in Tashkent and studied at the Gnesin Music Academy in Moscow. After her family migrated to Australia in 1975, she studied piano and composition at the Sydney Conservatorium of Music and won several prizes. She also did further study in Germany.

Tast-En 1991 (Australian Music Center) 7pp. 10½ min. "Tast-En means 'the keys' and at the same time 'to feel with the fingers.' I was interested in the game aspect of perception between the heard and the actually played tones. Also, the farewells to the sounds that don't want to end—thus a kind of funeral choral" (from the score). Much repetition, overtones, wide dynamic range. M-D to D.

Walter Kaufmann (1907–1984) USA, born Czechoslovakia

Sonata 1960 (Alfred) facsimile, 28pp. Moderato; Calmo e semplice; Moderato; Andante. Freely tonal around e, thin textures, parallel sonorities, highly effective writing. This work should become an important part of the repertoire. Pianistic expertise shows on every page. Alban Berg influence. M-D.

Ulysses Kay (1917–1995) USA

4 Inventions 1964 (MCA). 1: Transfer of line between hands is a problem. 2: Bouncy 5/8. 3: Melodic, large span required for tenths. 4: More like a true invention—imitation. M-D.

10 Short Essays 1939 (MCA). 1 or 2 pages each. Varied tempo and meter changes. Contrapuntal devices used.

First Nocturne (MCA 1974) 11 pp. 6 min. A tone row is heard at the opening and closing. Cantabile melodic treatment, meter changes, dissonant harmonies, uneasy rhythms, ostinati. M-D.

Donald Keats (1929–   ) USA

Sonata (Bo&H 1960) 28pp. Comfortably flowing: gentle, widely spaced, contrapuntal middle voices. Fast and precise: toccatalike, some hemiola, driving rhythms. Slow, in a free style: atmospheric, effective pedaling, wide registers, *pp* closing. Very fast and with vigor: Prokofieff style, percussive, energetic. Written in a freely tonal style; serial influence; powerful; large-scale, eclectic nature. D.

Wendell Keeney (1903–1982) USA

Mountain Tune (GS 1936). Catchy folk tune handled colorfully. Kind of a mountain "hoe-down"! Int. to M-D.

Sonatina (GS). A cheerful, witty, display piece. M-D.
> See: Bradford Gowen, "Neglected Repertoire: Some Contemporary Sona-
> tinas," AMT, 29/2 (November–December 1979):22–24. Discusses sonatinas
> by Keeney, Welcher, and Rawsthorne.

Spanish Capriccio (JF 1935). Allegro introduction leads to section based on "La
> cucaracha"; followed by "Boleras Sevillanas." Brilliant conclusion requires
> fine technique. M-D.

Milko Kelemen (1924–   ) Yugoslavia
Kelemen combines pointillistic technique with more conventional expressionistic usage.

Piano Sonata (H. Litolff 1954). Allegro veemente: flexible meters, staccato punc-
> tuation, thin texture. Andante sostenuto: three-part form, varied textures,
> extreme ranges. Presto: toccata-like, good octave and scale technique re-
> quired. Strong influence of Yugoslav folk music. M-D.

Dessins Commentés (CFP 1964). Seven pieces, avant-garde notation, clusters,
> glissandi on strings, extreme sonorities. D.

The Donkey Walks along the Beach (CFP 1961). Nine pieces. Picturesque titles,
> contemporary sonorities, sophisticated writing. Int.

Bryan Kelly (1934–   ) Great Britain
Sonata for Piano 1971 (Nov) 20pp. 13 min. Three movements, FSF. Traditional
> writing, thin textures. Large span required. M-D.

Walter Kemp (1938–   ) Canada
Five Latvian Folk Pieces (Waterloo 1971) 11pp. In addition to containing par-
> ticular technical problems, these pieces introduce the pianist to the rich,
> but relatively unfamiliar, heritage of Latvian folk song. Each song is iden-
> tified. Modal, lyric, attractive. Int.

Wilhelm Kempff (1895–1991) Germany
Sonata Op.47 (Sal 1959) 16pp. Praeambulum; Scherzo; Introduction and Toccata.
> Skillful pianistic writing, traditional harmonic vocabulary, weighty musical
> ideas, a convincing work. D.

Talivaldis Kenins (1919–   ) Canada, born Latvia
Sonata (F. Harris 1961). Three-movement work. Adagio introduction to first
> movement. Harmonic treatment merges post-Romantic and contemporary
> idioms. Well organized; fine craftsmanship. M-D.

Diversities (Leeds Canada 1968). 12 studies in contemporary styles for young
> pianists. Int.

Toccata—Dance (F. Harris 1971) 2pp. MC. Int.

The Juggler/Sad Clown (Bo&H). Original children's pieces. Easy to Int.

Kent Kennan (1913–   ) USA

Three Preludes (GS 1938) 9pp. Allegro scherzando: chromatic, arpeggio gestures, flexible meters, sudden *ff* ending. Lento, nello stile di un Chorale: freely tonal around e♭, four subtle phrases, thick textures. Allegro con fuoco: driving rhythms, repeated octaves in ostinato-like patterns, dramatic gestures, effective conclusion. Deservedly one of the most popular sets by a contemporary American composer. M-D.

Two Preludes (LG 1951) in collection *New Music for the Piano.* Rather freely; with a feeling of yearning and unrest: neo-Romantic, frequent motivic repetition, strong melodies. Massive and vigorous: two-part counterpoint punctuated with chords, contrary motion. M-D.

Louis Kentner (1905–1987) Great Britain, born Hungary

Sonatinas No.1 F, No.2 C, No.3. G (OUP 1939) published separately. All three Sonatinas are freely tonal and eminently pianistic and display a fine craft. M-D.

Johann Kaspar Kerll (1627–1693) Germany

Selected Keyboard Works DDT, II No.2. 8 Toccatas; 6 Canzonas; Capriccio Cucu; Battaglia; Ciaconna; Passacaglia; Ricercare in Cylindrum phonotacticum transferenda; Der steyrische Hirt. M-D.

Complete Works for Keyboard Instruments (Di Lernia—UE). Vol. 2: Toccata E; Canzoni. First complete edition.

Four Suites (Harris—BB). Critical-historical edition.

Eight Toccatas (Harris—BB). Critical-historical edition.

Aaron Jay Kernis (–   ) USA

Lullaby from *Before Sleep and Dreams* 1987. In collection *American Contemporary Masters* (GS 1995) 7pp. Opening and a later edition are similar to Liszt *Cradle Song* S.198. Builds to an intense pesante (nightmare?), arpeggiated passages; opening idea unifies piece. M-D to D.

Harrison Kerr (1897–1978) USA

Piano Sonata No.2 (Arrow 1943) 13 min. A one-movement work, tempo changes correspond with formal structure. Driving, biting dissonance, well written for piano. Ostinato, broad dynamic range, rhythmic element has most interest. M-D.

Joseph Christoph Kessler (1800–1872) Germany

Kessler knew Chopin and exerted considerable influence on the Polish master.

24 Préludes Op.31 (PWM 1994) 28pp. First published in 1835 by G. Ricordi and dedicated "to his friend Chopin." Perhaps these preludes served as an inspiration for Chopin's preludes: some striking similarities occur. Kessler's Preludes appear in random keys, are full of scalar figuration, arpeggios, mood changes, suggested improvisation. Some are as short as half a page. Related to the nineteenth-century style of preluding extempore. M-D.

Minuetta Kessler (1914–   ) USA, born USSR
Etude Brilliante 1948 (Transcontinental) 5pp. Energetic, requires firm and well-coordinated fingers. M-D.
Nocturne in Blue (Willis 1983). Chromatic melody, moves between hands, MC. Int.
Rustic Dance (Willis 1982). Modal, strong rhythms. Int.
Toccata in Red (Willis) 3pp. Brisk alternating hand figures, melodic mid-section. Int.

Otto Ketting (1935–   ) The Netherlands
Since 1957 Ketting has developed a style closely related to that of Webern.
Komposition mit zwölf Tönen (Donemus 1957). Seven short pieces in serial style. Repeated rhythmic pattern is employed. Ketting was one of the first to experiment in the Netherlands with parameters other than pitch. D.

Piet Ketting (1905–   ) The Netherlands
Praeludium en Fuga No.1 1940 (Donemus) 10pp. Short neoclassic prelude followed by an extensive three-voice fugue. Builds to strong climax. M-D.
Praeludium en Fuga No.1 1941 (Donemus) 18pp. Large prelude (Fransche Ouverture) followed by a three-voice fugue, Allegro con spirito (deciso). Neoclassic. M-D.

Nelson Keyes (1928–1987) USA
Three Love Songs for Piano Solo 1968 (Alfred 10114) in collection *Twelve by Eleven*. Gently, Johnny, My Jingalo: gently swinging, modal, four repetitions with varied treatment. Shenandoah: expressive melody accompanied by moving sixths; changing meters; requires large span. Lolly Too Dum: open-fifth accompaniment, bitonal, more development in this piece than in the other two, clever coda. An appealing set. Int. to M-D.

Aram Khatchaturian (1903–1978) Armenia
Nationalistic elements play a large part in the music of this Soviet Armenian composer. Rhapsodic freedom and colorful textures are characteristic.
Two Characteristic Pieces 1942, 1947 (MCA). A Glimpse of the Ballet: lyric. Fughetta: introspective. Two-part counterpoint, diatonic subjects, chromatic development are all part of these studies. M-D.
Two Pieces (MCA; CFP; K). Valse Caprice: rubato, capricious mid-section. Danse: strong rhythms; this piece could give the overworked *Toccata* a rest. M-D.
Poem 1927 (MCA; K; MMP) 7½ min. Long Allegro ma non troppo has a Scriabinesque flavor, exploits changing textures and unusual colors. M-D.
Adventures of Ivan (MCA). Eight varied pieces for students. Int.
Etude. In collection *Essential Keyboard Repertoire to Develop Technique and Mu-*

sicianship (Hinson—Alfred 4597). Motoric rhythms, repeated notes. A miniature toccata that is fine preparation for the 1934 *Toccata*. Int.

Recitatives and Fugues (Sikorski 1974) 50pp. Each Recitative serves as a prelude to a fugue of two to four voices. Best performed as individual pieces or groups of two rather than as a complete set. M-D.

Sonatina 1959 (MCA; CFP; K; Alfred; GS). Allegro giocoso: broken octaves are plentiful. Andante con anima, rubato: waltz. Allegro mosso: Impressionistic toccata. MC. M-D.

Sonata 1961 (MCA; CFP; K; GS) 25 min. Three movements. Colorful material is overworked, especially in the finale. M-D.

Toccata 1934 (Alfred; MCA; CFP; K; GS). Driving rhythm, brilliant, contrasting colorful mid-section, includes nationalistic elements. M-D.

Album for Young People, vol.1 (Palmer—Alfred) 32pp. Andantino; No Walking Today; Liado Is Ill; Birthday Song; Etude; A Musical Portrait; Invention; Fugue; Calvary March; Folk Song. Effective program pieces, worthy of performance by any serious music student, regardless of age. Int. to M-D.

Bruno Kiefer (1923–   ) Brazil, born Germany

Sonata I 1958 (Ric Brazil 1973) 17pp. 10 min. Com Energia; Saudoso; Fuga e Toccata. Preference for thin textures, subtle syncopation; neoclassic in conception. M-D.

Friedrich Kiel (1821–1885) Germany

Fugues Op.10 (Wollenweber 1981) 11pp. Four two-part fugues that are excellent for developing fluency in contrapuntal styles. M-D.

Wilhelm Killmayer (1927–   ) Germany

An John Field—Nocturnes (Schott 6688 1976) 27pp. Freely tonal, tremolo in inner voices, large left-hand skips, fast repeated chords and octaves, varied and contrasted figuration. M-D to D.

Earl Kim (1920–1998) USA

Two Bagatelles (LG). See Anthologies and Collections U.S.A., *New Music for the Piano, Guide*, pp.753–54. I. Allegro scherzando (1950): bold gestures, tremolando, expressionistic. M-D. II. Andante sostenuto (1948): expressive, changing meters not noticeable. M-D.

Johann Erasmus Kindermann (1616–1665) Germany

Tanzstücke für Klavier (R. Baum—Br 1950). 14 short dances including Ballets, A, C, S, and a Fuga. Int. to M-D.

Leon Kirchner (1919–   ) USA

Kirchner's style is characterized by strong dissonance; driving rhythms; rhapsodic, quasi-improvisational qualities; and a personal lyricism. Kirchner is a vital force in American music.

Sonata (Bomart 1948) 16 min. Lento—poco a poco doppio movimento: serves as
introduction and moves to a vigorous, rhythmic propulsive allegro, which
connects with an Adagio: a highly atmospheric movement. Allegro Barbaro: uses violent rhythmic patterns in a unique manner plus material
from the opening movement. The whole cyclic work pulsates with rubato
and requires a neurotic intensity. Exceedingly demanding. D.
See: David Burge, "Leon Kirchner's Sonata," *Keyboard*, 8/6 (June 1982):62.
Robert C. Ehle, "Romanticism in the *Avant-Garde*: Leon Kirchner's Piano
Sonata," AMT, 19 (April–May 1970):30.
Richard F. Goldman, "Current Chronicle: New York," MQ 35/4 (October
1949) for a review of the Sonata.

Little Suite (Mer 1950). Prelude; Song; Toccata; Fantasy; Epilogue. Brief sketches
of approximately one page each. Intense, flexible, resilient, serious. M-D.

Five Pieces for Piano 1986 (AMP 7979). Also in collection *American Contemporary Masters* (GS 1995) 13pp. These five pieces are to be played in one
movement. Broad gestures, intense yet songlike influence, expressionistic
harmonies, shifting meters, dramatic conclusion. Large span required. D.

Interlude 1989 (AMP) 6 min. Composed for Peter Serkin. Requires full range of
technique and tonal color. M-D to D.
See: Alexander L. Ringer, "Leon Kirchner," MQ, 43 (January 1957):1–20.

Theodor Kirchner (1823–1903) Germany

Most of Kirchner's compositions were workmanlike, small-scale pieces for the
piano. Although strongly influenced by Schumann, they show considerable inventiveness and possess a character of their own.

Nachtbilder Op.25 (Br&H 8131) 47pp. Night Scenes. Ten colorful character
pieces. Preface in German and English. Int. to M-D.

Spielsachen Op.35 (Schott 6876) 36pp. 14 light character pieces. Short, sincere,
some inspired. Similar to some of the more expressive pieces from Schumann's *Album for the Young*. Int.

Miniatures Op.62 (ABRSM) 27pp. 15 pieces with real charm and appeal. Int.

Variations on a Theme of Schumann 1878 (Schott). Kirchner condenses Schumann's duet version into a playable and effective piece. Ten variations, the
last a funeral march. Arrestingly beautiful. M-D.

New Scenes of Childhood Op.55 1881 (Salter—ABRSM 1986) 27pp. Title shows
that Kirchner was a disciple of Robert Schumann. 25 pieces. All display
polished craft and contain unexpected touches. Int.

Johann Philipp Kirnberger (1721–1783) Germany

Kirnberger was a theoretician and author of several temperament schemes, including one that claimed kinship with the practice of his teacher, J. S. Bach.

A Miscellany of Dances 1777 (R. Jones—ABRSM) Easier Piano Pieces No.9.
Contains two main groups: an *Entrée* followed by 18 short dances in D major and minor; and eight more in various keys, two of which are borrowed

(with acknowledgment) from Couperin and Handel. Delightful, technically undemanding, tasteful editorial suggestions. Int.

Acht Fugen für Cembalo oder Orgel (Ruf, Bemmann—Schott 6501). Eight thinly
textured fugues preceded by a short Prelude C. The three "jig" fugues are
the most attractive. No editing. Int.

Variationen "Ich schlief da traumte mir" ("I slept, then I dreamed") (Schott ED
7335). Published with C. P. E. Bach variations of this tune. See entry under
C. P. E. Bach.

Airs de danse (Mahlert—Br&H EB 8612). "Unlike Bach and Handel, whose
suites often left the basic form of the Baroque dance far behind them,
Kirnberger gives a brief and succinct illustration of their characteristics"
(from the Preface).

See Collections: *Le Trésor des Pianistes*, vol.14; and *Old Masters of the 16th, 17th
and 18th Centuries* (Niemann—K).

Stefan Kisielewski (1911–   ) Poland

Danse Vive (PWM 1939) 16pp. Vivacissimo; groups of notes alternate between
hands; extreme registers exploited; freely tonal around F; syncopated
rhythms; brilliant octaves at conclusion. M-D.

Prelude and Fugue (PWM 1943). The fast four-part fugue ends with a recitativo
cadenza. D.

Toccata (PWM 1943). Short, brilliant, much passagelike figuration. D.

Serenada 1945 (PWM 1973) 8pp. 4½ min. Descending staccato notes, arpeggio
gestures, chordal melody, recitative section, closing like opening. M-D.

Suite (PWM 1955). Melodic, uncomplicated texture. M-D.

Berceuse (PWM 1968) 11pp. 4 min. Allegretto moderato, fast chromatic figuration, 4 with 3, changing meters, trills in low register, many starts and stops,
ppp ending. M-D.

Giselher Klebe (1925–   ) Germany
Hindemith, jazz, Mahler, and Stravinsky influenced Klebe's early works. Twelve-
tone technique was incorporated into his style during the 1950s.

Wiegenlieder für Christinchen: Neun Stücke für Klavier Op.13 (Bo&Bo). Dedicated to Boris Blacher; makes use of his variable meter system. Rows are
also used. M-D.

Drei Romanzen Op.43 (Bo&Bo 1964). Influence of Berg, Schönberg, and Webern; mastery of free serial techniques. D.

Neun Klavierstücke für Sonja Op.76 1977 (Br 6195) 22pp. Short contrasting character pieces exploring contemporary techniques. Requires mature pianism
to exploit subtleties embedded in the work. M-D.

Oliver Knussen (1953–   ) Great Britain

Sonya's Lullaby Op.16 1977 (Faber) 8pp. 6 min. Built around a gently rocking
tritone in the middle register. Written on three staffs throughout. Many or-

namental notes; rich, warm harmonies; overtly emotional; expressionistic. M-D.

Erland von Koch (1910–   ) Sweden
Von Koch's style features rhythmic accentuation and variability, with a melodi-
ous sound reminiscent of folk music.
Monologue 13 (GM) 5 min. Opens with a cantabile part followed by a faster section. Each section may be performed separately. M-D.
Sonatina No.1 Op.41 (NMS 1950) 15 pp. Oriented toward Hindemith. M-D.
Varianti Virtuosi 1965 (Nov 1968) 9 min. No. 3 from Virtuoso Series, edited by
John Ogdon. Theme and 16 variations. Ogdon says in the notes: "The last
4 variants produce an escalation of virtuosity. Bartókian dance rhythms,
broken octaves, a decorated chorale, double octaves, compound arpeggi
and broken chord sequences vindicate the work's title and provide the
most testing technical demands in it." See Anthologies and Collections,
General: Contemporary. D.
Nordiska Impromptus 1–5 (NMS). Issued in the composer's manuscript. Short,
varied, and well conceived for the instrument. Would be most effective if
played as a complete set. M-D.

Frederick Koch (1924–   ) USA
Babette Piano Book (Gen 1969) 10pp. Five fresh-sounding pieces. Int.
Five Memories (CF). Five short contrasting pieces (graceful, lively, folk dance,
gentle, etc.), Romantic. Int.

Miklós Kocsár (1933–   ) Hungary
Improvisazioni 1972–73 (EMB) 16pp. Improvisatory, full of contrasting dynamics, no bar lines, great skips, aleatory sections, strong dissonance, effective
climax. Much experience is necessary to "bring off" this work. D.

Frantisek Kocvara (ca. 1750–1791) Bohemia
The Celebrated Battle of Prague 1788 (Musica Obscura) 9pp. An extraordinary
and musically quite worthless descriptive piece that was long a great favorite in London and was a forerunner of Beethoven's "Battle of Vittoria."
Fun for all! M-D.

Zoltán Kodály (1882–1967) Hungary
Kodály's style is mainly melodic and related to the Hungarian folk idiom. His
structures are always clear and well proportioned.
Nine Pieces Op.3 1909 (MCA; K; Ku; MMP). No.1: simple, solemn, and expressive. No.2: melismatic passages interrupted by bold chords. No.3: freely
moving accompaniment surrounds an expressive melody, big climax outlines the tritone, *pp* ending. No.4: vigorous Scherzoso. No.5: chordal Furioso,
Bartókian. No.6: slow, sad, modal. Nos.7 and 8: perpetual-motion studies.

No.9: a bold burlesco. The MCA edition contains a *Valsette*, in salon style, which is not up to the other pieces. Int. to M-D.

Twenty-four Little Canons on the Black Keys (Bo&H). The first 16 pieces are small studies in rhythms and syllables only, without complete staves. They can be sung as well as played. Int.

Seven Piano Pieces Op.11 1910–18 (UE). *Zongoramuzsika.* Folk-inspired, Impressionistic influence. See especially Nos.1, Lento; 3, Il pleut dans mon coeur comme il pleut sur la ville; and 5, Tranquillo. M-D.

Méditation sur un motif de Claude Debussy 1907 (UE). Impressionistic, improvisational, resonant, serious. M-D.

Gyermektáncok (Bo&H 1945). 12 children's dances on the black keys, based on Hungarian folk tunes. About same difficulty as Bartók *For Children.* Int.

Dances of Marosszek 1930 (UE). Based on peasant tunes, catchy rhythms, modal-tonal harmonies. Strong evocation of Hungarian folk music. Requires complete pianism. M-D to D.

12 Little Pieces (Bo&H 1973) 5pp. Nos.1–4 are to be played a half step lower and No.6 is to be played a half step higher, all on black keys. Also suitable for rote teaching. Easy.

See: Ylda Novik, "György Sandor Plays and Discusses Kodály," PQ, 88 (Winter 1974–75):14, 16. Prompted by Sandor's recording of the complete piano pieces of Kodály.

Edward Rath, "Kodály's Keyboard Compositions," *Clavier,* 21/10 (December 1982):18–21. Includes music to Op.11/7 from the *Seven Piano Pieces.*

Charles Koechlin (1867–1950) France

Koechlin's keyboard style combined a love of folk song, nursery rhyme, medieval music, free rhythms, and modal usage. Sometimes the writing may seem involved but the sonority always seems the "correct" thing at the moment. Koechlin experimented with many of the "isms" and "alities" in the early part of the twentieth century. Much charming music is listed below.

Douze Esquisses Op.41 (Sal). 2 series, 12 pieces in each of these varied "Songs without Words." Int. to M-D.

Ballade Op.50 1911–15 (Billaudot 1994) 30pp. Original version for solo piano; later orchestrated for piano and orchestra. One large movement in 8 sections. Beautifully flowing and supple lines, haunting melodies, modal flavor, cool and transparent harmonies. M-D.

Cinq Sonatines Op.59 (Sal). Three- and four-movement works written for the composer's children. Nursery rhymes and folk songs are suggested. Represents a microcosm of Koechlin's writing. Arranged in progressive order of difficulty. Int. to M-D.

Douze Petites Pièces Op.61d (Sal). Programmatic miniatures permeated with contrapuntal textures. Int.

Paysages et Marines Op.63 1918 (Sal). 2 collections, 6 pieces each. Lyric landscape and marine sketches. M-D.

See: Boaz Sharon, "Music of Charles Koechlin," *Clavier,* 20 (February

1981):14–19. Includes music of *Paysage d'October*, No.10 from *Paysages et Marines*.

Hommage à Gabriel Fauré 1922. No.5 in the set *Hommage à Gabriel Fauré, La Revue Musicale* 23 (October 1922), 2pp. Uses F-A-D-G-E 14 times, free rhythm, medieval modal cadences. Koechlin studied composition privately with Fauré and published a biography of his teacher. M-D.

Les heures persanes Op.65 1916–19 (ESC 1987) 82pp. Sixteen pieces, after Loti. M-D.

Nouvelles Sonatines Op.87 1926 (Sal). Four pieces, each in four movements, about 5 min. each. Strong links to French folk song. Progressively more difficult. Int. to M-D.

L'Anciènne Maison de Campagne Op.124 1932–33 (l'OL) 40pp. This suite of 12 pieces has bar lines that usually indicate phrase endings. Thin textures. Nos.6, 8, and 10 are especially recommended. M-D.

12 Petite Pièces Faciles Op.208 1946 (Heugel). Delightful pedagogic material, uses many contrapuntal devices. Easy to Int.

Danse Lente from *Danses pour Ginger, Clavier* 23/6 (July–August 1984):16–21. Includes the music and a lesson by Boaz Sharon. The music is Satie-like but has more tonal ambiguity. Calm, slow waltz mood in the mid-section, then assumes a languid and dreamy air as it drifts to a close. Int. to M-D.

See: Frank Cooper, "Sleeping Beauty: The Pianistic Legacy of Charles Koechlin," *Clavier*, 8 (December 1969):18–20.

Thomas H. McGuire, "Charles Koechlin," AMT, 25 (January 1976):19–22.

Hans Joachim Koellreutter (1915–   ) Germany
Musica 1941 (ECIC 1942). Tranquilo; Muy expresivo; Muy ritmado y destacado. 12-tone. M-D.

Jósef Koffler (1896–1943) Poland
Koffler was the only Polish composer to adopt serial techniques before World War II.
Sonatine Op.12 (UE). Highly chromatic, dissonant. Neither serial nor tonal. M-D.
15 Variations Op.9 (Senart). 12-tone technique. M-D.

Louis Köhler (1820–1886) Germany
Köhler wrote mostly studies.
12 Easy Studies Op. 157 (Palmer—Alfred 1972). All are in C and are 16 or 24 measures in length. Performance suggestions. Int.

Karl Kohn (1926–   ) USA, born Austria
5 Pieces for Piano (CF 1965). Contrasted pianistic ideas in a strong contemporary idiom. Short, freely atonal. Flexible rhythmic handling, no meter indications in Nos.2, 3, 4, or 5. Demanding musically. D.
Rhapsody 1960 (CF). Large scale, serial, intense. Sostenuto pedal required. D.
5 Bagatelles 1961 (CF). Contrasting colors and figurations. M-D.

Partita 1962–64 (CF 1972). Reproduced from composer's MS. Aleatoric; extensive diagram and directions are given so the performer can chart the course. Expressionistic style, avant-garde. D.

Ellis B. Kohs (1916–   ) USA

Kohs employs both tonal and atonal methods in his writing.

Toccata (Mer 1949). Free use of the row. Extended work employing canon, chorale, chordal sections, cadenzas, recitative, free passages. Form inspired by Baroque models. D.

Variations (Mer 1946). A basic set of four chords serves as the inspiration for this work. No break between variations, free use of the row technique. M-D.

Variations on "L'Homme Armé" (Mer 1946–47). 18 variations built on this famous Renaissance song. Advanced pianism required. M-D to D.

Joonas Kokkonen (1921–1996) Finland

Five Bagatelles 1968–69 (Fazer) 17pp. 13½ min. Praeambulum; Intermezzo; Aves; Elegiaco; Arbores. Contrasted pieces in a thoroughly contemporary idiom. M-D.

Sonatine (Fazer 1953) 11pp. 8½ min. Adagio; Allegro; Adagio-Allegro. Repeated chromatic chords ornate cantabile melody, octotonic. Good octave technique required. M-D.

Barbara Kolb (1939–   ) USA

Solitaire 1971 (CFP) 13½ min. For piano and tape. Dreamy, subtle coloristic contrasts. M-D.

Appello 1976 (Bo&H) 14 min. Appello is the Italian word for "call." Four highly contrasting movements, each of which embodies a specific type of call. Makes a strong impact by both the coherence of contrasting structures and a "furia," which exploits virtuoso pianistic percussion techniques; cascades of sound pour forth. Serial influence. D.

See: David Burge, "Barbara Kolb's *Solitaire* and *Appello*," CK, 6 (July 1980):65.

Mieczyslaw Kolinski (1901–   ) Poland

Sonata (Hargail 1972) 29pp. Lydian Theme and Variations: appealing and distinctive theme followed by seven contrasting variations. Chaconne: 13 short sections, variation treatment. Minuet: short, quiet. Rondo quasi Tarantella: metrical pattern based on three plus two, rousing concluding movement with propulsive forward motion. Traditional structures and musical treatment but a fresh, novel approach plus an inherent understanding of the piano's sonorities produce a first-class work of spontaneity and excitement. D.

Jo Kondo (1947–   ) Japan

Click Crack (Zen-On 381 1975) 11pp. Serial, harmonics, proportional rhythmic notation, avant-garde. D.

Sight Rhythmics 1975 (CFP 66791) 9pp. 13 min. A set of six pieces, the last entitled "Scholion" (a commentary or coda). First five pieces are each 27 bars long, contain similar rhythmic ideas as well as the same pitches in the same order. Tempo is nearly the same in all and each has a *mp* dynamic level throughout. Rhythms of first piece function like a theme. These rhythms are repeated in varied form in Nos.2–5. Subtle rhythmic metamorphosis takes place throughout Nos.2–5. Pointillistic, varied and unpredictable rhythms. A good example of minimalist music. M-D.

Paul Kont (1920–   ) Austria
12 Walzer mit Koda "Valses noires et lamentables" (Dob 1971) 26pp. Inspired by Schubert and Ravel. Twelve varied Valses in a mixture of neoclassic and Impressionistic style. Int. to M-D.

Yüksel Koptagel (1931–   ) Turkey
Koptagel studied at the Paris Conservatoire. She has won several prizes.
Tarnnzara 1958 (ESC 1980). A Turkish dance and regional dancing song from Anatolia, indigenous to the Turks, Armenians, and Kurds. In 9/8 divided into 4 + 5 eighth notes per measure. Requires precise rhythmic drive. The folk tune is heard from m. 17 forward. M-D.
　　See: Sahan Arzruni, "Let's Talk Turkey—The Music of Yüksel Koptagel," KC, 13/3 (May–June 1993):60–61. Includes score of *Tarnnzara* on pp. 56–59.
Brian's Diary (ESC). Children's album. Int.

Peter Jona Korn (1922–1998) Germany
Korn writes in a freely tonal style permeated with strong rhythmic counterpoint.
Eight Bagatelles Op.11 (Bo&H 1961). Not trifles but a difficult set with various moods and pianistic idioms. M-D.
Sonata No.1 Op.25 (Bo&H 1957). Three movements. Chromatic, preference for harmonic sevenths, persistent driving of the pulse in outside movements. Pedal points and ostinati stabilize tonalities. D.

Eric W. Korngold (1897–1957) Austria
Korngold was one of the most formidable composing prodigies in the history of music. By the time he was 11 he had already acquired his idiosyncratic style, which basically did not change during the rest of his life. It represents the last fling of the Romantic spirit in Vienna: big tunes with simple triads loaded with extra tones. His greatest success came in Hollywood, writing music for the movies.
7 Märchenbilder Op.3 (Schott; MMP) 44pp. *Fairy Tales*. Written and published when Korngold was 11 years old. Late-Romantic idiom. M-D.
Sonata No.2 E Op.2 (Schott 1911; MMP) 36pp. A large four-movement work in post-Romantic idiom. Richard Strauss's influence obvious yet Korngold was only 14 years old when he wrote it. Displays an emerging and determined musical voice. M-D.
Sonata No.3 C Op.25 (Schott 1931). Allegro molto e deciso: dramatic opening

leads to a cantabile section, gradually returns to the opening idea; broad sweeping close. Andante religioso: lyric idea broadly developed. Tempo di Menuetto molto comodo: full chords and Romantic harmonies. Rondo: Allegro giocoso; energetic theme treated to a variety of situations. A large work, anchored in post-Romantic techniques and sonorities. More developed than Op.2 and full of orchestral effects. D.

Don Quixote 1909 (Schott 8376 1995) 23pp. ca. 13 min. Character pieces written when Korngold was 12 years old. These early works already show his talent for painting pictures in sound. Don Quixote's dreams of heroic deeds; Sancho Panza on his grey donkey; Don Quixote goes forth; Dulcinea of Toboso; Adventure; Don Quixote's conversion and death. M-D.

Four Waltzes 1914 (Schott 8377 1996) 32pp. "These are not elementary piano pieces but rather little showpieces of Korngold's harmonic and dramatic skills" (from the score). Composed when Korngold was around 16 years old, they were written for four of his girlfriends. The pieces seem to reflect each girl's personality. Gretl; Margit; Gisi; Mitzi. M-D.

Gregory W. Kosteck (1937–1991) USA

Second Sonata for Piano (B&VP 1963) 9 min. Scintillating: toccata-like, equal interest between the hands. Sustained: contemporary lyric writing. Driving: opens with a pointillistic statement of the row, followed by lyric section with ostinato accompaniment; ends with brilliant octave passages. D.

Jun Kouda (1957–   ) Japan

Kouda is a graduate of the Tokyo College of Music.

Metamòrfosi 1994 (Japan Federation of Composers) 13 min. "The theme of this music, voiced in a poetic style by a feeling of free movement at the initial stage, gradually reveals its outline and is metamorphosed to a violent extent" (from the 1994 Japan Federation of Composers Catalogue, p. 12).

Boris Koutzen (1901–1966) USA, born Russia

Koutzen's style is almost exclusively polyphonic.

Sonatina 1931 (Gen) 12 min. Three movements in one. Vivo: marcato, chromatic, rhythmic punctuation. Andante pensieroso: quiet opening leads to energetic climax, calm closing. Allegro vivo: bitonal contrasted moods, extensive coda. M-D.

Eidolons 1953 (Gen) 13 min. One-movement poem for piano. Varied moods, tempi, and textures; repeated notes, grandiose climax, quiet close, neoclassic style. M-D.

Kiyoshige Koyama (1914–   ) Japan

Kagome Variations (Zen-On 316 1972) 6pp. Theme, 8 variations, and coda. Theme appears to be a Japanese folk song. Pentatonic usage throughout, attractive set. Int. to M-D.

Leopold Anton Koželuch (1747–1818) Bohemia
Koželuch, who wrote in almost all media, left over 100 solo piano sonatas.
5 Sonatas (Dana Setkova-Artia). No.1 c Op.2/3; No.2 g Op.15/1; No.3 d Op.20/3;
No.4 E♭ Op.26/3; No.5 f Op.38/3. Clean edition. M-D.
Sonata d Op.51/3 (K&S) Organum, Series V, No.23. 29pp. Largo: expressive, reminiscent of Beethoven; cadence on dominant leads to Allegro Molto e agitato: based on eighth-note figuration as found in Beethoven Op.31/2; interesting key relationships, foreign keys. Rondo: charming. M-D.

Leo Kraft (1922–   ) USA
Allegro Giocoso (LG 1957). See Anthologies and Collections, U.S.A. *New Music
for the Piano*. Changing rhythmic usage, syncopation, fun to play, jazz influence. M-D.
Partita I (Gen). Strong craft, lyrical, polished writing. M-D.

William Kraft (1923–   ) USA
Kraft's works have been influenced by his background as a jazz performer and
arranger and by his acquaintance with Stravinsky and Varèse.
Translucences 1979 (New Music West) 13pp. Clusters, harmonics, much sostenuto
pedal usage, motoric figuration, scherzando, recitative-like sections, rubato. D.

Jonathan Kramer (1942–   ) USA
Music for Piano No.5 1979–80 (GS) 32pp. 6–7 min. Shows Steve Reich influence.
Begins slowly and quietly, builds with brilliant figurations, some right-
hand boogie-woogie techniques. Built on a 6-note scale, constantly changing rhythmic flux. D.

Zygmunt Krauze (1938–   ) Poland
Triptych (PWM 1964) 9½ min. Employs a compositional notation that designates the precise tone and tempo but gives the performer an option of one
of 24 versions. The idea for the design of the notation comes from the
Gothic triptych. Contains one central panel and two moving side wings.
During performance the pianist may connect the central panel with the
side wings by opening or closing them. The parts may be connected in four
ways, thereby providing 24 different versions, depending on the order in
which the connections are made. Avant-garde. D.
Easy Pieces for Piano (UE 17264 1980) 26pp. A set of short contrasted pieces
written in an atonal style. Divided into six sections: the first, "Without
Contrast," has four pieces; then "5 Piano Pieces," "7 Interludes," Prelude,
Interlude, and Postlude. Varied meters; musical content is not obvious. Int.
to M-D.

Ernst Krenek (1900–1991) Austria
Krenek's compositional career was many-faceted. Opp.6–17 display an atonal
style. Opp.17–66 were written during a time of great experimentation, when

Krenek used ideas of jazz, Bartók, Hindemith, and others. The first 12-tone piano work was the *Zwölf Variationen* Op.79. Most of his works have since followed this style of writing but other experimentation has taken place, especially in electronic music. Krenek exerted influence on many younger composers through his teaching and writing.

Toccata and Chaconne Op.13 1922 (UE). Extended Toccata; Chaconne based on the choral "Ja, Ich glaub an Jesum Christum." Difficult, contrapuntal, atonal.

Little Suite Op.13A (UE). A supplement to Op.13 *Toccata and Chaconne*. Six small movements thematically related. Not as difficult as Op.13. M-D.

2 Suites Op.26 (UE 1924) 10 min. each. Five short movements in each suite. D.

5 Piano Pieces Op.39 (UE 1925) 10 min. Short mildly dissonant mood pieces. M-D.

Sonata No.1 Op.2 E♭ (UE 1921) 30pp. Three movements of intellectual, contrapuntal writing. M-D.

Sonata No.2 Op.59 1928 (UE) 20 min. Allegretto; Alla marcia, energico; Allegro giocoso. Freely tonal, chordal, driving and exhilarating. Needs rhythmic vigor and vitality. M-D.

12 Variations Op.79 1937 (H. Assmann) 25pp. Rev. 1940 and 1957. Krenek's first 12-tone work. For adventurous atonalists! M-D.

12 Short Pieces Written in the Twelve-Tone Technique Op.83 (GS 1938). Excellent introduction to 12-tone writing. All pieces written on same row. Explanation contained. M-D.

Sonata No.3 Op.92/4 (AMP 1943). Allegretto piacevole: lyrical. Theme, Canons and Variations: varying moods, textures. Scherzo: alternating moods and idioms. Adagio: thick textures build to climax, end *pppp*. 12-tone, atonal. M-D.

8 Piano Pieces Op.110 (Mer 1946). Etude; Invention; Scherzo; Toccata; Nocturne; Waltz; Air; Rondo. 12-tone works accompanied by the composer's analysis and interpretative suggestions. All pieces based on the same series. M-D.

Sonata No.4 Op.114 (Bomart 1948). Sostenuto—Allegro ma non troppo—Allegro assai: restless, introspective. Andante sostenuto, con passione: alternating contrasting sonorities. Rondo—vivace: Scherzando opening, wild rhythmic section, rolling ostinato figures. Tempo di minuetto, molto lento: 10-bar theme, variations, quiet close. 12-tone but the row seldom appears in its basic form. D.

George Washington Variations Op.120 (PIC 1950). 11 min. The main theme, Washington's Grand March, and the closing Martial Cotillion are from the eighteenth century. Six elaborate and contrasted variations including an Elegy, a Canon, and a Sarabande. Fine amusement! M-D.

Sonata No. 5 Op.121 1950 (Br 1992) 23pp. 18 min. Three movements, atonal, colorful textures, fast figurations, low trills, glissandi, dramatic and expressive gestures. D.

Sonata No. 6 Op.128 1951 (Br 1992) 21pp. Prelude: Introduction. Andante: moves mainly in eighth notes. Allegretto vivace: more grounded in sixteenth notes. Allegro drammatico, appassionato e molto rubato: dramatic, SA design. Epilogue: elegiac postlude. Angular writing. M-D to D.

20 Miniatures Op.139 (WH 1954). Strict 12-tone writing. All are based on the same row, some pleasant sounds. M-D.

Echoes from Austria Op.166 (Rongwen 1958) 12 min. Seven pieces based on folk song, revealing yet another facet of Krenek. The last one is the most difficult. M-D.

Sechs Vermessene Op.168 (Br 1958) 12 min. Vermessene is the German word for "completely measured." Directions describe the system of five layers in which the first has density, one tone at a time, the next has two tones together, the third three, etc. D.

See: David Burge, "Contemporary Piano—Ernst Krenek," CK, 6 (February 1980):80. A discussion of Krenek's piano music with special emphasis on the Fourth Sonata.

Ernst Krenek, *Horizons Circles: Reflections on My Music* (Berkeley: University of California Press, 1975), 167pp.

Georg Adam Kress (1744–1788) Germany

Klavierübungen des frankischen Dorfshulmeisters Georg Adam Kress (S. Kress— Schott). An eighteenth-century notebook of dances and pieces. Int.

Classical Study Pieces (Schott 6961 1981) 27pp. Short pieces in classical style, some dances (Polonaise, Menuet, Allemande). Similar in difficulty to Clementi Sonatinas Op.36. Int.

Edino Krieger (1928–   ) Brazil

Preludio (Cantilena) e Fuga (Marcha-rancho) (SDM 1954) 8pp. Colorful writing showing more nationalistic flavor than most of Krieger's other works. D.

3 Miniaturas (SDM 1952) 8pp. Moderato; Andante; Andante moderato. Skillful handling of pianistic techniques. Pieces are complementary and require mature pianism. D.

Sonata I (SDM 1953–54) 27pp. Andante-Allegro enérgico; Seresta—Lento (Homenàgem a Villa-Lobos); Variaçoes e Presto. Bravura writing requiring advanced pianistic equipment. D.

Sonatina (Vitale 1971) 13pp. Moderato; Allegro. Contemporary treatment of Alberti bass, neoclassic style. Second subject of first movement is well contrasted with the first by being more rhythmic. M-D.

Ton de Kruyf (1937–   ) The Netherlands

De Kruyf has used serial techniques in his writing since 1958.

Sgrafitti per Pianoforte (Donemus 1960). Free use of the row so that fewer than 12 tones may be used. The title of the work comes from the Italian "to steal, to pilfer," hence the relationship to the row usage. D.

Rafael Kubelik (1914–1996) Switzerland, born Czechoslovakia

Sonatina für Klavier 1957 (Litolff 1970) 20pp. Allegro: uses a double exposition. Arietta: expressive. Vivace: scherzolike. Toccata and Chorale: Toccata is percussive; repeated notes and chords. Classical forms and disciplined writing. M-D.

Gail Kubik (1914–1984) USA

Celebrations and Epilogue 1938–50 (PIC). Ten short pieces, fresh rhythms, varied moods, clear sonorities, clever titles such as: Birthday Piece; Wedded Bliss (parody on traditional wedding march); A Gay Time. See especially Movies; Saturday Night. Int. to M-D.

Sonatina (Mer 1941). Four short movements. Moderately fast; Lively; Very slowly; Toccata. Changing meters, repeated percussive notes, canonic writing, flowing melodies. M-D.

Dance Soliloquy (Mer 1942). Homophonic style, three-part form, ostinato under melody, clever rhythmic usage. Int.

Sonata 1947 (PIC). Four-movement work based on American idioms. Moderately fast, gracefully; Gaily; Slowly, expressively; Fairly fast: hard, bright, mechanical. D.

Whistling Tune (TP). Changing meters, crisp rhythms, polytonal. Int.

Juliasz Kuciuk (–   ) Poland

Children's Improvisations (PWM). Careful guidance will help young pianists enjoy these avant-garde pieces. Int.

Friedrich Kuhlau (1786–1832) Denmark, born Germany

Kuhlau moved to Denmark to avoid being drafted into Napoleon's army. He was the first flutist in the King's band in Copenhagen, Denmark, from 1810, becoming court composer and professor of music there. He composed operas and music for violin and flute, and is especially remembered for some fine sonatinas for the piano.

Six Sonatinas Op.55 (Alfred; GS; TP; Century). C, G, C, F, D, C. Nos.1 and 3 available separately (Alfred; GS) and in *World's Greatest Sonatinas* (Hinson—Alfred 4617). Fine teaching material. Int.

Three Sonatinas Op.59 (GS; TP; Century). A, F, C. Tuneful. Int.

Four Sonatinas Op.88. Available separately: No.1 (Delrieu); No.2 (Harris); No.3 (GS). Well-written. Int.

Sonatinas I Opp.20, 55, 59 (CFP; GS; K 3599). Int.

Sonatinas II Opp.60, 88 (CFP; GS; K 3600). These seven sonatinas are all fine pieces for this level. Int.

Nine Sonatinas Opp.20 and 55 (Alfred 4889). Kuhlau's finest sonatinas. Int.

Johann Kuhnau (1660–1722) Germany

Bach's predecessor in Leipzig at the Thomas Kirche occupies a special place in the history of keyboard music. His B♭ sonata in the appendix to his partitas (*Neue Clavier-Übung* Part II, 1692) is one of the earliest examples of the use of the term "Sonata." His complete keyboard works are contained in DDT, vol. 4, first series, as follows:

Neue Clavier-Übung Part I (1689). Seven suites (Partitas) in C, D, E, F, G, A, B♭. M-D.

Neue Clavier-Übung Part II (1692). Seven suites in c, d, e, f, g, a, b, plus the Sonata B♭. M-D.

Frische Clavier-Früchte (1696). Seven sonatas in g, D, F, c, e, B♭, a. M-D.

Musicalische Vorstellung einiger Biblischer Historien in 6 Sonaten (Musical Presentations of Some Biblical Stories) 1700 (Kurt Stone—BB). These multi-movement sonatas, Kuhnau's most effective for keyboard, are programmatic works based on scenes from the Old Testament. They employ many forms from the dance to the chorale prelude. Urtext edition. Includes English translation of Kuhnau's own essay to the "Gentle Reader." Published separately (CFP). Facsimile of the original 1700 edition (CFP) contains Kuhnau's preface and description of the pieces elegantly translated into English by Michael Talbot.

Sonata I C, "The Battle between David and Goliath" (Alfred; K).

Sonata II g, "Saul Cured through Music by David" (PWM). Daring chromaticism.

Sonata III G, "Jacob's Wedding."

Sonata IV c, "The Mortally Ill and Then Restored Hezekiah." In collection *Anthology of Baroque Piano Music* (Hinson—Alfred 4894).

Sonata V F, "Gideon, Saviour of Israel" (Alfred).

Sonata VI E♭, "Jacob's Death and Burial."

4 Selected Keyboard Works (K. Schubert—Schott). Partitas IV and III, F and e; *Biblical Sonatas* I and IV.

Easy Suite Movements (Frickert—Leuckart). 24 pieces. Int.

Franz Kullak (1844–1913) Germany

Son of Theodore.

Scenes from Childhood (K 3596). Worth an occasional hearing. Int.

Theodore Kullak (1818–1882) Germany

Scenes from Childhood Opp.62, 81 (CFP; Klauser—GS L365). 24 characteristic pieces. Int.

Air Bohemien (Musica Obscura) 7pp. Theme and variations in c. Contains some nice turns of phrases. Melodic. Int. to M-D.

Grandmother Tells a Ghost Story Op.81/3. In collection *Essential Keyboard Repertoire—95 Early/Late Miniatures* Vol. 8. One of the most attractive pieces from Opp.62 and/or 81. Int.

Rainer Kunad (1936–1995) Germany

Mozartparaphrase 1971–78 (DVFM 8047) 17pp. 10 min. The organ Fantasia in f for a musical clock (1791) K.608 is the basis for this work. Fast ornamental figuration supports tiny fragments that turn into fragments from the fantasia. Weird and curious, full of improvisatory chromatic ostinato patterns. M-D.

Jos Kunst (1936–1996) The Netherlands

Glass Music (CFP 7142 1977) 19pp. Includes notes for performers in English, Dutch, French, and German. Proportional notation; extreme ranges of keyboard and dynamics exploited; clusters; staccato sonorities suggest glasses tinkling; avant-garde. M-D.

Alfred Kunz (1929–   ) Canada

Music to Do Things By (Waterloo 1969) Vol.I: 7 short pieces. A collection of diverse pieces for all minutes, hours, days, seasons, and moods. Vol.II: 8 short pieces. Both volumes are written in a MC style with provocative titles, e.g., What to do till the Doctor comes; I Wonder?; Music to play when sad or in doubt; The strange people one meets when going for a walk. Int.

Louise Kupelian (1928–   ) USA

Theme and Variations on Happy Birthday (SB 1995) 11pp. Clever realizations in the style of Mozart, Chopin, George Shearing, à la Rag, à la Bebop, à la Bill Evans. M-D.

Meyer Kupferman (1926–   ) USA

Little Sonata (BMC 1947) 10 min. Three movements. Short, MC, fun to play, especially the final movement. Int. to M-D.

Recitative (BMC 1947). Highly chromatic. M-D.

Partita: Praeludium, Ariso and Toccata (BMC 1949). 29pp. 14 min. Outer movements require virtuoso techniques. Expressive writing in Arioso. Powerful closing to Toccata. D.

Variations (BMC) Set of serial variations, economical writing. M-D.

Sonata on Jazz Elements (Gen 1958). 13 min. Imaginative writing, avoidance of clichés. D.

Short Suite (Gen 1968). Prelude; Close-up; March; Canvas; Game. M-D.

14 Canonic Inventions for Young Composers (Gen 1966). Short contrapuntal models with analytical material. Can be used by student "to compose a set of his own original canons based on these models" (from the preface). Int.

Pico(—among the smallest particles) (Gen 1978) 1 min. Quiet bell-sonority opening, changes to agitated mood, ends with extravagant clusters. M-D.

5 Little Zeppelins 1976 (Gen). Ursa Major; Ursa Minor; Andromeda; Draco; Cygnus. Far-out harmonies and rhythms for these constellations. Zeppelins never got close to any of them! M-D.

Robert Kurka (1921–1957) USA

Kurka's style changed from a complex, intricate approach (*For the Piano*) to a more direct, clear style based on his growing preoccupation with folk music.

For the Piano 1949 (TP) 18pp. A virtuoso masterwork. Dazzling style; forthright and expressive writing supported by a sensitive and idiomatic understanding of the pianistic tradition, which makes it a performer's delight. Improvisations, no bar lines, numerous ideas. D.

Sonata Op.20 1954 (Chappell). Three fresh-sounding movements based on American folk materials, open fifths, percussive chords. Final movement requires bravura playing. M-D.

Yoshimitsu Kurokami (1933–   ) Japan

Wild Flowers 1965 (Zen-On 403) 4pp. Pentatonic melody. Contrasting mid-section, 3 against 2. Int.

Lyric Pieces for Children 1979 (Zen-On) 53pp. 15 solo pieces plus a duet. Shows much Western influence. Int.

Suite for Piano—12 Folk Songs in Southern Japan (Japan Federation of Composers 1969) 20pp. Merry Dance; Elegy; Rice Planting Song; Festival; Cradle Song; Among the Mountains; Barcarole; Rest; Ballad; Humming Song; Harvest Song; Fox Fire. Each piece uses harmonies based on pentatonic melodies. Requires an easy octave span. Int.

György Kurtag (1926–   ) Hungary
One of Hungary's significant post-Bartókian composers.

8 Piano Pieces Op.3 (EMB). Short pieces with complex problems. In the last piece, forearm clusters are called for in one hand while the other has to play pianissimo glissandi. Firm mastery and control of style. Worth exploring. Non-Bartókian in idiom. D.

Splinters Op.6D (UE 17070) 8pp. Four short, aphoristic pieces, Webernesque style. M-D.

Games 1973–81 (EMB) 4 vols. Vols.1–3 for solo piano; Vol.4 for piano four-hands. 164 miniatures inspired by observing children experimenting with the piano. Arranged in order of difficulty, both musical and technical. Similar to Bartók's *Mikrokosmos* but more avant-garde. Written to involve children in an unorthodox approach to the keyboard, where nothing is forbidden! Notes in English, German, and Hungarian. Easy to M-D.

Eugene Kurtz (1923–   ) USA
Kurtz has lived in Paris since 1949.

Four Movements (Jobert 1951). Prélude; Capriccio; Interlude; Allegro Martellato. M-D.

Le Capricorne (Jobert 1952, rev. 1970). Suite for Piano in Three Movements. Introduction; Intermezzo; Toccata.

Animations (Jobert 1968). Reproduction of MS, easy to read. Résonances: many avant-garde techniques, numerous special effects called for. "The performer will have to decide whether or not he will need some sort of protection for his wrists" (from description of special effects). D.

Rag: (à la mémoire de Scott Joplin) (Jobert). Ragtime rhythms in a contemporary harmonic setting. Cleverly changing meters. M-D.

Five-Sixteen 1982 (Jobert) 33pp. 12½ min. Gestures move all over keyboard, chromatic clusters, harmonics, unmeasured sections, changing meters and tempos, short and long fermatas, glissandos, expressionistic, complex rhythms. D.

Kei Kusagawa (1919–   ) Japan
Nine Pieces (Japan Federation of Composers 1970) 31pp. "I started writing these pieces in 1964. Feeling the change of seasons and observing nature in the neighborhood green foliage, I wrote these. These are to me a diary or essays" (from the composer's note). Prelude; Tiny Shock; Nocturne; Marianna; 1st Sonnet; Breezes; 2nd Sonnet; A Stir; To Pretend. Colorful, contrasted, some quartal harmony, extremes in ranges exploited. Int. to M-D.

Oddvar S. Kvam (1927–   ) Norway

Encyclopedia Op.31e (Musikk-Huset 1976). In this piece, two volumes of an encyclopedia are placed on the black keys. Avant-garde. M-D.

12 Proverbs Op.40 (Musikk-Huset 1976). Brief studies, simple yet elusive. Int. to M-D.

Johan Kvandal (1919–1999) Norway

Fem Sma Klaverstykker Op.1 (NMO 7194) 5pp. Five small pieces, MC. Would make a fine little suite. Int.

Fantasy Op.2 (NMO). Sounds like a nordic Brahms. M-D.

Tre Slätterfantasier Op.31 (NMO 1970) 14pp. Three pieces based on Norwegian folk songs. Jew's Harp Slätt: Lydian mode, strong rhythms. Langleik Improvisation: Mixolydian melody. Springleik for Fiddle: mixture of major and minor, irregular periodic construction. *Slätt* is the Norwegian word for peasant dance. M-D.

L

Wiktor Labuński (1895–1974) Poland
Easy Compositions (PWM). Four colorful miniatures. Int.
4 Variations on a Theme by Paganini (CF). Traditional harmonic language, attractive, especially for a good high school pianist. Int. to M-D.

Jiři Laburda (1931–   ) Czechoslovakia
10 Little Polyphonic Pieces (TP 1980) 14pp. Excellent for developing finger independence, musically fine. Int.

Osvaldo Lacerda (1927–   ) Brazil
Lacerda is a disciple of Camargo Guarnieri and lives in São Paulo.
Brasiliana No.1 (Vitale 1965). The *Brasiliani* are suites based on native Brazilian tunes and dances. Dobrado: a Brazilian march. Modinha: a love song treated linearly. Mazurca: with a Brazilian rhythmic twist. Marcha de Rancho: somewhat slow and sentimental. Contains a number of "wrong note" sounds. Int. to M-D.
Brasiliana No.2 (Vitale 1966). Romance: theme and four variations. Chote: Schottisch in ABA form. Moda: ABA. Côco: like a folk song. Int. to M-D.
Brasiliana No.5 (Vitale 1969) 4½ min. Desafio: two-voice fugue. Valsa: ABA. Lundu: ABA. (The Lundu was originally a rather lascivious dance in which the dancers touched belly buttons. It is a parent form of a number of other Brazilian dances and songs.) Cana-verde: green sugar cane dance, ABA. Int. to M-D.
Estudos (Vitale 1969) Book I:1–4; Book II:5–8. Each piece deals with certain pianistic problems and compositional techniques. 1. Melody and accompaniment in same hand. 2. Staccato and melodic playing. 3. Free, runs. 4. Divided between hands. 5. Intervallic study. 6. Broken octaves. 7. Tremolo. 8. Chromaticism. D.
Cinco Invenções a Duas Vozes (Ric Brazil 2701 1958) 13pp. Freely tonal, linear, some flexible meters. M-D.
Ponteio I (Ric Brazil 1955) 3pp. A Ponteio is kind of a Prelude in Brazilian style. Flowing melody, weaving accompaniment, freely tonal around d. M-D.
Ponteio III (Ric Brazil 1964) 3 min. Flexible rhythms, big climax, subsides to *pp* closing, colorful. M-D.
Ponteio V (Ric Brazil 1968) 2½ min. Linear, mostly thin textures, freely dissonant. M-D.

Suite Miniatura (Ric Brazil 1960) 5½ min. Chorinho; Toada; Valsa; Modinha; Cana verde. Influenced by Brazilian folk and popular music. M-D.

Variações sobre "Mulher Rendeira" (Vitale 1953) 12 min. Folk song theme followed by twelve variations that work to a strong closing. M-D.

Vinzenz Lachner (1811–1893) Germany
Organist, conductor, and composer whose four-part male choruses are well known in Germany. He also composed symphonies, string quartets, a piano quartet, and numerous songs.

42 Variations on the C-major scale (Schott ED 7555) 31pp. No. 10 in the series Journal für das Pianoforte. After a 16-measure theme, the 42 variations (mostly 8 or 16 measures each) unfold, offering a *tour de force* in ways to compose contrasted variations based on this scale. Nineteenth-century harmonic language. M-D.

Louis Lacombe (1818–1884) France
See below, "Collections," *Piano Music of the Parisian Virtuosos 1810–1860.*

Ezra Laderman (1924–   ) USA
Ladermann's writing is vigorous and Romantic; he sometimes mixes tonal, atonal, and aleatory materials.

Sonata No.1 (OUP 1967) 25pp. 13 min. Four movements, neoclassical in style. Based on a three-note motif. Effective. M-D.

Sonata No.2 (OUP 1966) 44pp. 22 min. Large four-movement work, neo-Romantic in style. The second movement, Romanza, shows Scriabin influence, effective large gestures. MC harmonic writing throughout. D.

Momenti 1976 (OUP) 8 min. Eight "moments." Varied moods, colorful performance instructions, dissonant and freely chromatic. Each "moment" is strongly characterized. Large span required; much use of clusters. D.

Joseph C. Lai (1970–   ) Canada, born Hong Kong
Lai studied at the University of Alberta and Concordia College.

Sarah's Solo 1988 rev. 1995 (Black Cat 1996) 4pp. Full chords, large pedals, impressionistic. A charming simplicity permeates the piece, MC. M-D.

Constant Lambert (1905–1951) Great Britain
Sonata 1928–29 (OUP). Three movements, based on jazz rhythms but a highly serious work. Ravelian in its harmonic richness and brilliant pianistic virtuosity. D.

Elegy 1938 (OUP). Short, energetic, improvisational Lento, molto rubato, introspective. M-D.

Elegiac Blues (MMP). Jazz influence, clever. M-D.

Phillip Lambro (1935–   ) USA
Toccata 1965 (Wimbledon 1977) 12pp. A virtuoso piece inspired by the Prokofiev *Toccata*. D.

John La Montaine (1920–   ) USA

La Montaine writes in a post-Romantic style influenced by the French School. His keyboard-oriented idiom is basically tonal, freely chromatic, and neoclassic in structure.

Toccata Op.1 1957 (BB). Short, brilliant, effective. M-D.

Sonata Op.3 1950 (Eastman School of Music Publications) 20pp. First movement: brilliant, alternates agitato and lyric ideas. Second movement: expressive and tranquil, interrupted bursts. Finale: sustained introduction followed by a virtuosic close. D.

12 Relationships for Piano Op.10 (CF). A set of canons, each at a different interval. Int. to M-D.

6 Dance Preludes Op.18 (BB) 10 min. Preamble; Aria; Burlesque; For Those Who Mourn; Intermezzo; For Those Who Dance. Well-conceived set; appropriate titles. Effective as complete set or as individual movements. M-D.

Fuguing Set Op.14 (CF 1965) 12½ min. Seven pieces. Three fugues, separated by Prologue, Pastorale, Cadenza, and Epilogue, each complete in itself. A miniature *Ludus Tonalis*. Advanced writing. Large span required, long pedals. D.

A Child's Picture Book (BB). Five imaginative pieces. Int.

Copycats Op.26 (Fredonia). Canons for young pianists. All are in five-finger positions; 13 are written at the octave, one at the fifth. Easy.

Elmar Lampson (1952–   ) USA

Drei Klavierstücke (PIC 1991) 28pp., holograph. Mixture of styles. M-D.

Serge Lancen (1922–   ) France

Domino-Suite Fantasque (Hin 57 1952) 15pp. Entree; Tango; Guinguette; Fumisterie; Music Hall. "This Suite is intended to be light and diverting in the French style. The title *Domino* was chosen to suggest that the music has no pretension to seriousness, for in addition to the actual game of Domino, the word itself also suggests a masquerade" (from the score). Each movement is briefly discussed. MC. Requires large span. M-D.

Fantaisen sur un thème ancien (Hin 1904 1959) 8pp. 7 min. Modal theme treated in various ways, freely tonal, quiet ending. Requires large span. M-D.

Moins Que Rien ("Less Than Nothing") (Hin 1901 1955) 4pp. A short MC character piece with a contrasting trio. Int.

Trois Impromptus (Hin 373 1953) 12pp. Written in a style reminiscent of Fauré with a bit more use of chromaticism. M-D.

Zwiefache (Folk Dances) (Hin 1902 1957) 19pp. A la mémoire de Franz Schubert. Six ländler-like pieces that use multiple meters (3/4 2/4), freely tonal, delightful. Int. to M-D.

Istvan Lang (1933–   ) Hungary

Intermezzi (EMB) 12pp. 10 min. Ten short contrasting pieces in MC idiom. Impetuous opening, subdued effects in No.4. Clusters, tremolandos, all add variety. M-D.

Walter Lang (1896–1966) Switzerland
Lang's style is full of rhythmic vitality and Impressionistic characteristics.
Bulgaria Op.16 (R&E). A small suite of ten movements. M-D.
Miniatures Op.17 (Hug 1927). Ten short alluring pieces. Int.
Variations Op.35 (Hug) 11pp. Introduction, theme, two variations, coda. Requires
    a fine octave technique. M-D.
Sonata Op.66 (Hug 1956) 16pp. Clear textures, well-developed ideas. Vivace; An-
    dante; Presto: changing meters. M-D.
Sonata Op.70 (UE 1958) 23pp. 13 min. Tumultuoso; allegro molto; Lento; Allegro
    energico. Thematic construction clearly delineated, fits fingers well, written
    in neoclassic style. D.
10 Klavier-Etüden Op.74 (Hug 1964) 16pp. Trill Study; Canon; Scales; For the
    Right Hand Alone; For the Left Hand Alone; Fughetto; Basso Ostinato; 2
    Against 3; Staccato; Legato. All written for two voices. Int.
Sonata III Op.75 (Hug 1965) 14pp. Praeludium; Sarabande; Finale. Continues the
    neoclassic style found in *Sonata II*; freely tonal with a very expressive slow
    movement. M-D.

Christian Lange (1946–   ) France
Ecoute 1979 (Leduc) 1½ min. Designed to familiarize young students with the
    styles, techniques, and graphic outlines of contemporary music. Requires
    subtle musicianship to make the piece "sound." Int.

Paul Lansky (1944–   ) USA
Modal Fantasy (CUMP 1970) 20pp. In three sections: Prelude (thick textures);
    Ludus (complex writing with corky rhythmic problems); Postlude (solemn,
    quiet). D.
Dance Suite 1977 (Boelke-Bomart 1982) 23pp. Preambulum; Allemande; Gal-
    liard; Sarabande; Air; Pavane; Capriccio. Traditional and nontraditional
    rhythmic patterns juxtaposed to effect metric modulation; melodies have
    little character. M-D to D.

Alcides Lanza (1929–   ) Argentina
Plectros II 1966–67 (Bo&H) for piano and electronic sounds, 16pp. Tape can be
    rented from publisher. Clusters, glissandos with fingers and palms, muted
    and plucked strings, pointillistic, proportional rhythmic notation. Numer-
    ous contemporary techniques fused with tape sonorities. M-D to D.

André Laporte (1931–   ) Belgium
Ascension (Tonos 1967) 8pp. Pointillistic, atonal, dynamic extremes, proportional
    rhythmic notation, aleatoric, clusters, contrary motion glissandi, plucked
    strings, changing meters, avant-garde. D.

Lars-Erik Larsson (1908–1986) Sweden
Larsson's style during the 1930s displayed clear classicist features but more recently
it moved into Nordic late Romanticism, classicism, and twelve-tone technique.

6 Croquises Op.38 (GM 1948). Capriccioso; Grazioso; Semplice; Scherzando; Espressivo; Ritmico. Hindemith influence. M-D.

Sonatine B Op.16 (UE 1936) 20pp. Four movements. Widespread broken chords. Second movement, Intermezzo, is romantic. Warm, lyric writing, effective. M-D.

Sonatine Op.39/2 (GM 1948) 10 min. Three movements. Mainly homophonic writing. MC. M-D.

12 Little Piano Pieces Op.47 (GM). 12-tone technique. M-D.

Five Pieces for Piano Op.57 (GM 1969). Humoresk; Barkarol; Burlesk; Valse-Caprice; Perpetuum Mobile. Neoclassic, simple structures, create immediate emotional response. M-D to D.

Jacques Lasry (1918–   ) France, born Algiers

Timbres et rythmes 1965 (IMP 675) 7pp. Timbres: Impressionistic play with colors. Rythmes: an impromptu echoing the composer's preoccupation with jazz. M-D.

Denise Lassimonne (–   ) Great Britain

Aubade on a Ground Bass 1981 (Musica Obscura) 2pp. The ground centers around C and D, which are the initials of His Royal Highness Prince Charles and Lady Diana Spencer. Fluid melodic line over recurring groups of eighth notes. MC. Int.

Berceuse 1982 (Musica Obscura) 2pp. To His Royal Highness Prince William. Flowing 6/8, freely tonal melody. Subtle pedaling required. Int.

Christian I. Latrobe (1757–1836) Great Britain

Latrobe was a Moravian clergyman and amateur musician. The influence of Joseph Haydn on the three sonatas listed below is the result of his friendship with the composer. Sensitive embellishments and keen development procedures contribute the imaginative qualities of these three works.

Three Sonatas for the Pianoforte Op.3 (Stevens—Bo&H 1970). Sonata I: Allegro; Lento; Menuetto; Finale—Presto. Sonata II: Allegro; Lento: an interesting Vivace mid-section provides contrast; Allegro molto. Sonata III: Adagio molto; Andante; pastorale serves as a poignant introduction to the Allegro. M-D.

See: SCE, pp. 765–67.

Carlos Lavín (1883–1962) Chile

Suite Andine 1926 (ESC). L'Aube (The Dawn); La Sieste (The Siesta); Paysage Lunaire (Moonlit Landscape). Mood pieces that depict scenes from the Andes Mountains. Int. to M-D.

Mario Lavista (1943–   ) Mexico

Pieza para Un(a) Pianista y un Piano (Collecion Arion 1970) 3 pages folded as one. Piece for one pianist and one piano. Performer decides the order of

the seven musical events. Tempi indicated quantitatively (in seconds) or quali-
tatively (grave, very slow, vivo, etc.), clusters, harmonics. Avant-garde. M-D.

Peter Lawson (1951–   ) Great Britain
Momenta 94 (CFP 1970) 14pp. 94 three-bar "moments" all evolve from the first
     moment. Varied sonorities in extreme registers, nonmusical objects used to
     pluck, brush strings, etc. Detailed instructions for performer. Composer
     states in the score that "there are no rules governing the relationship be-
     tween movements." Avant-garde. M-D.

José Clemente Laya (1913–   ) Venezuela
Sonata venezolana (Consejo Nacional de la Cultura: Editorial Latinoamericana
     de Música Simón Bolívar, Caracas, Venezuela 1992) 15pp. Includes two-
     page biographical sketch of composer. Colorful, some Latin rhythmic us-
     age, substantive writing. M-D to D.

Billy Jim Layton (1924–   ) USA
Three Etudes Op.5 1957 (GS). Serial technique brilliantly handled. Virtuosic ap-
     proach needed. D.

Henri Lazarof (1932–   ) USA, born Bulgaria
Lazarof composes in a full-blooded and highly international style.
Cadence IV 1970 (AMP) 9pp. For prepared piano. Uses a notation that leaves
     nothing to chance. With the exception of some dramatic plucked and hand-
     damped notes played directly on the strings, its technical context is con-
     ceived in a traditional way. This piece shares distinct thematic kinship with
     another Lazarof work, *Textures* (1971), for piano and 24 instruments. D.
Chronicles (Merion) 19pp. 15 min. Mixes fiery technical passages with pensive
     sections. D.

Ernesto Lecuona (1896–1963) Cuba
Lecuona's compositions personify the Spanish musical idiom and are basically
popular songs.
Suite Espagnole (EBM). Six pieces, all using Spanish rhythms and melodies. Int.
Danzas Afro-Cubanas (EBM). Six pieces with pianistic color and varied rhyth-
     mic background. Int. to M-D.
Danzas Cubanas (EBM) Seven pieces published together. All demand above-
     average technique.
19th-Century Cuban Dances (EBM). A suite of ten works, based on nineteenth-
     century dance tunes. Most are 2 pages in length. M-D.
Malagueña (EBM). Has become a "hit" in the USA, has enduring popularity,
     and is universally recognizable. Lecuona's most popular piano work. M-D.
Ernesto Lecuona Piano Music (EBM). 44 pieces. Int. to M-D.

Claude Ledoux (1955–   ) Belgium

Les Ephémérides Interrompues (Jobert) 17 min. Five movements, expressionistic and impressionistic influences. D.

Noël Lee (1924–   ) USA

Sonatine (OUP 1959) 5½ min. Allegretto; Song; Rondo—Presto. Neoclassic style, Impressionist influences especially in Song (molto lento ed espressivo). M-D.

Four Etudes Series I (Schott) 20pp. 11 min. Explanations in French, German, and English. On a Rhythm of Bartók; With Varied Sonorities (includes special explanation); With Acute Sounds; For Grave, Serious Sounds. Technical studies that explore different sonorities, including playing inside the piano. Much melodic and rhythmic interest, thoroughly contemporary, imaginative and colorful. M-D to D.

Four Etudes Series II (Schott 7068 1983) 24pp. For Legato Playing; Using Sonorous Effects; For Velocity; On Chords from Charles Ives. Calls for harmonics, playing inside the piano by plucking and damping strings, highly pianistic, pointillistic, clusters. Strong personality comes through. Requires large span. D.

Benjamin Lees (1924–   ) USA, born China

Lees's style mixes polyphonic textures with classic forms in a thoroughly contemporary idiom.

Fantasia 1953 (Bo&H) 6 min. Brilliant and fresh-sounding, minimum textural contrast. Makes a fine recital opener. M-D.

Kaleidoscopes 1959 (Bo&H). Ten short pieces, intriguing tonal sounds, few rhythmic problems. Int.

Sonata Breve 1955 (Bo&H) 11 min. One-movement work in three sections. Frequent mood changes, dissonant counterpoint mixed with octotonic passages, smooth pianistic chromatic figurations. M-D.

Toccata 1955 (SP) 6pp. Allegro con spirito, freely chromatic, explosive octaves, biting dissonance, accelerates to a brilliant closing, bravura writing. Sounds more difficult than it is. M-D.

6 Ornamental Etudes 1957 (Bo&H) 15 min. Incisive and robust style with a preference for ostinato; ornamental quality in melodic line. Freely tonal, variety of moods. M-D.

3 Preludes 1962 (Bo&H). Maestoso: rhythmic motives alternate with recitative passages, dramatic. Moderato: ABA, atmospheric, mid-section is declamatory. Tumultuoso: vibrant conclusion. M-D.

Sonata No.4 1964 (Bo&H) 22 min. Three movements of bravura keyboard style designed to show off virtuoso skills. Themes worked out thoroughly. D.

Odyssey 1970 (Bo&H) 12pp. Full resources of keyboard exploited; strong rhythms in this neo-Romantic ballade. Opens with "slow with strange foreboding." Accelerandi, leads to Tempo I with indication "from here to the end the feeling should be almost surrealistic." Ends with violent palm clusters. Pianistically grateful writing. D.

Fantasy Variations 1983 (Bo&H 1994) 30pp. ca. 28 min. "Consists of an original subject, 17 variations and a short coda. The word 'fantasy' was chosen because of the character of many of the variations" (from the score). Changing meters, strong contrasts between variations. Var. 1: Quickly. Var. 2: Slightly slower. Var. 3: Turbulently. Var. 4: Half note = 52; quietly, eerily. Var. 5: Fast. Var. 6: Calmly. Var. 7: Turbulently. Var. 8: Unhurried. Var. 9: Quickly. Var. 10: Calmly. Var. 11: Steady. Var. 12: Slower. Var. 13: Briskly. Var. 14: Smooth, strong. Var. 15: Soft, transparent. Var. 16: Boldly. Var. 17: Decisively. Full of emotion, tension, lyricism, and powerful excitement. A major work that is fresh but inevitable in its unfolding. D.

Reinbert de Leeuw (1938–   ) The Netherlands
De Leeuw teaches theory and composition at the Royal Conservatory in The Hague.

Music for Piano I (Donemus 1964). 12 structures, free in order except that the player must begin with I and end with XII. Spatial notation, aleatory, unusual sonorities. D.

Music for Piano II (Donemus 1966). Score is a graphic reproduction of the movements to be made on the keyboard, in and under the piano. Explanation of symbols, objects required to realize piece. D.

Ton de Leeuw (1926–1996) The Netherlands
De Leeuw is director of the Conservatory in Amsterdam. Many contemporary techniques are exhibited in his writing.

Men Go Their Ways (Donemus 1964) 14 min. Five interpretations of the Japanese haiku. Traditional and proportional notation used. Constantly changing permutations of the original rhythmic ideas characterize this work. Detailed instructions describe the proportional notation. M-D.

Drie Afrikaanse etudes (Donemus 1954) 7 min. Highly rhythmic. M-D.

Cinq Etudes pour le piano (Donemus 1951) 7 min. Pour les notes répétées; Pour l'unisson; Pour le main gauche; Pour les mains croisées; Pour l'agilité. These pieces are de Leeuw's most successful works for piano. M-D.

Lyric Suite 1953 (Donemus). Allegro: bell-like sounds. Andante tranquillo: short, leads to the lively Vivace: bitonal. Thin textures in outer movements; Andante is only lyric part, with full sonorities. M-D.

Nicola LeFanu (1947–   ) Great Britain
Chiaroscuro (Novello 1969) 12½ min. Seven short diversified sections (pieces) whose titles refer to the pictorial art that emphasizes light and shade: Exultate; Refrain; Sound and Silence; Epithalamion; Reflection and Cadenza; Refrain; Scherzo—Epilogue. MS reproduction but easy to read. Interpretative directions, rhythmic difficulties, sharp characterization and definition of musical ideas. Effective sonorities cleverly juxtaposed; variation concept permeates entire work. M-D.

See: Richard Cooke, "Nicola LeFanu," MT, 1593 (November 1975):961–63, for a discussion of the composer's works and career.

René Leibowitz (1913–1972) France, born Poland
Leibowitz's style reflects his dedication to twelve-tone technique.
Four Piano Pieces Op.8 1943 (UE). Highly organized serial writing, exploits full range of the keyboard. Thick textures, complex rhythmic treatment. D.
Toccata Op.62 1964 (Boelke-Bomart). Built on two contrasting 12-tone rows. Shows a wide range of imagination and strong craftsmanship. D.
See: Jan Maguire, "René Leibowitz (II): The Music," *Tempo* 132 (March 1980):2–10.

Kenneth Leighton (1929–1988) Great Britain
Leighton was an outstanding melodist who wrote in a freely tonal idiom. His style has its roots in Hindemith.
Sonata No.1 1950 (Lengnick) 35pp. 20 min. Four movements. Evocative Hindemith texture of harmony and polyphonic movement. Clever enharmonic modulations, vivid sense of color. M-D.
Sonatinas 1, 2 1946 (Lengnick) 10 min. each. Witty, appealing, MC. Int. to M-D.
5 Studies Op.22 1953 (Nov) 18 min. No.4 is a study in free declamatory style. All are freely tonal and brilliantly written. M-D.
Fantasia contrappuntistica Op.24 1958 (Ric) 12 min. "Homage to Bach." Toccata; Chorale; Fugue I and II. The four movements are linked by a motive heard in the opening section. Intervals of perfect and augmented fourths determine the melodic structure throughout and form the basis of the two fugues. Free; athletic linear movement of the music; deeply expressive. D.
Variations Op.36 1958 (Nov 1970). No.5 in Virtuoso Series. Nine variations. Straddles tonality and 12-tone writing, concludes with a fugue. Grateful writing, Lisztian piano style. Contains two pages of detailed commentary by the editor, John Ogdon. D.
Conflicts, Fantasy on Two Themes Op.51 1967 (Nov) 19 min. Variation principle subtly at work, passacaglia organization. Strongly contrasted moods. Virtuoso contemporary writing of the highest order.
Six Studies Op.56 (Nov 1971) 37pp. 18 min. These study variations are percussive and strongly dissonant and require a well-developed pianism. Expanded pitch phrases are tied to strong pedal points that create much tension. D.
Sonata Op.64 1972 (Nov). Compelling outer movements. "The heart of the work surely lies in the central 'chorale with contrasts.' Its masterly exploitation of the piano's resonances arouses an almost mystical state of sonic intoxication in the listener; . . . the valedictory atmosphere of Venice is suggested by the deep chiming clusters and shimmering hazes through which the poignantly insistent melodic lines wind in solitude" (Andrew Thomson, MT, 134/1804 [June 1993]:350).
Household Pets Op.86 (Nov 1983) 15 min. Cat's Lament; Jolly Dog; Goldfish; White Rabbit; Bird in Cage; Squeaky Guinea-Pig; Animal Heaven: "Here

they are. The soft eyes open." Programmatic, musical, and clever. Make a fine suite. Leighton concentrates on rhythmic patterns, keeps the textures thin, and imbues the music with a feeling of pity for the plight of animals subjected to the horrors of domesticity. Quotation from Blake for No.5 reads: "A Robin Red breast in a Cage Puts all Heaven in a Rage." Int. to M-D.

Guillaume Lekeu (1870–1894) Belgium

Lekeu studied with both Franck and d'Indy in Paris.

Sonate g (Lerolle 1891) 19pp. Five movements. More like a suite than a sonata. Fugal writing is supremely beautiful. Wagnerian harmonies. D.

See: O. G. Sonneck, "Guillaume Lekeu (1870–1894)," MQ, 5 (January 1919):109–47. Reprinted in *Miscellaneous Studies in the History of Music* (New York: Macmillan, 1921), pp. 190–240.

Alfonso Leng (1884–1974) Chile

Sonata 1951 (PAU) 17pp. Allegro con brio: militant. Andante: expressive. Allegretto: animated, energetic. No key signatures, chromatic, tonal centers vague. Well written; one of the finest works in Chilean piano literature. Large span required. MC. M-D.

4 Doloras 1916 (Instituto de Extension Musicale; IU). Doloras is derived from the Spanish word "dolor," meaning pain. Each of the pieces is reflective or somber in mood. Post-Romantic style similar to Scriabin *Preludes* Op.11. M-D.

John Lennon (1940–1980) Great Britain

Death Angel (Metamorphosis) (CUMP 1983) 19pp. No bar lines, complex rhythms, many tempo and texture changes, numerous performance directions, metronome indications. Static, dreamlike quality. Passes through various moods in linear style. Avant-garde. D.

Jacques Lenot (1945–   ) France

Sonata II 1978 (Sal) 18 min. Quiet and very fast; Very slow; Whimsical. Virtuosic writing requiring advanced pianism. D.

Sonata III 1979 (Sal) 20 min. One movement. Strength, speed, and flexibility alternate. D.

Leonardo Leo (1694–1744) Italy

Although mainly known for his sacred music and comic operas, Leo did write *13 Toccate per cembalo.* Some of them have been published as sonatas but Leo did not use this term.

Six Toccatas for Cembalo (M. Maffioletta—Carisch). Close to Scarlatti sonatas in style but easier. Fingered, editorial dynamic suggestions. Some errors in printing. M-D.

See: Anthologies and Collections, General, *Early Classics for the Piano* (Miro-vitch—GS) and Italian, *Clavicembalisti Italiani* (Montani—Ric).

Tania Leon (1944–   ) USA, born Cuba
Conductor and composer Leon is associated with the Dance Theater of Harlem and the Brooklyn Philharmonic. She is also composer-in-residence with the New York Philharmonic.
Ritual (PIC). Freely tonal, strong rhythms, exploits keyboard resources. M-D to D.

Theodore Leschetizky (1830–1915) Poland
Leschetizky's works for the piano were of the salon type, clearly reflecting the spirit of the time. The pieces listed below afford interesting material for all pianists.
Deux Alouettes ("Two Larks") Op.2 (GS; Cen). M-D.
Two Mazurkas Op.8 (Leuckart) 1. D♭, 2. f. M-D.
Andante Finale de "Lucia di Lammermoor" Op.13 (GS; Cen). For left hand alone. M-D.
Mazurka Op.24/2 (Cen). Int. to M-D.
4 Morceaux Op.36 (Rahter). Aria; Gigue (canon à deux voix); Humoresque; "La Source" etude. M-D.
Valse-Caprice Op.37 (Rahter). M-D.
Souvenirs d'Italie Op.39 (Bo&Bo). Barcarola (Venezia): 4. Mandolinata (Roma). 5. Tarantella (Napoli). M-D.
La Piccola Op.43/2. In KC, 13/5 (September–October 1993):18–24, with a master class on the piece by David Bradshaw:62–63.
Intermezzo in Octaves Op.44/4 (GS). A delicious musical study. M-D.
Two Arabesques Op.45 Arabesque en forme d'un etude (GS; Cen). À la taren-telle (Bo&Bo). M-D.
Trois Morceaux Op.48 (Bo&Bo). Prélude humoresque. Intermezzo scherzando. Etude Héroïque: a fine right-hand arpeggio study. M-D.
Deux Préludes Op.49 (Bo&Bo). Chant du soir-Prélude; Valse-Prélude. M-D.

John Lessard (1920–   ) USA
Lessard is a disciple of Igor Stravinsky. A French neoclassicism permeates much of his writing.
4 Preludes (ACA 1954). Contrasted ideas. Effective ostinato in No.3. M-D.
Perpetual Motion (Gen). Dissonant study in toccata style. M-D.
Toccata (Gen 1959) 20pp. Four movements. Moderato; Adagio; Allegro vivace; Adagio-Presto. For harpsichord or piano, more effective on harpsichord. Dramatic, tonal, MC. D.
Little Concert Suite (Gen 1964). Prelude; Dance; Lullaby; March; Pastoral; Proces-sion. Short, tonal, thin textures, contrasted movements and thematics. Int.
Mask (TP 1947) 6pp. Brisk; dissonant; dancelike; octaves and skips. M-D.

New Worlds for the Young Pianist (Gen 1966) Vol.I: 24 pieces, is "likened to the exploration of the new worlds still to be found in our old world." Vol.II: 16 pieces, is "a modest attempt at seeking out the planets" (from the score). MC sounds and idioms. Easy to Int.

Jean Yves Daniel Lesur (1908–1996) France
Lesur was a member of the group "Le Jeune France." His refined style is infused with lyrical and poetic qualities.
Suite Française (Amphion 1934–35). Divertissement; Menuet; Catilène et ronde pastorale. Pleasant, colorful writing, reflects influence of old French dance movements. M-D.
Les Carillons (Sal 1930). Experimentation in sonorities. M-D.
Trois Etudes (Durand). Hands crossing study; Sonorities study; Tremolando study. M-D.
Pastorale variée (Durand 1947). Eight variations on a whimsical theme. Final variation contains some choice writing. M-D.
Nocturne (Rongwen 1952). Romantic sounds. M-D.
Le Bal (EMT 1954) 18 min. A suite in seven movements: Préambule; Moment Musical; Valse; Mirages; Les Frénétiques; Idylle; Epilogue. Lyric and poetic qualities, sweeping gestures. Pianistic requirements vary; movements 1, 5, and 7 are the most demanding. M-D.

Alfonso Letelier (1912–   ) Chile
Letelier's style is clearly grounded in late Romanticism, with occasional hints at Impressionistic harmonies.
Variaciones en Fa 1948 (Bo&H). Romantic theme, ten variations, and a Finale. Similar to a Baroque suite of dances, each based on a common theme. Variations 6 and 7 especially resemble a neo-Baroque minuet and gavotte. Florid contrapuntal textures and spinning-out techniques of development. M-D.

Mischa Levitzki (1898–1941) USA, born Russia
Levitzki was an elegant, finished virtuoso; he was one of the world's leading pianists.
Valse de Concert Op.1 (Musica Obscura) 11pp. Sectionalized, brilliant, virtuosic, *ffff* ending. Requires large hand span. D.
Valse Op.2 (Musica Obscura) 4pp. Probably Levitzki's best-known piece. He often played it as an encore. Charming salon style, slithering chromaticism. M-D.
Gavotte Op.3 (Musica Obscura) 3pp. Part 2 is in the parallel minor; part 3 is a return of part 1, with thicker harmonies. Graceful. Int.
Arabesque Valsante Op.6 (Musica Obscura) 6 pp. Languishing, nostalgic, numerous chromatic inner voices, clever salon style. M-D.
The Enchanted Nymph 1927 (Musica Obscura) 8pp. Expressive melodic writing, graceful waltz mid-section. Opening section returns in a different key and with flowing accompaniment, but with same melody as in the beginning. M-D.

Valse Tzigane (SP). Exhibits Levitzki's Slavic temperament in high flair. M-D.

Burt Levy (1936–   ) USA
Six Moments (Smith Publications 1976) 8 min. Short character pieces, expressionistic, pointillistic. M-D.

Peter Tod Lewis (1932–   ) USA
Sweets for Piano (TP 1965). Ten short pieces, freely 12-tone, strong on color and dynamic contrasts, pointillistic textures. Various sized noteheads used to indicate dynamic range. Some serial technique (in No.3), same material used in outer movements. Metronome required for Sweet 3. Harmonics, clusters. M-D.

Robert Hall Lewis (1926–   ) USA
Serenades 1970 (CFP 66717 1983) 18pp. 10 min. Largo con tenerezza; Cantando molto; Poco allegro. White and black key clusters, pointillistic, expressionistic, abstract style, disjunct lines, absence of pulse, transparent textures, fermatas and long decays, nuances explored within quietest dynamics. Requires large span. D.

Bernhard Lewkovitch (1927–   ) Denmark
Lewkovitch's writing displays great delicacy, refinement, depth of feeling, and architectural strength.
Sonata Op.2 1949 (WH). First movement: energetic. Andante espressivo: lyrical. Finale: quasi-toccata, brilliant. M-D.
Sonata No.3 Op.4 1950 (WH) 19pp. One movement with three divisions. Outside divisions vigorous while the middle part is lyric and expressive. Strong polychordal approach. M-D to D.
Sonata No.4 Op.5 1954 (WH). First and third movements encompass an extended scherzo. Finely crafted. M-D.
Dance Suite Op.16 (WH 1956) 15pp. Introduction; Dance Song about a Bird's Wedding; Quiet Melody in the Field; Gopak; Cradle-song; Singing Game. MC. M-D.
Dance Suite No.2 Op.17 (WH 1960). Originally for orchestra, arranged by composer for piano. Influenced by N. V. Bentzon and Prokofieff. MC. M-D.

Salvador Ley (1907–1985) Guatemala
Danza Exótica (PIC 1959) 6 min. Concert piece written in a virtuoso style, energetic drive. M-D.
Danza Fantástica (EBM 1950) 3 min. Both pieces show black influence. M-D.

Anatol Liadoff (Liadov) (1855–1914) Russia
Liadoff's works range from single pedagogic pieces to extended compositions. They are written in a delicate, graceful style with Chopin influence, yet they retain a distinctive Russian character.

Biroulki (Children's Games) Op.2 (MMP). 14 short pieces carefully worked out. Int.

Ballad from Days of Old Op.21 1889 (Belaiev). Contains characteristics of Russian folk music. M-D.

La tabalière à musique (Musical Snuff-Box) Op.32 (GS; CF; Belaieff). Also in collection *Masters of Russian Piano Music* (Alfred 207). Imitates a music box by delicate tinkling in the upper register. Still fresh and attractive. Int.

Variations on a Theme of Glinka Op.35 (Beliaeff; MCA). 12 variations. Some virtuosic writing. M-D to D.

Etude Op.37 (Belaieff). Five sixteenth notes in right hand against two eighths in left hand. Inner melody. M-D.

Barcarolle Op.44 (Siloti—CF 1361) 7pp. F♯, rocking melody in thirds and sixths over arpeggio accompaniment. Mid-section in D. Concludes with melody in left hand. Lovely and expressive. M-D.

Preludes, Trifles and Other Pieces (ABRSM). Delightful miniatures; excellent for students to use after Tchaikovsky's *Album for the Young* but before they are ready for Rachmaninoff. Int. to M-D.

Liadov Album (G. Kováts—EMB Z.13776 1990) 44pp. Preludio Op.3/1; Mazurkas Op.3/4, 5, 6; Arabesques Op.4/2, 3; Impromptu Op.6; Valse Op.9/1; Mazurka Op.10/3; Etude Op.12; Petite valse Op.26; Une tabatière à musique Op.32. Chopin and Liszt influence present. Int. to M-D.

Piano Works (Y. Sasaki—Zen-On 1988) 97pp. Bagatelles Op.53/2, 3; Etudes Opp.37, 40/1; Preludes Opp.57/1, 40/2, 39/4; Mazurkas Opp.57/3, 42/3 (Mazurka on Polish Themes); Mazurka Op.11/3; The Musical Snuff-Box Op.32; Barcarolle Op.44; Variations on a Theme by Glinka Op.35; Variations on a Polish Song Op.51; Fugues Op.41/1, 2; Kanon Op.34/2. A superb collection. Opp.35 and 51 are among Liadov's finest compositions. All the others have much to recommend them. Int. to M-D.

30 Selected Pieces (C. Hellmundt—CFP 9193). Prefatory notes by the editor in German and English. Contains: Op.2/1, 2, 5, 6, 8; Op.3/4; Op.4/4; Op.7/2; Op.10/2; Op.11/1, 2; Op.15/2; Op.17/1, 2; Op.21; Op.26; Op.27/1; Op.31/2; Op.32; Op.40/1, 3; Op.44; Op.46/4; Op.57/1–3; Op.64/1–4. These pieces demonstrate nationalistic influence mixed with characteristics of Brahms, Chopin, Schumann, and Scriabin. Technically demanding. M-D.

Sergei Liapunoff (1859–1924) Russia

Liapunoff's style combines elements of folk music with the more traditional European training of his early studies. Liapunoff was also trained as a concert pianist and came under the influence of Liszt, to whom he dedicated his *Studies* Op.11. This influence is reflected in most of his piano works.

Etudes d'exécution transcendante Op.11 1897–1905 (Zimmermann). Vol.I: Berceuse. Ronde des fantômes. Carillon: has bell effects, sonorous, atmospheric. Vol.II: Terek. Nuit d'été. Tempête: influenced by Liszt's tenth etude. Vol.III: Idylle. Chant épique. Harpes éoliennes: exploits tremolando passages. Vol.IV:

Lesghinka (available separately EBM); Rondes des sylphes; Elégie en mémoire de Franz Liszt. Lesghinka is the finest of the set. It is based on folk material, is modeled on Balakirev's *Islamey*, and contains bravura writing throughout. D.

Sonata f Op.27 1906–1908 (Zimmermann). An intense and telling large one-movement work with a real scenario and apotheosis. Strong Liszt influence, cyclic construction. D.

Christmas Festivals Op.41 1910 (MMP). Christmas Night: first motive suggests quietness and wonderment; second motive suggests tinkling bells; third motive is a Russian church melody heard under quiet octave tremolo. Procession of the Magi: ostinato figure, Arab theme; final section has strong Liszt influence. Christmas Carolers: three motives, folklike melodies, rich harmony. Christmas Carol: two folk melodies alternated. An intimate work finely crafted. M-D.

See: Richard Davis, "Sergei Liapunoff (1859–1924): The Piano Works: A Short Appreciation," MR, 21 (August 1960):186–206. Contains a complete list of his piano works, with publishers.

David Kaiserman, "The Piano Works of S. M. Liapunov (1859–1924)," JALS, 3 (June 1978):25–26.

Heinrich Lichner (1829–1898) Germany

Lichner studied with Karov at Bunzlau, Dehen at Berlin, Mosewius and Adolf Hesse at Breslau. At Breslau he was cantor and organist of the Church of the Eleven Thousand Virgins and conductor of the Choral Society. He composed overtures, symphonies, songs, choruses for male voices, and much piano music.

Nine Sonatinas from Opp.4, 49, and 66 (GS; CF). Two- and three-movement works written in a pleasant nineteenth-century style; pianistic, scalar patterns, Alberti basses. Int.

Bunte Blumen (Colored Flowers) Op.111 (Schott 1680) 14pp. Short character pieces, chromatic. Int. to M-D.

Forget Me Not Op.160/6 (Zen-On 100) 4pp. Effective salon style. Int. to M-D.

Fantasie on Stille Nacht, heilige Nacht Op.269/3 (Schott 07149) 7pp. Five variations on this popular Christmas hymn with contrasting sections between them. M-D.

Pianoforte Album (Litoff 1558) 39pp. Salon Polka Op.101; Charakterstück Op.98; Mazurka Op.102; Idylle Op.97. Predictable salon writing with antiquarian charm. M-D.

Lowell Lieberman (1961–   ) USA

Piano Sonata I Op.1 1977 (TP) 11 min. An important first opus. Difficult but worth the effort.

Four Apparitions Op.17 1987 (TP). This set is prefaced by Walt Whitman's poem *Apparitions*: "A vague mist hanging 'round these pages: (Sometimes how strange and clear to the soul, that all these solid things are indeed but apparitions, concepts, non-realities.)" Starting with this as a commentary on the abstract, Liebermann has constructed these pieces, linking them with subtle rhythmic and motivic ideas. M-D.

Nocturne No. 2 Op.31 1990 (TP 1996) 7pp. 7 min. In memory of Steven De Groote. Intense, flowing lines, minor seconds used for color, dynamic extremes. M-D.

Nocturne No. 3 Op.35 1991 (TP 1994) 7pp. 6½ min. Unceasingly melodic, ranges from *fff* to *pppp*, arpeggiations with wave after gorgeous wave of sound, octotonic melody, repeated figures at quiet dynamic level. D.

Nocturne No. 4 Op.38 (TP) 6 min. MC, melodic. M-D.

Gargoyles Op.29 1989 (TP). Four contrasting movements requiring virtuosic technique. Highly effective. D.

Album for the Young Op.43 1993 (TP). A collection of 18 short one- and two-page vignettes. Arranged from easiest to more difficult. Int. to M-D.

Rolf Liebermann (1910–1999) Switzerland

Liebermann employs a variety of styles; tonal, polytonal, and atonal.

Sonata 1951 (UE) 19pp. 12 min. Four movements of masterly atonal and polytonal craftsmanship with some serial technique. This sonata was part of the opera *Leonora* (1940–45); it was played in Act 1, Scene 1 in which a piano recital takes place. The opera and the sonata share some of the same material. M-D to D.

Peter Lieberson (1946–   ) USA

Lieberson received degrees from New York University, Columbia University, and Brandeis University, where he received his doctorate. Influences of Brahms, Stravinsky, jazz, Broadway, and Buddhist philosophy are found in his music.

Breeze of Delight from *Fantasy Pieces* 1989. In collection *American Contemporary Masters* (GS 1995) 3pp. Shifting meters, freely tonal, opening right-hand figuration generates much of the piece. Large span required. M-D.

Memory's Luminous Wind from *Fantasy Pieces* 1989. In collection *American Contemporary Masters* (GS 1996) 2pp. First half is a chorale with contemporary harmonies, second half is a motet. Memoriam pieces for three named individuals. Large span required. M-D.

See: R. Dyer, "Peter Lieberson: A Composer Who Makes Music Talk," *Boston Globe* (April 17, 1983), A2.

Sharon Workman, "Travelling the Meditative Path," *The Globe and Mail* (April 14, 1997): A12–13.

Bertus van Lier (1906–1972) The Netherlands

Sonatine II 1930 (Donemus) 6½ min. Three movements. A pithy project that has the glow of important creativity. The middle movement is especially convincing, moving from *pp* to a violent *ff*, the latter section emphasized by chiseled use of diminished octaves and minor ninths. M-D.

György Ligeti (1923–   ) Austria, born Hungary
Influenced by Bartók and Kodály in his early works, Ligeti's style has been more adventurous since ca. 1957. He has experimented with slowly changing clusters, the "cloud" style, immobile drifts, mechanical processes, and tangled melody. His music exhibits highly controlled fantasy.

Musica ricercata 1951–53 (Schott 7718 1995) 37pp. ca. 23 min. Eleven varied pieces. No.9; Béla Bartók in memoriam. No.11: Omaggio a Giralamo Frescobaldi. Others not titled. Freely tonal, strong rhythms, post-Kodály style. M-D. to D.

Capriccio I 1947; Invention 1948; Capriccio II 1947 (Schott ED 7807 1991) 15pp., ca. 5 min. The capriccios are freely tonal with strong rhythms; the Invention is 12-tone and linear. Bartók-inspired. Written when Ligeti was studying at the Liszt Academy of Music in Budapest. Ideas in these pieces turn up in the later *Etudes*. M-D.

Passacaglia Ungherese 1978 (Schott). Form closely resembles the toccatas of Buxtehude. Theme is maintained throughout. Dramatic progression from large to small note values; some singable tunes. Properly for harpsichord but very effective on the piano. M-D.

Etudes for Piano (Schott 1988 facsimile ed.). Book I (1985). These may be the most important piano etudes written since Debussy's. Six richly varied pieces that explore compositional and pianistic techniques. They are almost impossible to play but enough pianists have mastered them for them to become a part of the standard repertoire. Polyrhythmic, simultaneous progressive layers of tempo. 1. Désordre (Disorder): bitonal, each hand assumes total rhythmic independence. 2. Cordes Vives (Open Strings): material mainly built on interval of the fifth. 3. Touches Bloquées (Blocked Keys): specific keys are depressed silently by one hand while the other hand plays chromatic figuration including some of the "blocked keys." 4. Fanfares: Latin American rhythms; requires total independence of hands and great rhythmic precision. 5. Arc-en-Ciel (Rainbow): delicate, lyrical, numerous expressive markings, almost tonal. 6. Automne à Varsovie (perhaps refers to the Warsaw Autumn Festival): chromatic melodic figuration supported by toccata-like sixteenths; enormous climax, then the piece simply collapses in a brusque and somewhat upsetting end. D.
See: Julian Jacobson, "György Ligeti: Etudes Pour Piano [premier livre]," *Piano Journal*, 9/25 (February 1988):11–12.

Etudes for Piano (Schott 1988–1993 facsimile ed.) Nos. 7, 8, and 9 issued together. 7. Galamb Borong. 6pp. To be played as legato as possible and vivacissimo luminoso. Each hand in different key; fast figuration with melody woven into the texture; careful pedal instructions. D. 8. Fem. 4pp. Very rhythmic and with an elastic swing; polyrhythmic, vigorous, gradually evolving chromatic figuration; concludes with slow chordal section. D. 9. Vertige. 6pp. Fast chromatic scales and figuration, no pedal is to be used; includes bar lines but sounds like there are none; melody evolves in outer voices, wide dynamic range *pppppppp* to *ffff*; evaporates to nothing. D. 10. Die Zauber-hehrling. 1994, 7pp. Prestissimo, staccatissimo, leggierissimo. No use of pedal until near the end, expanding diatonic then chromatic patterns, dynamic range *ppp* to *sfff*. D. 11. En Suspens. 1994. 4pp. Andante con moto (avec l'élégance du swing). Bitonal, graceful swinging chords, *ppp* glissandos (measured), dynamic range *ppp* to *mf*, melodic emphasis. D. 12. Entrelacs. 1993. 5pp. Vivacissimo molto ritmico. Melody and accompaniment in both hands, some parts bitonal, polyrhythmic, dynamic range is *pppp* to *fff*. D. 13. L'Escavlier du Diable. 1993. 7pp. Presto legato ma leggiero. *Mp* beginning, crescendos to *ffffff*; subito *p*; polyrhythmic, gonglike mid-section; polyrhythmic figuration and gonglike material used to the end. D. 14. Columna infinita. 1993. 6pp. Presto possible, tempestoso con fuoco. Chromatic figuration, polyrhythms; *fff* beginning leads to *ffffffff* conclusion "forza extreme al fine." D. Very few pianists in the world could play these etudes as indicated. Much similarity in the writing.

Dinu Lipatti (1917–1950) Rumania
Sonatine (Sal 1947). For left hand alone. Three movements in a clear neoclassic style. M-D.
Nocturne f♯ (Sal c. 1961) 3pp. Tonal, chromatic mid-section builds to climax, span of tenth required. M-D.
See: Walter Legge, "Dinu Lipatti," *The Liszt Society Journal*, 7 (Summer 1982): 45–48.

Franz Liszt (1811–1886) Hungary
Liszt was the quintessential modern of his time. As a performer, arranger, and general godfather, he nurtured the most progressive tendencies of his culture; as a composer, too, his music—both harmonically and structurally—was aggressively advanced, especially in his cryptic late works, which pushed well beyond the confines of traditional tonality. His music incorporated an attitude toward its basic materials that has become especially characteristic of the mid-twentieth century. The piano works of Liszt are an essential ingredient of the pianist's repertoire, and no pianist who desires to develop a complete equipment can ignore them. The complete gamut of pianistic resources is encountered in his works. "S" numbers refer to Humphrey Searle, *The Music of Liszt* (London: Williams & Norgate, 1954); 2d rev. ed. (New York: Dover, 1966). These numbers were adopted by *The New Grove Dictionary of Music and Musicians* (1980).

EDITIONS:

Collected Works (Gregg Press, reprint of Leipzig edition, 1901–36) 34 vols. bound as 33, including 12 vols. of piano works, all in Series II. The editors of this edition include Busoni, Bartók, Raabe, and da Motta. The final volume of the reprint edition incorporates a revised version by Humphrey Searle of his catalogue of Liszt's compositions and literary publications. The numbers in parentheses denote the series and volume numbers of the solo piano works in this edition: *Etudes* I, II, III (II/1, 2, 3); *Album d'un voyageur* (II/4); *Du temps de pèlerinage* (II/5); miscellaneous piano works I, II, III, IV (II/7, 8, 9, 10); *Hungarian Rhapsodies* (II/12).

New Edition of the Complete Works of Franz Liszt (Br and EMB through TP). Series I, Works for Piano Two Hands, 18 vols., edited by Zoltan Gardonyi and István Szelényi. Series II, Transcriptions and Arrangements of Original and Other Works for Piano Two Hands, projected to be about 6 vols. Hereafter referred to as NLE (New Liszt Edition).

Vol.I, *Studies I*: 12 Etudes d'exécution transcendante.

Vol.II, *Studies II*: 3 Etudes de Concert; Ab irato; 2 Concert Studies; 6 Grandes Etudes de Paganini.

Vol.III, *Hungarian Rhapsodies I*: 9 Hungarian Rhapsodies, including *Le Carnaval de Pesth*.

Vol.IV, *Hungarian Rhapsodies II*; 10 Hungarian Rhapsodies, including *Rákóczi-Marsch*.

Vol.V, *Piano Works*: Grosses Konzertsolo; Sonate; Fantasie und Fuge über das Theme B–A–C–H; Präludium und Fuge über das Motiv B–A–C–H.

Vol.VI, *Années de Pèlerinage I*: Première Année—Suiss; Appendix, including three pieces from *Impressions et poésies* and 9 pieces from *Fleurs mélodiques des Alpes*.

Vol.VII, *Années de Pèlerinage II*: Deuxième Année—Italie; Supplement of three pieces; Appendix of four pieces from *Venezia e Napoli* (1st version).

Vol.VIII, *Années de Pèlerinage III*: Troisième Année.

Available separately (BR and EMB, through TP): Après une Lecture de Dante; Au Bord d'une Source; Au Lac de Wallenstadt—Pastorale; Aux Cypres de la Ville d'Este I; Aux Cypres de la Ville d'Este II; Chapelle de Guillaume Tell; Chasse-neige; Les Cloches de Genève; Églogue—Le Mal du Pays; Eroica; 3 Études de Concert; Étude a; Étude f; Feux Follets; Grandes Études de Paganini; Harmonies du Soir; Les Jeux d'Eau à la Villa d'Este; Mazeppa; Orage; Il Penseroso—Canzonetta del Salvatore Rosa; Preludio—Paysage; Rhapsodies Hongroises I, II, III, IV, V, VII, X, XVI, XVII, XVIII, XIX (each individually); Ricordanza; Sposalizio; Sunt Lacrymae Rerum—Marche Funèbre; Tre Sonetti di Petrarca; Vallée d'Overmann; Venezia e Napoli; Vision; Wilde Jagd; Zwei Konzertetuden.

Vol.IX, *Various Cyclical Works I*: Huit Variations; Apparitions; Harmonies poétiques et religieuses; Consolations; Ballade I; Ballade II. Appendix: Harmonies poétiques et religieuses (first version); Invocation (first version); Hymne de la Nuit; Hymne du Matin; Klavierstück As-Dur No.2. Int. to D.

Vol.X, *Various Cyclical Works II*: Legendes; 5 Piano Pieces; Chorale; Historical Hungarian Portraits; Via Crucis; Legendes No.2 (simplified version); Elegies; Weihnachtsbaum. Int. to M-D.

Vol.XI, *Individual Character Pieces I*: Allegro di Bravura; Alleluja; Ave Maria (for the piano school of von Lenert and Stark); Berceuse (second version); Elegie on motives of Prince Louis Ferdinand of Prussia; Festvorspiel—Prelude; Piano Piece F♯; La Notte; Les morts; Romance; Rondo di bravura; Slavimo slavno slaveni!; 70 Bars on Themes from the First Beethoven Cantata. Int. to M-D.

Vol.XII, *Individual Character Pieces II*: Am Grabe Richard Wagners; Ave Maria (two versions); Carrousel de Madame P-N; Die Trauer-Gondel 1 and 2; En rêve; Epithalam; Impromptu; In festo transfigurationis Domini; Recueillement; Resignazione; Romanze oubliée; R.W.—Venezia; Sancta Dorothea; Schlaflos!; *Stabat mater*; Toccata; Trauervorspiel und Trauermarsch. Trübe Wolken; Unstern!; Un portrait en musique; *Urbi et orbi*; *Vexilla Regis prodeunt*; Wiegenlied. Int. to M-D.

Vol.XV, *Piano Versions of His Own Works I*: Am Rhein im schönen Strome; Angiolin dal biondo crin; Buch der Lieder für Piano allein; Der du von dem Himmel bist; Der König von Thule; Der Papst-Hymnus; Die Lorelei (first version); Die Lorelei (second version); Englein du mit blondem Haar; Es rufet Gott uns mahnend; Festmarsch nach Motiven von E. H. z. S. für das Pianoforte No.2; Geharnischte Lieder für das Pianoforte; Huldigungsmarsch; Ich liebe dich; Il m'aimait tant!; Inno del papa; Künstlerfestzug für das Pianoforte; Le roi de Thule; L'hymne du pape; Liebesträume; Marche héroïque pour piano; Mephisto-Walzer No.1; Mignons Lied; Nicht gezagt; Notturno No.1; Notturno No.2 (first version); Notturno No.2 (second version); Notturno No.3; Pastorale; Poésies; Vom Fels zum Meer!; Vor der Schlacht; Weihnachtslied; Weimars Volkslied No.1; Weimars Volkslied No.2. Int. to M-D.

Vol.XVI, *Piano Versions of His Own Works II*: Aus der Ungarischen Krönungsmesse; Ave Maris stella; Benedictus; Danse macabre; Die heiligen drei Könige; Drei Stücke aus der Legende der heiligen Elisabeth; Gaudeamus igitur (Humoreske); Gretchen; Hirtengesang an der Krippe; Interludium No.3; Le triomphe funèbre du Tasse; Marche hongroise (first version) No.2; Marsch der Kreuzritter No.2; Offertorium; Orchester Einleitung No.1; Szozat és Magyar Himnusz; Szozat und Ungarischer Hymnus; Totentanz; Ungarischer Marsch (zur Krönungsfeier am 8ten Juni 1867 in Ofen-Pest); Ungarischer Sturmmarsch (Neue Bearbeitung 1876); Ungarischer Sturmmarsch (first version); Zwei Orchestersätze aus dem Oratorium Christus. Each work is discussed in the Preface. Volumes XV and XVI contain some first printings and make a large number of works available that have been very difficult to come by. Int. to M-D.

Vol.XVII, *Piano Versions of His Own Works III*: A magyarok istene; A magyarok istene (transcription for left hand); A la tombe: berceau de la vie future; Cantico di San Francesco; Der blinde Sänger; Der Kampf um's Dasein; Deux polonaises (de l'oratorio St. Stanislas); Die Wiege; Die Zelle in Nonnenwerth (fourth version); Du berceau jusqu'à la tombe; Festpolonaise; Feuille d'album No.2; In domum Domini ibimus; Le berceau; Le combat pour la vie; Magyar király-dal; Mephisto-Walzer No.2; O Roma nobilis; San Francesco; Salve polonia; Ungarisches Königslied; Ungarns Gott;

Ungarns Gott (transcription for left hand); Von der Wiege bis zum Grabe; Zum Grabe: die Wiege des zukünftigen Lebens; Zum Haus des Herrn ziehen wir. Each work is discussed in the preface. Int. to M-D.
Vol.XVIII (Supplement). Étude Op.1 S.136, Étude en douze exercices. Magyar Dallok—Ungarische Nationalmelodien S.242, Nos.1, 2, 3, 8, 9, 10, 13, 15, 17, 20; S.243, Nos.1–3, easier version. Rákóczi-Marsch S.242, first version; easier version; popular edition; S.244/15,2, orchestral version arranged for piano, two hands; orchestral version in easier arrangement for piano. Comment, disaient-ils S.535. Enfant, si j'étais roi S.537. S'il est un charmant gazon S.538. La tombe et la rose S.539. Gastibelza S.540. Oh, quand je dors S.536. Also includes index of the New Liszt Edition, Series I, Vols.1–18. Many works are available separately from this edition.
Piano Works (Sauer—CFP) 12 vols. One of the most extensive accessible performing editions.
    Vol.I: *Hungarian Rhapsodies* Nos. 1–8.
    Vol.II: *Hungarian Rhapsodies* Nos. 9–15; *Spanish Rhapsody.*
    Vol.III: *12 Etudes d'exécution transcendante.*
    Vol.IV: *6 Paganini Etudes; 3 Concert Etudes; Waldesrauschen; Gnomenreigen.*
    Vol.V, *Original Compositions*, Vol.1: 2 Polonaises; 2 Ballades; Mephisto Waltz I; Valse-Impromptu; Première Valse oubliée; Grand Galop chromatique; Consolations, 2 Légendes.
    Vol.VI, *Original Compositions*, Vol.2: 3 Liebesträume; Harmonies poétiques (Bénédiction de Dieu dans la solitude; Funérailles; Cantique d'amour); Berceuse; Années de Pèlerinage, première année: Au Lac de Wallenstadt, Au bord d'une source; seconde année: Sonetto 47, 104, 123 del Petrarca; Venezia e Napoli: Gondoliera, Canzone, Tarantella; Sonata b.
    Vol.VII: *13 Transcriptions from Wagner Operas*: Rienzi; Tannhäuser (2); Lohengrin (4); Der Fliegende Holländer (2); Tristan und Isolde; Meistersinger; Ring des Nibelungen; Parsifal.
    Vol.VIII: *9 Transcriptions from various Operas*: Auber: La Muette de Portici; Bellini: Norma; Donizetti: Lucia di Lammermoor; Gounod: Faust; Mendelssohn: Midsummer Night's Dream; Mozart: Don Giovanni; Rossini: Stabat Mater; Verdi: Rigoletto, Trovatore.
    Vol.IX: *Song Transcriptions* of Schubert (19 Lieder); Schumann (2 Lieder); Beethoven (3 Lieder); Chopin; Lassen; Liszt; Mendelssohn.
    Vol.X: *Transcriptions*: Soirées de Vienne (Schubert); 6 Preludes and Fugues for organ (Bach); Variations on "Weinen, Klagen" (Bach); Fantasy and Fugue g for organ (Bach); La Regatta veneziana; La Danza (Rossini).
    Vol.XI: *Concerti* and other *Works with Orchestra.*
    Vol.XII: *Supplement*: Scherzo and March; Fantasy and Fugue on BACH; and transcriptions of Wagner, Tannhäuser-Ouverture; Meyerbeer, Prophet; Liszt, Faust-Symphonie; Schubert. 3 Marches.
Other editions: GS has most of the works in editions by Joseffy, Gallico, Hughes, Friedheim, Busoni, Deis, Pauer, and Fraemcke. The Br&H edition, well ed-

ited by Busoni, is no longer immediately available. Ric has a large selection, including all 20 *Rhapsodies* (19 Hungarian and one Spanish) and the 12 volumes of the *Technical Exercises* (Winterberger).

WORKS PUBLISHED SEPARATELY:

Album d'un Voyageur 1835–36 S.156. Some pieces in this early collection were reworked and finally appeared in the *Années de pèlerinage*. No.4 Les Cloches de G . . . (EMB 8542) 12pp. A great "bell piece" with an elegant barcarolle-like mid-section. M-D. No.7 Psaume (EMB 8543) 2pp. Inspired by Psalm 47, chorale-like. M-D.

Années de Pèlerinage. Three volumes of sensitive tone painting; prophetically utopian, kind of a musical scrapbook that reflect Liszt's years as a traveling virtuoso.

Vol.I S.160 Suisse 1835–52 (Herttrich—Henle 173). No.2, Au lac de Wallenstadt (At the lake of Wallenstadt): simple right-hand melody (later presented ingeniously in a rhythmic variation) over persistent accompanying figure. No.4, Au bord d'une source (At the spring) (Cortot—Sal; K; GS; Schott; EMB): ebullient and nostalgic with the melody cleverly distributed between the hands. No.5, Orage and no.6, Vallée d'Obermann (NLE, available separately). No.7, Eglogue (NLE; Ric): effective yet unpretentious. M-D to D.

See: Serge Gut, "Swiss Influences on the Compositions of Franz Liszt," JALS, 38 (July–December 1995):1–22.

Vol.II S.161 Italie 1838–49 (Herttrich—Henle 174). No.1, Sposalizio (Marriage) (NLE; GS): Raphael's painting *The Bethrothal of the Virgin Mary* inspired this piece; requires a fine left-hand octave technique. No.2, Il Penseroso (The Thinker): harmonically daring, solemn, marchlike. No.3, Canzonetta del Salvator Rosa (NLE): a vivacious march inspired by the verses printed with the tune. No.4, Sonetto 47 del Petrarca (Ric; NLE): cadenza in double notes, melodic material greatly syncopated. No.5, Sonetto 104 del Petrarca (Ric; GS; Schott; NLE): declamatory, agitated and emotional, contains some technical problems. No.6, Sonetto 123 del Petrarca (NLE; GS, includes the three poems illustrated in the Sonnets and their translations): lyric, melodious, imaginative, easier than Nos.4 and 5. No.7, Après une lecture de Dante (After reading Dante) (Cortot—Sal, available separately) subtitled "Fantasia quasi Sonata"; known as the "Dante Sonata"; three contrasting themes are developed in free rhapsodic style; many powerful octaves and repeated chords thicken the texture; shimmering treble tremolos depict Paradise.

See: Walter Robert, "Après une lecture de Dante," PQ, 89 (Spring 1975): 22–27.

David Yeagley, "Liszt's *Dante Sonata*: Origins and Criticism," JALS, 37 (January–June 1995):1–12.

Venezia e Napoli, supplement to Vol.II (Ric; Schott; EMB; NLE; Cortot—Sal). Gondoliera (Sal): simple tune treated in various fashions. Canzone: short Lento doloroso with a rhetorical cantilena leads to Tarantella (Sal): brilliant and full of display, many repeated notes, virtuosic chord passages; an elaborate fantasy in which the spirit of the tarantella is dissected and put back together in a variety of moods. M-D to D.

See: Joseph Banowetz, "A Liszt Sonetto: Sonnet 47 of Petrarch," *Clavier.* 17 (March 1978):12–21, including the music.

Ralph Neiweem and Claire Aebersold, "Liszt's Italian Years," *Clavier* 23/3 (March 1984):22–27.

Walter Schenkman, "The Venezia e Napoli Tarantella: Genesis and Metamorphosis," I: JALS, 4 (December 1979):10–24; II: JALS, 7 (June 1980):42–58; II: JALS, 7 (June 1980):35–41.

Sharon Winklhofer, "Liszt, Marie d'Agoult and the 'Dante' Sonata," *Nineteenth-Century Music,* 1 (July 1977).

Vol.III S.163 1867–77 (Herttrich—Henle 175). This volume is different in content and style from Vols.I and II. The pieces no longer cover travel impressions but serve as a means of expressing a religious pilgrimage. Nos.2 and 3, both entitled Aux cyprès de la Villa d'Este (NLE): two different musical paintings inspired by the cypresses at the villa where Liszt spent a part of each year when he was in Rome. No.4, Les Jeux d'eaux a la Villa d'Este (The Fountains at the Villa d'Este) (NLE; Ric; GS; Schott; Sal; CFP; CF; EMB): an important forerunner of Ravel's *Jeux d'eaux.* No.5, Sunt lacrymae rerum (NLE; EMB): in Hungarian modal style, contains some of the blackest sounds in the lowest register of the keyboard ever heard; no one was exploiting this register at this time as Liszt did. No.6, Marche funèbre: written in memory of Emperor Maximilian of Mexico, who died on June 19, 1867; octaves, left-hand tremolo, brilliant closing in F♯. No.7, Sursum corda (Lift Up Your Hearts): ringing bass pedal point supports tremendous sonorities to bring the set to a mighty climax. M-D.

Harmonies poétiques et religieuses S.173 1845–52 (K). Ten pieces inspired by a set of poems by Alphonse de Lamartine. Invocation: a pleading restless desire for the comforting presence of God. Ave Maria. Bénédiction de Dieu dans la solitude (God's benediction in the solitude) (Cortot—Sal): one of the most beautiful of Liszt's works. Pensée des morts (Thoughts of death). Pater Noster. Hymne de l'enfant a son réveil. Funérailles (Sal; Ric; EMB; K; Schott): somber and epic, a heroic lament for those killed in the 1848–49 Hungarian Revolution; harmonic clashes, stark fanfares, and the savage abruptness of the close are quintessential Liszt. Requires mature octave technique. Miserere d'après Palestrina. Andante lagrimoso. Cantique d'amour (GS). Int. to M-D.

See: Joan Backus, "Liszt's 'Harmonies poetiques et religieuses': Inspiration and the Challenge of Form." JALS, 21 (January–June 1987):3–21.

F. E. Kirby, "Liszt's Pilgrimage," PQ, 89 (Spring 1975):17–21.

Joan M. Pursewell, "The Travel Music of Franz Liszt," AMT, 32/3, (January 1983):30, 32, 34. Discusses the *Album d'un Voyager* and all three volumes of *Années de Pèlerinages*.

6 Consolations 1849–50 S.172 (Alfred; Henle; GS; K; Schott; UE; CFP; Sal; Durand; EMB; Br&H; S&B). E: 25 bars, chordal, legato, serves as an introduction to No.2. E: similar melodic features as No.1 but now the melody is divided between the hands. D♭: right-hand melody over a broken-chord accompanying left-hand figure; like a simpler Chopin nocturne. D♭: slow flowing theme with supporting chords, later dialogues between middle and low octaves of the keyboard. E: continuous melody with flowing accompaniment; texture remains constant. E: a fine pedal and touch study. Int. to M-D. See: John Diercks, "The Consolations: 'delightful things hidden away,'" JALS, 3 (June 1978):19–24.

Elizabeth Hobbs, "Some Points on Teaching the Liszt Consolations," *Quarterly Magazine* (February 1994):7–10; (May 1994):4–10.

Liebesträume (Dreams of Love) 1850 S.541 (CFP; Br&H; K; Schott; S&B; GS; WH; Ric; Sal). A♭ (K; UE): right-hand accompanied trills present a problem. E (K; UE; Willis): needs a broad singing quality, diversified accompaniment. A♭ (Alfred; K; UE; EMB; Schott): ingenious cadenzas are an extension of Chopin's ornamentation. M-D.

12 Etudes d'exécution transcendante 1851 S.139 (CFP; Br&H; Ric; K; EC; Sal; Durand). 1. Preludio: opening flourish, Cramer-like sequences. 2. [no title], in a (Br&H): fast chords and double notes require fleet fingers. 3. Paysage (Landscape) (NLE; Br&H): lyric and expressive, requires careful balancing and gradation of tone. 4. Mazeppa (NLE; Ric): fast and brilliant toccata chord-study suggested by the famous cossack's ride. 5. Feux follets (Will o' the wisp) (NLE): first 40 bars contain the greatest problem with double-note passages; must be light and delicate, like fireflies. 6. Vision (NLE): powerful chords tucked in sweeping arpeggios, double-note tremolos, crescendos add to the climax. 7. Eroica (NLE; Ric): bombastic, wide range of dynamics, less interesting material. 8. Wilde Jagd (Wild Chase) (NLE): taxing chord etude, requires great endurance. 9. Ricordance (Remembrance) (NLE): beautifully exploits the different registers of the keyboard, somewhat sentimental. 10. [no title] in f (NLE): on same level as No.5 as regards musical quality; persistent broken left-hand chord figures must be controlled evenly. 11. Harmonies du soir (Evening harmonies) (NLE): power required at climax; hand and weight control essential. 12. Chasse-neige (Snow plough) (NLE: Br&H): melody with rapid tremolo accompaniment in same hand; demands much physical endurance. These pieces might better have been named ballades or poems, since most of them are programmatic. D.

See: Joseph Banowetz, "Liszt Etudes d'exécution transcendante," AMT, 20 (January 1971):18–19, 38.

Alan Walker, "Liszt and the Keyboard," MT, 1615 (September 1977):717, 719–21. Deals mainly with the *Transcendental Etudes*.

12 Etudes Op.1 1826 S.136 (Hin, in 2 vols.; EC; Zen-On; EMB; Hofmeister). First
version of the *Transcendental Etudes*, numerical order corresponds to that
of the later set. No.4 is in collection *At the Piano With Liszt* (Alfred 2416).
In Nos.4 and 5 one can clearly see the themes and motives of "Mazeppa"
and "Feux follets." Int. to M-D.

Variation on a Waltz by A. Diabelli 1822 S.147 (Musica Obscura) 2pp. Mainly broken chords and arpeggios, hand-crossings. What a serious c-minor torrent
the ten-year-old Liszt lets loose on Diabelli's rollicking tune! Int.

Six Paganini Etudes 1851 S.141 (NLE; Sal; Br&H; CFP; Ric; K; GS; Durand). 1.:
an exacting study in playing melody and accompaniment (rapid tremolo)
with same hand. 2.: chromatic sixths for alternating hands; chromatic
scales in tenths for crossed hands; at the climax Liszt uses his "false octaves" with diabolical effect. 3.: La Campanella (Br&H; K; Schott; EMB;
Ric; WH): the most famous of the set; chiming chord effects, dazzling technical effects in upper register of keyboard, difficult repeated notes. 4.: imitation of a violinist's arpeggio staccato etude with passages conveniently
tossed between the hands. 5.: La Chasse (Ric, first and second versions):
horn effects in the main theme; divide the glissandos in the a section between the hands; the easiest of the set; compare with Schumann's version
in his Op.3. 6.: variations on the famous theme used by Brahms and Rachmaninoff; the most musical of the set. M-D to D.
See: Barbara Nissman, "Masterclass: Liszt's Paganini Etude No.4," KC
(May 1994):8.

Three Concert Etudes 1848 S.144 (NLE; Sal; Ric; K; Schott). 1. Ab, Il lamento:
repetitious, lyric melody with varied accompaniment. 2. f, La leggierezza
(GS): opening section displays a Chopinesque theme treated to graceful
arabesques, varied in repeats; rising and falling chromatic scales; chromatic
thirds at central climax; more delicate than powerful. 3. Db, Un sospiro
(CF; GS; Schott; Br&H; WH; Dob): broad pentatonic melody shared between hands, rolling arpeggios; main problem is maintaining evenness
when the left hand crosses over and back. M-D to D.

Two Concert Etudes 1862–63 S.145 (NLE; Henle; CFP; Schott; Ric; Sal; EMB;
Durand). 1. Waldesrauschen (Forest murmurs) (K): suave melody accom-
panied by rotational figures; later the right and left hands proceed in double
counterpoint; smashing climax. 2. Gnomenreigen (Dance of the Gnomes)
(Br&H): Puckish staccato theme alternates with a wild and whirling idea;
powerful climax then sneaks to a close. M-D to D.
See: Tedd Joselson, "Masterclass: Liszt's *Waldesrauchen* Etude," CK, 6
(July 1980):70.

Ab Irato 1852 S.143 (NLE). Written for Fétis's "Méthode des méthodes." A work
of great beauty, somehow neglected. Rugged conception. Concludes with
two pages of quiet loveliness. M-D.

Grosses Konzertsolo ca. 1849 S.176 (NLE Vol.5) 22½ min. Written for a piano
competition at the Paris Conservatory. Dedicated to Adolf Henselt, and
that alerts us to the virtuoso caliber of the work. In 1866 a two-piano

version by Liszt was published under the title *Concerto Pathétique*. The *Grosses Konzertsolo* is an integrated one-movement form that Liszt pioneered, using transformation of themes. The initial theme is characterized by the rise of a half step followed by the drop of an octave. It is worked up to a climax before the introduction of a lyrical theme *patetico, accentato assai il canto*, which also is characterized by a half-step interval at its opening. Other themes are introduced, and the remainder of the work presents development, combination, and recapitulation of these elements. D.

Sonata b 1852–53. S.178 (Henle; CFP; Sal; Ric; GS; Durand; K; EMB). (The Henle edition must be singled out as a magnificent facsimile in five colors that shows connected shorter passages and crossed-out sections followed by numerous pages with extensive revisions. Claudio Arrau adds "Some Final Thoughts" to this unusual edition.) Henle also has a study edition (9273). In a single span, Liszt enclosed the musical regions that previous composers had confined to separate movements, unifying this massive structure by concentrating on a small number of characteristic themes which are constantly transformed. Of special interest is the conclusion of the work: the original imposing conclusion of 25 bars rising to *fff* was replaced by an ending 32 bars longer, which gradually fades away to *ppp*. Technical demands are heavy—brilliant finger technique, glittering octaves at fast speed, accurate articulation in the fugato, rich tone in the soaring melodies, superb chord playing. D.

    See: Ray Longyear, "The Text of Liszt's B Minor Sonata," MQ, 60 (July 1974):435–50.

    ———, "Liszt's B Minor Sonata—Precedents for a Structural Analysis," MR, 34 (August 1973):198–209.

    Wadham Suttom, "Liszt: Piano Sonata in B Minor," *Music Teacher*, 52 (September 1973):16–17.

    Tibor Szasz, "Liszt's Symbols for the Divine and Diabolical: Their Revelation of a Program in the B Minor Sonata," JALS 15 (June 1984):39–95.

    Mikhail Voskressensky, Liszt's B Minor Sonata," MTA of New South Wales (November 1991):11–15. A master lesson on the work.

Two Legends 1863 S.175 (K; Ric; Sal; UE; GS; Schott; Durand; CFP). St. Francis preaching to the Birds (K; Heugel; Durand): combines melody with trills in same hand; delicate finger technique indispensable. St. Francis Walking on the Waves (NLE; K; EMB): broken octaves in left hand need much endurance, direct imitation of the rolling waves. Requires a fine bravura technique. Both are true program music. M-D to D.

Hungarian Rhapsodies S.244 (Dover, Nos.1–19; Ric, Nos.1–19 and *Spanish Rhapsody*, 2 vols.; NLE, Nos.1–19, 2 vols.; Durand, Nos.1–19, 5 vols.; CFP, Nos.1–15 and *Spanish Rhapsody*, 2 vols.; K, Nos.1–19, 2 vols.)

    Available separately: Nos. 2, 6, 9, 10, 11, 12, 13 (Sal). Nos. 2, 6, 9, 12, 13, 14, 15, 19, *Spanish Rhapsody* (EC). Nos. 6, 8, 9, 11, 12, 13, 14, 15, 16, 19 (NLE). Nos. 1, 2, 5, 6, 14, 15 (Schott). No.2 (CFP; WH).

    These pieces need no apology; they still provide dazzling pianistic brilliance and have much to recommend them. Their popularity seems to be returning in the last few years, as they are beginning to be programmed again.

Hungarian Rhapsody No.2. Familiar and effective, much use of alternating tonic and dominant harmony, strong suggestion of the circus. Good wrists and forearm rotation necessary. See especially the cadenza by Rachmaninoff (Mer). M-D.

Hungarian Rhapsody No.3. Uses the gypsy scale (using two augmented seconds). Short-long rhythmic treatment comes directly from the Hungarian language, large doses of rhapsodic improvisation. The shortest of the Rhapsodies. Int. to M-D.

See: Joseph Banowetz, "Master Lessons on a Liszt Hungarian Rhapsody," *Clavier*, 12 (March 1973):25–32. Includes score as edited by Banowetz.

Hungarian Rhapsody No.6. Opening declamatory sections are fascinating. The brilliant conclusion with octave passages in both hands requires endurance. M-D to D.

Hungarian Rhapsody No.11. Delicate and brilliant finger passages. Closing prestissimo is greatly effective without being too difficult. Shorter than most of the other Rhapsodies. M-D.

Hungarian Rhapsody No.12. High drama alternates with a relaxed charm, and the music's mercurial changes of mood and dress are accentuated by vivid contrasts of register, texture, and rhythm. Contains some tricky passages in two-note double-third slurs; needs plenty of power for the coda. M-D to D.

Hungarian Rhapsody No.13. One of the most musically valuable of the set. The opening Andante sostenuto is filled with great emotion, and the fast repeated notes of the concluding Vivace are strikingly effective. M-D.

Hungarian Rhapsody No.19. After a brilliant introduction the Rhapsody begins in true czárdás fashion, with a restrained, nobly paced section compounded of gypsy turns of phrase and unusual harmonies. Soon the lively *Friss* theme enters in bass octaves. From here to the end there is one exhilarating flight of virtuosity after another, building to a stupendous climax. M-D to D.

Spanish Rhapsody 1863 S.254 (CFP; Paragon; MMP). Free variations on two Spanish themes—*La Folia* in the first part and the *Jota Aragonesa* in the second, thus providing a brilliant contrast. The tunes are transformed to extraordinary effect. Opens with one of Liszt's finest cadenzas, using "blind" octaves. M-D to D.

Rumanian Rhapsody (Busoni—UE 10823) 31pp. Arranged, edited, and published by Busoni as the *Hungarian Rhapsody* No.20. Has all the tuneful verve and exotic moodiness of the most popular rhapsodies. "Bartókian element" can be detected in the oriental-sounding main section. M-D.

See: Alfred Brendel, *Musical Thoughts and Afterthoughts* (Princeton: Princeton University Press, 1976), pp.84–87. Offers penetrating insights on the Hungarian Rhapsodies.

Ballade No.1 D♭ 1845–48 S.170 (CFP; Schott; Ric; Henle has both Ballades 490).

A sweeping D♭ *con amore* melody, richly endowed almost from the opening, is prominent. It is relieved by the second, marchlike theme (in A), which is repeated in grand style in F. The D♭ theme reappears in bravura form, and the second closes in D♭. Brilliant, yet expressive and melodious. M-D to D.

Ballade No.2 b 1853 S.171 (Sal; CFP). Written in the grand manner, dramatic, with many passages of great beauty; needs imaginative and rhetorical treatment. Requires a technique that can handle broken and interlocking octaves and pedaling that can sustain chords while the accompaniment moves over the keyboard. M-D to D.

Polonaise No.1 c 1851 S.223/1 (Ric; Sal; Durand). Introspective, pessimistic mood; muttering sonorities in the bass are answered in the upper register. Sounds almost like an altercation, but a soothing *amorosamente* section in E♭ brings relief. Becomes attractive and finishes with strength. M-D to D.

Polonaise No.2 E 1851 S.223/2 (Ric; Durand; Sal; Schott). No.2 is the better known of the two Polonaises. Full of splendor and knightly pageantry, it shows Liszt at his greatest pianistic expertise. The opening sections have no great difficulties but the variation of the main idea near the end, with its delicate figures in the upper register, requires fleet fingers. M-D to D.

Mephisto Waltz No.1 1860 S.110 (CFP; Ric; Sal; GS; K; EMB; Schott; Durand). A virtuoso's delight, this picturesque music is one of the most effective of Liszt's compositions. Middle episode contains soaring melodies and rubato. Calls for a wide range of technical resources, including strong fingers, untiring broken octaves, granitic chord playing, accurate large skips. D.

Mephisto Waltz No.2 1881 S.111 (Fürstner). Less famous than No.1; at times more savage than No.1 but an equally powerful and disturbing work. Makes wide use of the tritone B–F. D.

Mephisto Waltz No.3 1883 S.216 Liszt Society Publications, Vol.1 (Schott). Carries even further the mood of cruelty, violence, and anger found in the first two *Mephisto Waltzes*, as Liszt seems progressively to suppress and erase lingering traces of erotic tenderness. The savage opening fanfare sets the mood for the entire work. As in No.1, the song of the nightingale is heard only once, immediately preceding the explosive outburst of the final page. D.

Mephisto Waltz No.4 1885 S.696 Liszt Society Publications, Vol.2 (Schott). Also in collection *The Final Years* (GS). Liszt never prepared this work for publication. Though it is complete in the sense that it is possible to play it through from beginning to end, there is a point marked with an asterisk and a note in the MS "about 60 bars Andantino," which Liszt evidently intended to insert at this point. Three pages of sketches, presumably for this passage, have been preserved and are included in this edition. Even in its embryonic state, this work has striking moments that have the glint of fire and diablerie so abundant in its three predecessors. M-D.

Apparitions 1834 S.155 (Nos.1, 2, 3 in Collected Edition II/5 Br&H; Nos. 1, 2 in Liszt Society Publications, Vol.2). The title of these pieces was suggested by a set of visionary songs, called *Auditions*, by Christian Urhan, a violinist of German origin with whom Liszt frequently played in Paris at this time. *Apparition* No.3 is a fantasy on a waltz by Schubert; it was later transformed into the fourth of the *Soirées de Vienne*. The writing in these pieces fully captures the warmth of the early Romantic movement. Nos.1 and 2 especially foreshadow the Italian *bel canto* style, which pervades so much of Liszt's later writing. M-D.

Christmas Tree Suite 1874–76 S.186 (Hin 88a, b) 2 vols., 6 pieces in each vol. Vol.1: An Old Christmas Carol; O Holy Night; The Shepherds at the Manger (Good Christian Men Rejoice); Ancient Provençal Christmas Carol; Evening Bells. Vol.2: Scherzoso—Lighting Candles; Carillon; Slumber Song; Formerly; Hungarian; In Polish Manner. Written for Liszt's granddaughter, Danelia. Nos.1, 3, 6, 10, 8 (Mer). Int. to M-D.

Variations on Weinen, Klagen (after J. S. Bach) 1862 S.180 (Cortot—Sal). Cortot considered these variations to occupy "an exceptional place next to the Sonata in B minor." Emotional gamut ranges widely from fear, pain, and desperation to the reconciling chorale, in which the grief is overcome. Formally, it is among Liszt's most imposing works, largely because of its tightly controlled, carefully graded levels of tension. M-D to D.
    See: David Bollard, "An Introduction to Liszt's Weinen, Klagen Variations," *Studies in Music*, II (1988):48–64.
    Michele Tannenbaum, "Liszt and Bach: 'Invention' and 'Feeling' in the *Variations on a Motive of Bach*," JALS 41 (January–June 1997):49–87.

Fantasy and Fugue on B A C H 1871 S.529 (Cortot—Sal) 12 min. No pianistic display; mainly in a chromatic chordal style. Opens with dark-sounding chords in low register over the notes BACH. The Fugue exposition verges at times on atonality and almost suggests the activity of a tone-row. Low chords in alternating hands with sustained pedal create a colossal effect. M-D.

Portraits of Hungarian Heroes 1885 S.205 (EMB; MMP). Seven pieces portraying Hungarian heroes. *Angst* has been worked to a stark visionary honor in these pieces ("drawn from life," Liszt said—an updated *Funerailles*). Gain in effect when played as a set. M-D.
    See: Linda W. Claus, "An Aspect of Liszt's Late Style: The Composer's Revisions for *Historische, Ungarische Portraits*," JALS, 3 (June 1978):3–18.
    Joy Wellings, "Liszt's 'Hungarian Historical Portraits," *Liszt Society Journal* (Centenary Issue 1986):88–92.

Fest Polonaise 1876 S.528 (Boccaccini & Spada 1981) 7pp. Originally composed for one piano four hands. This solo version is by Liszt. Polonaise rhythms, harmonically straightforward, colorful contrasting sections, octaves, large majestic chords. Int. to M-D.

San Francesco—Preludio per Il Cantico Del Sol 1881 S.499 (Boccaccini & Spada) 11pp. In four sections—Grave, Alla giubilante, Andante, and Andante. The melody "In dulci jubilo" weaves in and out of the unusually spare textures. M-D.

4 Valse Oubliées 1881–85 S.215. No.1 (NLE; EMB; Schott; Heugel): the most popular of the four "Forgotten Waltzes"; its charm is very effective. No.2 (Durand; Liszt Society Publications Vol.4). No.3 (Bo&Bo; Liszt Society Publications Vol.4). Nos.1, 2, 3 (Bo&Bo). No.4 (TP). These pieces are nostalgic evocations of the past, though it is not certain that they are based on themes from Liszt's earlier period. M-D.

Berceuse 1854 S.174 (EMB) first version, later version, 1863. Flowing melodies accompanied by broken chords. M-D.

Wiegenlied (Chant du Berceau) 1881 S.198 (Dob) 3pp. Reminiscent of the Brahms *Cradle Song*. Based on an ostinato rhythmic rocking figure; unison writing. Requires a carefully sustained light trill. M-D.

Czárdás Macabre (Dance of Death) 1884 S.225/1 (GS; EMB). Excellent for budding virtuosi. M-D.

Czárdás Obstiné 1884 S.225/2 (GS; EMB). An exciting Gypsy dance. Int. to M-D. See: Joy Wellings, "The Czardas Macabre," *Liszt Society Journal*, 7 (Summer 1982):2–6.

Lyon 1834 S.156 (NLE; Galaxy). This piece was originally part of the first book of *Années de Pèlerinage*, but it has disappeared from all subsequent editions. Liszt wrote this work in tribute to the silkworkers of Lyon, the "canuts," following the Lyon Revolution of 1834. M-D.
See: Alexander Main, "Liszt's *Lyon*: Music and Social Conscience," *Nineteenth-Century Music*, IV/3 (Spring 1981):209–27.

Romance Oubliée 1880 S.527 (Musica Obscura). In his old age Liszt's consent was sought for the publication of the *Romance in e*, S.169. Instead of agreeing, he wrote a new piece starting with a modified version of the opening bars of the original Romance, but with an entirely different ending. The piano solo version of *Romance Oubliée* was published in 1880 simultaneously with settings for piano and violin or viola or cello. Int. to M-D.

Rhapsodie Zingarese 1885 S.246 (Kreutzer—BMC; in CFP collection 4667). Original title was *Puszta—Wehmut*, which means "Longing for the Plains." A kind of miniature Hungarian Rhapsody. Int.

Bagatelle without Tonality 1885 S.216a (EMB). In waltz rhythm; originally conceived as the fourth of the *Mephisto Waltzes*. The sensual longing of Faust in the lyrical section and Mephisto's sardonic laugh at the end can easily be heard. The piece is so episodic in character that Liszt later felt that it did not belong with the other Mephisto Waltzes. He renamed it *Bagatelle without Tonality* since it constantly modulates toward a key that never materializes. M-D.

Die Zelle in Nommenwerth 1843 S.534 (EMB) 10pp. Elegie—Romance sans paroles. Also reproduced with an article about the piece by Joseph Bloch in PQ, 81 (Spring 1973):4–11. M-D.

Impromptu 1877 not listed in Searle (JALS, 3 [June 1978]:46–49). Known as the Gortschakoff Impromptu, this charming work is bathed in an atmosphere of Impressionism. M-D.

Hexameron Variations on the March from Bellini's I Puritani 1837 (K, with a short introduction by Eugene List; Paragon). Liszt, Thalberg, Pixis, Herz, Czerny, and Chopin each wrote one variation. Liszt also wrote the Introduction, several interludes, and the Finale. One of the grandest of the Romantic extravaganzas. D.

Piano Piece No. 1 A♭, 1866 R.44a, G. 189 (Roberton Publications Bardie Editions 1987) 3 pp. Also in collection *Franz Liszt—Masterworks Piano Library* (Bock Music Co. 1994). Lovely melody, chromatic harmony in arpeggiated figuration, six-measure coda. Int.

Waltz in A Major (Thorpe Music 1996) Foreword by Rena Mueller. This recently discovered piece was composed as an album leaf for the famous singer-pianist Pauline Viardot-Garcia, a student and friend of Liszt. Makes a fine encore. Int.

COLLECTIONS:

At the Piano With Liszt (Hinson—Alfred 2416) 63pp. Album Leaf S. 164; Christmas Song S. 502; Consolation I S. 172:1; Dedication, related to S. 566; Etude Op. I: 4 S. 136:4; Five Hungarian Folksongs S. 245 (See: Maurice Hinson, "Hungarian Folksong Settings for Piano by Franz Liszt," *Quarterly Magazine* of the MTA of New South Wales [1987]:3–10, 12–13); Forgotten Romance S. 527; Frühling S. 480: 2; Hungarian Rhapsody III S. 244: 3; La Cloche Sonne S. 238; Ländler in A♭ S. 211; Mazurka S. 384; Nocturne II; Piano Piece in A♭ S. 189: a; Psaume S. 156: 6; Sadness of the Puszta; The Shepherds at the Manger S. 186: 3. Also discusses Liszt as pianist and teacher, the Hungarian Rhapsodies, and performing Liszt today. Int. to M-D.

Il mio primo Liszt (Rattalino—Ric ER2702) 18pp. Andantino and Adagio, from *Four Little Pieces*. The Shepherds at the Crib, from the *Christmas Tree*. Consolation I. Lassan, Allegretto, Lassan, from *Five Hungarian Folk Songs*. Cradle Song. Sadness of the Puszta (Little Hungarian Rhapsody). Int.

Selected Works (Margaret Gresh—GS 1977) 159pp. Five Hungarian Folk Songs. Four Little Piano Pieces. Nuages gris. Abschied. En rêve. Csárdás obstiné. Csárdás macabre. Consolations 1–6. Liebesträume. *Années de Pèlerinage, 2. année*: Sonetto 47 del Petrarca; Sonetto 104 del Petrarca; Sonetto 123 del Petrarca. Two concert etudes: *Waldesrauschen; Gnomenreigen*. Two legends: *St. François d'Assise. La prédication aux oiseaux; St. François de Paule marchant sur les flots*. Int. to D.

Liszt (Gordon Green—OUP 1973) 63pp. Part of the *Oxford Keyboard Classics* series. Includes: Variation on a Waltz by Diabelli, S.147; Funeral March and Cavatina, S.398 from Donizetti's *Lucia di Lammermoor*; Chant Polonais V: Nocturne, S.480/5 (Chopin-Liszt); Consolation V, S.172/5; La Chasse, S.141/5 (Paganini-Liszt); Hungarian Rhapsody III, S.244/3; Eglogue, S.160/7; Hungarian Folksong, S.245/2; Andantino, S.192/4; Elegy II, S.197; Nuages gris, S.199. The introduction discusses Liszt as pianist, his attitude to his texts, playing Liszt today, Liszt's style of playing, his piano music, his achievement, the pedal, the una corda pedal, ornamentation, this edition. Notes on individual pieces. Int. to M-D.

Waltzes (USSR 1967) Vol.IV 121pp. Grand Valse di Bravura (first version 1836); Bravura Waltz (second version 1850); Valse Mélancolique (first version 1839); Valse Mélancolique (second version 1852); Ländler A♭ (1843); Petit Valse Favorite (1842); Valse-Impromptu (1850); Première Valse Oubliée (1881); Deuxième Valse Oubliée (1882); Troisième Valse Oubliée (1883); Quatrième Valse Oubliée (1885). M-D.

Liszt Society Publications (Schott; Vols.I, II, and IV available through K).

Vol.I, *Late Piano Works*: Csárdás Macabre; En Rêve; Nuages gris; La lugubre gondola I and II; Richard Wagner-Venezia; 4 Kleine Klavierstücke; Mephisto Waltz, Trauervorspiel and March; Unstern!

Vol.II, *Early and Late Piano Works*: Am Grabe Richard Wagner, piano or string quartet and harp; Apparitions Nos.1 and 2; Harmonies poétiques et religieuses, first version: Lyon; Méphisto Waltz No.4; Reminiscences de Boccanegra.

Vol.III, *Hungarian and Late Piano Works*: Csárdás obstiné: Elegy Nos.1 and 2; Funeral music to Mosonyi's death; 5 Hungarian folksongs; 2 Pieces in Hungarian Style (1828); Schlaflos, Frage und Antwort; To the memory of Petöfi.

Vol.IV, *Dances*: Valse mélancolique (1839–40); Valses oubliées Nos.2 and 3 (1884); Valse de concert; Galop a.

Vol.V: Mazurka brillante (1856); Mephisto-Polka (1883); plus works with some connection to the Swiss volume of *Années de Pèlerinage*: Fleurs mélodiques des Alpes Nos.3 and 2 were rewritten as Nos.3 and 8 respectively of the *Années*. The Swiss melodies of the Romantic Fantasy (Le mal du Pays and Ranz des vaches) were both used in the later collection. Also included are early versions of Vallée d'Obermann and Cloches de Genève. Interesting comparisons.

Vol.VI, *Liszt Songs*.

Vol.VII: *Unfamiliar Piano Works*: Magyar Dallok Nos.1, 2, 3, 6, 8, 9, 10; Sancta Dorothea; In Festo Transfigurationis Domini Nostri Jesu Christi; Piano Piece F♯; Romance e; Romance Oubliée; Die Zelle in Nonnenwerth (final version); Vive Henri IV (first publication); La Romanesca (first and second versions). M-D to D.

Franz Liszt, a Highlight Collection of His Best-Loved Original Works (C. Hansen 1972). Abschied; Au lac de Wallenstadt; Canzonetta del Salvator Rosa; Chapelle de Guillaume Tell; Consolations; En rêve; Hungarian Folk Song; Hungarian Rhapsody No.2; Il Penseroso; La lugubre gondola; Liebesträume; Little Piano Pieces; Mephisto Waltz; Nuages gris; Soirées de Vienne; Sonata; Sposalizio; Unstern.

Franz Liszt—An Introduction to the Composer and His Music (Joseph Banowetz —GWM 1973). Includes biography, pedagogical aids, and unusual photographs. Editing printed in red. Contains: Carrousel de Madame Pelet-

Narbonne; Sancta Dorothea; Wiegenlied; En Rêve; Five Hungarian Folk Songs; Abschied; Album Leaf; Album Leaf in the Form of a Waltz; Four Small Piano Pieces; Sospiri!; Ancient Provençal Christmas Carol; The Shepherds at the Manger; Etudes Op.1/4 d, 1/9 A♭; Variations on a Waltz Tune of Diabelli; Toccata. An outstanding broad introduction to Liszt's piano works. Int. to M-D.

The Twilight of Ferenc Liszt by Bence Szabolcsi. Reprint, Boston: Crescendo Publishers. Piano works (1880–1886) include: Abschied; Csárdás obstiné; László Teleki; Trübe Wolken; Unstern!

Liszt Album (EMB Z.4545) 67pp. Contains: Chant polonais (Chopin): Souhait d'une jeune fille (Op.47) R.145 (R stands for Peter Raabe, *Franz Liszt: Leben und Schaffen*, Stuttgart, 1931). Consolations Nos.3 and 4, R.12. La Pastorella dell'Alpa: G. Rossini Soirées Musicales No.6, R.236. La Regatta Veneziana: G. Rossini Soirées Musicales No.2, R.236. Rhapsodie Hongroise II, R.106 (transposed to C minor by Fr. Bendel). Soirées de Vienne No.6: Schubert: Wiener Abendgesellschaften, R.252. Trois Valses Oubliées I, R.66/b. Valse Impromptu, R.36.

The Final Years (J. Prostakoff—GS). These piano works of the late period include music written after 1861, when Liszt had retired from his duties at Weimar. Many have only been available in the complete edition (Liszt-Stiftung, Leipzig, 1908–33; reprint Gregg Press, 1966). Includes: Nuages gris (1885–86); Richard Wagner—Venezia (1883); Unstern! (1885–86); La Lugubre gondola I and II (1882); 5 Hungarian Folksongs (ca 1873); 2 Historical Hungarian Portraits (1870); Czárdás macabre (1881–82); Czárdás obstinée (1884); Mephisto Waltz No.4 (1885); Wiegenlied (1881); Abschied (1885); 4 little piano pieces (1865–76); 3 pieces from (Book III of *Années de Pèlerinage*: Sunt lachrymae rerum, Aux cyprès de la villa d'Este, Sursum Corda (1872 and 1877); Valses Oubliées Nos.2 and 3 (1882–83). Practical, discreetly edited. Int. to M-D.

Selected Works by Franz Liszt (Escandón—CPP/Belwin 1994). Vol. 1 of the Jorge Bolet memorial edition; Escandón was Bolet's student. The edition incorporates Bolet's markings and interpretative suggestions. Includes Sonata b; "Rigoletto," "Reminiscences of Norma," and "Overture" to *Tannhaüser*. D.

Franz Liszt. Consolations and Transcendental Etudes (Escandón—CPP/Belwin 1994). Vol. 3 of the Jorge Bolet memorial edition. 195pp. Int. to D. Vol. 5 (Escandón—CPP/Belwin 1995). Aprés une Lecture du Dante; Ballade II; Bénédiction de Dieu dans la Solitude; Mephisto Waltz; 3 Petrarch Sonnets; 3 Etudes de Concert; Venezia a Napoli. M-D to D.

Liszt. Selected Intermediate to Early Advanced Piano Solos (Hinson—Alfred 4887 1995) 64pp. Album Leaf S.164; Album Leaf in Waltz Form S.166; The Bell Tolls S.238; 7 Chorales: My Soul Exalts the Lord S.50:3; Now Thank We All Our God S.50:4; Now All the Forests are at Rest S.50:5; O Sacred Head and Wounded S.50:6; O Lamb of God! S.50:7; What God Does is Well Done S. 50:10; He Who Lets Only Beloved God Rule S.50:11; Christmas Song: Christ is Born S. 502; Consolation No. 1 S.172:1; Cradle Song S.198; Dedication: Liebeslied, related to S.566; Farewell: Russian Folk Song S.251; Four Short Piano Pieces S.192; Jesus, Word of God Incarnate: Ave verum corpus (Mozart, transcribed by Liszt); Ländler A♭ S.211; Madame Pelet-Narbonne's Merry-Go-Round S.214a; Nocturne No. 2 (first version), no S. No.; Piano Piece A♭ No. 2, S.189a; Serenade (F. Schubert, transcribed by Liszt) S.560:7; The Shepherds at the Manger: In Sweet Joy S.186:3; Spring (F. Chopin, transcribed by Liszt) S.480:2; Waltz A R.208a. Includes suggested teaching order. Int. to M-D.

Liszt Album I (K). Sonata b; Méphisto Waltz No.4; 6 Consolations; 3 Concert Etudes; La Campanella. M-D to D.

Liszt Album II (K). 3 Liebesträume; Nuages Gris; La Gondola Lugubre I, II; Hungarian Rhapsody II, Valse Mélancolique; Waldesrauschen; Les Jeux d'eaux à la Villa d'Este; St. Francis Walking on the Water. M-D.

Liszt Album (Compiled, edited, and fingered by Percival Garratt—Hin 1953). Feuille d'Album 1840, 1851): later became Valse mélancolique. Chanson d'Arcadelt—Ave Maria: a transcription of an Arcadelt three-voice chanson. Kleine Klavierstücke: moderato A♭, 1865; Appassionato, no date. Valse: first appeared under the title Albumblatt in Walzerform, 1842. En Mode Russe: No.22 of 24 pieces called *Bunte Reihe* for violin and piano, composed by the violinist Ferdinand David (1810–73). Csárdás: a Hungarian dance. Ave Maria. Int. to M-D.

Liszt Album (EMB 1966). Valse Impromptu (1850); Valse Oubliée No.1 (1880); Consolations 3 and 4; Rhapsodie Hongroise No.2 (1847) (transcribed Fr. Bendel); La Regatta Veneziana (1837); La Pastorella Dell'Alpi (1837); Chant Polonais (1860); Soirées de Vienne No.6 (1852). Int. to M-D.

In Various Moods (Kreutzer—BMC). Valse (1842); Album Leaf (ca. 1840); Nocturne (1883); Csárdás (1884); Hungarian Folksong Nos.1, 2, 5, (1875); Grey Clouds (1881). Technically, some of the easiest Liszt. Int.

Five Liszt Discoveries (Werner—Curwen). Ländler A♭; Wiegenlied; Ave Maria; Tyrolian Melody; La cloche sonne. Int.

Collection of Piano Works (Z. Gardonya and I. Szelenyi—EMB). Fifteen separate pieces covering 50 years of Liszt's career. Some familiar, some less known. Int. to M-D.

Fourteen Pieces for the Piano (F. Dillon—EBM). Excellent collection of easier works. 4 small Pieces (1865, 1873); Etude d (1827); Consolation E (1850); Pater Noster (1846); Nocturne (1885–86); Hungarian Folksongs I, II, IV; Gloomy Clouds (1881); Sancta Dorothea (1877); Dirge (The Funeral Gondola) (1882). "Each selection has the property of evoking in the performer the capacity to convey emotional shapes and patterns stimulated by the Master's conceptual pictures." Additional pedaling indicated by editor in dotted lines. Int. to M-D.

Liszt Klavierstücke (Hinze-Reinhold—CFP #4667). Vier kleine Klavierstücke (1865); No.8 from The Christmas Tree (1875); En Rêve (1885); No.8 from *Années de Pèlerinage*, first year (1835–36); No.7 from *Années de Pèlerinage*, first year; No.2 from *Années de Pèlerinage*, second year (1838–39); No.3 from

Années de Pèlerinage, second year (1849); Präludium on "Weinen, Klagen, Sorgen, Zagen" (1859); 5 Hungarian Folksongs (1873); Puszta-Wehmut (ca. 1885); Hungarian Rhapsody No.3 (1853); Csárdás macabre (1881–82). Reliable edition. Easy to M-D.

Miniatures (Prostakoff—GS). Contains 5 Hungarian Folk Songs, 4 Little Pieces, and 3 pieces from the later years. Int.

Rare and Familiar—28 Pieces for Piano (Mach—AMP 1982) 87pp. Contains: Carrousel de Madame Pelet-Narbonne, S.214a; Consolation E, S.172; Wiegenlied, S.198; Sancta Dorothea, S.187; En Rêve, S.207; Nuages Gris, S.199; Sospiri! (Sighing), S.192/5; Abschied, S.251; Ländler A♭, S.211; Album Leaf in the Form of a Waltz, S.166; Pater noster, S.173/5; Jadis (Formerly), S.186/10; Ancient Provençal Christmas Carol, S.186/8; The Shepherds at the Manger, S.186/3; Four Small Piano Pieces, S.192; Toccata, S.197a; Scherzo g, S.153; Zum Andenken (A Souvenir), S.241; 4 transcriptions on French National Themes: Vive Henri IV, S.239. La Cloche Sonne, S.238, La Marseillaise, S.237, Pastorale du Béarn, S.236; Siegesmarsch, S.233a; Etude d Op.1/4, S.136; Bagatelle sans Tonalité, S.216a. Some pieces published for first time. Includes facsimile of MS of Zum Andenken and a helpful preface. Int. to M-D.

21 Short Pieces (Ferguson—ABRSM 1982) 48pp. Includes: 6 Consolations, S.172; 4 Short Pieces, S.192; 5 Hungarian Folksongs, S.245; Chopin's Frühling, arranged by Liszt, S.480/2; En Rêve, S.207; Romance Oubliée, S.527; Abschied, S.251. Fingering, pedaling, metronome indications, and performance suggestions. Excellent editorial practice. Int. to M-D.

Franz Liszt Piano Compositions (Tucker—CPP/Belwin 1993) 32pp. Ave Maria; Etudes Nos. 3 and 4 (earliest version of *Transcendental Etudes*); Landscape; Lento assai from *5 Piano Pieces*; Liebesträume No.3; Three Consolations; Includes brief Introduction. Pieces not properly identified. Int. to M-D.

Mephisto Waltz and Other Works for Solo Piano (Dover). Fourteen pieces, including Fantasy and Fugue on BACH; Rapsodie Espagnole; Liebesträume; and Grand Galop Chromatique. M-D to D.

Technical Studies (Esteban—Alfred 1971). Contains 12 books (86 exercises) in one volume; excellent preface.

See: Julio Esteban, "On Liszt's Technical Exercises," JALS, 1 (June 1977): 17–19.

See: Alfred Brendel, "Liszt's 'Bitterness of Heart,'" MT (April 1981):234–35. Discusses Liszt's late piano works.

Elsie B. Barnett, "An Annotated Translation of Moriz Rosenthal's *Franz Liszt, Memories and Reflections,*" *Current Musicology,* 13 (1972): 29–37. "Rosenthal (1862-1946), one of Liszt's most famous pupils, describes Liszt as teacher, performer, and composer and gives his own opinions and impressions of Liszt and some of his contemporaries" (author).

France Clidat, "Interpreting Liszt's Piano Music," *Clavier,* 29/1 (January 1989):32.

Nancy Klenk Hill, "Landscape, Literature, and Liszt," JALS, 8 (December 1980): 15–24.

Maurice Hinson, "Liszt and His Hungarian Piano Music," *Music and the Teacher*, 18/1 (March 1992):7–13.

Istvan Kecskeméti, "Two Liszt Discoveries: 1. An Unknown Piano Piece; 2. An Unknown Song," MT, 1578, 1579 (August, September 1974): 646–48; 743–44. Contains a careful description of the MS of *Siegesmarsch*, a piano work virtually unknown until now, dated at about 1870 or later. Contains stylistic characteristics such as open fifths, ostinato structure, and extreme changes of register.

Ralph P. Locke, "Liszt's Saint-Simonian Adventure," *Nineteenth-Century Music*, IV/3 (Spring 1981):209–27.

William S. Newman, "Liszt's Interpreting of Beethoven's Piano Sonatas," MQ, 58/2 (April 1972):185–209. Concerns Liszt's special reverence for Beethoven and his position as the most important nineteenth-century interpreter of Beethoven. Discusses Liszt's playing of ten Beethoven sonatas (sometimes literally, sometimes freely), his comments on them, editing of them (especially as reflected in Bülow's celebrated edition), and teaching of them.

Piano Quarterly, 89 (Spring 1975). A special issue devoted to Liszt.

Nancy B. Reich, "Liszt's Variations on the March from Rossini's *Siege of Corinth*," JALS, 7 (June 1980):35–41.

Charles Timbrell, "Liszt and French Music," JALS, 6 (December 1979):25–33.

Mark Wait, "Liszt, Scriabin, and Boulez: Considerations of Form," JALS, 1 (June 1977):9–16.

Alan Walker, *Franz Liszt, The Virtuoso Years (1811–1847)*, vol.1 (New York: Alfred A. Knopf, 1983), 481pp.

———, ed., *Franz Liszt The Man and His Music* (New York: Taplinger, 1970).

Herbert Westerby, *Liszt, Composer, and His Piano Works* (London: W. Reeves, 1936; reprint, Westport, CT: Greenwood Press, 1970).

Konrad Wolff, "Beethovenian Dissonances in Liszt's Piano Works," JALS, 1 (June 1977):4–8.

Guy S. Wuellner, "Franz Liszt's Prelude on 'Chopsticks,'" JALS, 4 (December 1978):37–44.

Norman Lloyd (1909–   ) USA

Three Scenes from Memory (EV 1963). Winter landscape; Sad Carrousel; City Street. Each 2pp. Fresh, original recital material in contemporary idiom. M-D.

Episodes (EV 1964). Five pieces. Jazz influence, improvisatory style, varied moods. M-D.

Sonata (Mer 1964) 31pp. Four movements. Bitonal, polytonal writing, contrasted and developed ideas. Brilliant finale. D.

Jean-Baptiste Loeillet (1680–1730) Belgium

Much of Loeillet's music was erroneously ascribed to J. B. Lully and published under his name. The following works are contained in *Werken voor Clavicembel* (J. Watelet—De Ring 1932) (BB), which is in *Monumenta Musicae Belgicae*, Vol.1.

Lessons for the Harpsichord or Spinet. Suite No.1, e: A, Aire, C, M, Jigg. Suite No.2, D: A, C, Gavot, S, Minuet Rondo. Suite No.3, g: Aire, Hornpipe, Cibel.

Suites of Lessons. Suites g, A, c, D, F, E♭. Each suite contains an A, C, S, Aria, M, and Giga. Available separately: reprints of numerous movements from these suites (Durand; GS; UE; Br&H; Elkin; TP).

See: Brian Priestman, "Catalogue thématique des oeuvres de Jean-Baptiste, John et Jacques Loeillet," *Revue Belge de Musicologie*, 6 (October–December 1952):219–74.

———, "The Keyboard Works of J. B. Loeillet," MR, 16 (May 1955):89–95.

Matthew Locke (ca. 1622–1677) Great Britain

Melothesia (1673) (BB) Monuments of Music Literature Series. This treatise on music contains many of the compositions listed below. Emphasis on basso continuo realization.

Keyboard Suites from Melothesia (1673) (A. Kooiker—PSM 1968) 46pp. 34 pieces, including 5 suites and 11 other short pieces. Many have charm and interest, especially the jigs and hornpipes. Eight composers represented. Int. to M-D.

Seven Pieces from Melothesia (1673) (Gordon Phillips—Hin). Ornamentation, registration, and performance dealt with in a scholarly introduction. Urtext.

Suites (T. Dart—S&B). Contains all the known keyboard pieces by Locke: 5 suites, 11 other short pieces for harpsichord, and 7 organ voluntaries. Int. to M-D.

Theo Loevendie (1930–) The Netherlands

Strides 1976 (Donemus; PIC) 7 min. A dignified, idiomatic work with jazz-inspired elements woven into its musical fabric. Emphasis on bottom-register ostinatos and top-register repeated notes, an obvious polarization. The piece's references to Harlem "stride" piano (James P. Johnson, etc.) are difficult to detect. M-D.

Luca Lombardi (1945–) Italy

Variations on "Avanti Popolo alla riscassa" (Moeck 315179) 20 min. Performance instructions in Italian and German. Theme and 9 variations on a popular Italian song, "Before the Recovery of the People." The tune is metamorphosed in all its aspects—intervalically, rhythmically, melodically—but the variations are nondevelopmental overall. Exciting, full of energy and tension, even in its quiet moments. Moves over keyboard rapidly, many meter changes, large chords. D.

Robert Lombardo (1932–) USA

Laude, Fuga e Cavatina (CFP 1955). Laude: expressive, exploits open fifths. Fuga: energetic, many harmonic seconds and sevenths. Cavatina: short, melodic; contains some intense moments. M-D.

12 Contemporary Pieces for Children (PIC). Nontriadic, linear counterpoint, 12-tone suggestion. Easy to Int.

Ruth Lomon (1930–   ) USA

Five Ceremonial Masks 1980 (Arsis) 18pp. 14½ min. Changing Woman; Dancer; Spirit; Clown; Talking Power. Represents Navajo masks used in the Yeibichai Night Chant ceremonies. Features clusters using mallets, plucking strings, and enharmonics—all used to musical not theatrical ends. No.3 is partly aleatory with sonorous transformations, Impressionism of the 1980s. Effective. M-D.

Tom Long (–   ) USA

Alea: Music by Chance (Canyon Press 1974) 19pp. Includes instructions for performance. Melogic; Durations; Deceiving; Modulation; Maze; Random Density; Circulation; Contour. Eight aleatoric, or chance, music designs, introducing even the youngest students to creativity at the piano, using aleatoric experience. Easy to Int.

Nikolai Lopatnikoff (1903–1976) USA, born Russia

Lopatnikoff writes in a Russian Romantic style.

Sonatine Op.7 1926 (MCA) 10 min. (Editions Russe 1926). Allegro energico (Toccata): fugal, martellato touch, double notes, octaves, quartal harmony, brilliant climax. Andante; unmetered; expressive melodic writing; accompaniment relies on quartal outlines; builds to climax; subsides to quiet close. Allegro molto vivace: fugal texture, similar to opening movement. A strong work with some bravura writing. M-D.

Five Contrasts Op.16 1930 (Schott) 6 min. Five moods: impassioned; tender; agitated; expressive; energetic. Linear, dissonant, bravura writing. M-D.

Dialogues Op.18 1932 (Schott) 9 min. Moderato; Allegro molto; Vivace; Grave; Epilog. Two-part writing, linear, complex. M-D.

Variations Op.22 1933 (Schott). Six variations. Modal; short note values on strong beats; quartal and quintal harmony; highly contrasted. M-D.

Sonata E Op.29 1943 (AMP) 16 min. Allegro risoluto: toccata-like rhythm with cross accents. Andantino: elegiac, folklike melodies. Allegro molto vivace: vigorous rhythmic treatment, contrapuntal richness, bravura writing. D.

Dance Piece for Piano 1955 (TP) 3 min. Changing meters, bitonal mid-section. Int.

Intervals Op.37 1957 (MCA) 12 min. Seven studies based on intervals of the second, third, fourth, fifth, sixth, seventh, and octave. Contemporary techniques handled with much imagination. M-D.

Fernando Lopes-Graça (1906–1994) Portugal

Album for the Young Pianist (Nov). Vol.1 in series *Discovery*. 21 short pieces. Many seconds and asymmetrical rhythms. See especially No.13, Alla Bartók, with a folklike melody set to an interesting accompaniment, and No.16, Song Without Words. Portuguese folk elements subtly permeate these pieces. Int. to M-D.

Bent Lorentzen (1935–   ) Denmark

Five Easy Piano Pieces (WH 1971) 11pp. Explanations in English. Avant-garde notation, fist and forearm clusters. Look more difficult than they actually are. Int. to M-D.

Colori 1978 (WH 4346) 32pp. Suite in five colors. Conveys associations evoked by red, white, gold, azure, and black. Clusters; harmonics. Strings to be struck by fingers and palms, scraped horizontally and vertically, and stopped, with a grand final scrape using all ten fingernails! M-D.

Alexina Louie (b. 1949) Canada

Louie was born in Vancouver, British Columbia to parents of Chinese descent. She has degrees from the University of British Columbia and the University of California in San Diego. She presently lives in Toronto.

I Leap through the Sky with Stars 1991 (Gordon V. Thompson 1994) 8 min. Written in memory of Glenn Gould (1932–1982) and Claude Vivier (1948–1983). Based on a Zen poem. Combines consonant and dissonant sonorities, likes opposing white keys in one hand with black keys in the other, minimalistic, ideas not developed, "senza misura" passages, extremes of keyboard range and dynamics exploited, changing meters, octatonic, pentatonic, and whole-tone scales. Colorful and highly pianistic. D.

Alain Louvier (1945–   ) France

Etudes pour Agresseurs, Vols.I and II (Leduc 1969). Seven etudes in each volume. "These studies have been conceived for the training of pianists in view of the modern aggressive approach to the keyboard. We have at command a maximum of 16 'aggressors' (10 fingers, 2 palms, 2 fists, 2 forearms), individually treated" (from the Foreword). Traditional and avant-garde notation. Contains some clever, impressive, and wild sonorities. D.

Quatre Préludes pour Cordes (Pour les cordes du piano) (Leduc) 9pp. 10 min. For one or more pianos. Two pages each, four folded loose leaves in cover. Detailed instructions. Avant-garde. D.

Etude No.37 for Piano for Left Hand (Leduc 1973) 11 min. For 5 fingers, 1 palm, 1 fist, and 1 arm. Contains a chart of notations. Time changes in each bar. M-D.

Etudes pour Agresseurs No.38 (Choudens 1976) 6pp. Explanation in French. Pour 16 agresseurs apprivoises. D.

Trois gymnopédies automatiques (Leduc 1976) 4pp. 4 min. These pieces were written using a chart of numbers, a pocket computer, and a 1974 telephone directory. They are based on the pianistic style of Erik Satie, to whom they are dedicated. M-D. Int.

Juliusz Luciuk (1927–   ) Poland

Improvisations for Children (PWM 1962). Eight miniatures. Experimental work; aleatoric technique employed where improvisation on the given materials

is called for. Provides a good introduction to music of our time. Many young
pupils are more ready for this type of music than are their teachers. Int.

Lirica di timbri (PWM 1963). Five compositions for prepared piano. The composer says: "In this composition the substance of sound is derived directly
from the strings with all kinds of drum sticks and without the use of the
keyboard. The perpendicular line of the notations gives a faithful picture
of the movement of the sticks, in that the range of the strings set in vibration in a given register is not given precisely. Every performance may,
therefore, bring certain variations in sound and in individual accenting.
Two colors are used; red to denote the RH and green to denote the LH.
The scale of the piano strings is divided into four registers which correspond to the metal frames that extend through the length of the piano.
These are: registro basso, medio, alto and superiore" (from the score).
Somewhat similar to Henry Cowell's *The Banshee*. Avant-garde. D.

4 Sonatine (PWM 1966–69) 30pp. I: Three movements, freely tonal. Int. II: Three
movements, more chromatic than No.I. Int. III: Three movements, more
extensive and complex writing, dissonant, closer to M-D. IV: Three movements, clusters, extreme ranges exploited, short sections, experimental.
M-D.

Otto Luening (1900–1996) USA

Luening's early works made use of polytonal, atonal, and near-serial techniques
while much of his later writing involves the tape recorder. Luening taught many
of our younger American composers.

Eight Piano Pieces (Galaxy 1952) 15pp. 1. Intermezzo (free in time). 2. Inter-
mezzo. 3. Chorale. 4. Humoresque. 5. Prelude Starlight. 6. Prelude . . . The
Philosopher. 7. Prelude . . . Introspection. 8. Prelude . . . To the Warriors.
Varied sonorities but chordal preference is strong. M-D.

Five Intermezzos (Galaxy) 11pp. Allegro moderato: varied textures, exciting mid-
section, flowing arpeggiated chords in coda. Andante: flowing thirds, Romantic harmonies. Stars: two sixteenth-note figures in alternating hands,
fleeting. Birds: decorative lines. Swans: moving triplets plus chordal closing.
A very attractive set. M-D.

Four Preludes (Galaxy 1952) 7pp. Slow; Moderato; Andante; Andante. Freely tonal, motivic figures evolve, sensitive writing. M-D.

Two Preludes (Galaxy 1963) I. 2pp. Freely tonal in E♭, sixths and thirds in right
hand, broken-chord accompaniment in left hand. II. 4pp. Built on the half-
step; free dissonant counterpoint; varied rhythms; concludes in F. M-D.

Dance Sonata for Piano (Highgate 1952) 10pp. Grave; Alla breve; Andante; Allegro energico. Chordal, rhythmic, freely tonal. M-D.

Sonata in Memoriam Ferruccio Busoni (Highgate) 20 min. Eclectic, engaging.
A first-rate work; conventional material used in unexpected and original
ways; splashing virtuoso demands. Offers a fascinating play of a twentieth-
century mind on nineteenth-century ideas. "In my *Sonata* I have attempted

to assimilate and follow style he [Busoni] was interested in but without using direct quotes" (from jacket of recording of this work, CRI SD334). D.

First Short Sonata (Highgate 1958) 9pp. Allegro giusto: mainly linear, thickens at coda. Grave: chordal, builds to large climax. Vivace: contrasted with Andante section. M-D.

Third Short Sonata (Highgate 1966) 10pp. "Entertainment, That Glorious Science." Moderato un poco allegro; Molto moderato; eighth note equals 144–160; Allegro moderato. Delightful, witty, clever. M-D.

Fourth Short Sonata (Highgate) 10pp. Allegro moderato: flexible meters, clusters, varied textures. Adagio: built on same motive as first movement. Allegro: repeated notes, large span required. Allegro moderato: varied tempi, clusters, octotonic perpetual motion closing. M-D.

Phantasy (Highgate 1958) 8pp. Freely tonal; sections flow freely; chords alternate with contrary motion runs; quartal and quintal harmony. M-D.

2 Bagatelles (Highgate 1962) 5pp. Maestoso; Allegro. Fetching figurations. M-D.

Andante (Highgate 1958) 4pp. A freely tonal character piece that works to a large climax. M-D.

Music for Piano (A Contrapuntal Study) (CFE) 7pp. Requires fleet but expressive fingers. M-D.

6 Short and Easy Pieces (Highgate) 5pp. Linear, thin textures. Int.

Ray Luke (1928–   ) USA

5 Miniatures for Piano 1964 (FLP Music Publishing). Declamation: large octave gestures; mid-section drops back; builds to a dramatic close. Fugue: in a; three-voices; much rhythmic drive; last 12 bars use pedal point. Waltz: whimsical, uses 4/4 and 2/4 to break up triple meter; much chromaticism. Lament: built on rhythmic idea "short-long," quartal harmony. Toccata: driving work in 8/16; thin sonorities; requires close working together of hands. M-D.

David Lumsdaine (1931–   ) Great Britain, born Australia

Kelly Ground (UE 1966) 25 min. Avant-garde work in three cycles. Detailed notation and explanations. Cycle 1: five strophes in contrasting phrasing, texture, and rhythm; clusters. Cycle 2: short; exploits intervals of fourth and fifth. Cycle 3: built on intervals exploited in Cycle 2, but varied rhythmic patterns permeate harmonic structure. D.

Witold Lutoslawski (1913–1994) Poland

Album of Piano Pieces (PWM 1975) 51pp. Contains: 2 entiudy (1940–41); Melodie ludowe (1945); Bukoliki (1952); 3 utwory dla mlodziezy (1953); Inwencja (1968). Epilogue in Polish, English, and German. Illustrations, portrait. These 23 pieces of varying difficulty are the complete piano works of this eminent contemporary Polish composer. All the pieces are fingered and have pedal indications.

Available separately: *Two Studies* (PWM). Inspired by Chopin but display the composer's style even though they are early works. No.1 is very similar in figuration to the Chopin Etude Op.10/1. Both make use of all the instrument's potential and are full of accidentals. M-D.

Folk Melodies 1945 (PWM; MMP) 26pp. These twelve pieces were written primarily as teaching compositions, but their artistic value has brought them into the concert repertoire. Authentic folk tunes accompanied by harmonic and rhythmic subtleties. O my Johnny; Hey, down from Cracow; There is a path; The Shepherd Girl; An apple hangs on the apple tree; A river flows from Sieradz; Master Michael; The lime-tree in the field; Flirting; The Grove; A Gander; The Schoolmaster. Int.

Three Pieces for Young Performers (PWM). Four Finger Exercise; An Air; March. Int.

Invention (PWM 1968) in *Album of Piano Pieces* discussed above. Atonal, changing metrical units. M-D.

See: Mervyn D. Coles, "The Piano Music of Lutoslawski," *Music Teacher*, 60/4 (April 1981):17.

Elisabeth Lutyens (1906–1983) Great Britain

Lutyens, along with Humphrey Searle, introduced 12-tone writing to Great Britain about 1939.

5 Intermezzi Op.9 1942 (Lengnick). These pieces are based on a 12-note structure with traditional motivic shape. M-D.

Piano e Forte Op.43 1958 (Belwin-Mills) 12 min. A fantasia-like dramatic study in dynamics. Finale is rondo-like. M-D.

5 Bagatelles Op.49 1962 (Schott) 7 min. Miniature 12-note monodies that treat the note-order of the basic set with considerable freedom. M-D.

Frank Lynes (1858–1913) USA

Lynes studied at the New England Conservatory and with Karl Reinecke at the Leipzig Conservatory. He was one of the most outstanding piano teachers in the Boston area.

Four Analytical Sonatinas Op.39 (Olson—Alfred 2590) 32pp. C; G; C; G. Excellent pieces in classical style for teaching form. Each movement is analyzed. Easy to Int. No. 1 is in collection *World's Greatest Sonatinas* (Alfred 4617). Int.

M

John McCabe (1939–   ) Great Britain

McCabe has synthesized many contemporary influences into his extended tonal compositional style, including neoclassicism, Impressionism, serialism, Messiaenic rhythmic structures, clusters, and space-time notation. He uses the "Study" series to explore different aspects of contemporary piano writing.

Variations Op.22 1963 (Nov) 10 min. No. 1 in the *Virtuoso Series*. Unusual theme suggests an Indian Raga, Messiaen influence. 18 short variations built in a peculiar, steady, and exciting manner. Exotic music, demands advanced pianism. D.

See: Robert L. Reynolds, "Variations for Piano, Op.22—An Analysis," *Piano Journal*, 14 (June 1984):10–14.

5 Bagatelles Op.27 1964 (Elkin) 5 min. Capriccio; Aria; Elegia; Toccata; Nocturne. Short, spontaneous examples written to demonstrate certain aspects of serial writing. M-D.

3 Impromptus Op.4 1962 (OUP) 2½ min. Short neoclassic terse pieces. Nos.1 and 3 are highly rhythmic. No.2 is a Siciliano lento malinconico. An orchestral imagination will aid the performer. M-D.

Fantasy on a Theme of Liszt 1967 (Nov) 10 min. This one-movement form is in a neo-Lisztian idiom but stamped with McCabe's personal style, which is full of color and energy. Free 12-tone usage. M-D to D.

Capriccio 1969 (Nov) 6 min. Study No.1. Custers, harmonics, hammered octaves, printed on three staves. D.

Sostenuto 1969 (Nov) 8pp. 8 min. Study No.2. Widely spread sonorities, harmonics, varied figurations, extremes of keyboard used. Impressionistic. Evaporates "a niente." M-D.

Gaudi (Nov 1970) 25pp. 15 min. Study No.3. A tribute to the Spanish architect Antonio Gaudi. Sounds of bells and gongs; complex; highly contrasted sections; strong Messiaen influence; repeated cluster chords, irregular rhythms; flamboyant writing. D.

Aubade (Nov 1970) 8pp. 7 min. Study No.4. Slow, extended use of arpeggio figures and appoggiaturas; formally fairly free; concentrated thematic material; intended to conjure up the moment of stillness before dawn. Brief fragments of melodies are heard, but as if in recollection. Impressionistic. Requires an elegant legato. D.

Couples (Nov 1976) 2pp. Theme music from the Thames Television Series. Broad sweeping melody; seventh chords and octaves. Int.

Intermezzi 1968 (Nov) 16pp. 9 min. Five contrasted movements are linked by the opening fanfare-like passage, which appears again during the course of the piece and from which many of the themes derive. Each section presents problems of musicianship (e.g., phrasing and pedaling); all require careful rhythmic control. Eclectic, idiomatic style. M-D.

Paraphrase on "Mary Queen of Scots" 1979 (Nov) 17pp. 9 min. Study No.5. "This Study is, in its own way, a descendant of the type of operatic Paraphrase common in the nineteenth century and especially perfected by Liszt. In this case, however, the theatrical source is a ballet, the full-length work *Mary, Queen of Scots* for which I wrote the music in 1974–75. A further difference is provided by the actual form of this Paraphrase, which is that of a Prelude and Fugue. Although the themes of these two sections are to some extent related, they are derived from passages in the ballet which refer to two aspects of the life of Mary Stuart. The Prelude, which is partly a straightforward transcription, is taken from an Interlude depicting her in her domestic circle; in the ballet, this precedes a scene including *a Pas de Deux* for Mary and Darnley. The material of the Fugue is taken from a double *Pas de Trois* which represents the more public aspect, in this case the 'political' battle of wills and clash of interests between Mary and Queen Elizabeth I" (from the score). Flexible melodies, large arpeggiated chords, multi-layered textures, fast alternating octaves between hands, dynamic extremes. D.

Afternoons and Afterwards (Nov 1982) 17pp. 11 min. Seven pieces designed "for musicians of limited technical ability." Original ideas. Requires many subtle changes in hand position. Int.

Haydn Variations (Nov 1988) 53pp. 26 min. 17 variations (unnumbered) that begin with a brilliant octave cadenza, use varied techniques and figurations, end Andante *ppp*. The theme is eventually identified on p. 32. Dissonant, yet highly pianistic with lyric lines from time to time. Virtuosic. D.

Paul McCartney (1942–   ) Great Britain

Best known as a pop singer and songwriter, McCartney has composed a few "serious" music works.

A Leaf (Faber). 7 movements, reflective in character, some bravura passages. The fifth movement contains a complex climax; an alternative version is included for pianists not up to the original. M-D to D.

Bruce MacCombie (1943–   ) USA

MacCombie holds degrees from the universities of Massachusetts and Iowa and did postdoctoral work with Wolfgang Fortner at the Freiburg Conservatory. He presently teaches at Boston University.

Gerberau Musics, for partially prepared piano, 1976 (AMP 1979) 5pp. Prologue; Continuum; Antique Invention; Viel zu ernsthaft!; Blue Epilogue. The title *Gerberau Musics* refers to a street in Freiburg where the composer lived. This set of short pieces parodies different kinds of music and utilizes both normal and prepared piano sonorities. Sounds reminiscent of distant bells, unusual gongs, drums, and even gamelan music result from the careful placement of the 28 preparations used. Includes table of preparations and discussion of notation. Effective. M-D.

Byron McCulloh (1927–   ) USA
Spectra (CF 1980) 19pp. MS reproduction, readable. Dissonant, wild sonorities; rhythmic complexities; heavy technical demands. D.

Edward MacDowell (1860–1908) USA
Considered by many to be America's first truly professional composer, MacDowell was at his best composing miniatures. His piano writing shows that he understood the best styles and idioms in late-nineteenth-century writing. He left us 160 romantic character-pieces that have a poetic mastery about them.
Forgotten Fairy Tales Op.4 1897 (MMP). Sung outside the Prince's Door (Alfred 2629); Of a Tailor and a Bear; Beauty in the Rose-Garden; From Dwarfland. Int.
Six Fancies Op.7 1897 (Hinson—Alfred 10101). A Tin Soldier's Love; To a Humming Bird; Summer Song; Across Fields; Bluette; An Elfin Round. These pieces and the Op.4 set are endowed with sparkle and a charming Romantic atmosphere. Int.
First Modern Suite Op.10 1883. Prelude (AMP; SP); Intermezzo (AMP). The other movements are: Presto; Andantino and Allegretto; Rhapsody; Fugue. Well written and interesting as an early work. M-D.
Second Modern Suite Op.14 1883 (Br&H). Praeludium: contains an explanatory quotation from Byron's *Manfred*. Fugato. Rhapsody. Scherzino. March. Fantastic Dance. Teresa Carreño, MacDowell's teacher, performed this Suite frequently on her tours. M-D.
Serenata (Serenade) Op.16 1882. In collection *Nineteenth-Century American Piano Music* (Dover). The outer chordal sections feature left-hand syncopation on beat 1; the mid-section uses left-hand broken-chord accompaniment to support chordal melody; some arpeggiation. M-D.
Witches Dance Op.17/2 1884 (TP; K; CF). Colorful and imaginative. Int.
Moonlight Op.28/3 1887 (Anson—Willis). A Romantic American nocturne. Int. to M-D.
Scotch Poem Op.31/2 1887 (Alfred; GS; CF). A minstrel song. One of MacDowell's best. Int.
Four Little Poems Op.32 1887 (K). Pieces inspired by poems of Tennyson, Buliver, D. G. Rossetti, and Shelly. No.2, The Brook (in collection *Essential Keyboard Repertoire* vol. 5, Alfred 4574). Short, somewhat showy, good for small hands; fast and light figuration suggests the rippling brook. Int.
Etude de Concert Op.36 1887. In collection *Album of American Piano Music from the Civil War through World War I* (IMC 3367). A brilliant show piece written for Teresa Carreño. It was very popular during the early twentieth century. Requires a superb octave technique. M-D to D.

Marionettes Op.38 1901 (MMP). Prologue; Soubrette; Lover; Witch; Clown; Villain; Sweetheart; Epilogue. In their original form (1888) this charming set contained only six pieces. MacDowell afterward revised them extensively, rearranged the order, and added the Prologue and Epilogue. He uses descriptive English words rather than the usual Italian musical terms. This album comprises one of MacDowell's most interesting portrayals of everyday human nature camouflaged in the form of marionettes. Int.

See: Maurice Hinson, "Edward MacDowell: America's Great Tone Poet," *Clavier* 20 (April 1981):22–27. Includes music of Prologue and Clown, from *Marionettes* and a lesson on "Clown."

Twelve Studies Op.39 1890 (For the Development of Technique and Style) (GS; K; BMC; Elkin). Nos. 2, 8, and 12 available separately (Alfred). Hunting Song: a graceful accent study. Alla Tarantella (CF; in collection *Essential Keyboard Repertoire*, Vol. 5, Alfred 4574): a whirling dance, needs fluency and good finger staccato. Romance (BMC): a tune and touch study. Arabeske: a sparkling wrist study. In the Forest: development of rhythmic playing. Dance of the Gnomes: needs crisp articulation and perfect control of dynamics. Idyl: Lyric; charming; needs a singing tone and grace. Shadow Dance (IMC): needs agile fingers and a light touch. Intermezzo: excellent for developing independent fingers. Melodie: also fine for cultivating independence of fingers. Scherzino: tuneful; study in double-note playing for the right hand. Hungarian (IMC; CF): for dash, speed, and getting over the keyboard quickly. Int. to M-D.

See: Richard Bobo, "Edward MacDowell's Wonderful Etudes," *Clavier*, 33/4 (April 1994):22–29. Discusses this set and includes the music of *Alla Tarantella*.

Twelve Virtuoso Studies Op.46 1894 (AMP; K). More difficult than Op.39. Best are: Moto Perpetuo; Wild Chase; Elfin Dance (CF); March Wind (the very best!); Polonaise. All require a more mature technique and bold projection. M-D.

See: Richard Bobo, "MacDowell's Virtuoso Studies: A Closer Look," AMT, 42/2 (October–November 1992):32–35.

Etudes and Technical Exercises (Da Capo 1984) 140pp. "The Etudes were composed upon MacDowell's return to the U.S. after a period of 12 years in Europe, when he had decided to devote his talents to composition as well as performance. This reprint brings together for the first time his 25 piano etudes, which show the influence of various masters—in the easier ones most markedly Clementi and Mendelssohn, in the more difficult ones Chopin and Liszt. Exploring a range of moods, from introspective reflection to passionate drama, MacDowell challenges the pianist with technical hurdles such as simultaneous melody and accompaniment in the same hand and rapid figuration, always bending pedagogical purpose to an interpretive end" (from the score). M-D.

Ten Woodland Sketches Op.51 1896 (GS; BMC; EBM; K; Schott; IMC; Alfred; Elkin). The most characteristic are: To a Wild Rose (Alfred 876); In

Autumn; To a Water Lily (Alfred 2640); Will o' the Wisp; From Uncle Remus. This collection contains much variety and uses the piano delicately
and opulently. Int. to M-D.

Eight Sea Pieces Op.55 1898 (Alfred; GS; K; Elkin). To the Sea: clear chordal
writing spread over the keyboard. From a Wandering Iceberg: broad dynamic range, last seven bars are the finest. A.D. 1620: the Mayflower pic-
tured in rolling seas. Starlight: suggests a quiet, starlit sea. Song: cheerful,
with a rough and hearty chorus. From the Depths: calm and sinister sea
works to its full power in a storm. Nautilus: charming, fresh, and graceful.
In Mid-Ocean: noble, majestic, sweeping. Int. to M-D.
See: Dolores Pesce. "The Other Sea in MacDowell's *Sea Pieces*." *American
Music*, 10/4 (Winter 1992):411–40.

Six Fireside Tales Op.61 1902 (Hinson—Alfred 10139). Writing is more masterly
here than in any of the earlier sets. An Old Love Story: flowing melody,
new and expressive mid-section. Of Br'er Rabbit: catchy, humorous, and
vigorous. From a German Forest: lovely tunes, chromatic figuration, and effective changing meters. Of Salamanders: fanciful, delicate, intricate; demands fine control of fingers. A Haunted House: imaginative with ghostly
effects; requires fast fingers. By Smouldering Embers: short, quiet, tender;
masterful harmony and counterpoint. M-D.

Ten New England Idyls Op.62 1902 (GS; K; Schott). Imaginative but thematic
material is less inspired. The White Pine: stately, wide dynamic range. Joy
of Autumn: exhilarating, must leap along; final page with its whirl and rush
demands a polished technique. M-D.

Piano Sonatas (GS 3452 1984) 141pp. Available separately: *Sonata Tragica* Op.45
1893 g (GS). *Sonata Eroica* Op.50 1895 g (Br&H; GS; K): refers to King
Arthur legend. *Norse Sonata* Op.57 1900 d (K). *Keltic Sonata* Op.59 1901 e
(K; Elkin). Opp.50 and 57 owe much to the Liszt B minor Sonata. Opp.45
and 59 are consistently the finest. All involve idiomatic virtuoso writing
and require advanced pianism. D.
See: SSB, pp.760–77, for a good discussion of the Sonatas.
David Kaiserman, "Edward MacDowell—The Keltic and Eroica Piano Sonatas," MJ, 24 (February 1966):51, 76–77.

COLLECTIONS:

Piano Pieces Opp.51, 55, 61, 62 (Da Capo). Part of the Earlier American Music
series. A reprint of the first editions.

MacDowell Masterpieces (Schaum Publications 1973). Contents: Bluette; Of a
Tailor and a Bear; The Eagle; Improvisation; To a Wild Rose; In Autumn;
From an Indian Lodge; To a Water Lily; Starlight. Int. to M-D.

16 Selected Pieces (W. Weismann—CFP). Contains works from Opp.37, 51, 55, 61,
62. Preface in English and German.

Music by MacDowell (G. Anson—Schroeder & Gunther). Book 1: The Eagle,
Op.32/1; From a Log Cabin, Op.62/9; From a Wandering Iceberg, Op.55/2;

From Uncle Remus, Op.51/7; Humoreske, Op.24/1; Hungarian, Op.39/12; March Wind, Op.46/10; Novellette, Op.46/1; Of Br'er Rabbit, Op.61/2; Rigaudon, Op.49/2; Scotch Poem, Op.31/2; To an Old White Pine, Op.62/7; To the Moonlight Op.28/3.

Book 2: Alla Tarantella, Op.39/2; From an Indian Lodge, Op.51/5; Improvisation, Op.46/4; In the Woods, Op.28/1; Moonshine, Op.32/3; Song, Op.55/5; Soubrette, Op.38/2; Starlight, Op.55/4; Sung Outside the Prince's Door, Op.4/1; Tin Soldier's Love, Op.7/1; To a Water Lily, Op.51/6; To a Wild Rose, Op.51/1; Villain, Op.38/6; The Witch, Op.38/4.

Piano Works. Woodland Sketches, Complete Sonatas and Other Pieces (Dover 1990) 219pp. Woodland Sketches Op.51; Sea Pieces Op.55; Fireside Tales Op.61; New England Idylls Op.62; Sonata No. 1 (Tragica) Op.45; Sonata No. 2 (Eroica); Sonata No. 3 (Norse) Op.57; Sonata No. 4 (Keltic) Op.59. Reprinted from earlier editions. Int. to D.

Edward MacDowell Piano Compositions (Tucker—CPP/Belwin 1993) 32 pp. An Old Garden Op.62/1; Arabesque Op.39/4; The Flow'ret (from *Forest Idylls*) Op.19/2; Moonshine Op.32/3; Song Op.55/5; Starlight Op.55/4; To a Wild Rose Op.51/1; To an Old White Pine Op.62/7; Valse Triste Op.46/6. Includes an Introduction. Int. to M-D.

See: Richard Bobo, "Edward MacDowell as Pianist," AMT, 46/9 (February–March 1997):25–29, 75.

Francis Brancaleone, "Edward MacDowell and Indian Motives," *American Music*, 7/4 (Winter 1989):359–81.

Marian MacDowell, *Random Notes on Edward MacDowell and His Music* (Boston: A. P. Schmidt, 1950). Helpful as an aid to interpreting his piano works.

Teo Macero (1925–   ) USA

Flower Pieces (A. Broude 1980). Short colorful pieces describing flowers: Sea Pink; Japanese Anemone; Wormwood; Golden Marguerite; Butterfly Weed; English Daisy; Japanese Pearly Everlasting; Sweet Woodruff. Cool expressive writing, almost provides the aroma. Careful use of pedal necessary. Int.

Roman Maciejewski (1910–   ) USA, born Poland

Maciejewski's early works showed much Polish folklore influence. Later his compositions were affected by Impressionistic influences, and since the early 1950s he has written in a completely individual contemporary idiom.

Four Mazurkas (PWM 1952). Problems of form and construction are solved in a highly individual style. M-D.

Triptych (PWM 1948). Virtuoso treatment of the instrument. D.

Donald MacInnis (1923–   ) USA

Toccata for Piano and Two-channel Tape (EBM). Also published in Vol.III of American Society of University Composers Journal of Musical Scores (J. Boonin) 6pp. 8 min. Serial; dramatic octaves at opening; linear. The pianist is invited to respond to the sound events on the tape by improvising, from time to time, from a number of given tone-rows and short phrases. Some may be executed at the keyboard or inside the piano (plucking strings, strumming, rapping with the knuckles on resonant parts of the frame, etc.). Opens and closes on B♭. Avant-garde. D.

Dieter Mack (1954–   ) Germany
Chateau 1988 (Br 7218 1992) 12 leaves, photostat. With performance instructions in English. Avant garde.

Barton McLean (1938–   ) USA
Dimensions II 1974 (Tetra) for piano and tape, 23pp. 12 min. Tape on rental. Taped sonorities of mutated piano sounds surround and enclose the piano part; string scrapings; repeated notes. Some nontraditional notation. Can be poignantly beautiful with the proper performance and sound equipment and a good hall. A most evocative, even pretty, blend of ethereal and phantasmagorical tape sounds and hammering, tense figures from the pianist. M-D.

Edwin McLean (1951–   ) USA
Nightworks (CPP/Belwin c. 1993) 20pp. Five Star; Moonlight Tonight; Nightfall; Serenade; Fire and Shadows; Daybreak. Impressionistic. MC. Int. to M-D.

James MacMillan (1959–   ) Scotland
MacMillan puts together musical and extramusical devices that result in a unique style. He communicates a combination of Roman Catholic spirituality and Scottish nationalism—kind of a Scottish Messiaen.
Piano Sonata 1985 (Bo&H 1993) 20pp. 14 min. "I wrote my 'Piano Sonata' during a bitter Ayrshire [Scotland] winter and recall the barren trees and hard frozen ground of a landscape that was empty and silent but for the harsh, hollow cry from the rookeries. This is reflected in the Sonata's tolling, mournful chords, with its bursts of violent, or delicate and icy, figuration. Throughout the three movements the music conveys a mood of elegy, of despair and desolation" (from the score). Adagio; Grandioso ed affrettando; Adagio. Expressionistic, pedal marks, some "repeat ad lib." figuration; middle movement is virtuosic, intense dramatic writing. D.

Elizabeth Maconchy (1907–1994) Great Britain
Economy of thematic material characterizes Maconchy's work.
Sonatina (Lengnick 1972) 14pp. 6 min. Four movements. For a two-manual harpsichord, although the work sounds remarkably well on the piano. Questionable use of dynamics (e.g., quick accents and sforzandos) for harpsichord style. Many repeated patterns, short phrases, linear, forceful rhythmic treatment. Effective arpeggiando and legatissimo writing. M-D.

Boguslaw Madey (1932–   ) Poland
Sonatina (PWM 1952) 14pp. Allegro; Andante quasi rubato; Moderato-Allegro
   assai. Freely tonal, more interpretative problems than technical. Left-hand
   skips, thin textures. M-D.

Nikita Magaloff (1912–1992) Switzerland, born Russia
Magaloff was internationally known as pianist and pedagogue.
Toccata Op.6 (Edition Russe de Musique 1933). A virtuoso work by a virtuoso
   pianist emphasizing melodic fourths and fifths, glissandi, brilliant octave
   passages. Dedicated to Vladimir Horowitz.

Mary Mageau (1934–   ) USA
Australia's Animals (GS 19090 1978) 5pp. Sleepy Koala; Wandering Wombat;
   Ponderous Platypus; Silver Swan; Capering Kangaroo; Elegant Emu. Colorful and clever descriptive pieces. Excellent introduction to contemporary techniques. Int.

Robert Maggio (1964–   ) USA
Maggio graduated from Yale University and earned master's and doctorate degrees in music composition from the University of Pennsylvania. He teaches at
West Chester University.
Prelude, Hymn, and Toccata 1988 (TP 1996) 18pp. ca. 14 min. Prelude: enigmatic,
   tranquil; works to big climax; winds down to *ppp* ending. Hymn: very slow
   and distant opening, full chords, ethereal closing. Toccata: energetic, crisp,
   changing meters, rhythmically precise, furioso, *tutta forza* ending. MC.
   M-D to D.

Milosz Magin (1929–   ) France
Images d'enfants (Durand 1970). Seven short, clever, colorful movements. Int.
   to M-D.
Sonate (Durand 1972) 35pp. Four contrasting movements with the slow one the
   most successful. Long pedal points underlie changing Ravelian harmonic
   treatment. M-D.

Ernst Mahle (1929–   ) Brazil, born Germany
Mahle is founder and director of the Escola Livre de Música of Piracicaba in the
state of São Paulo.
As Melodias da Cecilia (Vitale 1971) 54pp. Forty short harmonizations of children's folk songs. Easy to Int.
As Músicas da Cecilia (Ric Brazil 1969) 8pp. Six short harmonizations of children's songs. Colorful, contrasted. No.6, O Gatinho Pega O Ratinho, is the
   trickiest. Int.
7 Pecas sôbre uma e duas notas só 1954 (Ric Brazil 1969) 7pp. Seven pieces, all
   on one or two notes each. Dynamic range exploited; pointillistic, harmonics, Webernesque. M-D.

Sonatina (Ric Brazil 1956) 6pp. A one-movement work with much driving rhythm in open fifths. A short Lento mid-section uses chordal sonorities. Driving rhythms return; a short reference to the Lento section appears before the final rhythmic conclusion. M-D.

Franz Anton Maichelbeck (1702–1750) Germany
8 Sonatas Op.1 1736 (Reichling—Merseburger 896) 86pp. Uses borrowed thematic material from G. F. Handel's 1720 suites. Maichelbeck's sonatas include many typical suite movements. Thin textures, performer needs to fill in some parts; idiom is similar to Telemann. Int. to M-D.

Samuil M. Maikapar (1867–1938) Russia
Maikapar taught piano at the St. Petersburg Conservatory for 20 years. His works are mainly for piano, and he was most successful with the miniature.
Pedal Preludes (SB). Romantic-flavored pieces designed to develop pedal technique. Mechanical action of pedals is discussed. Attractive recital pieces. Int.
18 Selected Pieces (A. Mirovitch—MCA 1956) 32pp. Genuinely fine and imaginative music for the early years of study. Annotations by the editor. Int.
Trifles Op.28 (GS). 26 short pieces. Int.

Martin Mailman (1932–   ) USA
Martha's Vineyard Op.48 (TP 1971) 8pp. Lazy Circles; Short Parade; Breezes; Walk on the Beach; Invention; Inside and Out; Sand Dance. Short, dissonant, clusters, contemporary techniques. Int. to M-D.
Petite Partita (Belwin-Mills). Prelude; Invention; Arietta; Toccatina; Chorale; Dance. Short, strong works. Int. to M-D.

Joseph Makholm (1954–   ) USA, living in France
Makholm studied at the New England Conservatory and moved to Paris in 1982 to study orchestral conducting with Léon Barzin. An accomplished jazz pianist and arranger, Makholm teaches arranging, composition, and jazz piano at the American School of Modern Music in Paris.
Trois Impressions (Billaudot 1994) 23pp., ca. 11 min. Preface: Concerning "Swing." 1. Mainstream Tune, Moderate Tempo: contrasted sections, performance directions, tempo changes, rubato. 2. Plaintive Blues: lyrical, "Dark, but precise, strident, calming gradually," and other terms, relaxed ending. 3. Bebop 'n You: varied jazz figurations, "On a roll!", freely tonal, tempo changes, "crumbling" ending. An effective group requiring advanced technique. M-D to D.

Gian Francesco Malipiero (1882–1973) Italy
Impressionist techniques are used extensively in Malipiero's writing. Many of his piano works are descriptive.
Poemetti Lunari (Sal 1909–10). Seven pieces. No.IV, Presto scherzando. No.VII: lengthy, agitated grotesque. M-D.

Preludi Autunnali (Sal 1914). Lento, ma carrezzevole: chromatic, flowing nocturne. Ritenuto, ma spigliato: horn calls, varied figuration, atmospheric, short. Lento, triste: solemn ostinato dirge. Veloce: bright, thin-textured scherzo. Varied and Impressionistic. M-D.

Barlumi (JWC 1917). Non lento troppo: atmospheric. Lento: somber, widely separated sonorities in parallel motion. Vivace: contrasting sonorities, double notes, effective ending. Lento, misterioso: broken chord sonorities. Molto vivace: vigorous dance with fast repeated chords. One of Malipiero's most successful sets. M-D.

Maschere che passano (JWC 1918). Five fantasylike sketches. D.

Hommage à Claude Debussy (JWC 1920). Short, parallel harmonies, quiet ending. M-D.

La Siesta (ESC 1920). Four delicate sketches. Much parallel usage, improvisational. M-D.

Tre Omaggi (JWC 1920). A un papagallo; A un elefante; A un idiota. Clever, amusing caricatures. M-D.

Cavalcate (Sal 1921). Three modes of four-legged locomotion. Somaro: Recalcitrant donkey: chords, octaves, broken rhythms, humorous. Camello: Swaying camel: a lyric Lento; flowing figuration. Destriero: Fiery steed: rhythmic emphasis, fast detached chords, climactic. M-D.

Il Tarlo (Sal 1922). Four short pieces. Impressionistic. M-D.

Pasqua di Risurrezione (Sal 1924). Extended, atmospheric, varied pianistic techniques. D.

3 Preludi a una Fuga (UE 1926). Three connected contrasted preludes lead to a legato three-voice fugue, sonorous ending. M-D.

Hortus Conclusus (Ric 1946). Eight sketches in contrasting styles: Prelude; Lento; Allegro; Andante; Tranquillo; Lentamente; Allegro moderato; extended Finale; variation-like. Int. to M-D.

Cinque Studi per Domani (UE 1954). Some imitation, transparent textures, 3 against 4. D.

Variazione (JWC 1960). Variations on Pantomine from *El Amor brujo* by Manuel de Falla. M-D.

Riccardo Malipiero (1914–   ) Italy

Inventions (SZ 1949). Nine pieces in serial technique intended as an introduction to this system. One-, two-, and three-voiced works. M-D.

Costellazioni (SZ 1965) 22pp. 12 min. Extensive directions. Pointillistic; flexible chord technique necessary. D.

Ursula Mamlok (1928–   ) USA

Grasshoppers. Six Humoresques (Casia Publishing Co. 1993) 9pp. Sunday Walk; Night Serenade; In the Rain; Minuet; In the Army; Hurrying Home. A good sense of humor is required to bring these off. Int.

Four Recital Pieces for Young Pianists (Casia Publishing Co. 1993) 8pp. The Sunken Bell; Throwing Pebbles; The Bewitched Pond; Revving up and Away. M-D.

Vincenzo Manfredini (1737–1799) Italy
Sei Sonate (Anna Maria Pernafelli—SZ 1975) 55pp. Well edited from the first
    edition of 1765. Preface in Italian, French, German, and an awkward En-
    glish translation. These six sonatas have real melodic charm and include a
    bit of dissonance from time to time. M-D.

Franco Mannino (1924–   ) Italy
Adolescenza (EC 1972) 28pp. Ideas, images, sensations in a collection of sixteen
    short pieces for piano, written when the composer was between 8 and 14
    years of age.
Sonata II Op.69 (EC 1972) 24pp. First movement: an eight-bar theme worked out
    in a short set of eight variations. Lento: broad gestures, unbarred, large dy-
    namic range (*pppp* to *fff*). Allegro: lengthy, demanding, driving rhythms in
    compound quadruple meter. D.
Sonata IV Op.208 (Boccaccini & Spada 1980) 34pp. Allegro appassionata; Ada-
    gio molto; Allegro Tumultuoso. Romantic, rhapsodic, extreme keyboard
    ranges, Lisztian, dramatic. M-D to D.
Sonata V "Ucraina" Op.210 (Boccaccini & Spada 1982) 18pp. A one-movement
    dramatic work with contrasting sections. Descriptive, post-Romantic and
    Impressionistic techniques, overtly glutinous melodies. M-D.

Jeff Manookian (–   ) USA
Twelve Etudes (WB 1993) 32pp. Each etude focuses on a special aspect of tech-
    nique. Titles are Debussy-inspired. 1. for the 5 fingers; 2. for arpeggios; 3.
    for chromatics; 4. for scales; 5. for repeated notes; 6. for two against three;
    7. for alternating hands; 8. for glissandos; 9. for thirds; 10. for octaves; 11.
    for grace notes; 12. for chords. Each piece is well put together and musi-
    cal. Int.

Benedetto Marcello (1686–1739) Italy
Two-part textures, harmonic interest, and balanced phrase structure are charac-
teristic of the music of Marcello. He may have left as many as twenty keyboard
sonatas.
Sonatas pour clavecin (Heugel). 12 sonatas in urtext edition. Helpful perfor-
    mance suggestions and historical background. M-D.
Sonata g (G. Taliapietra—Zanibon). Four movements, including some brilliant
    figuration. Int. to M-D.
Sonata B *Alte Meister*, Vol.V (Pauer—Br&H). Transcription by Bartók (CF;
    M. Maffioletti—Carisch). Three movements, straightforward, processional-
    like closing. M-D.
Toccata c. In collection *Early Italian Piano Music* (Esposito—OD). In collec-
    tion *Italian Masters* (I. Philipp—IMC). Effective study in repeated double
    notes. M-D.
Concerto d (CFP 217A). Contained in a volume of J. S. Bach concerto transcrip-
    tions. Transcribed by Bach from a work originally written for oboe in c. M-D.

See: W. S. Newman, "The Keyboard Sonatas of Benedetto Marcello," AM, 29 (January–March 1957):28–41.

Louis Marchand (1669–1732) France

Pièces de Clavecin (T. Dart—L'OL 1960). Suite I in d: A, C I and II, S, G, Chaconne, Gavotte en Rondeau. Suite II in g: Prelude, A, C, S, Gavotte, Menuet en Rondeau. Contains a table of ornaments. Performer is to make his own selection of movements. Int. to M-D.

See: Geoffrey B. Sharp, "Louis Marchand, 1669–1732. A Forgotten Virtuoso," MT, 110 (November 1969):1134–37.

Czeslaw Marek (1891–1985) Switzerland, born Poland

Variations on an Original Theme Op.3 (Amadeus) 22pp. Twelve variations on a choralelike Romantic theme. Variations alternate between quick and slow, calm and vigorous, brilliant and less involved. Last variation is powerful and effective. Whole work is basically Romantic in conception. D.

Sarabande and Toccata Op.27 (Amadeus ZB 10) 25pp. Late-Romantic style, broad lines, involved polyphonic textures, orchestral writing. Sarabande recalls the Debussy *Pour le Piano*, while the effective Toccata has affinities with *Islamey* and *Petrouchka*. M-D to D.

André F. Marescotti (1902–   ) Switzerland

Suite en sol (Jobert 1929) 17pp. Prélude; S; M; G. Captures the spirit of the Baroque suite with vigorous, rhythmic, colorful writing. D.

Croquis (Jobert 1946). Blue Girls; Rêverie; Fidelia (Bourrée). Free "sketches" in an unencumbered style. M-D.

Variations sur un thème de J. J. Rousseau 1978 (Joubert) 23pp. 11 min. Theme and 12 contrasting variations. Neoclassic, long trills, chromatic, glissandi. Colorful contemporary writing. M-D.

Massada (Joubert 1983) 15pp. "A lonely, majestic fortress atop an arid peak overlooking the Dead Sea. It was here that 967 Jews, under siege for 3 years, chose suicide rather than become Roman slaves" (from the score). Rhapsodic, many tempo and mood changes from violent to very calm; shows a strong sensitivity to timbre and high regard for purely musical relationships. M-D to D.

Pierrette Mari (1929–   ) France

Le Chardonet (Billaudot 1980). Reflects both its title, "The Goldfinch," and subtitle, "scaling a mountain," with its sections of swooping broken arpeggios alternating with running lines. Tense, insistent, contemporary writing. D.

Igor Markévitch (1912–1983) France, born Russia

Markévitch's style was basically tonal but laced with dissonant counterpoint. Markévitch was best known as a conductor and ardent champion of contemporary music.

Stefan la Poète: Impressions of Youth 1940 (Bo&H) 15 min. Seven-piece cycle. Romantic titles, lyric style; has affinities with the "new" classicism envisaged by Busoni. Especially effective is the fleet passage-work in "Snowflakes" and the cantilena of "Death of the Bird." Requires fine legato. Int. to M-D.

Variations, Fugue, and Envoi on a Theme of Handel 1941 (Bo&H) 15 min. Theme is from the *Harmonious Blacksmith*. The variations use all the grand and dramatic gestures composers have used since Beethoven. After an invigorating fugue, the Envoi makes a tranquil conclusion. A virtuoso bitonal blockbuster. D.

See: Alice Mavrodin, "Variations, Fugue, and Envoi on a Theme of Handel," *Tempo*, 133/4 (September 1980):61–67.

Rudolf Maros (1917–1982) Hungary

East European Folksong Suite (PIC 1971) 11pp. Nine short movements based on folklike material: Slovakian 1 and 2; Austrian; Hungarian; Croatian 1 and 2; Rumanian; Ruthenian [a province of Czechoslovakia] 1 and 2. Effective. Int.

Joaquin Marroquin (1933–   ) Guatemala

Chapiniana (PIC 1964) 19pp. Pastorale: features somber flute sounds. Burlesque: brusque humor. Nocturne: mysterious. Ronda: wistful. Fiesta: bright and colorful closing. The pieces in this suite relate to the moods and activities of certain areas of Guatemala.

Frank Martin (1890–1974) Switzerland

Bartók, Debussy, and Schönberg are the major influences on Martin's style.

Eight Preludes 1948 (UE) 20 min. 12-tone with the general tonality around c♯; prefers minor mode but ends in major. No.3 has similarities to the stark *Prélude* No.2 of Chopin. No.4, with its irregular meters, shows the influence of Dalcroze's rhythmic theories. No.6, mostly a two-part canon, is the most purely 12-tone. No.7 is the spiritual summit and includes an extended section for left hand alone which is later repeated with a right hand obbligato rising to a tremendous climax, all of this framed at beginning and end by an atmospheric study in chordal sonorities. A major contribution to twentieth-century piano literature. D.

See: David Burge, "Frank Martin's *Eight Preludes*," CK, 6 (March 1980): 58, 60.

Rhythmical Study 1965 (Gerig) 2½ min. In collection *Contemporary Swiss Piano Music*. A kind of homage to Dalcroze, pits 9/8 meter against 3/4. M-D.

Guitare. Four Short Pieces for Piano 1933 (UE 15041). Dedicated to Segovia, these pieces were originally written for guitar. Prelude: b. Air: slow, rhythmic, arabesques, flamenco influence. Plainte: widely spread chordal figures, repeated notes, Spanish influence. Gigue: cross rhythms. Musically interesting, sound well on piano. Not as difficult technically as the *Eight Preludes*. Large span required. M-D.

Fantaisie sur des rythmes flamenco 1973 (UE 15042) 17pp. Rumba lente–Rumba rapide–Soleares–Petenera. ". . . one day I stumbled on a series of chords which evoked sufficiently well the dreamy spirit of the romantics and immediately took on the slow rhythm of the rumba. The special character of this beginning informs the whole of the first part of the fantasia. The rhythm gets progressively faster until it bursts into the frenzy of a flamenco rumba. At its climax it breaks off abruptly. After a prolonged silence a different dance form appears—a 'Soleares.' Like most of the flamenco dances the 'Soleares' is based on an ostinato rhythm which has its complete exposition at the beginning of the dance. . . . The work ends with another dance, called the 'Petenera,' which is similarly based on a completely traditional, imperturbable rhythm. . . . the music, based on its traditional rhythms, expresses the character of flamenco without speaking the same musical language" (from the preface by the composer). Contains strong rhythms, trills, glissandi, fast repeating chords in alternating hands. Requires large span. M-D.

Esquisse 1965 (UE 16679) 5pp. Designed as a sight-reading study for a musical competition in Munich. A canny piece, beginning in a somewhat dry fashion but moving toward a menacing, almost martial climax. Cantabile melody, arpeggiated chords, Debussy-like. M-D.

Clair de Lune 1952 (Pierre Noël) 3 min. In collection *Les Contemporains*, book III. A highly chromatic modern counterpart of a Chopin nocturne. Int. to M-D.

See: Dolores Frederickson, "The Piano Music of Frank Martin," *Clavier*, 29/7 (September 1990):20–22.

Janet E. Tupper, "Stylistic Analysis of Selected Works by Frank Martin," diss., Indiana University, 1964. Includes the *Huit Préludes*.

Marianne Martinez (1744–1812) Austria

Martinez studied keyboard with Joseph Haydn and was sought out by Mozart as a partner in the playing of his four-hand music. She was considered one of the most outstanding pianist-composers of her day.

Sonata da Cimbalo G 1769 (Furore Verlag 148 1992) 15pp. First edition. For harpsichord. Preface in German and English.

Three Sonatas for Keyboard (Bean—Hildegard Publishing Co. 1994) 46pp. Preface by editor. These are Martinez' only known keyboard sonatas. No. 1, E ca.1763: Allegro, Andante, Allegro. First movement also in collection *At the Piano with Women Composers* (Alfred 428). No. 2, A ca.1765: Allegro, Adagio, Tempo de Minuetto. No. 3, G ca.1769: Allegro brillante, Andante, Allegro assai. The editor has added dynamics and much of the phrasing. The style suggests a mixture of C. P. E. Bach, Haydn, and Scarlatti plus influence from Baroque dance movements. M-D.

Padre Giambattista Martini (1706–1784) Italy

Famous throughout Europe, this composer and teacher of J. C. Bach and Mozart, among others, was highly respected by the musical world of his day. His sonatas were indicated for organ or harpsichord. Martini's music shows strong craft but the inspiration is less than impressive. The Sonatas range from two to five movements and include dance movements.

12 Sonatas Op.2 1742. In *I Classici della Musica Italiana*, Vol.XVIII. Two sonatas in TPA, Vol.XII. In *Le Trésor des Pianistes*, Vol.IX. M-D.

Sonate d'Intravolatura per l'Organo e l'Cembalo (BB). Facsimile of the 1742 Dutch edition. Contains 12 sonatas. Dance pieces and free movements form the basis of these works. Int. to M-D.

6 Sonatas 1747 (Hoffman-Erbrecht—Br&H; K). A; g; G; F; E; C. In two or three movements, graceful and spontaneous. M-D.

Prelude and Fugue e (Esposito—OD) In *Early Italian Music*. Flowing Prelude; academic Fugue. Int. to M-D.

Sonata E (de Paoli—JWC) In *Italian Sonatas of the 18th Century*. M-D.

Sonatas Nos.5, 7 (Busch—CFP N3659).

Sette composizioni inedite per il clavicembalo (Gabriele de Toma—Zanibon 1976) 16pp. Seven fluent, short, graceful pieces, but not the best of Martini. Preludio F; Rondeau; Sonatas in C, e, C, F, G. The title "Sonatas" was given by the editor; each sonata has only one movement. Excellent introduction; editorial additions carefully noted. One page in facsimile. M-D.

See: Howard Brofsky, "The Instrumental Music of Padre Martini," diss., New York University, 1963.

Donald Martino (1931–   ) USA

Martino's music is neo-Romantic and characterized by technical and intellectual rigor and a flair for instrumental virtuosity. It uses dense polyphony to support long melodic lines and is usually articulated by frequent rubato.

Piano Fantasy 1958 (Dantalian) 6 min. Serial, rigorous, and vital in its harmonies; free-flowing ideas well shaped. More difficult interpretively than technically. M-D to D.

Pianissimo (A Sonata for the Piano) 1970 (Dantalian) 43pp. 28 min. Four continuous movements, scrupulous craftsmanship. A solo sonata of Lisztian scope. As diverse in its expressivity as in its virtuosity. Difficult for performer and listener.

Fantasies and Impromptus 1981 (Dantalian) 32pp. 30 min. Nine emotionally charged pieces. The first, fifth, and ninth movements are called Fantasies and are large in scope and rich in varied material. The others, called Impromptus, are shorter and usually develop only one idea. Any of the pieces may be played separately, or the complete group may be played as a whole. Complex rhythmic and textural demands. This is Martino's most outstanding work for the piano. D.

Impromptu for Roger 1977 (Dantalian) 3 min. Dedicated to Roger Sessions at 80. Advanced contemporary style yet expressively varied, lyrical, and fantastical. Combines variety and concision. Pointillistic, expressionistic. M-D to D.

See: David Burge, "Notating Emotion," *Keyboard*, 8/7 (July 1982):61, 63. Discusses all of the above pieces.

Suite in Old Form 1982 (Dantalian) 15 min. Allemande Fantasy; Courante; Sarabande; Gavotte; Air; Gigue Fantasy. "Each movement admits a fairly wide range of interpretation as to basic tempo" (from the score). Single movements or groups of movements may be selected. Int. to D.
See: Leslie Amper, "Donald Martino's Sarabande," KC (July–August 1992):36. Includes music for Sarabande.

Twelve Preludes 1991 (Dantalian) 22 pp. ca. 20 min. Cycle of 12 short sonorous movements contains many moods and performance directions. Well integrated. Divided into two parts of six movements each. D.

Jean Martinon (1910–1976) France

Epilogue d'un conte d'amour Op.35/1 (Costallat 1948) 6pp. A berceuse. Many meter changes, added-note technique. Impressionistic. M-D.

Introduction et Toccata Op.48 (Costallat 1948). Biting dissonance, changing meters in Toccata, aggressive. D.

Sonatine No.3 Op.22 (Costallat 1945) 14pp. Three tightly knit movements. M-D.

Bohuslav Martinů (1890–1959) Czechoslovakia
Czech folksong, French clarity, modality, exactness, and rhythmic zest are all fused in the music of Martinů.

Eight Preludes (Leduc 1930). Blues; Scherzo; Andante; Danse; Capriccio; Largo; Etude; Foxtrot. Neoclassically oriented. M-D.

Borová: Seven Czech Dances (Leduc 1931). Borová was the name of Martinů's home town. Acerbic harmonic idiom. M-D.

Film en Miniature (Hudební Matice 1925). Tango; Scherzo; Berceuse; Valse; Chanson; Carillon. Amusing, sophisticated writing. Int. to M-D.

Marionettes (Artia; Br; MMP). 3 books of 5, 5, and 4 pieces. Graceful dance movements. Int.

Three Czech Dances (ESC 1929). Okračak; Dupák; Polka. Virtuoso writing including octaves, double notes, highly rhythmic. D.

Esquisses de Dances (Schott 1933). Five spirited dances, irregular meters. M-D.

Les Ritournelles (Schott 1933). Six varied etudelike pieces, very pianistic. M-D.

Etudes and Polkas (Bo&H 1946). 3 books, 16 pieces. Each Etude alternates with a Polka. Stamina is required for the Etudes, while the Polkas demand a flexible rhythm, sensitivity, and eloquent tonal balance. M-D to D.

Fables (Artia; MMP 1947). On the Farm; The Poor Rabbit; The Monkeys; The Chicken; The Angry Bear. Not the most interesting Martinů. Int. to M-D.

Les Bouquinistes du Quai Malaquais (Heugel 1954). Light lullaby, a kind of street song. Int.

Spring in the Garden (Artia; MMP 1948). Four easy children's pieces. Int.

Two Dances (Artia 1950). Valse; Polka. In the style of Ravel's *Valses Nobles*. M-D.

Fenêtre sur le Jardin (Leduc 1957). Four pieces. No.1 is the easiest, Int.; the others are M-D.

Sonata No.1 (ESC 1958) 19 min. Three movements, FSF. Bitonal, numerous figures, often developed from each other. D.

Fantaisie et Toccata (AMP 1940). Large-scale, bravura work; variety of textures exploited. Mature pianism required.

The Fifth Day of the Fifth Moon (Heugel 1951). Metrically free, Impressionistic. M-D.

Christmas (Le Noël) 1927 (Karel Solc—Artia). Sledding; A Child's Lullaby; Christmas Carol. Folksy flavor. Int. to M-D.

Dumka 1941 (ESC 1970). Easy flowing. Int.

Trois Esquisses 1927 (ESC) 6 min. Debussy style, especially in the second piece, which reminds one of "La Puerta del vino." M-D.

Klavirni skladby ("Piano Compositions") (Panton 1970) 21pp. Preface by Miloslav Nedbal. Contains: The Cats' Procession in the Solstice Night; Dumka; A Composition for Little Elves; Adagio; Prelude; Piece without Title. Int. to M-D.

Kleine Klavierwerke (Věra Zouharová—Panton AP2197 1974). Seven pieces written between 1913 and 1936. Preface by editor, in part translated into Russian, German, and English. Int.

Scherzo E and Eb 1924 (Joshua) 7pp. Humorous, dissonant, shifting meters, light repeated chords in alternating hands. M-D.

Butterflies and Birds of Paradise (Ars Polona 2194). Loosely constructed, dance influence. Int. to M-D.

Bozankovi A Sonicce 1932 (Bo&Bo 1992) 9pp. Little piano pieces for children. With colored pictures. Easy to Int.

See: Maurice Hinson, "Bohuslav Martinů—Czechoslovakia's Greatest 20th Century Composer," *Clavier*, 21 (October 1982):19–24. A discussion of the piano works.

Giuseppe Martucci (1856–1909) Italy

Martucci was a pioneer in restoring instrumental music to a place of prominence in nineteenth-century operatic Italy. He was oriented toward German music, especially to Schumann, Brahms, and Wagner. Fine craftsmanship is always in evidence. His collected piano works fill almost six volumes.

Tarantella Op.44/6 (Ric). In the Thalberg virtuoso tradition. M-D.

Variations Op.58 (Ric). Theme, 10 variations; extensive final variation. M-D to D.

Giga Op.61/3 (Ric). Vivacious, Scarlatti influence. M-D.

Notturno Op.70/1 (Ric). Lyrical, reminds one of Fauré. M-D.

Noveletta Op.82/2 (Ric). Deft, innocent charm; sounds like lightweight Elgar. M-D.

Daniel Gregory Mason (1873–1953) USA

Country Pictures Op.9 (Br&H). Book I: Cloud Pageant; Chimney Swallow. Book II: At Sunset; The Quiet Hour; The Whippoorwill; Night Wind. Descriptive works in Brahms and MacDowell tradition. Nos.2 and 6 demand facile technique. M-D.

Three Preludes (EMB 1943). Con fantasia, quasi improvvisata: nocturnelike. Tristamente, ma con moto: melodic line transferred between voices. Semplice: one page long, span of ninth required. M-D.

Color Contrasts. Appears in *U.S.A.: Compositions for Piano by Contemporary American Composers,* Vol. 2 (MCA), 1949. Charming without very strong individuality. Int. to M-D.

William Mason (1829–1908) USA

Mason's compositions are classical in form and refined in style and treatment. He is considered the "father of piano pedagogy" in the USA.

Dance Antique (Alfred 10102) in collection *Piano Music In Nineteenth Century America,* Vol.I. Contains some clever canonic writing. M-D.

Lullaby Op.10 1857. In collection *Masters of American Piano Music* (Alfred 4603). Chopinesque, ostinato left-hand figure. Int. to M-D.

Jules Massenet (1842–1912) France

Papillons Noirs (Heugel 1907). Lyric, salon-type pieces. Int.

Papillons Blancs (Heugel 1907). More difficult and more interesting. M-D.

Toccata (Musica Obscura) 7pp. Inspired by the Schumann *Toccata* but much easier. A flowing melody is tucked into the melodic figuration. Surprise ending. M-D.

Eduardo Mata (1942–1995) Mexico

Sonata (EMM 1960) 12pp. Serial, pointillistic, rhythmic proportional relationships, atonal, flexible meters, numerous dynamic and tempo changes, harmonics. Has no Latin American characteristics. D.

William Mathias (1934–1992) Great Britain

Mathias's style is essentially tonal, with influences of Bartók, Hindemith, Stravinsky, and Tippett.

Toccata alla Danza (OUP 1961) 3 min. Pianistic, brilliant, punctuated driving rhythms. Changing meters add a flexible rhythmic punch. Span of tenth required. M-D.

Sonata Op.23 (OUP 1963) 30pp. 18 min. Three movements. A large-scale work, free tonalities, bravura writing, harmonically lean. Well-contrasted ideas, interesting pedal notation. D.

Little Suite (OUP 1990) 12pp. 6 min. Prelude; Dance; Celtic Lament; Burlesque; Arietta; Finale. Freely tonal and effectively contrasted movements. Int.

See: Malcolm Boyd, *William Mathias* (Cardiff: University of Wales Press, 1978). Available in USA from Lawrence Verry, Inc., P.O. Box 98, Mystic, CT 06355.

Charles Henderson, "An Interview with William Mathias—Welsh Composer," M&M, 9 (July 1975):28–30.

Hugh Ottaway, "Some Thoughts on William Mathias—and Some of His Own," M&M, 26 (June 1978):28–30.

Yoritsune Matsudaira (1907–   ) Japan

Etudes pour piano d'après modes Japonais (Zen-On 1970) 67pp. A discussion of Japanese modes covers the first 9 pages. The first 17 pieces are studies in

Japanese modes, usually with two different key signatures (modes). This is followed by four sets of Themes and Variations, all in various Japanese modes. The final variation in the last Theme and Variation is a glissando study. Refreshing sounds. M-D to D.

Koromoi-uta (SZ 1972) 16pp. Twelve pieces based on popular tunes. Easy to Int.

Pièces de piano pour les enfants (Ongaku-No-Tomo-Sha 1969) 47pp. 32 short pieces based on Japanese children's songs and folk songs. Oriental harmonizations. Arranged by progressive difficulty. Easy to Int.

6 Préludes pour piano en Forme de Thème et Variations (Ongaku-No-Tomo-Sha 1976) 32pp. The player may begin the performance with any prelude and play the six pieces in any order. Inexact rhythmic notation, pointillistic, avant-garde. D.

Toshikatsu Matsuoka (1952–   ) Japan
Matsuoka has a master's degree in composition from the Tokyo University of Fine Arts and Music.

Music for Piano (Japan Federation of Composers 1994) 10 min. "These four movements demonstrate how the rhythmic elements and melodic elements are united into one after a repetition of mixture and dissociation. Echoes of the chords are dissimilated and the aftersound of the note C-sharp melts into time and space" (*1994 Japan Federation of Composers Catalogue*, p.14).

Tobias Matthay (1858–1945) Great Britain
Toccata 1888 rev. 1906 (Storm Clouds) Op.21 (Musica Obscura) 7pp. Arpeggios plus chromatic inflections, many rubato passages, dramatic closing; carefully edited. M-D.

Johann Mattheson (1681–1764) Germany
Pièces de Clavecin (1714) (BB, facsimile edition) 2 vols. Ouvertures, Preludes, Fugues, Allemandes, Courantes, Sarabandes, Gigues, and Aires. Int. to M-D.

Die wohlklingende Fingersprache (1735) (Hoffmann-Erbrecht—Br&H). 13 fugues and A, C, G, and Seriosita. The fugues are mainly in two and three voices. M-D.

See: Walter Schenkman, "Remembering Johann Mattheson," *Clavier*, 20 (December 1981):16–21. Includes *Suite* e.

Margaret Seares, "Johann Mattheson as Keyboard Composer," *Studies in Music*, II (1988):1–12.

Colin Matthews (1947–   ) Great Britain
Toccata, Nocturne and Scherzo 1977 (Faber) 14pp. 12 min. Toccata: brilliant, driving octaves on repeated E♭. Nocturne: static, octaves interspersed with flowing figure that develops. Scherzo: dissonant; declamatory; more relaxed trio section with an ostinato; leaping chords. M-D.

Berceuse and Sarabande 1978–79 (Faber) 13pp. 8 min. Conceived as the fourth and fifth parts of a Suite for piano; the first three parts are listed above. Expressionistic; well-ordered sonorities. M-D.

5 *Studies* (Faber 1977). 1. Quiet, slow chords in open fourths and fifths. 2. Fast alternating notes between the hands; right hand on black keys, left hand on whites; clever tunes emerge from these figurations. 3. Wispy, evaporates to nothing. 4. Angular and syncopated rhythms with alternating notes between the hands. 5. One-bar units of arpeggiation in contrary motion between the hands; many of the 270 bars are repeated numerous times; requires endurance. A well-crafted and varied set. M-D.

David Matthews (1943–   ) Great Britain

Piano Sonata Op.47 1989 (Faber 1994) 29 pp. 15 min. Recorded by William Howard on NMC DOZ15 (CD only). Allegro molto e ritmico: The sonata "may be heard either as three consecutive movements—sonata allegro, slow movement, scherzo plus coda—or as a piece in 15 sections each lasting roughly a minute, which is how I originally conceived it. Each section is based on a different tonality, beginning and ending on A. In the opening allegro the emphasis at first is on rhythm, but at its central point—the moment of recapitulation—there is a sudden eruption of melody, which then becomes dominant. Eventually the melodic line overflows into a 3-part slow movement, almost all quiet and lyrical. Then comes a miniature scherzo and trio, with jazzy rhythms, before a return to the music of the opening and an exuberant coda" (from the score). Schubert influence, lots of two-part writing, large distance between treble and bass, numerous rests. D.

David Maves (1937–   ) USA

Maves teaches at the College of Charleston in South Carolina.

Sonata I 1973 (CFP 1983) 27pp. 20 min. Tessitura; Tremolo; Attacca; Fioriture; Pianissimo; Finale. The first five movements are explorations of contrasting types of sonorities; the Finale sums up the other movements and adds strong emphasis on rhythm. Many directions for the performer. Avant garde. D.

Nicolas Maw (1935–   ) Great Britain

Personae 1973 (Bo&H) 13 min. 1. Free, improvisatory rhythm; quiet, harplike sonorities produced with arpeggiated chords surround little pieces of cadenza-like material. 2. Rhythmic but mainly concerned with "shades of soft." 3. Mainly two-part polyphony; agitated; contrasting sostenuto sections; concludes with a horrendous torrent of excitement. M-D to D.

See: Arnold Whittall, "Maw's 'Personae,' Chromaticism and Tonal Allusion," *Tempo*, 125 (June 1978):2–5, for a complete analysis of the piece.

Personae IV–VI 1985 (Faber) ca. 25 min. Wide expressive range, only for virtuosos. D.

William Mayer (1925–) USA

Sonata (CF 1961) 30pp. 18 min. Three movements. 12-tone idiom. Second movement has plucked string effects. Interlude appears between second and
third movements. Quintal and major-seventh harmonies, staccato chords,
bravura writing. D.

Trains and Things (TP 1971). Suite of four pieces, also available separately. Sub-
way in the Sunlight: ostinato-like bass; crisp, rhythmic melody; attractive.
Distance Times, Distance Places: 1. The Aging Troubadour: melody in left
hand, bitonal, flowing lines. 2. Cold of the Moon: recitative-like; short figures that press forward; long sustained chords; large span required. A Most
Important Train: heavy chords alternate between hands; repeated octaves;
arpeggi figures; repetitious left-hand figures give suggestion of moving
train; large span required. Int. to M-D.

Walter Mays (1941–) USA

Repetitions (Belwin-Mills 2150 1980) 9pp. 13 min. In three sections, one page of
performance notes, many directions in score. Aleatoric, avant-garde. M-D.

Kirke Mechem (1925–) USA

Suite Op.5 (ECS). Overture: cheerful, pompous. Elegy: cantabile, contrasting
middle section in octaves. Scherzo: spirited. Nocturne: Chopin style. Finale:
a brilliant presto, frequent meter changes. MC. M-D to D.

Sonata Op.26 (ECS). Three contrasted movements in traditional form. Neo-Romantic style. M-D.

Whims Op.31 (ECS 1972) 23pp. Fifteen short varied pieces in a neo-Romantic
style, strongly rhythmic. Cryptic titles, such as The Happy Drunken Organ
Grinder, Impertinence. Int.

Tilo Medek (1940–) Yugoslavia

Adventskalender (WH). 24 short pieces celebrating this joyous season. Opens with
Hunting Fanfare and closes with Christmas Eve. Contemporary throughout. Titles and comments in German only. Int. to M-D.

Meine Kleine Nostalgie 1974 (WH). Seven pieces reflecting moods and events re-
called from childhood. Reminiscent of Grieg's piano miniatures. German
titles only. Ranges from MC to avant-garde. M-D.

Nicholas Medtner (1880–1951) Russia

Medtner was a lapidarian craftsman who enlarged the piano repertoire considerably. 14 sonatas, some of imposing dimensions, 33 Fairy (Folk) Tales, 41 character pieces (Mood Pictures, Improvisations, Arabesques, Dithyrambs, Novels,
Lyric Fragments, Hymns, Romantic Sketches, Elegies, etc.), 3 volumes of *Forgotten Melodies,* and a set of variations make up the bulk of his solo piano writing.
His eclectic music is based on classic foundations, with a special fondness for
complex rhythmic procedure. A vivid imagination shows through in all his work.

All of the piano pieces require a well-developed pianism. Many can only be classified as difficult. A Medtner Society was formed in London in 1948 mainly to issue recordings of the composer playing his own works.

USSR has published the complete piano works in 4 vols. Vol.I: Opp.1–14: Vol.II: Opp.17–31: Vol.III: Opp.34–47: Vol.IV: Opp.47–59. Zimmermann also has a good selection of the piano works.

Sonata f Op.5 1904 (CFP) 44pp. Allegro: f. Intermezzo: c. Largo: E♭. Allegro risoluto: f. Many octaves and large chords. Influence of Brahms, Liszt, and Schumann in this portentous work. D.

Three Arabesques Op.7 (Benjamin 1925) 20pp. Allegretto tranquillo e dolce: left-hand melody, chromatic, *pp* closing. Andante con moto: chordal melody, chromatic accompaniment, big climax, then *ppp* closing. Allegro inquieto ma al rigore di tempo: syncopated accompaniment, soaring melody, many performance directions, virtuoso climax. M-D to D.

Two Fairy Tales Op.8 (Benjamin 1925) 19pp. Andantino: chordal melody laced with grace notes. Recitato—Allegro agitato: features 8/8 divided into 2 + 3 + 3, rich harmonies; scampers over keyboard. M-D.

Sonata-Triad Op.11 1907 (Frey—Simrock). No.1: Allegro non troppo, A♭. No.2: Andante molto espressivo, d; *Sonata elegie.* No.3: Allegro moderato, con passione innocente, C. Each movement is in SA design. Can be played as three separate pieces or as one work. M-D to D.

Sonata g Op.22 1911 28pp. 17 min. Tenebroso, sempre affrettando: Allegro assai. Interludium: Andante lugubre (leads to) Allegro assai. Written as a two-movement work but sounds like three with contrasting sections in a bravura-contrapuntal style. Fine motivic treatment, unusual rhythms. Excellent recital piece. M-D.

See: Harold Truscott, "Medtner's Sonata in G minor, Opus 22," MR (May 1961):112–23.

Märchen Sonata (Fairy Tale Sonata) Op.25/1c 1912 20pp. Allegro abbandonamente: c. Andantino con moto: E♭; cadenza leads to Allegro con spirito: c; in 5/2, 3/2. M-D.

Sonata e Op.25/2 1913 60pp. Introduzione: Andante con moto; Allegro; Tranquillo; Giocondamente; Stentato; Largamente; Allegro; Allegro molto sfrenatamente, Presto; Tenebroso tranquillo; Meno mosso, con meditazione; Concentrado, ma sempre con moto. These are some of the tempo-character directions used in this one-movement, diffuse work. M-D to D.

Sonata-Ballade F♯ Op.27 1913 41pp. Allegretto: F♯-f♯; large coda. Introduzione: Finale. Cyclic in form and more lyric than Op.22. M-D.

Sonata a Op.30 1914 27pp. Allegro risoluto. Many tempo-character directions. M-D.

Sonata b♭ Op.53/1 "Romantica" 48pp. Romance; Scherzo; Meditation; Finale. To be played without pause. Recurring reference to a single motive. A large work, somewhat similar in scope to Rachmaninoff's Sonata Op.36, composed 18 years earlier. Cyclic, cross-rhythms, complex harmonies, polyphonic textures. D.

See: SSB, pp.721–27, for a thorough discussion of the Sonatas.

SMALLER FORMS:

8 Mood Pictures Op.1 1902 (Forberg; Jurgenson) 30pp. Varied moods, all require facile technique. Int. to M-D.

3 Fairy Tales Op.9 1906. No.1 (Forberg) 8pp. Large span required for chord and octave passages. M-D.

3 Dithyrambs Op.10 1906 No.1 (Forberg; Jurgenson). No.1 is written in Brahmsian style, with rich harmonies, full chords, and octaves. M-D.

3 Pieces Op.31 1915. Improvisation: in the form of variations; brilliantly virtuosic and musically arresting. Funeral March. Fairy Tale. M-D to D.

Album of Selected Pieces (IMC). 4 Fairy Tales; Etude; Mood Picture; Idyll; Novelette; Dithyramb.

See: Eugene Barban, "In Praise of Medtner," *Clavier*, 19 (May–June 1980):14–21. Includes music of "Fairy Tale" Op.20/1.

Henry S. Gerstle, "The Piano Music of Nicolas Medtner," MQ, 10 (October 1924):500–10.

Sidney Miller, "Medtner's Piano Music," MT, 82 (October–November 1941):361–63, 393–95.

Etiènne Henri Méhul (1763–1817) France

Trois sonates pour le clavecin ou pianoforte Op.1 1783 (Minkoff) 24pp. While based on harpsichord style, the writing moves toward the Romantic piano. M-D.

Sonata A Op.1/3 1783 (Br&H 8108) 11pp. Allegro; Minuet and Trio; Rondo. Short movements that display a sensitive rococo style of form and expression. Good hand span required. M-D.

Sonata Op.2/3 in collection *Keyboard Music of the Baroque and Rococo* (Georgii —Arno Volk) Vol.3 contains Minuet A, second movement only. M-D.

Christopher Meineke (1782–1850) USA, born Germany

Meineke, a prolific composer, came to the U.S. in 1800 and lived and taught in Baltimore.

Rondo on "Polly Put the Kettle On" 1828. In collection *American Keyboard Music through 1865*, Vol.III (Clark—G. K. Hall 1990) 3pp. Simple classic style treatment. Int. to M-D.

Away with Melancholy 1827 In collection *American Keyboard Music through 1865,* Vol.III (Clark—G. K. Hall 1990). 4pp. 6 variations on the popular tune "Das klinget so henlich" from Mozart's *The Magic Flute.* Var. 6 is an "alla polacca" found in many variations sets of the day. This is one of 28 variation sets composed by Meineke. M-D.

Wilfrid Mellers (1914–   ) Great Britain

Natalis Invicti Solis (Nov 1969). No. 6 in *Virtuoso Series*. Canticle of the Waters: variations. Earth Rounds: requires electronic amplification, a rondo. Canticle of the Moon: static, derived from a single chord. Sun Rounds: interesting rondo technique. Reflects Mellers's interest in primeval rites and necromancy. Plucked strings, harmonics occasionally called for. Unusual. D.

Cat Charms 1965 (Nov) 11pp. Three times three pieces for piano. Morning: 1st charm—for walking to; 2nd charm—for hunting to; 3rd charm—for weaving to (at lunch time); 4th charm—for washing to; 5th charm—for dancing to in sunlight; 6th charm—for purring to at night; 7th charm—for keeping still in the dark to; 8th charm—for dancing to by midnight; 9th charm—for falling asleep to. Clever contemporary writing. These pieces could be mimed and danced to by a group of children. Suggested improvised added percussion is listed for such an occasion. Int.

Felix Mendelssohn-Bartholdy (1809–1847) Germany
One of the finest pianists of his time, Mendelssohn also had a remarkable memory and was probably one of the greatest of all improvisers. Synonymous with his style are well-thought-out ideas, smoothly flowing melodies, symmetrical designs, a highly individual scherzo style, and a complete familiarity with the piano. A sameness of harmonic idiom is sometimes brought about by his fondness for diminished and dominant sevenths. Opus numbers after 72 are assigned posthumously and are often incorrect chronologically.

Complete Piano Works (T. Kullak—CFP). Vol.I: Songs Without Words. Vol.II: Opp.5, 7, 14, 16, 33, 72. Vol.III: Opp.28, 35, 54, 82, 83, 104 (Book 2); Scherzo b; Etude f; Scherzo and Capriccio f♯. Vol.IV: Concerti; Capriccio Brilliant Op.22; Rondo Brilliant Op.29; Serenade and Allegro Op.43. Vol.V: Opp. 6, 15, 104 (Book 1), 105, 106, 117, 118, 119; Prelude and Fugue e; Gondellied A; 2 Piano Pieces B♭, g.

Complete Piano Works (K). Vol.I: Opp.5, 7, 14, 16, 33, 72; Andante Cantabile. Vol.II: Opp.28, 35, 54, 82, 104 (3 Etudes); Etude f; Scherzo b; Scherzo à Capriccio f♯. Vol.III: Opp.6, 15, 104 (3 Preludes), 105, 106, 117, 118, 119; Prelude and Fugue e; Barcarole A; 2 Piano Pieces B♭, g.
Available separately: Songs Without Words; Children's Pieces Op.72; Variations Sérieuses Op.54.

Complete Works for Pianoforte Solo (Julius Rietz—Dover) Reprint of the Br&H 1874–77 edition. Vol.I: Capriccio f♯ (1825); Sonata E (1826); Seven Characteristic Pieces; Rondo Capriccioso E (1824); Fantasy on "The Last Rose of Summer"; Three Fantasies or Caprices (1829); Scherzo b; Gondola Song A (1837); Scherzo a Capriccio f♯; Three Caprices (1833–35); Six Preludes and Fugues (1827–35); Variations Sérieuses d (1841); Fantasy f (1833); Andante cantabile e Presto agitato B (1838); Etude f (1836); Six Pieces for Children (ca. 1842); Variations E♭ (1841); Variations B♭. Vol.II: Three Preludes (1836); Three Etudes (1834–38); Sonata g (1821); Sonata B♭ (1827); Album Leaf (Song Without Words) e; Capriccio E/e (1837); Perpetuum Mobile C; Prelude and Fugue e (1827, 1841); Two Pieces; Songs Without Words (48 pieces in 8 books).

Complete Piano Works (Ravel—Durand) 9 vols.

Complete Piano Works (Falkenberg, Pierné—Heugel) 5 vols.

Selected Compositions (Romaniello—Ric) Vol.I: 48 Songs Without Words. Vol.II: Op.72; Gondellied A; 2 Piano Pieces B♭, g; Opp.117, 118, 119, 16, 15, 5, 14. Vol.III: Opp.28, 33, 7.

Miscellaneous Compositions (Kullak—GS). Opp.5, 7, 14, 16, 33, 72; Andante cantabile e presto agitato (no opus number).

SEPARATE PIECES:

Songs Without Words (Alfred 4860; Henle; CFP; GS; K; Ric; CF; Nov; EMB). The Alfred edition is complete and contains an analysis of each piece and a suggested teaching order. An immensely rich and varied collection of partly lyrical, partly virtuosic pieces, which, although short, are by no means simple. A suggested order of difficulty of a few selections might be: Op.19/6, Op.30/3, Op.19/4, Op.30/6, Op.19/2, Op.102/3, Op.38/2, Op.19/1, Op.67/5, Op.38/4, Op.53/2, Op.19/3, Op.30/1, Op.67/3, Op.102/2, 5, Op.38/3, Op.67/4, Op.62/5, Op.19/5. *Song Without Words* F (a 49th *Song*) (Werner—Curwen).

   See: Christine Brown, "Mendelssohn's *Songs Without Words*," *Piano Journal*, 14 (June 1984):15–17.

   Hans and Louise Tischler, "Mendelssohn's *Songs Without Words*," MQ, 33 (January 1947):1–16.

   Kenneth T. Williams, "A Teaching Guide to Mendelssohn's 'Songs Without Words,'" PQ, 141 (Spring 1988):48–55.

Capriccio f♯ Op.5 (Ric; Sal). Long, wide spectrum of technical requirements. M-D.

Andante and Rondo Capriccioso Op.14 (Alfred 3577; Henle; CFP; Schott; Sal; Ric; WH; GS; Durand; Nov). Still a fine work and one of Mendelssohn's most representative contributions, especially the elfin brilliance of the rondo. M-D.

3 Fantasies Op.16 (WH). a, e (deservedly the most popular) (Alfred), E. M-D.

   Available separately: Fantasy E (CF).

   See: John Horton, "Holiday Pictures from Wales—Mendelssohn's Three Fantasies, Op.16," *Music Teacher*, 60/2 (February 1981):22.

Fantasia f♯ Op.28 1833 (GS; Ric) 12½ min. Mendelssohn referred to this work as his "Scottish Sonata" (*Sonata ecossaise* has become affixed as a subtitle). First movement: slow tempo, preceded and several times interrupted by a rhapsodical introductory passage; grandiose return of the main theme. Second movement: a scherzo, opens with a somewhat Schubertian phrase. Finale: fiery and impetuous, in SA design. This major work deserves more playing; it seems to be finding its way back into the repertoire. M-D.

3 Caprices Op.33 a, E, b♭. Nos.1 and 3 have slow introductions and presto mid-sections. The mid-section of No.1 is a sonata-like movement mainly agitato in mood. M-D.

6 Preludes and Fugues Op.35 (ABRSM; Scharwenka—IMC; CFP; Sal). e, D, b, A♭, f, B♭. Prelude and Fugue No.1 (GS) is the most frequently played of the set. Prelude: melodic line moves through arpeggio figuration. Fugue: concludes on the chorale "Ein' feste Burg." M-D.

Andante cantabile and Presto agitato B 1838. No opus number. Lyric Andante followed by a SA Presto. Effective passage work. M-D.

Variations Sérieuses Op.54 1841 (Henle; Schott; CFP; GS; Sal; Ric; K; Durand). 17 continuous variations except for a short pause before and after the 14th, a major mode adagio of somewhat religious flavor. An intricate and tautly worked structure. Theme is one of Mendelssohn's most attractive; it provides the basis for some attractive piano writing. Notable among the beautifully conceived variations are the canonic No.4, the fugal No.10, the strongly Schumannesque No.11, and No.15, in which the rhythmic basis of the theme is emphasized. Ends with a tense coda. Mendelssohn's finest piano work. M-D.

See: George Kochevitsky, "A Discussion of Mendelssohn's Variations Sérieuses," *Clavier*, 22/3 (March 1983):26–30. Includes music of theme and first five variations.

Six Pieces for Children Op.72 1842 (Alfred; CFP; Durand; ABRSM; Hansen House; PWM; K). This set is sometimes titled *Six Christmas Pieces* (Alfred; ABRSM). Written to entertain performer and audience. Require neat and precise fingers. Nos.1, 5, and 6 make an appealing group. Int.

Variations E♭ Op.82 1841 (ABRSM; CFP; Sal; GS, with Opp.54 and 83). Smaller in dimension than Op.54 but similar figurations throughout. M-D.

Variations B♭ Op.83 1841. Five variations with a long finale. M-D.

3 Etudes Op.104a (GS; WH). b♭; F (Sal); a. Facile, perpetual motion studies with No.1 dividing melody between hands. Ingenious, charming. M-D.

See: Thomas Schumacher, "Performance Lesson on a Mendelssohn Etude," *Clavier*, 14 (February 1975):19–23. Discusses No.3 in a.

3 Preludes Op.104b (CFP; Ric). B♭, b, D. Single studies. M-D.

Sonata E Op.6 1826. Four movements to be played without a break. Allegretto con espressione: in SA design; recalls Beethoven Op.101. Tempo di menuetto; minuet tempo plus scherzo. Adagio e senza tempo: recitative, lengthy, free transition. Molto allegro e vivace: main theme of first movement requoted. M-D.

See: SSB, pp.299–300.

Sonata g Op.105 1821. Allegro: chromaticism recalls Mozart. Adagio: improvisatory. Presto: SA design. Earliest published work, but already shows Mendelssohn to be a master craftsman. M-D.

Sonata b♭ 1823 (CFP 66853 1981, first publication of this work). Composed when Mendelssohn was 14; strong Weber influence. More like a sonatina. Elegant pathos, displays facile compositional technique and grasp of form. Span of tenth required.

See: R. Larry Todd, "A Sonata by Mendelssohn," PQ, 112 (Winter 1980–81):30–41. Discusses Sonata b♭ and includes the music.

Sonata B♭ Op.106 1827. Allegro vivace: opening modeled after Beethoven Op.106.

Scherzo: Andante quasi allegretto followed by Allegro molto bridge. Allegro moderato: scherzo theme returns at Allegro non troppo. M-D.

Scherzo b. No opus number. Staccato study. M-D.

Scherzo à Capriccio f♯ (Ric). No opus number. Binary design. Pianistic demands vary from light staccato to demanding octaves. Melancholy undercurrent. M-D.

3 Posthumous Pieces (E. Walker—Nov). "Im Kahn"; Song Without Words d; Canon f♯. Int. to M-D.

Fantasy on the "Last Rose of Summer" Op.15 (Br&H). The Irish folk song is not elaborated but its simplicity is emphasized by other materials that contrast with it in tempo, mode, and figuration. To close the piece, rather than repeat the melody, Mendelssohn constructed an original Andante that reflects the folk song in general melodic shape. M-D.

COLLECTIONS:

Easy Piano Pieces and Dances (Töpel—Br 6568). Includes some of the "Songs without Words," two of which are published here for the first time. Int. to M-D.

Selected Works for the Piano (Eric Werner—Henle). Contains: Op.7; Op.35; Op.54; Op.106; Songs Without Words Op.19/6, Op.30/4, Op.38/6, Op.53/3, 6, Op.62/1, 3, 6, Op.67/3.

Il mio primo Mendelssohn (Pozzoli—Ric ER2447) 21pp. Contains: 6 pieces from Op.72; Andante sostenuto E♭; Andante con moto D; Allegretto G; Allegro non troppo G; Allegro assai g; Vivace F; 5 Songs Without Words; Venetian Barcarolle, Op.19/6; Op.30/3, 6; Op.85/2; Op.102/3. Int. to M-D.

The Young Pianist's Mendelssohn (Harry Dexter—Hansen House 1972) 33pp. A collection of the easier piano works in their original form. Int. to M-D.

Mendelssohn Album (EMB 1964). Songs Without Words Op.19/6, 3, Op.30/6, Op.67/34, Op.62/3, 6; Kriegsmarsch Op.61; Hochzeitsmarsch Op.61; Auf Flügeln des Gesanges Op.34/2 (arr. F. Liszt); Fantasies Op.16/1, 2, 3; Rondo capriccioso Op.14; Skizze from Zwei Klavierstücke Op.posth.; Scherzo Capriccioso f♯ Op.posth. Performing edition, tastefully edited.

Mendelssohn: An Introduction to His Piano Works (Halford—Alfred) 64pp. Contains: 6 Pieces for Children Op.72; Venetian Boat Songs Op.19/6 and 30/6; Songs Without Words Op.85/1, 2, Op.102/3, 6, Op.19/4, 8; Sonata E Op.6 (Tempo di Menuetto): Scherzo b no opus number; Fantasy or Caprice Op.16/1; Scherzo e Op.16/2. Int.

See: Joscelyn Godwin, "Early Mendelssohn and Late Beethoven," ML, 55 (July 1974):272–85. Discusses Mendelssohn's Sonata E Op.6 and Fantasies for piano f♯ Op.28 and E Op.15 and their inspiration drawn from Beethoven.

Robert Parkins, "Mendelssohn and the Érard Piano," PQ, 125 (Spring 1984):53–54, 56–59.

Hans and Louise Tischler, "Mendelssohn's Style," MR, 8 (1947):256–73.

Gilberto Mendes (1922–   ) Brazil
Prelúdio IV 1952 (Ric BR2548) 2pp. Hemiola accompaniment, wistful expressive
melody, attractive. Int. to M-D.

Jaime Mendozo-Nava (1925–   ) Bolivia
Three Bolivian Dances (Rongwen 1956). Lively, full sonorities, based on native
dance rhythms. M-D.
Gitana (BB 1957). Mixed meters, much glitter. M-D.

Misha Mengelberg (1935–   ) The Netherlands
Mengelberg has been involved with jazz since 1960.
3 Pianopieces and Pianopiece No.4 (Donemus 1966). Nos.1–3 are short with conventional notation, varied tempi, and mood. No.4: avant-garde, cluster technique emphasized. M-D to D.

Peter Mennin (1923–1983) USA
Mennin's music is characterized by propulsive rhythms, long flowing melodies,
effective treatment of dissonance, and linear writing of the highest order.
Five Piano Pieces (CF 1949). Prelude: short, transparent, perpetual motion. Aria:
tranquil adagio, sustained, sonorous. Variation—Canzona: contrapuntal
treatment of a rhythmic idea in 5/8. Canto: cantabile style, flowing andante.
Toccata: energetic rhythms, strongly accented, biting vigor, perpetual motion, most difficult of set. An eloquent and forceful work. D.
Sonata (CF 1967) 32pp. A large-scale three-movement work. Opening movement
characterized by frequent meter and tempo changes. Pedal point in the
second movement adds tonal stability. Third movement uses changing meters. Brilliant closing. D.

Gian Carlo Menotti (1911–   ) USA, born Italy
Poemetti (Ric). 12 pieces. Romantic, impressionist. Excellent teaching material.
Int.
Ricercare and Toccata, on a theme from "The Old Maid and the Thief" (Ric 1953).
Appealing melodic material, propulsive, "running" Toccata. M-D.
Amahl and the Night Visitors (GS 1978) 31pp. Eight opera excerpts arranged with
words printed as text. Attractive and pianistic. Int. to M-D.

Usko Meriläinen (1930–   ) Finland
Riviravi 1962 (Fazer) 15pp. Small pieces, sophisticated, clever and tricky. Int.
Sonata II (Weinberger 1966) 16pp. 17 min. A tempo variable lento—mosso; Lento;
Presto. A major work that uses clusters and experimental techniques in
sounding harmonics, atonal. D.
Sonata IV (Fazer 1975) 24pp. Epyllion II. Includes a table of notational devices.
Strings are to be plucked. Four movements; only the third is slow; the oth-
ers are full of pianistic acrobatics. Requires virtuoso technique. D.
Tre notturni (Fazer) 6 min. Expressionistic. D.

Michel Merlet (1939–   ) France

Jeu de quartes (Leduc 1973) 9pp. 4½ min. This "Play of Fourths" is constructed
on fourths in every conceivable way. Atonal, dynamic extremes, harmonics.
Large span required. D.

24 Preludes Op.31 1981 (Choudens). These pieces retain Chopin's idea of trying to extract from a single theme or cell everything that lends itself to its
enrichment while keeping it concise. Although relentlessly dissonant, the
work is tonal, Romantic in outlook, and eclectic. Influences of Wagner,
Scriabin, Prokofieff, Messiaen, Fauré (especially in the flowing opening
Prelude), Rachmaninoff, and Ives, whose dense Impressionistic harmonies
often cloud the music. M-D to D.

Sonatine 1966 (Leduc) 31pp. A substantial work. M-D.

Bors Mersson (1921–   ) Switzerland, born Germany

5 Pieces Op.23 (Eulenburg GM 886 1979) 19pp. MS reproduction, easy to read.
Capriccioso: fast perpetual motion. Sogno: lyric, varied meters. Inventio:
scherzolike. Intermezzo Tenebro: gentle suspension. Impromptu: perpetual
motion. MC; require dynamic control and facility. M-D.

Olivier Messiaen (1908–1992) France

Messiaen continued the development of the whole line of French piano music
from Debussy, beginning with the early *Préludes* and progressing to the unique
Catalogue d'oiseaux. His piano writing is built on the style of the late sonatas of
Beethoven and continued by Liszt and Ravel. Messiaen's style is best understood
and described in his own book, *Technique of My Musical Language* (Paris: Leduc,
1944). All his music is greatly influenced by his beliefs as a Catholic mystic. The
piano style is varied, with emphasis on multiple modality, free use of dominant
discords that often produce fresh sonorities, and use of the piano orchestrally.
Bird calls and Hindu ragas have also influenced Messiaen. His music is extremely
colorful. The emphasis on sonority is striking, and the musical gestures are generous and almost ritualistic in the obsessive use of characteristic rhythmic procedures. Messiaen juxtaposes ideas, but usually does not develop them. Most of
the piano works require advanced pianism, but a few of the earlier works, such
as *Fantaisie burlesque, Pièce pour le tombeau de Paul Dukas, Rondeau*, and a few
of the *Préludes*, are less involved. Messiaen has also influenced the composers
Boulez and Stockhausen, who studied with him.

Les Offrandes Oubliées 1930 (Durand) 8pp. A very pianistic transcription by
Messiaen of an orchestral work. The middle section shows the influence of
Dukas, both rhythmically and harmonically, but the language is still highly
personal. M-D.

Fantaisie Burlesque 1932 (Durand). ABA; the A sections are supposed to be
"burlesques." The B section is more interesting. Free, jazzy, polytonal
counterpoint, brilliant sonorities. M-D.

8 Préludes 1928–29 (Durand). La Colombe: short, expressive. Chant d'Extase
dans un Paysage triste: slow, somber. Instants Défunts: short, atmospheric.

Le Nombre Léger: melodic line over light, rapid figuration. Les Sons Impalpables du Rêve: complex, lengthy. Cloches d'Angoisse et Larmes d'Adieu: slow, complex, lengthy. Plainte calme: short, melodic, wistful. Un Reflet dans le Vent: flowing, climactic, long. M-D to D.

Comments by Messiaen about the *Préludes*:

"A work written in 1928–1929. I was then twenty. I had not yet embarked on those investigations of rhythm that were to change my life. I loved birds passionately without yet knowing how to set their songs down on paper. But I was already a sound-color composer. Through the use of harmonic modes, which were limited to a certain number of transpositions only and which drew their special colorations from that fact, I had succeeded in putting wheels of color in opposition, in interweaving rainbows, in finding 'complementary' colors in music. The titles of these Preludes conceal studies in color. And the sad tale implied by the sixth Prelude, *Cloches d'angoisse et larmes d'adieu* (Bells of Anguish and Tears of Farewell) is shrouded in sumptuous draperies of violet, orange, and royal purple.

"A few details on the colors of each Prelude:

"I. *La colombe* (The Dove): orange veined with violet. II. *Chant d'extase dans un paysage triste* (Song of Ecstasy in a Sad Landscape): grey, mauve, Prussian blue at the beginning and end; the middle section is diamonded and silvered. III. *Le nombre léger* (The Rapid Number): orange veined with violet. IV. *Instants défunts* (Dead Moments): velvety grey with mauve and green highlights. V. *Les sons palpable du rêve* (The Palpable Sounds of the Dreamworld): polymodal, super-imposing a blue-orange mode with ostinato and chord-cascades on a violet-purple mode treated like a brazen gong; note the pianistic writing: triple notes, stretches of chords, crab-canon, crossed hands, various staccatos, brassy legatos, jewel-effects. VI. *Cloches d'angoisse et larmes d'adieu*: The bells commingle several modes; the 'hum' (the deep-toned aftersound) and all the upper harmonics of the bells dissolve into each other in luminous vibrations; the farewell is royal purple, orange, violet. VII. *Plainte calme* (Quiet Moan): Velvety grey with mauve and green highlights. VIII. *Un reflet dans le vent* (A Reflection in the Wind): the little tempest with which this piece opens and closes alternates green-veined orange with several black patches; the central development section is more luminous; the second theme, quite melodic and wreathed in sinuous arpeggios, is blue-orange at its first appearance, green-orange at its second.

"Dominant colors of the work as a whole: violet, orange, royal purple."

Pièce pour le tombeau de Paul Dukas 1935 (*Supplément de la Revue Musicale*, May–June 1936). This "piece is very simple: it is the first transposition of Mode III whose orange, white, and gold light falls perpetually on a long dominant seventh. It is static, solemn, and unadorned like an enormous block of stone" (the composer, on Musical Heritage record jacket No.4423). M-D.

Vingt Regards sur l'Enfant Jésus ("Twenty Contemplations of Looking at the

Christ Child") 1944 (Durand). This pianistic marathon requires about 1¾ hours to perform the complete work. Messiaen lavishes his religious expression on the contemplations of the child Jesus by twenty different personages: the Father, the Virgin, the Star, etc. Leitmotifs represent the Cross and the heavenly arch, God, and the Star. Complex writing that requires virtuoso technique and musicianship. "More than in all my preceding works, I have sought a language of mystic love; at once varied, powerful, and tender, sometimes brutal, in a multi-colored ordering."

No.2, Regards de l'étoile: octotonic with the hands three octaves apart, shimmering arpeggio and chordal passages alternate, dynamics from *ppp* to *ff*. M-D. No.7, Regard de la Croix: colorful harmonic progressions in a slow, majestic mood. M-D to D. No.8, Regard de hauteur: bird calls find their way into this pianistic piece. D. No.10, Regard de l'Esprit: "dance of joy," octotonic opening, chain trills, chordal horn passage, "grand transport of joy" climax. D. No.13, Noël: crashing bell-like chords at extremes of keyboard contrast with ethereal meditative sections, exciting. No.16, Regard des prophètes, des bergers et des Mages: canonic rhythmic processional, picturesque throughout, orchestral. No.19, Je dors, mais mon coeur veille: meditation on "I sleep, but my heart watches"; rich and Impressionistic. M-D.

Available separately (Durand): VI. Par lui tout a été fait; X. Regard de l'esprit de joie; XI. Première communion de la Vierge; XV. Le baiser de l'enfant Jesus; XVII. Regard du Silence.

See: David Burge, "Olivier Messiaen's Vingt Regards sur l'enfant Jesus," *Keyboard*, 10/1 (January 1984):66.

Frank Martin, "Messiaen—A Brief Guide," *Piano Journal*, 43/15 (February 1994):13–18. Focuses on this work.

Michael Troup, "Regard sur Olivier Messiaen," *Piano Journal*, 11 (June 1983):11–13.

Quatre Etudes de Rythme 1949–50 (Durand) 17½ min. Published separately. Messiaen prefers the order listed. Ile de Feu I (Island of Fire I): dedicated to Papua (New Guinea), the themes have the violence of the magic cults of that country. Mode de valeurs et d'intensité (Mode of Values and Intensities): uses a pitch-mode (36 tones), a value-mode (24 note-lengths), an attack-mode (12 kinds of attacks), and intensity-mode (12 shades of intensity). Durations, intensities, and attacks are combined according to the tonal plan. Neumes rythmiques (Rhythmic Neumes): complex rhythmic study with fixed resonances and intensities. Ile de feu II (Island of Fire II): main theme, again violent and ferocious, has the same character of those of the first study; the variations of this theme alternate with permutations, always inverted in the same order of reading, and superimposed, one on another, in pairs; ends with a perpetual motion for crossed hands at the lower end of the keyboard. All four pieces contain unusual sonorities and a rhapsodic grandeur. D.

Cantéyodjaya 1953 (UE) 11½ min. This large work repeats the opening phrase extensively. Ragas, retrograde inversion, a six-voice canon, and fixed rhythms make this a most complex and vigorous work. Hypnotic. D.

Catalogue d'oiseaux 1956–58 (Leduc). 7 books. Large-scale pieces based on bird calls collected by Messiaen on travels throughout France. Includes list of the birds and a verbal description about each call. Book 1: Alpine Chough; Golden Oriole; Blue Rock Thrush. Book 2: Blackeared Wheatear. Book 3: Little Owl; Woodlark. Book 4: Reed Warbler. Book 5: Short-toed Lark; Cetti's Warbler. Book 6: Rock Thrush. Book 7: Buzzard; Black Wheatear; Curlew. A unique set of pieces, perhaps unprecedented in the history of music. Fascinating sonorities requiring the most advanced pianism. D.

La Fauvette des Jardin 1970 ("The Golden Warbler") (Leduc) 55pp. The composer's recreation of a peaceful summer day spent by the shores of a lake, colorfully enhanced with bird calls. Belongs in style to the *Catalogue d'oiseaux*. D.

See: Meri Kurenniemi, "Messiaen, the Ornithologist," MR, 41/2 (May 1980):121–26. A discussion of the bird-song influence mainly in the piano works.

Andrew Porter, "Messiaen's Wonderful World of Birds," *High Fidelity,* 23 (September 1973):79–80.

See: James Avery, "Olivier Messiaen—An Introduction to His Piano Music," CK, 5 (August 1979):36–40, 42.

Peter Hill, "Messiaen's Catalogue d'Oiseau," *Clavier,* 29/10 (December 1990): 20–22.

John M. Lee, "Harmony in the Solo Piano Works of Olivier Messiaen," *College Music Symposium,* 23/1 (Spring 1983):65–80. Concentrates on the earliest works through the *Quatre études de rythme.*

Alain Messiaen, "Olivier Messiaen's 'Message,'" MO, 103 (January 1980):133–34, 136.

Antonio Mestres (18th century) Spain

Doce Piezas (Francisco Civil—UME). Twelve pieces, most of them called Toccatas. No suggestions for performance. Mainly two-part textures, da capo form, syncopated rhythms, triplet figures. Appealing, colorful. Int.

Gérard Meunier (1928–   ) France

Meunier is a pedagogue, pianist, composer, and the director of the Aubervillers–La Courneuve Conservatory.

Sonate (Aux Oiseaux Victimes des Marées Noires) (Lemoine 1979) 17pp. Dedicated to bird victims of sea pollution. Three movements, bird calls, flutterings, dark colors, freely tonal. M-D.

L'Oiseau de Lumière (The Bird of Light) 1980 (Lemoine) 5pp. 5 min. Portrays a bird's fanciful flight. Impressionistic, sensitive, expressive, birdlike sounds. Many pedal instructions. Crashing cluster ends the piece. M-D.

Le chateau du Temps-Perdu (The Castle of Lost Time) (Lemoine 1980) 15pp. Six short colorful pieces with a story for each piece. Attractive. Int.

Krzysztof Meyer (1943–   ) Poland

24 Preludes Op.43 1978 (AA) 68 min. Varied contemporary textures, from simple two-voiced (No.8) to a chorale in whole notes (No.16) to the complex virtuoso (Nos.10, 13, 17). Moods range from the tragic and dramatic (Nos.12, 14, 16, 20, 22) to the playful and grotesque (Nos.17 and 19). Notation is precise and exact in some; others use various kinds of aleatorism. M-D to D.

See: Krzysztof Meyer, "My 24 Preludes," *Polish Music*, 14/3 (1979):12–16.

Second Piano Sonata 1963 (PWM). 16 min. First movement: a study in extreme dynamic contrasts. Second movement: a fast study in changing meters, mostly played softly and delicately. Finale: begins with new material in clusters, ideas from other two movements return, recognizable but in a new guise; concludes with repetition of soft theme from the first movement, now played softer than before and morendo. M-D to D.

See: David Burge, "Three Recent Piano Sonatas," *Keyboard*, 10/4 (April 1984): 64–65.

Nikolai Miaskovsky (1881–1950) USSR

Miaskovsky was a prolific composer for the piano. He wrote nine sonatas and numerous separate pieces. His style was essentially Romantic and is marked by a somber element. The harmonic and melodic fourth and imitative textures are common in his writing. All the piano music is contained in *Complete Edition* Vol.10 (USSR).

Complete Piano Sonatas (GS 6279).

Sonata No.2 f♯ 1912 rev.1948 (GS 528) 12 min. One movement. Short acerbic motives continually return and are developed by accumulation. Mid-section is built around the "Dies Irae" and takes the place of the development. The recapitulation leads to a fugue followed by a short coda. Virtuosic, sparkling passage-work. Scriabin influence minus his metaphysics. M-D to D.

Sonata No.3 C Op.19 (USSR). Large one-movement sectionalized work. Entire range of keyboard exploited; large span necessary. D.

Sonata No.4 c Op.27 (USSR). Allegro moderato: declamatory. Variations on a theme quasi-sarabanda. Finale: toccata-like, many double notes. D.

Yellowed Pages Op.31 (GS 532). Two short bagatelles, both poetic. Int.

4 Little Fugues Opp.43, 78 (K). In c, F, d, g. Excellent pedagogic material. Int.

Sonata d Op.83 (USSR). Three movements. More traditional, easier than other sonatas. M-D.

Sonata F Op.84 1949 (K 9545). Allegro non troppo; Andante sostenuto; Molto vivo. Pleasant, not taxing technically, requires nicely shaped phrasing, allows for exploring quieter tonal shades of the piano. M-D.

Francisco Mignone (1897–1986) Brazil

Mignone's music combines Portuguese, Indian, and African elements. His piano style is Romantic in conception and full of rich sonorities. Many other piano works are published by companies in Brazil.

Congada 1928 (EBM; Ric). Brilliant Brazilian dance. M-D.

Lenda Brasileira (EBM). No.1 (1923): atmospheric, restful, sonorous climax, quiet closing. No.2 (1923): short, arpeggio figuration, subtle. No.3 (1928): recitative-like passages, sudden dynamic changes, ferocious. No.4 (1930): flowing, brilliant climax, peaceful closing. These dramatic ballades are rewarding to study and play. M-D.

Tango Brasileira (EBM) Double sixths present problems. M-D.

4 Sonatinas 1949 (Ric). Short, in two movements. Clever rhythmic treatment contrasted with varied moods. Post-Impressionistic and highly nationalistic. Int.

Quasi Modinha (EBM 1940). Melodic, samba rhythms. Int.

Miudinho (EBM). Crisp, rhythmic. Int.

Crianças Brincando (EBM 1934). Brilliant, some dissonance, percussive, alternating hands. Int.

Six Preludes (Ric). Varied moods, mainly rhythmic. Int. to M-D.

Sonata No.1 (Ric 1941). Three movements, strong melodic writing, bitonal sonorities but tonal. M-D.

Sonata No.2 1962 (SDM) 19pp. 20 min. Three movements. Mignone's first attempt at atonal writing for the piano. All thematic ideas lean heavily on the interval of the third. Serialized melodies but not developed serially. D.

Sonata No.3 1964 (SDM) 15pp. 19 min. Four separate movements thematically related. Atonal, fragmentary texture, serial techniques. D.

Sonata No.4 1964 (Mangione) 15 min. One continuous atonal work in four sections. Texture is more cohesive than in Sonatas Nos. 2 and 3. Different from any other Mignone work; displays an integrated maturity not always seen in his other sonatas. D.

Twelve Studies (Columbia Music Co.) 2 vols. Recital pieces. M-D.

See: Sister Marion Verhaalen, "Francisco Mignone: His Music for Piano," *Inter-American Music Bulletin*, No.79 (November 1970–February 1971):1–36.

Georges Migot (1891–1976) France

Migot wrote in a highly linear style.

4 Nocturnes 1935 (Leduc). Interesting ideas, wandering, improvisatory style. M-D.

Preludes 1946–47 (Leduc). 2 books, 6 pieces in each. Poetic and expressive. M-D.

Le Zodiaque: 12 Etudes de Concert 1933 (Leduc). Migot's most solid contribution to piano literature. D.

Le Tombeau de Dufault jouer de luth 1923 (Senart). These three pieces (2pp., 2pp., 3pp.) utilize lute texture. Dedicated to Blanche Selva. M-D.

Marcel Mihalovici (1898–1985) France, born Rumania

Chanson, Pastorale and Danse Op.32 (Sal). In popular Rumanian style. M-D.

Quatre Caprices 1928 (ESC). Primitive rhythms exploited. M-D.

Cinq Bagatelles 1934 (ESC). Varied moods and difficulty. No.4, Toccata, is most effective.

Ricercari Op.46 1941 (Heugel) 21 min. Free variations on an eight-bar passacaglia theme, variations grouped into eleven movements. Broad scale, chromatic, sonorous. Virtuoso technique necessary. D.

Quatre Pastorales Op.62 (Heugel). Short, chromatic, colorful. No.2 is toccata-like. M-D.

Trois Pièces Nocturnes Op.63 1948–51 (Heugel). Impromptu; Rêve; Epilogue. Light, colorful sketches. M-D.

Sonate Op.90 1965 (Leduc) 18pp. 16 min. Allegretto piacevole; Lento, improvisando; Allegro giocoso. Special signs are explained. Written in a style that is developed from Enesco, Bartók, neoclassic Stravinsky, and Les Six. Large span required along with virtuoso technique. D.

Darius Milhaud (1892–1974) France

Milhaud used a variety of techniques, both old and new. Polytonality, contrapuntal textures, folksong, and jazz are all utilized in generous measure. Melody is very important in all his music. Formally, he was very much a classicist. Contrasting moods of tenderness and gaiety were popular with this prolific composer.

Suite en cinq partes Op.8 1913 (Durand; MMP). Lent; Vif et clair; Lourd et rythmé; Lente et grave; Modéré—animé. One of Milhaud's most successful pieces. M-D.

Sonata No.1 Op.33 1916 (ESC). Décidé; Pastoral; Rythmé. Polytonal treatment, folklike melodies. Exploits full use of keyboard, mainly chordal. M-D.

Printemps 1915–20 (ESC). Book I. Op. 25; Book II. Op.66, 3 pieces in each. Short, salon style with Debussy and Satie influence plus some dissonant originality. Int.

Saudades do Brazil Op.67 1921 (ESC; Ev). Vol.I: Sorocaba; Botafogo; Leme; Copacabana; Ipanema; Gavea. Vol.II: Corcovado; Tijuca; Paineras; Sumaré; Laranjeiras; Paysandu. Each 2pp. 12 dances in popular Brazilian style employing bitonality, tango and habanera rhythms, changing sonorities, varied figuration. Titles are names of different sections in Rio de Janeiro. Int. to M-D.

Trois Rag-Caprices Op.78 1922 (UE). Dated but clever rhythms in highly stylized ragtime style. No.2 is easiest. M-D.

L'Automne Op.115 1932 (Sal). Septembre; Alfama; Adieu. The first two pieces are brisk and require good double-note, broken-chord, and octave technique. Adieu is easier, somewhat contrapuntal, songlike. M-D.

Quatre Romances sans Paroles Op.129 1933 (Sal). Short, lyric. Int.

L'Album de Madame Bovary Op.128b (Enoch 1933). Seventeen short, sensitive pieces from the film *Madame Bovary*. Int.

Three Waltzes from Madame Bovary Op.128c 1933 (Enoch). Has subtle links with the movie. Int. to M-D.

Four Sketches Op.227 1941 (Mer). Eglogue; Madrigal; Alameda; Sobre la Loma. Rhumba rhythm in Sobre la Loma. M-D.

The Household Muse Op.245 1944 (EV). 3 vols. Fifteen short lyric sketches depicting activities such as Cooking, Laundry, The Son Who Paints. Int.

Une Journée Op.269 1946 (Mer). Five lyric miniatures representing various times of day. L'Aube; La Matinée; Midi; L'Après-Midi; Le Crépuscule. Int.

L'Enfant Aime (A Child Loves) Op.289 1948 (MCA). Five short children's pieces. Chromatic. Not easy. Int.

Sonata No.2 Op.293 1949 (Heugel). Alerte; Léger; Doucement; Rapide. Transparent textures, linear movement, arid. M-D.

Le Candélabre à Sept Branches (The Seven-Branched Candelabrum) Op.315 1951 (PIC). A suite based on the festivals that make up the Jewish Calendar: New Year; Day of Atonement; Feast of the Tabernacles; Resistance of the Maccabees; Feast of Esther; Passover; Feast of Weeks. Varied moods, styles, and difficulty. M-D.

Accueil Amical. Pièces enfantines Op.326 1943–48. (Heugel). Seventeen short easy pieces. In the same tradition as *Album for the Young.* Int.

Hymne de Glorification Op.331 1954 (ESC). Polytonal, bright, pretentious. M-D.

Sonatine Op.354 1956 (EMT). Décidé; Modéré; Alerte. More dissonance than in most of the other piano works. Each movement ends quietly. M-D.

The Joys of Life Op.360 1957 (Belwin-Mills) 23pp. Pastorale; The Indifferent; Rustic Pleasures; Serenade; Bagpipe; Masquerade. Composed in "Homage to Watteau," French painter of delicate, pastel-hued pictures (1684–1721), and takes its title from Watteau's celebrated "Les Charmes de la Vie." The Suite portrays scenes suggested by six of the artist's delightful canvasses. Milhaud evokes the gallant, cultured, and refined style of the rococo period in subtly spun, sensitive little tone-poems of almost Mozartean flavor. M-D.

The Globetrotter Suite Op.358 (Belwin-Mills) 28pp. France; Portugal; Italy; USA; Mexico; Brazil. Brilliantly colored vignettes of countries Milhaud knew intimately from his extensive travels. M-D.

La Libertadora Op.236 (Ahn & Simrock) 7 min. A set of five pieces. Light, deft, some fancy writing with some performing problems. Folklike tunes and samba rhythms used. Originally for two pianos, this arrangement is by the composer. M-D.

Polka Op.95 1929 (Heugel) 5pp. This spectacular piece is No.7 from *L'eventail de Jeanne,* a collaborative ballet by Ravel, Ferroud, Ibert, Roland-Manuel, Delanney, Roussel, Milhaud, Poulenc, Auric, and Schmitt. M-D.

See: Mary Jane Rupert, "The Piano Music of Darius Milhaud: A Survey," diss., Indiana University, 134 pp.

Akira Miyoshi (1933–   ) Japan

Miyoshi is Director of the Tojo Music School in Tokyo.

Sonate 1958 (Ongaku-No-Tomo-Sha) 34pp. 24 min. Composed in Paris. Allegro; Andante; Presto. This nontonal work requires virtuoso technique and mature musicianship. Big chords, fluid arpeggi passages, large skips, strong rhythmic drive, and a subtle sonority palette display a well-developed compositional talent. D.

Chaines 1973 (Chains) (Zen-On) 31pp. 21 min. A chain of 24 Preludes that lead directly from one to the next. In three parts. Flexible tempos, motivic development, harmonic richness, well-planned formal scheme, emotional appeal. Alternates between frantic activity and morose contemplation, uses "Dies Irae" theme. Interlocking materials (four small chainettes) fade out at conclusion. Messiaen influence; metric, spatial, and "do-it-yourself" notation used. Powerful and moving. D.

    See: David Burge, "Akira Miyoshi's *Chaines,*" *Keyboard*, 8/9 (September 1982):60–61.

En Vers (Zen-On 1980) 14pp. Flexible meters, dynamic extremes, serial influence, dramatic gestures, many starts and stops, expressionistic. Builds to climax with cadenza-like section. D.

See: Naomi Noro Brown, "Akira Miyoshi's Didactic Works for Piano," diss., Louisiana State University, 1994, 109 pp.

Robert Moevs (1920–   ) USA

Sonata 1950 (ESC). Preludio: toccata-like, modal. Aria: modal, melancholy, homophonic. Canone: tricky perpetual motion. Rondo: many skips, striking climax. D.

Fantasia Sopra Un Motivo 1951 (ESC) 6½ min. "The dotted upbeat containing a minor 2nd is the cause of all that follows. A downward drive persists until it attains a climactic low B. This then allows the minor 2nd to grow into a contrapuntal passage, affording temporary respite. The last part is an expanded recall of the processes carried out earlier" (composer, on CRI record jacket SD 404). D.

Phoenix 1971 (EBM1199) 5 min. Notated on three staves throughout. Serial, pointillistic, expressionistic, sensitive lyricism, an incredible study in counterpoint. Builds to dramatic intensity, fades away. M-D to D.

    See: David Burge, "New Pieces, Part II," CK, 4 (January 1978):50 for a discussion of this work.

Una Collana Musicale 1977 (TP) 23pp. 8 min. 12 brief pieces starting with a Praeludium that returns as a Postludium. In between are two sets of five pieces separated by an Interludium (à la *Ludus Tonalis* of Hindemith). Requires some inside muting and plucking. M-D.

Jérôme Joseph Momigny (1762–1842) France

Momigny is best known today for his theoretical writings, such as *Cours complet d'harmonie et de composition*, and his publishing activities.

Three Sonatas Op.7 (Albert Palm—Amadeus/Päuler 1973) 19pp. One page of notes. Sonatas in C, G, D, each two movements. Short, naive, charming classical style; similar to Clementi Sonatinas Op.36. Int.

Federico Mompou (1893–1987) Spain

Mompou's miniature Impressionist tone-poems are steeped in the folk music of his native Catalonia. Lack of bar lines, key signatures, and cadences are charac-

teristic of his style. His understatement recalls Satie. Mompou's piano music requires extensive yet subtle pedal usage.

Scènes d'enfants 1915 (Sal) 5 min. Five short, colorful, descriptive pieces of children's activities. No.5, Jeunes filles au Jardin, was a favorite encore of Gina
Bachauer. Int.

Suburbis 1916–17 (Sal). Five picturesque suburban scenes. The Street, the Gui-
tarist and the Old Horse. Gypsies I. Gypsies II. The Little blind Girl.
L'home de l'Aristo: describes a beggar playing the street organ with its
whining and somewhat out-of-tune sound. M-D.

Cants Magics (Magic Melodies) 1919 (UME). Five short varied pieces. Span of
tenth required. Int. to M-D.

Impressions Intimes 1911–14 (UME) 8½ min. Nine short charming pieces; much
flavor. M-D.

Fêtes lointaines (Far Away Festivals) 1920 (Sal) 9 min. Six dancelike pieces. No.1:
quiet, sad theme is interrupted by a cheerful simple melody; church bells
add to festive mood. Nos.2 and 3: suggest pictures of children playing and
singing. No.4: nostalgic. No.5: contrast of slow, solemn theme with one
more cheerful. No.6: a happy crowd portrayed with a suggestion of church
bells ringing in the distance. Int.

Trois Variations 1921 (ESC). Les soldats; Courtoisie; Le crapaud. Short, simple,
contrasted; mainly harmonized melodies. Int.

Dialogues 1923 (ESC). Four pieces. Declamatory, atmospheric, sonorous, brilliant, widely spaced figuration, Scriabinesque. M-D.

Quatre Préludes 1928 (Heugel). Short, varied moods, diatonic melodies, delicate,
folklike melodies. Int.

Variations on a Theme by Chopin 1961 (Sal). Twelve elaborate variations and a
final Lento, based on Prelude A. Var.3 is for left hand alone. Quotes from
the *Fantaisie-Impromptu*. The final epilogue is full of great beauty and tenderness. M-D.

6 Préludes 1962 (Sal). No.6 for left hand alone. M-D.

Charmes 1921 (ESC 1925). Six small hypnotic sketches that transport the listener
into the magical world of each title. To put suffering to sleep; To penetrate
the soul; To inspire love; For recovery from; To evoke past images; To call
in joy. Subtle, like primitive incantations. Int. to M-D.

Canción y Danza 1921–62. Nos.1–4 (UME); Nos.5–8 (EBM); Nos.5–12 (Sal). Includes some of the most beautiful folk tunes of Spain. See especially
Nos.4–6. M-D.

Música Callada (Quiet Music) 1959 (Sal). Book 1 and 2, nine pieces: chromatic.
Book 3 (Sal), seven pieces. Book 4 (Sal), seven pieces: somewhat Impressionistic, dedicated to Alicia de Larrocha. Int.

Pessebres (Crèches) 1914–16 (UME). Danza; L'Ermitage (The Hermitage); El
Pastor (The Shepherd). In Latin American countries people join together
at the Christmas season to sing and dance before the cradle to honor baby
Jesus. Int. to M-D.

Souvenirs de l'Exposition 1937 (ESC) in collection *Parc d'Attractions*. 1. untitled; 2. Tableaux de Statistiques; 3. Le Planétaire; 4. Pavillon de l'Elégance. M-D.

Chanson de Berceau 1951 (P. Noël 1962) in collection *Les Contemporains*. Quiet and elegant; middle part is like a minuet. Int.

See: Dean Elder, "Federico Mompou, Poet of the Soul's Music," *Clavier*, 17 (December 1978):14–20.

Stephen Montague (1943–   ) USA

Born in Syracuse, NY, Montague has lived in London since 1974.

Haiku 1987 (UMP) for piano, electronics, and tape; 13 min. Requires special lighting, a two- or four-channel sound system, a digital delay line, and two medium screws to "prepare" the piano. Full directions are included; the publisher must be contacted for the tape. Piano part is notated traditionally with careful pedal instructions; pianist must play *pppp* throughout! M-D to D.

After Ives 1991 (UMP 1992) 25 min. Piano, tape (optional flute, string quartet, live electronics). What a Friend We Have in Jesus; Songs of Childhood; Wayfaring Stranger; Shall We Gather at the River; The Grand Tour; Forever, J. P. S. (John Philip Sousa). Electronic and tape elements used only in last piece. These six studies are "inspired by some of the ideas and techniques of the American experimental composers from Ives to the present" (from the score). Avant garde. M-D to D.

Southern Lament 1997 (UMP) 16 min. "*Southern Lament* is just the sort of piece Liszt would have written had he endured to the present day and opted to draw on Negro spirituals for his thematic material. . . . It is, in its two frames of mind, a fascinating piece and one that demonstrates the composer's dynamic interest in piano sonorities and potential" (*The Daily Telegraph* [UK], n.d.; quoted in *News from United Music Publishers Ltd., November 1997–January 1998*).

Hélène Montageroult (1764–1836) France

Montageroult studied piano with Hüllmandel, Dussek, and Viotti. She taught at the Paris Conservatory from 1795 to 1798.

Sonatas (Johnson—Vivace) Vol.I, 60pp.: Sonata Op. 1/1; *Pièce pour le Fortepiano* Op.3. Vol.II, 52pp. ca.1810: Sonatas Opp. 1/2, 3. A mixture of classic and Romantic styles, unusual decorative melodies.

Xavier Montsalvatge (1912–   ) Spain

Tres Divertimentos (PIC 1942). Three divertissements on themes of forgotten composers. Brisk: marchlike. Tango: with a few unexpected twists. Spanish rhythms: polychords, fast tempo. M-D.

Sonatine pour Yvette 1962 (Sal) 9½ min. Vivo e spiritoso: lighthearted fluency. Moderato molto: expressive. Allegretto: vivacious rondo based on a popular theme. Virtuoso character. D.

Alegoría: Homenaje a Joaquín Turina 1989 (UME 1992) 8pp. Honored composer's style is suggested. M-D.

Elegía a Maurice Ravel 1945 (UME 1993) 3pp. Honored composer's style is suggested. M-D.

Douglas Moore (1893–1969) USA

Suite for Piano 1951 (CF). Prelude: changing meters; bright tune supported by two voices; con brio. Reel: complex 6/8, evolves into florid writing. Dancing School: thin textures, bouncing rhythms, melody in unison octaves, fresh. Barn Dance: involved, fun, skips, needs facility. Air: clear sonorities, sustained melody. Procession: marchlike allegro moderato requiring steady staccato octaves, good accentuation, energetic. A good piece of Americana. M-D.

Museum Piece (Alexrod). Tonal, colorful, short. Int.

Three Pieces from *Masters of Our Day* series (CF). Careful Etta: humorous minuet; easy. Fiddlin' Joe: captures spirit of an old New England folk dance; easy. Grievin' Annie: suggestive of an American folk ballad; easy.

Oscar Morawetz (1917–) Canada, born Czechoslovakia

Fantasy, Elegy and Toccata 1956 (Leeds 1968). A large, sonata-like tonal work, effective and colorful. Elegy is modal. Uses canon and chordal counterpoint. Exploits wide range of the keyboard. D.

Ten Preludes (CMC 1964). Large, contrasted pieces, each well developed. Too long as a complete set but a selection could be effective. M-D to D.

Suite for Piano 1968 (Leeds, Canada). Prelude: dissonant, changing meters, bold gestures. Nocturne: quiet opening; dramatic climax; *pp* closing; span of ninth required. Dance: rhythmic drive, martellato, changing meters. Extreme range and dynamics are exploited in most of this work. D.

Scherzino (F. Harris 1975) 2pp. MC, changing moods and meters. Fleet fingers required. M-D.

Four Contrasting Moods 1985 (Aeneas Publishing Co., 1990). Nos.1 and 3 are slow, Nos.2 and 4 are fast. Wide keyboard range exploited, careful pedal markings, conservative harmonies, "espressivo" used frequently points up emotional intent. M-D to D.

Makoto Moroi (1930–) Japan

Eight Parables 1967 (Ongaku-No-Tomo-Sha) 10pp. Based on the first eight letters of the Japanese alphabet and related to old proverbs. Preface gives background. Pages can be rearranged in any order. Pointillistic, harmonics, clusters. Int. to M-D.

Alpha und Beta Op.12 1953–54 (Ongaku-No-Tomo-Sha) 18pp. 13 min. A little sonata. Alpha: chromatic, dissonant, varied figurations. Beta: theme and twelve variations. Complex. D.

Klavierstück Op.14 1956 (Ongaku-No-Tomo-Sha) 9pp. 7 min. In one volume with *Alpha und Beta*. Strong Schönberg influence, involved, serial. D.

Ferdinand "Jelly Roll" Morton (1890–1941) USA
Morton was the first important jazz composer; he developed the New Orleans style to its finest expression.

The Best of Jelly Roll Morton (Hal Leonard 1993) 48pp. Billy Goat Stomp; Buffalo Blues; Chicago Breakdown; Dead Man Blues; Freakish; Frog-I-More Rag; Grandpa's Spell; Jelly Roll Blues; Kansas City Stomp; King Porter Stomp; London Blues; Milenberg Joys; Mr. Jelly-Lord; New Orleans Blues; The Pearls; Queen of Spades; Shreveport Stomp; Sidewalk Blues; Ted Lewis Blues; Wolverine Blues. M-D.

The Collected Piano Music (Smithsonian Institution Press and GS) 513pp. James Dapogny has transcribed 40 of Morton's piano pieces. Each piece is annotated in detail. Selections include King Porter Stomp; Jelly Roll Blues; The Pearls; and the virtuosic Fingerbuster. Morton deserves consideration beside the other major figures in American music—Joplin and Ellington, certainly; Sousa and Gershwin; and Thompson and Ives, too. M-D to D.

Ignaz Moscheles (1794–1870) Bohemia
Moscheles was one of the great piano virtuosi of the early nineteenth century.

Sonata mélancolique f♯ Op.49 (Newman, *13 Keyboard Sonatas of the 18th and 19th Centuries*—UNC). A one-movement work that approximates SA design. Clear tonal organization, eclectic. Maintains melancholy character throughout. M-D.

3 Concert Etudes Op.51 (CFP; K; MMP). La Forza; La Legerezza; Il Capriccio. Virtuoso, bravura. No.1 contains the qualities Moscheles considered most important in music: strength, agility, and caprice. This work inspired and influenced Liszt, Chopin, and Schumann. M-D to D.

24 Studies for Perfection Op.70 (UE; Ric; Zen-On). Chopin studied and taught these gymnastic pieces. They are Moscheles' most enduring works and helped prepare the way for the etudes of Chopin, Liszt, and Mendelssohn. M-D.

Grand Characteristic Studies Op.95 (K 9893) 77pp. Wrath; Reconciliation; Contradiction; Juno; A Nursery Tale; Bacchanale; Affection; Alla Napolitana; Moonlight on the Sea-Shore; Terpsichore; A Dream; Terror. These 12 studies still occupy a place in the classical literature of the instrument. A catalogue of period techniques and figurations. M-D to D.

See: Phillip Silver, "Ignaz Moscheles, Pianist, Composer, Educator," *Piano Journal*, 47 (June 1995):15, 17.

Mihály Mosonyi (1815–1870) Hungary
Romance (Sikesdi Press) 2pp. Elaborate melody with simple accompaniment, cadenza, chromatic, expressive. M-D.

Lawrence Moss (1927–   ) USA
Four Scenes for Piano 1961 (Seesaw) 10pp. 6½ min. Reproduction of composer's score. Allegro tempestoso; Adagio sostenuto; Allegro scorrevole; Epilogo.

Closely related pieces. Linear, changing meters. Liquid sound required in legato flowing counterpoint. Somewhat similar in style to Leon Kirchner's music. M-D.

Fantasy for Piano (EV 1973). 20pp. 11½ min. I. Very slowly and reflectively: Impressionistic. II. Adagio—as if still. III. Delicately, cloudlike. IV. Allegro ritmico: toccata-like. Written in a free serialistic style; subtly shaded; great delicacy; cascades from beginning to end. Reproduced from MS and not easy to read. A major work. D.

Moritz Moszkowski (1854–1925) Poland
Salon music of the excellent variety that Moszkowski composed can often be used to unravel thorny technical problems. This music is frequently more appealing than many etudes and technical studies. Moszkowski's piano music requires well-developed fingers that can execute spidery figurations and wide skips with delicacy and accuracy.

Hommage à Schumann Op.5 1875 (Hainauer 1573) 14pp. A seven-section fantasy featuring brilliant writing. M-D.

Spanish Dances Op.12 (CFP; K; Ric). Nos.1, 2, 4, 5 available separately (Century). Originally written for piano duet but by "popular demand" arranged for piano solo by the composer. Exotic superficial picturesque quality. Int. to M-D.

Polonaise D Op.17/1 (Musica Obscura). Many octaves, large skips. M-D.

3 Concert Studies Op.24 (Ric). No.1 is a fine left-hand study; good preparation for Chopin and/or Rachmaninoff. M-D.

6 Pieces Op.31 (MMP). Monologue E; Mélodie G; Valse mélancolique g; Scherzetto A♭; Impromptu D♭; Caprice G. Scintillating salon style. M-D.

Etincelles Op.36/6 (GS; APS; Century). Superb staccato study. M-D.

Caprice Espagnole Op.37 (CFP; Ric; CF; Century). Study for fast repeated notes. Long, effective dance piece. M-D.

Jongleurin Op.52/4 (CFP). Short, clever, descriptive, well structured. M-D.

Arabesken Op.61 (CFP 2944) 20pp. Allegretto animato; Allegro piacerole; Allegro. Fluent, flowing figuration, ingratiating melodies. M-D.

15 Virtuoso Etudes Op.72 (Alfred; GS; Enoch). Facile and fluent. Nos.6 and 12 are popular. M-D to D.

Carmen Fantasy (Musica Obscura). A brilliant and effective concert transcription. M-D.

Radio City Album of Selected Piano Compositions of Moszkowski (EBM). Mazurkas Op.10/3, Op.38/3; Scherzino Op.18/2; Etude Op.18/3; Melodie Op.18/1; Polonaise Op.18/5; Etincelles (Sparks) Op.36/6; Guitarre Op.45/2; Serenata Op.15/1; Valse Brillante A♭; Valse Mélancolique Op.31/3; Air de Ballet Op.36/5.

See: Gail Delente, "Solo Piano Music of Moritz Moszkowski," AMT, 32/2 (November–December 1982):19–21. Part 2, AMT, 32/4 (February–March 1983):22–24, 26–27.

José Vianna da Motta (1868–1948) Portugal
Da Motta studied with Liszt in Weimar and eventually became Director of the Lisbon Conservatory. During his life he was considered one of the leading musicians of Portugal.
Ballada Op.16 (Sassetti 1957). Romantic, bravura writing. For many years a required piece in piano exams at the Lisbon Conservatory. M-D.

Franz Xavier Mozart (1791–1844) Austria
W. A. Mozart's younger son. He studied piano with J. N. Hummel and voice with Antonio Salieri. This Mozart's style bridges the gap between his father and Chopin.
Four Polonaises Mélancoliques Op.22 (OUP 1975) 7pp. A facsimile of the first edition with a valuable introduction by Stoddard Lincoln. Somewhat representative of the earlier Romantic period, these pieces have something in common with Hummel, Schubert, and Weber and point stylistically to early Chopin. Graceful and charming. Similar in proportions to the W. F. Bach Polonaises. Int.
Variationen über eine Romanze von Méhul Op.23 1819 or 20 (Br&H 8150 1991) 17pp. Theme from Méhul's opera *Joseph in Egypt* (1807) is followed by five contrasting variations. Imaginative and brilliant writing, some of Mozart's best. M-D.

Leopold Mozart (1719–1787) Germany
Notebook for Nannerl (H. Schulungler—Schott). 16 pieces including Menuets, Marches, Scherzo, Allegro, Andante. Int.
Notebook for Nannerl (E. Valentin—Br) 72 pieces, text. (H. Kann—UE 17145; Zen-On) 41 pieces. Int.
      See: Alan Tyson, "A Reconstruction of Nannerl Mozart's Music Book (Notenbuch)," M&L, 60 (October 1979):389–400.
Notebook for Wolfgang (H. Schulungler—Schott). 32 pieces, some by other composers. Easy to Int.
Piano Pieces (Keller—CFP). Three suites from the Notebook for Wolfgang. Int.
12 Musikstücke für das Clavier (K. H. Taubert—R&E 1971). Preface and annotations in German. One short, charming, programmatic piece for each month in the year. Int. to M-D.
Der Morgen und der Abend (Franz Haselböck—Dob 1974) 15pp. Twelve short pieces, one for each month of the year; five by Eberlin; six by Mozart; and one anonymous, with variations by Mozart. Originally written in 1759 for the mechanical organ or horn-work that played every morning and evening from the heights of Salzburg Castle. Int.

Wolfgang Amadeus Mozart (1756–1791) Austria
Even though Mozart was one of the first virtuoso pianists, his solo piano music is frequently given a low rating. Much of it is up to the highest of his standards,

and its performance requires a special sensitivity and grace that most young students do not have. His solo piano music is so characteristic of his charm and seemingly effortless writing that we must survey most of it.

EDITIONS OF THE SONATAS:

Klaviersonaten (Herttrich—Henle; study edition) 18 sonatas in 2 vols. A comprehensive critical edition with suggestions for performance of ornaments; fingered; critical notes in French, German, and English.

Piano Sonatas (Füssl, Scholz—VU) 18 sonatas in 2 vols. Critical notes in German and English. Information about two or more traditional readings of the text is given. Conclusions are made on the basis of analogy, and musical quality sometimes substitutes for documentary evidence.

Sonatas (Plath, Rehm—Br 4861a and b 1986) 2 vols. Urtext of the New Mozart edition. 18 sonatas, critical notes. The latest critical thinking.

Sonatas (Thomson—Allans) 2 vols., 18 sonatas. Urtext.

Sonatas (Hinson—Alfred) 2 vols., 18 sonatas. Urtext with clearly indicated editorial suggestions. To be published in 2002.

Sonatas and Fantasies (Broder—TP) 18 sonatas. Comprehensive critical edition. Penetrating preface describes ornamentation practice of the period.

Sonatas (Sadie, Matthews—ABRSM) 19 sonatas in 2 vols. Contains performance directions. Each sonata is available separately.

Sonatas (Rudorff—K) 20 sonatas. A reprint of the 1895 Br&H edition. Omits many of Rudorff's footnotes.

Klaviersonaten (Teichmüller—Br&H). The first modern edition to distinguish three layers: the autograph, an authentic edition, and the editor's interpretations.

Sonatas (Martienssen—CFP) 20 sonatas in 2 vols. A good practical edition.

Sonatas (Koehler, Ruthardt—CFP) 18 sonatas in 2 vols. Outdated.

Sonate (E. Fischer—EC). A personal edition with text in French, English, German, and Italian.

Sonatas and Fantasies (Casella—Ric) 2 vols. Text in French, English, and Italian.

Sonaten, Fantasien und Rondi (Máriássy—Könemann Music Budapest 1993) 2 vols. Contains 18 sonatas, Präludium (Fantasie) und Fuge C K.394; Fantasie d K.397, c K.475; Rondo D K.485; Rondo F K.494; Rondo a K. 511. Urtext.

Sonatas (Georgii—Schott) 14 sonatas, published separately.

Sonatas (Parlow—WH).

Sonatas (M. Long—UMP). 17 sonatas plus 3 other pieces.

Sonatas (Saint-Saëns—Durand) 2 vols.

Twenty Sonatas (Bartók—K, 1 vol.; Bartók—EMB, 2 vols.). Interesting edition but contains excessive pedal markings.

See: M. Hinson, "Three Editions of the Mozart Piano Sonatas," PQ, 95 (Fall 1976): 33–35. Compares the Broder (TP), Henle, and Vienna Urtext editions.

F. Helena Marks, *The Sonata, Its Form and Meaning, as Exemplified in the Piano Sonatas by Mozart* (London: William Reeves, 1921).

Thomas Richner, *Orientation for Interpreting Mozart's Piano Sonatas* (New York: Columbia Teacher's College Press, 1953; reprint, Rexburg, Idaho: Ricks College Press, 1972).

The sonatas are identified by Köchel's original numbers (and Einstein's revisions). (See SCE, pp.482–89.) The first six sonatas were written in 1775–76. The first five were composed in Salzburg, the sixth in Munich. The early sonatas are based on the graceful Italian Rococo style.

Sonata C, K 279 (189d) (Henle; Georgii—Schott; WH). Allegro: improvisatory. Andante: expressive. Allegro: Haydn influence. M-D.

Sonata F, K 280 (189e) (Georgii—Schott; EMB). Allegro assai; Adagio; Presto. Haydn influence especially in slow movement. Effective use of rests in last movement. M-D.

Sonata B♭, K 281 (189f) (WH; EMB; Lemoine). Allegro; Andante amoroso; Rondo: Allegro. First two movements Haydn-like. Rondo has unusual dynamic markings and improvisatory passages. M-D.

Sonata E♭, K 282 (189g) (Henle; Schott; Lemoine; EMB; Durand). Adagio; Menuetto I and II; Allegro. Haydn influence, unusual form. Dynamic contrast in Minuets. Spirited finale. M-D.

See: Malcolm Bilson, "Execution and Expression in the Sonata in E-flat, K.282," *Early Music,* 20 (1992):237–43.

Sonata G, K 283 (189h) (Georgii—Schott; Podolsky, Jonas—SB; EMB). Allegro: graceful. Andante: flowing. Presto: delightful; SA design. J. C. Bach influence. M-D.

Sonata D, K 284 (205b) Allegro: orchestral. Rondeau en Polonaise: theme keeps returning in ever-more elaborate textures. Andante. Theme and (12) Variations: probably Mozart's finest set of variations. "This sonata sounds exquisite on Stein's fortepiano" (letter from Mozart to his father, October 17–18, 1777, translated by Emily Anderson in *The Letters of Mozart & His Family*, II [London: Macmillan, 1938], pp.479–80; Stein was Mozart's favorite fortepiano maker). More advanced virtuoso writing in this sonata than in the earlier sonatas. Unusually effective. M-D to D.

See: Donald Alfano, "An Interpretive Analysis of Mozart's Sonata No. 6," [K.284], *Clavier,* 34/10 (December 1995):17–21.

László Somfai, "Mozart's First Thoughts: The Two Versions of the Sonata in D Major, K.284," *Early Music,* 19 (November 1991):601–13.

The second group of sonatas dates from 1777–78 and was written in Mannheim and Paris. The left hand participates more fully in these sonatas and the middle register of the keyboard is cultivated in a new way.

Sonata C, K 309 (184b) (Schott; Lemoine; EMB). Allegro con spirito; Andante un poco adagio; Rondo: Allegretto grazioso. One of the most effective of the sonatas. Watch the *fp* markings in the middle movement: they mean only a small accent for expressive reasons. M-D.

See: John Horton, "A Portrait: Mozart's Piano Sonata in C, K.309," *Music Teacher,* 60 (May 1981):23.

Melvyn Tan, "Mozart's Sonata K.309," KC, 11/4 (July–August 1991):38–39.

Sonata a, K 310 (300d) VU 51010, urtext edition and facsimile of autograph; Schott; EMB; Durand). Allegro maestoso: broad, majestic, marchlike; sixteenth notes in second subject should not be played too fast. Andante cantabile con espressione: single-note repetition shows influence of Johann Schobert, an acquaintance of Mozart; Landowska thinks this movement "may be a minuet or a sarabande step" (*Landowska on Music*, edited by Denise Restout [New York: Stein and Day, 1964], p.321). Presto: an agitated rondo with tricky leaps and persistent breathless rhythmic pattern. Mozart's first sonata in minor. Tragic, pathetic in style, probably related to the death of Mozart's mother. M-D.

See: Kenneth Drake, "Mozart's Sonata in A Minor, K.310," PQ, 109 (Spring 1980):17–21.

Sonata D, K 311 (284c) (Schott; Lemoine; Durand). Allegro con spirito: brilliant; themes return in reverse order in recapitulation. Andante con espressione: childlike, innocent simplicity. Rondo: large, brilliant, many contrasts. M-D.

Sonata C, K 330 (300h) (Henle; Schott; EMB). Allegro moderato: SA design. Andante cantabile: minuet and trio. Allegretto: SA design; last four bars were added at a later time and are as elegant as anything Mozart ever wrote. Smaller dimensions than the preceding three sonatas. M-D.

Sonata A, K 331 (300i) (Schnabel—EMB; Henle; EMB; WH; VU; Prowse; SB). Andante grazioso; Menuetto; Alla Turca; Allegretto. Contains no movement in SA design. Careful attention to Mozart's articulation must be observed. Last movement must not go too fast or it loses its charm. M-D.

See: Maurice Hinson, "Mozart's Sonata in A Major, K.331," *Quarterly Magazine* of the MTA of New South Wales (November 1991):20–26.

Sonata F, K 332 (300k) (Henle). Allegro; change of mode plays a large part. Adagio: contains lavish ornamentation; influenced by J. C. Bach. Allegro assai: SA design; brilliant; contrasts dramatic and lyric elements. M-D.

See: Wilton Mason, "Melodic Unity in Mozart's Piano Sonata, K.332," MR, 22 (February 1961):28–33.

Sonata B♭, K 333 (315c). Allegro. Andante cantabile: contains some bold harmony. Allegretto grazioso: cadenza is a concerto characteristic; Wanda Landowska (BB) has written an effective cadenza for this movement. Lyric quality throughout. M-D.

Sonata c, K 457 (Henle; Schnabel—EBM; VU with Fantasie K 475; Georgii—Schott; WH). Allegro (autograph) Molto Allegro (first edition); Adagio; Molto allegro (autograph) Allegro assai (first edition). This work and the Fantasia c, K 475 were dedicated to a pupil, Thérèse van Trattner. They were originally conceived as two separate works but Mozart let them be published together. Opening and closing movement are intense and dramatic and carry over some of the character of the Fantasia. The middle movement is one of Mozart's finest slow movements: elaborate, florid, and highly expressive. D.

See: Betty C. Museus, "Mozart's Fantasia in C Minor, K.475," AMT, 26 (November–December 1976):31–32.

William S. Newman, "K457 and Op.13—Two Related Masterpieces in C Minor," PQ, 57 (Fall 1966):11–15.

——, MR, 28 (1967):38–44.

Lili Krauss, "Masterclass Lesson on Mozart Sonata c, K.457" [first movement], *Clavier*, 19 (September 1980):26–29.

Sonata F, K 533 and 494. Allegro (1788): broad; like a concerto; virtuoso arpeggio writing. Andante (1788): profoundly emotional with unusual harmonic clashes. Rondo: Andante (1786): may be performed separately. Mozart permitted these three movements to be published together. This conflation of movements written over several years becomes a sonata of unusual textural variety and thematic treatment. D.

See: Hans Neumann, "The Two Versions of Mozart's Rondo, K.494," *The Music Forum*, 1 (1967):1–34.

Sonata C, K 545 (Henle; Schott; EMB; Durand; VU; Ric; WH). Allegro; Andante; Rondo: Allegretto. This work was intended by Mozart for the instruction of beginners. It was not published during his lifetime. Int. to M-D.

See: Ilse G. Wunsch, "Mozart's 'Sonata Facile'—How Facile?," *Piano Guild Notes*, 24 (May–June 1975):14, 48–50.

Sonata F, K 547a (Anh. 135, Anh. 138a) (Schott; Durand). Allegro; Rondo: Allegretto; Thema: Allegretto. First and last movements come from a piano and violin sonata, K 547. Second movement is a transcription from K 545. It is likely that Mozart made the arrangements but we are not sure if he wanted them combined into a sonata. Einstein thinks he did. M-D.

Sonata B♭, K 570 (Schott; EMB). Allegro: monothematic. Adagio: rondo. Allegretto: rondo. Solo piano, and piano and violin versions exist. This is one of the most beautifully formed of all the sonatas. Contrapuntal interest throughout. M-D.

Sonata D, K 576 (Henle; EMB). Consciously contrapuntal. Allegro: imitative treatment recalls J. S. Bach, much modulation. Adagio: profound lyricism; contains some written-out ornaments, unusual for Mozart, nostalgic mood. Allegretto: free rondo form; main theme is simple, usually piano, and contrasts with the forte virtuoso passages. This sonata presents the most technical problems of all the sonatas. D.

Viennese Sonatinas (Rowley—Hin; IMC; Prostakoff—GS; Rehberg—Schott; Kann—VU; CFP 4615). These works were originally written for two clarinets and bassoon, *Wind Divertimentos*, K 439B. Editions for piano are transcriptions unknown to Mozart. They were possibly transcribed by Ferdinand Kauer (1751–1831). Int.

EDITIONS OF THE VARIATIONS:

Many of these sets were initially improvised at Mozart's concerts.

Variationen für Klavier (Zimmerman, Lampe—Henle). 15 sets, plus 3 sets in the Appendix, including a fragment consisting of a theme and 2 variations; Theme and 6 variations from the clarinet Quintet K 581 (K Anh. 137); 8

variations Come un agnello, K 460 (454a). Comprehensive critical edition with sources identified and suggestions for interpreting ornaments.

Variationen für Klavier (K. v. Fischer—Br). The *Neue Mozart Ausgabe*, Series 9, Part 26. 14 sets plus 4 fragments from incomplete sets.

Variations for Piano (Müller, Seemann—VU 1973). Vol.I: K 24, 25, 180, 179, 354, 265, 353. Vol.II: K 264, 352, 398, 455, 500, 573, 613. Preface, critical notes, and suggestions for interpretation in German and English.

Variations (CFP 273) 16 sets. Complete edition.

Variations (K 3694) 17 sets.

Variations (Bruell—IMC 458) 15 sets.

Mozart's early sets of variations mainly employ melodic embroidery. In a few later sets the melody is completely changed. The norm is for the next to last variation to be slow and the final variation fast. Usually one variation is in a minor mode if the theme is in major.

8 Variations G on a Dutch Song K 24 (K Anh. 208) (1766) (Br 4778; Nag). Baroque pattern employed: note values in each variation progress toward shorter durations. Lovely adagio. M-D.

7 Variations D on Willem van Nassau K 25 (1766) (Br 4778; Nag). Theme is the old Netherlands national anthem. More contrast between variations seen in this set. M-D.

6 Variations G on "Mio caro Adone" from *La Fiera di Venezia* of Salieri, K 180 (173c) (1773). Theme is transformed rather than embellished. M-D.

12 Variations on a Minuet of J. C. Fischer K 179 (189a) (1774). Fischer was a famous oboist who, for a while, was at the Mannheim Court. Theme comes from the final movement of his oboe concerto. Some virtuoso writing. M-D to D.

12 Variations Eb on the Air "Je suis Lindor" K 354 (299a) (1778). Theme comes from Count Almaviva's aria in the first act of Beaumarchais's *Le Barbier de Seville* by Nicholas Dezède (1745?–1792?). Each variation exploits a different figuration, melodic chromatic filler, broken octaves, cadenza passages. M-D.

12 Variations C on "Ah, vous dirai-je, Maman" K 265 (300e) (1778) Paris. (Alfred 899; Br 4779; Henle; CFP 273B; GS; Schott; K; IMC; Ric; VU; Durand; Hansen House). Pedagogic implication by use of scales, arpeggi, varying touches. One of the most charming sets and an artistic masterpiece. Int. to M-D.

12 Variations Eb on "La belle Françoise" K 353 (300f) (1778) Paris. All variations begin and end in similar fashion except Nos.1 and 9. M-D.

9 Variations C on "Lison Dormait" K 264 (315d) (1778) Paris. Theme comes from an air from the opera *Julie* by Nicholas Dezède. Exploits trill (Var.4), broken octaves (Vars.6 and 7), dramatic quality (Var.8), 2-octave glissando in sixths (Var.9). M-D.

8 Variations F on March from Grétry's opera *Les Mariages Samnites* K 352 (374c) (1781) Vienna. M-D.

6 Variations F on "Salve tu, Domine" from Paisiello's *I Filosofi Imaginarii* K 398 (416e) (1783) Vienna. Theme is in two sections. Last three variations are joined by cadenzas. An excellent program opener. M-D.

10 Variations G on "Unser dummer Pöbel meint" (What the Stupid Public Thinks) from Gluck's opera *Pilger von Mekka* K 455 (1784) Vienna. (Br; Zimmerman, Lampe—Henle; Nag). Much humor in this set, one of the very finest. Trills, cadenza, wide keyboard range, many contrasts. M-D to D.

12 Variations B♭ on an Allegretto K 500 (1786) Vienna. Theme is possibly by Mozart. Influence of Clementi may be observed in new idiomatic technique, triplet figuration, chords in upper register. M-D.

6 Variations F on an Allegretto K 54 (1788) Vienna. Third movement of violin sonata K 547 plus a new fourth variation arranged by Mozart for solo piano. M-D.

9 Variations D on a Minuet of Duport K 573 (1789) Potsdam (Henle). M-D.
    See: Eva and Paul Badura-Skoda, *Interpreting Mozart on the Keyboard* (New York: St. Martin's Press, 1957), p.133.

8 Variations F on "Ein Weib ist das herrlichste Ding K 613 (1791) Vienna. Theme from an operetta *Der dumme Gärtner oder Die zween Anton* by Benedict Schack and Franz Gerl. M-D.
    See: Eva and Paul Badura-Skoda, *Interpreting Mozart on the Keyboard*, pp.236–38.

8 Variations A on "Come un agnello" from Sarti's opera *Fra i due litiganti* K 460 (454a) (1784) Vienna. Brilliant passagework (Vars.1 and 3), bass melody (Var.5), left hand over right hand (Var.6), cadenza (Var.7). Kurt von Fischer doubts the authenticity of this work. M-D.

EDITIONS OF MISCELLANEOUS WORKS:

Klavierstücke (Wallner—Henle 22). Comprehensive urtext edition. Early works: Menuetts K 1, 2; Allegro K 3; Menuetts K 4, 5; Allegro K 9 (5a); Klavierstücke F; Menuetts K 61g II, 94 (73h). Mature works: Sonata movement g K 312; Fantasie C K 395 (300g); 8 Minuets K 315a (315g); Sonata movement B♭, K 400 (372a); Praeludium (Fantasie) and Fuge C, K 394 (383a); Fantasie c, K 396 (385f); Fantasie d, K 397 (385g); March C, K 408 (383e); part of a Suite C: Ouverture, A, C, K 399 (385i); March funèbre del Signor Maestro Contrapunto C, K 453a; Rondo D K 485; Rondo a, K 511; 6 Deutsche Tänze K 509; Adagio b, K 540; Gigue K 574; Menuett D, K 355 (594a); Andantino E♭, K 236 (588b). Appendix includes "The London Notebook" (1764–65), which contains 38 short works (minuettos, sonata movements, rondeaus, etc.), Sonata F, K 547 (Anh. 135); Andante F for a Waltz in a for small organ, K 616; Adagio for Glass Harmonica, K 356.
    See: Enrique Arias, "Exploring the Capriccios of the Great Composers," *Clavier,* 34/6 (July–August 1995):13–16, for a discussion of *Fantasie* K.395, also known as *Präludium* C, K.284a.

Klavierstücke (Müller, Kann—VU 50037). Contains: K 395, 394, 397, 485, 511, 540. Six of the more extensive pieces Mozart wrote partly for his sister and partly for his pupils. M-D.

Mozart: Selected Works for Piano Solo (Margaret Gresh—GS 1977) 160pp. Includes: Fantasias I K 397, II K 396, III K 394; Rondos I K 485, II K 577, III K 494, edited by G. Buonamici. Sonatas K 189f, K 189d, K 547a, K 300d, K 576, K 475; Fantasia and Sonata K 457; edited by Richard Epstein. M-D.

Mozart wrote very few miscellaneous pieces but they are of great importance and rank as masterpieces.

Fantasia c, K 396 (Schott; WH). An adagio in large SA design; should sound like a free improvisation but tests the performer's rhythmic control. Dignified in its Baroque grandeur. M-D to D.

Fantasia d K 397 (Henle; VU; Alfred; Leduc; Br&H 8139; Schott; Ric; Dob; WH). Also in collection *At the Piano with Mozart* (Alfred 2420). Three connecting contrasting movements. Easier technically than interpretatively. A fine introduction to Mozart for the sensitive student. Int. to M-D.

Fantasia c K 475 (Schott; Ric). The five separate sections of this great work are woven together to create one total sublime musical experience. Astonishing modulations, controlled improvisatory flights. More effective when played separately from the *Sonata* c K 457. D.

See: Paul Badura-Skoda, "A Master Lesson on Mozart's Fantasy in C Minor (K.475)," PQ, 125 (Spring 1984):36–39. Includes a record of the work with Badura-Skoda playing and speaking.

Jörg Demus, "Two Fantasies—Mozart's Fantasy in C Minor (K.475) and Schubert's Fantasy in C Minor (D.993)," PQ, 104 (Winter 1978–79):9–11. A perceptive comparison of these two works.

Rondo D, K 485 (Henle; VU 51018, urtext and facsimile edition; PWM). Set apart by its charm and simplicity. Each phrase is turned with distinction and taste. A one-movement sonata-rondo form based on one main subject; tender ending. Haydnesque. M-D.

See: Sandra Rosenblum, "Mozart's Masquerade," AMT, 40/3 (December–January 1990–91):30–33.

Rondo a, K 511 (Henle; VU 51019, urtext and facsimile edition; Schott). One of the most beautiful of all Mozart's works. Deceptive in its simplicity, especially in maintaining a legato beginning at bar 31. M-D to D.

See: Allen Forte, "Generative Chromaticism in Mozart's Music: The Rondo in A Minor, K.511," MQ, 64/4 (October 1980):459–83.

Paul Badura-Skoda, "Mozart's Rondo in A Minor, K.511," PQ, 95 (Fall 1976):29–32.

Adagio d, K 540 (Henle). SA, deeply emotional, one of the most profoundly moving of all Mozart's works. String quartet texture. M-D.

Gigue G, K 574. A three-voice fugue. Chromatic, delicate staccato study. Pure Mozart of the finest vintage. M-D.

Andante F, K 616 (Henle). This is not a waltz: *walze* (in the subtitle) refers to the revolving cylinder in a small mechanical organ. Expresses various moods. Very mature Mozart. M-D.

COLLECTIONS:

At the Piano With Mozart (Hinson—Alfred 2420) 64pp. Foreword; Mozart and the Clavier; Mozart as Performer; Mozart as Teacher; discussion of pedaling, ornamentation, varied repeats, articulation and phrasing; discussion of the pieces. Minuet F K.2; Allegro C K.1b; Andante C K.1a; Minuet II F from K.6; Allegro B♭ K.3; Andante B♭ K.5b; Minuet D K.315a; 9 pieces from "The London Notebook"; March F K.8; Klavierstücke F; Andantino E♭ K.236; Fantasy d K.397; Rondo D K.485; Twelve Variations on "Ah, vous dirae-je, Maman" K.300e.

Mozart at Eight—The Chelsea Notebook (Zalic Jacobs—TP 1972). Historical introduction by Paul Glass. Twenty short compositions selected from the original forty-three. Written during 1764–65, when Mozart was in London. Charming and surprising works for an 8-year-old, especially No.14. Unusual understanding of contrapuntal and harmonic techniques. Fingering included. (Henle has the complete London Notebook in Mozart: *Klavierstücke*.) Easy to Int.

London Musical Notebook (Ric 1975) 51pp. Contains K 15a-z, K 15aa-mm, K 1500-qq. Preface in Italian, English, and German.

London Musical Notebook (R. Risaliti—Ric 1975) 51pp. 39 pieces.

Prelude (EMB 1977) without K number. Preface by Imre Sulyok in German, English, and Hungarian. Facsimile edition of this modulating piano prelude of Mozart. "According to Wolfgang Plath, and judging by the writing, the MS might have originated around 1776–77. Up till now the prelude was unknown to research and thus it is not included in the Köchel list" (from the preface).

Selected Piano Pieces (CFP 4240). Fantasy and Fugue C, K 394; Fantasies C, D, K 396, 397; Rondos D, F, a, K 485, 494, 511; Andante F, K 616; Suite C, K 399; Adagio b, K 540; Minuet D, K 355; Gigue G, K574. M-D.

12 Piano Pieces (Klee—GS). Adagio b, K 540; Allegro g, K 312; Fantasias D, K 397, E♭, K 396, c, K 475; Gigue G, K 574; Minuetto K 355; Ouverture, Suite K 399; Romanza K 205; Rondos D, K 485, a, K 511, F, K 616. M-D.

The Easiest Original Mozart Pieces for the Piano (A. Rowley—Hin 5) 26pp. Minuet and Trio (*London Notebook*); Two Short Pieces (*London Notebook*); Two Minuets (1762); Ah! Vous dirai-je Maman (Theme with Variations) K 265; Andante Cantabile from Sonata C, K 330; Rondo D (1786); Romance A♭ (Mozart's authorship is not established); Minuet from *Don Giovanni*. Easy to Int.

Leichte Klavierstücke aus dem Londoner Skizzenbuch de achtjährigen Mozart (Br&H 6711). Nine short varied pieces. Easy to Int.

W. A. Mozart—An Introduction to His Keyboard Works (W. Palmer—Alfred). Excellent preface; fine, varied selection of pieces. Easy to M-D.

Mozart Album (M. Kiadas—EMB). 9 Variations on "Lison dormait" K 264; 12 variations on "Ah, vous dirai-je Maman" K 265; Fantasie c, K 396; Fantasie d, K 397; Rondo D, K 485; Rondo a, K 511; Adagio b, K 540; 9 Variations on a Menuet of Duport K 573. Performing edition, sensitively edited.

Mozart Easy Piano (Alfred). 14 pieces including short dances, arrangements of familiar opera arias and brief orchestral works, and two movements from an easy sonata. The short biography and notes on each piece are helpful. Easy to Int.

Mozart—Favorite Piano (Alfred). 24 pieces with eleven duplications in the above album. Fantasia d, K 397; Rondo D. Short biography and notes on each piece. Int. to M-D.

Easy Graded Mozart (J. Ching—K. Prowse) 32pp. Adagios C, D; Alla Gavotta; Allegrettos A, B♭; Allegro B♭; Minuet G; Minuettos from Sonata E♭, K 282; Minuettos A, B♭, C, C; Polonaise F; Rondo C; Theme and Variations from Sonata A, K 331; Waltz D. Highly edited. Int. to M-D.

Eight Minuets with Trios K 315a (B. Paumgartner—UE; Henle). Written in Salzburg, probably early in 1779. UE is attractive, with clean editing. Easy to Int.

Drei Klavierstücke (Karl Marguerre—Ichthys) 16pp. Allegro B♭, K 400; Allegro g, K 590d; Romanze B♭, K Anh. 205.

Easy Piano Pieces (Doflein—Br). The aim of this collection is to make Mozart's charming and noble music loved and known by every child. This first book contains a selection of pieces that Mozart composed when he was six to eight years old. Easy.

Zwei Divertimenti K 487 (Br&H 6712). I. Allegro; Menuetto; Polonaise. II. Andante; Menuetto; Allegro. A delightful set. Int.

Country Dances K 606 (CF). Transcribed by Wanda Landowska. Int. to M-D.

Young Pianist's Guide to Mozart (Y. Novik—Studio P/R 1977) 24pp. Includes 5 minuets; Allegro; Air; Little March; Burlesque (by Leopold); Country Dance; Polonaise; Allegretto; Presto; Adagio; Rondo; Andantino. Tastefully edited for the piano. Record of the contents included. Int.

Selected Pieces for the Piano (Henle 133). Adagio b, K 540; Adagio C, K 356; Andante F, K 616; Andantino E♭, K 236: Capriccio C, K 395; Gigue G, K 574; Fantasies c, K 396, d, K 397; Suite C, K 300; March funebre c, K 453a; Marcia C, K 408/1; Menuett D, K 355; Rondos D, K 485, a, K 511. M-D to D.

Mozart—Easiest Piano Pieces (Frey—CFP 5001). Dances and pieces from the Salzburg period including: March D; Minuets A, D, D, B♭, D, B♭, C, D; Passepied D; Contradance A, E♭, B♭; Gavotte gracieuse A; Gavotte B♭; Pantomime A. Int.

Mozart—The First Book for Young Pianists (Palmer—Alfred) 24pp. 12 easy pieces plus a brief discussion of ornamentation. Easy to Int.

The Young Mozart (Schüngeler—Schott 9008) 23pp. Pieces written by Mozart at the age of 6–8 years. Most are taken from the *London Sketch Book*. Int.

Mozart—A Commemorative Album (Tucker—WB 1991) 120pp. Adagio b K.540; Andante K. 616; Fantasy d K.397; Minuet D K.355; Rondo D K.485; 6

Variations on an Allegretto K.137; 6 Variations on "Mio caro Adone" by
Salieri K.180; Sonatas K.331, 309, 545, 457, and 332; 12 Variations on "Ah,
vous dirai-je, Maman" K.265; Viennese Sonatinas in B♭ and C. No distinction between composer's and editor's marks. No sources listed. Int. to M-D.

Mozart Piano Compositions (Tucker—CPP/Belwin 1993) 31pp. Adagio from Sonata K.331; Finale, from Sonatina No. 6; Menuet; Presto; Rondo alla Turca,
from Sonata K.331; Rondo, from Sonata.K.545; Sonatina No. 4; Theme and
Four Variations on "Ah, vous dirai-je, Maman" (Nos.5, 8, 9, and 12). Pieces
are not properly identified. Int. to M-D.

Variations, Rondos and Other Works for Piano (Dover 1991) 176pp. From complete edition (Br&H) 1878. 15 sets of variations; 2 Rondos; 6 Minuets; 3
Fugues; 3 Allegros; Capriccio K.395; Suite K.399; Contradance K.534; Adagio K.540; Gigue K.574; Andantino K.236. Int. to M-D.

See: Donald Alfano, "Three Mozart Sonatas in F," *Clavier,* 30/12 (December
1991):30–32.

——, "Landowska and Mozart," *Clavier,* 30/8 (October 1991):46–48.

Claudio Arrau, "The (Mozart) Piano Music," MA, (February 15, 1956):6–7, 124,
126.

Sol Babitz, "Modern Errors in Mozart Performance," *Mozart Jahrbuch*, 15 (1967):
62–89: "Clear metric accents in performance, with clear articulative silences between unslurred notes and slurred rubato within the beat were
characteristic of the Mozart era. The early style [in Mozart era] aimed at
the clarity and expressiveness produced by the use of hand-wrist control,
both in violin bowing and keyboard playing."

Eva and Paul Badura-Skoda, *Interpreting Mozart on the Keyboard*, translated by
Leo Black (New York: St. Martin's Press, 1957), 319pp.

——, "Some Technical Questions in the Piano Works of Mozart," *Piano
Teacher*, 5/2 (November–December 1962):5–11.

Malcolm Bilson, "Some General Thoughts on Ornamentation in Mozart's Keyboard Works," PQ, 95 (Fall 1976):26–28.

David Breitman, "Playing Mozart on Period Instruments," P&K, 187 (July–
August 1997):45–97.

A. Hyatt King, "Mozart's Piano Music," MR, 5 (1944):163–91.

John F. Russell, "Mozart and the Pianoforte," MR, 1 (1940):226–44.

Robert Muczynski (1929–   ) USA

Muczynski has a fundamentally neo-Romantic orientation and a penchant for
large instrumental forms.

6 Preludes Op.6 1961 (GS) 15pp. Percussive, staccato harmonies, mildly dissonant
à la Prokofieff. Five are fast, No.2 is solemn. Requires agility. M-D.

First Piano Sonata Op.9 1955–57 (SP). Two contrasting movements, brilliant figuration, imitation, effective dissonances, climactic conclusion. D.

Suite Op.13 1960 (GS) 9 min. Festival; Flight; Vision; Labyrinth; Phantom; Scherzo. Polytonal triads. All movements show fine craft and pianistic imagination. M-D.

Toccata Op.15 1971 (GS). Chromatic, driving, hemiola, thin textures, dramatic gestures, imposing climax. M-D.

A Summer Journal Op.19 1964 (GS). Seven pieces. Neoclassic, jazz influence, pristine melodies with unexpected leaps, builds to brilliant closing. M-D.

Fables Op.21 1965 (GS). Nine pieces in a fresh diatonic idiom. Int. to M-D.

Second Piano Sonata Op.22 1969 (GS) 33pp. Allegro: SA design. Con moto, ma non tanto: sombre, climactic, dirgelike. Allegro molto: monothematic. A strong work. M-D.

Diversions Op.23 1967 (GS). Nine short, varied, chromatic pieces, MC. Int.

Seven Op.30 1970–71 (GS) 23pp. Seven untitled contrasted pieces, varied styles, all technically well conceived, astringent dissonances coupled with lyric charm. The last piece requires a fine octave technique and provides a stunning conclusion to this fine suite. Rewarding. M-D.

Third Sonata Op.35 1973–74 (TP) 29pp. Allegro moderato: evolves from short opening fragment; great climax reached in coda before subsiding. Allegro grazioso: a happy 5/8 movement that has many delightful moments. Andante sostenuto: lyric and expressive, leads to a subito allegro to conclude the movement. Atonal, Prokofieff influence, powerful. D.

See: David Burge, "Five New Pieces," CK, 3 (December 1977):66. Discusses the Third Sonata.

Maverick Pieces Op.37 1976 (GS 1980). Twelve untitled pieces in a variety of styles and moods. Influence of blues and jazz, imaginative concepts. Int. to M-D.

Masks Op.40 1980 (TP) 10pp. 4½ min. Prefaced by a quote from Swift, "Harlequin without his mask is known to present a very somber countenance . . . ," which hints at a piece that ironically explores the dark edges of the commedia dell'arte character. Cold, powerful majesty of the introduction contrasts with the whirling, giddy playfulness of the ensuing frenzied allegro. A pianistic tour-de-force. D.

Desperate Measures (Paganini Variations) 1994 Op.48 (TP 1996) 12pp. 10 min. 12 variations on the famous Paganini etude, which is given as the theme. Contrasted, blues influence. No.8 is a tango, No.9 a waltz. Theme not always easily heard. D.

Sonatina F Op.1 1949 (AMP). Three cheerful movements. Large span required. M-D.

Gottlieb Muffat (1690–1770) Germany

French influence predominates in Muffat's writing. Thin textures are especially prevalent in his keyboard suites.

Componimenti Musicali per il Cembalo (1735–39). Facsimile edition (BB), DTOe Vol.7. Six suites and a Chaconne G with 38 variations (uses the same bass that Bach used in the first eight bars of the *Goldberg Variations*). Opening movements (Overture, Prelude, and Fantasie) precede the usual suite movements (A, C, S, G). Various optional dances are inserted before and sometimes after the Gigue, such as Air, M & Trio, Adagio, Finale, Rigaudon, Hornpipe, La Hardiesse, La Coquette, Menuet en Cornes de Chasse (Minuet in Imitation of Horns). Also contains a table of ornaments. Unusually fine suites. Suite II g is contained in *The Art of the Suite* (Y. Pessl), *Partitas and Pieces* (Georgii—Schott), *Old Masters* (K).

12 Toccatas and 72 Versetl (ca. 1726) (BB, facsimile edition, DTOe Vol.58; Upmeyer—Br). Each toccata is followed by six short fugues. Originally used for alternating with the choir during vesper services. Fine for teaching purposes, substantial music. Int. to M-D.

Collected Piano Works (K 9551) 80pp. Six suites (30 movements) and a Chaconne. No editorial additions. Table of ornaments and suggestions for interpreting the works are useful. Int. to M-D.

See: Susan Wollenberg, "The Keyboard Suites of Gottlieb Muffat (1690–1770)," PRMA, 102 (1975–76):83–91.

C. H. Müller (fl. ca. 1800) Germany

This set by an unknown composer (we know only his or her initials) was published ca. 1802.

Seize nouvelles variations sur l'air Ah! vous dirai-je maman (Paul van Reijen—Schott ED. 7806 1991) 31pp. Published with Louis Felix Despréaux (1746–1813), *Romance avec variations. Journal für das Pianoforte*; Heft 12. 16 variations. Counterpoint appears in the melody in Vars. 1, 4, 6, 9, 14, and 15; and the melody is transferred to a lower voice in 15; contrapuntal complexities abound in Var. 11. Vars. 3, 6, 9, 12, and 15 are in minor. A highly attractive set. Int. to M-D.

Thea Musgrave (1928–   ) Great Britain

Musgrave uses serial techniques with great flexibility.

Piano Sonata 1956 (JWC) 14 min. Freely tonal, linear, thin textures, secco, propulsive rhythms. M-D.

Monologue 1960 (JWC) 16pp. 5 min. Four variations (nocturne, cantabile, scherzo, fugue) with cadenza and coda. Theme is 12-tone but operates essentially in a tonal framework. Variations are highly concentrated and have an intensifying, culminating effect. Influenced by French music. Rhythms and contours must be strongly etched. M-D to D.

See: Susan Bradshaw, "Thea Musgrave," MT, 105 (December 1963):866–68.

Modest Mussorgsky (1839–1881) Russia

Pictures from an Exhibition 1874 (Schandert, Ashkenazy—VU; Henle; Lamm—IMC; Thumer—Schott; Casella—Ric; Dallapiccola—Carisch; Hellmudt—CFP 9585; Niemann—CFP 3727A; K; GS; USSR) 25 min. This unique cycle of ten pieces is by far Mussorgsky's most important work for piano. Musical representations of drawings and paintings by Victor Hartmann (all included in the USSR edition), a friend of the composer. The pieces are connected by a "Promenade" theme (which also appears in some of the pieces), a fine unifying device. These highly original character pieces are not always the most pianistic but they represent the greatest piece of piano writing to come from the nineteenth-century Russian national school. D. See: Tedd Joselson, "Master Class: Pictures at an Exhibition," Part 4, CK, 5 (June 1979):72. Part 5, CK, 5 (July 1979):87.

Mussorgsky Album (György Balla—EMB Z.7017) 60pp. Contains: Bydlo (excerpt from *Pictures at an Exhibition*); Capriccio "On the Southern Shore of the Crimea," No.2; Childhood Memory; Children's Games (Scherzo); First Punishment, from *Memories of Childhood*, No.1; Gurzuf "On the Southern Shore of the Crimea," No.1; Hopak (from the opera *Sorochintsy Fair*) arranged by the composer; Impromptu passionné; Meditation; Nurse and I from *Memories of Childhood*, No.1; Reverie; The Seamstress; Scherzo; Tear. A fine survey with some highly interesting pieces. Int. to M-D.

Compositions for Piano (Forberg 1971) Vol.I: En Crimée (Notes de voyage); Méditation; Une larme. Vol.II: La couturière; En Crimée; Au village. Int. to M-D.

8 Various Pieces (Br&H 8125 1981) 39pp. Preface in German and English. Intermezzo; Une plaisanterie; Une Larme; Ou Village; etc. Int. to M-D.

Memories of Childhood and Other Pieces (MMP). 13 pieces published posthumously. Int. to M-D.

Josef Mysliveček (1737–1781) Bohemia

Mysliveček's style is similar to Mozart's. Mozart knew and admired Mysliveček, whose name was so difficult for Italians to pronounce that they called him "the divine Bohemian."

Divertimento I F. In collection *Essential Keyboard Repertoire—95 Miniatures—One or Two Pages in Length* (Alfred 4619). A short rondo, Alberti bass with varied rhythms. Int.

Six Easy Divertimentos (Salter—ABRSM) 16pp. These short pieces (2 to 4 pages each with da capo) are written in a flowing classical style. They would make good substitutes for the Clementi Sonatinas Op.36. Int.

Selected Works (Racek, rev. Emingerova and Kredba—Czech State Music 1954). Rondos in A, B♭, F; Rondo from Divertimento G; Menuets D and A; Sonata D. A good survey of the keyboard music. Int. to M-D.

Sonatina D in Masters of the Sonatina, vol. 3 (Alfred 2208) 2pp. This is the Divertimento D from *Six Easy Divertimentos*. Int.

N

Zvi Nagan (1912–) Israel, born Germany
Five Bagatelles (Israeli Music Publications 195 1964) 7pp. A Town Is Awakening;
Strolling on the Boulevard; The Grasshopper; Boating; Quarrel and Reconciliation. Provides an introduction to contemporary techniques. Requires a sophisticated ear. Int. to M-D.

Isaac Nagao (1938–) Japan
Nagao graduated from Shimane University and studied at Tokyo University of
Arts for two years. He received his Master of Music Education degree from To-
kyo Gakugei University and his Ph.D. from Columbia Pacific University. He
presently teaches at Naruto University.
The Seasons (Ongaku No Tomo Sha 1987) 55pp. January: Alpha and Omega.
February: The Ice. March: A Chaos. April: Pistis, Elipis, Agape. May: A
Small Bird. June: U. F. O. July: The Rain. August: The Moth. September: A
Capella. October: The Sea (for left hand). November: A Blustery Day (for
right hand). December: The Christmas. Well written, MC. M-D.
9 Preludes 1970 (Ongaku No Tomo Sha 1992) 34pp. Contrasting, appropriate for
church use; some are tonal, others MC. Int. to M-D.
Echo Sonata (Ongaku No Tomo Sha 1996) 34pp. Ten pieces from the past based
on well-known Japanese children's songs. "I have altered the melodies in
order to be especially pleasing to the listener" (from the Preface). Full
chords, harmonic, rhythmic proportional notation, No. 3 for left hand, No.
4 for right hand. MC. Int. to M-D.

Masayuki Nagatomi (1932–) Japan
Trois Esquisses (Leduc 1982) 9pp. 5 min. Air; Fire and Water; Earth. Expressive,
improvisatory quality but contains motivic interrelationships. Flexible
rhythms, long pedals, tremolos, high and low registers exploited, Impressionistic. The middle stave of the first bar of p.8 should be read in the bass
clef instead of the printed treble, with the treble clef reserved for the next
bar. M-D.

Yoshino Nakada (1923–) Japan
Nakada is director of the Japanese Society of Rights of Authors and Composers.
Time 1952 (Ongaku-No-Tomo-Sha). Prelude. Harpsichord. Piano: Schuman-
nesque. Etude: Chopinesque. Romanticist: in style of Gershwin. Toyopet: in

a perpetual-motion Prokofieff style. The first two movements are for harpsichord. Int. to M-D.

Light and Shadow 1957 (Ongaku-No-Tomo-Sha). Published with the suite above. Highlight; A Story of Ocean; The Girl Playing the Koto; Electronic Calculator; Dirge; Labor. Tonal, modal, and atonal writing. Int. to M-D.

Sonata 1956 (Japanese Society of Rights & Composers) 32pp. Moderato gioviale; Agitato; Allegro ma non troppo. Full resources of the instrument are used in this freely chromatic, rhythmically driving work. D

Piano Pieces for Little Hands (Ongaku-No-Tomo-Sha 1976) 30pp. Covers a broad range of difficulty. Easy to M-D.

Japanese Festival (MCA). 17 pieces. Westernized sounds permeate these delightful pieces. Easy to Int.

Kenji Nakahara (1937–   ) Japan

Piano Sonata 1960 (Japan Federation of Composers 1978) 22pp. Moderato; Adagio; Allegro vivo Scherzando. Thin textures, many changing meters, freely tonal. The composer considers this work his "Opus 1." M-D.

Conlon Nancarrow (1912–1997) USA

Nancarrow's music and scores are among the most provocative and original in twentieth-century music. For 40 years he lived and worked in Mexico City, then returned to the United States. Most of his music involves the player piano.

Rhythm Study I for Player Piano (NME 1951) 22pp. This piece has been recorded by the composer on a piano roll by punching accurately spaced holes. In this way he is able to achieve rhythmic combinations that otherwise would be practically unplayable. Highly complicated rhythms. D.

Conlon Nancarrow: Selected Studies for Player Piano 1977 (EAM) 300pp. Contains numerous scores written for the player piano. There is some remarkably powerful and beautiful music embedded in these works. Complex rhythms, changing tempi, fast-moving lines. Also contains valuable essays on Nancarrow by Jim Tenney, Roger Reynolds, Gordon Mumma, and John Cage.

Collected Studies for Player Piano Vol.2 (Soundings Press). Some of these studies took a year to create. Irrational numbers relating the ratio of tempos of a first voice in a canon to a subsequent one require both mathematical computations and total accuracy. Some of the studies produce wild arpeggios and galloping tempos (up to 111 beats per second in Study No.21) that amaze the ear and defy any living pianist. The studies, now up to No.45, demonstrate imagination, sensitivity, and wit.

Study No.3 (Soundings Press). A boogie-woogie suite, in a rather surreal manifestation of the style—as if Jimmy Yancy, Fats Waller, James P. Johnson, and Art Tatum were all ecstatically "jamming" together in heaven!

Two Canons for Ursula 1988 (Bo&H 1992) 28pp. Canon A: left hand begins, right hand comes in faster and they get together in the middle—then the right hand concludes, then the left hand ends it. Canon B: again the right hand comes in later and faster than the left, and both hands meet at the conclusion. Old materials used in a new way. M-D. to D.

Sonatina (CFP 1986) 13pp. 4 min. Presto; Moderato più allegro; Allegro molto. Complex and original writing; metrical and rhythmic problems. Large span required. D.

Three 2-Part Studies (CFP 1993) 7pp. 5 min. Presto; Andantino; Allegro. Freely tonal, changing meters. M-D.

Emile Naoumoff (1962–   ) Germany

Sonate für Klavier (Schott 7004 1981) 32pp. Three movements with flashes of inspiration but uneven. Contains seemingly insurmountable obstacles for the pianist. Many tempo and mood changes. Pianist needs at least another five fingers to play this work! D.

Ernesto Nazareth (1863–1934) Brazil

Nazareth helped create a genuine Brazilian music. His works cover a wide variety of styles and include waltzes, marches, polkas, choros, and tangos.

Brejeiro (Tango) (Vitale 1940) 4pp. A Romantic Brazilian tango with the left hand providing the rhythm while the right dishes out the sentimental melody. Lilting and fun. M-D.

Nine Tangos (BME 1995). Daring 1913: introduces the maxixe, a popular Brazilian dance. Bicycle Club 1899. Dubious 1912: Liszt, Chopin, and ragtime influences. Sliding 1922: sophisticated piano techniques. Blatantly 1913. Warrior 1913: simple melody. Ninth of July 1917: Argentine tango. Dangerous 1911: title is a puzzle. Xangô 1921: sophisticated writing, fun, tricky. Available separately or in a collection. M-D.

Ernesto Nazareth—A Brazilian Piano Repertoire (BME 1996). Eleven pieces provide an introduction to some of Nazareth's most famous works, including tangos, waltzes, and polkas. Beija-Flor; Brejeiro; Nenê; Tenebroso; Julieta; Travesso; Odeon; Apanhei-te Cavaquinko; Tupinambá; Gotas de Ouro; Sarembeque. M-D.

25 Tangos Brasileiros (Schott 7561) 87pp. Colorful and exciting. Large span required. M-D.

Brazilian Tangos and Dances (D. Appleby—Alfred 16775 1997) 40pp. Ameno resedá; Brejeiro; Faceira; Ferramenta; Nenê; Odeon: Tango Brasileiro; Ouro sombre azul; Passaros em festa; Remando: Tango. Contains helpful introductions to the composer, the style, and to each piece. Int. to M-D.

Manuel Blasco de Nebra (ca.1750–1784) Spain

6 Sonatas for Harpsichord or Piano Op.1 (Robert Parris—UME 1964). The first edition of these sonatas appeared in Madrid in 1780. They seem to be the only extant works by this composer. They are musically and technically demanding. Excellent introduction; discussion of the works is particularly valuable because little is known about the composer. See especially Sonata No.5 f, a two-movement work in the style of early Haydn or Clementi. The first movement is brooding and expressive; the second is very brilliant in figuration. There are repeated-note passages that are reminiscent of Spanish guitar writing. All six sonatas are M-D.

See: Linton Powell, "The Sonatas of Manuel Blasco de Nebra and Joaquin Montero," MR, 41/3 (August 1980):197–206.

Christian Gottlob Neefe (1748–1798) Germany

Twelve Sonatas (1772) Vol.10 of the *Denkmäler Rheinischer Musik* (Musikverlag Schwann 1961). 2 vols. Critical edition. Mostly in three movements, a few sonatas in two. Rewarding material, should be investigated. Int. to M-D.

Vaclav Nelhybel (1919–1996) USA, born Czechoslovakia

Kaleidoscope (Gen 1968) 2 vols. 103 short pieces that introduce the young pianist to contemporary compositional techniques such as modal writing, changing meters, atonality, percussive usage, Bartókian style. Fine for developing quick responses to rhythm and articulation changes. Easy to Int.

Russian Folk Songs (E. C. Kerby 1972) 11pp. Black Beaver; Birch Tree; Glory to God; Christka; Luli, Lula; Christ Is Risen; The Volga Boatman; Kalinka. Easy to Int.

Isaac Nemiroff (1912–1977) USA

Piece for Solo Piano 1972 (McGinnis & Marx) 13pp. Expressionistic, long pedals, fast repeated notes, rhapsodic, dynamic extremes. D.

Edison Nenissow (–   ) USSR

Signes en blanc 1974 (Gerig 1353). A very quiet work using contemporary techniques. The loudest dynamic mark is *mp*, and the others go down to *pppp*. Carefully pedaled. M-D.

Dawn Nettheim (–   ) Australia

Nettheim lives in Sydney and many of her compositions have been written for students and school groups, often to commissions.

Six Piano Solos for Aussie Kids (The Keys Press 1996) 11pp. Here comes Ned Kelly!; An Outback Lullaby; At the Goldfields, I: Chinese Miners; At the Goldfields, II: Oh, that Squeaky Windlass!; Convicts at Moreton Bay; Fun at Luna Park. Involves clapping, clusters, irregular meters, glissando. Contains some harmonic and melodic surprises; no fingerings or pedal indications. Int.

Reid Nibley (1923–   ) USA

Reflections (GWM). Lyrical, expressive, undulating melodic turns, faster midsection, free cadenza, return of opening material, MC. M-D.

Carl Nielsen (1865–1931) Denmark

Nielsen, an uncompromising iconoclast, was not a brilliant pianist but the piano obviously interested him since he wrote for it throughout most of his creative life. His piano works have great originality and deserve more performance.

5 Pieces Op.3 1890 (WH; MMP). Folk Melody: the easiest of the set. Humoreske: a waltz in a. Arabeske: ambiguous tonality. Mignon: wistful, presto coda. Elf Dance: Grieg influence, most difficult of the set. Int.

Symphonic Suite Op.8 1894 (WH; MMP) 43pp. 16 min. Intonation—Maestoso, Quasi allegretto; Andante; Finale—Allegro. Brahms influence, especially in the thick chordal passages. Fresh tonal and harmonic treatment. Sparkling finale very effective, themes of the first three movements are reviewed. D.

Humoreske—Bagatelles Op.11 1894–95 (WH; MMP) 13pp. Dedicated to Nielsen's children. Good Morning! Good Morning! The Top. A Little Slow Waltz: contains the only instance in Nielsen's piano music of his own fingering indications. The Jumping Jack. Doll's March. The Musical Clock. Light and humorously innocent in character. Much of the humor is achieved through figurations and articulations imitating the children's subjects of the piece's titles. Similar to Schumann's *Album for the Young*. Int.

Chaconne Op.32 1916 (WH; MMP) 17pp. 10 min. Grows from a stark theme and displays a tremendous range of invention. Gritty sonorities, unsensuous. D.

Theme and Variations Op.40 1916 (WH 4387) 44pp. B minor is beautifully transformed into G minor. Theme is somber and choralelike. The 15 variations represent a wide diversity of moods, tempi, and styles. Counterpoint, contrasting tonalities and modes, and a great variety of textures and articulations add interest to this large-scale set. D.

Suite Op.45 1919 (WH; CFP) 55pp. 22 min. Six movements. Nielsen's greatest piano contribution. His "progressive tonality" is at work here: the key of B♭ gradually supplants the opening key of f♯; chromatic, polytonal and polyrhythmic treatment, bravura writing, percussive finale. D.

Music for Young and Old Op.53 1930 (WH; SM; MMP) 2 vols. 24 five-tone (in five-finger position) pieces in all keys. Varied textures, sophisticated and expressive writing. Easy to Int.

3 Piano Pieces Op.59 1928 (WH; CFP; MMP) 11 min. 1. Impromptu—Allegro fluente: grotesque. 2. Molto adagio: mysterious. 3. Allegro non troppo: brilliant. More independent motivic and rhythmic treatment of the left hand than in the earlier works. These pieces show the most-advanced aspects of Nielsen's writing. M-D.

Festival Prelude 1900 (WH 4383; CF) 2pp. A 39-bar trifle. Pompous, large chords, left-hand octaves. Could be effective in a school assembly. Freely tonal around E. M-D.

Complete Solo Piano Music (Miller—WH). A critically revised edition based on the editor's dissertation, "The Solo Piano Music of Carl Nielsen. An Analysis for Performance," New York University, 1978. In spite of all the commentary, Miller's text is kept clean.

See: Mina Miller, "Carl Nielsen's Tonal Language: An Examination of the Piano Music," *College Music Symposium*, 22/1 (Spring 1982):32–45.

Alfred Nieman (1913–1997) Great Britain

Sonata II (Gen 1975) 42pp. 23 min. Fantasy; Passacaglia; Music of Changes. A large introverted work in a neo-expressionistic vein. Clusters, polychords, thick textures contrasted with thin ones. One section requires holding the pedal down for five pages. Some serial usage, pointillistic. Stockhausen influence. D.

Two Serenades (Nov 1971) 7½ min. No.9 in Virtuoso Series edited by John Ogdon. Colombine and Pierrot. Two miniatures that employ delicate, free atonal writing. "Nieman is concerned to express not only the differences, but also the identity of the two characters from the renaissance 'Commedia dell' Arte.' The serenades are elegantly laid out for the piano and are not too difficult" (from editorial note by John Ogdon). M-D to D.

Arie Fantasie (Nov 1978). Displays constructional devices used by Stockhausen. M-D to D.

Walter Niemann (1876–1953) Germany

Ancient China Op.62 (CFP 3723). Five colorful pieces. M-D.

Barrel Organ Op.107/9 (CFP 3864B). Grotesquely out of tune. An encore piece, greatly indebted to Verdi. The tunes are very well known; the barrel organ effect is unmistakable. Int. to M-D.

Christmas Bells Op.129 (CFP 4272A). Eight little variations on an old English melody. Int. to M-D.

Janmaaten Op.136 (CFP 4277). Two Humoresques from the Port of Hamburg. M-D.

Yule Slumber Lilt Op.143 (CFP 4279). Six easy Christmas pieces. Int.

Serge Nigg (1924–   ) France

Nigg studied with both Messiaen and Leibowitz and has evolved a very complex musical idiom.

Deux Pièces for Piano Op.5 (Le Chant du Monde 1946). 5 min. 12-tone writing with jazz rhythms appearing infrequently. M-D.

Deuxième Sonate pour Piano (Jobert 1965) 37pp. Written especially for piano competition at the Paris Conservatory. Tempo I-II-III-IV: virtuoso writing. Theme and Variations: five very free variations on a row. Allegro ruvido e marcato: idea of non-retrogradable rhythms exploited. D.

Variations (Jobert 1964) 9pp. 10 min. Serial, lyric lines. D.

Sonate I 1943 (Billaudot 1993) 25pp., 11 min. Tres lent: a very free introduction leads to *peu à peu sauvage, primitif, farouche,* with strong octatonic writing punctuated with syncopated chords, glissando, gigantic conclusion. Adagio: this delicate and transparent movement shimmers with chromatic beauty and leads attaca to the finale, Allegro: vigorous, brilliant, parts are toccata-like, some bitonal feeling. D.

Tolia Nikiprowetzy (1916–   ) France, born Russia

Treize Etudes (Bo&H 1973) 31pp. Each of these thirteen pieces deals with some problem of contemporary music. Some are highly dissonant. New symbols are used for pedal markings: full pedal, half pedal, combinations of both. Directions in French. Nos.1, 3, 5, and 11 are well balanced between form and content and display ingeniously developed rhythmic ideas. Somewhat reminiscent of Scriabin *Etudes*. M-D to D.

Tatiana Nikolaeva (1924–1993) Russia

Nikolaeva was a renowned Russian pianist who played the world première of the Shostakovich 24 Preludes Op.87, in Leningrad in 1952.

24 Concert Etudes, Op.13 1951–53 (USSR 1955) Vol.I: 1–12, 87pp. Vol.II: 13–24, 106pp. Writing seems to be influenced by Shostakovich with MC sonorities. Prefers full sonorities à la Rachmaninoff. Large span required. M-D to D.

Album for Children 1959 (Zen-On 1992). March; Music Box; Old Waltz; Polka; Etude; Little March; Mazurka; Harlequin Dance; The Little Waltz; Doll's Romance; Galop; Tarantella; Elegy; Gallop. Tarantella is found in *Piano & Keyboard*, 167 (March–April 1994):37–39, along with an article on Nikolaeva's performing career. Int.

We Draw Animals 1984 Op.31 (Zen-On 1993). 14 pieces and pictures. Pussy Cat; Little Lamb; Billy-Goat; Cocks and Hens; Geese; The Bull; The Horse; Pigeon; etc. Precocious children's music of the highest order. Int.

Bo Nilsson (1937–   ) Sweden

Nilsson is a disciple of Karlheinz Stockhausen.

Quantitäten (UE). A series of 12 phrases arranged on facing pages to be played in a set order. No tempo marks are given but tempo is determined by speed at which the smallest note values can be played. High pitches sound longer than low pitches. A dynamic scale of 20 steps from 1.0 to 10.5 for *p* and *f* is indicated. Nilsson suggests that at concerts the piano should be "equipped with one or more loudspeakers." Avant-garde. D.

See: David Burge, "Scandinavian Composers," CK, 4 (November 1978): 84, for an analysis of this work.

Joaquín Nin (1879–1949) Spain

Nin's style is Romantic and permeated with Spanish harmonic idioms and guitar and other coloristic effects.

Cadeña de Valses (ESC 1927). A chain of waltzes in Spanish dance style with musical commentary between the first six. An Invocation à la valse is followed by "Messages" to Schubert, Ravel, and Chopin. Concludes with a Spanish national dance, Homenaje à la Jota. M-D.

Message à Claude Debussy 1925 (ESC 1929). An extensive "symphonic sketch," moody Tempo di Habanera. M-D.

Trois Danses Espagnoles (ESC 1938). M-D. Danza Murciana: 5½ mins., 6/8 and 3/4 alternating rhythm, cadenzas. Danza Andaluza: brilliant, fast rhythmic dance on El Vito; repeated notes. Secunda Danza Ibérica: guitar effects, ornamental cadenzas. M-D.

Iberian Dance (ESC 1925). Lengthy, percussive Allegro vivace, sonorous Lento, recitatives, exciting ending. M-D.

Canto de cuña para los Huérfanos d'España (ESC 1928). Long, ornamental berceuse for the orphans of Spain. M-D.

Joaquín Nin-Culmell (1908–   ) Cuba, born Germany

Nin-Culmell is the son of Joaquín Nin.

Sonata Brève 1932 (Broude). 7½ min. Three neoclassic movements employing Impressionist techniques, thin textures. Sinewy and rhythmic. Large span required. M-D.

Three Impressions 1929 (Broude). Habanera; Las mozas del cantaro; Un jardin de Tolède. Spanish idioms plus MC harmonies. M-D.

Tonadas (Broude 1956–61) 4 vols. 48 short evocative pieces; colorful, pianistic. Based on folk songs and dances from many regions of Spain. Int.

Alejandro y Luis 1983 (Billaudot) 2 min. A teaching piece based on two Catalonian folksongs published in Book I of *Collection Panorama*, a series of contemporary pieces for young musicians written by several composers in various styles. Int.

Twelve Cuban Dances 1985 (ESC) Written as an homage to Ignacio Cervantes, these pieces evoke aspects of nineteenth-century Cuban dances. M-D.

Three Homages for Piano 1941–90 (ESC). 9 min. In Memoriam Paderewski: a pavane. Canción de cuna para el sueño de Federico Mompou: evokes Mompou's late style in his treatment of Catalonian folk melodies. 3er Sonata de El Escorial: evokes the music of both Rudolfo and Ernesto Halfter, who wrote several works in the style of the Spanish composer Antonio Soler. M-D to D.

See: Arlene B. Woehl, "Nin-Culmell: España me persigue," *Clavier*, 26/1 (January 1987):20–27.

I am indebted to Professor Woehl for help with this section.

Herbert Nobis (1941–   ) Germany

Hommage à Jelinek (Moeck 5210 1979) 8pp. Invention; English Waltz; Siciliano; Bolero; Epilog. Subtitled "Five Piano Pieces on a Row." A gracious, witty, and accessible set of little melodic pieces based on a 12-note row built from a sequenced four-note motive. Octaves and large chords. Int. to M-D.

Marlos Nobre (1939–   ) Brazil

Nobre writes in a free serialistic style. His works display aleatoric structures and indigenous Afro-Brazilian influences.

Nazarethiana Op.2 1960 (Vitale) 4pp. 3 min. Written in the style of Ernesto Nazareth. Light, popular, and classical. M-D.

1° Ciclo Nordestino Op.5 1960 (Vitale) 7pp. 6 min. A suite based on folk materials from northeast Brazil. Samba Matuto; Cantiga; E Lamp; Gavião; Martelo. Clever; contrapuntal style. Tonal and modal combinations. Int. to M-D.

Tema e Variações Op.7 1961 (Vitale) 11pp. 4 min. Theme and six variations. Folk-like theme with contrasted variations; thoroughly contemporary treatment. M-D.

16 Variações sôbre un tema de Frutuoso Vianna Op.8 1962 (Ric Brazil 1973) 19pp. 11 min. Vianna is a contemporary Brazilian composer. A large, thoroughly contemporary work. Highly pianistic. D.

Tocatina, Ponteio e Final Op.12 1963 (Vitale) 10pp. 4 min. Fast, Slow, Fast. Quasi expressionistic treatment. M-D.

2° Ciclo Nordestino Op.13 1963 (Vitale) 10pp. 6 min. Folklike dances from northeast Brazil. Batuque; Praiana; Carretilha; Sêca; Xenhenhém. Pedal instructions. The music of northeastern Brazil contains a mixture of African and Gregorian elements. Int.

3° Ciclo Nordestino Op.22 1966 (Vitale) 10pp. 5 min. Capoeira; Côco I; Cantiga de Cego; Côco II; Candomblé. Special notation for clusters. Right hand taps different rhythm from what left hand plays. M-D.

Homenagem a Arthur Rubinstein Op.40 (Tonos 1973) 11pp. Free 32nd-note Presto con fuoco figuration alternates with slower Violento sections. Flexible meters; recitativelike Lento section with long pedals. Con fuoco-più vivo-prestissimo conclusion. Notational peculiarities. D.

Ichiro Nodaïra (–   ) Japan

Arabesque II 1979/89/91 (Lemoine 1995) 19pp. Atonal, changing meters, many tempo changes, much use of sostenuto pedal, expressionistic, clusters, pointillistic, wide dynamic range. Requires advanced pianism. D.

A. Theodoro Nogueira (1928–   ) Brazil

9 Danças Brasileiras (Ric BR 1497 1973) 28pp. 17 min. Maxixe; Maracatu; Lundu; Samba; Baião; Cateretê; Marcha Carnavalesca; Jongo; Frevo. Contrasting, colorful, chromatic, strong syncopation. All require a well-developed technique and a rhythmic drive. M-D.

Luigi Nono (1924–1990) Italy

Sofferte Onde Serene 1976 (Ric 132564) 14pp. For piano and tape. Reproduced from holograph. Bell influence. Subdued, varied, and grateful writing that shows the composer's meticulous control of his material. The lyricism characteristic of Nono's vocal lines has been transferred here to the keyboard in the gently lapping lines of the opening and the interlaced high-register arabesques of the work's climax. The title refers to Nono's Venetian home and to the requiem-like character of the work. M-D.

Pehr Henrik Nordgren (1944–   ) Finland

Nordgren studied at Helsinki University and in 1970–73 at Tokyo University of Arts and Music. Though he does make use of 12-tone technique, free application of both clusters and traditional harmonies are also found in his music.

Hoichi the Earless Op.17 1972 (Fazer) 7pp. 9 min. Clusters, widely spread gestures, dynamic extremes, involved rhythms. D.

Arne Nordheim (1931–   ) Norway
Since 1968 Nordheim has been interested in experimental music, particularly music that is to be performed outside a concert hall.

Listen 1971 (WH 4237) 4pp. 10 min. Contrary-motion chromatic figures repeated for suggested number of seconds or times at extreme dynamic ranges (crescendo-decrescendo). After these sections the pianist is to listen (silence) for indicated length of time. Pointillistic, long trills, tremolos, harmonics. Avant-garde. M-D.

Per Nörgaard (1932–   ) Denmark
Nörgaard bases his work on short tonal motives treated in contrapuntal style. Motives undergo rhythmic displacement and several forms of contraction or expansion.

Sonata in One Movement Op.6 (WH 1952, revised 1956) 13 min. Contemporary contrapuntal style, thematic material deftly manipulated. D.

Sonata No.2 Op.20 (WH 1956) 25 min. Three movements. Dynamic contemporary writing. D.

4 Fragments 1959–61 (WH) 9pp. Special rhythmic and pedal notation, Webernesque. M-D.

Sketches 1959 (WH) 2pp. Four short pieces. Varied moods, textures, and figurations. Dissonant. M-D.

Grooving 1968 (WH) 14 min. Variations, no time or key signatures. Unusual pedal effects. Minimalist influence. M-D.
   See: David Burge, "Contemporary Piano," CK, 4 (November 1978):84, for an analysis of this work.

Nine Piano Pieces Op.25 (WH). Ostinato technique, principal theme varied in such a way that it logically returns to its starting point. Contemporary treatment of isorhythmic technique. M-D.

Journeys 1971 (NMO) in collection *Scandinavian Aspects*, 13 min. For prepared piano. Hand damping and harmonics, metal rod, teaspoon, spike. "Opening the top of a grand piano or removing the front panel of an upright reveals the secret places where piano tone is produced . . ." (from the score). Notes notated graphically, strings struck and strummed. Three sections, numerous pieces, a compendium of contemporary piano effects notations. Int. to M-D.

Ib Norholm (1923–   ) Denmark
Strofer og marker (Stanzas and Fields) Op.33 (Engström & Södring). Two types of textures: pointillistic, conventional. Two contrasting cycles of six pieces make up the design. M-D.

Christopher Norton (1953–   ) New Zealand
Norton graduated from Otago University. He went to Great Britain in 1977, where he is currently a free-lance composer. He is best known for his "Micro-jazz" series.

Latin Preludes (Bo&H 1990) 22pp. Seven preludes based on a variety of Latin

American styles, including the samba, beguine, and bossa nova. Available with a MIDI disc and/or cassette tape. Int.

Yankee Doodles (Bo&H 1993) 19pp. 9 improvisations on American folk tunes. Polly Wolly Doodle; Dixie; Carry me back to Old Virginny; Camptown Races; Yankee Doodle; Turkey in the Straw; Dreadful Sorry; Clementine; Alabama Rag. Clever, attractive. Int.

Rock Preludes (Bo&H). Seven preludes based on the strong rhythms of rock music. Effective separately or as a suite. Int.

Latin Preludes 2 (Bo&H 1995) 22pp. Seven preludes, in same style as earlier volume but slightly more difficult. Int. to M-D.

Vítězslav Novák (1870–1949) Czechoslovakia

Novák used folk inspiration in classic forms, such as the variation, chaconne, and fugue.

Variations on a Theme of Schumann 1893 (Artia) 19 min. Based on Schumann's Op.68/34. M-D.

Sonata Eroica Op.24 (Artia). Romantic emotionalism, folksong influence. M-D.

Pan: Symphonic Poem Op.43 (Artia 1963) 66pp. Preface in English. Prolog; Berge; Meer; Wald; Weib. Monothematic; everything comes from single-note rhythmic motive. D.

Slowakische Suite Op.32 (Artia). In the Church; Amongst the Children; In Love; With the Dancers; At Night. Int.

Lionel Nowak (1911–1995) USA

Nowak's music is serious, uncompromising, and significant, displaying high craft and original ideas.

Soundscape One (ACA 1964). Four well-contrasted sections, energetic conclusion. Pianistically conceived, full sonorities. First-rate concert material. M-D to D.

Capriccio (ACA 1962) 6pp. The first section to be played "hard and dry"; granitic punched sounds. A lyric section leads to a toccata-like finale. M-D.

Fantasia (CFE 1954). Impressive, large-scale, imposing work demanding complete equipment. Worth exploring.

Four in a Row (CFE). Easy 12-tone pieces.

Emmanuel Nunes (1941–   ) Portugal

Litanies du Feu et de la Mer (Jobert 1972) 2 separate sheets, 4pp. each. 25 min. A full page of directions is included. Aleatoric, extremes in dynamics and range, clusters, some unusual notation. D.

José Maurício Nunes-Garcia (1767–1830) Brazil

Nunes-Garcia was born in Rio de Janeiro, the son of a black Brazilian woman. He became a priest in 1792 and was acclaimed for his musical ability, intellect, and spirituality. He wrote mainly music for the church. His few works for keyboard are based on Viennese Classical style.

Twelve Lessons. Part One of the *Compendio de Musica: Methodo de Pianoforte* 1821 (Neal Richardson-Africanus Editions AE-0441-02 1999) 15pp. 12 short contrasting pieces. Int. to M-D.

Twelve Lessons. Part Two of the *Compendio de Musica: Methodo de Pianoforte* 1821 (Neal Richardson-Africanus Editions AE-0441-03 1999) 22pp. 12 pieces, slightly more difficult than the set discussed above. Various groupings make attractive recital repertoire. M-D.

Six Fantazias. Part Three of the *Compendio de Musica: Methodo de Pianoforte* 1821 (Neal Richardson-Africanus Editions AE-0441-04 1999) 16pp. Contrasting pieces in same style as discussed above. No. 6, a theme and set of variations, is the most difficult. M-D.

O

Lev Oborin (1907–1973) USSR

Oborin taught piano at the Moscow Conservatory and was a distinguished pedagogue. He also had a fine career as a concert pianist.

Quatre Morceau Op.2 1927 (USSR) 27pp. Non allegro—Inquieto—Rubato: outer sections are thin textured and chromatic; mid-section is a flexible melody accompanied by dense full chords at *ppp* dynamic level. Molto allegro—Affanato: driving rhythmic chromatic chords with brief Lento *pp* melodic interruptions. Molto allegro: contrary-motion arpeggios; fluent melodies over expressive but vigorous chordal accompaniment. Lento—Pesanto—Funebre: chromatic and turgid. Style is a mixture of Scriabin and Shostakovitch. M-D to D.

Sonata eb Op.3 192607 (UE) 47pp. Three movements, FSF. Virtuosic writing, same style as described for Op.2 but with even more Prokofieff-like toccata touches. D.

Siegfried Ochs (1858–1929) Germany

Ochs was an outstanding choral director as well as a composer.

S'kommt ein Vogel geflogen (Schott 7165 1983) 19pp. Book 7 of *Journal für das Pianoforte*. Published with Cornelius Gurlitt, humorous variations on *Ach du lieber Augustin*. Ochs treats this German folk tune in the style of various composers, such as J. S. Bach, Haydn, Mozart, Johann Strauss, Verdi, etc. Clever and most appealing. M-D.

John Ogdon (1937–1989) Great Britain

Ogdon was regarded as Britain's most outstanding pianist of his age group. Much of his composing was naturally directed toward his chosen instrument. His style is eclectic and highly pianistic.

5 Preludes 1965 (Ascherberg) 10 min. Bagatelle; Pensée héroïque; Hommage; Pensée militaire; In modo napolitano. Pianistically expert ideas directly expressed. Final piece is a kind of modern tarantella. M-D.

Sonatina (Ascherberg 1965) 20pp. 10 min. Four movements. Freely moving tonalities, rhythmic problems, linear texture, M-D.

Theme and Variations 1966 (Ascherberg) 6 min. Complex theme followed by 10 variations, each complete in itself. Bravura style, rhythmic complexities. Liszt influence. D.

Dance Suite 1967 (Ascherberg) 20pp. 6½ min. Prelude; Sarabande; Arabesque; Cortège; Finale. Arabesque is pianistically colorful. M-D.

Michal Kleofas Ogiński (1765–1833) Poland

Ogiński was a diplomat who left Poland after its partition. He agitated in Turkey and France for the Polish cause.

Polonaise a (Les Adeux à la Patrie) (PWM 1956) 2pp. This piece was also known as "Death Polonaise" and was very popular during the nineteenth century. The Trio is very similar to Chopin's early *Polonaise* B♭, BI 3. Int.

Maurice Ohana (1914–1992) France

Ohana was one of France's most respected composers. He was of Spanish extraction and created a highly personal style rooted in the mysteries of folk music and bathed by the Mediterranean sun and sands.

24 Préludes (Jobert 1974) 47pp. 42 min. Performance directions in French. Clusters, harmonics, careful pedal indications, mostly unmetered, black- and white-key glissandi together. These pieces are conceived as a unit with immediate attacas. Some improvisation is called for. Wide variety of rhythmic patterns; dynamics and range exploitation evident. Double-note percussive effects are highly effective in No.13. Some of the pieces are very short (No.23 is 1⅓ lines). Only a pianist with highly developed technique and interpretive powers could bring these off in performance. D.

Sonatine Monodique (Billaudot 1945) 17pp. 12 min. Allegretto con motto: unisons, chromatic, thin textures, uses wide ranges. Vif: 5-flat signature; scampering 16ths broken up by Lento sections; moves to three sharps, concludes by cancelling all. Andante: single-line introduction leads to thicker textures and faster tempi, *fff* climax. Animé: shifting tempi; slow, sonorous, cadenza-like section; returns to opening textures; drives to final climax. D.

12 Etudes D'Interpretation (Jobert). Book I: Nos.1–6; Book II: Nos.7–12. Explore different pianistic techniques and textures. Nos.11 and 12 with percussion. D.

Hajime Okumura (1925–   ) Japan

Japanese Children's Songs for Piano 1964 (Ongaku-No-Tomo-Sha) 27pp. 14 charming songs; original flavor and sentiments retained. Includes information about each song as well as an English translation. Easy to Int.

Japanese Folk Songs 1964 (Ongaku-No-Tomo-Sha) 2 vols. Int. to M-D.

Odori 1961 (Ongaku-No-Tomo-Sha) 2 min. Bound with *Sonatine IV*. A short dance. Changing meters, octotonic lines juxtaposed with repeated chromatic chords, più lento mid-section. M-D.

Toccata under Construction (Zen-On 307 1972) 13pp. Energetic rhythms, contrasting sections, fast alternating hands, clusterlike chords, bitonal. M-D to D.

Preludes to Three Flowers (Zen-On 287 1971) 8pp. Anemone; Hyacinth; Tulip. Clever, colorful characterizations. Int. to M-D.

Dance Impromptu (Zen-On 277 1970) 7pp. Brilliant, glissandi, appealing. M-D.

Capriccio (Zen-On 270 1969) 10pp. Broken-chord figuration, octaves, punctuated syncopation. M-D.

Two Sonatas (Zen-On 1970) 51pp. Three-movement works. Prokofieff influence. Require much stamina. M-D to D.

Kevin Oldham (1960–   ) USA

Oldham received his bachelor's and master's degrees from The Juilliard School.

Variations on a French Noel Op.7 (La Jolla 1989) 20pp. Noel followed by 14 contrasting variations, some very difficult. Builds to a powerful climax, then ends *ppppp*, with final pedal held for 20 measures. Effective. D.

Fernando Corrêa de Oliveira (1921–   ) Portugal

O Principe do Cavalo Branco ("The Prince of the White Horse") Op.6 (Parnaso) 22pp. 16 short colorful pieces. Clusters, galloping effects, effective. Int. to M-D.

50 Peças para os 5 Dedos ("50 pieces for 5 fingers") Op.7 (Parnaso) 62pp. Composed in the author's harmonic system, called "Symmetric Harmony," which has a new nomenclature for intervals; black keys are indicated by oblique crosses. Short, a kind of contemporary "Album for the Young." Easy to Int.

Variaçoes classicas Incompletas Op.10 (Parnaso) 9pp. Theme and 13 contrasting variations. Modal. M-D.

20 Peças em Contraponto Simétrico Op.15 (Parnaso) 24pp. MC, linear, twentieth-century inventions. Int.

Sete Estudos de Pequena Virtuosidade Op.18 (Parnaso) 22pp. Each study emphasizes particular pianistic problems. M-D.

Willy Correa de Oliveira (1938–   ) Brazil

Oliveira is resident composer at the University of São Paulo. He is presently working on musical structures at the levels of syntax and semantics. Aleatory processes occur in his works though always under the control of all parameters.

Cinco Kitschs 1967—68 (Ric BR) 12pp. 14 mins. Back-ground; Nocturne; Make It Yourself; Jazztime: uses a drummer for assistance. Narcisus: to be taped; the pianist is to sit in the audience and applaud himself! Avant-garde writing aptly named (*Kitsch*=trash, or trifle, a doo-dad). Problematical concepts with each kitsch built on a series. Detailed directions. D.

Impromptu para Marta 1971 (Ric BR) 4pp. 4 min. New notation. Basically in two parts. Aleatoric, form left to performer. Extensive instructions for pianist. Improvisation required. The piece can never be played as it is written. D.

Two Intermezzos (Ric BR 1973) 5pp. 3 min. New notation. Intermezzo I: predetermined intensity levels, such as right hand piano, left hand mezzo forte; square black notes performed at forte level; other gradations are to be developed from these intensities. Intermezzo II: revolves around rhythm and meter problems. D.

Harold Oliver (1942–   ) USA

Piano Etude (CF 1969) 8pp. Reproduced from holograph. Varied moods and tempi, pointillistic, broad gestures, expressionistic. Wide span required. D.

Betty Olivero (–   ) Israel
Sofim (Endings) 1991 (IMI 1992) 12pp., ca. 9 min. Very free, no meter, many vio-
lent outbursts followed by subito *pp* sonorities, pointillistic, repeated notes.
The piece does not end, it just stops. D.

Sparre Olsen (1903–1984) Norway
Norwegian Folk Songs (NMO 1946) 15pp. 19 folk songs from Gudbrandsdal.
Winsome and racy tunes, whimsical and touching poems. Much expressed
in little. Foreword by Percy Grainger. Easy to Int.

Carl Orff (1895–1982) Germany
Klavier-Übung 1933 (Schott). Easy children's pieces. MC.
The Orff Collection (Hinson-Schott 546 1998) 26pp. Contains 40 short piano
pieces from his *Schulwerk*, kind of a miniature piano method covering
Orff's approach to the instrument. The complete piano works of Orff! Int.

Leo Ornstein (1892–   ) USA, born Russia
Ornstein's music requires a pianist with formidable technique, a flair for the ex-
troverted, and great power.
Burlesca (A Satire) (Joshua 1041 1976) 18pp. Fast figurations, irregular note
groupings, relentless driving rhythms, ironic humor. D.
A Chromatic Dance (Joshua 1980). Wild chromaticism; fast and gets faster as
piece proceeds; highly dissonant. M-D to D.
Danse Sauvage (Wild Men's Dance) Op.13/2 1915 (Joshua 1080). Much dissonance in many bunched clusters. Requires sustained percussive playing.
M-D to D.
À la Chinoise Op.39 1928 (Br&H). Simple pentatonic melody accompanied by
dissonant, motoric tone clusters and swirling arpeggios. More polytonal
keyboard beating; handled correctly it can be a brilliant concert piece. D.
Epitaph (Joshua 1026). Expressive, rubato, lyric flowing lines. Large span re-
quired. M-D.
Impressions de Notre Dame Op.16/1 1913, 41, 79 (Joshua 1079). Bell effects cre-
ated by clusters and thick dissonance, heavy percussive use. D.
Impromptu (A Bit of Nostalgia) (Joshua 1027). Waltzlike, reminiscent of other
composers' music, brilliant conclusion. M-D.
Memories from Childhood (Joshua 1042). Eight pieces describe scenes in the life
of an imaginative child. Int.
À la Mexicana Op.35 1919, 1947, 1979 (Joshua 1081). Three pieces in folk style.
Romantic and pianistic, unlike most of Ornstein's other pieces. M-D.
Poems of 1917 Op.41 (CF) Ten movements. Strong hypnotic element. Written as
a reaction to the horrors of World War I. Requires brute force. D.
Valse Diabolique (Joshua 1022). A devilish and dissonant frantic waltz. D.
Sonata No.4 1919 19 min. (Poon Hill Press). Moderato con moto; Semplice;
Lento; Vivo. Traditional design, uses idioms of Liszt, Debussy, Scriabin, and
Bartók. Debussy is quoted in the first movement, Borodin in the second

movement; third movement recalls Schumann's "Prophet Bird"; fourth movement "challenges the virtuosity of Scriabin's *Fifth Sonata*" (from record notes, Albany Records, CD Troy 070). Ornstein used to play this sonata on his tours. D.

Arabesques, Op.42 1918 9½ min (Poon Hill Press). The Isle of Elephants; Primal Echo; Chant of Hindoo Priests; Shadowed Waters; A Melancholy Landscape; Pompeian Fresco; Passion; The Basoche; The Wailing and Raging Wind. This gallery of expressionistic tone-pictures is full of tone clusters and ear-splitting sounds. Some critics thought Ornstein was temporarily insane when he composed these pieces! D.

See: Vivian Perlis, "The Futurist Music of Leo Ornstein," *Notes*, 31 (June 1975): 735–50.

Buxton Orr (1924–1997) Great Britain

Bagatelles 1952 (Eulenberg 1973) 24pp. 12 min. MS. reproduction. Four contrasted pieces. Light style, complexities infused with numerous unison passages. Effective when played as a group; engaging and usable. M-D.

Juan Orrego-Salas (1919–) USA, born Chile

A neoclassical craftsmanship is found in all of Orrego-Salas's works.

Variaciones y Fuga sobre el Tema de un Pregón Op.18 (Hargail 1946). Eight variations and fugues on a street cry. Diatonic, parallel chords, modal repeated notes, bravura writing. Three-voice fugue. D.

Suite No.2 Op.32 (Bo&H 1951). "In the Baroque Style." Five movements. Vigorous, arresting writing. Any movement could be played separately. M-D.

Rústica Op.35 (PAU 1952). Rustic dance, joyous, meter changes, rhythmic bounce. M-D.

Sonata Op.60 1967 (PIC) 21pp. Libero e mesto; Maestoso; Prestissimo; Violento e cangiante. Based on the idea of repeated notes and contrast of two different melodic styles: a flexible recitative and a strongly rhythmic toccata style. The form of each movement is developed on the element of contrast. 12-tone, atonal, thoroughly authoritative contemporary writing. D.

Léon Orthel (1905–) The Netherlands

Orthel composed 28 compositions for piano solo and piano duet over a 59-year period. He was well known in The Netherlands as a composer and concert pianist. He was Professor of Piano at the Royal Conservatory in The Hague from 1941 to 1971.

Preludes Op.7 1925 (Albersen). Four short unpretentious pieces. Orthel played these pedagogic studies in numerous concert performances. M-D.

Tien Pianostukjes Op.14 1933 (Albersen). Ten short pieces that explore various pianistic techniques. Int.

Epigrammen Op.17 1938 (Albersen). Five short pieces inspired by a visit to a World War I cemetery. Many pianistic demands. M-D to D.

Twee Preludes Op.27 1944–45 (Alsbach). Quiet, requires large span. M-D.

Deux hommages en forme d'etude Op.40 1957–58 (Donemus). Dedicated to Debussy: impressionistic, whole-tone scale, sweeping arpeggios. Dedicated to Ravel: writing similar to Ravel's *Une barque sur l'océan* from *Miroirs* is used. Both suggest sounds related to the dedicatees. M-D to D.

Sonatine No. 6 Op.70 1974 (Donemus). Three movements, resolute character, bitonality, brilliant conclusion. M-D.

Sonatina No. 7 Op.73 1975 (Donemus). Four movements: 1. short hymnic prelude; 2. scherzolike; 3. chordal; 4. fast scalar passages. M-D.

Sonatina No. 8 Op.78 1975 (Donemus). Three movements: 1. fast changing styles; 2. more traditional treatment; 3. bitonal. M-D.

Jens-Peter Ostendorf (1944–   ) Germany

Transkription für Klavier (Sikorski 1970) 7pp. Tonal, large skipping chords, fast octaves, flexible tempi and meters, tremolando, waltz section, Liszt-like. M-D.

Trauer (Sikorski) 10pp. An oversize print in the composer's handwriting; many directions in German only. Numerous avant-garde techniques. Requires a wooden wedge (for plugging the pedal), a baton (to strike the interior of the instrument), a music case, and gym shoes. D.

Robert Owens (1930–   ) USA

California Sonata Op.6 (Sikorski 565 1958) 13pp. Allegro cantabile: flowing melodies accompanied by leggiero broken seventh chords; an Andante espressivo mid-section is more chordal and returns at end of movement like a coda. Andante: chordal and octotonic; più mosso section more melodic. Vivace: ostinato-like left-hand figure supports right-hand melody. The whole sonata is freely tonal and displays Impressionistic influence. M-D.

Carnival Op.7 (Sikorski 661 1962) 25pp. Arrival; Merry-Go-Round; Roller-Coaster; Clowns; Valse; Promenade; Trapeze Artists; Acrobats. This MC, freely tonal suite is attractive and well written for the instrument. Programmatically conceived. M-D.

P

Luis de Pablo (1930–   ) Spain
De Pablo has written in a serial style from his earliest works.
Sonata para Piano Op.3 1960 (UME). Considered to be the first serial work written in Spain. Thin textures; silence used effectively; original rhythmic treatment. Style akin to late Webern. M-D to D.
Libro para la Pianista Op.11 1964 (Tonos Verlag) 12 min. Partially serial, partially aleatory. Material is well developed. D.

Johann Pachelbel (1653–1706) Germany
An important precursor of J. S. Bach, Pachelbel composed in all the usual genres of his day. His keyboard compositions may be found in DTB Vol.2 and DTOe Vol.17.
Hexachordum Apollinis (1699) (Moser, Fedtke—Br). Six arias with figural technique in d, e, F, g, a, f. This edition also contains an Ariette F and 2 Chaconnes C, D. The Ariette has 9 variations. The C Chaconne has 24 variations, D Chaconne has 12 variations. Introduction in English by Hans J. Moser. Int. to M-D.
7 Selected Pieces (Döflein—Schott). Phantasie D; Fuga a; Aria con variazioni g; Aria mit Variationen A (Fragment); Aria mit Variationen a; "Werde munter, mein Gemüte" from *Musikalischen Sterbensgedanken* (Musical Meditations on Death); Suite e. Int. to M-D.
Selected Keyboard Works (H. Schultz—CFP) Twelve works including Suites; Choralthema D with 8 variations; Fantasia g; Prelude and Fugue f♯; Ciacona d. Int. to M-D.
17 Suites (DTB Vol.2). Short, in usual order of A, C, S, G with some optional dances. Int. to M-D.

Steen Pade (1956–   ) Denmark
Florilegium (WH 4368 1981) 12pp. 8 min. Three movements of mental and digital challenges. Many changing meters, pointillistic, insistent rhythms. Complex figures such as quintuplets, sextuplets, and more awkward units are juxtaposed against each other, and usually at a fast tempo. Exact and demanding pedal markings. Also includes a few moments of silence. Stamina required. D.

Ignace Jan Paderewski (1860–1941) Poland
Paderewski is best known for his outstanding playing, but a few of his works still turn up on programs.

Menuet G Op.14/1 (GS; TP; CF). Famous salon piece with lyric charm. Int.

Caprice à la Scarlatti Op.14/3 (EBM; Musica Obscura). Sparkling salon pianism required. M-D.

Nocturne B♭ Op.16/4 (Willis). Rich Romantic sonorities. M-D.

Légende A♭ Op.16/1 (GS). Attractive. Requires octave technique. M-D.

Theme and Variations Op.16/3 (GS; Schott). Embraces conventional techniques of pianism—a bit of left-hand scale work, some octaves rather reminiscent of Chopin's F♯ minor *Polonaise* Op.44 (which Paderewski must surely have played many times)—and a discreet avoidance of legato double notes. The conservative nobility and quiet serenity of this work are a tribute to Paderewski's memory. Reposeful conclusion. M-D.

Cracovienne fantastique Op.14/6 (BMC; Musica Obscura; PWM). Facility and scale passages in thirds required. M-D.

Sonata e♭ Op.21 (Bo&Bo) 30 min. Allegro con fuoco: folklike theme, modal flavor, forceful rhythm, muscular character. Andante ma non troppo: rippling, filagree figuration, interesting colors. Allegro vivace: begins as a three-part scherzo in perpetual motion, enclosing an imitative section and concluding with a vigorous Presto, vigorous and dazzling. D.

See: Bryce Morrison, "Paderewski's Sonata," M&M, 23 (July 1975):18.

Variations and Fugue e♭ Op.23 (Bo&Bo) 26 min. Alkan, Chopin, Liszt, and Schumann influence; runs a wide gamut of colors and styles. Opening theme is similar to the opening theme of the *Sonata*, especially in its modal and strongly rhythmic character. Theme takes on many varied moods from a nocturne to a virtuoso etude. The 20 variations and fugue are similar in approach to Brahms's Handel variations (Op.24). D.

Selected Compositions of Moderate Difficulty (Ashdown) 22pp. Menuet G Op. 14/1; Sarabande Op.14/2; Au Soir Op.10/1; Melodie Op.8/3; Un Moment Musical Op.16/6; Mazurka Op.9/2. Int. to M-D.

Album per pianoforti (Z. Sliwinski—PWM 1973) 67pp. Krakowiak E; Mazurek; Krakowiak B♭, Op.5/1–3; Album de Mai, Op.10/2; Op.14/1, the famous Menuet; Cracovienne fantastique, Op.14/6; Op.16/1. Légende, 2. Mélodie 3. Thème varie, 4. Nocturne, 6. Moment musical. These pieces were composed between 1880 and 1890. Pedaling and some fingering are indicated. Also contains a photograph of Paderewski and editorial notes. Int. to M-D.

See: A. M. Henderson, "Paderewski as Artist and Teacher," MT, 97 (August 1956): 411–13.

John Knowles Paine (1839–1906) USA

Paine was one of the foremost New England composers of the nineteenth century. A Professor of Music at Harvard University for over 30 years, he strongly influenced the academic study of music in the USA. His finely crafted and restrained music was greatly affected by the German Romantic tradition.

Complete Piano Music (Da Capo 1984) 105pp. Introduction by John C. Schmidt. Includes A Christmas Gift Op.7; A Funeral March in Memory of President Lincoln Op.9; Romance Op.12; Four Characteristic Pieces Op.25: Dance;

Romance; Impromptu; Rondo Giocoso. In the Country—Ten Sketches for piano Op.26: Woodnotes; Wayside Flowers; Under the Lindens; The Shepherd's Lament; Village Dance; Rainy Day; The Mill; Gipsies; Farewell; Welcome Home. Romance Op.39; Three Piano Pieces Op.41: A Spring Idyl; Birthday Impromptu; Fuga Giocosa; Nocturne Op.45.

Village Dance Op.26/5 (Hinson—Alfred 4603). In collection *Masters of American Piano Music*. Light-hearted and cheerful. Int.

Fuga Giocosa Op.41/3. Based on the baseball refrain "Over the fence is out, boys." A sprightly fugue shows Paine's love for Bach and identifies him as an American composer. M-D.

Dance Op.25/1 1876. The good humor recalls the Intermezzi of Brahms. M-D.

Under the Lindens Op.26/3 1876. The third of *10 Sketches for Piano*. Delightful miniature, especially well made in its melodic contours. M-D.

A Funeral March Op.9 (in memory of President Lincoln) 1865. A fine example of Paine's classical restraint and economy of form and expression. M-D.

A Christmas Gift Op.7 1889. This piece was written for Paine's sister. Shows thorough workmanship. A delightful scherzo feeling permeates its entirety and gives it a kinship with Mendelssohn. M-D.

See: Maurice Hinson, "A Christmas Gift from John Knowles Paine," *Clavier*, 26/10 (December 1987):14–15.

Giovanni Paisiello (1740–1816) Italy

The sonatas listed below were probably written between 1776 and 1784, when Paisiello was living in St. Petersburg, Russia.

Six Sonatas (C. Mola-Carisch; MMP). One-movement works in spirited rococo style. From Paisiello's 19 sonatas. Not sonatas, even in the sense of the day, but closer to the rondo idea. f, E♭, G, D, F, E♭. Int. to M-D.

See: Jon L. Hunt, "The Keyboard Works of Giovanni Paisiello," MQ, 61 (April 1975):212–32.

Manuel Palau (1893–1967) Spain

Homenaje a Debussy (UME 1957) 7pp. Romantic style interlaced with a few dissonances. Tuneful, showy. M-D.

Marcha burlesca (UME 1960) 13pp. Requires plenty of rhythmic control. M-D.

Roman Palester (1907–   ) Poland

Preludes 1963 (PIC) 26pp. 12 min. Ten short works. Introspective, highly chromatic, 12-tone, no meter or bar lines. Some are slow and poetic, others sparkling and exciting. A selection could be made but it is more rewarding to play them as a whole. M-D to D.

József Pálfalvi (1928–   ) Hungary

Four Pieces for Piano (EMB 1974) 9pp. Lullaby; March; Air; Waltz. Technical demands are minimal. Music has much to recommend it. Int.

Robert Palmer (1915–   ) USA

Palmer's style is based on melodic thematic material, asymmetric rhythmic patterns, and varied processes of motivic expansion.

Three Preludes 1941 (PIC). Vivace con grazia: lyric, changing meters, ideas well developed. Molto tranquillo e cantabile: flowing, legato, in 17/16. Molto pesante—Allegro con energia: dissonant; heavy; broken figuration in left hand requires stamina. M-D.

Toccata Ostinato 1945 (EV). Displays a driving, relentless energy, harmonically conservative, marked by clean and brittle textures, continuous metric displacement, rhythmic variety, ostinato bass, sturdy writing. M-D.

Three Epigrams (PIC 1960). Allegretto grazioso: meter changes, contemporary sonorities. Agitato ma leggiero: flexible meters, tricky tonal balance in a few passages. Andante con moto: musically the most interesting. M-D.

Evening Music (TP). Expressive, Lydian and Mixolydian modes. M-D.

See: William Austin, "The Music of Robert Palmer," MQ, 42 (January 1956)35:50.

Selim Palmgren (1878–1951) Finland

Palmgren's music is highly pianistic and written in a nineteenth-century idiom with mildly innovative harmonies and figuration.

May Night Op.27/4 (Alfred 6353; GS; BMC; WH; Willis). Impressionistic, atmospheric, colorful pedal effects. Int.

24 Preludes Op.17 1907 (Fazer) 52pp. Andante; In Folk Style; Allegretto con grazia; Tempo di Valse; Presto; Sarabande; Un poco mosso; Allegro feroce; Cradle Song; In Folk Style; Dream Picture; The Sea; Veloce; Pesante; Round Dance; Andante con moto; Allegro agitato; Duo; Bird Song; In Memoriam; Un poco mosso; In Folk Style; Venezia; The War. Palmgren was an excellent pianist, and these little pieces lend themselves admirably to performance on the piano. Many of them evoke an immediate response with their sensitively felt northern mood. In spite of the Impressionistic lyrical style reflecting the period during which they were composed, the composer's personal idiom is at all times clearly recognizable. Int. to M-D.

6 Lyric Pieces Op.28 (WH, published separately; BMC). Prelude; The Isle of Skuggornas; Legend; A Mother's Song; The Swan; Roundlay. The Swan requires a large span and is similar to *May Night*. Int.

5 Sketches from Finland Op.31 (BMC; WH). Karelian Dance; Minuet; A Guilty Conscience; Waltz; Finlandish Dance. Int. to M-D.

Sonatine F Op.93 (GM 1935) 11pp. Allegro vivace; Andantino; Allegro vivace. Tuneful, flowing, more rhythmic finale. M-D.

Palmgren Album (BMC). Twelve pieces including: Prelude; Dalliance; Intermezzo; Waltz; Berceuse; Humoresque; Gavotte and Musette; Sarabande; The Dragon-fly; The Sea; May-night. Int. to M-D.

See: Anne Christiansen, "Palmgren, the Finnish Impressionist," *Clavier*, 17 (January 1978):12.

Robert Palmieri (1928–   ) USA

20 Piano Exercises 1971 (OUP) 21pp. "Problems of bi-rhythms in one hand, legato-staccato, 2-note patterns played at triplets or 3-note patterns played as quadruplets are some of the difficulties involved" (from the score). Highly musical. Would make fine recital pieces. Int. to M-D.

Andrzej Panufnik (1914–1991) England, born Poland

Panufnik composed in an advanced musical style. His *Miniature Studies* are a valuable contribution to modern piano technique.

Suite A La Quinte (PWM 1949) 20 min. 12 pieces in variation form. Prelude c♯; Interlude f♯; Study b; Interlude e; Study a; Interlude d; Study g; Interlude c; Study f; Interlude b♭; Study e♭; Postlude a♭. D.

6 Miniature Studies (Bo&H 1955). Vol.1: one technical problem per study. No.1: alternating chromatic and diatonic passagework. No.2: three layers of simultaneous contrasting dynamics. No.3: study in octaves and thirds. No.4: melody in tenor and bass accompanied by seconds. No.5: study in fifths and thirds. No.6: contrasted sonorities. M-D.

6 Miniature Studies (Bo&H 1966). Vol.2: various problems in each piece. No.7: rhythm study in 3/8 plus 2/8 plus 3/8. No.8: expressive pedaling called for. No.9: groups of five eighths, many ninths embedded into figuration. No.10: study in tonal balance. No.11: perpetual motion, tonal balance, melody in left hand. No.12: in time signature 1/2, crescendo from beginning to end, shifted accents. Fascinating textures. M-D.

Reflections (Bo&H 1971) 12pp. 12 min. Improvisatory, no bar lines, pointillistic, atonal, mixture of Impressionist and MC style, echo phrases, *pp* opening and closing, sparse textures. A three-note cell is subjected to varied treatment. Avant-garde. D.

Pentasonata 1984 rev. 1987 (Bo & H 1992) 15pp., ca. 15 min. A single-movement work based on the pentatonic scale. Two allegrettos and two andantinos frame a mid-section *contemplativo*. Harmonics, strong rhythms, wide dynamic range. M-D to D.

See: Andrzej Panufnik, *Impulse and Design in My Music* (London: Boosey & Hawkes, 1974), 27pp., for brief descriptions of Panufnik's works.

Jean Papineau-Couture (1916–   ) Canada

Mouvement Perpetuel (BMI Canada). Much left-hand passage-work. M-D.

Suite (BMI Canada 1959). Prelude. Bagatelle No.1. Aria: requires sensitivity. Bagatelle No.2: whimsical. M-D.

Rondo (BMI Canada 1951). Toccata-like character. Neo-Romantic style. Large span required. D.

Etude B♭ (PIC 1959). Effective concert etude. M-D.

Complementarité 1971 (CMC) 25pp. Clusters, harmonics, plucked strings, half pedals, un-metered. Extreme ranges and dynamics exploited; many avant-garde techniques creatively explored. D.

Yoram Paporisz (1944–   ) Israel, born Poland

Discoveries (PIC). 3 vols., graded. Based on idioms from around the world: fifth-century Ambrosian hymn, Hindu ragas, Mozarabic cantillation, etc. Excellent pedagogic material; compares favorably with Bartók *Mikrokosmos* in scope and quality. Easy to Int.

Horla 1970 (Moeck) 13pp. 8 min. Sectionalized, rhapsodic, expressionistic, some unusual notation. Sonorous Choral booms out near conclusion; aphoristic coda. D.

Indische Musik (Impero 1977) 26pp. 18 pieces based on ragas or "in the style of" certain ragas. Fluid rhythms and varied textures. Int. to M-D.

Lajos Papp (1935–   ) Hungary

Variazioni 1968 (Bo&H) 11pp. Theme and 9 variations, final one a partial repeat of the theme. Chromatic harmony, preference for seconds and sevenths. Contemporary sounds. Large span required. M-D.

27 Small Piano Pieces (EMB). Short, musical, five-finger position. Easy.

Improvvisazione 1965 (EMB 6383). Five short contrasted colorful sections; moves over keyboard. M-D.

3 Piano Pieces (EMB 5703). Two Burlesques; theme with five variations. Bartók- and Kodály-inspired. M-D.

Aquarium 1987 (EMB 1994) 19pp. Tropical Dark Water; Water Fleas; Salt-water Crab; Sea Horse; Lobster; Bubbles with Characins; Sunfish; Butterfly perch; Pebbles in the Water; Starwort with Rubybarbel; Leaping Fish. Short pieces, requiring nothing larger than an octave, move around keyboard; much use of the whole-tone scale and varied articulations, large skips. M-D.

Pietro Domenico Paradies (Paradisi) (1707–1791) Italy

Paradies was one of the strongest composers of the eighteenth century. His sonatas were admired by Clementi, Cramer, and Mozart. Each sonata, in two movements, demonstrates an amazing variety of figural treatment, rhythmic vitality, unusual dissonances, and idiomatic keyboard style. The writing is masterly and deserves more performance.

12 Sonate di Gravicembalo 1754 (Ruf, Bemmann—Schott) 2 vols. *I Classici della Musica Italiana* Vol.XXII. Of special interest are No.1 G (Br&H), No.6 A (CF), No.10 D (CF; Litolff). See TPA, XII, and *Le Trésor des Pianistes* XIV (contains 10 sonatas). *Sonata* B♭ in *Italian Sonatas of the 18th Century* (de Paoli—JWC). *Toccata* e (Vitali—Ric).

Toccata A (Alfred; CF; Schott; GS; Durand; Br; Delrieu) 3pp. Continuous sixteenths in one voice or another throughout. Attractive and flowing. Would make a fine recital opener. Int.

Album per Pianoforte (PWM 8258 1980) 90pp. Sonatas. Based mainly on the first English editions by Johnson & Welcker. Commentary in Polish, English, and German.

Paul Paray (1886–1979) France
Paray's works are sincere and well written, if occasionally somewhat academic.
Portraits d'Enfants 1910 (Jobert) 7pp. Très calm opening leads to a piquant Allegro. M-D.
Prelude 1913 (Jobert) 4pp. Like a pastorale. M-D.
Thème et variations 1913 (Jobert) 15pp. Flowing theme (Fauré-like) and ten contrasting variations. Tends towards academic propriety. M-D.
d'une âme 1914 (Jobert) 27pp. A suite of nine short contrasting character pieces. A few added sixths and seventh chords. Int. to M-D.

Maria Hester Park (1760–1813) Great Britain
Park was a singer and pianist as well as a composer.
Sonata Eb Op. 4/2 ca. 1790 (Harbach—Vivace) 16pp. Three movements, galant style, varied rhythms, energetic. M-D.

Robert Parris (1924–   ) USA
Variations (ACA 1958) 4 min. Simple octave theme, each variation colorfully treated (including a fugato). Final statement dramatically conceived. D.

Ian Parrott (1916–   ) Great Britain
Theme and Six Variants 1945 (Lengnick) 23pp. 12½ min. Well-developed and contrasted variations. Requires fine pianistic equipment. M-D to D.
Westerham 1940 (Lengnick) 7pp. 4 min. A freely tonal colorful rhapsody. Large span required. M-D.

Arvo Pärt (1935–   ) Estonia
Pärt's music is reflective and meditative. Characteristic of his style are modal usage and hypnotic rhythms.
Variationen zur gesumdung von arinuschka (UE 1980) 4pp. Four variations on a continuous moving melody: melodic pattern moves up an octave and returns. Harmonics, one dynamic mark (*p*) in piece. Int. to M-D.
Für Alina (VE 1990) published with the above-listed piece. Also in collection *The Century of Change* (EAMC 772 1996) 2pp. Ethereal, restful, to be played with inner resignation, long pedals. Each measure contains one more beat than the last one, to measure 8; then each measure is reduced by one beat to measure 14. Int.
Zwei Sonatinen Op.1 1958 (UE 30411 1997) 20pp. I. Allegro: two-part invention with contrasted sections. Larghetto: nocturne-like, short recitative ends with recap of two-part invention idea from first movement. II. Allegro energico: détaché subject sets mood for strong rhythmic use, Attacca Largo: lyric, chordal, tonal. Allegro: a miniature toccata with contrasting *pesante* chords. Toccata figuration concludes movement. M-D.
Partitur Op.2 1959 (UE 30410 1997) 10pp. Toccatina: single-line sixteenth-note figuration; chordal support of rhythmic melody; ends with opening idea.

Fughetta: like a two-part invention; imitative. Larghetto: nocturne-like, sustained. Ostinato: portamento left-hand ostinato supports changing right-hand figuration. Freely tonal. M-D.

Oedoen Partos (1907–1977) Israel, born Hungary

Prelude 1960 (IMI). Rhapsodic, large musical gestures, short. M-D.

Metamorphoses 1971 (IMI) 12pp. 8 min. Includes biographical and program notes in Hebrew and English. Motives expand and contract; proportional rhythmic notation; expressionistic. D.

Thomas Pasatieri (1945–   ) USA

Pasatieri's music is all highly dissonant and intense and reveals a unique compositional personality.

Cameos (Belwin-Mills 1975). Six short pieces. Contrasting moods and tempi. M-D to D.

Sonata I 1969 (Belwin-Mills 1975) Allegro: broad, builds to huge climax. Lento: slow, cantabile, strong conclusion. Third movement: motoric, driving, toccata-like, double octave passage-work. Moderato: moderate opening, ends slowly. Employs a repeated-note figure throughout; strong rhythmic drive, complex polyrhythms. D.

Sonata II 1974 (Belwin-Mills). Opening movement is agitated; middle movement is scherzo- and toccata-like; finale opens in a dark brooding mood but closes with a dramatic climax. M-D.

Claude Pascal (1921–   ) France

L'Album de Lisette et Poulot (Durand). Twelve exercise pieces exploiting different pianistic problems. Int.

La bal improvisé (Durand). Nine varied pieces. MC. M-D.

Le cahier du lecteur (Durand). Vol.I: 24 varied pieces. Vol.II: 12 pieces in canon form. Vol.III: 18 varied pieces. Easy to M-D.

Douze Dechiffrages 1963–69 (Durand, first part). Twelve pieces. Varied moods, MC, appealing. Int.

Quatre études 1980 (Durand 14079) 19pp. 6½ min. En ut majeur: octotonic, chromatic, changing meters, parallel chords, ostinato-like figures, octaves in imitation. En ré bémol majeur et en forme de Toccata: alternating chords in sixteenths between hands, motoric, contrasted with thin two-voice textures. En ut majeur: secco, agitated, skipping tenths in left hand, chromatic. En sol majeur, et en forme de Mouvement perpétuel: chromatic melody embedded in first note of four sixteenths. Fast and fleeting. This MC set makes a nice group. M-D.

Portraits d'enfants (Durand). Twelve small sketches. Easy to Int.

Toccata (Durand 1952). Brilliant and short. M-D.

Suite 1970 (Durand) 13½ min. Prélude; Fugue; Interlude; Canon; Finale. Neobaroque. D.

Bernardo Pasquini (1637–1710) Italy

Pasquini was one of the finest Italian keyboard composers of the second half of the seventeenth century. His music is vigorous and terse, yet it abounds in melodic grace. Pasquini wrote suites consisting of allemandes, courantes, and gigues, using the term "sonata." In some ways he anticipated techniques of D. Scarlatti.

Complete Keyboard Works (Hänssler). 7 vols.

Toccata sul Canto del Cucu in I Clavicembalisti (Rossi—Carisch 1946). Programmatic and charming writing. M-D.

3 Arias (Rehberg—Schott). Lyric, flowing. Int. to M-D.

Works in *L'Arte Musicale in Italia* III; TPA VIII; *Le Trésor des Pianistes* III; *Selection of Pieces composed for the Harpsichord* (Shedlock—Nov 1895). Still a fine source. Int. to M-D.

Opera per cembalo e organo, Vol.I (Transcribed and revised by Hedda Illy—Edizioni de Santis 1971) 90pp. Introduction in English and Italian. 15 selections: Fantasia; canzone francese; ricercari; variations; and a few dance movements, including a charming and rhythmically unusual Bergomasca. M-D.

Boris Pasternak (1890–1960) Russia

Prelude g♯ 1906 (*Tempo*, 121:20–25). Early in his life Pasternak had planned to be a musician. He was close friends with Alexander Scriabin, and this Prelude shows that influence strongly along with a few Wagnerisms. M-D.

See: Christopher Barnes, "Pasternak as Composer and Scriabin-Disciple," *Tempo* 121 (June 1977):13–19. Discusses the Prelude and surviving piano pieces and fragments of Pasternak.

Stephen Paulus (1949–   ) USA

Paulus earned three music degrees from the University of Minnesota.

Dance. In collection *Changing Faces* (EAMC 1987) 4pp. Energetic, long pedals in middle section provide a sonorous atmosphere; outer sections should be light and bouncy. Numerous variations on melodic fragments, clear tonalities plus chromatic coloration. M-D.

Preludes Book I (EAMC 1994) 30pp. Spirited; Mysterious; Sprightly; Serene; Rollicking. Varied idioms, colorful writing, harmonics, strong gestures; an outstanding set. Large span required. D.

Translucent Landscapes 1978 (EAMC 498) 48pp. Gossamer; Summer's Dance; Meadow Winds; Tarn; Starry Night. Contrasting moods and textures, impressionistic influence, octotonic, freely tonal. Large span required. D.

Paul Paviour (–   ) Australia

Paviour studied in London at the Royal College of Music and at London University. He is an organist, choral conductor, and music educator who has written over one hundred works in many different forms.

Let's Go Walkabout (The Keys Press 1996) 14pp. The Property at Tunganoo (an old farm house); Under the stars on the Nullarbor (a desert stretching for many miles); The game reserve; Midnight on the Olgas (a series of giant monoliths in central Australia); Rock Pools (found on the beach). Attractive suite, colorful, refreshing. Int.

Anthony Payne (1936–   ) Great Britain
Paean 1971 (JWC) 15pp. 10½ min. Eloquent; explosive; variation procedures; rapidly evolving ideas with a considerable degree of conscious numerical manipulation. This conscious control is not inhibiting but is used as a dramatic device. D.
See: Susan Bradshaw and Richard Rodney Bennett, "Anthony Payne and His 'Paean,'" *Tempo*, 100 (Spring 1972):40–44.

Juan Carlos Paz (1897–1972) Argentina
Paz was the first South American composer of renown to adopt 12-tone technique.
Sonatina No.3 Op.25 1933 (ECIC). Three atonal movements. Thin textures, severe writing. M-D.
Diez Piezas Sobre una Serie dodecafónica Op.30 (Editorial Politonia). Strict use of the row, but rather easy works. Int.
Canciones y Baladas Op.31/1 in *Música Viva*, 10 (1941) (Rio de Janeiro). No.2 (GS) in album *Latin American Anthology of Music*. Short, 12-tone. M-D.
At the Cost of Parana (CF). Seven colorful variations on a tango theme. M-D.

Russell Peck (1945–   ) USA
Suspended Sentence (Jobert 1973) 12pp. In part graphic notation; aleatoric. Notation carefully explained in French and English. Numerous sonorities and keyboard effects investigated, including: black and white chromatic clusters, sometimes rolled with both hands and arms; extreme dynamic treatment; glissandi in various speeds; rhythmic figuration, sometimes free sometimes strict. All over keyboard. D.

José Enrique Pedreira (1904–1959) Puerto Rico
Plénitude (Nocturne) (EBM). Smooth modulations. M-D.
Tus Cariccas (EBM). Popular dance style. M-D.
Vals en La Mayor (EBM). Appealing. M-D.
Ritmo (Zapateado) (EBM). Forceful dance rhythms. M-D.

Carlos Pedrell (1878–1941) Uruguay
A Orillas del Duero (ESC 1922). Colorful suite of four pieces depicting musical pictures "On the Outskirts of Duero." Good technique required. M-D.

Flor Peeters (1903–1986) Belgium
Sonatina I Op.45 (CFP 66553 1975) 5pp. Three short movements originally composed for carillon but effective on the piano. Int.

Sonatina II Op.46 (CFP 66554 1975) 7pp. Allegretto semplice: modal. Aria: melodic. Finale on "Lord Jesus Has a Garden": charming rondo. The changes (tremolos) are best played as mordents. Originally composed for carillon. Int.

Toccata Op.51a (CFP). Effective perpetual-motion writing, hands close together. M-D to D.

10 Bagatelles Op.88 1958 (CFP). Short, MC, varied styles and moods. Int.

12 Chorale Preludes Op.114 1966 (CFP) 2 vols. MC treatment of twelve fairly well-known chorales in three and four parts. Includes: A Mighty Fortress Is Our God; O Sacred Head: O God Thou Faithful God; Wake, Awake for Night Is Flying. Int. to M-D.

20 Divertimenti Op.121 1974 (Lemoine). Conservative idiom with some Impressionistic influences. Int. to M-D.

Guerra Peixe (1914–   ) Brazil

Peixe has studied Brazilian music all his life. His compositions use folk music materials as the basis for much of his inspiration. Sonatinas I and II and Sonata I are based on nationalistic styles employing folk materials.

Musica II 1942 (SDM) 9pp. I. Allegro. II. Largo. Serial, harmonics. M-D.

Sonatina I 1951 (SDM) 22pp. Three movements. D.

Sonatina II 1969 (SDM) 17pp. Three movements. D.

Sonata I 1950 (SDM) 27pp. Three movements. D.

Sonata II 1967 (SDM) 34pp. Vivace: ostinato-like left hand, driving chordal figuration in right hand, contrasting second tonal area in brillantissimo treatment of coda. Largo: calm; melodic; chordal usage in mid-section rises to climax; concludes *pp*. Allegro: in a quasi march style, à la Prokofieff; bravura passages. Vivace coda. D.

Suite II *Nordestina* 1954 (Ric BR) 27pp. Violeiro (The Guitar Player): ostinato-like left-hand syncopated accompaniment; color chords in right hand decorate melody. Cabocolinhos (The Little Half-Breed): burlesque, vigorous melody, repeated chords. Pedinte (The Beggar): diatonic melody, chordal accompaniment, bravura return of opening section. Polaca (Polka): graceful; works to climax and recedes to *pp* closing. Frêvo (Brazilian Dance): vigorous, rhythmic, dashing climax. This suite displays Peixe's maturity in using folk materials for his inspiration. M-D to D.

Suite II *Paulista* 1954 (Ric BR2257) 28pp. Catereté; Jongo; Canto-de-Trabalho; Tambu. Nationalistic style based on native materials. Requires a big technique with strong rhythmic drive. D.

Prelúdios Tropicais No.4 (Ponteado de Viola) (Vitale 1979) 4pp. "Ponteado" means to play a string instrument finger style in a melodic and improvisatory manner. "Viola" is a folk guitar with five or six double strings and a full, melodious sound. In 5/8, ABA plus coda, Gregorian mode. Fluid, repeated fast chords between hands, bitonal, free B section, colorful. M-D.

See: Ruth Serrão, "Guerra-Peixe's 'Ponteado de Viola,'" *Clavier*, 23/2 (February 1984):16–21; includes music.

Samuel Pellman (1953–   ) USA
Silent Night 1976 (A. Broude) 8 min. For prepared piano; uses screws, bolts, clothespins, rubber wedges, and erasers. Highly elaborate preparation. Effectively dramatic. D.

José Penalva (1924–   ) Brazil
Sonata I (Seresta e Desafio) 1970 (Ric BR3186) 7pp. 5 min. A one-movement work, Moderademente: 12-tone with row given at the opening. Clusters, long trills, toccatalike passages, lento, *ppp* ethereal closing. M-D.
3 Versetos 1963 (Ric BR) 2½ min. 12-tone. M-D.
Mini-Suite 1 1968 (Ric BR) 2½ min. 12-tone. M-D.
Mini-Suite 2 1969 (Ric BR) 2½ min. 12-tone. M-D.
Mini-Suite 3 1971 (Gerig) in collection *New Brazilian Piano Music*. 2 min. M-D.

Craig A. Penfield (1948–   ) USA
Penfield's work reflects both French (Debussy, Ravel) and Russian (Rebikov) influence.
From a 19th Century Toy Box (Willis 1991) 15pp. The Wooden Horse; Fanfare for a Tin Soldier; Jumeau Doll; The Train; Fish Whistle; The Magic Lantern; Mandarins. Varied character pieces make up this attractive suite. Int.
New England Winter Pictures (Willis 1992) 20pp. On a Bright Winter's Morning; Skating in the Park; Sleigh Ride; Winter Starlight; Snow Flurries; Children at Play; Fireside Dreams. Colorful character vignettes. Int.

Barbara Pentland (1912–2000) Canada
Pentland's style is strongly influenced by Schönberg and Webern.
Studies in Line 1941 (BMI Canada) 6 min. "Four studies from single ideas developed in four short movements. Each is headed by a sketch rather than a title. The contours of each sketch are descriptive not only of the general contour of the following study but of the emotional effect as well" (from the score). Clever. M-D.
Fantasy 1962 (BMI Canada) 7 min. Serial, harmonics, specific and unusual directions (white tone). M-D to D.
Dirge 1948 (BMI Canada). Polytonal, dissonant contrapuntal usage, portentous sonorities. M-D.
Toccata 1957–58 (BMI Canada). Propulsive and driving rhythms, 12-tone, calm adagio mid-section, brilliant ending. D.
Maze-Puzzle (Waterloo 1969). Two short, freely chromatic pieces with shifting five-finger positions. Int.
Music of Now (Waterloo 1970) 3 vols. Based on contemporary techniques. 1: Intervals; tapping rhythms; student should try to feel the shape of the music and express it with gestures. 2: More black keys used: dotted notes and tone clusters. 3: Simple part playing introduced; triads; use of damper pedal. Main concern in all three volumes is the development of a sensitivity to rhythm and line. Easy to Int.

Shadows (Waterloo 1964) 3pp. Long pedals, serial, pointillistic, subtle sonorities. M-D.

Space Studies (Waterloo 1968) 7pp. Frolic: study in the use of wide compass (moving over keyboard). From Outer Space: 1. In Space (study in use of pedal connecting widely spaced melody and of vibration of overtones to enrich harmony); 2. Beeps (rhythm study); 3. Quest (contrapuntal phrasing); 4. Balancing Act (rhythm study). Int.

Clermont Pépin (1926–   ) Canada

Short Etudes 1, 2, 3 (Western Music). Impressionistic; individual ideas well worked out. M-D.

Trois Pièces pour la Legende Dorée (Leeds Canada). Three short pieces based on the legend of an early French pirate: Prelude; Interlude; Toccata. MC. Int.

Ernst Pepping (1901–1981) Germany

Pepping preferred Baroque forms and linear textures.

Sonate 1 1937 (Schott) 20pp. Three movements. Neoclassic, euphonious. Second movement is especially delightful. M-D.

Sonate 2 1937 (Schott) 22pp. Canzona con variazioni: expressive. Rondo pastorale: flowing. Finale alla marcia: rhythmic. M-D.

Sonate 3 D 1938 (Schott) 31pp. Cheerful throughout. M-D.

Sonate 4 1948 (Br) 43pp. 24 min. Similar to the others but broader in scope. M-D to D.

Tanzweisen und Rundgesang 1939 (Schott). Dances and Rounds. Large amiable work. M-D.

12 Phantasien 1949 (Br). One-movement pieces, varied moods. M-D.

Ronald Perera (1941–   ) USA

Piano Suite 1966 (ECS 1973) 12pp. Three atonal pieces to be played together. Prelude: mood contrasts, meter and tempo changes. Nocturne: mainly quiet but contains quick figuration near end. Toccata: free, some brilliant and driving effects, harmonics. D.

Giovanni Battista Pergolesi (1710–1736) Italy

Complete Edition (Amici della Musica da Camera, Rome). Vol.I contains 6 sonatas and 3 suites. Sonatas are short, one movement each, homophonic. Spurious works permeate this edition.

See: Frank Walker, "Two Centuries of Pergolesi Forgeries and Misattributions," ML, 30 (October 1949):297–320.

Sonata D (Azzoni—Carisch) 11pp. Larghetto: melodic, flowing. Minuetto: rhythmic, graceful. Gavotta con Variazioni: square Gavotte theme followed by five contrasting and highly attractive variations. Over-edited. Int. to M-D.

Sonata F (Zecchi, Fazzari—Carisch) 9pp. A one-movement Allegro with interesting and effective treatment of ideas. M-D.

See: C. L. Cudworth, "Notes on the Instrumental Works Attributed to Pergolesi," ML, 30 (October 1949):321–28.

Lothar Perl (1910–1975) USA, born Germany
Perl wrote piano novelties influenced by jazz. They were very popular in the 1930s.
Syncopated Impressions (R. Walker—Schott SMC 543) 35pp. Cowboy; Hollywood Stars; The Last Mohican; Rondeau; Tim & Tom; Rockinghorse; Crazy Top; Zebra Stripes. Clever and fun to play but require solid technique. M-D.

George Perle (1915–   ) USA
Perle writes in a freely or intuitively conceived style that combines various serial procedures with melodically generated tonal centers, intervallic cells, and symmetrical formations.
Sonata Op.27 (ECIC 1950) 8pp. First movement: dissonant, major sevenths and minor seconds; requires large span and fine octave technique. Second movement (1 page): thorny and sonorous. Serial writing. M-D.
6 Preludes in album *New Music for the Piano* (LG 1958). Combination of atonal and 12-tone technique. M-D.
Short Sonata (TP 1964) 16pp. 8 min. Three movements, FSF. A tightly knit work, extreme dynamic changes, flexible meters. Specific pedaling required in the Impressionist second movement. Invigorating writing. D.
Toccata 1969 (TP) 19pp. 6 min. Bristling intellectuality that displays changing meters, a few slower contrasting sections, restless qualities, and a soft and tonal conclusion. Based on two sets of inversional chromatic scales. Toccata-like figuration. Opening material is most interesting. D.
Six Etudes 1973–76 (Margun) 26pp. 12 min. These pieces have become modern classics. Each etude is associated with a problem of instrumental technique i.e., No.1 is concerned with interlocking staccato passage-work; No.3 involves fast repeated notes inserted into skipping figurations played by a single hand. Each piece has a limited repertoire of sonority. Carefully controlled choice of pitches, rapid rhythmic changes, serious writing combined with subtle and dry wit. These pieces seem to bridge gaps among the primary forces of our century's musical thought. They show us that there are more similarities in the harmonic systems of the modern classicists than dissimilarities. Virtuosity required. D.
See: David Burge, "George Perle's *Six Etudes*," *Keyboard*, 9/9 (September 1983):66, 69.
Pantomime, Interlude, and Fugue 1937 (Boelke-Bomart 1982) 11pp. Charming neoclassic writing, excellent craft, thin textures, amusing two-voice fugue, a winning combination. M-D.
Ballade 1981 (CFP 66895) 24pp. 9 min. Built on serpentine flowing opening motive, chromatic, luxuriant harmonies, changing meters, seven basic tempos, strong lyric element. D.
Six New Etudes 1984 (Gunmar). Similar to the first set with same kind of technical requirements. D.

Phantasyplay 1994 (Galaxy). Displays Perle's debt to Alban Berg. M-D to D.
See: Michael Boriskin, "Saving More Music for the Piano," P&K, 174 (May–June 1995):32–35. At 80 Perle was writing and keeping twice as much music as he used to.
Leo Kraft, "The Music of George Perle," MQ, 57 (July 1971):444–65.
Bruce Livingston, "A Perle Without Price," P&K, 174 (May–June 1995):36–37. A discussion of Perle's *Phantasyplay*.

Vincent Persichetti (1915–1987) USA
Persichetti was an outstanding pianist who gave us twelve sonatas and numerous smaller works for piano. His writing displays a superb technique for exploiting the keyboard. Much of his music sounds difficult but is only moderately so because it "fits" the fingers so well. Persichetti's style displays a vertical progression of harmonies rather than the interplay of contrapuntal line. His writing is mainly homophonic with a strong, freely tonal base. All works listed below are published by Elkan-Vogel unless otherwise indicated.
Serenade No.2 Op.2 1929. Three short movements: Tune; Strum; Pluck. Textural rather than melodic in emphasis, a characteristic of almost all Persichetti's music. Int.
Poems Opp.4, 5 1939. 2 vols. Titles come from twentieth-century poets. Wide range of technical and interpretative problems. Versatile, delicate, imaginative; captures fragmentary moods. Int. to M-D.
Poems Op.14 1981. Five pieces. This is the third and final volume of short pieces inspired by poetic images. Long lyric lines, abstruse harmonic idiom, melodic vagueness. My favorite is No.5, "Each gay dunce shall lend a hand"; good humor. M-D.
Variations for an Album Op.32 1947 (Mer). Theme and five melodic variations in free style. M-D.
Serenade No.7 Op.55 1952. Six short pieces "that are distillations of a musical expression that has undergone clarification to the point of great simplicity" (personal communication from Mrs. V. Persichetti). Int. to M-D.
Parades Op.57 1952. March; Canter; Pomp. Sprinkled with ostinati and simple polychordal combinations. Int.
Little Piano Book Op.60 1953. Fourteen short pieces displaying many characteristics of the composer in distilled form. A "classic" with many teachers. Easy to Int.
Sonatinas Vol.1: No.1, Op.38; No.2, Op.45; No.3, Op.47. 1950. Sonatina No.2 is the most difficult in Vol.1. Vol.2: No.4, Op.63; No.5, Op.64; No.6, Op.65. Int. to M-D.
See: Vincent Persichetti, "The Modal Sonatina," *Staff Notes*, 13, Holiday Edition (1974):2–5. Discussion of Sonatina No.3.
Sonata 1 Op.3 1939 15 min. Allegro: SA; 12-tone introduction, which returns at end of sonata. Adagio: a sensuous song. Scherzo and trio: comical and contrapuntal. Andante passacaglia: climactic. M-D.
Sonata 2 Op.6 1939 11 min. Moderato; Sostenuto; Allegretto; Allegro. Sonatina-like, all four movements are thematically linked, amiable and attractive,

strong melodies and rhythms. Introspective earlier movements, ends with an emphatic rondo. M-D.

Sonata 3 Op.22 1943 13 min. Declaration; Episode; Psalm. Chordal, melodic, grandiose closing. One of the most frequently performed sonatas. M-D.

Sonata 4 Op.36 1949 17 min. Solid and varied work requiring superb finger legato, strong octaves, and plenty of drive. D.
    See: David Burge, "Persichetti's Fourth Sonata," CK, 7 (April 1981):48.

Sonata 5 Op.37 1949 12 min. With motion. Tenderly: a lyric berceuse. Briskly: ebullient. M-D.

Sonata 6 Op.39 1950 12 min. Short finale. Large span required. M-D.

Sonata 7 Op.40 1950 7 min. Three movements. Thin textures. Large span required. M-D.

Sonata 8 Op.41 1950 9 min. Three movements. More melodically conceived than the other sonatas. M-D.

Sonata 9 Op.58 1952 9 min. Moderato; Allegro agilité; Larghetto; Allegro risoluto. M-D.

Sonata 10 Op.67 1955 22 min. Adagio; Presto; Andante; Vivace. Four movements played without interruption, based on the opening Mixolydian motive. Full piano range is exploited within the Sonata's tight construction to express varied emotions, vibrant colors, full sonorities, lyrical melodies, and driving rhythms. This work is one of the very finest contemporary American piano sonatas. D.

Sonata 11 Op.101 1965 16 min. Risoluto; Articulato; Sostenuto; Leggiero. Nonmetrical, strong contrasting rhythms, sonorous pedal effects, strong dissonance. A somewhat new style emerges in this work. Requires endurance and powerful drive. D.
    See: David Burge, "Persichetti's Eleventh Sonata," CK, 7 (May 1981):52.

Sonata 12 Op.145 ("Mirror") 1982 13 min. Sostenuto: toccata-like. Amabile: expressive, varied moods, emotional. Scherzo: bouncing staccato chords; scales and trills. Brioso: toccata-like. Every note in the right hand is perfectly balanced and reflected in the left hand. A strong work, powerfully designed. Stylistic evolution in Sonatas 11 and 12 point toward increasingly advanced contemporary compositional techniques. D.

Parable for Piano Op.134 1976. 10½ min. (Parable XIX). Uses thematic ideas from three folk songs: Waillie, Waillie; Who Will Shoe Your Pretty Little Foot?; De Blues Ain Nothing. Flexible tempi and meters, improvisatory, changing moods, Impressionistic. Interpretive problems, pointillistic melody in alternating hands, hypnotic effects. M-D to D.
    See: David Whitehouse, "Learning Techniques for Contemporary Music," *Clavier*, 20 (March 1981):20–26; includes a lesson and four pages of Persichetti's *Parable for Piano*, Op.134.

Reflective Keyboard Studies Op.138 1981. 48 miniature studies to obtain simultaneous development of both hands. Uses symmetrical inversion, or, as Persichetti calls it, mirror music: exact intervals duplicated in each hand. Much rhythmic variety. These are preparatory studies for the *Mirror Etudes*. Int.

Little Mirror Book Op.139 1983 4½ min. Magnifying Mirror; Makeup Mirror;

Magic Mirror; Mirror Lake; Rearview Mirror. One hand plays exactly what the other hand plays, in contrary motion and at the same time. Fingering is always the same in both hands. Carefully pedaled; clever and attractive for the strict techniques used. Int.

Four Arabesques Op.141 1982 3½ min. Refined and delicate works that feature a clear, elegant interplay between the hands, effortless counterpoint, neoclassic. Int. to M-D.

Three Toccatinas Op.142 1979 6 min. Sparse neoclassic style "touch pieces" to be played with a "gentle touch." Brilliant short group. Passage-work divided between hands; facile pianism and firm rhythmic control required. M-D.

Mirror Etudes Op.143 1980 14 min. Seven concert pieces in different styles of playing, i.e., Affabile, Delicatissimo, Vigoroso, etc. One hand mirrors the actions of the other by repeating the same intervals and patterns in inversions. D.

See: Valerie O'Brien, "Look into the Mirror," *Keyboard Classics*, 2/5 (September–October 1982):42. An analysis of the *Mirror Etudes*.

See: Maurice Hinson, "The Solo Piano Works of Vincent Persichetti," AMT, 15 (April–May 1966):38–39, 59.

Morris Pert (1947–   ) Great Britain

Voyage in Space (J. Weinberger 1978) 38pp. Twenty pieces. "This collection of miniature pieces is intended to introduce some of the freedoms of contemporary notation, expression and sound production to the adventurous and imaginative piano student. The most important aspect of each piece is its evocative and sonic nature and the player must be primarily concerned with quality of sound and the creation of atmosphere. In addition to performance of the complete collection, suites of varying length can be drawn from the set for concert purposes" (from the score). Easy to M-D.

Sonores—5 Studies in Miniature 1973 (Weinberger) 9pp. Facsimile edition. Five untitled pieces. Contemporary techniques, some sections are to be ad libbed for a specified number of seconds or minutes. Changing meters, dramatic cross-hand gestures, "continuous hand to hand tremolo." Avantgarde. M-D.

Giovanni Battista Pescetti (ca. 1704–1766) Italy

Pescetti studied with Antonio Lotti and Baldassare Galuppi. For several years Pescetti was director of both Covent Garden and King's Theaters in London. He returned to Italy in the 1740s and was organist at St. Marks in Venice until his death.

Sonata c, *Cembalisti Italiani del Settecento* (Benvenuti—Ric). Three movements, FSF, lovely slow movement. M-D.

Allegretto C, *Italian Harpsichord Compositions* I (Vitali—Ric). Single sonata movement, Scarlatti style, perpetual motion. M-D.

Sonatas—*Selections* (Arnaldo Forni 1977) 59pp. Facsimile edition. Reprint of the London 1739 edition. Includes 9 sonatas plus Ouverture, nel vello d'oro, per il cembalo; Ariette nell' opere del Sigr. Pescetti (continuo or string orchestra accompaniment). Sonatas have several movements. Early classic style, little use of Alberti bass. Int. to M-D.

Sonata in c (P. Hurford—OUP 1977) 7pp. Allegro ma non piesto; Moderato; Presto. Attractive galant style; imitation, dynamic contrasts. Int.

Selected works found in *Clavecinistes Italiens* (Heugel).

Alexander Peskanov (1953–   ) USA, born Russia

Peskanov received a master's degree from The Juilliard School.

Prelude in D (Willis 1994) 6pp. Attractive impressionistic writing, except for a too predictable ending. Int.

Intermezzo (Willis 1994) 3pp. Expressive, a fine study in tied notes. Int.

John David Peterson (–   ) USA

Peterson teaches at the University of Memphis, Tennessee.

Camptown Mozart (Drew Publishing 1994) 7pp. This piece will surely make audiences smile. It is a humorous arrangement of Stephen Foster songs interspersed with fragments of Mozart's *Andante* K. 616. M-D.

Goffredo Petrassi (1904–   ) Italy

Partita 1926 (De Santis) 10pp. Preludio: dramatic scales and arpeggi in outer sections; contrasting expressive chromatic melody in mid-section. Aria: flowing, melodic. Gavotta: secco, à la Prokofieff. Giga: vivace eighths contrasted with melodic octotonic thirds; rousing. M-D.

Toccata 1933 (Ric). Diatonic harmony and melodic idiom, neo-Baroque contrapuntal style, linear excursions out of established tonality. Different from later works. M-D.

See: Olga Stone, "Goffredo Petrassi's Toccata for Pianoforte: A Study of Twentieth-Century Toccata Style," MR, 37 (February 1976):45–51.

8 Inventions 1944 (SZ) 20 min. Varied moods and characterizations skillfully worked out in a personal contemporary style; unusual lyric quality. Int. to M-D.

See: Olga Stone, "Goffredo Petrassi's Eight Inventions for Pianoforte," MR, 33 (August 1972):210–17.

Oh les beaux jours! 1942–76 (SZ) 13pp. Two pieces. An athletic Bagatelle and an impetuous interpretation of Miró's *Le petit chat*, displaying kittenish humor and mobility. Int. to M-D.

Petite pièce 1950 (SZ 1978) 4pp. Agile, graceful, fluid melody, delicate repeating figures, neoclassic, witty. Int. to M-D.

Allan Pettersson (1911–   ) Sweden

Lament (WH). Short (30 bars), thin textures, much use of interval of the octave, tragic and desolate mood created by understatement. M-D.

Felix Petyrek (1892–1951) Austria

24 Ukrainische Volksweisen (UE 1920). Polyphony is especially effective in Nos.2, 3, and 10. Could be performed as a suite. M-D.

Chorale, Variations and Sonatina (UE 1924). Theme in Chorale. Six variations, utilizing advanced pianistic devices follow. Sonatina attacca, theme still present. Var.7 becomes the second movement of the Sonatina and concludes the work *ppp*. A successful, curious mixture of formal structures. D.

Sechs Griechische Rhapsodien (UE 1927). Each utilizes full chords, free dissonant treatment, syncopated rhythms, interesting sonorities. None are easy and all require fine pianistic background. M-D.

6 Grotesques (UE 1914–20). Picturesque titles such as Procession By Night, Excentric, The Official Reception, Night Adventure. Colorful even though not so "unusual" sounding today. M-D.

Irena Pfeiffer (1912–   ) Poland

Let Us Hasten to the Stable (PWM 1972) 29pp. Twenty short attractive Christmas carols and pastorales, MC. Int.

Hans Pfitzner (1869–1949) Germany

Fünf Klavierstücke Op.47 (Johann Oertel Verlag, 1941). Last Effort; In High Spirits; Hieroglyphics; Anxious Restlessness; Melody. Late-nineteenth-century-sounding character pieces involving considerable technical difficulties. Highly chromatic. M-D.

6 Studien Op.51 (Oertel 1943). No.6 is a trill study. Slightly more difficult than Op.47. M-D.

Nicole Philiba (1937–   ) France

Jubilé (Billaudot 1975) 8pp. 42 min. Vivacious opening; then moves to a toccata style full of octaves and unison figuration. Brilliant with some dissonance. D.

Isidor Philipp (1863–1958) France, born Hungary

Philipp, eminent teacher and pianist of international renown, left a number of salon pieces of high quality in addition to his numerous etudes and finger exercises. An Isidor Philipp Archive and Memorial Library have been established by The American Liszt Society at the School of Music, University of Louisville, Louisville, KY 40292. The Archive and Memorial Library welcome any memorabilia related to Philipp. Further information can be obtained from Music Librarian, Dwight Anderson Memorial Music Library, University of Louisville.

Feux-follets Op.24/3 (GS). Jack-o'-lanterns. Effective. M-D.

Deux Etudes d'après Fr. Chopin Op.25/6 (Leduc). No.1 is based on chromatic sixths in the right hand. No.2 inverts the hands as contained in the original Chopin. D.

12 Preludes in Double Notes Op.85 (Sal). All are short but fairly demanding. M-D.

See: Maurice Hinson, "Isidor Philipp—An Appreciation," PQ, 88 (Winter 1974–75):20.

Isidor Philipp, "Some Reflections on Piano Playing," PQ, 88 (Winter 1974–75): 21–28.

Charles Timbrell, "The Isidor Philipp Archives at the University of Louisville," JALS, 35 (January–June 1994):59–60.

Michel Philippot (1925–1996) France
Sonate II (Sal 1973) 18pp. 15 min. One movement. No metric directions, pointillistic, dynamics for almost every note. Exploits full range of keyboard. Avant-garde. D.

Burrill Phillips (1907–   ) USA
Phillips's neoclassic style is permeated with American rhythms.
A Set of Three Informalities 1945 (GS). Blues: chordal accompaniment to melody. Scherzo: short; fast; passages alternate between hands; parallel triads. Sonatina: Romantic melodic treatment, fast mid-section, most difficult of set. M-D.
Three Divertimenti (EV 1946). Fancy Dance; Homage to Monteverdi; Brag. Brief pieces that exploit single ideas. Int.
Toccata (EV 1946). A boogie-woogie bass ostinato supports two voices throughout; distribution between hands. M-D.
Five Various and Sundry (EV 1961). Short, varied character pieces. Effective as a set or individually. Int.
Sonata No. 3 (Fallen Leaf Press 1991) 16pp.

Giovanni Picchi (1500?–1600?) Italy
Complete Keyboard Works (Ferguson—Zen-On 1979) 72pp. 14 works including 8 dance movements, 3 Passamezzos (2 paired with Saltarellos) and a Toccata. Some of the dance movements are in Polish, German, and Hungarian style. The Toccata (which appears in the FVB) is earliest in style and dates from before 1619. Editorial ornaments realized, chordal basses. Practical edition with all the musicological information required. Surprisingly effective on the piano. Not a lot of notes but requires real musicianship and an affinity with the period to make the music come alive. Int. to M-D.
Tänze für Klavier (G. Wohlgemut—Mitteldeutscher Verlag). Dances in different styles: German Dance, Hungarian Dance, Gagliarda con variazioni, Corrente con variazioni, Hungarian Pavan, Dance in Polish style, etc. Modal harmonies add interest to this early example of dance forms. Also found in TPA, V.

Karl-Heinz Pick (1929–   ) Germany
Kleine Märchensuite für Klavier (CFP 1973) 19pp. Seven lively and varied titles from fairy tales. Folklike tunes with sudden harmonic twists. Frequent use of augmented fourths. Int.

Riccardo Pick-Mangiagalli (1882–1949) Italy
Toccata A♭ Op.7 (Carisch 16173 1930) 8pp. Rondo with main idea in left-hand octaves, constant eighths throughout, fluent and facile, *pp* coda, *ppp* ending. M-D.
2 Lunaires Op.33 (Ric 1916; MMP). Colloque au clair de lune: a sensuous nocturne. La danse d'Olaf: a difficult but rewarding piece. M-D.
Capriccio Op.65 (Carisch 19979 1941) 10pp. 5 min. Vivace, sectionalized, secco, harmonic fourths, fleeting, left-hand melody under right-hand broken-chordal accompaniment, *ff* coda, *ff* ending. M-D.

Tobias Picker (1954–   ) USA

Andrew Porter praised Picker as "a genuine creator with a fertile, unforced vein of invention . . . one of the most gifted, individual, and unschematic of our young composers" *The New Yorker* (20 November 1978):10; (15 January 1979):94.

Three Pieces 1988 (Helicon EA 722 1988) 15pp. 6 min. Written for Peter Serkin. Svelto; Liberamente; Feroce. The outer pieces are fast and short while the second is long and slow. "The harmonic materials of the slow piece, a multi-layered landscape, consisted of the fast pieces slowed down, magnified and fitted together in different ways. But if the slow piece could be squeezed, at both ends would pop two very short, fast pieces which are contained in the slow piece, though not recognizable as such. I had thought of calling the pieces *Inside Out*. The fast pieces are spotlights which throw the slow piece into relief" (the composer). Changing meters, pointillistic, wide dynamic range, widely spread sonorities. D.

The Blue Hula 1990 (Helicon 1990) 5pp. Changing meters, much syncopation, ragtime influence, lyric and rhythmic passages juxtaposed. Requires large span. D.

Old and Lost Rivers. In collection *Changing Faces* (EAMC 1987) 4pp. Inspired by the calm dry tributaries of Houston's Trinity River. Upper range exploited expressively; widely spread over keyboard; more rubato can be used than indicated; *pp* throughout. A sense of meandering and wandering is appropriate for the flexible phrasings. Much pedal required. M-D.

Alexandra Pierce (1934–   ) USA

Pierce is a member of the music faculty at the University of Redlands.

Blending Stumps 1976 (Seesaw) 10pp. 11 min. For prepared piano. Preparation materials require: 7 bamboo wedges, 19 blending stumps (blending stumps, or tortillions, are made in France and consist of tightly wound paper in the shape of short pencils), 1 brass shoulder hook, 1 thin rubber washer, 1 Faber-Castell "Magic-Rub" eraser. Includes careful preparation directions. Plucked strings, pedal effects, harmonics, pointillistic, chromatic coloring in a basically diatonic idiom. D.

Coming to Standing 1975 (Seesaw) 11pp. 8 min. Performance directions include: "use abundant pedal, keep melody notes clear, ad lib unless otherwise shown; legato ½ pedal, clearing incompletely." Thin textures are increased to thicker ones. "During a sensory awareness workshop with Charles Brooks and Charlotte Selver I was struck by their frequent use of the direction, 'Come to standing.' They never discussed the expression, yet it was richly suggestive in the context of their work. It meant to me . . . bring oneself to the full presence of the process of one's own simple actions—standing, sitting, etc." (from a letter to the author, July 7, 1977). M-D.

Dry Rot (Seesaw 1977) 17pp. 15½ min. For prepared piano. Includes 4 pages of directions and preparation instructions. Preparations include: Magic Rub erasers, bamboo stalk, large hook screw, rubber tuning damper. Marimba mallet is used to strike strings. No bar lines, pointillistic. "There is a quote from Virgil which almost seems a paraphrase of 'Dry Rot': 'The wound unuttered lives deep within the heart'" (from a letter to the author, November 13, 1977). M-D.

Greycastle 1974 (Seesaw) 13pp. 8½ min. For prepared piano. Preparation materials require 4 piano tuner's rubber wedge mutes, 8 bamboo wedges, 3 pencil erasers, screws, 6 pennies, 2 dimes. Careful preparation instructions included. Repeated notes, pointillistic, trills, effective pedal usage, fast dynamic changes, thin textures. M-D.

Orb 1976 (Seesaw) 13pp. 9 min. For prepared piano. Preparation materials required: 1 piano tuner's rubber mute, 7 wooden clothespin halves, 6 rubber plumbing washers, 2 screws, 1 brass shoulder hook. Careful preparation instructions included. Ideas and fragments are repeated and expanded; no meters indicated; thin textures; varied pedal effects; subtle sonorities emerge from trills. Highly effective. M-D.

Spectres 1976 (Seesaw) 12pp. 8 min. For piano with five easy eraser preparations. Includes careful preparation instructions. A study in repeated notes; very few bar lines; much use of alternating hands; subtle pedal effects; MS easy to read. M-D.

Transverse Process (Seesaw 1977) 13pp. 11 min. No bar lines; varied textures; harmonics; freely expressionistic; sumptuous sonorities. Virtuoso pedaling requires flutter, ½, ¼, blurred releases. M-D.

Offering to Birdfeather 1974 (Seesaw) 7pp., ca. 5 min. "The title refers to a recurrent visualized image from that period of an inner teacher whose form took that of an Indian medicine-man: Birdfeather. The intermittent tonally askew trills, quick arpeggios and tremolos, and dancelike sections with uneven and shifting meters suggest the contrast of unpredictable and dreamlike states with the more comfortable and known reality of the stable outer portions of the piece" (from the score). Freely tonal. M-D.

Soundings 1978 (Seesaw) 7pp. 11 min. "In *Soundings* the image is the ocean. The idea of surface tension is suggestive of the musical shape. The horizontal surface of the piece is the tone, 'A-flat.' Its tones ramify" (from the score). Includes detailed remarks on notation, many performance directions. Avant garde. M-D to D.

Gabriel Pierné (1863–1937) France

Album pour mes petis amis Op.14 (Leduc; MMP). Six charming teaching pieces on level of Chopin Prelude A. Int.

Trois Pièces Formant Suite de Concert Op.40 (Hamelle 1906; MMP). Preludio e fughetta: D. Nocturne en forme de valse: M-D. Etude symphonique: D.

Variations c Op.42 (Hamelle 1918; MMP) 36pp. Large work, bravura writing. Alfred Cortot considered this one of the most important works in twentieth-century French pianism. M-D.

Willem Pijper (1894–1947) The Netherlands

Pijper was a much-respected composer, a craftsman of high quality.

Three folk dances of the world (Donemus 1926). De Boufon; Dutch children's dance; Scharmoes. M-D.

Sonatine No.2 1925 (OUP; B&VP). One movement. Short, changing meters, scherzo quality. M-D.

Sonatine No.3 1925 (OUP; B&VP) 5 min. Impressionist and jazz influences, irregular meters, whimsical. M-D.

Sonata 1930 (OUP; Donemus) 5 min. Allegro: short and rhythmic. Adagio molto: atmospheric and serious. Allegro volante: bright. M-D.

See: Alexander L. Ringer, "Willem Pijper and the Netherlands School of the 20th Century," MQ, 41 (October 1955):427–45.

Daniel Pinkham (1923–   ) USA

The music of Pinkham is always accessible technically. He constantly keeps the performer in mind in his writing.

Prelude (ACA 1946). Presto, changing meters, about 30 seconds long, ostinato effect. M-D.

A Song for the Bells (CFP 1962) 3 min. Written for carillon. Freely flowing, comes off surprisingly well on the piano, especially when pedal is used liberally. No time signatures but many instructions for tempo changes. Atmospheric, Impressionistic. M-D.

Preludes for Piano (Ione Press 1997) 21 min. 12 preludes that can be played as a group or separately; varied material, MC. Int. to M-D.

George Frederick Pinto (1785–1806) Great Britain

Pinto's works, with a wide range of expression, astonishingly anticipated the compositions of Beethoven and Schubert. These works have extraordinary merit.

Four Sonatas and a Fantasia (John McCabe—Allans 1206 c. 1985).

Sonata e♭ Op.3/1 1803 (S&B 1963) 16pp. 17 min. Allegro moderato con espressione; Adagio con gusto; Allegro con brio. Style shows something in common with Dussek and the three early sonatas of John Field. Emotional intensity and melodic and harmonic resources place Pinto among the masters of the Classical period. M-D.

Sonata A Op.3/2 1803. Schubert-like, especially the lyric writing. M-D.

Sonata c 1803. Passionate writing. M-D.

Fantasia and Sonata c Op. posth. A fugue appears in the Fantasia section, showing Pinto's great interest in the music of J. S. Bach. M-D.

The London Pianoforte School 1770–1860, in Anthologies and Collection section. *Complete Works for Piano Solo* are located in Vol. 14.

See: Nicholas Temperley, "George Frederick Pinto," MT, 106 (April 1965):265–70; with related correspondence on 446 and 523–24.

Octavio Pinto (1890–1950) Brazil

Dança Negreira (GS 1945). Constant sixteenth-note motion, energetic, syncopated. Requires rhythmic vitality. M-D.

Marcha do Pequeña Polegar (GS). Crisp, short. Int.

Scenas Infantis (GS). Five descriptive scenes for childhood. Int.

Festa de crianças (Children's Festival) (GS). Five easy, attractive children's pieces.

Georg Pirckmayer (1918–1977) Austria

Transitionen für Anfänger (Dob 1973) 12pp. Five pieces, each notated twice: once to show what is done at the keyboard; once to show the musical results when the pedal is used. Interpretive problems. Int.

Transitionen (Dob 1972) 27pp. Book III. Five "Transitions" in 12-tone writing. Requires full resources of the keyboard; includes thorough pedal indications. Individual handling of dodecaphonic technique. M-D.

Paul A. Pisk (1893–1990) USA, born Austria

Vier Klavierstücke Op.3 (UE) 9 min. Short, freely tonal. M-D.

Sechs Konzertstücke Op.7 (UE 1922) 11 min. Atonal, chromatic, rhapsodic, D.

Speculum Suite Op.17 (ACA). Toccata; Sarabande; Intermezzo; Menuet; March. Chromatic, tightly organized, turbulent. D.

5 Sketches Op.39 (NME 1936) 9½ min. Short, contrasted, contemporary, brilliant close. M-D.

Engine Room (MCA) A "Motor Study for Piano." Vigorous perpetual motion. M-D.

Dance from The Rio Grande Valley (LG 1957). Attractive. Int.

Nocturnal Interlude (LG 1963). Well-written mood music. M-D.

Caribbeana (ACA) 3pp. Three-section work. Bitonal, tango rhythm.

Sonatina E Op.94 (CFE 1958) 6½ min. Three movements, FSF. Neoclassic, numerous chromatics, fluctuating tonalities, much imitation. M-D.

Walter Piston (1894–1976) USA

Piston was often characterized as America's leading neoclassicist.

Passacaglia (Mer 1943). Short, grows in intensity with each variation to sonorous climax, involved textures, chordal counterpoint, excellent craftsmanship. M-D.

Improvisation (MCA). In *U.S.A. Vol. I* with works of other American composers. Short, lyric, quartal harmony, peaceful closing. Int.

Thomas B. Pitfield (1903–1999) Great Britain

Homage to Tschaikowsky 1963 (OUP) 3pp. Uses a theme from Tchaikovsky's *Serenade for Strings* Op.40. Int. to M-D.

Johann Peter Pixis (1788–1874) Germany

The Pixis Waltz (Musica Obscura) 2pp. Sections in thirds, sixths, and octaves; chromatic; scherzando ending. M-D.

See below, "Collections," *Piano Music of the Parisian Virtuosos 1810–1860,* vol. 7.

Ildebrando Pizzetti (1880–1968) Italy

Three Pieces 1911 (Joseph Williams). Da un autunno gia lontano: 1. Sole mattutino sul prato del roccolo; 2. In una giornata piovosa nel bosco; 3. Al fontanino. Lyrical throughout. M-D.

Sonata 1942 (Curci) 21 min. First movement: lengthy; some Arioso style. Adagio: thick chordal writing; arpeggi. Turbinoso: many octaves; variety of mood. D.

Giovanni Benedetto Platti (ca. 1697–1763) Italy

G. B. Platti E La Sonata Moderna. Vol.II Istituzioni Dell' Arte Musicale Italiana (Nuova Serie) edited by Fausto Torrefranca (Ric 1963). A scholarly work with 211 pages of introduction and all 18 extant sonatas for the cembalo (188 pages). A handsome work, with index, 413 pages. Int. to M-D.

12 Sonatas (K 9495). Most have four short movements. Concise, lucid, often with dignified slow movements. Their grace and spontaneity make them a welcome change from Scarlatti and Bach in a recital. See especially No.5 c and No.10 A. Good for small hands. Int. to M-D.

6 Sonatas (Pestelli—Ric 132617) 66pp. Preface and commentary in Italian, English, and German. First published in 1742. At their best they are graceful, even beguiling. The sonatas in D, g, and c are the finest. Careful edition. M-D.

Sonata A (Boccaccini & Spada 1982) 11pp. First edition. Preludio; Allemanda; Minuet—Minuet Alternativo; Giga. Suitelike; excellent contrasting movements; would make a fine recital-opener. M-D.

Sonata No.11 c (G. Scotese—GS 1975) 14pp. Adagio; Allegro; Allegro. Each movement is in binary form. Ornaments are realized. A very beautiful work. M-D.

Hubert du Plessis (1922–   ) Union of South Africa

Preludes Op.18 (Galliard). Seven pieces. Linear writing in a Romantic idiom. Imaginative pianism. M-D.

Raoul Pleskow (1931–   ) USA, born Austria

Three Bagatelles 1969 (CFE) 8pp. Harmonics, stopped strings. Tightly knit. Keyboard exploited elastically from bottom to top. D.

Pentimento 1974 (Gen) 9pp. In five movements. Pointillistic, serial influence, changing meters and tempi, expressionistic, wide dynamic range, strong in statement. Radical restatement in final two movements of material from first three movements. D.

Alessandro Poglietti (?–1683) Italy

Poglietti, an Italian, worked in Vienna and died there during the Turkish siege.

Harpsichord Music (W. E. Nettles—PSM 1966). Suites a and C; Capricietto sopra il Cu Cu; Toccata del 7 tuono; Canzon Teutsch; Trommel; Canzon Francaix Trommel; Toccata fatta sopra L'Assedio. Descriptive works: bird calls, battle sounds, droning bagpipes, etc. Fascinating notes by the editor. Int. to M-D.

Capricietto also in W. Georgii's *Keyboard Music of The Baroque and Rococo I*. M-D.

Il Rossignolo (F. Goebels—Br). Set of variations. M-D.

Aria Allemagna con alcuni Variazoni (DTOe XXVII, 13–22). Written in 1677 as a birthday present for the Empress of Austria, Eleonora Maddalena Theresa. 20 variations, one for each year of her age, based on programmatic connotations, such as Bohemian Bagpipe, Hungarian Fiddles, Bavarian Shawn, French Kiss-the-Hand, Juggler's Rope-dance, Old Hag's Procession, Dance of the Honor-guard. Delightful picturesque music. Also found in *Alte Meister des Klavierspiels* (W. Niemann—CFP) Vol.I. Int. to M-D.

Suite F in anthology series *The Suite*, pp.113–17. Toccata; A; Double; C; S. M-D.

See: Friedrich W. Riedel, "Ein Skizzenbuch von Alessandro Poglietti," *Essays in Musicology—A Birthday Offering for Willi Apel* (Bloomington: School of Music, Indiana University, 1968), pp.145–52.

Franz Xaver Pokorny (1728–1794) Bohemia

Sonata F (Bosse BE 709 1978) 11pp. Allegro spiritoso; Adagio; Allegro molto. Early Viennese classic style. M-D.

Eduard Poldini (1869–1957) Hungarian

Poupée valsante (Dancing Doll) (Alfred 4623). Poldini's best-known piece; fleet, graceful melody contrasted with colorful countersubject. Int.

Claire Polin (1926–1995) USA

Out of Childhood (Seesaw 1973) 8pp. Variations on Russian-Turkish folk songs. The Six Kings of Turkey; The Orchard; Rocking Chair Song; Sing, Birdie, Sing; The Rooster; A Gypsy Song; The Sleigh. Chromatic, freely dissonant. For adults thinking back on their childhood. Int. to M-D.

Laissez sonner 1975–76 (Seesaw) 12pp. 15 min. Piano sonata. Inventio: chromatic; expressionistic; glissandi. Fabula: for prepared piano; subtle, misterioso; arpeggi gestures; remove preparation at conclusion of this movement. Parodia: rhythmic; flexible tempi at places; staccato style; thin textures. Strong writing throughout. M-D.

Robert Pollock (1946–   ) USA

Bridgeforms 1972 (Boelke-Bomart) 35pp. 17 min. Eight pieces. Serial, complex and thorny, pointillistic, contrasting tempi and dynamics, involved, expressionistic. D.

Manuel M. Ponce (1886–1948) Mexico

Ponce composed in a popular, nationalistic style.

Gavota (PIC 1941). Refined, lyric dance. Int.

Elegía de la Ausencia (PIC 1959). Melody accompanied by rhythmic ostinato. M-D.

Preludio Trágica (PIC 1950). Expressive but full of fast repeated double notes. M-D.

Tema Mexicano Variado (PIC 1960). Sentimental theme, four variations, much use of shifting rhythms. M-D.

Sonata No.2 (PIC 1968) 33pp. Revised, fingered, and edited by Carlos Vazquez. First movement; much rhythmic drive. Allegro Scherzo; contains a contrasting trio section. Romantic and Impressionist idiom. M-D.

Momento Doloroso (PIC 1960). Short, expressive. Int.

Twenty Easy Pieces for Piano (PIC). Based on folk tunes, many Indian. Charming and clever writing throughout. Easy to Int.

Quatre Pièces (Senart 1930) 12pp. Preludio Scherzoso; Arietta; Sarabande; Giga. Bitonal; right hand written in one key, left hand in another; uses pentatonic scales. M-D.

Marcel Poot (1901–1988) Belgium

Poot's style is full of facile lyricism, naturalness, and spontaneity.

Suite (UE 1943) 10½ min. Preludio; Fughetta; Passacaglia; Toccata. Excellent for concert use. M-D.

Sonate C (ESC 1927). Three movements. The Andante has a Menuet as B section, then returns to Andante. Much rhythmic vitality. M-D.

Etude (ESC 1951). Written for the Brussels competition. Technical and lyrical display. M-D to D.

Variationen (UE 1952). Finely contrasted moods. M-D.

On the Spanish Border. Towards Avignon. In collection *The Century of Invention* (EAMC). Folksong oriented. Int.

Quincy Porter (1897–1966) USA

Sonata 1929–30 (CFP) 15 min. Three movements. Outer movements are lively and rhythmic (syncopation and cross accents), while the middle one is more like a fantasia. MC. M-D.

Day Dreams (Merion 1958) 2pp. Delicately tinted, wistful; requires evenly balanced chords. Int.

Marcos Portugal (1762–1830) Portugal

Sonata y variaciones (Lemmon—UME 1976) 24pp. Sonata D: opening movement (untitled) suggests concerto grosso style. Rondo C: ornamental and free, with cadenzas; triolike section in E♭ leads to six Variations in E♭: displays strong rhythmic and technical expertise. Viennese classic style. Int. to M-D.

Hans Poser (1917–1970) Germany

Sonata No.1 Op.7 (Sikorski 1953). Three movements. Free linear writing. Second movement contains a fugue. M-D.

Musik für Ursula Op.10 (Sikorski 1950). Seven easy pieces in style of Gretchaninoff. Int.

2 Sonatinas Op.12/1, 2 (Sikorski 1950). In A, G. No.2 a little more difficult. Int.

Musik für Klavier Op.24 (Sikorski 1957). Pastorale-Recitative, Aria-Allegro rubato. 12-tone technique. M-D.

Sonatine No.3 Op.44/1 (Sikorski 1959). Linear. Int.

Sonatine No.4 Op.44/2 (Sikorski 1959). More difficult.

Alte Volkslieder (Sikorski). Easy settings.

Cipriani Potter (1792–1871) Great Britain

Potter went to Vienna in 1817 to study composition with Aloys Förster and was advised by Beethoven. Potter taught at the Royal Academy of Music in London from 1822 and was director from 1832 to 1859. He introduced Beethoven's piano concertos Nos. 1, 3, and 4 to England and composed three piano concertos of his own and much other music.

Selected Piano Pieces 1816–1848. In *London Pianoforte School 1766–1860,* vol.14 (Garland Publishing 1986).

Francis Poulenc (1899–1963) France

It is possible that Francis Poulenc's music will prove to be the most durable of all the group known as "Les Six." His music is characterized by unpretentiousness, wit, freshness, and accessibility. It bespeaks the "music hall" and all that it implies. Poulenc's spontaneous melodic writing is one of his unique and easily identifiable qualities. Poulenc wrapped his music in a halo of pedals; he said: "Do not analyze my music, love it!" He considered Erik Satie his mentor.

Mouvements Perpétuels 1918 rev. 1962 (Alfred; JWC; MMP). Three homophonic pieces. Assez modéré: ostinato bass, sans nuances. Très modéré: casual mood. Alerte: bright, more energetic than the others. Int.

Suite C 1920 (JWC). Presto; Andante; Vif. Short movements, mainly diatonic, busy. M-D.

Five Impromptus 1920–21 (JWC). Short parody pieces in varied moods. M-D.

Promenades 1921 (JWC). The title explains the significance of the ten pieces. A pied; En auto; A cheval; En bateau; En avion; En voiture; En chemin de fer; A bicyclette; En diligence. Contains moments funnier than anything else Poulenc ever devised, including a wicked distillation of seasickness. M-D.

Pastourelle 1927 (Heugel). Transcription from the ballet *L'Eventail de Jeanne.* Enticing melody, saucy asides. Int.

Feuillets d'Album 1923 (Sal). Ariette; Rêve; Gigue. Interesting part writing in the outside movements. Int.

Napoli 1925 (Sal). Barcarolle: lyric, mixed meters, unusual harmonies. Nocturne: short, rich harmonies, contrasting mid-section. Caprice Italien: brilliant Presto tarantella; cadenza; long; considerably more difficult than the first two movements. One of Poulenc's best piano works. M-D.

Trois Novelettes 1927–28 (JWC). C, b, e. No.3 published separately (JWC). No.1 is best known. No.3 based on a theme by Manuel de Falla. M-D.

Trois Pièces 1928 (Heugel). Pastorale: most characteristic. Toccata: brilliant perpetual motion; restlessness created by vague tonality, "scissors and paste" compositional structure. Hymne: chordal, powerful, introspective, ornamental melody, quiet close. M-D.

Huit Nocturnes 1929–38 (Heugel). C, A, F, c, d, G, B, E♭, coda to the cycle. Popular melodic style, rich harmonies, some of Poulenc's most beautiful writing. See C, A, G, E♭ especially. Nos.4 5, 6, and 8 available separately. M-D.

Hommage à Albert Roussel 1929 (Leduc). Short, lyric, quiet ending. Name "Albert Roussel" is treated forward and in retrograde. M-D.

Villageoises 1933 (Sal). Five pieces for young people. Attractive melodic and harmonic writing. Int.

Presto B♭ 1934 (Sal). Fresh, whimsical staccato etude. Written for Vladimir Horowitz. Excellent encore. Requires facility. M-D.

Suite Française (after Claude Gervaise) 1935 (Durand). Seven sixteenth-century French dances freely arranged in Poulenc's harmonic and modal language. Diatonic. Int. to M-D.

Intermezzi 1934 (Sal). No.1 c: delightful Presto con fuoco. No.2 D♭: quiet. M-D.

Badinage 1934 (Sal). A salon piece. M-D.

Improvisations (Sal). Book I: 6 pieces (1932). Book II: 6 pieces (1933–34, 1941). Nos. 13, 14 (1958). No.15, Hommage à Edith Piaf (1959): an accompanied vocalise, rich harmonies support a sequential tune. Nos. 1–10 available separately. Informal, moderate length, varied moods. See especially Nos.1, 3, 5–8, 10. Nos.4 and 9 are brilliant and expressive. Nos.13 and 14 go together well as a group. M-D.

Les Soirées de Nazelles 1930–36 (Durand) 30 min. Préambule; 8 Variations; Cadence; Finale. Poulenc said of this work: "The variations which form the center of this work were improvised at Nazelles during the course of long soirées in the country when the author played at 'Portraits' with friends grouped around the piano. We hope today that, presented between a Préambule and a Finale, they will evoke the memory of this game played in the setting of a Touraine salon, a window opening onto the night." Poulenc's most important solo piano work. Complete pianism required. D.

Mélancolie 1940 (ESC). A Romantic pastorale. M-D.

Intermezzo A♭ 1943 (ESC). Fauré influence, melody supported by widely spaced figuration. Romantic, salon style. M-D.

Thème Varié 1951 (ESC). A banal theme with eleven well-crafted variations. M-D.

Bourée au Pavillon d'Auvergne in album *A l'Exposition* and separately (Sal). Melody over drone bass, drum effects, short, attractive. Int.

Histoire de Babar (le petit éléphant) 1940 (JWC). For narrator and piano. 22 min. Contains some of Poulenc's most charming piano writing. An English translation of the text is available through the publisher. Sections may be excerpted. Excellent musical vaudeville. M-D.

Humoresque 1935 (Sal). Short. Two main themes are brilliant; insouciant but full of grace and spirit. M-D.

Caprice C (Sal). Based on the Finale of *Bal masqué*, a secular cantata. "Music hall" style, contrasting habanera mid-section. Effective. M-D.

Album of Six Pieces (JWC). Revised and corrected by the composer. Mouvement perpétuel No.1 (1918); Presto, from Suite in C (1920); Impromptu No.3:

Française (d'après C. Gervaise) (1939); Novelette No.1 C (1927); à Pied (Promenade No.1) (1921). M-D.

Valse C 1919 (Schott) 2 min. An endearing miniature full of echoes of the Parisian *Café Concert*, capturing in its few bars the feeling of a Toulouse-Lautrec painting. Composed when Poulenc was greatly influenced by Igor Stravinsky, this piece displays Stravinskian brittleness (wrong notes!) and is Poulenc's witty homage to this popular dance. Fetching tunes and rhythms. M-D. Also contained in collections *L'Album des 6* (ESC 1920) and *The Century of Invention* (EAMC). M-D.

Les Biches 1923 (Heugel). Ouverture; Rondeau; Adagietto; Andantino. Based on popular French songs and transcribed by Poulenc. See especially Adagietto. M-D.

Valse—Improvisation sur le nom de Bach 1932 (Sal). Waltzlike, witty, Gallic charm, exciting conclusion. M-D.

Piano Album (Sal 1989) 89pp. Caprice en ut majeur; Intermède en ré mineur; Valse-improvisation sur le nom de BACH; Villageoises; Feuillets d'album; Badinage; Humoresque; Ier intermezzo en ut majeur; IIème intermezzo en réb majeur; Presto en sib; Bourrée, au pavillon d'Auvergne. Int. to M-D.

See: Laurence Davies, "The Piano Music of Poulenc," MR, 33 (August 1972): 195–203.

Linda P. Stutzenberger, "Poulenc's Tempo Indications: To Follow or Not to Follow," AMT, 31/3 (January 1982):26.

W. Kent Werner, "The Piano Music of Francis Poulenc," *Clavier*, 9 (March 1970): 17–19.

Henri Pousseur (1929–   ) Belgium

Pousseur was the first Belgian composer to work with electronic music.

Exercices pour piano: Variations I 1956 (SZ) 24pp. 10 min. Serial, thick textures, expressionistic, variation technique apparent throughout. D.

Exercices pour Piano: Impromptu et Variations II (SZ 1955–56). Webern influence, with thicker textures. D.

Caractères I (UE 1961). Unusual notation, including inexact metric indications, which are to represent values "felt as units, whose relations are of a qualitative nature. . . . This notation presupposes in the interpreter both an understanding of the 'semantic kernel' from which all structural principles are derived (i.e., integral aperiodicity) and a clear idea of what, as a means of fulfilling this demand, is in fact possible with our sensory apparatus." The performer can begin with any one of six pages. D.

Caractères II (UE). Three pieces. Nos.1 and 3 have variable forms, as found in *Caractères* I. No.2 (La Chevauchée fantastique) begins in an early classic style and progresses to 12-tone technique. D.

Apostrophe et 6 Réfléxions 1964–66 (UE 894). Apostrophe is a collection of themes (structural motives) in a neo-Impressionistic vein that is full of potential development. Each Réfléxion (variation) is built on a complete fragment from Apostrophe. See especially the variations "Sur le phrase," "Sur le toucher," and "Sur les octaves." Avant-garde. D.

Ballade Berlinoise 1974–77 (SZ 8373) 9pp. This haunting and intriguing Berlin style Ballade is dedicated to the memory of Brahms, Mahler, Schönberg, and J. S. Bach. Strong Romantic influence, but Schönberg has the last word. Freely tonal with key signatures throughout. A change in Pousseur's style. M-D.

John Powell (1882–1963) USA

At the Fair (John Powell Foundation 1912, Box 37711, Richmond, VA 23211) 35pp. Hoochee-Coochee Dance; Circassian Beauty; Merry-Go-Round; Clowns; Snake-Charmer; Banjo-Picker. These sketches of American fun are delightful and develop from the Gottschalk and MacDowell tradition. Folklike tunes permeate the pieces, and color from the old South is apparent on every page. Also available separately. M-D.

Sonate Psychologique Op.15 1905 (MS available from the Manuscripts Dept., University of Virginia Library, Charlottesville, VA 22901) 31½ min. Uses as motto: "On the text of St. Paul: 'The Wages of Sin is Death'" 1. Kampf (Struggle), Grave—Allegro agitati; 2. Nocturne, Hingebund (Submission), Andante—Allegro brioso; 3. Scherzo diabolique, "In den Klauen" (In the Clutches), Allegro con fuoco; 4. Thanatopsis (Contemplation of death), Tempo di Marcia Funebre, un poco meno mosso. Shows Liszt, Richard Strauss, and Rachmaninoff influence. Written while Powell was studying piano with Theodor Leschetizky in Vienna. D.

In the South Op.16 (John Powell Foundation 1910) 25pp. Humming Birds: fast-moving chromatic and diatonic lines. Love Poem: Romantic harmonies, dramatic mid-section in ragtime style. Negro Elegy: "My Mother's dead and gone" is the theme; mid-section dreams of the past; then opening section returns. Pioneer Dance: based on tune "Howdy Stranger," which is similar to "The Arkansas Traveler"; mid-section based on "Over the Fence." This brilliant piece requires virtuoso octave technique. M-D to D.

Variations and Double-Fugue on a Theme of F. C. Hahr, Op.20 1907 (A. Z. Mathot; also available from Manuscripts Dept., University of Virginia Library, Charlottesville, VA 22901) 21 min. Reveals a change in musical style from the earlier works. "In addition to its 17 variations (the 16th of which is entitled *Canon*) and an extended, thoughtful *Finale*, the piece has three fugues: the first and third are on a variation of Hahr's theme; the second uses one of the third's counter-subjects. The influence of Leopold Godowsky, who liked to play informally for Leschetizky's classes, can be seen in Variation 8, which is for left hand alone. The theme is in the Aeolian mode (b-flat); its choice foreshadows Powell's later (after 1931) exclusive use of modal materials" (from CRI SD jacket 505, notes by Roy Hamlin Johnson; record contains Opp.15 and 20). M-D to D.

See: Roy Hamlin Johnson, "John Powell's *Sonata Psychologique* and *Varia-*

tions and Double Fugue on a Theme of F. C. Hahr," AMT, 35 (January 1986):34–35.

Sonata Noble Op.21 1907 (GS 1921) 37pp. Allegro moderato: based on folk tunes or melodies suggested by folk tunes in the mountain areas of western Virginia, West Virginia, Tennessee, and Kentucky; SA. Theme and (7) Variations: in Var.5 the spirit of the dead returns. Minuetto—Allegretto sostenuto: this is the most intimate and contrapuntal movement. Inscribed with a quotation from the poet Sidney Lanier, "Vainly might Plato's head revolve it, Plainly the heart of a child could solve it." Displays a sophisticated contrapuntal technique and a disarming simplicity. M-D.

Sonata Teutonica Op.23 1913 (R. H. Johnson—OUP 1983) 69pp. Notes, performance edition with biographical and editorial commentary. Allegro, molto sostenuto; Andante sostenuto; Tempo di marcia. "Teutonic" refers to Anglo Saxon as much as, if not more than German. Inspired by philosophical ideas, Powell combined a kind of Wagnerian leitmotif technique with cyclical technique and fit them into extensive classical forms. This performance edition is an abridgement of the original score as transcribed in a copy prepared for Benno Moiseiwitch's premiere of the work in 1914. An American masterpiece. Requires tremendous virtuosity combined with a singing, Romantic tone and an intellectual approach. D.

See: Roy Hamlin Johnson, "John Powell's Sonata Teutonica," AMT, 28 (November–December 1978):34–36.

See: Mary Helen Chapman, "The Piano Works of John Powell," thesis, Indiana University, 1968. "A survey of Powell's life, emphasizing his political, cultural, and aesthetic values, serves as a background for a stylistic analysis of the complete works for keyboard" (from author's abstract).

Mel Powell (1923–1998) USA

Powell was an outstanding jazz pianist before study with Ernst Toch in Los Angeles and Paul Hindemith at Yale University. He taught at the California Institute of the Arts.

Prelude. In collection *American Contemporary Masters* (GS 1995) 5pp. Vivid 12-tone writing, rhythmic proportional relationships, expressionistic organic imagery. D.

Sonatina (Ric 1951). Vivace: free moving counterpoint, light, fleeting touch exploited. Chorale-Variations: mixed meters, chorale intricately woven into texture, big climax exploits melody. Largo assai—Allegro: brief introduction requiring large span leads to Allegro that uses repeated notes in percussive fashion; Animato ending. M-D.

Ettore Pozzoli (1873–1957) Italy

Pozzoli's style is highly attractive, and his pieces for younger students contain sterling qualities.

Berceuse (Ric 128153) 3pp. Melody thins and thickens over supporting broken-chordal bass. M-D.

Easy Sonatina in the Classic Style (Ric 129753). One movement in SA design. Int.

15 Easy Pieces (Ric 436). Delightful, charming. Easy.

Impressions (Ric 127900) Book I. (Ric 127177) Book II. 12 short colorful character pieces. Int. to M-D.

Pinocchio Suite (Ric 129061) 18pp. 12 short pieces describing events in the life of the famous wooden doll. Charming. Int.

Riflessi del Mare 1929 (Ric 121108) 17pp. Three beautiful character pieces. M-D.

See: Riccordo Castagnone, "Ettore Pozzoli," PQ, 82 (Summer 1973):34–36.

Almeida Prado (1943–   ) Brazil

Prado is associated with the music vanguard in Brazil. Along with other young composers, he left behind the nationalist school of Camargo Guarnieri and his disciple Osvaldo Lacerda.

Sonata I 1965 (Tonos) 22pp. 14 min. Luminoso, Solar; Improvizando; Energico (Fuga). Strong Schönberg and Villa-Lobos influence. D.

VI Momentos 1969 Book II (Ric BR) 14pp. 10 min. Two types of motion: a. rapid fluid motion; b. slow dense motion; uses a series throughout this piece. 2. Pedal changed on each chord. 3. Free repetitions, unusual metrical notation, clusters. 4. Nocturnal: exploits soft sonorities, night sounds. 5. Primitivo: imitation of a native instrument. 6. Tenso, heróico: dramatic, harmonics. D.

Taaroá 1971 (Tonos) 12pp. 7 min. Theme and (5) Magic Variations. Theme is divided into chords (thème d'accords) and single line (thème mélodique), flexible meters. Taaroá II ends the piece. Complex writing, involved organization, avant-garde. D.

Ilhas 1973 (Tonos) 23pp. 13 min. Six pages of explanation; a catalogue of avant-garde techniques full of dense and explosive volcanic sonorities. D.

Cartas celestes ("Celestial Charts") 1974 (Tonos) 15 min. Pieces are: Doors of Sunset; Night-Milky Way; Nebulae and Constellations; Milky-Way; Doors of Dawn. The work was originally composed to accompany a show at the São Paulo Planetarium; it was later developed into a concert work. The sky is depicted during the Brazilian springtime (September to November). There are twenty-four different chords, each related to a letter of the Greek alphabet, which is utilized for the classification of stars, constellations, galaxies, and nebulae. The celestial bodies of the Southern Hemisphere are musically interpreted through the combination of the chords. The piano language is deliberately luminous and brilliant, with emphasis on resonance and on the complexity of several simultaneous "clusters"; these generate both vertiginous brightness and thick sonoric vagueness. The musical structure is very free, "like a promenade through the skies in Brazil." There are, however, certain fixed elements, the repetition of which results in the punctuation of the musical text. M-D to D.

Rios 1975–76 (Tonos) 38pp. 20 min. Three movements. Includes three pages of notes, thematic indexes, and explanation. Very involved and complex rhythmic structures, strong Messiaen influence. A catalogue of avant-garde techniques. Virtuoso technique required. D.

Anthony Powers (1953–   ) Great Britain
Powers studied at Oxford University, in Paris with Nadia Boulanger, and at York with David Blake and Bernard Rands. He teaches at the University of Wales, College of Cardiff.
The Memory Room 1991 (OUP 1994) 17pp., ca. 17 min. 16 short contrasting atonal pieces. Various contemporary techniques are used. Strong rhythms. Int. to M-D.
Sonata No. 1 1983 (OUP 1989) 28pp., ca. 17 min. Allegro energico; Lento sereno; Lento moderato—Allegro. "Immediately impressing in this work was the sonata style opening movement, where the ideas were gripping, well contrasted and presented with a classical sense of proportion and pianistic flair" (Meirion Bowen, in *The Guardian,* from OUP brochure on Powers). D.
Sonata No. 2 1985–86 (OUP) 24 min. A substantial work. Shows mastery of the instrument and the form as well as economy of material; well developed; full of dramatic intensity. D.

André Previn (1929–   ) USA
Impressions (MCA). 20 short pieces in a combination of styles. Pianistic. Int.
Birthday Party (Robbins 1949). A suite of eight short descriptive pieces, each employing at least one contemporary device of composition. Int.
Five Pages from My Calendar 1976 (Bo&H). "The dates which form these five preludes are the birthdates of my five children. The pieces are in no way meant as portraits of their complex personalities; rather they are simply birthday greetings from me to them" (from the score). Contrasted, chromatic, jazz influence, sophisticated. D.
Paraphrase on a Theme by William Walton 1971 (Nov) 8pp. 4 min. No.10 in Virtuoso series, editorial note by John Ogdon. Based on a theme from Act 2 of *Troilus and Cressida.* "Pianistically, the *Paraphrase* is very sharply etched and needs for its performance the staccato effects . . . almost a stencilled style, which Gershwin asked for in his music" (editorial note). Contains much dissonance, but basically the piece is a lyric and tonal arabesque. Debussy influence is noted toward the conclusion in consecutive sevenths and other chordal structures. M-D.
The Invisible Drummer 1974 (Bo&H) 18 min. Written for Vladimir Ashkenazy. Five preludes in an improvisatory jazz dissonant style. Polyrhythms, large leaps, rich harmonies. Title implies an invisible drummer is necessary at all times to maintain absolutely steady tempi. Dazzling pieces of concert jazz for the more advanced pianist. M-D to D.
Matthew's Piano Book (Magnamusic-Baton). 10 pieces. Colorful, strong jazz influence, witty. Juxtaposition of Bachian cadences with light dissonances in No.7 is most attractive. Makes a fine "suite" for an outstanding performer. M-D.

Deon Nielsen Price (1934–   ) USA
Price earned music degrees at Brigham Young University and the University of Michigan, and her DMA from the University of Southern California.

Diversions 1961 (Culver Crest 1984) 22pp. Freeway Fugue; Desert Impression; Surf Dance; Quake Fantasy. "The 4 pieces are tightly crafted. The initial chromatic subject in No. 1 reappears in the last phrases of No. 3 and is heard throughout No. 4. The tonal levels extend from C to F-sharp (G-flat). This tritone functions as a dominant in both Nos. 1 and 4. No. 2 begins with a lyrical melody accompanied by the quiet color of a minor 2nd harmonic dissonance. The repeated intervals in the accompaniment gradually expand to the consonance of thirds. In No. 3 the folklike melody is based on F-sharp Mixolydian and its lively rhythm includes a palindrome pattern" (abridged, from the score). M-D.

Angelic Piano Pieces (Culver Crest 1995) 30pp. Pink Clouds and Harps: major triads in root position. Angel Cookies: seventh chords in jazz rhythms. Descending Night: avant garde notation, groups of 3 and 2 black keys. Cupid's Darts: right hand plays on white keys, left hand plays on black keys. Snow Angels: pentascales and white key clusters. Angels Dancing: right hand plays black keys, left hand white keys. Green Tara: legato melody in thirds and sixths, irregular meter. Cherubic Messenger: impressionistic. This set provides a fine introduction to innovative contemporary techniques. Int.

Florence Price (1887–1953) USA

Price grew up in Little Rock, AR, graduated from the New England Conservatory, and taught in Little Rock and Atlanta colleges before moving to Chicago. She was a prolific and versatile composer in many media and genres. Her piano works are available through Special Collections, University of Arkansas Libraries, Fayetteville, AR 72701.

Sonata in E Minor 1932, 27pp. 25 min. Andante-Allegro: heroic opening, exposition with two main themes, development moves towards B minor, recap returns to E minor. Andante: rondo with two episodes, cakewalk influence. Scherzo: two parts, powerful, MacDowell influence. M-D to D.

The Cotton Dance 1931 (OUP) 3pp. In *Oxford Piano Course,* Book 5. Five-part rondo form, syncopation, clever melodic turns. Int. to M-D.

Dances in the Canebrakes 1953 (Mills Music). Nimble Feet; Tropical Moon; Silk Hat and Walking Cane. All three offer contrasting moods and are based on "authentic Negro rhythms" (from the score). Int. to M-D.

Maria Teresa Prieto (1910–1982) Mexico

24 Variaciones (EMM 1964) 30pp. Consists of twelve tonal variations (one each in twelve different keys) and twelve serial variations. The tonal set seems to unfold more naturally. Concludes with an exciting fugue. M-D to D.

Serge Prokofieff (1891–1953) Russia

Prokofieff's nine sonatas (now firmly established in the pianist's repertoire) and the approximately one hundred smaller pieces constitute a treasured contribution to twentieth-century piano literature. Prokofieff developed an individual, percussive style, which was probably the most significant innovation in piano technique since Chopin. His percussive manner of treating the piano is uniquely blended with a lyric element frequently accompanied by strong dissonance, yet his basic arsenal of figuration stems directly from the nineteenth century. Influences of Russian folksong are evident in his melodies and energetic rhythms. The pianistic demands vary, from the *Music for Children* Op.65 to the highly motoric *Toccata* Op.11 and the virtuosic *Sonatas* Nos.6, 7, and 8. Biting percussive effects, physical endurance, and a fine octave technique are requirements for many of Prokofieff's works.

Complete Piano Works (K). Vol.1: Opp.2, 3, 4, 11. Vol.2: Opp.12, 17. Vol.3: Opp.22, 31, 32, 59, 65. Vol.4: Opp.1, 14, 28. Vol.5: Opp.29, 38, 135. Vol.6: Opp.82, 83. Vol.7: Opp.84, 103. Vol.8: Classical Symphony (No.1), Op.25; March and Scherzo from *The Love for Three Oranges*, Op.33; Six transcriptions for piano, Op.52, from Opp.46, 48, 35, 50. Vol.9: Opp.75, 77. Vol.10: Opp.95, 97, 102. Vol.11: Organ fugue d by Buxtehude, arr. for piano, Op.96; Waltzes by Schubert, transcribed and combined into a suite for two pianos, four hands.

Sonatas (Bo&H 1985). Introduction and performance notes by Peter Donohoe. Vol.1: Nos.1–5. Vol.2: Nos.6–9.

Sonatas (Sandor—MCA; Freundlich—Leeds; IMC; K). Available separately (MCA; K).

Sonata No.1 Op.1 f 1909 (CFP; Simrock; Rahter). One movement, Romantic, enthusiastic. M-D.

Four Etudes Op.2 1909 (MCA; IMC; CFP; K). d, e, c, c. Involved studies in double notes, octaves, running figuration, broken octaves. D.

Four Pieces Op.3 1907–11 (Rahter; GS, in collection *Selected Works for the Piano*; K, has two). Conte; Badinage; Marche; Fantôme. M-D.

Four Pieces Op.4 1910–11 (Bo&H; MCA; IMC; K; EMB, has No.4). Réminiscence: melody accompanied by chromatic harmony. Elan: short, energetic. Désespoir: chromatic ostinato. Suggestion diabolique: mocking, bravura, driving, most difficult of set. M-D.

Toccata Op.11 1912 (MCA; IMC; K). SA, motoric perpetual motion, skips, double notes, chromatic chords in contrary motion, virtuosic, insistent ostinatos all set in a percussive and dissonant framework. D.

Ten Pieces Op.12 1913 (Freundlich—MCA; CFP; IMC; K). Marche; Gavotte; Rigaudon; Mazurka; Caprice; Légende; Prelude A; Scherzo humoristique; Scherzo. Neoclassic influence. M-D.

   Available separately: Nos.1, 2, 3, 7, 9, 10 (CFP). Nos.1, 2, 6 (EBM).

Sonata No.2 Op.14 d 1912 (CFP; Simrock). Allegro ma non troppo: lyric. Scherzo: motives crossing hands. Andante: melodic. Vivace: tarantella-like. M-D.

Sarcasms Op.17 1912–13 (Freundlich—MCA; Bo&H; EBM; Simrock; K). Tempestoso; Allegro rubato; Allegro precipitato; untitled; Precipitosissimo. Five pieces that storm, rage, and thunder throughout. Bitonal, brusque, percussive, much rhythmic motion. D.

Visions fugitives (Fleeting Visions) Op.22 1915–17 (MCA; GS; Bo&H; EMB; K; IMC). 20 short aphoristic pieces, Prokofieff's "Preludes." Lyric; varied moods and difficulty. For a suite of tiny bits—not one is as much as 2 mins.

long—this set has, when played complete, a glowing unity that too few pianists have explored. M-D.

See: Tedd Joselson, "Master Class—Prokofieff's Vision Fugitives," Part 1, CK, 5 (September 1979):74. Part 2, CK, 5 (October 1979):87. Part 3, CK, 5 (November 1979):78. Part 4, CK, 5 (December 1978):86. Part 5, CK, 6 (January 1980):64. Part 6, CK, 6 (February 1980):83.

Sonata No.3 Op.28 a 1917 (IMC; Simrock; Bo&H). One movement, Allegro tempestuoso, based on earlier sketches (1907). Bravura, rhythmic drive. Requires power and great energy. D.

Sonata No.4 Op.29 c 1917 (Bo&H). Allegro molto sostenuto: mainly lyric, ponderous. Andante assai: enticing melody with rich figurative accompaniment. Allegro con brio, ma non troppo: a facile rondo. Based on earlier sketches (1980). D.

Tales of the Old Grandmother Op.31 1918 (MCA; IMC; K; Bo&H; MMP). Four short, melodic pieces. Int.

Four Pieces Op.32 1918 (MCA; IMC, No.3; K; MMP; Bo&H, Nos.3 and 4). Dance; Minuet; Gavotte; Waltz. Neoclassic influence. Gavotte is finest in the set. Int. to M-D.

Sonata No.5 Op.38 C 1925 (Bo&H). Also exists as Op.135 (K) in a second version. Allegro tranquillo: forceful melodic writing, parallel harmonies. Andante: dancelike, mocking. Un poco allegretto: requires large span. M-D to D.

See: Frank Merrick, "Prokofieff's Piano Sonatas One to Five," MT, 86 (January 1945):9–11.

Divertissement Op.43B 1925–26 (Bo&H; MCA). Four pieces arranged by Prokofieff from his other works. Divertissement (from *Trapèze*); Nocturne; Dance (*Trapèze*); Epilogue. M-D.

Things in Themselves Op.45 1928 (Bo&H; K). Allegro moderato; Moderato scherzando. Lengthy, somewhat involved pieces with strong lyric overtones. M-D.

Six Transcriptions Op.52 1931 (Bo&H; AMP). Both editions publish these separately. Intermezzo; Rondo; Etude; Scherzino; Andante; Scherzo. M-D to D, the Scherzo especially difficult.

Two Sonatinas Op.54 e, G. 1931 (Bo&H; K). Each in three movements, short but not easy. Diatonic, linear, sophisticated writing. M-D.

Three Pieces Op.59 1934 (Bo&H; MMP). Promenade; Paysage; Sonatine pastorale. Available separately. The one-movement Sonatine is somewhat easier than Op.54. Int. to M-D.

Pensées Op.62 1933–34 (Bo&H). Adagio penseroso, Moderato: double melody two octaves apart, ornamental right hand. Lento: choralelike. Andante: longest of the set, melodic, chromatic. Simple, melodic, and beautiful. M-D.

Music for Children Op.65 1935 (Bo&H; IMC; Ric; Alfred; GS). Twelve pieces involving a variety of problems. Provides an excellent introduction to the composer. Easy to Int.

Peter and the Wolf Op.67 1936 (MCA; CFP). Arranged by Prokofieff. M-D.

Ten Pieces Op.75 1937 (MCA; CFP; MMP). From the ballet *Romeo and Juliet*. Short sketches: Danse populaire; Scène; Menuet; Juliette jeune fille; Masques; Mercutio, etc. Effective as a group or separately. Most of the melodies are direct and uncomplicated, utilizing harmonies and chromatics not associated with Prokofieff's piano sonatas. Int. to M-D.

Gavotte Op.77 E♭ 1938 (K). From music to *Hamlet*. Forceful, effective. M-D.

Sonata No.6 Op.82 A 1939–40 (CFP; Sikorski; Bo&H) 26 min. Allegro moderato: biting, dissonant, driving, SA. Allegretto: marchlike, staccato chords, lyric mid-section. Tempo di valzer lentissimo: long, slow, Romantic waltz. Vivace: brilliant rondo, sparkling melodic treatment, sonorous climax. Largest of the sonatas. Requires virtuoso equipment. D.
> See: Frank Merrick, "Prokofieff's Sixth Piano Sonata," MT, 85 (January 1944):9–11.

Sonata No.7 Op.83 B♭ 1939–42 (IMC; CFP; Bo&H; Sikorski; K). Allegro inquieto: bare, percussive. Andante caloroso: lush harmonic treatment. Precipitato: perpetual-motion toccata, one of the finest ever written. Most popular of the sonatas. D.
> See: Tedd Joselson, "Master Class: Passages from Prokofiev's 7th Sonata," CK, 6 (March 1980):70.

Sonata No.8 Op.84 B♭ 1939–44 (CFP; Bo&H: Sikorski; K). Andante dolce: melodic but includes a powerful climax. Andante sognando: lyric intermezzo. Vivace: lengthy rondo leads to a highly spirited Allegro ben marcato. Most lyrical of the sonatas. D.
> See: Malcolm H. Brown, "Prokofieff's Eighth Piano Sonata," *Tempo*, 70 (Autumn 1964):9–15.
> Tedd Joselson, "Master Class—Prokofiev's Sonata No.8," CK, 4 (November 1978):87.

Three Pieces Op.95 1942 (Bo&H; CFP; K). From ballet *Cinderella*. Intermezzo; Gavotte; Valse Lente. M-D.

Three Pieces Op.96 1941–42 (CFP; K). Transcriptions from *War and Peace* and the film *Lermontov*. Waltz (*War and Peace*): lengthy, octaves, large chords. Contradance (*Lermontov*). Mephisto Waltz (*Lermontov*). Displays the ever-changing style of this composer. M-D.

Ten Pieces Op.97 (K). From *Cinderella*. Colorful moods. M-D.

Sonata No.9 Op.103 C 1947 (CFP; Bo&H; Sikorski; K). Four movements. A strange mixture of styles pervades this work, neoclassic plus Romantic. Less difficult than *Sonatas* 6 and 7. M-D.
> See: Lawrence Chaikin, "The Prokofieff Sonatas: A Psychograph," PQ, 86 (Summer 1974):9–19.
> Frank Merrick, "Prokofieff's Piano Sonatas," PRMA, 75 (1948–49):13–21.

First Piano Compositions (Sikorski 2276 1977). 13 short pieces by the teenaged composer; first publication. Int. to M-D.

Works, Piano, Selections (EMB Z8289 1979) 52pp. Works transcribed by the composer from film scores and ballets including *Romeo and Juliet, War and Peace, Lermontov, Cinderella*. Waltz Op.96/1; Contredanse Op.96/2; Zho-

luska's Variation Op.102/2; Quarrel Op.102/3; National Dance Op.64/2:
Scene, Minuet, Dance, Romeo and Juliet; Op.65/6. M-D.

March and Scherzo from *The Love for Three Oranges* Op.33-ter transcribed by
the composer (K) Vol.8 of *Complete Piano Works*. Prokofieff wrote this opera in America in 1919. It was initially a failure but the fantastical *March
and Scherzo* achieved considerable popularity and was later quoted in his
Cinderella ballet. The piano version has long been a favorite encore. M-D.

Selected Works for the Piano (Balogh—GS). Op.2/3, 4; Op.3/1, 2, 3, 4; Op.4/4;
Op.11; Op.12/1, 7; Gavotte from *Classical Symphony* Op.25; March from
The Love for Three Oranges Op.33; Op.45/1; Op.52/6; Op.54/2; Op.59/3;
Op.62/1, 2, 3,; Op.77/4; Contradance from the film *Lermontov* Op.96/2;
Mephisto valse from film *Lermontov*.

Album of Prokofieff Masterpieces (EBM). Includes original works for piano:
Etude Op.2/4; Conte Op.3/1; Devilish Inspiration Op.4/4; Marche Op.12/1;
Gavotte Op.12/2; Prelude Op.12/7; Sarcasms Op.17/3, 5; and transcriptions
from Opp.25, 33, 48, 67, and 75. Int. to M-D.

Six Pieces for Piano (GS 1978) 23pp. Specially edited by Prokofieff. Includes:
Etude c Op.2/4; March Op.12/1; Gavotte Op.12/2; Prélude Op.12/7; Sar-
casme Op.17/3; Vision Fugitive, Op.22/16. M-D.

Album (K). Etude Op.2/3; March Op.12/1; Sarcasms Op.17; Sonatinas Opp.54
and 59; Toccata Op.11; Visions Fugitives Op.22. M-D to D.

Shorter Piano Works (D. Feofanov—Dover 1992) 293pp., 79 pieces. Reprinted
from various Russian editions. 4 Etudes Op.2; 4 Pieces Op.3; 4 Pieces Op.4;
Toccata Op.11; 10 Pieces Op.12; Sarcasms Op.17; Fugitive Visions Op.22;
Tales of the Old Grandmother Op.31; 4 Pieces Op.32; Things in Themselves Op.45; 2 Sonatinas Op.54; 3 Pieces Op.59; Thoughts Op.62; Children's Music Op.65; Dumka. Commentary by editor.

See: Stephen C. E. Fiess, *The Piano Works of Serge Prokofiev* (Metuchen, NJ:
Scarecrow Press, 1994), 252pp.

Carlo Prosperi (1921–   ) Italy

Fantasia 1973 (SZ 7767) 11pp. Many tempo, mood, and meter changes. Octotonic,
expressionistic. M-D.

Joseph Prostakoff (1911–1980) USA, born Asia

Two Bagatelles (LG) in collection *New Music for the Piano*. Adagio molto e
espressivo: 12-tone, quiet, meanders. Con moto: changing meters, 12-tone,
much 16th-note figuration. M-D.

Kazimierz B. Przybylski (1941–   ) Poland

Tema con variazioni (PWM 1964) 11pp. Chromatic theme, seven contrasting
variations. 1. Contrapuntal. 2. Lyric and free. 3. Fast, light, chromatic skips
and runs. 4. Heavy syncopated chords; stems without notes denote repetition of the last note or chord. 5. March, imitative octaves. 6. Harmonics. 7.
Theme heard forward, backward, inverted, etc. M-D.

Marta Ptaszyńska (1943–   ) USA, born Poland
Ptaszyńska is also widely known as a virtuoso percussionist.
Journeys into Space (PWM 1981) 19pp. Charming pieces full of simple contemporary techniques. Easy to Int.
Miniatures for Young Pianists (EBM 1983) 16pp. Similar to above collection. Also contains notes on each piece describing techniques used. Enormously attractive to both player and listener. Easy to Int.

Henry Purcell (ca 1659–1695) Great Britain
French and Italian influences are evident in the keyboard works of Purcell. He left eight suites and a few separate pieces, all thinly textured. Three or four movements make up the suites; they usually begin with Preludes, followed by Almands, Corants. Sarabands, and sometimes a Hornpipe, a Minuet, etc. Z. numbers refer to Franklin B. Zimmermann, *Henry Purcell (1659–1695): A Thematic Index to his Complete Works* (Philadelphia: Pennsylvania Pro Musica, 4816 Beaumont Avenue, Philadelphia, PA 19143).
8 Suites 1696 (Ferguson—S&B 1964) 30pp. 1. G, Z.660: Prelude; Almand; Corant; Minuet. 2. g, Z.661: Prelude; Almand; Corant; Saraband. 3. G, Z.662: Prelude; Almand; Courante. 4. a, Z.663: Prelude; Almand; Corante; Saraband. 5. C, Z.666: Prelude; Almand; Corant; Saraband. 6. D, Z.667: Prelude; Almand; Hornpipe. 7. d, Z.668: Almand ("Bell-barr"); Corant; Hornpipe. 8. F, Z.669: Prelude; Almand; Courante; Minuet. Editorial and textual notes. Also includes a few alternative versions of some of the pieces to show how they may be stylishly varied. Int. to M-D.
8 Suites 1696 (C. Kite—JWC) 2 vols. The text is virtually the same as the 1964 Ferguson edition. Includes the recently discovered "Prelude for the Fingering." Eminently serviceable and highly recommended edition, especially for teaching purposes. Int. to M-D.
     See: Arthur Steiger, "Purcell Called His Suite a Lesson," *Clavier*, 14 (November 1975):21–23. Suite I G is analyzed. Music included.
The Second Part of Musick's Handmaid (Dart—S&B; SZ 8652). 35 easy keyboard pieces mostly by J. Blow and H. Purcell. Includes Purcell's settings of *Lilliburlero* and *Sefouchi's Farewell*. Int. to M-D.
Selected Pieces for Piano Solo (K 9537). Includes 9 pieces from *A Choice Collection of Lessons* and 3 pieces from *Musick's Handmaid* II. Based on Howard Ferguson's 1964 edition (according to the anonymous editor). Be careful of the advice to use the pedal. Metronome marks, essential fingering, and interpretation of ornaments included. Int. to M-D.
See: Thurston Dart, "Purcell's Harpsichord Music," MT, 100 (June 1959):324–25.
Gloria Rose, "Purcell, Michelangelo and J. S. Bach: Problems of Authorship," AM, 40 (1968):203–19.

Eduard Pütz (1911–   ) Germany
Pütz delights in mixing serious and light music styles. He frequently incorporates elements of pop music and jazz in his writing.

Jazz Sonata 1988 (Schott ED 7954 1993) 23pp. Includes preface by the composer in German and English. Toccata in Rhythm; Ballad; Waltz; Play Bass. Good introduction to jazz styles. Based on improvised jazz figures and jazz formulas. Int. to M-D.

Waltzing the Blues: 3 Jazz Waltzes (Schott ED 8033 1993) 8pp. Valsette; Sentimental Lady; Waltzing the Blues. Contrasting, attractive. Int.

How About That Mr. Offenbach! Can-can fantasy (Schott 8496 1995) 7pp. Seconds, Bossa nova section. The famous Offenbach theme appears at the end. Lots of fun. M-D.

Let's Swing, Mr. Bach! 1991 (Schott 8003) 19pp. Six pieces in "play-Bach" style. When Mr. B. goes Marching in; Invention in C; Invention in Blue; Interlude; Siciliano; Invention in F. Clever, fun. Int.

Q

Marcel Quinet (1915–　　) Belgium

Trois Préludes (CeBeDeM 1970) 17pp. 10 min. 1. Somewhat Impressionistic, spread over wide range of keyboard. 2. Broken-seventh figuration, perpetual motion, upper register exploited. 3. Broken figurations accompany upper register chords; eighth-note motion maintained. M-D.

Hommage à Scarlatti 1962 (CeBeDeM) 20pp. 7 min. Three movements, much two-voice texture, upper register staccato writing, dissonant, many accidentals. M-D.

Hector Quintanar (1936–　　) Mexico

Sonidos für Klavier 1970 (Tonos) 6pp. Explanations for performance in Spanish and English. Plucked strings, clusters, metallic comb and ruler used on strings, aleatoric, avant-garde. M-D.

R

Jan Rääts (1932–   ) Estonia
Toccata (GS 1977) 14pp. Fast repeated thin textures grow into fast repeated chords. Clusters, glissandi, cadenza. ABA, exciting close. Prokofieff influence, but more contemporary sounding. M-D.

Sergei Rachmaninoff (1873–1943) USA, born Russia
The piano music of Rachmaninoff is written in an eclectic individual style derived from Chopin, Liszt, Schumann, Tchaikovsky, and Brahms and is flavored with Russian nationalism. Rachmaninoff's melodic writing is of the highest order and is supported by sonorous harmonies with florid decoration, resulting in unusually effective music for the instrument. A breathless motion permeates most of his writing. Many character pieces are contained in his works.
3 Nocturnes 1887 (Sorel—EBM 1973). 1. f♯: longest, dramatic. 2. F: melodically oriented. 3. c: mid-section resembles early c♯ Prelude. Slavic melancholy; hint at Rachmaninoff later style. Large span required. M-D.
5 Pieces Op.3 1892 (MMP; GS, published separately). Elegie (Belwin-Mills; CF): lush harmonies, sweeping Chopinesque and Tchaikovsky-like melodies. Prelude c♯ (Schott; CFP; IMC; Bo&H; CF; WH; Leduc): original, powerful and expressive, deserves its popularity. Polichinelle (CF; Leduc): puckish, trilled chords, melody in octaves, busy inner voices. Melodie (CF): lyric. Serenade (Belwin-Mills): Spanish inflections. Int. to M-D.
See: Ruth Laredo, "New Discoveries about Rachmaninoff's Prelude Op.3, No. 2." KC, 611 (January–February 1986):34–35, with the music on pp. 24–28.
Prelude F 1891 (Musica Obscura 1983) 4pp. This early work has many characteristics of the later Rachmaninoff: flowing melody, chromaticism, lush harmonies. The mid-section in D♭ requires careful control of legato harmonic thirds in the right hand. M-D.
4 Pieces 1887 (Dowd—Musica Obscura 1983) 14pp. Romance f♯; Prelude e♭; Gavotte D; Melodie E. "This Romance . . . is the first of four works composed in [1887] by the fourteen-year-old Russian prodigy for a composition class, and demonstrates more than any other early work the already blooming talent for lyricism and the building of powerful climaxes that would later become his trademark. . . . At the audition to be accepted into either the advanced composition or theory class . . . Tchaikovsky was present. On the basis of his class work, Rachmaninov had already received the highest grade possible with the additional 'plus' beside the grade. After the exami-

nation, Tchaikovsky was asked if he would like to hear Rachmaninov play some of the pieces in three-part form that he had composed that year (presumably these four works). . . . Sometime later, Rachmaninov discovered that the older composer had added plusses above, below, and before the grade in addition to the one already present" (Editor's note). M-D.

7 Pieces Op.10 1894 (K; Willis; Century). Nocturne (WH; Willis): limpid, nostalgic melodic lines. Valse (Schott; Leduc; Century): lilting and with technical embellishments. Barcarole: flowing, with motion. Melodie (GS): cantabile, rich sonorities. Humoreske (Belwin-Mills; GS; Leduc; WH; CF): opening theme echoes the First Symphony; witty—a quality that is rare in Rachmaninoff. Romance: imaginative mood. Mazurka: effective. M-D.

4 Improvisations 1896 (Hinson—Hinshaw 1985). Brief pieces, each using themes by the four composers Arensky, Glazunov, Rachmaninoff, and Taneyev. Interest is more for melodic and pastiche qualities than for breaking any new ground in pianism, but the writing is charming and refined. Requires large span. Int. to M-D.

6 Moments musicaux Op.16 1896 (GS; K; IMC; Simrock). bb; eb (Belwin-Mills); b; e; Db; C. Brilliant salon pieces written in a full-blown late-Romantic style. See especially e and eb. More difficult than Opp.3 and 10. M-D to D.

2 Fantasy-Pieces g 1899; d 1884 (Hinson—Hinshaw 1985). Youthfully exuberant character, sketchy, improvisational structure. Already contain a number of Rachmaninoff characteristics, i.e., idiomatic piano writing and a striking gift for melody. M-D.

Variations on a Theme by Chopin Op.22 1903 (IMC; MMP). Based on Chopin's *Prelude* c Op.28/20. 22 variations with a wide diversity of mood and texture. D.

Preludes Op.3/2, Op.23, Op.32 (Bo&H 1985). Introduction and performance notes by Peter Donohoe. A reissue of the original Russian edition (Gutheil) of all 24 Preludes. It was scrupulously corrected and edited by the composer.
See: Jeremy Norris, "Rachmaninov's First and Last Preludes," *Piano Journal,* 6/18 (October 1985):11–13.

10 Preludes Op.23 1903–4 (Bo&H; CFP; GS; IMC; EBM; K; Hansen House). 1. f#: Chopinesque, sweeping emotions, chordal closing. 2. Bb: brilliant, sonorous, hammered chordal motif; difficult especially for a small hand. 3. d: staccato-chord study, overflowing with rhythmic vitality and contrapuntal interest. 4. D: serene, nocturnelike. 5. g (CF; WH): military character, big repeated chords. 6. Eb: lyric and sweet, careful tonal balancing necessary. 7. c: broken-chord sequences, exhilarating. 8. Ab: sparkling, built on one figure. 9. eb: double-note study very difficult. 10. Gb: melodic, sensuous harmonies, shortest and simplest. M-D to D.
See: Ruth Slenczynska, "Master Class on Rachmaninoff's Prelude Op.23/4," *Clavier,* 18 (December 1979):20–24. Includes the music.

Sonata No.1 d Op.28 1907 (Bo&H; IMC; K; MMP) 33 min. Allegro moderato;

Lento; Allegro molto. A brilliant, well-wrought work of epic proportions with lush, sensuous harmonies and haunting melodies reminiscent of the Russia of Tchaikovsky. Because the work is awesomely difficult and very long, it is rarely performed and has been unjustly neglected. The extreme demands on the pianist's technical skills and the relentless emotional intensity make this Sonata one of the most challenging works in the solo piano repertoire. D.

13 Preludes Op.32 1910 (Bo&H; CFP; IMC; Hansen House; EBM; K). 1. C: brilliant, quiet closing. 2. bb: dotted triplet rocking figure, brilliant climax, fanciful figuration. 3. E: motif hammered out in octaves, no melody. 5. G: lovely theme, variations, bridges, and coda; tops! 7. F: duet between outer voices. 8. a: effective, similar to No.3. 10. b: perhaps the finest of all the 24 Preludes. 11. B: rhythmic motif in a restrained mood. 12. g#: ingratiating textures. 13. Db: sums up by quoting from several of the preludes, ingratiating themes beautifully worked out, a glorious conclusion. Rachmaninoff patterned his key relationships after Chopin and wrote one prelude in each major and minor key. The famous Prelude c#, published separately (Op. 3/2), is No.24. It has become the most assaulted piano piece in the world. M-D to D.

See: Morton Estrin, "Playing the Preludes, Op.32," *Clavier*, 12 (October 1973):19–20, 30.

Ruth Slenczynska, "Rachmaninoff's Preludes," *Clavier*, 2 (November–December 1963):27–30. Includes music for Prelude g# Op.32/12.

Etudes-Tableaux Op.33 1911 (GS; IMC; K; Bo&H, with Op.39; Belwin-Mills, Nos.2 and 6; Gutheil, Nos.2, 3, 4, and 6; MCA, Nos.2, 3, 4, and 6; Nos.3 and 4 published in USSR, 1947). 1. f: a march, staccati bass ostinati, sustained melody, ringing upper sonorities. 2. C: melody reigns over slow rolled chords, trills, Chopinesque closing. 3. c: nocturne-like; remained unpublished during Rachmaninoff's lifetime; his refusal to publish it probably stems from the fact that its final bars, in a slightly altered form, were inserted in the slow movement of Piano Concerto No.4, and Rachmaninoff had no desire to repeat himself. 4. d: brilliant staccato study. 5. eb: chromatic, shifting rhythms and harmonies. 6. Eb: strong rhythms and broad melodic line. 7. g: elegiac melody, broken chords, cadenza climax, ends with *fff* scale passage. 8. c#: declamatory, five themes worked out, major-minor shifting. These miniature tone-poems are "studies" in sheer pianism in the same tradition as the Chopin *Etudes*. They are also poetic "studies" or "pictures" in the tradition of the descriptive character pieces of Schumann and Liszt. D.

Sonata No.2 bb Op.36 (Bo&H; IMC; MMP). Allegro agitato; Non allegro; Allegro molto. Rachmaninoff originally wrote this work in 1913 but revised it in 1931, tightening the structure while simplifying some of the performance problems. Although it is a three-movement work, at first hearing it gives the impression of having only one. As involved and difficult as the first sonata. D. Original and revised editions published together (Bo&H).

See: Geoffrey Norris, "Rachmaninoff's Second Thoughts," MT, 114 (April 1973):364–68. Discusses Rachmaninoff's revisions to the Second Piano Sonata, the first and fourth piano concertos, and several other works.

9 Etudes Tableaux Op.39 1916–17 (Bo&H, with Op.33; available separately MCA; IMC; GS; K). 1. c: propulsive, flying figurations, dramatic chordal closing. 2. a: lyric, quiet, tenuous. 3. f♯: unusual metrical groupings, cadenza leads into doubled staccato chords closing. 4. b: staccato chord study, no meter signature, powerful rhythmic surges. 5. e♭: best known of the set; an expansive, somber tone poem; epic themes couched in a grand dramatic style; groups well with the E♭ (Op.33/7), c (Op.33/3), or c (Op.39/7). 6. a: chromatic figuration binds entire piece together. 7. c: funereal; elegant chordal passages; builds to large climax. 8. d: lush harmony, no distinctive melody. 9. D: pulls together material from the others, dramatic, formidable. M-D to D.

Prelude 1917 (Belwin-Mills) 3pp. Andante ma non troppo. This beautiful posthumous work has many characteristics of other works composed at the same time. It is full of rich harmonies, cantabile melodies, and somber sonorities. M-D.

Variations on a Theme of Corelli Op.42 1932 (Belwin-Mills). Based on "La Folia" Op.5/12. Rachmaninoff erroneously attributed the "La Folia" tune to Corelli. This set of 20 variations is in reality two sets of variations, generally of parallel construction, separated by an "Intermezzo" and concluded by a Coda. Less complicated than Op.22. Displays a more imaginative treatment of the theme than in the earlier Chopin Variations. D.

Polka de W. R. (Bo&H). Written for Wassili Rachmaninoff, Sergei's father, an amateur pianist. M-D.

Oriental Sketch 1917 (Foley) 4pp. Octotonic, octaves, full chords, cantabile melody, some of the chromaticism sounds slightly Oriental. M-D.

COLLECTIONS:

Sergei Rachmaninoff; a highlight collection of his best-loved original Works (C. Hansen Educational Music and Books 1973). Notes on the life and times of Rachmaninoff by H. Dexter. Includes: Op.3/1, 2, 3, 4, 5; Op.10/2, 3; Op.23; Op.32; Op.33; Second Piano Concerto arranged for piano solo.

A Commemorative Collection—Original Works and Transcriptions (Belwin-Mills 1973) 115pp. A centennial edition. Original works include: Fragments; Humoresque Op.10/5; Mélodie Op.3/3; Polichinelle Op.3/4; Oriental Sketch; Prelude (Posthumous). Transcriptions include: J. S. Bach, Suite from Partita E for violin (Preludio, Gavotte, Gigue); Bizet, Minuet from *L'Arlesienne Suite*; Mendelssohn, Scherzo from *A Midsummer Night's Dream*; Mussorgsky, Hopak; Rimsky-Korsakoff, The Bumblebee; Schubert, The Brooklet; Tchaikovsky, Lullaby. Most of these transcriptions are available separately (Belwin-Mills). M-D to D.

Sergei Rachmaninoff, Anton Rubinstein, Nicholas Rimsky-Korsakov—Their Great-

est Piano Solos (Shealy—Copa). Rachmaninoff: Barcarolle Op.10/3; Elegie Op.3/1; Humoreske Op.10/5; Melodie Op.3/3; Piano Concerto II theme (simplified); Polichinelle Op.3/4; Prelude c♯ Op.3/2; Preludes Op.23 and Op.32; Serenade Op.3/4; Valse Op.10/2. M-D.

Album (Schott). Nine selected pieces. From Op.3: Elégie, Prelude c♯, Mélodie, Sérénade, Polichinelle. From Op.10: Nocturne, Valse, Humoreske, Romance. M-D.

Album (GS). Barcarolle g; Elégie e♭; Mélodie E; Polichinelle; Prélude c♯; Prélude g; second piano concerto, third movement condensed and arranged by C. Deis; Sérénade b♭; Valse A. M-D.

Radio City Album of Selected Composition for Piano by Rachmaninoff (EBM). Etude-Tableau f Op.33/1; Moment Musical D♭ Op.16/5; Polichinelle Op.3/4; 3 Preludes Opp.3/2, 23/5, 32/5; Romance Op.10/6; Valse Op.10/2; themes from Concerti Nos.1 and 2. Practical collection. M-D.

See: Francis Crociata, "The Piano Music of Sergei Wassilievitch Rachmaninoff," PQ, 82 (Summer 1973):27–33.

Joseph Yasser, "Progressive Tendencies in Rachmaninoff's Music," *Musicology* 2/1 (1948):1–22.

Joachim Raff (1822–1882) Germany, born Switzerland

La Fileuse Op.157/2 (GS; Schott; Musica Obscura). Facile melody, broken-chord accompaniment. Int. to M-D.

Octaven Etude (Musica Obscura) 4pp. g, Allegro, octave scales, chromatic arpeggios, octaves in both hands. M-D.

Sonatina Op.99/1 (CFP 2558). Thick textures, Brahms influence, surging Romantic melodies. Int.

Erhard Ragwitz (1933–   ) Germany

Sonate Op.19 (DVFM 1968). Grave: built on springy, dissonant figuration; lyrical episodes. Allegro con fuoco: much use of triplet figure; leads to marcato section with melody in bass; triplet figure returns and leads to clashing conclusion. Hindemith influence. D.

David Rakowski (1958–   ) USA

Rakowski studied at Princeton and the New England Conservatory. He has taught at Columbia and Stanford Universities.

Trillage 1993 (Etude 4) (CFP 1995) 4 min. Theme and 6 imaginative variations that view the trill in numerous ways, including double and triple trills. Theme emerges in the variations; changing meters and textures. Written for Alan Feinberg. D.

Jean-Philippe Rameau (1683–1764) France

Rameau's 53 pieces for keyboard show dramatic sweep, boldness, and an art more firmly rooted in the Baroque than that of his older contemporary François

Couperin. Rameau's keyboard works have a more sustained quality and are more suited to the piano than Couperin's. Rameau uses some or all of the four basic movements of the suite and adds other movements with illustrative titles.

Pièces de Clavecin (K. Gilbert—Heugel 1979) Le Pupitre, vol.59. Includes 25 pieces that have never been available in a modern edition. They consist of Rameau's own keyboard arrangements of "symphonies" (i.e., instrumental dances and interludes) from his opera-ballet *Les Indes galantes* 1735. In three of the pieces a second player is required. Resolves the disputed question of Rameau's ornament changes. Int. to M-D.

Pièces de Clavecin (Jacobi—Br 1958). 4 books of pieces dating from 1706 (10 pieces), 1724 (21 pieces), 1736 (16 pieces), and 1741 (5 arrangements from *Pièces en Concert*), and *La Dauphine* (1747). Also contains Rameau's treatise *On the Technique of the Fingers on the Harpsichord* and a table of ornaments from the 1724 and 1731 editions of *Pièces de Clavecin*. Expertly translated. Urtext edition. Int. to M-D.

Pièces de Clavecin (Saint-Saëns—Durand; K, in minature score and in Lea Pocket Scores).

Complete Works for Solo Keyboard (Dover). No fingerings or dynamic suggestions.

Nouvelles Suites de Pièces de Clavecin ca. 1727 and *Pièces de Clavecin* 1731 (BB; facsimile editions; Lea Pocket Scores, reprint of Durand).

Les Indes Galantes 1735 (Sadler—OUP 1979) 34pp. Selected movements from Rameau's celebrated opera-ballet, in his own keyboard arrangements. In these transcriptions Rameau adds ornaments, altered textures, harmonies, and even melodic lines in order to create idiomatic keyboard music. Int. to M-D.

The Easier Rameau (Barsham—Novello) 23pp. 16 pieces, mostly short dance forms. Sources listed, includes table of ornaments. Int. to M-D.

See: Kathleen Dale, "The Keyboard Music of Rameau," MMR (December 1947; January 1948).

Cuthbert Girdlestone, *Jean-Philippe Rameau: His Life and Works* (London: Cassell & Co., 1957).

Gerald Hendrie, "Some Reflections on the Keyboard Music of Jean Philippe Rameau (1683–1764)," *Studies in Music*, II (1988):17–38.

Philip Ramey (1939–   ) USA

Epigrams 1968 (Bo&H). 11 short unrelated pieces showing various influences and pianistic effects of the twentieth century from serialism to pointillism. Each has a distinctive mood: sarcastic, dreamlike, jaunty, etc. M-D.

Leningrad Rag 1972 (EBM) Mutations on Scott Joplin. 7pp. 5 min. Freely based on Joplin's *Gladiolus Rag*. The two might be performed together. Bitonal, biting dissonances, in true rag style. D.

Memorial (In Memoriam Alexander Tcherepnin) 1977 (CFP 66773) 6pp. 6 min. Dedicated to Tcherepnin and makes use of themes from his Symphony

No.4, Op.91. Atonal, thin textures, slow tempos; chant combined with main theme of Symphony. M-D.

Piano Fantasy 1969–72 (GS 3458 1984) 16pp., 10½ min. Four sections, played without pause. Exposition with variations. Scherzo; expressive interlude; finale with further variation. The scherzo is built on new material and there is a new theme at the beginning of the third section, but the main materials are presented in the first eight bars of the work. The writing is very difficult, not only in the scherzo but in the finale, where the sonorities are orchestral. In a sense, the piece is a concerto without orchestra. A concentrated, highly organized score built in large part on the principle of cumulative variation. Attempts for long stretches to avoid rhythmic regularity and to establish an over-the-barline feeling. Serial influence. D.

Shulamit Ran (1947–   ) Israel

Ran teaches composition at the University of Chicago and is composer-in-residence with the Chicago Symphony Orchestra and the Lyric Opera of Chicago.

Piano Sonata No.2 1967 (IMI) 21pp. 10 min. Moderato: thin textures, linear. Lento: Impressionistic, colorful pedal effects. Vivo (Rondo): folk influence. M-D.

Hyperbole (IMI 6070) 12pp. 7 min. This was the required piece at the second Arthur Rubinstein International Piano Master Competition in Israel in 1977. The first few bars supply the material for the entire piece. Uses a few avant-garde notational signs. Pointillistic, spacious writing, virtuosic, Messiaenic. D.

Verticals 1982 (TP 4010-41308 1995) 23pp. 17 min. Based on an opening 8-tone ("vertical") chord, pointillistic. Dramatic gestures. Ran says this work is "inspired by pianistic style and textures, indeed by the sheer physical sensation experienced by the performer...." Cast in a very free SA form. Chromatic clusters; accidentals apply to the following note only; careful pedal indications. *ppp* ending suggests distant bell sounds. Includes performance notes. D.

Bernard Rands (1935–   ) Great Britain

Tre Espressioni 1960 (UE 14229) 7pp. Serial technique handled with much freedom. Aleatoric, exploits pointillistic technique. The first piece, the most highly ordered, is interchangeable with the third, the least structured. Proportional notation used in the third piece. Includes extensive directions. D.

György Ranki (1907–   ) Hungary

Sonata II (EMB 1964) 12pp. Allegro Capriccioso: energetic theme, exploited in opening and closing sections; mid-section not developed but a new rhythmic figure serves as the inspiration. Largo espressivo: choral, intense, many seconds, fourths, and fifths. Allegretto "al" bulgarese: in Bulgarian dance style, accelerando to *pp* closing; bold colors. M-D.

Scherzo 1962 (EMB 4096) 15pp. Allegro giocoso, secco, contrasting sections and textures, capricious ending. A fine recital number in a MC Hungarian flavor. M-D.

Sam Raphling (1910–1988) USA

American Album (Mer). Eight cleverly written portraits of Americana. Redskin; Cowboy; Jitterbug; Square Dance; Introduction and Rag; etc. MC. Int. to M-D.

Sonata No.1 (Belwin-Mills 1961). Three movements. Contemporary idiom. Clever rhythms, free tonality. Last movement is a perpetual motion, mixed meters. M-D.

Sonata No.3 (Edition Musicus 1958). First movement: chromatic, transfer of register. Second movement: expressive theme with interesting contour. Third movement: agitato, rhythmic, energetic, percussive chords. Quartal and quintal harmony. M-D.

Sonata No.5 (Gen 1966) 24pp. Slow Introduction to Agitato section: many sequences. Lively: alternating 4/8 and 3/8; slower mid-section; return to opening idea. Moderately Slow: expressive harmonic and melodic writing. Lively: maintains basic exciting tempo, chromatic. M-D.

24 Etudes (Gen 1965). 2 vols., 12 in each vol. Contemporary techniques, wide skips, dissonant harmonic and melodic intervals. Some etudes are lyric. Pedal and tone production problems. M-D to D.

7 Mobiles (Gen 1968). Chordal, trills, varied moods. Span of tenth required. Int.

Passacaglia Ebraica 1973 (Gen) 9pp. Varied moods, colored with Hebraic influences. A few involved rhythms, flexible tempos. M-D.

Six Tiny Sonatas (Gen 1971) 13pp. Each short sonata has three or four movements. MC, clever. Not as easy as they look. Int.

12 Indiscretions (Gen 1978) 17pp. Dedicated to "Georges," "Edward," and other famous musicians who have composed hackneyed piano pieces. Witty and clever parodies. M-D.

Karl Aage Rasmussen (1947–) Finland

Min forars dagbok ("My Spring Diary") (WH 1975) 15pp. Vol.2. Explanations in Danish and English. Depicts the progress of the day from afternoon to night. Nine pieces, contemporary notation. Vol.1 is a set of duets with the same title. Int. to M-D.

Karol Rathaus (1895–1954) USA, born Poland

Sonata No.1 Op.2 c (UE 1920). A large four-movement work, bravura style, highly chromatic. D.

Sonata No.2 Op.8 (UE 1924). Post-Romantic, contrapuntal, well formed. M-D.

Five Pieces Op.9 (UE 1920). Linear, rhythmically strong, thick textures. M-D.

Six Little Pieces Op.11 (UE 1926). Miniatures grotesques. M-D to D.

Sonata No.3 Op.20 (UE 1927). A work of much intensity and sweep, fine skill displayed. D.

Three Mazurkas Op.24 (UE 1928). Follows the Chopin tradition. Flexible tempo in No.2 especially effective. Szymanowski influence. M-D.

Ballade Op.40 (Bomart 1936). Variations on a Hurdy-Gurdy Theme. M-D.

Mazurka (CF). Modal. Int.

Cross Talk (CF). Polytonal, humorous. Int.

Three Polish Dances Op.47 (Bo&H 1942). Oberek; Kujawiak; Mazurka. Long dances, varied moods. Demand mature pianism. D.

Four Studies after Domenico Scarlatti Op.56 (TP 1945–46). Stinging dissonance, sharp rhythms, modern commentary on an eighteenth-century style. D.

See: Boris Schwarz, "Karol Rathaus," MQ, 41 (October 1955): 481–95. A survey of his life and music.

Einojuhani Rautavaara (1928–   ) Finland

Rautavaara's works reveal not only a discriminating control of technical resources but also the effects of a personal struggle for artistic expression, as in his solutions to the problems of form and in his intelligent organization of symbolistic devices. In spite of his conscious modernism Rautavaara's output up to now is also marked by an adherence to conservative principles, which is reflected in his scores primarily by a cultivated taste.

Pelimannit ("Fiddles," or "Folk Musicians") Op.1 1952 (Fazer) 11pp. 8 min. Six free fantasies based on dances written by an eighteenth-century Finnish fiddler, Samuel Rinda-Nickola. A colorful set that begins with a procession and concludes with a stamping, jumping dance. M-D.

Ikonit ("Icons") Op.6 1956 (Fazer) 13pp. 12 min. The Death of the Mother of God; Two Village Saints; The Black Madonna of Blakernaya; The Baptism of Christ; The Holy Women at the Sepulchre; Archangel Michael Fighting the Antichrist. Notes in the score describe the background of each icon (piece). Full sonorities, many texture contrasts, freely chromatic, an impressive suite. M-D.

Seven Preludes Op.7 1957 (Fazer) 11pp. 11 min. Elastically Hammering; Slowly Enough; Nervously But in Rhythm; Choral and Variation; Fugato; Shivering; Alla Finale. Strong gestures, dissonant, free rhythms. M-D.

Three Symmetric Preludes Op.14 1949 (Fazer 1972) 7pp. 6 min. 1. Contrary chromatic lines; tremolo; large span required. 2. Syncopated chords, hand-crossings, broken-chord figures. 3. Contrary motion figuration, mixture of styles. M-D.

Partita Op.34 1958 (Fazer 1967) 5pp. 5 min. Three short contrasting movements. Freely chromatic, mild dissonance. M-D.

Etudes Op.42 1969 (Fazer) 19pp. 13 min. 1. Thirds, broken and solid, chromatic and diatonic. 2. Sevenths, melodic treatment. 3. Tritones. 4. Fourths, arpeggi, and chords. 5. Seconds, harmonic treatment. Freely dissonant. M-D.

Sonata I "Christus und die Fischer" Op.54 1969 (Fazer) 8pp. 13 min. 1. Based on three contrasting tempi with contrasting ideas and figuration; clusters; large span required. 2. Cluster sonorities in changing meters, frequent alternation of hands, harmonics. 3. Chromatic chords, different meters for each hand, freely dissonant counterpoint. M-D.

Sonata II "The Fire Sermon" Op.64 1970 (Fazer) 15pp. Molto allegro: 8/8 divided into groups of 3+2+3, freely chromatic, fast alternation of hands, clusters. Andante assai: quiet melodic opening; appassionato mid-section made of arpeggi and chords; clusters; quiet opening returns and then concludes with clusters. Allegro brutale: fuguelike opening, parallel chords, driving rhythms, crushing clusters at conclusion. Individual idiomatic writing. D.

Music for Upright Piano (GS 1978). Four staves, top one for string use, next one for dampers, bottom two for keyboard. Only playable on an upright piano. Avant-garde. M-D.

Second Music for Upright Piano (GS 1978). More of the same, but shorter than the above work. Avant-garde. M-D.

Matti Rautio (1922–   ) Finland

Suita per Piano 1951 (Fazer). Preludio: pays homage to Czerny. Intermezzo: dancelike. Ostinato ritmico: tricky rhythms. Intermezzo: quiet and mysterious. Toccata: driving, some melodic interest. Int. to M-D.

Hanoniana 1971 (Fazer) 13pp. Pianistic games on the white keys in honor of Charles-Louis Hanon (1820–1890). Int. to M-D.

Maurice Ravel (1875–1937) France

The piano music of Ravel is characterized by precise attention to detail, sharp outlines, and clear forms. There is a tapestry-like beauty in his pianistic textures. His chordal harmonies usually play a subordinate role to line and rhythm. A classicist with Romantic tendencies, Ravel extended the pianistic traditions of Franz Liszt. Ravel's *Jeux d'Eau* had a profound influence on the piano writing of Claude Debussy.

Sérénade grotesque 1893 (Sal). Guitar sounds, Chabrier influence. The guitarlike pizzicatissimo chords of the opening bars and the alternation of triads between the hands foreshadow *Alborado del gracioso*. The nascent fantastic irony found in the *Sérénade grotesque* appears later in the "Scarbo" from *Gaspard de la Nuit*. M-D.

Minuet antique 1895 (Enoch; K; IMC). Foreshadowing of things to come. M-D.

Pavane pour une Infante défunte 1899 (Alfred; CFP; GS; Schott; ESC; EBM). Grave, stately, diatonic, a few widely spread chords. Requires steady tempo. Original edition listed quarter note at 54. Not easy to project on the piano. M-D.

See: Michael de Cossart, "Ravel, the Pavane and the Princess," MO, 1159 (May 1974):323–25.

Dean Elder, "Perlemeter on Ravel," *Clavier*, 21/3 (March 1982):18–25. Includes the music to *Pavane pour une Infante défunte*.

Jeux d'Eau 1901 (Alfred; CFP; GS; K; Schott; ESC; EBM). SA design, fluid arpeggio figures, watery cadenza. Lies under the fingers but demands much
facility. The title means "Play of the Water" and the epigraph states: "The
River God laughs at the water, which tickles." Liszt influence. Ravel
viewed this work as "the point of departure for all new pianistic expressions one may find in my work." He recommended the use of the pedal in
high passages to produce, instead of clear notes, the vague impression of
vibrations in the air. D.

Sonatine f♯ 1905 (Alfred; CFP; Durand; EBM; GS; CF; IMC; K). Modéré: melody
in the outside fingers, SA design, neat and thoroughly finished. Mouvement
de Menuet: charming, nostalgic, playful and teasing. Animé: dazzling, subtle rubato, careful pedaling required. One of the best Sonatines ever written. M-D.

See: Saul Dorfman, "Ravel's Sonatine—A New Edition," *Clavier*, 16 (October 1977):16–22. Includes the first and second movements; the third
movement is contained in the November 1977 issue. Careful fingering, pedaling, and redistribution of parts are included since Ravel indicated practically nothing in these areas. M-D to D.

Edwin Smith, "Ravel: Sonatine," *Music Teacher*, 55 (March 1976):13–15. An
analysis of the work.

Miroirs 1905 (Alfred; CFP; ESC; EBM; GS; Schott; K). Available separately
(EBM; K). Noctuelles: "moths" flit in delicate figures, evasive, scurrying
figuration. Oiseaux tristes: these "sad birds" evoke a melancoly lament;
needs sensitive balance of tone; "somber and distant" ending; perhaps the
finest of the set. Une barque sur l'ocean: a consummate barcarolle, broad
arpeggi; changing rhythms make continuity difficult; lengthy. Alborado del
gracioso (IMC): Spanish guitar serenade, repeated notes, double glissandi;
most difficult of the set. La vallée des cloches: syncopated bell sonorities;
melody passes between hands; careful pedaling required for this atmospheric study.

See: Dean Elder, "According to Gieseking—A Master Lesson on 'La
vallée des cloches'," *Clavier*, 14 (October 1975):29–33. M-D to D.

Charles Timbrell, "Ravel's *Miroirs* with Perlemuter," PQ, 111 (Fall 1980):
50–52. Perlemuter is the only pianist Ravel taught his complete solo works.

Roy Howat, "Debussy, Ravel and Bartók: Towards Some New Concepts of
Form," M&L, 58 (July 1977):285–94. Contains a penetrating analysis of
"Oiseaux Triste."

Gaspard de la Nuit 1908 (Alfred; CFP; Durand). Ondine: opening accompanying
figure must be *pp*; flowing left-hand melody rhythmically free so as to
evoke the fluid surroundings of the water sprite. Le gibet: a dirge over a
hypnotic pedal point; tonal balance is a problem; varied layers of sonorities; large span helpful. Scarbo: diabolic scherzo, great contrast, sweeping
gestures; a major challenge to the pianist, most difficult of set. These three
poems for piano are based on poems of Louis Bertrand, an early contributor to nineteenth-century works about scary fantasies and ghost stories.

This set is one of the peaks in twentieth-century French piano music. Transcendentally difficult.

See: Irwin Freundlich, "Maurice Ravel's Gaspard de la Nuit," PQ, 53 (Fall 1965):19–21.

Andrew Fletcher, "Ravel's 'Gaspard de la Nuit,'" *Music Teacher*, 64/6 (June 1983):12.

Menuet sur le nom de Haydn 1909 (Alfred; Durand). Short, unpretentious, lightweight. Written for the one hundredth anniversary of Haydn's death. The Haydn motto appears eleven times. Int. to M-D.

Valses nobles et sentimentales 1911 (Alfred; Durand; MMP). This set derives its name from Schubert. Eight glittering connected pieces ranging from a forceful opening to a delicate closing that recapitulates the previous waltzes. More chordally oriented than most of Ravel's works. M-D.

Prélude a 1913 (Alfred; Durand). Relaxed tempo, interesting inner voices. Int.

See: Robert Dumm, "Enjoying the Paradoxes of Maurice Ravel," *Clavier*, 34/8 (October 1995):28–31. Includes the *Prelude*.

A la manière de—E. Chabrier 1913 (Sal). Strangely, this is a paraphrase of the famous "Flower Song" from Gounod's *Faust*. Its haunting tunes are lovingly sung by the fingers. Int. to M-D.

A la manière de—Borodin 1913 (Sal). A charming waltz "in the style of Borodin," flowing, colorful harmonies. Int. to M-D.

Le Tombeau de Couperin 1914–17 (Alfred; CFP; MMP; K; Durand) 26 min. Prélude: fast finger figuration, mordents, 6/8. Fugue: lyric, concentrated, 26 subject entries, rather static. Forlane: modal, dotted 6/8 rhythm, skips in melody, wistful harmony; filagree ornamentation adds much charm. Ragaudon: vigorous; mostly diatonic; mid-section more chromatic; sections open with a flourish; snappy and bristling throughout. Menuet: lyric, prominent use of mordant, modal, parallel chords in Musette (Trio), upper register tinkling melody. Toccata: SA, virtuoso piece, repeated notes, pentatonic theme, imposing climax, uses all three pedals, SA design, martellato chords, brilliant ending. Six large pieces related to the clavecin suite of the eighteenth century. M-D to D.

See: The Alfred edition includes much information about the style and background of the suite and each piece.

La Valse 1920 (Durand). Ravel's own solo version. Highly effective but requires virtuoso technique. D.

Album (Durand). Prélude a; Menuet sur le nom Haydn; Transcriptions; Les Entretiens de la Belle et de la Bête, Danse de Daphnis, Habanera; Menuet from the Sonatine. Int. to D.

Album of Maurice Ravel Masterpieces (EBM). Miroirs, Jeux d'Eau, Pavane; Lento (excerpt from the string quartet). M-D to D.

Ravel Album (K 3826). Miroirs; Sonatine; Jeux d'eau.

At the Piano with Ravel (Hinson—Alfred 1986). Menuet antique; Pavane pour une infante défunte; Jeux d'eau; Sonatine; Oiseaux tristes; La Vallée des Cloches; Menuet sur le nom d'Haydn. Includes discussion and analysis of each work, fingering and pedaling, plus performance instructions. Int. to M-D.

Piano Masterpieces of Maurice Ravel (Dover) 128pp. Menuet antique; Pavane pour une infante défunte; Sonatine; Menuet sur le nom d'Haydn; Miroirs; Gaspard de la nuit; Jeux d'eau. Reprint of Durand with mistakes. Int. to D.

Pièces (MMP). Pavane pour une infante défunte; Menuet antique; Habanera. M-D to D.

Ravel. Selected Favorites (Alfred 4865) 64pp. In the Style of Borodin; In the Style of Chabrier; Conversations between Beauty and the Beast; Forlane, Menuet, and Rigoudon from *Le Tombeau de Couperin*; Habanera from *Rapsodie espagnole*; Mouvement de menuet from *Sonatine*; Sad Birds from *Miroirs*; Pavane for a Dead Princess; Prélude; Nos.1, 2, and 6 from *Valses Nobles et Sentimentales*. Includes discussion of each piece, Ravel's pianistic style, his musical influences, and suggested teaching order. Int. to M-D.

See: *Clavier*, 14 (October 1975). A special issue devoted to Ravel.

Stelio Dubbioso, "The Piano Music of Maurice Ravel, an Analysis of the Technical and Interpretative Problems Inherent in the Pianistic Style of Maurice Ravel," diss., New York University, 1967.

James Keller, "Unraveling Ravel," P&K, 161 (March–April 1993):53–56. A discussion of Jean-Yves Thibaudet's performance (in two recitals) of the complete piano works of Ravel.

Marguerite Long, *At the Piano with Ravel* (London: Dent, 1974).

Arbie Orenstein, "Scorography: The Music of Ravel," *Musical Newsletter*, 5 (Summer 1975):10–12. Includes a list of corrections for most of the piano works. Especially helpful for *Gaspard de la nuit*.

Frans Schreuder, "Ravel According to Ravel," PQ, 110 (Summer 1980): 37–39. Ravel's advice on performing his own piano music.

Lee P. Yost, "A Ravel Masterclass," *Clavier*, 21/7 (September 1982):23–25. Based on masterclass of Horacio Gutierrez.

Alan Rawsthorne (1905–1971) Great Britain

Influenced by Hindemith, Rawsthorne developed an abstract style through highly crafted procedures that suggest 12-tone technique although he always attached great importance to tonal centers.

4 Bagatelles (OUP 1938) 6 min. Allegro: scherzando. Allegretto: siciliano. Presto non assai: sprintlike. Lento: serious. Set of short pieces. M-D.

See: Edwin Smith, "Rawsthorne: Bagatelles," *Music Teacher*, 55 (January 1976):13–14.

Sonatina (OUP 1949) 11 min. Allegro sostenuto e misterioso. Lento ma con movimento: dramatic climax, quiet closing. Allegretto con malinconia. Allegro con brio: energetic, poco brusco, some alternating hands, broad gestures close movement. Freely chromatic. First three movements subdued.

See: Bradford Gowen, "Neglected Repertoire: Some Contemporary Sonatinas," AMT, 29/2 (November–December 1979):22–24. Discusses the Rawsthorne Sonatina.

4 Romantic Pieces (OUP 1953) 10 min. Accessible textures and colorful harmony. "Romantic" refers more to style than to material. M-D.

Ballad (OUP 1967) 16pp. 12 min. Commissioned by Cardiff Festival of Twentieth-
Century Music and first performed by John Ogdon in March 1967. Tightly
constructed, mainly from two figures in the quiet and reflective introduction. Ternary form, contrasted sections. Virtuoso technique required, effective display piece. D.

Theme and Four Studies (OUP 1973) 15pp. 9 min. The fourteen-bar theme in C
major is in 5/4 and is simple and haunting. It is followed by four contrasted
variations with a quiet closing. The second study occupies the center of the
work. Recalls the style of the earlier *4 Bagatelles*. M-D.

Gardner Read (1913–   ) USA

American Circle (SB). Short, varied settings of a folklike melody. Int.

Poem Op.20 (JF 1945). Short, romantic. Int.

Capriccio Op.27/3. See Anthologies and Collections, USA, *U.S.A.*, II (MCA). Int.
to M-D.

Intermezzo Op.42a (SB 1959). Short, lyric, open fifths. Int.

Sonata da Chiesa Op.61 1945 (Seesaw 1971). Rather free interpretation of Baroque style in movements entitled Intrada, Canzona, and Ricercare. M-D.

Vladimir Rebikov (1866–1920) Russia

The Christmas Gift (K 9475). Suite of 14 pieces for young people, but includes
some octaves and large chords. Pieces are mainly one page long. Int.

See collection *Contemporary Piano Repertoire* (Hinson, Glover—Belwin-Mills)
Level 5. Includes The Tin Soldier; Oriental; The Grumpy Bear. Attractive
and clever writing. Int.

H. Owen Reed (1910–   ) USA

3 Nationalities (Belwin-Mills 1951) 4pp. Suite. El Muchacho: melodic, syncopated. Le Sonneur: bitonal, harmonic vocabulary most interesting. Mr.
Jazz: most difficult. Int.

Max Reger (1873–1916) Germany

Reger's style favors thick textures, leaps, intricate polyphony, bravura playing,
wide dynamic range, and delicate balance of parts. The page is often crowded
with details. The piano pieces range from short one-page sketches to fifty-page
fugues.

Complete Edition (Br&H 1954). Vols.IX-XII: piano solos. Vol.XIII: piano duets.
Vol.XIV: two-piano music.

7 Waltzes Op.11 1891 (Schott; Augener). A, c♯, D, A♭, E, f♯, A. M-D.

Lose Blätter Op.13 1895 (Schott; Augener). 14 sketches in salon style. See especially No.2 Valsette A♭; No.5 Petite caprice b♭, Danse des Paysans A. M-D.

Aus der Jugendzeit Op.17 1895 (Schott). 2 books of 7 pieces each from the original 20 pieces. In the tradition of Schumann's *Album for the Young*. See

No.6 Cheerfulness, No.8 Anxious Question, No.9 Almost Too Bold, No.10 First Quarrel. Int.

Improvisationen Op.18 1895 (Schott; Augener). 2 vols., 4 pieces in each. See Nos.2, 3, 4, 6 and 7. M-D.

5 Humoresken Op.20 1898 (UE). Some of the best pieces in the early works. No.2 b (in Magyar style) and No.6 Vivace assai g are outstanding. M-D.

6 Morceaux Op.24 1898 (CFP). Valse-impromptu; Menuet; Rêverie fantastique; Un moment musical; Chant de la nuit; Rhapsody e (in style of Brahms). Elegant writing. M-D to D.

Aquarellen Op.25 (Augener). Five small sketches. See No.2 Humoreske and especially No.3 Impromptu. M-D.

7 Fantasiestücke Op.26 (CFP). See No.4 Humoreske c and No.6 Impromptu b. M-D.

7 Charakterstücke Op.32 (UE). Book 1: Nos.1–4. Book 2: Nos.5–7. Brahms influence. D.

Bunte Blätter Op.36 (UE). Book 1: Nos.1–4. Book 2: Nos.5–9. See No.2 Albumblatt, No.3 Capricietto e, No.6 Elegie. Int. to M-D.

10 Little Instructional Pieces Op.44 (UE). In progressive order: Albumblatt; Gigue; Scherzo; Burletta; Es war einmal; Moment musical; Capriccio No.4; Fughette; Capriccio No.10; Humoreske. Int.

6 Intermezzi Op.45 (UE; MMP). Title is misleading. Nos.2, 4, and 6 are virtuoso pieces. Some are influenced by Brahms's later music, and they throw light on a crucial period in the development of German music. D.

Silhouetten Op.53 (UE). e, D, F♯, A, C, E, B♭. No.2 shows Brahms influence; No.3 is reminiscent of Grieg. M-D to D.

10 Klavierstücke Op.79a (Sikorski). Short and relatively uncomplicated for Reger. See Nos.2, 3, 6, 7, 8. Int.

Variationen und Fuge über ein Thema von J. S. Bach Op.81 1904 (Bo&Bo; CFP; MMP). Probably Reger's masterpiece for piano. 14 variations and fugue on a theme from Cantata No.128. Bravura writing of the highest order, involved and lengthy fugue, gigantic conclusion. D.

Aus meinem Tagebuch Op.82 (Bo&Bo; MMP; CFP, 1 vol. of 10 pieces). Vol.1: 12 pieces. Vol.2: 10 pieces. Vol.3: 6 pieces. Vol.4: 7 pieces. Contains some of Reger's most beautiful lyric writing. See Vol.1 No.5 Gavotte; Vol.2 No.4 Andantino, No.7 Larghetto, No.8 Vivacissimo; Vol.3 No.4 Romanze, No.2 Albumblatt, No.6 Humoreske; Vol.4 No.5 Silhouette, No.7 Humoreske. Vols.3 and 4 are more difficult than the first two. Int. to M-D.

4 Sonatinas Op.89 (Henle; Bo&H). No.1 e 1905; No.2 D 1905; No.3 F 1908; No.4 a 1908. All are long and in three movements, except for No.2 which has four movements and is a little less involved. M-D.

6 Preludes and Fugues Op.99 (Bo&Bo). 2 vols. Comparable in difficulty to Bach's *Well-Tempered Clavier*. M-D.

Episoden Op.115 (Bo&Bo). 8 pieces for big and little people. Published in 1 as well as in 2 books. In the same style as Op.82. M-D.

Variationen und Fuge über ein Thema von Telemann Op.134 (CFP) 32 min. Based on a theme from Telemann's *Hamburger Tafelkonfekt*. As difficult as Op.81 but more classic in structure and style. Contains some very beautiful music with extraordinarily fine craft and poetic sensibility. D.

Träume am Kamin 1916 Op.143 (CFP). 12 short pieces. No.12 *Studie* based on Chopin's *Berceuse*. M-D.

Blätter und Blüten (Leaves and Blossoms) 1898–1902 (Henle 615). No opus number. 12 titled pieces, written in "end of the century" Romantic style. Int. to M-D.

6 Pieces 1899 (Greeting to the Young) (Br&H 8103 1981) 27pp. Preface in German and English. Fughetta: based on the name Edvard Grieg. Caprice fantastique (Danse macabre): animated, with much contrast, cross-rhythms plus bittersweet harmonic language. Abenddämmerung (Dusk): requires chord control. Albumblatt: expressive. Scherzo; Humoreske: both lively and require deft fingerwork. M-D.

Selected Works (Schott ED 7336 1986) 107pp. Preface in German and English. Includes pieces from Opp.11, 13, 17, 18, 20, 24, 36, 44, 79a, 82 Book I, 99, and 143; and Two-Part Invention and Fughetta über das Deutschlandlied (both without opus number). Provides a broad spectrum of Reger's piano music. Int. to M-D.

See: Harold Truscott, "Max Reger," MR, 17 (May 1956):134–52. Also see reply by E. Wellesz, MR, 17 (August 1956):272.

Anton Reicha (1770–1836) Bohemia

Selected Works for Piano (Dana Zahn—Henle 254). Fingering by Hans-Martin Theopold. Edited after the first editions. Contains: Sonata E♭ Op.43; L'Art de varier ou 57 variations F Op.57; Fantaisie E Op.61. Representative works from three genres cultivated by Reicha. M-D.

36 Fugues Op.36 ca.1805 (V. J. Sykora—Br). Book I: Fugues 1–13. Book II: Fugues 14–24. Book III: Fugues 25–36. Preface in French, German, and English. Bold writing for the period. Makes high demands on the pianist's interpretive powers. Kind of a later *Well-Tempered Clavier*. Some fugues are based on subjects by other composers, such as J. S. Bach, Mozart, Haydn, and Scarlatti. Excellent urtext-performing edition. M-D.

L'Art de varier Op.57 (Artia). Contained in Vol.50 MAB. Theme and 57 variations. Introductory notes by Jan Racek and Dana Setkova. M-D.

10 Fugen (Artia). A; D (Cercle harmonique); g (On a theme of D. Scarlatti); C; f (On a theme of Haydn); Fuga-fantasia d (On a theme of Frescobaldi); c; G; a; C. M-D.

Sonata B♭ Op.46/2 (Artia). Rondo only. Well written. M-D.

Paul Reif (1910–   ) USA, born Czechoslovakia

Pentagram 1970 (Bo&H) 18pp. Fast; Calmly; Slow; Fast; Fairly Fast. Five pieces in contemporary idiom to be played without a break. Free in style; includes improvised cadenzas. Large span required. D.

7 Musical Moments (Gen). Pensive; Impatient; Friendly; Fickle; Sleepy; Laughing; Heroic. Provides an introduction to contemporary writing. Int.

Aribert Reimann (1936–   ) Germany
Spektren 1967 (Ars Viva) 19pp. 9 min. Unbarred, pointillistic, flashy piano writing, athematic, antirhythmic. Mainly on three staves except for final climax, which calls for four. Some notational problems. Avant-garde. D.

Alexander Reinagle (1756–1809) USA, born England
Reinagle spent his early years in England and Scotland, where he studied with Raynor Taylor. He met C. P. E. Bach during a visit to the Continent. Reinagle came to Philadelphia in 1786 and became a major influence in shaping the musical life of that city. He was probably the most important composer in America during the early life of our country. His contribution to the musical life of America was significant.
Six Scots Tunes (Krauss, Hinson—Alfred) 19pp. Lee Rig; East Nook of Fife; Malt Man; Black Jock (Gypsy Laddie); Laddie Lie Near Me; Steer Her Up and Had Her Gawn. Thin textures, unusual modulations, strong Scottish flavor. Int. to M-D.
Twenty-Four Short and Easy Pieces Op.1 (Krauss, Hinson—Hinshaw 1975) 19pp. Short pieces used by Reinagle in his teaching. Simple classic style, highly attractive writing for this level. Easy.
    See: Anne McClenny Krauss, "More Music by Reinagle," *Clavier*, 15 (May–June 1976):17–20. Includes "Lee Rigg" and excerpts from *24 Short and Easy Pieces*.
A Second Set of Twenty-Four Short and Easy Lessons Op.2 (Hinson, Krauss—Alfred 10107) 28pp. Short pieces used by Reinagle in his teaching. Simple classic style that introduces sonata form and minor mode. Includes small suites. Int.
The Philadelphia Sonatas ca.1790 (Robert Hopkins—A-R Editions 1978). Sonata I D; Sonata II E; Sonata III C; Sonata IV F. Scholarly edition, extensive preface, sources identified. Reinagle composed these sonatas after he arrived in the U.S. They "may well be the first real piano music, as well as the first sonatas for any instrument, written in the United States" (from the preface). M-D.
Sonata No.1 D (McClenny, Hinson—Willis). In *Collection of Early American Keyboard Music*. Allegro con brio; Allegro. Written in Philadelphia. Both movements are in abbreviated SA design, the first theme being omitted in the recapitulation. In classic style. M-D.
Sonata No.2 E (JF). A shortened form is contained in the album *Early American Piano Music*. Allegro: bright, facile. Adagio: long, florid, improvisatory. Rondo: in style of Haydn, cheerful.
    See: Ross Wesley Ellison, "The Piano Sonatas of Alexander Reinagle," AMT, 25 (April–May 1976):23.

Theme with Variations 1787 (Hinson; Krauss—EAM 1998) 8pp. Based on a theme from the slow movement of Joseph Haydn's Symphony Hob. I:53 in D "L'Imperiale," 4 variations in classic style. Would make a fine program opener. Int. to M-D.

Shorter pieces in collection *Early American Music* (McClenny, Hinson—Belwin-Mills).

Theme with Variations (Hinson, Krauss—EAMC) 8pp. An adaptation of the slow movement from Haydn's Symphony No. 53 ("L'Imperiale") in D. It makes a fine recital opener. Theme and four variations. M-D.

See: Anne McClenny, "Alexander Reinagle," AMT, 19 (September–October 1969): 38, 50.

Ernst C. Krohn, "Alexander Reinagle as Sonatist," MQ, 18 (1932):140–49.

Katherine Hines Mahan, "Hopkinson and Reinagle: Patriot-Musicians of Washington's Time," *Music Educators Journal*, 62 (April 1976):40–50.

John F. Strauss, "Alexander Reinagle—Pianist—Composer—Impresario in Federalist America," *Clavier*, 15 (May–June 1976):14–16. Pp.25–27 contain the final movement of the F major Sonata.

Carl Reinecke (1824–1910) Germany

Reinecke was a prolific composer, influenced to some extent by Schumann and Mendelssohn. He wrote operatic, choral, orchestral, and chamber works as well as music for the piano. Much of his output was of an instructional nature.

5 Serenades for the Young Op.183 1885 (ABRSM 1983) 28pp. Each Serenade contains three or four short movements. Not important music but attractive and engaging. Fit the fingers splendidly. Int.

Suite à la Rococo Op.173/3 (Br&H 8109) 11pp. Gavotte; Madrigal; Menuetto. Part of the cycle "Für Kleine Hände"; archaic dance forms in Romantic dress. Int. to M-D.

6 Miniature Sonatinas Op.136 (Br&H 8110) 23pp. Although written for the student, these sonatinas are fully developed Romantic works, if a little dull and repetitive. Well contrasted in use of keys, no octaves, adequately fingered. Int.

6 Liedersonatinen (Br&H; Zen-On). Miniature sonatinas, each in three movements. Int.

Libro di musica per piccola gente (Carisch). 30 short pieces in the style of Gurlitt. Easy.

Christmas Sonatina Op.251/3. In collection *World's Greatest Sonatinas* (Hinson—Alfred 4617) 6pp. Three contrasting movements using familiar Christmas material: motive from Bach, *Christmas Oratorio*, "Silent Night," Chorale "From Heaven Above to Earth I Come," "Every Valley" from Handel, *Messiah*, and Sicilian Hymn, "O How Joyfully." Int.

Who Has the Whitest Lambkins (Holland—SB) 10pp. The theme comes from a set of children's songs written by Reinecke with words by Hoffman von Fallersleben. Reinecke especially liked this tune and used it for a set of variations in his Sonatina Op.47/2. An attractive solo with four variations written in nineteenth-century style. Int. to M-D.

Jay Reise (1950–   ) USA
Rhythmic Garlands (Merion 1994). Universe-shattering, energetic, based on rhythmic patterns with brutally counterpointed accents from which the melodic style evolves naturally; suggestions of tonality, written in a kind of dissolved SA design. D.

Franz Reizenstein (1911–1968) Great Britain, born Germany
Reizenstein was a fine pianist and always had a dual interest in performance and composing.
Scherzo Fantastique Op.26 (Lengnick 1952) 8 min. Grateful to play, full of so-phisticated harmonies, Chopinesque in design. M-D to D.
Scherzo A (Lengnick). Lively recital repertoire. M-D.
12 Preludes and Fugues Op.32 (Lengnick 1955). 2 books, 6 in each. 50 min. Lin-ear, transparent textures. Regerian, Hindemithian style. In each pair the fugue subject is presented in the prelude, an interesting unifying device. D.
The Zodiac Op.41 (Leeds). 12 pieces, available in 3 books or one. A suite using the signs of the Zodiac: Aries, Aquarius, etc. Various styles, fine recital ma-terial. Int.
Sonata No.2 A♭ Op.40 (Galliard 1966) 34pp. 26 min. Three movements. Dramatic, Romantic writing. Many moods: somber, passionate, delicate, fiery. Virtuoso technique required. D.

Sándor Reschofsky (1887–1972) Hungary
Reschofsky was an eminent pianist, pedagogue, and composer. He collaborated with Béla Bartók in writing a *Piano Method*.
Sonata No.3 f (Kultura 1966) 14pp. Three movements. Interesting tonal writing, well-developed material. M-D.

Ottorino Respighi (1879–1936) Italy
Canone 1905 (Bongiovanni) 4pp. Lyrical canonic writing, contrasting sections. M-D.
Ancient Dances and Airs (Ric; MMP). Inspired by Renaissance forms, effective. M-D.
Notturno (GS; Willis). Flowing melody over a gently lapping chordal accompani-ment. Respighi's finest work for piano. M-D.
Etude A♭ (Bongiovanni). Interlocking hands and double-note technique re-quired. M-D.
3 Preludes on Gregorian Melodies (UE). Decorated plain-song, elaborate and florid. M-D.
Pieces (MMP). Valse caressante; Canone; Notturno; Minuetto; Studio; Inter-mezzo-Serenata. M-D.

Rudolph Reti (1885–1957) USA, born Yugoslavia

Terassen: drei Stücke Op.2 (UE 1922) 14pp. Ausdrucksvoll, bewegt: dissonant, sixteenth-note runs in sevenths. Burleske: rhythmic, brusque. Im charakter eines ruhigen Tanzes: syncopation, dramatic sweep (arpeggi, 64th-note scale passages), demanding. D.

Träume, Liebe, Tänze Op.4 (UE 1923). More extensive than Op.2, many of same devices and techniques. Interesting sonorities. D.

The Magic Gate (BB 1957) 22pp. 15 min. Through a Glass Darkly; The Gate Opens; Of Demons and Angels; The Dead Mourn the Living; March and Transcendence. 12-tone technique, flowing counterpoint. Large work. D.

Julius Reubke (1834–1858) Germany

Grosse Sonate b♭ (Musica Obscura) 55pp. Large virtuoso work in the style of Reubke's teacher, Franz Liszt. Similar in plan to Liszt's *Sonata* b. Reubke's work provides a striking example of originality through metamorphosis and contains interesting anticipations of Mahler and Reger. D.

See: Roy A. Johnson, "Julius Reubke—A Promise Unfulfilled," *Clavier*, 20 (April 1981):33–35. Focuses mainly on the organ sonata but has some reference to the *Piano Sonata* b♭.

Raymond Songayllo, "A Neglected Masterpiece," JALS, 18 (December 1985):122–28. Deals with *Piano Sonata* b♭.

Hermann Reutter (1900–1985) Germany

Reutter wrote in a neoclassic style and followed Hindemith in his treatment of musical materials.

Fantasia apocalyptica Op.7 (Schott 1926) 23pp. Two familiar chorales, "A Mighty Fortress" and "O Sacred Head," form the basis of this work. D.

Die Passion in 9 Inventionen Op.25 (Schott). Short descriptive pieces on biblical scenes. No key signatures but all are tonal. Interpretative sensitivity required. D.

Roger Reynolds (1934–   ) USA

Reynolds majored in engineering and then pursued his interest in music.

Epigram and Evolution 1959 (CFP). 6½ min. This work "develops a certain row in a strict and then in a free manner. A playful characteristic found throughout other scores appears in several sections" (BBD, p.145).

Fantasy for Pianist 1964 (CFP). 17 min. "A more advanced work, based on permutation of a segmental row (hexachords or tetrachords). The serial concept is also extended to the time structure of all four movements. The method used to create this proportional time structure derives the rhythmic patterns from the row by numbering up by semitones from the lowest tone of a transposition" (BBD, p.145). Sympathetic vibrations, arm clusters, and other effects are achieved by plucking, rasping, and muting the strings. These effects are combined with sonorities produced at the keyboard by complex and lavish configurations of notes enhanced by subtle pedal effects. D.

Alan Richardson (1904–1978) Scotland

Sonatine F Op.27 (Weinberger 1960) 13pp. Three movements. Post-Romantic in style. Fine for small hands. M-D.

Rhapsody (JWC 1959) 8 min. Effectively designed. M-D.

4 Romantic Studies Op.25 (Augener). More emphasis on pedaling and phrasing than on facile fingers. M-D.

3 Pieces Op.35 (JWC 1959) 6 min. Tableau; Silver Night; Fantasy-Study. Imaginative, eminently playable. The Fantasy-Study, in constant motion, makes most demands. M-D.

Frederico Richter (1932–   ) Brazil

O Esplendor do Folchore Brasileiro (The Splendor of Brazilian Folklore) (BME 1995). This folk suite is a fine introduction to the various aspects of Brazilian folklore. Seven movements. Evokes some of Brazil's dances and the world of enchanted characters from that country. M-D.

Marga Richter (1926–   ) USA

Richter's style is guided by her ear and not by adherence to any doctrine or technique. Her piano works sound contemporary but without an overabundance of dissonance.

8 Pieces (CF FE135 1978) 11pp. Short, contemporary techniques, expressionistic. M-D.

Remembrances (EV 1979). An 82-bar delicate piece blending a floating decorative melody over soft dissonances; ostinato figures evolve. Helpful directions for the performer, well fingered. M-D.

Sonata for Piano 1954 (CF 1980) 37pp. A somber, often sinister mood permeates this work; and there is a sense of dark, forbidding power. Angular and dissonant harmonic language, compelling and demanding writing. D.

Requiem 1978 (CF 1986) 21 min. Evocative, intense writing, long pedals, enormously effective. D.

Alan Ridout (1934–1996) Great Britain

Dance Bagatelles 1959 (Thames) 5 min. 7pp. Allegro molto: rondo. Andante: "blues" quality. Vivace: driving rhythm, percussive, most difficult. M-D.

Sonatina 1968 (Thames) 8 min. 12pp. First movement: broad unison melodic writing; no key signature. Second movement: 3/4 pulse with third beat shortened. Third movement: 4/4 plus 3/4 syncopated dissonant treatment. M-D.

Portraits (Weinberger). Eight pieces. Composer suggests he is on holiday; these are musical portraits of some of his friends (similar to pieces on same idea by Bernstein, Couperin, and Virgil Thomson). D. J. M. and T. W. seem to be the most interesting friends! Tonal. Int.

Wallingford Riegger (1885–1961) USA

Blue Voyage Op.6 (GS 1927). Impressionist, rhapsodic piece, after poem of Conrad Aiken. M-D.

4 Tone Pictures Op.14 (CFP 1932). Prelude: atmospheric, Impressionistic. Angles and Curves: bouncing rhythmic idea contrasted with melodic idea. Wishful Thinking: two-bar ostinato supports melody. Grotesque: rhythmic emphasis, tone clusters, pentatonic scale. M-D.

New Dance Op.18 (AMP 1935). South American rhythms incorporated into brilliant bravura writing. A fine closing number. D.

New and Old Op.38 1944 (Bo&H). 12 imaginative pieces full of attractive discourse that illustrate contemporary compositional techniques. Excellent recital pieces. Analytical notes. Int. to M-D.

Toccata 1957 (Bo&H). No.12 of the above collection with a brilliant new closing. M-D.

Petite Etude Op.62 1956 (Merion). Bitonal study. Int.

Carlos Riesco (1925–   ) Chile

Semblanzas Chilenas (PIC) "Chilean Sketches." Zamacueca: gay and rhythmic, many seconds. Tonada: richly harmonized folksong. Resbalosa: begins as a waltz then moves to a lively dance. M-D.

Sonata 1959–60 (Universidad de Chile, Facultad de Ciencias y Artes Musicales y de la Representación 1975; IU) 21pp. Allegro: changing meters, polyrhythmic, unified by frequently repeated and thematic material. Lento: somber, moody, chordal texture, syncopated rhythms, much use of interval of fourth. Allegro ruvido: 5/8 with constantly shifting units of 2 and 3, energetic bass melody, textures vary from linear to chordal, perpetual-motion effect. M-D to D.

Vittorio Rieti (1898–1994) Italy, born Egypt

Rieti embraced the neoclassic cause and always remained faithful to it.

Poema Fiesolana (UE 1921). Large dramatic work requiring bravura technique. D.

Sonatina (UE 1925). March. Theme and Variations. Finale: infused with lightness and vitality. M-D.

Suite (UE 1926). Preludio; Valzer; Barcarola; Canzonetta; Rondo variato. Clever, rewarding work. M-D.

Sonata A♭ 1938 (Gen 1966). First movement: moderate tempo with modulatory excursions. Second movement: slow and expressive, frequent meter changes. Third movement: rondo, perpetual motion, clever rhythmic rumba idea near middle of movement. MC, traditional tonal relationships, emphasis on melodic writing. M-D.

Variations Académiques (F. Colombo 1950). Theme and 8 variations, a fugue, and a chorale. Classical method combined with contemporary vitality and humorous character. Thunderous closing. M-D.

Sonata all'Antica for Harpsichord or Piano (BB 1957) 11 min. Three movements. Well-defined ideas, excellent craftsmanship. Imitative counterpoint, repeated chords, brisk closing Rigaudon. Works well on either instrument. M-D.

Sonata (F. Colombo 1966) 24pp. Three movements. MC, based on a three-note motive heard at opening. M-D.

Medieval Variations (Gen). Theme and seven variations. Quick mood changes, catchy tunes, fine recital piece. M-D.

5 Contrasts (Gen 1967). Preludio; Variazioni; Bagatella; Elegia; Girandola. Short. Int. to M-D.

Dodice Preludi 1979 (Gen 1215) 29pp. 12 tiny preludes. Sparse textures, lyric, dance rhythms, many modulations. Int. to M-D.

Wolfgang Rihm (1952–   ) Germany

Klavierstück No.1, Op.8a 1970 (UE 19594) 19pp. 13 min. Sectional, extreme dynamics, damper and sostenuto pedal indications, widely arpeggiated chords, shifting meters, wide-interval melodies. Large span required. First publication of this 1970 work.

Ländler 1979 (UE 17860 1979) 8pp. Proportional rhythmic relationship, shifting meters, leisurely tempo, no dynamics, chromatic. Large span required. M-D to D.

Klavierstück No. 4 1974 (UE). Dramatic, enormous contrast. D.

Klavierstück V 1976 (Tombeau) (UE 16608) 21pp. In three sections. Powerful and at times brutal. Built on a series of dissonant chords having middle C as a common tone. D.

Klavierstück No. 6 1978 (UE 17057) 10pp. Dynamic extremes (*pppp* to *sffffz*), tremolo, shifting meters, exploits extreme ranges, harmonics, expressionistic. Large span required. D.

Klavierstück No. 7 1980 (UE 17216) 16pp., ca. 10 min. Dynamic extremes: many two-note patterns indicated by *sfffz ppp*, with the direction "The second note always like a shadow of the first one"; long trills, shifting meters, exudes much nervous energy, expressionistic. D.

Dennis Riley (1943–1999) USA

Six Canonic Variations: Piano Piece I Op.2a (CFP 1963) 4pp. Serial, expressive, short, Webern influence. M-D.

Five Little Movements: Piano Piece II Op.2b (CFP 1963). Short, serial, pointillistic, contrasted moods and dynamics. Evocative of Schönberg's Op.19. Firm rhythmic control necessary. M-D.

Piano Piece III 1964 (CFP 1978) 3 leaves, 3½ min. Similar in style to Stockhausen's *Klavierstücke*, aleatoric, atonal. Graduated table of pause symbols. D.

Nicolas Rimsky-Korsakov (1844–1908) Russia

4 pieces Op.11 (Belaieff 1974). Impromptu; Novelette; Scherzino; Etude. An effective recital set. M-D.

S. Rachmaninoff, A. Rubinstein, N. Rimsky-Korsakov—Their Greatest Piano Solos (Shealy—Copa) 192pp. Rimsky-Korsakov: Festival at Bagdad (from *Sche-*

herazade); Flight of the Bumble Bee; Hymn to the Sun; Romance A♭ Op.15/2; Song of India. M-D.

Six Variations on BACH Op.10 1878 (WB) 22pp. Variations are entitled Valse; Intermezzo; Scherzo; Nocturne; Prelude; Fugue. Contained in *Piano Solos*, Vol. II. M-D.

Rimsky-Korsakov Album for Piano (Gabor Kovats—EMB). Part of the new Composers Album series, this volume includes 6 Variations on the theme of B-A-C-H and—of course—the Flight of the Bumblebee! Plus pieces from Opp.11 and 15.

Jean Rivier (1896–1987) France

Rivier was one of the most progressive younger composers of the interwar years. His style was strongly purposeful and tonal.

Cinq mouvements brefs (Sal 1931) 9½ min. Prélude; Caprice; Berceuse; Ronde; Final. Amusing, light, witty. M-D.

Musiques pour piano (Sal 1937–38) 14½ min. Printemps; Jeux; Les bouffons; Tumultes. Fresh, brilliant, rumba rhythms, ostinati. M-D.

Nocturne sur le nom de Marquerite Long 1957 (Sal). Subtle harmony and melody. M-D.

Pour des mains amies (EMT 1956). Suite Nostalgie; Confidence; Danse triste; Crépuscule; Cabrioles. Dance qualities, MC, bright. Last dance requires a big technique. D.

Torrents (EMT 1960) 4½ min. Dancelike, many fourths, full resources of keyboard explored. D.

Tornades (Sal 1952). Formidable octave technique required. D.

Alternances (EMT 1975) 8pp. 5½ min. An exciting contemporary work in freely chromatic style. Highly sectionalized, each section dealing with a single idea. Written for the Marguerite Long and Jacques Thibauld Concours International 1975. D.

Sonate en cinq mouvements 1969 (EMT) 21 min. Fluide: chromatic, octaves, skips. Incisif: scherzolike, many dynamic changes. Concentré: imitative; large span required in left hand. Souple: syncopated; fast-moving full chords. Violent: frenetic, toccata-like, glissandi. Facile, colorful writing. D.

Edwin C. Robertson (1938–   ) USA

Robertson teaches at the University of Montevallo, Alabama.

Mountain Brook (CPP/Belwin 1990). In *Musical Pictures,* Vol. 3. 2 pp. Mixed meters, sustained lower notes support moving notes, MC. Int.

Going Places (Willis 1993) 3pp. Modal, clever, attractive, jazz influence. Int.

Antón Roch (1915–   ) Spain

Roch is a pseudonym for Antonio García Rubio.

Consonantes (UME 1973) 8pp. Four bagatelles to be played together. Each one short and effective in performance. Nos.1 and 3: Impressionistic. No.2:

highly rhythmic. No.4: brilliant and in Spanish style. Wide dynamic contrast. D.

George Rochberg (1918–   ) USA

Rochberg has moved from serial writing to incorporating Ivesian simultaneities of original and preexisting material. He has recently tended toward more tonal writing. I am indebted to Dr. Joan D. Dixon for assistance with this section.

Arioso ca. 1956 (TP) 3 min. Tender, Italianate, three-voiced, modified Phrygian mode. Int.

12 Bagatelles 1952 (TP). Only four of the possible 48 forms of the 12-tone set are used in these character pieces. Intense serial writing. A significant work. D. See: David Burge, "George Rochberg's *12 Bagatelles*," *Keyboard*, 9/5 (May 1983):67.

Bartókiana ca. 1956 (TP) 1½ min. Joyous, Lydian, and Mixolydian modes, ABA forms, mixed meter. M-D.

Carnival Music 1971 (TP 1975) 39pp. Fanfares and March; Blues; Largo Doloroso; Sfumato; Toccata—Rag. Amalgamates original music and quotations from other music in a hallmark of Rochberg's extroverted style. Multilayered. D. See: Daniel Paul Horn, "Carnival Music—An Introduction to the Piano Music of George Rochberg," *Clavier*, 27/9 (November 1988):17–21.

Nach Bach (After Bach) 1966 (TP) 8 min. This improvisatory fantasy contains abrupt changes in dynamics, articulation, and tempo and uses a combination of direct quotations from J. S. Bach's *Partita* No.6 and unmeasured ideas, many of which are pointillistic. Includes specifications regarding the relative length of fermatas and detailed markings of the number of seconds between blocks of sound. Very difficult to memorize. M-D to D.

Partita Variations 1976 (TP). 13 continuous sections, extreme eclecticism, tonal and atonal juxtaposed with contrapuntal and homophonic styles, summation in final section. Uses material from some of his other works. A *tour de force*. D.

Prelude on "Happy Birthday" 1969 (TP) 3pp. (For almost two pianos.) Big sound, great fun. Uses another piano if available (playing different music at the same time) and possibly a radio. Large span required. M-D.

Sonata-Fantasia 1956 (TP) 23 min. Prologue, three cyclical movements separated by interludes, and Epilogue, played without a break. Serial, ingenious piano writing, intricate structure, wide range of mood and expression. Incorporates excerpts from Schoenberg's Op.23/1, references to B-A-C-H, and the rhythms and beat of ragtime. D.

2 Preludes and Fughettas 1946 (TP 1980) 11pp. 10½ min. In d, c. From Rochberg's very early tonal period. In the style of the *Well-Tempered Clavier*. Preludes: lyric and expressive. Fughettas: triple counterpoint, highly chromatic. Int. to M-D.

Four Short Sonatas 1984 (TP 1986) 20pp., ca. 12 min. Contrasting separate atonal movements share ideas from other Rochberg pieces. They are to be played together as a set. SA design is clear in No. 1 and gradually less clear in the others. M-D to D.

Joaquín Rodrigo (1901–1999) Spain

Rodrigo is recognized as one of Spain's outstanding contemporary composers. Gilbert Chase, in his survey of Spanish music, credits Rodrigo with the most interesting work between Falla and Carlos Surinach.

A l'ombre de Torre Bermeja 1957 (Sal) 9pp. To the memory of Ricardo Viñes. Much alternation of hands in various figurations, rhapsodic, parallel chords, some bitonality, highly pianistic. Coda requires span of tenth in left hand. M-D.

Bagatela 1926 (Schott) 7pp. Strong rhythms, light and gracious, accelerando and crescendo to big ending. M-D.

Berceuse d'Automne 1923 (Schott) 2pp. Calm, nostalgic, Impressionistic. M-D.

Berceuse de Printemps 1928 (Schott) 3pp. Tender and gay, luscious. Int. to M-D.

Danza de la Amapola ("Dance of the Poppy") (UME) 5pp. A lively 3/8 dance. Excellent for fast fingers and small hands. Int.

Un Album de Cecilia (UME 1953). Six refined pieces in treble clef. Int.

Quatre Pièces (ESC 1948) 18pp. Hommage à chueca; Petit Fandango; Prière de l'Infante de Castille; Danse Valencienne. Effective; in style of Granados. M-D.

Sarabande Lointaine 1926 (ESC) 3pp. Colorful and tuneful. M-D.

Serenata española 1931 (Schott 1994) 11pp. 4 min. To José Iturbi. Sectional, creates a Spanish ambience, unusual picturesque ending. M-D.

Sonada de Adios (ESC 1966) 5pp. Open texture, mournful. Requires fine tonal balance for rich sonorities. Int.

Suite 1923 (Schott) 16pp. Prélude: bitonal, scampers. Sicilienne: Lento, many added seconds in chordal melody. Bourrée: delicate, staccato. Minué: thin textures, requires span of ninth for left hand. Rigodón: sectional, most involved movement, *pp* closing. M-D.

Preludio al Gallo Mañanero 1926 (Schott 7938) 11pp. 4 min. A colorful concert solo, a *tour de force*. Much use of patterns where one hand leads and the other follows immediately, bitonal, glissandos. Prefaced with: "And Mother Hen had said to her chicks: 'Do not wander off, or the old and ugly fox will eat you. . . .'" M-D to D.

Deux Berceuses 1923, 1928 (Schott 7915) 7pp. 6 min. Berceuse de Printemps; Berceuse d'Automne. Beautiful atmospheric lullabies. M-D.

Bagatela 1926 (Schott 7914) 7pp. 3 min. Fast, graceful, dancelike, brilliant ending. M-D.

Tres Danzas España 1941 (Schott; MMP). Inspired by poems of Victor Espinós. Short; Spanish atmosphere. M-D.

Sonatas de Castilla con Toccata a modo de Pregón 1950–51 (Schott 7453) 40pp. Colorful, contrasting, atmospheric, abstract sonorities. M-D.

The Rodrigo Collection (Hinson—Schott 535) 32pp. Maria of the Kings; Dance of the Doves; Song of the Blond Sprite; Song of the Brunette Sprite; El Negrito Pepo; The Little White Donkey on His Way to Bethlehem; Rustica; Dance of the Three Maidens; Dance of the Poppy; Night on Guadal-quiver River. Refreshing and rewarding to play. Int.

See: Linton Powell, "Spanish Treasure: The Piano Repertoire of Joaquín Rodrigo." PQ, 157 (Spring 1992):27. Includes music to *Danza Valenciana*.

Jean Jules Roger-Ducasse (1873–1954) France

Arabesque 1917 (Durand) 9pp. Sectional, freely tonal, numerous moods. M-D.

Arabesque II 1919 (Durand) 8pp. Frequent mood and tonal changes, Impressionistic. M-D.

Barcarolle II 1920 (Durand) 12pp. Flowing figuration, changing dynamics; builds to large climax. M-D.

Barcarolle III 1921 (Durand) 13pp. Contrasting tempos, moods, figuration, *ppp* ending. M-D.

Esquisses 1917 (Durand) 7pp. Four short contrasting pieces, chromatic. M-D.

Variations on a Chorale 1915 (Durand). Contrapuntal, classical tendencies. D.

Lionel Rogg (1936–   ) Switzerland

Etudes pour piano (Leduc 1992) 29pp. Eight etudes emphasizing improvisation rather than technical difficulty from a master of improvisation himself. Rogg is a most distinguished organist teaching at the Geneva Conservatory. M-D.

Ned Rorem (1923–   ) USA

Rorem is best known for his songs, but he has written for different media in a personal style that recalls Poulenc and Satie.

Sonata No.1 1948 (CFP 66355) 20pp. 13 min. Half note = 72: hard and driving opening, tranquil section, many fourths. Tema and 5 contrasting variations; var.4 is the climax of the movement; var.5 is a calmato coda. Clear, fast, and hard: a toccata tour-de-force, traditional modulation; full keyboard exploited; published separately as "Toccata" (CFP). M-D.

Sonata No.2 1949–50 (Noël Edition). Large four-movement neoclassic work. First and third movements melodic; brilliant Scherzando; flexible Finale. D.

Sonata No.3 1954 (CFP 66356) 26pp. Quarter-note = 144: like a motor, with no alteration of tempo, minimum use of pedal, secco. Slow: simple melody expands and is treated variously, Impressionistic. Scherzando: always muted, never louder than *mp*, non-legato. Molto Allegro: dramatic, passionate, con tutta forza ending. D.

3 Barcarolles 1949 (CFP). These "songs without words" are pianistic and spontaneous. No.3 is the most extensive and most exciting. M-D.

A Quiet Afternoon 1949 (PIC) 10½ min. Nine pieces. Varying moods in this contemporary "Scenes from Childhood." Good musicianship and technique required. Int.

Eight Etudes 1976 (Bo&H) 35pp. 20 min. An outstanding set of virtuoso studies, written in an Impressionistic idiom that has interest melodically, rhythmically, and texturally. Conceived as a suite. Each study focuses on a different technical problem. D.

See: Dolores Fredrickson, "Ned Rorem and Emmanuel Ax," *Clavier*, 26/5 (May–

June 1987):14–19. A conversation with Rorem and Ax about Rorem's *Eight Etudes*. Pp. 20–23 include Etudes 5 and 7.

Maurice Hinson, "Ned Rorem," an interview, and "The Keyboard Music of Ned Rorem," PQ, 110 (Summer 1980):6–7, 9–11, 13–16.

Horacio Lopez de la Rosa (1933–   ) Argentina

Invenciones Op.34 (Barry 1978). Six short contemporary pieces. Conventional keyboard writing in all but No.6, which requires a pencil to be bounced on the keys without depressing them to produce a unique percussion effect. M-D.

B. Jeannie Rosco (1932–   ) USA

Spectrums Op.9 (WB 1980) 11pp. Evolution: tender, slow. Equinox: veiled. Imminencies: graceful and cheery. Abstractions: lively. Includes discussion of composer's purposes with each piece. The title means "a range of characteristics" (from the score). M-D.

Michael Rose (–   ) Great Britain

Ten Dances in a Popular Latin-American Style (ARRSM 1993 AB 2328) 19pp. Clever characterizing of the Zortzico, Tango, Habanera, Pasodolbe, Cha-Cha, Bolero, and Samba. Three pieces are untitled. Int.

Thomas Roseingrave (1690–1766) Great Britain

The major influences on Roseingrave's compositions were the music of Palestrina and the harpsichord playing of Domenico Scarlatti. While visiting Italy Roseingrave became a close friend of Scarlatti; later, when he had returned to London, he edited a collection of Scarlatti's sonatas. Roseingrave developed a fine contrapuntal technique. His powers of improvisation were widely known.

Compositions for Organ and Harpsichord (D. Stevens—PSM 1964). Vol. Two of the Penn. State Music series. Voluntary IV. Fugue X. Double Fugue V. Introduction to Scarlatti's "Lessons." First Suite of Lessons Eb: Overture, A, C, Presto, Chaconne. Third Suite d: A, C, S, G. Sixth Suite e: A, C, S, G, M. Eighth Suite g: A, S, G. Int. to M-D.

Hilding Rosenberg (1892–1962) Sweden

Rosenberg was influential in introducing new musical resources into Swedish musical life during the first quarter of this century.

Sonata No.3 (NMS; MMP 1926) 18 min. Andantino: no key signatures, centers around F♯, flowing theme, thin textures. Lento: much doubling of part writing, many seconds, elegant. Scherzo: many tempo changes, not true scherzo, Valse tempo used part time, variable tonal areas. Finale: Allegro energico: sixteenth-note motion, thematic material resembles first movement, thin textures, *pp* ending. M-D.

Improvisationer (NMS 1939). Seven variations on opening marchlike ideas. Contemporary harmonic and melodic language, mood changes with each variation. Large span required. M-D.

Tema con Variazioni (NMS 1941). Large-scale work with 17 variations on theme in a. All types of pianistic treatment involved. D.

Manuel Rosenthal (1904–   ) France
Rosenthal writes in the tradition of Chabrier and Ravel and is a superbly refined craftsman.

Huit bagatelles (Senart 1924). Most are 2pp. long. Pastorale; Berceuse; Remember; Le joli jeu; Romance; Rag; Romance; Finale. Clear, bright textures. M-D.

6 Caprices 1926 (Heugel) 27pp. Ouverture: syncopated, ragtime influence. Pastorale: flowing outer sections, texture change for mid-section. Impromptu: light and easy. Soirée chez le Colonel: animated outer sections, waltz-like mid-section. Hommage à Debussy: slow, sweet, melodic. La belle Italienne: sectional, à la Poulenc. MC. M-D.

Serenade 1927 (Heugel) 23pp. Sinfonia; Nocturne; Scherzo; Rondo. A short suite with contrasting movements that show Ravel influence; noble neoclassic style. M-D.

Moritz Rosenthal (1862–1946) Poland
Rosenthal was one of the supervirtuosos of all times. He studied with Liszt for six years.

Papillons (Musica Obscura) 7pp. Staccato study employing alternating hands, much tempo elasticity. M-D.

Carnaval de Vienne (CF 1925) 21pp. A pianistic jigsaw puzzle of themes by Johann Strauss the Younger. This Gobelin tapestry of *schlagobers* by the Waltz King is known to have pleased Strauss himself. He regularly visited the young Rosenthal's apartment to hear his latest paraphrases and to put his seal of approval on them. M-D to D.

Walter Ross (1936–   ) USA
6 Shades of Blue (Bo&H 1979) 19pp. 11 min. Separate movements that can be performed individually or as a set. Blues character permeates all six preludes; atonal, but the blues focus is made clear by the melodic rhythm and the voice leading. Inspired by the Gershwin *Preludes*. Int. to M-D.

Prelude, Nocturne and Dance (Bo&H 1974) 5pp. Nontonal and nonmeasured pieces. D.

Lorenzo de Rossi (1720–1794) Italy
"His music is light, fresh, skillful and convincing" (SCE, p.202).

Sei Sonate per Cembalo (R. Tenaglia—Ric). Edited and transcribed by Tenaglia. Two-movement works on the slow–fast order; early classic style. Int. to M-D.

Michelangelo Rossi (ca. 1600–1674) Italy
Bold chromatic alterations, virtuoso scale passages, and polyphonic treatment account for the unusual expressiveness in these works. Toccata style continued from Frescobaldi. Some of Rossi's works are found in the following collections.

L'Arte Musicale in Italia III (Torchi—Ric).

Antologia de musica antica e moderna per il pianoforte VI (G. Tagliapietra—Ric).

10 Toccatas (Torchi—Ric; CF, Nos.1 and 9 transcribed by Bartók).

6 Toccatas (Boghen—Heugel). C, a, e, g, B, f. Tasteful edition with only phrasing and a few dynamics added. M-D.

10 Correnti for cembalo or organ (Torchi—Ric; CF, Nos.1, 2, and 5 transcribed by Bartók). M-D.

Gioacchino Rossini (1792–1868) Italy

Most of Rossini's piano music dates from the last eleven years of his life. Many pieces are very humorous, and some of the titles anticipate Satie. Most require a secure technique.

5 Original Pieces (CFP 1952). Selected from *Sins of Old Age*. Fun pieces, pianistic. See especially No.3 Capriccio. Large span required. Int.

Pieces for Piano (G. Macarini—Carminignani Fondazione Rossini 1954). Vol.1: Petit Caprice; Prélude inoffensif; L'innocence italienne—La candeur française, Ouf!; Les petits pois: Une caresse à ma femme; Un petit train de plaisir—Comique imitatif; Spécimen de l'ancien régime; Tarantelle pur Sang; Echantillon du chant de Noël à l'italienne; March et réminiscence pour mon dernière voyage. Int. to M-D.

Fanfare pour Chasse (J. Werner—Curwen). Brilliant, witty, charming. M-D.

Une réjouissance September 20, 1868. (Faber). Probably Rossini's last composition. In waltz style, Neapolitan flavor, some right-hand glissandi. Int. to M-D.

Piano Pieces (K). Vol.1: 6 pieces. Vol.2: 3 pieces. Vol.3: 4 pieces. Vol.4: 5 pieces. Broad selection. Int. to M-D.

Ten Selections (Fondazione Rossini 1975) Preface in Italian by Bruno Cagli, rev. by Sergio Cafaro. Contains: Prélude blaguer; Des tritons s'il vous plaît (Monté-Descente); Petite pensée; Une bagatelle; (Mélodie italienne-Descente), une bagatelle: In nomine patris; Canzonetta "La Venitienne"; Une réjouissance (pour album); Encore un peu de blague (Montée-Descente); Tourniquet sur la gamme chromatique (Ascendante et descendante); Ritournelle gothique. M-D.

Five Pieces for Piano (Marcello Abbado—Ric). Introduction in French, German, and English. Une caresse à ma femme; Un petit train de plaisir; Momento homo; Petite [sic] caprice; Marche et réminiscenses pour mon dernier voyage. In the last piece Rossini quotes fragments from some of his operas. M-D.

Original Piano Pieces (P. Zeitlin—TP 1976). Six pieces from *Les Riens* and *Pièces Diverses*, including Bagatelles in A♭ and E♭; Entr'acte; Waltz E♭; Regret; and Austrian Waltz. Int. to M-D.

Piano Pieces 1857–68 (Br 6546 1992) 23pp. Introduction. Selections from piano pieces *Péchés de Vieillesse*. Postface. Contents: Petite pensée; Une caresse à ma femme; Une bagatelle; Valse lugubre; Chansonette. Composed for performance at Rossini's famous salons. Witty, will add interest to a recital program. Int. to M-D.

See: Marvin Tartak, "Sinful Little Nothings," P&K, 160 (January–February 1993):44–45, 49–50. Discusses Rossini's piano music. Focuses mainly on the 13-volume *Péchés de Vieillesse* (Sins of Old Age), characterized as a "treasure trove of wit." Includes a copy of the music "Un Rien" (A Nothing).

Nino Rota (1911–1979) Italy

7 Pieces for Children (Ric 133342). Short, colorful, and fun to play. Int.

Variazioni e Fuga nei dodice toni sul nome di BACH (Carisch 1972) 31pp. Cadenza-like opening leads to 12 contrasting variations; expansive fugue begins tranquil and builds to enormous chromatic, chordal climax. Freely tonal abound B♭, post-Romantic idiom. M-D to D.

15 Preludes 1964 (Creazioni Artistche Musicali). Lyrical but mixed with a bit of Prokofieff irony and wit; like improvisations. M-D.

Christopher Rouse (1949–   ) USA

Little Gorgon. In collection *Changing Faces* (EAMC 1986) 3pp. Fast and violent, exploits bass register with strong percussive treatment. Obsessive rhythmic drive, hand crossings, wrenching brutality. Tritone usage adds to unstable tonal feeling. Cluster ending. The physical feel of this piece makes it fun and exciting to play. M-D.

Albert Roussel (1869–1937) France

Roussel composed music for solo piano from the suite *Des Heures Passent*, Op.1, published in 1896, to the *Prélude et Fugue*, Op.46, completed in 1934, three years before his death. His music reflects his free spirit and uncompromising nature. He is a composer who merits further exploration.

Des Heures Passent Op.1 (Hamelle 1896). Suite with each mood of the "hour" related to it. Graves—légères: choralelike introduction leads to the légères (Allegretto scherzando); figure from bars 13–14 is transformed into a transitional motive not heard again; impression of SA form without development. Joyeuses: jolly, ABA, rhythmic figures tossed from hand to hand. Tragiques: bell-like opening, irregular phrase lengths, most dramatic movement with contrasting themes. Champêtres (Rustic) Animé: fugal, three main sections. Contains some forced and pedantic writing. M-D.

Rustiques Op.5 1904–6 (Durand; MMP). Danse au bord de l'eau (Dance at the Water's Edge): solemn dance in lilting 5/8 meter with waves lapping at the shore; Dorian mode. Promenade sentimentale en forêt (Sentimental Forest Walk): ABA, coda, bird-call motive. Retour de fête (Return of the Festival): full sonorities, motives, rhythms, and tonalities tossed about; naively sincere writing. Advanced pianism for its period. M-D to D.

Suite Op.14 1910 (Sal; MMP). Prélude: bravura writing. Sicilienne: built on three themes, treated extensively, whole-tone scale. Bourrée: style of Chabrier. Ronde: SA, a "tour de force," highly effective. Requires thorough pianistic equipment. D.

Sonatine Op.16 1912 (Durand; MMP). Modéré—Vif et très leger: combines SA and scherzo; fast-moving, thick harmonies. Très lent—très animé: square chordal textures lead to light energetic finale. Contains some awkward pianistic spots. Cyclic use, transitional work. M-D.

Petit canon perpétuel 1913 (Durand). Short, lyric. "Go back to the da capo, transposing the three voices up an octave and continue thus as far as the range of the keyboard will permit" (from the score). M-D.

L'Accueil des Muses (The Greeting of the Muses) 1920 (Durand). Lament for Debussy, uses various techniques associated with Debussy's piano style such as bitonal effects, wide spacing on the keyboard. Chordal and broken harmonies. Big climax. M-D.

Prélude et Fugue Op.46 1932–34 (Durand). Homage to Bach. The fugue on BACH takes the final "H" up a seventh, an unusual approach. Uncompromising in its angularity; a model of contrapuntal skill. M-D.

Trois Pièces Op.49 1933 (Durand). Toccata C: rhythmic, octaves, driving, music-hall atmosphere. Valse lente F: dainty, two- and three-voice texture, humorous. Scherzo et trio C: jolly opening, ABA, brilliant lyric mid-section with large climax, longest of set. M-D to D.

Francis Routh (1927–   ) Great Britain

Routh's accessible contemporary style has much logic and conviction.

Little Suite Op.28 1974 (Redcliffe) 18pp. 12 min. Choreographic scenes. March—Prelude; Waltz; Serenade; Dance of the Shadows; The Piano Lesson; March—Postlude. Listener is to think of this suite as an imaginary ballet. The titles are self-evident; the music has a certain subtlety beneath the surface and is full of expressive nuance and wit. M-D.

Scenes for Piano. To the Evening Star Op.37/2 1979 (Redcliffe) 8pp. Facsimile edition. Title is from a poem of William Blake by same name. Slow, expressive, long pedals, chromatic lines, wispy ending. M-D.

Gaspard Le Roux (ca. 1660–1707) France

Fuller points out in his introduction that the works of Le Roux "may very well be considered in retrospect as a summing up of the French keyboard traditions and the springboard for the final brilliant and consummate splash of François Couperin himself."

Pieces for Harpsichord 1705 (A. Fuller—Alpeg 1959). Suites in d, D, a, F, f♯, and g; plus arrangements for two harpsichords of five pieces from the suites (Allemande La Vauvert, Gavotte en rondeau, Menuet, Second Menuet, Courante) and a Gigue that does not appear anywhere else in the collection. Elaborate introduction with bibliographical and critical notes, facsimiles, and translations. The editor's fine notes are often applicable to the works of other French harpsichordists. Le Roux's style most resembles that of d'Anglebert. There is a close relationship with French lute music, even in some of the titles, e.g., "Courante luthée." In the usual manner of the French clavecinistes, Le Roux gives fanciful titles to some of his pieces, e.g., "Allemande l'Incomparable." His music has an individuality that lifts it above the conventional level of some of his contemporaries.

Howard Rovics (1936–   ) USA

3 Studies for Piano 1964–66 (Seesaw). For Robert Goldsand. Well contrasted. No.2 uses string tapping, plucking, sliding finger on string, etc. Advanced pianism required. M-D to D.

Poul Rovsing-Olsen (1922–   ) Denmark

Nocturnes Op.21 1951 (WH 29397 1977) 13pp. For Debussy; For Ali Akbar Khan; For Chopin. Styles match titles. D.

David Rowland (1939–   ) Great Britain

Partita 1974 (Donemus) 33pp. Photostat of MS. Prelude; Fanfare; Barcarolle; Dirge; Finale. Expressionistic, pointillistic, long pedals, avant-garde. D.

Alec Rowley (1892–1958) Great Britain

Rowley is primarily known for his fine contribution to pedagogical piano music.

Twelve Little Fantasy Studies Op.13 (Bo&H 1917). For the first year. Attractive, five-finger studies, trill study, easy arpeggi, chord study, etc. Easy.

Etudes in Tonality (CFP 1937). Prologue; Modal; Pentatonic; Diatonic; Chromatic; Whole-tone; Polytonal; Atonal. Each piece follows the title, clear forms. Int.

Polyrhythms Op.50 (CFP 1939). 7 Pieces. M-D.

2 Sonatinas Op.40 (CFP). Spring-Summer. Easy to M-D.

2 Sonatinas Op.40 (CFP). Summer-Winter. Easy to M-D.

5 Miniature Postludes and Fugues (JWC). Fine for small hands, simple two-voice fugues. Easy.

Edwin Roxburgh (1937–   ) Great Britain

Roxburgh is the director of The 20th Century Ensemble of London.

Labyrinth 1970 (UMP) 12pp. A quick-witted fantasy that contains some sensuous piano sonorities with many patterns and clusters. Precise directions given for speed, notation, and pedal. Extended lower keyboard required (only an Imperial Bösendorfer has it!). Moves through numerous textural changes. Outbursts are interspersed with moments of graceful, almost Impressionistic sonorities. D.

Les Miroirs de Miró (UMP 1981) Four one-page pieces based on paintings by Miró. Harlequin's Carnival: bright; romps in compound time; jiglike. The Nightingale's Song at Midnight and Morning Rain: expressive, trills in upper register, layers of sound. Dialogue of the Insects: dissonant seconds, sudden tempo changes, unusual grace-note usage. Spanish Dancer: rhythmical quirks, flamenco rhythms, most difficult of set. Pairing these pieces with reproductions of the companion paintings would make an interesting program. Int. to M-D.

Six Etudes (UMP 1983) 42pp. Vivace ed incisivo: many free bars, widely spread gestures. Flautando, leggiero: fast, thin textures gradually thicken. Adagio piagnevole: cantabile, fast mid-section with chords in alternating hands. Allegro ritmico: as fast as possible, toccata-like. Impetuoso e pesante: octonic passages juxtaposed with splashing chords and fast scalar passages. Tempo giusto e deciso: broken chords, chromatic, ferocious closing. This set generally focuses on textural, expressive, and dynamic contrast. M-D to D.

Miklós Rózsa (1907–1995) USA, born Hungary

Rózsa studied at the Leipzig Conservatory from 1925 to 1929. He eventually settled in Hollywood and is best known for his outstanding film scores. He was influenced by Hungarian folk music although he does not quote folk material directly.

Variations Op.9 1932 (Salabert). Theme is folklike, 12 variations. Var. 5 is elegiac; Var. 6 is a rhythmic presto with syncopations. Finale resembles a folk dance. M-D.

Bagatelles Op.12 (Br&H 1932). Little March: bitonal. Novellette. Valse Lente. Hungarian: folksong quality. Canzone. Capriccietto. Usable as a group or separately. M-D.

Kaleidoscope Op.19 (AMP 1945). March; Zingara; Musette; Berceuse (easiest); Chinese Carillon; Burlesque. MC recital pieces effective as a set or individually. Int.

Sonata Op.20 (Br&H 1948). First movement: energetic. Second movement: Romantic, pensive Andante. Third movement: vigorous, earthy dance. Bartók influence. Strong rhythms and rhythmic ideas. Displays excellent contrapuntal craft and emotional intensity. D.

The Vintner's Daughter Op.23 (BB 1953) 15 min. Twelve variations on a French folk song, each of which is related to a verse of the text. Tonal but freely chromatic. Hungarian folk element gently permeates the work. M-D.

See: Christopher Palmer, *Miklós Rózsa: A Sketch of His Life and Works* (Wiesbaden: Breitkopf & Härtel, 1974), 80pp.

Edmund Rubbra (1901–1986) Great Britain

Prelude and Fugue on a theme by Cyril Scott Op.69 (Lengnick 1950) 5 min. The theme is from the slow movement of Cyril Scott's first *Piano Sonata* Op.66. Romantic treatment of a Romantic theme. Fugue: chromatic. M-D.

Children's Pieces (Lengnick 1952). 3 vols. Easy to Int.

8 Preludes Op.131 (Lengnick 1966) 10 min. See especially Nos.1 and 6. Prefers low registers, No.6 especially thick. No.3: 16 bars, solemn, charming. Some of Rubbra's best piano writing. M-D.

Invention on the Name of Haydn Op.160 (Lengnick) 2pp. Dignified, pianistically laid out, explores the sonorities of the instrument. Requires a warm cantabile touch to express the melodic character. M-D.

See: Michael Dawney, "Edmund Rubbra and the Piano," MR, 31 (August 1970): 341–48.

Marcel Rubin (1905–1995) Austria

Klaviersonate 1925 (Dob 1985) 14pp., ca. 10 min. Impetuoso; Molto tranquillo; Allegro vivace. Diatonic motives fed into bitonal harmonies, strong rhythms, expressive melodies. M-D to D.

Anton Rubinstein (1829–1894) Russia

Rubinstein was one of the keyboard giants of the nineteenth century. He wrote with a powerful, craggy lyricism. He sings like Mendelssohn, thunders like Liszt, but always remains himself. His piano works prove that he always played better than he composed.

Sonata I e Op.12 1848 (CFP 1169) 39pp. For a teenager, impressively written; the youthful ardor of the first movement being well contrasted with the improvisatory musings that follow in the slow movement. An academic fugue breaks the grotesque character of the propulsive finale of this four-movement piece. Probably the first Russian piano sonata. Reminiscent of Mendelssohn's early works. M-D.

Etude Op.23/2 (Ashdown). In this "Staccato Etude" we find an unceasing wrist motion at a terrifying Allegro Vivace. Increased reliance on shoulder and back muscles for hitherto undreamed-of power and sonority. Linearity completely gives way to ruddy strength and rotund texture. M-D to D.

6 Preludes Op.24 1854 (CFP 1170; GS 8069) 42pp. A♭, f, E, b, G, c. Fine ideas developed in a trivial manner; too much note-spinning! Strong Mendelssohn influence. M-D.

Sonata III F Op.41 1853–54 (Br&H) 39pp. Allegro risoluto a con fuoco: powerful rhetorical opening, genuine lyricism in the second subject. Scherzo: original, but strange and marchlike. Andante: quasi-religious cloying sentimentality. Tarantella: interesting. Designed to show off Rubinstein's skills as both composer and performer. M-D to D.

Valse Caprice E♭ 1870 (GS; Allans; Zen-On; Century) 6 min. A delightful salon piece, very popular during the first half of the twentieth century; an excellent encore. M-D.

Rubinstein Album (G. Kovats—EMB). A new addition to the Composers Album series. Includes three miniatures, two melodies, impromptus, and a polka.

S. Rachmaninoff, A. Rubinstein, N. Rimsky-Korsakov—Their Greatest Piano Solos (Shealy—Copa). Rubinstein: Kamennoi Ostrow (Eastern Star) Op.10/22; Melody in F; Romance Op.44; Staccato Etude Op.23/2; Valse Caprice. M-D.

Album of Selected Piano Compositions by Anton Rubinstein (EBM). Barcarole f Op.30/1; Ondine Op.1; Polka Op.82; Aubade Op.75/22; Fourth Barcarole G; Third Barcarole g Op.50; Valse Caprice E♭; and other works.

See: Charles MacLean, "Rubinstein as Composer for the Pianoforte," PRMA, 39 (1912–13):129–51.

Ernest Lubin, "The Other Rubinstein—Anton," *Clavier*, 16 (April 1977):14–17.

Kassimira Jordan, "The Legacy of Anton Rubinstein," *Clavier*, 31/10 (December 1992):24–27.

David Swift and Maurice Hinson, "The Legacy of Anton Rubinstein," *Clavier*, 33/10 (December 1994):20–24. Part I: Titan of a Bygone Age; Part II: Exploring Rubinstein's Works, Joseph Banowetz on Rubinstein.

Beryl Rubinstein (1898–1952) USA

Rubinstein was Director of the Cleveland Institute of Music for many years.

Two Etudes (OUP 1929). Ignis Fatuus: *Will o' the Wisp*; short, presto staccato, double notes. Whirligig: continuous right-hand figuration, light, brilliant. M-D.

A Day in the Country (CF). Five impromptus, varied moods. Int.

Sonatina c♯ (OUP 1929). First movement: brisk, cheerful. Adagio: atmospheric with French influence in the harmonic treatment. Allegro vivace: tarantella-like, brilliant. M-D.

Twelve Definitions (GS 1950). A set of character pieces portraying the following moods: Gently moving; Animated; Lightly; Decisive; Gay; Lyric; Serene; Spritely; Graceful; Agitated; Expressive; Spirited. Int. to M-D.

Scenes from Carroll's Alice in Wonderland (Chappell 1951) 19pp. Alice Falls Asleep: peaceful and rather drowsy. The White Rabbit: lively, don't rush. Father William: four statements, each treated differently. The Dormouse: hesitatingly, gently. The Lobster Quadrille: lively and rhythmic. The Queen of Hearts: loud and fierce. Alice Wakens: gently and leisurely, brings back ideas from each movement. Charming and imaginative. Int. to M-D.

Poul Ruders (1949–   ) Denmark

Tre Breve dra den ukendte soldat ("Three Letters from the Unknown Soldier") (Engstrom & Sodring 1973) 6pp. Explanations in English and German. March: brutal; primitive force required with some impossible muting effects. Bells: tension of the piano's lowest strings is changed by pushing with thumb or pulling with fingers of one hand while other hand plays on the keyboard. Prayer: chromatic scale in major seconds *pppp*; concludes with a cluster played "tutta forza" seven times! D.

Dane Rudhyar (1895–1985) USA, born France

In some ways Rudhyar's works anticipate Messiaen, and Rudhyar was a spiritual confrère of Scriabin in their mutual mystical interests.

Granites (Merion). Published with *Three Paeans*. Five sketches in different moods. Granitic dissonances, dynamic extremes. Writhes in quartal-quintal harmonic structures. Large span required. D.

Three Paeans (Merion 1927). Three hymns, Scriabin-like ideology, lofty works, panchromatic. Requires virtuoso technique. D.

Pentagrams One and Two (CUMP 1974) 24pp. No.1: The Summons. No.2: Enfoldment. Anachronistic and naive writing, static rhythms. Poetic fantasy in the directions, but instructions are impossible to incorporate into the music. D.

Pentagrams Three and Four (CUMP 1974) 34pp. No.3 (Release): Gates, The Gift of Blood, Pentecost, Stars, Sunburst. Intriguing harmonic and timbral spectrum. No.4 (The Human Way): Pomp, Yearning, Irony, Overcoming, Peace. These poems are strongly dissonant and display complex writing at every turn. D.

Tetragrams, 1st Series 1920–27 (Joshua 1021) 27pp. The Quest; Crucifixion; Rebirth. Each piece is subdivided into smaller units. Dissonant and rugged writing. D.

Archduke Rudolph of Austria (1788–1831)

Theme and 40 Variations on a Theme by Beethoven (A-R Editions; S. A. Steiner 1819; LC) 32pp. 30 min. Beethoven's little square-cut theme (WoO 200), composed especially for the Archduke, is treated with much ingenuity and imagination, utilizing every conceivable method of variation technique. While most of the 40 variations are very short, like the theme, the introduction and some of the last variations are tediously drawn out. A curiosity worth investigating. M-D.

See: Susan Kagan, "The Archduke Rudolph, Beethoven's Patron and Parnassan Pupil," *The Beethoven Newsletter*, 7/3:62–67.

Witold Rudzinski (1913–   ) Poland

Quasi una Sonata 1978 (AA). Dramatic in form, capricious and rhapsodic in character. Powerful chords interspersed with lyrical fragments, recitativos, and improvised richly embellished themes. Romantic influence toward the end. M-D to D.

Carl Ruggles (1876–1971) USA

The mysterious and reclusive Ruggles worked out his own particular method of composing a unique form of atonal music.

Evocations, 4 Chants (AME 1937–43). Highly dissonant and complex works, profuse chromaticism. Style similar to Charles Ives yet distinctive. Fondness for constantly changing meters, tritone, thick colors, legato melodies, brooding intensity. No.4 is dedicated to Ives. Advanced pianism required. D.

See: David Burge, "Carl Ruggles' *Evocations*," *Keyboard*, 10/2 (February 1984):73, 89.

Steven E. Gilbert, "The 'Twelve-Tone System' of Carl Ruggles: A Study of the *Evocations* for Piano," *Journal of Music Theory*, 14/1 (Spring 1970): 68–91.

See: Dave R. Harman, "The Musical Language of Carl Ruggles (1876–1971)," AMT, 25 (April–May 1976):25–27, 31.

John Kirkpatrick, "The Evolution of Carl Ruggles," PNM, 6 (Spring–Summer 1968):35–41.

Gordon Rumson (1960–   ) Canada

Rumson has degrees from the University of Calgary and the University of Michigan. He studied further at Bowling Green State University and the University of Wisconsin, where he researched the music of Gunnar Johansen.

Threnody for John Ogdon in the form of Chorale Variations with Introduction and Finale 1990 (Sikesdi Press 1991) 25pp. Dramatic introduction leads to a solemn chorale, 5 contrasting variations. Quasi-presto finale includes the "Dies Irae" theme; concludes with a coda (*pp* and *ppp*) Adagio, molto sereno. Virtuosic, freely tonal. D.

Three Preludes (Sikesdi Press 1993) 14pp. Violenta: furious full chords in both hands contrasted with quiet chorale-style harmonies. Arioso: Adagio, flowing melody. "In Modo Ironico": varied textures and dynamics; Prokofieff influence. M-D.

Fantasy 1994 (Sikesdi Press) 10pp. Opening motive provides the basic material for the work. Chromatic, sectional, large gestures. M-D.

Poem for Emil Gilels 1995 (Sikesdi Press) 8pp. Contrasting sections, chromatic, includes a few fingerings, *ppp* closing. M-D.

Sonata I 1994 (Sikesdi Press) 14pp. A quasi-andante e misterioso opening leads to a più mosso furioso climax that quickly diminishes and moves into a *pppp* Adagio. The rest of the movement features a middle-voice melody with accompanimental figuration. The final page and a half build to a *fff* climax. Sonata form is difficult to decipher. Virtuosic, freely tonal. D.

Christian Friedrich Ruppe (1753–1826) The Netherlands

Variations for Piano on "Willem van Nassau" (Paul van Reijen—Vereniging voor Nederlandse Muziekgeschiedenis 1993) 13pp. Published with the next entry.

Sicco Albertus Hempenius (1785–1849). "Air varié Wilhelmus van Nassauen." Notes in Dutch and English. (Exempla musica Neerlandica 17.) Both sets are written in a refined classic style. M-D.

Loren Rush (1935–   ) USA

Oh, Susanna (Jobert 1970) 10 min. Amusing treatment of material tucked in with complex rhythmic and harmonic usage. Refers to Susanna in Mozart's opera *Marriage of Figaro*. Upper range of the keyboard is exploited in a pointillistic manner. ¼ pedal is required throughout. Cool, unpretentious avant-garde writing played *p* throughout. Ends with quotation from "Look What They Have Done To My Song, Ma" in an innocent C major. M-D to D.

Oswald Russell (1933–   ) Jamaica

Three Jamaican Dances (Henn 1976). These pieces are sometimes sassy, sometimes flavored with a sly touch of sentiment or nostalgia, but continuously light-hearted and alert. Based on slim melodic materials, full of vigor. M-D.

Friedrich Wilhelm Rust (1739–1796) Germany

Twelve Sonatas (V. d'Indy—Rouart, Lerolle). Mainly in three movements. Effective pianistic writing. No.9 *Sonata* G imitates the Timpanum, Psaltery, and Luth and anticipates a few twentieth-century devices, including the right hand touching a string while the left hand depresses the key. These sonatas resemble the pianism of Clementi. Also available separately. Int. to M-D.

Giovanni Rutini (1723–1797) Italy

Rutini composed about 88 keyboard sonatas, mainly published in sets. Most contain two movements, some have three, and a few have four. Main ideas incorporate modulatory figuration, fragmentary in character. Rutini is fond of trills, turns and appoggiaturas, runs, arpeggios, and alternation and crossing of hands.

18 Sonatas (Hedda Illy—De Santis) 3 books, 6 sonatas in each opus. Op.3 (1757): see especially No.3 D. Op.5 (1759): the strongest of the set. Op.6 (1760). Int. to M-D.

Peter Ruzicka (1948–   ) Germany
Ausgeweidet die Zeit . . . Drei Nachtstücke für Klavier (Sikorski 1969) No.16 in Exempla Nova. 8 min. Based on poems from the cycle *Glühende Rätsel* by Nelly Sachs (1891–1970). Molto calmo, quasi meditativo: clusters, dynamic range *ppppp* to *sfff*, plucked strings. Molto agitato: wide dynamic range, pointillistic, free rhythms, dramatic gestures. Elegiaco: complex metrical patterns, tiny bits from Beethoven Op.110 (III) and Schönberg Op.19 (VI). Pedal directions are carefully notated. Avant-garde. D.

Feliks Rybicki (1899–   ) Poland
I Begin to Play Op.20 (PWM 1946) 35pp. 26 short pieces, many in five-finger position. Titles in Polish, English, and German. Clever illustrations. Easy.
I Am Already Playing Op.21 (PWM). 18 pieces. Provides ample opportunity for developing musical and pianistic abilities. Easy to Int.
The Young Modernist Op.23 (PWM 1947) 25pp. 15 MC pieces with colorful illustrations. Easy to Int.
Folk Songs Op.46 (PWM). 16 miniatures that introduce basic piano problems. Easy to Int.
Etudes for the Left Hand Op.54 (PWM). Three books, ranging from easy to difficult. There are few comparable collections in the available pedagogical literature for piano. Skillful use of a number of technical problems.
This Is Our Garden-Fair Op.58 (PWM 1971) 17 Czech and Slovak folk songs attractively arranged for piano. Easy to Int.
I Can Play Anything (PWM). 14 varied pieces, fingered and pedaled. Int.

Frederic Rzewski (1938–   ) USA
Rzewski has tried, in his more recent works, to integrate the European classical tradition with the American popular/folk tradition and the avant-garde. He represents the latest installment in musical Marxism.
The People United Will Never Be Defeated 1975 (Zen-On 179) 92pp. 50 min. A set of 36 variations on a famous revolutionary song (by Sergio Ortega), which has come out of the Chilean new-song movement. Since the overthrow of the Allende government this song has become a kind of symbol or anthem of the Chilean resistance movement. Composed in the late-Romantic vein of Brahms and Busoni on a broad canvas of brilliant color. At the premiere of this work, the *New York Times* critic Harold Schonberg called it "a landmark in the history of piano music." Recalls the architecture of the *Goldberg* Variations and the variation techniques of Brahms; parody techniques are also used. The pianist is called on to whistle a few times. Clusters, lid-slamming, unwritten cadenza, and harsh dissonances are mixed with luscious nineteenth-century harmonies. D.

See: David Burge, "Rzewski's *The People United*," CK, 6 (December 1980):63.

4 Pieces for Piano 1977 (Zen-On 192) 37pp. 32 min. Really a sonata but without the title. Clear formal structures, makes use of wide dynamic range, extremes in pitches and textures, virtuosic. Includes all sorts of elements: purely tonal melodies, thunderously undulating clusters, bouncy jazzlike riffs, strictly rhythmic sections and others that are rhythmically and tonally amorphous. A freshness and urgency make the music compelling. D.

4 North American Ballades 1978–79 (Zen-On). 64pp. Squall: based on "Dreadful Memories." Hyenas: based on "Which Side Are You On?" (a Kentucky mine-union song of the 1930s). Noctamble: based on "Down by the Riverside." Sideshow: based on "Winnsboro Cotton Mill Blues." Each piece is based on an American work song and begins with simple statements of the folk themes, then subjects them to complex development, drawing motives from the themes and twisting them into thundering virtuoso displays. The last is the most remarkable; it begins with several minutes of thick, rhythmic banging that mimics the sound of a cotton mill; gradually the clusters thin out and become the basis for the tune, and we have some bluesy variations. Neo-Ivesian sounds. D.

See: Joshua Rosman, "Improvising with a Pencil, The Piano Music of Frederic Rzewski," P&K, 161 (March–April 1993):30–34, 36–37. Includes piano piece "A Life."

S

Guy Sacre (1948–   ) France

Thème Varié 1979 (Leduc 1981) 8pp. 5½ min. Flowing theme followed by 11 contrasting variations. The style sounds like a MC Fauré. Efficient writing, especially beautiful conclusion. M-D.

24 Préludes 1980–83 (Durand 1993) 27pp. 22 min. These highly contrasted character pieces are short, say what they have to say, and end—no padding anywhere. Freely tonal. Some are pedaled; all contain metronome indications. M-D.

Piccolissima—Sérénade 1979 (Durand 1988) 15pp. 11 min. Preludio; Barcarola; Quasi Minuetto; Berceuse; Madrigale (based on Ganymède); Notturno; Finale. Neotonal (almost impressionistic at moments), freely chromatic, flowing lines. M-D.

Deuxième Sérénade 1981–82 (Durand 1988) 20pp. 14 min. Ligurienne; Gondoliere; Scherzo; Cazone; Mandoline; Autre Canzone; Saltarello. Attractive suite, freely tonal, some surprising harmonies, refined ear. M-D.

Harald Saeverud (1897–1992) Norway

Saeverud is the best known composer in Norway, after Grieg.

Siljuslatten Op.17 (NMO). From "Siljustöl," the name of the composer's home in Bergen. Short character pieces. M-D.

Tunes and Dances from "Siljustöl" (EMH). Vol.1: Op.21, 5 pieces; clever, No.5 the most adventurous. Vol.2: Op.22, 5 pieces; four charming pieces plus No.5 "Ballade of Revolt," which was the rallying cry of the Norwegian underground during World War II. Vol.3: Op.24, 5 pieces; more contemporary style; "Beware Bear!" is most appealing. Vol.4: Op.25, 5 pieces. Expanded tonal usage. Int. to M-D.

6 Sonatinas Op.30 (EMH 1948–50) 29pp. Some have two, some three movements. All are short, with thin textures. Many moods, MC. Contains fresh teaching material. Int.

See: Lorentz Reitan, "Harald Saeverud (1897–1992) Born in a Graveyard," *Listen to Norway,* 5/1 (1997):34–38.

Ketil Saeverud (1939–   ) Norway

Rondo con Variazioni 1970 (Lysche 1973) 14pp. Theme, rondo, theme repeated, three variations, finale. Chromatic, sudden dynamic changes, fast alternating hands, expressionistic. Theme played backward ends the piece. M-D to D.

Tormod Saeverud (1938–   ) Norway
Saeverud is the son of Harald Saeverud.
Five Small Tone Poems (NMO 1969). Short attractive settings. Easy to Int.
Three Novelettes (NMO). Capriccio; Elegi; Humoreske. Freely dissonant, neo-classic. M-D.
Tide Rhythm (NMO). Race; Tune; Springtime; Footprints in the Sand; Happy Lovers; Tide Rhythm. Jazz influences, freely tonal. M-D.

Joseph Boulogne, Chevalier de Saint-Georges (c. 1739–1799) Guadeloupe
Boulogne was the son of an African mother and a French Parliamentary councillor. His family moved to Haiti, and then in 1749 to Paris, where he became an expert fencer as well as one of the most romantic and memorable figures of the age. It is believed that he studied violin with Leclair and composition with Gossec. Boulogne composed concertos, sonatas, string quartets, seven *symphonies concertantes,* a ballet, and two operas. His works are vibrant and well-written.
Adagio f (Merion 1981) 5pp. Mournful melody, ostinatos, frequent rests, subtle. Anticipates Beethoven and the Romantics to a certain degree. Performance notes by Natalie Hinderas. Int.
Collection of Pieces for the Countess of Vauban (Richardson, Bauer—Africanus Editions AE-0141-15 1999) 26pp. 8 pieces in classical style. Allegro. Andantino. Adagio. Grazioso. Grazioso. Tempo di Menuetto. La Vauban: a charming character piece. Les Badinages de L'Amour. Int. to M-D.

Camille Saint-Saëns (1835–1921) France
Saint-Saëns was a brilliant pianist with a fine sense of style. He was an excellent craftsman—facile, elegant, and well grounded. His piano writing can always be counted on to glitter and flow without much emotional depth. He has been called the "French Mendelssohn." Saint-Saëns's works are published by Durand unless otherwise noted.
6 Bagatelles Op.3 1856. Like some of the Chopin *Impromptus*; already display the clarity which distinguished the works that followed. One of the few sets of Bagatelles composed at this time. M-D.
6 Etudes Op.52 1877 (K) 22 min. Prélude. Pour l'indépendance des doigts. Prélude et fugue f. Etude de rythme. Prélude et fugue A. En forme de valse: more Valse influence than Etude; long 422 bars; brilliant. M-D to D.
Album of 6 pieces Op.72 1884. Also published separately. Prélude. Carillon. Toccata: requires a diligent staccato touch. Valse. Chanson napolitaine. Finale. M-D.
Allegro Appassionata c Op.70 1884. Toccata-like style modeled on the Schumann *Toccata*, which Saint-Saëns so greatly prized. M-D to D.
Rhapsodie d'Auvergne Op.73 1884. 17pp. Three contrasting sections in a setting of folk songs from this province. Thematic material is very tuneful and attractive. The fast passage figuration of the brilliant Finale (Allegro) presents the only technical problems. M-D.
Suite Op.90 1892. Prélude et fugue; Menuet; Gavotte; Gigue. Uses eighteenth-

century models filled with "harmonic" counterpoint. Displays a command of formal symmetry, a simple harmonic system, and a well-wrought melodic line throughout. M-D.

Valse nonchalant Op.110. Charming, in the style of Liszt's *Valse oubliée*. M-D.

6 Etudes Op.111 1899. Tierces majeures et mineures. Traits chromatiques. Prélude et Fugue. Les Cloches de Las Palmas. Tierces majeures chromatiques. Toccata d'après le 5ème concerto (IMC): treats an Algerian theme brilliantly. Virtuosity required throughout. D.

Caprice on airs from Gluck's Alceste. (Also GS). One of the composer's most brilliant and most frequently performed works. The central theme and variations is often played separately. M-D to D.

Choeur from the "Ruins of Athens" (Beethoven) (Musical Scope) 7pp. Whirling figuration builds to an effective climax. M-D.

Danse Macabre (K 9555) arranged by Liszt. See entry under Liszt.

Piano Works (Rolf-Dieter Arens—CFP 9295) 104pp. Contains: 6 Bagatelles Op.3; Allegro appassionato Op.70; Album pour piano Op.72 (six separate pieces); Les cloches du soir Op.85; Suite pour piano Op.90 (four separate pieces). Preface by Reiner Zimmerman in German, French, and English; critical note in German.

Album de Six Morceaux Choisis (Durand) 29pp. 1re Mazurka; Valse Mignonne; Rêverie du Soir; Valse Langoureuse; Gavotte; Les Cloches du Soir. M-D.

Marina Saiz-Salazar (1930–   ) Panama

Sonata 1954–55 (PAU). First movement: punctuated rhythmic drive, disjunct motion. Second movement: big sonorities, disjunct writing. Third movement: thin-textured mid-section before driving opening ideas return. Dramatic ending. Much dissonance and drive to this work. Neoclassic handling of key centers, chromaticism. Some 12-tone techniques used. All meters are duple. M-D to D.

Erkii Salmenhaara (1941–   ) Finland

Sonata I e♭ 1965–66 (Fazer) 27pp. Allegro; Recitativo-Notturno; Intermezzo-Wiegenlied; Introduzione-Finale. Bitonal, square rhythms, Romantic outlook, simple neoclassic style, excellent development of ideas. M-D.

Sonata II (Fazer). Four movements, not closely related; many repeated patterns infused with strong dissonance. M-D to D.

Sonatina 1979 (Fazer) 10pp. Nocturne: slow, mysterious, repeated figurations and patterns rather than melody, bitonal. Scherzo: endless bass ostinato under a high, thin melody. Menuetto: unconventional design; much repetition of thematic material; borrows from the Bach *Minuet in G* theme, altering notes here and there. M-D.

Franz Salmhofer (1900–1975) Austria

All these pieces show Salmhofer's music to be firmly rooted in the traditions of the Viennese Romantics.

Drei Klaverstücke Op.2 (UE 7139 1923) 8pp. Präludium; Poèm; Menuett. In a style similar to that of Bruckner and Reger. M-D.

Klavierstück in Quarten Op.3 (UE 7140 1923) 8pp. Large character piece, full chords, thick textures, Richard Strauss overtones. M-D to D.

Scherzo Op.4 (UE 7141 1923) 10pp. Fleeting, moody, chordal melodic Trio. M-D.

Sonate C 1952 (UE 12129) 32pp. 21 min. Allegro con brio; Adagio; Vivace. Freely tonal around C. Shows a vigorous invention and a sure instinct for dramatic effect. M-D.

Gustave Samazeuilh (1877–1967) France

Samazeuilh's style reflects the early works of Debussy and Ravel.

Esquisses (Durand 1948). Dédicace. Luciole. Sérénade: left hand only. Souvenir: right hand only. Colorful and contrasting. M-D.

Le Chant de la Mer (Durand 1919). Prélude: full chords over pedal point. Clair de lune au large: evocative. Tempête et lever du jour sur les flots: influence of Ravel and Dukas. Imaginative virtuoso program music. Warm Impressionist pianism that requires expert use of the sostenuto pedal. D.

Evocation (Durand). Slow and calm, freely tonal around F$\sharp$, Impressionistic. M-D.

Naiades au soir (Durand) 7pp. Requires rhythmic suppleness. M-D.

Chanson a ma poupée (Durand). Simple tune, colorfully treated. Int.

Chant d'Espagne (Lemoine). In a habanera rhythm, De Falla influence. M-D.

Pierre Sancan (1916–) France, born Morocco

Sancan is a distinguished pianist and a member of the faculty of the Conservatoire National in Paris.

Dusting 1950 (Durand) 4pp. With fantasy, many glissandos and acciaccatura chords, sprightly. M-D.

Mouvement 1946 (Durand) 11pp. Animated; contrasting sections, but always returns to toccata-like opening style; fast repeated notes; glissandos. M-D.

Pièces enfantiles (Durand). Vol.1: 5 pieces. Vol.2: 6 pieces. Easy to Int.

Pedro Sanjuan (1886–1976) USA, born Spain

Toccata (Mercury 1949) 10pp. Lyric passages alternate with toccata ideas. Freely tonal, exciting, brilliant conclusion. M-D.

Domingo Santa Cruz (1899–1987) Chile

Santa Cruz has played a large role in the development of music in Chile.

4 Viñetas (Casa Amarilla 1927) 9 min. Conceived in the spirit of an early suite. M-D.

5 Poemas Trágicas (Casa Amarilla 1929) 14 min. Contains touches of atonality. M-D.

Imagenes Infantiles (PIC 1960) 13 min. Book 1, Op.13a: 4 pieces. Book 2 Op.13b: 4 pieces. Varied moods and devices, bitonal preferences. Int. or above.

Claudio Santoro (1919–1988) Brazil

2 Dansas Brasileiras 1951 (PIC). Fascinating rhythmic interest, three-staff notation, No.1 easier. Int. to M-D.

Frevo 1953 (Ric BR 1601) 6pp. 3 min. Syncopated octaves and chords, 16th-note
figuration. An exciting dance. Large span required. M-D.

7 Paulistanas 1953 (Vitale) 21 min. Seven short pieces with rhythmic elements
characteristic of São Paulo dances. Int. to M-D.

Toccata 1954 (Ric). Demands endurance and energy. D.

Sonata No.3 1955 (Ric) 16 min. Allegro energico: displaced accents, bolero
rhythm. Adagio (Espressivo): samba rhythm in ostinato. Moderato: alternating rhythms. Clear textures, expanded tertian harmony. M-D.

Sonatine II 1964 (Tonos) 6pp. 6 min. Allegretto moderato; Andante; Vivo. MC,
neoclassic. Int.

Mutationen III (Tonos 1970) 8pp. For piano and tape. Extensive explanations in
English. Preface in German. Study score. Clusters, nontraditional notation.
Avant-garde. D.

Sonata IV (fantasia) 1957 (Tonos) 20pp. 16 min. Allegro deciso; Andante; Allegro molto. Well crafted, serially oriented. Allegro molto contains highly effective toccata-like writing. D.

Murillo Santos (1931–   ) Brazil

The Insects (BME 1995). Curious and sophisticated writing. An interesting view
of Brazil's multifaceted piano tradition. M-D.

Vassily Sapellnikoff (1868–1941) Russia

Dance of the Elves Op.3 (Musica Obscura). This was a favorite of Ossip Gabrilowitsch, who played it with great success. A bravura piece requiring nimble
fingers. M-D.

Gavotte D Op.5/2 (André). Also contained in collection *Twenty-Six Romantic
and Contemporary Piano Pieces* (GS). M-D.

Tibor Sárai (1919–   ) Hungary

Distances (EMB Z8278 1978) 10pp. Frequent meter changes, agitated mood with
many alternating notes between hands, exploits middle and outer ranges
of the keyboard, white- and black-key clusters. M-D.

József Sári (1935–   ) Hungary

Episodi (EMB 1968) 10pp. Serial, strongly contrasted moods, hammered repetitions, wide skips. M-D.

Giuseppe Sarti (1729–1802) Italy

3 Sonatas (Degrada—Ric 132952). Light 2-part textures, perky little rhythmic
figurations, conventional tunes, Alberti bass. Designed for the amateur of
Sarti's day. Int. to M-D.

László Sary (1940–   ) Hungary

Collage 1974 (EMB Z8021). A deliberately chance succession of tiny elements. Each parameter except pitch is fixed. Can be played with or without accidentals. M-D.

Andrés Sás (1900–1967) Peru, born France

Sás went to Peru in 1924. His style incorporates Impressionism with nationalism.

Melodía y Aire Variado Op.18 (PIC). A north Peruvian love song is the basis for the melody. The variations (on a Peruvian Indian dance) are very rhythmic, use double melodies with inner voices and irregular skips. Dissonant harmony. M-D.

Preludio y Toccata (PIC 1952). Peruvian folk tune is the basis of the Prelude. Toccata ends softly. M-D.

Arrulo y Tondero Op.39 (EV). Opening Lullaby in 5/4 with lovely melody followed by a Creole Dance. Quick Tondero in 6/8, very rhythmic. M-D.

Sonata Op.47 (PIC 1964). Four movements. Much play on bitonal relationships. Second movement: an expressive canon. Third movement: a Vals. Fourth movement: a humorous skippy Rondo. Neoclassic. M-D.

Himno y Danza (GS 1942). Short, chordal procession leads to a driving Danza with ostinato rhythms. M-D.

Aires y Danzas Indios del Peru (Lemoine 1934) 17pp. 11 pieces based on Peruvian folktunes. Highly interesting material, basically tonal plus some bitonal and dissonant usage, pianistic and effective. Int. to M-D.

Suite Peruana (A La Flûte de Pan 1935) 17pp. Yaravi: Indian cantilena. Kcashwa: Indian dance. El Caballito: tune from Titicaca lake (Peru-Bolivia). Little Variations on an Indian Theme: theme, 11 variations, and coda. Colorful, tasteful use of ethnic material. M-D.

Erik Satie (1866–1925) France

Satie was one of music's greatest originals. His influence on other composers was more important than his music but his music is unique in many ways. An antiquarian quality surrounds some of his early works. After a period of study at the Schola Cantorum, his style became more linear and infused with humorous, satirical, and cynical overtones. He parodied styles of well-known composers, quoted from their works, and deliberately attached comical names to his pieces. Fun seemed to be the essence of his aesthetic. Satie despised all Germanic Romantic music, and his own compositions negated any kind of sentimentality. He said the French needed a music of their own—without sauerkraut! He was a precursor of Debussy's Impressionism. Most of his works present no great difficulties, but they must be played almost perfectly or they run the strong risk of failure. His compositions clearly reveal the early development of twentieth-century French music. At one period in his life he coined the phrase "musique d'ameublement" (background or furniture music) to characterize his aesthetic conception. The pieces are transparent in texture, have fresh harmonies and simple melodies, and completely avoid any type of complexity or histrionics.

Ogives 1886 (MCA; Sikorski). Four short pieces, parallel chords. Int. to M-D.

Trois Sarabandes 1887 (Sal; MMP). Published separately. Somber, graceful, harmonic innovation. Int. to M-D.

Deux Oeuvres de Jeunesse: Valse-Ballet Op.62 and *Fantaisie-valse* 1885 (Sal). Satie's first compositions for piano. Salon style. Romantic, graceful. Int.

Trois Gymnopédies 1888 (B&VP; GS; Sal; K) Gymnopédies are ceremonial dances performed at ancient Greek festivals. Each piece is a different approach to the same idea, sad and languorous. Int.
See: Eric Frederick Jensen, "Satie and the 'Gymnopédie'," M&L, 75/2 (May 1994):236–240.

Trois Gnossiennes, Book I, Nos.1–3 1890 (GS; Sal; MMP). "Gnossienne" is most likely a vague allusion to Gnossos, an ancient city on the island of Crete—the site of the mythical King Minos. Repeated melody, basic bass rhythm. Int. to M-D.

Trois Gnossiennes, Book II, Nos.4–6 (B&VP 1968). Each has a different mood. Int.
Available separately: Nos.1–6 (Sal).

Chorals ca.1906 (Sal 1968). Twelve small chorals. Int. to M-D.

Première Pensée Rose-Croix (Sal). Plodding, mystical, dull. Int.

Danses gothiques 1893 (Sal). Nine pieces. Int. to M-D.

Le fils des étoiles 1892 (Sal 1972; MMP) 8pp. Preludes for piano. Wagnérie Kaldéenne du Sar Péladan. M-D.

Musique intimes et secrètes (Sal 1968). Nostalgie—Froide Sogerie. Fâcheux Exemple. Int. to M-D.

Sonneries de la Rose-Croix 1892 (Sal). Air de L'Ordre; Air du Grand Maître; Air de Grand Prieur. Static chords, modal, melody in octaves. M-D.
See: Wilson Lyle, "Erik Satie and Rosicrucianism," MR 42/3–4 (August–November 1981):238–42.

Quatre Préludes 1893 (Sal). Chordal, fourths, fifths, sevenths, ninths, floating effect. M-D.

2 Rêverie Nocturnes (Sal). Simple, restful. Int.

Le Piccadilly 1904 (Sal 1975; B&VP). In collection *Masters of the Character Piece* (Alfred 1856). A march, similar to a cake-walk, rhythmic, would make a good substitute for the Debussy *Le Petit Nègre*. Int.

Pièces froides 1897 (Sal; MMP). Available separately. Airs à faire fuir ("Three Airs Put to Flight"); Danses de travers ("Crooked Dances"). Barless notation. Basic ideas viewed differently. M-D.

Prélude en tapisserie 1906 (Sal). Neoclassic in style. M-D.

Passacaille 1906 (Sal). Neoclassic in style, chordal. M-D.

Véritables préludes flasques 1912 (ESC; MMP). Four "Flabby Preludes" with ridiculous Latin directions, delightful. Terse, bony, and highly contrapuntal. M-D.

Descriptions automatiques 1913 (ESC; MMP). Alludes to a number of popular songs. Fun; lively and naughty. M-D.

Embryons desséchés 1913 (ESC). Three imaginary crustaceans accompanied by silly descriptions, somber character. In No.2, Chopin's *Funeral March* is parodied and called a "quotation from the celebrated Mazurka of Schubert." M-D.

Croquis et agaceries d'un gros bonhomme en bois ("Sketchings and Provocations of a Big Wooden Boob"). 1913 (ESC; MMP). Parodies of Mozart, Chabrier, Cyril Scott, and Debussy. M-D.

Chapitres tournés en tous sens ("Chapters Turned Every Which Way") 1913 (ESC; MMP). No.1: parody on a wife who talks too much. No.2: a porter who carries heavy stones. No.3: uses "Nous n'irons plus au bois" (see Debussy *Jardins sous la pluie*). M-D.

Vieux Sequins et Vielles Cuirasses ("Old Sequins and Armor") 1914 (ESC; MMP). Allusions to Gounod, King Dagobert, and "Malbrouck s'en va-t-en guerre." The first piece describes a gold merchant. M-D.

Menus Propos Enfantines 1913 (ABRSM; ESC). Three sets of children's pieces, for small hand, no thumb crossings, comical commentary. A good example of the aesthetic of the "new simplicity" popular at this time. Easy to Int.

Heures séculaires et instantanées ("Old Age and Instantaneous Moments") 1914 (ESC; MMP). Obstacles vénimeux; Crépuscule matinal (de midi); Affolements granitiques. Grotesque narratives; in a footnote, Satie forbids the player to read the text aloud during performance. M-D.

Nouvelles pièces froides (Sal). Sur un mur; Sur un arbre; Sur un pont. Simple and strong. Int.

Petite Ouverture à Danser (Sal; B&VP 1288). Dull exercises. Int. to M-D.

6 Pièces de la Période 1906–13 (B&VP). Désespoir agréable; Effronterie; Poésie; Prélude canin; Profundeur; Songe creux. Int. to M-D.

Trois Valses distinguées d'un précieux dégoûté ("Three Distinguished Waltzes of a Disgusted Dandy") 1914 (Sal; MMP). His Waist; His Spectacles; His Legs. A collage of quotations from Bruyère, Cicero, and Cato. Short waltzes involving bitonality, with running commentary by Satie. Ingenious, delightful. Int. to M-D.

2 Nocturnes and a Minuet 1919 (ESC). Two of Satie's best works. M-D.

Sports et Divertissements 1914 (Sal, *Piano Music*, Vol.III; Cramer; Dover). Sal has a regular edition and a deluxe version, a facsimile of the manuscript with colored drawings by Charles Martin. It includes an English translation by Virgil Thomson. According to Satie's wish, the texts are to be read between the pieces, and not during their performance. The Swing; Hunting; Italian Comedy; The Bride; Blind Man's Bluff; Fishing; Yachting; Bathing; Carnival; Golf; The Octopus; Racing; Puss in the Corner; Picnic; Water Slide; Tango; The Sledge; Flirt; Fireworks; Tennis. Twenty brief sketches of fantasy and delicate charm. "I recommend that you turn its pages with a tolerant thumb and with a smile, for this is a work of fantasy. Let no one regard it otherwise. For the 'dried-up' and the 'stultified' I have written a chorale, sober and suitable. This makes a sort of bitter prelude, a kind of introduction quite austere and unfrivolous. Into it, I have put all I know about boredom. I dedicate this chorale to those who do not like me. And I withdraw" (from the preface). The summation of Satie's piano music. Int. to M-D.

See: David H. Porter, "Recurrent Motifs in Erik Satie's *Sports et Divertissements*," MR (August–November 1978):227–30.

Avant-dernières Pensées ("Next-to-Last Thoughts") 1915 (Sal; MMP). Aubade à Paul Dukas; Idylle à Debussy; Meditation à Albert Roussel. Short pieces. M-D.

Nocturnes 1919 (Sal, Nos.1–3; ESC, Nos.4, 5). Each one page long. Among Satie's best works. M-D.

Jack in the Box Op. posth. (UE). Originally music for a pantomime. Satie said this little "pantaloonery" was his "way of making faces at the evil men who live in this world" (Gillmor, p.118). Prelude; Entr'acte; Finale. Written in a stylized music-hall style. Int. to M-D. Int.

Grimaces Op. posth. (UE). Five pieces, originally incidental music for a Cocteau production of a Shakespeare play. Int. to M-D.

Pages Mystiques (ESC). Three one-page fragments. Prière: choralelike. Vexations. Harmonies: sparse chords. Int.

Sonatine bureaucratique 1917 (Alfred; Consortium; EV; B&VP; MMP; Sal). The Alfred and Sal editions have commentary in English translation. Three colorful neoclassic movements. In style of Clementi. Satirical comments relate to an office worker. Int.

Le Piège de Méduse ("Medusa's Snare") (Sal). Seven short delicious pieces based on an operetta of the same name (1913), for which Satie also wrote the libretto. Quadrille; Valse; Pas vite; Mazurka; Un peu vif; Polka; Quadrille (different from the first one). Modal, no key signatures or bar lines, added-note chords, varied textures. Anticipates Dada. Int.

Children's Pieces for Piano (Nov 1976; MMP) 16pp. Nine pieces for beginners published for the first time as a complete collection. Contains: Menus propos enfantines ("Children's Chatter"); Enfantillages pittoresque ("Child's Play"); Peccadilles importunes ("Silly Pranks"). Easy.

See: Marcelle Vernazza, "Erik Satie's Music for Children," *Clavier*, 18 (January 1979):39–40.

Piano Music Vol.I (Sal). Selected works 1887–94; Sarabandes 1, 2, 3; Gymnopédies 1, 2, 3; Gnossiennes 1, 2, 3; Les fils des étoiles—preludes; Sonneries de la rose e croix; Prélude de la porte héroïque du ciel. Int. to M-D.

Piano Music Vol.II (Sal). Selected works 1897–1919. Pièces froides; Airs à faire fuir; Danses de travers; Je te veux; Poudre d'or; 3 Valses distinguées du précieux dégoûté; Avant-dernières pensées; 3 Nocturnes. Int. to M-D.

Piano Works Vol.I (Maurice Rogers—Cramer) 75pp. Contains 34 works including: 3 Gymnopédies; 3 Gnossiennes; Embryons Desséches; 3 Sarabandes; 5 Nocturnes; Sonatine Bureaucratique; Véritables préludes flasques. Int. to M-D.

Piano Works Vol.II (M. Rogers—Cramer). Croquis et agaceries d'un gros bonhomme en bois; Chapitres tournés en tous sens; Vieux séquins et veilles cuirasses; Heures séculaires et instantées; Les trois valses distinguées du précieux dégoûté; Valse-Ballet; Fantaisie-Valse Op.62; Premier Menuet. Contains an erudite introduction. Int. to M-D.

Petite Musique de Clown Triste (ESC 8398 1980) 3pp. A colorful picture of a sorrowful clown but with humor. Faster metronome marks than indicated are suggested. Int.

Vexations (Musica Obscura; ESC). To be played 840 times! Int.

See: Melanie Haiken, "Vexatious Marathon," P&K, 160 (January–February 1993). A report on a 26½-hour performance of the piece.

The Piano Music of Erik Satie (AMP). A collection of thirty piano pieces including the famous 1912–1914 piano works.

The Satie Collection (Hinson—EAM 1999). Contains 21 works at the intermediate and moderately difficult levels. Selected and introduced by the editor.

A Satie Entertainment (D. Ratcliffe—Nov 1976). Contains three piano pieces Satie used in the nightclub where he was pianist and three short love songs accompanied by chromatic harmonies. Other piano solos include 3 Sarabandes; 3 Gymnopédies; 3 Gnossiennes; Airs à faire fuir from Pièces froides. The three nightclub piano pieces are Je te veux; Poudre d'or; Le Piccadilly. Editorial additions given in square brackets. Int. to M-D.

3 Gymnopédies & 3 Gnossiennes (Baylor—Alfred 2501) 23pp. Includes performance directions. Int.

Gymnopédies, Gnossiennes, Sonatine bureaucratique (Schott 9013 1996) 45pp. Includes glossary for French words. Int. to M-D.

Music for Piano in 2 Vols. (R. Nichols—CFP). Vol I: 3 Gymnopédies; Je te veux; 3 Sarabandes; 3 Pieces Froides. Vol. II: Gnossiennes; 3 Avant-Dernières pensées; Sonata bureaucratique; 5 Nocturnes.

Je te veux (MMP). A charming waltz. Int.

Gymnopédies, Gnossiennes and other Works for Piano (Dover 1989) 172pp. Also includes 3 Sarabandes; The Son of the Stars: A Chaldean Wagnery by Sâr Péladan; Trumpet Calls of the Rose and Cross; The Heroic Gate of Heaven; Cold Pieces; Gold Dust; 3 Pieces: The Pear (for 4 hands), In Riding Habit (4 hands), Unpleasant Observations (4 hands); Genuine Flabby Preludes for a Dog; Automatic Descriptions; Dried Embryos; Sketches and Provocations of a Partly Wooden Mannikin; Chapters Turned Every Which Way; Old Sequins and Armor. Int. to M-D.

See: Alan M. Gillmor, *Erik Satie* (Boston: Twayne Publishing, 1988). Analyzes all of Satie's piano music as well as his other works.

Emil Sauer (1862–1942) Germany

Boîte à Musique (Spieluhr) (Schott 1913) 5pp. Effectively imitates a music box. Subtler and more flexible mid-section with fast scale passages adds color. M-D.

Frisson de Feuilles (Espenlaub) (Schott 1897) Etude de Concert No.6. ABA, Presto fleeting triplets in b minor in A sections, poco meno mosso cantando B section; elegant salon style. M-D.

Henri Sauguet (1901–1989) France
Sauguet described himself as a "traditionalist, though strongly anti-academic." His style is characterized by spontaneous and unpretentious writing that seeks to please rather than to be profound.
Sonata D (Sal 1926) 19pp. Three movements. Cheerful writing with a few unconvincing modulations. M-D.
Feuillets d'Album (Jobert 1928). Une valse; Un nocturne; Un scherzo. M-D.
Romance C (Jobert). 3pp. Unpretentious character piece, tuneful. Int. to M-D.

Manuel Saumell (1817–1870) Cuba
Contradanzas (Editorial Letras Cubanas 1980) 134pp. 51 contradanzas in the style of Gottschalk. Charming. Int. to M-D.

Jane Savage (fl. 1780–1790) Great Britain
Six Sonatas for Piano or Harpsichord (Harbach—Vivace) 40pp. Strong galant style; full of energetic rhythms and flowing lines. M-D.

A. Adnan Saygun (1907–1991) Turkey
Although Saygun studied in France, he exploits native folk music extensively.
Sonatina Op.15 (PIC 1938). First movement: Impressionistic. Second movement: Adagio con moto, uses ostinati and highly embellished melodic ideas. Horon: a dance from the Black Sea area; brilliant, driving rhythms. M-D.
Anadolu'dan Op.25 (PIC 1945). Meseli: 9/8 in 2+2+2+3. Zeybek: 9/4 in 4+5; Romantic treatment. Halay: 4/4, 10/8 in 2+3+2+3. Interesting rhythmic patterns. M-D.
Inci'nin Kitabi (PIC 1934) (Inci's Book). Character pieces of Turkish origin: Inci; Playful Kitten; A Tale; The Giant Puppet; A Joke; Lullaby; A Dream. A shortened contemporary "Turkish Album for the Young." Easy to Int.
10 Etudes on Aksak Rhythms (PIC 1969) 51pp. A fine foreword throws light on these rhythmic studies. Unusual works. D.
12 Preludes on Aksak Rhythms (PIC 1969). The term *Aksak* designates a special category of rhythms, a few specimens of which were made known by Béla Bartók under the denomination "Bulgarian rhythm." Foreword explains the use of the rhythms. Interesting sonorities and rhythmic treatment. M-D.

Alessandro Scarlatti (1660–1725) Italy
Father of the great and better-known Domenico.
Composizioni per Clavicembalo (A. Longo—Ric). Minuett C; Balletto a; Adagio; Allegretto; Aria alla francese; Corrente (in 4/4 time); 2 Fugues g, a. Int. to M-D.
Primo e Secundo libro de Toccate in *I Classici Musicali Italiani* XIII (R. Gerlin—Fondazione Eugenio Brevi). Ten toccatas. Sectionalized, virtuoso figuration, modulations. M-D.
7 Toccatas for Clavier (R. Nardi—Br). Nos.2, 4 (Tureck—CF) available separately. Multi-sectioned, include a few dance elements. Int. to M-D.

Variations on "Follia di Spagna" (Tagliapietra—Ric). Colorful treatment of this popular theme. M-D.

Collected Works Vol. I (MMP). 7 Toccatas and Fugues. M-D. Vol. II (MMP) 5 Toccatas and Fugues; Partita alla Lombarda; 2 Fugues; 6 Little Pieces. Int. to M-D.

See: Julio Esteban, "On the Neglected Keyboard Compositions of Alessandro Scarlatti," AMT, 18 (January 1969):22–23.

John Shedlock, "The Harpsichord Music of Alessandro Scarlatti," SIMG, 6 (1904–5):160–78, 418–22.

Domenico Scarlatti (1685–1757) Spain, born Italy

Scarlatti composed more than 550 keyboard sonatas for the musically gifted Portuguese Princess Maria Barbara. For nearly ten years he served as her music teacher, and upon her marriage in 1729 to the heir of the Spanish throne, he moved with her court to Spain, where he spent the rest of his life. Most of these sonatas were collected toward the end of his life in a series of volumes for his former pupil, now Queen of Spain. Evidence indicates that more than half of them were composed when Scarlatti was between the ages of 67 and 72. In these sonatas, which show a constantly developing style and an abundance of creativity, Scarlatti gave the binary form a variety and expressive range that has never been surpassed by any other composer. Their originality and emotional range span every mood and temperament and often require all the talent and skill the most virtuosic performer can deliver.

Complete Keyboard Works (Kenneth Gilbert—Heugel) 11 vols. Preface in English, French, and German. Critical note in French. This scrupulous new edition has much to recommend it. Based on the Venice manuscripts. Vol.1: Sonatas K.1–52. Vol.2: Sonatas K.53–103. Vol.3: Sonatas K.104–55. Vol.4: Sonatas K.156–205. Vol.5: Sonatas K.206–55; Vol.6: Sonatas K.256–305. Vol.7: Sonatas K.306–57. Vol.8: Sonatas K.358–407. Vol.9: Sonatas K.408–57. Vol.10: Sonatas K.458–506. Vol.11: Sonatas K.507–55.

Complete Keyboard Works (Johnson Reprint Corporation) 18 vols. Facsimile from the Parma manuscript and printed sources, compiled and annotated by Ralph Kirkpatrick. Each volume contains a preface, notes on sources, notes on texts, catalogue of sonatas, table of sonatas in the order of Longo's edition, listing of sonatas in the order of tonalities and time signatures. Vol.I: Sonatas K.1–42 (1–30 are the thirty *Essercizi* [1738–39] and 31–42 are the twelve sonatas that Thomas Roseingrave added in his 1739 printing of forty-two sonatas). Vol.II: Sonatas K.43–68, Appendix of K.8, 31, 33, 37, 41. Vol.III: Sonatas K.69–97, Appendix with variants of K.52, 53. Vol.IV: Sonatas K.98–123. Vol.V: Sonatas 124–47. Vol.VI: Sonatas K.148–76. Vol.VII: Sonatas K.177–205. Vol.VIII: Sonatas K.206–35. Vol.IX: Sonatas K.236–65. Vol.X: Sonatas K.266–95. Vol.XI: Sonatas K.296–325. Vol.XII: Sonatas K.326–57. Vol.XIII: Sonatas K.358–87. Vol.XIV: Sonatas K.388–417. Vol.XV: Sonatas K.418–53. Vol.XVI: Sonatas K.454–83. Vol.XVII: Sonatas K.484–513. Vol.XVIII: Sonatas K.514–55.

See: William S. Newman, "Kirkpatrick's Facsimile Edition of Scarlatti's Keyboard Sonatas," PQ, 79 (Fall 1972):18–21.

Complete Edition of the Sonatas (Emilia Fadini—Ric). Vol.1: Sonatas 1–50. Vol.2: Sonatas 51–97. Vol.3: Sonatas 98–153. Vol.4: Sonatas 154–213. Vol.5: Sonatas 214–273. This new edition prints an accurate and elegant text. Fadini uses her own numbering system and ignores some of the more recent fully documented studies of Scarlatti's sonatas and their sequence. She collates all available sources and bases her order on the Venice Manuscript. Kirkpatrick and Longo numbers are given. Apart from the confusion caused by the various numbering systems, the edition is admirable.

Complete Edition of the Sonatas (Allessandro Longo—K 1978) 10 vols., 50 Sonatas in each, plus Supplementary Volume containing 45 Sonatas; Sonatas numbered consecutively. This American reprint makes easily available a series first published in the early part of the twentieth century. Also available is a complete thematic index to the entire series (K).

Sixty Sonatas (Kirkpatrick—GS). Exemplary edition. In the following table, the first column refers to the order of the Sonatas in this edition, the second (K) to Kirkpatrick's chronology, and the third (L) to Longo's. See Ralph Kirkpatrick, *Domenico Scarlatti* (Princeton: Princeton University Press, 1953), Appendix II, for a complete catalogue of the 545 sonatas, listing the Kirkpatrick and Longo numbers.

Schirmer	K	L	Schirmer	K	L
1	3	378	22	140	107
2	7	379	23	208	238
3	16	397	24	209	428
4	18	416	25	215	323
5	28	373	26	216	273
6	29	461	27	238	27
7	44	432	28	239	281
8	46	25	29	259	103
9	54	241	30	260	124
10	57	S.38	31	263	321
11	84	10	32	264	466
12	52	267	33	308	359
13	96	465	34	309	454
14	105	204	35	366	119
15	115	407	36	367	172
16	116	452	37	394	275
17	119	415	38	395	65
18	120	215	39	402	427
19	132	457	40	403	470
20	133	282	41	420	S.2
21	175	429	42	421	252

Schirmer	K	L	Schirmer	K	L
43	426	128	52	493	S.24
44	427	286	53	494	287
45	460	324	54	513	S.3
46	461	8	55	516	S.12
47	470	304	56	517	266
48	471	82	57	518	116
49	490	206	58	519	475
50	491	164	59	544	497
51	492	14	60	545	500

200 Sonatas (Gyorgy Balla—EMB) 4 vols., 50 Sonatas in each. Exciting new urtext edition. Helpful performance suggestions in English, German, and Hungarian; convenient thematic index. Critical note in German. English translation of the preface is awkward, but the information is helpful. Excellent fingering provided. Vol.I: Sonatas K.1, 9, 11, 20, 24–27, 29, 30, 37, 43, 51–53, 55, 64, 69, 72, 78, 82, 96, 98, 102, 103, 106, 107, 113, 114, 119, 120, 121, 122, 124, 125, 129, 132, 133, 140, 141, 145, 146, 148, 149, 150, 151, 154, 155, 158, 159. Vol.II: Sonatas K.175, 177, 178, 181, 182, 185, 186, 187, 201, 202, 208, 209, 211, 212, 213, 214, 221, 222, 223, 224, 232, 233, 238, 239, 240, 241, 246, 247, 256, 257, 261, 262, 266, 267, 268, 269, 270, 271, 277, 278, 281, 282, 283, 284, 296, 297, 298, 299, 302, 303. Vol.III: K.308, 309, 318, 319, 320, 321, 322, 323, 335, 336, 337, 338, 343, 344, 347, 348, 358, 359, 366, 367, 376, 377, 378, 379, 380, 381, 386, 387, 402, 403, 404, 405, 406, 407, 408, 409, 415, 416, 420, 421, 422, 423, 430, 432, 433, 434, 435, 436, 441, 442. Vol.IV: K.443, 444, 445, 446, 449, 450, 456, 457, 460, 461, 466, 467, 472, 473, 476, 477, 478, 479, 480, 484, 488, 489, 490, 491, 492, 497, 498, 501, 502, 507, 508, 513, 514, 515, 518, 519, 520, 521, 524, 525, 530, 531, 532, 533, 542, 543, 544, 545, 550, 551.

100 Sonatas (Eiji Hashimoto—GS 1985) 3 vols. Contains a six-page preface and seven pages of textual notes in an English translation, as well as two pages of facsimiles. No fingering. Vol.1: Sonatas K.6, 9, 24, 25, 26, 30, 49, 87, 99, 100, 104, 113, 114, 123, 126, 127, 128, 141, 147, 173, 179, 180, 181, 182, 183, 184, 201, 211, 212, 213, 214, 225, 226. Vol.2: Sonatas K.232, 233, 240, 241, 246, 247, 248, 249, 261, 262, 298, 299, 318, 319, 320, 321, 347, 348, 364, 365, 368, 369, 380, 381, 424, 425, 430, 434, 435, 436, 437, 438, 443, 444. Vol.3: Sonatas K.445, 446, 447, 448, 454, 455, 466, 467, 468, 469, 474, 475, 478, 479, 485, 486, 487, 497, 498, 499, 500, 511, 512, 520, 521, 526, 527, 532, 533, 546, 547, 550, 551. Scholarly and performing edition.

36 Sonatas (Leon Kartun—Les Editions Ouvrières). Book I: L.488, 366, 338, 370, 104, 487, 449, 415, 224, 8, 486, 462, 429, 374, 407, 390, 158, 416. Book II: L.413, 475, 465, 499, 48, 383, 171, 241, 375, 33, 461, 391, 14, 32, Supplement 26 (K.337), Supplement 40 (K.172), 382, 345. Edited for the piano in good taste.

Scarlatti Album I (Zbigniev Drzewiecki—PWM). Contains: K.1, 2, 9, 19, 20, 33, 125, 132, 159, 259, 377, 380, 430, 533. Clean edition.

27 Selected Sonatas (BMC). L.201, 286, 268, 249, 262, 24, 6, 15, 10, 11, 3, 481, 496, 457, 302, 406, 126, 127, 187, 383, 366, 378, 390, 385, 360, 263, 376. Edited.

5 Pairs of Sonatas (S. Rosenblum—ECS). The excellent preface includes a discussion of stylistic considerations. L.24, 61, 64, 88, 93, 95, 322, 359, 454, 483. A careful, clean edition. Int. to M-D.

Scarlatti—An Introduction to His Keyboard Works (Margery Halford—Alfred 1974). Includes a discussion of the manuscripts, style and form, interpretation, ornamentation, rhythmic alterations, phrasing, articulation and fingering, dynamics, pedal, figured bass. Includes: K.32, 63, 77b, 80, 83b, 391, 44e, 40, 42, 73b, 73c, 415, 81d, 88c, 90d, 431, 89b, 34, and a thematic index. A most useful volume. Int. to M-D.

Ausgewählte Klaviersonaten (Johnsson, Kraus—Henle 395). Vol I: Sonatas K.30, 47, 54, 82, 88, 127, 149, 159, 197, 261, 268, 291, 294, 302, 307, 380, 386, 415, 430, 520. C, G, g, C First Editions. Vol. II (Henle 451): Sonatas K.4, 9, 58, 64, 72, 96, 125, 141, 200, 238, 265, 270, 278, 280, 347, 377, 396, 397, 417, 423, 426, 477, 513, 544. A different version of K.96 is contained as an Appendix. Vol. III (Henle 476): Sonatas K.13, 24, 25, 98, 101, 122, 169, 170, 205, 215, 240, 263, 297, 298, 305, 351, 353, 365, 382, 420, 442, 483, 516, 545. All three volumes are urtext editions and are well fingered by Kraus.

At the Piano With Scarlatti (Hinson—Alfred 109) 63pp. Includes discussion of Scarlatti as performer, teacher, and composer; his influence and reputation; guide to performance practice in the Scarlatti sonatas; explanation of K. and L. numbers; and information about each sonata. Includes Sonatas G K.2 L.388; a K.3 L.378; d K.34 L.Supplement 7; G K.63 L. 84; F K.78 L.75; C K.95 L.358; D K.178 L.162; D K.277 L.183; A K.323 L.95; C K.330 L.55; G K.391 L.79; B♭ K.393 L.74; G K.431 L.83; B♭ K.440 L.97; A K.453; f K.481 L.187.

Twelve Sonatas (Ferguson—ABRSM). Includes K.289, 259, 335, 60, 198, 408, 206, 323, 304, 309, 69, 446. Int. to M-D.

Nine Sonatas (Ferguson—ABRSM) 40pp. A fine collection that includes K.159, 462, 86, 103, 87, 318, 142, 402, and 531. Int. to M-D.

Eleven Sonatas (Ferguson—ABRSM). Includes K.172, 424, 149, 279, 277, 424, 425, 144, 178, 197, 284.

Domenico Scarlatti Piano Compositions (Tucker—CPP/Belwin 1993) 30pp. Sonatas L.193, K.499; L.243, K.451; L.151, K.464; L.339, K.512; L.413, K.9; L.187, K.481; L. 388, K.2. No way to distinguish editorial markings from composer's. M-D.

Domenico Scarlatti—An Introduction to the Composer and His Music (J. Banowetz—GWM 1978) 80pp. Highly informative preface with discussion of the sources used for this edition. Scarlatti's Grouping of the Sonatas, Playing Scarlatti on the Piano, Ornamentation, and other topics. Includes: Sonatas K.63 G L.84; K.64 d L.58; K.78 F L.75; K.178 D L.162; K.208 A L.238; K.274 F L.297; K.275 F L.328; K.277 D L.183; K.322 A L.483; K.323 A L.95; K.330 C L.55; K.391 G L.79; K.393 B♭ L.74; K.431 G L.83; K.440 B♭ L.97;

K.453 A (no L no.); K.481 f L.187. Also includes notes for each sonata. An exemplary edition with all editorial marks in red. Int. to M-D.

48 Sonatas and Pieces (Schott). No. K. or L. numbers, fingerings added, no sources listed. Attractive collection with fine music. M-D.

37 Pieces and Sonatas (Arnold Goldsbrough—ABRSM 1962). Vol.1: Pieces K.80, 40, 34, 32, 42, 81, 88, 83, 163, 322, 377, 95, 74, 88 (another part), 512, 471, 63. Vol.2: Sonatas K.389, 342, 123, 278, 67, 102, 537, 25, 427, 11. Vol.3: Sonatas K.9, 481, 535, 436, 140, 525, 4, 380, 8, 38. Includes source identification, fingering, and a preface that discusses ornamentation, tempi, and touch. The three volumes are graded and range from Easy to Int. in Vol.1 to M-D in Vol.3.

Il mio primo Scarlatti ("My first Scarlatti") (R. Risaliti—Ric 1976) 21pp. Includes: K.32 D L.423; K.34 d L. S.7; K.40 c L.357; K.42 B♭ L. S.36; K.78 F L.75; K.80 G; K.94 F; K.95 C L.358; K.332 A L.483; K.391 G L.79; K.431 G L.83; K.440 B♭ L.97; K.453 A. Int.

A Scarlatti Notebook (Christina Emra—McAfee 1977) 2 vols. Sixty of the easier sonatas. Int. to M-D.

Scarlatti, the First Book for Young Pianists (M. Halford—Alfred 1977) 24pp. Int.

60 Sonatas (K) 2 vols. Sonatas L.366, 388, 378, 390, 367, 479, 379, 488, 413, 370, 352, 489, 486, 387, 374, 397, 384, 416, 383, 375, 363, 360, 411, 495, 481, 368, 449, 373, 461, 499, 345, 104, 463, 338, 128, 180, 447, 465, 340, 290, 282, 205, 433, 175, 260, 430, 395, 343, 432, 266, 497, 500, 283, 188, 475, 396, 235, 103, 490, 263. Int. to M-D.

26 Sonatas (E. Granados—UME). 2 vols. Highly edited for performance on the piano. Int. to M-D.

10 Sonatas (A. Loesser—Music Press 1947). Contains some less familiar Sonatas: L. 46, 49, 131, 203, 204, 212, 289, 380, 405, 416. Int. to M-D.

35 Sonatas (CF) after the Longo Edition. Vol.I: Sonatas L.104, 187, 188, 256, 331, 338, 345, 368, 375, 407, 413, 422, 424, 490, 498, 499, Supp. 39. Vol.II: Sonatas L. 23, 33, 58, 128, 263, 324, 370, 381, 396, 416, 429, 430, 433, 434, 465, 475, 486, Supp. 3. Int. to M-D.

12 Easy Sonatas (A. Mirovitch—EBM). Some sonatas only one page long. Excellent collection of the easiest sonatas. Highly edited. Int.

10 Sonatas (W. Georgii—Arno Volk Verlag). Sonatas L. 430, 139, 461, 231, 287, 499, 498, 384, 476, and Sonata D. Sources and performance suggestions given. M-D.

9 Selected Sonatas (I. Philipp—IMC). Sonatas L. 97, 486, 488, 490, 465, 463, 487, 413, 375. M-D.

6 Selected Sonatas (I. Philipp—IMC). Sonatas L. 33, 483, 23, 25, 209, 430. M-D.

30 Sonatas (Gregg Press 1967). A beautiful reprint of a 1739 London edition. Contains an interesting selection of Sonatas, the *Essercizi per gravicembalo*. M-D.

24 Sonatas (J. Friskin—JF 1938, 1945). 2 vols., 12 Sonatas in each. Edited and fingered. M-D.

2 Sonatas (E. Hashimoto—Zen-On 221). Sonatas K.380, 381 (L.23, 225). M-D.

10 Sonatas (B. Bartók—MMP) 42pp. Overedited but interesting fingerings. M-D.

2 Sonatas (E. Hashimoto—Zen-On 222). Sonatas K.499, 500 (L.193, 492). M-D.

10 Selected Sonatas (Wouters—Zephyr 1975) 32pp. Sonatas L.213, 345, 358, 375, 388, 413, 461, 486, 495, 499. M-D.

2 Sonatas (APS). Sonatas K.34, 42. Highly edited. Int.

Album for Keyboard (Alfred A. Kalmus). 14 sonatas with editorial additions of fingering, dynamics, and interpretation of ornaments. Also contains an account of Scarlatti's life, his contribution to the repertoire, and his technique of composition. Int. to M-D.

Sonata g K.30 (L.499) (Alfred) "The Cat's Fugue." M-D.

5 Klaviersonaten (W. Gerstenberg—Gustave Bosse 1933). Sonatas K.452, 453, 204a, 204b, 357. M-D.

Sonata d K.9 (L.413) (Alfred). One of the finest sonatas. M-D.

Essercizi 1738 (F. Valenti—GS) 30 sonatas first published in 1738. Contains no editing or K. numbers but they are K.1–30. Not as useful a collection as it could have been. Valenti has added very little personal contribution outside of a few footnotes and a foreword. These Sonatas are not the first 30 Scarlatti wrote, but his first printed collection. The Sonatas display a great variety, ranging from extrovert pieces to more personal, inward-looking ones. M-D.

Easiest Piano Pieces (Weismann—CFP 5009) 27pp. 14 pieces, no K. numbers. Int. to M-D.

Sonatas, Book 1 (C. Kite—S&B). A new purified edition of the Thomas Dunhill practical edition (1917). Book 1 contains 15 of the original 29 selected by Dunhill. Carefully edited with fine annotations. Book 2 will contain the other 14 Sonatas. Kite plans to offer a Book 3 of his own, "presenting a broader picture of the composer's style." It will contain Sonatas K.87, 219, 220, 270, 271, 281, 282, 370, 371, 439, 440, 501, 502. Int. to M-D.

5 Pieces (K 3858) 23pp. Transcribed by Béla Bartók. Allegro; Molto moderato; Vivace; Moderato; Allegro molto. These transcriptions attest to Bartók's great interest in Baroque literature. All are expertly worked out but are overpedaled. M-D.

Scarlatti. Piano Sonatas. Vol. I (Hinson—Alfred 29) 64pp. Includes a Foreword and a guide to performance practice, and discusses playing Scarlatti on the piano, the influence of Spanish folk music and dance on Scarlatti, his pairing of sonatas, and the character of each sonata. Contains Sonatas c K.11 L.352; a K.54 L.241; d K.64 L.58; a K.148 L.64; a K.149 L.93; A K.208 L.238; A K.209 L.428; F K.274 L.297; e K.291 L.61; F K.275 L.328; c K.302 L.7; E K.380 L.23; C K.421 L.252; D K.430 L.463. Int. to M-D.

Scarlatti. Piano Sonatas. Vol. II (Hinson—Alfred 107) 65pp. Includes same information in front matter as Vol. I plus information about each sonata. Contains Sonatas A K.74 L.94; G K.105 L.204; c K.116 L.452; G K.427 L.286; F "Pastorale" K.446 L.433; G K.471 L.82; D K.490 L.206; D K.492 L.14; C

K.502 L.3; C "Pastorale" K.513 L.Supplement 3; f K.519 L.475; E K.531 L.430; B♭ K.551 L.396. Int. to M-D.

Scarlatti. Selected Sonatas (Hinson—Alfred 108) 63pp. Includes a Foreword, an explanation of K. and L. numbers, and information about each sonata. These are the editor's favorite Sonatas: F K.6 L.479; d K.9 L.413; G K.14 L.387; E K.20 L.375; D K.29 L.461; D K.96 L.465; A K. 113 L.345; C K.132 L.457; G K.146 L.349; C K.159 L.104; G K.260 L.124; A K.322 L.483; C K.420 L.Supplement 2; G K.455 L.209; g K.476 L.340. Int. to M-D.

Sonata D K.29 (L.461). Presto, repeated notes in alternate hands, melody in right hand over chordal left hand with seconds and sevenths, flamenco guitar mood. M-D.

Sonata c K.84 (L.10). Brilliant arpeggio style. M-D.

Sonata b K.87 (L.33). Flows with limpid poignancy and scrupulous concern for the supporting melodies. M-D.

Sonata D K.96 (L.465). One of the most popular. Keep in mind terrace dynamics and use echo effects for the numerous repeated parts. M-D.

Sonata G K.125 (L.487). Glints and dazzles like a crystalline bell chiming in bright sunlight. M-D.

Sonata C K.132 (L.457). One of the finest. Unusual dissonances. M-D.

Sonata a K.175 (L.429). Left-hand clusters add considerably to the effectiveness of the piece. Avoid editions that "clear out" these dissonances (CF and Ric). M-D.

Sonata G K.259 (L.103). Slow and melodious. M-D.

Sonata G K.394 (L.275). Mid-section is an arpeggiated fantasy with canonic imitation and a bagpipe trio. M-D.

Sonata C K.461 (L.8). Popular and appealing. M-D.

Sonata D K.492 (L.14). Full of Spanish poignancy, found in many collections. M-D.

Sonata C K.513 (L.Supp.3). First section is based on a pastorale-like "Pifferari" theme that was also used by Berlioz in *Rustic Serenade to the Virgin.* The second part is a fleeting Presto. M-D.

See: Joseph Banowetz, "A Close Look at Scarlatti Sonatas," *Clavier,* 17/8 (November 1978):18–20. Includes music and lesson on Sonata f♯ K.447 (L.294), pp.21–24.

Rita Benton, "Form in the Sonatas of Domenico Scarlatti," MR, 13 (November 1952):264–73.

Massimo Bogianckino, *The Harpsichord Music of Domenico Scarlatti* (Kassel: Barenreiter, 1967). Translated from the Italian by John Tickner. Contributi di Musicologia I.

Kathleen Dale, "Domenico Scarlatti: His Unique Contribution to Keyboard Literature," PRMA, 74 (1947–48):33–44.

Stephen Daw, "Clementi as a Performer of Scarlatti," M&M (October 1985):6–9. Also includes Clementi's edition (London, 1791) of the Scarlatti Sonata in E, K.206.

Robert Dumm, "A Performer's Analysis—A Scarlatti Sonata," *Clavier*, 14 (February 1975):27–30. Discusses the "Pastorale Sonata d," K.9.

——, "The Keyboard Sonatas of Domenico Scarlatti," *Clavier*, 35/4 (April 1996):20–23. Includes Sonata E K.380.

Barbara Sachs, "Scarlatti's *tremolo*," *Early Music* (February 1991):91–93. Suggests repeated notes be used for this indication found in K.96, 114, 115, 118, 119, 128, 132, 136, 137, 172, 175, 183, 187, 194, 203, 204a, 208, 272, 291, 296, 510, 525 and 543.

Joel Leonard Sheveloff, "The Keyboard Music of Domenico Scarlatti: A Reevaluation of the Present State of Knowledge in the Light of the Sources," diss., Brandeis University, 1970.

Edwin Smith, "Four Scarlatti Sonatas," *Music Teacher*, 53 (June 1974):20–21. Discusses K.113, 159, 426, 96.

Fernando Valenti, *The Harpsichord: A Dialogue for Beginners* (Hackensack, NJ: Jerona, 1982), 92pp. An informal guide for the player at any level, with a special chapter on the music of Scarlatti.

Giacinto Scelsi (1905–1988) Italy

Scelsi made a special study of Sanskrit literature and Indian culture, which influenced and inspired his creative work.

Sonata II 1939 (GS 1979) 29pp. Composer's autograph series. An impressive work in three movements that owes its inspiration to the piano music of Bartók and Scriabin. Repeated notes, minor seconds, and major sevenths are some of the ingredients from which much of the thematic material emerges. M-D.

Suite X (Ka) 1954 (GS 1979) 36pp. Composer's autograph series. "Ka" is a Sanskrit word that means "essence," among other things. Seven-movement suite of short pieces. Thematic material is derived throughout from the repeated use of certain intervals, mainly half-steps. Similar in some ways to the work of Boulez and other composers whose avant-garde piano music emerged in the 1950s. M-D.

Boguslaw Schäffer (1929–   ) Poland

Musica per Pianoforte 1949–60 (PMP). 24 pieces. Uses graphic notation, analytic geometry, and the colors red and green to indicate sound intensities, duration, and placement of notes. These pieces trace Schäffer's style from conservative to radical. Int. to D.

R. Murray Schaffer (1933–   ) Canada

Polytonality (Berandol 1648 1974). The left hand seldom varies the pattern of a G/a broken-chord figure, kind of a hillbilly accompaniment. The right hand has a clever melody. No fingering, key signature, time signature, or tempo indications. A cheerful work, would be excellent for an encore. M-D.

Philipp Scharwenka (1847–1917) Poland

Moment Musical (Musica Obscura) 3pp. In A; Allegretto con grazia; salon style,
    melody in right hand then left hand. Int.

Xaver Scharwenka (1850–1924) Poland

Polish Dance e♭ Op.3/1 (Br&H 1980). A favorite on student recitals for years. Int.
Album for Young Pianists Op.62 (Musica Obscura) 25pp. Contains some attrac-
    tive pieces. Int.
Four Polish Dances Op.47 (Musica Obscura) 23pp. Contrasted, spirited. Int.
    to M-D.

Peter Schat (1935–   ) The Netherlands

Schat, a pupil of Boulez, was a seeker of musical and social utopias during the
1970s and 80s.
Anathema Op.19 1969 (Donemus 1980) 13pp. 8 min. Title suggests something
    violent but the aggression is inward and ironic. Uses techniques that were
    anathema for composers in the 1950s and early 60s: repetition pursued to
    the extent of rugged ostinato, simple harmonies, regular rhythms, clear
    modality, and harshly hammered chords. Expressive but downbeat ending.
    Work was finished "on the day Ho Chi Minh died . . . and with him the
    revolutionary fervour of the 60s." New notational signs used. D.

Heinrich Schenker (1867–1935) Austria

Zwei Klavierstücke Op.1 1892 (Dob 01610). Etude; Capriccio. Lively pieces that
    show the influence of Bruckner (Schenker's teacher). Interesting melodies
    and rhythmic shape. Franz Eibner has written interesting commentary
    about Schenker. M-D.

Armin Schibler (1920–1986) Switzerland

Schibler wrote in many styles, including neo-Baroque, late-Romantic, expres-
sionistic, 12-tone.
Nobody Knows (Eulenberg). 12 pieces based on Negro Spirituals. Int.
Rhythmisches Kaleidoskop Op.36 (Kahnt). The composer advises "much expres-
    sion and much rubato." Int.
Aphorismen Op.29 (Ahn & Simrock 1960). Nine short expressive pieces using
    "dodecaphonic tonality," which the composer defines as tonal equality of
    the 12 tones without the use of a series. M-D.
Aufzeichnungen Op.86 (Eulenberg 1967). Eight short pieces. Advanced harmonic
    idiom. M-D.

Peter Schickele (1935–   ) USA

Three Folk Settings (EV 1963) 7pp. Henry Martin; Turtle Dove; Old Joe Clark.
    Octotonic, modal, thin textures, attractive. Int.
The Household Moose 1965 (EV 1975) 9pp. Written in tribute to Darius Milhaud,

especially for his piano suite *The Household Muse*. Seven colorful, inventive pieces, MC. Suitable for sophisticated young players as well as for more advanced pianists. Int. to M-D.

Presents I (EV 1974) 4pp. Celebration; Peaslee Porridge Hot; Crab Game; Song for Susan; Remembrance; Berceuse; Notes from Underground. Atonal, serial, pointillistic, contrasted. M-D.

Three Piano Sonatinas (EV 1974) 16pp. Three movements each, in contemporary idiom. Sonatina II is the shortest and easiest. Dissonance, wide leaps, and changing meters require good pianistic equipment. Some bitonality used. Sonatina III is based on poems by American poets. Large span required for all three. M-D.

Little Suite for Josie 1958 (EV) 4 min. Seven short movements arranged symmetrically: the first and last are identical, Nos. 3 and 4 are solos for right and left hand respectively; the remaining three pieces are like two-part inventions. Linear, atonal, sparse style. Fingered. Fine introduction to MC idiom. Int.

Epitaphs 1966–79 (EV) 11pp. Orlando di Lasso; Michael Praetorius; Domenico Scarlatti; Frédéric Chopin. Imitations of these composers' styles. Program notes describe each piece. Int. to M-D.

Small Serenade (EV). Six rhythmical studies. Long phrases, rhythmic challenges. Int.

Little Suite for Susan (EV) 12pp. 7½ min. Seven short pieces written for the composer's wife. Changing meters, requires a good hand span, tricky in spots. Int.

Hollers, Hymns and Dirges 1988 (EV) 12 min. 8 clever folksong settings. Int.

Lalo Schifrin (1932–   ) USA, born Argentina
Schifrin is best known for his music for films and television.

Jazz Piano Sonata 1961 (MJQ) 46pp. Allegro. Andante molto espressivo. Presto: theme, 9 variations, and finale. This work is a catalogue of jazz techniques. Much is left to the performer: to ad lib the right hand, improvise over a walking bass, combine freely with the Hypodorian mode, repeat four times, etc. Chord identification (e.g., C maj 7, Dm 7) is frequently used. Requires mature pianism, but more important, a "feel" and love of the style. M-D to D.

Mima (EBM 1958). Progressive jazz suite. El Jefe; Mima; Buenos Aires Minuit; Blues for Berger; Silvia. Short movements. Int. to M-D.

Karl Schiske (1916–1969) Austria, born Hungary
Schiske's style is basically polyphonic.

Sonata Op.3 (Dob 1936) 25pp. Four movements. One of the composer's strongest works. M-D.

Dance Suite Op.23 (Dob 1945) 20pp. Foxtrot; Langsamer Walzer; Tango; Schneller Walzer. M-D.

Sonatina Op.42 (Dob 1954). Three movements. Frequently changing meters, neo-classic style. Int. to M-D.

Gustav Adolf Schlemm (1902–   ) Germany

Fünf Klavierstücke (Tonos 7002 1968) 17pp. 15 min. Präludium; Ciaconnetta; Nächtliche Vision; Impression; Impromptu. Freely tonal, neoclassic. M-D.

Sieben Klavierstücke nach Albrecht Dürer's Kupferstich-Passion (Tonos 1954, rev. 1974) 11pp. Christus als Schmerzensmann; Jesus in Gethsemane; Die Gefangennahme; Die Geisselung; Die Kreuztragung; Die Kreuzigung (a three-voice fugue); Die Beweinung. Chromatic, somewhat in Frank Martin's early style, full chords, octaves, flexible meters. M-D.

Julius Schloss (1902–1972) USA

23 Pieces for Children in 12-Tone Style 1958 and 1965 (PIC). Provides a fine introduction to this technique. Pieces are short and highly musical. Interesting titles. Easy to Int.

23 Studies for Children in 12-Tone Style 1962 and 1965 (PIC). Slightly more difficult than the above volume. A fine follow-up. Int.

Franz Schmidt (1874–1939) Austria

Toccata for Left Hand (Dob 1979) 12pp. Preface in German and English. Dedicated to Paul Wittgenstein, the Austrian pianist who lost his right arm in World War I. Molto vivace: fast 16ths, scalar, broken chords, melodic line brought out in the treble. M-D. Also available in a version for two hands (Dob 01553).

Yves Rudner Schmidt (1933–   ) Brazil

Dois Ponteios 1954–55 (Vitale) 9pp. 1. Groups of five notes in broken chordal figuration serve as accompaniment to left-hand melody. 2. Ideas are inverted so left hand has broken chordal figuration. Post-Romantic sonorities. M-D.

Toada II 1954 (Vitale 1975) 2pp. Brazilian rhythms and melodies. Int.

Hoje eu mesmo, amanhã o mundo ("Today, I Myself, Tomorrow the World") 1967 (Ric BR) 4pp. 2 min. National Brazilian influences mixed with an international style. Sonorities are explored by playing with all the fingers, the arms, and the palms; and finally the pianist sits on the keyboard with a fermata! Traditional notation. D.

Diálogo triste 1965 (Ric BR 1973) 2 min. Unusual chromatic ostinato treatment. M-D.

Florent Schmitt (1870–1958) France

Schmitt used only the small forms for his solo piano works. The pianistic layout often resembles that of his teacher Fauré but his accompanimental writing is more ample than Fauré's. His harmony is expressive. Schmitt was a meticulous editor of his own works.

Ballade de la Neige Op.6 1896 (Sal). 7pp. Expressive, 2 against 3, parallel broken chords float through closely related harmonies. M-D.

Sept Pièces Op.15 (Durand 1928) 32pp. Shows influence of German Romanticism, some picture painting, especially in "Promenade à l'Etang." M-D.

Musiques Intimes Op.16 1890–1900 (Heugel; MMP). Six pieces. Delicate, Romantic plus Impressionistic sonorities. M-D.

Musiques Intimes Op.29 1898–1904 (Sal; MMP). Dreamy atmospheric effects, shimmering sonorities. M-D.

Ombres Op.64 1916–17 (Durand) 36pp. J'entends dans le lointain; Mauresque; Cette ombre mon image. Effusive lyricism, contains a rainbow of timbres. M-D to D.

A la Mémoire de Claude Debussy Op.70/1 1920 (Durand) 8pp. Shows Schmitt's admiration for Debussy; looks and sounds somewhat like Debussy. M-D.

La Tragique Chevauchée Op.70/2 1921 (Durand) 16pp. Strong rhythms, violent ending. M-D.

Trois Danses Op.86 1935 (Durand) published separately. Montferrine: full chords, strong rhythms. Bocane: Impressionistic. Danse de corde: tango rhythm. M-D.

Enfants Op.94 (Durand). Eight short pieces. Technical requirements vary. Int.

Scènes de la vie moyenne Op.124 (Durand 1952). La Marche au Marché; Anséanic Dance; Castles in Spain; Saut périlleux du poulet. A most attractive suite. M-D.

Artur Schnabel (1882–1951) Germany

Drei Klavierstücke Op.15 (Verlag Dreililien 1907; LC). Rhapsodie C; Nachtbild f♯; Walzer C. These works sound like a mixture of Brahms, Reger, and Richard Strauss. M-D.

Piece in Seven Movements (EBM 1947) 33½ min. Moderato semplice; Vivace un poco resoluto; Allegretto piacevole; Allegretto agitato; Vivacissimo; Adagio (a variation of No.1). A lengthy, involved work reflecting the influence of Schönberg. Requires the most advanced pianism and mature musicianship. D.

Douce tristesse, Rêverie. Diabolique, Scherzo. Valse mignonne (Simrock). Early works with a "turn of the century" Viennese flavor. Originally titled *Three Piano Pieces*; the publisher supplied these names. M-D.

Alfred Schnittke (1934–1998) Russia

Sonata II (Sikeski). Clusters, strong dynamics contrasts, improvised finale. D.

Johann Jean Schobert (1720–1767) Germany

In Dr. Burney's *A General History of Music* Vol.II, p.957, the author noted that the main merit of Schobert's music was to bring "the symphonic, or modern overture style" to the harpsichord. Nevertheless, his keyboard writing is very pianistic and had some influence on the young Mozart, who arranged a movement of a Schobert sonata as the second movement of his Concerto K.39, (1767). A selection of Schobert's compositions is found in DDT, Vol.39, which also includes a thematic index.

Sonata F Op.8 (Saint-Foix—Senart 1923) 11pp. Allegro moderato; Andante; Polonaise; Minuetto (and Trio). Spontaneous and fresh but lacks thematic development. Lines flow easily. M-D.

Sonata Eb Op.10 in collection *Keyboard Music of the Baroque and Rococo* (Georgii—Volk), Vol.III. Originally for keyboard with accompaniment of a violin and possibly two horns. Schobert was a pioneer in making optional the accompaniment in the accompanied keyboard sonata. Elements of SA design. M-D.

See: Herbert C. Turrentine, "Johann Schobert: A Reappraisal of His Musical Style and Historical Significance," AMT, 19 (January 1979):20–22.

Othmar Schoeck (1886–1957) Switzerland
Schoeck's style is conservative and contrapuntal with strong Reger influence.

Klavierstücke Op.29 1919–20 (Br&H). Consolation and Toccata. Toccata much more difficult. M-D.

Ritornelle und Fughetten Op.68 1953–55 (Hug). Neo-Baroque; scholarly and academic exercises; idiomatic and ultraconservative writing. M-D.

Robert Schollum (1913–1987) Austria
Sonata III (Pastorale) Op.46/3 1952–63 (Dob 1975). First movement: flowing, with dancelike figuration. Second movement: a Lied; contains a few meter changes, short. Finale: quick, active octave passages; fast fingers and strong rhythmic drive are required. Nontonal. M-D to D.

24 Preludes Op.113 (Dob 01.604). Book I: 12 Preludes, varied, short, offer strong contrast to Preludes of the Baroque. Book II: 12 Preludes, more difficult than Book I. Tempo indications and interpretation directions are mainly in German. Nontonal, exploit purely pianistic sonorities. Int. to M-D.

Erwin Christian Scholz (1910–1977) Austria
Kaleidoscope. American Rhythms for Piano (Dob 1959). Book 1: Easy. Book 2: Int.

Aller Anfang ist nicht schwer (Dob 1951). 82 short, easy, musical pieces.

Pieces for Children (Dob 1960). Short, original. Easy to Int.

Sonata No.3 Op.52 (Dob 1954) 38pp. Three movements, FSF. Tonal. Last movement meter 5/8, 3/8 effectively handled. D.

Toccata (Dob 1959). Brilliant writing with a contrasting mid-section. D.

Arnold Schönberg (1874–1951) Austria
Schönberg's piano works were composed during crucial periods in his general development. They are among the most significant contributions to the repertoire. His keyboard style stresses wide-interval melodies, subtle rhythmic usage, and sonorities that require the most careful balancing of parts. Schönberg's indications are minute, verge on the finicky, and are often explained at the start of

a work. His metronome marks are only suggestions and should not be followed slavishly. An understanding and analysis of the 12-tone system used is highly desirable for analysis is a guide to performance. A complete edition is in progress with Josef Rufer as editor-in-chief. The piano works are contained in Series A, Vol.2, Part 4 (UE and Schott) with Edward Steuermann and Reinhold Brinkmann the editors.

Drei Klavierstücke 1894 (Belmont). Andantino: 41 bars; a 3/8 pulse but notated in 2/4. Andantino grazioso: 72 bars. Presto: 101 bars. Post-Romantic techniques with strong Brahms influence. More interesting than effective, and yet there are some lovely sonorities in all three pieces. M-D.

Three Piano Pieces Op.11 1908 (UE; MMP). Extensions of the Romantic character piece with a special kinship to Brahms, but Schönberg is already beginning to reject the classical principle of repetition in favor of continuous organic growth. Atonal. No.1 is powerful and expressive. No.3 is the most involved and completely unpredictable according to established principles. D.

    See: David Burge, "Schoenberg's Op.11/3," CK, 7 (July 1981):70.

    Allen Forte, "The Magical Kaleidoscope: Schoenberg's First Atonal Masterpiece, Op.11/1," *Journal of the Arnold Schoenberg Institute* (November 1981):127–68.

Six Little Piano Pieces Op.19 1911 (UE; Belmont; MMP). Least complex of the piano works. Aphoristic miniatures held together by extreme brevity and concentrated psychological content. Subtle, fleeting sketches. M-D.

    See: Hugo Leichtentritt, "Schönberg and Tonality," MM, 5 (May–June 1928):3–10. Contains an analysis of Op.19.

Five Piano Pieces Op.23 1923 (Belmont; WH). No.1: somewhat like a three-part invention. No.2: small three-part form. No.3: demonstrates various ways of using a short series as the basis for the whole piece. No.5 (Walzer): employs, for the first time, a 12-tone row as basis for both linear and vertical content of a composition. All pose difficult interpretative problems. D.

    See: Elaine Barkin, "A View of Schoenberg's Op.23/1," PNM (Fall–Winter 1973, Spring–Summer 1974):99–127.

Suite for Piano Op.25 1924 (Belmont; UE). Prelude; Gavotte; Musette; Intermezzo; M; G. All movements are built on the same row. More complex treatment than the earlier works. D.

    See: David Burge, "Schoenberg's Op.23 and 25," *Keyboard*, 7 (August 1981):56–57.

Piano Piece Op.33a 1932 (UE; Belmont). More vertically structured than earlier works; sharp contrasts, both dramatic and lyrical, elaborate use of the row. D.

    See: Eric Graebner, "An Analysis of Schoenberg's *Klavierstück* Op.33b," PNM (Fall–Winter 1973, Spring–Summer 1974):128–40.

Piano Piece Op.33b 1932 (Belmont; UE). Thinner texture than Op.33a, extended melodies. D. Both Op.33a and b are outstanding examples of abstract twentieth-century expressionism.

Selected Works (VU 50195 1995) 93pp. Drei Klavierstücke Op.11 (rev. 1924); Sech kleine Klavierstücke Op.19; Suite Op.25; Klavierstück Op.33a; Klavierstück Op.33b; Drei Klavierstücke 1894. Includes Critical notes and "Interpreting Schönberg at the Piano" and "Detailed Notes on Interpretation" by Peter Roggenkamp. Edited from the autographs, MS copies, and original editions by Rienhold Brinkmann. M-D to D.

Selected Piano Music (R. Brinkmann; P. Roggenkamp—Vienna Urtext). Includes all the solo piano music except Op.23 *Five Piano Pieces,* which could not be included because of copyright complications. Also includes three early pieces (1894) in the mode of Brahms's late piano works. Includes Opp.11, 19, 25, and 33. M-D to D.

See: David Burge, "Interpreting Schoenberg," CK, 7 (June 1981):62.

Patricia Carpenter, "The Piano Music of Arnold Schoenberg," PQ, 41 (Fall 1962):26–31; 42 (Winter 1962–63):23–29.

Ruth Friedberg, "The Solo Keyboard Works of Arnold Schönberg," MR, 23 (1962):83–96.

Philip Friedheim, "Tonality and Structure in the Early Works of Schoenberg," diss., New York University, 1963.

Dika Newlin, "The Piano Music of Arnold Schoenberg," PQ, 105 (Spring 1979): 38–43.

T. T. Tuttle, "Schönberg's Compositions for Piano Solo," MR, 18 (November 1957):300–18.

Avi Schönfeld (–   ) The Netherlands

Evocations—3 Pieces for Piano (Partitura, Utrecht, Holland). No.1: Gentle, austere with a few outbursts; needs careful pedaling and tonal control. No.2: "May be conceived as a sad, solemn and noble procession" (from the score). Dramatic mood changes. No.3: Varied textures, moods, and colors; impressing ending. M-D to D.

Animato 1994 (ESC 1995) 13pp. 3 min. Contrasting sections and textures, freely tonal, strong rhythms. M-D to D.

Ruth Schonthal (1924–   ) USA, born Germany

Schonthal is a composer of real expressive impetus.

Potpourri (CF). 10 short, bright pieces. MC. Int.

Sonata Breve (OUP 1976) 8pp. 7½ min. Fresh harmonies; silent clusters add unusual harmonics; chromatic, a warmly Romantic work. Interesting recital possibilities. M-D.

Variations in Search of a Theme (OUP) 16 min. 15 individual and contrasting sections that are to function as variations on an unstated theme. The cumulative effect of these sections (episodes) should imply a suggestion of the theme. Brittle gestures, dissonant harmonies. M-D.

Near and Far (CF). 13 musical scenes. For the more sensitive student. Int.

Gestures (Hildegard). 11 short pieces using traditional and experimental keyboard techniques. Int.

Self Portrait of the Artist as an Older Woman (Hildegard). M-D.

Pentatonics (CF 1996). 11 imaginative pieces exploiting the pentatonic scale, bi-tonality, changing meters, and parallelism. Int.

Hermann Schroeder (1904–1984) Germany
Schroeder's style leans towards neo-Baroque writing.
Minnelieder 1939 (Schott). Variations on 5 old German songs. Int. to M-D.
Sonata a 1952 (Schott). Praeludium; Fugue; Aria; Capriccio. More like a suite than a sonata. Preference for quartal harmony. M-D.
Sonata II f♯ 1953 (Schott). Three movements. Fluent, facile, thin textures, attractive harmonic and melodic construction, MC. M-D.
Sonata piccola (Gerig 1039 1974) 18pp. Allegro; Andante; Poco Allegretto; Molto Vivace. Freely tonal, quartal and quintal harmonies. M-D.

Heinz Schröter (1907–1974) Germany
Reflections 1973 (Gerig 1060) 28pp. 17 min. Praeludium: dramatic gestures in Allegro deciso outer sections. Andante espressivo mid-section. Romanze: tranquil and rubato melody spread over keyboard. Toccata: Vivace agitato e ritmico, many seconds used to provide rhythmic drive. Epilog: varied figurations, dissonant. Actually a four-movement suite. MC. M-D.

Franz Schubert (1797–1828) Austria
Schubert was equally at home in piano, vocal, and chamber music. Great lyric beauty, bold harmonic vocabulary, natural spontaneity, and intimate writing, sometimes coupled with large spatial design, characterize Schubert's unique keyboard style. A few of the outer movements in the sonatas may seem long, but as Robert Schumann said, they are of "heavenly lengths" and under no circumstances should any of these movements be cut. According to Walther Dürr, MT, 1619 (January 1978):68, in Schubert's autographs *decrescendo* means "getting gradually softer," while *diminuendo* means "getting gradually softer and slower," the latter indication customarily being followed by *a tempo*. The piano music falls into three broad categories: dances, piano pieces, and sonatas. D. numbers refer to O. E. Deutsch, *Schubert: Thematic Catalogue of All His Works in Chronological Order* (New York: W. W. Norton, 1951). See also Reinhard van Hoorickx, "Thematic Catalogue of Schubert's Works: New Additions, Corrections and Notes," *Revue Belge Musicologie*, 28–30 (1974–76):136–71, which lists more than a hundred new pieces—either omitted previously or discovered since the Deutsch Catalogue appeared—with corrections and additional notes.
Complete Piano Music (Dover). Reprint of Vol.V of the critical edition of 1884–97 (Epstein—Br&H). Divided into *Complete Sonatas* and *Shorter Works for Pianoforte Solo* (34 pieces).

DANCES:

Schubert wrote 452 short dances, including Menuetts, German Dances, Ländler, Waltzes, Ecossaises, and Galops. The easiest are *20 Minuette* (D. 41); *Ländler* (D. 378, 679, 681); *17 Ländler* (D. 145); *Ecossaises* (D. 421, 511, 529, 299, 781). Slightly more difficult are the *Waltzes* Opp.9, 18, 33, and *Kleine Deutsche Tänze* (D. 722). More difficult are the *34 Valses sentimentales* Op.50; 16 *Waltzes* Op.33; 12 *Ländler* Op. 171. Finally, the most difficult of the dance pieces are 6 *German Dances* (D. 820); 12 *Grazer Waltzes* Op.91; and the 12 *Valses nobles* Op.77.

Dances (P. Mies—Henle). Vol.I: 20 *Menuette* (D. 41); 2 *Menuette* (D. 91); 12 *Little German Dances* (D. 128); *Waltz* c♯ (D. 139); 12 *Waltzes*; 17 Ländler; 9 *Ecossaises* Op.18 (D. 145); 20 *Easy Waltzes* Op. 127 (D. 146); *Ecossaise* D (D. 158); 12 *Ecossaises* (D. 299); *Menuette* A, E, D (D. 334–36); 36 *Erste Walzer*, Op.9 (D. 365); 17 *German Dances* (D. 366); 8 *Ländler* (D. 378); 3 *Menuette* (D. 380); 12 *German Dances* (D. 420).

Vol.II: 6 *Ecossaises* (D. 421); *Ecossaise* E♭ (D. 511); 8 *Ecossaises* (D. 529); *Menuett* c♯ (D. 600); *Trio* (D. 610); *German Dance, Ecossaise* (D. 643); 2 *Ländler* (D. 679); 8 *Ländler* (D. 681); 5 *Ecossaisen* (D. 697); *Variation c on a Waltz of Diabelli* (D. 718); *German Dance* G♭ (D. 722); 16 *Ländler*; 2 *Ecossaises* Op.67 (D. 734); *Galop, 8 Ecossaises* Op. 49 (D. 735); 2 *German Dances* (D. 769); 34 *Valses sentimentales* Op.50 (D. 779); 11 *Ecossaisen* (D. 781); *Ecossaise* D (D. 782); 16 *German Dances, 2 Ecossaisen* Op.33 (D. 783); 12 *Ländler* Op.171 (D. 790); 6 *German Dances* (D. 820); 2 *German Dances* (D. 841); *Albumblatt* G (D. 844); 12 *Grazer Walzer* Op.91 (D. 924); *Grazer Galop* (D. 925); 12 *Valse nobles* Op.77 (D. 969); 6 *German Dances* (D. 970); 12 *German Dances* (D. 971–75); *Cotillon* (D. 976); 8 *Ecossaisen* (D. 977); 4 *Walzer* (D. 978–80); 3 *Ecossaisen* (D. 816); Appendix containing 32 pieces from D. 354, 355, 370, 374, 640, 680, 995. Int. to M-D.

Dance Album (P. Mies—Henle). 12 *Waltzes* from Opp.18, 9, 67; 18 *Waltzes* from Opp.50, 33, 171; D. 820, Op.91, D. 610, D. 718. Int. to M-D.

Complete Dances for the Piano (A. Weinmann, H. Kann—VU 1973) Preface, critical notes, and sources in English and German. Vol.I: works published during Schubert's lifetime or shortly thereafter. Vol.II: later sets and smaller individual pieces. Some dynamic and phrasing marks are found in parentheses with no explanation. Few critical notes. Remarks on musical details contained in footnotes at bottom of page. Int. to M-D.

Dances (GS L1537). German dances and écossaises Op.33; Ländler Opp.67, 171, and posthumous; Last Waltzes from Op.127; Minuets (posthumous); Trio E; Valse nobles, Op.77; Valses sentimentales from Op.50; Waltzes, Opp.9a, 9b, 91a; Waltzes and écossaises from Op.18a. Int. to M-D.

33 Dances (Ferguson—ABRSM 1983) 28pp. Two sets of waltzes, 16 in each, divided by a Minuetto that serves as an interlude. Many of these were probably improvised at social evenings with Schubert's friends. The editor has chosen a sequence in which the dances follow one another smoothly as far as key and contrast are concerned. Each set may be played separately, or the two may be joined to form an unbroken whole. Includes Deutsch and opus numbers. Helpful introduction. Int. to M-D.

Dances for Piano (P. Zeitlin—TP 1976) 19pp. Original dances through the twelve major keys with an introduction and finale in minor keys (fourteen dances in all). Int.

See: Lynn Rice-See, "Schubert's Wonderful Dances," *Clavier*, 36/1 (January 1997):14–17.

The Easier Schubert (Eve Barsham—Elkin). 45 pieces, mainly écossaises, minuets, ländler, waltzes, and other dances. Serves as an excellent introduction to Schubert. Fingering and pedaling as well as some dynamics have been added. Concise and helpful preface on the dance forms. Int.

Il mio primo Schubert (Pozzoli—Ric 1956) 17pp. 2 Scottish Dances G, B♭; Little Waltz D; Ländler A; Waltzes Op.9/2, 3, 11, 12; Op.67/15; Sentimental Waltzes Op.50/3, 11, 13, 17; Dance A♭; Moment musical Op.94/3. Int.

My First Schubert, Book 2 (Rattalino—Ric). 12 pieces including two duets. Mainly dances such as Minuetto, Ländler, Danza tedesca, Walzer sentimental, and Galop. The duets are of the student–teacher type, with one part more difficult than the other. Easy to Int.

PIANO PIECES:

Impromptus, Moments Musicaux (Gieseking—Henle; Badura-Skoda—VU 50001, published with *Drei Klavierstücke*).

4 Impromptus Op.90 (D.899) (Badura-Skoda—VU50001, includes pencil sketch of No.1; Ferguson—ABRSM). c: continuous variations on two alternating themes; many repeated chords for left hand. E♭: calls for brilliant finger work in outer sections with strongly contrasted mid-section and coda; one of the most popular of both sets. G♭: title given by original publisher; unique melodic and harmonic usage; requires a beautiful singing legato line. A♭: right-hand rotation study, lyric mid-section. M-D.
See: David Goldberger, "A Posthumous Lesson with Artur Schnabel," *The Piano Teacher*, 7/6 (July–August 1965):5–7. On *Impromptu* Op.90/4.

4 Impromptus Op.142 (D.935) (Badura-Skoda—VU 50001, urtext edition plus facsimile of autograph of Op.142/2). Both Robert Schumann and Alfred Einstein believed this work to be a sonata. f: lengthy, a combination of rondo and SA designs. A♭: easiest of the set; a lyric quality permeates the work. B♭: one of Schubert's most beautiful sets of variations; theme and 5 variations. f: most difficult of the set; requires even scale work and a fine staccato. M-D.
See: Valerie Dyke, "Schubert Impromptus," *Music Teacher*, 58 (August 1979):16–18. A discussion of Op.142/2,3.

The Impromptus D. 899 (Op.90), D.935 (Op. posth. 142) (C. Landon—Br 5611) from the New Schubert Edition.

Schubert's naïveté leaves room for a good deal of sophistication, nowhere more clearly confirmed than in such cameolike works as the *Impromptus* and the *Moments Musicaux*. And nowhere are the exquisitely concentrated moments of poignancy and charm more difficult to capture in performance.

Drei Klavierstücke (D.946) 1828 (Mies—Henle; Ferguson—ABRSM; CFP). e♭: energetic Allegro assai contrasts with two Andante sections. E♭: 5-part form with two episodes. C: allegro with sharply accented syncopations and interesting harmonies. Approximate difficulty of the Impromptus.

6 Moments Musicaux Op.94 (D.780) 1823–27 (Henle and Study Edition with Opp.90 and 142; Badura-Skoda—VU; Ferguson—ABRSM; CFP; Lympany—Hansen House; Krust—Lemoine). C: lyric mid-section requires fine legato line. A♭: lyric, sustained, requires good pacing. f: pianissimo staccato and careful balance of hands required; enharmonic modulations. c♯: clean unaccented right-hand passage-work required; Bachlike. f: powerful chord and octave figuration. A♭: poetic, chordal legato required. Among the earliest and finest examples of Romantic miniatures, pieces of exquisite perfection. Can be played in isolation or in sequence. Int. to M-D.

Variation on a Waltz by Diabelli (D.718) 1821. Short, Schubertian harmonies. In collection *Small Works* (Pauer—Br&H) Int.

Albumblatt G (D.844) (Pauer—Br&H). In collection *Small Works*. Sometimes listed as *Waltz* G. Int.

Allegretto c (D.915) 1827. In preceding Pauer collection and *400 Years of European Keyboard Music*. Similar to a *Moment Musical*. Int.

2 Scherzi B♭, D♭ (D.593) 1817 (Schott; Ric). The first one is easier. Int.

5 Klavierstücke (D.459) 1816 (Henle 150; ABRSM; Dover 22648-4 Pa). See *Sonata* E (D.459).

Klavierstück A (D.604) 1818? (Dover 22648-4 Pa). Alfred Einstein suggests this movement was originally written for *Sonata* D Op.53 (D.850) (1825). M-D.

Adagio E (D.612) 1818 (Dover 22648-4 Pa). Chromatic vocabulary. M-D.

10 Variations F on an Original Theme (D.156) 1815 (EMT). Also available with *13 Variations on a Theme of Anselm Hüttenbrenner* (Ferguson—ABRSM). D.156 was composed when Schubert was 18. It is based on a 21-bar theme; Var.4 is in the tonic minor key; Var.8 ends with cadenza-like passages; Var.9 has trills and fast scalar passages; Var.10 is full of drama, an exciting conclusion. M-D.

13 Variations on a Theme of Anselm Hüttenbrenner (D.576) 1817 (Br&H). Also available with *10 Variations F on an Original Theme* (Ferguson—ABRSM). Theme is from Hüttenbrenner's first String Quartet E Op.3 published in 1816 or 1817. Not as difficult as D.156. Fingering is included in the Ferguson edition. M-D.

Adagio and Rondo D♭, E (D.505–6) Op.145 1816 (Dover 22648-4 Pa). Deutsch says the association of these two works is spurious. The original form of the Adagio seems to be the second movement of the *Sonata* f (D.625) 1818. M-D.

March E (D.606) 1818 (Dover 22648–4 Pa). Trio in A♭. M-D.

Walzer (R. Strauss—UE 1970). A simple waltz Schubert improvised at a wedding. Int.

Ungarische Melodie D.817 1824 (Dob 831) Preface in German and English. The original shorter version of the third movement of the *Divertissement à la hongroise* for Piano Duo, D.818. Right hand has many dotted rhythms and grace notes to give the Hungarian flavor. Some octave leaps but no large chords. Fine encore. Int.

9 Short Piano Pieces (Ferguson—ABRSM). These pieces cover most of Schubert's life from the Andante C (D.29), composed at age 15, to the Allegretto c (D.915), written 18 months before his death. Fingering added. Int.

Klavierstücke; Klaviervariationen (Haberkamp—Henle 444 1992) 71pp. Andante D.29 (1812); Zehn Variationen D.156; Adagio D.178; Variations on a theme of Anselm Hüttenbrenner D. 576; Two Scherzos D.593; Fantasie D.605; Marsch D.606; Hungarian Melody D.915 (1827). Several of these works were discovered relatively recently. D.156 was Schubert's first large piano work. Int. to M-D.

Franz Schubert Piano Compositions (Tucker—CPP/Belwin 1993) 32pp. Andante; Four Dances from Op.33; Four Ecossaises; Impromptu Op.142/2; Marche Militaire; Menuetto from Sonata Op.78; Minuet F; Moment Musical Op.94/3; Scherzo B♭; Two Ländler from Op.171; Waltz a. Does not distinguish between composer's and editor's markings.

Moments Musicaux D.780 (Op.94), *Hungarian Melody* D.817, *Allegretto* c D. 915, *Three Piano Pieces* D. 946 (Br 5615) from the New Schubert Edition. 44pp. Int. to M-D.

EDITIONS OF THE SONATAS:

Klaviersonaten, Vol.I (Mies, Theopold—Henle 146): Sonatas A Op. posth. 120 D.664; a Op.42 D.845; a Op. posth. 143 D.784; a Op. posth. 164 D.537; D Op.53 D.850; E♭ Op. posth. 122 D.568; B Op. posth. 147 D.575. Based on autographs and first editions. M-D to D. Vol.II (Mies, Theopold—Henle 148): Sonatas G Op.78 D.894; c, A, B, D.958–60. Based on autographs and first editions. Vol.III (P. Badura-Skoda, Theopold—Henle 150): Contains the early and unfinished sonatas: Sonatas A♭, D.557; C, D.279/346; C, D.613/612; C ("Reliquie") D.840; D♭, D.567; E, D.157; E (5 Klavierstücke) D.459; e, D.566/506; f, D.625/505; f♯ D.571/604/570; and Appendix containing early sketches for D.154, D.157, D.279. Preface in German, French, and English. Critical note in German and English. Badura-Skoda has completed the movements of the incomplete works for practical use, basing his work on available fragments. Based on autographs and first editions.

Other editions: Ferguson—ABRSM, 3 vols.; Tirimo—VU, 2 vols.; Weismann, Erber—CFP, 2 vols.; E. Ratz—UE, 2 vols.; Dover, reprint of Br&H 1888 edition; Pauer—Br&H, 3 vols.; Köhler, Ruthardt—CFP, 2 vols.; K, 2 vols.

Sonata 1 E (D.157) 1815 17 min. Planned as a four-movement work but only three movements exist. Allegro ma non troppo. Andante: elegiac. Menuetto —Allegro vivace: vigorous. M-D.

See: Paul Badura-Skoda, "Paul Badura-Skoda on the Schubert Sonatas," an interview with Dean Elder, *Clavier*, 12 (March 1973):7–16. Also includes score to Schubert Sonata E, D.157 edited by Elder.

Sonata 2 C (D.279) 1815 15 min. Unfinished, three movements exist. Allegro moderato; Andante; Minuetto: Allegro vivace. In the opening movement daring modulation and thematic development are important; recapitulation begins on the subdominant rather than the tonic, a device Schubert used in later works. M-D.

Sonata 3 E (D.459) 1816 27 min. Published as *Fünf Klavierstücke*. The autograph with "Sonate" written on it was discovered later. Allegro moderato: concise; alternation of major and minor, interesting modulations in the development. Scherzo—Allegro: more interesting than second scherzo but lengthy. Adagio: the finest movement. Scherzo con trio—Allegro. Allegro patetico. M-D.

Sonata 4 a (D.537) Op.164 1817 17 min. Allegro ma non troppo; Allegretto quasi Andantino; Allegro vivace. First movement has an energetic opening, unequal phrase lengths, whimsical development. Second movement appears later in *Sonata* A (D.959) in a more spacious conception. M-D.

See: Harold Truscott, "Organic Unity in Schubert's Early Sonata Music," MMR, 89, N.992 (March–April 1959):62–66. Deals primarily with *Sonata* Op.164.

Sonata 5 A♭ (D. 557) 1817 9½ min. Allegro moderato; Andante; Allegro. Begins A♭, ends E♭. Haydn influence. M-D.

Sonata 6 e (D. 566) 1817 16 min. Moderato; Allegretto; Scherzo—Allegro vivace; Allegretto moto (D. 506, Kathleen Dale—British and Continental Agencies 1948). Vintage Schubert. Deserves performance. M-D.

See: Robert Simpson, "Schubert. Pianoforte Sonata in e minor, edited by Kathleen Dale," MR, X (May 1949):147–48.

Sonata 7 E♭ (D.568) Op.122 1817. 24 min. (Swarsenski—CFP). Allegro moderato; Andante molto; Allegro moderato. Light, charming, well unified in mood. Smooth piano writing. Originally in D♭ (D.567) (Dover). In the E♭ version, the outer movements have shorter and sometimes different development sections; the slow movement is in the tonic minor; there is no Menuet movement; and the last movement is incomplete. M-D.

See: Harold Truscott, "The Two Versions of Schubert's Op.122," MR, 14 (May 1953):89–106.

Sonata 8 f♯ (D.570-1) 1817? Scherzo, fragment of Allegro f♯ with the bare possibility that the isolated Andante A (D.604) supplies the missing slow movement. Completed by Walter Rehberg in 1927 (Steingraber 1928) as well as by Vernon Duke (Chappell 1968).

See: SSB, p.208.

Sonata 9 B (D.575) Op.147 1817 21 min. Allegro ma non troppo: unusual key relationships and abrupt modulations. Andante: anticipates Mendelssohn; encloses a dramatic mid-section. Scherzo—Allegretto: contrapuntal textures. Allegro giusto: motivic development plays a large part; restless.

See: Maurice J. E. Brown, "An Introduction to Schubert's Sonatas of 1817," MR, 12 (1951):35–44.

Sonata 10 C (D.613) 1818. Only second movement, Moderato, is complete.

First and last movements incomplete; no tempo indicated in final movement.

Sonata 11 f (D.625, 505) 1818 19 min. Allegro: stops abruptly at the end of the development section after some bold modulations. Scherzo—Allegretto. Adagio (D.505): highly colored. Allegro: remarkable energetic drive. All four movements are not published together. In his edition of the Sonatas (UE, 2 vols.), Erwin Ratz has supplied the recapitulation of the first movement and other short missing passages. Walter Rehberg also completed this sonata (Steingraber 1928).

Sonata 12 c♯ (D.655) 1819. Contains only a sketch of the first movement.

Sonata 13 A (D.664) Op.120 1819? 22 min. (Mies, Theopold—Henle). One of the most compact, technically easy, and frequently performed sonatas. Allegro moderato: mainly lyric, octaves in development present the most technical difficulty; little contrast in this SA design. Andante: a persistent rhythm, often found in the faster movements; characteristic alternation of major to minor and reverse. Allegro: SA design; the most animated and taxing movement. M-D.

See: Christine A. Nagy, "Masterclass with John Browning," *Clavier*, 20 (January 1981):24–25. Focuses on the first movement of Op.120 and includes the music, pp.26–30.

Sonata 14 a (D.784) Op.143 1823 (Henle) 21 min. Robert Schumann considered this one of Schubert's best sonatas. Allegro giusto: lean textures, broken octaves, and powerful development make this one of the most original movements in all of the sonatas. Andante: songlike, punctuated by curious rhythmic *ppp* octaves. Allegro vivace: constructed around three contrasted figures—a triplet idea, a vigorous rhythmic idea, and a lyric tune—which are worked into a strong concluding movement; octaves in the final ten bars formidable. M-D to D.

Sonata 15 C (D.840) 1825 (Reliquie) 34 min., with the Krennek completion. Only the first two movements are complete. Probably Schubert's most important unfinished sonata. Completed by Armin Knab (1881–1951) (CFP), Ernst Krenek (UE 1921), Walter Rehberg (Steingraber 1927), and Einfeldt (PIC 1991). Moderato: SA design with the two main ideas not greatly contrasted but spread out spaciously. Andante: c, rondo with second episode a recapitulation of the first. Menuetto—Allegretto. Rondo—Allegro. M-D.

See: Harold Truscott, "Schubert's Unfinished Piano Sonata in C (1825)," MR, 18 (1958):37–44.

Sonata 16 a (D.845) Op.42 1825 31 min. (Mies, Theopold—Henle; Bischoff—WH). This large-scale work was Schubert's best-known sonata during his lifetime. Moderato: consistently fine throughout with two highly contrasted ideas that must progress at basically the same tempo. Andante poco moto: set of 5 variations, displays some of Schubert's finest contrapuntal writing. Scherzo—Allegro vivace: with Trio. Rondo—Allegro vivace: thin textures, varied phrase lengths, unusual economy of material; calls for most skillful handling of the piano. M-D to D.

See: David Goldberger, "An Unexpected New Source for Schubert's A Minor Sonata, Op.42, D.845," *19th Century Music* (Summer 1982):3ff. The new source is a copy of the Pennauer edition in the collection of pianist Jacob Lateiner that differs quite markedly from the 1826 publication.

Brian Newbould, "A Schubert Sonata," *Music Teacher*, 56 (November 1977): 14–16. Discussion and analysis of D.845.

Sonata 17 D (D.850) Op.53 1825 31 min. Written for the virtuoso pianist Karl Maria Bocklet, and Schubert treats the piano as a virtuoso instrument. Allegro vivace: SA design worked out in a masterly way even though the thematic material is not Schubert's best. Andante con moto: rich texture, spacious lay-out, and harmonic interest make this rondo with a returning second episode one of Schubert's finest slow movements. Scherzo—Allegro vivace: energetic; linked to the Austrian dances Schubert loved so much; the trio includes some marvelous modulations. Rondo—Allegro moderato: happy, with two lengthy episodes; has deservedly been called "the crown of the sonata" by Alfred Einstein. Great vitality. M-D to D.

Sonata 18 G (D.894) Op.78 1826 29 min. (Br; Bischoff—WH; British Library, facsimile edition). First published under the title of "Fantasie, Andante, Menuetto und Allegretto." Schumann called this Schubert's "most perfect sonata in form and spirit." Molto moderato cantabile: effective long crescendo in the development section provides a needed contrast to the lyric serenity in the rest of the movement. Andante: similar in form to those in Sonatas D.840 and 850. Menuetto—Allegretto moderato: dancelike. Allegretto: spaciously conceived Rondo with two episodes. Exciting work but difficult to sustain. D.

See: Delia Calapai, "Schnabel and Schubert," *Piano Journal*, 2/5 (June 1981):7–9; and *Clavier*, 22/1 (January 1983):20–22. Emphasize *Sonata* G, Op.78.

Sonata 19 c (D.958) 1828 (Br) 28 min. This work as well as D.959 and 960 were all composed in less than four weeks. They were first published as "Drei grosse Sonaten." This somber work is probably the least known of the three. Allegro: stormy, should not go too fast, an "Allegro Moderato" warning appears on the sketch. Adagio: expressive rondolike design as used in D.840, 850, and 894. Menuetto—Allegro: spontaneous and wistful. Allegro: SA-like finale. D.

Sonata 20 A (D.959) 1828 (Br) 35 min. Allegro: opens solemnly with brilliant but controlled passage-work; development is based on a small theme from the codetta. Andantino: opens as a barcarolle but soon moves to more improvisatory section and works to a great climax; one of the most difficult movements in all of Schubert. Scherzo—Allegro vivace: playful. Rondo—Allegretto: lengthy and lyrical, of great beauty; theme was used in the Allegretto of D.537. D.

See: Martin Chusid, "Cyclicism in Schubert's Piano Sonata in A Major (D.959)," PQ, 104 (Winter 1978–79):38–40.

Adele Marcus, "Performance Hints on a Schubert Sonata," *Clavier*, 15 (March 1976):27–29. Discusses *Sonata* A D.959.

Sonata 21 B♭ (D.960) 1828 (Br) 32 min. A transcendental work of unique individuality. Molto moderato: one of the quietest and longest of Schubert's first movements. Andante sostenuto: in the unusual key of c♯, evolves a poetic and religious atmosphere of great beauty. Scherzo—Allegro vivace con delicatezza: exploits a varied harmonic range and utilizes bold chromaticism. Allegro ma non troppo: Beethoven influence, opening centered on the dominant of c, as in the beginning of the finale of Beethoven's Op.130 string quartet. D.

See: William G. Hill, "The Genesis of Schubert's Posthumous Sonata in B♭," MR, 12 (November 1951):269–78.

Walter Klein, "Masterclass on Sonata B♭, D.960, first movement," *Clavier*, 20 (April 1981):18–21.

Konrad Wolff, "Observations on the Scherzo of Schubert's B♭ Sonata Op. posth. D.960," PQ, 92 (Winter 1975–76):28–29.

Maurice J. E. Brown, *Essays on Schubert* (New York: St. Martin's Press, 1966). See especially "Towards an Edition of the Pianoforte Sonatas," pp.197–216.

———, "Schubert's Piano Sonatas," MT, 1592 (October 1975):873–75.

Arthur Satz, "Alfred Brendel: The Playing of Schubert Sonatas Is a New Art," *Musical America* 23 (August 1973):12–13.

Miriam K. Whaples, "Schubert's Piano Sonatas of 1817–1818," PQ, 104 (Winter 1978):34–37.

Arnold Whittal, "The Sonata Crisis: Schubert in 1828," MR, 30 (1969):124–30.

Fantasia C (D.760) Op.15 1822 "Wanderer Fantasia." (Badura-Skoda—VU; Herttrich—Henle 282; Georgii—Schott; Cortot—Salabert; Liszt—Augener; Niemann—CFP; Bischoff—WH). Allegro con fuoco ma non troppo; Adagio; Presto; Allegro. Here Schubert writes for the piano in a grandiose, orchestral style. All themes (except the first subsidiary theme of the Scherzo) are derived from the song "Der Wanderer." Each movement deals with its various transformations, anticipating similar procedures in Liszt's *Sonata* b. Projection of epic power is needed and virtuoso octave technique is required briefly in this very forward-looking work. D.

See: Elaine Brody, "Mirror of His Soul—Schubert's Fantasy in C (D.760)," PQ, 104 (Winter 1978–79):23–24, 26, 28, 30–31.

Charles Fisk, "Questions about the Persona of Schubert's 'Wanderer Fantasy,'" *College Music Symposium*, 29 (1989):19–30.

Ted Joselson, "Schubert's Wanderer Fantasy," CK, 4 (December 1978):63. Examines the Adagio movement from a performer's point of view.

Fantasie C (D.605) 1818? "Grazer Fantasie." (Walter Dürr—Br 19101). Moderato con espressione; Alla polacca; Moderato con espressione. This work was found in 1962. It is not based on SA design but section follows section until the end, when the introduction is repeated, as in Mozart's *Fantasy* c K.

475. Some stylistic points might possibly tie the work to Anselm Hütten-brenner or other composers. Dürr does point out similarities to D. 605, 612, and 613. It is a brilliant work and could appeal to contemporary tastes, as it did in Schubert's day. Not as difficult as D. 760. M-D.

See: Miriam K. Whaples, "Style in Schubert's Piano Music from 1817 to 1818," MR, 35 (1974):260–80. Discusses the "Graz" Fantasy and the eight piano sonatas of these years.

Fantasy c, Largo, D.993 (J. Demus—TP 1979; PQ, 104 [Winter 1978–79]:12–17) 4½ min. This first publication commemorates the 150th anniversary of Schu-bert's death. It is of major interest in that it represents a rare composition for the keyboard from Schubert's mid-teens (ca.1812). Listed in the Schu-bert Foundation catalogue as "Largo for Clavicembalo." The editor, Jörg Demus, has titled the piece *Fantasy*, because of its resemblance to the fa-mous Mozart C-minor *Fantasy* (K.475). The Schubert work is a three-part song form Largo-Andantino-Largo. Motives evolve into melodies; fluctu-ating tonalities; third-relationships. M-D.

See: Jörg Demus, "Two Fantasies—Mozart's Fantasy in C Minor (K.475) and Schubert's Fantasy in C Minor (D.993)," PQ, 104 (Winter 1978–79):9–11. A perceptive comparison of these two works.

COLLECTIONS:

Schubert—An Introduction to His Piano Works (Margery Halford—Alfred 1977) 64pp. Includes: facsimile of an Album Leaf; Allegretto D.915; Andante D.29; 8 Ecossaises; 2 German Dances Op.33/2, 15; Impromptu Op.142/2; Ländler, from 17 Ländler No.13; Moments Musicaux Op.94/3, 5; Scherzo I & II D.593; Scherzo con Trio from Five Pieces, No.4; Variations on a Theme by Anselm Hüttenbrenner D.935 (7 variations omitted); 4 Waltzes. Subjects discussed in the foreword include Schubert's biography, style and interpre-tation, ornamentation, origin and sources. An altogether excellent contri-bution. Int. to M-D.

6 Popular Pieces (CFP 1825a). Theme from Bb Impromptu Op.142/3; Scherzo Op. posth.; Moment Musical Op.94/3; Andante from Sonata A Op.120; 2 Waltzes from Op.9a; 6 German Dances from Op.33. Int. to M-D.

Schubert (Stephen Bishop—OUP 1972) 58pp. Part of the *Oxford Keyboard Clas-sics* series. Includes: Sonata Db D.567; two movements from unfinished Sonata C ("Reliquie") D.840; Variation c (on the Diabelli waltz) D.719; Al-legretto c, D.915; Valse sentimentale A, D.779/13. Also contains notes on interpretation, including instruments of the period, dynamics, pedaling, or-namentation. Int. to M-D.

Schubert. The First Book for Young Pianists (M. Halford—Alfred 1977) 24pp. Many of the selections included are taken from *Schubert—An Introduction to His Piano Works*. Contains 3 Ländler; 3 Menuets and Trios; 7 Ecossaises; 2 German Dances; 4 Waltzes. Int.

Schubert—Easiest Piano Pieces (Volger—CFP 5015). Easy Viennese dances and pieces including: 3 Minuets; Valse noble; 7 Waltzes; 6 German Dances; 2 Ländler; 4 Valses sentimentales; 3 Ecossaises; Impromptu; Moment musical f. Int.

Schubert—Easier Favorites (Heinrichschofen—N4051) 39pp. 9 pieces ranging from 7 Viennese Dances to Impromptu B♭ Op.142/3. Int. to M-D.

See: Paul Badura-Skoda, "Textual Problems in Schubert—Discrepancies Between Text and Intention," PQ, 104 (Winter 1978–79):49–55.

Malcolm Bilson, "Schubert's Piano Music and the Pianos of His Time," PQ, 104 (Winter 1978–79):56–61.

Alfred Brendel, "Schubert's Piano Sonatas, 1822–1828," in *Musical Thoughts and Afterthoughts* (Princeton: Princeton University Press, 1976), pp.57–74.

Maurice J. E. Brown, "Schubert's Piano Sonatas," MT, 1592 (October 1975):873–75.

Josef Dichler, *Interpretationsprobleme bei Schuberts Klaviermusik* (Problems of interpretation in Schubert's piano music), *Osterreichische Musikzeitschrift* 27 (April 1972):200–207. In German. The author claims that in general Schubert's music poses no stylistic difficulties for the present-day interpreter, but that in his piano music there are problems of a technical and notational nature. Since Schubert, in contrast to Chopin, for example, provided no pedal indications, several entirely different-sounding performances of a particular passage are possible, and the difficulty is compounded by the fact that the sense of Schubert's pause and staccato marks is not always clear. Moreover, the value of dotted notes is ambiguous when triplet rhythms are present in another voice.

Stewart Gordon, "Anniversary Reflections on Schubert's Solo Keyboard Music," AMT, 28 (November–December 1978):20, 22.

Maurice Hinson and F. E. Kirby, "A Schubert Bibliography," PQ, 104 (Winter 1978–79):63–64.

Christa Landon, "New Schubert Finds," MR, 31 (August 1970):215–31.

Ernest G. Porter, *Schubert's Piano Works* (London: Dobson, 1980).

Olga Samaroff, "The Piano Music of Schubert," MQ, 14 (October 1928):596–609.

Walter Schenkman, "Impromptu Thoughts on a Schubert Anniversary," *Clavier*, 17 (October 1978):24–33. Includes "A Lesson on a Schubert Impromptu" (Op.90/2).

Harold Truscott, "Organic Unity in Schubert's Early Sonata Music," MMR, 89 (March–April 1959):62–66.

Richard Van Hoorickx, "Fugue and Counterpoint in Schubert's Piano Music," PQ, 105 (Spring 1979):48–51. Also includes a Fugue of Schubert, D.24D, written in 1811(?).

Konrad Wolff, "Schubert's 'L'istesso Tempo,'" PQ, 106 (Summer 1979):38–39.

Manfred Schubert (1937–   ) Germany

Variazioni 1960 (DVFM 8039) 19pp. 11 min. Theme and 14 contrasting variations (each metronomically indicated), including a waltz, minuet, boogie, and tango. Extremely musical and well made. No fingering or pedaling included. M-D.

Erwin Schulhoff (1894–1942), Czechoslovakia

Schulhoff studied with Max Reger and associated with the German dadaists. He died in a concentration camp. His music is having a renaissance because of the interest in musicians and artists whose lives were cut short by the Nazis.

11 Inventions Op.36 1921 (Schott 1993) 16pp. 10 min. Preface in German and English. Influence of French impressionists, Schönberg, and Scriabin. Atonal, interesting sonorities, no meter indicated. M-D.

Ostinato 1923 (UE 7933) 10pp. "Six delightful piano pieces for large and small children" (from the score). Papa; Mama; —da . . . . da—; —hopp . . . . hopp— ; —a . . . . a— : —trara—. MC. Int. to M-D.

Suite II (UE 7934 1925) 16pp. Preludio; Melodia; Toccatina; Pastorale; Gigue. Neoclassic style. M-D.

Suite III for Left Hand 1926 (Schott). Displays an abundance of color and a flow of musical ideas, especially in the contrasting dance elements. Motoric rhythm in finale. M-D to D. M-D if played by both hands.

5 Études de Jazz 1926 (UE 8954–58) 27pp. Charleston; Blues; Chanson; Tango; Toccata sur le Shimmy "Kitten on the Keys" de Zez Confrey. Clever and tricky, but also has an emotional directness. Attractive. M-D.

Hot Music. 10 Syncopated Études (UE 8643 1929) 19pp. Contrasted, varied syncopations. M-D.

Gunther Schuller (1925–   ) USA

Standpoint Rag (Margum). Mixture of Stravinsky and jazz styles; more difficult than it looks. M-D.

Peter Schulthorpe (1929–   ) Australia, born Tasmania

Schulthorpe is a major force in creating a truly Australian contemporary musical language.

Night Pieces 1971 (Faber 1973) 4½ min. Snow, Moon and Flowers: delicate; ephemeral; black-key glissando. Night: quiet, languorous, short. Stars: dart about in calmness. Mysterious and subtle sonorities; should be played directly on the strings; harplike textures. Exact sense of timing required for these short, descriptive, and evocative little pieces. Int. to M-D.

Sonatina 1954 (Leeds) 7½ min. Fast, ritualistic, nonmelodic and nonharmonic textures and slow harmonically static melodies. In place of developing ideas, there are many repetitive variational patterns and taut miniature forms. Contains strong extra-musical associations with Australia and the legends of the Aboriginal people. M-D.

Mountains 1981 (Faber) 6pp. 5 min. Proportional rhythmic relationships, broad gestures, very sustained, dissonant. "The work is a response to the mountainous terrain of Tasmania, often known as 'Isle of Mountains,' where the composer was born" (from the score). M-D to D.

Callabonna 1962 (Faber 1989) 4pp. 4½ min. This piece started out as the first movement of a piano sonata. "While the sonata was abandoned, I kept playing this particular movement. Almost 30 years later, I finally decided officially to 'reinstate' the piano version. I called the piece *Callabonna* because it was written at the time of the beginning of my friendship with the painter Russell Drysdale, who often said that my music reminded him of the outback Lake Callabona" (from CD 3031 Move Records jacket). Mysterious, brooding mood. M-D.

Djilile 1986–89 (Faber 1989) 4pp. 4½ min. Based on Schulthorpe's adaptation of an Aboriginal melody. The composer says of the piece: "I have a special fondness for this melody, having used it in my music for the feature film *Essington* (1974); for the string orchestra work derived from it, *Port Essington* (1977); and recently in the orchestral work *Kakadu* (1988). I made this piano arrangement of it, with common material, simply for my own pleasure, and, perhaps for the pleasure of others." The title "Djilile" means "whistling duck on a billabong." The 12-bar melody, presented alone at the beginning, is the basis for the whole piece. (From CD 3031 Move Records jacket.)

Piano Music Selections (Faber) 6pp. *Landscape* 1971 12½ min.: suggests a terrain of pianistic effects ranging from flat to jagged. M-D. *Koto Music I*: in six sections, aleatoric, based on the notes of the *hirajoshi* scale. M-D. *Koto Music II*: uses the lowest five notes of the *kumoijoshi* scale, aleatoric. M-D.

Nocturnal 1989 (Faber) 6pp. 7 min. A version of the solo piano part of the slow fourth section (*Come notturno*) from the composer's *Piano Concerto* (1983). Uses toccata-like alternation of hands. No attempt is made to include any of the orchestral music. Casts a hypnotic mood over listeners. M-D.

Two Easy Pieces (Faber) 3pp. *Sea Chant* 1971; *Left Bank Waltz* 1958. Titles and moods are evocative of Paris's Left Bank cafes; clever harmonies. Int.

Robert Schultz (1948–   ) USA

Schultz earned B.M. and M.M. degrees in theory and composition from West Virginia University. He is a music editor at Warner Brothers Publishers in Miami, FL.

Ballade Op.17 (WB 1984) 6 min. A fine piece for an advanced high school student, MC, mixed meters, lyrical midsection. Makes an excellent impression if well performed. M-D.

Montage Op.20 (WB 1986) 15 min. One movement, sectional, bold and dramatic, strong rhythms, musically challenging, pianistic, brilliant conclusion. M-D.

Five Impromptus Op.23 (WB 1993) 24pp. Contrasting, repeated patterns and groupings. Some sound more difficult than they are. MC. Int.

Winter Scenes 1975 (WB 1982) 13pp. Waiting; The Death of Autumn; Another Window. "Each of the three sketches depicts a different scene on the day of the first snowfall in a rural area of Western Pennsylvania" (from the score). Colorful, impressionistic; pieces complement each other. M-D.

Adolf Schulz-Evler (1852–1905) Poland

By the Beautiful Blue Danube. Concert Arabesque (GS; CF). This effective period piece with its virtuoso encore writing still deserves to be mentioned. D.

William Schuman (1910–1992) USA

Three-Score Set 1945 (GS). A tiny suite of three short contrasting pieces. Triadic, nonfunctional harmony, rhythmic alteration of melodic lines. M-D.

Voyage 1954 (TP). Anticipation; Caprice; Realization; Decision; Retrospection. Contrasting pieces that require more musical than technical demands. Taut, chromatic. M-D.

3 Piano Pieces (Merion). Lyrical. Pensive. Dynamic: ostinato-like, irregular rhythm, in mode that resembles Mixolydian. M-D.

Chester: Variations for Piano (Merion). Commissioned for the Eighth Van Cliburn International Piano Competition. Originally written as an overture for band. Schumann transcribed the work for solo piano, and it is awkward for the piano and unpianistic although it does contain some effective moments. D.

Clara Wieck Schumann (1819–1896) Germany

Clara Schumann's euphuistic compositions have been overshadowed by her husband's works and her own pianistic virtuosity. Her piano works display a variety of emotions including enthusiasm, melancholy, passion, and sometimes sparkle.

Quatre Polonaises Op.1 1830 (Hierholzer—R&E 1987; CF) 8pp. plus introduction in German. Composed when Clara was 11 years old. Shallow ideas, some hand-crossing, designed to show off her technical facility. One wonders how much her father, Wieck, had to do with this set. Int. to M-D.

Quatre Pièces Caractéristiques Op.5 1835–36 (Da Capo 1979) 17pp. In collection *Clara Wieck Schumann. Selected Piano Music.* Impromptu: Le Sabbat (The Witches' Sabbath): fast repeated notes and chords; requires good rebound while moving quickly over keyboard; careful pedal marks by composer. Caprice à la Boleros: opening of repeated note pattern suggests the dance, lyrical mid-section, brilliant closing. Romance: wistful and melancholy, perhaps the best piece in the set. Scène Fantastique: Le Ballet des Revenants (Ballet of the Ghosts): motifs from this piece are used in Robert Schumann's Sonata in f♯ Op.11 (1835); active figuration throughout, *pp* ending. M-D. Impromptu available separately (Lienau 1993) 6pp.

Soirées Musicales Op.6 1835 or 1836 (Glickman—Hildegard) 20pp. Toccatina: outer sections must be light and clear, lyric mid-section. Notturno: Chopin influence, requires well-projected melodic lines. Mazurka: chromatic turns, frisky grace notes, unexpected chords. Ballade: warm harmonies, varied figurations. Mazurka: Robert Schumann quotes this opening material in his *Davidsbündlertanz* Op.6; tricky grace notes. Polonaise: dance rhythm supports florid melodies; rich harmonies. M-D.

Variations de Concert sur la Cavatine du Pirate, de Bellini Op.8 1837. In collection *Clara Wieck Schumann. Selected Piano Music* (Da Capo 1979) 16pp. Clara had seen the opera in 1832 and played this work on her concert tours of 1837 and 1837–38. This piece contains large leaps, fast passages in thirds and sixths, and full arpeggiated chords. The brilliant closing made it a real crowd pleaser. M-D to D.

Souvenir de Vienne Op.9 1837–38 (Diabelli 6530 1838). Written when Clara was

18 years old and in Vienna on a concert tour. Based on Haydn's "Emperor's Hymn" and written in the brilliant style of the then popular salon music. Clara wrote to Robert from Graz in April 1838: "I am playing among others a 'Souvenir à Vienne' which I started in Vienna and finished here. It is only a little impromptu, but impressed enormously since the Austrians are quite delighted with their Folk song" (Weissweiler I, p.167). Clara had just been named Royal and Imperial Virtuosa to the Austrian Court in Vienna. M-D.

Scherzo d Op.10 1839 9pp. In collection *Clara Wieck Schumann. Selected Piano Music* (Da Capo 1979). A great dramatic display piece with two contrasting trios. Very popular with Parisian audiences. M-D.

Trois Romances Op.11 1839 10pp. In collection *Clara Wieck Schumann. Selected Piano Music* (Da Capo 1979). Andante e♭: serves as a prelude to the others. Andante g: melancholy, much rubato required, Allegro passionato midsection. Moderato A♭: waltzlike, moves through numerous keys. All in ternary form. M-D.

Quatre Pièces Fugitives Op.15 1840–44 (Draheim—Br&H). Dedicated to Marie Wieck, Clara's half-sister who was then about 13 years old. Larghetto F; Un poco agitato a; Andante espressivo D. These three character pieces are similar to the Romances Op.11. Scherzo G: sprightly; same piece is in the sonatina written for Robert at Christmas 1841. This set contains some of Clara's finest writing for the piano. M-D.

Sonata g 1841–42 (Nauhaus—Br&H 7445 1991) 32pp., first printing. Allegro; Adagio; Scherzo; Rondo. This work began as a sonatine for Robert and was presented to him at Christmas 1841; it contains only the Allegro and Scherzo. The present editor calls the work a sonata, and his preface details good reasons for this decision. Clara finished the work in January 1842 by adding the Adagio and the Rondo finale. The Scherzo is probably the most attractive movement and should not go too fast. The Rondo contains thematic references to the Allegro movement. It is good that this work is finally available. Eminently pianistic. M-D to D.

Three Preludes and Fugues Op.16 1845 (Glickman—Hildegard; Harbach—Vivace Press). Also in *Clara Wieck Schumann. Selected Piano Music* (Da Capo) 13pp. 1. g: Prelude: Andante, syncopated melody; Fugue: Allegro vivace, long subject in quarter and sixteenth notes, labored. 2. B♭: Prelude: Allegretto, flowing melody, chromatic harmony, best of the three preludes; Fugue: Andante, chromatic legato subject worked out neatly. 3. d: Prelude: Andante, imitative voices, leads attacca to the Fugue: Andante con moto, terse and turgid. Fugues have three and four voices. Written while Clara and Robert were studying the fugues of J. S. Bach. Lively subjects and arpeggios are favored, tender melodies. M-D.

Variations on a Theme by Robert Schumann Op.20 (Alfred 1200; Süddeutscher). Based on the first of the five *Albumblätter* Op.99. Brahms used this same theme for his *Variations on a Theme by Schumann* Op.9. Clara elaborates the theme considerably as the basis for her set with varied harmonies. Pianistically imaginative. M-D.

See: Maurice Hinson, "Varying Schumann's Theme," *Clavier*, 25/10 (December 1986):9–12. Discusses Clara Schumann's "Variations on a Theme of Robert Schumann" Op.20 and Johannes Brahms's "Variations on a Theme of Robert Schumann" Op.9.

Selected Piano Music (Da Capo 1979) 95pp. plus introduction. Includes: Quatre Pièces caractéristiques Op.5. Soirées Musicales Op.6: 6 pieces. Variations de Concert Op.8: based on a theme by Bellini; flashy. Scherzo Op.10. Trois Romances Op.11. Drei Praeludien und Fugen, Op.16. Salon style, Romantic writing, a valuable anthology of representative works long unavailable. Also contains a helpful essay on Clara by Pamela Susskind. M-D.

Romantic Piano Music. Book 1 (Br 6550): 3 Preludes and Fugues Op.16; Variations on a Theme by Robert Schumann Op.20; Romance g Op.21/3. Book 2 (Br 6556): Romance variée Op.3: a fairly extended work with Introduze, Romanza (with cadenza), 2 Brillante sections, Espressivo and pesante, Adagio, Allegro, Vivo, Presto. Trois Romances Op.11: No.1 D♭, Andante; No.2 g, Andante; No.3 A♭, Moderato. Scherzo Op.14c, con fuoco. Pièces fugitives Op.15: No.1 F, Larghetto; No.2 a, Un poco agitato; No.3 D, Andante espressivo; No.4 Scherzo, G. Romanze a Op.21/1. Romanze b, Christmas 1856. Book 2 is a selection of Clara Schumann's work before and after her marriage to Robert. As the editor explains, her various personal relationships and reflections are revealed; her development from superficial fashionable trends of her youth to an independent poetry inspired by Schumann and also by Brahms. Of special note are the first and last pieces (published here for the first time): Andante con sentimento, 1838; and Romanza b, 1856. Most of the pieces contain octaves and large chords. No fingering or pedaling given. M-D.

Three Kleine Klavierstücke (Marciano—Dob DM 812) 16pp. Preface in English and German. 2 Romances, 1885–86: first publications. Andante con sentimento, 1838: charming, idyllic, amiable character. M-D.

See: Donald Bea Isaak, "Clara Schumann as a Composer," *Clavier*, 15 (February 1976):22–24. Also includes Prelude and Fugue B♭ Op.16/2.

Carlos Juris, "Stylistic Links in the Piano Music of Robert and Clara Schumann," *Piano Journal*, 13/39 (October 1992):15–17, 19–22.

Pamela Susskind Pettler, "Clara Schumann's Recitals, 1832–50," *Nineteenth-Century Music*, IV (Summer 1980):71–76.

Nancy B. Reich, *Clara Schumann: The Artist and The Woman.* Ithaca, NY: Cornell University Press, 1985. 346pp.

———, "Clara's Art," *Piano Today,* 16/3 (May–June 1996):4–7. On *Andante and Allegro*, or Romance II g, from Op.11.

Eva Weissweiler, ed. *The Complete Correspondence of Clara and Robert Schumann* (New York: Peter Lang Publishing, 1994).

Robert Schumann (1810–1856) Germany

Schumann was the Romantic composer "par excellence." His creative and fresh output for piano has provided some of the most imaginative and touching music in the pianist's repertoire. The first twenty-three opera are devoted to the piano.

His creative energy flourished early and then decreased. Throughout his career Schumann was occupied writing character-pieces, and though he wrote in larger forms, he continually favored that genre. Characteristic of Schumann's piano writing was his use of fast harmonic rhythm, unusual pedal effects, syncopation and cross-rhythms, varied accompanimental figurations, chord doublings, and a unique exploitation of contracting and expanding the pianist's hand.

EDITIONS:

Piano Solos Vol.1 (W. Boetticher, W. Lampe—Henle 108): Scenes from Childhood Op.15; Album for the Young Op.68; Colored Leaves Op.99; Album Leaves Op.124. Vol.II (W. Boetticher, W. Lampe—Henle 110): Abegg-Variations Op.1; Fantasy Pieces Op.12; Arabesque Op.18; Flower Pieces Op.19; Novelettes Op.21; Night Pieces Op.23; 3 Romances Op.28; Forest Scenes Op.82; 3 Fantasy Pieces Op.111. Vol.III (W. Boetticher, H.-M. Theopold—Henle 112): Papillons Op.2; Intermezzi Op.4; Davidsbündlertänze Op.6; Carnaval Op.9; Symphonic Etudes Op.13; Kreisleriana Op.16; Carnaval Prank from Vienna Op.26. Vol.IV (W. Boetticher, H.-M. Theopold—Henle 114): Toccata Op.7: Sonatas Opp.11 and 22; Fantasie Op.17; Concerto without Orchestra Op.14. All four volumes are based on autographs and early editions.
  Available separately: Opp.1, 2, 4, 6, 7, 9, 12, 13, 14, 15, 16, 17, 18, 19, 20, 21, 22, 23, 26, 28, 68, 68 with 15, 82, 99, 111, 124 (Henle).Opp.1, 2, 4, 5, 6, 7, 8, 9, 11, 12, 13, 14, 15 with 68, 16, 18 and 19, 20, 21, 22, 23, 26, 28, 32, 99, 111, 118, and 124 (Hans Joachim Köhler—CFP), with detailed critical commentaries in English, German, and French. Köhler's editions present a convincing and comprehensive account of how this music is best interpreted. All editorial additions are carefully indicated. Opp.2, 12, 15, 18, 19, 68, 82 (VU). Opp.1, 2, 6, 7, 9, 11–15, 16, 17, 18–22, 26, 82 (Cortot—Sal). Opp.1, 2, 6, 7, 9, 11, 12, 13, 15–18, 20, 21, 22, 26, 28, 32, 68, 82 (Carlo Zecchi—EC). Opp.6, 12, 13, 15, 18, 21, 82, 124 (Bischoff—WH). Opp.2, 12, 17, 21, 68 (Ric).
Complete Piano Works (Sauer—CFP) Vol.I: Opp.15, 18, 19, 28, 68, 82, 99, 124. Vol.II: Opp.6, 9, 12, 16, 21. Vol.III: Opp.1, 2, 4, 5, 7, 8, 13, 17, 20, 26. Vol.IV: Opp.3, 10, 23, 32, 72, 76, 111, 118, 126, 133. Vol.V: Opp.11, 14, 22, 54, 92, 134, Op. posth. Scherzo f; Presto g.
Sämtliche Klavierwerke (C. Schumann, W. Kempff—Br&H). Vol.I: Opp.1–8. Vol.II: Opp.9–13. Vol.III: Opp.14–19. Vol.IV: Opp.20–23, 26, 28, 32. Vol.V: Opp.56, 58 (*Studies and Sketches for pedalpiano*), 68, 72, 76, 82. Vol.VI: Opp.99, 111, 118, 124, 126, 133. Vol.VII: Op.54 *Concerto*.
Complete Works (C. Schumann—K). More of Clara Schumann's interpretation comes through in this edition than Robert's. Vol.I: Opp.1–8. Vol.II: Opp.9–13. Vol.III: Opp.14–19. Vol.IV: Opp.20, 21, 22, 23, 26, 32. Vol.V: Opp.56, 58, 68, 72, 76, 82. Vol.VI: Opp.99, 111, 118, 124, 126, 133. Vol.VII: works for piano and orchestra. Many of these works are available separately in the above complete editions.
Complete Works (C. Schumann—Dover). Vol.I: Opp.1, 2, 3, 6, 7, 8, 9, 10, 11, 12, 14,

15, 16, 18, 19. Vol.II: Opp.20, 21, 22, 23, 26, 68, 72, 82, 99, 118. Vol.III: Opp.4, 13, 17, 28, 32, 76, 111, 124, 126, 133. Also includes various supplementary movements to other works, e.g., to Opp.13, 14, and 22.

SEPARATE WORKS (listed numerically by opus number):

Variations on the name Abegg Op.1 1830. Theme on the name of Countess von Abegg, three variations with brilliant finale, effective pianistic figuration in Hummel style. M-D.

Papillons Op.2 1829–31 (Hinson—Alfred 4800; Ferguson ABRSM; VU 51021, urtext edition and facsimile of autograph). Cycle of twelve imaginative dance movements, employs chromatic weaving of inner parts and canonic devices. Work concludes with the "Grossvaterlied" and the clock striking while the dancers disperse. M-D.
See: Edith Cornfield, "The World of Schumann. *Papillons*, Op.2," MTA of NSW (November 1991):2, 4–6, 8–10.

Six Studies after Caprices by Paganini Op.3 1832. a, E, C, B♭, E♭, g. Literal transcriptions of the Paganini works originally for violin alone. Schumann included a set of exercises to help solve technical problems and suggested these pieces were written to supply material of more interest than the studies of Czerny, Clementi, Hummel, and Kalkbrenner. No.2 is the most musical and was also set by Liszt. M-D to D.

Intermezzi Op.4 1832. A, e, a, C, d, b. Schumann called these works "longer *Papillons*." Six pieces in ternary form written in a free improvisatory style. No.2: the most involved. No.4: consists of parts of three different discarded works. No.5: has great beauty. No.6: contains the "Abegg" theme in measure 43. M-D.

Impromptus on a theme of Clara Wieck Op.5 1833. A second and later version (1850) is superior to this one. Free set of nine variations handled in a fluent and ingenious manner; closes with an extensive fugue. M-D.
See: Claudia S. Becker, "A New Look at Schumann's Impromptus," MQ, 67 (October 1981):568–86.

Davidsbündlertänze Op.6 1837 (Ferguson—ABRSM). Two versions of this work exist. The second gives Schumann's final ideas. This cycle of 18 "characteristic" pieces contains indications that underlie the mood of each piece. Subtle key and tempo shifts are found throughout. Technical problems of special note are left-hand skips in Nos.3 and 9, complex left-hand part in No.6, and fast chords in No.13. D.
See: Roger Fiske, "A Schumann Mystery," MT, 105 (August 1964):574–78.

Toccata C Op.7 1833. This virtuoso masterpiece of the young Schumann is in SA design. Double notes and octave passage-work account for much of the difficulty. First written in D then transposed to C. D.

Allegro b Op.8 1831. Uncharacteristic work, shows the influence of Hummel. M-D.

Carnaval Op.9 1834–35 (Hinson—Alfred 4576; G. Fauré—UMP). Variegated suite of 22 pieces with the subtitle "Little Scenes on Four Notes." Most of

the pieces are variations on the four notes A E♭ C B (A S C H in German) or alternatively A♭ C B, the musical letters in Schumann's name. Opening and closing movements are the most extensive. Special technical problems are encountered in *Papillons, Reconnaissance* (fast thumb repetitions), *Pantalon et Columbine* (finger staccato), and *Paganini* (left-hand skips). D.
See: Joseph Bloch, "The Piano Cycles of Robert Schumann," *Etude* (July–August 1956):19, 49, 62–63.
Catherine Kautsky, "Musical Masks in Schumann's *Carnaval*," *Clavier,* 30/6 (July–August 1991):26–29. In keeping with the theme of a masquerade, Schumann creates ambiguity in tonality, meter, and even the identity of composer and composition.
Moritz Rosenthal, "A Master Lesson on *Carnaval*, Op.9 by Robert Schumann," *Etude,* L/11 (November 1932):765–66, 816.
Six Studies after Caprices of Paganini Op.10 1833. A♭, g, g, c, b, e. More imaginative settings than Op.3. The *Paganini* movement in *Carnaval* refers to No.1 in this set. No.2 was also set by Liszt. D.
Sonata f♯ Op.11 1835. Introduction and Allegro vivace: frequent tempo and key changes, staccato chords. Aria. Scherzo and Intermezzo: two contrasting subjects alternate in the Scherzo; Intermezzo has an unusual recitative. Finale: loosely organized. Orchestrally conceived and demands much physical stamina. Cyclic overtones permeate this work. Moments of rare beauty throughout. D.
See: Gregory W. Harwood, "Robert Schumann's Sonata in F-Sharp Minor: A Study of Creative Process and Romantic Inspiration," *Current Musicology*, 29 (1980):17–30.
Ian Parrott, "A Plea for Schumann's Op.11," ML, 33 (January 1952):55–58.
Fantasiestücke Op.12 1837 (Hinson—Alfred 4850). Eight contrasting pieces with individual descriptive titles, planned as a complete unit. By their individual titles and expressive directions to the player they attempt pointedly to evoke the capricious and illusory dream world of the imagination. Des Abends D♭ (In the Evening): exploits a cross-rhythm. Aufschwung f (Soaring): requires firm rhythmic control. Warum? D♭ (Why?): needs an even, singing tone. Grillen D♭ (Whims): requires a strong rhythmic drive. In der Nacht f (In the Night): one of Schumann's finest inspirations; a passionate piece that requires sensitive handling of multiple layers of melodic writing in the same hand. Fabel C (Fable): alternates capricious and lyric moods. Traumes Wirren F (Restless Dreams): right-hand rotation technique and sturdy outside fingers are required. Ende vom Lied F (End of the Song): sturdy chordal writing; an uninterrupted succession of pleasures. No.9 Feurigst (Fiery) (Werner—Curwen) in this series was discarded by Schumann but is now available. Although characteristically Schumannesque it is not up to the quality of the first eight pieces. M-D.
Etudes en forme de variations (Etudes Symphoniques) c♯ Op.13 1834 (Hinson—Alfred 4847). There are 12 etudes in this set but only 9 are based on the theme (Etudes 3, 9, and the Finale are not). Five additional variations were

rejected by Schumann but are contained in the Br&H and Henle editions. A gloomy theme lends coherence to the work. Mood and figuration of each etude varies considerably. Schumann's most important technical explorations and one of his most artistic creations. Staccato chord technique, wide skips for left hand, and perpetual motion writing are some of the difficulties encountered in this highly effective masterpiece. D.

See: John L. Kollen, "Tema, Op.13, Robert Alexander Schumann (1810–1856)," in *Notations and Editions* (Dubuque: Wm. C. Brown, 1974; reprint, New York: Da Capo Press, 1977), pp.163–71.

Thomas Warburton, "Some Performance Alternatives for Schumann's Opus 13," JALS, 31 (January–June 1992):38–46.

Exercises (Beethoven-Etüden) 1833 (Robert Münster—Henle 298 1976) 15pp. Seven studies based on a theme in the form of variations from Beethoven's Seventh Symphony (second movement). These pieces reveal a marked affinity to the *Symphonic Etudes* Op.13, a very close relationship existing between Op.13/6 and study No.3 of the *Exercises*. The character of the *Exercises* is more pianistic than that of variation techniques. Schumann adheres closely to Beethoven's theme. An excellent preface and critical notes in French, German, and English provide great detail. Serious musical character; written during the year Schumann attempted suicide. D.

Sonata f Op.14 1835–36. Named "Concerto without Orchestra" by publisher Haslinger. Allegro f. Scherzo D♭. Andantino f: four variations on a theme by Clara Wieck. Finale f: sonata-rondo. The theme of the Andantino provides a motto for the entire cyclic work. This sonata is loosely organized and was revised by Schumann. Provides some effective, brilliant, and demanding writing. Broad and grand conception is necessary to "bring off" this work. Requires command of long form and inner relationships. D.

See: Linda Correll Roesner, "The Autographs of Schumann's Piano Sonata in F Minor, Op.14," MQ, 61 (January 1975):98–130.

Kinderszenen (Scenes of Childhood) Op.15 1838 (Draheim—VU; Steiglich—Br; Lympany—Hansen House; Ferguson—ABRSM). In one of his letters, Schumann said these pieces were about children, not for them. Programmatic connotations are contained in each individual title although they were added after the completion of the pieces. Beguilingly deceptive. Von fremden Ländern und Menschen G (From Foreign Lands and People): cantabile melody, accompaniment divided between hands. Curiose Geschichte D (Curious Story): animated chordal writing. Hasche-Mann b (Catch Me): playful etude in finger staccato. Bittendes Kind D (Entreating Child): sweet tears, melody accompanied in same hand. Glückes genug D (Perfect Happiness): sensitive phrasing in right-hand melody and left-hand imitation required. Wichtige Begebenheit A (Important Event): heavy chords. Träumerei F (Dreaming): needs flexible phrasing and sensitive legato. Am Kamin F (By the Fireside): expressive cantabile; some rearrangement by voicing is appropriate for a small hand. Ritter vom Steckenpferd C (Knight of the Rocking-Horse): syncopated rhythm; keep arms free. Fast zu ernst g♯ (Almost Too Serious): needs good tonal balance between syncopated melody and bass. Fürchtenmachen G (Frightening): careful dynamic details, contrasted phrases. Kind im Einschlummern e (Child Falling Asleep): gentle imagination needed. Der Dichter spricht G (The Poet Speaks): firm control of tempo required. Int. to M-D.

See: Irwin Freundlich, "Robert Schumann's 'Scenes from Childhood'—A Discussion," PQ, 22 (Winter 1957):15–18, 28.

MT, (February 1974):146 for a review of the VU edition and a comparison with the Clara Schumann edition.

Robert Polansky, "The Rejected *Kinderszenen* of Robert Schumann's Opus 15," JAMS, 31 (Spring 1978):126–31.

Kreisleriana Op.16 1838. The title refers to Kapellmeister Kreisler, a character in several of the tales by E. T. A. Hoffman. Schumann dedicated this work to Chopin. It consists of eight untitled pieces of widely varying moods, many of them in da capo form. Ausserst bewegt d: precise melodic slurring will be facilitated by a carefully controlled rotation technique. Sehr innig und nicht zu rasch B♭: octave and double-note legato technique are essential; the two intermezzi require quicker tempi. Sehr aufgeregt g: repeated four-note figures move to an animated climax; mid-section is in a contrasting cantilena style. Sehr langsam B♭: calls for sensitive tonal control. Sehr lebhaft g: opening subject needs a light touch; numerous rhythmic repetitions test the performer's interpretive powers. Sehr langsam E♭: expressive tonal quality demanded. Sehr rasch c: vigorous, energetic; calls for facile, yet strong fingers. Schnell und spielend g: light pianissimo touch is appropriate for the opening, great power for the climax. D.

See: James L. Martin, "Schumann, Hoffmann, and Kreisleriana," *Clavier*, 30/6 (July–August 1991):20–25. A familiarity with *Kreisleriana's* literary antecedents can help performers and audiences understand Schumann's eccentric masterpiece.

Charles Timbrell, "Really Wild Love—Schumann's Kreisleriana Then and Now," P&K, 172 (January–February 1995):26–29.

Fantasia C Op.17 1836 (Hinson—Alfred 4843). Dedicated to Franz Liszt. Durchaus fantastisch und leidenschaftlich vorzutragen C: modified SA design; requires special sustained quality; great extremes in the dynamic range. Mässig, durchaus energisch E♭: scherzo quality, requires big technique, sensitive approach to the middle section, and ability to manage the unusually difficult skips in the coda. Langsam getragen, durchweg leise zu halten C: flowing poetical piece with two powerful climaxes. Schumann's greatest large-scale piano work; a landmark of nineteenth-century piano literature. Contrasting movements make the utmost demands on the musical sensibilities and technical equipment of the performer. D.

See: Nicholas Marston, "Im Legendenton. Schumann's Unsung Voice," *19th Century Music*, XVI/3 (Spring 1993):227–41.

Alan Walker, "Schumann, Liszt and the C Major Fantasie, Op.17: A Declining Relationship," M&L, 60/2 (April 1979):156–65.

Arabesque C Op.18 1839 (Palmer—Alfred 3298). Cantabile and graceful piece. Rondo form with two contrasting episodes. Reflective coda marked "Zum Schluss" employs new material. M-D.

Blumenstück D♭ Op.19 1839. A theme remodeled in numerous guises moves through five sections, all in similar mood. The final cadence introduces the opening theme of *Humoresque* Op.20. M-D.

Humoresque B♭ Op.20 1839. Six connected pieces and epilogue. Long improvisatory, cyclelike work. Exploits many features of Schumann's piano style. Loose organization and numerous themes make it difficult for the listener to follow. In bars 251–74 an "inner voice [is] not to be played." This work is related to one by Clara Schumann (part of which is reproduced at the end of the Köhler—CFP edition). M-D to D.

See: Walter Schenkman, "A Study of Schumann's Humoresque," diss., Indiana University, 1963.

Novelletten Op.21 1838. Schumann described these eight untitled pieces as "longish connected tales of adventure." Dance influence is obvious. No.1 F: march in full chords with a lyric contrasting section. No.2 D: grateful bravura writing utilizing many thumb repetitions. No.3 D: jolly waltz using staccato chords. No.4 D: waltz with cross-rhythms and lively syncopations. No.5 D: uses polonaise rhythm, staccato chord figuration. No.6 A: staccato chords in opening followed by more lyric sections, increasing tempo, short coda. No.7 E: brilliant octaves contrasted with cantabile writing. No.8 f♯: most effective of the set, two works in one; contrasting in meter 2/4, 3/4, the two works are linked by a Romantic episode "Voice from afar." M-D.

Sonata g Op.22. First movement (1833): SA design with coda; rotation technique. Andantino (1830): one of Schumann's loveliest lyrical inspirations. Scherzo (1833): snappy persistent rhythms. Rondo (1838): continuous broken octaves require some stamina. Most tightly organized of the three sonatas. M-D to D.

See: Linda Correll Roesner, "Schumann Revisions in the First Movement of the Piano Sonata in G Minor, Op.22," *19th Century Music*, I (November 1977):97–109.

Wadham Sutton, "Schumann: Piano Sonata in G Minor, Op.22," *Music Teacher*, 52 (April 1973):14–15.

Nachtstücke Op.23 1839. In their final form these pieces are untitled, but originally they were conceived as "Funeral Procession," "Strange Company," "Nocturnal Carouse," and "Round with Solo Voices." No.1 C: detached chords support a marchlike subject that contrasts with legato writing, dark and foreboding. No.2 F: fast chords, monotonous rhythmic repetition needs relief by varied tonal coloring. No.3 D♭: scherzo with two trios; right thumb playing melody presents a legato problem; sonorous beginning, evolves into some strange harmonies. No.4 F: melody is heard at the top of the arpeggiated chords; tonal balance in the lower register presents a problem. Unusual color, rhythmic vitality, and harmonic and contrapuntal ingenuity. M-D.

Faschingschwank aus Wien (Carnaval Prank from Vienna) Op.26 1839. This suite of character pieces is a direct result of Schumann's visit to Vienna in the interests of his publication *Neue Zeitschrift für Musik*. Allegro B♭: long, robust movement, main idea contrasted with six episodes. Romanze g: wistful, florid melody, inconclusive ending. Scherzino B♭: two-bar rhythmic repetition, no trio. Intermezzo e♭: the finest movement, passionate and noble, can be performed separately. Finale B♭: SA design animated, similar problems in opening movement. M-D.

Three Romances Op.28 1839. No.1 b♭: melody is supported by a running figuration divided between hands. No.2 F♯: duet, melodic writing in rich register of the piano; careful pedaling and phrasing required. No.3 B: animated rondo infused with too many interesting ideas. M-D.

Scherzo, Gigue, Romanze and Fughetta Op.32 1838–39. Scherzo B♭: playful, impetuous, short. Gigue g: light, whimsical, dance-like. Romanze d: a short study. Expressive, soaring melody accompanied by brilliant figuration divided between hands. Fughetta g: subject is tossed between hands with accompanying chords, dancelike, athletic gestures. M-D.

Six Studies for Pedal Piano Op.56 1845 (Henle 367; Heinrichshofen D2960). C, a, E, A♭, b, B. Two-part accompanied canons. See especially the ones in A♭ and b. Four have been arranged for piano (Clara Schumann—K). M-D.

Four Sketches for Pedal Piano Op.58 1845 (Henle 367; Heinrichshofen D2959). c, C, f, D♭. Less use of a pedal part is made here. Not canonic. M-D.

Werke für Orgel oder Pedalklavier (Henle 367 1987) 82pp. Includes *Six Studies for Pedal Piano* Op.56; *Four Sketches for Pedal Piano* Op.58; *Six Fugues on the Name BACH* Op.60. At the beginning of 1845 Schumann, together with Clara, embarked on an intense course of contrapuntal studies in Dresden. These pieces are the result of that study. The Op.60 fugues are more suited to the organ than to the pedal piano; pedal parts are well developed. M-D.

Album for the Young Op.68 1848 (Palmer—Alfred; Ferguson—ABRSM; VU 50049; Banowetz—GWM). 43 charming pieces. Some require a good hand span. Easy to Int.

3 Very Easy Pieces from the Album for the Young (Rönnau, Kann—VU 51002). No.1, Melody. No.8, The Wild Horseman. No.10, The Merry Peasant. Urtext edition with facsimile of the autograph. Easy.

For Younger People. Part I of *Album for the Young* Op.68 (Ferguson—ABRSM). Contains the first 18 pieces only. Easy to Int.

Unpublished Pieces from Album for the Young Op.68 (J. Demus—Ric). Contains 17 pieces originally intended for Op.68. Some are surprisingly fine while others are not up to the standards of those included in the original collection. Require a good hand span. Easy to Int.
See: Eric Sams, MT (June 1974):488.

Four Fugues Op.72 1845. d, d, f, F. Skillful contrapuntal treatment. Bach's *Well-Tempered Clavier* I/22 inspired the theme of No.2, and Chopin's posthumous *Etudes*, No.1 inspired the theme of No.3. M-D.

Four Marches Op.76 1849. E♭, g, B♭, E♭. No.3, "Camp Scene"; others untitled.

Written during the "troubles" of 1848, these pieces were Schumann's way of showing his sympathy for the revolutionists. Schumann wrote that they were "written with really fiery enthusiasm." M-D.

Waldszenen Op.82 (1848–49) (Ferguson—ABRSM). Eintritt (Entrance) B♭: asymmetrical phrasing. Jäger auf der Lauer (Hunter in Ambush) d: spirited, some technical problems. Einsame Blumen (Solitary Flowers) B♭: carefully balance the two lines in same hand. Verrufene Stelle (Haunted Spot) d: misterioso, double-dotted chords, staccato phrases. Freundliche Landschaft (Friendly Landscape) B♭: rubato, poetic. Herberge (At the Inn) E♭: tonal balance is important. Vogel als Prophet (The Prophet Bird) g: cross-relations, incomplete phrases, questioning melodic line requires great delicacy. Jagdlied (Hunting Song) E♭: wrist and arm endurance needed. Abschied (Farewell) B♭: 2 against 3, melody and accompaniment in same hand; a touching, liedlike conclusion. About the same difficulty as Op.15. Int. to M-D.

See: Robert Dumm, "Interpreting Robert Schumann," *Clavier*, 34/4 (April 1993):22–25. Focuses on No.4, Haunted Spot.

Eric F. Jensen, "A New Manuscript of Robert Schumann's *Waldszenen* Op.82," *The Journal of Musicology*, 3/1 (Winter 1984):69–89.

Nita Laurie, "Teaching Schumann's *Waldszenen* Op.82," *The Studio*, 2/1 (February 1996):23–33.

Bunte Blätter (Colored Leaves) Op.99 1839–49. A heterogeneous collection of 14 pieces containing some prime material. Three small works: A, e, E. Five were titled "Album Leaves": f♯, b, A♭, e♭, E♭; Brahms used theme of the first one in his *Variations* Op.9. Six titled pieces: Novelette b. Prelude b♭: turbulent. March d: slow, impressive. Evening Music B♭. Scherzo g: satisfyingly live. March g: quick. Novelette is the most significant work in the set, and the five miniature "Album Leaves" are exquisite. Int. to M-D.

Fantasiestücke Op.111 (1851). Three short pieces that continue the same idea as Op.12 but have no descriptive titles. No.1 c: powerful sweep. No.2 A♭: lyric, engaging. No.3 c: robust, marchlike, graceful middle section. Int. to M-D.

Three Sonatas for the Young Op.118 1853. Dedicated to Schumann's three daughters. Each is in four movements, some with descriptive titles. The first two were intended as teaching pieces for his daughters. No.1 G, In memory of Julie: G, e, C, G. No.2 D, In memory of Elisa: D, b, G, D. No.3, C Dedicated to Mary: C, F, C, C; final movement contains a reference to the opening of the first sonata. Int. to M-D.

Album Blätter Op.124 1832–45. Twenty titled unrelated short pieces written over a period of years. See especially Nos.4, 5, and 17, which were rejected from *Carnaval*. Also see No.16. Int. to M-D.

Seven Pieces in Fughetta Form Op.126 1853. a, d, F, d, a, F, a. Overactive subjects and restricted tonal schemes lead to monotony. Nos.1, 4, and 5 have the most interest. M-D.

Gesänge der Frühe (Songs of the Dawn) Op.133 1853 (Henle) D, D, A, f♯, D. Schumann conceived these short pieces as "Characteristic pieces depicting the approach and waxing of the morning but more an expression of feeling than painting." Int. to M-D.

Variations on an Original Theme 1854 (K. Geiringer—Hin 1939). Schumann's last piano composition. Theme and five variations. Brahms used the theme for his *Variations for piano duet* Op.23. Also published as "Ghost Variations" (Henle 482 1995). More accurate than the 1939 edition. Written just prior to Schumann's entering an insane asylum; Schumann thought he had ghosts around him playing music. This music comes from that experience. Int. to M-D.

Variationen über ein Nocturne von Chopin 1835-36 (Draheim—Br&H 8151 1992) 11pp. Three variations, the last not complete (8 measures completed by Draheim). Based on Chopin's Nocturne g Op.15, No.3, which Schumann called "one of my favorite pieces." Not completely successful: too short (97 measures with 27 measures being the theme). Style is similar to *Carnaval*. Preface in English and German, critical notes in German. M-D.

COLLECTIONS:

The Easiest Original Pieces for the Piano (A. Rowley—Hin 7) 19pp. A Little Cradle Song Op.124/6; Album Leaf Op.99/4; Solitary Flowers Op.82/3; Waltz Op.124/4; A Country Dance Op.124/7; Fantastic Dance Op.124/5; Grief's Forebodings Op.124/2; Album Leaf Op.99/8; Gipsy Dance from Op.118; To a Flower from Op.19; Fughetta Op.126/1; Canon from Op.118. Int. to M-D.

Schumann—An Introduction to His Piano Works (Palmer—Alfred 1976) 63pp. Selections from Opp.68, 124, 15, 82, 99, 118a. Excellent choice of repertoire. A most helpful preface includes a brief biography, comments about the music, identification of sources, and discussion of ornamentation, pedaling, and metronome markings. Int.

Schumann Easy Piano (Alfred). 18 pieces, mainly from *Album for the Young*; plus three from *Scenes from Childhood* and two from other works. Includes a short biography and a note about each work. Easy to Int.

Schumann—Favorite Piano (Alfred). 29 pieces, some of which duplicate selections in *Schumann Easy Piano*. Also includes four pieces from *Carnaval*, *Arabesque*, *Forest Scenes*, as well as pieces from *Album for the Young* and *Scenes from Childhood*. Biography and notes on each piece. Int. to M-D.

Piano Works—Selections (J. Antal—EMB 1974) Book I, 56pp. Book II (EMB 1976) 59pp. Contains works from Opp.21, 22, 26, 28, 82, 99, 111, 118, 124.

Young Pianist's Guide to Schumann (Y. Novik—Studio P/R 1978) 31pp. Includes 13 easy works from Opp.15, 68, 99, 124. Tastefully edited for the piano. Record of the contents included. Int.

Easiest Piano Pieces (Weismann—CFP 5029). Includes selections from Opp.15, 68, 99, and 124. Int.

Schumann—Easier Favorites (Heinrichshofen N4052) 39pp. 17 pieces ranging from Cradle Song Op.124 to Soaring Op.12. Int. to M-D.

Schumann Album (EMB Z7293) 56pp. Includes: Papillons Op.2/5, 8, 11; Intermezzi Op.4/4, 5; Davidsbündlertänze Op.6/2, 10–12, 18; Carnaval Op.9, 7 movements; Sonata f♯ Op.11, second movement, Aria; Fantasiestücke Op.12, 3 movements; Scenes from Childhood Op.15, 4 movements; Kreisleriana Op.16/4, 6; Fantasie C Op.17, third movement. Int. to M-D.

12 Cameos from Robert Schumann as dictated to Rosemary Brown. See more complete entry under Brown, Rosemary.

Robert Schumann Piano Compositions (Tucker—CPP/Belwin 1993) 32pp. Arabesque Op.18; Berceuse Op.124/6; Entrance Op.82/1; Fantastic Dance Op.124/5; Finale from *Papillons* Op.2/12; From Foreign Lands and People Op.15/1; Grillen Op.12/4; Knight Rupert Op.68/12; Novelette Op.21/7. No distinction is made between composer's and editor's markings. Int. to M-D.

Virtuosic Music for Piano (C. Schumann—GS No.1997). Includes *Davidsbündlertänze, Toccata, Carnaval, Symphonic Etudes, Kreisleriana,* and other works. M-D to D.

Sonatas for Piano (C. Schumann—GS No. 1997). Includes Opp.11, 12, and 14. M-D to D.

See: William Black, "Robert Schumann's Fantasy World," KC, 1115 (September–October 1991):42–43.

Elaine Brody, "Schumann's Legacy in France," *Studies in Romanticism*, 13/3 (Summer 1974):189–212. List of works.

Fanny Davies, "About Schumann's Pianoforte Music," MT, 51 (1910):493–94.

J. Fuller-Maitland, *Schumann's Pianoforte Works* (London: Oxford University Press, 1927; Reprint, St. Clair Shores, MI: Scholarly Press, 1972), 59pp.

Peter F. Ostwald, "Florestan, Eusebius, Clara, and Schumann's Right Hand," *19th Century Music*, IV (Summer 1980):17–31.

Brian Schlotel, "Schumann and the Metronome," in *Robert Schumann: The Man and His Music*, edited by Alan Walker (London: Barrie & Jenkins, 1972), pp.109–19.

Linda Siegel, "The Piano Cycles of Schumann and the Novels of Jean Paul Richter," PQ, 69 (Fall 1969):16–22.

L. A. Whitesell, "E. T. A. Hoffmann and Robert Schumann," JALS 13, (June 1983):73–101.

Gerard Schürmann (1928–   ) Great Britain, born Indonesia

Bagatelles 1945 (Novello 10025101 1983) 16pp. 8 min. Allegro volante; Allegretto scherzando; Presto; Poco lento; Allegretto. Octotonic, thin textures, neoclassic, MC. M-D.

Contrasts (Nov 1975) 28pp. 15 min. A colorful suite that displays both Liszt and Ravel pianistic influence. Cumulonimbus: many sevenths, dramatic, driving rhythms, majestic opening. Summer Rain: capricious, long melodic lines punctuated by scalar interjections, clever pedal effects. Becalmed: expressive, slow-moving, chromatic; rises to furioso climax and then subsides. Undersun: similar to opening movement in rhythmic treatment; chordal tremolos; dashing arpeggi figures; a ma flessibile mid-section leads to a toccata-like coda. Keyboard fully explored. D.

Leotaurus 1975 (Nov 12022110) 23pp. 15 min. Theme and ten variations. A prickly eight-bar introduction leads to a tranquillo dolcissimo cantabile theme that is freely tonal around b. Contrasted variations range from simple textures (No.5) to Allegro toccata-like (No.10) with a crashing conclusion. Neoclassic orientation. M-D.

Two Ballades (Novello 2934-10) 15 min. Hukvaldy; Brno. These technically demanding pieces pay tribute to the musical legacy of the Czech composer Leoš Janáček. The first takes its title and inspiration from the Moravian village in which he was born, the second from the town in which he spent most of his working life. D.

Giora Schuster (1915–   ) Israel, born Germany

Splinters 1974 (IMI 317) 9pp. 12 min. Three contrasting expressionistic movements. Exploits quiet dynamics. M-D.

Eduard Schütt (1856–1933) Austria, born Russia

Schütt studied at the St. Petersburg and Leipzig Conservatories and piano privately with Leschetizky in Vienna. He toured Central Europe as accompanist and performed his first piano concerto in St. Petersburg in 1882. He composed two piano concertos, numerous piano miniatures, chamber music, and a comic opera; and he prepared Robert Schumann's piano works for the Universal edition.

19 Romantic Pieces (Johnson ABRSM 1987) 32pp. A Journey into the Country Op.105/1; A Child Asleep Op.102/2; An Idea Op.68/2; A Mother's Cares Op.105/2; In the Garden Op.108/1; A Moment of Sadness Op.60/7; Album Leaf Op.68/1; Evening Stillness Op.105/6; Solitude Op.60/8; Dance Tune Op.108/2; A Trifle Op.31/1; In a Gondola Op.105/4; Village Merriment Op.105/5; A Word of Love Op.60/4; Confession Op.30/2; Little Cradle Song Op.108/3; In the Country Op.60/5; Elegy; Friendly Meeting Op.103/1. Attractive tunes and ideas cleverly crafted. Int.

Paraphrases on "Die Fledermaus" (Cranz). Schütt wrote paraphrases on many other Strauss waltzes as well as innumerable other salon pieces of good quality.

Joseph Schwantner (1943–   ) USA

Schwantner teaches at the Eastman School of Music in Rochester, N.Y.

Veiled Autumn. In collection *Changing Faces* (EAMC 1987) 4pp. Impressionistic, subtle sonorities, careful use of damper pedal required (use more than indicated), clear but changing tonal centers, ringing sounds. Hold final three measures until all sound has disappeared. M-D.

See: Maurice Hinson, "Commissioned by Clavier," *Clavier,* 27/3 (March 1988):18.

Elliott Schwartz (1936–   ) USA

Schwartz has worked in electronic music studios since 1963. His works for piano solo and prerecorded tape attempt, using electronic means, to enhance, expand, obscure, develop, or otherwise modify the piano sonority and the act of piano performance.

Music for Prince Albert on His 150th Birthday 1969 (Bowdoin College Music Press) 13pp. 9 min. For pianist and two tape tracks (consisting mostly of piano sounds). Two prerecorded tapes come with the score. Lighting effects (optional) are called for. Some traditional writing appears in the body of the work. Avant-garde. M-D to D.

Mirrors 1973 (CF) 12pp. 7 min. For piano and two-channel tape. Tape is prepared by the pianist. Pointillistic; some improvisation required. Mallet used to strike different parts inside the piano; plucked and strummed strings; harmonics; fist clusters; drum-stick is to be thrust into piano lower register; keyboard cover is slammed; pianist must hum at conclusion. Aleatoric. Avant-garde notation is similar to *Music for Prince Albert*. D.

A Dream of Bells and Beats 1977 (AMC) 1 p. of music, 5pp. of directions, 10 min. For solo piano and 11 members of the audience. Requires 4 music boxes, 3 metronomes, 3 radios, 3 alarm clocks. The pianist performs the given effects (a series of fragments in separate boxes) as a continuum, with no breaks, in any sequence, according to instructions. Auxilliary performers execute their events (as directed), with extended periods of silence in between. The pianist finishes the piece alone. Avant-garde but not terribly involved, fun for all. M-D.

Pentagonal Mobile 1977 (AMC) for 5 pianos or for piano solo and a quadraphonic tape. 12pp. 12 min., 1p. for each minute of the piece; 5pp. of performance directions. It is preferable for the "live" pianist to make his/her own tape (by recording the other four parts); however, a tape is available. Clusters, harmonics. Requires improvisation and humming and singing in lyric style. Avant-garde. M-D to D.

Four Maine Haiku 1984 (Norruth Music 1987) 11pp. Based on a method of predetermined pitch selection and phrase arrangement. Score contains explanation of this serialistic approach. Highly chromatic, diverse rhythms, technically not very difficult. 1: Quiet, lyrical, changing meters, free choice of repeated chords. 2: Changing meters, jumps, trills, sweep of strings. 3: Dancelike, meter changes, octaves, legato and staccato. 4: No meter, muted tones, ostinato, free choice regarding certain figures (number of repetitions), melody in the accompaniment. A fine set for introducing contemporary techniques. Int. to M-D.

Ludwig Schytte (1848–1909) Denmark

Schytte studied composition with Liszt. His most interesting works were in miniature form.

Sonata B♭ Op.53 (Henri Gregh; SBTS) 23pp. Allegro brioso; Intermezzo—Moderato e cantabile; Finale—Allegro molto agitato. Effective derivative Romantic style, pianistic, virtuoso toccata finale. M-D.

Salvatore Sciarrino (1947–   ) Italy
De la nuit; alla candida anima di Federico Chopin, da giovane (Ric 1971) 29pp. Scurries dissonantly all over the keyboard; very quiet; wanders; requires enormous control. D.
Sonata I 1976 (Ric 132489) 65pp. Swirling chromatic figures become more furioso and dramatic as this one-movement work unfolds. Harmonics, glissandos. Terribly difficult for performer and audience. D.

Cyril Scott (1879–1970) Great Britain
Scott's originality earned him the title "the English Debussy."
Three Little Waltzes (Elkin). Short, simple. Int.
Pastorale Suite (Elkin). Courante; Pastorale; Rigaudon; Rondo; Passacaglia. The Passacaglia theme is built on a folklike tune. M-D.
Impressions from Kipling's Jungle Book 1912 (Schott). The Jungle; Dawn; Rikki-Tikki-Tavi and the Snake; Morning Song in the Jungle; Dance of the Elephants. Int. to M-D.
Lotus Land Op.47/1 (CF; Elkin; Schott). Atmospheric, pentatonic, sonorous, pseudo-oriental, fine climax. M-D.
Poems 1912 (Schott; MMP). Five of Scott's finest short pieces. Poppies; The Garden of Soul-Sympathy; Bells; The Twilight of the Year; Paradise-Birds. M-D.
Sonata III 1956 (Elkin 26240600) 20pp. 16½ min. Molto tranquillo. Scherzo Patetico. Finale—Grave con moto: concludes with a fugue; improvisatory; driving climax. A different style from Scott's earlier works; more advanced harmonic ideas. Not altogether successful. M-D.
Sonata No.1 Op.66 1909 (Elkin; MMP) 27½ min. Allegro con spirito; Adagio; Scherzo; Fugue. These movements are uninterrupted except by tempo changes and transformations of the main theme. The fugue requires virtuosic technique. Irregular rhythms occur throughout in the original version. Scott later revised the work by replacing some of the changing meters. Percy Grainger said of this sonata: "In our own time the outstanding vehicle of musical progress has been the Cyril Scott *Piano Sonata*, Op.66, with its irregular rhythms (originally an Australian invention), its 'nonarchitectural' flowing form, its exquisite discordant harmonies. The Scott *Sonata* is as significant artistically, emotionally and pianistically as it is historically" (from notes of Albany Records, CD Troy 070).
Dance Negre Op.58/5 (Alfred 6399). Brilliant, short, strong ragtime influence, perpetual motion. Fine encore. Requires facility and accuracy. Int. to M-D.
Egypt (Schott 1436 1913) 21pp. An album of five impressions. In the Temple of Memphis; By the Waters of the Nile; Egyptian Boat Song; Funeral March of the Great Ramses; Song of the Nile. Colorful, Impressionistic. Large span required. M-D.

For My Young Friends (Elkin). Ten attractive pieces. Int.

Indian Suite 1922 (Schott). The Snake Charmer; Juggernaut; Indian Serenade; Dancing girls. M-D.

Valse Caprice Op.74/7 (Elkin). Impressionistic, *pp* ending. Span of ninth required. Int.

Four Pieces (MMP). Asphodel Op.50/2; Dance Negre Op.58/5; Bergeronnette Op.71/3; Intermezzo Op.67/3. Fine examples of Scott's exotic lyricism. M-D.

Alexander Scriabin (1872–1915) Russia

Scriabin was an outstanding pianist with a fluent and spontaneous style of playing that was recognized throughout Europe. His early piano works owe much to Chopin and Liszt. The etudes, impromptus, mazurkas, nocturnes, preludes, and valses all show an affinity with Chopin in his preference for miniature forms. A chromatic harmonic vocabulary later evolved into a highly individual style, closely related to his mystic-theosophic interests. Almost all of Scriabin's piano music is difficult. A few easier works are Opp.2/1; 8/11; 9/1; 11/3, 9, 10, 14, 17; 32/1; 47; and 57. The piano works generally require a large span and a fine sense of pedaling. Widely spaced writing, melodic leaps, irregular metric and rhythmic groupings, much use of the trill, and lush sonorities are characteristic of his style. His infinite exploration of technical means makes new demands on the pianist, especially in his use of fourths, which require a new type of digital skill. Ten piano sonatas form the core of Scriabin's creative output. They provide an accurate chronicle of his evolution from the "Russian Chopin" to the mystical innovator of the avant-garde.

Selected Piano Works (G. Philipp—CFP) Vol.1: Etudes Opp.8, 42, 65. Vol.2: Preludes, Poems and Other Pieces, Part 1, Opp.11, 27, 32, 47, 56, 72, 73, 74. Vol.3: Preludes, Poems and Other Pieces, Part 2, Opp.13, 16, 38, 45, 48, 49, 51, 52, 57, 58, 59, 61, 63, 67, 69, 71. Vol.4: 21 Mazurkas Opp.3, 25, 40. Vol.5: Sonatas Nos.1–5. Vol.6: Sonatas Nos.6–10.

Sonatas (Sheldon—MCA; IMC; GS). Opp.6, 19, 23, 30, 53, 62, 64, 66, 68, 70.

The Complete Preludes and Etudes (Dover 1973). Reprint of Moscow 1966, 1967 editions. Opp.8, 11, 33, 42, 48, 65, 74, and the Preludes and Etudes from Opp.2, 9, 13, 15, 16, 17, 22, 27, 31, 35, 37, 49, 51, 56, 59, 67. 108 pieces in all. Editorial marks in English. Presents a complete spectrum of Scriabin's work.

    See: Simon Nicholls, "The Etudes of Alexander Scriabin," *Piano Journal*, 1/3 (1980):22–24.

    Hilda Somer, "Scriabin's Complete Preludes and Etudes," PQ, 94 (Summer 1976):46–47.

Selected Works (Murray Baylor—Alfred 1974). 30 pieces, including: 6 etudes; 11 preludes; 2 Poems Op.32/1, 2; Mazurka Op.40/1; 4th Sonata Op.30; Quasi valse Op.47; Album Leaf Op.45/1; Winged Poem Op.51/3; Languorous Dance Op.51/4; Ironies Op.56/2; Nuances Op.56/3; Desire Op.57; Strangeness Op.63/2; Garlands Op.73/1. Includes discussions of the music and the playing of Scriabin, and photographs. Contains some of the technically easiest pieces. An excellent introductory anthology. Int. to M-D.

33 Selected Piano Pieces (CFP). Preludes, Poems, Mazurkas, and other pieces from Opp.9 (for left hand), 11, 13, 16, 25, 27, 31, 33, 37, 40, 44, 45, 46, 47, 48, 51, 56.

Mazurkas, Poèmes, Impromptus and Other Works for Piano (Dover 1991) 309pp. Republication of earlier Russian editions. The other works are 3 Valses Opp.1, 38, 47, Op. Posth. Allegro appassionato Op.4. Allegro de concert Op.18. Polonaise Op.21. Fantaisie Op.28. Nocturne for left hand Op.9. Morceaux Op.2/3; Op.45/1, 2; Op.49/3; Op.51/1, 3, 4; Op.52/1, 2, 3; Op.57/1, 2; Op.59/1. 2 Nocturnes Op.5. Scherzo Op.46. 4 Pieces Op.56/2, 3. Feuillet d'album Op.58. Poème Nocturne Op.61. Ver la flamme Op.72. 2 Dances Op.73. Canon Op. Posth. Contains a glossary of French terms. Int. to D.

Keyboard Essentials (GS). Easier short pieces. M-D.

SEPARATE WORKS (listed numerically by opus numbers):

Waltz Op.1 f (CFP). Derivative but charming. M-D.

Three Pieces Op.2. Study c♯ (CFP; GS; CF); Prelude B (Simrock); Impromptu à la Mazur C (Simrock). Chopinesque. M-D.

Ten mazurkas Op.3, b, f♯, g, E, d♯, c♯, e, b♭, g♯, e♭.

Allegro appassionato e Op.4 (Bo&H). Liszt influence. M-D to D.

Two Nocturnes Op.5, f♯, A (JWC). Charming. M-D.

Sonata No.1 f Op.6 1892 (Belaieff). Allegro con fuoco: chordal, dramatic arpeggi gestures, *pppp* ending. No title: slow, improvisatory movement. Presto: fast octaves in low register, agitated; leads to Funèbre: pedal point on F, chordal mid-section at *pppp*, surprise final bar. Romantic. Chopin influence. M-D.

Two Impromptus à la Mazur Op.7 g♯, f♯ (CFP). Light, chromatic pieces. M-D.

Twelve Studies Op.8 (Belaieff; CFP; IMC). Chopinesque treatment. C♯; f♯; b; B; E; A; b♭; A♭; c♯; D♭; b♭; d♯ (GS): vibrant and stormy. M-D.

Available separately: E, D♭, d♯ (Belaieff)

Two Pieces for the Left Hand Op.9 (Bo&H). Prelude c♯: requires sensitive control. Nocturne D♭: a ravishing, Romantic display piece. M-D.

Available separately: Prelude, Nocturne (GS; CF). Prelude (TP).

See: Samuel Randlett, "Scriabin's Prelude for the Left Hand," *Clavier*, 17 (April 1978):23–29.

Two Impromptus Op.10 (Belaieff) f♯, A. Imaginative, musical. M-D.

Twenty-four Preludes Op.11 (Henle; Belaieff; CFP; IMC; EBM). Through the cycle of keys. Varied moods, Chopin influence, charming. See especially D, f♯, D♭, f, d. M-D to D.

Two Impromptus Op.12 (Bo&H). F♯, b♭. Colorful. M-D.

Six Preludes Op.13 (Belaieff). C, a, G, e, D, b. Easier than some of the other Preludes.

Two Impromptus Op.14 (Bo&H). B, f♯. Post-Romantic sonorities. M-D.

Five Preludes Op.15 (Belaieff). A, f♯, E, E, c♯. Lyrical, Romantic. M-D.

Five Preludes Op.16 (Belaieff; CF). B, g♯, G♭, e♭, F♯.

Seven Preludes Op.17 (Bo&H; Belaieff). d. E♭: octave study. D♭. b♭. f: brilliant Prestissimo. B♭: quiet Andante doloroso. g: nervous Allegro assai. M-D.

Concert Allegro Op.18 b♭ (Belaieff). Showy concert piece. M-D.

Sonata No.2 Op.19 g♯ 1892–97 (Belaieff; K; IMC) 12 min. Subtitled *Sonata-Fantasy*. Andante: melancholy, melody rises out of widely spaced figuration, reflective. Presto: constant triplets, sweeping melodies. The entire work is memorable melodically and sophisticated pianistically. M-D to D.

Polonaise Op.21 b♭ (Belaieff; IMC). Contains some brilliant octaves. M-D to D.

Four Preludes Op.22 (GS; Belaieff). g♯, c♯, B, b. Very lyrical.

Sonata No.3 Op.23 f♯ 1897 (Belaieff; CFP; IMC). Drammatico; Allegretto; Andante; Presto con fuoco. More interesting for the manner in which ideas are developed than for the ideas themselves. Four large movements that pass through many states. One of Scriabin's most accessible works. M-D to D.

Nine mazurkas Op.25 (Bo&H). Scriabin's personality is beginning to show. M-D.

Two Preludes Op.27 (GS; Belaieff). g, B.

Fantasy Op.28 b (IMC; Belaieff; K). Liszt and Wagner influence. A work of great complexity and subtlety. Virtuoso demands. D.

Sonata No.4 Op.30 F♯ 1903 (Belaieff; IMC). Andante: delicate, shimmering; leads to a Prestissimo volando: driving, enormous climax that reworks the opening Andante theme. One of the shortest but one of the most grandiose and remarkably unified of the sonatas; sheer sensuousness becomes a prominent element. A progression from melancholy and languor through struggle and flight to luminosity takes place in the two connected movements. Scriabin prefaces the sonata with a poem that serves as a program for the composition. M-D to D.

Four Preludes Op.31 (Belaieff). D♭-C, f, E♭, C. Characteristics of early and later styles. M-D.

Two Poems Op.32 (Belaieff; K; IMC). F♯ (CF), D (CFP). The second Poem points toward future harmonic and thematic treatment. M-D.

Four Preludes Op.33 E, F♯, C, A♭ (Belaieff). A varied, well-balanced set. M-D.

Tragic Poem Op.34 B♭ (Belaieff; IMC; K). Liszt influence, use of the ninth with raised fifth used more and more. D.

Three Preludes Op.35 (Belaieff). D♭, B♭, C. Chopin, Wagner, and Schumann influence. M-D.

Satanic Poem Op.36 C (Belaieff; IMC; K). Virtuoso writing, terms "riso ironico" and "ironico" suggest mood of the work. D.

Four Preludes Op.37 (Belaieff). b♭, F♯, B, g. Mesto: expressive. Maestoso; chordal. Andante: lyric. Irato impetuoso: angry. M-D.

Waltz Op.38 A♭ (Belaieff). Advanced harmonies, a favorite with Scriabin. Rich tapestry, dense figuration; provides a rarefied atmosphere. M-D.

Four Preludes Op.39 (CFP; Belaieff). F♯, D, G, A♭.

Two Mazurkas Op.40 D♭, F♯ (CFP; Belaieff). Delicate, elegant. M-D.

Poem Op.41 D♭ (Belaieff). Less demanding than other Poems, Liszt influence. M-D.

Eight Studies Op.42 (Belaieff; IMC; K). No.5 c♯ (Belaieff).

Two Poems Op.44 (Belaieff). C: 2/4, Lento. C: 3/8, Moderato. Well-contrasted pieces. M-D.

Three Pieces Op.45 (Belaieff; K). Album leaf E♭; Poème Fantasque C; Prelude E♭. Delightful set of miniatures. Early style. Int. to M-D.

Scherzo Op.46 C. 6/8 Presto.

Quasi-Valse Op.47 F.

Four Preludes Op.48 (Bo&H: Belaieff). No.1: F♯, impetuous. No.2: C, a delightful eight bars. No.3: D♭, restless. No.4: C, a celebration.

Three Pieces Op.49 (Belaieff). Etude E♭; Prélude F; Rêverie C. Full chords, large span required. M-D.

Four Pieces Op.51 Fragilité E♭: frequent meter changes. Prelude a: sober. Poème ailé B. Danse languide G: especially appealing. M-D.

Three Pieces Op.52. Poem C: meter changes. Enigma: no definite tonality. Poème languide B. M-D.

Sonata No.5 Op.53 1908 (Bo&H; CFP; IMC; MMP). One movement, fantasy-like, mystical, orchestrally conceived. Prefaced with lines from "Le Poème de l'Extase." Requires a rhythmic fluidity and an acute sensitivity to Scriabin's unique methods of voicing chords whereby tones that outline the sonata's harmonic structure must be stressed.

Four Pieces Op.56 (Belaieff). Prelude E♭; Ironies C; Nuances; Etude.

Two Pieces Op.57 (Bo&H; Belaieff). Desir: many augmented sonorities. Caresse Dansée: delicate. Two of Scriabin's best small works. M-D.

Album Leaf Op.58, 3/4. Con delicatezza, steamy mysticism somewhat similar to *Träumerei*. Int.

Two Pieces Op.59. Poème; Prélude. Early and late Scriabin characteristics. M-D.

Poème-Nocturne Op.61 (K). Complex harmonic usage, interesting scale passages. M-D.

Sonata No.6 Op.62 1911–12 (Bo&H). One movement, no key signature, dissonance exploited, strikingly ominous quality, judgment-day music, with fleeting suggestions of heavenly bliss. D.

Two Poems Op.63. Masque: 6/8, Allegretto. Etrangeté: 9/8, Gracieux, Délicat. M-D.

Sonata No.7 Op.64 1911 (Bo&H). Subtitled "White Mass." One movement, terms such as "mystérieusement sonore," "menaçant," "impérieux," and "comme des éclairs" point out the mystical element. The most elusive, intuitive, and technically complex of all the sonatas. D.

Three Studies Op.65 (CFP). B♭, C♯, G. In ninths, sevenths, and fifths: no key signatures. No.2 is perhaps Scriabin's most serenely beautiful piece. No.3 is loaded with electric energy that borders on the psychotic. M-D.

Sonata No.8 Op.66 1913 (Bo&H; CFP). Longest of the sonatas. One movement, two development sections, built on a basic chord. Lowered tenth plays an important role. Dancelike coda, subtle. A bewitching and multilayered work, full of polyrhythms, textural entanglements, and difficult passage-work. D.

Two Preludes Op.67 (Rahter). Andante: 5/8. Presto: 4/8.

Sonata No.9 Op. 68 1913 "Black Mass" (CFP; IMC). Diabolical element, markings such as "perfide" and "avec une douceur de plus en plus caressante et empoisonée." Presents a clear structural profile plus continuous development of four contrasting musical ideas. Twisting melodies and chords. One of the most successful sonatas, perhaps the greatest. D.

Two Poems Op.69 (Simrock). Allegretto: 3/4. Allegretto: 6/8. These pieces are almost too subtle to be appreciated in a normal concert-hall setting. They require an amazing dynamic control through a myriad of levels between *pp* and *mf* and a velvet, gossamer tone. M-D.

Sonata No.10 Op.70 1913 (CFP; IMC). A complex and diffuse structure posing great problems in performance. The trill plays such an important role that the composer referred to this work as his "sonata of insects." Resembles a tapestry of improvisation. Fluid polyrhythms and layered sonorities. Enigmatic. D.

Two Poems Op.71 (CFP; Rahter). Fantastique (CFP); En revant. M-D.

Poem vers la flamme Op.72 1914 (CFP; K; IMC) 5 min. One chord generates this work; it begins in darkness and moves inexorably toward dazzling light. Great climax, intense, totally bizarre. D.

Two Dances Op.73 (IMC; Rahter). Guirlandes: built on the opening upward figure. Flammes sombres: descriptive. M-D.

Five Preludes Op.74 (IMC). Douloureux, déchirant; Très lent, contemplatif; Allegro drammatico; Lent, vague, indécis; Fier, belliqueux. Some of Scriabin's finest shorter pieces, intense, highly personal creations. M-D.

COLLECTIONS:

Sixteen Preludes (Deis—GS). Opp.15/1–5; 22/1–4; 27/1–2; 35/1–3; 51/2; 56/1.

Album of Twelve Selected Preludes (Philipp—IMC). From Opp.11, 13, 15, 16, 27, 48, 51, 59, 67.

Album of Six Pieces (IMC). Albumleaf Op.58; Désire Op.57/1; Etude Op.2/1; Guirlandes Op.73/1; Masque Op.63/1; Poem Op.59/1; Tragic Poem Op.34.

Album of Scriabin Masterpieces (Sugarman—EBM). Preludes Op.11/9, 13, 15; Op.16/4; Op.27/2; Op.45/3; Op.48/4, Op.74/2; Etudes Op.2/1; Op.8/5, 10, 12; Op.42/4; Nocturnes Op.5/2; Op.9/2 (for left hand alone); Poème Op.32/1; Poème tragique Op.34; Poème fantasque Op.45/2; Poème ailé Op.51/3; Poème Op.69/2; Feuillet d'Album Op.45/1; Scherzo Op.46; Quasi Valse Op.47; Danse languide Op.51/4; Ironies Op.56/2.

Etudes (K 3941). Includes Op.2/1; Op.8/1–12; Op.49/1; Op.56/5; Op.65/1, 2.

Ten Preludes Opp.15, 74 (K 9492).

Twelve Preludes for the Intermediate Pianist (Dorff—TP). Excellent for adults.

Youthful and Early Works of Alexander and Julian Scriabin (D. Garvelmann—

MTP). Foreword by Faubion Bowers. A lavishly produced volume of unknown piano works by father and son. Several manuscript facsimiles are published for the first time. 157 pp. Includes: Canon (1883); Nocturne A♭, 2 versions; Sonate-Fantasie g♯ (1886); Valse g♯; Valse D♭; Variations sur un thème de Mlle. Egoroff (1887); Mazurka F (1889); Mazurka b (1889); Feuillet d'album (1889); Sonata e♭ 3 movements (1887–89); Allegro appassionato Op.4 (1892); Fantasy for 2 pianos (1889); Aria from the Opera *Keistut and Beirut* (1891); Fuga (1892); Romance for Voice and Piano (1893); Romance for Waldhorn and Piano (1893); Etude Op.8/12 alternate version (1894–95); Variations sur un thème populaire russe pour quatuor d'archets (1898); Feuille d'album F♯ (1905). Works by Julian Scriabin, son of Alexander: 3 Preludes: Op.2 (1918); Op.3 (1918); The last prelude (1919). M-D.

See: John Rodgers, "Four Preludes Attributed to Julian Skriabin," *Nineteenth-Century Music*, IV/3 (Spring 1983):213–19.

See: Faubion Bowers, *Scriabin*, 2 vols. (Tokyo and Palo Alto: Kodansha International Ltd., 1969).

——, "How To Play Scriabin," PQ, 74 (Winter 1970–71):12–18.

A. Eaglefield Hull, "Survey of the Pianoforte Works of Scriabin," MQ, 2 (October 1916):601–14.

Edwin Hymnovitz, "Playing the Scriabin Etudes: Problems of Keyboard Technique and Style," JALS 14 (December 1983):43–58.

M. Montagu-Nathan, *Handbook of the Pianoforte Works of Scriabin* (London: Chester, 1922).

Samuel L. Randlett, "Elements of Scriabin's Keyboard Style," PQ, 74 (Winter 1970–71):20–25; PQ, 75 (Spring 1971):18–23; and PQ, 77 (Fall 1971):24–27.

——, "The Nature and Development of Scriabin's Pianistic Vocabulary," diss., Northwestern University, 1966. Scriabin's pianistic vocabulary is divided into twenty-four devices, and the use of each device is traced in detail.

Jay Reise, "Late Skriabin: Some Principles behind the Style," *19th Century Music*, IV/3 (Spring 1983):220–31.

Humphrey Searle (1915–1982) Great Britain

After 1946 Searle used 12-tone technique in all his compositions. He and Elisabeth Lutyens were the first English composers to use it.

Vigil Op.3 1949 (Lengnick) 7 min. "France, 1940–44," Three main sections, thick textures, pianistic sonorities, fine craftsmanship. M-D.

Ballade Op.10 1943 (J. Williams) 7 min. Liszt influence, strong virtuoso writing. D.

Threnos and Toccata Op.14 1948 (Lengnick) 6 min. 12-tone. D.

Piano Sonata Op.21 1951 (OUP) 16 min. Based on thematic transformation within the 12-tone system. Great variety of styles are contained in this one-movement architectural structure. Begins with a statement of the row and soon develops into a virtuoso display of Romantic exhibitionism. Liszt *Sonata* b is the model. D.

Suite for Piano Op.29 1955 (Schott) 10 min. In album *Contemporary British Piano Music*. Atonal. Third movement contains some serial techniques. M-D to D.

Prelude on a Theme of Alan Rawsthorne Op.45 1965 (Faber) 3½ min. Theme comes from Rawsthorne's *Elegiac Rhapsody*. Searle's piece is short, 12-tone, with varied meters, yet it retains the lyrical character of the original theme. M-D.

Pia Sebastiani (1925–   ) Argentina

4 Preludes 1944–47 (PIC). Published separately. Nos.1 and 3: technically the easiest, with No.3 (Lento) freer. No.2: vigorous and rhythmic, ends quietly. No.4: bright and festive. M-D.

Simon Sechter (1788–1867) Bohemia

Franz Schubert studied with Sechter.

Hommage à Franz Schubert (Schott) Vol.I in *Journal for the Pianoforte*. Three elegiac pieces in honor of Schubert. Int. to M-D. For full description see Collections: Tombeau, Hommage section.

Ruth Crawford Seeger, see Crawford Seeger, Ruth

Mátyás Seiber (1905–1960) Great Britain, born Hungary

Gregorian chant, sixteenth-century vocal polyphony, folk music, jazz, and 12-tone technique all played a part in the music of Seiber. He was extremely versatile as a musician, adapting many musical styles, past and present, into his own.

3 Hungarian Folksongs 1922 (WH 4003) 5pp. Modal. In a style between Kodály and Bartók. Thoroughly attractive. Int.

Scherzando Capriccioso (Schott 10247 1953) 6pp. Jazz influence, syncopation, accented full chords, many tempo changes; a quirky humor comes through. M-D.

Rüdiger Seitz (1927–1991) Austria

Aperçus 12 transparent Stücke. Epigramme (Dob 1974) 15pp. Lucid, fresh style in Hindemith idiom. M-D.

Epigramme (Dob 1974) 11pp. Ten pieces. Similar to the *Aperçus*. M-D.

Sonatine 1955 (Dob) 7pp. Alla marcia. Scherzo. Espressivo. Rondo: especially attractive. Short playable movements influenced by Hindemith, some counterpoint. Int. to M-D.

Carlos Seixas (1704–1742) Portugal

Seixas, one of the most important Portuguese keyboard composers of the eighteenth century, was probably a student of Domenico Scarlatti. Seixas's sonatas differ from Scarlatti's in their use of two themes. In addition to the collection *Cravistas Portugueses*, which contains 12 Toccatas and 12 Sonatas, the following publications make most of Seixas's keyboard compositions available in modern editions.

80 Sonatas para Instrumentos de Tecla. Transcribed and edited by M. S. Kastner. Vol.X, *Portugaliae Musica,* Serie A (Gulbenkian Foundation 1965). Also available in 4 vols: Sonatas 1–18, 19–39, 40–60, 61–80. Excellent commentary in English and French. Int. to M-D.

25 Sonatas para Instrumentos de Tecla (Kastner, Valeriano—Gulbenkian Foundation 1980) 112pp. Most of the binary first movements are followed by Minuets. There are also cases where the beginnings of both movements are related by a common motive. Thematic development is used more frequently than with D. Scarlatti and A. Soler. Int. to M-D.

See: Elyse Mach, "Rediscovering an Old Master—Carlos Seixas," *Clavier,* 8 (November 1969):36–37. Also includes a reprint of *Sonata* e No.14, pp.24–27.

José Serebrier (1938–   ) USA, born Uruguay

Sonata 1957 (PIC). Allegro molto vivace: animated, meter changes, percussive. Andante: tender, expressive, large dynamic range. Moto perpetuo: driving Presto with much two-part texture. Effective tonal writing in three contrasting movements. M-D.

David Serendero (1934–   ) Chile

Reinhild: Rapsodía para piano (PAU 1961). Sectionalized by varied tempi and textures. Harmonics and tapping on wood of piano employed. Freely chromatic. Chords of sevenths and ninths used extensively in concluding section. Requires advanced pianism. D.

Tibor Serly (1900–1978) USA, born Hungary

Sonata in Modus Lascivus 1973 (PIC) 26pp. 15 min. Three movements, MC, many accidentals. Modus Lascivus is a system of composition Serly developed over a period of years. D.

Kazimierz Serocki (1922–1981) Poland

Krasnoludki (The Gnomes) 1953 (PWM). Seven miniatures in a freely tonal style. Int.

Suite of Preludes for Piano (PWM 1952) 10 min. "The fourth, fifth, and sixth preludes represent the first dodecaphonic post-war writing in Poland. The composer noted that the Suite does not fully comply with the Schönberg practices" (BBD, p.157).

A Piacere (PWM 1963). Combines serial and aleatory practices, in three sections, ten structures for each section. Preliminary remarks, table of abbreviations, and symbols in Polish, English, and German. D.

Juan de Sessé y Balaguer (1736–1801) Spain

Seis fugas (Almonte Howell—UME 22159 1976) 40pp. For keyboard instruments. Preface in Spanish and English. Sonorities varied through freely voiced changes of register and texture. Capricious and good-humored writing. M-D.

Roger Sessions (1896–1985) USA

The music of Sessions has a weighty philosophic character, full of long phrases, extended expressive gestures, complex counterpoint, motivic development, and traditional forms. He has influenced countless younger composers in the USA. His music for the piano offers a microcosm of his complete works.

Sonata No.1 1930 (Schott). Andante—Allegro; Andante; Molto vivace. In three large movements plus the opening cantilena. Involved, neoclassic, connecting movements, substantial, compact and strong ideas, clearly defined. D.

From My Diary 1937–40 (EBM). Poco adagio: mainly three voices, serious, melodic. Allegro con brio: ABA, fast passage-work, strong climactic points, peaceful mid-section, quiet close. Larghissimo e misterioso: short, atmospheric, sensitive. Allegro pesante: vigorous, sharp rhythmic chordal accents, rhythmic syncopation of a main theme in 3/8 set against a basic meter of 2/4. Intense character pieces (like a small suite) in contrasting moods. Linear. M-D.

Sonata No.2 1946 (EBM). Allegro con fuoco; Lento; Misurato e pesante. Large-scale work to be played without pause, highly chromatic. Contains broad ideas and is intellectually complex; wears well. Outer movements are built on relentless development of ideas and explosive contrast of sections. Probably one of the most important piano sonatas by an American composer of the twentieth century. A challenge to the finest pianist. D.

Sonata No.3 1964–65 (EBM). Adagio e misterioso—Sostenuto; Molto allegro e con fuoco; Lento e molto tranquillo (In memoriam: Nov. 22, 1963). Large, complex, and expressionistic work; dark, uneasy, troubling. Serial, with the same row used in all movements. The middle movement is the most demanding; three separate lines must be voiced simultaneously at some places, fluctuating densities, continuous unfolding. Of transcendental difficulty. D.

Five Pieces 1974–75 (Merion) 23pp. 13 min. Atonal, brooding, contrasting (slow, fiery, light, agitated, very slow), imaginatively shaped. The powerful fourth movement and the elegaic fifth movement are very special. Written in memory of Luigi Dallapiccola. Thorough pianism and mature musicianship required. D.

Waltz 1978 (Merion 1983) 3pp. Originally contained in collection *Waltzes* (CFP) 66735 1978). Freely tonal around b, a few changing meters from the original 3/8: 4/8, 5/8, 9/16; built from thematic germ of b, c♯; more difficult than it looks. M-D.

See: David Burge, "Piano Music of Roger Sessions," CK, 6 (October 1980):61.

Arvi Sinka, "The Piano Music of Roger Sessions," diss., Indiana University, 1965.

Mordecai Seter (1916–1994) Israel, born Russia

Chaconne and Scherzo (IMI 1956). A misty theme, five variations, and a scherzo, which is a sixth variation. The variations are in turn figurative, florid, in two voices, canonic, etc. Theme reappears at end of Scherzo. The music dissolves at the conclusion. D.

Sine Nomine 1973 (IMI 274) 12pp. 10 min. In three parts. 1. Slow chords in low register, enigmatic. 2. An "amabile" in a lively 6/8. 3. Armonioso: sustained notes, returns to opening large bass chords. Int. to M-D.

Janus 1972 (IMI 249) 15pp. 13 min. In two sections, the second of which is the shortened inversion of the first. Musical elements are based on an original diatonic scale of 12 notes, as well as its inversion and its retrograde progression, including its transposition at the interval of a fifth. The material undergoes a free development. M-D to D.

Soliloquio 1972 (IMI 246) 11pp. 13 min. Note in Hebrew and English. In two sections. Sequence of long chords leads to unresolved dissonances. Second section is a vigorous left-hand exercise with ostinato triplets supporting a sparse right-hand part. At end the two hands mirror each other. Requires great sensitivity to nuance in phrasing. M-D.

Improvisation 1983 (IMI 1992) 15pp. "The work consists of three contrasting movements. It is based on common material—the following original 21-tone diatonic mode and its inversion" (from the score, which includes the 21-tone diatonic mode). Unbarred, shimmering sonorities, freely tonal. M-D.

Presence 1986 (IMI 1992) 9pp. "The material of the composition is based on the following original 23-tone diatonic mode and its inversions, starting with a large tenth" (from the score, which includes the 23-tone diatonic mode). Three contrasting sections, varied figurations, impressionistic influence. M-D.

Kilza Setti (1932–   ) Brazil

8 Variações Sobre um tema popular "Onde Vais, Helena" (Ric BR 1972) 19pp. 15 min. Eight variations in individualistic style, strongly contrasted. Fondness for chromaticism noted. M-D.

Valsa (Ric BR 1970) 9pp. 5 min. Calmo: chromatic; thin textures; builds to climax in mid-section; ends *ppp*. M-D.

Déodat de Sévérac (1872–1921) France

Sévérac's piano music is descriptive, mainly of events and local places in his native Languedoc. Elements of improvisation as well as sonorous harmonies and traditional pianism are present.

Chant de la Terre: Poème géorgique 1900 (Sal; MMP). Four movements, Impressionist. See especially the Prologue, Intermezzo, and the sprightly Epilog, which is in Chabrier style. M-D.

En Languedoc 1904 (Sal). A suite of five pieces depicting scenes and events in the composer's home town. Movements 1, 2, 3, and 5 are available separately (Sal). An extended work. M-D.

Baigneuses au Soleil 1908 (Sal; MMP). Varied sonorities, lengthy. M-D.

Cerdaña 1910 (Sal) 61pp. Five extended movements. Four movements are available separately (Sal). M-D.

En Vacances 1912 (Sal; MMP). Two collections of seven and three pieces respectively. All the pieces in the first book and two in the second are available separately. Romantic. M-D.

Stances de Madame de Pompadour (Sal 1921) 4pp. A short character piece that is mainly Romantic in style and character with a few Impressionistic touches. M-D.

Peppermint—Get (Sal 1907; MMP). A valse brillante de concert, salon style, full of Gallic charm although not very brilliant. Three contrasting sections. Int. to M-D.

Sonata b♭ 1900 (EmM 1990) 54pp. Introduction in French and English. Style alternates between descriptive Romanticism and embryonic Impressionism. M-D to D.

Giovanni Sgambati (1841–1914) Italy
Sgambati was a virtuoso pianist who studied with Liszt.

Gavotte a♭ Op.14 (Schott). Exuberant rhythmic vitality. M-D.

Vecchio minuetto Op.18/2 (Schott). Graceful dance. M-D.

Raccolta di Pezza (Schott 2678 1939) 23pp. Album of pieces. Campane a festa Op.12 (Joy Bells): a short nocturnelike piece, ends with bell-like sounds in upper register. Idillio: ABA with an Alla marcia as the B section, pleasing, flowing. Berceuse-Rêverie Op.42/2: sectionalized, languid cantabile melodies. Preludio Op.18: agitated and impassioned. Alla Fontana Op.23/2: octotonic melody, chromatic accompaniment. Toccatina Op.12: con fuoco octaves and chords in 16ths tossed between hands. M-D.

Stephen K. Shao (–   ) China
Chinese Folk Songs for the Young Pianist (EBM 1973) 32pp. 14 folk songs skillfully arranged by retaining an Eastern flavor of melodic development with simple harmonic accompaniment, striking rhythms. Int.

Harold Shapero (1920–   ) USA
Three Sonatas (GS 1944). Cast in a modern idiom. Transparent works inspired by principles of the eighteenth century. No.3 is the most difficult but all require sensitive pianistic equipment. M-D.

Sonata f (PIC) 64pp. First movement: clear SA design. Second movement: a set of variations ("this movement may be performed separately under the title 'Arioso Variations'"). Third movement: perpetual-motion study with large skips and biting chordal sonorities. Large-scale work, employs bold gestures. Virtuoso technique required. D.

Variations c (PIC 1947). Jagged textures, large gestures, unusual sonorities. D.

Song Without Words (TP). Short, bitonal implications. Int.

Staccato Dance (TP). Sprightly, short. Careful articulation required. Int.

Ralph Shapey (1921–   ) USA
Shapey's craggy style features an internal play of energies that results from the continuous redefinition of fixed material, which remains in a constant state of tension. He calls himself a "radical traditionalist" (Anthony Tommasini, *New York Times*, May 14, 1996, page H-31).

3 Essays on Thomas Wolfe 1948–49 (TP 1980) 47pp. Quotations from Wolfe precede each Essay. Dazzling, angular, sharply etched ruminations on selections from Wolfe. Rushes forth in dramatic pianistic gestures. D.

7 Little Pieces 1951 (TP 1979) 11pp. Each piece demonstrates a special technical demand: legato without pedal, sudden dynamic shifts, repetition, etc. Expressive and effective contemporary writing that needs careful penetration to extract what is there. Serial influence. M-D.

21 Variations 1978 (TP) 36pp. 28 min. Reproduction of the composer's MS is difficult to read. Tables of comparative tempi. A difficult series of elaborations, highly complex rhythms, dissonant, well-paced variations, broad emotional range, somber and austere. D.

Arnold Shaw (1909–   ) USA

A Whirl of Waltzes (TP 1974). Seven MC waltzes with attractive titles, e.g., The Waltzing Walrus, Waltz for a Piano Teacher, A Waltz in Space. Int.

Mobiles (Tp 1966). Ten graphic impressions. Short, imaginative, written in a jazz style. Int. to M-D.

Plabiles (TP 1971) 23pp. Twelve Songs without Words composed to help develop phrasing and a singing line. Pieces are linked, with each new selection taking off from the terminal notes of the preceding piece. Int.

Allen Shawn (1948–   ) USA

Shawn attended Harvard and Columbia Universities, where he studied composition with Leon Kirchner, Earl Kim, and Jack Beeson; and he spent two years in Paris studying with Nadia Boulanger. Since 1985 he has been a member of the music faculty of Bennington College, Vermont.

Four Jazz Preludes 1980 (Galaxy 1985) 17pp. 14 min. These pieces "look more like jazz compositions than they really are . . . they are impressions of improvisation, and belong to the tradition of works such as Copland's *Four Piano Blues* or the ragtime movement in Ives' First Sonata. In short, they are molded from motives and intervals and have no trace of jazz form" (letter to the author, June 15, 1995). No.3 is subtitled "Spiritual." All are attractive, MC sounding. Require large span. M-D to D.

Improvisation No.3 1984 (Galaxy 1987) 8pp. 4 min. Style is somewhat similar to the *Four Jazz Preludes*: syncopation, seventh chords, choralelike section, lilting swing, glissando, strong conclusion. M-D.

Valentine 1984 (Galaxy 1987) 5pp. 4 min. Freely tonal with many accidentals, jazz influence. Large span required. M-D.

Rodion Shchedrin (1932–   ) Russia

Shchedrin's music shows a fine melodic gift and exuberance, coupled with intelligent and sensitive craftsmanship.

Toccatina (MCA). Triplet figuration, chromatic color, pianistic, *pp* ending. M-D.

Sonata (C. A. Rosenthal—MCA 1962). Allegro da Sonata: tone clusters, much dissonance. Variazioni Polifonici: seven variations, melodic interest resolves around a five-note theme. Rondo—Toccata: astringent sonorities, virtuoso writing, taxes both performer and audience. Cacophonous but exciting atonal writing. D.

Polyphonic Notebook 1972 (AMP 7762; MMP) 58pp. Cycle of 25 short polyphonic preludes, may be played as a complete work or as separate pieces, or in a group of two or more. Various titles, i.e., Invention in Two-Parts; Canon at the Octave; Toccatina-Collage; Passacaglia; Polyphonic Mosiac, etc. A fine collection for developing hand and finger independence, MC varied textures. Int. to M-D.

Sonata 1962 (GS). Three movements of strong dissonant writing. The second movement is a set of contrapuntal variations. D.

Pieces (MMP 2001). Poem; The Humpback Horse; Humoresque; A la Albéniz; Troika; Two Polyphonic Pieces. M-D.

24 Preludes and Fugues (MMP) in 2 vols., 12 in each. Illustrates numerous aspects of polyphonic writing. M-D.

Bright Sheng (1955–   ) China
Sheng survived the Chinese Cultural Revolution and came to the USA in 1982. He attended Columbia University and Queen's College.

My Song for Piano 1988 (GS 1994) 10 min. Suitelike. Section 1: two melodies gradually grow into four; rhythms of 5 vs. 6 and 6 vs. 7; builds to climax then slows to closing with performer tapping on low strings. Section 2: impressionistic treatment of pentatonic melody. Section 3: toccata-like, percussive treatment. Section 4, "Nostalgia": lyrical, quiet dynamic level. Sheng says "the phonetic pronunciation of 'My Song' (m'ai-sang) in Chinese can coincidentally be translated as 'pulsating voices.' And my 'm'ai-sang' (pulsating voices) is the folk music and dance of my native land." D.

Arthur Shepherd (1880–1958) USA
Gay Promenade (CF 1936). For young pianists. Rhythmic trouble spots. Easy.
Autumn Fields (CF 1936). For young pianists. Two-part melodic writing. Easy.
Second Sonata f (OUP 1930). Moderato, ma deciso; Moderato, cantabile ma semplice; Enfatico ed affrettato—Toccata. Impressionistic influences, well-constructed work. Stamina, brilliant playing, and a facile technique are required. M-D.
Eclogue (TP 1956). A Romantic character piece requiring considerable facility. M-D.
Capriccio II (Ric 1954). A large-scale work conventionally written but showing skill and an unusual understanding of the instrument. D.
In Modo Ostinato (TP 1956). 7/4 meter, lyric, on quiet side, ostinato transferred between hands, sophisticated elegance. M-D.
Gigue Fantasque (TP). Mainly two-part writing; interesting syncopations. Int.
Exotic Dance (OUP 1930). Short, effective, reflects a ghostly pallor. Int.
Lento Amabile (TP 1956). Freely chromatic, left hand frequently over right hand, sensitive voice leading necessary, asymmetric phrasing. M-D.

Noam Sheriff (1935–   ) Germany
Klaviersonate 1961 (Bo&Bo) 18pp. Molto moderato e giusto; Vivace. Freely tonal with many fast chromatic melodic groupings, echo imitation between hands, intense and dramatic, changing tempos, clusters. M-D to D.

Seymour Shifrin (1926–1979) USA, born Austria
4 Cantos (Merion 1949). Lento; Allegro; Largo Rubato e Espressivo; Vivace. 12-tone, heavily drenched with accidentals and dissonances. All are short. No.3 is barless, and No.4 uses clusters. M-D.
Responses 1973 (CFP 66622) 11pp. 6 min. Pointillistic, long-lined sense of growth from phrase to phrase, delicate staccato figures, phrase structure delineation very important, abstract and rhythmically varied texture. M-D to D.
Trauermusik 1956 (CFP). Focuses on intense lyrical expression. M-D.

Edward Shipley (–   ) Great Britain
La luna 1978 (Fentone) 16pp. 10 min. The composer says La luna "drains away both motivation and life, until only an empty shell is left," and "Everything is seen as allusion." Impressionistic, tightly controlled thematic and motivic material, many similar arabesques, short-winded phrases. M-D.

Dmitri Shostakovitch (1906–1975) Russia
Shostakovitch's early works show traces of urban folk music and of Bartók's general approach to folk music. His compositions contain sarcasm, pastiche, the grotesque, and the imitation of natural sounds. The piano music is never bombastic or overloaded.
Complete Edition (USSR). The piano works are found in Vols.39 and 40.
3 Fantastic Dances Op.5 1922 (Alfred 3597; Bo&H; MCA; K; IMC; CF; EBM). Light, charming, excellent for students. March: droll. Waltz: lyrical and capricious. Polka: unexpected harmonic changes. Int.
Sonata No.1 Op.12 1926 (Bo&H; CFP; MCA; K; Sikorski; USSR) 14 min. Cyclic one-movement work, brilliant virtuoso writing, highly dissonant, vigorous. Schönberg and Prokofieff influence. D.
Aphorisms Op.13 1926–27 (GS; MCA). 10 short character pieces. Highly experimental, clear textures, idiomatic, many ideas, adventurous harmonies. M-D.
24 Preludes Op.34 1932–33 (GS; CFP; IMC; MCA; K; BMC). Nos.14 and 24 available together (MCA). Follows key scheme of Chopin's Op.28 set. No.4: two-part fughetta. No.5: dashing etude. No.14: somber adagio rises to great climax, probably the best in the set. No.15: a delightful waltz. No.24: a gavotte à la Prokofieff. Idiomatic writing, varied moods. M-D to D.
See: Robert Dumm, "Performing Shostakvich's Prelude in A Minor, Op.34/2," *Clavier*, 35/2 (February 1996):20–24. Includes the music.
Sonata No.2 Op.64 1943 (Bo&H; CFP; MCA; K; MMP) 60pp. Allegretto; Largo; Moderato. Easier on performer and audience than No.1. Finale is a set of 9 variations with a quiet ending. M-D to D.
24 Preludes and Fugues Op.87 1951 (Bo&H; CFP; MCA; K; Sikorski). Nos.5, 11,

and 18 available separately (CFP). Baroque inspired, a contemporary *Well-Tempered Clavier* but with close affinity to *The Art of Fugue*. A few of the preludes are technically easier than those from Op.34. M-D to D.

See: Dean Elder, "Lesson on Performance of a Shostakovich Prelude and Fugue (No.17 of Op.87)," *Clavier*, 13 (September 1974):25–33.

5 Preludes (MCA; Sikorski). Short, technically easier than the Op.34 set and the Preludes from Op.87. No.3 requires a good octave technique. A fine recital group. Int. to M-D.

Doll's Dances (Alfred; CFP; MCA). Seven easy pieces. Called *Puppet Dances* in Alfred edition.

6 Children's Pieces (Alfred; MCA). Written for Shostakovitch's daughter. Easy miniatures, mainly 2 voices.

Melodic Moments (MCA 1969). Eight pieces selected from ballet, operetta, and film scores. Beautifully arranged by Denes Agay. An interesting collection, generally easier than Op.1. Attractive addition to the sparse Shostokovitch pedagogic repertoire. Int.

Album of Selected Piano Works (IMC). 12 Preludes from Op.34; 3 Fantastic Dances Op.1; Polka from "The Golden Age" ballet.

A Childhood Notebook (Ric). Six easy pieces.

Easy Pieces for Piano (Prostakoff—GS 1972). Excerpts from films, ballets, and operettas, transcribed in simplified versions. Also includes two pieces for piano duet. Easy.

Dmitri Shostakovitch, Igor Stravinsky, Alexander Scriabin: Their Greatest Piano Works (Copa 1973). See under Collections, General: Contemporary USSR.

Selected Preludes (EBM). Op.34/13, 16, 17, 24. Published together as a set. M-D.

Piano Compositions (CFP 5717). Three Fantastic Dances Op.1; Aphorisms Op.13; Five Preludes, without opus number. Int. to M-D.

Shostakovitch Album I (K). 3 Fantastic Dances; 4 Preludes Op.34/13, 16, 17, 24; 24 Preludes and Fugues Op.87/1–5, 6–9; Sonata No.I.

5 Miniatures from *Miniatures chorégraphiques* (Atoumian—MMP). Easy to Int.

Selected Works (MMP 7080). Three Fantastic Dances; Dances of the Dolls; Sonata I Op.12; 4 Preludes from Op.34; 9 Preludes and Fugues from Op.87. Int. to M-D.

Jan Sibelius (1865–1957) Finland

Sibelius's piano style is always definitely conceived for the piano, although most of his 117 piano pieces are insignificant when compared to the rest of his output.

6 Impromptus Op.5 1893 (Br&H; MMP). Experiments in capturing and sustaining a mood or atmosphere, whether brooding, like the first (a preview of the opening of the Symphony No.4); energetic, like the second (a dance reminiscent of the Russian dance in the finale of Beethoven's Quartet Op.130), or songful, like the fifth and sixth. M-D.

Sonata F Op.12 1893 (Br&H). Allegro molto: modeled after Beethoven's "Hammerklavier" Sonata but sounds as if Schubert and Grieg had done the rewriting. Andantino: alternately static and volatile. Vivacissimo: Brahmsian, ambitious; if its reach exceeds its grasp, it isn't by much. M-D to D.

Romance Db Op.24/9 (Alfred 3602; CF; Br&H; BMC; SP). Romantic, pianistic, effective recital piece. Int. to M-D.

Bagatelles Op.34 1914–16 (Br&H 8156) 28pp. Preface in English and German. 10 contrasted pieces. Int.

Kyllikki Op.41 1904–1906 (Br&H). Lyric pieces based on Kalevala legends (Finnish mythological inspiration). Largamente: stormy. Andantino: bardic, mystical. Commodo: dizzily energetic. M-D.
See: Glenn Gould, "Sibelius and the Post-Romantic Piano Style," PQ, 99 (Fall 1977):22–24. Includes the Andantino Op.41/2 and a discussion of this work and other piano works of Sibelius.

Valse Triste Op.44/1 (Alfred 3598) 7pp. Includes information about the music and performing suggestions. This piece and Romance Op.24/9 are the best-known piano works by Sibelius. M-D.

Ten Pieces Op.58 1909 (Br&H). Richly dissonant without taxing the layman's level of tolerance. A collection of Impressionistic sketches, including a night piece in tribute to Schumann ("Rêverie"), a striking "Fischerlied" (Sibelius's evocation of Venice), a beautiful "Air varié," and a "Serenade" that could have been written by Granados. Int. to M-D.

Three Sonatinas Op.67 f#, E, bb 1912 (Br&H; Fazer). Almost neoclassical; have the same Spartan concision as in Sibelius's symphonies. Highly evocative melodies and darkly hued harmonies will appeal to pupils with more than usual interpretative insight. Though titled *Sonatinas* their structure has little in common with formal sonatina design. Fine interpretative ability required to create an intelligent musical performance. M-D.
See: Cedric T. Davie, "Sibelius's Piano Sonatinas," *Tempo*, 10 (March 1945).

Two Rondinos Op.68 1912 (MMP). Similar to the sonatinas in style; like improvisations. M-D.

The Trees Op.75 1914 (WH). Suggest varied moods of nature; the set is one of the composer's best-known works. When the Rowan is in Bloom: delicate. The Lonely Pine: serious. The Aspen: delicate, perhaps the best of the set. The Birch: suggests the rustling leaves in the blowing wind. The Spruce: pianistic. M-D.
See: Robert Dumm, "A Tribute from Jean Sibelius," *Clavier*, 36/7 (September 1997):29–35. Includes the music to "The Spruce."

Five Sketches Op.114 (Fazer). Landscape; Winter Scene; Forest Lake; Song in the Forest; Winter Scene. Lovely scenes of Finland painted with effective Romantic chromatic colors. M-D.

Six Finnish Folksongs 1903 (Br&H). Miniatures, experiments in tonalities. Goes as far as bitonality in No.3 and some relatively daring modal harmonies in Nos.1 and 4. Int. to M-D.

See: Eric Blom, "The Piano Music," in *Sibelius, A Symposium*, ed. G. Abraham (New York: Norton, 1947; reprint, New York: Da Capo Press, 1975), pp.97–107.

Harold Levin, "Sibelius's Neglected Piano Music," *Clavier* (July–August 1994): 33–35. Contains music for *Sonatine* No.1.

Alec Rowley, "The Pianoforte Works of Jan Sibelius," *Musical Mirror* (May 1929):121.

Elie Siegmeister (1909–1991) USA

American Sonata (EBM 1944). Three movements based on popular American materials. Outside movements are highly rhythmic while the middle movement is lyric. M-D.

Sunday in Brooklyn 1946 (CF). Five Americana scenes: Prospect Park; Sunday Driver; Family at Home; Children's Story; Coney Island. Varied moods and techniques. M-D.

Americana Kaleidoscope (Sam Fox). 19 pieces, varied moods and techniques, suitable for teenage pianists. Int.

Toccata on Flight Rhythms (EBM 1942). From "Air Plane Suite," driving rhythms in 3 + 3 + 2 sequence, effective. M-D.

The Children's Day (MCA). Six children's pieces. Easy.

Sonata No.2 (MCA 1968). 18pp. One movement, dissonant, virtuoso writing, harmonics, clusters, plucked strings, nervous quality, polyrhythms, driving tempos, drastic register changes. D.

A Set of Houses 1978 (CF). Impressions of a country house, a two-story house, a city house, a monkey house, an old stone house, and a penthouse. Descriptive. Int.

Our Cat 1953 (CF 1996) 8pp. Catching a Mouse; Unravelling a Ball of Thread; Sleepy Time (All Day). This delightful miniature suite is colorful and somewhat suggestive of Copland's *The Cat and the Mouse*, but much easier. Int.

Robert Sierra (–   )

Tres Inventos 1987 (Subito Music Publishing 1992) 7pp. Each invention exploits a specific compositional device. Style is a mixture of jazz influence coupled with the improvisatory. Violento: alternation between octaves and single notes generates a new rhythm. Naive: a self-devouring canon flows over a Caribbean-like ostinato. Ritmico: Explores "truncated" rhythms, which compress or stretch the pulse by freely combining triplets, sixteenth notes, and quintuplets. Manic, restless rhythms. Effective group. M-D.

Paul J. Sifler (1911–   ) USA, born Yugoslavia

Three Tall Tales (Fredonia Press) with optional narration. Jack and the Beanstalk; The Frog Prince; The Three Bears. Humorous. Based on sound musical writing, effective. Easy to Int.

Thorkell Sigurbjörnsson (1938–   ) Iceland

Das Wohltemperierte Pianist 1971 (Iceland Music Information Center) 6 min. Concerned with musical abstractions, with careful references to Bach; octotonic; nationalistic overtones. M-D.

Thomasz Sikorski (1939–   ) Poland

Sonant (PWM). The elementary levels of attack and decay (action and consequence) are repeated until they become confused in the listener's mind. M-D.

Two Preludes (PWM). Short, contrasting character. M-D.

Hymnos 1979 (AA) 10pp. Consists mainly of loud chords interspersed with soft dissonances. Overly long and simplistic in form and content, alternating spurts of sound with long, awkward silences; seems like a meandering improvisation. D.

Friedrich Silcher (1789–1860) Germany

Sämtliche Klavierstücke: Original-kompositionen und Bearbeitungen (M. Frank —Carus Verlag 1992) 71pp. Contains all his original compositions and transcriptions for piano. Extensive preface and critical notes. Variations and single pieces. Int. to M-D.

Ann Silsbee (1930–   ) USA

Doors 1976 (ACA) 12 min. Beautiful and delicate clusters, filigree, "Parlando" style, unique. D.

Netty Simons (1913–   ) USA

Night Sounds (TP). Evening Haze; Thinking of Past Things; Stars on the Pond; The Rain Beats on the Rain. Short, atonal pieces that are evocative and contain sensitive harmonic, dynamic, and rhythmic colorations as well as dissonant counterpoint. M-D.

Time Groups No.1 (ACA 1964). Consists of 84 short sections that can be arranged in a number of different ways. Some unconventional notation and numerous directions for performance. Can be longer or shorter, depending on the arrangement of groups. Avant-garde. M-D to D.

Ralph Simpson (–   ) USA

Simpson teaches at Tennessee State University

Impromptu and Presentiment (Vivace) 16pp. Challenging and instinctive writing. Impromptu: unusual and effective rhythms. Presentiment: based on spiritual "Everybody Talking About Heaven Ain't Going There." M-D.

Robert Simpson (1921–1997) Great Britain

Sonata (Lengnick 1944) 34pp. Three movements. Well written, closely knit ideas, traditional style. M-D.

Variations and Finale on a Theme of Haydn (Lengnick 1948). Theme is a reversible minuet. 12 short variations and a lengthy finale. MC.

See: Wadham Sutton, "Robert Simpson's Piano Sonata," *Music Teacher,* 50 (February 1971):11.

Christian Sinding (1856–1941) Norway

Marche grotesque Op.32/1 (GS; CFP; Musica Obscura). Rhythmic, alternating-hand technique, fast scales. Int. to M-D.

Rustle of Spring Op.32/3 (Alfred 3604; CF; GS; Musica Obscura). Arpeggio figuration, effective. Probably the most popular piece describing this season. Int. to M-D.

Moods Op.103/5 1910 (Br&H 8117). Reminiscent of Liszt and Wagner. Large chords require large hand span. M-D.

Alvin Singleton (1940–   ) USA

Changing Faces. In collection *Changing Faces* (EAMC 1987) 4pp. Legato, thin textures, many repetitions of short figures ("minimal music"), evolving tonalities, many effective shifting accents. Subtle pedal use desirable. M-D.

Larry Sitsky (1934–   ) Australia, born China

Sitsky's style is described as "expressionistic (i.e., dealing with extreme emotional states) and influenced by the music of Bartók, Berg, and Bloch and by the esthetics of Busoni, on whom he has done extensive research" (DCM, p.684). Sitsky studied piano with Egon Petri from 1958 to 1961.

Bagatelles for Petra (Ric). 17 contemporary pieces for young pianists to introduce them to contemporary signs and sounds. Elbow clusters, boxed ostinato figures, free notation, and continuous pedal are some of the devices encountered. Int. to M-D.

Little Suite 1958 (Allans 1062) 6pp. Improvisation (Jazz Waltz); Folk Song; Nocturne; Two-Part Invention on a Name; Elegy. Clever, clusterlike chords, attractive. Int.

Sonatina Formalis 1960 (Allans 9038) 5pp. Melody with Accompaniment; Canon at the Tritone; Preludio; Fuga (on the name Egon Petri). MC, effective fugue. Int. to M-D.

Fantasia No.10 (Sikesdi Press 1996) 12pp. For the Emanuel Moór double keyboard piano. Written "in a freeflowing, quasi-improvisational style, attempting to exploit the particular characteristics of this piano. It cannot be performed on a normal piano" (from the score). D.

Fantasia No.8 on D. B. A. S. 1990 (The Keys Press 1996) 10pp. Written to commemorate the ten years since the passing of Australian composer Don Banks. The pitches D, B, A, S (E♭) are derived from the names Don Banks and Larry Sitsky. The piece requires great freedom and much rubato. Many performance directions, harmonic, one flat (E♭) for key signature, MC. M-D to D.

Nikos Skalkottas (1904–1949) Greece

Skalkottas studied with Arnold Schönberg. He used 12-tone technique strictly from 1925 to 1927 but gradually began to employ this technique much more freely in a personal, expressive manner. For a fine discussion of this development see BBD, pp.159–61.

15 Little Variations (UE 1927) 6½ min. Modified 12-tone technique closely constructed around two chord progressions. M-D.

10 Piano Pieces. (UE). From *Music for Piano Solo* (32 pieces for the piano, never completed). Andante Religioso; Rêverie in the Old Style; Rêverie in the New Style; Gavotte; Menuetto; Tango; Romance; Little Peasant March; Marcia Funebre; Greek Folk Dance. The composer emphasized that "The difficulties in these pieces can all be overcome and are nearly always there for the sake of some special virtuoso angle." M-D to D.

See: Misha Donat, "Skalkottas's 32 Piano Pieces," *Tempo*, 135 (December 1980):48–49.

Passacaglia (UE 1940). Free 12-tone organization. 20 short "variations" greatly contrasted. Impressive climax. Advanced pianism required. D.

Piano Pieces (Margun). 3 vols. From the *32 Klavierstücke*, which is one of the composer's most monumental creative achievements. Large in scope and imagination. Notes by Gunther Schuller. D.

Suite for Piano No.3 (UE 1962). Minuet and Trio; Variations on a Greek Song; Funeral March; Binary movement in 2/4. Free serial treatment. D.

Suite for Piano No.4 (UE 1941). 7 min. Toccata: bristling. Andantino: lyrical. Polka with Trio: clever. Serenade: Romantic. Free dodecaphonic writing. D.

Howard Skempton (1947–   ) Great Britain

Piano Pieces 1967–73 (Faber) 12pp. First Prelude: 5/4, repeated chords that gradually change each measure. One for Molly: melody embedded in tremolos. Simple Piano Piece: unbarred, chromatic, choralelike. Intermezzo: tremolo in right hand over moving chord in left hand. Riding the Thermals: extremely slow, quiet, formal, unbarred. Slow Waltz: for three hands. Quavers: repeated chords in eighth notes. A Humming Song: "play as slowly and quietly as possible, black notes should be hummed as well as played" (from the score). September Song: as slowly and quietly as possible. A fine introduction to avant-garde technique. Easy to Int.

Images 1989 (OUP 1994) 28pp. Commissioned by HTV West for a six-part television series entitled "Images." It was shown in 1989 to mark the 150th anniversary of the invention of photography. Music was required to complement the many sequences of evocative photographs. Barrie Gavin, the producer, had in mind something akin to Satie's *Gymnopédies*, like a sculpture viewed from different angles in a changing light, hence the remarkably similar character of the eight Preludes. Unlike most of the Interludes, they were composed without a specific sequence in mind (from the score). 8 Preludes. The Cockfight: a traditional song. Song 2. Variations. 8 Interludes. Postlude: The Keel Row. Pieces may be played in any order. Short, tonal, thin textures. M-D.

Nicolas Slonimsky (1894–1995) USA, born Russia

51 Minitudes 1972–76 (GS). A collection of erudite and witty miniatures, many of which are spoofs of more familiar pieces. Titles and details are often amusing: *Borborygmus*, the medical term for a rumble in the stomach; *Anabolism*, constructive metabolism; *Catabolism*, destructive metabolism. Each piece is "quite cachinogenic" (from the preface). Int. to M-D.

Haskell Small (1948–   ) USA

3 Impressions (EV 1979) 5pp. 2½ min. Andantino: bouyant. Misterioso: witty. Giocoso: charming. Show a fine sensitivity to tone color and atmosphere. Well fingered and pedaled. Int.

Roger Smalley (1943–   ) Great Britain
Piano Pieces I–V 1962–65 (Faber) 11pp. 6 min. These short epigrammatic studies are essays in concentrated, concisely thought-out, expressionistic piano
writing. Full of technical ingenuity (rhythmic formulae, space-time notation, and isorhythm), but technique is at the service of expression. Each
parameter is strictly controlled. Dynamics and pitch serialized. M-D.
See: Stephen Walsh, "Roger Smalley," M&M 17 (June 1969):37–40. Nos.1
and 4 of the above are printed and the works are discussed.
Missa Parodia I 1967 (Faber) 10 min. A sort of parodic intabulation of the composer's earlier *Missa Brevis*; utilizes techniques of variation and isorhythm.
M-D to D.
Monody 1972 (Faber) 10pp. 12 min. For piano and electronic modulation (one
player). Includes notes for performer. Like a fantasy, some unusual harmonic effects created by a ring modulator. Grave, fiercely embellished,
strong character. In 21 short sections, uses four different types of material,
strong rhythmic patterns. Some percussion: 4 triangles, 2 congas, 2 large
bongos or timbales. D.

Bedřich Smetana (1824–1884) Czechoslovakia
Smetana treated the Czech national dance form the way Chopin treated the ma-
zurka. All of Smetana's polkas are an important and too much neglected part of
the nationalistic piano repertoire.
6 Characteristic Pieces. Op.1 1848 (Artia; MMP). In the Forest; The Curious One;
Shepherdess; Longing; Warrior; Despair. Contains Lisztian overtones with
numerous octave leaps, canonic passages, and often rhapsodic format. M-D.
Bagatelles and Impromptus 1844 (Artia). Eight light character pieces that suggest
Chopin and Schumann. M-D.
Sketches Opp.4, 5 1858 (Artia). Four pieces in each opus. Delightful, intensely
lyrical. If any music can put melancholy to flight, it is this. Int. to M-D.
6 Dreams 1875 (Artia). Combines Lisztian chromatic melody with Chopin's keyboard sonorities. Frequently echoes other composers' work (the last piece,
Harvest Home, almost sounds like a cheery Bohemian paraphrase of the
finale of Brahms's Piano Concerto No.1). But the pieces are entirely original, with marvelous flow of melody, transparent harmony, and piquant
rhythms. M-D.
Sonata g 1849 (Artia). One long movement. The broadly conceived Adagio shows
considerable resource and imagination in the use of variation technique;
87 bars from the finale were borrowed for the Piano Trio in g. M-D.
3 Poetic Polkas Op.8 1855 (Artia). E♭, g, A♭. Many excellent melodic ideas with
which Smetana paints a charming tonal portrait of Bohemian village and
country life. M-D.
3 Wedding Scenes 1849 (Artia; MMP). Wedding Procession; Bridegroom and
Bride; Wedding Feast. From the same lovely, amiable folklike world of the
Bartered Bride. M-D.

Czech Dances Books I and II 1877 (Artia; MMP). Nationalistic flavor, harmonic ingenuity. Make considerable demands on the pianist. M-D to D.

Concert Study On the Seashore 1862 (GS; Artia). Virtuoso tone-poem. D.

6 Bohemian Dances (K 3980; CFP 4435; MMP). Display much variety and pianistic ingenuity within the restricted meter. M-D.

10 Polkas (CFP 4455). Taut and brilliant. M-D.

Selected Piano Works (Schott 7079) 55pp. 15 pieces that reflect the development of Smetana's creative inspiration, spanning over 30 years. Includes bagatelles, impromptus, Chanson Op.2/2, and polkas. The Polka F (1877) has unforgettable rising and falling figurations. M-D.

See: David Yeoman, "Smetana's Piano Music Reflects Bohemian Culture," *Clavier,* 35/3 (March 1996):16–18, 22. Includes music of *Polka* a, Op.12/1.

Michael Smetanin (1958–   ) Australia

Smetanin was born in Sydney. After studying at the Sydney Conservatorium of Music and winning numerous prizes and fellowships, he spent three years in Amsterdam studying composition with Louis Andreissen. Since then he has been living in Australia.

Stroke 1988 (Australian Music Center) 12pp. 8 min., 14 sec. "A stroke: a violent blow or a gentle caress; take your pick, either way it can be a sudden affliction" (from CD Tall Poppies 040 "Lisa Moore Stroke"). Fast alternation of hands, chromatic, glissandos in both hands in opposite directions, cluster sonorities, wide dynamic range, 2 pages of directions for pianist. Sounds more like a violent blow than a gentle caress. D.

Leo Smit (1921–1999) USA

Rural Elegy 1950 (Bo&H). Rondel; Toccata Breakdown; Hymn. Pleasing pieces. Int.

Sonata in One Movement 1951–55 (Belwin-Mills). In actuality, three short movements played without a break. Neoclassic, contrapuntal lines, direct harmonic and melodic usage. M-D.

Variations G 1954 (Bo&H). 12 variations that use many devices, quiet close. A distinguished large-dimension work. M-D to D.

Fantasy: The Farewell 1957 (BB). Sad, somber introduction; lively farewell and return of introduction. MC. M-D.

5 Pieces for Young People 1947 (CF). Linear, contrasted, appealing. Int.

7 Characteristic Pieces 1959 (BB). Suite of short pieces for concert use. Nos.1, 3, and 6 are especially interesting. M-D.

Dance Card 1986 (TP). Exhilarating; dance influence permeates entire work. M-D to D.

Hale Smith (1925–   ) USA

Evocation (CFP). "The entire piece derives from the row exposed in the first stave, and in several places has faint but definite rhythmic affinities with jazz phrasing. This doesn't mean that it's supposed to swing—it isn't, but the affinities are there" (from the Preface). A work of lyrical gesture and chordal sonorities. M-D.

Faces of Jazz 1968 (EBM) 16pp. Twelve short pieces, each titled; clever and effective. Int.

Anticipations, Introspections and Reflections 1971 (Merion) 10pp. 6 min. One movement in free SA design, changes of mood, kind of an expressionistic fantasy, tends to ramble, rhythmic difficulties, large chords. M-D to D.

Julia Smith (1911–   ) USA

Characteristic Suite (TP 1967) 16pp. 10 min. Canon; Waltz; Passacaglia (with 5 variations and coda); March; Toccata. MC. M-D.

Leland Smith (1925–   ) USA

Six Bagatelles 1965 (San Andreas Press) 6pp. Graphic realization by POP 10 computer. Strong voice-leading, contrapuntal textures, freely tonal, short, expert craft displayed. Expressionistic, careful and unusual notation used for pedal indications. M-D.

Sonata (ACA 1954). March; Fast (Rondo); Coda. Serial organization. March displays humor in Prokofieff vein. Mature pianistic equipment required. M-D.

4 Etudes (Merion 1952). Each one page. Disjunct, pointillistic writing. Preference for fourths, sevenths, and ninths. Requires large span. M-D.

Stuart Smith (1948–   ) USA

Pinetop 1976–78 (Lingua) 8pp. A tribute to Pinetop Smith. Contains no quotes from boogie-woogie. Freely improvisatory full of digressions and right and wrong turns. Should be played with a rough, strong touch. There should be no feeling of sections, just keep going. Proportional rhythmic relationships, pointillistic, B♭ opening and closing. M-D to D.

Naresh Sohal (1939–   ) Great Britain, born India

A Mirage 1974 (Novello 10025003) 9pp. 12 min. Composer's facsimile. Freely repeated notes, extreme registers and dynamics, proportional rhythmic relationships, mixture of Impressionistic and expressionistic characteristics. D.

Padre Antonio Soler (1729–1783) Spain

Soler wrote many sonatas in a one-movement design similar to those of Domenico Scarlatti. Later in his career he wrote sonatas in three and four movements. Frederick Marvin, in a letter to the author, stated that, "My belief is that he [Soler] was not a pupil [of Domenico Scarlatti]. He admired Scarlatti greatly (quoting him in his book *Key to Modulation* but does not in this book refer to him as his teacher). He does however mention his other teachers. His contact with Scarlatti would have been limited to a few weeks a year when the Royal family visited Escorial." Marvin claims to have collected over 200 sonatas, the last 20 after 1957.

Sonatas, Complete Edition (S. Rubio—UME). Vol.1: Sonatas 1–20. Vol.2: Sonatas 21–40. Vol.3: Sonatas 41–60. Vol.4: Sonatas 61–68. Vol.5: Sonatas 69–90. Vol.6: Sonatas 91–99. Vol.7: Sonatas 100–120.

Sonatas (F. Marvin—A. Broude). M=Marvin Catalogue number. Vol.I: Sonata c M.1; Sonata c M.2; Sonata g M.3; Sonata c M.4; Sonata C M.5; Sonata e M.6; Sonata f M.7; Sonata d M.8; Sonata 9 M.9. Vol.II: Sonata C M.10; Sonata c M.11; Sonata c M.12; Sonata B♭ M.13; Sonata E♭ M.14; Sonata D♭ M.15; Sonata b M.16; Sonata e M.17; Sonata F♯ M.18; Sonata f♯ M.19; Sonata g M.20; Sonata g M.21. Vol.III: Sonata g M.22; Sonata c M.23; Sonata c M.24; Sonata B♭ M.25; Sonata B♭ M.26; Sonata F M.27; Sonata a M.28; Sonata F M.29; Sonata D M.30; Sonata a M.31; Sonata G M.32; Sonata f♯ M.33; Sonata D M.34. Vol.IV: Sonata G M.35; Rondo e M.36; Sonata F♯ M.37; Sonata g M.38; Sonata F M.39; Sonata f M.40; Sonata A M.41. Vol.V: Sonata B♭ M.42 (four movements). Vol.VI: Sonata F M.43; Sonata c M.44. Vol.VII: Sonata C M.45 (four movements). Vol.VIII: Sonata (Rondo) G M.46; Sonata D♭ M.47.

See: Richard S. Hill, *Notes*, 16 (December 1958):155–57 for a review that compared all editions available at that time.

Selected Sonatas (F. Marvin—Henle 475) 84pp. Urtext edition with fingerings by the editor. Includes Sonatas G R.12; G R.14; c♯ R.21; G R.13; D♭ R.88; E♭ R.105; D no R.No.; E R.34; G no R.No.; d R.24; d R.49; G R.31; c no R.No.; c no R.No; G R.33; e R.26; F R.5; C R.9. M-D.

14 Sonatas (K. Gilbert—Faber) 70pp. From the Fitzwilliam Collection. Urtext edition. Includes Sonatas A R.1; G R.4; C R.8; C R.9; B R.11; E♭ R.16; c R.18; c R.19; c♯ R.20; c♯ R.21; d R.24; d R.25; e R.26; e R.27. Editorial notes. M-D.

Fandango Mia (Marvin—A. Broude; UME) 21pp. Colorful and exciting writing. Remarkable for its time. Wild dance that demands accuracy (especially for fast hand-crossings), drive, and endurance. D.

Sonata c M.1. Vivacious allegro, 3/8; bold opening, interesting transitions and codas, unusual phrase lengths. M-D.

Sonata B♭ M.13. Allegro spiritoso, 3/8; a playful rondo that is more difficult than it looks. M-D.

Sonata e M.17. Adagio, has four themes, trill chains, remarkable modulations, short development. One of the most expressive of all the sonatas. M-D.

Sonata f♯ M.19. Spanish character, many repeated figures, unexpected developments. M-D.

Sonata g M.21. Brilliant prestissimo alternates with a flowing cantabile, colorful trills, involved but effective cadenza. M-D to D.

Sonata F R.83. In collection *Masters of Spanish Piano Music* (Alfred 434) 4pp. Sounds like a fascinating Spanish folk dance. M-D.

See: Frederick Marvin, "An Almost Forgotten Composer," MJ, 18 (February 1960):34–36.

———, "On the Trail of Padre Antonio Soler," PQ, 80 (Winter 1972–73):17–19.

———, "Discovered Treasure: The Music of Antonio Soler," *Clavier*, 19 (July–August 1980):22–29. Includes Sonata d, M.28.

Reah Sadowsky, "Antonio Soler: Creator of Spain's Fifth Century of Musical Genius," AMT, 28 (September–October 1978):10, 12, 14–15. Contains an excellent discussion of the sonatas and the *Fandango*.

Harry Somers (1925–1999) Canada

3 Sonnets (BMI Canada 1958). Prelude; Lullaby to a Dead Child; Primeval. Each piece deals with a single idea. Complex, advanced harmonic idiom. Lullaby is written in 4/4 rather than usual 3/4. M-D.

12 × 12 Fugues (BMI Canada 1951). 12 short fugues using dodecaphonic technique. No.1 appears in the album *14 Pieces by Canadian Composers*. M-D.

Sonata III 1950 (Berandol 1813) 28pp. Large four-movement work in the classic-Romantic tradition, sharply defined thematic material. Virtuoso technique required. D.

Sonata V 1957 (Berandol). Three movements. Beautiful logical sense of phrase development and dramatic contrast. D.

Öistein Sommerfeldt (1919–   ) Norway

Sonatina No.1 Op.4/1 (NMO 1964) 17 pp. Three movements, FSF. Clear textures, solid sonorities; not difficult but some facility required. Int.

Sonatina No.2 Op.4/2 (NMO 1961). First movement: SA. Second movement: ABA. Third movement: Rondo (scherzo character). Prefers parallel thirds in bass. Carl Nielsen influence. Attractive. M-D.

Sonatina No.3 Op.14 (NMO 1968) 12 min. Three movements, FSF. Slow movement based on ground bass. Contrapuntal. M-D.

Suite No.1 Moods (NMO 1967) Five short movements. Inspired by Norwegian landscape. Highly contrasted are No.1, like a folk dance, and No.5, a vigorous dance. Neat fingerwork required in these largely two-part, linearly conceived movements. MC. M-D.

Fables Op.10 (NMO). Five pieces, two-part design, freely tonal. M-D.

Fables Op.15 (NMO). Five movements, contrapuntal throughout. M-D.

3 Sma Valser Op.17 (NMO 1971). 7pp. Small, freely tonal waltzes. Int.

Sonatina IV Op.20 (NMO 1970). 15pp. Largo—Allegretto; Adagio; Presto. Clear, linear, and attractive writing. M-D.

Sonatina V Op.31 (NMO 1972) 11pp. Allegretto grazioso; Adagio cantabile; Presto scherzando. Colorful, unusual harmonic progressions, thin textures in outer movements. M-D.

Short Seasonal Suite Op.49 (NMO). Four contrasting movements, each representing a season. Int. to M-D.

József Soproni (1930–   ) Hungary

Incrustations 1973 (EMB) 12pp. Freely dissonant and chromatic, pointillistic, proportional rhythmic relationships, much use of rubato, improvisational. Large span required. D.

Invenzioni sul B-A-C-H 1971 (EMB) 18pp. Six short pieces. Pointillistic, fast repeated notes, highly organized, clusters, strong dissonance. D.

Note Pages (EMB Z7672, Z7735) Vol.1: 44 pieces. Vol.2: 23 pieces. In the tradition of Bartók's *Mikrokosmos*; deals with the technique and performance of many of the compositional devices that are becoming a standard part of today's musical language. Easy to Int.

Kaikhosru Shapurji Sorabji (1892–1988) Great Britain
Sorabji's piano music presents a complex picture. Polyphonic writing is combined with decorative tendencies that produce music of the utmost difficulty. This, plus the fact that many of his works are unusually long, has made his music almost unplayable. In 1977 Sorabji lifted the ban on the performance of his works. In the same year he completed his Sixth Symphony (*Sinfonia Magna*) for piano solo but it is not yet published. He has also recently finished *Sinfonia Notturno* (also unpublished), which is supposed to be of epic dimensions! The young American pianist Michael Habermann is a strong champion of Sorabji's music.
Opus Clavicembalisticum (Curwen). In three parts, 12 subdivisions, 252pp. Requires more than five hours to perform. Described by the composer as "the most important work for piano since *The Art of Fugue*." Pars prima: 1. Introito; 2. Preludio corale; 3. Fuga 1; 4. Fantasia; 5. Fuga a due soggetti. Pars altera: 6. Interludium primum (Thema cum XLIV variationibus); 7. Cadenza 1; 8. Fuga a tre soggetti. Pars tertia: 9. Interludium alterum (Toccata: adagio passacaglia cum LXXXI variationibus); 10. Cadenza 2; 11. Fuga a quattro soggetti; 12. Coda stretta.
Three Piano Sonatas (OUP). These works display many rhythmic intricacies and an oriental luxuriance of detail and textural density. Varied sonorities, inventive figuration, and imaginative decoration are unequaled by any other composer of the contemporary or any other period. Sonata No.3 lasts about 1½ hours. It is totally athematic and defies analysis! Exhausting physical demands on the performer. D.
Prelude, Interlude and Fugue (Curwen 1920) Prelude: 5 pages of unmeasured sixteenth notes. Interlude: written on three staves, imitative; full chords require large span. Fugue: thick textures in flexible meters. Highly individual work, unusually difficult both technically and interpretively. D.
Pastiche on the Minute Waltz of Chopin (Music Treasure Publishers 1969) 5 min. Contrapuntal, interweaves melodic strands, is spread over the entire keyboard. Trill on A♭ builds to huge chordal tremolos. Probably the ultimate in a keyboard transformation of this waltz. D.
Le Jardin Parfum (OUP) 15–20 min. A tropical nocturne, exotic and richly creative, polytextural textures, trancelike. D.
Fantaisie Espagnole 1919 (OUP). In three major contrasting sections separated by cadenzas. A brilliant virtuoso piece on the grand scale. D.
Two Piano Pieces (OUP). In the Hothouse (1918): delicate effects within a narrow dynamic range. Toccata (1920): a bouncy perpetual motion, unusual rhythms. Debussy and Scriabin influences. A fine introduction to Sorabji's work. D.
Valse Fantaisie—Homage to Johann Strauss (OUP) 15 min. Lighthearted piece, explores and pays tribute to the waltz rhythms of Strauss. Ends *ffff* in seven registers (octaves). D.

4 Frammenti Aforistici 1977 (Sikesdi Press 1991) 2pp. For Alistair Hinton. 1: Uses BACH motive; 2 lines. 2: Dramatic gestures; 1 line. 3: *ppp*, proportional rhythmic relationships; 1 line. 4: Long left-hand trill under legatissimo moving chords; subito *sfffz* ending. M-D.

Passeggiata Variata 1981 (Sikesdi Press 1994) 7pp. Dedicated to Clive Spencer Bentley. Widely spread chordal and single-line figurations, rhythmic proportional relationships, dramatic gestures, *ppp* ending. D.

Gulistan (The Rose Garden) 1940 (Alistair Hinton, Sorabji Archive, Easton Dene, Bailbrook Lane, Bath BAI 7AA, England) 28pp. "A post-impressionistic 'nocturne.' It is a superb, luscious piece featuring slow successions of diatonic chords (generally in broken form) in the lower regions and shimmering chromatic figures in the upper registers. In the midrange we hear hypnotic chantlike melodies. The title *Guilistan* refers to the verse and prose *The Rose Garden* (1258) by the Sufi Persian poet Sandi (1213–1291)" (Michael Habermann, "Strange Music—the World of Kaikhosru Sorabji," *Piano Today,* 15/6 [November–December 1995]:56). Contains dazzling difficulties. D.

Quaere reliqua hujus materiei inter secretiora (Seek the rest of this matter among the things that are more secret) 1940 (available from Sorabji Archive listed above). 14pp. This "is a programmatic piece depicting sinister events and a horrific climax. It is based on a ghost story, *Count Magnus*, by M. R. James. Its numerous contrasts form an interpretive challenge. One of its themes bears resemblance to the 'Dies Irae,' a powerful symbolic chant" (Michael Habermann, op. cit.).

Fantasiattinia sul nome illustre dell'egregio poeta Christopher Grieve ossia Hugh M'Diarmid 1961 ca. 3 min. (available from Sorabji Archive, listed above) 10pp. "A tiny work which reveals two sides of Sorabji. In the first half we feel the 'volcanic' character of the composer. The second part is visionary, and quite soothing as well. Hugh M'Diarmid was a poet and close friend of Sorabji" (Michael Habermann, op. cit.). D.

Nocturne "Djami" 1928 (available from Sorabji Archive, listed above) 28pp. This "deeply solemn composition pays homage to Persian poet Nuru'd-Din Abdu'r-Rahman Jami (1414–92). It is meant to be played in an intentionally restricted dynamic range throughout (*ppp–mp*). One critic, stirred to a state of elation by this work, wrote, '*Djami* moves my soul as few other works for piano ever have. It will surely be the state ceremonial music of Heaven once things settle down up there after the last judgment . . .'" (Michael Habermann, op. cit.). D.

Habermann has recorded these four works on Elan CD 82264 plus three other recordings of Sorabji's piano music on MusicMasters MMD 60118W and ASV CD AMM 159. He is one of the few pianists in the world able to perform this music magnificently.

See: Donald Garvelmann, "Kaikhosru Shapurji Sorabji," JALS, 4 (December 1978):18–22.

Robert J. Gula, "Kaikhosru Shapurji Sorabji (1892–   ): The Published Piano Works," JALS, 12 (December 1982):38–51.

Michael Habermann, "Kaikhosru Shapurji Sorabji," PQ, 122 (Summer 1983):36–37.
Michael Habermann talks to Martin Anderson. "Sorabji and Habermann: A
Composer and His Interpreter," *Fanfare,* 19 (January–February 1996):89–92.

Claudette Sorel (1934–1999) USA

Fifteen Smorgasbord Piano Solos (EBM 1974). Music plus recipes! Pieces are MC
and introduce varied rhythmic and melodic ideas. The Hungarian recipes
sound delicious. Int.

João Souza Lima (1898–   ) Brazil

Prelúdios, 1.ª série 1954 (Vitale) 25pp. 14 min. Five preludes. Colorful post-Romantic writing. No.2 Humoristicamente is especially attractive. M-D.

Leo Sowerby (1895–1968) USA

Florida 1929 (Sowerby Foundation). Program suite: River Night; St. Augustine;
Cypress Swamp; Sun-Drenched Palms; Pines at Dusk. Varied moods and
techniques. Three middle movements are especially demanding. M-D.

From the Northland (Sowerby Foundation). Five movements in a program suite.
Sowerby's impressions of the Lake Superior area converted into musical
expression. M-D.

Toccata (Mer 1941). Quartal harmony, driving rhythms, martellato playing required. D.

A Fancy (TP). Modal, clever modulations, no key signature. Int.

The Irish Washerwoman (BMC 1920). Varied harmonizations and treatment of
the tune, a fine concert piece. M-D.

Sonata in D 1948 rev. 1963 (Sowerby Foundation) 31pp. Boldly; Moderately fast:
dramatic octotonic writing, themes well contrasted, brilliant conclusion.
Slowly with Intensity of Expression; ostinato-like left-hand opening, builds
to big climax, recedes and closes *pp* with opening material. With verve;
Fairly fast: The most distinctive feature is its rollicking fugue, about which
Sowerby commented "is not only a pretty good fugue, but tears the place
apart." Not published during Sowerby's lifetime. D.

For other unpublished piano works of Sowerby write the Leo Sowerby Foundation, 135 Wintergreen Way, Rochester, NY 14618.

Summer-Beach Sketches 1915 (TP 1996) 16pp. Light; Water; Sand. Impressionistic gestures throughout, widely spread over keyboard. Pieces are effective
individually or as a group. M-D to D.

Claudio Spies (1925–   ) USA, born Chile

Bagatelle (Bo&H 1970) 4pp. 12-tone. Extensive directions for all three pedals.
Fluid meters, pointillistic, quiet, and cantabile. Carefully realized dynamics
will reveal imbedded rows. Large span required. D.

Impromptu (EV 1963) 2pp. 12-tone, changing meters, gently gestural, dynamic
range *p–ppp*, sophisticated writing. M-D.

Three Intermezzi 1950–54 (EV) 11pp. I. Quarter note=66: varied textures, inner
lines, freely tonal. II. Non troppo adagio: delicate cantando lines, three

staffs used to notate ⅔ of piece. III. Allegretto capriccioso: octotonic, repeated chords, secco style, big conclusion. M-D.

Verschieden 1979 (A Lament for Seymour Shifrin) (PNM [Spring–Summer
1979]:1–8). Serial, pointillistic, harmonics, expressionistic, proportional
rhythmic relationships, highly organized. D.

See: Paul Lansky, "The Music of Claudio Spies—An Introduction," *Tempo*, 103
(1972):38–44.

Leopold Spinner (1906–1980) Austria, born Poland
Spinner studied with Anton Webern from 1935 to 1938, an influence that is
clearly noticeable in his writing.

Sonata Op.3 (UE 1953). Three-part work in 12-tone writing. Transparent textures. D.

Fantasy Op.9 (Bo&H). A minor serial "tour de force." There is a refreshing humorous quality about this piece, very different from most serial works. D.

Inventions Op.13 (Bo&H 1958). Five pieces. Delicate serial ideas move from one
hand to the other in complex manner. D.

Louis Spohr (1784–1859) Germany

Sonata A♭ Op.125 1843 (Ric) L'Arte antica e moderna, scelta di composizioni
per pianoforte, 21 vols., Vol.IV, pp.180ff. Allegro moderato: chromatic suspensions, harmonic flow in triple meter, well organized, some surprising
harmony, unpianistic—written more in quartet style. Romanze: cloying
chromaticism. Scherzo: most successful movement. Finale: refined writing
but melodic ideas are weak; hints at Weber in the figuration; well-designed
form. M-D.

Alojz Srebotnjak (1931–   ) Yugoslavia

Macedonian Dances (GS 1975) 20pp. Five elaborate transcriptions of Macedonian folk tunes à la Bartók. Interesting rhythms and sonorities, modal,
repeated notes. M-D.

Patric Standford (1939–   ) Great Britain

Variations Op.23 1969 (Nov) 8pp. Reproduction of MS, not easy to read. Style
is based on the nineteenth century. Well-etched theme is always present
(in different guises) in the varied variations. No meter indications, some
double octaves. M-D.

Sonata II 1979 (Redcliffe Edition) 19pp. Tranquillo; Scherzo; Very slow, meditative; Finale—Vivace. Neoclassic, octotonic, freely tonal, strong lyric emphasis. An exciting performance could arouse some apocalyptic frenzy. M-D.

Robert Starer (1924–   ) USA, born Austria
Starer's music reflects his varied background through a stylistic blend of European, Hebraic, and American elements.

5 Preludes 1952 (MCA). 2 pp. each. Atonal, contrasting movements within a miniaturist framework. Requires facility and some experience in this idiom. M-D.

Five Caprices (PIC 1948). Varied moods, from No.1, a light scherzando, to No.5, a burlesque rapid toccata. M-D.

Seven Vignettes (MCA). Short, colorful, easy.

Prelude and Toccata (MCA 1946). Prelude: chordal, lyric. Toccata: in perpetual motion with changing meters. M-D.

Sonata (MCA 1949). Allegro; Andante; Allegro frivole. The outer movements are strongly rhythmic while the middle movement is lyric. Large-scale work. Advanced pianism required. D.

Sonata No.2 (MCA 1965). A serially organized one-movement work of three contrasting tempi and ideas. Intervals of minor second and seventh exploited, biting dissonance, vigorous rhythmic drive. Large span required. M-D.

Sonata No.3 (MCA). Sophisticated and challenging writing throughout. D.

Excursions for a Pianist (MCA). One movement with varied moods, jazzy to dramatic. M-D.

Sketches in Color (MCA). Book 1: 7 clever works, each allied with a particular color, exploit different twentieth-century techniques. Int. Book 2: 7 pieces, more advanced technically and musically than the first book. Int. to M-D.

Hexahedron 1971 (MCA). Six short characteristic mood pieces, interesting, imaginative. Int.

Evanescents 1975 (MCA) 19pp. An extensive, unfolding piece, like a collage fantasy. Expressionistic, contrasting sections and character, difficult to hold together. Requires large span. D.
See: David Burge, "New Pieces, Part II," CK, 4 (January 1978):50.

At Home Alone (MCA 1980) 23pp. 12 pieces in varied styles. Serious contemporary writing, imaginative, thin textures. Written "for people who play the piano when they are at home alone." I especially like Herman the Brown Mouse and Steps to the Attic. Delicate sonorities in Opening Petals. Int. to M-D.

Twilight Fantasies 1985 (MMB 1986) 15pp. Title comes from Shelley: "hopes and fears, and Twilight Fantasies." Uses bell-like effects to unify the piece, contrasting sections, unusual scale, impressionistic effects, serial influence, strong rhythmic chords; two sections near the end build to strong climaxes and subside to *ppp*. M-D to D.

The Contemporary Virtuoso (Alfred Publishing 1996) 15pp. "7 pianistic studies for the intermediate student" (from the score). Each 2-page study focuses mainly on a single technical problem, such as hand crossing over hand, repeated notes, singing tone, thirds, dots, dashes and slurs (articulation), scales, skips, all supported by Starer's MC harmonic, melodic, and rhythmic usage.

Album for Piano (H. Leonard 1992) 237pp. Contains all of Starer's piano music composed between 1946 and 1991.

Peter Pindar Stearns (1931–   ) USA

Toccata (ACA 1961) 5 min. ABA design, use of thirty-second notes, effective syncopation, highly chromatic. D.

Adagio with Variations (ACA 1962) 13 min. Six adventurous variations, well organized and contrasted, worth exploring. M-D to D.

Partita (AMP 1961). Introduction and 4 variations. Flexible meters, irregular rhythms, dramatic. Large span required. D.

Christopher Steel (1939–1992) Great Britain

Sonatina No.1 (Nov 1960) 14pp. 7 min. Movement called Greek Dance could be performed by itself. Entire work needs fluent pianism. M-D.

Sonatina No.2 (Nov 1962) 11pp. 5½ min. Delightful writing. M-D.

Jacobean Suite (Nov 1961) 6 min. A pastiche. Fanfares at opening and closing surround some untitled pieces. Lute inspired? Not as pianistic as the two *Sonatinas*. M-D.

Fjölner Stefánsson (1930–   ) Iceland

Five Sketches 1958 (Iceland Music Information Center). 12-tone. M-D.

Wolfgang Steffen (1923–1993) Germany

Sonata Op.21 (Bo&Bo 1956). Aggressive free-voiced motion in outer movements. Lyrical mid-section spiced with atonal counterpoint. M-D.

Walter Steffens (1934–   ) Germany

Steffens likes to incorporate the visual into his scores. Sometimes they bear the literal impression of art.

Pluie de Feu Op.22 (PIC 1970). One folded leaf. Based on a fire-graphic by B. Aubertin. "Touch durations are schematically fixed; note entries are freely interpretable. Definitely fixed notes within the fire centre should be regarded as central tones" (from the score). Avant-garde. M-D.

Gottfried Stein (1932–   ) Germany

Character Pieces. (Br&H 8101) 11pp. Preface in German and English. A set of 9 pieces that look back to the nineteenth century but are more modern in content. No.6 Oriental and No.7 Toccata will give much pleasure to the student. Int. to M-D.

Leon Stein (1910–   ) USA

Toccata I (Cole 1981) 4pp. A short brilliant work utilizing a perpetual-motion pattern of predominantly quartal and bitonal harmonies. Int. to M-D.

Toccata II (Cole 1981) 20pp. Begins with a broad declaratory introduction. Main theme is a reiterated 16th-note pattern which sets the propulsive character. This theme recurs, alternating with episodes in which the driving 16th-note rhythm is maintained. A recitative-like Andante leads to the return of the introduction. A variant of the main theme follows and reestablishes the 16th-note pattern. Gradually tension increases. A section of alternating chords leads to a brilliant descending octave passage and the concluding bars, in which a last reminiscence of the introduction is heard. An extension of Ravel and Prokofieff toccata technique. Virtuosic. D.

Gitta Steiner (1932–   ) USA

Sonata 1964 (Seesaw). Tightly knit work built on 12-tone technique. One continuous movement with changing tempi and a rich harmonic palette. D.

Fantasy Piece 1966 (Seesaw). An essay in variegated splashes of sound, clusters, expressionistic. Directions are given for performance and notation. Highly exciting. M-D.

Greg A. Steinke (1942–   ) USA

Six Pieces 1964 (Seesaw 1972) 20pp. Lento interotto; Andante con moto e linea; Quieto e tranquillo; Allegro martellato; Adagio con frase larga; Allegro. Flexible meters, atonal, four staves required for some notation, harmonics, dynamic extremes, clusters. Contains some very subtle and compelling sonorities, an effective set. D.

Wilhelm Stenhammar (1871–1927) Sweden

Stenhammar was one of the most distinguished figures in Swedish music. He began as a national Romantic in the neo-Romantic vein but gradually achieved simplicity, refinement, and concentration in his musical language.

Tre Fantasien Op.11 (WH 1895). Deep emotional undertones permeate these pieces. Strongly derivative of Chopin and Schumann, well constructed, inventive. Sonorously written for the instrument, but lack individuality. M-D.

Nights of Late Summer Op.33 1914 (WH). Five Romantic pieces that depict latesummer Scandinavian evenings. Alternate between scenic and dance movements, slow-moving harmonically but generate strong tension. M-D.

Three Piano Pieces 1895 (ELK). Chopinesque miniatures, expertly composed nugacities. Int. to M-D.

Josef Anton Štěpán (Steffan) (1726–1797) Bohemia

Composizioni per piano solo Vol.64 MAB (Artia). Introduction in English. Divertimentos I–IV: similar to Haydn's Divertimentos for keyboard; multicontrasting movements. Sonatas. Some exceptionally fine writing. Int. to M-D.

Capricci (A. Weinmann—Henle 227). Five pieces. Rhapsodic fantasy style. Based on earliest sources. M-D.

Edward Steuermann (1892–1964) USA, born Poland

Steuermann's style included delicate shadings, smooth transitions, and mosaics of contrasting bits of material. Short strands of contrasting intervallic, rhythmic, timbral, and dynamic content produce flexible and expressive phrases.

Suite 1953-54 (Schuller—Margun 1980) 24pp. 14½ min. Prelude; Melody; Misterioso; Chorale; March. Interesting treatment of the row in which the 12 tones are subdivided into three groups of four notes each, a grouping functionally exploited throughout. The final movement contains reminiscences of themes from the first four. Both hands move over a wide range, all registers of the instrument are constantly engaged. Includes a biographical sketch and extensive performance directions. D.

Bernard Stevens (1916–1983) Great Britain

Stevens was professor of composition at the Royal College of Music in London for many years. He was a musical craftsman of considerable stature.

Five Inventions Op.14 (Lengnick 1950) 13pp. Contrasting, freely tonal, thin textures except for No.4 (Adagio), neoclassic. M-D.

Ballad Op.17 (Lengnick 1953) 13pp. 12 min. Laid out in a post-Brahms pianism with MC harmonies. Arrives at a dramatic climax before concluding *pp* in G♭. M-D to D.

Fantasia on "Giles Farnaby's Dreame" Op.22 (Lengnick 1953) 14pp. 13 min. Variation treatment, quasi cadenza, fugal conclusion, Romantic harmonies. M-D.

Ballade II Op.42 1969 (Roberton) 12pp. 7 min. Static introduction, returns four times; rhythmic Allegro; Adagio reminiscent of C. Franck. Many tempo changes, large chords and octaves, scalar movements, mechanical patterns, loud and showy ending. M-D.

Four Concert Pieces (Robertson). Aria: Subtle tonal shifts, marchlike mid-section. Nocturne on a note-row by Ronald Stevenson: harmonic shifts dictated by row; chromatic but never atonal. Fuga alla saraband a: three-part fugue on a 12-tone row. Elegiac fugue on the name "Geraldine": free treatment of subject, more diatonic harmonies than the other fugue. M-D to D.

Halsey Stevens (1908–1988) USA

Stevens has written a great deal for the piano. Folk music, Brahms, Hindemith, and the Baroque have all played a part in the development of his style. There is a spontaneous flow to his piano music.

Intrada 1949–54 (ACA) 3½ min. An adagio 4/8 meter using dotted rhythms begins quietly in the lower register of the piano, works to climax with dramatic arpeggi gestures in upper register, subsides briefly and returns to climactic treatment before returning to a calm conclusion in lower register of piano. This would make an excellent opening recital number. M-D.

Preludes (First Series) 1952 (ACA). Written for Lillian Steuber. 1. Poco lento: legato; inner voices require careful balance; works to a suonando climax assisted by sostenuto pedal; mid-section uses left hand to provide a contemporary Alberti bass for the right hand; cantando melody; effective chordal ending. 2. Andante con moto, quasi menuetto: long, semi-contrapuntal lines between the hands treated in a highly expressive manner is the basis for this 80-bar piece. 3. Allegro, in modo burlando: a driving, well-accented 5/8 rhythm opens this Prelude; at bar 20 a cantando espressivo melody takes over; these two elements treated in various guises make up the piece; brilliant coda in octaves and a dashing arpeggio conclude the work. M-D.

Preludes (Second Series) 1952–56 (ACA). 4. Moderato: legato octaves interspersed with well-articulated broken chromatic chordal figures work to a *ff* climax at bar 54; music quickly subsides and concludes with the broken chordal figure in the lower register. 5. Andante con moto; accompanied melody in left hand is reversed at bar 18; mainly a very sustained work; accompaniment rocks back and forth between small and large intervals. 6. Andante quasi allegretto: broken fourths in left hand accompany an expressive right-hand melody; figuration becomes more chromatic and dramatic, is extended over a broad area of the keyboard, and leads to a dashing close. All M-D.

Nepdalszvit, Zongorára 1950 (ACA) Eight Magyar Folk Songs. Based on melodies collected by Bartók and Péczely. Short, original, and fresh sounding. Could be played as a complete group or a selection could be made from them. Mode for each piece is listed. Int. to M-D.

Piano Music Vol.I 1948–49 (ACA). Toccata: shifting meters, chromatic textured melodic writing, tonal orientation. M-D. Inventions 1, 2, 3: two-voiced; display attractive contrapuntal chromatic writing; notes not difficult but solid pianism and sensitive interpretative equipment are required. Int. to M-D. Improvisation: Andante, giusto e con moto: very lyric and expressive; builds to *ff* climax; concludes *pp* in lower register. M-D. Scherzo: Quasi presto tagliente: a bouncing light diatonic figure evolves into punctuated octaves; both ideas cleverly treated in this lively short setting. M-D.

Four Improvisations on Javanese Themes 1951 (ACA) 4pp. 4 min. "Closely akin to the children's songs are the dongèng-songs; they are very ancient ditties, usually containing only a few tones, and intoned every now and then during dongèng (i.e., the telling of fairy-tales). . . . According to Radèn Kodrat [this song] No.1 (which occurs in a story that strongly reminds one of 'Hop o' me thumb'), is neither sléndro nor pelóg—although perhaps tending toward the latter . . ." (from the score). 1. Poco andante: based on four notes only—b, c♯, d, f♯; melody in octaves in mid-section. 2. Allegro: pentatonic; lacks fourth and seventh; has much rhythmic vitality, melody in left hand in mid-section. 3. Andante: pentatonic; charming setting with melody treated between hands as well as given to right hand; unique harmonizations. 4. Quasi parlando: based on five notes—e, f, g, b, c; melody treated octotonically and in octaves over low pedal open fifths; recitative-like. Colorful treatment of all four pieces. Strong oriental flavor. Would make a highly effective and unusual recital group. Int. to M-D.

Notturno "Bellagio Adagio" 1971 (Alfred) in collection *Twelve by Eleven*. 2pp. 3 min. ABA, expressive and chromatic, short motives, transfer of line between hands, a beautiful work. Notes not difficult but piece requires mature musicianship. M-D.

3 Ukrainian Folk Songs 1960 (ACA) 2 min. All three are short and modal. Nos.1 and 2 are slow and linear with melody in left hand some of the time. Control of inner voices in No.2 is important. No.3 is quick and rhythmic and uses harmonic seconds, thirds, fourths, and fifths; alternating hands with left-hand octaves. Int.

Fantasia 1961 (Helios) 4 min. Grows from opening motif e, f, d. Varied figuration; treatment held together by subtle permeation of motif; spread over keyboard. Fine octave technique required. M-D.

Study in Irregular Rhythms (Helios) 2 min. Flexible meters, hands work close together, octotonic. Requires strict time. M-D.

Sonatina II (Helios 1975) 7 min. Allegro moderato; Canon; Rondo. Int. for notes, M-D for interpretive problems.

Sonatina III 1950 (ACA) 9 min. Allegretto semplice: thin textures thicken during second tonal area; some contrapuntal writing; centers around E. Lento, parlando (Elegy) in memory of Bartók: molto espressivo writing, chromatic coloration, poignant treatment. M-D.

Music for Ann 1954 (Helios) 5½ min. Modal elements combined with traditional harmonic functions. Int. to M-D.

Ritratti per pianoforte 1959–60 (Helios) 24pp. 12 min. Intrada; Arietta; Tema con quattro variazioni. All the materials are derived from music themes present in the painting that inspired the respective piece. Contains some of the finest writing by Stevens. M-D.

4 Bagatelles 1960 (Helios) 8pp. 5 min. MC, short, contrasting. M-D.

See: Maurice Hinson, "The Piano Music of Halsey Stevens," PQ, 96 (Winter 1976–77):32–34.

Jeanette C. Wong, "An Introduction to the Piano Music of Halsey Stevens," AMT, 42/5 (April–May 1993):18–25.

Ronald Stevenson (1928–   ) Scotland

Prelude, Fugue and Fantasy on Themes from Busoni's Doktor Faust Op.51 1949–59 (Nov) 29 min. No.4 in Virtuoso series, a modern piano series edited by John Ogdon, the English pianist. Based on themes from Busoni's *Faust*. Extensive demands are made on performer. Three basic motives from *Doktor Faust* are put to cyclic use. All three are introduced in the Prelude, while the Fugue is based on the third motive. Fantasy appears to be a telescoped SA design. The tonal centers (C for the Prelude and Fugue and E for the Fantasia) are the same key relations used in Busoni's piano concerto. This also exists in another version entitled *Piano Concerto No. 1: Faust Triptych*. A two-piano reduction of this version is available (Nov). D.

Passacaglia on D-S-C-H Op.80 (OUP 1963). 151pp. 80 min. Built on the subject D E♭ C B. Contains such elements as a Fandango, Pibroch, Triple Fugue, March, Sonata, and Waltz. The subjects of the triple fugue are D S C H, B A C H, and the Dies Irae. D S C H (in their German counterpart) form the initials of Dmitri Shostakovitch, to whom the work is dedicated. "This is possibly the most concentrated expression of motif development in the history of music" (Ates Orga, M&M, 17/2 [October 1968]: 29; Stevenson's creative philosophy is summed up in this article). *Passacaglia* is an attempt to achieve a synthesis of "world music." Technical demands are not staggering but great stamina on the part of the pianist is required. D.

A Wheen Tune for Bairns tae Spiel Op.84 (Schott 1967). A suite of four Scottish pieces written for Stevenson's youngest daughter. Influence of Percy Grainger in this miniature "Scottish Mikrokosmos." Easy.

Peter Grimes Fantasy (Bo&H 1972) 12pp. 6½ min. On themes from Benjamin Britten's opera. This powerful operatic transcription follows in miniature form the design of the opera. Full sonorities, bravura octaves, and arpeggi passages; some Impressionistic effects; eclectic style. Free recitativo middle section, more strict outer sections. Effective calm ending. Requires virtuoso technique. D.

Sounding Strings (UMP). Album of Celtic music for piano or harp. Int. to M-D.

Numerous other solo piano works are available from The Ronald Stevenson Society, 3 Chamberlain Road, Edinburgh EH10 4DL Scotland.

See: Ates Orga, "The Piano Music of Ronald Stevenson," MO, 92 (March 1969):292–95.

William Grant Still (1895–1978) USA

Copies of the JF publications are available from: Mrs. William Grant Still, 1262 Victoria Avenue, Los Angeles, CA 90019.

3 Visions (JF 1936) 11 min. Dark Horseman; Summerland; Radiant Pinnacle. Short character pieces in varied moods that reflect Still's thoughts on life after death. A mixture of styles. M-D.

7 Traceries (JF 1939) 17 min. Cloud Cradles; Mystic Pool; Muted Laughter; Out of the Silence; Woven Silver; Wailing Dawn; A Bit of Wit. Somewhat Impressionistic. M-D.

Fairy Knoll (MCA) A filigree tinkling scherzo. Int.

Phantom Chapel (MCA). Deep, sonorous, bell-tone qualities. Int.

Marionette (MCA) in collection *U.S.A. 1946* 1 min. Int.

Quit dat fool'nish (Belwin-Mills 1938) 3pp. 2 min. Rapid 16th-note figuration accomplished by staccato chords, alternating hands. M-D.

Frank Stewart (1920–   ) USA

Toccata 1976 (GWM) 15pp. From collection *Seven Americans*. Brilliant and effective with strong, incisive rhythms. M-D.

Suite for Piano based on American Indian Songs 1949 (Seesaw) 8 min. Mojave-Apache Medicine Song; Hopi Lullaby; Cheyenne and Arapaho; He-Hea Katzina Song (Hopi Rain Dance). Colorful, contrasting. Int. to M-D.

Karlheinz Stockhausen (1928–   ) Germany

Stockhausen's music is about people. The relationships between composer and public, performer and composer, public and performer have never been so thoroughly explored as by Stockhausen, but using his works as tools for exploration. In 1952 Stockhausen began a cycle of 21 piano pieces, but to date only 11 have been completed. In many ways the writing is pianistic, usually taking advantage of the entire range of the keyboard and the dynamics, using overtones most effectively with subtle pedal effects. It is conceivable that these pieces might eventually be considered twentieth-century piano classics.

Klavierstücke I–IV 1952–53 (UE). "The tempo of each piece, determined by the smallest note-value, is 'as fast as possible.' When the player has found this tempo and determined it metronomically, all the more complicated time proportions . . . can be replaced by changes of tempo" (from the score). M-D to D.

Klavierstücke V–VIII (UE 1965). No.V (954): emphasizes the great range of the keyboard to heighten the sense of space; uses silence effectively to accentuate the sense of motion. D. No.VI (1955): 48pp., extremely complex. D. No.VIII (1954): might appeal to the very adventurous pianist. D. No.VIII (1954): contains the fewest technical problems. M-D.

See: G. W. Hopkins, "Stockhausen's Piano Pieces," MT, 107 (April 1966):331 for an analysis of Nos.V–VIII.

Klavierstücke IX & X (UE c.1967). No.IX: exploits a single sonority; technically the easiest of all the *Klavierstücke*. No.X: 38 separate pages, contains detailed comments and instructions to the pianist; requires fist glissandi and forearm cluster trills among other virtuoso requirements; one of Stockhausen's most important pieces. D.

See: David Burge, "Karlheinz Stockhausen," CK, 4 (May 1978):58. Includes a discussion of *Klavierstück* X.

The first ten *Klavierstücke* may be played as a cycle, in groups, or separately.

Klavierstück XI (UE 1956). Comes in several versions: one is a cardboard tube with a strip of paper (with or without rack) and 19 sections of music. These sections are to be performed at random but each is to be performed according to directions contained in the preceding section. The work is to end whenever one section has been played for the third time. Tone clusters of different sizes are mixed with regular chords. Both free and rigid methods of notation are employed. D.

A progressive change of notation takes place throughout these eleven works, as Stockhausen continues searching for the "correct" notational form of each piece.

Zodiac (UE). 12 movements named after the signs of the Zodiac. The upper register of the piano is exploited. In Virgo the right and left hands outline 2 separate tonal centers. D.

See: Jonathan Harvey, *The Music of Stockhausen* (Berkeley: University of California Press, 1976), 143pp. The analysis of Stockhausen's piano pieces and his work with electronic composition will be of the most interest to pianists.

Robert Craft, "Boulez and Stockhausen," *The Score*, 24 (November 1958):54–62.

Roger Smalley, "Stockhausen's Piano Pieces," MT, 110 (January 1969):30–32.

Richard Toop, "Stockhausen's Other Piano Pieces," MT, 124 (June 1983):348–52. Deals with *Klavierstücke* V–X and a set of piano pieces never published.

Simon Stockhausen (1967–   ) Germany

Musik für Junge 1974–76 (Stockhausen Verlag). Twelve charming and imaginative pieces for piano and/or melody instrument written by Karlheinz Stockhausen's son when he was 7 or 8 years old. Int.

Sigismond Stojowski (1869–1946) USA, born Poland

Orientale No.2 (Caprice) Op.10/2 (Musica Obscura) 9pp. Etudelike, sectional, chromatic. M-D.

Einsamkeit (Solitude) Op.24 (Musica Obscura; Willis) 2pp. A quiet flowing "Song Without Words." M-D.

Chant d'Amour Op.26/3 (Musica Obscura) 4pp. Romantic style. M-D.

Aspirations. Vers l'azur Op.39/1 (Musica Obscura) 7pp. Chopin influence, salon style. M-D.

Richard Stoker (1938–   ) Great Britain

A Poet's Notebook 1969 (MCA). Six pieces. Neoclassic style, no key signatures, bitonally flavored. Int.

Fireworks 1970 (Ashdown). Six little pieces. Triads with superimposed fourths, bitonal implications. Int.

Piano Sonata I Op.26 1966 (CFP 1973) 11pp. 12 min. Ritmico: *pp* to explosive *fff*s, much impetuosity, big gestures. Reposo: varied meters, broader mid-section with widely spaced chords, octave passages. M-D.

Zodiac Variations 1963 (Ashdown) 10 min. Twelve pieces. Theme and 11 simple transformations, all of which retain the thematic melodic shape. Some rhythmic, register, touch, mood, and meter changes. A fine suite for student recitals. Int. to M-D.

See: "Richard Stoker Talks to Christopher Norris," M&M, 23 (February 1975): 16, 18, 20, 22.

Robert Stolz (1880–1975) Austria

Stolz was one of the great Viennese composers. He wrote operettas and salon music.

Valse brillante Op.4 1898 (Schott 7952 1993) 7pp. Originally published in 1898. Delightful writing, requires sensitivity as well as good technical facility. M-D.

Sherman Storr (–   ) USA

Aegean Adventure of Mode, Mood and Myth (Alacran Press) 15pp. Twelve attractive descriptive pieces, MC. Int.

8 Variations on an Aria of Domenico Scarlatti (Alacran Press) 14pp. Contrasting, traditional harmonies. Var.8 is an exciting Tango! M-D.

Zodiac Suite (Alacran Press) 32pp. Vigorous MC pieces portraying the 12 signs of the Zodiac. A verse before each piece describes the best and worst traits of each sign. M-D.

Alan Stout (1932–   ) USA

Stout is a member of the music faculty at Northwestern University.

For Prepared Piano Op.23 1956 (ACA). Four movements, a sonata in the truest sense. Complex preparations; bolts, screws, erasers, wood, rubber, nuts. D.

Music for Good Friday Op.24 1955–58 (ACA). Five movements. Abstruse, complex writing. Some sections are spread over four staves. D.

Sonata Op.45/1 (ACA 1958). One movement. Serial, frequent tempo and meter changes, unbarred, stylistically conservative. More idiomatic for the piano than many serial works. D.

Joep Straesser (1934–   ) The Netherlands

Straesser teaches theory at Utrecht Conservatory.

Intersections III 1971 (Donemus) 6pp. "Hommage à Bach; if it were a fantasia and fugue." Facsimile of the composer's MS. Two dissimilar movements. I: chromatic groupings evolve into clusters. II: performer may vary interpretation. Avant-garde. M-D.

See: Daan Manneke, "About Joep Straesser's Intersections III for Piano," *Sonorum Speculum*, 53 (1973):24–36.

Five Close-ups 1960–61, rev. 1973 (Donemus) 4 min. Based on a 12-tone row by Pierre Boulez. D.

Just Signals—Sonata for Piano 1982 (Donemus) 19pp. 13½ min. A one-movement work (Deciso) in which the "bar lines" have no metric significance but make the score surveyable. The distances between bar lines vary. "The quasi-romantic tendency in the music of the pages 12 and 13—it seems as if, for a moment, Schumann were present in frozen-in condition—may not be over-emphasized. The music at issue, which appears in the piece at a later stage, must be played in a clear and simple way" (from the score). Webernesque, many repeated fast notes, spread over keyboard, rhythmically complex, a strong sonic edifice. D.

Willard Straight (1930–   ) USA

Structure (Bo&H). Commissioned for the Van Cliburn Competition, 1966. A virtuoso-bravura piece designed to display the pianist's skills. Exciting ending consists of a double glissando, black and white notes together. Pianistic. D.

Richard Strauss (1864–1949) Germany

5 Klavierstücke Op.3 1880–81 (UE; MMP). Sturdy little pieces in intermezzo style, Schumann influence. Look forward to the finer music which is to come. M-D.

Sonata b Op.5 1880–81 (UE; MMP). Allegro molto appassionato; Adagio cantabile; Scherzo (Presto); Allegretto marcatissimo. Derivative style that contains some effective writing and some notably Romantic melodies (see the Adagio cantabile). Inspiration from Beethoven and Mendelssohn. M-D.

5 Stimmungsbilder Op.9 1882–84 (K 9234; UE; MMP) (Moods and fancies). In

Silent Forests; Beside the Spring; Intermezzo; Träumerei; On the Heath. The best of Strauss's character pieces. No.4 anticipates certain accompanimental characteristics demonstrated more fully in his later songs. Int. to M-D.

Enoch Arden Op.38 (Forberg) 63 min. Recitation with piano. With German and English words. Based on Tennyson's "Enoch Arden." Could be performed by solo piano. M-D.

Igor Stravinsky (1882–1971) USA, born Russia
Stravinsky's piano works, while varied and interesting, are not as important as his works in other media.

Four Etudes Op.7 (CFP; IMC; AMP; K, separately; Rahter; Bo&H, in collection *The Short Piano Pieces*; No.4 EBM) 8 min. Nos.1, 2, and 4 are involved with metrical problems. No.4 is a brilliant perpetual-motion study. Effective and strong post-Romantic studies in polyrhythms. M-D.
See: W. Kenton Bales, "The Unknown Stravinsky," AMT, 34/5 (April–May 1985):38–39. Focuses on these etudes.

Scherzo 1902 (Faber) 7pp. A kind of salon piece; coda is most interesting part. M-D.
See: Charles M. Joseph, "Stravinsky's Piano Scherzo (1902) in Perspective," MQ, 67 (January 1981):82–93.

Sonata f♯ 1903-4 (Faber) 42pp. Allegro: melody in dotted rhythms with accompanying left-hand octaves. Scherzo: quiet and fast, clever syncopation. Andante: Romantic, in D, leads to Allegro: F♯, opposing D and F♯ sonorities. The entire work is something of a mixture of Beethoven, Liszt, Brahms, and Rachmaninoff. Displays a fine grasp of idiomatic piano writing. An excellent example of late Russian Romanticism and a document of emerging creativity. D.

Valse pour les enfants 1917. Published in *Le Figaro* in 1922. Contained in Eric Walter White's book *Stravinsky* and in *The Short Piano Pieces*, listed below. Int.

Piano Rag-Music 1919 (Bo&H) 9pp. Syncopation, changing meters, inner melodies. Large span required. M-D.

Les cinq doigts 1921 (Mer; JWC; MMP). Eight easy pieces on five notes.

Trois Mouvements de Petrouchka 1921 (Bo&H; IMC). Danse Russe; Chez Petrouchka; La Semaine grasse. Virtuoso paraphrases of three scenes from the ballet. Brilliant orchestral writing for the piano that requires prodigious stretches and glittering display. Highly effective and demanding. D.
See: Christopher O'Riley, "A Piano Lesson with C. O'Riley," P&K, 166 (January–February 1994):37, on this piece.

Sonata 1924 (Bo&H; MMP). Objective, short, neoclassic, chamber style. "I have used the term 'Sonata' in its original sense, deriving from the word 'sonare'. . . ." Three movements, FSF; thin textures. The second movement is a florid Adagietto in Baroque style while the concluding movement is a toccata-like rondo. M-D to D.

See: David Burge, "Stravinsky's Piano Sonata," CK, 5 (April 1979):69.

Sérénade en la 1925 (Bo&H; MMP). Four movements written in the spirit of the eighteenth century. Hymne: processional, somber. Romanza: elegant, opening and closing cadenzas. Rondoletto: dry, impersonal. Cadenza finale: quiet, moving eighth notes. M-D to D.

See: Angeline Schmid, "Stravinsky's Sérénade en la," *Clavier*, 21/10 (December 1982):29–30.

Margaret Tolson, "Shipboard Lesson with Stravinsky," *Clavier*, 21/10 (December 1982):31. On the *Sérénade en la.*

Tango 1940 (Schott). Syncopated tango rhythm. Romantic trio. Int.

Circus Polka for a Young Elephant 1942 (Schott). Humorous, rhythmic, like a military march. M-D.

The Short Piano Pieces (Soulima Stravinsky—Bo&H 1977) 55pp. Includes: Piano Rag Music (1919); Tango (1940); The Five Fingers (1920–21); Valse and Polka (1915); Valse pour les enfants (1917); Four Etudes Op.7 (1908). Foreword by the editor includes background information on the works. This edition differs in some minor respects from other printed versions in performance suggestions since the editor had personal advice from his father regarding some of the works. Easy to M-D.

See: David Evenson, "The Piano in the Compositions of Igor Stravinsky," PQ, 118 (Summer 1982):26–31.

Charles M. Joseph, "Igor Stravinsky—The Composer and the Piano," AMT, 25 (April–May 1976):16–17, 21.

Dika Newlin, "The Piano Music of Igor Stravinsky," PQ, 106 (Summer 1979):27, 30–33. Focuses on the solo works.

John Ogdon, "Stravinsky and the Piano," *Tempo*, 81 (Summer 1967):36–41.

Joan Pursewell, "Stravinsky's Piano Music," *Clavier*, 18 (January 1979): 24–31, 51. Also includes *Valse pour les enfants* and *Les cinq doigts.*

Marlene Thal, "The Piano Music of Igor Stravinsky," thesis, University of Washington, 1978.

Soulima Stravinsky (1910–1994) USA, born Switzerland

Sonata B♭ (JWC 1947) 32pp. 13 min. Cheerful writing that requires much keyboard facility. D.

Art of Scales, 24 Preludes (CFP). A "modern" Clementi that makes scale practice more interesting. M-D.

6 Easy Sonatinas for Young Pianists (CFP 1967). Vol.I: Nos.1–3. Vol.II: Nos.4–6: Very pianistic. Int.

Piano Music for Children (CFP). Vol.I: 19 pieces. Vol.II: 11 pieces. Easy.

Piano Variations (CFP 1970). First series: 18pp. 12 min. Prelude; Forlane; Stanza; Piccolo Divertimento (theme and 3 variations); In Modo Russo (theme and 3 variations); Les Valses (theme and 4 variations). Neoclassic. Int. Second series: 16pp. 13 min. 11 Tones (theme and 6 variations); Metrics (theme and 6 variations); 12 Tones (theme and 7 variations); Pavana (theme and 3 variations) and Pavana returns more fully harmonized. Int. to M-D.

3 Fairy Tales 1976 (CFP 66692) 36pp. 21 min. Cinderella; Jack and the Beanstalk;

The Sleeping Beauty. Subtitles tell the stories. Fresh and delightful, enchanting melodies, arresting gestures, pianistic sonorities. Int.

6 Sonatinas (CFP 6590a & b) 2 books. Clear forms, driving rhythms. Wide range of styles from Gregorian chant to Quodlibet, to Machaut, to canons. Int.

15 Character Pieces (CFP 66441) 33pp. 22½ min. In various moods and styles, sophisticated writing, Hindemith style. Int. to M-D.

The Art of Fingering (CFP 10010 1995). *The Art of Fingering* falls "between Czerny's *The Art of Finger Dexerity* and Bartók's *Mikrokosmos*" (from the score). Contains 12 short preludes, each offering specific technical challenges. M-D.

20 Etudes Pittoresques 1994 (CFP 67392) 20pp. 27½ min. Contains brief references to Gregorian chant, Bach inventions, Scarlatti sonatas, a little waltz, and jazz. Int.

Aurel Stroe (1932–   ) Rumania

Sonate 1972 (Sal) 28pp. Moderato: changing meters, chromatic, quartal and quintal harmonies, main subject identified, serial-like. Andante: quintal harmony emphasized; chromatic arpeggi-like figuration; cadenza with trills; glissando; opening section returns; large span required. Fuga—Allegro energico: changing meters; marcato handling of subject; one statement of subject in octaves accompanied by clusterlike chords; same compositional techniques as in first movement utilized; tranquillo closing without rallentando. M-D.

Folke Strömholm (1941–   ) Norway

Etude Fantastique 1964 (NMO 1971) 6pp. Molto presto: alternating hands with harmonic seconds, full chords, glissandi, strong driving rhythms, freely tonal. M-D.

10 Sma Pianostykker for Barn og Ungdom Op.17 (NMO 8674 1970) 11pp. Varied short pieces, contemporary techniques. Duggdräper has left hand on all black keys, right hand on white keys. Not easy. Int.

Sonatina Op.25 (NMO 1977) 14pp. Two movements, harmonics, delightful melodic and rhythmic material used. M-D.

Morton Subotnick (1933–   ) USA

Prelude No.3 for Piano and Electronic Sounds 1964 (MCA). 2 scores, 7pp. each. Aleatoric in part, many clusters, avant-garde. D.

Prelude No.4 for Piano and Electric Sounds (MCA 1966). Some parts are not strictly measured ("beat bars") but are not improvisational either. The notated tape part is a series of cues for coordination. Atonal sonorities are used for color only. Experimental but highly expressive. Sensitive, thought-provoking work. M-D.

Dia Succari (1938–   ) Syria

Suite Syrienne 1976 (Jobert) 28pp. Nida; Samah; Dabké. Colorful and intriguing music based on Syrian tunes, complex rhythms, recurring motif. Dabké ends with a brilliant and driving climax. May be played individually or as a suite. D.

La Nuit du Destin (Jobert 1978) 18pp. Expressionistic, improvisatory, strings strummed, performance directions. M-D to D.

Robert Suderburg (1936–   ) USA

Six Moments for Piano 1966 (TP) 3pp. Six brief sketches. Atonal, pointillistic, contrasts in mood and tempo, flexible rhythmic flow. D.

Rezsö Sugár (1919–   ) Hungary

Hungarian Children's Songs (Bo&H). 25 short pieces. Various moods and keys with melodic and rhythmic interest, varied harmonizations. Contains sources from which the folk material is taken. Handsomely illustrated, expertly written. Int.

Baroque Sonatina (EMB Z8916) 12pp. Three movements. Hungarian in character; strongly linked with the Baroque style through its kinetic rhythm and counterpoint technique. Int. to M-D.

Josef Suk (1874–1935) Bohemia

Suk studied composition with Dvořák and married his daughter. Suk's music contains expressive Slavonic warmth and melting, dreamy melodies. He wrote inventive polyphony, and his unique rhythmic use is significant.

Piano Works, Vol. 1 (Simrock). 6 Pieces Op.7; Humoresque; Album Leaf; 8 Pieces Op.12; and other works.

Piano Works, Vol. 2 (Simrock).

Piano Works, Vol. 3 (Simrock).

These three volumes contain most of what Suk wrote for solo piano. They range from classically based tonal writing to more MC examples. Folk music influenced him very little. Int. to M-D.

Toshiya Sukegawa (1930–   ) Japan

Two Pieces from "Little Poems of Four Seasons" (Zen-On 315 1970) 3pp. Short, thin textures, MC, oriental flavor. Int.

Sonatina (Zen-On 213 1975) 17pp. Poems in Blue. Three contrasting movements, contemporary writing, serial influence. M-D.

Arthur Sullivan (1842–1900) Great Britain

Sullivan Piano Music (Chappell 1976) 55pp. Ten short pieces. Edited with an introduction and notes by John Parry and Peter Joslin. Contains: Thoughts I and II; Day Dreams 1–4; Allegro risoluto; Twilight. Shows both Mendelssohn and Schumann influences; charming if shallow. Contains an introduction and a few photographs. Int. to M-D.

Fernando Sulpizi (1936–   ) Italy

Album per Daniela Op.15 (Berben). Eleven easy pieces.

Album secondo per Daniela 1975 (Berben) 9pp. Seven contemporary pieces. The last two (one for each hand) are unmetered and contrapuntal. Notes are easy but interpretive problems abound. Int. to M-D.

Epigrammata Alia Op.21 (Berben) 12pp. Five sonority studies. 1. Webernesque. 2. Continuous motion, pointillistic. 3. Three layers of contrasting textures. 4. Heavy chordal outer sections, toccata-like mid-section with alternating hands. 5. Study in trills, frequently punctuated with punched chords. D.

Carlos Surinach (1915–1997) USA, born Spain

Three Spanish Songs and Dances (PIC 1951) 8½ min. Colorful harmonies, exacting rhythms, superbly written, effective as a group. Int. to M-D.

Sonatina (PIC 1943) 19pp. 10 min. Three movements, lean textures, excellent concert piece. M-D.

Acrobats of God: Five Dances (AMP) 12 min. Transcribed from Surinach's ballet of the same title. Fanfare; Antique Dance; Bolero; Minuet; Spanish Galop. Rhythmic emphasis in the faster movements while the slower ones emphasize much embellishment in the melodic treatment. Int. to M-D.

Tales From the Flamenco Kingdom (AMP 1955). Pepper King: Use of seconds harmonically and melodically, syncopation, accented dissonance, synthetic scale. Sweet Beauty: chromatic, many minor seconds, wide dynamic range, four sixteenths followed by triplet eighths, pedal points. Witch Dance: 3/8 and some use of 3/4, accented rhythmic treatment, Gypsy scale. Attractive suite. Int.

Heinrich Sutermeister (1910–1995) Switzerland

Sutermeister's style is basically diatonic and shows a preference for parallel, moving streams of unrelated harmony.

Sonatina E♭ (Schott 1948). Three movements. Felicitous musical invention in all movements. Irregular meters, healthy contemporary language. M-D.

Acht Kleine Stücke (Schott 2881 c. 1940) 15pp. Contrasted, would appeal to precocious young person, MC. All titles in German. Int.

12 Two-Part Inventions (Schott). Varied styles. Effective in groups or complete. Int. to M-D.

Hommage à Arthur Honegger 1955 (Schott 1967) 11pp. 9½ min. This four-section work uses two mottos: A–B and A–B♭ which correspond to the initials of Arthur Honegger. M-D.

Thomas Svoboda (1939–   ) USA, born Czechoslovakia

Svoboda writes extremely well for the instrument. His style is MC but individual. His works deserve investigating. Strangeland publishes all the music.

A Bird Op.1 1949. Andante, flexible meters, many seconds, a sad murmuring bird. Int.

Prelude Op.3a 1954. Quiet contrapuntal study, two and three voices. Int.

Bagatelles "In a Forest" Op.45 1965. Trails; Aspens; Rocks; Holy Cross; Forest and Meadows. A contemporary "Forest Scenes." Int. to M-D.

9 Etudes Op.44 1965. (No.4, PQ, 114 [Summer 1981]:51–55). A four-voice fugue beautifully worked out, expressive. M-D.

Nocturne Op.84 1977. Slow, dissonant, changing meters; builds to a large climax before subsiding. M-D.

Children's Treasure Box Vols.1–4. Explores various aspects of contemporary piano technique, in order of difficulty. Easy to Int.

Howard Swanson (1909–   ) USA

The Cuckoo (MCA 1949). Short scherzo inspired by the cuckoo call. M-D.

Sonata (Weintraub Music 1950). Allegro risoluto; andante cantabile; Allegro vivo. Linear two- and three-part writing, strong rhythmic treatment in outer movements. Arresting, relevant writing. D.

Giles Swayne (1946–   ) Great Britain

Zebra Music (Nov). 12 pieces written in layers of black and white keys: one hand may be playing the white keys while the other plays the black. Or both may be on white, or both on black. All possible combinations are used. Rich modal melodies and interesting African rhythms. Int.

Richard Swift (1927–   ) USA

Summer Notes 1966. (PNM, 15 [Spring–Summer 1977]:97–114). Three movements separated by two Interludes. Notation directions, clusters and harmonics, pointillistic, exploits extreme ranges, highly organized, unusual sonorities. D.

See: Thomas Stauffer, "Richard Swift's *Summer Notes*," PNM, 15 (Spring–Summer 1977):115–21. A thorough analysis and discussion of this work.

William Sydeman (1928–   ) USA

Sydeman's music is clearly conceived, colorful, and linear. His works are effective, clever, and direct.

Sonata (Ione Press). 36pp. 14 min. Three movements. Thoughtfully organized. Not always pianistic. D.

Variations (MCA). Diffuse quasi-recitativo theme is thoroughly worked out in 6 variations. Abbreviated return of theme closes the work. Preference for sevenths. M-D.

Witold Szalonek (1927–   ) Poland

Mutanza 1968 (JWC) 9pp. 18 min. For prepared piano. Precise explanation of diagrammatic notation. Strings to be struck with nonmusical objects (4 steel rods, 30 steel balls, 20 sticks of plasticene, etc.). Score is reproduction of MS. Sound is only that made by dropping, brushing, rolling objects inside the piano. Avant-garde. D.

István Szelényi (1904–1972) Hungary

42 Preludes (EMB 1978) 36pp. Short, brilliant, varied moods and tempos. Can make up groupings or use all on same program; somewhat reminiscent of Chopin's *Preludes*. M-D.

Georg Szell (1897–1970) USA, born Hungary
Drei Kleine Klavierstücke Op.6 (UE 1922). Skizze; Sarabande; Capriccio. Written in post-Romantic tradition, attractive. M-D.

Erzsebet Szönyi (1924–   ) Hungary
Szönyi has been a member of the faculty of the Franz Liszt Academy of Music in Budapest since 1948.
Five Preludes 1963 (EMB) 11pp., 7 min. 1. Ostinato. 2. Maestoso: reminiscent of the Copland *Piano Variations*. 3. Variazioni. 4. Grazioso. 5. Dotted eighth-note equals 165. Short contrasted pieces with dodecaphonic traits; all show solid craftsmanship. Impressionist and contemporary idioms also blended. M-D.

Maria Szymanowska (1789–1831) Poland
Szymanowska was an important precursor of Chopin and wrote Romantic salon music. Robert Schumann spoke highly of her in his *Music and Musicians*. Chopin was familiar with her music.
Maria Szymanowska Album (Josef and Maria Mirsy—PWM). Biographical material in Polish. Polonaise f; Menuet E; Le Murmure; Song Setting; Etude F; Etude E♭; Etude d; a revised version of Etude d; Etudes in E, C, and E♭. Interesting and musical writing. Int. to M-D.
Nocturne B♭ (PWM). Beautiful and effective but oriented more toward John Field than Chopin. Also in collection *At the Piano With Women Composers* (Alfred 428). Int.
Five Dances (PWM 1975). Contredanse: has a march, *Jean of Paris*, in the mid-section. Anglaises in B♭, E♭, A♭. Quadrille: lively, attractive, simple. All are tuneful and are about the scope of Schubert's waltzes. The collection contains a delightful portrait of the young composer. Int.
Music for Piano (Glickman—Hildegard) 38pp. Contradance A♭; Menuet E; Polonez f; Etudes f, d, C; Four Valses for 3 Hands. Int. to M-D.
25 Mazurkas (Poniatowska—Hildegard). Short, charming, based on popular folk material. Int. to M-D.
See: Joan Davies, "Maria Szymanowska," *The Consort*, 23 (1966):167–74.

Karol Szymanowski (1882–1937) Poland
Chopin, Scriabin, Richard Strauss, Debussy, and Stravinsky all influenced Szymanowski, and yet he was an original composer. In the 1920s Szymanowski began to employ Polish folk elements in his music. Many of his piano works are virtuosic and use most of the resources of the instrument. The later compositions, which became very personal and unique in style, dissonant, and rhythmically complex, emerged to stamp Szymanowski as one of the most creative artists in the early twentieth century. Opp.1, 4, and 10 provide an excellent introduction to his works.
Nine Preludes Op.1 (1900–1902) (PWM; UE; MMP). Chromatic, quartal har-

mony, Chopin and Scriabin influence, varied moods. Nos.1 and 8 are the most popular. Set is dedicated to Artur Rubinstein. M-D.

Theme and Variations b♭ Op.3 1901 (PWM). Twelve variations, rich harmony, flowing and florid. D.

Four Etudes Op.4 (1903) (PWM; MMP; UE, also available separately). Romantic harmony, double notes, octaves, broken-chord figuration. No.4 b♭ (PWM) is the best piece in this set. M-D to D.

Sonata No.1 c Op.8 1905 (Piwarski). Chopin and Scriabin influence. In 1910 received first prize in a competition organized by the Chopin Centenary Committee at Lwów. Large Romantic virtuoso four-movement work, closes with a fugue. Dramatic ending. D.

Variations on a Polish Folk Song Op.10 1903 (PWM; UE; MMP). 10 variations, post-Romantic, elegant, virtuoso writing, brilliant closing. D.

Prelude 1905 *and Fugue* 1909 (PWM). Won a second prize in 1909 in a competition sponsored by the Berlin musical journal *Signale für die Musikalische Welt*. Influenced by R. Strauss and Wagner. M-D.

Sonata No.2 a Op.21 1910 (UE; MMP). Reger influence. Climax of the composer's earlier period. Appassionato, followed by variations on a sprightly theme, concluded by a fugue. D.

Métopes Op.29 1915 (UE; PWM). L'isle des Sirènes; Calypso; Nausicaa. Three mythological poems, florid, Impressionist, varied tonalities, orchestrally conceived, late Scriabin influence. D.

Twelve Etudes Op.33 1916–18 (UE; PWM, facsimile). Short pieces intended to be played as a set. Scriabin and Ravel influence. Each has a different tempo and color. D.

Masques Op.34 1915–16 (UE; PWM; MMP). Shéhérazade; Tantris le bouffon; Sérénade de Don Juan. Thick textures, complex writing. D.

Sonata No.3 d Op.36 1916–19. (UE; MMP). One movement, episodic, leans toward Scriabin. Delicate Presto opening leads to an Adagio, culminates in a grotesque Fugue, scherzando e buffo. Mature pianism required. D.

Twenty Mazurkas Op.50 1923–29 (UE; PWM). 5 vols., 4 Mazurkas each. Intense, improvisatory, subtle works. Varied in style, type, and tonality. Require sensitive pianism. M-D to D.

The Szymanowski Collection (Mattingly—UE 70002) 68pp. Foreword by Nelita True explores the music of Szymanowski and the composer; performance notes. Part I, Late Intermediate Level: Preludes Op.1/1, 3, 6; Mazurkas Op.50/1, 6. Part II, Early Advanced Level: Etude Op.4/3; Preludes Op.1/7, 2, 5, 4, 8. Sources listed.

See: Gwilym Beechey, "Karol Szymanowski (1882–1937) and His Piano Music," *Musical Opinion*, 106 (October 1982):5–9, 16.

B. M. Maciejewski, *Karol Szymanowski, His Life and Music* (London: Poets and Painters' Press, 1967).

T

Michel Tabachnik (1942–   ) Switzerland
Frise 1969 (Nov) 25 min. Triglyphes 1-A, 2-A, 1-B, 2-B, 1-C, 2-C, and Métope are
    to be played in various orders suggested by the composer, who says, "The
    title of this work (and its construction) is based upon architectural termi-
    nology." Written in a similar vein to that of the Boulez *Third Piano Sonata.*
    Sometimes spread out over four staves. Contrast lacking. Avant-garde. D.

Germaine Tailleferre (1892–1983) France
Dance rhythms permeate most of Tailleferre's writing.
Fleurs de France (Lemoine 1962). Eight short, charming pieces. Int.
Pastorale A♭ 1928 (Heugel). Smooth, graceful melody. M-D.
3 Sonatines (Lemoine 1993) 9pp. Probably composed between 1975 and 1978, de-
    lightful. Each has three short movements. E.

Marko Tajčević (1900–   ) Yugoslavia
Tajčević approaches Yugoslavian folk music much as Bartók approaches Hun-
garian folk music.
Seven Balkan Dances (Schott 1957). Colorful, contrasted dances, technical prob-
    lems. M-D.
Serbian Dances (Rongwen 1959). Tuneful, graceful, attractive. Excellent peda-
    gogic material. Int.
Lieder von der Murinsel (Henle). Folksong settings. Easy to Int.

Jenö Takács (1902–   ) Hungary
From Far and Wide Op.37 (UE) 20 pieces representing many countries. Folk ele-
    ment permeates some of them. Easy to Int.
Rhapsodie Op.43/1 (Dob 01595) 12 pp. 5½ min. Declamatory opening, toccata-
    like scherzando, slow improvisatory section, vivace ending; witty and bril-
    liant. Requires good hand span and the ability to cope with widely spread
    notes in the left hand. M-D.
Little Sonate Op.51 (Dob) 7pp. In Hungarian folk music style. Int.
Toccata Op.54 (Dob 1946). Exhibits elements of the pianistic styles of both De-
    bussy and Ravel. Effective bitonal writing. Interesting mid-section ca-
    denza marked Quasi Fantasia. Requires fast fingers.
Doubledozen for Small Fingers (UE 1965). 24 short pieces employing many MC
    idioms. Very original. Easy to Int.

Partita Op.58 (Dob 1954). Five movements with the Toccata Burlesca the most successful; 12-tone, tightly constructed. M-D.

Sounds and Silences Op.78 (Dob). Atonal, improvisatory, no bar lines, aleatory. Effective. D.

For Me. Little Recital Pieces Op.76 (Dob). 22 short pieces, clever. Easy to Int.

4 Epitaphs Op.79 1964 (Dob). Homage to 4 composers: Hindemith, Debussy, Berg, Bartók. Characteristics of each composer appear in each piece. M-D.

Sonatina 1923 (Dob). First movement: f♯, strong melody, lively. Second movement: a short nocturne, Lento dolente. Finale: rondo with a series of shifting fifths for the left hand and a folklike melody in the right hand. M-D.

Twilight Music Op.92 (Dob 1973) 8pp. 9½ min. 1.Molto rubato: recitative-like, trills, repeated notes, chordal punctuation. 2.Tranquillo: flowing, fast pedal changes; dies away in upper register. 3.Rapidamente: secco, pointillistic, Lento chordal section, rests indicated by number of seconds. 4.Lento, dolente: legato choralelike melody followed by quiet clusters in upper register. 5.Presto, volative: cadenza-like passages in upper register, Largo section uses low register chords to support free melody. 6.Thoughtful: pointillistic, dynamic mark on each note, long pedals, dies away. Impressionistic sonorities using expressionistic techniques. M-D.

Sounds and Colours Op.95 (Dob 1977) 20pp. Notes in German and English. 15 miniatures that explore avant-garde techniques. Int.

  See: Jerry Perkins, "Teaching *For Me* and *Sounds and Colours*," *Clavier,* 20 (October 1981):47–49.

Le Tombeau de Franz Liszt Op.100 1977 (Dob 1979) 15pp. 10½ min. Lacrimoso: Grave, lento, doloroso, low dissonant tolling fifths with lamenting octaves that become more intense. Dies Irae (Totentanz): fast, energetic, left hand underscores open fifth outlining the Dies Irae, repeated octaves, hammered chords, one large cluster. D.

When the Frog Wandering Goes (Dob 1970). Six pieces with clever titles. MC and not easy. Int. to M-D.

  See: Mary Greenhoe, "Jenö Takács, Contemporary Sounds for Piano," *Clavier,* 20 (October 1981):45–46.

Noriaki Takahashi (1948–   ) Japan

Takahashi is a graduate of the Kunitochi Music College.

Lyric Flight II (Japan Federation of Composers 1994) 10½ min. 12-tone but rows are arranged tonally; Alban Berg influence. M-D.

Yuji Takahashi (1938–   ) Japan

Takahashi is considered one of Japan's leading exponents of contemporary piano music.

Metathesis (CFP 1968) 5 min. "The structure is based on the subgroups of a permutation group of 6 and Order 24, which are applied to the various factors of the tone events for piano, such as the density, the duration, the dynamic form, the tone form (all of them are extratemporal structures). The temporal structures are stochastic" (from record jacket, Mainstream MS/5000, recording of the work by the composer). D.

Three Poems of Mao-tse Tung (Zen-On 404 1976) 6pp. Tapoti; Ode to the Plum Tree; Reply to Comrade Kuo Mo-Jo: English translation of poems included. Barless; arpeggiated chords; ideas inspired by poems. The first two are for right hand alone and contain sound patterns essentially Oriental in flavor. The third is a more violent movement with many half-step clashes and a sense of buzzing energy. M-D.

Chained Hands in Prayer (Zen-On 416 1979) 6pp. Includes poem and musical setting of text on separate page. Post-Romantic and Impressionistic sonorities, some changing meters. Based on the deeply religious writing of Kim Chi Ha, this moving, passionate work is an eloquent plea for release. It is simple in structure and language yet has immense power. M-D.

Rosace II (CFP 1969) 7pp. 9½ min. 34 pitches are to be tuned with a strobotuner, some ⅓ pedal usage, thin sonorities, constantly changing rhythms, avant garde. M-D.

Chromamorphe II (CFP 1969) 10pp. 9 min. *Chroma* means color; *Morphe* means shape. "Two sets (a, B) and the logical operations based on them are defined in the abstract. They are applied then to the various ranges on the keyboard. . . . Melodic and time intervals are formed stochastically" (from the score). Avant garde. D.

Saburo Takata (1913–   ) Japan

Preludes 1947 (Ongaku-No-Tomo-Sha 1964) 22pp. 16 min. Colorful titles, e.g., By the Dark-blue Marsh; The Sunlight Dances in the Wind; The Wild Pigeon; Down in the Blue Valley; Mountains Fading into the Twilight. The composer hopes "that one does not become overly conscious of these titles as they merely function as a sort of key to the music" (from the score). Freely tonal; fondness for seconds, fourths, and fifths; Impressionistic. M-D.

Toru Takemitsu (1930–1996) Japan

Takemitsu has perhaps emerged as Japan's leading avant-garde composer. His music reminds this writer of a Buddhist rock garden. It has floating, static, and sonorous qualities that suggest Morton Feldman's music. It may seem formless but is rigidly controlled. "In my music there is no constant development, as in the sonata. Instead, imaginary soundscapes appear. A single element is never emphasized by development through contrast. My music is composed as if fragments were thrown together unstructured, as in dreams. You go to a far place and suddenly find yourself back without noticing the return" (from *Dream and Number,* in Takemitsu's *Confronting Silence* [Berkeley, CA: Fallen Leaf Press, 1995]).

Pause Ininterrompue ("Uninterrupted Rest") 1952–60 (Sal). Three short atonal pieces: Slowly, sadly and as if to converse with; Quietly and with a cruel reverberation; A song of love. To be played as a group. Dynamics attached to almost every note. Great contrast of sounds from brutal to genial. Fascinating sonorities. D.

Piano Distance 1961 (Sal) 4pp. Many interpretative problems and strong dissonances but extraordinarily beautiful. Precise dynamic and pedal indications. A note in the score suggests this piece "could be interpreted as expressing the various and multiple tones of the piano."

For Away 1973 (Sal) 6 min. The composer talks about "inner, personal" qualities, about "nature," about not being afraid of the past, about the unknown, about East and West, about new freedoms. Maybe that is what this piece is all about. Makes great use of all three pedals. The dynamic range leans to the quieter side. Pointillistic delicate treatment, serene, great metric freedom. Many passages have a dynamic mark for each note. D.

Les Yeux Clos 1979 (Sal) 10pp. Written as a memorial to the poet Shuzo Takiguchi, who Takemitsu says "influences [him] a great deal as an artist." An exploration in rhythm, dynamics, and color. Requires great sensitivity. M-D to D.

Les yeux clos II 1989 (Schott 1990) 10pp. 7 min. Commissioned by and dedicated to Peter Serkin. The inspiration for this piece arose from the composer's visceral reaction upon seeing a series of lithographs by the French painter Odilon Redon, entitled *Les yeux clos*. It consists of a black-and-white lithograph juxtaposed with two others in varying colors. In this musical composition, the composer attempts to convey the sense of movement created by Redon's particular use of color. Very slow tempo, proportional rhythms relationships, harmonics, pedal notation for all three pedals. D.

Litany In Memory of Michael Vyner 1950–89 (Schott 1990) 10pp. 6 min. A recomposition of "Lento in due Movimenti (1950) from the composer's memory since the original score has been lost" (from the score). Adagio: con rubato, octotonic, changing meters, pedal carefully marked; large span required. Lento misterioso: changing tempi, chromatic, contrasting sections, tranquil *ppp* ending. D.

Rain Tree Sketch II in Memoriam Olivier Messiaen (Schott 1992) 5pp. 5 min. Celestially light (Tempo I): slow moving, chromatic chords, contrasts with Tempo II: thinner, more varied texture and a little slower than Tempo I. Proportional rhythmic relationships, some pedal indications, some pedal ad lib. Tempo I turns to Joyful before returning to celestially light; contains suggestions of impressionistic sonorities. M-D. to D.

See: David Burge, "Oriental Composers," CK, 4 (December 1978).

Joseph Tal (1910–   ) Israel, born Poland

Sonata (IMP) Three movements. Thick textures. Theme of bass ostinato in second movement is based on a Rahel song. Final movement is a fast Rondo. M-D.

Dodecaphonic Episodes (IMI 1963). "Based on a 12-tone row and use many of the 48 forms. The first episodes also introduce a rhythmic series with its R and I forms. In the second episode the rhythmic row is developed according to Boris Blacher's variable meter system, the form being dependent on the continuous time flow thus created. The third episode features motivic exploitation. The fourth and last permits improvisation which is controlled by the rhythmic proportions derived from the pitch row" (BBD, p.170). D.

Louise Talma (1906–1996) USA

Talma is a composer of authority and high professional skill. Her output for piano is not large but is interesting and significant. The style is oriented toward Stravinsky and, in the case of the second Sonata, toward Ravel.

Sonata No.1 (CF 1943). Largo—Allegro molto vivace: short introduction leads to a driving rhythmic staccato movement in 6/8, ostinato figuration. Larghetto: serene melody, quartal and quintal harmonic usage, homogeneous texture. Presto: toccata-like rhythmic finale, ostinato, changing meters, dramatic closing. Serious large-scale work. D.

Alleluia in Form of Toccata (CF 1947). Lengthy, cheerful, flexible meters, staccato style, fresh melodies. Requires firm rhythmic control, agility, and stamina. D.

Six Etudes (GS 1953–54). Impressive virtuoso writing. No.3, a sostenuto pedal study, is of special interest. D.

Pastorale Prelude (CF 1952) 3pp. Quiet, ABA, conjunct motion and wide leaps, pentatonic mid-section. Would make a good combination with the *Alleluia in Form of Toccata.* Int. to M-D.

Sonata No.2 1944–55 (CF 1977) 17pp. 16 min. Effective large-scale work demanding bravura and complete musicianship. Neoclassical with serial elements. A rewarding piece to play. D.

Sawako Tamaru (1956–   ) Japan

Tamaru is a graduate of Kunitachi Music College

Suishôren (Japan Federation of Composers 1994) 8 min. The title means Chinese blind, or shade, with crystal beads. Influenced by traditional Chinese music, especially the sounds of the pipa, liuqin, and yangqin. M-D.

Akira Tanaka (1947–   ) Japan

Sonate (EMT 1654 1981) 18pp. Être; L'Ombre; Réflexions. Highly organized writing with each subject identified in all its forms (retrograde, retrograde inversion, etc.). Octotonic, lyric quality. M-D.

Sergei I. Taneive (1856–1915) Russia

Taneive was one of the greatest theoretical contrapuntists of all time. Much of his music has no trace of nationalism.

Prelude and Fuge g♯ Op.29 (USSR). A Chopinesque prelude in the grandest style followed by a fugal essay remarkable in its imagination and dramatic ferocity. This work startlingly reveals where both Scriabin and Rachmaninoff came from—Taneive taught them during their teens in the 1880s in Moscow. M-D.

Elias Tanenbaum (1924–   ) USA

Sonata (ACA 1959) 25pp. Dissonant counterpoint, atonal, melodic skips, polyrhythms, harmonics, quiet closing. D.

Music for Piano (ACA 1963) 10 min. Serial, preference for sevenths, use of overtones (depress thick chords silently, sound higher notes), pointillistic. M-D.

Hilary Tann (1947–   ) Wales

Ms. Tann chairs the Performing Arts Department, Union College, Schenectady, N Y.

Doppelgänger 1984 (OUP 1992) ca. 5½ min. Explores the potential for *rapprochement* between two contrasting types of musical continuity. During its course a rather formal, bravura character gradually dissolves into its more lyrical counterpart (from the composer's notes). M-D to D.

Alexandre Tansman (1897–1986) Poland

Tansman, like his compatriot Frédéric Chopin, lived most of his life in Paris. His style varied from early pieces definitely influenced by Chopin to Impressionist and neoclassic writing. Jazz also played a large part in some of his music. The piano writing is always idiomatic.

Mazurkas 1918–28 (ESC). Vol.I: 10 pieces of varied difficulty. Vol.II: 9 pieces of varied difficulty. Vol.III: 8 pieces. Vol.IV: ca. 1990. Some of Tansman's best works.

Petite Suite 1919 (ESC). Seven short movements, lyric. M-D.

Trois Études transcendantes 1922 (Sal). Chromatic, pianistically interesting. M-D to D.

Sonatine 1924 (Sal). Well worked-out. M-D.

Cinq Impromptus 1926 (ESC). Varied moods. No.5 Toccata is most difficult. M-D.

Sonatine transatlantique 1930 (Leduc). Fox-trot; Spiritual and Blues; Charleston. Attractive jazz improvisation. "This work does not propose to realize an 'American Music,' but simply to put down the 'reaction' of a European musician to contact with the dance rhythms from across the sea" (composer's note). Large span required. M-D.

Arabesques 1931 (ESC). No.6 Danza is the best of the set. Int. to M-D.

Troisième Sonatine 1933 (ESC). Pastorale: animated. Hymne: chordal. Rondo: perpetual motion. M-D.

Cinq Impressions 1934 (ESC). Calme; Burlesque; Triste; Animé; Nocturne. Short, varied. Int. to M-D.

Pour les Enfants 1934 (ESC). Four graded collections, 12 pieces in each except the final collection, which has 10. Attractive, conventional settings.

Trois Préludes en forme de Blues 1937 (ESC). Uncomplicated, convincing settings. M-D.

Intermezzi 1939–40 (ESC). 4 series, 6 Intermezzi in each. More dissonant than Tansman's usual style. M-D to D.

Les Jeunes au Piano 1951 (ESC). Vol.I: Mireille et les animaux. Vol.II: Marianne devant le kiosque aux journeaux. Vol. III: L'Autobus imaginaire. Vol.IV: Au télescope. Graded pieces. Easy to M-D.

Four Nocturnes 1952 (UE). Each one page in length. Large span necessary. Int.

Prelude et Toccata 1943 (ESC). Scriabinesque prelude; perpetual motion toccata reminiscent of Ravel. Varied rhythmic usage, warm and incisive, fine showpiece. M-D to D.

Six études de virtuosité pour piano 1941 (ESC 1995). Contrasted, light textures, MC, delightful. M-D.

Suite variée 1952 (UE). Seven short pieces, chromatic. The four-voice fugue is difficult. Int. to M-D.

Sonata No.5 1955 (UE). To the memory of Bartók. Allegro deciso; Lento; Molto vivace; Largo—Allegro con moto. Terse, expressive. M-D.

11 Interludes 1955 (ESC). Varied moods and styles. M-D.

Four Impressions 1945 (MCA). Impressionistic. M-D.

Eight Novelettes (ESC). Accessible, moderate length. M-D.

Eight Cantilenas (MCA). Homage to Bach. M-D.

3 Ballades (ESC 1942) published separately. 1. 8pp. Moderato: chromatic. 2. 8pp. Andante cantabile: improvisatory opening, Allegro con moto mid-section, Allegro giusto closing, wide dynamic range *(pppp-ff)*. 3. 14pp. Andante comodo: dramatic opening leads to Allegro scherzando; Andante sostenuto, followed by a Presto mecanico closing. These pieces are too extended for their ideas; Tansman is more successful with the shorter character piece. M-D.

Hommage à Arthur Rubinstein 1973 (ESC) 9pp. 7 min. Tempo di Mazurka: Andantino malinconico, melody in left hand, graceful and tranquil. Toccata: Allegro moderato, risoluto groups of 16ths are interspersed with con forza chords in both hands, syncopated and punctuated lines, subtle rhythmic shifts, chromatic, dramatic ending on C. M-D.

10 Easy Pieces (UE 14559 1994) 16pp. Hungarian Mood; Toccata; Meditation; Gigue; Echo; Two-Part Gavotte; Siciliana; Study; Fughetta; Vienna. Charming, ingratiating. Int.

Sonata No.3 1932 (ESC 1992) 29pp. Introduzione e Fugato; Notturno; Toccata finale. Excellent ideas, natural gestures, facile and brilliant finale, extremely pianistic. M-D to D.

The Tansman Collection (Hinson—UE 1997) 28pp. 15 charming pieces, contrasting moods, bitonal influence. Int.

20 Easy Pieces on Polish Folksongs (MMP). Refreshing, nimble writing. Int.

Piano Album (Sal). Contains Sonatine, 3 Etudes Transcendantes, 4 Danse Miniatures, 20 Pièces Faciles, and Etude-Scherzo.

Album d'amis 1980 (ESC 8430) 17pp. Nine miniatures, warm harmonies, expressive and atmospheric, style of Debussy and Ravel. Int.

Phyllis Tate (1911–1987) Great Britain

Explorations Around: A Troubadour Song for Piano Solo 1976 (OUP) 47pp. 20 min. The theme is "Chevalier, mult este guariz" (1147). Intrada; Antiphon; Impromptu; Canzonetta; Epitome. Variation treatment. In the first and last movements the pianist must place a small drum between his knees. Photographed MS is not easy to read. M-D.

Bruce J. Taub (1948–   ) USA

Preludes 1987 (CFP 1990) 44pp. 40 min. 12 contrasting pieces. Passacaglia; "jazzy"; Furioso; rubato; poco rubato; Passacaglia; rubato; misterioso; Quasi meccanicamente: somewhat playful; Agitato: "sweeping"; rubato; rubato. Conceived as a group, freely tonal, frequent meter changes. Large span required. D.

Toccata (Etude IV) 1981 (CFP 1989) 10pp. 10 min. Four sections: the first is motoric and features strong rhythms; section two is slower, expressive, and rubato with widely spread sonorities. Section one is repeated, followed by a lontano and misterioso coda, *ppp* ending. Extremely affecting writing. M-D to D.

Antonio Tauriello (1931–   ) Argentina

Tauriello writes in a slightly atonal, linear, often pointillistic style.

Toccata (Bo&H). Polytonal usage blended into fine toccata style. M-D.
   See: Ylda Novik, "A Display of Touch," *Clavier,* 8 (January 1969):29–31, for a lesson on this piece. The music is printed on pp.23–28.

4 Sonatinas 1956 (Barry). No key signatures, does not display any nationalistic elements, fond of skips, MC. Each sonatina is short enough for all four to be played as a larger "sonata." Int.

Carl Tausig (1841–1871) Germany, born Poland

Tausig studied with Liszt from the time he was 14 and almost equaled him in grandeur of interpretation and technique. Tausig left more transcriptions than original works for the piano.

Zwei Konzertetüden Op.1 (H. M. C. Linden—Eulenburg 1975) 20 pp. Published separately during Tausig's lifetime under the titles *Impromptu* and *Das Geisterschiff.* The former contains many repeated notes, while the latter is built on arpeggi and is rhythmically flexible. Both breathe more Chopin influence than Liszt and are eminently worthy of performance. M-D to D. Available separately: *Das Geisterschiff* (Musica Obscura).

Ballade (Musica Obscura).

Reminiscences de Halka—Moniuszko Op.2 (Musica Obscura). A glittering virtuoso work. D.

10 Preludes (Musica Obscura) 10pp. Each prelude is about a page in length and is devoted to a particular pianistic problem: double notes, pedal, broken octaves in tenths, etc. Contains some lovely pieces. M-D.

3 Valses-Caprices d'après J. Strauss (Musica Obscura). Nachtfalter; Man Lebt nur Einmal; Wahlstimmen. Sparkling concert arrangements. These pieces are positive proof of F. Busoni's statement that "the piano can do anything." Also published separately. M-D to D.

Ungarische Zigeunerweisen (Musica Obscura) 23pp. One of the finest paraphrases of Gypsy tunes. Requires dazzling pianism. D.

Raynor Taylor (1747–1825) USA, born Great Britain

Taylor arrived from England in 1792 and was active along the East Coast. He was one of the most important eighteenth-century American musicians.

Rondo 1794 (Willis) in *A Collection of Early American Keyboard Music.* Many characteristics of light, eighteenth-century opera can be found in this piece. The graceful rondo theme employs imitation, a technique rarely used in American works of this period. M-D.

Variations to Adeste Fidelis (Hinson, McClenny—Alfred 11131). A simple, naive, and charming setting of the familiar tune with two variations and a Largo andante coda. Int.

Divertimento II 1797. In collection *Anthology of Early American Keyboard Music 1787–1830,* Part I (A–R Editions 1977) 3pp. Somewhat like a two-movement sonatina with a Rondo as the second movement. Classic style. Int.

Peter Ilich Tchaikovsky (1840–1893) Russia

Tchaikovsky was much more successful with ballet and symphonic scores than with works for the piano, although some of them do have a certain "period charm."

Complete Edition (USSR). All works for solo piano are contained in Vols.51A, 51B, and 53. Separately in octavo size (K).

Selected Piano Works (CFP). Vol.1: Op.1/1 Scherzo à la russe; Op.8 Capriccio; Op.19/6 Theme and Variations; Op.21 Six Pieces on a Theme (Suite): Prelude, Fugue, Impromptu, Funeral March, Muzurka, Scherzo; Op.59 Dumka. Vol.2: Op.2/1 The Castle Ruins; Op.2/3 Chant sans paroles; Op.5 Romance; Op.7 Valse-Scherzo; Op.9/2, 3 Polka, Mazurka de salon; Op.10/1, 2 Nocturne, Humoresque; Op.19/1, 3, 4 Rêverie du soir, Feuillet d'album, Nocturne; Op.40/2, 6, 9, 10 Chanson triste, Chant sans paroles, Valse, Danse russe; without opus number: Impromptu—Caprice; Valse—Scherzo; Impromptu; Aveu passionne. Vol.3: Op.51/2, 4, 5, 6 Polka peu dansant, Nata Valse, Romance, Sentimental Valse; Op.72/1–4, 8, 9, 12, 13, 15, 16 Impromptu, Cradle Song, Tender Reproaches, Characteristic Dance, Dialogue, Un poco di Schumann, L'Espiègle, Rustic Echo, Un poco di Chopin, Valse à 5/8.

Theme and Variations F Op.19 1873 (Hin; K). 12 variations and coda. Simple, expressive 16-bar theme is expansively developed through various contrasting moods and figurations. Var.1: adds more motion. Var.2: left hand has theme under right-hand triplets. Var.3: quirkily brilliant. Var.4: triplet staccato chords, more dashing and bravura. Var.5: mood and key change (D♭). Var.6: jaunty, snappy staccatos. Var.7: calm, quasi-religious chordal procession. Var.8: high-stepping and brilliant. Var.9: Alla mazurka: includes a miniature cadenza before the reprise of a mazurka-metamorphosis of the original theme. Var.10: original theme returns under quietly florid arabesque-passage-work. Var.11. "Alla Schumann": sounds like Tchaikovsky's idol in one of his most exuberant moods. Var.12: ostinato tonic pedal-point in the bass; coda works fleetly up to a bring-the-house-down conclusion. M-D.

6 Pieces on a Theme Op.21 1873 (K). The main changes in this suite are in the settings and moods rather than in the theme itself, although it is altered to some extent, especially in rhythm, to suit its various metamorphoses. M-D.

Sonata G Op.37 1878 (CFP; Simrock; Rahter; USSR; K). Moderato e risoluto: in

G, SA, big, bold, powerfully proclaimed first subject; second theme, Tranquillo, is lyrical and unusual only in some of the modulations it undergoes in its working-out. Andante non troppo, quasi moderato: in e, plaintive meditative main theme alternates with two other themes. Scherzo—Allegro giocoso: G, athletic first subject, exuberant passage-work, graceful mid-section with running left hand and melodic right hand. Allegro vivace: G, rondo, a bravura showpiece; main subject features big, declamatory, syncopated chords and swiftly dashing runs; followed by a quieter, meandering lyrical episode; the longer second episode is more insistent and expansive; a quiet coda with a slowing-down pedal-point concludes with the final chords. Tchaikovsky's largest and most ambitious solo piano work. Requires eloquence and virtuosity. D.

The Seasons Op.37b 1875–76 (Alfred; CFP; GS; K; Br&H; WH; EMB; Leduc). Twelve pieces, one for each month. More effective when performed individually. M-D.

Album for the Young Op.39 1878 (CFP; GS; EBM; Br&H; Ric; K; Alfred; ABRSM). Tchaikovsky was influenced by Schumann's Opp.15 and 68. Tchaikovsky knew how to write for young people without writing down to them. Ranges from easy (No.12) to fairly difficult (No.4). Int. to M-D.
See: W. G. Robertson, "Tchaikowsky's *Album for the Young,*" *Piano Journal*, 41 (June 1993):17–19.

12 Etudes Op.40 1876–78 (Henle; K). Dedicated to the composer's brother. Mostly short. No.1: brilliant study. No.2 Chanson triste (Henle, separate). No.7 Au village: a miniature *Dumka*. No.9 Waltz f♯: Schumannesque. No.10 Danse russe. These five are the best of the set. Int. to M-D.

Dumka Op.59 1886 (IMC; K) 10 min. This concert fantasy is probably Tchaikovsky's most substantial and successful piano solo. Contrasting mournful and wild episodes; has a certain Russian rustic scene about it. M-D.

Sonata c♯ Op.80 1865 (Posth) (K; USSR). Less demanding technically and more rewarding musically than Op.37. Allegro con fuoco: sufficiently superior to the rest of the sonata to warrant performance on its own. Andante: short, Schumannesque, agreeable without being distinguished. Scherzo: charming, turned up in the composer's First Symphony, with a waltz substituted for the original trio. Allegro vivo, alla breve: noisy and empty; this movement probably accounts for the relative neglect of this work. M-D.

Easiest Piano Pieces (Niemann—CFP 5013). Nine pieces from *Album for The Young,* Op.39. Int.

Il mio primo Ciakovski (Pozzoli—Ric 2599) 14pp. Nine pieces from *Album for the Young,* Op.39. Int.
See: A. E. F. Dickinson, "Tchaikowsky, The Piano Music," in *The Music of Tchaikowsky,* edited by Gerald Abraham (New York: Norton, 1946): pp.114–23.

André Tchaikowsky (1935–1982) Great Britain

Inventions Op.2 1961-2 (Nov 1975; Weinberger) 36pp. 20 min. Ten pieces. Dedicated to fellow concert pianists Peter Feuchtwanger, Fou Ts'ong, Stefan

Ashkenazy, Tomás Vasary, Ilona Kabos, and others. Varied styles and moods. Astringent harmonies, atonal. Large span required. M-D to D.

Alexandre Tcherepnin (1899–1977) USA, born Russia
"A fecund and expert composer internationally successful in classical forms and also theatrically. Initially inspired by the Russian Romantic masters, he developed in France from medieval sources an original approach to modality and rhythm, later in East Asia was influenced by classical Chinese music. His work has at all periods been filled with poetry and bravura" (Virgil Thomson, *American Music since 1910* [New York: Holt, Rinehart and Winston, 1971], p.177).
Toccata No.1 Op.1 1921 (Belaieff) 6 min. Bravura writing. M-D to D.
Nocturne g♯ Op.2/1 1919 (Belaieff) 5 min. Short, poetic, stormy. M-D.
Dance Op.2/2 1919 (Belaieff) 4 min. Martellato writing, sharp changes of registers, interlocking hand technique. M-D to D.
Scherzo c Op.3 1917 (Durand) 3 min. Chordal, double notes. M-D to D.
Sonatine Romantique Op.4 1918 (Durand) 11 min. Uses a 9-step scale, in cyclic form. Main theme is similar to Russian chant for the dead. M-D to D.
    See: Enrique Alberto Arias, "Tcherepnin's Sonatine Romantique," *Clavier,* 31/10 (December 1992):36–41. Includes music of the first movement.
10 Bagatelles Op.5 1913–18 (Heugel; GS; MCA; TP; IMC) 12 min. Some of the composer's finest writing. Int. to M-D.
    See: Guy Wuellner, "A. Tcherepnin's Bagatelles, Op.5," PQ, 99 (Fall 1977): 46–48.
Episodes 1912–20 (Heugel) 12 min. Twelve sketches, 1 or 2 pages in length, varied moods, MC. Int.
Petite Suite Op.6 1918–19 (Durand). March: Chant sans paroles; Berceuse; Scherzo; Badinage; Humoresque. Concert pieces. Int. to M-D.
Pièces sans titres 1915–19 (Durand) 12pp. Eight short character pieces exploiting various pianistic devices: staccato chords in fifths in No.1; arpeggi in bass register accompanying single-note right-hand melody in No.3; chromatic runs in No.5; inner voices in No.6. Int. to M-D.
Nocturne Op.8/1 1919 (Durand). A concert piece, full sonorities. M-D to D.
Danse Op.8/2 1919 (Durand) 4 min. Toccata-like figuration with interwoven melody. Brilliant arpeggi and octave passages lead to a cadenza. *Pp,* grave, chordal conclusion. Large span required in both hands. M-D to D.
8 Preludes Op.9 1919–20 (Heugel) 8 min. Short, facile, varied, chromatic, subtle. Good concert pieces. M-D.
Feuilles libres Op.10 1920–24 (Durand) 9 min. Four short concert pieces. D.
5 Arabesques Op.11 1920–21 (Heugel) 6 min. Similar to subtle chromatic style found in Op.9. Nos.1–4 for piano solo; No.5 for piano and violin. M-D to D.
9 Inventions Op.13 1920–21 (ESC) 8 min. Freely chromatic, clear textures, short. M-D.
Etude de Concert b 1920 (Hamelle). Virtuosic, arpeggi, perpetual motion idea. D.
10 Etudes Op.18 1915–20 (Heugel) 25 min. More character pieces than studies. M-D to D.
2 Novelettes Op.19 1921–22 (Heugel). Large concert pieces. M-D to D.

Toccata No.2 Op.20 1922 (Simrock) 6 min. New edition (1974) revised by the composer. Wide stretches and skips are prevalent. Good concert piece. D.

Six Etudes de travail Op.21 1922–23 (Heugel) 12 min. Each etude exploits a specific aspect of piano technique. Also good as recital pieces. D.

Sonata No.1 Op.22 1918 (Heugel) 16 min. Allegro commodo; Andante; Allegro; Grave. Cyclic form, dark sonorities, unusual quiet closing movement. M-D to D.

4 Nostalgic Preludes Op.23 1922 (Heugel) 6½ min. One work in free form consisting of four movements. Effective improvisational style. M-D.

4 Préludes Op.24 1922–23 (Durand). One work in free form made up of four movements. Polyphonic textures. M-D to D.

Transcriptions Slaves Op.27 1924 (Heugel) 12½ min. Les Bateliers du Volga: paraphrases "Song of the Volga Boatmen." Chanson pour la chérie: tune stated seven times; textures thicken during repetitions. Chanson-grande-russienne: tune in different registers, repeated chords. Le Long du Volga: shortest of the set. Chanson Tchèque: Slovakian tune, off-beat rhythms. Effective concert pieces. M-D to D.

Canzona Op.28 1924 (Simrock) 5 min. Based on a nine-step scale, style similar to Op.13 and Preludes of Opp.23 and 24. Subdued, extreme registers used. M-D.

4 Romances Op.31 1924 (UE). Four movements. Good concert piece. M-D to D.

Histoire de la petit Thérèse de l'Enfant Jésus Op.36 bis 1925 (Durand). A set of thirteen pieces that survey the saint's life. Like a suite. Good for recital. Int.

Message Op.39 1926 (UE). Has the dimensions of a sonata in a free, one-movement form. D.

Voeux (Prayers) Op.39 bis 1926 (Durand). Six small concert pieces. No.4, "Pour le bonheur bourgeois," is best known. Like a suite. Good for recital. M-D.

Entretiens (Conversations) Op.46 1930 (Durand). Ten short pieces, experimental harmonies. M-D.

Etude de Piano sur la gamme pentatonique Op.51 1934–35 (Heugel). 3 sets. The last set of twelve short pieces (Bagatelles Chinoises) is the best known. Easy to Int. Opp.51, 52, and 53 could be called a "Chinese Mikrokosmos" (Wuellner, diss., p.223; see reference given at end of Tcherepnin listing). See: Ming Tcherepnin, "Tcherepnin's Chinese Bagatelles: A Master Lesson," *Clavier,* 22/7 (September 1983):26–27. Includes Nos.1, 7, and 8.

5 Etudes de Concert Op.52 1934–36 (Schott). Varied textures and sonorities. Nos.2 and 3 draw upon Chinese instruments (the lute for No.2, Pi-Pa for No.3). Nos.1 and 4 draw upon Chinese folk character music. Like a suite. Good concert pieces. D.

Technical Studies on the Five-Note Scale Op.53 1934–36 (CFP). Based on pentatonic scale. Explores many aspects of piano technique. M-D.

Autour des montages russes 1937 (ESC) 1 piece: Le guichet; Les "on dit"; Le Swing; Et voilà. Int.

Sept Etudes Op.56 1938 (Belaieff) 14 min. Some reveal an interest in oriental music. Good recital pieces. M-D to D.

Pour petits et grands Op.65 1940 (Durand) 26 min. 2 vols. 12 student character pieces. Also good for recital. Int.

Chant et Refrain Op.66 1940 (Durand) 7 min. Chant: homophonic. Refrain: polyphonic. The two pieces are unified by one tonal center. Large concert pieces. D.

Badinage 1941 (CFP; Harald Lyche). Effective encore. M-D.

Polka 1944 (SP) 2 min. Effective encore. M-D.

Le Monde en Vitrine (Showcase) Op.75 1946 (Bo&H). Romantic character pieces. Like a suite. Good for recital. D.

La Quatrième 1948–49 (Heugel) 3 min. "Title alludes to the Fourth Republic of France and the difficulties which followed World War II" (Wuellner, diss., p.223; see citation below).

Expressions Op.81 1951 (MCA). Ten short character pieces, transparent writing. Like a suite. Good for recital. M-D to D.

Songs without Words Op.82 1949–51 (CFP). Five fine recital pieces. In the form of a suite. M-D to D.

12 Preludes Op.85 1952–53 (EBM; new edition revised by composer, Belaieff) 25 min. Chromatic, complex harmonies, rhythms, extreme registers used. Good for recital. D.

8 Pieces Op.88 1954–55 (TP). Like a suite. Good for recital. D.
    See: Richard Zimdars, "Eight Pieces for Piano, Op.88," *Clavier,* 24/2 (February 1985):26–27.

Contemporary Piano Literature 1954 (SB). 17 easy pieces for the Francis Clark series. Easy to Int.

Sonata No.2 Op.94 1961 (Bo&H). Three connected movements, lightly contrapuntal and percussive textures, highly chromatic. D.

Rondo à la Russe 1946 (Gerig 1975) 7pp. M-D to D.

Sunny Day (Bagatelle Oubliée) 1915 (TP 1977). Also published in PQ, 100 (Winter 1977–78):34–35. Easy.

See: Gerry Wallerstein, "Happy Birthday to A. Tcherepnin," *Clavier,* 13 (January 1974):10–17. An interview with the composer.

Guy Wuellner, "Alexandre Tcherepnin 1899–1977," PQ, 100 (Winter 1977–78): 29–33.

——, "The Complete Piano Music of Alexandre Tcherepnin: An Essay together with a Comprehensive Project in Piano Performance," DMA diss., University of Iowa, 1974, 487pp.

——, "The Theory of Interpoint," AMT, 27 (January 1978):24–28.

——, "Alexander Tcherepnin, in Youth and Maturity: *Bagatelles* Op.5 and Expressions, Op.81," JALS, 9 (June 1981):88–94.

——, "The Piano Etudes of Alexander Tcherepnin," JALS, 35 (January–June 1994):1–22.

——, "A Sampler of the Piano Music of Alexander Tcherepnin," *Piano Journal,* 27 (October 1988):13, 15, 17–19.

Special appreciation goes to Guy Wuellner for his help with this section.

Ivan Tcherepnin (1943–1998) USA, born France
Son of Alexander Tcherepnin.
4 Pieces from Before (Belaieff) 11pp. For Christmas (1958); Valse (1959); Vernal

Equinox (1961); Riding the Clouds (1962). Contrasting, MC, glissandos, large span required. M-D.

Nikolai Tcherepnin (1873–1945) Russia
Father of Alexander Tcherepnin. He studied with Rimsky-Korsakov.
Six Pieces 1923 (MMP). Colorful, Romantic harmony. Int. to M-D.

Serge Tcherepnin (1941–   ) USA, born France
Son of Alexander Tcherepnin.
Inventions 1961 (Belaieff) 8pp. 1: fluid chromatic horizontal continuity through a basic motive. 2: harmonic and rhythmic confrontation of two five-note motifs. 3: builds diagonally, through a wall-of-brick interlay of the six basic unchanging motifs. Neoclassic. M-D.

Georg Philipp Telemann (1681–1767) Germany
Telemann, one of the most prolific composers of all time, was inspired by Couperin, Lully, and Rameau. Much of his keyboard writing employs thin textures that contribute to the freshness and charm of his rococo miniatures.
Fantaisies pour le Clavecin; 3 Douzaines (BB; Br; Dover). Three dozen small pieces, each dozen reflects a different national style: German, French, and Italian (ABRSM). They are precursors of the classical sonata form. Int. to M-D.
Fantasies (K 9538) 36pp. 16 Fantasies, each of two or three short movements. Ornaments realized and essential fingering added. Int.
Klavierbüchlein (von Irmer—Schott). 4 dance suites; 4 separate pieces: Moderato, Cantabile, Aria, Praeludium; 2 fugues a, e, for two players (duets). Int.
6 Overtures (Fischer and Oberdoerffer—Vieweg) in *German Keyboard Music of the 17th and 18th Centuries,* Vols.4 and 5 (MMP). All have the same form: a French Overture with two following movements, slow and fast. M-D.
Spielstücke für Klavier. (Degen—Br). 36 pieces from *Getreuen Musikmeister,* partly for lute. Also includes works by Weiss, Baron, Kreysing, Haltmeier, Goerner, and C. Petzold. M-D.
Easy Fugues and Short Pieces (IMC; MMP). 6 fugues from *20 Little Fugues,* each followed by short homophonic movements. Int. to M-D.

Sigismond Thalberg (1812–1871) Austria, born Switzerland
Thalberg was undoubtedly a man of great talent. He was highly esteemed by Anton Rubinstein and was called by Schumann a "god at the keyboard." He was famous for bringing out the melody with the thumbs while surrounding it with elaborate figuration. It sounded as though he had three hands. The Sigismund Thalberg Society in the United States has done much to refocus and bring renewed interest to this composer. Most of his piano works were fantasies on popular operas of the day.
12 Studies Op.26 (Ric). Contain many tricks of the trade. Most require a virtuoso technique. M-D to D. No.3 available separately (Musica Obscura).

Grande Sonate c Op.56 1844 (Musica Obscura) 47pp. Allegro moderato; Scherzo Pastorale; Andante; Finale—Agitato. Makes heavy demands on the performer. D.

Grazioso—Romance sans Paroles (Musica Obscura) 2pp. Andantino, e♭-E♭. Lovely character piece, salon style. Int. to M-D.

"Don Pasquale" Fantasy Op.67 (MTP). Published with two other operatic fantasies: *Moses,* Op.33, and *Barber of Seville,* Op.63. Thalberg was nicknamed "Old Arpeggio" by his contemporaries because he specialized in arpeggio passage-work. The Op.67 fantasy is a good example to demonstrate the "3 hand" illusion that Thalberg frequently produced. This device (achieved by dividing a third voice between the hands) had come to be considered his private property, as he used it so much. Thalberg was among the new order of pianists who loved special effects and *misterioso* suggestion. He purposely avoided transparent textures, which formerly were deemed a prerequisite for good piano playing. M-D to D.

Transcription of Pergolesi's "3 Days My Nina" (Musical Scope). Once a repertoire piece of Joseffy and Busoni. M-D.

See below, "Collections," *Piano Music of the Parisian Virtusoso 1810–1860.*

See: Daniel L. Hitchcock, "Sigismund Thalberg 1812–1871, An Evaluation of the Famous Composer-Pianist, on the 100th Anniversary of His Death," PQ, 77 (Fall 1971):12–16.

Timothy K. Thompson (–   ) USA

Duologues 1964–65 (CF 1982) 19pp. Facsimile edition. Many expansive processes at work, i.e., melodic units expand intervalically and lengthwise, and the rhythmic units progress from eighth notes to quarter notes to half notes and even to whole notes. Octotonic, long bars (13/8, 7+5/8), player free to combine various rhythmic units, ad lib sections. M-D.

Toccata-Pastorale 1965 (CF 1982) 20pp. Long bars are true (23/8, 31/8, etc.), not just sums of shorter units. Freely tonal, anchor chords support more adventurous melodies. Refreshing, much air space for sonorities to sound. M-D.

Virgil Thomson (1896–1989) USA

Brilliant and objective, Thomson is a musical commentator on America.

Five Two-Part Inventions 1926 (EV). Tonal essays in two-part writing with a spicy contemporary flavor. Int. to M-D.

Sonata No.1 1929 (MCA) 3½ min. Original solo version of Symphony No.2. Allegro con brio; Andante; Allegro non troppo. Genial, sunny and extrovert; cyclical in thematic content and asymmetrical in form. Thomson calls it "a panoramic landscape drawn in France." Int.

Sonata No.2 1929 (Belwin-Mills 1982) 11pp. Cantabile; Sostenuto; Leggiero brilliante. Mixture of styles, withdrawn, poetic, reflective, witty. Int.

Sonata No.3 1930 (TP) 5pp. Four movements. Uses only white keys; a dialogue between two voices. Int.

Sonata No.4 1940 (EV). Short, humorous, Int.

10 Etudes 1943–44 (GS). Variegated set of clever pieces designed to work out specific technical problems. Repeating Tremolo. Tenor Lead. Fingered Fifths. Fingered Glissando. Double Glissando. For the Weaker Fingers. Oscillating Arm. Five Finger Exercise. Parallel Chords: highly rollicking. Ragtime Bass: deliberate evocation of ragtime style, like a barn dance, a fine encore. Practicable and engaging, wonderfully imaginative. M-D.

9 New Etudes 1954 (GS). With Trumpet and Horn; Pivoting on the Thumb; Alternating Octaves; Double-Sevenths; The Harp; Chromatic Major Seconds; Chromatic Double-Harmonies (Portrait of Sylvia Marlowe); Broken Arpeggios; Guitar and Mandoline. Graceful, witty, with unusual results. M-D.

Portraits (GS) 4 albums, 8 pieces on each. Some of Thomson's best compositions are in the form of musical portraits of his friends. These works reveal his darting, quixotic sense of humor; clarity of form and content, and mastery of his craft. "The subject sits for his likeness as he would for a painter. An effort has been made to catch in all cases a likeness recognizable to persons acquainted with the sitter" (from the Preface). Somewhat humorous, but for more serious moments see the neoclassic portrait of Nicolas de Chatelain in Album 3. Many famous people included, from Pablo Picasso (Album 1, No.1) to Lou Harrison (Album 1, No.5). Int. to M-D.

9 Portraits (PIC 1974). More of Thomson's friends depicted by musical portraits. M-D.

Edges. A musical portrait of Robert Indiana 1966 (GS) 5pp. Opposing harmonies move over keyboard; much use of chromatic seconds; mirror effects between hands. M-D.

13 Portraits (Bo&H 1981) 44pp. Each of the subjects is briefly identified. Int. to M-D.

Man of Iron (GS 1978). A musical portrait of Willy Eisenhart. Dissonant, frenetic arpeggios. M-D.

10 Easy Pieces and a Coda 1926 (PIC 1972) 8pp. Clever introduction to contemporary styles. Easy to Int.

See: Anthony C. Tommasini, "The Musical Portraits by Virgil Thomson," MQ, 70/2 (Spring 1984):234–47.

Francis Thorne (–   ) USA
Thorne is Executive Director of the American Composers Orchestra.
Seven Simple Sincopations (TP). Colorful, clever writing, easy-to-play style. Int.

Ton-Thât Tiêt (1933–   ) Viet Nam
Trung Dzuong 1980 (Jobert) 12pp. 12 min. Performance directions in French and English. Clusters, harmonics, proportional rhythmic relationships, changing and unusual meters (5/4+1/8). Repeat sections a specified number of times, very free sections. Performer can repeat in irregular rhythm, use free permutation of sounds, vary order of chords. Expressionistic and avant-garde. D.

Michael Tippett (1905–1998) Great Britain

Tippett's dissonant style stems from Bartók and Hindemith. It also displays wide skips and other gesticulative thematic elements as well as occasional use of texture and sonority for their own sake.

Sonata G 1942 (Schott). Allegro: Theme and 5 variations, brilliant, vigorous, poco maestoso, scherzando, toccata in alternating octaves, theme returns. Andante molto tranquillo: unassuming melody followed by contrapuntal treatment, quiet closing. Presto: octaves, cross-rhythms, thin textures, quiet closing. Rondo giocoso con moto: complete rondo, various difficult pianistic figurations. D.

Sonata No.2 1962 (Schott). A one-movement work, mainly lyrical, thoroughly worked out. Little development. Variation and repetition very important. D.

Sonata No.3 1973 (Schott 11162) 42pp. 25 min. Allegro: changing meters, three opening ideas, close imitation, extremes in range exploited. Lento: shifting chords evolve into fascinating patterns. Allegro vivace: a virtuoso rondo. A large but taut work; a valuable and important addition to the repertoire. D.

Sonata No.4 1984 (Schott 12250) 58pp., ca 35 min. I: ABCAB form, 5-note figure, B♭, C, A, C♯, D, is important in unifying the movement. II: "Crisp and dancing" mood mixed with more serious quality. III: begins and ends on A, 5 parts, complex rhythms, hammered material. IV: C♯ is the first and last note, mid-section in slower canonic style, busy and exciting movement. V: theme and 4 variations, theme returns. Much cohesiveness throughout this work. D.

Roger Green, "Tippett's Fourth Piano Sonata," *Piano Journal*, 7/19 (February 1986):12–13, 15.

See: Andrew Ball, "Tippett's Piano Sonatas: A Pianist's Reactions," *Music and Musicians* (January 1985):6.

Roger Green, "Tippett Piano Sonatas," *Piano Journal,* 2/5 (1981):19–21.

Wadham Sutton, "Contemporary British Piano Sonatas 4: Michael Tippett Sonata No.2," *Music Teacher,* 45 (January 1966):23.

Clive Swansbourne, "The Piano Music of Sir Michael Tippett," PQ, 147 (Fall 1989):53–56, 58.

———, "The Piano Music of Michael Tippett," *Clavier*, 29/6 (June 1990):12.

Heuwell Tircuit (1931–   ) USA

Bartók Variations, set II (AMP 1976) 25pp. The theme is the sixth piece of Bartók's *Sketches,* Op.9, subtitled "Rumanian." Composer's notes, performance suggestions, and biographical note. A well-developed set in post-Bartók style. M-D.

Boris Tishchenko (1939–   ) USSR

In the sonata genre, it may be that Tishchenko is well on his way to composing the most important body of works in Russia since Prokofieff. He has composed four piano sonatas.

Sonata II Op.17 1960 (USSR). Three movements. Opening theme of the first movement is a wild, quasi-fugal, quasi-atonal invention that sends the pianist all over the keyboard. At the same time the performer must coordinate split-second micro-rhythms between the hands. Second theme is dreamy, moves in Impressionistic parallel thirds. Dazzling virtuosity is put to the service of exciting and absorbing musical ideas. M-D to D.

Sonata III Op.32 1965 (Sovetskii Kompozitor 1974) 62pp. Dissonant writing that reflects dark, harsh colors. Freely tonal, flexible rhythms, violent, jagged conclusion. D.

Antoine Tisné (1932–1998) France

Boréal (Billaudot 1984) 15pp. 13 min. This "north wind" begins mysteriously and *ppp lointain*, builds to gargantuan sonorities (repeated clusters) before it eventually evaporates; dramatic gestures all over the keyboard. D.

Loris Tjeknavorian (1937–   ) Iran

Armenian Miniatures 1975 (Ramsey). Nine pieces based on Armenian folk and dance melodies, free arrangements. Unusual key signatures, contemporary idiom, modal. Look more difficult than they are. M-D.

Armenian Sketches (Novello 1975) 32pp. 26 short, pleasant pieces illustrating traditional Armenian rhythms and modes. Wide variety of keys, modes, time signatures, and difficulty. Interesting lyric quality. Mainly cast in two-part texture. Unusual rhythms will perhaps be a problem. Fine for small hands; outstanding for developing rhythmic independence. Int. to M-D.

See: Denby Richards, "Loris Tjeknavorian," MO, 100 (December 1976):135–36.

Ernst Toch (1887–1964) USA, born Austria

Toch utilized all tones of the chromatic scale in a free way and emphasized linear writing. In many ways his music reminds one of Hindemith.

Burlesken Op.31 (Schott 1923). Three scherzi. No.3 *Der Jongleur* is best known. Facility and rhythmic drive required. M-D.

Three Piano Pieces Op.32 (Schott 1925). Quiet; Delicate without haste; Allegro moderato. Short, require subtle tonal balance and, in the last one, some bravura playing. M-D.

Five Capriccetti Op.36 (Schott 1925/1936). Short, require sensitivity and facility. M-D.

Kleinstadtbilder Op.49 (Schott) (*Pictures of a Small Town*). 14 small pieces that require subtle phrasing and different kinds of touch. Easy to Int.

Five Times Ten Studies (Schott 1931). A collection dealing with various facets of contemporary piano writing. The pieces are chromatic and atonal; a wide range of problems are investigated. *10 Concert Studies* Op.55, 2 vols. *10 Recital Studies* Op.56. *10 Studies of Medium Difficulty* Op.57. *10 Easy Studies* Op.58. *10 Studies for Beginners* Op.59.

Sonata Op.47 (Schott 1928). Quasi Toccata; Intermezzo; Allegro. Variety of techniques from two-part writing to thunderous climax of the last movement. Imaginative. M-D.

Profiles Op.68 (AMP 1948). A cycle of six pieces. Calm: flowing dissonant counterpoint. Moderato: changing meters, free counterpoint. Calm, Fluent, Tender: simple lullaby. Merry: scherzo in 5/4, rhythmic, staccato. Slow, Pensive,
Very Tender: flowing melody, thin accompaniment. Vigorous, Hammered:
perpetual motion, octaves, strong climax. M-D.

Ideas Op.69 (MCA). Calm: free, linear two- and three-part writing. A Black Dot
Dances in My Closed Eyes: melody, flowing figuration. Vivo: crisp and
legato playing required. Allegro: "each note hammered." Short sketches.
M-D.

Diversions Op.78a (MCA 1956). Five pieces. M-D.

Sonatinetta Op.78b (MCA 1958). Three short movements, clever linear writing.
M-D.

Three Little Dances Op.85 (Belwin-Mills). No.1 on black keys; No.2 on white
keys; No.3 on black and white keys. Dissonant, vigorous. Int. to M-D.

Reflections Op.86 (Belwin-Mills 1961). Five pieces, each one page. Int.

See: Wilton Mason, "The Piano Music of Ernst Toch," PQ, 41 (Fall, 1962):22–25.

Johann Wenzel Tomáschek (1774–1850) Bohemia

Sonatina G (NV). Homophonic, melodic. Int.

Tre Ditirambi Op.65 (MAB Vol.29) c, E, F. Early examples of the dramatic character piece. M-D.

Eclogues Vol.I (MAB Vol.73); Vol.II (MAB Vol.74) Poetic, somewhat smaller
than the *Ditirambi*, in ternary form and pastoral in character. M-D.

Sonata F Op.21 (Anthology Series *The Solo Sonata* pp.98–108). Adagio—Allegro
moderato cantabile. Only one movement of this work is available in a modern edition. The Adagio serves as introduction. Form is clear-cut: moments
of brilliant figuration. M-D.

Ausgewälte Klavierwerke (Dana Zahn—Henle 260). Fingering by Hans-Martin
Theopold. Preface in German, English, and French. Variations on an Unknown Theme G Op.16; 6 Eclogues Op.35; 3 Ditirambi Op.65; 3 Allegri
Capricciosi de Bravura Op.84. All these works were composed between
1805 and 1818. Excellent urtext edition. Int. to M-D.

9 Variations on the song "O du lieber Augustin" (Goebels—Schott 6875 1980)
14pp. Contrasted variations infused with a certain amount of humor and
Romantic touches. Var. 9 is a canon. Many octaves, requires flexible wrists.
M-D.

Henri Tomasi (1901–1971) France

In his attempt to appeal to the general public, Tomasi wrote music that is frequently rich in color, lyrical, pleasant to the ear, and easily understood. He often
borrowed from folklore, especially that of Corsica and Provence, in his desire to
preserve native forms and melodies, but other more exotic cultures are also represented. Tomasi's style is eclectic and individual, though many influences from
his contemporaries can be noticed, and it is impossible to put his music into one
specific category.

Pièces brèves (Lemoine). Suite I. 7pp. Et s'il revenait un jour; Menuet; Le lied que chante mon coeur. Suite II. 8pp. Parade; Air à danser; espiègleries. Mildly Impressionistic sonorities, attractive. Int. to M-D.

Paysage 1930 (Lemoine) published separately. Marine (mouettes); Clairière (matin d'été); Forêt (chants d'oiseaux). Infused with modal flavor and supple rhythms. M-D.

Scènes Municipales (Leduc 1932) 11pp. Le garde champêtre; Danse des charretiers; La timide rosière; Le défilé des pompiers. Mood contrasts, bright and cheerful with angular rhythms. M-D.

Sampiero Corse (Marche Corse) (Lemoine 1933) 5pp. A pleasant march with a vivid rhythmic Trio. M-D.

Tarentelle (Leduc 1936) 8pp. Flowing triplets with rhythmic melody contrast with light, scherzando chordal sections. Contains some unexpected rhythmic twists. M-D.

Le coin de Claudinet 1948 (Leduc) 9pp. Twelve short attractive pedagogic pieces. Int.

Berceuse 1959 (Leduc) 3pp. Modal melodies answered by bitonal sonorities that surround and drown (like distant bells), fairylike on p.2, improvisational. Int. to M-D.

I am grateful to Jane Eschrich for help with Tomasi's music.

Michael Torke (1961–   ) USA

Torke studied at the Eastman School of Music.

Laetus 1981 (Hendon Music 1995) 16pp. 8 min. Mildly dissonant, exciting gestures, strong percussive usage, pianistic, accessible but challenging. M-D to D.

Hector Tosar Errecart (1923–   ) Uruguay

Danza Criollas 1947 (BB) 4 min. Continuous running eighth notes; a few lyric passages but rhythmic treatment is most interesting. M-D.

Sonatina No.2 1954 (Ric) 12 min. Three movements, FSF. Large atonal work with passages of quartal harmony, well-defined themes, rousing conclusion. M-D.

Improvisation 1941 (ECIC). Extended, ambling "poco animando," 4 against 3, broken-chord figuration, expressive mid-section. M-D.

Habib Touma (1934–   ) Israel

Arabic Suite (IMP 169) 15pp. Three highly contrasted movements. Strong melodies, exploits melodic half and whole steps, colorful harmonies. M-D.

Charles Tournemire (1870–1939) France

Douze Préludes-Poèmes Op.58 (Heugel 1932) 86pp. Untitled; some require four staves to notate; virtuoso figuration, avant-garde for its day. D.

Joan Tower (1938–   ) USA

Tower's music is extremely evocative and features strong rhythms. She teaches at Bard College in New York.

"Or like a . . . an engine." In collection *American Contemporary Masters* (GS 1995) 10pp. Also in P&K, 171 (November 1994):36–41. "A propulsive toccata that traces the spatial, easily visualized choreography of tones" (James M. Keller, P&K, p.35). Continual triplet and sixteenth-note figuration throughout most of the piece. Slight tempo changes return to original tempo. Eminently pianistic. D.

Roy Travis (1922–   ) USA
Travis teaches at UCLA, where he has drawn inspiration from African music at the Institute of Ethnomusicology.
African Sonata (Sonata II) 1966 (University of California [Berkeley] Press 1973) 44pp. Sikyi: a coquettish and attractive Ashanti dance, SA design. Bambara Dance-Song: intricate rhythms, chromatic major second runs. Sohu: an Ewe dance, scherzolike, many perfect and augmented fourths. Adowa: an Ashanti funeral party dance; introduction followed by 15 variations. Based on rhythms, melodic motives, and sonorities derived from traditional West African dances. Because it is difficult for the piano to sound like the original sources, much musical content has been lost, but this is still an unusual and stimulating work. D.
Five Preludes (TP 1966) 9pp. Marcato; Andante sostenuto; Grazioso; Barcarola; Con fuoco. Freely tonal; each piece develops one main idea; borders on the expressionistic. Large span required. M-D.

Arkady Trebinsky (1897–   ) France
Suite française Op.20 (EMT 1971) 14pp. Gavotte: mainly two voices, chromatic coloration, witty. Gigue: thin textures, detached touch. Sarabande: sustained, accompanied melody, more tonal than first two movements. Bourrée: kind of a perpetual-motion idea, some melodic emphasis with arpeggio accompanimental style. Int. to M-D.

Karl Ottomar Treibmann (1936–   ) Germany
Klavierzyklus II 1978 (Br&H). Five short atonal improvisatory pieces, each exploiting one idea; linked by permanently depressing the sustaining pedal; metrically free. Interesting if uninspired effects. Mushed sonorities accumulate in each movement. Int. to M-D.

Ronald Tremain (1923–   ) USA, born New Zealand
Prelude, Aria and Variations (Price Milburn). Cerebral 12-tone writing, clear and concise structure, variations flow convincingly into one another. M-D.

Gilles Tremblay (1932–   ) USA, born Canada
Deux Pièces 1956–58 (Berandol) 8 min. All directions in French. Phases: short, slow, brutally dissonant. Réseaux: more involved, longer, changing tempi, extremes of keyboard used, very contemporary-sounding (this title might be translated as "tangles" or "webs"). D.

Tracantes 1976 (Sal) 5 min. Reproduced from holograph. 14 sheets with varied figures, one page of performance directions. Clusters, harmonics, proportional rhythmic relationships, pointillistic, avant-garde. M-D to D.

Christos Tsitsaros (1961–   ) USA, born Cyprus
Tsitsaros is assistant professor of piano pedagogy at the University of Illinois.
Six Autumn Sketches 1993 (Hal Leonard 00290418) 31pp. After the Rain; Mists; Night Train to Tokyo; Perpetuum Mobile; Sunset. "The Autumn Sketches were composed as an attempt to create interesting and challenging teaching materials for the upper intermediate and early advanced level. Musically, they represent the European post-romantic and early twentieth century pianistic idiom, infiltrated by American harmonic, melodic, and rhythmic influences. At the pianistic level, they deal with specific technical aspects. For example, *Sunset* is a study in legato 'singing' double notes over extended arpeggiated figures in the left hand. *Mists* deals with repeated notes, while *Toccata* is based on a left hand detached ostinato and alteration of meters. All this is done with special attention 'not to make it sound like an etude'" (program notes from recital at the University of Illinois, November 12, 1993).
Cinderella Suite (F. Harris 1996) 30pp. 8 colorful movements, MC, well written. Int.
Blackbirds at Ueno (H. Leonard 1992) 9pp. Changing meters, trills, chromatic, alternating octaves between hands, *fff* ending. Int. to M-D.
The Bike Ride (H. Leonard 1992) 3pp. Light, staccato, jaunty, catchy tune, glissando ending. Int. to M-D.
Nine Tales (F. Harris 1996) 36pp. A colorful and contrasting set of late-intermediate character pieces.

Antonin Tučapský (1928–   ) Czech Republic
Fantasia Quasi una Sonata (Roberton 1992) 15pp. 15 min. A one-movement work with contrasting *attacca* sections: Largo e sereno: tranquil; con moto—impetuoso: strong rhythms. Adagio: expressive tension; Animato: a fluttering build-up to: con moto—impetuoso; Adagio e tranquillo: melodic and delicate; Allegro: varied melodic figuration over contemporary Alberti bass, secco style; Adagio e molto tranquillo da lontano: serene, dreamy. Freely tonal, melodic continuity, ends in C major. D.

Fisher Tull (1934–1994) USA
Two Fabrications (Bo&H 1980) 11pp. 5 min. Prelude: fantasy-like, filmy texture, delicately pedaled 16th-note arpeggios. Toccata: percussive passage-work, highly rhythmic, left-hand ostinato. Both pieces are freely tonal and use clever rhythmic interplay between the hands. M-D.

Joaquín Turina (1882–1949) Spain
Turina spent some time in France and was influenced by Impressionism. He has written a large repertoire for the piano. Most of his works are in a semipopular style, always colorful, exhibiting a fine mastery of form.

Suite Pittoresque—Sevilla Op.2 1909 (K 9239; Schott; MMP) 24pp. Sous Les Orangers (Under the Orange Trees): combines malagueña and habanera rhythms. Le Jeudi Saint à Minuit (Holy Thursday at Midnight): remarkable nocturnal images evoked, the best piece of the set. La Feria (Holiday): two contrasting elements, one outgoing and joyous, the other a graceful tango. The entire suite is rhythmic and colorful and contributed largely to Turina's early fame. The big splashy sounds are a pleasure in themselves. M-D.

Sonata romántica (sur un thème espagnol) Op.3 (ESC 1910). Theme and variations; Scherzo; Final. Extended work, a theme and variations throughout. M-D.

Coins de Séville Op.5 1911 (Schott; MMP) 1st suite. Soir d'été sur la terrasse; Rondes d'enfants; Danse des seises dans la cathédrale; A los toros. Vibrant. M-D.

Tres danzas andaluzas Op.8 1912 (Sal). Petenera. Tango. Zapateado: shoe-dance. Rhythmic vigor plus vivid color produce a sense of physical immediacy in these pieces. M-D.

Album de Viaje Op.15 1916 (IMC; K; UME). Five pieces. Descriptive "Travel Impressions." M-D.

Mujeres españolas (Femmes d'Espagne) Op.17 1917 (Sal; MMP) Set I, three portraits. Musical portraits of Spanish ladies. M-D.

Cuentos de España Op.20 1918 (Sal; MMP) Set I, seven pieces. Full of profound musical poetry. M-D.

Niñerías Op.21 1919 (Sal). Set I, eight pieces. Casual, flowing. See especially Prelude and Fugue No.1. Int. to M-D.

Danzas Fantásticas ("Imaginary Dances") Op.22 (UME; MMP). Pictorial excerpts from the Spanish poet José Más are used to preface each of the three dances. Exaltación ("Ecstasy") (IMC; K 9499). "It seems as if the figures in that incomparable picture were moving like the calix of a flower." Ensueño ("Daydream"): "The guitar strings, when struck, sounded like the lament of a soul that could no longer bear the weight of bitterness." Orgía ("Revel"): "The perfume of flowers, mingled with the fragrance of mansanilla, and the lees of a splendid wine, was like an incense that inspired joy." M-D.

Sanlúcar de Barrameda (Sonata pintoresca) Op.24 1922 (IMC; UME; MMP). Four movements. En la torre del castillo ("In the Tower of the Citadel"); Siluetas de la calzada ("Portrait of a Woman in Shoes"); La Playa ("The Beach"); Los pescadores en Bajo de Guia ("The Fisherman of Bajo de Guia"). Sanlúcar de Barrameda is a fortified seaport near Cádiz made picturesque by its ancient Moorish citadel and colorful fishing fleets. Turina spent his summer vacations there. This work, one of his most ambitious, describes the atmosphere of the town. The third and fourth movements combine to make an Impressionistic prelude and fugue. M-D to D.
See: Linton Powell, "Cyclical Form in a Forgotten Sonata of J. Turina (1882–1949)," AMT, 27 (September–October 1977):23–25.

El Barrio de Santa Cruz Op.33 1925 (Sal). Rhythmic variations for piano. Theme and seven variations. M-D.

Miniatures Op.52 1930 (Schott). Eight little pieces with Impressionistic overtones. Int.

Danzas Gitanas Set I Op.55 (Sal). Five pieces. Interesting rhythmically. See especially No.5 "Sacromonte," which describes the mystery of the jagged, holy mountain of Montserrat near Barcelona. Int. Set II Op.84 (Sal). Five pieces based on Gypsy themes. Int. to M-D.

Niñerías Op.56 (Sal). Eight pieces. See especially Carnaval des enfants. Int. to M-D.

The Circus Op.68 (Schott). Fanfare; Jugglers; Equestrienne; The Trained Dog; Clowns; Trapeze Artists. Attractive recital pieces, appropriate for an accomplished teenage student. Int. to M-D.

Silhouettes Op.70 (Sal). Available separately. L'aqueduc. La tour de la véla: a light dance. La puerta del sol: two contrasting moods. La tour de l'or. Le phare de Cadix: brilliant. Descriptive pieces. Int. to M-D.

Préludes Op.80 1928 (Heugel). Five pieces. Delicate sounds, based on folk songs, diatonic melodies. Int.

Trois Variations 1926 (ESC). Varied simple harmonizations of a melody. Int.

Variations on a theme of Chopin (Sal). Romantic variations on Prelude A. M-D.

Femmes d'Espagne Op.73 (Sal). Five more musical portraits of Spanish ladies. Int. to M-D.

Piano Music. Selections (Sal 1991) 378pp. Contains Contes d'Espagne; Danses gitanes; Buñerias; and others.

The Turina Collection (Hinson—Schott SM6534) 52pp. Contains 20 of his finest intermediate works, including selections from *The Circus*; *Miniatures*; *At the Shoemakers*; *Postcards.*

See: Linton Powell, "Joaquin Turina. Another of the Spanish Nationalists," *Clavier,* 17 (October 1976):29–30.

——, "The Influence of Dance Rhythms on the Piano Music of Joaquin Turina," MR, 37 (May 1976):143–51.

——, "The Piano Music of Spain (Joaquin Turina)," PQ, 98 (Summer 1977): 45–48.

Daniel Gottlob Türk (1756–1813) Germany

Türk, a famous pedagogue, published 48 sonatas for keyboard between 1776 and 1793. He is best known for his well-organized *Klavierschule* of 1789, which is available in a fine English translation by Raymond H. Haggh (Lincoln: University of Nebraska Press, 1983), 563pp. Only a few of Türk's sonatas are available in contemporary editions.

Sonatas e, C, A, D (K&S). Available separately. Each work contains some fine moments interlacing the more academic passages. Int. to M-D.

COLLECTIONS OF TEACHING PIECES (all Easy to Int.):

29 Easy Pieces (Döflein—Schott).
46 Pieces for Beginners (Döflein—Schott).

49 Pieces for Small Hands 1792 (Auerbach—Nag).
60 Handstücke für angehende Klavierspieler 1792 (Serauky—Litolff).
12 Pieces (Litolff).
49 Pieces for Beginners (K).

Elizabeth Turner (active 18th century) Great Britain

Turner was active in choral activities in London in the 1750s. During this time
she published *A Collection of Songs With Symphonies* and a *Thorough Bass With
Six Lessons for the Harpsichord.*

Six Lessons for Harpsichord or Piano (Barbara Harbach—Vivace Press 1994)
68pp. Suites ranging from three to five movements each, including andantes, gavottes, gigues, minuets, and a few unusual titles such as savoyard,
scotaza, and tambourine. Textures are thin; pleasant galant style. Int. to M-D.

Paul Turok (1929–   ) USA

Little Suite Op.9 (GS). Prelude; Arabesque; Toccata. Effective dissonant writing.
M-D.

Passacaglia Op.10 (A. Broude 1977) 4pp. Contemporary look at a baroque form.
Essentially lyrical. Explores basic piano sonorities, dissonant, bitonal influence. M-D.

Geirr Tveitt (1908–1981) Norway

Danse du Dieu Soleil ("Dance of the Sun God") Op.91/15 (NMO 1952) 16pp.
Ornate figures develop into strong rhythms and full chords; thick textures;
tonal. D.

50 Hardanger Op.150/50 (NMO 1951) 7pp. The final piece in a set of fifty popular Norwegian tunes developed into varied character pieces. Full chords,
fast repeated notes, clusters. M-D.

U

Ernst Ludwig Uray (1906–   ) Austria
Thema, Variationen und Fuge 1933 (UE). In Brahms-Reger tradition. Especially brilliant fugue. D.

Erich Urbanner (1936–   ) Austria
Urbanner is professor of composition and harmony at the University of Music and Performing Arts in Vienna.
Sonatina 1956 (Dob 1983). Strongly chromatic, nonserial use of 12-note patterns, thin textures, gentle and lyric. M-D.
13 Charakterstücke 1988–89 (Dob 1991) 26 min. Contrasted moods (from humorous to grotesque) and textures, changing meters, atonal. Could be performed individually, in groups, or as the whole work. M-D to D.

V

János Vajda (1949–   ) Hungary
Light Sonatina 1988–89 (EMB 13840 1994) 11pp. Allegro moderato; Un peu triste . . . Satie—manie; Des garçons joyeux. Strong dance rhythms, ragtime influence. M-D.

Fartein Valen (1887–1952) Norway
Valen's style is an attempted synthesis of polyphony, traditional Viennese classical forms, an inconsistent 12-tone technique, and his own characteristically melodic and sonorous mode of expression.
Legende Op.1 1907 (Lyche). A piece of late Romanticism, ABA design, chromatic decoration. M-D.
Sonata No.1 c♯ Op.2 1910–12 (WH) 27 min. Large three-movement work in Brahms-Reger style. Complex, moments of great beauty. See opening of Adagio movement. M-D.
Variations Op.23 1935–36 (Lyche). Twelve serial variations. Blends neoclassic sense of structure, Impressionistic feeling for atmosphere, expressionistic intensity of emotion, and polyphony into a personalized atonal style. D.
Gavotte and Musette Op.24 1936 (Lyche). An embroidered 12-tone theme is broken into four cells, repeated notes. M-D.
Prelude and Fugue Op.28 1937 (Lyche). Two-voice Prelude, three-voice Fugue, both atonal, contrapuntal interplay—strict, yet ambient. M-D.
Intermezzo Op.36 1939–40 (Lyche). Uses the 12 notes of the chromatic scale to develop a thematic sequence of five germ motives. Intense yet subdued. M-D.
Sonata No.2 Op.38 1940 (Lyche) 20 min. Subtitled "The Hound of Heaven." First movement: restless, atonal. Andante: pensive, ponderous. Toccata: motoric, ends in atypical solitude and resignation. D.

Michael Valenti (1942–   ) USA
5 Sonatinas (AMP 1979) 45pp. Contemporary sonorities in classical forms. Elements of blues, jazz, ragtime, and rock are present. Fresh writing for the middle teenage group. Int. to M-D.
Piano Preludes (AMP 7780) 32pp. A set of twelve pieces, rich harmonies, plenty of fireworks, easily assimilated tunes. M-D.
10 Nocturnes (AMP 1981) 32pp. Broadway musical influence, more nineteenth- than twentieth-century style. Int. to M-D.

The Musical Telephone Book (Schroeder & Gunther). Twelve pieces for young
pianists. Musical anagrams—telephone numbers of famous places and in-
stitutions are translated into music. Int.

Mary Jeanne Van Appledorn (1927–   ) USA
A Light Fantasie 1984 (Sisra Publications 1992) 12pp. 5 min. Includes tune index.
M-D
Set of Five 1953 (OUP 1978) 15pp. 8 min. Ostinato; Blues; Improvisation; Elegy;
Toccata. Improvisation and Toccata are available separately. Freely tonal,
well conceived for the instrument, effective as a group. M-D.

Nancy Van der Vate (1930–   ) USA
Sonata 1978 (Arsis Press) 15pp. 14 min. Very slowly; Slow; Fast. A structurally
clean and sensitively shaped work, sharply sculpted lines, subtle coloristic
voicing required in some of the chordal sections of the opening movement.
The Finale is full of motoric excitement with ostinatos and interlocking
octaves. D.

Jan Vaňhal (1739–1813) Bohemia
Easy Sonatinas. 16 Little Pieces (Millerova—Artia). Excellent teaching material.
Int.
Two Sonatinas (Vol.17 MAB, Artia). Same level as above. Also contained in this
volume are sonatinas by Fr. X. Dussek, Benda, and Worzischek.

Frederik Van Rossum (1939–   ) Belgium
Little Style Studies Op.41 (Roberton). Five short studies (about 1 min. each) of
mikrocosmic elegance. The first English publication of a composer highly
regarded in France and his native Belgium.

Nicholas Van Slyck (1922–1983) USA
Fingerpaints (Gen 1981). Vol.I: 23 short, varied pieces with a number of twentieth-
century techniques: mirror writing, clusters, dissonant harmonies. Easy to
Int. Vol.II: not so easy; imaginative. Int.

Ralph Vaughan Williams (1872–1958) Great Britain
The Lake in the Mountains (OUP 1947) 4 min. From the film music for *49th Par-
allel.* Linear, unusual key changes, atmospheric, quiet. M-D.
Suite of Six Short Pieces (S&B). Prelude; Slow Dance; Quick Dance; Slow Air;
Rondo; Pezzo ostinato. Unpianistic. M-D.
Hymn Tune Prelude on Gibbons Song 13 (OUP 1936) 3½ min. Legato is a prob-
lem. Int.
Piano Concerto (OUP). Original version for one piano dates from 1933. Joseph
Cooper, in collaboration with the composer, made a two-piano version in
1946. This score includes both versions. Toccata: animated. Romanza: lyric.

Fuga chromatica con finale alla Tedesca: chromatic; Romantic; cadenza precedes Tedesca. M-D.

Six Teaching Pieces 1934 (OUP; MMP). Three two-part Inventions; Valse lente; Nocturne; Canon. The Nocturne is the most effective piece of the set. The OUP collection is titled *Little Piano Book*. Int.

Elizabeth Vercoe (1941–   ) USA

Fantasy (Arsis Press 1978) 14pp. Features some playing inside the piano (plucked harmonics), vigorous keyboard writing, clusters, trills, many arpeggiated sonorities, angular, final two pages unbarred, impressive conclusion. M-D.

Three Studies (Arsis Press 1978) 5pp. Mirrors: hands take turns mimicking each other. Daydreams: a small mood piece. Fugue: perpetual motion. MC. Int.

Giuseppe Verdi (1813–1901) Italy

Valzer in Fa Magg (Musica Obscura; Boccaccini & Spada). An early work. Melody in octaves, waltz accompaniment figure, glamorous with a grand sweep. Int.

Marion Verhaalen (1930–   ) USA

Fantasy Suite (H. Leonard 1983) 8pp. Fanfare; Chorale; Aria; Toccata. "Improvise on the black key pentatonic scale as long as you like"; "Improvise on the Phrygian Mode" (from the score). Free and dramatic sections guide the improvising. Effective, MC. M-D.

John Verrall (1908–   ) USA

Préludes en Suite (AMC). Seven short pieces, varied moods. Pianistic, require more effort than appears necessary. Int.

Theme and Variations (ACA 1944) 8 min. Ten variations in neoclassic style. Finale consists of last four variations in rondo form. M-D.

Sonata (ACA 1951) 15 min. First movement: many tempo changes. Vivace: 3/4–2/4 meter. Adagio e serioso: movement ends with return to tempo of first movement but slows down to a *ppp* ending. MC. M-D.

Hélio Bacelar Viana (1954–   ) Brazil

Micro Pieces Vols.1 and 2 (BME). For beginning piano students; introduces some of the wealth of Brazilian rhythms. Easy to Int.

Miniature Suite (BME). Based on fragments of Brazilian rhythms. Int.

Miniatures (BME). 17 short pieces. Int.

Fructuoso Vianna (1896–1976) Brazil

7 Miniaturas sobri temas Brasileiros (Vitale 1979) 15pp. Children's Song. Dance of the Negroes: grotesque, lively, and invigorating. Song of the Negroes: sauntering. Work Song: slow and monotonous. Hillbilly Dance (a Hoe Down!). The Street Vendor. Little Tango. A charming set that should be performed as a group. Int. to M-D.

Laszló Vidovszky (1944–   ) Hungary

The Death of Schroeder 1974–75 (EMB Z8423) for pianist and 3 assistants. The title is a reference to Charles M. Schulz's cartoon series, *Peanuts,* and its character Schroeder, who practices the piano incessantly. During the course of the piece, the assistants gradually transform the sound of the piano. Meanwhile the pianist continously plays scales, taking in turn the 61 possibilities listed in the score, then starts all over again playing them in reverse order. Great fun! Int. to M-D.

Louis Vierne (1870–1937) France

Suite Bourguignonne Op.17 (MMP). Late-nineteenth-century style. M-D.

Anatol Vieru (1926–1998) Rumania

Nautilos 1968 (Sal) for piano and tape (tape on rental) 9pp. 9½ min. Divided into five sections, scrupulously notated with performance instructions in French. Requires normal keyboard playing as well as the use of a plastic stick, a small heavy glass, keys and other metal objects on the strings; clusters, glissandi, striking with the fist, etc. The tape is used in the fourth section. Dynamic marks for each note, pointillistic, some improvisatory sections. Timings in seconds are coordinated with the tape. D.

Heitor Villa-Lobos (1887–1959) Brazil

Villa-Lobos was one of the most prolific composers of the twentieth century. Vol.3 of *Composers of the Americas* (Washington, D.C.: Pan American Union, 1957) lists 727 compositions written by him. Villa-Lobos once told the late Olin Downs, "I compose in the folk style. I utilize thematic idioms in my own way, and subject to my own development. An artist must do this. He must select and transmit the material given him by his people. I have always done this and it is from these sources, spiritual as well as practical, that I have drawn my art" (Marcos Romero, ibid., p.9). This great Brazilian artist began composing in a post-Romantic style, moved to Impressionism and folklore, later experimented with classicism, and finally synthesized all these elements. Some works are simple and easily understood, while others are abstract and highly complex. It is helpful to remember that Villa-Lobos wrote for many different publics. His keyboard style often involves a wide dynamic range, complex cross-rhythms, improvisatory sweeps, lush sonorities, and a unique manner of handling the pedals. Much of his music that is published in Brazil is available from Music Imports, 2571 N. Oakland Ave., Milwaukee, WI 53211.

Amazonas 1932 (ESC). Almost all the melodic material in this work is based on indigenous themes from the Amazon, collected by Villa-Lobos. The main melodic motives represent the themes of the invocation, the surprises of the mirage, the slithering and galloping of the legendary monsters of the Amazon River, the sensuousness of the Indian priestess, the heroic song of the Indian warriors, and the precipice. M-D.

Cirandinhas (Little round dance) 1912–14 (ESC; MMP). Suite of 12 pieces based on popular children's themes, written as teaching pieces. Int.

Ciclo Brasileiro 1936–37 (Consolidated Music Publishing). A series of impressions of a trip through Brazil. Based on local color and on original themes from some North East Brazilian birds. Native Planting Song: quiet, melody in tenor, widespread chordal figuration in right hand. Minstrel Impressions: lengthy, rich sonorities, waltz, improvisatory treatment. Jungle Festival: alternating hands, octaves, cross-rhythms, brilliant right-hand figuration. Dance of the White Indian: alternating chords and octaves, energetic, bravura. M-D.

Bachianas Brasileiras No.4 1930–36 (Consolidated Music Publishing 1941). Brazilian and Bach-like elements combined. Preludio—Introdução; Coral; Aria; Dansa. Dansa is in collection *Latin American Art Music* (GS). Some of Villa-Lobos's best. M-D.

Carnaval das Crianças Brasileiras (Arthur Napoleão 1919–20; MMP). Eight pieces. Nos.2 and 3 published separately (EBM; Consolidated Music Publishing). No.2 O Chicote do Diabinho (The Devil's Whip): short, light, brilliant, trills, fast, repeated chords. M-D. No.3 A Manha da Pierette (Pierette's Hands): playful, attractive. Int.

Ten Pieces on Popular Children's Folk Tunes of Brazil (Mer). 2 vols., 5 pieces in each. Short, simple settings, traditional harmony. Int.

Guia Prático 1932–35. Eleven collections containing about half a dozen pieces in each. Settings of popular Brazilian children's songs. Album I (Consolidated Music Publishing): see especially No.1 Dawn. Album II (ESC; MMP): see No.4 Samba. Album III (ESC): see No.1 Le Petit berger. Album VI (Mer): see No.4 Anda a roda. Album VII (Mer): see No.5 O Corcunda. Album VIII (Consolidated Music Publishing): see No.1 O limao and No.4 Pai Francisco. Album IX (Consolidated Music Publishing): see No.3 O ciranda, a cirandinha. Album XI (Southern): see No.6 Long Live the Carnival: colorful virtuoso writing. Int. to M-D.

Francette et Piá 1929 (ESC). Suite of ten pieces based on the story of little Brazilian Indian who went to France and met a little French girl. French and Brazilian tunes are combined in each piece. Requires imagination. Int.

The Three Maries. 1939 (CF). Inspired by the stars commonly called "The 3 Marias"; based on one of Villa-Lobos's own poems. Alnitah: requires brilliance and facility. Alnilam: lyric, short staccato contrasting mid-section. Mintika: facility, careful tonal balance, and free pedaling required. Int. to M-D.

Cirandas 1926 (Arthur Napoleão; MMP). Collection of 16 pieces loosely based on popular Brazilian themes. But this is music of great sophistication that combines simple melodies with rich harmonic and rhythmic ideas. Experiments with a different form in each piece. Large span required. Int. to M-D.

Prole do Bébé (The Baby's Dolls) Series I 1918 (Appleby—Alfred; EBM; ESC;

K). This set of pieces came into being as a result of the composer's meeting Artur Rubinstein. They are based on Brazilian folklore and have an imaginative Impressionistic flavor. Branquinha (The Porcelain Doll): bell-like sonorities, pedaling and balance problems. Moreninha (The Paper Doll) (EBM, separately): cross-rhythms, brilliant, 16th-note tremolos. Caboclinha (The Clay Doll): samba rhythm, chordal, steady 16ths. Mulatinha (The Rubber Doll) (EBM, separately): varied textures and tempi, improvisatory. Negrinha (The Wooden Doll): brisk, alternating hands in 16ths. A Pobrezinha (The Rag Doll): short, chordal, ostinato harmonies, melancholy. O Polichinello (Punch) (Ric; CF, separately): fast alternating hands in 16ths, breathless. A Bruxa (The Witch Doll): lengthy, broad scope, varied textures, climactic. M-D.

Prole do Bébé (The Little Animals) Series II 1921 (ESC). More difficult, more adventurous, and longer than Series I. Each piece has its own character. A Baratinha de Papel (The Little Paper Bug): study in cross accents. O Gatinha de Papelão (The Little Cardboard Cat): atmospheric, ostinato figures, limping half-step figure. O Camondongo de Massa (The Little Toy Mouse): brilliant, bravura playing required. O Cachorrinho de Borracha (The Little Rubber Dog): slow, moves to sonorous climax, short. O Cavalinho de Pau (The Little Wooden Horse): lively, rocking-horse patterns, cross-rhythms, *ffff* climax, ends softly. O Boizinho de Chumbo (The Little Tin Ox): large scope, octaves, double notes, big chords. D. O Passarinho de Pano (The Little Cloth Bird): cross-rhythms, trills in both hands. D. O Ursinho de Algodão (The Little Cotton Bear): lively, alternating hands, double notes. D. O Lobozinho de Vidro (The Little Glass Wolf): a ferocious toccata, broad sweeps, obsessively recurring theme. D.

Suite Floral Op.97 1916–17 (Consolidated Music Publishing; MMP). Idílio no Rêde (Summer Idyll): lyric, broken-chord figuration divided between hands. Camponeza Cantadeira (A Singing Country Girl): melodic, irregular groupings, quiet close. Alegria na Horta (Joy in the Garden) (IMC): lively, colorful dance, varied textures; Rubinstein played this frequently. M-D to D.

Saudades Das Selvas Brasileiras (Brazilian Forest Memories) (ESC). No.1: lively mosaiclike melodies over ostinato bass figures, exotic. No.2: brisk, rhythmic, chordal, 4 against 3. M-D.

Alma Brasileira—Choros No.5 (Brazilian Soul) 1925 (EBM; ESC; MMP). Syncopations, lament over chord and broken-chord accompaniment, rubato, atmospheric. Suggests the essence of Brazilian character, with its gentleness and generosity combined with explosions of furious energy. M-D.

Rudepoema 1921–26 (ESC) 18 min. The "rude" in the title refers to the rough, unpolished nature of the sentiments the composer wished to express. In one movement (Villa-Lobos's most extended piano solo), several short opening motives alternate and interweave continuously in varying tempos, colors, and rhythms. Rhythms, tune, and harmonies of a Brazilian flavor overwhelm at certain points. Harmonics, obligatory use of the sostenuto pedal, and a final fist cluster to be repeated four times. Virtuosic writing. D.

Hommage à Chopin 1949 (Merion; ESC). No.1 Nocturne: lyric Impressionism. M-D. No.2 Ballade: broad scope, Romantic, brilliant. D.

Petizada (PIC 1954). Six delightful 2-page works, published separately. Simple tunes, mainly two voices. Easy to Int.

Poema Singelo 1942 (Consolidated Music Publishing). Variations on a simple tune, alternating chordal treatment between hands, vivace chromatic triplets, opening Andantino closes piece. M-D.

Caixinha de Música Quebrada (The Broken Little Music Box) 1931 (Consolidated Music Publishing). Syncopated chromatic right-hand accompaniment over broken-chord figuration in left hand, large sweeps, catchy closing. M-D.

Simples Colentânea 1917 (Consolidated Music Publishing; MMP). No.1 Valse Mística: fast, broken melodic figuration, expressive mid-section, *fff* closing. M-D. No.2 Um Berço Encantado: improvisatory, atmospheric, broad sweeps. M-D. No.3 Rhodante: fast triplet figuration, glissandi, repeated notes, double trills, brilliant closing. D.

Brinquedo De Roda (The Toy Wheel) (PIC). Six pieces, published separately. Charming realizations based on Brazilian children's tunes, contrasted, clever. Int.

A Lenda do Cabocla (Napoleão 1920; MMP) 5pp. Syncopated chordal accompaniment, gently flowing melody, lush harmonies. M-D.

Suite infantile I 1912 (Schott ED 7569; MMP) 15pp. Dancing; The child goes to sleep; Cunning; Reflections; On the Swing. Int.

Suite infantile II 1913 (Schott ED 7570; MMP) 11pp. Allegro; Andantino; Allegretto; Allegro non troppo. Int.

Both suites sound MC and contain little or no folk music influence.

Historia da carochinha (Napoleao; MMP) 10 min. No palcio encantado; A cortesia do principezinho; E o pastorzinho cantava; E a princezinha dançava. Attractive but contain tricky spots. Int. to M-D.

Piano Music (Dover). 50 piano pieces including Prole Do Bebe No.1. Int. to M-D.

Valsa da Dor (Waltz of Sadness) (ESC 1932) 5pp. 5½ min. Luxuriant Romantic style. Published posthumously. M-D.

The Piano Music of Heitor Villa-Lobos (Consolidated 1972) 166pp. *Music for Millions,* Vol.62. Contains a broad range of Villa-Lobos's music.

See: Randall Bush, "Heitor Villa-Lobos," AMT, 30/4 (February–March 1981):20–21. Mainly a discussion of the piano works.

——, "The Piano Works of Heitor Villa-Lobos," *Clavier,* 24/2 (February 1985): 18–21. Includes music to and discussion of *A Pombinha Voou* (The Little Dove Flew Away).

Laurence Morton, "Villa-Lobos: Brazilian Pioneer," *Clavier,* 16 (January 1977): 29–32. Contains pieces from *Guia Prático* Nos. 8, 97, and 137.

Roberta Rust, "Interpreting the Music of Villa-Lobos," *Clavier,* 33 (October 1994):20–23.

Madame de Villeblanche (18th century) France
Four Sonatas for Piano or Harpsichord (C. Johnson—Vivace Press 1994) 60pp.
Virtuosic passages, weak harmonic usage, interesting rhythms; galant–
early classic style. Originally published ca. 1789. M-D.

Carl Vine (1954–   ) Australia
Piano Sonata 1990 (JWC 1990) 33pp., ca. 18 min. 1: Half note = 48. 2: Leggiero e
legato. "Tempo markings throughout this score are not suggestions but indications of absolute speed. Rubato should only be employed when directed, and then only sparingly. Romantic interpretation of melodies,
phrases and gestures should be avoided whenever possible" (from the
score). Harmonics, glissandos, forearm clusters. The second movement contains many tempo changes, double tempo, *pppp* ending. Virtuosic. D.

Roman Vlad (1919–   ) Italy, born Rumania
Vlad began utilizing serial techniques in 1939.
Studi Dodecafonici per Pianoforte (SZ 1943, revised 1957). Four contrasted 12-
tone studies. In these pieces "a segment of the basic row recurs in the
transpositions so frequently that it provides a source of structural unity.
Vlad frequently creates a complex of two rows; at such times this recurring
segment of the basic row is conspicuous" (BBD, p.176).
Sognando il sogno; variazioni su di una variazione per pianoforte (Ric 1973) 22pp.
Subtitled "Variations on the First Variation." The first variation uses a 12-
note row whose first seven pitches make up the F-major scale. This allows
for a varied version of Schumann's "Träumerei" for the second variation.
Final variation is effective, but the whole piece involves many double
sharps and flats, making for difficult reading. D.

Ernst Vogel (1926–1990) Austria
Motivation I–V 1972 (Dob) 13pp. 9 min. Mildly dissonant, varied meters. M-D.

Moritz Vogel (1846–1922) Germany
Magic Flute Sonata Op.48/3 (Br&H 8111 1980) 13pp. A turn-of-the-century trifle
based on themes from Mozart's opera. Three movements with the first
based on the "Birdcatcher's Song." Written only for a performer with a
sense of humor! Int. to M-D.

Wladimir Vogel (1896–1984) Switzerland, born Russia
Vogel was the first Swiss composer to use 12-tone technique.
Etude-Toccata 1926 (Bo&H). Virtuoso writing. D.
Variétude 1931–32 (Bo&H). "Contains chaconne-like repetitions of the principal
theme, suggestive of a rhythmic series" (BBD, p.178). D.
Epitaffio per Alban Berg 1936 (Ric). The tone row is a series of 23 tones using 9
pitches derived from the words "Alban Berg auf's Grab Friede!" (Alban
Berg upon the grave's peace). Develops in the manner of a passacaglia.

The row appears continuously in one or the other voices. Very expressive in spite of strict control. "The brilliance of much of the figuration is typical of Vogel's style. The work is an effective example of application of serial writing to a traditional form" (BBD, p.178). D.

Nature vivante (HV 1962) 8pp. Strophe d'album; Prélude gris; Nettement désagréable; Morceau poétique; Lasse et plaintif—Joyeaux. Expressionistic pieces. M-D.

Dai Tempi più Remoti 1921–47 (Eulenburg GM803) 10pp. Three pieces in Bergian style. M-D.

Hans Vogt (1911–1978) Germany

Sonata alla toccata (Bo&Bo 1971) 20pp. 13 1/2 min. Molto allegro: broad gestures, contrasted moods, sudden closing. Andante: suggested pedal points. Presto: brilliant secco writing. Neoclassic orientation. M-D to D.

W

Bernard Wagenaar (1894–1971) USA, born The Netherlands
Ciacona (EBM 1942). A four-bar chordal phrase varied seven times. Chordal
  with florid melodies, short, dissonant, dramatic closing. M-D.
Sonata (AMC 1920). First movement: broad, large scale. Improvisation: atmospheric, lyric. Rondoletto. Widely spaced sonorities, complete exploitation
  of instrument's resources. D.
Saltarello (TP). Polytonal, two voices, gay, dancelike. Int.

Georg Christoph Wagenseil (1715–1777) Austria
Wagenseil is one of the most important influences to have shaped the Viennese
classical keyboard sonata.
Six Divertimenti Op.1. 1753 (Helga Scholz-Michelitsch—Dob 1975) Vol.I: Nos.1–
  3. Vol.II: Nos.4–6. Preface in German and English. Charming and unpre-
  tentious rococo three- or four-movement works in expanded binary form.
  Int. to M-D.
4 Divertimenti (Nag No.36). Similar to C. P. E. Bach *Prussian* and *Württemberg*
  Sonatas. Three and four movements, homophonic, thin textures, pianistic
  figuration. M-D.
Sonata F Op.4 (Köhler—Litolff). Also in collection *Alte Meister,* Vol.II (Pauer).
  M-D.

Joseph Wagner (1900–1974) USA
Sonata b 1946 (PIC) 24pp. Three movements. Well-contrasted ideas, shifting accents, quartal and quintal harmonies, some jazz syncopation. Advanced
  pianism required.
Pastorale and Toccata 1948 (PIC). Pastorale: lyric, melodic. Toccata: highly rhythmic. M-D.
Four Miniatures 1959 (PIC). Preface; S; Berceuse; March. Tonal and polytonal,
  humorous, clever. M-D.

Richard Wagner (1813–1883) Germany
Wagner composed at the keyboard, and, in spite of his brilliant achievements in
orchestration, his music always sounds good on the piano.
Complete Works, Piano Works Vol.19, Series A. (Dahlhaus—Schott 1970). Sonata
  B♭ Polonaise D for four hands; Fantasia f♯; Grosse Sonate A; Albumblatt
  für Ernst Benedikt Lietz (Lied ohne Worte); Polka G; Eine Sonate für das

Album von Frau M. W.; Züricher Vielliebchen—Walzer; In das Album der Fürstin M; Ankunft bei den schwarzen Schwänen; Albumblatt für Betty Schott.

Sonata Bb Op.1 1831 (Br&H; Musica Obscura; MMP) 25 min. Allegro con brio: 4/4, SA design. Larghetto: 3/8. Minuetto and Trio: Bellini-like. Finale— Allegro Vivace: Rondo. Classic sonata form, Beethoven influence, outer movements use much Alberti bass. M-D.

Grosse Sonata A Op.4 1831 (Gerig) 28pp. Pleyel influence—written on assignment from Wagner's teacher Weinlig. Wagner tried his hand at fugal writing in the last movement. M-D.

Album-Sonate Ab 1853 (Br&H; Musica Obscura) 16pp. Written for Mathilde Wesendonck. Bears a spiritual relation to the "Love-Dream" music of *Tristan und Isolde* as well as the song "Träume," No.5 of the Wesendonck cycle. Int. to M-D.

See: John A. Dowd, "The Album-Sonata for Mathilde Wesendonck: A Neglected Masterpiece of Richard Wagner," JALS, 10 (December 1981):43–46.

Fantasia f# Op.3 (Musica Obscura; Kahnt; MMP) 20pp. Sectionalized, recitativo passages, chromatic, quite lovely, many starts and stops. Sounds more like the operatic Wagner. M-D.

Ankumft bei den schwarzen Schwänen (Musica Obscura) 2pp. Langsam, Ab. Charming character sketch, somewhat Schumannesque. Int. to M-D.

Klaviermusik aus der Zuercher Zeit (Labhart—Hug GH 11209) 14pp. Eine Sonate für das Album Frau. M. W. 1853. Polka 1853. Zuericher Vielliebchen-Walzer. Short pieces from the Zürich period. Int. to M-D.

Polonaise D 1831 (Walker—Nov 1973). A sketch for the *Polonaise* D for 4 hands. Has much vitality, octaves, chording. Would make a good encore. Int.

See: R. S. Furness and A.D. Walker, "A Wagner Polonaise," MT, 114 (January 1973):26, with the *Polonaise* printed on p.27.

In das Album der Fürsten Metternich 1861 (Musica Obscura) 4pp. Charming salon character piece. Numerous written-out turns. A superb encore. Int. to M-D.

Richard Wagner Klavierwerke (Schott 7000). Wagner's complete piano works, 11 pieces, background material. Int. to M-D.

Wagner. Piano Music Inspired by Women in His Life (Alfred 264). Polka; Sonata for the Album of Mrs. M. W.; Züricher Vielliebchen—Walzer; Album Leaf; Arrival at the Black Swan; Album Leaf for Mrs. Betty Schott. Int. to M-D.

See: Jonathan Bellman, "Wagner Pianiste?" P&K, 175 (August 1995):50–54. Includes a copy of *Albumblatt für Ernst Benedikt: Lied ohne Worte.*

W. S. Newman, "Wagner's Sonatas," *Studies in Romanticism,* 7/3 (Spring 1968): 128–39. A discussion of the circumstances, dates, publication, and content of five known piano sonatas by Wagner, with special reference to Wagner's relation to Liszt and the Wesendonck family.

Charles W. Timbrell, "Wagner's Piano Music," Part I, AMT, 23 (April–May 1974): 5–9; Part II, AMT, 23 (June–July 1974):6–9.

Rudolf Wagner-Régney (1903–1969) Germany
The Collected Piano Works (Tilo Medek—DVFM). Foreword and commentary in
    German. Contains all the piano music, including many short pieces, suites,
    sonatinas, and fugues. Much use is made of flexible meters. Int. to M-D.
Spinettmusik 1934 (UE). Six pieces in a contrapuntal idiom. Int.
2 Sonatas (UE 1943). Published together. Sonata I: four movements, 9pp. Sonata
    II: three movements, 10pp. Both are neoclassic in style. M-D.
Hexameron (UE 1943). Six moderately easy pieces.
Zwei Tänze für Palucca (UE 1950). Clever studies in variable meters. 12-tone. M-D.
Klavierstücke für Gertie (Bo&H 1951). Variable meters. M-D.
5 French Pieces (Bo&Bo 1951). Meter studies. Free 12-tone techniques. D.
7 Fugues (Bo&Bo 1953). Concise. Each one dedicated to a well-known friend
    whose style is imitated in the writing: Carl Orff, Boris Blacher, G. von
    Einem, Kurt Weill, Paul Hindemith, Ernst Krenek, Darius Milhaud. M-D.

George Walker (1922–   ) USA
Walker's compositions display striking gestures and strong rhythms.
Prelude and Caprice 1941 (Gen 1975) 7pp. 8 min. Prelude: lyric, freely tonal, flow-
    ing. Caprice: flexible meters, syncopation, fast octaves in both hands re-
    quired in coda. A fine combination. M-D.
Sonata I 1953 rev. 1991 (MMB 1972) 27pp. 15 min. Allegro energico. Moderato:
    a theme and six variations built more on intervals and timbres than on
    melodic lines. Allegro con brio: sensationally exciting. An ambitious and
    deserving work tinged with classical touches of Ravel and Prokofieff. Con-
    trasting movements, dissonant, virtuosic. D.
Sonata II 1957 (Galaxy) 19pp. 10 min. Adagio non troppo: four-bar theme and
    ten short contrasting variations inventively manipulated. Presto: rhythmic
    two- and three-voice textured scherzo; exploits opening two-bar staccato
    figure. Adagio: changing meters; builds to dramatic climax; *ppp* close; per-
    haps the finest movement. Allegretto tranquillo: requires fine left-hand oc-
    tave technique; most technically difficult of all movements. Written in a
    biting contemporary idiom, freely tonal. D.
    See: Wilfrid J. Delphin, "A Comparative Analysis of Two Sonatas by George
    Walker: Sonata I and Sonata II," DMA diss., University of Southern Mis-
    sissippi, 1976, 118pp.
    D. Maxine Sims, "An Analysis and Comparison of Piano Sonatas by
    George Walker and Howard Swanson," *The Black Perspective in Music,* 4
    (Spring 1976):70–81.
Spatials 1961 (Gen) 7pp. 4 min. Six variations, serial, flexible meters, expressive.
    M-D.
Spektra 1971 (Gen) 12pp. 7 min. Serial, pointillistic. Five staves required for some
    notation; rhythmic proportional relationships. D.
Sonata III 1976 (MMB) 13pp. 12 min. Fantoms: rhapsodic, surging sonorities.
    Bell: a widely spread dissonant chord is repeated seventeen times in con-

trasting dynamics and note values. Chorale and Fughetta: gyrating gymnastics, bristling figurations, dissonant. D.

Bauble 1980 (Gen) 6pp. Tranquillo indication at opening but glittering sonorities move over the entire keyboard, expressionistic. Brilliant full chords at conclusion. Requires large span. D.

Guido's Hand 1986 (MMB) 16pp. Five contrasting pieces, atonal, dramatic gestures, complex rhythms, serial influence. M-D to D.

Sonata No.4 (MMB 1985) 19pp. Maestoso: dramatic introduction leads to "a tempo" section that features strong rhythms and tempo changes; cluster-like sonorities, striking textures, much octave use. Tranquillo: Expressive opening leads to motoric rhythm section (a tempo), *pp* ending. Both movements are intense, exploit the entire keyboard, and are eminently pianistic. D.

See: David Burge, "New Pieces, Part II," CK, 4 (January 1978):50.

Jeffrey Chappell, "From Sonata to 'Satin Doll,'" P&K, 189 (November–December 1997):42–45. Examines Walker's piano music.

Gwyneth Walker (b.1947) USA

Cantos for the End of Summer (ECS 1993) 19pp., ca. 15 min. Prelude; Caper; Evensong. MC. Can be performed individually but are more effective when played as a group; no fingerings. M-D.

Robert Walker (1946–   ) Great Britain

Twelve O (Novello 1979) 27pp. Symbolic titles for each piece refer to the 12 apostles. Each piece covers specific areas of piano technique: legato chords, glissandos, 2 against 3, contrasted touches. Unusual collection. Int.

Friedrich K. Wanek (1929–   ) Germany

A Propos Haydn (Schott 6909 1980) 12pp. The first movement of Haydn's *Sonata* G, Hob.XVI/27 is dressed up in contemporary garb. A sizzling fantasy piece. M-D.

Robert Ward (1917–   ) USA

Lamentation (Mer 1948). Somber largo builds to a sonorous climax; quartal harmony; a few brilliant octaves. M-D.

David Ward-Steinman (1936–   ) USA

Latter-day Lullabies (EBM 1972) 7pp. 7 min. Jenna—Matthew—David—Meredith—Karen. Contemporary sounds including clusters produced by using a twelve-inch ruler. M-D.

3 Lyric Preludes (Highgate 1965). For piano or organ. Moderately Fast. Very Slow. Not Too Slow: contains a few clusters. Clear textures, rhythmic interest. M-D.

Elegy for Martin Luther King (Galaxy 1969) 3 min. Short, poignant processional ode. Uses palm clusters as an accompaniment. Mainly diatonic melody. Part of "We Shall Overcome" is worked in. M-D.

Improvisations on Children's Songs (Lee Roberts). Contemporary treatment of "Twinkle, Twinkle, Little Star," "Happy Birthday," and "Frère Jacques." Int.

Sonata 1956–57 (Music Graphics Press) 23pp. Very slow, foreboding. Fast, light: changing meters, octotonic, strong rhythmic gestures. Slow: thin textures, chromatic, builds to violent climax then subsides. Fast and brilliant: concludes with a capricious fughetta, freely tonal. M-D to D.

Sonata for Piano Fortified 1972 (Music Graphics Press) 23pp., 12 min. Maestoso: only essential meters are indicated, one clave is on strings, fingernail string plucking. Slow: claves moved to another section of strings, strings are tapped with fingernails, string glissandi. Giocoso, tempo giusto: claves moved to another section of strings, ends mechanically à la "General Lavine-eccentric." Toccata: fast and rhythmic, one clave moved to another section of strings, xylophone mallets used on strings, *pp* ending. Includes instructions for fortifying the piano; indicated pitches prepared with bolts, screws, washer, rubber wedge, etc. Avant-garde. D.

Peter Warlock (1894–1930) Great Britain

5 Song Preludes (Thames Publishing; MMP) 9½ min. Convincing writing but does not always lie well under the hands. "I am also experimenting with Celtic folk songs, endeavouring to do for them what Grieg did for the Norwegian, Bartók for the Hungarian in his children's pieces . . . to set each tune in a short, straightforward manner but without the usual idiotic harmonic restrictions that fadists like Cecil Sharp, V. Williams and Co. like to impose upon themselves" (from the preface). Good hand span and careful pedaling required. Int. to M-D.

Valses Rêves d'Isolde 1917 (Thames Publishing 1976) 6pp. A parody on Wagner's *Tristan und Isolde*. "These slow valses hit off to a nicety the characteristic Valse de Salon at its most glutinous" (from the preface). Large chords and plenty of octaves require a large span. A fine encore. M-D.

Scott Watson (–   ) USA

Seven Variations on a Theme by Haydn 1956 (GS) 5pp. Clever variations on the famous theme from the *Surprise Symphony*. Delightful. Int.

John Watts (1930–1982) USA

Sonata 1955–58, rev. 1960 (Joshua) 16 min. Allegretto leggiero: mild dissonances, Impressionistic harmonies. Andante sostenuto: fugal; concludes with great climax; classical textures; large span required. Andante semplice: Romantic-sounding harmonies; careful voicing needed. Allegro giocoso: eighth-note ostinato bass effectively unfolds; final six bars have direction "Pound the hell out of it!"; large span required. Solid technical equipment necessary for entire sonata. D.

Donald Waxman (1925–   ) USA

Fifty Etudes (Galaxy 1976) Book 1, Nos. 1–14, Int. Book 2, Nos. 15–27, upper Int. Book 3, Nos. 28–39, M-D. Book 4, Nos. 40–50, D. An outstanding set of contemporary pedagogical etudes, each focusing on a particular problem or problems of technique related to conservative twentieth-century literature. Expressive titles. Those listed below are available separately.

Etude of Sixths in Wrist Staccato (Galaxy). The subtitle, "Motto: II—Greetings to Loeschhorn" pays homage to this composer of piano studies. Staccato sixths are used throughout. Int. to M-D.

Etude in Octaves (Galaxy). "Motto: IV—Greetings to Concone." Brilliant and bravura playing required in this strong rhythmic study. D.

Etude of Alternating Double Notes (Galaxy). This "Confetti" is light and fast. Various intervals in double notes are tossed between hands. Bright and sprightly. M-D.

See below, "Collections," *A Dance Pageant. Renaissance and Baroque Keyboard Dances* (ECS).

Alain Weber (1930–   ) France

Etudes acrostiches 1973 (Leduc) 33pp. 34 min. Explanations in French, German, and English. In the form of variations. Possibilities of a fragmentary performance set up by the composer on the third preliminary page. Choral et variation; Acrostiche 1; Résonance 1; Acrostiche 2; Mouvement perpétuel; Acrostiche 3; Résonance 2; Acrostiche 4; Mobile. Fiery rhetoric alternates with steamy Impressionism. Musical acrostic construction and solution are at their best in these difficult contemporary settings. D.

Ben Weber (1916–1979) USA

Weber's style combines atonal chromaticism with the 12-tone system.

5 Bagatelles Op.2 1938 (TP). Short and amiable pieces in clear 12-tone technique. These were the first published American works for piano in a serial style. M-D.

3 Piano Pieces Op.23 1946 (Bomart) 11pp. Written in a serious, Bergian style. Problem lies in following every melodic line through its entire trajectory. D.

Fantasia Op.25 1946 (EBM). Large-scale set of variations built on an 11-tone row. The first statement introduces the row in a chordal scheme, the second part is rhapsodic and exploits the full range of the keyboard, the third is a scherzo, the fourth is a passacaglia. The last part uses the original row as a melodic theme against a quasi-improvised accompaniment figure; leads into a rather jabbing, terse-sounding coda. Expressionistic, complex textures, full of personality, Weber's most important solo piano work. D.

See: David Burge, "Ben Weber's *Fantasia* (Op.25)," *Keyboard*, 9/1 (January 1983):58, 65.

Humoresque Op.49 1963 (LG) in collection *New Music for the Piano* 2 min. Economical use of material, poignant wistfulness, lyrical with some wryness. M-D.

Variazioni quasi una fantasia Op.65 1974 (Mobart) 12pp. 8 min. For piano or harpsichord. Chromatic theme (serial) and eight variations. First half of theme is linear; second half is more chordal. Contains a few character indications. Expressionistic. Seems to exploit serial technique, piano sonority, and just plain dissonance rather than carry forward any strong musical impulse. D.

Carl Maria von Weber (1786–1826) Germany

The piano works of Weber may be considered period pieces of charm and imagination showing how well he explored the potential of the instrument during his day. A fluent technique is required to perform any of the representative works, and a large span is frequently needed. Orchestral influence often shows in Weber's piano writing, which is characterized by large skips; brilliant passages in thirds, sixths, and octaves; dramatic crescendos; and awkward stretches.

Piano Works (CFP). Vol.I: Four sonatas Opp.24, 39, 49, 70. Vol. II. Variations Opp.7, 40; Momento Capriccio Op.12; Grande Polonaise Op.21; Rondo brillante, Op.62; Polacca brillante Op.72; Concertstück for piano and orchestra Op.79. Vol. III: Variations Opp.2, 5, 6, 9, 28, 55; Concertos Opp.11, 32.

Four Sonatas (CFP; K 9516; Durand; Ric; Heugel). These works were once held in high regard and often heard in recitals. They have much to offer the enterprising pianist.

Sonata No.1 C Op.24 1812 (Henle). Allegro: C; symmetrical thematic structure and lack of tonal integration hinder effectiveness. Adagio: F, contains some dramatic moments; variation technique; unconvincing formal design. Menuetto: Allegro, e; Trio E: fast, more like a Scherzo. Rondo: Presto, C; perpetual motion (available separately: Durand; CF; Ric; GS; Schott; O. Jonas—Simrock, includes versions by Brahms and by Tchaikowsky for left hand). M-D to D.

Sonata No.2 A♭ Op.39 1814–16 (Cortot—Sal). Allegro moderato con spirito ed assai legato: A♭: rich texture in this noble and original movement; orchestrated with highly contrasting figuration, tremolos, and arpeggiated chords. Andante: C, c; expansive; lyric in conception although a large climax provides strong contrast. Menuetto capriccioso: A♭; vivacious and whimsical. Rondo—Moderato e molto grazioso: A♭; graceful, contains some beautifully "elided" sections. Artur Schnabel frequently performed this work in his programs. M-D to D.

Sonata No.3 d Op.49 1816 (GS). Allegro feroce d-D: has Beethoven characteristics, especially the contrast of thematic material. Andante con moto B♭: simple structure and ornamental decoration. Rondo—Presto D: in 3/8, contains five different ideas, one an elegant waltz rhythm, leads to one of Weber's most effective conclusions; effective played separately; also known as "Allegro di Bravura." This work is subtitled "Demoniac," but not by Weber. M-D to D.

Sonata No.4 e Op.70 1819–22. Moderato e: built on two contrasting ideas. Minuetto—Presto vivace ed energico e-D: leggermente murmurando is called for in the Trio. Andante quasi Allegretto, consolante C: a Schubertian quality pervades this movement, which resembles a rondo but is more mosaic in actual design. Finale (La Tarantella): a unique piece of whirlwind virtuoso writing. Finest of the four sonatas, this work shows refinement of numerous elements seen in the earlier sonatas. M-D to D.

　　See: Stephen Marinaro, "Carl Maria von Weber: His Pianistic Style and the Four Sonatas," JALS, 10 (December 1981):48–55.

Momento capriccioso B♭ Op.12 1808 (Cortot—Sal). Sparkling pianissimo staccato study, highly effective. M-D.

Grande Polonaise E♭ Op.21 1808 (Georgii—Schott; Seak—Ric). Florid pianistic writing, dotted notes, contrasted second episode. M-D.

Rondo Brillante "La Gaieté" E♭ Op.62 1819 (Cortot—Sal; Georgii—Schott; Kroll—Ric; Durand; Zanibon; CF). Inspired by the dance, includes a variety of technical problems, effective. M-D.

Invitation to the Dance D♭ Op.65 1819 (Henle 415; Cortot—Sal; Georgii—Schott; CFP; Br&H; CF; GS; Durand). Weber's most popular piano work, a rondo design with numerous thematic fragments woven into a successful whole. Brilliant. Exquisite when properly performed. M-D to D.

Polacca Brillante E Op.72 1819 (Cortot—Sal; Georgii—Schott; Kroll—Ric). Dotted rhythms, similar to Op.62 but less difficult. M-D.

Variations on an Original Theme C Op.2 1800 (CFP). Straightforward treatment.

Variations on a Theme from Castor and Pollux F Op.5 1804. (CFP)

Variations on a Theme from Samori B♭ Op.6 (CFP). With violin and cello ad lib.

Variations on Bianchi's 'Vien' quà, Dorina Bella' C Op.7 1807 (CFP; GS).

Variations on an Original Theme F Op.9 1808 (CFP).

Variations on a Theme from Méhul's 'Joseph' C Op.28 1812 (CFP). More virtuoso.

Variations on "Schöne Minka" c Op.40 1815 (CFP). Weber's longest set of variations.

Variations on a Gipsy Air C Op.55 1817 (CFP). Effective dance rhythms.

Weber's eight sets of variations are less interesting than his Sonatas and occasional pieces. The variations employ mainly melodic decoration and they are highly sectionalized.

Seven Ecossaises (Werner—Curwen). Excellent teaching material.

Two Waltzes (Werner—Curwen). Tuneful, easy.

Twelve German Dances Op.4 (1801) (Frey—Schott). Int.

Book of Dances (Wolters—Schott). Contra-Dances; Waltzes; German Dances; Max-Waltz. Int.

Twenty Easy Dances (Frickert—Mitteldeutscher Verlag). German Dances; Waltzes; Ecossaises; two four-hand German Dances. Attractive format. Int.

Miscellaneous Compositions (Mason—GS). Opp.12, 21, 62, 65, 72; Les adieux Op.81; Opp.7, 37. Includes biographical sketch. Int. to M-D.

Complete Sonatas, Invitation to the Dance, and Other Piano Works (Kohler, Ruthardt—Dover) 242pp. Includes most of Weber's solo piano works, including his four piano sonatas. A reprint of parts of the three-volume Peters edition. Includes Opp.12, 21, 62, 72, 2, 5, 6, 7, 9, 28, 40, and 55.

Ausgewählte Klavierwerke (Gerlach, Viertel—Henle 414, 1987) 70pp. Includes Weber's five brilliant large-scale concert pieces and his last two sets of variations. These seven works constitute his most significant compositions for piano two-hands, apart from his four sonatas. Includes Momento capriccioso Op.12; Grand Polonaise Op.21; Air russe varié . . . Schöne Minka Op.40; Variationen über ein Zigeunerlied Op.55; Rondo brillante Op.62; Invitation to the Dance Op.65; Polacca brillante Op.72. Int. to D.

4 Selected Works (K 9483) 61pp. Rondo from Sonata C, Op.24; and as transcribed by Brahms, Tchaikowsky, and A. Michalowski. M-D to D.

Master Series for the Young (Hughes—GS). Andante with variations; Andantino; March; Mazurka; Minuet; Original theme; Rondo; Sonatina; Theme from *Invitation to the Dance*; Theme from Sonata Op.70; 3 Waltzes. Int.

Anton von Webern (1883–1945) Austria

Webern's influence on twentieth-century composition cannot be overemphasized. Webern is a seminal figure of the century. However, his contribution to piano literature is small. He first used serial technique as advocated by Schönberg in 1924.

Sonatensatz (CF 1906). This rondo movement "belongs to a large group of works, written about 1906, that are indicative of the ferment in harmonic concepts soon to lead to the abolition of traditional tonality" (from the Preface by Hans Moldenhauer). A key signature is present; more traditional in harmonic and melodic treatment than Webern's later style. M-D.

Satz für Klavier (CF 1906). Fine example of SA design, tonality present although in a very fluid state, chromatic, post-Romantic qualities. M-D.

Klavierstück 1925 (UE 1966). Short minuet, sparse textures, pointillistic writing. M-D.

Kinderstück 1924 (CF). 17 bars. Provides an excellent introduction to serialism. Based on 12-tone row, one of Webern's earliest examples of this technique. Webern had intended to write a series of pieces for children but this was the only one finished. Int.

Variations Op.27 1936 (UE 10881; Stadlen—UE 16845 1979). The Stadlen edition sets out, for the first time, Webern's ideas on the work's interpretation, using a facsimile of the working copy containing his instructions for the world premiere. Preface in English and German. Webern once described this work as "kind of a suite." The "theme," based on a row, is stated in bars 1–7 of the opening movement; the rest of the work explores every facet of this material in terms of melody, harmony, pitch, rhythm, and dynamics. Mirror canon is in use throughout. There is endless variation of the opening statement, which is expressed in the work as a whole in a continuous pattern. The three self-contained variations are expressed in three basic and different tempi. A unique work with the barest sonorities, extreme skips, and changeable rhythms and dynamics.

See: David Burge, "Webern's Variations," CK, 6 (May 1980):50.

Mary E. Fiore, "Webern's Use of Motives in the Piano Variations," in *The Computer and Music* (Ithaca and London: Cornell University Press, 1970), pp.115–22.

Walter Kolneder, *Anton Webern, An Introduction to His Works,* translated by Humphrey Searle (Berkeley: University of California Press, 1968).

Karl Weigl (1881–1949) Austria

Bilder und Geschichten (Pictures and Tales) Op.2 (UE 1910). Six pieces. Late-nineteenth-century approach to folklike tunes. Attractive titles and music. No.3 "Stork, lanky long-legs" is clever. Int.

28 Variations über ein achttaktiges Thema Op.15 (UE). Schönberg influence. D.

5 Nachtphantasien Op.13 (Leuckart; Joshua 1977) 25pp. In Nos.3 and 4 the music achieves considerable eloquence and beauty. M-D.

Leo Weiner (1885–1960) Hungary

Weiner's works are not "modern" in the sense that we apply the term to his compatriot Bartók. Nevertheless, Weiner is revered in Hungary as a musician who exerted immeasurable influence on an entire generation of musicians.

31 Hungarian Peasant Songs (Gen). Vol.I: Nos.1–19; Vol.II: Nos.20–31. Some are short, others extended; all have melodic and rhythmic charm. See especially No.17. Easy to Int.

Stanley Weiner (1925–   ) Belgium, born USA

Sonata Op.5 (MCA 1972) 26pp. Allegro: SA; opens with a tranquil 6/8; freely tonal; broken-octave and chordal figuration; octotonic; chromatic cadenza. Un poco lento: ABA; active melodic line; a tempo con brio mid-section works to large climax. Presto: running two-voice octotonic opening punctuated with chromatic chords; left-hand skips; changing meters. M-D to D.

Louis Weingarden (1943–   ) USA

Triptych 1969 (Bo&H). Abraham and Isaac. David the Shepherd: a spiritual etude. The Three Marys Lamenting and the Angel Describing the Resurrection. Large-scale virtuoso work, freely atonal, ample romantic structures, serious in intent, of imposing dimensions. Well worth exploring, for mature pianists. D.

John Weinzweig (1913–   ) Canada

Weinzweig introduced 12-tone technique to Canada in 1939.

Berceuse (OUP 1950). Serial, a 5-note series. M-D.

Toccata Dance (OUP 1950). 12-tone.

Conversation Piece (OUP 1950). 12-tone.

Sonata 1950 (Cramer 1981) 18pp. Clear textures, modest in design and pianistic demands. M-D.

Hugo Weisgall (1912–1997) USA, born Bohemia

Sine Nomine 1966 (TP). Graven Images No.3. A small, rounded binary piece constructed on a bass pattern of six bars. Int.

Two Improvisations (TP 1969). Graven Images No.6. Serial, short. Large span required. M-D.

Sonata 1982 (TP) 21pp. 17 min. Allegro impetuoso: changing meters, strongly punctuated lines, three contrasted tempi. Adagio molto: cantabile and expressive, evolves to big climax and subsides, proportional rhythmic relationships. Rondo—Quasi presto: Scherzando, rhythmic and contrasting tranquillo sections, chromatic. For adventurous virtuosos. D.

Four Birthday Cards 1978–83 (TP 1986) 8pp. 8 min. Billy's Belated Birthday Ray: easy going, quartal harmony. For Randy at 70: freely tonal, cantabile and expressive. Valse Oubliée: a slow waltz, changing meters. Rückblick: serial influence. M-D.

See: Bruce Saylor, "The Music of Hugo Weisgall," MQ, 59 (April 1973):239–62.

Harold Weiss (1949–   ) Germany

My Blue Diary Op.118 (Schott 8288 1995) 47pp. 16 varied pieces, a cycle (diary) "in the form of an album of poetry" (from the score). MC with a few avant-garde notations, minimal effects. Int.

Dan Welcher (1948–   ) USA

Welcher is professor of composition at the University of Texas–Austin.

Sonatina 1972 (TP 1979) 14pp. Vigoroso; Lento; Presto. Carefully balanced between linear and homophonic writing. Shows a fondness for octotonic techniques. Freely tonal, shifting meters, exciting and brilliant conclusion, effective gestures. M-D.

See: Bradford Gowen, "Neglected Repertoire: Some Contemporary Sonatinas," AMT, 29/2 (November–December 1979):22–24. Discusses this piece.

Dance Variations 1979 (EV 1984) 40pp., 20 min. Dramatic (noble, liberamente) and multi-sectioned opening is followed by six contrasting variations. Var.6 serves as an Epilogue and uses material from the opening. Harmonics, muted strings, clusters on keys and strings, knocking on frame and upper soundboard, string glissandi, strong rhythmic usage. Radiant writing. D.

Egon Wellesz (1885–1974) Austria

Der Abend Op.4 1909–10 (Dob 1971) 19pp. A cycle of four impressions. M-D.

Drei Skizzen Op.6 (Dob 1911). Similar to the Schönberg Op.11. Requires subtle shading. M-D.

Epigramme Op.17 (UE 1914). Danse; Capriccio; Vision; Notturno; Elégie fantastique. More accessible style than Op.6. M-D.

Idyllen Op.21 (UE 1917). Five pieces. Impressionist style. Beautiful melodic writing. M-D.

Zwei Studien Op.29 (Dob 1921) 3 min. Atonal. Langsam: restricted dynamic range, study in tonal balance. Sehr ruhig: repeated notes, chords, and octaves, light. Requires a supple wrist. M-D.

Fünf Tanzstücke Op.42 (UE 1927). Harsh dissonances. No.4 is most appealing. D.

5 Piano Pieces Op.83 (Simrock 1962). Skillful miniatures. Int.

Triptychon Op.98 (UE 1967) 4 min. Grazioso; Cantabile; Appassionata. Atonal, but accessible. The last is most difficult. M-D to D.

Studien in Grau Op.106 (Dob). Five serial studies. D.

Chiang Wen Yeh (1910–1983) Taiwan

Wen Yeh studied at the Tokyo Music Academy. All his works were either destroyed or prohibited during the cultural revolution in China.

Bagatelles Op.8 (SP) 27pp. Originally published in 1936 by Alexandre Tcherepnin. 16 pieces, some titled. 1: Green Leaves Young Leaves; 4: Charmela; 7: Epitaph; 9: I Remember; 11: Er'khu; 15: Pi'ba; 16: Peiking Gate. Some pentatonic usage, impressionistic influence; pieces have varied moods and lengths. Int. to M-D.

Frederick Werlé (1914–1997) USA

Sonata brevis No.2 (Rongwen) 11pp. Based on short opening motive of D—C♯–G♯. Changing tonalities. Formally balanced by eight different tempo sections. Economy of material. Large span required. M-D.

Toccata (Rongwen 1949). Neo-Romantic style, Impressionist treatment, Ravel influence, dramatic closing. M-D.

Pastorale (TP) 2pp. Melody in thirds, rocking rhythmic motion, tonal, pianistic. Int.

Six Fancies (A. Broude 1977). Short pieces to relieve a young pianist's doldrums; Romantic and contemporary sonorities. Int.

Sarabande (CF). A stately pedal study. Slow, sustained chords support a flowing melody. Int.

Piano Sports (McAfee) Ten pieces that describe various sports: tennis, basketball, boxing, baseball, billiards, football, etc. Descriptive and MC writing. Int.

Jean-Jacques Werner (1935–   ) France

Première Sonate (EMT 1962) 15pp. Allegro Moderato: tonal, freely chromatic; large span required. Adagio: dissonant cantabile writing. Allegro con moto: rhythmic, repeated notes and chords; large span required. M-D.

Richard Wernick (1934–   ) USA

Sonata 1982 "Reflections of a Dark Light" (TP) 30pp. Reflections of a Dark Light: dramatic chordal gestures, changing meters, rubato, pointillistic, extremely slow section, "bring out trill on changes of pitch," "becoming more and more bell-like and agitated," spacious and con tutta forza ending. Fragments of Things Remembered: slow, glacial, timeless, large dynamic range, *ppp* to *ffsz,* pressando to third movement. "—in the forehead of the morning sky": three variations followed by a theme (slightly slower than the beginning), followed by five variations; Var.8 serves as an Epilogue; variations are strongly contrasted and exploit most of the instrument. Highly organized, expressionistic. Gains fluency and strength as work progresses. D.

Graham Whettam (1927–   ) Great Britain

Prelude and Scherzo Impetuoso (Meriden Music 1990) 11pp., ca. 10 min. A slow, impressionistic Prelude leads to an *Allegro assai con precipitazione* section that is full of strong rhythmic usage; alternating octaves between hands, dramatic closing. MC. M-D.

John White (1937–   ) Great Britain

White has composed 53 piano sonatas, which have become increasingly simpler and even fragmented.

First Sonata (Leduc 1961) 15pp. 10 min. Three movements FSF. Opening movement: striking. Slow movement: expressive with thin textures, clear ideas. Third movement: semi-ostinato. Not overly difficult, highly concentrated work. M-D.

Fifth Sonata (Leduc 1961) 7 min. One movement. Numerous tempo changes, keen sense of keyboard sonorities and contrapuntal textures. Fondness for low sonorities. Big technique required. D.

See: Brian Dennis, "The Music of John White," MT, 112 (May 1971):453–57.

Gillian Whitehead (1941–   ) New Zealand

Voices of Tane 1975 (Price Milburn). Short, contrasted six-movement set, Satie influence. Final movement contains aleatory elements and staccato figures; it is the antithesis of the first movement. Displays impressive invention in a slightly superficial context. M-D.

Charles Whittenberg (1927–   ) USA

Three Compositions for Piano (CFP 1972). Short, contrasting, varied meters, pointillistic. These pieces show the composer's interest in 12-tone classicism within the strict application of the 12-pitch class systems. Babbitt influence noted. D.

Ernst Widmer (1927–   ) Brazil, born Switzerland

Widmer is Dean of the School of Music and Performing Arts of the Federal University of Bahia.

Ludus Brasiliensis Op.37 (Ric BR 1965–66) 2 hours 10 min. Vol.I: Nos.1–55. Vol.II: Nos.56–95. Vol.III: Nos.96–125. Vol.IV: Nos.126–53. Vol.V: Nos.154–62. Progressive pieces of pedagogical character. Similar to Bartók's *Mikrokosmos.* Includes objectives for the series, pieces for sight-reading and instructions for sight-reading, pieces for improvisation and directions on how to improvise. Also contains observations for the teacher, explanation of pieces on three staves (ensemble pieces for teacher and student). Some pieces are very contemporary-sounding, and a few employ avant-garde techniques and notation. Easy to M-D.

Charles Marie Widor (1845–1937) France

Waltzes, Vol.I (K 9812) 91pp. Introduction; 1ᵉ Valse, Op.11/1: Intermezzo. Valse Laendler, Op.11/2. Valse caprice, Op.11/3. Valse rêverie, Andantino, Op.26/3. 1ᵉ Rhapsodie, Op.26/1. Valse romance, Op.26/2. Valse slave, Op.26/4. Valse élégante, Op.26/5. Papillons bleus, Op.31/2. Ciel gris, Op.31/10. Valse-Impromptu, Op.15/6. 2ᵉ Rhapsodie, Op.26/6. Entrée de la reine, Op.20/2. Airs de Ballet, Op.4. Wide range of style and mood, lush sonorities. M-D.

Jean Wiener (1896–1982) France

Wiener's style exhibits a facile technique strongly influenced by jazz.
Sonatine Syncopée 1923. (ESC). Lourd; Blues; Brillant. Extended work employing stylized jazz. D.
Sonate 1925 (ESC). Three movements. Juxtaposed sonorities. Requires facile pianism. D.
Deuxième Sonatine 1928 (ESC). Popular style, involved, jouncing finale. M-D.
Quatre petites pièces Radio (Jobert). Popular style, attractive. Int.
Trois Moments de Musique (EMT 1983). Three Impressionistic tone paintings, polychromatic. Blend kaleidoscopic tonalities with changing number of beats per measure. An interesting set of "water-colors." Int. to M-D.

Johan Wikmanson (1753–1800) Sweden

Sonata for piano forte 1784 (Autographus Musicus) 12pp. This sonata was called "Divertissement at Söderfors" and dedicated to Anna Johann Grill, who lived at Söderfors, Sweden. Classic style. Int. to M-D.
36 Pages; Pieces for piano forte 1796 (Autographus Musicus). Written for the composer's daughter Christina when she was 14 years old. Int.

Alec Wilder (1907–1980) USA

Pieces for Young Pianists (Margum 1978). Vols.I and II. Imaginative and entertaining. Easy to Int.
Suite for Piano (Margum) 14 min. Imaginative contemporary writing that includes a fugue and a passacaglia. M-D.

Raymond Wilding-White (1922–   ) USA, born England

Character Sketches—Study Pieces (Galaxy) in collection *Piano Music for the Young,* Book 2. Jacques Tati; Inspector Lestrade; Miss Prism; Truman Capote; Leonide Massine; Uriah Heep; Cesar Romero; Erik von Stroheim; Nobody at All; Stuart Little; Mack Sennett. Clever characterizations. Int.

Malcolm Williamson (1931–   ) Great Britain, born Australia

Williamson has an eclectic style that ranges from austere serialism to pop tunes.
Sonata No.1 1953–55 (Bo&H). Three movements, FSF. Thin textures, more

pandiatonic than chromatic, centers around F in a kind of Stravinskian sense. Eclectic style, witty rhythms, some serialism in slow movement. One of the finest piano sonatas from the 1950s. M-D to D.

Traval Diaries (Chappell 1961). 5 books. In order of difficulty: Sydney; Naples; London; Paris; New York. Excellent series of pedagogic music. Easy to M-D.

The Bridge that Van Gogh Painted (EBM 1976). Nine moods of southern France inspired by impressions of the French Camargue region, where Van Gogh frequently worked. Impressionistic; MC sonorities; descriptions add interest to the imaginative titles. Int.

Haifa Watercolors (EBM). Ten short descriptive pieces with playing and technical suggestions. Composer gives notes about each piece. Well fingered. Int.

Piano Impressions of New York (EBM). Six descriptive pieces. Part of the series Travel Diaries. Int.

Sonata No.2 1958, rev. 1970–71 (Weinberger) 20pp. 16 min. Quasi lento; Poco Adagio; Allegro assai. Contrasting movements. Severe, deeply expressive, dark coloration, intense. A work of major proportions; large span required. D.

Richard Wilson (1941–   ) USA

Wilson was born in Cleveland, OH. He graduated from Harvard University, studied piano and composition in Europe, received a master's degree from Rutgers University, and has taught at Vassar College since 1966.

Eclogue 1974 (Bo&H) 23pp. 12 min. Composer's note: *"Eclogue,* written for the Colombian pianist Blanca Uribe, is a work in one movement that is comprised of three parts. There is an introductory section, contrapuntal and motivic, proceeding on a high level of energy and intensity. This is followed by a much more drawn-out, atmospheric kind of music, in which thematic material—chords and a brief melodic figure—is projected against different sorts of trills. This thematic material becomes the basis for a succession of connected, textural variations, which build in dynamics to a high point, after which quiet, muted sounds, become the basis of a variation. The final section is a reflection on what has come before. In general, I was trying to make my *Eclogue* a celebration of the traditional resources of the piano, both the kinds of sounds it is capable of producing and the variety of styles of playing that its vast literature reveals." Wilson has an unerring ear for the right sound and a fabulous command of the instrument. If there must be a "standard repertoire," *Eclogue* should be part of it. Very beautiful, expressionistic, avant-garde. D.

See: David Burge, "Contemporary Piano—Composition Contest Winner," CK, 5(January 1979).

Sour Flowers 1979 (Bo&H). Eight short movements each prefaced by a description of the relevant herb from Banckes's *Herbal* (1525); this passage provides the key to the movement's character. Not difficult to play but written in a strongly dissonant (sour!) idiom with frequent touches of subtle humor. Int. to M-D.

Fixations 1985 (PIC 1991) 22pp. Birds in Space: inspired by Brancusi sculptures. Shadowings: parallel motion. Flashback: parenthetical structure. This piano piece gives shape to musical ideas that are amorphous and fleeting in their incipient state. Nos.2 and 3 "take their titles largely because of musical procedures employed" (from the score). Expressionistic. D.

Intercalations 1986 (PIC 1991) 32pp. The title refers to a day added to a calendar (like February 29). A varied four-movement work. Interspace: alternates passages of imitative counterpoint with excursions that often involve figuration or ornamentation rather in the manner of a preludial ricercare. Interplay: toccatalike, with steady rapid motion that features repeated notes. Interlacing: a song without words. Interaction: the most orchestral of the four; a narrative perhaps akin to the ballade or tone poem (from the score). D.

Three Short Pieces 1964 (PIC 1991) 7pp. 1. ♩ = ca. 72. 2. ♩ = ca. 60. 3. ♩ = ca. 88. Pointillistic, expressionistic. D.

A Child's London 1984 (PIC 1990) 11pp. London Bus; Primrose Hill Park; On Regent's Canal; Mrs. Orang-outang; Costumes at the Victoria and Albert; Roundabout. Varied styles, attractive. Int.

Robert Barclay Wilson (1913–   ) Great Britain

Sonata (Cramer). First movement: restless. Interlude: slow and expressive with poignant dissonances. Allegro giocoso: in rondo form, pulls together the previous thematic ideas. M-D.

Thomas Wilson (1927–   ) Great Britain, born USA

Piano Sonata 1959, rev. 1964 (S&B) 14pp. 8 min. Reproduction of composer's score. Two movements: Adagio introduction leads to a taut Allegro, which is a set of variations on a free ground-bass. D.

Geoffrey Winter (1928–   ) Great Britain

Studies from a Rainbow Op.71 (Anglican 1981) 18pp. 10–19 min., depending on performance method selected. This piece may be played in four ways. Seven colors identified, each conjures a specific mood (red for strong, strident; green for limpid, fresh; blue for cool, crystal, etc.). Chords plus ornamental flourishes. Short, well unified until a colorless coda. M-D.

Bruce Wise (1929–   ) USA

Four Piano Pieces (Hinson—Alfred) in collection *Twelve by Eleven*. The pieces use a four-note motive as the basis of the work: G, F♯, E, and F. Each piece has its own tempo and mood as well as its own treatment of the basic musical idea. As the music unfolds, a 12-tone series is arrived at in the fourth piece. Every voice participates in the texture of these short and pointillistically conceived pieces. M-D.

Joseph Woelfl (1773–1812) Austria

In his day Woelfl was one of Europe's most acclaimed musicians. As a concert pianist he was a rival of Beethoven. All three sonatas listed below are enjoyable and well worth performing, and have real charm and personality.

Sonata Op.25 c (W. Newman—UNC) in collection *Thirteen Keyboard Sonatas of the 18th and 19th Centuries.* Similar to Mozart's K.475 and Beethoven's Op.13 in that it opens with an Introduction. Includes a four-voice fugue. M-D.

Sonata Op.33/2 d (LC). Juxtaposition of lyric and dramatic seem to be presaging Schubert. Keyboard figuration also suggests Schubert. M-D.

Sonata Op.33/3 E (LC). Color, finesse of style, and lyricism are a part of the success of this piece. M-D.

See: SCE, pp.562–64.

Ernst Wilhelm Wolf (1735–1792) Germany

Five Sonatas (Fritz Oberdoerffer 66934). Classic style infused with sensitive melodies. Int. to M-D.

Hugo Wolf (1860–1903) Austria

Klavierkompositionen (Hans Jancik—Musikwissenschaftlicher Verlag 1974, through AMP), Sämtliche Werke, Vol.18 v + 143pp. Critical Edition. Published by the International Hugo Wolf-Gesellschaft. Preface in German and English, critical notes in German. Variationen Op.2 1875: Viennese classic influence here and in Op.8. Sonate G Op.8 1876: last leaf is lost. Rondo capriccioso Op.15 1876: Mendelssohn influence. Humoreske 1877: Schumannesque. *Aus der Kinderzeit:* Schlummerlied 1878, Scherz und Spiel 1878. Paraphrase über *Die Meistersinger von Nürnberg* ca.1880. Paraphrase über *Die Walküre* ca.1880. Albumblatt 1880. Kanon 1882. Contains all of Wolf's complete piano works, which are mainly early pieces and provided the distillation necessary to arrive at Wolf's lied style. Int. to M-D.

Ermanno Wolf-Ferrari (1876–1948) Italy

Impromptus Op.13 (Elite Ed.3458/D Rahter). 1: D♭, Andante, suave melody. 2: B♭, Romantic, much rubato required, chordal. 3: F♯, impassioned, interval of sixth exploited. Some pedaling included. Brahmsian sonorities, lush and full. M-D.

Three Piano Pieces Op.14 (Elite Ed.3459/D Rahter). Melodie: f♯, left hand accompanies sweeping, decorated melody. Capriccio: b♭, scherzo section requires nimble fingers and control of leaps. Romanze: E, cantabile style, requires careful pedaling. M-D.

Christian Wolff (1934–   ) USA, born France

The music of Webern, Varèse, and Boulez has strongly influenced the development of Wolff's style. No matter how intricately structured his music may be, it always allows the performer(s) varying kinds of choice.

For Piano I 1952 (CFP). "The pitches, durations, and dynamics are each based on a pattern of 9 components, repeated with such re-ordering and over-lapping as is necessary to compensate for a structural length of 16 beats" (BBD, p.186). An extract of this work is found in M&M, 17 (May 1969): 42–43.

Suite No.1 *for Prepared Piano* 1954 (CFP). This work requires 6 screws, 2 bolts (small), a strip of tin (from a tin can cover) about 2″ × ½″, a penny, a small stick of wood, 3 strips of jar rubber, and 3 rubber wedges. D.

For Prepared Piano 1951 (NME). Wolff tells performer more how to play than what to play. He also notes how to listen. M-D.

Bread and Roses 1976 (CFP 66751) 5pp. Reproduced from MS. Based on the work song written in 1912, during the great mill strike at Lawrence, MA. Tempo, ways of playing, and dynamics are free and variable. Parallel chords in 20ths; sections of the tune appear very simply, followed by complex figurations. M-D to D.

Hay Una Mujer Desaparecida (After Holly Near) 1979 (CFP 66892) 14pp. 11 min. A set of free variations on a Holly Near song; the work commemorates the Chilean women who have disappeared in political prisons. Only fragments of the song are used. Intense, difficult to grasp on first hearing. D.

Three Studies 1976 (CFP). Tempos are free, barlines can be read sometimes as pauses (not too long); these are really studies in rhythm. M-D to D.

Preludes 1–11 1981 (CFP 66916) 28pp. "Tempi can shift at structural points within a prelude (marked by double lines). Some material is drawn from songs, for instance, Hallelujah I'm a bum (No.3), Rock About (No.4), Abi Yoyo (No.7), Po' Lazarus (No.9), Big Rock Candy Mountain (No.10), Acres of Clams (No.11)" (from the score). Pointillistic, octotonic. No.1 is unbarred; No.5 requires whistling or humming. Avant garde. D.

See: Jack Behrens, "Recent Piano Works of Christian Wolff (1972–76)," *Studies in Music,* 2 (1977):1–7. Descriptions of *Accompaniments, Three Studies,* and *Bread and Roses,* including extensive quotations from conversations with the composer about his compositional process.

Christian Wolff, "Taking Chances," M&M, 17 (May 1969):38–40.

——, "On Form," *Die Reihe,* 7 (1965):26–31.

——, "On Movement," *Die Reihe,* 2 (1959):61–63.

Edward Wolff (1816–1880) France, born Poland
See below, "Collections," *Piano Music of the Parisian Virtuosos 1810–1860.*

H. A. Wollenhaupt (1827–1863) Germany
5 Morceaux caractéristiques en forme d'Etudes Op.22 (GS). A certain charm about these pieces still makes them welcome in the pianist's repertoire. M-D.

Nocturne Op.29/10 (GS). Brooding intensity and melodic invention permeate this piece. M-D.

Stefan Wolpe (1902–1972) Germany
Wolpe was a powerful musician who strongly influenced many American composers. His style incorporates elements of the European mainstream, folk and Hebrew music, and jazz.

Early Pieces for Piano 1924 (McGinnis & Marx). MC with improvisatory character. Content stretched. M-D.

Dance 1941 (Arrow). In the form of a chaconne. Short, rhythmic vigor, percussive. M-D.

Form 1959 (Tonos). Serial, harmonic experimentation, restless. Rich in rhythmic variations on the musical line as well as in a continuous reshaping of the texture of the music. D.

See: Martin Brody, "Sensibility Defined: Set Projection in Stefan Wolpe's *Form* for Piano," PNM, 15 (Spring–Summer 1977):3–22.

2 Studies for Piano Part 2 1955 (McGinnis & Marx) 7pp. 1. Vivid and Enraged; 2. Broad, with a Feeling of Profound Intensities. Complex rhythmic procedures, full use of keyboard. D.

Passacaglia 1936 (AMC). A major work of virtuoso proportions on a theme utilizing all the intervals. Powerful, demanding. D.

Form IV: *Broken Sequences* 1969 (CFP). Compact, great structural continuity. Opening chord in quarter notes Ab—F—Bb—A—G—E provides basis of the work. Many augmentations and diminutions. D.

Four Studies on Basic Rows 1935–36 (Merion 1974) 76pp. Study of Tritones. Study of Thirds. Presto Furioso: expanding and contrasting intervals. Passacaglia: highly complex study on all-interval row in conjunction with eleven basic rows. Almost a tone-row textbook. Pieces are probably better played separately or in sets of two. Complex and difficult writing, but overall structural drama, exciting pacing, and inherent sense of sonorities are always present. D.

Hugh Wood (1932–   ) Great Britain

3 Piano Pieces Op.5 1960–63 (UE) 10 min. Strongly lyrical, Bergian expressionism, uses a free 12-tone idiom. Unity is aided by a motivic and intervallic structure of considerable strictness. The first piece is unified by thematic interrelations and by the integrating force of the minor second. Material in the second piece, a scherzo in extended ritornello form, binds it to the third piece, a sort of postlude. M-D.

See: Leo Black, "The Music of Hugh Wood," MT, 1572 (February 1974): 115–17.

James Woodard (1929–   ) USA

Nocturne 1974 (MMB 1984) 12pp. Molto rubato e cantabile, flexible meters, freely tonal, neoclassic, broad gestures, exploits resources of the keyboard.

Wladimir Woronoff (1903–1980) Belgium, born Russia

Sonnet pour Dallapiccola (NME April 1950) 10pp. In four sections with subdivisions. Serial; notes marked with an asterisk form the bell motif from *Parsifal*; flexible meters. D.

Johann Hugo Woržischek (Voříšek) (1791–1825) Bohemia

Woržischek represents in the Czech musical context a transition between the piano styles of Tomasek and Smetana, and can be regarded as the direct precursor of the latter. Woržischek's piano works are of much interest, especially the *Rhapsodies* and *Impromptus,* because they strongly influenced Franz Schubert.

Piano Works (Vol.52 MAB Artia). Contains a biography and excellent comments on the music in English. 2 Rondos Op.18, G, C: light, short, virtuosic. 2 Impromptus. Eclogue. Le plaisir Op.4. Le désir Op.3. 6 Variations Op.19: Andante, Mozartian piano texture. M-D.

Sonata b♭ Op.20 1820 (Vol.4 MAB Artia) 15 min. Allegro con brio; Allegro; Allegro con brio. Uses keys up to seven sharps and five flats; Beethoven characteristics (Woržischek was an intimate friend of Beethoven), somber moods. The finale is based on Hummelian virtuosity, but foreshadows the future Chopin and Liszt virtuoso movements. Woržischek's best-known work. M-D.

Selected Pieces of Piano Music (Dana Zahn—Henle 278). Based on the earliest sources, critical edition. Excellent preface. Contains: Impromptu B♭; 6 Impromptus Op.7; Fantaisie Op.12; 6 Variations Op.19; Sonata Quasi una Fantasia Op.20. Appendix: Adagio b♭, which in the autograph was between the first and second movements of Sonata Op.20. A valuable anthology of a most interesting composer. M-D.

See: Ates Orga, "Schubert's Bohemian Contemporary," M&M 21 (February 1973):30–40. Outlines Woržischek's career; Rondo C, Op.18, given on pp.42–45.

12 Rhapsodies Op.1 1818 (Vol.78 MAB; Supraphon, 2 vols.) Preface in Czech, German, and English. Most are in ABA form and are relatively fast with little contrast. Middle parts are somewhat more leisurely with much chord writing. Large span required. M-D.

See: Kenneth de Long, "The Piano Rhapsodies of Vorisek," JALS, 26 (July–December 1989):12–28.

Rhapsodie g Op.1/9 (UE). See Anthologies and Collections, General: in album *Viennese Masters from the Baroque, Classical and Biedermeier Periods* (Voříšek). M-D.

See: Joseph Smith, "Vorisek's Rhapsody, Op.1, No.9," KC, 14/1 (January–February 1994):14–19. Includes the music.

6 Impromptus Op.7 1822 (Artia). First examples of the title. Ideas repeated rather than developed. No.4, especially, demonstrates an original style. M-D.

Friedrich Wührer (1900–1975) Austria

18 Studies on Chopin Etudes in Contrary Motion (Süddeutscher Musikverlag 1958) 65pp. Devised to promote equal facility in the two hands. D.

Charles Wuorinen (1938–   ) USA

Wuorinen is a recognized innovator whose works provide constantly fascinating sound experiences. He represents all that is avant-garde: distinctive individualism, atonalism, and electronics, while seeking to generate the most musical material, values, and traditions as he works.

Sonata 1969 (CFP) 41pp. 20 min. In two large parts. Highly complex and only for the most adventurous pianist, uncompromisingly abstract. Based on eleven intervals in a series. Each section is twice subdivided by the same intervals. Dense textures, opening rhythmic figuration appears at end of piece to be performed "out of time." A major work that does not easily give up its secrets. D.

Second Piano Sonata 1976 (CFP 1979). This work is a Triple Discourse, containing a Prelude, three movements intermixed, a Pause, the same resumed, and the whole completed with a Postlude. Pointillistic, governed by serial principles, sometimes acerbic, mellifluous, and often sonorous. Small motives commingle, expand, and gain impetus; springy and spiky writing. Only for the most venturesome virtuoso. D.

12 Short Pieces for Piano 1973 (CFP 66579) 7pp. 4½ min. These little pieces (basically, a theme and variations on a 12-note row), were composed to provide an easy, accessible avenue into the world of atonal music. They illustrate certain compositional techniques, yet are intended for concert purposes. Webern-like, dissonant, austere. Int. to M-D.

Piano Variations 1963 (McGinnis & Marx) 17pp. A highly dramatic work with the variation technique difficult to follow. Webernesque in spirit. Constantly changing meters; a few extra-musical effects such as stopping, plucking strings; clusters; jagged; brilliant gestures. Virtuoso technique required. D.

The Blue Bamboula 1980 (CFP 66532) 28pp. 10½ min. Pointillistic, many types of varied figurations. Pedal is to be used a lot, especially in single-line passages where the harmony requires overlapping pitches. Extreme dynamic range, some sections repeated a number of times, expressionistic. Metrically, it willfully rejects any regular rhythmic sense; melodically, it is almost entirely fragmented and disjunct. D.

Capriccio 1981 (CFP CC428) 23pp. 13 min. Granitic, glittering sonorities, register extremes, contrasting speeds and textures in one over-all tempo. Superb craft. D.

Arnold Van Wyk (1916–1983) Union of South Africa

Night Music (Galliard) 24 min. Extensive nocturne, closer to a symphonic rhapsody. Contemporary idiom. Virtuoso technique required. D.

Pastorale e Capriccio (Bo&H 1956) 19pp. 8 min. Contrasting; demanding technically and interpretatively. D.

4 Piano Pieces (Bo&H 1965) 21pp. Written for the piano examination of the University of South Africa. Dumka. Scherzino: marchlike. Romanza: many dynamic levels. Toccata: 5/8 meter. Displays a wide variety of pianistic techniques. Irregular rhythms. M-D.

Ruth Shaw Wylie (1916–1989) USA

Wylie's style ranged from conservative to experimental, but it always had a creative honesty and aesthetic communicativeness.

Psychogram 1968 (CUMP 1995) 16pp. A curious blend of atonal, serial, and aleatory elements with fist and forearm clusters forming a climax that concentrates on extremes—of pitch, volume, and textural density. Free meter, thin textures develop into thick dissonances, fluid alteration of hands required, rhythmic complexities, rhapsodic, *pppp* ending. M-D.

The White Raven Op.37/2 (CFP 66976 1983) 8pp., 9½ min. Numerous figural gestures to be played by "alternate hands at will throughout." Chromatic lines and chords interspersed with dramatic figuration, carefully pedaled, colorful Impressionistic and expressionistic sonorities. M-D.

Yehudi Wyner (1929–   ) USA, born Canada

Wyner's early style was neoclassic and influenced by Hindemith and Stravinsky. Chromaticism has also played an important part in his stylistic development, and Wyner now uses improvisation and flexible rhythmic and melodic elements in his colorful instrumental writing.

Partita 1952 (AMP 1976) 24pp. 5 min. Overture: first half in French Overture rhythm, major-minor sonorities mixed, then an allegro with ostinato-like bass. Aria: melodic, use of ninths. Allemande. Minuet. Gigue: fugal. Derivative but highly successful neo-Bachian writing. The suite is infused with charm, grandeur, and lyric beauty. M-D.

Sonata per Pianoforte (CFE 1954). First movement: thin textures; use of ninth, both harmonically and melodically; lower register used for single-note rhythmic punctuation. Second movement; juxtaposes major-minor sonorities. Final movement: ninth again prominent. Widespread thin textures and important use of the trill. Striking work. 12-tone but with tonal orientation. M-D.

Three Short Fantasies 1963, 1966, 1971 (AMP 1973) 11pp. 6 min. Serial, contrasted, highly melodic, much repetition, ostinato-like motives, improvisatory, successful miniatures. To be played together. Large span required. D.

Ivan Wyshnegradsky (1893–1979) USSR

Deux Préludes Op.2 1917 (Belaieff) 3½ min. Strong Tchaikowsky influence. M-D.

Etude sur le Carré magique sonore Op.40 1956 (Belaieff) 9 min. Based on ultrachromatic scales (quarter tones, sixth tones, etc.). The principle of nonoctavian spaces (a system of control over the extremes of ultrachromaticism as well as sixth and twelfth tones) is at work in this piece. D.

Jürg Wyttenbach (1935–   ) Switzerland

Drei Klavierstücke (Ars Viva 1969) 7pp. Short pieces. Directions (in German) explain notation. Harmonics, strings stroked with a wooden hammer. Avantgarde. M-D.

X

Iannis Xenakis (1922–   ) France, born Rumania

Xenakis is of Greek descent and has worked in many countries. He is one of the truly innovative intelligences in today's musical world. He has incorporated computer-determined probabilities and transferred certain architectural structures into his music.

Herma—"Musique symbolique" 1960–61 (Bo&H). *Herma* means "bond," "foundation," "embryo." The rhythm is stochastic, that is, the notation is only an approximation. Based on logical operations imposed on classes of pitches. A dazzling diffusion of notes. Preface describes work. Notation and sound are unusual. Avant-garde. D.

Evryali 1971 (Sal) 28pp. Literal accuracy is almost impossible because of the required speed. Notes are scattered all over the keyboard. Super-Lisztian virtuosity and an acrobatic performer are required. When "brought off," there will be plenty of dazzled listeners; otherwise it could sound like a lot of primitive banging. Contains a dense, rapid-fire series of chord combinations. The rhythm is deterministic, the evenness of attacks being the decisive factor to achieve the continuity. A kind of imaginary music from an imaginary performer! Extravagantly difficult.

See: Peter Hill, "Xenakis and the Performer," *Tempo*, 112 (March 1975): 12–22. Contains helpful discussions of both *Herma* and *Evryali*.

Mists 1980 (Sal 17492) 4pp. 12 min. Photostat of MS, ring binding. Austere and lucid, opens with a sequence of canonic entries or "the unfolding of 'arborescences,' that is, of bushes of melodic lines all originating from the same branch, therefore of the same shape, but of a different time-structure, so that the phasing is dislocated" (Brigitte Schiffer, *Tempo*, 137, p.35). Stochastic, arborescent; looks as unplayable as other Xenakis scores. Widely disseminated notes assemble like drops of dew, in formations of ever-changing density, varying between haze, mist, and cloud, with the pedal used as an additional parameter. D.

See: Mario Bois, *Iannis Xenakis—The Man and His Music, a Conversation with the Composer and a Description of His Works* (New York: Boosey and Hawkes, 1967).

David Jones, "The Music of Xenakis," MT, 107 (June 1966): 495–96.

Iannis Xenakis, *Formalized Music* (Bloomington: Indiana University Press, 1971).

Y

Tadasi Yamanouchi (1935–　　) Japan
Métamorphose 1971 (Japan Federation of Composers) 15pp. Moderato: presents
main idea and its development in two parts. Andante: continued harmonic
development of main ideas, ternary form. Presto: melodic development of
main ideas, sonata-rondo form. Same thematic material varied throughout
piece, contemporary treatment. M-D.

Masahiro Yamauchi (1960–　　) Japan
Yamauchi is a graduate of the Tokyo National University of Fine Arts and
Music.
Dislocation of Time (Japan Federation of Composers 1994) 12 min. This piece
"consists mainly of fast repetition of figures, and most of its tempos and
rhythms should be decided by the natural breath of the performer" (from
1994 Japan Federation of Composers catalogue, p.26).

Yehuda Yannay (1937–　　) Israel, born Rumania
Music for Piano 1962 (IMI). Three short movements oriented toward Schönberg
demanding sophistication and knowledge of the style. M-D to D.
7 Late Spring Pieces 1973 (IMI 335) 15pp. 9 min. Introduces new and precise
pedal notation; expressionistic and Impressionistic characteristics. M-D.

Richard Yardumian (1917–1985) USA
Yardumian's style has a Middle Eastern color that comes from his Armenian
background.
3 Preludes (EV 1945). The Wind; The Sea; The Sky. Short, expressive, refined. M-D.
Chromatic Sonata (EV 1947) 20 min. First movement: dancelike. Second movement: introduced by slow chorale. Third movement: varied tempi; ends quietly. M-D.
Prelude and Chorale (EV 1949) 3 min. Prelude: melodic line is embedded in accompaniment of sixteenth notes. Chorale: chordal; long, sustained sonorities. M-D.

Akio Yashiro (1929–1977) Japan
Yashiro was one of the most brilliant young Japanese composers.
Sonate 1960 (Ongaku-No-Tomo-Sha) 25pp. 17 min. Agitato: numerous slow-fast
tempo changes. Toccata: fast alternation of hands, pointillistic, octaves and

repeated chords. Thème et Variations: chordal chromatic theme, large climax, subsides, closes *ppp.* D.

Yip Wai Hong (1931–   ) China
Memories of Childhood. See collection *Chinese Contemporary Piano Pieces,* Vol.I. 13pp. A suite. Morning Haze; Having Fun; The Voice of Old Grandmother; Dance of the Puppets; Afternoon Nap; Picnicking. Impressionistic expressivity, clever, contrasting, some pentatonic influence, MC. Requires subtleties. Int.

Joji Yuasa (1929–   ) Japan
On the Keyboard. Projection Topologic. Cosmos Haptic (Ongaku-No-Tomo-Sha 1973) 26pp. Bound in one volume. Strongly avant-garde throughout. Requires virtuoso technique and an inquiring mind. *Cosmos Haptic* contains nostalgic and abstract Scriabinisms. D.
Chant pour "Do" (Zen-On). Exquisite! Hypnotic repetition of C. M-D.

Isang Yun (1917–1995) Germany, born Korea
Fünf Stücke 1958 (Bo&Bo). Displays strong Schönberg and Berg influence; fluctuating meters; extreme ranges exploited, emotional overtones. D.
   See: David Burge, "Isang Yun's *Five Pieces*," *Keyboard,* 9/6 (June 1983):69.
See: David Burge, "Contemporary Piano—Oriental Composers," CK, 4 (December 1978):60.

Akira Yuyama (1932–   ) Japan
Children's Land (Ongaku-No-Tomo-Sha 1967) 46pp. Twenty pieces for small hands, no octaves. Provides a good introduction to contemporary piano sonorities. Int.
Sunday Sonatina 1969 (Ongaku-No-Tomo-Sha) 55pp. Consists of a Prelude and a series of sonatinas from Sunday to Saturday. Saturday Sonatina is the most difficult. Linking each piece with a day of the week has no special meaning. Bitonal, alternating hands, freely tonal, Impressionistic sonorities. Each sonatina contains two or three movements. Int. to M-D.

Z

Harold Zabrack (1929–1995) USA

Zabrack was an exceptionally fine pianist, and his performance expertise comes through in his writing at all times.

Contours (Kenyon 1978) 23pp. Eight contemporary pieces in contrasting style, mood and length. A brilliant Etude exploits alternating notes and chords; a showy Toccata and an expressive Elegy for the left hand are particularly fine. Dialogue and Introspection are 12-tone. M-D.

Etudes (Kenyon 1979) 17pp. Allegro scherzando: light and rhythmic, flowing thirds. Andante expressivo: rhapsodic, glorious mid-section. Allegro: octaves, light and fast. M-D.

Piano Variations (Kenyon 1981) 12pp. Modal 16-bar theme, 11 contrasting variations with the final one the most difficult, MC, thoroughly pianistic, austere tension. Large span required. M-D.

Sonata I 1965 (Kenyon 1978). Allegro con brio: percussive, virtuosic. Adagio espressivo: atonal, calm. Interlude. Finale: impetuous, changing tempi, atonal, brilliant closing. A bravura work of symphonic proportions. D.

Sonata II (Kenyon 1981) 25pp. Allegro moderato; Andante espressivo; Allegro con brio. Freely tonal, filled with soaring melodies and incisive rhythms. Requires bravura. M-D to D.

Preludes (Kenyon Publications 1979) 16pp. 1: Quartal and quintal harmony, flowing melody, gentle rocking motion. 2: Strong rhythms, freely tonal, tempo fluctuations. 3: Expressive melody over contemporary Alberti bass. 4: Exploits bass register. 5: Attractive melody over broken-chord accompaniment. 6: Light allegro opening section returns after more melodic mid-section. A fine set displaying first-rate writing in a MC style. M-D.

Mario Zafred (1922–1987) Italy, born Trieste

Zafred had considerable technical skill, and his compositional goal was the ideal of immediate communicability.

Third Sonata (Ric 1950) 23pp. Two movements. MC. M-D.

Fourth Sonata (Curci 1964). Three movements. Effective writing. M-D.

Fifth Sonata 1976 (Boccaccini & Spada 1026) 30pp. Moderamente mosso: changing meters, restless, large chordal skips. Sostenuto e cantabile: subtle contrapuntal texture surrounds melody. Finale: arpeggio figures; tension and tempi increase. D.

Judith Lang Zaimont (1945–   ) USA

Calendar Collection 1976 (Vivace) 26 min. Twelve prelude-etudes, one for each month, each written during the month described. July and December seem to be inspired by Ives, a windy etude for October, Ice for February, all with quotations to clarify the composer's intent. These pieces display a sensitive, Romantic temperament with a mixture of dissonance and humor. M-D.

Suite Impressions (Vivace) 12pp. Folk song; In Pop Style; Jazz Waltz. Wonderfully contrasted moods: serene to stormy. M-D.

Nocturne La fin de siècle 1978 (Galaxy). The composer's gesture to nineteenth-century pianism and style of composition. Three-part design, flowing MC sonorities, mid-section surprises with virtuosic splashes, relaxed ending. M-D to D.

See: Clinton Adams, "All-American Appeal," *P&Q* No. 195 (November–December 1998): 39–43. A discussion of Zaimont's piano music.

Arlene Zallman (1934–   ) USA

Zallman studied at the Philadelphia Conservatory of Music and The Juilliard School, and for composition, with Luigi Dallopiccola and Vincent Persichetti. She is chair of the Music Department, Wellesley College.

Variations on the Villanella "Alma, che fai?" by Luca Marenzio (CFP 67656 1996) 15pp. 11½ min. Text of the Italian song is given at beginning. Contrasting variations flow into each other, changing meters, MC, tune of song heard at opening and closing. M-D.

Luigi Zaninelli (1932–   ) USA

Fantasia (EV 1973) 9pp. Brilliant writing, requires first-rate pianist to bring it off. Toccata-like passages contrasted with freer, recitative-like sections, freely tonal. M-D.

Commedia (E. C. Kirby 1980). Varied meters, brilliant scales and triads, lively rhythms, a circus of sonorities. M-D to D.

Julien-François Zbinden (1917–   ) Switzerland

Jazz Sonatina Op.11 (Br&H 1949–50). Blues; Improvisation. Zbinden played in a jazz orchestra for a while and readily absorbed the style. M-D.

4 Solitudes Op.17 (SZ). Contrasted, pianistic. No.2 asks to be played "with desperate energy." M-D.

Album pour mon chien Op.19 (Foetisch). Amusing, rhythmical. Int.

Ruth Zechlin (1926–   ) Germany

Kontrapunkte 1969–70 (DVFM) 8pp. For harpsichord or piano. Biographic note in German. Consists of a preludium, four inventions (mainly two-part), and postludium. Hindemith influence. M-D.

Lubomir Zelezny (1925–1979) Czech Republic

4 Polkas 1948 (Panton). Cheerful, chromatic, folk influence, large chords, octaves, lively. No fingering or pedaling. M-D.

Carl Friedrich Zelter (1758–1832) Germany
Rondo mit Variationen (K. H. Taubert—R&E). Graceful, in the style of Mozart variations. Int. to M-D.

Alexander von Zemlinsky (1872–1942) Austria
Zemlinsky was Arnold Schönberg's teacher, and his sister married Schönberg.
Country Dances Op.1 1892 (Br&H 8105) 19pp. Preface in German and English. Twelve short pieces (the last two performed without pause), all in 3/4. Moods vary: No.2 is elfin, almost Mendelssohnian; No.5 reserved; No.6 dramatic; No.7 tender; No.8 jovial; No.9 a peasant dance. Some hand-crossings, motivic repetition, interesting tonal relation and harmonic progressions. Int. to M-D.
Fantasien Op.9 (Dob). Actually four "songs without words" inspired by texts by Dehmel. Written in the German Romantic character-piece tradition (Richard Strauss, Franz Schreker), they are rewarding to perform. M-D.

Pierre-Joseph-Guillaume Zimmerman (1785–1853) France
See below, "Collections," *Piano Music of the Parisian Virtuosos 1810–1860*.

Bernd-Alois Zimmermann (1918–1970) Germany
Extemporale 1943 (Gerig 1950) 16pp. Sarabande: quiet, chordal. Invention: quick, two-part. Siciliano: contrasted character, sweet with harsh. Bolero: mostly left-hand rhythmic figuration. Finale: gains in intensity to closing heavy chords. Large span required. D.
Enchiridion 1949–51 (Schott). Bartók, Hindemith, and Schönberg influence. Great concentration needed for these 13 short introspective pieces. M-D.
8 Configurations (Schott 1956). Dynamics exploited, pointillistic. Clever 12-tone studies; row is treated as a unit. Dissonant and percussive. D.

David Zinn (1953–   ) USA
The Awakening (Excelsior 1983) 8pp. Romantic style, "object was to subject a stylistic genre to varying degrees of modern linear and harmonic complexity. . . . The objective of my system is to transcend style" (from the score). Uses techniques from the composer's system of "Structural Free-Form Musical Composition." M-D.
Transformation (Excelsior 1983) 20pp. "The objective was to subject certain thematic material to different compositional treatment, resulting in a total musical transformation of the original statement" (from the score). Freely tonal, interesting developmental procedures. M-D to D.
Scottish Trilogy (Excelsior 1984) 57pp. The Homecoming: joyous and festive, varied figurations, contrasting sections. The Scot's Life: "representative of day to day living in a small Scottish village" (from the score); folklike themes; extended. The Final Journey: traditional folk flavor coupled with modern compositional treatment, overly long. M-D to D.
Fusion Sonata (Excelsior 1984) 103pp. plus 44pp. of analysis. With musical tech-

nique derived by Zinn from his systems of composition and improvisation. Three main movements, each containing several sections in varied tempo. Analysis should be read carefully before beginning this work. Freely tonal, octotonic, chromatic, overly long. D.

Ramon Zupko (1932–   ) USA

Zupko is director of the Studio for Electronic Music and of the New Music Ensemble at Western Michigan University, Kalamazoo. He has become increasingly concerned over the past several years with a more ecumenical approach to musical materials, which embraces not only the spectrum of contemporary compositional techniques, but also those of the past and of other cultures.

Fluxus II 1978 (CFP 66865) 9pp., 13½ min. "The expressive and dramatic flow of the work was inspired by the poem of Dylan Thomas entitled 'In the Beginning,' the poet's personal expression of the story of Genesis. The musical materials employed in this piece reflect a predilection towards the reinterpretation of musical gestures, figurations, and technics of older music within my own tonal style and sound-mass texture. The work is concerned throughout with Baroque and Classical keyboard embellishment, Romantic keyboard figuration and bravura, and with the relationships among static tonal centers. The 'genesis' of *Fluxus II* derives from the melodic growth and expansion of a three-note cell. It approaches the piano as a polyphonic 'color' instrument, with many gradations of attack and dynamic, 'orchestrated" textures with foreground accompanied by one or more layers of background, various 'echo' effects, and the rapid alternation of differing textures and shapes" (the composer in a letter to the author). Avant-garde. D.

Samuel Zyman (1956–   ) Mexico

Zyman studied at the National Conservatory of Music in Mexico City and received his MM and DMA degrees in composition from The Juilliard School. He is a member of the Juilliard faculty in the Department of Literature and Materials.

Two Motions in One Movement 1996 (Merion Music) 9pp., ca. 7 min. Agitato, contrasting moods, octotonic, parallel chords, changing meters, exciting conclusion. M-D to D.

Part II

Anthologies
and Collections

This section is divided into four groupings, each arranged alphabetically by title. "General" includes music from different countries written over a period of one to three centuries. "General: Contemporary" lists collections of piano music primarily of the twentieth century from different countries. The "Tombeaux, Hommages" section catalogs those collections written in honor of a composer. The last and largest category consists of collections of various nationalities, sometimes divided into pre–twentieth century and twentieth century. The "Bach" section (under "German") lists collections which include music by more than one member of the Bach family. Single-composer collections are listed under the composer's name in the main part of the book.

Initial articles and Arabic numerals (A, An, Das, Der, I, Le, Les, The, 15, 24, 30) are ignored in alphabetization. Composers' names are given in the spelling used in the collection being described. The Title Index of Anthologies and Collections at the end of the volume lists all the collections in one alphabetic sequence.

General

The Age of J. S. Bach (CFP 4452a) 43pp. Includes original pieces by J. S. Bach, C. P. E. Bach, Handel, Krebs, Pergolesi, Rameau, Scarlatti, Telemann, and others, plus a table of ornaments. Int. to M-D.

Alicia de Larrocha Favorite Encores for Piano (Daniel Gerard) 64pp. J. S. Bach: *Sanctify Us By Thy Goodness* (arr. by Harriet Cohen); *Beloved Jesu We Are Here*; *Fantasia* c. Granados: *Andaluza*; *Zapateado*. Soler: *Sonatas* D and g. I. Albeniz: *Tango*; *El Puetro*; *Leyenda*; *Seguidillas*. M. Albeniz: *Sonata* D. Includes biographical sketches of each composer and a brief biography of de Larrocha. Many typographical errors. M-D.

Alte Meister der Klaviermusik des 16–18 Jahrhunderts (H. Keller—CFP).
Vol.1: German Masters: Froberger, Buxtehude, Pachelbel. J. K. F. Fischer, Mattheson, Händel, J. S. Bach, Muffat, Krebs, Kirnberger, W. F. Bach, C. P. E. Bach.
Vol.2: French Masters: Chambonnières, D'Anglebert, Lully, Le Bègue, F. Couperin, Marchand, Dieupart, Rameau, Dandrieu, Daquin, Duphly.
Vol.3: Italian Masters: Frescobaldi, Pasquini, Pollarolo, A. Scarlatti, Zipoli, D. Scarlatti, Platti, Martini, Galuppi, Paradies, Vento, Turini.
Vol.4: English, Dutch, Spanish Masters: Byrd, Farnaby, Johnson, Anony-

mous, Hooper, Philips, Bull, Purcell, Sweelinck, Reinken, Cabézon, Milan, Soler.

Alte Meister des Klavierspiels (W. Niemann—CFP) *Old Masters of the 17th and 18th Centuries*

Vol.1: English, French, Italian Masters: 11 pieces by Byrd, Bull, F. Couperin, Daquin, Durante, Frescobaldi, Galuppi, Marchand, Martin, Paradisi.

Vol.2: German Masters: 19 pieces by Böhm, Fischer, Froberger, Graun, Kerll, Kirnberger.

Vol.3: German Masters: 15 pieces by Krieger, Kuhnau, Marpurg, Mattheson, Muffat, Pachelbel, Murschhauser, Scheidt.

Alte Programmusik (F. Reuter—Mitteldeutscher Verlag). Banchieri: *La Battaglia*. F. Couperin: *Les Papillons*. Rameau: *Tambourin*. Byrd: *The Battle*. Munday: *The Tempest*. Kuhnau: *The Battle between David and Goliath*. An unusually fine collection, not edited.

Alte Tänze des 17. und 18. Jahrhunderts (Dana Setkova—Br). 27 works by Chambonnières, D'Anglebert, Rameau, Dandrieu, Zipoli, Froberger, Pachelbel, Kuhnau, J. S. Bach, Purcell, Croft, Handel.

The George Anson Anthology of Piano Literature (EV). 17 pieces from The Fitzwilliam Book through Mozart to Grieg by 16 composers. Selected from the Anson "Survey of Piano Literature." Int.

Anthology of Music (Karl G. Fellerer—Arno Volk Verlag). This is the English edition of *Das Musikwerk*, a collection of 37 volumes with complete musical examples illustrating the history of music. Volumes of special interest to the pianist are: Vol.1: 400 Years of European Keyboard Music (Georgii). Vol.6: The Classics (Stephenson). Vol.8: The Character Piece (Kahl). Vol.11: The Variation (von Fischer). Vol.12: Improvisation (Ferand). Vol.15: The Solo Sonata (Giegling). Vol.17: The Toccata (Valentin). Vol.19: The Fugue, I (Adrio). Vol.21: Romanticism in Music (Stephenson). Vol.25: The Solo Concerto (Engel). Vol.26: The Suite (Beck). Vol.27: The Dance (Reichert). Vol.33: The Fugue, II (Müller—Blattau).

An Anthology of Piano Music (Agay—YMP 1971). Comprehensive coverage of the periods. Ranges in difficulty from easy to D. with most material Int.

Vol.I: *The Baroque Period*. Scholarly introduction by Louis L. Crowder, editorial notes, biographical sketches of composers, glossary. Works by d'Anglebert, C. P. E. Bach, J. S. Bach, W. F. Bach, Blow, Buxtehude, Byrd, Chambonnières, F. Couperin, Dandrieu, Daquin, Durante, J. K. F. Fischer, Frescobaldi, G. Gabrieli, Gibbons, Graupner, Händel, Hurlebusch, Kinderman, Kirnberger, Krebs, Krieger, Kuhnau, Leo, Loeillet, Lully, Maichelbek, Marcello, Martini, Mattheson, Muffat, Nichelman, J. Pachelbel, Paradisi, Pasquini, Pergolesi, Purcell, Rameau, Rathgeber, D. Scarlatti, Scheidt, Seixas, Soler, Sweelinck, Telemann, Tischer, Trabacci. Walther, Weckmann, Witt, Zipoli. Superb survey of the period.

Vol.II: *The Classical Period*. Scholarly introduction by Louis L. Crowder, biographical sketches of composers, glossary. Works by J. C. Bach, J. C. F.

Bach, Beethoven, J. A. Benda, Clementi, Cramer, Diabelli, Dittersdorf, Dussek, Hässler, Haydn, Hüllmandel, Hummel, Kuhlau, Mozart, Reichardt, Türk, Weber. Superb survey of the period.

Vol.III: *The Romantic Period*. Scholarly introduction by Louis L. Crowder, biographical sketches of composers, glossary. Works by Albeniz, Alkan, Brahms, Chopin, Dohnányi, Dvořák, Fauré, Franck, Gade, Glinka, Grieg, Heller, Liszt, MacDowell, Mendelssohn, Moussorgsky, Rachmaninoff, Reger, Schubert, Schumann, Sibelius, Smetana, Tchaikovsky, Volkmann, Wolf. Superb survey of the period.

Vol.IV: *The Twentieth Century*. Scholarly introduction by Louis L. Crowder, biographical sketches of composers, glossary. Works by Antheil, Bartók, Casella, Cowell, Creston, Debussy, Einem, Granados, Gretchaninoff, Hauer, Hindemith, Ives, Jelinek, Kabalevsky, Kadosa, Khatchaturian, Kodály, Krenek, Lutoslawski, Martin, Milhaud, Palmgren, Piston, Prokofieff, Ránki, Ravel, Rebikoff, Rieti, Satie, Schuman, Schönberg, Scott, Shostakovich, Scriabin, Starer, I. Stravinsky, Swanson, Tcherepnin, Toch, Villa-Lobos, Webern.

Antologia di Musica Antica e Moderna (Tagliapietra—Ric 1931-32). The second largest anthology of keyboard music. Extends from the sixteenth century to the twentieth. Includes bio-bibliographical notes in Italian, French, English, and Spanish.

Vol.1: F. Verdelotto, A. Willaert, L. Molan, G. Cavazzoni, A. de Mudarra, M. de Fuenllana, G. Bermudo, C. de Rore, A. Gabrieli, A. de Cabézon, A. Padovano.

Vol.2: C. Merulo, L. Luzzaschi, W. Byrd, T. Morley, G. Gabrieli, F. Richardson, P. Philips, G. Farnaby.

Vol.3: J. P. Sweelinck, J. Mundy, J. Bull, J. Titelouze, H. L. Hässler, A. Banchieri, C. Erbach, B. Praetorius, O. Gibbons.

Vol.4: Giorolamo Frescobaldi: *Fiori Musicali*; *Il primo Libro di Capricci*.

Vol.5: G. Frescobaldi, G. M. Trabani, G. Picchi, A. Gabrieli.

Vol.6: S. Scheidt, H. Scheidemann, G. B. Fasolo, M. A. Rossi, T. Merula, F. Fontana, J. J. Froberger.

Vol.7: D. Stungk, W. Ebner, J. E. Kindermann, F. Roberday, J. C. de Chambonnières, H. Dumont, J. A. Reinken, N. Gigault, J. R. von Kerll, J. d'Anglebert, G. B. de Lully, J. Gaultier (le "Vieux").

Vol.8: A. Poglietti, A. Le Bègue, L. Couperin, G. Muffat, D. Buxtehude, B. Pasquini.

Vol.9: J. C. Bach, J. Krieger, C. F. Pollaroli, A. Corelli, J. Pachelbel, H. Purcell, A. Scarlatti.

Vol.10: J. Kuhnau, F. X. A. Murschhauser, J. K. F. Fischer, J. B. Loeillet, F. Couperin, L. Marchand, A. B. Della Ciaja, D. Zipoli. A. Vivaldi, G. Ph. Telemann, J. Mattheson.

Vol.11: J. Ph. Rameau, J. F. Dandrieu, F. Durante, G. F. Händel, J. S. Bach, D. Scarlatti, B. Marcello, N. Porpora.

Vol.12: G. Muffat, L. C. Daquin, L. Leo, J. A. Hasse, G. B. Sammartini, G. A. Paganelli, G. B. Pescetti, G. B. Martini, B. Galuppi, W. F. Bach, P. A. Paradies, J. L. Krebs.

Vol.13: K. P. E. Bach, F. W. Marpurg, J. P. Kirnberger, G. Benda, J. E. Bach, F. Bertoni, G. P. Rutini, J. Haydn, S. Sacchini, J. C. Bach, J. W. Hässler, F. Turini, G. B. Grazioli, M. Clementi, W. A. Mozart.

Vol.14: L. Cherubini, J. L. Dussek, F. Pollini, D. Steibelt, L. v. Beethoven, J. B. Cramer, J. N. Hummel, J. Field, F. Ries, K. M. v. Weber.

Vol.15: F. W. M. Kalkbrenner, K. Czerny, I. Moscheles, F. P. Schubert, J. C. Kessler, F. Mendelssohn, F. Chopin.

Vol.16: R. Schumann, F. Liszt, S. Thalberg, H. Kjerulf, S. Golinelli.

Vol.17: J. Raff, A. Fumagalli, A. Rubinstein, J. Brahms, G. Sgambati, M. Esposito, G. Martucci, C. Albanesi, N. v. Westerhout, A. Longo, G. Orefice.

Vol.18: F. Busoni, F. Cilèa, A. Zanella, A. Savasta, D. Alageona, R. Pick-Mangiagalli, L. Perrachio, A. Casella, F. Santoliquido, P. Coppola, A. Voretti, M. Castelnuovo-Tedesco, S. Musella, E. Masetti, M. Pilati.

Anthology of Baroque Keyboard Music (Hinson—Alfred 4894 1998) 248pp. An up-to-date, comprehensive survey of keyboard music written between 1590 and 1750, with works by 42 composers. Works are in their original form, with clearly identified editorial markings. Contains a useful foreword with historical information and performance notes on each piece. Every ornament is realized at least once in the footnotes. Int. to M-D.

Two video cassettes, *Baroque Dance and Baroque Keyboard Music* (Alfred VHS 12116) and *Performance Practices in Baroque Keyboard Music* (Alfred VHS 12117) are available separately.

The Art of the Suite (Yella Pessl—EBM). Eight suites of dances by seventeenth- and eighteenth-century composers, including works by Chambonnières, Froberger, Purcell, J. K. F. Fischer, F. Couperin, Dieupart, Daquin, and Gottlieb Muffat. The edition is tastefully done, with biographical notes, essay on the suite, and a table of ornaments.

At the Piano with Women Composers (Hinson—Alfred 428) 65pp. Contains a Foreword, information about the composers, and a discussion of each piece. Marianna von Auenbrugger: *Sonata* Eb, Rondo: Allegro. Agathe Backer-Grondahl: *Song of Youth* Op.45/1; *Summer Song* Op.45/3. Amy Marcy Beach: *Promenade* Op.25/1; *Scottish Legend* Op.54/1; *Waltz* Op.36/3. Teresa Carreño: *Le Sommeil de l'Enfant* (Berceuse) Op.35. Cecile Chaminade: *Scarf Dance* Op.37/3. Louis Farrenc: *Impromptu*. Elisabetta de Gambarini: *Gigue*; *Tambourin*. Fanny Mendelssohn Hensel: *Mélodie* Op.4/2; *Melodie* Op.5/4. Wanda Landowska: *Berceuse*. Marianne Martinez: *Sonata* E, Allegro. Clara Wieck Schumann: *Mazurka* Op.6/5. Adaline Shepherd: *Wireless Rag*. Maria Szymanowska: *Nocturne* Bb. Sources listed.

The Baroque Era—An Introduction to the Keyboard Music (W. Palmer and M. Halford—Alfred 1976) 64pp. Foreword discusses such subjects as the Baroque era, ornamentation, free ornamentation, "good taste," the theory of affects, pedaling, keyboard instruments of the Baroque era, and time signatures. Pieces from the Italian Baroque include works by Salvator Rosa, A. Scarlatti, Pasquini, and D. Scarlatti; from the English Baroque, works by John Blow, Henry Purcell, and Jeremiah Clark; from the French Baroque, works by L. Couperin, Chambonnières (and a section on inequality), Rameau, M. Corrette, and F. Couperin; from the German Baroque, works by Pachelbel, Telemann, Böhm, Handel, and J. S. Bach. A fine compendium with much useful information. Easy to Int.

Baroque Masters—Easiest Piano Pieces (CFP 5028) 24pp. Works by Böhm, Fischer, Froberger, Krieger, Kuhnau, Pachelbel, and Weckmann, plus biographical notes. Int.

Beethoven and His Circle: An Anthology of Music by Beethoven and His Contemporaries (Ernest Lubin—Amsco Music 1974) 160pp. Annotations by the compiler. Bibliography. Contains: C. G. Neefe, *Sonata* XI; Beethoven, *Sonatina* f, first movement; German Song and Romanza from the *Ritterballett*; Variations on a theme by Count Waldstein; 10 Variations on the theme "La stessa, la stessissima," from the opera *Falstaff* by Salieri (for piano duet); Largo from *Sonata* E♭ Op.7. D. Steibelt, Romance from *Sonata* G. L. Cherubini, Overture from *The Water Carrier* (for piano duet). J. Wölfl, *Introduction and Allegro* c. J. N. Hummel, *Un scherzo all'antico* from *Sonata* D Op.106. Beethoven: *Sonata* Op.54, first movement. C. Czerny: *Toccata* C Op.92. *Variations on Diabelli*, Waltz C, by Hummel, Moscheles, Schubert, Liszt. Beethoven: *Variations on a theme by Diabelli* (excerpts); *Bagatelles*, Op.126. Int. to M-D.

The Birds in Piano Music (PWM 5564) 40pp. Also available as *Bird Calls in Piano Music* (UE 18580). A collection of pieces that include the name of a bird in the title. F. Couperin: *Le Rossignol en amour*. L. C. Daquin: *Le Coucou*; *L'Hirondelle*. B. Pasquini: *Toccata con lo Scherzo del Cuculo*. J. P. Rameau: *La Poule*. A clever and interesting collection. Int. to M-D.

Black Women Composers: A Century of Piano Music (1893–1990) (Walker-Hill—Hildegarde). Includes works by Aldridge, Bailey, Baiocchi, Bonds, Capers, Goodwin, King, Kinney, León, McLin, D. R. Moore, U.S. Moore, J. Perry, Z. P. Perry, Price, Ricketts, Schuyler, Solomon, and Williams. Int. to M-D.

Celebri composizioni per pianoforte (Ric). Book I. A varied collection of favorite classics in chronological order ranging from Albinoni; Adagio g; D. Scarlatti; *Sonata* C, L.104; J. S. Bach, *Jesu Joy*; Paganini-Liszt, *Capriccio* E; to a little-known work by Giuseppe Martucci (1856–1909), *Nocturne* G♭ Op.70/1. Also contains short works by Haydn, Mozart, Schumann, Grieg, and Rachmaninoff. Int. to M-D. Book II. Works by Alberti, Beethoven, Casella, Chopin, Dvořák, Paradisi, Rameau, Rossini-Liszt, Scarlatti, Schubert, Schumann. M-D.

The Century of Invention (Hinson—EAMC 772 1996) 70pp. Piano music of the twentieth century, works by 18 composers from 14 countries. Includes composer biographies. A fine survey of some of the best from the twentieth century.

Part I: Richard Rodney Bennett: *Two Diversions*. Alban Berg: *Menuette*

F. Ross Edwards: *Little Piano Piece I*. Jean Françaix: *Dreamy; Playing Soldier*. Paul Hindemith: *Marsch*. Witold Lutoslawski: *Bukoliki*. Darius Milhaud: *Romance*. Arvo Pärt: *Für Alina*. Marcel Poot: *On the Spanish Border; Towards Avignon*. Joaquim Rodrigo: *A la Jota*; El Negrito Pepo. Arnold Schönberg: *Kleines Klavierstücke* Op.19/2. Matyas Seiber: *Argentine Tango; Cakewalk*. Joaquin Turina: *Clowns; Fiesta*.

Part II: Belá Bartók: *Allegretto* Op.14. Alban Berg: *Klavierstück* b. Luciano Berio: *Wasserklavier*. Lili Boulanger: *D'un vieux jardin*. Aaron Copland: *Sentimental Melody*. Jean Françaix: *The Tender One*. Peggy Glanville-Hicks: *Prelude for a Pensive Pupil*. Paul Hindemith: *Foxtrot*. Györgi Ligeti: *All'ungherese*. Bohuslav Martinů; *Intermezzo I*. Ernest Pepping: *Poco Lento*. Francis Poulenc: *Valse*. Erik Satie: *Jack in the Box*. Joseph Schwantner: *Veiled Autumn*. Tong Shang: *Dance*. Kurt Weill: *Tango-Ballade*.

The Century of Dance (M. Hinson—Schott 2000) 48pp. The dance has inspired some of our finest twentieth-century piano repertoire. This collection contains 19 dances composed by 16 outstanding twentieth-century composers including: Part I. Intermediate Level: Béla Bartók, *Two Old Dance Tunes*, Sz. 71: 9, 10. Claude Debussy, *The Little Negro* (Cakewalk). Alexander Gretchaninoff, *Russian Dance*. Eduard Pütz, *Sentimental Lady* (Jazz Waltz). Joaquin Rodrigo, *A la jota* (Dance of the Doves). Mátyás Seiber, *Charleston; Mazurka; Polka; Tango* (Habanera). Tong Shang, *Chinese Dance*. Alexander Tansman, *Vienna Waltz*. Joaquin Turina, *The Trained Dog*. Part II: Moderately Difficult Level: Jean Françaix, *Dancer* (Waltz). Paul Hindemith, *Foxtrot*. Scott Joplin: *Rag Time Dance*. Ernesto Nazareth, *Striking* (Tango Brasileiro). Erik Satie, *Gold Dust* (Waltz). Kurt Weill, *Tango-Ballade*. Also includes composer biographies.

The Character Piece (W. Kahl—Arno Volk) Vol.8 of the "Anthology of Music Series." Includes an aesthetic and historical introduction and notes on the music and sources. Solo keyboard pieces include: Johann Kotter: *Carmen in sol*. Thomas Mulliner: *Since thou art false to me; When shall my sorrowful sighing*. Johann J. Froberger: *Lamentation faite sur la mort très douloureuse de Sa Majesté Impériale Ferdinand le troisième*. J. S. Bach: *Prelude* b♭, WTC, I. F. Couperin: *Les Langueurs tendres*. C. P. E. Bach: *Abschied vom Silbermannschen Clavier in einem Rondeau*. J. F. Reichardt: *Rondo*, after a Poem by Petrarch. A. Hüttenbrenner: *Nachruf an Schubert in Trauertönen am Pianoforte*. W. Taubert: *Minnelied*. S. Heller: *Wanderstunden*, from Op.80; *Präludien* e, from Op.81. A. Jensen: *Abendlied*. J. Rheinberger: *Two Pieces in Canonic Form*, Op.180. F. Liszt: *Sonetto 123 Petrarca; Consolation* E. R. Strauss: *Träumerei*. J. Haas: *Mummenschanz*. E. Sjögren: *Elegy*. Z. Fibich: three pieces from *Stimmungen, Eindrücke und Erinnerungen, Morgenunterhaltung*. Int. to M-D.

Chopin and His Circle (Ernest Lubin—Amsco 1975) 159pp. An anthology of music by Chopin and his contemporaries. A perspective of the time, with works by composers who influenced him and by composers Chopin influenced. Includes works by Chopin, J. Field, J. N. Hummel, J. Elsner, F. Liszt, S. Thalberg, H. Herz, F. Kalkbrenner, J. Kessler, R. Schumann, F. Mendelssohn, I. Moscheles, and A. Scriabin. Annotations by Lubin. Bibliography. Better editions of some of the pieces are available. Int. to D.

Classic Sonatas for Piano (Podolsky—CF). Vol.I: Arne: *Sonata* g. Grazioli: *Sonata* G. Hässler: *Sonata* C, No.3 from *Six Easy Sonatas*. Paradisi: *Sonata* D. Vol.II: Méhul: *Sonata* A, Op.1/3. Hässler: *Sonata* C, No.1 from *Six Easy Sonatas*. Hasse: *Sonata* d. Paradisi: *Sonata* A. Vol.III: Arne: *Sonata* A. Galuppi: *Sonata* D. C. P. E. Bach: *Sonata* A. Vol.IV: Scarlatti: *Sonata* f. Rust: *Sonata* f#. Arranged in progressive order of difficulty. Well fingered. Int. to M-D.

The Classical Era—An Introduction to the Keyboard Music (Palmer—Alfred 1977) 64pp. A foreword covers subjects such as the classical era; classicism in architecture, art, and music; the new classical performer; and ornamentation. Includes works by W. A. Mozart: *Two Minuets* (with suggested ornamentation); *Divertimento* from *Viennese Sonatina* I. J. C. Bach: *Minuetto* from *Sonata* II in D. C. P. E. Bach: *Arioso* C from *Sonatas with Varied Reprises*. Domenico Alberti: *Theme and Variations from Sonata* F. Op.1/7. G. C. Wagenseil: *Sonatina* C, Allegro, F. J. Haydn: *Air*; *Sonata* C, *Moderato*; *Menuet*; *Finale*. M. Clementi: *Sonatina* D Op.36/6, Allegro con spirito. Beethoven: *Bagatelle* D Op.33/6; *Sonata* G Op.49/2, Allegro ma non troppo. An excellent introduction to the period. Int.

Classical Masters (CFP 5044) 24pp. Works by Beethoven, Diabelli, Haydn, Mozart, including arrangements from a symphony, an oratorio, an opera, and a piano trio. Int.

Classical Music for the Church Service
Vol. 1 (Hinson—Alfred 452) 64pp. 42 pieces appropriate for the worship service from J. S. Bach through Granados. Early int.
Vol. 2 (Hinson—Alfred 453) 63pp. 34 pieces from J. S. Bach through Khachaturian. Int.
Vol. 3 (Hinson—Alfred 460) 63pp. 27 pieces from J. S. Bach through Sibelius. Late int.

Classical Music for the Wedding Service (Hinson—Alfred 447) 64pp. 29 pieces from J. S. Bach through Granados. Int.

Classical Music for the Worship Service (Hinson, Boozer—GS 19092 1980) 24pp. 17 pieces by J. C. Bach, J. S. Bach, Grieg, Gurlitt, Handel, Heller, Kohler, Kuhnau, L. Mozart, Nichelmann, D. Scarlatti, Schumann, and Tchaikowsky. All are appropriate for effective use in the worship service. Preface provides criteria for selection. Easy to Int.

The Classical Period (CFP 4453) 41pp. Works by J. C. Bach, Beethoven, G. Benda, Clementi, Diabelli, Dittersdorf, Eberl, Haydn, Hässler, Hoffmeister, Hummel, Mozart, Tomaschek, Weber. Int. to M-D.

Classics for the Young Pianist (Grace Lankford—GS). Unusual and lesser-known pieces for young players. Book I: 26 pieces for early grades. Works by J. S. Bach, Beethoven, Blow, Böhm, Corelli, Eccles, Handel, Haydn, Loeillet, Leopold Mozart, W. A. Mozart, Daniel Purcell, Henry Purcell, A. Scarlatti. Book II: 21 pieces for intermediate grades. Works by J. S. Bach, Beethoven, Exaudet, Handel, Haydn, Hook, Hullmandel, Kirnberger, Kuhnau, Leo,

Marais, Leopold Mozart, W. A. Mozart, Paradisi, A. Scarlatti, Türk, and an anonymous composer.

Classics to Moderns in the Early Advanced Grades (D. Agay—CMP). Vol.47 of *Music for Millions* series. Contains 54 original works from three centuries, Baroque to present. Based on urtext or other reliable scores. Works from Purcell, Rameau, Bach to Bartók, Ravel, Prokofieff, and others.

Classics to Moderns in the Intermediate Grades (D. Agay—CMP). Vol.37 of *Music for Millions* series. Contains 115 original pieces from nearly three centuries. Some unfamiliar and fine works by Pasquini, C. P. E. Bach, Villa-Lobos, Kirnberger, Kodály, Stoelzel, Scriabin, and Granados make this a desirable collection.

Composers for the Keyboard (TP). Vol.1: *Beethoven to Shostakovich* 72pp. 50 original piano solos, compiled and edited by George Walter Anthony. Easy II. Vol.2: *Byrd to Beethoven* 71pp. 27 original piano solos, compiled and edited by George Walter Anthony. Int. I. Vol.3: *Purcell to Mozart* 72pp. 50 original piano solos, compiled and edited by George Walter Anthony. Easy I. Vol.4: *Schubert to Shostakovich* 72pp. 39 original piano solos, compiled and edited by George Walter Anthony. Int. II. All four volumes contain brief biographies and notes concerning the works. The insides of the covers contain photographs and brief comments about the development of keyboard instruments.

A Dance Pageant. Renaissance and Baroque Keyboard Dances (Waxman—Galaxy 1992) 80pp. With illustrated descriptions and historical notes on the dances by Wendy Hilton. Includes groups of dances—Courante, Minuet and Passepied, Gavotte, Bourrée and Rigaudon, Saraband, Gigue, Allemande, Pavane, Galliard and Volta—with four or five excellent examples of each dance form. Many illustrations. An outstanding collection. Int. to M-D.

Dances and Ancient Melodies for the Beginner (K 9482) 93pp. 90 pieces by composers ranging from H. Purcell to Beethoven. Clean editing. Easy to Int.

Early Dances (Lakos—Könemann Music Budapest 1994) 156pp. Numerous musical examples of: A, C, S, G, B, Gavottes, M, Passepieds, Hornpipes, Rigaudons, Loure (one by Telemann), Polonaise, Suites, Deutscher Tanz, Ecossaise, Walzer, by composers from Froberger to Beethoven. Int. to M-D.

Easy Keyboard Music—Ancient to Modern (Palmer—Alfred). Easy original works by Bartók, Beethoven, Kabalevsky, Rameau, and others. Earliest piece is "Sumer is Icumen In." Easy to Int.

Easy Piano Music from the Vienna Classicism (EMB 1982). 20 selections from lesser-known composers, including Dusik, Dittersdorf, Hoffmeister, Hummel, and Tomasek, among others. All are melodic. Int.

Easy Sonatinas and Short Recital Pieces (CFP 3195 a, b). Vol.1, 47pp. Vol.2, 41pp. Arranged in progressive order. Works by Beethoven, Bertini, Clementi, Corelli, Diabelli, Dussek, Gayrhos, Grieg, Haydn, Köhler, Kuhlau, Kullak, Lemoine, Locatelli, Mayer, Mozart, Schubert, Schumann, Sternberg, Volkmann, Wilm, and others. Easy to Int.

Eighteenth Century Women Composers for the Harpsichord or Piano (Harbach—Vivace Press 1992) Vol. I, 32pp. Elisabetta de Gambarini (1731-1765): *Aria;*

Gavotte and Variations; Gigue. Maria Hester Park (1775–1822): *Sonata in F*;
A Lady; Lesson VI in D. Vol. II. Marianne Martinez (1744–1812): *Sonata A.*
Maria Hester Park: *Sonata C.* No articulation, phrasing, or fingerings. Int.
to M-D.

Encores of Great Pianists (Raymond Lewenthal—GS). 34 pieces by 27 well-
known composers that have been used as encores by some of the greatest
pianists from the past. An essay on the art of the encore and notes about
each piece and who has performed it make this a most interesting collection. Beethoven: *Polonaise* Op.89; *Ecossaises.* Borodin: *Scherzo.* Busoni:
Turandots Frauengemach ("Greensleeves"). Chaminade: *Autrefois* Op.87/4.
Clementi: *Finale* from *Sonata* B♭ Op.47/2. Czerny: *Etude* A♭ Op.740/33. Delibes: *Passepied* from *Le Roi l'a dit; Pizzicato* (Pizzicato Polka from *Sylvia*)
(Joseffy). Godowsky: *Alt Wien.* Granados: *Quejas ó la Maja y el Ruiseñor*
("Laments, or the Maiden and the Nightingale" from *Goyescas*). Grieg: *An
der Wiege* ("By the Cradle"). Guion: *Turkey in the Straw.* Leschetizky: *Arabesque en forme d'Etude* Op.45/1. Levitski: *Arabesque valsante* Op.6. Lewenthal: *Toccata alla Scarlatti.* Liszt: *Valse Oubliée* No.1. Medtner: *Fairy Tale*
Op.34/2. Mendelssohn: *The Joyous Peasant* Op.102/5. Moszkowski: *The Jug-
gleress* Op.52/4; *Etude* F Op.72/6. Mozart: *Serenade* from *Don Giovanni* (Busoni). Philipp: *Feux-Follets* ("Jack o'Lanterns") Op.23/4. Prokofieff: *March*
from *The Love of Three Oranges.* Raff: *La Fileuse* ("The Spinner"). Schumann: *Nachtstück* Op.23/4; *Romance* Op.28/2; *Contrabandista* ("The Smug-
gler") (Tausig); *Widmung* ("Dedication") (Liszt). Shostakovitch: *Polka* from
the ballet *L'Age d'or.* Smetana: *Polka* Op.7. Weber: *Momento capriccioso*
Op.12. Most of the music is showy and difficult but highly effective. Int. to D.

Essential Keyboard Repertoire

Vol. 1 (Olson—Alfred 501c) 143pp. 100 Early Intermediate selections in
their original form, baroque to modern. CD and cassette tape available.

Vol. 2 (Olson—Alfred 503) 143pp. 75 Intermediate selections in their
original form, baroque to modern. CD and cassette tape available.

Vol. 3 (Olson, Hilley—Alfred 505) 152pp. 16 Popular sonatinas in their
original form. Early-late intermediate. CD and cassette tape available.

Vol. 4 (Hinson—Alfred 4556) 128pp. 85 selections in their original form,
baroque to modern. Divided into three levels: Early intermediate, intermediate, late intermediate. 2 CDs and 2 cassette tapes available.

Vol. 5 (Hinson—Alfred 4574) 161pp. Requiring a Handspan of an Octave
or Less. 85 Intermediate Level selections in their original form, baroque to
modern. Divided into three levels: early intermediate, intermediate, late intermediate.

Vol. 6 (Hinson—Alfred 4597) 144pp. 75 Early to Late Intermediate selections in their original form, baroque to modern. Divided into three levels:
early intermediate, intermediate, late intermediate.

Vol. 7 (Palmer—Alfred 2093) 160pp. 85 Early Intermediate Selections
Spanning Seven Centuries.

Vol. 8 (Hinson—Alfred 4619) 143pp. 95 Early-Late Intermediate Miniatures One or Two Pages in Length, Baroque to Modern, in their original

form. Divided into three levels: early intermediate, intermediate, late intermediate.

Five Eighteenth-Century Sonatas (Stoddard Lincoln—OUP 1975). Johann Samuel Schroeter (ca.1752–1788), *Sonata* Op.1/1 C: three movements; expressive slow movement; could almost have been written by J. C. Bach. Johann Jacob Paul Küffner (1727–1786), *Sonata*: two movements; displays refined taste and a gift for creating sensitive and subtle melodies. Leopold Anton Kozeluch (1747–1818), *Sonata* Op.2/3 c: slow, symphonic introduction returns at the end of the first movement; this is perhaps the finest work in the collection. Christian Ignatius Latrobe (1757–1836), *Sonata* Op.3/1 A: four movements; well constructed and charming. Jacob Kirkman (?–1812?), *Sonata* Op.3/3 E♭: two movements; fuses development and recapitulation in the main Allegro. (Kirkman's Op.3 is a collection of Six Lessons in an unusual arrangement of three neo-Handelian suites and three more modern sonatas in a true piano style.) These works, all dating from the 1780s, form a valuable addition to the repertoire of the early piano. They display characteristics of the English and Viennese styles. The increasing interest in the field is well served by illuminating comments on the music, its interpretation, and the types of instruments that were used. Sources are listed, and editorial marks are easily identified. An altogether fine collection of unknown and rarely heard music that can be most effectively realized on the fortepiano. M-D.

Folies d'Espagne (F. Goebels—Schott). Three sets of variations based on *La Folia*. Bernardo Pasquini: simple elaboration of harmonic scheme. Alessandro Scarlatti: more brilliant figuration. C. P. E. Bach: finest of the three, some expressive writing. M-D.

Four Keyboard Sonatas by Early English Women Composers (S. Fortino—Hildegarde). Includes Elizabeth Weichsell Billington (ca. 1765–1818): written at age 8. Cécilia Maria Barthelemon (1770–?): dedicated to Haydn. Veronica Dussek Cianchettini (1779–1833): with variations on "Adeste Fidelis." Maria Hester Parke (Beardsmore) (1775–1822). Int. to M-D.

Four Hundred Years of European Keyboard Music (W. Georgii—Arno Volk). Vol.I of the Anthology of Music Series. Includes a historical introduction, suggestions on performance, list of sources consulted, over 50 pieces representing 47 composers from Johann Kotter (ca. 1485–1541) to Schönberg. Includes works not often performed and some not easily found in other editions. Some works by Kotter, B. Schmid, Byrd, Bull, Purcell, Couperin, Rameau, Poglietti, Scarlatti, Martini, Galuppi, Paradisi, Froberger, Pachelbel, Kuhnau, Buxtehude, Böhm, Fischer, Muffat, Telemann, Bach, Handel, sons of Bach, Schobert, Wagenseil, Clementi: *Sonata* A, Op.50/1; Haydn: *Presto* D; Mozart: *Adagio* b; Beethoven, Op.126/4, 5; Weber: *Menuet* from Op.24; Schubert: *Allegretto* c; Schumann Op.16/1, 4; Mendelssohn: Op.7/1; Brahms: Op.118/2; Chopin: Op.68/4; Smetana: Op.13/1; Mussorgsky: *In the Village*; Liszt: *Provenzal*; *Christmas Song*; Grieg: *Norwegian Spring Dance*; Debussy: *Clair de Lune*; Scriabin: Op.51/4; Reger: Op.143/3; Hindemith: *Sonata* I; C. Scott: *Rainbow Trout*; Schönberg: Op.19/2. Int. to M-D.

Great Women Composers (Gail Smith—Mel Bay). 27 works by 11 composers from Hildegard von Bingen (d. 1179) to Gail Smith. Also includes Elizabeth-Claude Jacquet de La Guerre, Amy Beach, Cécile Chaminade, Lili Boulanger, Clara Schumann, Maria Szymanowska, Fanny Mendelssohn Hensel. Int. to M-D.

Humor in Piano Music. Character and Content (Hinson—Alfred 4526) 96pp. Baroque to Modern. Section on Humor in Music (what makes some music amusing?); Suggested Teaching Order. Bartók: *Bear Dance* Sz.39. Beethoven: *Bagatelle* C Op.33/2, *Ecossiase* Wo023; *The Rage over the Lost Penny* Op.129. Debussy: *Doctor Gradus ad Parnassum; Jimbo's Lullaby; The Toy Box; Le petit Nègre.* Farnaby: *His Humour.* Grieg: *Humoreske* Op.6/3. Haydn: *Moderato from Sonata B♭*, Hob.XVI: 2; *Presto from Sonata G* Hob.XVI: 40; *Presto, ma non troppo from Sonata D* Hob.XVI: 37. Joplin: *Gladiolus Rag.* Kirchner: *Humoresque* Op.29/3. Prokofiev: *March of the Grasshoppers* Op.65/7. Ravel: *In the Style of Borodin.* Satie: *Silly Pranks.* D. Scarlatti: *Sonata B♭* K.248. Schumann: *Whims* Op.12/4. Shostakovich: *Prelude* Op.34/17. Description of each piece describes how humor is created. Int. to M-D.

An Introduction to Pianistic Styles (Motchane—Bourne) 3 books, each 39pp. 1. Pre-classic Style: an introduction for elementary levels using examples by Bach, Corelli, Couperin, and others. 2. Classical: examples by Clementi, Haydn, Mozart, Beethoven, and others. 3. Romantic: examples by Brahms, Chopin, Grieg, Schubert, and others. Each piece is a paradigm of its composer's style. Easy to M-D.

Introduction to the Keyboard Sonatina (Halford—Alfred 2218) 64pp. Discusses the age of the sonata, the classical era, the keyboard sonatina, sonatina form, ornamentation, other performance practices, performance style. Includes works by Attwood, Beczwarzowsky, Beethoven, Benda, Biehl, Camidge, Diabelli, Haydn, Hook, Kollmann. Int.

Introduction to the Masterworks (Palmer, Lethco—Alfred 1976). A survey of the major periods: Baroque, classical, Romantic, and modern. Includes works from some of the major composers in each period. Also contains short discussions of musical practices. Includes pieces by J. Clarke, J. S. Bach, F. Couperin, D. Scarlatti, Händel, Haydn, W. A. Mozart, Clementi, Beethoven, Chopin, Schumann, Grieg, Bartók, Satie, Prokofieff, and Palmer. Int.

The Joy of Baroque (D. Agay—YMP 1974). 45 pieces of Baroque keyboard music, mostly written for the harpsichord, but much of it would sound well on the piano. An outstanding survey including many familiar names but some less familiar, such as: Daniel Speer, Johann H. Buttstedt, Valentin Rathgeber, John C. Pepusch, Johann Tischer, Johann Goldberg, Mattia Vento, and Leonardo Leo. A few editorial marks have been added. Int.

The Joy of Classics (D. Agay—YMP). 71 pieces including some time-honored original shorter works from the eighteenth and nineteenth centuries: Scarlatti and Purcell to Brahms and Tschaikowsky. Broad range of selections. Int. to M-D.

The Joy of Romantic Piano (Denes Agay—YMP 1976). A unique collection of appealing solo pieces in their original form, including many unusual works from the nineteenth and early twentieth centuries. Vol.I: Easy to Int. Vol.II: Int. to M-D.

A Keyboard Anthology (H. Ferguson—ABRSM) 1st series: Book 1: 23 pieces from Handel to Schumann. Book 2: 20 pieces from Bach to Tchaikovsky. Book 3: 16 pieces from Couperin to de Severac. Book 4: 10 pieces from Farnaby to Dvorak. Book 5. 10 pieces from Scarlatti to Debussy. Int. 2nd series: Book 1: 21 pieces from John Blow to Alexander Goedicke. Book 2: 19 pieces from Anon. (seventeenth-century) to Genari Karganoff. Book 3: 13 pieces from Telemann to Tchaikovsky. Book 4: 16 pieces from D. Scarlatti to Scriabin. Book 5: 14 pieces from D. Scarlatti to Max Reger. Int. to M-D. Meticulous and tasteful editing. Refreshing choice of literature.

Keyboard Music of the Baroque and Rococo (W. Georgii—Arno Volk).

Vol.I: Music before Bach and Handel. Contains works by Byrd, Bull, Farnaby, Purcell, Sweelinck, Chambonnières, L. Couperin, Le Bègue, Frescobaldi, Pasquini, Poglietti, A. Scarlatti, Froberger, G. Muffat, F. T. Richter, Pachelbel, J. K. F. Fischer, Kuhnau.

Vol.II: Music of Contemporaries of Bach and Handel. Contains works by D. Scarlatti, F. Couperin, Rameau, Daquin, Dandrieu, Telemann, Muffat.

Vol.III: Music after Bach and Handel. Contains works by D. Scarlatti, F. Couperin, Rameau, Méhul, Wagenseil, Schobert, J. C. Bach, W. F. Bach, G. Benda, J. W. Hässler. Int. to M-D.

Keyboard Sonatas of the 18th Century (Smart—GS 1967). Contains sonatas by J. C. Bach, Pleyel, Schobert, Platti, G. Berg, von Ferguson, de Nebra, Holder, Bull, Horsley. Unusual collection. M-D.

Keyboard Works: 4 Baroque Masters (Gresh—GS 1976) 159pp. Works by F. Couperin, Handel, H. Purcell, and D. Scarlatti. M-D.

Klassische Klavier-Sonaten (W. Georgii—Henle 62) 87pp. with fingering added by Georgii, C. Hansen, and W. Lampe. Preface and commentary in English, French, and German. Urtext edition. C. P. E. Bach: *Prussian Sonata* I F. W. A. Mozart: *Sonatas* K.280 F, K.283 G, K.545 C. Beethoven: Op.49/2 G; Op.14/1 E; Op.14/2 G. An appendix contains a possible realization for the Andante of the C. P. E. Bach sonata. Int. to M-D.

Klaviermusik der Romantik (K. Herrmann—Hug 1960). 19 original works by J. P. E. Hartmann. Heller, Jensen, Kirchner, MacDowell, Raff, Smetana, Mussorgsky. M-D.

Der Kreis um Telemann (At the Time of Telemann) (Frey—CFP). 28 dance movements (M, Gavotte, Air, Loure, Rigaudon, etc.) by Dieupart, Marchand, Graupner, Grünewald, Krebs, Muffat, Stölzel, J. S. Bach, Telemann. All are short dances, easier to perform than the suites of Bach and Händel. Some of these works appear in no other contemporary collection. Excellent introduction to musical life in the first half of the eighteenth century. Int.

Leichte Klaviermusik aus zwei Jahrhunderten (W. Georgii—Henle 167/168). Fingering added by Hans-Martin Theopold. Urtext edition.

Vol.I: W. F. Bach: *Fugue* E♭ from 8 Fugues. C. P. E. Bach: *La Stahl*. J. W. Hässler: *Allegro* B♭ from 6 Easy Sonatas. W. A. Mozart: *Andantino* E♭ K.236;

Courante E♭ from fragment of a suite K.399. Beethoven: *Bagatelles* Op.33/6 D and 119/4 A♭. Schubert: *Scherzo* B♭ D.593. R. Schumann: *Eintritt* and *Einsame Blumen* from *Waldszenen* Op.82. Mendelssohn: *Allegretto* G from *Kinderstücke* Op.72. Heller: *Etude* A♭ from 25 Etudes Op.47. A. Jensen: *Intermezzo* G from *Lieder und Tanz* Op.33. Chopin: *Prélude* b Op.28/6; *Mazurka* a Op. posth. 68/2. Liszt: *Hymn de l'enfant à son réveil* from *Harmonies poétiques et réligieuses*. Mussorgski: *Eine Träne* Op.70/8; *Meditation* Op.70/17. Grieg: *Vöglein* from *Lyric Pieces* Op.43. MacDowell: *From an Indian Lodge*; *A Deserted Farm*, from *Woodland Sketches* Op.51. Marko Tajčević: 2 pieces from *Lieder von der Mur-Insel*. Int.
Vol.II: W. F. Bach: *Polonaise* c from 12 Polonaises. C. P. E. Bach: *Abschied vom Silbermannschen Clavier in einem Rondeau*. W. A. Mozart: *Menuett* D K.355. Beethoven: *Bagatelle* C Wo056: Schubert: *Menuett* E♭ from *Sonata* Op. posth. 122, D.568. Mendelssohn: *Allegro non troppo* G from *Kinderstücke* Op.72. R. Schumann: *Walzer, Larghetto und Elfe* from *Albumblätter* Op.124. Chopin: *Nocturne* g Op.37/1; *Muzurka* g Op.24/1; *Waltz* b Op.69/2. Liszt: *Il Pensieroso* from *Années de Pèlerinage*.
Vol.III. Brahms: *Intermezzo* a Op.76/7. Mussorgski: *Im Dorf* Op.70/15. Smetana: *Polka poétique* g Op.8/2. Dvořák: *Humoreske* A♭ Op.101/3. Albeniz: *Zortziko* from *España* Op.165. Milo Cipra (1906–   ): *Alter Tanz* Int. to M-D.
Leichte Klavierstücke des Klassischen und Romantischen Zeitalters (W. Georgii —Henle 134/135). Fingering added by W. Georgii, W. Lampe, and Hans-Martin Theopold. Urtext. Preface and commentary in French, German, and English.
Vol.I: Türk: *Elf Handstücke für angehande Klavierspieler*. W. A. Mozart: *Menuetts* G K.1, F K.2, F K.5, and A♭ K.Anh. 109 b No.8; *Allegro* B♭ K.3. Clementi: *Sonatinas* C Op.36/1 and G Op.36/2. J. W. Hässler: 9 pieces from Op.38. J. Haydn: *Sonata* G Hob.XVI/8; *Sonata* C Hob.XVI/7. Beethoven: *Allegro* C Wo051; *Lustig und traurig* Wo054; *Bagatelles* F Op.33/3 and g Op.119/1. Schubert: *Ecossaise* Op.18/4 D.145; *Waltzes* Op. posth. 127/15 D.146, Op.9/3 D.365, and Op.9/16 D.365; *Ländler* Op.67/5 D.734; *Deutscher Tanz* Op.33/2 D.783. R. Schumann: *Album for the Young* Op.68/2, 10, 14, 16; *Wiegenliedchen* Op.124/6. Easy to Int.
Vol.II: Fingering by W. Georgii, W. Gieseking, W. Lampe, and H. Keller. J. W. Hässler: 6 pieces from Op.49. W. A. Mozart: *Sonata* movement g K.312; *Marcia* C K.408. Beethoven: *Menuett* E♭ Wo082; *Für Elise* Wo059. Schubert: *Allegretto* c D.915; *Moments musicaux* f Op.94/3 D.780 and A♭ Op.94/3 D.780. Mendelssohn: *Song without Words* Op.30/3. T. Kirchner: 6 *Präludien* from Op.65. Tchaikovsky: 3 pieces from *Kinderalbum* Op.39. R. Schumann: *Träumerei* Op.15/7; *Phantasientanz* Op.124/5; *Romanze* F♯ Op.28/2. Brahms: *Waltz* E Op.39/2 (easy version). Liszt: *Consolation* I. Chopin: *Préludes* e Op.28/4 and D♭ Op.28/15; *Mazurkas* g Op.33/1 and g Op. posth. 67/2; *Waltzes* a Op.34/2 and f Op. posth. 70/2. Int. to M-D.
Leichte Klaviervariationen aus Barock und Klassik (G. Lorenz—Henle 26) 39pp.

Fingering added by Hans-Martin Theopold. Urtext. Commentary in French, German, and English. Handel: 5 Variations B♭ (the ones Brahms used in his Variations Op.24). C. P. E. Bach: 6 Variations C (first time this set has been printed). J. Chr. Bach: 4 Variations G Op.5/3. J. Haydn: Variations E♭ Hob.XVII/3. W. A. Mozart: 7 Variations on "Willem van Nassau" K.25. Beethoven: 9 Variations on "Quant'è più bello" by Paisiello, Wo069. Int. to M-D.

Lied- und Tanzvariationen der Sweelinck-Schule (Werner Brieg—Schott). Song and dance variations by Sweelinck and other composers of the "Sweelinck School."

Masters before J. S. Bach (Hermann—CFP 4451) 36pp. 34 pieces by composers from seventeenth-century Germany, France, England, and Italy, such as F. Couperin, Frescobaldi, Froberger, Loeillet, Purcell, Sweelinck, Zipoli. Int.

Masters of Impressionism. A Guide to Style and Interpretation (Hinson—Alfred 455) 64pp. Includes a discussion of Impressionism, musical techniques, and information about each piece. Bartók: *Dawn* Sz.39/7. Chopin: *Mazurka* a Op.17/4. Debussy: *Arabesque I; Bruyères; The Girl with the Flaxen Hair; Footprints in the Snow; Voiles; Gardens in the Rain.* Grieg: *Bell Ringing* Op.54/6. Liszt: *Evening Bells* G.186/9. Palmgren: *May Night* Op.27/4. Ravel: *Sad Birds.* Scott: *Lotus Land.* Scriabin: *Desire* Op.57. Int. to M-D.

Masters of Piano Program Music (Hinson—Alfred 4572) 64pp. Foreword, a brief history and description of piano program music, and discussion of each piece. J. S. Bach: *Theme that Imitates Hens' Cackling and Cuckoos' Cries* BWV 963. Brahms: *Intermezzo* E♭ Op.117/1. Chopin: *Berceuse* Op.57. Debussy: *To Invoke Pan, God of the Summer Wind.* Gottschalk: *O My Charmer, Spare Me.* Granados: *Enchanted Palace in the Sea—Legend.* Grieg: *Bridal Procession* Op.19/2. Liszt: *Eglogue* S.160. MacDowell: *To the Sea* Op.55/1. Mussorgsky: *The Old Castle.* Saint-Saëns: *Evening Bells* Op.85. Satie: *Fishing.* Schumann: *Playing Tag* WoO 16/3. Tchaikovsky: *November* Op.37b/11. Int. to M-D.

Masters of Polyphonic Piano Music. A Guide to Style and Interpretation (Hinson—Alfred 435) 64pp. Foreword plus a discussion of types of polyphonic piano music and of each piece. J. S. Bach: *Bourrée* BWV 831/8; *Gavotte* BWV 816/4; *Invention 13* a BWV 784; *Little Prelude* BWV 941. W. F. Bach: *Fuga* D. Bartók: *Canon* Sz.42; *Two Conversations* Sz.52. Beethoven: *Fuga, Piano Piece for Ferdinand Piringer* WoO61; *Presto from Sonata* F Op.10/2. Brahms: *Sarabande.* Chopin: *Mazurka* c♯ Op.63/3. Fischer: *Fugue* C. Franck: *Canon.* Handel: *Air; Allemande; Fugue; Moderato; Passepied.* Haydn: *Minuetto al rovescio* from *Sonata* A Hob.XVI: 26. Hiller: *Duet.* Kabalevsky: *Dance* Op.27/15; *Twins* Op.39/7. Kirnberger: *Chimes.* Lindemann: *Anglaise.* Mozart: *Courante* K.399; *Menuet* K.94. Nichelmann: *Polonaise.* Pachelbel: *Gigue.* Rachmaninoff: *Fugal Sketch.* Reger: *Kanon.* Schubert: *Valse Sentimentale* D.779/13. Schumann: *Canonic Song* Op.68/27; *Waltz in Canonic Style.* Stanley: *Invention.* Weber: *A Little Fugue.* Int. to M-D.

Masters of the Character Piece: A Guide to Style and Interpretation (Hinson—Alfred 1856) 48pp. A brief history of the character piece and a discussion of each piece. C. P. E. Bach: *Les Lagueurs tendres* Wq.117: 30. Brahms: *Ballade* d Op.10/1. Chopin: *Prelude* g Op.28/22. Debussy: *Clair de lune.* Fibich: *Morgenunterhaltung* (Morning Conversation). Field: *Nocturne II* c. Franck: *Prayer.* Heller: *Prelude* e Op.81/4. Hüttenbrenner: *Lamentation on Schubert's Death by His Friend.* Jensen: *Evensong* Op.33 Book II, No.4. Liszt: *Sonetto 123 del Petrarca* S.161/6. MacDowel *Smouldering Embers* Op.61/6. Mendelssohn: *Hunting Song* Op.19/3. \ *: Le Piccadilly.* Schumann: *Entrance into the Forest* Op.82/1. Sjögren: *Elegy on the Motif e b b a* Op.41. Smetana: *Innocence.* R. Strauss: *Traümerei* Op.9/4. Int. to M-D.

Masters of the Classical Period. A Guide to Style and Interpretation (Hinson— Alfred 1199) 64pp. Foreword includes a discussion of classical style and tempo, the difference between the fortepiano and the pianoforte, and performance practice: ornaments, dynamics, pedal, etc. Beethoven: *Bagatelle* B♭ Op.119/11; *Bagatelle* C WoO56; *Six Variations* Op.76. Clementi: *Sonatina* G Op.36/5; *Allegretto moderato* (6th edition), *Sonata* B♭ Op.24/2; *Rondo.* Haydn: *Adagio* F Hob.XVII: 9; *Partita (Sonata)* G Hob. XVI: 6. Mozart: *Adagio* b K.540; *March funèbre del Signor Maestro Contrapunto* K. 453a. Schubert: *Hungarian Melody* D.817; *Impromptu* A♭ Op.142/2; *Moments musicaux* Op.94/3. Int. to M-D.

Masters of the Piano Ballade. A Guide to Style and Interpretation (Hinson— Alfred 513) 64pp. Includes a foreword, a discussion of the ballade, and notes for performance. Arensky: *Little Ballade* Op.36/4. Bartók: *Ballade* (from 15 *Hungarian Peasant Songs*). Brahms: *Ballade* Op.10/4. Chopin: *Ballade II* Op.38. Debussy: *Ballade.* Grieg: *Ballade* Op.65/5. Liszt: *Ballade I* (Song of the Crusader) G.170. Schumann: *Balladenmässig.* Int. to M-D.

Masters of the Piano Fantasy. A Guide to Style and Interpretation (Hinson— Alfred 751) 64pp. Includes Foreword, history of the fantasy, and a discussion of each piece. C. P. E. Bach: *Fantasia* d Wq.117/12. J. S. Bach: *Fantasia* g BWV 917. Bartók: *Fantasy* No.2. Brahms: *Phantasie* (Intermezzo a) Op.116/2. Haydn: *Fantasia* C Hob.XVII: 4. Mendelssohn: *Fantasia on "The Last Rose of Summer"* Op.15. W. A. Mozart: *Fantasie* c K.475. Rachmaninoff: *Fantasy Piece.* Franz Schubert: *Fantasy* c D.993. Schumann: *Fantasiestück: Aufschwung* Op.12/2. Scriabin: *Poème fantasque* Op.45/2. Sources listed. Int. to M-D.

Masters of the Romantic Period. A Guide to Style and Interpretation (Hinson— Alfred 1183) 64pp. Foreword plus a discussion of the Romantic Period and performance suggestions for each piece. Berlioz: *Rustic Serenade on the theme of the Roman Pifferari.* Brahms: *Ballade* D Op.10/2; *Intermezzo* Op.116/6. Chopin: *Etude* A♭ from *Three New Etudes; Mazurka* f Op.63/2; *The Wish* Op.74/1. Field: *Nocturne V* (new edition). Liszt: *Consolation III* D♭ G.172/3; *Il Penseroso* G.161/2. Mendelssohn: *Andante and Rondo Capriccioso* Op.14. Schumann: *Fantastic Dance* Op.124/5; *Night Piece* Op.23/4; *Romance* Op.28/2. Int. to M-D.

Masters of the Sonatina

Vol. I (Hinson—Alfred 2206) 31pp. Introduction, brief analysis of the keyboard sonatina, articulation and notation guides, and biographical notes on each composer. Bertini: *Sonatina* C. Biehl: *Sonatina* G Op.57/4. Diabelli: *Sonatina* F. Duncombe: *Sonatina* C. Gurlitt: *Sonatina* C. Kabalevsky: *Sonatina* a Op.27/11. Le Couppey: *Sonatina* C. Pleyel: *Sonatina* C. Reinecke: *Sonatina* F. Spindler: *Sonatina* C. Steibelt: *Sonatina* a. Vanhal: *Sonatina* F. S. Wesley: *Sonatina* D. Early-Int.

Vol. II (Hinson—Alfred 2207) 32pp. C. P. E. Bach: *Sonatina* E Wq.63/8. Beethoven: *Sonatina* F Anh.5/2. Benda: *Sonatina* G. Camidge: *Sonatina* G. Cimarosa: *Sonatina* B♭. Czerny: *Sonatina* C Op.163. Haslinger: *Sonatina* C. Khachaturian: *Sonatina*. Paganelli: *Sonatina* A. Int.

Vol. III (Hinson—Alfred 2208) 63pp. Bartók: *Sonatina*. Cimarosa: *Sonatina* g. Clementi: *Sonatina* D Op.36/6 (5th edition). Handel: *Sonatina* a. Haydn: *Sonatina* C Hob.XVI: 7. Hewitt: *Sonatina* D. Jones: *Sonatina* C. Kabalevsky: *Sonatina* a Op.13/1. Mozart: *Sonatina* C. Mysliveček: *Sonatina* D. E. D. Wagner: *Sonatina* C Op.67/1. Late-Int.

Masters of the Sonatina (EMB) Book I: 18 lesser-known sonatinas of Vanhal, Benda, Kohler, Camidge, Hook, Cimarosa, Andre, Diabelli. Book II: 10 sonatinas by Kuhlau, Diabelli, Benda, Cimarosa, Handel. Both books are fingered and well edited. Int.

Masters of the Suite. A Guide to Style and Interpretation (Hinson—Alfred 1800) 64pp. Foreword, short history of the suite, and discussion of each movement of each suite. J. S. Bach: *Suite* f BWV823. Handel: *Suite 13* B♭. Mozart: *Suite* C K.399. Purcell: *Suite* I G Z.660. Satie: *Chapters Turned Every Which Way*. Schumann: *Forest Scenes* Op.82. Int. to M-D.

Masters of the Theme and Variations. A Guide to Style and Interpretation (Hinson —Alfred 2209) 64pp. A brief history of variation as a form, techniques and types of variation, and discussion of each piece. C. P. E. Bach: *Variations on the Song "I Slept, Then I Dreamed."* Bartók: *Variations on a Slovakian Folk Tune* Sz.42/II/5. Beethoven: *Six Variations on a Swiss Song* WoO64; *Six Variations on the Duet "Nell cor più non mi sento"* WoO70. Dussek: *Menuet* G. Granados: *Theme, Variations and Finale*. Handel: *Sarabande* d. Haydn: *Air with Variations from "La Roxolane" Symphony* Hob.I: 63/2. Hummel: *Tyrolean Variations*. Kuhlau: *Variations on an Austrian Folk Song*. Mozart: *Six Variations on an Allegretto* K.54. Müller: *Allegretto with Variations*. Pachelbel: *Gavotte* a. Schumann: *Quasi Variazioni on a Theme by Clara Wieck* Op.14. Int. to M-D.

The Mediterranean Baroque (Gabor—EMB Z8972 1980) 42pp. M. Rossi: *Andantino-Allegro* G. B. Pasquini: *Sonata* d. Durante: *Sonata* D. D. Scarlatti: *Sonata* F, K.85. Zipoli: *Preludie e Corrente* b. Pescetti: *Allegro* C. Soler: *Sonatas*, e, G. Freivanet: *Sonata* A. J. de S. Carvalho: *Toccata* g. Jacinto: *Sonata* d. Seixas: *Sonata* f. Int. to M-D.

Meister der Romantik—Leichte Klavierstücke (W. Weismann—Litolff CL5033) 32pp. 24 short pieces by Brahms, Chopin, Grieg, Mendelssohn, Schubert,

Schumann, Smetana, Tchaikovsky, and Weber. Contains some unusual literature, e.g., Brahms: *Sarabande* a; *Sandmännchen*. Smetana: *L'Innocence*. Schubert: *Theme* E. Int.

More German Masters of the 18th Century (K 9543). Seven complete works by Benda, Hasse, Telemann, etc. M-D.

More Select Sonatinas (Podolsky—Belwin-Mills) 3 vols. Useful for students not ready to play Haydn and Mozart sonatas. Int.

New Recital Repertoire by Masters of the 17th, 18th, and 19th Centuries (A. Mirovitch—EV). Telemann: *Fantasies* D, B♭. J. Pachelbel: *Fugue* c. F. J. Kuhnau: *Prelude* b. J. C. Bach: *Allegretto* from *Sonata* Op.5/1; *Tempo di Minuetto* from *Sonata* Op.5/5; Giovanni Giornovichi (1745–1804): *Tempo di Gavotta* (arr. for piano by S. Dussek). J. F. Reichardt: *Aria*. M. Clementi: *Waltz* No.24. J. L. Dussek: *Larghetto, Quasi Andante*. J. Haydn: *La Roxolane* (Air Varié). An unusual collection of repertoire for Int. level.

Nine Little Lyric Pieces of the 19th and 20th Centuries (H. Kreutzer—BMC). 12pp. Z. Fibich: *In the Morning*. A. Gretchaninoff: *An Ancient Poem* Op.119/2. E. Grieg: *Cradle Song for Gjendine* Op.66/19. S. Heller: *Prelude* Op.81/4. D. Kabalevsky: *Lullaby*. T. Kirchner: *Miniature* Op.62/8. R. Schumann: *Little Folk Song* Op.68/9. D. Shostakovitch: *Romanze*. E. Sjögren: *Elegy* on the name "EBBA" Op.41. Int.

Nineteenth-Century European Piano Music (John Gillespie—Dover 1977) 343pp. M. Clementi: *Exercises* 12–15 of *Gradus ad Parnassum*. C. Czerny: *Song without Words* Op.795/1; *Etude mélodieuse* Op.795/3; *Toccata* C Op.92. J. L. Dussek: *Sonata* A♭ Op.70 ("The Return to Paris"). A. Dvořák: Nos.1–6 *Silhouetten* Op.8. G. Fauré: *Thème et Variations* Op.73. J. Field: *Nocturnes* Nos.2 c, 4 A. N. Gade: *Arabeske* Op.27. E. Granados: selections from *Spanish Dances*. S. Heller: *Drei deutsche Tänze*; *Toccatina*. J. N Hummel: *Variations sur un thème d'Armide de Gluck* Op.57. Short, distinctive, and idiomatic works not often found in other anthologies. Includes bibliographic references and translations of tempi. M-D.

Old Masters of the 17th and 18th Centuries (W. Niemann—CFP).

Vol.1: England, France, Italy. 11 pieces. Byrd: *The Bells*. Bull: *King's Hunting Jigg*. Couperin: *Little Windmills*. Daquin: *Cuckoo*. Durante: *Studio*. Frescobaldi: *Due Canzone*. Galuppi: *Sonata* D. Marchand: *Gavotte*. Martini: *Gavotte*. Paradisi: *Sonata* A.

Vol.2: Germany. 19 pieces. Böhm: *Presto*. Fischer: *Praeludium and Rondeau; Sarabande; Praeludium and Chaconne*. Froberger: *Suite* (Variations) "Auf die Mayerin"; *2 sarabandes; Toccata*. Graun: *Gigue*. Kerll: *Capriccio* "Cucu"; *Canzone*. Kirnberger: 6 pieces.

Vol.3: Germany. 15 pieces. Krieger: *Partita* No.11. Kuhnau: *Prelude and Gigue; Bourrée; Gavotte; Presto*. Marpurg: *Menuet; La Badine; La Voltigeuse*. Mattheson: *Allemande*. Muffat: *Air; Menuet*. Pachelbel: *Fugue on the Magnificat*. Murschhauser: *Aria pastoralis variata*. Scheidt: *Passamezzo Variations*. M-D.

Organum. Series 5, Piano Music (K&S). Each number is available separately. 1.

Muzio Clementi: *Sonate* C. 2. Carl Philipp Emanuel Bach: *Sonata* G. 3. Johann Ladislaus Dussek: *Sonata* g, Op.10/2. 4. Muzio Clementi: *Sonata* B♭, Op.10/3. 5. Leopold Anton Kozeluch: *Sonata* E♭, Op.51/2. 6. Johann Ladislaus Dussek: *Sonata* E♭ (The Farewell), Op.44. 7. Ernst Wilhelm Wolf: Two easy *Sonatas* d, E♭. 8. Johann Nepomuk Hummel: *Variations on a Theme from Gluck's Armida*. 9. Daniel Gottlob Türk: *Sonata* e. 10. Johann Baptist Cramer: *Les menus plaisirs*. 11. Johann Nikolaus Forkel: *Sonata* D. 12. Johann Ladislaus Dussek: *Sonata* B♭, Op.45/1. 13. Daniel Gottlob Türk: *Sonata* C. 14. Daniel Steibelt: *Rondo* C. 15. Muzio Clementi: *Sonata* g, Op.7/3. 16. Muzio Clementi: *Sonata* f, Op.14/3. 17. Johann Nikolaus Forkel: *Sonata* d. 18. Muzio Clementi: *Sonata* B♭, Op.14/1. 19. Daniel Gottlob Türk: *Sonata* a. 20. Muzio Clementi: *Sonata* b, Op.40/2. 21. Ernst Wilhelm Wolf: Two easy *Sonatas*, G, F. 22. Johann Ladislaus Dussek: *Sonata* c, Op.35/3. 23. Leopold Anton Kozeluch: *Sonata* d, Op.51/3. 24. Daniel Gottlob Türk: *Sonata* D. 25. Ernst Wilhelm Wolf: Two easy *Sonatas* c. 26. Johann Wilhelm Hässler: Two easy *Sonatas*. 27. Wilhelm Friedemann Bach: *Solo Concerto* G. 28. Johann Wilhelm Hässler: Two easy *Sonatas*. 29. Johann Gottfried Müthel: *Sonata* B♭ with six Variations. 30. Johann Wilhelm Hässler: Two easy *Sonatas*. 31. Wilhelm Friedemann Bach: *Fantasie* C.

Original Airs and Dances—A Collection of Short and Easy Eighteenth Century Pieces (H. Kreutzer—BMC) 23pp. J. S. Bach: *Bourrée; Gigue; For Anna Magdalena; Aria*. J. C. F. Bach: *Menuet*. Christoph Graupner: *Air en Gavotte*. G. F. Handel: *Menuet; Passepied*. J. W. Hässler: *Allegro*. Leopold Mozart: 6 pieces from *Notebook for Wolfgang*. W. A. Mozart: *Menuet* from Violin Sonata K.6; *Air* E♭; *Menuet* B♭; *Menuet* F; *Andante; Contretanz* G. Easy to Int.

Oxford Keyboard Classics (OUP). Howard Ferguson, general editor of the series. Based on the same didactic method of presentation as Ferguson's *Style and Interpretation* volumes. Each volume is devoted to a roughly chronological selection of works, edited from original MSS and first editions by a great keyboard composer. Each volume also provides an essay on the composer's stylistic background together with detailed notes on each work. See individual volumes listed under composers: J. S. Bach, Haydn, Liszt, Schubert.

The Performer's Analysis (Robert Dumm—Schroeder & Gunther 1972) 22pp. A series of analytic-interpretive lessons of piano masterworks. J. S. Bach: *Scherzo* S.844; *Minuet* S.843. G. F. Handel: *Capriccio*. M. Mussorgsky: *Niania and I*, Op. posth./1 from *Souvenirs d'enfance*. R. Glière: *Album Leaf* Op.31/11. E. MacDowell: *An Elfin Round*, Op.7/6 from *Six Fancies*. Each piece is carefully analyzed, and directions for study are most helpful. A fine series. Int.

Le Petit Classique (M. Morhange-Motchane—Sal) 30pp. 22 short pieces from the Baroque and classical periods, each with technical exercises. Directions in French and English. Easy to Int.

Le Petit Romantique (M. Morchange-Motchane—Sal) 39pp. 20 short pieces from this period, each with technical exercises. Familiar and unfamiliar works. Int.

The Pianist's Book of Baroque Treasures (Banowetz—GWM GP 330) 79pp. Works by Arne, C. P. E. Bach, J. C. Bach. J. S. Bach, W. F. Bach, Buxtehude, L. Couperin, Daquin, Handel, Platti, Rameau, D. Scarlatti, Seixas, Soler. Fingered, editorial additions indicated in brackets. Includes colorful biographies of the composers and a running commentary throughout the volume. Excellent edition. Int. to M-D.

The Pianist's Book of Early Contemporary Treasures (Banowetz—GWM GP 334) 78pp. Works by Bartók, Debussy, Dohnányi, Kabalevsky, Kodály, Nielsen, Prokofieff, Rachmaninoff, Ravel, Satie, Scriabin, Shostakovitch, Strauss, Tcherepnin. Fingered, editorial additions in brackets. Includes colorful biographies and pictures of the composers and a running commentary throughout the volume. Int. to M-D.

The Pianist's Book of Early Romantic Treasures (Banowetz—GWM) 80pp. Works by Chopin, Field, Gottschalk, Heller, Kalkbrenner, Liszt, Mendelssohn, Schumann, Weber. Includes some popular teaching pieces and unfamiliar works. Fingered, editorial additions in brackets. Includes colorful biographies and pictures of the composers and a running commentary throughout the volume. Int. to M-D.

The Pianist's Book of Late Romantic Treasures (Banowetz—GWM 333) 79pp. Works by Albéniz, Brahms, Dvořák, Fauré, Franck, Grieg, MacDowell, Mussorgsky, Saint-Säens, Smetana, Tchaikovsky. Fingered, editorial additions in brackets. Includes colorful biographies and pictures of the composers and a running commentary throughout the volume. Int. to M-D.

The Piano and Its Ancestors (F. Gunther—AMP). 14 selected works from 1563 to 1800 by Scheidt, J. S. Bach, C. P. E. Bach, Bull, Farnaby, Purcell, Rameau, Couperin, Telemann, W. F. Bach, Haydn, Mozart. One page of photographs of early keyboard instruments. Brief biographies and notes about the pieces. Int.

Piano Literature (Glover, Hinson—Belwin Mills 1984) 4 vols. Each volume contains original compositions by masters from the baroque, classical, Romantic, and contemporary periods. Includes both familiar and unfamiliar works. Easy to Int.

Piano Master Lessons with Jerome Rose (CPP/Belwin). Compiled in collaboration with Joanne Smith. Includes cassette of the pieces with commentary on form, style, and interpretation of each piece. Beethoven: *Allegretto.* Mozart: *Six Variations on an Allegretto* K.54. Saint-Saëns: *Romance sans Paroles.* Scriabin: *Prelude* Op.11/13. M-D.

Piano Music of the Parisian Virtuosos 1810–1860 (J. Kallberg—Garland Publishing 1993) 10 vols. "Throughout the first part of the 19th century, Paris was a mecca for pianists. Not only the likes of Chopin and Liszt, but such then-renowned figures as Thalberg, Kalkbrenner, Herz, and Moscheles found their way to the French capital. Pianos, pianists, and piano music captured the attention of the 19th-century Parisian musical public to a degree scarcely imaginable today. With the exception of such major figures as Chopin and Liszt, most of the piano music written by the virtuosos of this epoch remains accessible only in specialized collections of various European and

American libraries. The present series corrects this situation by making available a large and fascinating selection of piano music published in Paris between roughly 1810 and 1860. Reproducing over 180 pieces, its sampling is truly representative. The series spans operatic fantasies, rondos, and sonatas, a wide array of such briefer genres as the nocturne, romance, barcarolle, mazurka, waltz and polonaise, a number of extended sets of etudes and preludes, and a sprinkling of unusual or curious genres. The series surveys a wide gradation of pianistic technique, from the fiendishly difficult to the relatively simple and reveals the range of compositional skills possessed by the virtuosos" (from the Introduction).

Vols. 1, 2: Sigismond Thalberg (1812–1871). *Selected Works.* "These volumes offer an abundant selection of compositions by the pianist generally regarded, along with Liszt, as the greatest virtuoso of his time. While perhaps best known today for his operatic fantasies (with their famous third hand technique featuring melodies surrounded above and below by arpeggios and other virutosic passage work), Thalberg in fact worked in a wide array of genres, including the caprice, nocturne, romance, scherzo, ballade, barcarolle, and sonata. All the different facets of Thalberg's compositional career are represented here" (from the Preface).

Vol. I: *Grande Fantaisie sur des motifs de l'Opéra Norma* Op.12. *Grande Fantaisie et Variations sur deux motifs de l'Opera Don Juan* Op.14. *1er Caprice* Op.15. *Deux Nocturnes* Op.16. *2 Airs Russes Variés* Op.17. *Les Soirées Musicales, Divertissement sur des motifs favoris de Rossini* Op.18. *Trois Nocturnes* Op.21. *Grande Fantaisie* Op.22. *Sept Romances* Op.25. *Nocturne* Op.28. *Scherzo* Op.31. *Andante* Op.32. *Grand Nocturne* Op.35. *Impromptu en forme d'Étude* Op.36. *Mi Manca la Voce: Quatour de Rossini. Romance et Étude* Op.38. *Souvenirs de Beethoven, Grande fantaisie sur la 7e Symphonie de Beethoven* Op.39. *3 Romances. Grande Fantaisie sur La Sérénade et Le Menuet de Don Juan* Op.42. *Andante Final de Lucie de Lamermoor Varié* Op.43. *Thème et Étude en La Mineur* Op.45. *Graziosa, Romance sans paroles. La Romanesca fameux air de danse du XVIe siècle. 6 Romances sans paroles.*

Vol. II: *Fantaisie sur l'Opéra Lucrezia Borgia* Op.50. *Nocturne* Op.51bis. *Le Départ, Fantaisie-Étude* Op.55. *Grande Sonate* Op.56 [sic]. *Décaméron*: No.4, *Fantaisie sur Norma*; No.5, *Fantaisie sur des mélodies de F. Schubert* Op.57. *Marche Funèbre Variée* Op.59. *Barcarolle* Op.60. *Grande Fantaisie sur le Barbier de Seville* Op.63. *Souvenir de Pesth, Airs Hongrois Variés* Op.65. *Tarentelle* Op.56 [sic]. *Fantaisie sur la Fille du Régiment* Op.68. *The last Rose of Summer, Air Irlandais Varié* Op.73. *Ballade* Op.76. *Il Trovatore, Fantaisie pour piano* Op.78. *Romance Dramatique* Op.79. *La Napolitaine Danse* Op.80. *Un Ballo in Maschera, Fantaisie pour piano* Op.81. *Rigoletto Opéra de Verdi, Souvenir pour le piano* Op.82.

Vol. 3: Fredric Kalkbrenner (1785–1849). *Selected Works.* "One of the most powerful figures in Parisian musical life after settling there in 1824, Kalkbrenner so strongly influenced the course of piano playing that the young

Chopin once aspired to study with him. This volume reproduces a selection of compositions written throughout his career" (from the Preface). *Trois Grandes Sonates* Op.4. *1ʳᵉ Fantaisie Avec Six Variations sur l'Air: Il Pleut Bergère* Op.5. *Troisième Fantaisie Suivie d'une Fugue* Op.8. *Effusio Musica: Grande Fantaisie* Op.68. *24 Préludes dans tous les Tons* Op.88. *Romance et Rondo Brillant* Op.96. *La Brigantine: Fantaisie Romantique* Op.103. *Caprice* Op.104. *Les Soupirs: Deux Romances* Op.121. *La Crainte et L'Espérance: Rondo Brillant* Op.130. *Le Fou: Scène Dramatique* Op.136. *Causerie de Jeunes Filles: Pensée Fugitive. Grande Sonate* Op.177. *Les Nationalités musicales: Six Esquissess* Op.184. *3 Nocturnes de Salon* Op.187. *3 Romances sans paroles*, Op.189.

Vol. 4: Henri Herz (1803–1888). *Selected Works.* "Epitome of the 19th-century pianist-entrepreneur, favorite whipping boy of the critic Schumann, author of a defamation suit against the publisher Maurice Schlesinger, Henri Herz elicits more commentary on his flamboyant reputation than on his music. This volume offers a corrective in the form of a sampling of works from his long career, including several written during his tours of the Americas" (from the Preface). *Rondo alla Cosacca* Op.2. *Fantaisie et Rondeau brillant sur La Zelmira* Op.12. *Primo Divertimento* Op.15. *Exercises et Préludes* Op.21. *Polonaise Brillante* Op.25. *1ᵉʳ Caprice* Op.32. *Grandes Variations Sur le Choeur des Grecs du Siège de Corinthe* Op.36. *Rondo-Capriccio sur la Barcarolle Favorite de la Muette de Portici* Op.44. *Trois Nocturnes Caractéristiques* Op.45. *Variations brillantes sur la dernière Valse de C. M. de Weber* Op.51. *Marche et Rondo sur la Clochette de Paganini* Op.63. *Variations brillantes d'une coupe nouvelle* Op.78. *2 Ballades* Op.117. *Variations caractéristiques sur un Thême Arabe* Op.137. *Variations brillantes et grande fantaise sur des airs nationaux américains* Op.158. *Fantaisie méxicaine* Op.162. *La Californienne, Granda Polka Brillante* Op.167. *Le chant du pélerin, Elégie* Op.187. *Rêverie Nocturne* Op.194.

Vol. 5: *Two Bohemians in Paris. Selected Works of Ignaz Moscheles* (1794–1870) and *Alexander Dreyschock* (1818–1896). "Two different generations of Bohemian composers whose works were popular in Paris are represented in this volume. The more senior Moscheles, though by temperament more at ease with the music of Mozart, Hummel, and Beethoven than with that of Chopin, Thalberg, and Liszt, nonetheless wrote in both the older and newer styles. The younger Dreyschock wrote strictly in the newer *brillante* style, and was perhaps best known for his stupendous technique (J. B. Cramer remarked "The man has no left hand! Here are two *right* hands!")" (from the Preface). Moscheles: *Rondo Espagnol* Op.24. *Grande Variations sur un Thême Militaire* Op.32. *La Tenerezza: Rondeau* [Op.52]. *Polonaise Brillante* [Op.53]/Schlesinger 17. *Les Charmes de Paris: Rondeau Brillant Précédé d'une Introduction* Op.54. *Rondoletto sur un Theme du Cinquième Nocturne Français de Mr Paër* [Op.61]. *Souvenirs d'Irlande: Grande Fantaisie* Op.69. *Nocturne*, Op.71. *Bijoux à la Malibran: Trois Fantaisies sur les airs les plus Favoris chantés par Mme Malibran* Op.72 Nos.1–3. *50 Préludes ou Introductions* Op.73. *La Gaité: Rondeau Brillant* Op.85. *Souvenir d'Anna Bolena: Fantaisie Dramatique* Op.86. *Impromptu,* Op.89. Dreyschock: *Trois Andante et Quatre Impromptu caracteristiques* Op. 3. *L'Absence, Romance sans paroles avec de nouveaux effets acoustiques. Bluette* Op.16. *Fantaisie Andante, Veloce et Allegro spiritoso* Op.31. *Morceau caractéristique* Op.45.

Vol. 6: Edward Wolff (1816–1880). *Selected Works.* Born and raised in Poland, Edward Wolff studied composition with Chopin's teacher, Józef Elsner. Although much of his career followed the path blazed by his illustrious compatriot (he emigrated to Paris in 1835, cultivated many of the same genres as Chopin, and often used particular Chopin works as models for his own), Wolff nevertheless was a serious and interesting composer in his own right" (from the Preface). *Trois Romances* Op.11. *5 Mazurkes* Op.12. *24 Études en forme de Préludes* Op.20. *Souvenir de Benvenuto Cellini, Caprice Brillant* Op.21. *Deux Nocturnes* Op.27. *Scherzo* Op.28. *Quatre Rapsodies en forme de Walses* Op.29. *Grand Allegro de Concert* Op.39. *Nocturne en forme de Mazurke* Op.45. *Nocturne* Op.46. *6 Mélodies caractéristiques* Op.60. *Ballade* Op.62. *2 Morceaux de Salon* Op.95. *Nocturne et Romanesca* Op.109. *5 Valses brillantes* Op.112. *3 Chansons Polonaises* Op.136. *2 Polonaises caractéristiques* Op.137. *Tarentelle* Op.148. *La Marseillaise variée* [Op.149]. *Hommage à Chopin: Rêverie-Nocturne* Op.169.

Vol. 7: Johann Peter Pixis (1788–1874). *Selected Works.* "Pixis, born in Mannheim, spent some 17 years in Paris from 1823 to 1840 and was active as both a piano virtuoso and teacher. As one of the early popularizers of the kind of operatic fantasy that was to become the rage in Paris in the 1830s and 40s, his works take on particular historical and musical significance. Included in the selection printed in this volume are several editions that Pixis himself presented as gifts to acquaintances" (from the Preface). *Polonaise Sur la Cavatine di tanti palpiti de Tancrede de Rossini* Op.27. *Grandes Variations sur un Thême favori de l'Opéra le Barbier de Séville* Op.36. *Premier Mélange ou Choix d'Airs Favoris de l'Opéra du Freyschütz* Op.71. *Impromptu sur an Air favori de l'Opéra II Crociato in Egitto* Op.79. *Exercises en forme de Valse* Op.80. *Rondo Brillant* Op.84. *Mélange sur des Motifs Favoris du Siège de Corinthe* Op. 91. *Ballande Écossaise Variée* Op.96. *Caprice Brillant Sur une Tarantelle favorite Napolitaine* Op.108. *Fantaisie Composée sur la dernière pensée Musicale de Weber* Op.109. *Caprice Dramatique (Scène de la Cavatine de Robert le Diable)* Op.116. *Second Caprice Dramatique sur des motifs de Ludovic* Op.125. *Souvenir de Tradate. Nocturne et Variations sur un motif favori de la Pazza per amore, Opéra de Coppola* Op.135. *Valse du Couronnement. Fantaisie sur des motifs de l'Opera La Vestale de Mercadante* Op.141. *Toccata* Op.147.

Vol. 8: François Hünten (1793–1878). *Selected Works.* Hünten, like Pixis, cultivated his reputation more in Paris than in his native Germany. During two extended sojourns in the French capital (1821–1835, 1839–1848) he was in demand both as a fashionable teacher and as a composer of music for the salon. Indeed, G. W. Fink in 1837 described Hünten as the favorite piano composer of the day, played by more pianists than any other composer at that time. In addition to the expected array of rondeaus, etudes, and fantasies, this volume reproduces such interesting curiosities as the 'Virelay et Rondeau Martial' and the 'Fantaisie Arabe sur l'air Kradoudja'" (from the Preface). *Rondoletto* Op.15. *Quatre Rondino* Op.21. *Trois Bagatelles* Op.52. *Premier Quadrille de Contredanses Variées Suivi d'un Galop* Op.63. *12 Études Mélodiques* Op.81. *Bluettes musicales: Rondo et airs varié sur deux Thèmes de Caraffa* [Op.82]. *Suisse & Tyrol: Deux Airs Favoris Suivis de Rondos* Op.89. *Virelay et Rondeau Martial sur l'Opera de G. Onslow Guise on les États de Blois* Op.100. *Rondeau* Op. 110 No. 1. *Les Perles: 3 Rondos* Op.117. *Les Caractères: 3 Airs Variés* Op.118. *Fantaisie brillante sur l'Opéra Nabucodonosor de Verdi* Op.127. *Les Topazes: Grande Valse Brillante et Trois Reveries Mélancoliques* Op.129. *Fantaisie Arabe sur l'air Kradoudja* Op.136. *Au Gré des Ondes, Fantaisie-Barcarolle sur un thème Français* Op.195.

Vol. 9: Henri Bertini (1798–1876) and Théodore Döhler (1814–1856). *Selected Works.* "Henri Bertini is one of the few Parisian Virtuosos actually born in France. Among the works reproduced in this volume is his substantial set of *50 Préludes* Op.141. Théodore Döhler studied piano with Czerny and composition with Sechter, and developed his reputation through a series of international tours (a concert in 1838 at the Paris Conservatoire significantly boosted his stature in the French capital). Döhler wrote for both skilled and less-skilled pianists; compositions of both types are reproduced in this volume" (from the Preface). Bertini: *Air Allemand, Varié et Précédé d'une Introduction* Op.18. *Trois Nocturnes* Op.87/7. *Polacca. Grande Fantaisie sur l'Opera L'Elisire d'Amore de Donizetti* Op.127. *2 Nocturnes* Op.130. *50 Préludes* Op.141. *Les deux Soeurs: 2 Romances sans Paroles* Op.158. Döhler: *Deux Fantaisies sur des motifs favoris de l'Opéra I Puritani* Op.14. *Demière Pensée Musicale de V. Bellini Variée* Op.15. *Deux Nocturnes* Op.25. *Valses Brillantes* Op.26. *Andantino* Op.32. *Tarentelle* Op.39. *Ballade* Op.41. *Romances sans paroles. 6 Romances sans paroles* Op.44. *Deux Fantaisies sur les motifs de Nabucodonosor* Op.48. *3 Mazurkas* Op.53. *Grand Galop Brillant* Op.61. *Une Promenade en Gondole: Nocturne* Op.64. *Les Sirènes: Valses dansantes* Op.67.

Vol. 10: Native and Foreign Virtuosos. *Selected Works of Zimmerman, Alkan, Franck and Contemporaries.* "This volume collects little known or otherwise unavailable works by some of the more famous Parisian virtuosos . . . as well as selected compositions by some of the lesser composers active in Paris during this period . . ." (from the Preface). Pierre-Joseph-Guillaume Zimmerman (1785–1853): *Sonate* Op.5. Louise Farrenc (1804–1875): *Rondeau sur un Choeur du Pirate, de Bellini* Op.9; *Encouragement aux jeunes pianistes: 3 Rondinos.* Ferdinand Hiller (1811–1885): *La Danse des Fantômes; La Danse des Fées* Op.9; *Six Suites d'Etudes* Op.15. Leopoldine

Blahetka (1811–1887): *Trois Rondeaux Élégans sur des Mélodies Favorites Allemandes* Op.37. Charles Valentin Alkan (1813–1888): *Les Omnibus: Variations* Op.2. Stephen Heller (1813–1888): *Scherzo* Op.24; *Capriccio* Op.65. Louis Lacombe (1818–1884): *Le Retour de Guerrier: Fantaisie dramatique*, Op.14. Charles Hallé (1819–1895): *Esquisses* Op.2. César Franck (1822–1890): *Fantaisie sur deux Airs Polonais*, Op.15.

Piano Recital (D. Agay—Amsco 1975). 54 varied pieces, most no longer than 4pp. each. Practical edition containing some unusual repertoire (e.g., Beethoven: *Rondo* Wo048; Heller: *Etude Héroïque*; Moszkowski: *Second Spanish Dance*) in an attractive format. Int. to M-D.

Piano Sonatas of the Early Classical Period (Smart—GS). J. Schobert, *Sonata* c Op.14: three movements, fiery and impetuous. George Berg, *Sonata*: Prelude, Menuet, Gigue; suite-like. Quintin Buée, *Sonata* II a: intense, dramatic, and expressive. Joseph W. Holder, *Sonata* E♭: three movements; the middle one is a Siciliano. William Horsley, *Sonata* II: represents the mature classical sonata. Ornaments are written out in footnotes and metronome marks are included. Int. to M-D.

Preromantic Age (Kovats—EMB Z7976) 36pp. Beethoven: *Für Elise*; *Rondo a capriccioso* Op.129. Schubert; *Scherzo* B♭; *Valses sentimentales* Op.50; *German Dances* Op.33; *Ländler* Op. posth. Weber: *6 German Dances*; *6 Ecossaises*. Int. to M-D.

Progressive Romanticism (Gabor—EMB X8477) 43pp. Works of Chopin and Liszt. Chopin: several of the easier and familiar *Mazurkas* and *Preludes*; *Valse* Op.62/2; *2 Valses*, 2 *Polonaises*, Op. posth. Liszt: *Scherzo* g; *Consolation* II; *Christmas Tree Suite* III (a transcription of "Good Christian Men Rejoice"); No.8 from same suite (a transcription of "Ancient Provençal Christmas Carol"); three of a group called *4 Small Piano Pieces*; *Etude*, Op.1. Int. to M-D.

Recital Repertoire for Pianists (Waterman, Harewood—Faber) Book I. 28 Pieces that span 200 years and show different styles and forms of composers from D. Scarlatti through de Séverac. Well fingered and pedaled. Easy to Int.

Renaissance to Rock: An Annotated Keyboard Collection of Renaissance, Baroque, Jazz and Popular Music (Nathan Bergenfeld—Hyperion 1975) 160pp. Everybody's Favorite Series No.157. In part with chord symbols. Works by Byrd, Couperin, Rameau, Scott Joplin, Cy Oliver, John Mehegan, Paul McCartney. Contains much commentary about each composer and his music. Styles are compared by pairing old with new. Bibliography and indexes. Int. to M-D.

The Rococo (Kovats—EMB) 40pp. 17 representative pieces by Loeillet, J. C. Bach, Hässler, Cimaroso, Türk, Mozart, and Haydn. Original sources and editorial additions not identified. M-D.

The Romantic Era: An Introduction to the Piano Music (Palmer, Halford—Alfred 1978) 64pp. Excellent preface provides introduction to performance practices of the period. Works by Weber, Schubert, Beethoven, Field, Mendelssohn, Schumann, Chopin, Grieg, Liszt, Brahms. Int. to M-D.

Romantic Masters (Weismann—CFP 5033) 32pp. 24 short pieces by Brahms, Chopin, Grieg, Mendelssohn, Schubert, Schumann, Smetana, Tchaikovsky, Weber. Int.

The Romantic Period (Herrmann—CFP 4454) 36pp. Short works by Borodin, Brahms, Chopin, Dvorak, Gade, Grieg, Jensen, T. Kirchner, Liszt, Mussorgsky, Raff, Schubert, Schumann, Smetana, Tchaikovsky, Wagner. Int.

The Romantic Pianist (Johnson—CFP 7188A) Vol.I, 24pp. Works by Hiller, Godard, Jensen, Moszkowski, Rheinberger, Nicole, Raff, Moscheles. Preface in English, notes by the editor. Essential fingerings given. Int.

Romantische Klaviermusik II: Clara Schumann (Goebels—Müller 1976) 57pp. *Romance variée*, Op.3. *Andante con sentimento* (posth.). *Trois romances*, Op.11. *Scherzo*, Op.14. *Quatre pièces fugitives*, Op.15. *Romanze* a, Op.21/1. *Romanze* b (posth.). M-D.

Select Sonatinas (Podolsky—Belwin-Mills) 5 vols. In progressive order of difficulty. Biographical notes on composers. Highly edited, fine selection. Easy to Int.

Selected Piano Sonatas by Classical Composers (W. Georgii—Henle).
    Vol.I: C. P. E. Bach: *Prussian Sonata* F. Clementi: *Sonata* G. Op.39/2. Haydn: *Sonatas* C No.35, G No.40. Mozart: *Sonatas* F (280); G (283); C (545). Beethoven: Op.49/1, 2, Op.14/1, 2.
    Vol.II: J. C. Bach: *Sonata* G Op.17/4. Clementi: *Sonata* D Op.39/3. Haydn: *Sonatas* D No.37; E♭ No.52. Mozart: *Sonatas* A (331); F (332). Beethoven: *Sonatas* Op.2/1; Op.13; Op.27/2.

Selected Pre-Classical Sonatas (PWM). Eighteenth-century German and Italian compositions which, in the history of the development of the sonata for solo instrument, form a link between one-movement sonatas (e.g., those of D. Scarlatti) and sonatas in cyclic form (of the classical period). All performing indications are the editor's suggestions. J. C. Bach: *Sonata* c. M. P. Cherubini: *Sonata* B♭. B. Galuppi: *Sonata*. J. Hässler: *Sonata* a. P. D. Paradies: *Sonata* D. G. B. Pescetti: *Sonata* c.

Seven Centuries of Keyboard Music (Palmer—Alfred 1981) 160pp. A selection of easy to intermediate works, from the fourteenth to the twentieth centuries, with editorial suggestions in gray print and brief biographical sketches of the composers.

Silhouetten—Old and New Dances for Piano Solo (F. Hirsch—Br&H). Dance movements from the time of Bach to the present, including boogie-woogie, rumba, cha-cha, mambo, and carioca. Short movements. M-D.

Six Keyboard Sonatas from the Classic Era (W. S. Newman—CFP 66587). Six little-known sonatas. Urtext edition with critical annotations. Heinrich Joseph Riegel (1741–1799): *Sonata* D, Op.13/3. Nicolas Séjan (1745–1819): *Sonata* c, Op.1/6. Nicolas Joseph Hüllmandel (1756–1823): *Sonata* g, Op.10/3. Giovanni Marco Placido Rutini (1723–1797): *Sonata* d, Op.3/4. Ferdinando

Turini (ca.1749–ca.1812): *Sonata* IV g. Ernst Wilhelm Wolf (1735–1792): *Sonata* II g. Int. to M-D.

Slavic Romanticism (Gabor—EMB Z7981) 49pp. Works by Chopin, Tchaikovsky, Mussorgsky, Dvořák, Smetana, Glier, A. Rubinstein, Liadow, Cui. M-D.

The Solo Sonata (F. Giegling—Arno Volk) Vol.15 of Anthology of Music Series. Includes historical survey, list of sources consulted, checklist of modern editions of sonatas of the seventeenth and eighteenth centuries, and bibliography. Johann Kuhnau: *Suonata Seconda* ("Frische Clavierfrüchte" 1696). Francesco Geminiani: *Pièce de Clavecin* (1762). Domenico Alberti: *Sonata* F (before 1740). Georg Benda: *Sonata* IX a (ca. 1780). Anton Eberl: *Sonatina* Op.6 C (1796). Wenzel Johann Tomaschek: *Sonata* Op.21 F (1806). Robert Schumann: *Sonata* Op.118/2 D (1853). Paul Hindemith: *Second Sonata* (1936).

Sonatas: Classics to Moderns (D. Agay—CMP 1974) 208pp. Vol.67 of *Music for Millions*. 17 sonatas by as many composers from D. Scarlatti to D. Kabalevsky. Each work is complete, in its original form, and is based on an authentic text. C. P. E. Bach: *Sonata* G W.62. J. C. Bach: *Sonata* B♭ Op.5/1. Beethoven: *Sonata* c Op.10/1. D. Bortniansky: *Sonata* F. D. Cimarosa: *Sonata* B♭. M. Clementi: *Sonata* D Op.26/3. J. L. Dussek: *Sonata* G Op.39/1, C.166. E. Grieg: *Sonata* e Op.7. G. F. Handel: *Concerto* G. J. Haydn, *Sonata* F Hob.XVI/23. D. Kabalevsky: *Sonata* III Op.46. W. A. Mozart: *Sonata* G K.283. S. Prokofieff: *Sonata* III (from *Old Notebooks*) Op.28. D. Scarlatti: *Sonata* E L.23. F. Schubert: *Sonata* A Op.120. R. Schumann: *Sonata for the Young* G Op.118a. E. W. Wolf: *Sonata* E. An outstanding survey of the development of one of the most important of all instrumental forms. Int. to M-D.

Sonatina Album (CFP 5003) 28pp. Haydn: *Sonatina* F, Hob.XVI/9. Mozart: *Viennese Sonatina* I, C. Beethoven: *Sonatina* V, G. Int.

Sonatinas for Piano (Glover, Hinson—WB)

Book I, 62pp. Sonatinas by Albert Biehl, Thomas Attwood, Tobias Haslinger, Johann B. Wanhal, Jean Latour, Beethoven, Koehler, Haydn, Gurlitt, Charles Wilton, G. Benda, Jacob Schmitt, James Hook. Easy to Int.

Book II, 62pp. Sonatinas by G. Benda, Pleyel, Kabalevsky, Clementi, Cimorosa, Reinecke, Mozart, Diabelli, Kirchner, Handel and Beethoven. Int.

Each volume contains a brief discussion of the sonatina form.

Sonatinas, Sonatas, Pieces from the 18th through the 20th Centuries (Hans-Georg Schwerdtner—Schott 6695 1977) 115pp. Preface in English and German. Contains works by Handel, D. Scarlatti, Couperin, Galuppi, C. P. E. Bach, Benda, Cimarosa, J. C. Bach, Mozart, Haydn, Clementi, Beethoven, Kuhlau, Schubert, Mendelssohn, Chopin, Reger, Fibich, Kadosa, Bartók, Hindemith, Honegger, Françaix, Prokofiev, and Ligeti. Int. to M-D.

Sonatinas, the First Book for Young Pianists (M. Halford—Alfred 1977) 24pp. Sonatinas by Thomas Attwood, George Berg, Theodore Latour, and Matthew Camidge. Int.

Sonatinen für Klavier I (E. Herttrich—Henle 339 1982). This is the first in a series of three volumes containing sonatinas covering a span of two centuries. Contains 26 sonatinas representing the late-baroque and pre-classical era. D. Scarlatti: K.34, 40, 42, 67, 169, 446. C. P. E. Bach: W. 63/7–12; 53/1, 3. Georg Benda: *Sonatinas* c, G, a. Handel: *Sonatina* d. L. Guistini da Pistoia: *Sonata* B♭. Platti: *Sonata* F. J. C. F. Bach: *Sonata* C. Haydn(?): *Sonata* E♭ Hob.XVI/16. Excellent fingering. Int. to M-D.

The Student's Essential Classics (CFP 6173 1981) 103pp. J. S. Bach: *Two-Part Inventions* 1, 4, 6, 8. Beethoven: *Für Elise*. Chopin: *Etudes* Op.10/1; Op.25/1, 9; *Nocturne* c♯ Op. Posth: *Prelude* Op.28/7; *Waltzes* Op.64/1, 2, 3; Op.69/1. Debussy: *Clair de Lune*; *Reflets dans l'eau*; *Sarabande*. Liszt; *En Reve*; *Liebestraum* No. 3. Mendelssohn: *Rondo capriccio*. Mozart: *Fantasy* K.396. Rachmaninoff: *Prelude* c♯ Op.2/1. D. Scarlatti: *Sonata* a K.208 (L.238). Scriabin: *Etude* c♯ Op.2/1. With commentary and performance suggestions by David Bar-Ilan, Jorge Bolet, Gilbert Kalish, Ruth Laredo, Santiago Rodriguez, Earl Wild. These pieces have also been recorded on the Baldwin "Essential Classics Series." An exemplary collection. Int. to M-D.

Style and Interpretation (H. Ferguson—OUP).
  Vol.1: Early Keyboard Music I: England and France.
  Vol.2: Early Keyboard Music II: Germany and Italy.
  Vol.3: Classical Piano Music.
  Vol.4: Romantic Piano Music.
  54 pieces from the sixteenth to the nineteenth century. Designed to illustrate the way in which style and interpretation change from century to century, and from country to country. Each volume contains detailed essays on the conventions governing performance, and on the instruments of the periods and countries concerned, as well as a short introduction to each work. Int. to M-D.

Themes and Variations (D. Agay—CMP 1974). Vol.77 of *Music for Millions.* 28 compositions by 24 composers representing a broad survey of theme and variation techniques. Agay: *Variations on a Hebrew Folk Theme* from *Mosaics*. J. S. Bach: *Aria Variata alla Maniera Italiana*. Bartók: *Variations on a Slovakian Folk Tune* from *For Children*, Book II. Beethoven: *7 Variations on "God Save the King"* WoO 78; *32 Variations* c WoO 80. Brahms: *Variations on an Original Theme* Op.21/1. Byrd: *The Carman's Whistle*. Jean F. Dandrieu: *Wedding Feast of the Birds*. Glinka: *Variations on a Russian Folk Song*. Goedicke: *Theme and Variations* Op.46. Granados: *Theme, Variations and Finale* from *Seis Estudios Espresivos*. Handel: *Passacaglia* from *Suite VII* g. Haydn: *Variations "Un Piccolo Divertimento"* Hob.XVII/6. Earl Hines: *Jazz Improvisation on the Song "Smoke Rings."* Kabalevsky: *Variations* Op.40/2; *Toccata Variations* Op.40/1. Kuhlau: *Variations on an Austrian Folk Song*. Liszt: *Praeludium* ("Weinen, Klagen, Sorgen, Sagen") on an ostinato bass after J. S. Bach. Mendelssohn: *Variations Sérieuses* Op.54. Mozart: *6 Variations on an Air* ("Mio Caro Adone") by Salieri, K.180; *Variations on an Allegretto* K.54. J. Pachelbel: *Chorale and Variations* ("Werde Munter Mein Gemute"). J. P. Rameau: *Gavotte Variée*—Gavotte with Variations. Sam Raphling: *Improvisations on 2 American Folk Tunes*. Schubert: *Impromptu* Op.142/3. Villa-Lobos: *Preludio* from *Bachianas Brasileiras* IV. Leo Weiner: *Variations on a Hungarian Peasant Song* Op.22. Tempo, dynamic, and expression marks added by the editor are discreet and tastefully handled. Int. to M-D.

Thirteen Keyboard Sonatas of the 18th and 19th Centuries (W. S. Newman—UNC 1947). A fine collection of unfamiliar sonatas with critical commentaries. Includes sonatas by Jean Barrière (1720–50), Platti, Alberti, Georg Benda (1722–95), J. J. Agrell (1701–65), C. G. Neefe (1748–98), Manuel Blasco de Nebra (ca. 1750–1784), Dittersdorf (1739–99), Joseph Wölfl (1773–1812), E. T. A. Hoffman (1776–1822), J. F. Reichardt, Loewe, Moscheles. M-D.

Three Centuries of the Waltz (Bradley). Works by Beethoven, Brahms, Dvořák, Granados, Gurlitt, Haydn, Mozart, Prokofiev, Schubert, J. Strauss. Includes some music that precedes the waltz. Int. to M-D.

Three Hundred Years of Keyboard Music (Anthony—TP 1984) 32pp. 28 pieces in their original form from Arcangelo Corelli to Dmitri Kabalevsky. Easy to Int.

Toccata Album (E. Balogh—GS). 18 Toccatas by Antheil, J. S. Bach, Buxtehude, Czerny, Frescobaldi, Gabrieli, Hoiby, Khachaturian, Padovano, Paradisi, Pollini, Prokofieff, Purcell, Rheinberger, A. Scarlatti, D. Scarlatti, Schumann, Froberger. Points up the variety of forms included in this term. M-D to D.

Le Trésor des Pianistes (compiled by Jacques and Louise Farrenc—Leduc 1861–72; reprint Da Capo 1977). The most complete collection of keyboard music ever assembled. About 250 of the works are available separately (Leduc).
    Vol.I: Preliminaries, History of the Piano, Treatise on Ornaments.
    Vol.II: *Parthenia* (1611): 18 pieces by William Byrd (1542–1623), John Bull (1562–1628), Orlando Gibbons (1583–1625). Various English composers. Claudio Merulo (1533–1604): *Toccatas*. Girolamo Frescobaldi (1583–1643): *Three Fugues* (spurious); *6 Canzoni*; various pieces. Georg Muffat (1645–1704): 12 *Toccatas*. Jacques Champion de Chambonnières (ca 1602–1672): *Pièces de Clavecin*, 2 Books. Jean Henri d'Anglebert (1635–1691): *Pièces de Clavecin*.
    Vol.III: Johann Kuhnau (1660–1722): 7 *Sonatas*; *Neue Clavier Übung*; *Toccatas*. Henry Purcell (1658–1695): collection of pieces. Johann Jakob Froberger (1616–1667): 5 *Capricci*, 6 *Suites*. Louis Couperin (1626–1661). Antoine Le Bègue (1631–1702). Bernardo Pasquini (1637–1710). Johann Kaspar Kerll (1627–1693). Alessandro Scarlatti (1659–1725).
    Vol.IV: François Couperin (1668–1733): *Pièces de Clavecin*, 3 Books.
    Vol.V: François Couperin: *Pièces de Clavecin*, Book 4. George Frederick Handel (1685–1759): *Suites*, 3 Books; 6 *Fugues*.
    Vol.VI: Domenico Scarlatti (1685–1757): 77 pieces.
    Vol.VII: Domenico Scarlatti: 75 pieces.
    Vol.VIII: J. S. Bach (1685–1750): 6 *Partitas*; 6 *English Suites*. Jean Philippe Rameau (1683–1746): *Pièces de Clavecin*, 2 Books. Nicolo Porpora (1686–1766): 6 *Fugues*.

Vol.IX: Francesco Durante (1684–1755): 6 Sonatas. François Dandrieu (1682–1738). Benedetto Marcello (1686–1739). Georg Telemann (1684–1740). Giovanni Pescetti (ca. 1704–1766). Claude Daquin (1694–1772): *Pièces de Clavecin*. Padre Martini (1706–1784): 12 *Sonatas*. Johann Ludwig Krebs (1713–1780): 3 *Fugues*.

Vol.X: Wilhelm Friedemann Bach (1710–1784): 12 *Polonaises*; *Sonata*; 8 *Fugues*, *Suite*, 4 *Fantasies*. Gottlieb Muffat (1690–1770): collection of pieces. Christoph Nichelmann (1717–1762): 11 *Sonatas*.

Vol.XI: Johann Gottlieb Goldberg (ca 1720–?): *Prelude and Fugue*. Johann Ernst Eberlin (1702–1762): 6 *Preludes and Fugues*. Johann Mattheson (1681–1764): various pieces. Domenico Zipoli (1688–1726): pieces for organ and harpsichord. John Christopher Smith (1712–1795): 9 *Suites*. Chr. Schaffrath (18th cent.): 2 *Sonatas*.

Vol.XII: C. P. E. Bach (1714–1788): 30 *Sonatas*.

Vol.XIII: C. P. E. Bach: 35 *Sonatas*; 4 *Rondos*.

Vol.XIV: Domenico Paradies (1707–1791): 10 *Sonatas*. Duphly (1715–1789): *Pièces de Clavecin*. Johann Philipp Kirnberger (1721–1783): 6 *Fugues*; various pieces. Johann Buttstedt (1666–1727): 2 *Sonatas*. Georg Benda (1722–1795): 6 *Sonatas*.

Vol.XV: Christoph Friedrich Bach (1732–1795): *Sonatas*; various pieces. Joseph Haydn (1732–1809): 10 *Sonatas*. J. G. Albrechtsberger (1736–1809): 30 *Fugues*. Karl Fasch (1736–1800): 2 *Sonatas*; one piece.

Vol.XVI: Muzio Clementi (1752–1832): 3 *Sonatas* Op.2; 2 *Sonatas* Op.7; 3 *Sonatas* Op.8; 4 *Sonatas* and a *Toccata* Opp.9, 10, 14. Johann Wilhelm Hässler (1747–1822): 2 *Fantasies*; 9 *Sonatas*; 4 *Solos*. O. A. Lindemann (1769–1859): various pieces.

Vol.XVII: W. A. Mozart (1756–1791): 10 *Sonatas*; Romance.

Vol.XVIII: Johann Christian Bach (1735–1782): 7 *Sonatas*. Johann L. Dussek (1760–1812): 3 *Grandes Sonatas* Op.35; *Sonata* Op.64. J. G. Wernicke (?): 5 pieces. Johann Schwanenberg (1740–1804): 2 *Minuets*. Daniel Steibelt (1765–1823): *Grande Sonate* Op.64. J. B. Cramer (1771–1858): 3 *Sonatas*.

Vol.XIX: L. van Beethoven (1770–1827): *Sonatas* Op.2 to Op.27.

Vol.XX: Beethoven: *Sonatas* Op.28 to Op.90.

Vol.XXI: Beethoven: *Sonatas* Op.101 to Op.111; 6 sets of *Variations*.

Vol.XXII: Johann Nepomuk Hummel (1778–1837): 7 sets of *Variations*; *Introduction and Rondo* Op.19; *Rondo brilliant* Op.109; *Sonatas* Opp.13, 20, 81; *Adagio* from Op.38; *Fantasie* Op.18.

Vol.XXIII: Ferdinand Ries (1784–1838): *L'Infortunée*; *Sonata* Op.26. Carl Maria von Weber (1786–1826): 4 *Sonatas*. Felix Mendelssohn (1809–1847): *Rondo capriccioso*; 3 *Fantasies* or *Caprices* Op.16. Frederic Chopin (1810–1849): 9 *Nocturnes*.

See: Maurice Hinson, "Le Trésor des Pianistes," PQ, 72 (Summer 1970): 20–21, for a discussion of the background and development of the collection.

Twenty-Six Pieces from Three Centuries (Scarlatti to Prokofiev) (Karl Bradley—GS 1975) 106pp. Music by Albeniz, Blood, Bruckner, Chaminade, Dello

Joio, German, Granados, Helm, Henselt, Herbert, Holst, Mozart, MacDowell, Moszkowski, Muczynski, Pachulski, Poldini, Prokofiev, Saint-Saëns, Schütt, Surinach, Turina. Contains a wide variety of repertoire with some unusual items. Int. to M-D.

Twenty-Six Romantic and Contemporary Piano Pieces (Karl Bradley—GS 1975) 106pp. A fine collection of popular and some unusual works by Albeniz, Barber, Cowell, Debussy, Dvořák, Godard, Grainger, Griffes, Guion, V. Herbert, MacDowell, Muczynski, Nevin, Prokofiev, Rachmaninoff, Rossini, Sapellnikoff, Sarasate, Satie, R. Schumann, Scriabin, A. Tcherepnin, Warlock. Int. to M-D.

Two Hundred Years of Piano Music (Christopher—McAfee 1984) 259pp. 112 pieces from the Baroque, Classical, and Romantic periods. Contains mostly well-known pieces by Bach, Beethoven, Chopin, Clementi, Grieg, Handel, Haydn, Mendelssohn, Schumann, Tchaikovsky. Not well documented. Int. to M-D.

Vienna Classics (Kormel—EMB). Haydn: *Fantasia* C, Hob.XVII/4; *Variations* C, Hob.XVII/5. Mozart: *Rondo*, K.511; *Adagio*, K.540; *Andantino*, K.236. Beethoven: *Rondo* C, Op.51; *Polonaise*, Op.89. M-D.

Viennese Masters from the Baroque, Classical and Biedermeier Periods (H. Kann —UE). Haydn: *Capriccio*. Mozart: *Rondo* K.511. Schubert: *Eccossaises*. Fux: *Sonata* No.4. Muffat: *Fantasia*. Wagenseil: *Ricercata*. Albrechtsberger: *Galanterie fuga*. Czerny: set of *Variations* and a sequence of *Waltzes*. Voříšek (Woržischek): *Rhapsody*. Hummel. Froberger. Kann's editorial work is excellent. There are also useful notes about the composers and the music. M-D.

World's Greatest Classical Sonatas. Vol. 1 (Hinson—Alfred 4593) 168pp.; Vol. 2 (Hinson—Alfred 4594) 180pp. These pedagogical-performance editions contain some of the greatest Classical sonatas ever written. Graded volumes. Each sonata appears in its original form, with performance notes and editorial markings.
Vol. 1: Haydn: Sonatas C, G, and D, Hob.XVI: 35, 27, and 37. Mozart: Sonatas C, F, G, A, and B♭, K.545, 547a, 283, 331 and 570. Beethoven: Sonatas g, G, G, and E, Opp.49.1, 2, 79 and 14/1.
Vol. 2: Haydn: Sonatas b, G, and E♭, Hob.XVI: 32, 40, and 49. Mozart: Sonatas F, a, and F, K.280, 310, and 332. Beethoven: Sonatas f, c, A♭, and c♯, Opp.2/1, 13, 26, and 27/2.

World's Greatest Melodies (Hinson—Alfred 203) 160pp. Contains some of the greatest melodic treasures from the piano repertoire. Special attention is given to Chopin, Grieg, Schubert, and Tchaikovksy. Organized in order of increasing difficulty. Int. to M-D.

World's Greatest Sonatinas (Hinson—Alfred 4617) 144pp. 22 sonatinas from C. P. E. Bach to Kabalevsky. Editing easily distinguished from composers' indications. Each sonatina analyzed. Includes two unusual works—Reinecke: *Christmas Sonatina* Op.255/3; and Satie: *Bureaucratic Sonatina*.

General: Contemporary

All Time Favorite Piano Pieces from the Modern Repertoire (GS 3489 1984) 94pp. Bartók: *Bagatelle*; *Valse Ma mie que danse*. Bloch: *Chanty*. Carpenter: *Impromptu*. Chavez: *Prelude* (from *10 Preludes*). Debussy: *Valse romantique*. DeFalla: *Serenata Andaluza*. Fauré: *Impromptu* Op.31/2. Foss: *Grotesque Dance*. Godowsky: *Nocturnal Tangier*. Harris: *Little Suite*. Křenek: *The Moon Rises*. Pinto: *Marcha do Pequeno Polegar*. Prokofiev: *Marche*; *Vision Fugitive* Op.22/16. Ravel: *Pavane pour une Infante défunte*. Satie: *Gymnopédie*. Scriabin: *Poëme* Op.69/1. Shostakovitch: *Polka* Op.22. Igor Stravinsky: *Etude* Op.7/2. Int. to M-D.

The Carnegie Hall Millennium Piano Book (2000) (Bo&H 2000). Ten works by contemporary composers commissioned by Carnegie Hall. The score is packaged with a CD of all ten works recorded by pianist Ursula Uppens and featuring liner notes by each composer. Contents: Louis Andriessen (1939–   ) *Images de Noreau*; Milton Babbitt (1916–   ) *The Old Order Changeth*; Elliott Carter (1908–   ) *Two Diversions*; Tan Dun, *Few-Drops-Fall*; Hannibal, *John Brown and Blue*; John Harbison (1938–   ) *On an Unwritten Letter*; Wolfgang Rihm (1952–   ) *Zwiesprache*; Frederic Rzewski (1938–   ) *The Days Fly By*; Chen Yi, *Ba Ban*; Ellen Taafe Zwilich (1939–   ) *Lament*. Int. to M-D.

Collection Panorama (Billaudot 1984) 9pp. Jacques Chailley: *À 12 doigts*. Odette Gartenlaub; *Prélude et récréation*. Betsy Jolas; *Petite suite sérieuse pour concert de famille*. Bozidar Kantuser: *Il était une fois*. Joachin Nin-Culmell: *Alexandre et Louis*. Writing ranges from fairly traditional to freely tonal. Clever and attractive. Easy to Int.

Composer-Pianists (J. Schaum 1971) 32pp. Ten compositions in their original form. Eugen d'Albert: *Blues*. Ossip Gabrilowitsch: *Oriental Melody*. Walter Gieseking: *Jazz Improvisation*. Leopold Godowsky: *Meditation*. Wanda Landowska: *En Route*. Gustav Mahler: *I Walk with Joy through the Green Forest*. Tobias Matthay: *Movement Musical*. Emil Sauer: *Petite Etude*. Arthur Schnabel: *Valse Mignonne*. Alec Templeton: *Springtime in the Village*. Contains some interesting and unusual pieces. Int. to M-D.

Contemporary Composers (Schaum Publications 1976) 31pp. Twelve compositions in their original form. Granville Bantock: *Chanticleer*. Eric Coates: *By the Sleepy Lagoon*. Claude Debussy: *Album Leaf*. Eugene Goossens: *Tugboat*. Arthur Honegger: *Study in Cacophony*. John Ireland: *Reapers' Dance*. Leoš Janáček: *Moravian Dances*. Zoltán Kodály: *Furioso* Op.3/5. Vladimir Rebikov: *Dervish*. Erik Satie: *Gymnopédie*. Florent Schmitt: *Petit Musique* Op.33/8. Cyril Scott: *Lento*. Int. to M-D.

Contemporary Music and the Pianist (Alice Canady—Alfred 1974). Examples of some of the best contemporary music arranged in graded order. Includes a list of valuable source books and a graded list of other recommended contemporary music. It is as its subtitle claims, "A Guidebook of Resources and Materials." Some of the composers include Hindemith, Schönberg, Krenek, Dello Joio, Finney, La Montaine, and Helps. Six grading levels. Level 1 is not for a beginner, and level 6 would be material for an advanced high school student who had studied 8–10 years.

Contemporary Piano Repertoire (Hinson, Glover—WB) Level 5. Bartók: *Let's Dance*; *Peasant Dance*; *The Fox*; *Scaredy Cat!* Gretchaninoff: *Trumpets*; *Out for a Stroll*; *Secrets*. Kabalevsky: *Guessing Game*; *Happy Times*; *Miniature Waltz*; *Little Toccata*. Rebikov: *The Tin Soldier*; *Oriental*; *The Grumpy Bear*. Also contains biographies aimed at the piano works. Int.

Contemporary Piano Repertoire (Hinson, Glover—WB) Level 6. Khachaturian: *Horseman's Gallop*; *Scampering*. Prokofiev: *Promenade*; *Fairy Tale*. Shostakovitch: *Gavotte*; *Waltz*; *Tricks*. Stravinsky: *Pastorale*; *In the Garden*. Also contains biographies pertinent to these piano works. Int.

Easy Contemporary Piano Music (Lueck—Gerig HG 1363) 35pp. Contains over 20 short pieces by contemporary composers such as Bjelinski, Burkard, Constantinidis, Kabalevsky. Notes in German and English. Arranged in order of difficulty with new techniques of composition progressively introduced. Easy to Int.

Masters of the Early Contemporary Period (1890–1914) (Hinson—Alfred 4579) 64pp. Includes Foreword; discussion of performance practices, 1890–1914; suggested teaching order; and discussion of each piece. Bartók: *Bagatelle* Op.6/4; *Bear Dance* Sz.39: 10. Bruch: *Swedish Dance* Op.63/7. Debussy: *Le petit Nègre*; *Rêverie*. Dohnányi: *Postludium* Op.13/10. Grainger: *The Sussex Mummer's Christmas Carol*. Joplin: *Pine Apple Rag*. MacDowell: *From a Wandering Iceberg* Op.55/2. Prokofiev: *Humoreske* Op.3/2. Rachmaninoff: *Romance* Op.10/6. Ravel: *Menuet sur le non d'Haydn*. Satie: *Of the Edriophthalma*; *Sea Bathing*. Schönberg: *Short Piano Piece* Op.19/2. Scriabin: *Nuances* Op.56/3; *Prelude* Op.31/4. de Severac: *An Old Music Box*. Sibelius: *Impromptu* Op.5/1. Stravinsky: *Etude* e Op.7/3. Int. to M-D.

Meet Modern Music (Esther Abrams—Mer 1943). Almost all of the original titles have been changed.

Vol.I: Bartók: *Not Too Fast*; *Peasant's Song*; *Song of the Tramp*. Goedicke: *In a Quiet Mood*. Gretchaninoff: *Holidays*; *Mommy*. Liapounov: *Lullaby for a Doll*. Prokofieff: *Fairy Tale*; *Promenade*. Rebikoff: *Children Skating*; *Hurdy Gurdy*; *Playing Soldiers*. Rhené-Baton: *A Little Song*; *A Little Waltz*. Satie: *The Tulip Princess Says*; *Waltz of the Chocolate Bar*; *War Song of the Bean King*. Sibelius: *Valsette*. Stravinsky: *Just Walking*. Easy to Int.

Vol.II: Bartók: *Dance Tune*; *Energy*. Amado Carvajal: *Miniature*; *Tristeza*. René de Castera: *The Cat Is Dead*. E. Granados: *Theme and Two Variations*; *The Last Pavanne*. Jaques-Dalcroze: *The Battle*. Samuel Maykapar: *The Blacksmith*. Prokofieff: *Morning*; *Parade of the Grasshoppers*. Abel Rufino: *Campestre*. Domingo Santa-Cruz: *March of the Kittens*. Stravinsky: *Heavily*. Int.

Modern Pieces for the Young Artist in Recital (Amsco) 95pp. Works by Albeniz,

Bartók, Kabalevsky, Rachmaninoff, Ravel, Shostakovitch, and others. Not terribly modern but contains a broad spectrum of works. Fingered, no editor given. Int. to M-D.

Music Without Borders (Karabyts—Duma Music 1996). A collection of twentieth-century piano music by six Ukrainian and six American composers: Virko Baley, Aaron Copland, Emma Lou Diemer, Morton Gould, Darrell Handel, Leonid Hrabovsky, Ivan Karabyts, Borys Lyatoshynksy, Richard Nanes, Leo Revutsky, Valentin Silvestrov, and Myroslav Skoryk. M-D to D.

Das Neue Klavierbuch I (Schott 6010/1) 31pp. Henk Badings: *Air*; *Scherzo pastorale*. Béla Bartók: *Dudelsack*; *Allegro ironico*. Conrad Beck: *Für eine stille Stunde*. Wolfgang Fortner: *Serenata*; *Lied*; *Elegie* No.IV. Harald Genzmer: *Präludium*; *Andante*. Kurt Hessenberg: *Invention*. Paul Hindemith: *March*; *Zwei leichte Fünftonstücke*. Wilhelm Maler: *Drei kleine Stücke*. Bohuslav Martinù; *Intermezzo* II. Ernst Pepping: *Tanzweise*. Herman Reutter: *Lustiges Stück*. Mátyás Seiber: *Ap agapak*; *Toccatina*. Igor Strawinsky: *Allegro*, Bernd Alois Zimmermann: *Aria*. Int.

Das Neue Klavierbuch II (Schott 6011) 33pp. Béla Bartók; *Volkslied*. Boris Blacher: *Sonatine*. Wolfgang Fortner: *Präludium*. Jean Françaix: *La Tendre* Harald Genzmer: *Präludium*. Paul Hindemith: *Tanzstück*; *Interludium*; *Fuga*. Arthur Honegger: *Sarabande*. Witold Lutoslawski; *Bukolische Weisen*. Darius Milhaud: *Mazurka*. Francis Poulenc: *Valse*. Igor Strawinsky: *Walzer*. Alexander Tcherepnin: *Intermezzo*. Int. to M-D.

Das Neue Klavierbuch III (Schott 7095) 55pp. Frank Michael Beyer: *Ragtime*. Hans-Jürgen von Bose: *Drei kleine Klavierstücke*. Aaron Copland: *Sentimental Melody*. Wolfgang Fortner: *Epigramm* IV. Jean Françaix: *En cas de succès*. Peter Michael Hamel: *Schwarz-weiss*. Hans Werner Henze: *Ballade*; *Allegro con grazia*. Paul Hindemith: *In einer Nacht* Op.15/3, 4. Bertold Hummel: *Notturno*. Wilhelm Killmayer: *Nocturne* III (*An John Field*). Noël Lee: *Intervalle*. György Ligeti: *Musica ricercata*, Nos.5 and 6. Emile Naoumoff; *Burlesque*. Karl Heinz Wahren: *Tango-Rag*. Friedrich K. Wanek: *Elegie*. M-D.

New Piano Music for Study and Teaching (Roggenkamp—Br&H 1990) 52pp. "Contains pieces by 11 contemporary composers born between 1925 (Boulez) and 1956 (Babette Koblenz); the works are organized according to the year of the composer's birth. All of the pieces were written after 1945, most of them in the 1980s" (from the score). Pierre Boulez (1925–   ): *From 12 Notations*, Nos.3 and 4. Hans Otte (1926–   ): *The Book of Sounds* No.2. Dieter Schnebel (1930–   ): *Bagatelles* Nos.4 and 6. Marek Kopelent (1932–   ): *Song for Piano*. Helmut Lachenmann (1935–   ): *Child's Play*; *Akiko*; *Filter Swing*. Friedhelm Döhl (1936–   ): *4 Bagatelles*. Hans-Joachim Hespos (1938–   ): *Stimulus for a Pianist*. Graciela Paraskevaidis (1940–   ): *One Side, Another Side*. Coriun Aharonian (1940–   ): *What Now?* Theo Brandmuller (1948–   ): *Memento*. Babette Kohlenz (1956–   ): *Piano Piece I*. A supplement includes remarks and explanation of signs. Some avant garde notation. M-D to D.

New Piano Pieces for Children (Schott 7392 1986) 47pp. Pieces by Henk Badings (1907–1987), Jan Novák (1921–1984), Jean Françaix (1912–1997), Henning Brauel (1940–   ), Frank Michael Beyer (1928–   ), Friedrich Zehm (1923–   ), Wilfried Zehm (1923–   ), Wilfried Hiller (1941–   ), Erich Wolfgang Korngold (1897–1957). Int. to M-D.

Piano Music Inspired by Folklore (P. Arma—Lemoine 1959). 24 pieces by contemporary composers based on popular themes of 14 nationalities. Includes works by Arma, Bartók, Sas, Tansman, Viski, and others. Easy to Int.

Pro Musica Nova (Alfons Kontarsky—Hans Gerig 1972) 47pp. Studies for playing avant-garde music for piano written since 1950. Contains works by Pavle Merkù, Lucia Alcalay, Tilo Medek, Bojidar Dimov, Norbert Linke, Yannis Ioannidis, Werner Heider, José Luis de Delás, Günther Becker, Helmut Lachenmann, and Friedhelm Döhl. Two valuable appendixes with explanations in German and English. Some of the pieces are highly suitable for public performance. M-D to D.

Styles in 20th-Century Piano Music (UE). An outstanding collection of 24 pieces by 24 European composers from the first half of this century. Ranges from Sibelius (post-Romantic) to Schönberg (12-tone). Points up the multiplicity of styles and moods already heard in this century. This is a revised and extended version of a volume published in 1951 on the occasion of the 50th anniversary of the Universal Edition. A note on each composer and some commentary on unusual notation add to the fine qualities of a first-rate collection. M-D to D.

Thirty-Six Twentieth-Century Piano Pieces (GS). A collection of contemporary works for recital and study. Works by Antheil, Barber, Bartók, Bernstein, Bloch, Carpenter, Chavez, Creston, Debussy, Dello Joio, Fauré, Fine, Grainger, Griffes, Kabalevsky, Khachaturian, Krenek, MacDowell, Muczynski, Prokofieff, Rachmaninoff, Ravel, W. Schuman, Scott, Shostakovich, Tcherepnin. Contains some important twentieth-century piano works. D.

Treize Danses (T. Harsányi—ESC 1930). 13 mildly contemporary dances by Beck, Delannoy, Ferroud, Harsányi, Larmanjat, Lopatnikoff, Martinù, Migot, Milhaliovici, Rosenthal, Schulhoff, Tansman, and Wiener. Varied influences and styles. The "official" existence of a group of young musicians who resided in Paris in the 1920s, known as the "Ecole de Paris," was signalized by the publication of this collection. Each member had a composition included. M-D.

20th Century Keyboard Masters (M. Nevin—Schroeder & Gunther 1972). Original piano works by modern composers for intermediate and early advanced levels. Compositions by Bartók, Debussy, Kabalevsky, Prokofieff, and others. Int. to M-D.

Twenty-Six Romantic and Contemporary Piano Pieces (Karl Bradley—GS 1975) 106pp. A fine collection of popular and some unusual works by Albeniz, Barber, Cowell, Debussy, Dvořák, Godard, Grainger, Griffes, Guion, V. Herbert, MacDowell, Muczynski, Nevin, Prokofiev, Rachmaninoff, Rossini, Sapellnikoff, Sarasate, Satie, R. Schumann, Scriabin, A. Tcherepnin, and Warlock. Int. to M-D.

The World of Modern Piano Music (Agay—MCA). 42 easy original pieces by contemporary composers of nine different countries.

The Young Pianist's Anthology of Modern Music (AMP 1972) 65pp. 42 works by contemporary composers, including Bartók, Bernstein, Cowell, Creston, Grainger, Guarnieri, Harris, Haufrecht, Hovhaness, Kabalevsky, Krenek, George List, Muczynski, Pinto, Rodrigo, W. Schuman, S. Strohbach, Surinach, Takacs, Tansman. No commentary on composer's style or technical problems. Diverse styles. Easy-Int.

Tombeaux, Hommages

Ein Haydnpass! (Goebels—Schott). A collection of works inspired by a work of Haydn or by his life and example. In honor of the 250th anniversary of Haydn's birth. Includes works by Debussy, Ravel, Widor, Czerny, Ernst Pfiffner, Wolfgang Hochstein, Friedrich Wanek and Glen Buschmann. M-D to D.

Homage to Haydn (MMP). Three pieces for the Haydn Centenary 1909 by Debussy, Dukas, and Ravel.

Hommage à Franz Schubert (Goebels—Schott 6874 1980) 17pp. Simon Sechter (1788–1867), *Fugue* c on Schubert's name: chromatic contrapuntal web. Carl Czerny (1791–1857), *Variations über den beliebten Trauerwalzer* (based on Schubert's "Mourning Waltz"): the most successful in the set. Anselm Hüttenbrenner (1794–1868): *Nachruf an Schubert* ("Remembering Schubert"): one-page character piece. Int. to M-D.

American

The American Book for Piano (William Deguire—Galaxy 1975). Contains original piano compositions, vocal and choral works transcribed for piano, and well-known tunes of traditional music freely arranged for piano by the editor. Solo piano works include: Benjamin Carr, *Sonata* I (from *A New Assistant for the Pianoforte or Harpsichord*, 1796). Philip Phile: *The President's March*. Raynor Taylor: *The Subject from "Adeste Fidelis."* William Mason: *Lullaby* Op.10 (1857). Stephen Foster: *Soirée Polka* (1850). John Knowles Paine: *The Shepherd's Lament* Op.26/4 (1875). George Chadwick: *The Cricket and the Bumble Bee* (1903). Arthur Foote: *Prelude* e Op.52/10 (1903). Amy Beach: *Waltz* Op.36/3 (1897). W. Iucho: *The Arkansas Traveller* (1879). Ethelbert Nevin: *Narcissus* Op.13/4 (1891). Edward MacDowell: *To a Wild Rose* Op.51/1 (1896). Harvey W. Loomis: *Prayer to Wakonda; Offering of the Sacred Pipe* Op.76, Book 2, No.1 (1904). Int. to M-D.

American Composers of the Twentieth Century (Schaum Publications 1969). Twelve compositions in their original form: Samuel Barber: *Love Song*. Cecil Burleigh: *Mazurka*. Abram Chasins: *Prelude* c. Zez Confrey: *After Theater Tango*. James Francis Cooke: *Twilight at Carcassonne*. James P. Dunn: *Be-*

witched. Howard Hanson: *Impromptu.* Edward B. Hill: *March of the Mountains.* Alan Hovhaness: *Fire Dance.* Henry H. Huss: *Gipsy Dance.* A. Walter Kramer: *Silhouette.* Nicolas Slonimsky: *Dreams and Drums.* Int.

American Contemporary Masters (GS 1996) 152pp. Contains works by John Adams, Dave Brubeck, John Corigliano, Richard Danielpour, Anthony Davis, Norman Dello Joio, Phillip Glass, Morton Gould, John Harbison, Lee Hoiby, Aaron Jay Kernis, Leon Kirchner, Peter Lieberson, Mel Powell, and Joan Tower. See, above, under individual composer, for discussion of each entry. An outstanding collection of late-twentieth-century works. M-D to D.

American Piano Music from the Civil War to World War I (Dubal—IMC 3367 1995) 154pp. 22 works by 18 composers, from Gottschalk (1826–1869) to Mana-Zucca (1887–1981). Good variety of repertoire from the period. Louis Moreau Gottschalk: *Tournament Galop.* Richard Hofman: *Impromptu c*; *Polka de Concert.* Homer Bartlett: *Grand Polka de Concert* Op.1. Arthur Foote: *Pierrot* Op.34/1; *Pierrette* Op.34/2. George W. Chadwick: *Chanson Orientale*; *Nocturne.* Reginald de Koven: *Andante Classique* Op.93. Victor Herbert: *The Mountain Brook.* Edward MacDowell: *Concert Etude* Op.36. Ethelbert Nevin: *Mazurka*; *Narcissus* Op.13/4. Henry Holden Huss: *Three Intermezzi*: No.1 *Allegretto con graza*; No.2 *The Twilight*; No.3 *Allegro moderato e gioioso.* Horatio W. Parker: *Valse Gracile* Op.49/3. Amy Marcy Beach: *Dreaming* Op.15/3. Arthur Farwell: *Raising the Pipes* Op.21. Fred S. Stone: *Silks and Rags.* Daniel Gregory Mason: *Night Wind* Op.9/6. Nathaniel Dett: *Juba Dance.* Charles T. Griffes: *The Fountain of the Acqua Paola.* Mana-Zucca: *Valse Brillante* Op.20. Int. to M-D.

American Sonatinas (Schaum Publications 1963) 31pp. Six original sonatinas by American composers. Edward Holst (1843–1899): *Pilgrim Sonatina.* Hans Engelmann (1872–1914): *Colonial Sonatina* Op.372/12. Frank Lynes (1858–1914): *Spirit of '76 Sonatina* Op.39/1. Frank Addison Porter (1859–1911): *New England Sonatina.* William Dawson Armstrong (1868–1936): *Rustic Sonatina.* Frederick N. Shackley (1868–1937): *Spinning Wheel Sonatina.* Also contains brief information on the background of each composer. Int.

American Women Composers: Piano Music from 1865–1915 (Glickman—Hildegard Publishing Co.) 75pp. Mazurkas, marches, polkas, rags, variations, and waltzes by May Aufderheide, Amy Beach, Celeste Heckscher, Faustine Hasse Hodges, Helen Hopekirk, Carrie Jacobs-Bond, Sadie Koninsky, Margaret R. Lang, Julia Niebergall, Eliza Pattiani, Clara Gottschalk Peterson, Clara K. Rogers, Clara Scott, Adeline Shepherd, and Jane Torry Sloman. Includes a brief biography of each composer. Int. to M-D.

Anthology of Early American Keyboard Music 1787–1830 (J. Bunker Clark—A–R Editions 1977).

Vol.I: William Brown: *Rondo* III. Benjamin Carr: *The Siege of Tripoli, an Historical Naval Sonata*; *Sonata* VI; *Voluntary for the Organ*; *The Maid of Lodi with Variations.* Charles Gilfert: *Ah! What is the Bosom's Commotion with Variations.* James Hewitt: *The New Federal Overture*; *Sonatina* III;

Theme with 30 Variations; Yankee Doodle with Variations; Trip to Nahant. T. L. Holden: *The Copenhagen Waltz.* John Christopher Moller: *Meddley; Rondo.* Eliza Crawly Murden: *March.* Mr. Newman: *Sonata* III. Stephen Sicard: *The President of the United States' March.*

Vol.II: Arthur Clifton: *An Original Air with Variations.* Frederick A. Getze: *Saxon Rondo.* James F. Hance: *2d Grand Fantasie.* Anthony Philip Heinrich: *The Debarkation March; Toccatina Capriciosa.* Charles F. Hupfield: *A Favorite Waltz with Variations.* Francis Johnson: *Honour to the Brave; Johnson's New Cotillions.* Christopher Meineke: *Divertimento; Variations to the favourite air Au clair de la lune.* Julius Metz: *Petit Pot Pourri.* Peter K. Moran: *A Fantasia; Moran's Favorite Variations to the Suabian Air.* Oliver Shaw: *Welcome the Nation's Guest.* William Taylor: *Clinton's Triumph.* Charles Thibault: *L'Adieu à Rondo.* Charles Zeuner: *Grand Centennial March.* Contains a most helpful preface, biographical notes on each composer, and sometimes a discussion of the pieces. Int. to M-D.

Best of Ragtime (Max Morath—Cherry Lane Music 1993) 54pp. 12 pieces, including The Entertainer; Dill Pickles; Ragtime Nightingale; Grizzly Bear Rag. Fine discussion of tempos in ragtime, suggested dynamics. M-D.

The Bicentennial Collection of American Keyboard Music (Edward Gold—McAfee 1975). Covers the period from 1790 to 1900 and represents a wide variety of styles. Alexander Reinagle: *La Chasse.* James Hewitt: *Yankee Doodle with Variations.* Frederick Damish: *President Adams Grand March and Quick Step.* Anthony P. Heinrich: *The Maiden's Dirge.* Charles Grobe: *Variations on My Old Kentucky Home* Op.385. Stephen C. Foster: *Holiday Scottish.* H. A. Wollenhaupt: *Etude* A♭ Op.22/1. Louis M. Gottschalk: *The Dying Swan* RO 76. Richard Hoffman: *Chi-ci Pipi Nini* (Cuban Dance). Frederick Brandeis: *Still Life* Op.85/2. George W. Chadwick: *Caprice* No.2. Edward MacDowell: *A.D. 1620* Op.55/3; *Starlight* Op.55/4. Ethelbert Nevin: *Alba (Dawn)* Op.25/1. Harvey W. Loomis: *Music of the Calumet* Op.76/1. Mrs. H. H. A. Beach: *Scottish Legend* Op.54/1. Scott Joplin: *The Easy Winners.* Arthur Farwell: *Dawn* Op.12. Also contains notes on the composers and the individual pieces. Int. to M-D.

The Bicentennial Collection of American Music Vol.I, 1698–1800 (Compiled by Elwyn A. Wienandt—Hope 1974) 240pp. William Brown: *Rondo* III G (1787). Alexander Reinagle: *Federal March* (1788). Raynor Taylor: *An Easy and Familiar Lesson for Two Performers on One Piano Forte* (1793?) consisting of a Menuetto, Gavotta and Fandango. Franz Kotzwara: The *Battle of Prague* (1793) (incomplete). Francis Linley: *Two Selections (Tempo di Gavotta, Tempo di Minuetto)* from *A New Assistant for the Piano-Forte* (1796), the first piano instruction book printed in America. James Hewitt: *The Battle of Trenton* (1798) (incomplete, 249 bars omitted). Commentary by the compiler. Int. to M-D.

Changing Faces (Hinson—EAMC 591) 34pp. New piano works by American composers. Robert Beaser: *Landscape with Bells.* Kamran Ince: *My Friend Mozart.* Stephen Paulus: *Dance.* Tobias Picker: *Old and Lost Rivers.* Chris-

topher Rouse: *Little Gorgon*. Joseph Schwantner: *Veiled Autumn*. Alvin
Singleton: *Changing Faces*. Each piece is discussed. M-D.

Classic Piano Rags (Dover 1973) selected and with an introduction by Rudi
Blesh. 364pp. Contains 81 piano rags by Scott Joplin, James Scott, Joseph
Francis Lamb (50 pieces by these three composers), Charles Hunter, Percy
Wenrich, Thomas Turpin, Arthur Marshall, Artie Mathers, and several others. Provides a wide and diverse selection of rags from the earliest period
of ragtime, when it was associated with folk songs and dance, to its later
classical period. Contains the original covers on the sheet music. M-D.

A Collection of Early American Keyboard Music (Hinson, McClenny—Willis
1971). Anonymous: *Yankee Doodle Arranged with Variations*. Raynor Taylor: *Rondo* G. Christopher Moller: *Sonata* VIII D. William Brown: *Rondo* I
G. Mr. Newman: *Sonata* Op.1/1 C. James Hewitt: *Mark My Alford With
Variations*. Alexander Reinagle: *Sonata* I, D. Also includes preface, comments on composers and works, and editorial additions in red type. Int. to
M-D.

Contemporary American Piano Music (J. Prostakoff—Morris 1956). 29 pieces by
19 American composers. Wide range of contemporary idioms and wide
range of difficulty. Int. to M-D.

Early American Music (A. McClenny, M. Hinson—WB). Reinagle, Hewitt, Carr,
Taylor, anonymous dances. Discussion of the works, composers, keyboard
instruments. Easy to Int.

Easy American Piano Classics (Stuart Isacoff—Consolidated Music Publishers
1978) 80pp. Vol.76 in series *Music for Millions*. Rags, blues, early jazz,
marches, dances, and modern music from the Revolutionary War to the
1970s. Int. to M-D.

Four Piano Rags (Margun). Four new works by Gunther Schuller, Robert Car-
riker, Stefan Koznski, and Kenneth Laufer, all composed between 1977 and
1981. The style continues to fascinate composers. M-D.

Great American Piano Works (D. Tucker—WB 1992) 128pp. Leroy Anderson:
Forgotten Dreams; *Jazz Legato*; *Serenata*; *The Typewriter*. William Bergsma:
Fantasie No.3. Paul Creston: *Burlesk*; *Interlude*; *Salve Regina*. Norman
Dello Joio: *Sonata* I. Louis M. Gottschalk: *The Banjo* Op.15; *Scherzo Ro-
mantique* Op. posth. Morton Gould: *Boogie Woogie Etude*; *Pavanne*. Scott
Joplin: *Bethena*; *The Cascades*; *Elite Syncopations*; *Harmony Club Waltz*;
Maple Leaf Rag. Edward MacDowell: *Arabesque* Op.39/4; *At an Old Tryst-
ing Place* Op.51/3; *Romance* Op.39/3; *Sonata* Op.57 (1st movement); *To the
Sea* Op.55/1; *Told at Sunset* Op.51/6. Ethelbert Nevin: *Narcissus* Op.13/4.
No distinction between composers' and editor's marks. No sources listed. Int.
to D.

Masters of American Piano Music (Hinson—Alfred 4603) 64pp. Foreword, discussion of three periods of American piano music, suggested teaching order, and discussion of each piece. Barber: *Love Song*. Beach: *In Autumn*.
B. Carr: *Yankee Doodle arr. as a Rondo*. Crumb: *Dream Images*. Faith: *Souvenir*. Finney: *Medley*. Gottschalk: *Ojos Criollos*. Harrison: *Reel*. Heinrich:

Philadelphia Waltz. Hoffman: *Dixiana*. Joplin: *Gladiolus Rag*. MacDowell: *To an Old White Pine* Op.62/7. Mason: *Lullaby* Op.10. Paine: *Village Dance* Op.26/5. Reinagle: *East Nook of Fife*. Int. to M-D.

Masters of Our Day (Saminsky, Freed—CF 1963). 18 pieces in contemporary idiom from the series bearing the same title, also published separately in the 1950s. This entire series is still available separately. The collection contains: A. Copland: *Sunday Afternoon Music*; *The Young Pioneers*. H. Cowell: *The Harper Minstrel Sings*; *The Irishman Dances*. I. Freed: *Jeneral Jerry's Jolly Jugglers*. H. Hanson: *The Bell*; *Dance of the Warriors*; *Enchantment*. D. Milhaud: *Touches Blanches*; *Touches Noir*. D. Moore: *Careful Etta*; *Fiddlin' Joe*; *Grievin' Annie*. R. Sessions: *March*. D. Taylor: *The Smugglers*. R. Thompson: *Little Prelude*; *Song After Sundown*. V. Thomson: *A Day Dream*. Easy to Int.

Mosaics (Marguerite Miller—Alfred 10156). Pieces by Paul Creston, Vincent Persichetti, Paul Cooper, Ross Lee Finney, Merrill Bradshaw, and others. Short pieces by some of the finest contemporary American composers that demonstrate new notation and "far out" sounds. Recording included. Editor encourages students to make up their own compositions using techniques employed in the various compositions. Int.

Music from the Days of George Washington (U.S. George Washington Bi-centennial Commission 1931; reprint AMS Press 1970) 61pp. Introduction by Carl Engle. In addition to other items this collection contains the following piano music: Philip Phile: *The President's March*; *Washington's March*; *General Burgoyne's March*; *Brandywine Quick-Step*; *Successful Campaign*. James Hewitt: *The Battle of Trenton* (abbreviated form). Alexander Reinagle; *Sonata* D (first movement); *Menuet and Gavotte*. Pierre Duport: *Two Minuets*. William Brown: *Rondo*. Int. to M-D.

New Music for the Piano (J. Prostakoff—LG 1963). 24 pieces by 24 contemporary American composers. A fine collection representing many styles of writing. Samuel Adler: *Capriccio*. Josef Alexander: *Incantation*. Milton Babbitt: *Partitions*. Ernst Bacon: *The Pig-Town Fling*. Arthur Berger: *Two Episodes: 1933*. Sol Berkowitz: *Syncopations*. Mark Brunswick: *Six Bagatelles*. Norman Cazden: *Sonata*. Ingolf Dahl: *Fanfares*. Vivian Fine: *Sinfonia and Fugato*. Miriam Gideon: *Piano Suite* No.3. Peggy Glanville-Hicks: *Prelude for a Pensive Pupil*. Morton Gould: *Rag—Blues—Rag*. Robert Helps: *Image*. Alan Hovhaness: *Allegro on a Pakistan Lute Tune*. Kent Kennan: *Two Preludes*. Earl Kim: *Two Bagatelles*. Leo Kraft: *Allegro Giocoso*. Hall Overton: *Polarities* No.1. George Perle: *Six Preludes*. Paul A. Pisk: *Nocturnal Interlude*. Mel Powell: *Etude*. Joseph Prostakoff: *Two Bagatelles*. Ben Weber: Humoreske. M-D to D.

Nineteenth-Century American Piano Music (Gillespie—Dover 1978) 323pp. Contains 40 works by 27 composers, a chronological list, and introductory notes. Some of the composers are Mrs. H. H. A. Beach, Dudley Buck, Victor Herbert, Ethelbert Nevin, L. M. Gottschalk, Edgar S. Kelly, Harvey W. Loomis, Edward MacDowell, John Knowles Paine. The earliest work dates from 1808, the latest from 1906. Some pieces are fingered and pedaled. Int. to M-D.

Northwest Passages (Permanent Press 1992) 52pp. Music by six composers from the Northwest United States: Dorothy Cadzow, Gerald Kechley, Gloria Swisher, John Verrall, James Beale, and John Cowell, collected by Jane Guthrie Beale. The pieces show "a broad span of expressive content. They are in turn, rollicking, intense, dreamy, driving, atmospheric, philosophical, jazz-tinged, nostalgic, melodious and witty" (from the score). All of the composers have been associated with the University of Washington in Seattle. Int. to M-D.

Piano Music from New Orleans 1851–1898 (Baron—Da Capo 1980) 168pp. 30 pieces, including mazurkas, polkas, waltzes, a varsovia, dances from Mexico and Cuba, celebrations of Mardi Gras, Creole melodies, marches, a 2-step, a cakewalk, and pieces on contemporary social issues. M-D.

Piano Music in Nineteenth Century America (Hinson—Alfred 10102) Vol.I: Thomas Bethune (Blind Tom): *Battle of Manassas*. Richard Hoffman: *In Memoriam L. M. G.* William Wallace: *Nocturne* II. Anton Philip Heinrich: *Song without Words* (for Jenny Lind). William Mason: *Dance Antique* Op.38. MD.

Ragtime Classics (Paxton 1976) 36pp. Introduction by Charles Wilford. Scott Joplin: *The Easy Winners*; *Heliotrope Bouquet* (with Louis Chauvin). Tom Turpin: *St. Louis Rag*. Charles Hunter: *Cotton Bolls*. Arthur Marshall: *Kinklets*. Joe Jordan: *Nappy Lee*. Joseph F. Lamb: *Sensation*. James Scott: *The Ragtime Betty*. Lucian P. Gibson: *Jinx Rag*. J. Hubert (Eubie) Blake: *Fizz Water*. M-D.

The Ragtime Current (EBM 1976) 56pp. Piano solos by a mainstream of today's ragtime composers. Foreword by Rudi Blesh. William Albright: *Sweet Sixteenths*. Donald Ashwander: *Astor Place Rag Waltz*; *Friday Night*. William Bolcom: *Last Rag*. Kathy Craig: *Romantic Rag*. Milton Kaye: *Amatory Hallucination Rag*. Max Morath: *One for Norma*; *The New Black Eagle Buck*. William Rowland: *Tickled Pink*. Thomas A. Schmutzler; *Shootin the Agate*. Trebor Jay Tichenor: *The Show-Me Rag*. Terry Waldo: *Yellow Rose Rag*. M-D.

Ragtime Rediscoveries (Tichenor—Dover 1979) 269pp. A selection of 64 works dating from 1879 to 1921, the golden age of rag; reprints the original sheet music. M-D.

Ragtime for Piano (G. Kaluza—Furore Edition 1994) 31pp. Rags by American women composers. May Aufderheide: *Dusty*; *The Thriller*. Imogene Giles: *Red Peppers*. Grace M. Bolen: *The Smoky Topaz*. Bess Rudisill: *The Thriller*. Julie Lee Niebergall: *Chicken Chowder*. Irene Cozad: *Eatin Time*. Preface in German and English. Int. to M-D.

Seven Americans (Banowetz—GWM). Works by Reid Nibley, Merril Ellis, Felix Powell, Frank Stewart, John Kimmey, William Latham, and David Wheatley. Available separately. Varied styles that include most recent trends. Includes pictures and short biographies of each composer. M-D to D.

Three Centuries of American Music. Vol. 3, *American Keyboard Music Through*

1865 (J. Bunker Clark—G. K. Hall 1990) 442pp. Includes works (in chronological order in book) by James Bremner, Alexander Reinagle, Benjamin Carr (?), James Hewitt, John Christopher Moller, Joanetta Catherine E. van Hagen, Mr. Newman, Philip Laroque, Julius Metz, Peter K. Moran, Arthur Clifton, Charles F. Hupfeld, Charles Thibault, Anthony Philip Heinrich, Joseph C. Taws, Christopher Meineke, Charles Zeuner, Charles Hommann, Leopold Meigen, George Frederick Bristow, Leopold Herwig, William Henry Fry, Edward L. Walker, James G. Maeder, Charles Balmer, William Iucho, Max Tzorr, Oliver J. Shaw, Charles Wels, William Henry Fry, Carl Wolfsohn, Richard Hoffman, Michael Hurley Cross, Charles Kunkel, Theodore von La Hache, Charles Grobe, Samuel Sebastian Mills, Robert Goldbeck, William Mason, Karl Merz, Charles Jerome Hopkins. Includes comments about composers and works.

Vol. 4, *American Keyboard Music 1866 Through 1910* (Sylvia Glickmann—G. K. Hall 1990) 482pp. 1. Early Concert Music: Composers Born 1820–50. Blind Tom, George Frederick Bristow, Dudley Buck, Jr., William Wallace Gilchrist, Louis Moreau Gottschalk, William Mason (Joseph Noll, arranger). 2. Some Women of the Early Period. Faustina Hasse Hodges, Adele Hohnstock, Eliza Pattiani, Clara Kathleen Rogers, Clara Scott, Jane Sloman. 3. Boston Classicists: Composers Active in New England. Amy Marcy Cheney (Mrs. H. H. A. Beach), George Whitfield Chadwick, Arthur Foote, John Knowles Paine, Horatio W. Parker, Arthur Whiting. 4. Contemporaries of the Boston Classicists. Arthur Bird, Victor Herbert, Edward MacDowell, Daniel Gregory Mason, Ethelbert Nevin. 5. The Early Twentieth Century: American Folklore. Frederic Ayers, John Parsons Beach, Charles Wakefield Cadman, John Alden Carpenter, Frederick Shepherd Converse, Arthur Farwell, Silas Gamaliel Pratt. 6. More Women. Celeste Heckscher, Helen Hopekirk, Carrie Jacobs-Bond, Margaret Rutlven Lang, Clara Gottschalk Peterson. 7. Into the Twentieth Century: Descriptive Music and Rags. J. C. Capron, William H. Fry, E. Mack, Father V. De Marzi, E. T. Paull, H. H. Thiele, Septimus Winner. 8. Ragtime. May Aufderheide, Gus W. Bernard, Axel Christensen, Raymond W. Conner, Abraham Holzmann, Sadie Koninsky, Frederick Allen, Julia L. Niebergall, James Scott, Adaline Shepherd, Tom Turpin, Percy Wenrich. Includes comments about composers and works.

Twelve by Eleven (Hinson—Alfred 10114). 12 original compositions by 11 contemporary composers of the U.S. Stylistically, the pieces range from the Romantic heritage to post-serial techniques. Challenging and exciting new piano repertoire. Milton Babbitt: *Playing for Time*. Leslie Bassett: *Mobile*. Fred Coulter: *Variations for Agnes*. George Crumb: *Dream Images*. David Diamond: *Prelude and Fugue* II c. Richard Faith: *Souvenir*. Ross Lee Finney: *Medley*. Lou Harrison: *Homage to Milhaud, Reel*; *Homage to Henry Cowell*. Nelson Keyes: *Three Love Songs*. Halsey Stevens: *Notturno—Bellagio Adagio*. Bruce Wise: *Four Piano Pieces*. For descriptions of each piece, see listing under composer's name. Int. to M-D.

Twentieth Century Composers: Easiest Piano Pieces (CFP 5065) 12pp. 19 pieces. Charles Wuorinen, *Short Pieces* Nos.1 and 2: the most abstract and uncluttered items in the collection. Alan Hovhaness, *Mystic Flute*: the most rhythmically vexing. Soulima Stravinsky, 4 pieces: the most conservative. Katrina Knerr, 4 programmatic works: the most evocative. Ross Lee Finney, 8 brief offerings: the most successful. Int.

Twentieth Century Composers: Intermediate Piano Book (CFP 4199) 39pp. Ross Lee Finney: pages from *24 Inventions*; *32 Piano Games*; and *Youth's Companion*. Alan Hovhaness; *Macedonian Mountain Dance* Ned Rorem: *Barcarolle* I. Soulima Stravinsky: 14 *Preludes* (from *24 Preludes*). Charles Wuorinen: 8 *Short Pieces* (from *12 Short Pieces*): the most difficult; serial and vivid writing.

Various Leaves (Fallen Leaf Press 1993). 35 short works by 31 (mostly living) contemporary American composers in the San Francisco area. Includes works by Leo Ornstein, Lou Harrison, Andrew Imbrie, Richard Felciano, Robert Basart, Robert Greenberg (1954–   ), Peter Josheff (1954–   ), Elinor Armer, Marta Ptaszynska, Douglas Leedy, Robert Strizich, Richard Festinger, and Anthony Gnazzo, among others. Excellent introduction to contemporary styles. Int. to M-D.

Waltzes (CFP 66735 1978). A collection of contemporary waltzes by Ashforth, Babbitt, Busby, Cage, Constanten, Felciano, Fennimore, Finney, Gena, Glass, Harrison, Felps, Imbrie, Kohn, Krauze, Mellnaes, Moran, Sessions, Shifrin, Stout, I. Tcherepnin, Thomson, Thorne, Tower, and Wuorinen. These pieces show that there is still plenty of excitement and dash in this old dance form. Int. to M-D.

World Collection of Piano Pieces for Children, Vol.2, *by American Composers* (M. Hinson—To-oN Kikaku 1984) 44pp. Includes: A. Reinagle: 7 pieces. Raynor Taylor: *Variations to Adeste Fideles*. Edward MacDowell: *Beauty in the Rose-Garden*; *From Dwarf-land*; *An Elfin Round*; *Clown*; *By Smouldering Embers*. Arthur Farwell: *Approach of the Thunder God*; *The Old Man's Love Song*. Nelson Keyes: 3 *Love Songs*. A survey of American piano music since the late eighteenth century. Easy to Int.

World's Greatest Ragtime Solos (Hinson—Alfred 4615) 172pp. Contains over 40 rags by 20 different ragtime masters, including Scott Joplin (18 rags), W. C. Handy, and Eubie Blake, as well as "classic rags" by Debussy and Satie. All pieces appear in their original form. Background information and performance notes given. Int. to M-D.

Australian

Australian Piano Music (Sally Mays—Currency Press 1990, 1994) An outstanding survey of twentieth-century piano music from this great country. Covers a wide variety of styles and techniques. Vol. 1, 51pp., Easy to Int.; Vol. 2, 60pp., Int. Contains notes on each composer and about each piece. Composers: Barry Anderson (1935–1987), Edwin Carr, Ann Carr-Boyd, Ross Edwards, Eric Gross, Michael Hannan, Wendy Hiscocks, Matthew Dylan Jones, Don Kay, Sally Mays, Rosalind Page, Haydn Reeder, Peter Schulthorpe, Larry Sitsky, Martin Wesley-Smith, Lawrence Whiffen.

Austrian

Klaviermusik aus Österreich (H. Kann—UE 1965). Works by Froberger; Fux; Muffat; Wagenseil; Monn; Haydn. *Capriccio* G; Albrechtsberger, *Fugue* F; Mozart, *Rondo* a, K.511; Hummel, *Rondo* Op.11; Woržischek, *Rhapsody* Op.1/9; Czerny, *La Ricordanza* Op.33, *Valses di Bravura* Op.35; Schubert, *Klavierstück* A, *Ecossaises*. Preface and notes about the composers in English, German, French, and Italian. Contains unusual as well as well-known pieces. Clean text and attractive collection. Int. to M-D.

Styrian Composers: Works for Piano (Marckhl—OBV). Six sonatas and two sets of pieces by contemporary Austrian composers.
Vol.1: Waldemar Bloch, Max Haager, H. F. Aigner.
Vol.2: Karol Haidmayer, Gunther Eisen, Walter Kainz.
Vol.3: Evany Mixa, Erich Marchl. M-D.

Belgian

Album I (Metropolis E. M. 4269) 15pp. Contemporary Belgian Music. Richard de Guide: *Nocturne*. Louis de Meester: *Toccata*. R. Van der Velden: *Andante espressivo*. Willem Pelemans: *Allegro flamenco*. All pieces require well-developed technique. M-D to D.

6 Piano Sonatinas by Belgian Composers (Huybregts—AMP 7758 1979) 43pp. Original works by Jean Absil, Victor de Bo, George Lonque, Armand Lonque, Flor Peeters, Marcel Poot. MC with Impressionistic influence. Contains short biographies of all the composers and generally helpful fingering. My favorites are those by de Bo and G. Lonque. All require efficient fingers. Int. to M-D.

Brazilian

Bravo Brazil! (Appleby—Kjos West WP93 1983) Book I 16pp. Osvaldo Lacerdo: *Cana verde*; *Valsa*. Ernst Mahle: *Hoppla, hoppla, bum bum bum*. Francisco Mignone: *Dorme bonequinha*. Marlos Nobre: *Samba matuto*. Heitor Villa-Lobos: *A moda da carranquinha*. A fine introduction to the rich ethnic heritage of Brazil. All the pieces are full of rhythmic vitality and have the universal attractiveness of folk music. Unusual and delightful literature. Int.

Contemporary Brazilian Piano Music (Gerig HG 1068/9 1978) Vol.1: 42pp. Vol.2:

41pp. Preface includes a historical introduction and a discussion of piano music in Brazil by Paulo A. M. Ferreira and biographical notes in German and English. Works by Armando Albuqueque, Heitor Alimonda, Jorge Antunes, Dinorá de Carvalho, Sérgio O. de Vasconcellos Corrêa, Henrique de Curitiba, Alyton Escobar, Mario Ficarelli, Camargo Guarnieri, Osvaldo Lacerda, Souza Lima, Ernst Mahle, Francisco Mignone, Marlos Nobre, Jamary Oliviera, Guerra Peixe, José Penalva, Almeida Prado, Claudio Santoro, Guerra Vicente, Heitor Villa-Lobos. Pieces range from the Romantic (Souza Lima) to the avant-garde (Antunes), broad survey. Int. to M-D.
See: David Appleby, "The Piano Music of Brazil," PQ, 106 (Summer 1979):47–50.

Bulgarian

Bulgarian Miniatures (Kasandjiev—Litolff 1979) 2 vols., each 18pp. 15 pieces in each. Explores entire keyboard, encourages experimentation. Uses conventional articulations, dynamics, pedaling, rhythms, and meters with inventiveness. Clusters, improvisation, free tempo changes explained in the signs chart. Unusual treatment of folksongs and dances; imaginative settings. Arranged in order of increasing difficulty. Int.
Contemporary Bulgarian Piano Music (Otto Daub—Gerig 1965).
Introduction and biographical sketches in English.
Vol.I: Konstantin Iliev (1924–   ): *The Cuckoo*; *The Hen Laid an Egg.* Dimiter Nenov (1902–   ): *Melody*; *Musette*; *Pastorale.* Ljubomir Pipkov (1904–   ): *Spring Dance.* Alexander Raitschev (1922–   ): *The Angry Rooster*; *The Old Water-Mill.* Dimiter Tepkov (1929–   ): *Grandfather's Glove.* Int. to M-D.
Vol.II: Marin Goleminov (1908–   ): *Bulgarian Dance.* Bojan Ikonomov (1900–   ): *Horo.* Vasil Kasandjiev (1934–   ): *The Jolly Sparrow; Nightmare.* Krassimir Kürktschijski (1936–   ): *Elegy.* Pantscho Wladigerov (1899–   ): *Lullaby.* M-D.

Canadian

Alberta Keys (Oil City Press). Order from V. R. Stewart, 68 Cherovan Drive S. W., Calgary, Alberta T2V2 P2 Canada. Contains 45 solos by 17 composers, all members of the Alberta Registered Music Teachers' Association. Reproduced from MS but easy to read. Mainly traditional writing. Int.
The Canadian Musical Heritage. Piano Music (Elaine Keillor—Ottawa 1983). A survey of Canadian piano music written up to the last decade of the nineteenth century.
Vol. I, 246pp. George Pfeiffer (ca. 1790–after 1827): *Canadian Dance.* T. F. Molt (1795–1856): *Post Horn Waltz, with variations.* Alex Duff (died before October 1840): *The Canada Waltz*; *The Montreal Bazaar Waltz*; *A Canadian*

Lady; *The Canada Union Waltz*. A. H. Lockett: *Centenary, or Fancy Fair Polka and Galop*. J. P. Clarke (1807 or 1808–1877): *The Burlington Polka*; *The Janus Minuet*; *The Royal Welcome Waltzes*. J. C. Braunirs, Jr. (1814–1871): *Marche de la St. Jean Baptiste*; *The Monklands Polka*; *The Royal Welcome Waltzes*. G. W. Strathy (1818–1890): *The Magic Bell Polka*; *The National Lancers*; *Joy and Grief*; *Wedding March*; *Brilliant Contradance and Polka*; *Caprice* (d: bravura); *Modulation Sketch*. C. W. Sabatier (1819–1862): *Mazurka Caprice*; *Mazurka Caprice* Op.190. Antoine Dessane (1826–1873): *Quadrille canadien*. Ernest Gagnon (1834–1915): *Le Carnaval de Québec*; *Stadaconé*; *Souvenir de Venise*. Gustave Gagnon (1842–1930): *Reflet du passé*. R. O. Pelletier (1843–1919): *Scherzo*. Damis Paul: *Scintillation*. Gustave Smith (1826–1896): *La Comète*; *Air Savoyard*. Calixa Lavallée (1842–1891): *The War Fever*; *The First Welcome*; *The Ellinger Polka*; *L'Oisau mouche*; *Grande Marche de concert*; *Première Valse de salon*; *Marche funèbre*; *Une Couroune de louriers*; *Vole au vent*; *Le Papillon* (The Butterfly). Solomon Mazurette (1847–1910): *Home, Sweet Home*. W. H. Clarke (1840–1913): *A Storm on the Lake*. Includes information on each composer and piece. The music is pretty trite but this volume gives a good overall view of where Canadian music began. Int. to D.

Vol. II, 282pp. Alexis Contant (1858–1918): *La Lyre enchantée*; *Valse nationale*; *Yvonne*. Susie Frances Harrison (1859–1935): *Chant du voyager*. W. O. Forsyth (1859–1937): *Wiegenlied* Op.12/1; *Evening Song* Op.14/3; *Through the Fields* Op.34/1; *A Song of Summer* Op.38/1; *On the Highway* Op. 40; *Confession* Op.45/2; *In the Vale of Shadowland* Op.50/2; *Prelude* Op59/2. C. A. E. Harriss (1862–1929): *Happy Moments*. J. Humfrey Anger (1862–1913): *Tintamarre*. W. Caven Barron (1866–1956): *Prosodion* Op.2/2; *Deux Mazurkas* Op.13; *Praeludio con Fuga* Op.32; *Valse Impromptu* Op.44; *Ariel* Op.55. Byron C. Topley (1866–1939): *Sonata* A♭. Arthur Letondal (1869–1956): *Mazurka Sentimentale* Op.2/2. Edward Manning (1874–1948): *Fugue*. Emiliano Renaud (1875–1932): *Berceuse*; *"A l'Aurore"*; *Souvenir*. Edmund Hardy (1876–?): *To Daffodils*. Gena Branscombe (1881–1977): *Cavalcade*; *Valse-Caprice*. Leo Smith (1881–1952): *Suite for Piano*; *The Concertina*. Léo Roy (1887–1974): *Serenade*. Henri Gagnon (1887–1961): *Deux Pièces de genre*. George M. Brewer (1889–1947): *Trois Préludes*. Rodolphe Mathieu (1890–1962): *Trois Préludes*; *Sonate*. Claude Champagne (1891–1965): *Prélude et Filigrane* Op.4. Georges-Emile Tanguay (1893–1964): *Trois Pièces brèves*; *Gavotte pompadour*; *Pavane*. Léo-Pol Morin (1892–1941): *Suite canadienne*. Colin McPhee (1901–1964): *Four Piano Sketches* Op.1. Barbara Pentland (1912–   ): *Rhapsody 1939*. John Weinzweig (1913–   ): *Dirgeling*. Better music than in Vol. I. Int. to D. Only after 1940 did Canadian composers "begin to create decidedly original organizations of sounds" (from the Introduction).

Horizons—Music by Canadian Composers (Waterloo 1973) Book I. Nine pieces aimed at acquainting the beginning piano student with the sound of music that is not based on the traditional major or minor scale. Materials drawn from various sources: modes, non-Western scales, synthetic scales. Certain keyboard styles prevalent in twentieth-century idioms are introduced. Explanatory notes and performance suggestions are included for most pieces. Composers include: George Fiala, Louis Applebaum, Violet Archer, Robert Fleming, Carleton Elliott, Brian Cherney, Richard Johnston, Robert Turner, and Murray Adaskin. Int. Book II. Slightly more difficult, follows same format. Composers include: Anne Eggleston, John Beckwith, Samuel Dolin, and Gerhard Wuensch. Int. to M-D.

Meet Canadian Composers at the Piano (Thompson 1968) 24pp. Pieces by Boris Berlin, Claude Champagne, Eileen Ruthven Gilley, William Lea, Leonard Leacock, Godfrey Ridout, and Healey Willan. Easy to Int.

Chinese

Chinese Contemporary Piano Pieces Vol.I (Karlsen Publishers, Hennessy Plaza, Gr/Fl., 164 Hennessy Road, Hong Kong 1979) 88pp. Ah Ping: *The Moon Mirrored in the Pool*. Wang Chien Chung: *Plum Blossom Melody; Sakura*. Yip Wai Hong: *Memories of Childhood* (6 miniatures). Kwo Chi Hung: 2 *Yi Li Folk Songs*. Chu Wang Hua: *Sinkiang Capriccio*. Lui Shi Kuen and Kuo Chi Hung; *Battling the Typhoon*. Post-Romantic pianistic figurations, much pentatonic usage, some charming and interesting moments. This collection is a good example of the type of piano writing going on in this area of the world today. Int. to M-D.

Chinese Piano Music for Children (N. Liao—Schott 7652 1990) 55pp. Written between 1973 and 1986 when Chinese music "increasingly absorbed the influences and ideas current in the new music of the West, without sacrificing its own tradition and national style" (from the score). Luting He (1903–   ), *The Young Shepherd with his little Flute* 1934: tender, artistic simplicity, national style. Shande Ding (1911–   ), *Suite for Children* (5 pieces) 1953: folklike but no folksongs are quoted. Tong Shang (1923–   ), *Seven little Pieces after Folk Songs from Inner Mongolia* 1953: a charming suite of folksong arrangements. Lisan Wang (1953–   ), *Sonatine* 1957: three titled movements, cheerful, displays spirited humor. Int. to M-D.

Chinese Piano Pieces (Chow Shu-San—The New Music Society, P.O. Box 30955 CWB, Hong Kong) 61pp. 10 contemporary pieces by Chinese composers. Heh Lu-Ting: *Buffalo Boy's Flute*. Chow Shu-San: *Dragon Dance; Meditation*. Chan Pui-Fan: *The Pedlar; To Spring*. M. S. Dow: *Water Grass*. C. C. Wu: *Wedding Dance*. Chen Chien Hua: *Love Dance of Yi Tribe*, etc. Most pieces are short (4 or 5pp.) and use some form of the pentatonic scale. All are colorful. Int. to M-D.

The Dream of Heaven, New Piano Music from China 1992 (Naixiong Liao—Schott) 55pp. 10 works by 6 contemporary Chinese composers. All the pieces (except one from 1934) have been composed since 1972. Luting: *Berceuse* 1934. Jianzhong Wang: *All the Birds Gather Before the Phoenix* 1973. Yinghai Li: *Flute and Drum at Sunset* 1979. Lisan Wang: *The Dream of*

Heaven 1980. Jihoa Quan: *Combination of Long and Short* 1984. Zhongrong Luo: *Three Piano Pieces* Op.50, 1986. A fine collection showing present-day thinking in China as regards the piano. No masterpieces here but rather mostly colorful writing showing folk influences. Recorded on Wergo 60138-10 (cassette) and 60137-50 (CD) by pianist Chong Liao. M-D.

Selected Piano Pieces by Contemporary Chinese Composers (Ts'enyu Music Publishing Co., 7, Macdonnell Rd., 2/F, Hong Kong 1974) 58pp. Lin Sheng-shil (1915–   ): *Thailand Fantasy*. Hwang Yau-tai (1912–   ): *Aria and Fuga*. Chen Chien-Hua (1935–   ): *Adagio für Klavier*. Wong Yok-Yee (1924–   ): *St Lukas Church*. Ts'ao Yuen-Sheng (1940–   ): *Lamp and After* (3 *Little Pieces*); *Festival*. Most are written in a post-Impressionistic idiom with much pentatonic usage. Colorful. M-D.

Czech

Czech Classics (Artia). Two large series, Musica Antiqua Bohemica (MAB) and Musica Viva Historica (MVH) are available. The following volumes are of interest to the pianist:
MAB Vol.14: *Classici Boemici I*. Works by Benda, Brixi, J. A. Stepan, F. X. Dussek, Kozeluh, Becvarovsky, Vranicky, Cibulka, Jirovec, Held and Vitášek.
MAB Vol.20: *Classici Boemici II*. Works by J. L. Dussek, Reicha, Tomášek and Voříšek. Vols.14 and 20 each contain biographical and analytical notes in English.
MAB Vol.17: *Sonatine Boemiche* (Bohemian Sonatinas). Sonatina movements and sonatinas by J. Benda, F. X. Dussek, J. L. Dussek, L. A. Kozeluh, J. Mysliveček, J. B. Vanhal, J. Voříšek.
MVH Vol.15: *Czech Variations of the 18th Century for Piano*. Works by Stepan, Becvarovsky, Vanhal, Kozeluh, J. L. Dussek, Lipavsky.
MVH Vol.5: *Ceske Sonatiny* alter tschechischer Meister (Czech Sonatinas) (O. Kredba).

Czech Piano Music: 42 Works by Dussek, Dvorák, Janácek, Martinu, and Smetana. Selected and introduced by Rudolf Firkushny (Dover 1995) 181pp. Includes excerpts Dvorák: *Poetic Tone Pictures* Op.85; Janáček: *On the Overgrown Path*, Books 1 and 2. Martinů: *Puppets*, Books 1 and 2. J. L. Dussek: *Leaving for Syria* (Theme and 8 variations). Smetana: *Czech Dances*, 5 excerpts; *Festival of the Bohemian Peasants* (*Dreams*, Op.6/6); and 3 excerpts from *Memories of Bohemia in the Form of Polkas*. Int. to M-D.

Czech, Twentieth Century

Contemporary Czechoslovakian Piano Music (Jan Matějček—Gerig 1978). Introduction in English, biographical sketches.
Vol.I: Viktor Kalabis (1923–   ): *About a Fountain*. Dezider Kardoš (1914–   ): *Bagatella*. Jaroslav Křička (1882–   ): *Scherzino*. Bohuslav Martinů

(1890–1959): *A Composition for Little Elves.* Jan Novák (1921–   ): *Allegretto.* Klement Slavický (1910–   ): *A Ballad.* Luboš Sluka (1928–   ): *Two Merry Pieces for Piano.* Eugen Suchoň (1908–   ): *Arietta.* Václav Trojan (1907–   ): *The Bells of Prague.* Int. to M-D.

Vol.II: Jan Klusák (1934–   ): *Rondo.* Marek Kopelent (1932–   ): *For Arnošt Wilde.* Juraj Pospíšil (1931–   ): *Monologue.* Zbyněk Vostřak (1920–   ): *Essay.* Ilja Zeljenka (1932–   ): *Three Pieces for Piano.* M-D to D.

Czechoslovak Album for the Young (CFP 9418). 40 easy, progressive pieces by nineteenth-century and contemporary composers from Smetana, Dvořák, Fibich, Janáček, and Martinů to present-day writers such as Sarauer, Batńy, and Schåfer. Many folk-dance rhythms, much lyricism, and varied moods. Contains a short note about each composer. Easy to Int.

Dutch

Dutch Piano Album No.2 (B&VP). 13 compositions by H. Andriessen, W. Andriessen, Felderhof, de Groot, Hengeveld, Meenwisse, Mul, Mulder, Stokvis, Strategier, Van Der Bilt, Van Hemel. M-D.

Dutch Piano Album No.3 (Homage to Willem Pijper) (B&VP). 10 compositions by Van Baaren, Bosmans, Dijk, Dresden, Escher, Henkemans, Van Lier, Mengelberg, Wijdeveld. M-D.

The Most Beautiful Pages from Dutch Harpsichord Music (P. Montani—Ric 1969). J. P. Sweelinck: *Capriccio* a. Heinrich Weissenburg: *Suite* g. Elias Bronnemüller: *Toccatina and Fugue* d. R. P. van Oevering: *Suite* IV. Christian F. Ruppe (1753–?): *Sonata.* M-D.

English

Contemporary British Piano Music (Schott 1956). Works by Don Banks, P. Racine Fricker, Iain Hamilton, and Humphrey Searle. M-D.

English Piano Music 1780–1800 (T. Roberts—ABRSM 1985) 35pp. Entertaining teaching pieces by English composers written "for a public that increasingly regarded piano playing as an essential social grace" (from the Introduction). Matthew Camidge (1764–1844): Sonata D. Stephen Storace (1762–1796): Sonata No.2 G; Sonata No.4 F; Sonata No.5 D. Samuel Wesley (1766–1837): Sonata A Op.5/1; Sonata Bb, Op.5/2. Samuel Arnold (1740–1802): Aria from Sonata a Op.12, Bk. 2 No.11; Sonata D Op.12, Bk. 2 No.3. George Frederick Pinto (1785–1806): Minuetto in Ab. Int. to M-D.

Four Keyboard Sonatas by Early English Women Composers (S. Fortino—Hildegard). Includes works by Cecilia Maria Barthelemon (1770–?): dedicated to Haydn. Vernoica Dussek Cianchettini (1779–1833): with variations on "Adeste Fideles." Maria Hester Parke (1775–1822). Elizabeth Weichsell Billington (ca. 1765–1818): written at age 8. Biographical sketches; early Classic style. Int. to M-D.

Great English Piano Works (D. Tucker—WB 1991) 144pp. Thomas Arne: *Sonata IV* d. John Blow: *Almand I*; *Chaconne*. Frank Bridge: *Capriccio I* a. John Bull: *Courante Jewel*; *Galiardo*; *The King's Hunt*. William Byrd: *The Carman's Whistle*; *Preludium* C; *Sellenger's Round*; *Victoria*. Edward Elgar: *Dance I*, from "The Bavarian Highlands"; *Enfants D'un Rêve*; *Pomp and Circumstance I*. Giles Farnaby: *Fantasia*; *Paroles Wharfe*; *The Land of Salisbury Pavan*; *Preludium* G. Thomas Morley: *Alman* C; *Fantasia* a. Henry Purcell: *Overture* D; *Suite V*; *Toccata* A. Cyril Scott: *Chimes* Op.40/3; *Impromptu* Op.41; *Lotus Land*; *A Song from the East* from "Summerland." Thomas Tallis: *Felix Narnque II*. No distinction between composers' and editor's marks. No sources listed. Int. to M-D.

The London Pianoforte School 1770–1860 (N. Temperley—Garland Publishing). Over 400 individual pieces by 44 composers, including the complete works for piano solo by Clementi, Cogan, Field, Pinto, and Sterndale Bennett. Reproduced in facsimile from the first or other authentic editions with editorial corrections and interpretations entered directly on the page.

Vols.1–5. Muzio Clementi: complete works for piano solo.

Vol.6. Continental composers in London: Haydn, Dussek, and contemporaries (1770–1810).

Vol.7. Late Georgian composers: Samuel Wesley and contemporaries (1776–1830).

Vol.8. Philip Cogan (c.1748–1833): complete sonatas for piano solo.

Vol.9–11. John Baptist Cramer; selected works.

Vols.12–13. John Field; complete works for piano solo.

Vol.14. George Frederick Pinto: complete works for piano solo. Cipriani Potter: selected piano pieces.

Vol.15. Continental composers in London: Ries, Moscheles, and contemporaries (1810–1850).

Vol.16. Early Victorian Composers: William Wallace, S. S. Wesley, and contemporaries (1830–1860).

Vol.17–18: William Sterndale Bennett, complete works for piano solo.

Vol.19. A selection of duets (1777–1838).

Vol.20. Sonatas for two pianos (1775–1815).

Masters of English Piano Music (Hinson—Alfred 4505) 64pp. Foreword, discussion of the English keyboard idiom, suggested teachings order, and discussion of each piece. Arne: *Gigue* G. Arnold: *Song of the Shepherd Boy*. Attwood: *Sonatina* G. Bantock: *Chanticleer*. J. Barrett: *The St. Catherine*. Blow: *Air*. Byrd: *Wolsey Wilde*. Clarke: *The Duke of Glocester's March*. Croft: *Trumpet Tune*. d'Albert: *Blues*. Elgar: *Skizze*. Farnaby: *A Maske*. Field: *Nocturne* e. Gibbons: *Pavane Lord Salisbury*. Hook: *Sonatina* F Op.12/9. Ireland: *Reapers' Dance*. R. Jones: *Brisk Air in G*. Matthay: *Moment Musical* Op.11/6. Purcell: *Hornpipe* B♭. Scott: *Lento*. Templeton: *Springtime in the Village*. Wesley: *Sonatina* G Op.4/10. Sources listed. Int. to M-D.

Spectrum. 20 Contemporary Works (T. Myers—ABRSM 1996) 71pp. All composers live in Great Britain. Diversity of styles is noted in the moderately short pieces. Eleanor Alberga (1949–   ): *If the Silver Bird Could Speak*.

David Bedford (1937–   ): *Toccata*. Diana Burrell (1948–   ): *Constellations I and II*. Philip Cashian (1963–   ): *Landscape*. Brian Elias (1948–   ): *Moto perpetuo*. Michael Finnissy (1946–   ): *Yvaropera 5*. Graham Fitkin (1963–   ): *Sazz*. Michael Zev Gordon (1963–   ): *Far Away*. Jonathan Harvey (1939–   ): *ff*. Alun Hoddinott (1929–   ): *Dark March*. Gabriel Jackson (1962–   ): *Memorial Blues*. Stephen Montague (1943–   ): *Mira*. Anthony Payne (1936–   ): *Song Without End*. Roger Redgate (1958–   ): *Trace*. Jeremy Dale Roberts (1934–   ): *Stele for John Lambert*. Edwin Roxburgh (1937–   ): *Moonscape*. Timothy Salter (1942–   ): *Lutie's Arabesque*. David Sawer (1961–   ): *Diversion*. Howard Skempton (1947–   ): *Cantilena*. Andrew Toovey (1962–   ): *Still*. Int. to M-D.

English Virginalists

Anne Cromwell's Virginal Book 1638 (Transcribed and edited by Howard Ferguson—OUP 1975). Anne Cromwell was the first cousin of Oliver Cromwell, and this edition of her Virginal Book provides a revealing glimpse of the kind of keyboard music that was played in the home during the second quarter of the seventeenth century. The collection, which consists of 50 short arrangements of songs, dances, and masque music, is a personal anthology of enjoyable keyboard pieces. It is an important link between *Parthenia* (1612) and *Musick's Hand-Maide* (1663). Some chording and octaves. Int. to M-D.

At the Court of Queen Anne (Fuller-Maitland—JWC). Contains smaller pieces by many of the composers listed in *Contemporaries of Purcell*. Trumpet Tunes, Minuets, Marches, Aires, a Serenade, and two song transcriptions by W. Croft, J. Clarke, John Blow, John Barrett and Richard Jones. Contains some delightful literature. Highly edited. Int.

Clement Matchett's Virginal Book (1612) (T. Dart—S&B). 12 pieces by Byrd, Bull, Wilby, and others, from a manuscript written by a young musician in 1612. Excellent scholarly editorial notes. Int. to M-D.

Contemporaries of Purcell (Fuller-Maitland—JWC).
Vols.I,II: works of John Blow (1648–1708).
Vols.III,IV: works of William Croft (1678–1727).
Vol.V: works of Jeremiah Clarke (ca. 1675–1707).
Vol.VI: works by Benjamin Rogers (1614–1698), Mark Coleman, Gerhard Diesner, Robert King, Daniel Purcell, John Eccles.
Vol.VII: works by Francis Piggott (?–1704), William Turner (1651–1740), John Barrett (1674–1735), and Anonymous. Int. to M-D.

Early English Keyboard Music (Barsham—JWC 1980). Useful semi-urtext teaching material, well-chosen pieces; emphasizes lighter textures that transfer better to the piano. Ornaments are realized in a rationalized system, essential fingering included. Book 1: 25 pieces by Arne, Byrd, Purcell, Gibbons,

Blow, Clark, Barrett, Farnaby, Green, Peerson, Croft, Stanley, Johnson. Book 2: 26 pieces from similar sources, a little more difficult. Int.

Early English Keyboard Music (H. Ferguson—OUP). Scholarly notes on the music, ornamentation, rhythmic conventions, interpretation. No editorial phrasing, dynamics or fingering added. Arranged in order of technical difficulty.

Vol.I: 19 pieces by Tallis, Newman, Byrd, Tavener, Farnaby, Bull, Munday, etc.

Vol.II: 23 pieces by Tomkins, Gibbons, Locke, H. Purcell, and D. Purcell, Clarke, etc.

Early English Music (Halford—Alfred 1979) 24pp. 15 dances by Byrd, Farnaby, Purcell, and "Anonymous." Prefatory notes for the teacher, information on the period, and a discussion of ornaments. Int.

English Keyboard Music 1663–1702 (R. Jones—ABRSM 1990) 24pp. Contains keyboard pieces from the last half of the seventeenth century: the post-Restoration period, which was dominated by Henry Purcell (1659–95). Includes: William Lawes (1602–45): *Golden Grove, Coranto.* Benjamin Rogers (1614–98): *Jigg.* Matthew Locke (1621–77): *Alman.* Albertus Bryne (ca. 1621–71): *Sarabande.* Anonymous: *Italian Rant; The English Paspy.* Thomas Pratt (17th century): *Sarabande to "Corke."* John Blow (1649–1708): *Round O.* Henry Purcell: *Prelude* Z.660: 1; *Minuet* Z.649; *March* Z.647; *Minuet* Z.T.688; *Song Tune* Z.T694; *Minuet* Z.650; *Riggadoon* Z.653; *Corant* Z.660:3; *A New Scotch Tune* Z.655; *Sarabande* Z.665: 4; *Jigg* Z.665: 5. Jeremiah Clarke (ca. 1674–1707): *Round O.* Robert King (ca. 1676–1728): *Air.* (Thomas?) Morgan (fl.1691–99): *Twas When the Sheep was Shearing.* John Barrett (ca. 1676–1719): *Minuett.* Ralph Courteville (d. ca. 1735): *Minuett; Air.* Daniel Purcell (ca. 1660–1717): *Hornpipe.* William Croft (1678–1727): *Aire.* Charming. Int.

English Piano Music for the Young Musician (György Balla—EMB) 49pp. Contains one work from the Robertsbridge Codex, fourteen other short anonymous pieces, and works by Hugh Ashton (*Hornepype*), J. Barrett, Blow, Bull, Byrd, Clarke, Croft, Eccles, Giles Farnaby, Richard Farnaby, Edmund Hooper, R. Johnson, Morley, Peerson, Daniel Purcell, Henry Purcell, Tisdall. A few ornaments have been realized; clean edition. Int. to M-D.

15 Pieces from Elizabeth Rogers' Virginal Book (1656) (F. Dawes—Schott 1951). Anonymous: *Nanns maske; Almaygne; The Nightingale; Almaygne; Corrant; Selebrand; A Maske; The Chestnut; Corrant; Selebrand; Mock-Nightingale; Corrant; Phill Porters Lamentation.* Beare: *Selebrand.* Robert Johnson (Orlando Gibbons): *Almaygne.* Int. to M-D.

Fitzwilliam Virginal Book (Fuller-Maitland, Barclay Squire—Br&H; reprint, Dover, 1964). 2 vols. The most comprehensive and extensive collection of keyboard music from the period 1550–1620; in fact, it is one of the greatest keyboard collections of all time. Contains 297 compositions, representing practically every composer of the virginal school: over 130 dances, 46 arrangements of 40 songs, 9 arrangements of madrigals, 22 fantasias, 19 preludes, 6 sets of hexachord variations, and 7 fancy pieces descriptive or otherwise. The majority of works were written by four composers: 72 by Byrd, 52 by Farnaby, 45 by Bull, 19 by Peter Philips. Int. to M-D.

See: Elizabeth Cole, "7 Problems of the Fitzwilliam Virginal Book, an Interim Report," PRMA, 79 (1952–53):51–64.

Howard Ferguson, "Repeats and Final Bars in the Fitzwilliam Virginal Book," ML, 43 (October 1962):345–50.

Guy Wuellner, "The Fitzwilliam Virginal Book," MR, 32/4 (November 1971):326–48. An excellent discussion of textural procedures of the English Virginalists.

The Mulliner Book (D. Stevens—S&B 1954) Vol.1 of *Musica Britannica. Pieces from The Mulliner Book* (CFP). The manuscript of this work was compiled around 1550 and contains works by John Tavener, Richard Farrant, John Redford, Thomas Tallis, and others. In the introduction Stevens says: "The Mulliner Book alone runs the whole gamut of 16th-century music. Latin motets, English anthems, arrangements of part-songs, transcriptions of consort music, plainsong, fantasias for organ, dance music for clavichord or virginals, music for cittern and gittern."

See: D. Stevens, *The Mulliner Book: A Commentary* (London: Stainer and Bell, 1952).

Musick's Hand-Maid (T. Dart—S&B). First published in 1663. Contains approximately 80 miniatures, including works by Locke, Purcell, and others. Represents some of the finest harpsichord music of the period. Scholarly edition.

Parthenia (K. Stone—BB 1951; T. Dart—S&B 1960). When first printed in 1611 this collection was called "Maydenhead of the first Musicke ever printed for the Virginals." It contained 21 pieces by Bull, Byrd, and Gibbons.

See: Hilda Andrews, "Elizabethan Keyboard Music," MQ, 16 (January 1930):59–71.

Otto E. Deutsch, "Cecilia and Parthenia," MT, 100 (November 1959):591–92.

Charles W. Timbrell, "Performance Problems of English Virginal Music," PQ, 77 (Fall 1971):20–23.

Finnish

Finnish Piano Music for the Youth (Fazer 117341 1978) 37pp. Contains works by 9 Finnish composers, of whom only Selim Palmgren and Jean Sibelius are well known. Provides an introduction to early-twentieth-century Finnish piano music. Int. to M-D.

French

L'Album des Six (ESC 1920). Durey: *Romance sans paroles*. Honegger: *Sarabande*. Poulenc: *Valse*. Milhaud: *Mazurka*. Auric: *Prelude*. Tailleferre: *Pastorale*. This collection proclaimed the existence of the French group known as "Les Six," although they never had identical aesthetic views or artistic aims. Contains pieces in varied styles and techniques.

A l'Exposition (Sal 1937). Contains eight piano works by Auric, Delannoy, Ibert,

Milhaud, Poulenc, Sauguet, Schmitt, Tailleferre. Wide scope of idioms and difficulty.

French Piano Music of the Early 20th Century (Martin Canin—Sal 1976). 74pp. Déodat de Séverac: *En Vacances* ("Holiday Time") (suite of seven short Romantic pieces). Charles Koechlin: *Petites Pièces faciles* Op.41/1 (suite of ten pieces); *1ère Sonatine* Op.59/1. Darius Milhaud: *4 Romances sans paroles*. Florent Schmitt: *Musiques Intimes* Op.29/1, 3, 5 (suite of three pieces). Francis Poulenc: *Improvisations* Nos.3, 5, 6, 8, 12; *Badinage*. Excellent anthology of recital and teaching repertoire by five French composers who were all major figures during their lifetime. M-D.

French Piano Music: An Anthology (I. Philipp—Dover 1977) 188pp. 44 short works from 1670 to 1906 representing 28 composers. Includes a wide range of compositions: courantes, passepieds, sarabandes, gigues, gavottes, preludes, minuets, waltzes, romances, scherzos, and caprices. Works of special interest include: Lully: *Courante* in e; F. Couperin: *Les Papillons*; Rameau: *The Hen*; Gossec; *Gavotte*; Saint-Saëns: *Song without Words*; Delibes: *Passepied*; Bizet: *Le Retour*; Massenet: *Toccata*; Fauré: *Fourth Barcarolle*; d'Indy: *Scherzo* from *Sonata* C. Other composers are J. C. de Chambonnières, André Campra, André-Cardinal Destouches, J. B. Loeillet, François Dagincourt, Louis-Claude Daquin, Johann Schobert, C. -H. Valentin Alkan, Georges Mathias, Théodore Dubois, Emmanuel Chabrier, Charles-Marie Widor, Benjamin Godard, Cécile Chaminade, Camille Erlanger, Gabriel Pierné, Isidor Philipp. Int. to M-D.

French Piano Music 1784–1845 (M. Cauchie—l'OL 1957). This fine collection gives an excellent account of French piano repertoire from this period. Brief biographies in French. Contains 12 works: Nicolas Séjan (1745–1819): *Pièces dans le genre gracieux, gai* Op.11/1–2 (1784). Charles Bonjour: *Prélude en sol mineur* Op.8/8 (around 1791). G. P. Repichet: *Première Sonate* Op.1/1 (around 1795). Hyacinthe Jadin (1769–1802); *Andante de la dixième Sonate* Op.4/1 (around 1795); *Dix-septième sonate* Op.6/2 (around 1800). Alexandre Boëly (1785–1858): *Caprice* No.5/2 (around 1810). Leon Kreutzer (1817–1868): *Valses* Op.3 (1830 or 31). Ambroise Thomas (1811–1896): *Fantaisie sur un air ecossais* Op.5 (1835); *Valse caractéristique* No.6 Op.4 (1835). Felix le Couppey (1811–1887): *Troisième étude de salon* (1842). Emil Prudent (1817–1863): *Scherzo* Op.19/2 (1845).

Great French Piano Works (Tucker—WB 1990) 136pp. Georges Bizet: *Intermezzo* from "L'Arlesienne Suite II." Cécile Chaminade: *Air de Ballet; Scarf Dance. Ernest Chausson: *Pavane* Op.26/3. François Couperin: *La Diligente*; *Soeur Monique*. Claude Debussy: *En Bateau*; *Golliwogg's Cake Walk*; *La Cathédrale Engloutie*; *Prelude* a from "Pour le Piano." Paul Dukas: *Sonata* eb *(second movement)*. Gabriel Fauré: *Barcarolle VII* Op.90; *Valse-Caprice* Op.30. Henri Lemoine: *Etudes Enfantines* Op.37/23, 50. J. P. Rameau: *Les Tourbillons*. Maurice Ravel: *La Vallée des Cloches*; *Le Jardin Féerique*; *Pavane de la Belle au bois dormant*. Camille Saint-Saëns: *Etude de Rythme* Op.52/4; *Tierces Majeures et Mineures* Op.111/1. Erik Satie: *Gymnopédie I*. Charles Emile Waldteufel: *Bella Polka* Op.113; *Dolores Waltz* Op.170.

Charles-Marie Widor: *Valse Slave* Op.26/4. No distinction between composers' and editor's markings. No sources listed. Int. to M-D.

Masters of French Piano Music (Hinson—Alfred 4503) 64pp. Foreword, discussion of the French idiom, suggested teaching order, analysis of each piece. Alkan: *Les Cloches.* Anonymous French (early 16th century): *Branle.* Campra: *L'Europe Galante.* Chabrier: *Feuillet d'Album.* Chausson: *Dédication* Op.26/1. F. Couperin: *La Pastourelle.* Daquin: *Noël.* Debussy: *Jimbo's Lullaby; General Lavine—eccentric.* Delibes: *Passepied.* Destouches: *Amadis de Grèce.* Fauré: *Romance sans Paroles* Op.17/3. Franck: *Noël Angevin.* Gossec: *Rosine.* Gounod: *Musette.* Lully: *Air.* Marais: *Romance.* Mouret: *The Highlander.* Rameau: *Tambourin; Le Lardon.* Ravel: *Emmanuel Chabrier: Paraphrase sur un air de Gounod.* Satie: *Gymnopédie* No.3. Schmitt: *Valse Viennoise.* de Séverac: *The Little Girls from Next Door.* Sources listed. Int. to M-D.

Piano Works by French Composers (Margaret Gresh—GS 1977) 159pp. Bizet: *L'Arlésienne*: suites de concert Nos.1 and 2. Debussy: *Suite bergamasque.* Fauré: *Romance sans paroles; First Barcarolle* Op.26; *Third Impromptu* Op.34; *Fourth Nocturne* Op.36; *Fourth Barcarolle* Op.44; *Sixth Barcarolle* Op.70; *Clair de lune* Op.46/2; *Improvisation* Op.34/5; *Berceuse* Op.56/1. Ravel: *Sonatine.* Satie: *Three Gnossiennes; Three Gymnopédies.* Int. to M-D.

French Clavecinists

Early French Keyboard Music (Barsham—JWC). Book 1: 17 pieces by some of the greatest eighteenth-century French composers, such as Chambonnières, F. Couperin, Dandrieu, Daquin, Rameau. Well edited; helpful preface includes instructions on ornaments. Int. Book 2: 17 pieces, including works by Balbastre, Clerambault, Couperin, Daquin, Dandrieu, Dieupart, Rameau. Int. to M-D.

Early French Keyboard Music (H. Ferguson—OUP). 2 vols. Scholarly introduction discusses complete editions of some of the composers included and provides a table of ornaments by seven different composers spanning the years 1670 to 1724. Contains 50 pieces by Attaingnant, Chambonnières, L. Couperin, d'Anglebert, de la Guerre, F. Couperin, Marchand. M-D.

Early French Masters Miniatures (O. v. Irmer—GS). Works by d'Anglebert, F. Couperin, Dandrieu, Daquin, Loeillet, Lully, Marchand, de Neufville, Rameau. Smaller and easier works, often selected from larger works. Includes a brief section on ornaments and their realization.

The French Baroque (EMB Z8764) 47pp. 17 pieces by F. Couperin, Dandrieu, Daquin, Dagincourt, Destouches, Marais, Rameau. Ornaments are written out, includes essential fingering. Int. to M-D.

French Baroque Music for the Young Pianist (P. Zeitlin—EBM). 21 pieces by nine French composers of the seventeenth and eighteenth centuries. Editorial markings are distinguished from composer's text. Execution of ornaments indicated in footnotes; variety of styles demonstrated in various pieces.

The same fifteen keys that J. S. Bach used in the *Inventions* are represented in this volume. Brief biographies. Easier works by Chambonnières, Louis Couperin, François Couperin, Le Bègue, d'Anglebert, Rameau, Dandrieu, Boismortier, and Daquin.

French Piano Music of the 18th Century (W. Georgii—Arno Volk). Contains mainly excerpts from Couperin's 6th, 8th and 11th ordres; examples from Rameau's *Nouvelles Suites de Pièces de Clavecin*; and works by Daquin and Dandrieu.

See: Beverly Scheibert, *Jean-Henry D'Anglebert and the Seventeenth-Century Clavecin School* (Bloomington: Indiana University Press, 1986).

German

Early German Keyboard Music (Barsham—JWC 55273 1980) Vol.1, 28pp. Pieces by Handel, Kuhnau, Pachelbel, J. S. Bach, Fischer, C. P. E. Bach, Telemann, and others. Vol.2 (JWC 55274) 29pp. Pieces by Krebs, Speer, J. S. Bach, Handel, Muffat, Kirnberger, and others. Clear indications of editorial and original markings. A good blend of well-known favorites and less-familiar items. Also excellent for undergraduates who are studying the history of the period. The pieces sound well on the piano. Int. to M-D.

Early German Keyboard Music (H. Ferguson—OUP 1970). 2 vols. Scholarly introduction that includes a discussion of early sources of German keyboard music, four different systems of notation found in early German keyboard music, forms, tempo, the interpretation of preludes and fugues, ornamentation, rhythmic conventions, and a table of suggested ternary-rhythm interpretation of binary-rhythm gigues. 30 pieces by Anonymous, Kotter, Ammerbach. Paix, Sweelinck, Scheidt, Froberger, Kerll, Buxtehude, Johann Christoph Bach, Krieger Muffat, Pachelbel, Kuhnau, Böhm, J. K. F. Fischer, Telemann. M-D.

Early German Piano Music (Fodor Akos—EMB 1974) 52pp. Works by C. P. E. Bach, J. C. Bach, J. C. F. Bach, W. F. Bach, G. Böhm, J. J. Froberger, K. H. Graun, J. P. Kirnberger, J. L. Krebs, C. G. Neefe, J. Pachelbel, J. F. Reichardt, C. F. Schale, G. P. Telemann, G. C. Wagenseil, E. W. Wolf. A collection of some unusual Baroque keyboard works. Int.

German Late Baroque (Gabor—EMB Z8913 1980) 42pp. J. S. Bach: *Overtures* F S.820, G S.822; *Allemande and Courante* S.838; *Scherzo* S.844; *Fuga* S.952; *Fughetta* S.961. G. F. Handel: *Lesson* a; *Sonatinas* d, a; *Capriccio* F; *Concerto* G; *Toccata* g. M-D.

German Romanticism (Gabor—EMB Z7554) 46pp. R. Schumann; *Album Leaves* Op.124/3–6, 10; *Colored Leaves* Op.99/1–3; *Forest Scenes* Op.82/3; *Album for the Young* Op.68/1, 2, 7, 8, 12, 23, 25, 29. Mendelssohn: *Songs Without Words* Op.19/2, 4, Op.30/3, 6, Op.53/3, Op.102/3; *Character Piece* Op.7/1; *Children's Pieces* Op.72/5, 1. Brahms: *Waltzes* Op.39/5, 9, 11, 15. Int. to M-D.

See: Willi Apel, "Early German Keyboard Music," MQ, 23 (April 1937):210–37.

German: Bach Family

Bach (K. Geiringer—Harvard University Press 1955). 27 compositions by 14 different Bachs. Includes biographies, bibliographies, and source notes. Int. to M-D.

The Bach Family 1604–1845 (K. Geiringer—UE 1936). 14 pieces by 12 members of the Bach family. The earliest Bachs: *Chorales*; *Rondeau*. J. S. Bach: *Capriccio on the Departure of His Beloved Brother*. W. F. Bach: *Polonaise*. C. P. E. Bach: *Farewell to My Silbermann Clavier*. J. E. Bach: *The Bees*. J. C. Bach: *Sonata* Op.5/6. W. F. E. Bach: *Waltzes*. This collection not only reveals the development of the Bach family but also the progress of music over two centuries. Int. to M-D.

A Bach Family Album (R. Jones—ABRSM 1989) 20pp. 20 pieces. Minuets, polonaises, and an Aria from a Hamburg MS. ca. 1780s. 7 pieces are among Johann Christian Bach's earliest compositions. The collection was probably compiled in 1744–48, when J. C. Bach would have been 9–13 years old —possibly a kind of "Notebook for J. C. Bach." Also includes 3 compositions by J. S. Bach, 2 pieces by C. P. E. Bach, 5 pieces by J. C. F. Bach, 1 piece by J. C. Altnickol (J. S. Bach's son-in-law), and 2 anonymous pieces. Pieces are similar to shorter pieces in the *Anna Magdalena Bach Notebook*. Int.

Clavier Music from Johann Sebastian Bach's Circle (Rüdiger Wilhelm—Br&H 8454 1993) 47pp. Anonymous: *Concerto del sign. Telemann*. Johann Peter Kellner (1705–1772): *Fuga* G. Johann Philipp Kirnberger (1721–1783): *Praeludium* c. Johann Christopher Kellner (1736–1803): *Sechs Fugen; Fantasie und Fugue* g. David Traugott Nicolai (1733–1799): *Fuga* B. Wilhelm Hieronymus Pachelbel (1686–1764): *Fuga* F. All pieces can be played on one keyboard. Nuanced and precise phrasing; colorful treatment of motives. M-D.

Sons of Bach (Soldan—CFP 5011 1980) 32pp. 18 short pieces. W. F. Bach: 6 pieces. C. P. E. Bach: 5 pieces. Johann Christoph Bach: 5 pieces. Johann Christian Bach: 2 pieces. Int. to M-D.

Sons of Bach (W. Newman—TP 1957). J. C. Bach: *Sonata* B Op.17/6. C. P. E. Bach: *Sonata* g No. 65 (Wotquenne's Catalogue). W. F. Bach: *Sonata* E. Fine text with excellent preface. Int. to M-D.

The Sons of Bach (EMB Z7517 1979) 52pp. C. P. E. Bach: *Sonata* e is in three movements and only 4 pages long. More representative of his style are the delightful *Rondo* G and *Fantasia* C. W. F. Bach: *Sonata* D (three movements, 11pp.); *Fugue* f (three voices); 2 short *Polonaises* d, E♭. Johann Christian Bach: *Sonata* c. Johann Christoph Frederich Bach: *Sonata* E♭. Includes a table of ornaments. Int. to M-D.

The Sons of Bach (W. Rehberg—Schott). 13 works (sonatas, single movements and pieces) by W. F., C. P. E., J. C. F., and J. C. Bach. Also contains suggestions for practicing. Int. to M-D.

Greek

Contemporary Greek Piano Music (Gerig 1967). Fine survey of younger Greek composers.
Vol.I: Michael Adamis (1929–   ): *Epitymbio*. Stephanos Gazouleas (1931–   ): *Piano Piece*. Jannis Joannidis (1930–   ): *Little Fantasia*. Georgios Léotsakos (1935–   ): *Sérenade*. Jannis A. Papaioannou (1910–   ): *Oraculum*. Yorgo Sicilianos (1922–   ): *Miniature* No.7, Op.23/7. Nikos Skalkottas (1904–1949): *Little Peasant March*. Int. to M-D.
Vol.II: Theodor Antoniou (1935–   ): *Syllables*. Arghyris Kounadis (1924–   ): *Three Idiómela*. Jannis Konstantinidis (1903–   ): *Greek Island Dance* No.2. Dimitri Mitropoulos (1896–1961): *Piano Piece* I. Georges Poniridy, (1892–   ): movement from *Sonata* 1961. Georges S. Tsouyopoulos (1930–   ): *Toccata* III. M-D to D.

Hungarian

Hungarian Piano Music (M. Szavai—EMB). A collection of short pieces by twentieth-century Hungarian composers. Contains works by Zoltan Gardonyi, Mihaly Hajdu, Pal Kadosa, Istvan Lang, György Ranki, Tibor Sarai, Rezso Sugar, Erzsebet Szonyi, and Béla Tardos. Folksong influence in many of the pieces. Int. to M-D.

Hungarian Piano Music for the Young Musician (Hambalko—EMB 8796/7) Vol.1: works by Bartók, Farkas, Liszt, and others. Vol.2: works by Kodály, Bartók, and others. Attractive collections of original, lesser-known piano solos. M-D.

Piano Sonatas of Hungarian Composers of the 18th Century (F. Brodszky—ZV 1962). Anonymous: *Suite*. Jozsef Csernak: *Partita*. Pantaleon Roskovszky: *Divertimento*. Anonymous: *Sonata*. Ferenc Pokorny: *Sonata; Aria*. Anonymous: *Suite*. Ferenc Ninger: three organ pieces. M-D.

Szonatina Albuma (EMB 1963). 10 Sonatinas by contemporary Hungarian composers. Unusually fine collection. Int.

Tarka-Barka 1977 (Teöke—EMB) 47pp. A collection of about 90 avant-garde miniatures, some only 2 lines long, by six contemporary Hungarian composers. Contemporary notation, inside-the-piano techniques, clusters, varied pedal techniques. A significant volume. Int. to M-D.

Irish

Six Irish Pieces (Breen—ESC). A collection of works from the seventeenth and eighteenth centuries. Int. to M-D.

Israeli

Contemporary Israeli Piano Music (Gradenwitz—Gerig 1976) 2 vols. Preface and biographical notes in English and German. Contains works by Menahem Avidom, Paul Ben-Haim, Yehuda ben Conhen, Abraham Daus, Ram Da-Oz, Sergiu Shapira, Yoram Paporisz, Verdina Shlonsky, Habib Hassan Tourna, Erich Walter Sternberg, and Joachim Stutschewsky. Int. to M-D.

Italian

Antichi Maestri Italiani (Zanibon). 10 pieces by Corelli, D. Scarlatti, Rossi, Zipoli, Pasquini, and Santelli. Contrapuntal writing, some octaves and spread chording. Edited with fingering, metronome marks, and ornaments written out. Int.

Barockmusik Italiens (Fedtke—Litolff EP 8374 1978) 30pp. Works by Aresti, Bassani, Colonna, Guistiniani, Gerll, Monari, Pasquini, Pollaroli, Schiava di Lucca, Ziani. Preface in German and English. Int. to M-D.

Early Italian Keyboard Music (H. Ferguson—OUP). 2 vols. 35 pieces ranging from anonymous music of the sixteenth century to Domenico Scarlatti. Ferguson provides notes on ornamentation, rhythmic conventions, and other points of interpretation. Includes works by Cavazzoni, Della Ciaja, Facoli, Frescobaldi, A. Gabrieli, G. Gabrieli, Luzzaschi, Merulo, Picchi, Poglietti, Rossi, A. Scarlatti, D. Scarlatti, Trabaci, and others.

Italian Keyboard Music (Andras Pernye—EMB through TP) Vol.I. 29 pieces from the sixteenth and seventeenth centuries. Includes a few anonymous and little-known compositions. Carefully edited. Appendix lists other references. Int.

Italian Masters of the 17th and 18th Centuries (I. Philipp—IMC). Galuppi: *Sonata*. Grazioli: *Sonata*. Marcello: *Toccata on a Song of a Cuckoo*. Rossi: *Andantino*. Zipoli: *Suite*. M-D.

Italian Piano Music for the Young Musician (István Mariassy—EMB 1974) 54pp., colored illustrations. Anonymous: *Gagliarda veneziana*. Anerio: *Gagliarda*. D. Cimarosa: *Sonata* c. Clementi: *Valse "il eco."* Corelli: *Gigue*. Durante: *Studio*. Frescobaldi: *Aria detta "La Frescobalda."* Galuppi: *Variazioni*. Martini: *Gavotte*. Pergolesi: *Allegretto*. Rossini: *Énchantillon du Chant de Noël a l'Italienne*. D. Scarlatti: *Sonatas* f♯, g. Zipoli: *Suite*. The Clementi and the Rossini works are the only true piano music. The two Scarlatti Sonatas, the delightful Gigue by Corelli, and the Frescobaldi variations have the most interest. No fingering given. Int. to M-D.

33 Italian Harpsichord Compositions (K 9494) 100pp. Works by Croce, Durante, Galuppi, Grazioli, Legati, Martini, Pampani, Porpora, Paradisi, Rutini, D. Scarlatti, Turini, Zipoli, and others. Contains arias, allemandes, gigues, sarabandes, toccatas, etc. Ornaments are realized above the staff. Heavy editing, nineteenth-century trappings added. Int. to M-D.

Italian: Twentieth Century

Antologia Pianistica di Autori Italiani Contemporanei (Montani—SZ). 2 vols. 81 pieces by contemporary Italian composers, including Casella, Dallapiccola, Petrassi, and others.

Autori Italiani Contemporanei: Composizione Pianistiche (P. Montani—Ric 1955). Piano works by nine contemporary Italian composers: Fuga, Farina, Ghiglia, Gentilucci, Gargiulo, Micheli, Quaranta, Silvestri, and Tedoldi. The works by Ghiglia, a 12-tone *Esercizio Per l'Espressione* and *Quaranta* (in Modo di Novelletta), are of special interest.

Composizioni di Autori Contemporanei per Pianoforte (Carisch 1959). Contains: F. Ghedini: *Allegretto*. J. Napoli: *Ninna-Nanna Campana*. E. Porrino: *Dancing*. T. Alati: *Senza nome*. B. Bettinelli: *Preludio*. T. Gargiullo: *Canzonetta*. F. Margola: *Danza e Notturno*. G. Piccioli: *Il pescatore solitario*. G. Viozzi: *Ninna-nanna*. MC. Int.

Il Pianistica Italiano Moderno (Carisch 1944). Gorini: *Perpetuum mobile*. Margola: *Leggenda*. Pick-Mangiagalli: *La Ronda d'Ariel*. Casella: part of *Toccata* Op.59. A curious mixture of styles. Int. to D.

Japanese

Haru No Yarjoi (Anthology of Japanese Piano Music) (Ongaku-No-Tomo-Sha) Vol.60 Sekai Dai Ongaku Zenshu, 225pp. Contains a broad sampling of twentieth-century Japanese piano music ranging from traditional to expressionistic (à la Schönberg). Shukichi Mitsukuri (1895–   ): 3 pieces after the *Flower* Op.16 (1. *Night Rhapsody*; 2. *Sakura-Sakura*; 3. Es ist März, der Frühling). Toroque Takagi (1904–   ): *Five Homages* (to Tchaikovsky, Waltar, Gershwin, Albeniz, Khachaturian). Toshitsugu Ogihara (1910–   ): *Moderato*; *Allegro*; *Andantino*. Taminosuke Matsumoto (1914–   ): 7 pieces. Toshio Kashiwagi (1914–   ): *Moderato*; *Allegro moderato*; *Lento tranquillamente con espressione*; *Tranquillamente*; *Delicatamente*; *Molto tranquillo*. Akira Ifukube (1915–   ): *Bon-Odori* (Nocturnal dance of the Bon-Festival); *Tanabata* (Fête of Vega); *Nebuta* (Festal Ballad). Roh Ogura (1916–   ): *Sonatine* (Allegro moderato; Canzonetta; Rondo). Minao Shibata (1916–   ): *Improvisation for Piano*. Shinichi Matsushita (1922–   ): 3 pieces. Takanobu Saitoh (1924–   ): *Prelude and Fugato*; *Promenade* (3 movements). Hajime Okumura (1925–   ): *Capriccio pour Piano*. Yasushi Akutagawa (1925–   ): *La Danse* Op.1 (Suite pour piano—deux danses avec un intermezzo). Michio Mamiya (1929–   ): 3 *Inventions*. Mutsuo Shishido (1929–   ): 2 *Dances*. Yutaka Makino (1930–   ): *Pre-*

lude and Fugue. Thoru Takemitsu (1930–   ): 3 pieces. Makoto Moroi (1930–   ): *Suite Classique* (*Allemande*; *Courante*; *Sarabande-fantastique*; *Gavotte* I & II; *Menuet sentimental*; *Gigue.* Akira Miyoshi (1933–   ): *Suite in Such Time* (*So Merry Is Dabbling!*; *A Witch Will Give You Some Sweets*; *Well Let's Play in the Garden*; *Lions Live in Far and Away Lands*; *For His Mamma*). Contains biographical information in Japanese. Int. to D.

Japanese Folk Airs on the Piano (Zen-On 1960) Vol.1: 13 pieces. Vol.2: 14 pieces. Varied moods, lengths, and figurations in these expressive, original, and effective folk tunes. Titles given in Japanese and English. Tempo markings included. The four arrangers are: R. Ito, K. Koyama, Y. Makino, and A. Tsukatani. Int. to M-D.

Latin American

Latin-American Art Music for the Piano (Curt Lange—GS 1942). An anthology by twelve contemporary composers from seven countries; includes preface and biographical data. José María Castro: *Cuatro Piezas*, from *Diez Piezas Brevas.* Alberto E. Ginastera: *Piezas Infantiles.* Roberto García Morillo: *Canción Triste y Danza Alegre.* Juan Carlos Paz: *Balada* No.2 from *Canciones y Baladas.* Carlos Suffern: *Danza.* Camargo Guarnieri: *Toada Triste.* Heitor Villa-Lobos: *Dansa* (Miudinho), *Bachianas Brasileiras* No.4. René Amengual: *Astaburuaga*; *Burlesca* Op.5. Manuel M. Ponce: *Deux Etudes pour Piano.* Andrés Sás: *Hymno y Danza.* F. Eduardo Fabini: *Triste* No.2. Juan B. Plaza: Sonatina Venezolana. Int. to M-D.

Piano Music of Viceregal Mexico (Hinson, Martin—Alfred 10119). Anonymous (ca. 1790): *Sonata en Mi.* Jose Aldana (1758–1810): *Minuet with Variations*; *Polaca.* Much of the music heard in Mexico during the late eighteenth and early nineteenth centuries conformed with European standards. The music in this collection exudes charm and elegance but does not exhibit traits that later came to be classed as characteristically Mexican or Latin American. Aldana's Minuet and Variations aptly represents this late viceregal music. The Polaca is a most unusual example in that it is a simplified keyboard arrangement of a movement from Beethoven's Serenade for String Trio Op.8. The anonymous Sonata comes the closest to containing elements associated with music by known Mexican-born composers of the period; influences of Scarlatti and Soler are evident. An altogether unusual collection. Int.

New Zealand

Four Piano Pieces (Price Milburn 1977) by New Zealand composers. Christopher Norton, *Four-three*: meter changes on almost every bar, lively. David Griffiths, *Equation*: chordal, carefully pedaled. Jack Speirs, *Metamorphoses*: strong contemporary writing, the most difficult of the four pieces. John M.

Jennings, *Abstract One*: repeated notes, alternating quintal and quartal chords. M-D.

Polish

Bitonal Etudes by Contemporary Polish Composers (Z. Romaszkowa—PWM). This selection of etudes calls for advanced technique and a certain freedom of interpretation. M-D to D.

Eight Etudes by Contemporary Polish Composers (PWM 1959). Compiled by Zofia Romanszkowa. Contains works by Grazyna Bacewiczowna, Zafia Iszkowska, Tadeusz Paciorkiewicz, and Tadeusz Szeligowski. Each piece involves a particular problem or set of problems. Most are tonal but are liberally sprinkled with accidentals, adhere to the key signature, and are eminently pianistic.

Four Pieces by Modern Polish Composers for Young Pianists (Compiled by Emma Altberg—PWM 1972) 31pp. Short compositions by Tadeusz Paciorkiewicz, Zofia Iszkowska, Feliks Radzkowski, and Hanna Skalska. Interesting pedagogic material. Easy to Int.

Polish Contemporary Piano Miniatures 1939–1964 (PMP). Beautifully printed book representing contemporary Polish composers' approach to the keyboard. D.

Portuguese

Cravistas Portugueses (Kastner—Schott 1935, 1950). A collection of old Portuguese keyboard music. Works by Coelho, Correa de Araujo, Seixas, Jacinto, Carvalho. Int. to M-D.

The Most Beautiful Pages from Portuguese Harpsichord Music (P. Montani—Ric 1963). Padre M. R. Coelho (1583–ca.1633): *Primeiro Tento*. J. A. Carlos de Seixas (1704–42): *Sonata Prima* a; *Toccata* C, *Sonata seconda* a. Fra Jacinto (? – ?): *Toccata* d. J. de Sousa Carvalho (? –1798): *Toccata* g. Biographical notes in English. Int. to M-D.

Sonatas Para Tecla (Kastner—Fundacao Calouste Gulbenkian 1982) 53pp. Includes: Carlos Seixas: *Sonata* F. Frei Jacinto do Sacramento: *Sonatas* d, g. Frei Jose de Sant'ana: *Sonata* d. Frei Manuel de Santo Elias: *Sonatas* D, F, E♭, g. Francisco Xavier Bachixa: *Sonatas* D, F. Quality varies but these are unusually interesting works. M-D.

Rumanian

Contemporary Rumanian Piano Music (Alexandre Hrisanide—Gerig 1971). 2 vols. Techniques and styles range from late Romantic to avant-garde. Introduction and biographical sketches in English.

Vol.I: Ludovic Feldman (1893–   ): *The Stubborn One*; *Catch as Catch*

Can. Vasile Spătărelu (1939–   ): *Rubato.* Nina Cassian (1930–   ): *Scherzo.* Nicolae Brânduž (1935–   ): *Klavierstücke* I. Anatol Vieru (1926–   ): *The Chinese Bird*; *Taboo!*; *The Monkeys.* Myriam Marbe (1931–   ): *Allegro.* Vasile Herman (1929–   ): *Birds in the Meadow.* Liviu Comes (1918–   ): *Melopee.* Sandu Albu (1897–   ): *Valse pour Alice.* Sigismund Toduță (1908–   ): *Trenia.* Dan Constantinescu (1931–   ): *Nocturne.* Zoltán Aladar (1929–   ): *Làhaut le sommet.* Int. to M-D.

Vol.II: Nicolae Coman (1936–   ): *The Ancient Clock.* Zeno Vancea (1900–   ): *Fuga.* Horațiu Rădulescu (1942–   ): *Cradle to Abysses.* Ştefan Zorzor (1932–   ): *Acuta.* Iancu Dumitrescu (1942–   ): *Diacronies* II. Tudor Ciortea (1903–   ): *Weihnachtslied.* Cornel Țăranu (1932–   ): *Dialogues* II. Liviu Dandara (1933–   ): *Structura I . . . Quasi preludio.* Andrian Rațiu (1928–   ): *Mónosonata* I. Eugen Wendel (1934–   ): *Per pianoforte* I. M-D.

Rumanian Piano Miniatures (Comes—CFP 9634 1976) 57pp. Works by Jora, Petra, Constantinescu, Pascanu, Stroe, and others. Contains biographies of the composers in German, English, and French. Int. to M-D.

Russian

Contemporary Soviet Piano Music (R. Luck—Gerig). Works by Soviet composers since World War I.

Vol.I: Devoted to easier pieces for students and amateurs: Arno Babajanian (1921–   ): *Picture No.4; Intermezzo.* Reinhold Glière (1875–1956): *Song from the East.* Dimitri Kabalevski (1904–1987): *Ball Game* Op.27/4. Aram Khachaturian (1903–1978): *Ljado Is Ill.* Nodar Mamisashvili: *Prelude No.1; Whole-Tone Scales.* Anti Marguste (1931–   ): *The Weasel.* Arvo Paert (1935–   ): *Fughetta; Toccatina.* Valentin Silvestrov (1937–   ): *Serenade.* Georgi Sviridov (1915–   ): *Toccatina.* Vladimir I. Tsytovich (1931–   ): *Prelude* No.4.

Vol.II: Concert material: Edison Denisov (1929–   ): *Variations.* Vitali Godziatski (1936–   ): *Surface Scratches.* Alemdar Karamanov (1934–   ): *Prologue, Idea and Epilogue.* Alfred Shnittke (1934–   ): *Variations on a Chord.* Dmitri Shostakovich (1906–1975): *Aphorisms* Op.13 (10 pieces, 7 included in book).

Easy Russian Piano Music (Maisie Aldridge—OUP) Book I: 14 appealing, short pieces based on folk tunes and dances. Book II: slightly more difficult; contains pieces by Russian composers not too familiar in the U.S.A., e.g., L. Vlasova, A. Baltin, L. Revutsky. Easy.

Educational Series of Russian Music for Piano (JWC).

Vol.1: 20 pieces, including works by A. Goedicke, K. Eiges, W. Landstein, W. Rebikov, S. Pantchenko, N. Ladoukhin, V. Selivanov. Easy.

Vol.2: 13 pieces, including works by A. Goedicke, N. Amani, S. Pantchenko, K. Eiges, S. Maykapar, R. Glière, H. Pachulski, N. Ladoukhin. Int.

Vol.3: 11 pieces, including works by S. Maykapar, N. Ladoukhin, N. Amani, R. Glière, H. Pachulski, A. Goedicke. M-D.

Vol.4: 9 pieces, including works by A. Arensky, R. Glière, A. Goedicke, S. Maykapar, H. Pachulski. M-D.

Eleven Variations on a Theme by Glinka (AMP 7729 1976) 24pp. The theme is Vanya's song from the opera *Ivan Susanin*. "This set of eleven variations on a theme from the opera *Ivan Susanin* is meant to be a musical homage to Michael Glinka, the father of Russian music, on the occasion of the one hundredth anniversary of his death in 1957. The first composer to do so was Dmitri Shostakovitch, who wrote three variations for this cycle. The contributions of Shostakovitch and the seven other musicians are a lasting tribute to a composer who, like Verdi, is beloved by all his countrymen for his patriotic fervor as well as his musical genius" (from the score). Other composers represented are Kabalevsky, Eugen Kapp, Vissarion Shebalin, Andrei Eshpai, Rodion Shchedrin, Georgi Sviridov, and Yuri Levitin. M-D.

From Russia for Youth—Contemporary Piano Music by Russian Composers (Boris Berlin—Harris 5044 1971) 24pp. Pieces by E. Aglinzev, K. Akimov, L. Barenboim, V. Gerstein, A. Goedicke, D. Kabalevsky, A. Khachaturian, S. Liakhovitskaya, N. Lubarsky, L. Lukomsky, Y. Medin, T. Salutrinskaya, P. Tchaikovsky, and other less-known composers. Easy.

Great Russian Piano Works (D. Tucker—WB 1990) 136pp. Anton Arensky: *Nocturne* Op.36/3; *Prelude* Op.38/1. Alexander Borodin: *Intermezzo* from "Petite Suite." Alexander Glazunov: *Grand Valse de Concert.* Alexander Gretchaninoff: *Nocturne* Op.3/5; *Plainte* Op.3/1. Dmitri Kabalevsky: *Rondo* Op.30; *Slow Waltz* Op.39/23; *Sonatina* Op.13/1 (1st movement). Aram Khachaturian: *Toccata.* Anatole Liadow: *Theme and Variations* (Nos.1 and 10). Nikolai Miaskowsky: *Sonata* Op.82 (3rd movement). Modeste Mussorgsky: *Great Gate of Kiev*; *Promenade.* Sergei Prokofiev: *March* Op.12/1; *The Montagues and the Capulets* from "Romeo and Juliet." Sergei Rachmaninoff: *Nocturne* I. Vladimir Rebikoff: *Max and Moritz* from "The Christmas Gift." Nicolai Rimsky-Korsakov: *Mazurka* Op.38/2; *Variations on a Russian Theme* (Theme and Variation 1). Alexander Scriabin *Poeme Satanique* Op.36; *Valse.* Dmitri Shostakovitch: *Lyric Waltz*; *The Mechanical Doll*; *Romance.* Peter Tchaikovsky: *Waltz of the Flowers.* No distinction between composers' and editor's marks. No sources listed. Int. to M-D.

Masters of Russian Piano Music (Hinson—Alfred 207) 60pp. Foreword, discussion of the Russian idiom, suggested teaching order, discussion of each piece. Arensky: *Arabesque* Op.67/1. Borodin: *In the Monastery.* Cui: *Berceuse* Op.20/8. Glière: *Harlequin* Op.34/8. Glinka: *Mazurka* a; *Mazurka* c. Goedicke: *Sonatine.* Kabalevsky: *Prelude* Op.38/2. Khachaturian: *Cat on a Swing.* Liadov: *A Musical Snuff-Box.* Miaskosvky: *Faded Page* Op.31/1. Mussorgsky: *Ballet of the Chickens in Their Shells.* Prokofiev: *Promenade* Op.65/2. Rachmaninoff: *Four Improvisations.* Rebikov: *Danse Orientale* Op.2/5. Rimsky-Korsakov: *Miniature.* A. Rubinstein: *Romance* E♭. Shostakovich: *A Funny Story*. Scriabin: *Prelude* Op.16/4. Tchaikovsky: *Reverie* Op.39/21. Tcherepnin: *Bagatelle* Op.5/1. Sources listed.

Paraphrases on an Easy Theme (A. Tcherepnin—Belaieff 1959) 47pp. 24 variations and 17 small pieces based on the theme "Chopsticks." Composers who contributed to this unique collaborative collection include: Rimsky-Korsakow: *24 Variations* and *Finale*. Liszt: *Prélude*. Borodin: *Polka; March funèbre; Requiem; Mazurka*. Cui: *Valse*. Liadow: *Valse; Galop; Gigue; Cortège triomphal*. Rimsky-Korsakow: *Berceuse; Fughetta on* BACH *Tarantelle; Menuet; Carillon; Fugue grotesque*. N. Stcherbatcheff: *Bigarrures*. Also contains Petit supplément. Int. to M-D.

See: Guy Wuellner, "Franz Liszt's Prelude on Chopsticks," JALS, IV (December 1978):37–44.

Piano Music of the Russian Five

Vol. 1. (Rüger—CFP 9286a 1983) 96pp. Mili Balakirew: *Polka; Paraphrase on Glinka's Romance "The Lark"; In the Garden—Idyll* (Study). Alexander Borodin: *Rêverie*, from the *Petite Suite; Scherzo*. César Cui: *Mazurka* Op.20/11; *Polonaise* Op.94/3; *Valse* Op.95/1; *Nocturne* Op.95/3. Modest Mussorgski: *Scherzo* (second version); *On the South Crimean Coast; In the Village*. Nikolai Rimski-Korsakow: *Waltz* Op.15/1; *Romance* Op.15/2; *Impromptu* Op.11/1; *Novelette* Op.11/2; *Small Song*. Appendix contains Glinka's "The Lark" arranged by N. Tiwolski. This fine survey contains excellent repertoire for the above-average high school student and for the college student. Some unusual and highly colorful writing. Int. to M-D.

Vol. 2 (Rüger—CFP 9286b 1985) 103pp. Modest Mussorgsky: *Souvenir d'enfance; Seamstress*. Nikolai Rimski-Korsakov: *3 Variations* from *6 Variations on BACH* Op.10/1; *Intermezzo* Op.10/2; *Scherzo* Op.10/3; *Prélude Impromptu* Op.38/1; *Mazurka* Op.38/2. Alexander Borodin: *Serenade* and *Mazurka* from *Petite Suite*. César Cui: *8 Preludes* from *25 Preludes* Op.64/4, 6, 8, 9, 13, 15, 17 and 25. Mili Balikirew: *Memories of Glinka's Opera* "A Life for the Tsar" (*Ivan Sussanin*); *Toccata*.

Both volumes of this fine survey contain excellent repertoire for the above-average high school student and for the college student. Some unusual and highly colorful writing. Int. to M-D.

Piano Pieces by Soviet Composers for Children (Leonid Roisman—CFP) Edited with biographical notes in German, French, and English. Most of the composers are unfamiliar in the USA; among them are: Yossif Neumark, Moissej Weinberg, Grigori Frid, Dmitri Blagoi, and Alexander Pirumow. Among the better-known composers included are Khatchaturian, Shostakovich, Maikapar, and Glière. Vol.I: 40 pieces and biographies of the 30 represented composers. Easy to Int. Vol.II: 27 pieces and biographies of 23 composers. Int. Vol.III: 22 pieces with biographical notes on the composers. A brilliant Toccata by Andrej Eschpai and an Impromptu for left hand by Glière are two of the most interesting works. Most of the pieces are short and effective. Int. to M-D.

PKK Their Greatest Piano Solos (Prokofieff, Kabalevsky, Khachaturian) (A. Shealy—Ashley 1972) 192pp.

Kabalevsky: *Sonatina* C Op.13/1; 8 pieces from Op.27: *Dance*; *Dance in the Garden*; *Etude* A; *Etude* a; *Scherzo*; *Sonatina* a; *Toccatina*; *Waltz*; *Rondo* Op.59; *A Warlike Dance*; *Preludes* 1 and 2.

Khachaturian: *Dance* g; *Sabre Dance* (*Gayne* Ballet); *Sonate*; *Sonatinas* a, C; *Toccata*; *Valse Caprice*.

Prokofieff: *A Story* Op.3/1; *Humoreske* Op.3/2; *Fantasy* Op.3/4; *Diabolical Suggestion* Op.4/4; *Toccata* Op.11; *Gavotte* Op.25; *March* (from *The Love of Three Oranges*) Op.33; *Paysage* Op.59/2; *Sonatina Pastorale* Op.59/3; *Moments Musicaux* 1 and 2, Op.62/2, 3; *Tarantella* Op.65/4; *Triumphant March* (from *Peter and the Wolf*) Op.67; *Mephisto Waltz* Op.96/3; *Etude* c; *Morning*; *Waltz* (from the ballet *Cinderella*). Int. to M-D.

Rare Masterpieces of Russian Piano Music (D. Feofanov—Dover) 144pp. Works by composers from the eighteenth to the late twentieth century. Balakirev: *Reverie*. Glazunov: *Prelude and Fugue* d Op.62. Kalinnikov: *Nocturne* f♯. Liadov: *Prelude* Op.11/1. Griboyedev: *Two Waltzes*. Medtner: *Sonata* g Op.22. Schlözer: *Etude* A♭ Op.1/2. Taneyev: *Prelude and Fugue* Op.29. Glinka: *Prayer*. Hassler: *Sonata-Fantasie* Op.4. Liapunov: *Transcendental Etude* Op.11/10. Int. to D.

Russian Music for the Young Pianist (P. Zeitlin, D. Goldberger—MCA 1967–68). 6 vols., graded. Well edited, excellent variety of material. Some of the composers included are Rimsky-Korsakov, Prokofiev, Tschaikovsky, Glinka, Shostakovich, Gretchaninoff, Scriabin, Hosenpud, Glière, Laskovsky, Rachmaninoff, Borodin, A. Rubinstein, Liadov, Maykapar, Kabalevsky, Arensky, Cui, A. Tcherepnin, Medtner, Mussorgsky, Rebikov, Gnessina, Khachaturian, Goedicke, Miaskovsky, Shchedrin.

Russian Piano Music for the Young Musician (Lehel Both—EMB 1973) 50pp. Attractive collection featuring a number of miniatures by some of Russia's greatest Romantic composers, including Borodin, Mussorgsky, Tchiakovsky, Rachmaninoff, as well as less-known writers such as Dimitry Arakishvile (1873–1953), Sogomon Komitas (1869–1935), Miaskovsky, Maikapar, Goedicke, Liapounov (with an *Allegretto* that is fairly easy, for once), Drozdov, and Kopilov. Fingering added. Int. to M-D.

Russische Klaviermusik, 1780–1820 (Lubimow—Heinrichshofen 1983).

Vol.1: 32pp. Dmitry S. Bortnyansky: *Sonata* C (three movements, large scale); *Sonata* F (one movement); *Sonata* B♭ (one movement). All date from 1784. The Sonatas provide the most substantial music in these two volumes. The quality of the writing is consistently high. Vasiliy F. Trutovsky (1740–1810), *Variations* in G: opening theme begins in G and cadences on C; the subsequent 12 variations follow the same pattern, and the work ends in C. Writing varies from fast right-hand melodic arabesques and scales to syncopated interlocking and repeated patterns.

Vol.2: 32pp. Variation sets by Lev S. Gurilëv (1782–1844), Ivan E. Khandoshkin (1747–1804), and Anonymous. Catherine de Licoschin (ca. 1780–1840): *Polonaise* a. Brief program notes in German. M-D.

Scriabin, Shostakovich, Stravinsky—Their Greatest Piano Solos (Alexander Shealy—Copa 1973) 192pp. A comprehensive collection of these composers' most famous works. This writer was not able to determine if all the pieces were definitely in their original form. Contains 16 works by Stravinsky (including pieces from *Petrushka, Firebird, L'Histoire du Soldat*, and *Le Sacre du Printemps*), 18 works by Scriabin, and 44 works by Shostakovich (including pieces from *L'Age d'or* and Fifth Symphony). Int. to M-D.

Sergei Rachmaninoff, Anton Rubinstein, Nikolas Rimsky-Korsakoff—Their Greatest Piano Solos (Alexander Shealy—Copa 1972) 192pp. A comprehensive collection of these composers' world-famous works in their original form. Contains original works and arrangements.

Scandinavian

Ancient Danish Piano Music (E. Winkel—SM 1943). 2 books. Works by Johan Foltmar (1714–1794). F. L. A. E. Kunzen (1761–1817), Claus N. Schall (1757–1835), J. A. P. Schulz (1747–1800), J. A. Scheibe (1708–1776). M-D.

Norwegian Pianorama (C. Ore—WH). 25 pieces by contemporary Norwegian composers. In various styles, ranging from folktune influence through freely tonal, 12-tone, and aleatoric writing to jazz and ragtime. Works by Albertsen, Fongaard, Hovland, Larsen, Mortensen, Orbeck, and Sommerfeldt. Contains a brief biographical note under each composer's photograph and an introduction to each piece. M-D.

Pepparrot (New Scandinavian Piano Music) (B. Nordenfelt—NMS 1949). Foreword in English. Contains photographs of each composer plus biography in English. Works by Lidholm, K. B. Blomdahl, Bäck, Riisager, Holmboe, Hoffding, and Saeverud. The *Sonatina* by Lidholm is especially appealing. Includes one duet, *Minuett*, by Hoffding. "This collection of modern Scandinavian music is intended for a more or less advanced stage of teaching, to be played *to* the pupils and *by* the pupils themselves" (from the Foreword). M-D.

Pianolyric. (Swedish Piano Album) (F. Kjellberg—NMS 1949). Contains works by Erik Alvin, Margit E. Anderson, Tor Bengtson, Nils Björkander, Harry Danielsson, Ejnar Eklöf, Gunnar de Frumerie, Wilhelm Göransson, Axel Hambraeus, Ingemar Liljefors, Carin Malmlof-Forssling, Friedrich Mehler, Gustaf Norqvist, Albert Runbäck, Gerda Söderberg, Gunnar Thyrestam, Rune Wahlberg. M-D.

Piano Spectrum (Herbert Connor—Reuter & Reuter 1966) 31pp. 26 original compositions for piano by 10 contemporary Scandinavian composers. Introduction and instructions for study included. Contains a cross section of styles from polyphonic to dancelike. Gottfrid Berg (1889–1970): *Five Pieces.* Laci Boldemann (1921–   ): *Two Piano Pieces without Pedal.* Hans

Eklund (1927–   ): *To an Obtuse Common Chord*; *Swatting Flies*. Hallgrimur Helgason (1914–   ): *A New Song*; *Icelandic Song*; *From a Fairytale Isle*. Daniel Hellden (1917–   ): *Rondo giocoso*. Finn Höffding (1899–   ): 5 pieces. Edvin Kallstenius (1903–   ): A 400-Year-Old Miners' Hymn. Matti Rautio (1922–   ): *Berceuse*; *Little Study in Boogie Woogie*. Knudåge Riisager (1897–   ): *Sarabande*; *Polytonal*; *Duet in Canon*; *Duet*. MC. Int. to M-D.

Scandinavian Aspect (Kjell Baekkelund, Bengt Johnsson—WH 1971) 46pp. Works by contemporary composers from Norway, Sweden, Denmark, and Finland. Egil Hovland: *Raindrop Study*. Tage Nielsen: *Sun, Moon and Stars*. Per Nørgård: *Journeys*. Poul Rovsing Olsen: *Three Etudes—Ride Through a Comet's Tail, The Asteroid's Song, Death Dance of a Variable Star*. Erik Bergman: *Spectrum*, from the suite *Aspekter*. Einojuhani Rautavaara: *Quinte*. Sigurd Berge; *Chorale*. Finn Mortensen: *Nocturne*. Bengt Hambraeus: *Musical Box*. Arne Mellnäs: *For You and Me*. An interesting and valuable collection showing the great variety of stylistic and technical elements being used by contemporary Scandinavian composers. Most pieces contain detailed performance instructions. Varied keyboard techniques required. Most are avant-garde. M-D to D.

Swedish Profile (Trygve Nordwall—NMS 1974) 36pp. Ten pieces for piano by Blohmdahl, Bäck, Hambraeus, Johanson, Maros, Mellnäs, Nilsson, Rabe, Werlin, Werle. M-D.

Scottish

Early Scottish Keyboard Music (K. Elliot—S&B 1967). Second revised edition. Contains 10 keyboard pieces, Pavans, Galliards, etc.; 8 Scottish national airs on folksongs, 5 for cittern and 3 for violin. Most of the keyboard pieces come from Duncan Burnett's music book of about 1610, mainly works by William Kinloch. Excellent and unusual collection with fine historical notes. Int. to M-D.

Spanish

Colección-Piano (Schott 8245 1993) 44pp. Joan Guinjoan (1931–   ): *Celulas No.3* (1968). Tomás Marco (1942–   ): *Le Palais du Facteur Cheval*. Josep Soler (1935–   ): *Soneto 295 del Michelangelo* (1992). Alfredo Aracil (1954–   ): *Ottavia Sola* (1986). Ramón Barce (1928–   ): *Tango para Yvar*. A broad mixture of styles from the avant garde (Guinjoan) to more traditional style (Barce). M-D to D.

Collection Espagnole (Colección de obras españolas e iberoamericanas) from Albéniz to Villa-Lobos (F. Guenther—EBM 1941). Works by Albéniz, Cha-

varri, de Falla, O. L. Fernandez, E. Granados, V. Granados, Isamitt, Lecuona, Longas, Robles, Sandoval, Suffern, Turina, Villa-Lobos.

Early Spanish Keyboard Music (B. Ife and R. Truby—OUP 1986) 3 vols. Vol. III:
The Eighteenth Century, 49pp. Introduction includes a discussion of ornamentation and instruments. Vicente Rodriguez Monllor (1690–1760): *Sonata* A♭. Sebastian de Albero (1722–1756): *Sonata* g; *Sonata* g; two separate one-movement sonatas. Antonio Soler (1729–1783): *Preludio*; *Sonata* d
R.115; *Sonata* d R.117; *Sonata* c♯ R.21; *Sonata* c R.100; *Sonata* c R.19. Felix
Maximo Lopez (1742–1821): *Sonata* c. José Ferrer (ca. 1745–1815): *Adagio*
g; *Sonata* g. Critical notes. An outstanding edition. Int. to M-D.

Great Spanish Piano Works (CPP/Belwin 1991) 143pp. Works by four Spanish
composers and two Brazilian composers. Isaac Albeniz (1860–1909): *Coti-
llon Valse*; *Gavotta*, from "Troisieme Suite Ancienne"; *Granada*, from
"Suite Española"; *Mallorca* Op.202; *Rumores de la Caleta*; *Seguidillas*
Op.232/5; *Sevilla*, from "Suite Española"; *Spanish Dance No.3*; *Tango in D*
Op.165/2. Manuel de Falla (1876–1946): *Andaluza* and *Aragonesa* from
"Four Spanish Pieces"; *Serenata Andaluza*. Enrique Granados (1867–1916):
Berceuse and *Danza de la Rosa* from "Escenas Poéticas"; *Epílogo* from
"Goyescas"; *Jota, Playera,* and *Villanesca* from "Andaluza Suite"; *Valse
Poéticas II*. Francisco Mignone (1897–1986): *Microbinko*. Joaquin Turina
(1882–1949): *El Casino de algeciras* and *Paseo Nocturno* from "Album de
Viaje"; *Exaltación* from "Danzas Fantásticas." Heitor Villa-Lobos (1887–
1959): *Coborlinha, Negrinha*, and *O Polichinelo* from "Prole de Bebe," Vol.
I; "Mischievous Little Imp." No distinction between composers' and edi-
tor's markings. No sources listed. Int. to M-D.

Llibre per a Piano (Piano Anthology of Catalonian Composers) (Associació
Catalana de Compositors 1980, through Seesaw). 357pp. A sumptuous collection of modern Catalonian piano music. For each of 34 composers it
includes a complete work, often of large scale, a list of works, and a discography. Some well-known names—Balada, Mompou—and many lesser-
known figures. An unusual and important collection. Int. to D.

Masters of Spanish Piano Music (Hinson—Alfred 434) 64pp. Foreword, discussion of the Spanish idiom, suggested teaching order, and discussion of each
piece. I. Albeniz: *Preludio* Op.165/1; *Capriccio Catalano* Op.165/5. M. Albeniz: *Sonata* D. de Falla: *Montañesa*. Granados: *The Bell of the Afternoon;
Coming from the Fountain; Dance of the Rose; The Phantom; March; May
Song; Memories of Youth; Old Man's Tale; Spanish Dance* Op.5/1; *Spanish
Dance* Op.5/5. Rodriguez *Rondo* B♭. Soler: *Sonata* F R.83. Sources listed.

The Most Beautiful Pages from Spanish Harpsichord Music (G. Marchi—Ric
1955). Edited in accordance with the originals. Padre Vicente Rodriguez
(1685–1761): *Sonata* F. Padre Antonio Soler (1729–1783): *Sonatas* a, D♭.
Padre Felipe Rodriquez (1759–1814): *Rondo* B♭. Mateo Albéniz (17 ? –
1831): *Sonata* D. Cantallos (1760– ?): *Sonata* c. Padre José Galles (1761–
1836): *Sonatas* c, f. Int. to M-D.

New Library of Spanish Keyboard Music, 16th to 18th Centuries (A. Baciero—

UME). A series of 180 scholarly performing editions including works by Hernando de Cabezon, Antonio Soler, Joseph Ximenez, D. Scarlatti, and many others; all previously unpublished.

Piano Music from Spain (AMP 1971). 15 pieces by Albéniz and Granados. Albéniz: *Sevilla*; *Asturias*; *Córdoba*; *Rumores de la Caleta*; *Pavana-Capricho*; *Zortzico*; *Triana*. Granados: *Quejas ó la Maja y el Ruiseñor*; *Andaluza* (*Playera*); *Rondalla Aragonesa*; *El Invierno*; *Barcarola*; *Añoranza*; *Ecos de la Parranda*; *Zapateado*. Excellent collection of some of the most popular pieces by these composers. Int. to M-D.

17 Sonatas of Old Spanish Masters (J. Nin-ESC). Sonatas by V. Rodriguez, Soler, Freixanet, Casanovas, Angles, R. Rodriguez, Galles.

16 Sonatas of Old Spanish Masters (J. Nin-ESC 1925). Sonatas by Soler, M. Albéniz, Cantallos, Serrano, Ferrer. All the works in both collections are in one movement and most are moderately easy to Int.

Spanish Music from the Old and New Worlds (AMP 7961–3) 56pp. Albéniz: *Cordova*, from *Songs of Spain*, Op.232/4. Chávez: Nos.1 and 8 from *Ten Preludes*. Nos.1, 8. Granados: *El Pelele* from *Goyescas*. Mompou: *Canta Mágics*. Pinto: *March, Little Soldier!*; *Sleeping Time*, from *Scenas Infantis*. Turina: *La Oración del Torero*, Op.34. A collection of favorite Spanish pieces. Int. to M-D.

Spanish Piano Music (Dover). 24 works by Albéniz, de Falla, Granados, Soler, and Turina. Int. to M-D.

Spanish Piano Music for the Young Musician (György Balla—EMB 1974) 56pp. 14 works by Isaac Albéniz, Mateo Albéniz, Cabezón, Cantallos, Ferrer, Freixanet, Milán, Narváez, Felipe Rodriguez, Vicente Rodriguez, Serrano, Soler. The *Sonata* by Cantallos (born 1770?) is excellent though reminiscent of D. Scarlatti. The collection covers the sixteenth to the twentieth century, concluding with *Sevilla* by I. Albéniz. Includes reproductions of paintings by Alonso Cano and Velazquez. M-D.

See: Willi Apel, "Early Spanish Music for Lute and Keyboard Instruments," MQ, 20 (July 1934):289–301.

Olga Llano Kuehl, "The Piano Music of Spain, Its Flavor and Interpretation," *Clavier*, 15 (October 1976):17–18, 20.

Swiss

Contemporary Swiss Piano Music (Charles Dobler—Gerig 1973). Introduction provides a good background of the development of Swiss music, which did not develop any great individuality until around 1800. A short biographical note is included on each composer. None of these pieces have been published before. Stylistically they range from the Romantic to post-serial techniques. To some extent they are arranged progressively according to degree of difficulty and style.

Vol.I: Willi Burkard (1900–1955): *Intermezzo*. Martin Wendel (1925–   ):

Lullaby. Peter Mieg (1906–   ): *At Montsouris Park.* Othmar Schoeck (1886–1957): *Piano Piece.* Henri Gagnebin (1886–1960): *The Two Gossips.* Rudolph Ganz (1887–1972): *Three Rubes.* Roger Vuataz (1898–   ): *Question—Answer.* Richard Sturzenegger (1905–   ): *Hommage à Paul Sacher.* Hugo Pfister (1914–1969): *Crystallisations.* Raffaele d'Alessandro (1911–1959): *Vision* III. Albert Moeschinger (1897–   ): *Implacable.* Rudolf Kelterborn (1931–   ): *The Little Mirror.* Wladimir Vogel (1896–1984): *Loneliness Falling in Drops.* Hans Eugen Frischknecht (1939–   ): *Music for Piano.*

Vol.II: Hermann Haller (1914–   ): *Intermezzo.* Alban Roetschi (1922–   ): *Lasolfation.* Julien-François Zbinden (1917–   ): *Pianostinato.* Frank Martin (1890–1974): *Rhythmical Study.* Alfred Keller (1907–   ): *Flageolett.* Edward Staempfli (1908–   ): *Sonority Study.* Robert Suter (1919–   ): *White and Black.* Jacques Wildberger (1922–   ): *Vision Fugitive.* Ernst Widmer (1927–   ): *Rondo Mobile.* Klaus Huber (1924–   ): *Ein Hauch von Unzeit* II. Han Ulrich Lehmann (1937–   ): *Piano Piece* Int. to M-D.

Swiss Piano Music from the Classic and Romantic Era (W. Frey, W. Schuh—Hug). X. Schnyder von Wartensee (1786–1868): *Scherzo* E; *Andante* F. H. G. Naegeli (1773–1836): *Toccata.* Theodor Fröhlic; *Finale* from *Sonata* Op.11. M-D.

Yugoslavian

Contemporary Yugoslavian Piano Music (R. Luck—Gerig 1966). Introduction and biographical notes in English.

Vol.I: Bruno Bjelinsky: *Alarm*; *Fog Creeps Up*; *Song of the Little Emigrant.* Dejan Despić: *Duo Pastorale*; *Fanfare*; *Waltz.* Jakob Jež: *The Little Boat Is Departing.* Ivo Lhotka: *Kalinski*; *Microforms.* Božidar Kunc; *The Favorite Fairy Tale.* Janez Matičić (1926–   ): *Pavane.* Dušan Radić (1929–   ): *Rondino.* Josip Slavenski (1896–1955): *Song from Medjimure.* Marco Tajčević (1900–   ): *First Suite.* Int. to M-D.

Vol.II: Natko Devčic (1914–   ): *Micro-Suite.* Ivo Malec (1925–   ): *Dialogues.* Slavko Osterc (1895–1941): *Arabesque* No.3. Boris Papandopulo (1906–   ): *Dance Study.* Primož Ramovš (1921–   ): *Prelude.* Branimir Sakać (1918–   ): *Variation.* M-D.

Yugoslav Youth Album (Lipovsek—CFP 9633a 1975)

Book 1. Preface in German and French. 37 works by such composers as Matija Bravnicar, Marijan Lipovsek, Marko Tajcevic. Includes biographies and essential fingering. Wide variety of keys and moods. Int. to M-D.

Book 2 (CFP 9633b 1977) 40pp. Pieces by Ivana Lang, Pavel Sivic, Vlastimir Nikolovski, and others. Preface in German and English. M-D.

Bibliography

This extension of the references that appear after individual composers or compositions concentrates on English-language books, periodicals, and dissertations. These sources are most helpful when used in conjunction with the musical score. Careful attention has been directed toward dissertations, some of which are annotated. As a general rule, biographies have been excluded, except for those that focus on the composer's music. For a more complete list of books related to keyboard accompanying, aesthetics, analysis, biographies, group piano, construction and design, history, lists of piano music, ornamentation, pedagogy, performance anxiety, stress and tension, performance techniques, piano duets, transcriptions, two or more pianos, performance practice, and video cassettes, see Maurice Hinson, *The Pianist's Bookshelf* (Bloomington: Indiana University Press, 1998).

Denes Agay. "The Search for Authenticity." *Clavier*, 14 (November 1965):29–31.

Cathy Albergo and Reid Alexander. *Intermediate Piano Repertoire*. Oakville, Canada: The Frederick Harris Music Co., 2000.

Putnam Aldrich. "The 'Authentic' Performance of Baroque Music." In *Essays on Music in Honor of Archibald T. Davison*. Cambridge: Department of Music, Harvard University, 1957. Pp.161–71.

George Anson. "Contemporary Piano Music of the Americas." *Inter-American Music Bulletin*, 13 (September 1959):19–20.

Willi Apel. *The History of Keyboard Music to 1700*. Bloomington: Indiana University Press, 1972.

——. *Masters of the Keyboard*. Cambridge: Harvard University Press, 1947.

Dean Luther Arlton. "American Piano Sonatas of the Twentieth Century: Selective Analyses and Annotated Index." Diss. Columbia University, 1968.

William Austin. *Music in the 20th Century*. New York: Norton, 1966. Contains an extraordinary annotated bibliography.

Beatrix Baas. "Dutch 20th-Century Piano Music in Development—The Renovators born before World War I," Part 1, *Key Notes*, 13 (1981):28–38.

Sol Babitz. "A Problem of Rhythm in Baroque Music." MQ, 38 (October 1952):533–65.

Eva Badura-Skoda. "Textural Problems in Masterpieces of the Eighteenth and Nineteenth Centuries." MQ, 51 (April 1965):301–17.

George Barth. *The Pianist as Orator: Beethoven and the Transformation of Keyboard Style*. Ithaca: Cornell University Press, 1992.

Gerald S. Bedbrook. *Keyboard Music from the Middle Ages to the Beginnings of the Baroque*. New York: Macmillan, 1949. Reprint, New York: Da Capo, 1968.

R. Beer, "Ornaments in Old Keyboard Music." MR, 13 (February 1952):3–13.

David Blum. *Casals and the Art of Interpretation*. New York: Holmes & Meier, 1977. 223pp.

Rita Benton. "Some Problems of Piano Music Editions." AMT, 6 (November–December 1956):6–7, 21.

Oscar Bie. *A History of the Piano and Piano Players*. London: J. M. Dent, 1899. Reprint, New York: Da Capo, 1966.

Joseph Bloch. "Some American Piano Sonatas." JR, 3 (Fall 1956):9–15.

Eric Blom. *The Romance of the Piano*. London: Foulis, 1928. Reprint, New York: Da Capo, 1968.

Dean E. Boal. "A Comparative Study of Existing Manuscripts and Editions of the Robert Schumann Sonata in F Sharp Minor, Op.11, for Piano." Diss., University of Colorado, 1959.

Kenwyn G. Boldt. "The Solo Clavier Sonatas Attributed to J. S. Bach." DMA paper, Indiana University, 1967.

———. "The Solo Piano Ballade in the Nineteenth-Century." DMA paper, Indiana University, 1967.

———. "The Solo Piano Variations of Rachmaninoff." DMA paper, Indiana University, 1967.

David A. Boltz. "The Solo Piano Works of M. Camargo Guarnieri." Paper, Indiana University, Latin American Music Center, 1965.

Bonnie Cave Bradley. "The Compositions for Piano Solo by Antonin Dvorak." Thesis, University of Kentucky, 1969.

Alfred Brendel. *Musical Thoughts and Afterthoughts*. Princeton: Princeton University Press, 1976.

Nathan Broder. "Mozart and the Clavier." MQ, 27 (October 1941):422–32.

Maurice J. E. Brown. "Schubert: Discoveries of the Last Decade." MQ, 47 (July 1961): 293–314.

———. "Schubert: Discoveries of the Last Decade." MQ, 57 (July 1971):351–78.

———. "Schubert's Manuscripts: Some Chronological Issues." MR, 19 (August 1958): 180–85.

———. "Schubert and Some Folk Songs." ML, 53 (April 1972):173–78. Discusses the use of folk songs in Schubert's piano and chamber music, citing two dances (D.529 and D.146), *Divertissement a l'hongroise* (D.818m), Adagio (D.879), and the unfinished Sonata in C major (D.845). Reports recent discoveries by the Neue Schubert Ausgabe.

———. *Schubert's Variations*. New York: Macmillan, 1954.

Thomas Alan Brown. "The Aesthetics of Robert Schumann in Relation to His Piano Music, 1830–1840." Diss., University of Wisconsin, 1965.

Conrad Bruderer. "The Studies of Charles Ives." DM paper, Indiana University, 1968.

Siglund Bruhn. *Guidelines to Piano Interpretation*. Hong Kong: Penerbit Muzical, 1989.

Barbara Jeanne Brynie. "The Nineteenth-Century Piano Ballade." Thesis, University of Hawaii, 1968. Nineteen ballades by eleven composers are analyzed and reveal elements that differentiate the ballade from other one-movement genre pieces.

Richard Bunger. *The Well-Prepared Piano*. Pedro, CA: Litoral Arts Press, 1981.

David Burge. *Twentieth-Century Piano Music*. New York: Schirmer Books, 1990.

John Butt. *Bach Interpretation: Articulation Marks in Primary Sources of J. S. Bach*. New York: Cambridge University Press, 1990.

John C. Byrt. "Form and Style in the Works of J. S. and C. P. E. Bach." Ph.D. diss., Oxford University, 1970. 2 vols., 380pp.

Mosco Carner. "Some Observations on Schumann's Sonata Form." MT, 76/1112 (1935): 884–86.

Alvan D. Cazedessus. "The Study and Performance of Selected Contemporary Piano Sonatinas." Diss., Teacher's College of Columbia University, 1967. Part I includes an annotated bibliography of 98 sonatinas, written between 1900 and 1963, considered suitable for performance by advanced students or concert artists. Part II consists of structural analyses and comments on the performance of nine of these sonatinas.

David Charlton. "Performance Practice around 1800." M&M, 23 (January 1975):22–24. A discussion of the pros and cons of using contemporary instruments of the period.

Gilbert Chase. *The American Composer Speaks*. Baton Rouge: Louisiana State University Press, 1966.

———. *America's Music*, 2d rev. ed. New York: McGraw-Hill, 1966.

———. *The Music of Spain*, 2d rev. ed. New York: Dover Publications, 1959.

———. "Piano Music by 12 Contemporaries." *Inter-American Monthly*, 1 (September 1942):32–33.

Abram Chasins. *Speaking of Pianists*, 3d rev. ed. New York: Da Capo, 1981. 312pp.

J. Bunker Clark. "The Renaissance of Early American Keyboard Music: A Bibliographic Review." *Current Musicology*, 18 (1974):127–32.

———. *The Dawning of American Keyboard Music*. Westport, CT: Greenwood Press, 1988.

Ernest Closson. *History of the Piano*, new ed. St. Clair Shores, MI: Scholarly Press, 1977.

C. F. Colt. "Early Pianos: Their History and Character." *Early Music*, 1 (January–February 1965).

Herbert Colvin. "Contemporary American Piano Music." AMT, 14 (January–February 1965).

Barry A. R. Cooper. "English Solo Keyboard Music of the Middle and Late Baroque." Ph.D. diss., Oxford University, 1974. 517pp.

———. "The Keyboard Suite in England before the Restoration." ML, 53 (July 1972):309–19.

Martin Cooper. *French Music from the Death of Berlioz to the Death of Fauré*. London: Oxford University Press, 1951. See especially pp.1–7, where the "esprit de la musique française" is characterized.

Alfred Cortot. *French Piano Music*. London: Oxford University Press. Reprint, New York: Da Capo Press, 1977. 208pp.

Anthony Cross. "The Significance of Aleatoricism in Twentieth-Century Music." MR, 29 (1968):305–22.

Kathleen Dale. *Nineteenth-Century Piano Music*. London: Oxford University Press, 1954. Reprint, New York: Da Capo Press, 1972.

———. "The Three C's (Clementi, Czerny, Cramer): Pioneers of Pianoforte Playing." MR, 6/3 (1945):138–48.

Thurston Dart. "Handel and the Continuo." MT, 106 (May 1965):348–50.

———. *The Interpretation of Music*. London, New York: Hutchinson's University Library, 1954. Reprint, New York: Harper & Row, 1963.

John Daverio. "Reading Schumann by Way of Jean Paul and His Contemporaries." *College Music Symposium* (Fall 1990):28.

Laurence Davies. "French Piano Music." *Music*, 3/2 (April 1969):30–32.

Gail B. Delente. "Selected Piano Music in France Since 1945." Diss., Washington University, 1966. Devoted to the piano works of Bienvenue, Boutry, Castérède, Constant, Dutilleux, Hugon, Jolivet, and Ohana. Special emphasis is given Dutilleux, Castérède, and Jolivet.

Norman Demuth. *French Piano Music. A Survey with Notes on Its Performance*. London: Museum Press, 1959.

J. M. Dent. "The Pianoforte and Its Influence on Modern Music." MQ, 2 (April 1916):271–94.

Benning Dexter and George Loomis, "Choosing the Best Edition," *Clavier*, 8 (September 1969):50–52.

Benning Dexter and Charles Timbrell. "Another Look at Editions—The Piano Works of 12 Important Composers." PQ, 116 (Winter 1981):39–41.

Robert Donington. *The Interpretation of Early Music*. London: Faber & Faber, 1963.

John R. Douglas. "The Composer and His Music on Record." *Library Journal*, 92 (March 15, 1967):1117–21. A discography of 115 composers conducting or performing their own works.

Kenneth Drake. *The Beethoven Sonatas and the Creative Experience*. Bloomington: Indiana University Press, 1994.

Robert Dumm. "A Schubert Symposium." *Clavier*, 34/10 (December 1995):10–16. Report of the symposium held in Washington, D.C., in April 1995. Contains excellent comments on performance practices in Schubert's piano music.

Robert Ehle. "20-Century Music and the Piano." PQ, 96 (Winter 1976–77):28–31.

Jean-Jacques Eigeldinger. *Chopin: Pianist and Teacher as Seen by His Pupils*. Cambridge: Cambridge University Press, 1986. 324pp.

Dean Elder. "Bach Talk with Rosalyn Tureck." *Clavier*, 18 (January 1979):18–23.

Mildred Katharine Ellis. "The French Piano Character Piece of the Nineteenth and Early Twentieth Centuries." Diss., Indiana University, 1969.

Herbert Elwell. "A Composer Evaluates Twentieth-Century Piano Music." *MTNA Proceedings* (1950):42–47.

Winsome Evans. "The Influence of the Pianoforte on 18th-Century Keyboard Style." *Musicology*, 3 (1968–69):49–68.

Albert Faurot. *Concert Piano Repertoire*. Metuchen, NJ: Scarecrow Press, 1974. 337pp.

———. "Hunting the Rara Avis of the Repertoire." *Clavier*, 20 (October 1981):43–44. A discussion of some unusual (in the composer's view) piano repertoire.

Edwin Fischer. *Reflections on Music*. London: Williams & Norgate, 1951. See chapters on interpretation of Mozart, Chopin, Schumann, Beethoven, and J. S. Bach.

I. P. Fletcher. "An Analytical Study of the Form and Harmony of the Pianoforte Music of Chopin, Schumann, and Liszt." Diss., Oxford University, 1963.

Lukas Foss. "The State of Piano Playing in the Twentieth Century." *MTNA Proceedings* (1948):158–67.

Andrew Fowler. "Robert Schumann and the 'Real' Davidsbündler." *College Music Symposium* (Fall 1990):19. Addresses four composers close to Schumann—Felix Mendelssohn, William S. Bennett, Stephen Heller, and Clara Wieck. Analyzes "salient compositional features of a selected work" by each one and "interprets each piece" as a model for a specific Davidsbünd ideal.

Irwin Freundlich. "Neglected Works in the Earlier Keyboard Repertoire." PQ, 59 (Spring 1967):158–67.

James Friskin and Irwin Freundlich. *Music for Piano: A Handbook of Concert and Teaching Material from 1580 to 1952*. New York: Rinehart, 1954. Reprint, New York: Dover, 1974.

Thomas Lee Fritz. "The Development of Russian Piano Music as Seen in the Literature of Mussorgsky, Rachmaninoff, Scriabin, and Prokofiev." Diss., University of Southern California, 1959.

Virginia H. Gaburo. "Notes from Inside the Piano." PNM, 16/2 (Spring–Summer 1978):3–18. A performer's view of the interaction between present-day composers and performers. Criticizes many composers for being satisfied with inadequate performances and suggests that raising expectations would serve both performer and composer.

Saloméa Gandelman. *36 Compositores Brasileiros obras para piano (1950–1988)*. Rio de Janeiro: Ministério da Cultura Funarte Relume Dumará, 1997. 336pp.

Peter F. Ganz. "The Development of the Etude for Pianoforte." Diss., Northwestern University, 1960.

Rudolph Ganz. *Rudolph Ganz Evaluates Modern Piano Music.* Evanston: The Instrumentalist Co., 1968.

Willis C. Gates. "Mozart's Articulation Signs: A Dilemma for Editors." AMT, 19 (September–October 1969):20–23.

Walter Georgii. *Klaviermusik*, 2d ed. Zürich: Atlantis-Verlag, 1950.

Reginald R. Gerig. *Famous Pianists and Their Technique.* Bethesda, MD: Robert B. Luce, 1974.

John E. Gillespie. *Five Centuries of Keyboard Music.* Belmont: Wadsworth, 1965. Reprint, New York: Dover, 1972.

Henri Gil-Marchev. "French Piano Music Since Fauré." AMT, 13 (March–April 1964):10–11, 31–33.

Elfriede Glusman. "The Early Nineteenth-Century Lyric Piano Piece." Diss., Columbia University, 1969.

Scott Goddard. "The Evolution of the Pianoforte Concert." *The Listener* (London), 19 (1938):437.

Laurette Goldberg. *The Well-Tempered Clavier of J. S. Bach: A Handbook for Keyboard Teachers and Performers.* 2 vols. Berkeley, CA: Music Sources, 1996.

Walter Goldstein. "The Rhythmic Tricks of Chopin and Schumann." *MTNA Proceedings* (1924):63–73.

George S. Golos. "Some Slavic Predecessors of Chopin." MQ, 46 (October 1960):437–47.

Roger Goodman. "Choosing Editions of Baroque Keyboard Music." *Clavier*, 25/5 (May/June 1985):20–25.

Katherine Goodson. "English Pianists and the Development of Piano Playing in England." *Etude*, 29/1 (1911):9–10.

Stewart Gordon. *A History of Keyboard Literature.* New York: Schirmer Books, 1996.

Paul Griffiths. *British Music Catalogue 1945–1981. Works for Piano*, Vol.1. London: The Warwick Arts Trust, 1983. 39pp.

"Guide for Selecting Editions." PQ, 56 (Summer 1966):14–36. Most of this issue, compiled by the editors, is devoted to this subject.

Serge Gut. "Swiss Influences on the Compositions of Franz Liszt." JALS, 38 (July–December 1995):1–22.

Robert A. Hagopian. "The Confluence of Artistic and Literary Sources in the Creation of Ravel's Gaspard de la Nuit." DMA project, Indiana University, 1975. 37pp.

———. "The d'Indy and Dukas Piano Sonatas." DMA project, Indiana University, 1975. 53pp.

Margery Halford. "Editing: Some Problems, Puzzles and Solutions." PQ, 114 (Summer 1981):32–34.

Hal Haney. "Conversation with Harpsichordist Rosalyn Tureck." *Harpsichord*, 8 (February–March–April 1975):8–11, 14–22.

Albert L. Hanna. "A Statistical Analysis of some Style Elements in the Solo Piano Sonatas of Franz Schubert." Diss., Indiana University, 1965.

Rosamond E. M. Harding. "The Earliest Pianoforte Music." ML, 13/2 (1932):194–99.

———. "Experimental Pianofortes and the Music Written for Them." PRMA, 57 (1930–31).

John Harris. "Thematic Catalogs for Pianists." *Clavier*, 20 (April 1981):38–39. A discussion of the most frequently used thematic catalogues involving composers of piano music: Deutsch, Köchel, Kirkpatrick, etc.

Doris Hays. "Noise Poise." MJ, 35 (February 1977):14–17, 42. A discussion of avant-garde techniques used in playing the piano.

Arthur Hedley. *Chopin*. London: J. M. Dent and Sons Ltd., 1947. Rev. ed. 1963.

——. "Some Notes on Chopin Biography," ML, 18/1 (1937):42–49.

——. "Some Observations on the Autograph Scores of Chopin's Works," in Zofia Lissa, ed., *The Book of the First International Musicological Congress* [February 1960], *Devoted to the Works of Frederick Chopin*. Warsaw: Polish Scientific Publishers, 1960, pp.474–77. Throws fascinating new light on distinctions between Chopin's autographs and Fontana's contemporary copies.

Sarah Carson Hegmann. "The Latin-American Piano Sonata in the Twentieth Century." Ph.D. diss., Indiana University, 1975. 142pp. "A study of sonatas or sonatinas representing most of the major countries and twentieth-century composers of Latin America; some are nationalistic in character, and others represent major twentieth-century compositional techniques. Categorizes the countries according to those of Indian, Negro, or cosmopolitan cultural influences; summarizes elements of tonality, harmony, melody, texture, rhythm, and form; and examines the position of the sonatas within the international musical sphere" (author, abridged).

William H. Heiles. "Rhythmic Nuance in Chopin Performances Recorded by Moritz Rosenthal, Ignaz Friedman, and Ignaz Jan Paderewski." Diss., University of Illinois, 1964.

A. M. Henderson. "Old English Keyboard Music (Byrd to Arne)." PRMA, 64 (1937–38).

Julius Herford. "Bach's Models of 'Good Inventiones'—How to Develop the Same Well." *Bach*, 4 (January 1973):16–20.

——. "J. S. Bach's Fugue in C Minor from *The Well-Tempered Clavier*, Book I." *Bach*, 4 (July 1973):36–40. An analysis.

Albert G. Hess. "The Transition from Harpsichord to Piano." *Galpin Society Journal*, 6 (1953):75–94.

Karin Heuschneider. *The Piano Sonata of the 18th Century in Germany*. Cape Town and Amsterdam: A. A. Balkema, 1970.

——. *The Piano Sonata of the 18th Century in Italy*. Cape Town: A. A. Balkema, 1966.

Maurice Hinson. "Keyboard Music in the Colonies and the United States of America to 1800." PQ, 123 (Fall 1983):40–42. Includes recording of the examples.

——. "Published Piano Sonatas and Sonatinas by American-Born Composers, 1900–1960." AMT, 10 (July–August 1961):10–11, 14, 35–36.

——, with H. Wiley Hitchcock. "Piano Music." *New Grove Dictionary of American Music*, 3 (1986):562–65.

Jan Holcman. *The Legacy of Chopin*. New York: Philosophical Library, 1954.

Charles A. Horton. "Serious Art and Concert Music for Piano in America in the 100 Years from Alexander Reinagle to Edward MacDowell." Diss., University of North Carolina, 1965.

Louis Horst. *Pre-Classic Dance Forms*. New York: Kamin Dance Publications, 1953.

Madeleine Hsu. *Olivier Messiaen. The Musical Mediator. His Major Influences: Liszt, Debussy and Bartók*. Cranbury, NJ: Associated University Presses, 1996.

Frederick Iliffe. *Analysis of Bach's Forty-eight Preludes and Fugues*. London: Novello, 1897.

Jeffrey Kallberg. *Chopin at the Boundaries: Sex, History, and Musical Genre*. Cambridge, MA: Harvard University Press, 1996.

Keyboard Solos and Duos by Living British Composers: A Catalogue. London: Composers' Guild of Great Britain, 1974. 63pp.

Frank E. Kirby. *Music for Piano: A Short History*. Portland: Amadeus Press, 1995.

——. "A Typology of Beethoven's Piano Sonatas." PQ, 73 (Fall 1970): 12–15.

John Kirkpatrick. "American Piano Music: 1900–1950." *MTNA Proceedings* (1950):35–41.

——. "United States Piano Music as Recital Literature." *MTNA Proceedings* (1941):70–78.

Ralph Kirkpatrick. "Eighteenth-Century Metronomic Indications." *Papers of the AMS* (1938):30–50.

B'jarn Korsten. *Contemporary Norwegian Piano Music*. Oslo: Norsk Komponistforening, 1965. 3d enlarged and revised ed. 1976.

Anne McClenny Krauss. "Alexander Reinagle, His Family Background and Early Professional Career." *American Music*, 4/4 (Winter 1986):425–56.

Siegfried Kross. "Brahms and E. T. A. Hoffmann." *19th Century Music*, V/3 (Spring 1982): 193–200. Discusses the biographical-literary analysis of the relationship between Brahms and Hoffmann.

Patrick La Cerra. "The Keyboard Alman in Elizabethan England." *Clavier*, 16 (September 1977):24–34. Includes scores of seven almans.

Harry B. Lincoln, ed. *The Computer and Music*. Ithaca: Cornell University Press, 1970. 372pp. See essay on experiments in analyzing and identifying the keyboard styles of Haydn, Mozart, and Beethoven.

Mark Lindley. "Authentic Instruments, Authentic Playing." MT, 118 (April 1977):285, 287–88.

Albert Lockwood. *Notes on the Literature of the Piano*. Ann Arbor: University of Michigan Press, 1940. Reprint, New York: Da Capo Press, 1968.

Arthur Loesser. *Men, Women, and Pianos: A Social History*. New York: Simon and Schuster, 1954.

——. "A Pianist Views Contemporary Piano Music." *MTNA Proceedings* (1950):48–52.

——. "Playing Bach on the Modern Piano." *Piano Teacher*, 1 (January–February 1959):5.

Bobby H. Loftis. "The Piano Sonatas of Nicolai Medtner." Diss., West Virginia University, 1970.

Ricardo Lorenz, ed., with Luis R. Hernández and Gerardo Dirié. *Scores and Recordings at the Indiana University Latin American Music Center*. Bloomington: Indiana University Press, 1995.

Ernest Lubin. "Another Look at the Urtext." PQ, 98 (Summer 1977):24, 16–17.

Francis F. McGinnis. "Chopin: Aspects of Melodic Style." Diss., Indiana University, 1968.

Sister Mary de LaSalle McKeon. "Stylistic Tendencies in Mid-Twentieth-Century American Piano Music." Diss., University of Rochester, 1957.

Duncan R. McNab. "A Study of Classic and Romantic Elements in the Piano Works of Mozart and Schumann." Diss., University of Southern California.

Jane Magrath. *The Pianist's Guide to Standard Teaching and Performance Literature*. Van Nuys, CA: Alfred Publishing Co., 1995.

Robert L. Marshall, ed. *Eighteenth-Century Keyboard Music*. New York: Schirmer Books, 1994. A collection of essays by various authors.

Mischa Meller. "Some Critical Comments on Modern Editions of the Piano Classics." AMT, 4 (September–October 1954):1, 16–17.

Wilfrid Mellers. *Percy Grainger*. New York: Oxford University Press, 1992.

MENC. "Selective List of American Music for the Bicentennial Celebration—Piano." *Music Educators Journal*, 62 (April 1976):87–89, 98–104. A graded list by various contributors.

Newton W. Miller. "On Taking the Repeats." AMT, 28 (February–March 1979):40–44.

Ricardo Miranda-Perez. "Piano Music by Mexican Composers," *Quarterly Magazine* (November 1992):31–33. Discusses piano music of Felipe Villanueva, Ricardo Castro,

Jose Rolon, Miguel Bernal-Jimenez, Blas Galindo, Pablo Moncay, and Eduardo Hernandez Moncado.

Patricia Montgomery. "The Latin American Piano Suite in the Twentieth Century." Diss., Indiana University, 1978. 129pp.

Robert P. Morgan. "Towards a More Inclusive Musical Literacy: Notes on Easy 20th-Century Piano Music." *Musical Newsletter* (January 1971):8–12.

Hans-Christian Müller. "Sources and Their Line of Descent (Sources and Urtext)." PQ, 97 (Spring 1977):43–45.

Donald Arthur Myrvik. "Musical and Social Interaction for Composers and Performers: Differences between *Source* Music and the 1950 Avant-Garde." Diss., University of Minnesota, 1975. In 1970, in a significant number of new compositions—those published in *Source*—the relationship between the composer and the performer was substantially different from what it was for compositions written around 1950. Highly interesting dissertation.

Paul Nettl. *Forgotten Musicians.* New York: Philosophical Press, 1951. See especially "Schubert's Czech Predecessors, Johann W. Tomáscheck and Hugo Voříšek," pp.91–109.

Frederick Neumann. *Ornamentation in Baroque and Post-Baroque Music with Special Emphasis on J. S. Bach.* Princeton: Princeton University Press, 1978. Neumann makes many musicians and scholars revise their pet ideas on this subject.

———. *Essays in Performance Practice.* Ann Arbor: UMI Research Press, 1982.

———. *New Essays on Performance Practice.* Ann Arbor: UMI Research Press, 1989.

———. *Ornamentation and Improvisation in Mozart.* Princeton University Press, 1986.

William S. Newman. "Beethoven's Pianos Versus His Piano Ideals." JAMS, 23 (Fall 1970): 220–24.

———. "The Pianism of Haydn, Mozart, Beethoven, and Schubert . . . Compared." PQ, 105 (Spring 1979):14–16, 18–27.

———. *The Pianist's Problems.* New York: Harper & Row, 1950. 4th rev. ed., New York: Da Capo Press, 1984.

———. *The Sonata in the Baroque Era.* Chapel Hill: University of North Carolina Press, 1959. 4th rev. ed., New York: W. W. Norton, 1983.

———. *The Sonata in the Classic Era.* Chapel Hill: University of North Carolina Press, 1963. 3d rev. ed., New York: W. W. Norton, 1983.

———. *The Sonata Since Beethoven.* Chapel Hill: University of North Carolina Press, 1969. 3d rev. ed., New York: W. W. Norton. 1983.

———. *Beethoven on Beethoven. Playing His Piano Music His Way.* New York: W. W. Norton, 1988. 336pp.

Randolph Nicholas. "Tempo and Character." *Clavier,* 15 (March 1976):46–47. Discusses Chopin's Prelude e and Beethoven's use of tempo and character terms.

Frits Noske. "Dutch Piano Music from the 16th and 17th Centuries." *Sonorum Speculorum,* 14 (March 1963):14–18.

Fritz Oberdoerffer. "On Urtext Editions." *Peters Notes 'The Newsletter of C. F. Peters,'* 1 (Fall/Winter 1976–77):5.

———. "Urtext Editions." AMT, 10 (July–August 1961):2, 15–18.

Joan Orvis. "Technical and Stylistic Features of the Piano Etudes of Stravinsky, Bartók, and Prokofiev." DM diss., Indiana University, 1976. 89pp. Presents some of the stylistic and technical features in the piano etudes of three of the giants of twentieth-century music.

Carl Parrish. "The Early Piano and Its Influence on Keyboard Technique and Compositions in the Eighteenth Century." Diss., Harvard University, 1939.

Ernst Pauer. *Ernst Pauer's Six Historical Performances of Pianoforte Music . . . April 20, 27, May 4, 11, 18, June 1, 1861 with Comments and Critical Remarks, Biographies, etc.* London: W. J. Golbourn, 1863.

Jerry Ross Perkins. "An Examination of the Solo Piano Music Published by the Wa-Wan Press." Diss., Boston University, 1969.

Charles P. Phillips. "Latin American Art Music for the Piano. A Catalogue of Representative Graded Teaching Materials." *Inter-American Music Bulletin*, 85–86 (November–June 1972–73):1–11. A catalogue of Latin American piano music, graded according to difficulty. Indicates basic or frequently used rhythmic patterns in the repertory listed.

Marc Pincherle. "On the Rights of the Interpreter in the Performance of 17th and 18th Century Music." MQ, 44 (April 1958):145–66.

Linton Powell. "Guitar Effects in Spanish Piano Music." PQ, 92 (Winter 1975–76):40–44.

Johann J. Quantz. *On Playing the Flute.* Translated by Edward Reilly. New York: The Free Press, 1966. Reprint, New York: Schirmer Books, 1975. One of the best sources for study of Baroque performance practices for all instruments.

Eduard Reeser. *The Sons of Bach.* Translated by W. A. G. Doyle-Davidson. Stockholm: The Continental Book Co., 1949.

Rita Reymann. "Spanish Teaching Pieces." AMT, 29 (April–May 1980):30, 32.

Joseph Rezits and Gerald Deatsman. *The Pianist's Resource Guide: Piano Music in Print.* Park Ridge, IL: Pallma Music Corp., 1974, 1978. 1491pp.

H. Riley. "Aleatoric Procedures in Contemporary Piano Music." MT, 107 (April 1966): 311–12.

Walter Robert. *From Bach to Brahms: A Musician's Journey through Keyboard Literature.* Bloomington, IN: Brown Composition Systems, 1993.

Stephen Roe. *Keyboard Music of J. C. Bach: Source Problems and Stylistic Development in the Solo and Ensemble Works.* New York: Garland Publishing Co., 1989.

Charles Rosen. *The Classical Style: Beethoven, Haydn and Mozart.* New York: Viking, 1970. Reprint, New York: W. W. Norton, 1972.

——. "When Ravel Ends and Debussy Begins." HF, 9 (May 1959):42–44.

——. *The Romantic Generation.* Cambridge, MA: Harvard University Press, 1995.

Lydia Rosen. "Guide to the Understanding and Performance of Contemporary Piano Literature of Holland, with Selective Analysis." Diss., Columbia University, 1959.

Sandra P. Rosenblum. "Calando: The Life of a Musical Term." PQ, 134 (Fall 1987):60–65.

——. *"Performance Practices in Classic Piano Music.* Bloomington: Indiana University Press, 1988. 516pp. The finest book in English on the subject. Contains many musical examples.

——. "The Use of *Rubato* in Music, Eighteenth to Twentieth Centuries." *Performance Practice Review*, 7/1 (Spring 1994):33–53.

Fritz Rothschild. *Musical Performance in the Times of Mozart and Beethoven.* London: Adam & Charles Black, 1961.

——. *Stress and Movement in the Works of J. S. Bach.* London: Adam & Charles Black, 1966. This is the final chapter of *The Lost Tradition in Music* (New York: Oxford University Press, 1953), with additional material, a lengthy Introduction, and an Appendix.

Felix Salzer, ed. *The Music Forum*, Vol.IV. New York: Columbia University Press, 1976. 403pp. Articles of special interest to pianists: "Ornamentation," by Heinrich Schenker (originally published some 75 years ago; not previously available in English), which discusses the appoggiatura, trill, and turn, with many examples from the Baroque and classical literature; "Aspects of the Recapitulation in Beethoven's Piano Sonatas," by Roger Kamien; and "The Musical Significance of Beethoven's Fingerings in the Piano Sonatas," by Jeanne Bamberger. Also contains other highly interesting articles by Schenker, Carl Schacter, and Felix Salzer.

Walter Schenkman. "Beyond the Limits of Urtext Authority." *College Music Symposium*, 23/2 (Fall 1983):145–63. A contemporary record of early-nineteenth-century performance practice based on Hummel's *Piano Method* of 1828.

———. "Clementi, Cramer, Czerny, Composers of Valuable Etude Material." CK, 3 (September 1977):14–16, 43.

Angeline Schmid, "Schubert's Early Sonatas." *Clavier* 36/10 (December 1997):20–25. Includes Menuetto from Sonata C, D.279.

Artur Schnabel. *Music and the Line of Most Resistance*. Princeton: Princeton University Press, 1942. Reprint, New York: Da Capo Press, 1969.

———. *My Life and Music*. New York: Longmans, 1961.

Harold Schonberg. "The Far-Out Pianist." *Harper's Bazaar*, 130 (June 1960):49.

———. *The Great Pianists*. New York: Simon & Schuster, 1963. From Mozart to the 1960s.

David Schulenberg. *The Keyboard Music of J. S. Bach*. New York: Schirmer Books, 1992.

Rudolph Serkin. "Some Thoughts on Editions for the Artist Student." In *Comprehensive Guide for Piano Teachers*. New York: The Music Education League, 1963. Pp.94–95.

John Shedlock. *Beethoven's Pianoforte Sonatas; the Origin and Respective Value of Various Readings*. London: Augener, 1918.

———. *The Piano Sonata*. London: Methuen, 1895. Reprint, New York: Da Capo Press, 1964.

Joel Sheveloff. "Domenico Scarlatti—Tercentenary Frustrations." MQ, 71/4 (1985):399–436.

Alexander Siloti. *My Memories of Liszt*. JALS, 15 (June 1984).

Adrienne Simpson. "Bohemian Piano Music of Beethoven's Time." MT, 1553 (July 1972):666–67. Deals with the four volumes of piano works published by Henle under this same title (Reicha, Steffan, Tomášek, and Voříšek).

Pamela Snow. "Analytic Study of Selected Piano Literature, 1949–1972." DM document, Indiana University, 1980. 79pp. Discusses George Crumb, *Makrokosmos* II; Mario Davidovsky, *Synchronisms* No.6; Olivier Messiaen, *Mode de Valeurs et d'intensités*; Karlheinz Stockhausen, *Klavierstuck* XI.

Ellsworth Snyder. "Avant-garde Piano: Non-traditional Uses in Recent Music." CK, 3 (April 1977):12–13.

Laszlo Somfai. *The Keyboard Sonatas of Joseph Haydn: Instruments and Performance Practice, Genres, and Styles*. Chicago: University of Chicago Press, 1994.

Erwin Stein. *Form and Performance*. London: Faber, 1962.

Leonard D. Stein. "The Performance of Twelve-tone and Serial Music for the Piano." Diss., University of Southern California, 1965.

Madeau Stewart. "Playing Early Pianos—A Lost Tradition?" *Early Music*, 1 (1973):93–95.

Hope Stoddard. "The 3 C's—Immortals Anonymous." *Musicology*, 2/1 (1948):59–66. Concerns Clara (Schumann), Constanza (Mozart), and Cosima (Wagner).

David Stone. "The Italian Sonata for Harpsichord and Pianoforte in the 18th Century (1730–90)," 3 vols. Diss., Harvard University, 1952.

Kurt Stone. "Urtext." PQ, 55 (Spring 1966):22–25.

Robin Stowell. *Performing Beethoven*. Cambridge: Cambridge University Press, 1994.

Charles R. Suttoni. "Piano and Opera: A Study of the Piano Fantasies Written on Opera Themes in the Romantic Era." Ph.D. diss., New York University. 494pp. "A study of the piano fantasy on opera themes, particularly from 1830 to 1850. Relates the fantasy to the technical development of the piano and to the tradition of improvisation in the Classic and Romantic eras. Discusses Mozart, Clementi, Cramer, Beethoven, Hummel, Moscheles, Joseph Gelinek, Daniel Steibelt, Franz Hünten, Kalkbrenner, Henri Herz, Czerny, Thalberg, Liszt, and Busoni" (author, abridged).

Richard Taruskin. *Text & Act: Essays on Music and Performance*. New York: Oxford University Press, 1995.

Betty Jean Thomas. "Harmonic Materials and Treatment of Dissonance in the Pianoforte Music of Frederic Chopin." Diss., University of Rochester, Eastman School of Music, 1963. An objective investigation of the harmonic and non-harmonic materials in Chopin's piano music.

Virgil Thomson. *American Music since 1910*. New York: Holt, Rinehart & Winston, 1970.

Alf Thoor. "Modern Swedish Piano Music." *Musikrevy International* (1954):16–18.

John Tilbury. "The Contemporary Pianist: An Interview with Michael Parsons." MT, 110 (February 1969):150–52.

R. Larry Todd. *Schumann and His World*. Princeton: Princeton University Press, 1994.

———, ed. *Mendelssohn Studies*. New York: Cambridge University Press, 1992.

———, ed. *Nineteenth-Century Piano Music*. New York: Schirmer Books, 1990.

Gennadi M. Tsipin. Trans. by Beatrice L. Frank. "Chopin and the Russian Piano Tradition." JALS, 38 (July–December 1995):67–82. An investigation of the problems of interpretation of the music of Chopin by Russian and Soviet pianists.

Rosalyn Tureck. "Toward a Unity of Performance and Musicology." *Current Musicology*, 14 (1972):164–72.

Daniel Gottlob Türk. *School of Clavier Playing or Instructions in Playing the Clavier for Teachers and Students*. Translation, Introduction and Notes by Raymond H. Haggh. Lincoln and London: University of Nebraska Press, 1983. 653pp.

Hubert Unverricht. "Urtext for Practical Use." PQ, 88 (Winter 1974–75):46–47.

Fernando Valenti. *A Performer's Guide to the Keyboard Partitas of J. S. Bach*. New Haven: Yale University Press, 1989.

John Verrall. "American Composers and the Piano." *MTNA Proceedings* (1949):23–30.

Helen Walker-Hill. *Piano Music by Black Women Composers*. Westport, CT: Greenwood Press, 1992.

Bernhard D. Weiser. *Keyboard Music*. Dubuque, IA: W. C. Brown Co., 1971.

Herbert Westerby. *The History of Pianoforte Music*. New York: Dutton, 1924. Reprint, New York: Da Capo Press, 1971.

———. *Introduction to Russian Piano Music*. London: Reves, 194–.

Emanuel Winternitz. *Musical Autographs from Monteverdi to Hindemith*. Princeton: Princeton University Press, 1955. Reprint, New York: Dover, 1965. See especially Vol.I, p.16, for an account of Beethoven's use of < > sign.

Henry S. Wolf. "The 20th Century Piano Sonata." Diss., Boston University, 1957.

Konrad Wolff. *Masters of the Keyboard*. Bloomington: Indiana University Press, 1983. A close look at individual style elements in the piano music of Bach, Haydn, Mozart, Beethoven, and Schubert.

Klaus Wolters. *Handbuch der Klavierliteratur*. Vol.I, *Klaviermusik zu zwei Händen*. Zürich: Atlantis, 1967. Rev. ed., 1994. The foremost work in its field. An outstanding achievement in thoroughness, detail, scope, and organization.

Byron A. Wolverton, "Keyboard Music and Musicians in the Colonies and United States of America before 1830." Diss., Indiana University, 1966.

Appendix: Historical Recital Programs

Anton Rubinstein

Programs given in 1885–1886, designed to exhibit the scope of piano literature.

PROGRAM 1

William Byrd
  The Carman's Whistle
John Bull
  The King's Hunting Jig
François Couperin
  La Ténébreuse
  Le Réveil-matin
  La Favorite
  Le Bavolet flottant
  La Bandoline
Jean P. Rameau
  Le Rappel des oiseaux
  La Poule
  Gavotte and Variations
Domenico Scarlatti
  Cat's Fugue, Sonata, A
J. S. Bach
  Preludes and Fugues, c and D
    (*Well-tempered Clavichord* [*sic*])
  Chromatic Fantasia and Fugue
  Gigue, B♭
  Sarabande
  Gavotte

Georg F. Handel
  Fugue, e
  The Harmonious Blacksmith
  Sarabande and Passacaglia,
    from Suite in g
  Gigue, from Suite in A
  Lied with Variations
Carl P. E. Bach
  Rondo, b
  La Xenophon
  Sybille
  Les Langueurs tendres
  La Complaisante
Joseph Haydn
  Theme and Variations, f
Wolfgang A. Mozart
  Fantasia, c
  Gigue, G
  Rondo

PROGRAM 2

Ludwig van Beethoven
  Seven Sonatas:
    Op.27, No.2
    Op.31, No.2
    Op.53
    Op.57
    Op.90
    Op.101
    Op.111

PROGRAM 3

Franz Schubert
   Fantasia, C ("Wanderer")
   Moments musicales, Nos.1–6
   Minuet, b
   Impromptus, c and E♭
Felix Mendelssohn
   Variations sérieuses
   Capriccio, e♭
   Ten Songs Without Words
   Presto and Capriccio

Carl Maria von Weber
   Sonata, A♭
   Momento capriccioso
   Invitation to the Dance
   Polacca brilliant, E

PROGRAM 4

Robert Schumann
   Fantasia, Op.17
   Kreisleriana, Nos.1–8
   Etudes symphoniques
   Sonata, f♯
   Des Abends

In der Nacht
Traumeswirren
Warum
Vogel als Prophet
Romanza, b♭
Carnaval, Op.9

PROGRAM 5

Muzio Clementi
   Sonata, B♭, with the Toccata for
   closing movement
John Field
   Three Nocturnes, E♭, A, and B♭
Ignaz Moscheles
   Etudes caractéristiques
   Reconciliation
   Juno
   Conte d'enfant
Adolf Henselt
   Poème de'amour
   Berceuse
   Liebeslied
   La Fontaine
   "If I Were a Bird"
Sigismund Thalberg
   Etude, a
Fantasia on "Don Juan"

Franz Liszt
   Etude, D♭
   Valse caprice
   Consolations in E and D♭
   Au bord d'une source
   Rhapsodies hongroises, Nos.6 and 12
   Soirées musicales (after Rossini)
   La Gita in Gondola
   La Danza
   La Regatta
   Transcriptions of Schubert's Songs:
      Auf dem Wasser zu singen
      Ständchen
      Der Erlkönig
   Soirée de Vienne in A
   Fantasia on "Robert the Devil"

PROGRAM 6

Frédéric Chopin
   Fantasia, f
   Preludes: e, A, A♭, b♭, D♭, d
   Barcarolle
   Waltzes: A♭ (the small one), a,

Berceuse
Impromptus: F♯, G♭
Scherzo, b
Nocturnes: D♭, G, c
Mazurkas: b, f♯, A♭, b♭

Ab (the large one)
Sonata, bb

Ballades: g, F, Ab, f
Polonaises: f#, c, Ab

PROGRAM 7

Frédéric Chopin
  Etudes: Ab, f, c, eb, Eb, b, Ab, c#, c
Anton Rubinstein
  Sonata in F
  Theme and Variations from
    Sonata in a
Michael Glinka
  Tarantella
  Barcarolle
  Souvenir de Mazurka
Mili Balakirev
  Scherzo
  Mazurka
  Islamey

Peter Tchaikovsky
  Chant sans paroles
  Valse
  Romance
  Scherzo à la russe
César Cui
  Scherzo-Polonaise
Nikolai Rimski-Korsakov
  Etude
  Novelette
  Valse
Anatol Liadov
  Etude
  Intermezzo
Nicholas Rubinstein
  Feuillet d'album
  Valse

Ferruccio Busoni

Devoted to the Piano Works of Franz Liszt, October 31–December 12, 1911, Berlin, Germany.

PROGRAM 1

Grandes Etudes d'Exécution Transcendante
Fantasie über 2 Motive aus Mozart's Die Hochzeit des Figaro

PROGRAM 2

Années de Pèlerinage, Première Année. La Suisse
Legendes
  St. François d'Assisi. La prédication aux oiseaux
  St. François de Paule marchant sur les flots
Adelaide von Beethoven
Réminiscences de Don Juan

PROGRAM 3

Années de Pèlerinage, Deuxième
  Année. Italie
Gondoliera
Tarantella
Sérénade de Rossini

Il Trovatore (Verdi)
Valse a capriccio sur *Lucia e
  Parsina* (Donizetti)
Fantasie über *Norma* (Bellini)

PROGRAM 4

Années de Pèlerinage, Troisième
   Année
Deuxième Ballade
Bénédiction de Dieu dans la
   solitude

Valse oubliée
Die Zelle in Nonnenwerth
Polonaise, c
Galop chromatique

PROGRAM 5

Variationen über "Weinen, Klagen,
   Sorgen, Zagen" und das "Crucifixus"
   aus Bach's H-moll-Messe
Sonate H-moll

Transcriptionen nach Schubert:
   Erlkönig
   Die Forelle
   Ungarischer Marsch
   Ungarische Rhapsodien
   Héroïde élégiaque
   XIII. Rhapsodie
   XII. Rhapsodie

PROGRAM 6

Grandes Etudes d'Après les Caprices de Paganini
Transcriptions by Busoni:
   Fantasie und Fugue über "Ad nos ad salutarem undam"
   Mephisto-Walzer
   Polonaise E-dur

Ossip Gabrilowitsch

Programs given in New York, Boston, and Chicago, in 1915–1916, showing the development of piano music from the days of the clavichord and harpsichord to "the present time."

PROGRAM 1

Clavier composers of the sixteenth, seventeenth, and eighteenth centuries

English School:
   William Byrde (1538–1623) [*sic*]
     Pavane, a (composed for the
     Earl of Salisbury)
   Henry Purcell (1658–1695)
     Minuet from the Suite in G
French School:
   François Couperin (1668–1733)
     Les Moissonneurs (The
     Harvesters)
   Claude Daquin (1694–1772)
     Le Coucou (The Cuckoo)
   Jean Philippe Rameau (1683–1764)

   Domenico Scarlatti (1683–1757) [*sic*]
     Sonata (Allegro vivace), A
North-German School:
   Johann Sebastian Bach (1685–1750)
     Prelude and Fugue in b♭
     (*Well-tempered Clavier*, Vol.1,
     No.22)
     Prelude from 2d English Suite, a
     Sarabande from 5th English Suite, e
     Chromatic Fantasy and Fugue, d
   Georg Friedrich Händel (1685–1759)
     Variations (The Harmonious
     Blacksmith)

PROGRAM 1 — CONTINUED

Le Tambourin
Italian School:
    Padre Michel-Angelo Rossi
    (1620–1660)
    Andantino, G
Viennese School:
    Joseph Haydn (1732–1809)
    Sonata No.2, e

Allegro from 2d Suite, F
Carl Philipp Emanuel Bach
    (1714–1788)
    Rondo in b
Wolfgang Amadeus Mozart
    (1756–1791)
    Variations, F
    Marcia alla Turca
    (Turkish march)

PROGRAM 2

Ludwig van Beethoven (1770–1827)
    Sonata, A, Op.2, No.2
    Thirty-Two Variations, c
    Rondo, G, Op.51, No.2

Sonata, f, Op.57
    ("Sonata Appassionata")
Sonata, A♭, Op.110

PROGRAM 3

Romantic Composers

Franz Schubert (1791–1828)
    Moment musical, A♭, Op.94
    Menuet, b, Op.78
    Impromptu, B♭, Op.142
Carl Maria von Weber (1786–1826)
    Invitation to the Dance
Felix Mendelssohn-Bartholdy (1809–1847)
    Four Songs without Words: E, Op.19, No.1; A, Op.102, No.5; E♭, Op.53, No.2; F, Op.53,
        No.4
    Variations sérieuses, Op.54
Robert Schumann (1810–1856)
    Des Abends ⎫
    Aufschwung ⎬ from Fantasy-Pieces, Op. 12
    Nachtstück, F, Op.21, No.4
    Carnaval, Op.9

PROGRAM 4

Frédéric Chopin (1810–1849)
    Ballade, A♭, Op.47
    Etudes: E, Op.10, No.3; F, Op.10, No.8; c♯, Op.25, No.7; C, Op.10, No.7
    Sonata, b♭, Op.35
    Twelve Preludes, Op.28
    Nocturne, G, Op.37, No.2
    Mazurka, b, Op.33, No.4
    Polonaise, A♭, Op.53

PROGRAM 5

Johannes Brahms (1833–1897)
 Variations and Fugue on a Theme
  by Händel, Op.24
 Intermezzo, A, Op.118
 Intermezzo, e, Op.119, No.2
 Rhapsodie, E♭, Op.119, No.4

Franz Liszt (1811–1886)
 Sonata, b
 Dance of the Gnomes
  (Gnomenreigen)
 Love-Dream (Liebestraum)
 Etude, f (from *Etudes d'exécution
  transcendante*)

PROGRAM 6

Modern Composers

César Franck (1822–1890)
 Prelude, Choral et Fugue
Edvard Grieg (1843–1907)
 Lyrical Pieces: Nocturne, Op.54,
  No.4; Butterfly, Op.41, No.1;
  To Spring, Op.43, No.6
Edward MacDowell (1861–1908)
 To the Sea, Op.55, No.1
 Witches' Dance (Hexentanz)
Peter Tschaikovsky (1840–1893)
 Chant d'automne, Op.37, No.10
 Humoresque, Op.10, No.2
Anton Rubinstein (1830–1894)
 Barcarolle, g, Op.50
 Valse, Op.14
Serge Rachmaninov (born 1873)
 Prelude, c♯, Op.3, No.2
Alexander Skriabin (1872–1915)
 Etude, Op.42, No.5
Alexander Glazunov (born 1865)
 Gavotte, D, Op.49
Theodor Leschetizky (born 1830)
 Gigue à l'antique, Op.44

Ignace Jan Paderewski (born 1859)
 Melodie, G♭, Op.16
Maurice Moszkowski (born 1854)
 Etude de Concert, G♭, Op.24
Max Reger (born 1873)
 Sarabande, Op.13, No.7
Richard Strauss (born 1864)
 Intermezzo (from "Stimmungs-
  bilder"), Op.9
Arnold Schoenberg (born 1874)
 Clavierstücke, Op.19
Claude Debussy (born 1862)
 Clair de Lune (from "Suite Berga-
  masque")
 L'Isle joyeuse
Maurice Ravel (born 1875)
 The Fountain (Jeux d'Eau)
Cyril Scott (born 1879)
 A Pierrot-Piece, Op.35, No.1
Percy Grainger (born 1884)
 Shepherd's Hey

Indexes

Alphabetical List of Composers under Nationality Designations

Black Composers

Women Composers

Compositions for Piano and Tape

Compositions for Prepared Piano

Title Index to Anthologies and Collections

Initial articles and Arabic numerals (A, An, Das, Der, Die, I, La, Le, Les, The, and numbers) are ignored in alphabetization.

Title Index to **Anatomy of a Classic, Virtuoso Series,** *and Van Cliburn Competition* **Commissioned Works and Publishers**

Anatomy of a Classic (Hinson—Alfred). A series of piano classics. Beethoven: *Variations* c. Chopin: *Fantaisie-Impromptu.* Debussy: *Pour le piano*. Haydn: *Variations* f. Mendelssohn: *Variations Sérieuses* Op.59. Mozart: *Sonata* A, K.331. Ravel: *Valses nobles et sentimentales*. Schumann: *Carnaval* Op.9.
Van Cliburn Competition Commissioned Works.
1962   Lee Hoiby, *Capriccio on Five Notes* (Bo&H).
1966   Willard Straight, *Structure* (Bo&H).
1969   Norman Dello Joio, *Capriccio on the Interval of a Second* (EBM).
1973   Aaron Copland, *Night Thoughts* (Bo&H).
1977   Samuel Barber, *Ballade* Op.46 (GS).
1981   Leonard Bernstein, *Touches* (Bo&H).

1985   John Corigliano, *Fantasia on an Ostinato* (GS).
1989   William Schuman, *Chester: Variations for Piano* (TP).
1993   Morton Gould, *Ghost Waltzes* (GS).
1997   William Bolcom, *Nine Bagatelles* (EBM).
Virtuoso (Ogdon—Nov). A modern piano series. Jean Coulthard: *Variations on BACH* 1972. Richard Hall: *Suite* 1971. Alun Hoddinott: *Sonata* No.3 Op.40 1966. Erland von Koch: *Varianti virtuosi* 1968. Kenneth Leighton: *Nine Variations* Op.30 1970. John McCabe: *Variations* Op.22 1966. Wilfrid Mellers: *Natalis invicti solis* 1969. Alfred Nieman: *Two Serenades* 1971. André Previn: *Paraphrases* 1973. Ronald Stevenson: *Prelude, Fugue and Fantasy on BACH* 1968.

MAURICE HINSON, Senior Professor of Piano at the Southern Baptist Theological Seminary, was founding editor of the *Journal of the American Liszt Society* and is a contributor to the *New Grove Dictionary of American Music.* He is known for his many books on piano repertoire, editions, more than 100 articles, videos, and lecture recitals, especially on early American piano music.